# 1001 MOVIES
## YOU MUST SEE BEFORE YOU DIE

GENERAL EDITOR
STEVEN JAY SCHNEIDER

CASSELL ILLUSTRATED

# THE CONTRIBUTORS

**Geoff Andrew (GA)** is Senior Film Editor of *Time Out* London, Head of Programming at the National Film Theatre, and the author of numerous books on film, including studies of Nicholas Ray, U.S. "indie" filmmakers of the 1980s and 90s, and Krzysztof Kieslowski's *Three Colors Trilogy*.

**Linda Badley (LB)** is Professor of English at Middle Tennessee State University, where she also teaches film studies. She is the author of *Film, Horror, and the Body Fantastic* (Greenwood) and has published essays on fantasy, science-fiction, and horror literature, film, and TV.

**Kathryn Bergeron (KB)** is a graduate student in Media Arts at the University of Arizona. Her work focuses primarily on the representation of race and the themes of marginalization in film.

**Joanna Berry (JB)** began her career as a film critic for *Time Out* before becoming reviews editor for *Empire* magazine. She has written for a host of magazines and newspapers including the *The Observer*, *Maxim* Magazine, and *Radio Times*.

**Edward Buscombe (EB)** was formerly Head of Publishing at the British Film Institute. He is the author of volumes on *Stagecoach* and *The Searchers* in the BFI's Film Classics series. *Cinema Today*, his history of World Cinema since 1970, comes out in 2003.

**Garrett Chaffin-Quiray (GC-Q)** has sponsored film festivals, taught TV and cinema history, and published book, movie, video, and event reviews, several scholarly essays and book chapters, and one short story.

**Tom Charity (TCh)** is Film Editor of *Time Out* London magazine. He is the author of *John Cassavetes: Life Works* (Omnibus Press) and *The Right Stuff* (BFI).

**Travis Crawford (TCr)** is a curator for the Philadelphia Film Festival. His festival programs, "New Korean Cinema" and "Danger After Dark," highlight the best in Asian genre filmmaking. He has written for *Film Comment, The Village Voice, Fangoria*, and is a regular contributor to *Filmmaker* and *Moviemaker* magazines.

**Adrian Danks (AD)** is the Head of Cinema Studies in the School of Applied Communication, RMIT University (Australia). He is currently President and cocurator of the Melbourne Cinémathèque, and coeditor of the journal supplement *Cteq*, published in the on-line journal *Senses of Cinema*.

**Ethan de Seife (EdeS)** is a Ph.D. candidate at the University of Wisconsin-Madison. He is currently at work on a dissertation about the films of Frank Tashlin.

**David Del Valle (DDV)** has been Hollywood correspondent for *Films and Filming* (U.K.) and *L'Ecran Fantastique* (France). He has written for *Video Watchdog, Psychotronic, Films in Review*, and *Scarlett Street* among others. His definitive interview with Vincent Price appears on DVD: *Vincent Price: The Sinister Image* (AllDay Entertainment) and he has a column, *Camp David*, on *www.filmsinreview.com*.

**Roumiana Deltcheva (RDe)**, Ph.D., is an independent scholar in new media technology in Montreal, Canada. With numerous publications, she engages in cross-cultural, interdisciplinary research in literature, film, and print media, focusing on the cultural paradigms defining posttotalitarian East Central Europe.

**Dana Duma (DD)** teaches film history at Hyperion University and the National University of Cinema and Theatre in Bucharest. She has written the books *Self-Portraits of the Movie, Gopo*, and many articles for film and cultural periodicals.

**Rachel Dwyer (RDw)** is Senior Lecturer in Indian Studies at SOAS, University of London. Her publications include *Pleasure and the Nation: The History, Politics, and Consumption of Public Culture in India* (with C. Pinney; OUP), *Yash Chopra* (BFI), and *Cinema India: The Visual Culture of Hindi Film* (with D. Patel; Rutgers UP).

**Angela Errigo (AE)** studied film and journalism at San Francisco State University. She is a freelance writer and broadcaster, a contributing editor on *Empire*, and film critic for the BBC Radio 2 *Arts Programme*.

**Chiara Ferrari (CFe)** is a Doctoral candidate in the Department of Film, Television, and Digital Media at the University of California-Los Angeles. Her research includes culture, media, and society, Latin American cinema, and new media theory.

**Cynthia Freeland (CFr)** is Associate Professor of Philosophy and Director of Women's Studies at the University of Houston. She has published widely on ancient philosophy and aesthetics, is the author of *The Naked and the Undead: Evil and the Appeal of Horror* (Westview Press) and *But is it art?* (OUP), and is coeditor of *Philosophy and Film* (Routledge).

**Jean-Michel Frodon (J-MF)** is the Senior Editor on cinema at the French daily *Le Monde* and teaches at the Institut de Sciences Politiques. He created L'Exception, a think tank about cinema, and has published several books, including *L'Age Moderne du Cinéma Français* (Flammarion), *La Projection Nationale* (Odile Jacob), and *Conversation avec Woody Allen* (Plon).

**Chris Fujiwara (CFu)** is the author of *Jacques Tourneur: The Cinema of Nightfall* (Johns Hopkins UP). He is a contributing editor of *Hermenaut* and a regular contributor to *The Boston Phoenix*.

**Tom Gunning (TG)** is a Distinguished Service professor in the Department of Art History and the Committee on Cinema and Media at the University of Chicago. He is the author of *Fritz Lang: Allegories of Vision and Modernity* (BFI) and *D.W. Griffith and the Origins of American Narrative Film* (University of Illinois Press).

**Rahul Hamid (RH)** is a Doctoral candidate in the Department of Cinema Studies at New York University, writing his thesis on Iranian film. He has written on contemporary international film in various publications, including *Cineaste* magazine.

**Ernest Hardy (EH)** is a film/music critic and poet. He is a Sundance Fellow whose work has appeared in the *New York Times, LA Times, Village Voice, Rolling Stone*, and *Vibe*. He is a member of LAFCA (Los Angeles Fim Critics Association).

**Bernd Herzogenrath (BH)** is the author of *An Art of Desire: Reading Paul Auster* (Editions Rodopi) and editor of *From Virgin Land to Disney World: Nature and Its Discontents in the USA of Yesterday and Today* (Editions Rodopi). He is currently teaching at the University of Cologne.

**Anikó Imre (AI)** teaches film studies in the Department of Interdisciplinary Arts and Sciences of the University of Washington, Tacoma. She has published on East and Central European cinemas, race and gender in cinema, violence, and postcoloniality.

**Jyotsna Kapur (JKa)** teaches in the Department of Cinema and Photography at Southern Illinois University. She is currently working on a book-length study on the redefinition of childhood in contemporary American children's cinema, the public debate on children and television, and children's marketing.

**Philip Kemp (PK)** is a writer and film historian, a regular contributor to *Sight and Sound, Total Film*, and *International Film Guide*, among others. He is the author of *Lethal Innocence: The Cinema of Alexander Mackendrick* (Heinemann) and is currently working on books about Michael Balcon and the Coen brothers.

**James Kendrick (JKe)** is an associate instructor in the Department of Communication and Culture at Indiana University, Bloomington. His research interests include violence in the media, cult and horror films, and postclassical Hollywood film history. He is also the resident film critic at *www.QNetwork.com*.

**Joshua Klein (JKl)** is a Chicago-based freelance writer and DVD columnist whose work has appeared in the *Chicago Tribune*, *Washington Post*, and *The Onion*.

**Mikel J. Koven (MK)** is lecturer in Film and Television Studies at the University of Wales, Aberystwyth. He is the author of the *Pocket Essentials guide on Blaxploitation Films*, and is currently working on a study of the giallo film.

**Karen Krizanovich (KK)** has reviewed films for a variety of publications, including *Empire*, *NME*, *Word* magazine, *Ms London*, and *Cosmopolitan UK*.

**Andrea F. Kulas (AK)** recently obtained her MA in Media Arts from the University of Arizona and is the coeditor of *Ridley Scott: Interviews* (University Press of Mississippi).

**Frank Lafond (FL)** is Doctora candidate studying aesthetics at Lille University, France. He has written essays on horror and film noir, has edited a book on the modern American horror film (*Cauchemars américains*). He is the editor of an annual journal entitled *Rendez-vous avec la peur*.

**Colin MacCabe (CM)** is Distinguished Professor of English and Film at the University of Pittsburgh. His most recent books are *Godard: A Portrait of the Artist at 70* (published January 2004), *The Eloquence of the Vulgar* (BFI), and a revised edition of *James Joyce and the Revolution of the Word* (2nd edition, Palgrave).

**Adrian Martin (AM)** is film critic for *The Age*, author of *The Mad Max Movies* (Currency), *Once Upon a Time in America* (BFI), and *Phantasms* (Penguin), and coeditor of *Movie Mutations* (BFI) and *Rouge* (www.rouge.com.au). He is a Doctoral candidate at Monash University, Faculty of Art and Design.

**Ernest Mathijs (EM)** is lecturer in film at the University of Wales, Aberystwyth. His recent research concerns the reception of David Cronenberg, Low Countries cinema, and a study of the cross-cultural impact of *The Lord of the Rings*.

**Annalee Newitz (AN)** is founder of the webzine *Bad Subjects*, and has written *White Trash: Race and Class in America* (Routledge) and *The Bad Subjects Anthology* (New York UP). Her work has appeared in *Feed*, *Gear*, *Alternative Press Review*, *New York Press*, *The San Francisco Bay Guardian*, and several academic journals.

**Kim Newman (KN)**, novelist, critic, and broadcaster, is the author of *Nightmare Movies* (Bloomsbury), *Wild West Movies* (Bloomsbury), *Apocalypse Movies* (Griffin), and *BFI Classics: Cat People*, and is editor of *The BFI Companion to Horror* (Continuum). His novels include *The Night Mayor*, *Anno Dracula*, *The Quorum*, and *Life's Lottery*.

**Devin Orgeron (DO)** is an Assistant Professor of Film Studies at North Carolina State University. His book-in-progress is *Road Pictures: The Transportation of American Cinema*. His writing has appeared in *CineAction*, *COIL*, *Film Quarterly*, *College Literature*, and *Post Script*.

**Marsha Orgeron (MO)** is an Assistant Professor of Film Studies at North Carolina State University. Her book-in-progress addresses the impact of the film industry on American culture. She has recently been published in *Cinema Journal*, *American Literature*, *Quarterly Review of Film & Video*, and *COIL*.

**Corinne Oster (CO)** recently completed her dissertation on new representations of marginality in contemporary French women's cinema, for the Department of Comparative Literature at the University of Massachusetts, Amherst.

**R. Barton Palmer (RBP)** holds Ph.Ds. from Yale University (Medieval Studies) and New York University (Cinema Studies). He is Calhoun Lemon Professor of Literature at Clemson University and Director of the South Carolina Film Institute. He has published on Hollywood cinema and film theory, including *Hollywood's Dark Cinema: The American Film Noir* (Twayne).

**Richard Peña (RP)** is an Associate Professor of Film Studies at Columbia University and the Program Director of the Film Society of Lincoln Center.

**Murray Pomerance (MP)** is Professor and Chair of the Department of Sociology at Ryerson University. His books include *Ladies and Gentlemen, Boys and Girls: Gender in Film at the End of the Twentieth Century* (State University of New York Press), and *Sugar, Spice, and Everything Nice: Cinemas of Girlhood* (Wayne State UP). He is coeditor of the *American Decades* series (Rutgers UP).

**Phil Powrie (PP)** is Director of the Centre for Research into Film and Media, University of Newcastle upon Tyne. He has published widely on French cinema, most recently a book on Jean-Jacques Beineix (Manchester UP).

**Bérénice Reynaud (BR)** is the author of *Nouvelles Chines, nouveaux cinémas* (Editions du Jeu de Paume) and *A City of Sadness* (BFI). She teaches at the California Institute of the Arts.

**David Robinson (DR)** is the former film critic of *The Times* (London), an independent film historian, and Director of the Giornate del Cinema Muto (Pordenone Silent Film Festival). His many publications include *World Cinema 1895-1980* (Eyre Methuen), and *From Peepshow to Palace: The Birth of American Film* (Columbia UP).

**Jonathan Romney (JRom)** is the *Independent on Sunday* film critic and writes for *Sight and Sound*, *Film Comment*, and other publications. His books include *Atom Egoyan* (BFI), and *Short Orders*, a volume of collected writing.

**Jonathan Rosenbaum (JRos)** is film critic for the *Chicago Reader*; his recent books include *Abbas Kiarostami* (with Mehrnaz Saeed-Vafa; University of Illinois Press), *Dead Man* (BFI), and *Movies as Politics* (University of California Press).

**Martin Rubin (MR)** programs films at the Gene Siskel Film Center in Chicago. He has written on Busby Berkeley (Columbia UP) and thrillers (Cambridge UP).

**Marc Siegel (MS)** writes about queer theory and experimental film. He is currently a Visiting Lecturer in Film Studies at the Free University in Berlin.

**Adam Simon (AS)** is a writer and director whose work includes *Braindead* (1990), *Carnosaur* (1993), *The Typewriter, The Rifle and the Movie Camera* (1996), *The American Nightmare* (2000), and *Bones* (2001).

**Peter Stanfield (PS)** is Senior Lecturer in Media Arts at Southampton Institute, England. His books include *Hollywood, Westerns and the 1930s: The Lost Trail* (University of Exeter Press).

**David Sterritt (DS)** is film critic of *The Christian Science Monitor*, Professor of Theater and Film at the C.W. Post Campus of Long Island University, a member of the Film Studies Faculty at Columbia University, and Co-Chair of the Columbia University Seminar on Cinema and Interdisciplinary Interpretation.

**Adisakdi Tantimedh (AT)** is a writer and filmmaker. He has written radio plays and television scripts for the BBC and various screenplays for Britain and Hollywood, including the BAFTA award winner *Zinky Boys Go Underground*. His most recent work includes the short film *Open House*.

**Michael Tapper (MT)** is editor of *Film International*. He has contributed to various publicatons including *Lars von Trier: Interviews* (University of Mississippi Press).

**Ella Taylor (ET)** is a film critic for *LA Weekly*. A former academic, she has also written about film for a wide range of newspapers and magazines.

**Ginette Vincendeau** is Professor of Film Studies at the University of Warwick. Among her recent books on French cinema is *Jean-Pierre Melville: An American in Paris* (BFI).

**Josephine Woll** teaches at Howard University and writes about Russian film and literature, most recently *Real Images: Soviet Cinema and Thaw* (I.B. Tauris).

A Quintet Book

First published in Great Britain in 2003 by Cassell Illustrated
a member of Octopus Publishing Group Limited
2-4 Heron Quays
London E14 4JP



A CIP catalogue record for this book is available from the British Library.

ISBN 1 84403 044 X

This book was designed and produced by
Quintet Publishing Limited
6 Blundell Street
London N7 9BH

Associate Publisher: Laura Price
Project Editor: Catherine Osborne
Researcher: Richard Guthrie

Designers: Ian Hunt, James Lawrence
Creative Director: Richard Dewing

Publisher: Oliver Salzmann

Manufactured in Universal Graphics Pte Limited, Singapore.
Printed by Midas Printing International Limited, China

CASSELL ILLUSTRATED

# WELCOME TO 1001 MOVIES YOU MUST SEE BEFORE YOU DIE

To help you navigate through the book, here are a few points about the structure and information given for each film.

- Each English-language film is listed under its main release title. Non English-language films are listed by the original title, followed by the main English-language release name.
- Original titles in languages that do not use the Roman alphabet, such as Cantonese and Russian, have been transliterated in standard phonetic spelling.
- Films are dated by the year of their general release.
- The country of origin is the producer's base at the time of the making of the film, followed by and abbreviation of the production company or companies, the length of the film in minutes, whether the film was shot in black-and-white or color, and if the film was silent.
- The language spoken in the film is only mentioned when it is either not in English or is in English in combination with other languages.
- A list of the major creative contributions is listed under: Director, Producer, Screenplay, Photography (Director of Photography), Music, and Cast (main performers only).
- Hollywood awards are listed under Oscar and Oscar nomination, followed by awards and citations presented at the annual International film festivals of Cannes, Berlin and Venice. All award titles and categories have been abbreviated.
- On pages 12–25 are a series of indices divided by genre. Many films fall into more than one genre and you will find them under each genre. For example: the 1940 film *Fantasia* is listed in four genre categories: animation, musical, fantasy, and family.
- At the end of the book is a complete Title Index that lists, where applicable, both original language and English language titles. This is followed by a full Index of Directors whose films appear in the book.
- Some entries include information about the plot or ending of the films. Film ratings have not been given.

# CONTENTS

**FOREWORD** 6
**GENRE INDEX** 12
**FILM ENTRIES** 26
**FILM TITLE INDEX** 950
**DIRECTOR INDEX** 956
**PICTURE CREDITS** 959

# FOREWORD

*1001 Movies You Must See Before You Die* is, as the title suggests, a book that seeks not just to inform and to prescribe, but to *motivate*: To turn its curious readers into ardent viewers and to make it obvious that the pressure is on, that time is short, and that the number of films eminently worth watching has become very long indeed.

Nowadays, "Top 10 Movie" lists survive almost exclusively as annual critics polls; and talk of "The 100 Greatest Films" tends to be restricted either to specific genres, such as comedy, horror, sci-fi, romance, or the western, or to particular national cinemas, such as France, China, Italy, Japan, or the U.K. All of this points to the impossibility—or at least the irresponsibility—of selecting a number less than (oh let's just say) a grand to work with when it comes to preparing a list of "best," or most valuable, or most important, or most unforgettable movies; a list that aims to do justice and give coverage to the entire history of the medium.

With this latter goal in mind, even 1001 can quickly start to seem like way too small a number. Maybe not so small if silent movies were kept off the list; or avant-garde films; or Middle Eastern films; or animated movies; or documentaries; or shorts...but these strategies of exclusion are in the end all just ways of taking the pressure off, of drawing arbitrary lines in the cinematic sand, and refusing to make the heap of difficult decisions necessary to end up with a limited selection of films that treats *all* the heterogenous types and

traditions comprising motion picture art with equal and all due respect. The book you are holding in your hands takes a great risk in offering up an all-time, all-genre, all-world, must-see films list. But it is a risk well worth taking, and if you make the effort to go and see the films discussed herein you can be sure to die a happy moviegoer. In short: The more you see, the better off you'll be.

So how to determine which 1001 movies must be seen before dying? How much easier, and less controversial, it would be to come up with 1001 movies that should be avoided at all costs! It is no surprise to learn that film criticism hardly qualifies as an exact science—Roger Ebert's infamous formula "Two thumbs up, way, way up!" notwithstanding—and it is hardly an exagerration to claim that one person's *Midnight Cowboy* may well be another one's *Ishtar*. Perhaps there are ways of objectively comparing, even ranking, highly codified and historically specific cycles, movements, or subgenres, such as the 1970s Italian thriller, in this case on the basis of the form's aestheticized violence, labyrinthine narratives, and psychological resonance. And maybe it really is legitimate to separate out Hitchcock's indisputable classics (*North By Northwest*, *Rear Window*, *Vertigo*, *Psycho*, *The Birds*, etc.) from what are often held to be the director's weaker efforts (*Torn Curtain*, *Family Plot*, *Topaz*, *The Paradine Case*). But what basis could there possibly be for deciding between Tsai Ming-liang's *What Time Is It There?* and Robert Aldrich's *What Ever Happened to Baby Jane?* Or between George Méliès' *A Trip to the Moon* and

Marleen Gorris's *A Question of Silence*? If the goal of this book is indeed to include a little bit of everything, then what is to prevent the resulting list of 1001 films from being just a cinematic smorgasbord—a case of mere variety taking precedence over true value?

Good questions all. The first step in determining the 1001 movies to be included here involved taking a close look at a number of existing "greatest," "top," "favorite," and "best" film lists, and prioritizing titles based on the frequency with which they appeared. This allowed us to identify something like a canon of classics (including modern and contemporary classics) that we felt confident warranted a spot in this book on the joint basis of quality and reputation. By no means did *every* film that turned up on these shorter, occasionally idiosyncratic lists make our cut of 1001, but the exercise at least gave us some key reference points and reduced to a significant extent the unavoidably subjective nature of the selection process.

After we tentatively settled on an initial batch of around 1300 titles, we proceeded to go through the list again (and again, and again, and again...) with the dual—and conflicting!—aim of reducing the overall number while still achieving sufficient coverage of the medium's various periods, national cinemas, genres, movements, traditions, and notable auteurs. With respect to the latter, we took the notion of an "auteur" in the loosest possible sense to include not just directors (Woody Allen, Ingmar Bergman, John Cassavetes, Federico Fellini,

Jean-Luc Godard, Abbas Kiarostami, Satyajit Ray, etc.), but also actors (Humphrey Bogart, Marlene Dietrich, Toshiro Mifune), producers (David O. Selznick, Sam Spiegel, Irving Thalberg), screenwriters (Ernest Lehman, Preston Sturges, Cesare Zavattini), cinematographers (Gregg Toland, Gordon Willis, Freddie Young), composers (Bernard Herrmann, Ennio Morcicone, Nino Rota), et al.

We were also mindful of not giving automatic preference—free passes, as it were—to self-consciously "quality" productions or high cinematic art (historical epics, Shakespeare adaptations, Russian formalist experiments) at the expense of ignoring the so-called "low" genres (slapstick comedy, 1930s gangster films, blaxploitation cinema), or even movies that are of somewhat questionable aesthetic merit (*Pink Flamingos, Saturday Night Fever, The Blair Witch Project*), wholeheartedly populist appeal (*Top Gun, Rain Man, Big, E.T.: The Extra-Terrestrial*), or dubious ideological or ethical value (*The Birth of a Nation, Freaks, Triumph of the Will, Salo, or The 120 Days of Sodom*). Instead we endeavored to adjudge each of our candidate selections on their own terms, which meant, to begin with, figuring out as best we could just what the "terms" in question consisted of—not always an easy or obvious task, as in the case of *Pink Flamingos*, the infamous tagline for which read "An exercise in poor taste"—and then coming up with ways of separating the wheat from the chaff (even when the difference between the two might seem so slight as to be indiscernible or irrelevant).

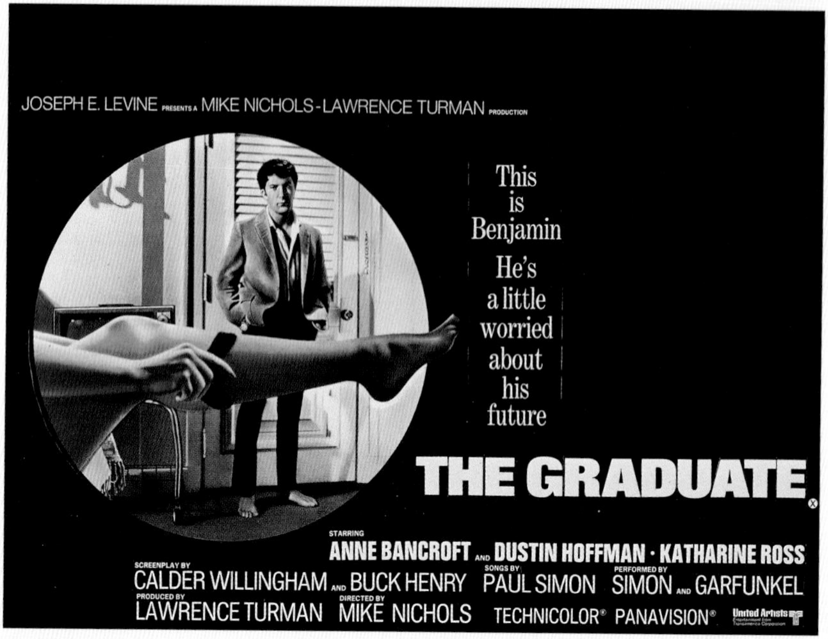
JOSEPH E. LEVINE PRESENTS A MIKE NICHOLS-LAWRENCE TURMAN PRODUCTION
This is Benjamin He's a little worried about his future
THE GRADUATE
STARRING ANNE BANCROFT AND DUSTIN HOFFMAN · KATHARINE ROSS
SCREENPLAY BY CALDER WILLINGHAM AND BUCK HENRY
SONGS BY PAUL SIMON
PERFORMED BY SIMON AND GARFUNKEL
PRODUCED BY LAWRENCE TURMAN
DIRECTED BY MIKE NICHOLS
TECHNICOLOR® PANAVISION®
United Artists

What's the old saying, something along the lines of "even if you could have filet mignon every single day, once in a while you're bound to crave a hamburger?" The point here is, even if your filmgoing preferences lie heavily on the side of acknowledged world classics (the *Citizen Kane*s, the *Rashomon*s, the *Raging Bull*s, the *Battleship Potemkin*s) or the treasures of European art cinema (the *L'Avventura*s, the *Hiroshima mon amour*s, the *Last Tango*s *in Paris*), there is sure to come a time when you long to see a movie with a wholly different agenda, whether it's a Hollywood blockbuster (*Jurrasic Park, The Empire Strikes Back, Titanic*), an underground oddity (*Scorpio Rising, Flaming Creatures, Hold Me While I'm Naked*), or a cult curiosity piece (*El Topo, Seconds, Slacker, Mondo cane, Tetsuo*). As we envisioned it, our main task was to make sure that whatever your cinematic tastes—in general, or on those days when you feel like trying something new—this book would be a menu where every dish is a winner.

Finally, after making the last agonizing cuts that were required to bring the list down to a "mere" 1001, the remaining step was for us to tweak the results based on the feedback and suggestions offered by our esteemed group of contributors, whose collective experience, expertise, and passion for watching, discussing, and writing about motion pictures has ensured that, while no list of all-time-greatest anythings can possibly be perfect (whatever that means) or utterly uncontroversial (and wouldn't that be dull?), the one you have before you is, to be sure, as good as it gets. But it isn't just the list itself that makes this book so special: It is also the specially-commissioned entries that accompany each of the 1001 movies included on that list—concise, thoughtful, stimulating essays that seamlessly combine important plot details, insightful commentary, cultural and historical context, and a fair share of trivia besides (so George Lucas was originally set to direct *Apocalypse Now*? Who knew?). Don't be fooled by the ease with which these essays are digested. There is a definite skill—one might even say an art—to writing a profound, engaging piece of only five hundred words on a film like *Casablanca*, *The Searchers*, or *The Rules of the Game*, much less three hundred and fifty words on *Boogie Nights*, *Cries and Whispers*, or *The Night of the Hunter*, or (gasp!) two hundred words on *Marketa Lazarova*, *The Pianist*, or *Cleo from 5 to 7*. Somehow, with great aplomb, these authors have managed to pull it off, and brilliantly.

As for my own experience working on this book, I can only say that the pains of having to cross several personal favorites off the list was more than made up for by the pleasures of admiring the resulting medley, of reading so many wonderful film entries by so many wonderful writers on film, and of finding out so much about the history, traditions, and secret treasures of the cinema that I never knew before. Even if you have already seen all 1001 movies discussed and paid tribute to in these pages (congratulations, though I seriously doubt it), I'm sure you will benefit tremendously from reading about them here.

But the clock continues to tick away... So start reading already, and keep watching!

***

As general editor of *1001 Movies You Must See Before You Die*, I have the honor and the privilege of being able to give thanks in print to all the individuals responsible for ensuring the timely completion and inevitable success of this ambitious, enjoyable, eminently worthwhile project. My sincerest gratitude goes out to Laura Price, Catherine Osborne, and the rest of the remarkably industrious and conscientious staff at Quintet Publishing, a division of the Quarto Group; to Andrew Lockett of the British Film Institute; to the close to sixty contributors from eight different countries who worked under tight deadlines and a slave-driving editor (me) to produce the entertaining and educational film entries which make up this volume; and, as always, to my family, friends, and colleagues, whose support and encouragement continues to be my not-so-secret weapon.

**STEVEN JAY SCHNEIDER**
GENERAL EDITOR

# GENRE INDICES

## ACTION


'A' Gai Waak Juk Jaap 748
Adventures of Robin Hood, The 146
Akira 764
Alien 653
Aliens 737
Apocalypse Now 658-659
Batman 776
Ben-Hur 371
Beverly Hills Cop 713
Big Red One, The 670
Blade Runner 684-685
Braveheart 854
Captain Blood 126
Captains Courageous 138
Cidade de Deus 945
City of God 945
Come Drink With Me 460
Crouching Tiger Hidden Dragon 920-921
Da Zui Xia 460
Die Hard 771
Die Xue Shuang Xiong 781
Do Ma Daan 742
Easy Rider 512-513
Empire Strikes Back, The 668
Enter the Dragon 569
Faster Pussycat! Kill, Kill! 453
Fight Club 904
Five Deadly Venoms 640
Full Metal Jacket 750-751
Gangs of New York 942
Get Carter 544
Gladiator 915
Goldfinger 429
Great Train Robbery, The 28-29
Harder They Come, The 582
Heat 856
Hsia Nu 505
Independence Day 866
Jaws 612
Killer, The 781
King of New York 791
Lola Rennt 889
Mad Max 662
Matrix, The 911
Mononoke Hime 876
Natural Born Killers 842
Once Upon a Time in China 799
Peking Opera Blues 742
Planet of the Apes 490
Potomok Chingis-Khana 76
Princess Mononoke 876
Project A, Part II 748
Public Enemy, The 95
Pulp Fiction 843
Raiders of the Lost Ark 674
Resevoir Dogs 818
Return of the Jedi 697
Rio Bravo 375
Rocky 615
Romper Stomper 819
Run Lola Run 889
Saving Private Ryan 886-887
Seven Samurai, The 304-305
Shaft 546
Shao Lin San Shih Liu Fang 647
Shaolin Master Killer 647
Spartacus 392
Star Wars 622-623
Storm over Asia 76
Strange Days 853
Superfly 564
Terminator 2: Judgment Day 808
Terminator, The 708-709
Thelma and Louise 808
Thief of Bagdad, The 50
Thin Red Line, The 892-893
Three Kings 902
Top Gun 743
Total Recall 799
Touch of Zen, A 505
Untouchables, The 756
Who Framed Roger Rabbit 773
Wo Hu Cang Long 920-921
Wong Fei-Hung 799
Wu Du 640


## ADVENTURE


2001 498-499
Adventures of Robin Hood, The 146
African Queen, The 267
Aguirre, Der Zorn Gottes 552
Aguirre: The Wrath of God 552
Akira 764
Back to the Future 723
Beat the Devil 295
Beauty and the Beast 221
Ben-Hur 371
Black Cat, The 121
Bridge on the River Kwai, The 345
Captain Blood 126
Captains Courageous 138
Close Encounters of the Third Kind 624
Crouching Tiger Hidden Dragon 920-921
Deliverance 555
Dersu Uzala 583
E.T. the Extra-Terrestrial 682
Easy Rider 512-513
Empire Strikes Back, The 668
Fitzcarraldo 690-691
Five Deadly Venoms 640
Goldfinger 429
Great Escape, The 421
Gunga Din 161
Hill 24 Doesn't Answer 315
Hsia Nu 505
It Happened One Night 122-123
Jaws 612
Jurassic Park 830
La Belle et la Bête 221
Lawrence of Arabia 406-407
Lion King, The 840
Lord of the Rings: The Fellowship of the Ring, The 940
Man Who Knew Too Much, The 331
Mononoke Hime 876
Monty Python and the Holy Grail 601
Mutiny on the Bounty 126
North By Northwest 361
O Brother, Where Art Thou? 926
Princess Bride, The 755
Princess Mononoke 876
Raiders of the Lost Ark 674
Return of the Jedi 697
Right Stuff, The 703
Salaire De La Peur, La 287
Sen To Chihiro No Kamikakushi 930-931
Shanghai Express 105
Spirited Away 930-931
Stand By Me 732
Star Wars 622-623
Sullivan's Travels 180-181
Thief of Bagdad, The 50
Total Recall 799
Touch of Zen, A 505
Treasure of the Sierra Madre, The 244
Wages of Fear 287
Wizard of Oz, The 154-155

Wo Hu Cang Long 920-921
Wu Du 640

## ADULT
Ai No Corrida 619
In the Realm of the Senses 619

## ANIMATION
Akira 764
Alice 776
Animal Farm 299
Dumbo 178
Fantasia 166
Fantastic Planet 579
Grave of the Fireflies 768
Heaven and Earth Magic 412
Hotaru No Haka 768
Jungle Book, The 483
Lion King, The 840
Mononoke Hime 876
Neco z Alenky 776
Pinocchio 169
Planète Sauvage, La 579
Princess Mononoke 876
Sen To Chihiro No Kamikakushi 930-931
Snow White and the Seven Dwarfs 143
Spirited Away 930-931
Toy Story 853
Who Framed Roger Rabbit 773

## ART
Flaming Creatures 420
Koyaanisqatsi 704
Spring in a Small Town 237
Vinyl 442
Xiao cheng zhi chun 237

## AVANT-GARDE
Blonde Cobra 415
Deseret 851
Flaming Creatures 420
Hold Me While I'm Naked 455
Koyaanisqatsi 704
Még Kér A Nép 544
Meshes of the Afternoon 191
Red Psalm 544
Report 471
Scorpio Rising 430
Too Early, Too Late 681
Vinyl 442
Wavelength 479
Zu Fruh, Zu Spat 681

## COMEDY
'A' Gai Waak Juk Jaap 748
À Nous la liberté 89
Adam's Rib 249
Adaptation 947
Age d'or, L' 84-85
Age of Gold, The 84-85
Airplane! 671
All About My Mother 900-901
Amarcord 580-581
Amélie 927
American Beauty 906-907
American Graffiti 568
American Werewolf in London 679
And Your Mother Too 928
Annie Hall 626-627
Apartment, The 390-391
Archangel 795
Ariel 762
Artists and Models 310
Atalante, L' 120
Attack the Gas Station! 908
Awful Truth, The 144
Babbete's Gaestebud 749
Bab El Hadid 352
Babe 852
Babette's Feast 749
Back to the Future 723
Baker's Wife, The 148
Band Wagon, The 282
Bank Dick, The 171
Beat the Devil 295
Being John Malkovich 905
Being There 656
Beverly Hills Cop 713
Big 767
Big Chill, The 697
Blazing Saddles 591
Boogie Nights 879
Boudu Sauvé des Eaux 101
Boudu Saved from Drowning 101
Brave-Hearted Will Take the Bride, The 860
Brazil 724-725
Breakfast at Tiffany's 396
Breakfast Club, The 717
Breaking Away 654
Bringing Up Baby 149
Broadcast News 754
Buffalo 66 888
Bull Durham 762
Butcher Boy, The 877
Cairo Station 352
Campanadas a Medianoche 449
Caro Diario 850
Carrosse d'or, Le 281
C'est arrivé près de chez vouz 825
Charme Discret de la Bourgeoisie, Le 560
Chicago 949
Chimes at Midnight 449
Christmas Story, A 695
City Lights 95
Clerks 839
Closely Watched Trains 486-487
Clueless 855
Crimes and Misdemeanors 778
Daisies 460
Dance, Girl, Dance 169
Dear Diary 850
Déclin de l'Empire Américain, Le 735
Decline of the American Empire 735
Deconstructing Harry 874
Delicatessen 802
Demoiselles de Rochefort, Les 474
Destry Rides Again 156
Dilwale Dulhaniya le Jayenge 860
Diner 688-689
Discreet Charm of the Bourgeoisie, The 560
Do Ma Daan 742
Do the Right Thing 782-783
Down By Law 738
Dr. Strangelove 434-435
Duck Soup 112-113
Fabuleax Destin d'Amélie Poulain 927
Fargo 864-865
Fast Times at Ridgemont High 681
Femme du Boulanger, La 148
Ferris Bueller's Day Off 737
Firemen's Ball, The 484
Fish Called Wanda, A 766
Forrest Gump 838
Four Weddings and a Funeral 839
Freedom for Us 89
General, The 66
Gentlemen Prefer Blondes 289
Ghost Busters 713
Gigi 353
Giulietta deglie Spiriti 451
Gold Rush, The 60
Golden Coach, The 281
Good Morning Vietnam 752
Graduate, The 468-469
Grease 644
Groundhog Day 828
Gunga Din 161
Hable con ella 944
Hannah and Her Sisters 734
Happiness 891
Hard Day's Night, A 436
Harold and Maude 542-543
Hayno 385
Heartbreak Kid, The 551
High Society 336
His Girl Friday 164
Horí, Má Panenko 484
Housemaid, The 385
Hsi Yen 834
Idioterne 894
Idiots, The 894
It Happened One Night 122-123
Jerk, The 660
Judge Priest 121
Juliet of the Spirits 451
Jungle Book, The 483
Juyuso Seubgyuksageun 908
Kid Brother, The 71
Kind Hearts and Coronets 247
King of Comedy, The 702
Kingdom, The 849
Ladies Man, The 399
Lady Eve, The 174
Ladykillers, The 316
Lavender Hill Mob, The 266
Little Big Man 527
Lucía 504
M*A*S*H* 530
Man Bites Dog 825
Manhattan 661
Me and My Gal 107
Meet the Parents 919
Million, Le 90
Million, The 90
Modern Times 131
Mon oncle 357
Monsieur Verdoux 230
Monsoon Wedding 936
Monty Python and the Holy Grail 601
Monty Python's Life of Brian 657

Moonstruck 756
Mr. Deeds Goes to Town 134
M. Hulot's Holiday 291
Mujeres al Borde de un Ataque de Nervios 759
Muppet Movie, The 660
Murmur of the Heart 547
My Fair Lady 433
My Man Godfrey 133
My Uncle 357
Naked Gun, The 767
Network 618
Night at the Opera, A 127
Ninotchka 161
No Man's Land 933
Nutty Professor, The 414
O Brother, Where Art Thou? 926
Once Upon a Time in China 799
One Flew Over the Cuckoo's Nest 596
Ostre Sledované Vlaky 486-487
Our Hospitality 49
Paleface, The 241
Palm Beach Story, The 183
Peking Opera Blues 742
Philadelphia Story, The 167
Pink Flamingos 563
Player, The 817
Playtime 470
Pretty Woman 794
Princess Bride, The 755
Prizzi's Honor 728
Producers, The 496
Project A, Part II 748
Purple Rose of Cairo, The 722
Quiet Man, The 271
Rain Man 774
Raising Arizona 749
Real Life 651
Règle du Jeu, La 162-163
Riget 849
Rocky Horror Picture Show, The 598-599
Roger & Me 784
Roman d'un tricheur, Le 138
Roman Holiday 286
Room with a View, A 739
Royal Tennenbaums, The 939
Rules of the Game, The 162-163
Rushmore 890
Saturday Night Fever 631
Sedmikrasky 460
Seven Brides for Seven Brothers 298
Seven Chances 56
She Done Him Wrong 111
Sherlock Jr. 54-55
She's Gotta Have It 735
Singin' in the Rain 274-275
Slacker 812
Sleeper 575
Smiles of a Summer Night 322
Smoke 858
Some Like it Hot 362-363
Sommarnattens Leede 322
Sons of the Desert 116
Souffle Au Coeur, Le 547
Steamboat Bill, Jr. 76
Sting, The 564
Story of a Cheat, The 138
Stranger than Paradise 715
Strictly Ballroom 816
Sullivan's Travels 180-181
Sunset Blvd. 260-261
Swing Time 132
Talk to Her 944
Tampopo 741
Terms of Endearment 701
There's Something About Mary 896
Thin Man, The 124-125
This is Spinal Tap 712
Three Kings 902
Three Lives and Only One Death 863
To Be or Not to Be 186
Todo Sobre Mi Madre 900-901
Tootsie 686
Top Hat 130
Toy Story 853
Trainspotting 871
Trois Vies & Une Seule Mort 863
Trouble in Paradise 102-103
Trust 795
Unbelievable Truth, The 787
Underground 860
Up in Smoke 647
Vacances de M. Hulot, Les 291
W.R.—Misterje Organizma 534
W.R.—Mysteries of the Organism 534
Wedding Banquet, The 834
When Harry Met Sally 777
Whiskey Galore! 250
Who Framed Roger Rabbit 773
Willy Wonka and the Chocolate Factory 538
Withnail and I 752
Women on the Verge of a Nervous Breakdown 759
Wong Fei-Hung 799
Y tu mama tambien 928
Young Frankenstein 587
Young Girls of Rochefort, The 474
Zéro de conduite 107
Zero for Conduct 107

## CRIME

12 Angry Men 337
400 Blows, The 360
All the President's Men 614
American Friend, The 635
Amerikanische Freund, Der 635
Angels with Dirty Faces 146
Argent, L' 699
Ariel 762
Asphalt Jungle, The 255
Atlantic City 665
Badlands 566-567
Batman 776
Beat the Devil 295
Big Heat, The 290
Bird with the Crystal Plumage, The 533
Black Cat, The 121
Blue Velvet 733
Bob le flambeur 318
Bob the Gambler 318
Body Heat 677
Bonnie and Clyde 480-481
Boyz N the Hood 800-801
Breathless 370
Bring Me the Head of Alfredo Garcia 595
Casino 850
C'est arrivé près de chez vouz 825
Chicago 949
Chinatown 588-589
Cidade de Deus 945
City of God 945
Clockwork Orange, A 536-537
Come Drink With Me 460
Conformist, The 511
Conformista, Il 511
Conversation, The 584
Cyclo 859
Da Zui Xia 460
Daybreak 160
Detour 214
Die Xue Shuang Xiong 781
Dirty Harry 547
Dog Day Afternoon 595
Double Indemnity 204-205
Dr. Mabuse, der Spieler 43
Dr. Mabuse, Parts 1 and 2 43
Drugstore Cowboy 779
Enter the Dragon 569
Farewell My Lovely 206
Fargo 864-865
Fish Called Wanda, A 766
Force of Evil 237
French Connection, The 545
Gangs of New York 942
Get Carter 544
Godfather, Part II, The 592-593
Godfather, The 558
Goodfellas 790
Great Train Robbery, The 28-29
Gun Crazy 248
Harder They Come, The 582
Heat 856
Heavenly Creatures 847
Henry: Portrait of a Serial Killer 798
Hole, The 376
I Am a Fugitive from a Chain Gang 101
JFK 810-811
Jour se lève, Le 160
Killer, The 781
Killers, The 223
King of New York 791
Klute 541
L.A. Confidential 874
Lady from Shanghai, The 240
Ladykillers, The 316
Last Seduction, The 842
Lavender Hill Mob, The 266
Little Caeser 88
Lock, Stock, and Two Smoking Barrels 888
Lone Star 870
Long Goodbye, The 572
M 96-97
Man Bites Dog 825
Manchurian Candidate, The 409
Mean Streets 570-571
Memento 924
Money 699
Murder, My Sweet 206
Natural Born Killers 842
Neuve Reinas 912
Nine Queens 912
O Brother, Where Art Thou? 926
Odd Man Out 232
On the Waterfront 296-297

Once Upon a Time in America 705
Out of the Past 231
Pépé le Moko 145
Pickpocket 372-373
Pink Flamingos 563
Point Blank 478
Postman Always Rings Twice, The 217
Prizzi's Honor 728
Public Enemy, The 95
Pulp Fiction 843
Quatre Cent Coups, Les 360
Question of Silence, A 693
Rashomon 256-257
Resevoir Dogs 818
Rope 239
Scarface 706
Scarface: The Shame of a Nation 104
Serpico 575
Shaft 546
Stilte Rond Christine M., De 693
Sting, The 564
Straw Dogs 550
Superfly 564
Targets 501
Taxi Driver 616-617
Thelma and Louise 808
Touch of Evil 350-351
Traffic 922
Trou, Le 376
Uccello dalle Piume di Cristallo, L' 533
Untouchables, The 756
Usual Suspects, The 862
Vampires, Les 32-33
White Heat 251
Wrong Man, The 335
Xich Lo 859


## DOCU-DRAMA


Close-up 796
Kandahar 929
Louisiana Story 245
Nema-Ye Nazdik 796
Safar e Ghandehar 929
W.R.—Misterje Organizma 534
W.R.—Mysteries of the Organism 534


## DOCUMENTARY


Aileen Wuornos: The Selling of a Serial Killer 824
Battle of San Pietro, The 207
Chagrin et la Pitié, Le 538
Chelovek s kinoapparatom 78-79
Chronicle of a Summer 401
Chronique d'un été 401
Crumb 846
Deseret 851
Dog's Life, A 403
Fast, Cheap & Out of Control 877
Fires Were Started 192
Gimme Shelter 532
Glaneurs et la Glaneuse, Les 923
Gleaners and I, The 923
Häxan 48
Hearts of Darkness: A Filmmaker's Apocalypse 814-815
High School 514
Histoire de Vent, Une 772
Hoop Dreams 836-837
Hôtel Terminus:Klaus Barbie et Son Temps 765
Hotel Terminus:The Life and Times of Klaus Barbie 765
House is Black, The 425
Hurdes, Las 114
In the Year of the Pig 515
Khaneh Siah Ast 425
Koyaanisqatsi 704
Land Without Bread 114
Mad Masters, The 315
Maîtres fous, Les 315
Man with a Movie Camera, The 78-79
Méditerranée 425
Mondo cane 403
Nanook of the North 44-45
Night and Fog 323
Nuit et Brouillard 323
Olympia 1: Teil—Fest Der Volker & Olympia 2: Teil—Fest Der Schönheit 147
Olympia Part 1: Festival of the Nations & Part 2: Festival of Beauty 147
Roger & Me 784
Sans Soleil 698
Sherman's March 744
Shoah 730
Sorrow and the Pity, The 538
Sunless 698
Tale of the Wind, A 772
Thin Blue Line, The 763
Tokyo Olympiad 445
Tokyo Orimpikku 445
Tongues Untied 813
Triumph des Willens 118-119
Triumph of the Will 118-119
Woodstock 524-525


## DRAMA


1900 620
2 ou 3 Choses Que Je Sais D'Elle 467
8½ 416-417
À Ma Soeur! 937
A One and a Two 916
Accidental Tourist, The 775
Actor's Revenge, An 428
Actress, The 826
Adaptation 947
Affair to Remember, An 340
Affaire de Femmes, Une 775
Age of Innocence 831
Aguirre, Der Zorn Gottes 552
Aguirre: The Wrath of God 552
Ai No Corrida 619
Albero degli Zoccoli, L' 641
Ali Zaoua, Prince de la Rue 914
Ali Zaoua, Prince of the Streets 914
Ali: Fear Eats the Soul 594
All About Eve 259
All About My Mother 900-901
All Quiet on the Western Front 89
All That Heaven Allows 332-333
All That Jazz 655
Alphaville 448
Alphaville, une Étrange Aventure de Lemmy Caution 448
Amadeus 707
Amélie 927
American Beauty 906-907
American Friend, The 635
American Graffiti 568
Amerikanische Freund, Der 635
Amores Perros 918
Anatomy of a Murder 364
Andrei Rublev 518
Andrei Rublyov 518
And Your Mother Too 928
Angst Essen Seele Auf 594
Animal Farm 299
Aparajito 344

Apartment, The 390-391
Apocalypse Now 658-659
Apur Sansar 368-369
Ariel 762
Artificial Intelligence: A.I. 944
Ascent, The 619
Ashes and Diamonds 356
Astenicheskij Sindrom 785
Asthenic Syndrome, The 785
Au Hasard Balthazar 466
Au revoir les enfants 753
Autumn Afternoon, An 405
Ba Wang Bie Ji 827
Babbete's Gaestebud 749
Bab El Hadid 352
Babe 852
Babette's Feast 749
Bad and the Beautiful, The 278
Bad Ma Ra Khahad Bord 902
Badkonake Sefid 858
Badlands 566-567
Ballad of Narayama, The 707
Balthazar 466
Barefoot Contessa, The 302
Barren Lives 424
Barry Lyndon 602
Battaglia di Algeri, La 446
Battle of Algiers, The 446
Battleship Potemkin 58-59
Beau travail 897
Beauty and the Beast 221
Before the Revolution 438
Being There 656
Beiqing Chengshi 788
Belle de Jour 472-473
Belle noiseuse, La 805
Ben-Hur 371
Bharat Mata 346
Bicycle Thief, The 233
Big Chill, The 697
Big Red One, The 670
Bigamist, The 281
Bigger Than Life 335
Birth of a Nation, The 30-31
Biruma No Tategoto 327
Bitch, The 98
Bitter Tea of General Yen, The 116
Bitter Tears of Petra von Kant, The 561
Bitteren Tränen der Petra von Kant, Die 561
Black God, White Devil 441
Black Narcissus 227
Black Orpheus 366
Blade Runner 684-685
Blaue Engel, Der 82-83
Blechtrommel, Die 654
Blowup 456-457
Blue Angel, The 82-83
Blue Kite, The 834
Boat, The 675
Boogie Nights 879
Boot, Das 675
Boucher, Le 519
Bram Stoker's Dracula 822
Brave-Hearted Will Take the Bride, The 860
Breakfast at Tiffany's 396
Breakfast Club, The 717
Breaking Away 654
Breaking the Waves 867
Bridge on the River Kwai, The 345
Brief Encounter 216
Brighter Summer Day, A 803
Broadcast News 754
Broken Blossoms 38
Bronenosets Potyomkin 58-59
Büchse der Pandora, Die 80-81
Buffalo 66 888
Bull Durham 762
Burmese Harp, The 327
Butcher Boy, The 877
Butcher, The 519
Cabaret 553
Cairo Station 352
Camille 135
Campanadas a Medianoche 449
Captive, La 912
Captive, The 912
Caravaggio 741
Carmen Jones 307
Caro Diario 850
Carrosse d'or, Le 281
Casablanca 184-185
Ceddo 635
Celebration, The 885
Celine and Julie Go Boating 590
Céline et Julie Vont en Bateau 590
Chant of Jimmy Blacksmith, The 640
Chariots of Fire 676
Charme Discret de la Bourgeoisie, Le 560
Chienne, La 98
Children of a Lesser God 739
Children of Paradise, The 210
Chimes at Midnight 449
Chong Qing Sen Lin 845
Chuen Gwong Tsa Sit 875
Chungking Express 845
Cidade de Deus 945
Cinema Paradiso 765
Citizen Kane 172-173
City of God 945
City of Sadness, A 788
Cléo de 5 à 7 404
Cleo from 5 to 7 404
Clerks 839
Close Encounters of the Third Kind 624
Closely Watched Trains 486-487
Cloud-Clapped Star, The 384
Color of Pomegranates, The 520
Color Purple, The 731
Come and See 720
Come Drink With Me 460
Condamné à Mort s'échappé ou Le Vent Souffle où Il Veut, Un 330
Conte d'hiver 823
Contempt 418
Conversation, The 584
Cook, the Thief, His Wife, & Her Lover, The 779
Cool Hand Luke 476-477
Cool World, The 415
Cow, The 489
Cría Cuervos 609
Cria! 609
Cries and Whispers 559
Crimes and Misdemeanors 778
Crouching Tiger Hidden Dragon 920-921
Crowd, The 72
Crying Game, The 824
Csillagosok, Katonák 482
Czlowiek Z Marmuru 630
Czlowiek z Zelaza 680
Da Hong Deng Long Gao Gao Gua 802
Da Zui Xia 460
Daisies 460
Dance, Girl, Dance 169
Dancer in the Dark 925
Dangerous Liaisons 768
Dao Ma Zei 745
David Holzman's Diary 496
Day for Night 573
Day in the Country, A 130
Days of Heaven 645
De Man Die Zijin Haar Kort Liet Knippen 455
Dead, The 757
Dear Diary 850
Decalogue, The 770
Déclin de l'Empire Américain, Le 735
Decline of the American Empire 735
Deep End 526
Deer Hunter, The 642-643
Deewar 600
Defiant Ones, The 353
Dekalog, Jeden 770
Dernier Metro, Le 665
Dersu Uzala 583
Deserto Rosso, Il 437
Deus E O Diabo Na Terra Do Sol 441
Diary of a Country Priest 268
Dilwale Dulhaniya le Jayenge 860
Diner 688-689
Discreet Charm of the Bourgeoisie, The 560
Do the Right Thing 782-783
Docks of New York, The 73
Dodsworth 136
Dog Star Man 404
Dolce Vita, La 378-379
Double Life of Veronique, The 816
Double Vie de Véronique, La 816
Down By Law 738
Dr. Zhivago 444
Dut Yeung Nin Wa 913
Madame de... 283
Ear, The 528-529
Earth 86-87
Earth Entranced 485
Eclipse, The 405
Eclisse, L' 405
Edward Scissorhands 797
Ehe Der Maria Braun, Die 650
El Norte 695
Elephant Man, The 669
Enfants du Paradis, Les 210
English Patient, The 868
Eraserhead 634
Espíritu del la Colmena, El 579
Europa '51 277
Europa Europa 793
Eyes Wide Shut 909
Fabuleax Destin d'Amélie Poulain 927

Faces 491
Fanny and Alexander 694
Far from Heaven 948
Farewell My Concubine 827
Fast Times at Ridgemont High 681
Faster Pussycat! Kill, Kill! 453
Fat City 560
Fat Girl 937
Faustrecht Der Freiheit 603
Festen 885
Fight Club 904
Fitzcarraldo 690-691
Five Easy Pieces 522
Floating Weeds 377
Foolish Wives 49
Forbidden Games 272
Forbidden Planet 326
Fox and His Friends 603
Full Metal Jacket 750-751
Funny Games 881
Gaav 489
Gabbeh 869
Gallipoli 676
Gangs of New York 942
Garden of the Finzi-Continis, The 535
Gattopardo, Il 422-423
Gertrud 439
Ghandi 692
Giant 331
Giardino dei Finzi-Contini, Il 535
Giulietta deglie Spiriti 451
Gladiator 915
Glengarry Glen Ross 819
Glory 784
Gohatto 899
Golden Coach, The 281
Golden River 454
Goodbye Children 753
Gospel According to St. Matthew, The 440
Graduate, The 468-469
Grand Illusion 140
Grande Illusion, La 140
Grapes of Wrath, The 168
Grave of the Fireflies 768
Great Expectations 224-225
Greed 52-53
Guling Jie Shaonian Sha Ren Shijian 803
Hable con ella 944
Happiness 891
Happy Together 875
Harder They Come, The 582
Hayno 385
Heat 856
Heiress, The 246
Henry V 202
Hill 24 Doesn't Answer 315
Himmel über Berlin, Der 746-747
Hitlerjunge Salomon 793
Hong Gao Liang 757
Horse Thief, The 745
Hotaru No Haka 768
Housekeeping 755
Housemaid, The 385
How Green Was My Valley 182
Hsi Yen 834
Hsimeng Jensheng 831
Hustler, The 402
I Am a Fugitive from a Chain Gang 101
Ice Storm, The 878
Idi I Smotri 720
Idioterne 894
Idiots, The 894
If... 494
Ikiru 276
In the Heat of the Night 461
In the Mood for Love 913
In the Realm of the Senses 619
India Song 604
Intolerance 34-35
It's a Gift 117
Ivan Groznyj I 203
Ivan the Terrible, I 203
Jalsaghar 358-359
Jazz Singer, The 70
Jean Dielman... 597
Jeux interdits 272
Jezebel 145
Journal d'un curé de campagne 268
Joven, La 384
Jules and Jim 398
Jules et Jim 398
Juliet of the Spirits 451
Keeper of Promises 410
Kes 521
Killer of Sheep 632-633
Killing Fields, The 716
Killing of a Chinese Bookie, The 613
King of Comedy, The 702
King of New York 791
Kippur 916
Kiss of the Spider Woman 726
Kjælighetens Kjøtere 856
Körkarlen 41
Kramer vs. Kramer 657
Kumonosu Jo 343
Kundun 880
La Belle et la Bête 221
Ladri di biciclette 233
Landscape in the Mist 769
Lan Feng Zheng 834
Last Chants for a Slow Dance 628
Last Laugh, The 56
Last Metro, The 665
Last Picture Show, The 549
Last Seduction, The 842
Last Tango in Paris 553
Lawrence of Arabia 406-407
Le Mépris 418
Leopard, The 422-423
Letter from an Unknown Woman 234-235
Letzte Mann, Der 56
Life of Emile Zola, The 141
Lola 396
Lola Montès 326
Lolita 409
Lost Weekend, The 212-213
Loulou 670
Lucía 504
Ma Nuit Chez Maud 504
Magnificent Ambersons, The 188-189
Magnolia 896
Make Way for Tomorrow 142
Maman et la Putain, La 565
Man Escaped, A 330
Man in Grey, The 193
Man of Iron 680
Man of Marble 630
Man who had his hair cut short, The 455
Man Who Knew Too Much, The 331
Manhattan 661

Manila in the Claws of Brightness 605
Marketa Lazarová 483
Marriage of Maria Braun, The 650
Marty 316
Masculine-Feminine 466
Masculin-Féminin 466
Mat I Syn 883
Maynila: Sa Mga Kuko Ng Liwanag 605
Még Kér A Nép 544
Meghe Dhaka Tara 384
Memorias del Subdesarrollo 495
Memories of Underdevelopment 495
Metropolis 62-63
Midnight Cowboy 507
Mirror 586
Mishima: A Life in Four Chapters 728
Monsoon Wedding 936
Mortal Storm, The 170
Mother and Son 883
Mother and the Whore, The 565
Mother India 346
Moulin Rouge! 934-935
Mr. Smith Goes to Washington 153
Mujeres al Borde de un Ataque de Nervios 759
Murmur of the Heart 547
Music Room, The 358-359
Mutiny on the Bounty 126
My Brilliant Career 651
My Left Foot 780
My Life to Live 412
My Night with Maud 504
My Own Private Idaho 806-807
Naked Lunch 804
Napoléon 71
Narayama Bushi-Ko 707
Nashville 608
Nattvardsgästerna 419
Natural Born Killers 842
Natural, The 716
Network 618
Ni Neibian Jidian 928
Night of the Shooting Stars, The 693
Night, The 397
Nights of Cabiria, The 342
No Fear, No Die 789
No Man's Land 933
Notte di San Lorenzo, La 693
Notte, La 397
Notti of Cabiria, Le 342
Novecento 620
Now, Voyager 183
Nuit Américaine, La 573
Nuovo Cinema Paradiso 765
O Pagador De Promessas 410
October 68-69
Official Story, The 721
Oktyabr 68-69
Olvidados, Los 262
On the Waterfront 296-297
One Flew Over the Cuckoo's Nest 596
Only Angels Have Wings 157
Open City 211
Obchod Na Korze 443
Ordet 317
Ordinary People 664
Orfeu Negro 366
Orphans of the Storm 42
Ossessione 197
Ostre Sledované Vlaky 486-487
O Thiassos 610-611
Out of Africa 721
Paisà 217
Paisan 217
Pandora and the Flying Dutchman 266
Pandora's Box 80-81
Papillon 569
Paris, Texas 710
Partie de Campagne, Une 130
Pasazerka 418
Passage to India, A 714
Passenger 418
Passion de Jeanne d'Arc, La 75
Passion of Joan of Arc, The 75
Pather Panchali 312-313
Paths of Glory 348
Patton 530
Performance 531
Persona 464-465
Phantom Carriage, The 41
Philadelphia 829
Pianist, The 943
Pianiste, La 932
Piano Teacher, The 932
Piano, The 833
Picnic at Hanging Rock 604
Pierrot le Fou 452
Pillow Book, The 863
Platoon 740
Player, The 817
Playtime 470
Popiól I Diament 356
Potomok Chingis-Khana 76
Prima Della Rivoluzione 438
Prizzi's Honor 728
Public Enemy, The 95
Pulp Fiction 843
Puppetmaster, The 831
Queen Christina 114
Quiet Earth, The 727
Raging Bull 672-673
Rain Man 774
Raise the Red Lantern 802
Ran 718-719
Rapture, The 805
Rebel Without a Cause 320-321
Red and the White, The 482
Red Desert, The 437
Red Psalm 544
Red Shoes, The 242-243
Red Sorghum 757
Reds 678
Règle du Jeu, La 162-163
Rekopis Znaleziony w Saragossie 447
Requiem for a Dream 917
Reversal of Fortune 789
Right Stuff, The 703
Road, The 303
Rocco and his Brothers 377
Rocco e i suoi fratelli 377
Rocky 615
Roma, Città Aperta 211
Roman Holiday 286
Romper Stomper 819
Room with a View, A 739
Roseaux Sauvages, Les 844
Rosemary's Baby 492-493
Rosetta 899
Roue, La 50
Royal Tennenbaums, The 939
Rules of the Game, The 162-163
Russian Ark 946
Russkij Kovcheg 946
Safe 854
Salò o le centoventi giornate di sodoma 606-607
Salo, or The 120 days of Sodom 606-607
Salt of the Earth 310
Salvador 742
Sanma No Aji 405
Sans Toit Ni Loi 729
Sanshô Dayû 308-309
Sansho the Baliff 308-309
Saragossa Manuscript 447
Såsom I En Spegel 400
Sátántangó 841
Saturday Night and Sunday Morning 380
Saturday Night Fever 631
Satyricon 508-509
Saving Private Ryan 886-887
Sayat Nova 520
Say Anything 787
Schindler's List 832
Se7en 857
Secrets & Lies 866
Sedmikrasky 460
S'en Fout La Mort 789
Sen To Chihiro No Kamikakushi 930-931
Senso 306
Sergeant York 178
Servant, The 428
Seven Samurai, The 304-305
Seventh Seal, The 338-339
Sex, lies, and videotape 786
Shadows 367
Shadows of Our Forgotten Ancestors 437
Shaft 546
Shame 497
Shanghai Express 105
Shao Lin San Shih Liu Fang 647
Shaolin Master Killer 647
Shawshank Redemption, The 844
Shock Corridor 421
Shop on Main Street, The 443
Short Cuts 829
Signs & Wonders 919
Sin of Lola Montes, The 326
Sjunde Inseglet, Det 338-339
Skammen 497
Slacker 812
Smiling Madame Beudet, The 42
Smoke 858
Smultronstället 341
Snake Pit, The 240
Solaris 556-557
Soldaat Van Oranje 638
Soldier of Orange 638
Solyaris 556-557
Sombre 894
Son's Room, The 932
Souffle Au Coeur, Le 547

Souriante Madame Beudet, La 42
Spartacus 392
Spider's Stratagem, The 526
Spirit of the Beehive, The 579
Spirited Away 930-931
Splendor in the Grass 392
Spring in a Small Town 237
Stachka 51
Stagecoach 150-151
Stand By Me 732
Stanza del Figlio, La 932
Star is Born, A 302
Stella Dallas 141
Storm over Asia 76
Story of the Late Chrysanthemums, The 152
Story of Women, The 775
Strada, La 303
Stranger than Paradise 715
Strategia del Ragno, La 526
Streetcar Named Desire, A 264
Strike 51
Stroszek 629
Subarnarekha 454
Suna No Onna 433
Sunrise 64-65
Superfly 564
Sweet Hereafter, The 880
Sweet Sweetback's Badasssss Song 548
Tabu 91
Tale of Winter, A 823
Tales of Ugetsu 293
Talk to Her 944
Ta'm e Guilass 882
Taste of Cherry 882
Taxi Driver 616-617
Temps retrouvé, Le 904
Ten Commandments, The 336
Terms of Endearment 701
Terra Em Transe 485
The 39 Steps, The 128
The Beautiful Troublemaker 805
The Wall 600
Thelma and Louise 808
Thin Red Line, The 892-893
Thirty Two Short Films About Glenn Gould 827
Three Brothers 679
Three Colors: Blue 833
Three Colors: Red 835
Throne of Blood 343
Through a Glass Darkly 400
Through the Olive Trees 848
Time Regained 904
Time to Live and the Time to Die, The 723
Tin Drum, The 654
Tini Zabutykh Predkiv 437
Titanic 884
To Kill A Mockingbird 408
To Live 276
Todo Sobre Mi Madre 900-901
Tokyo Story 285
Tong Nien Wang Shi 723
Too Early, Too Late 681
Top Gun 743
Topio Stin Omichli 769
Trainspotting 871
Travelling Players 610-611
Tre Fratelli 679
Treasure of the Sierra Madre, The 244
Tree of Wooden Clogs, The 641
Tristana 521
Trois Couleurs: Bleu 833
Trois Couleurs: Rouge 835
Trust 795
Turkish Delight 578
Turks Fruit 578
Two or Three Things I Know About Her 467
Two-Lane Blacktop 551
Ucho 528-529
Ugetsu Monogatari 293
Ukigusa 377
Ultimo Tango a Parigi 553
Umberto D 280
Unbelievable Truth, The 787
Untouchables, The 756
Unvanquished, The 344
Utu 700
Vagabond 729
Vangelo Secondo Matteo, Il 440
Vidas Secas 424
Viridiana 399
Viskingar och Rop 559
Vivre Sa Vie: Film en Douze Tableaux 412
Voskhozhdenie 619
Voyage in Italy 292
Walkabout 540
Wanda 535
Way Down East 39
Wedding Banquet, The 834
Week End 474
West Side Story 402
What Time Is It There? 928
Wheel, The 50
White Balloon, The 858
Who's Afraid of Virginia Woolf 462-463
Wild Reeds 844
Wild Strawberries 341
Wind Will Carry Us, The 902
Wings of Desire 746-747
Winter Light 419
Within Our Gates 40
Wo Hu Cang Long 920-921
Woman in the Dunes, The 433
Woman Under the Influence, A 587
Women on the Verge of a Nervous Breakdown 759
World of Apu, The 368-369
Written on the Wind 330
Wuthering Heights 164
Xiao cheng zhi chun 237
Y tu mama tambien 928
Yi yi 916
Yol 687
Young and the Damned, The 262
Young One, The 384
Yuen Ling-yuk 826
Yukinojo Henge 428
Zabriskie Point 533
Zangiku monogatari 152
Zemlya 86-87
Zerkalo 586
Zero Kelvin 856
Zire Darakhatan Zeyton 848
Zu Fruh, Zu Spat 681


## EXPERIMENTAL


Blonde Cobra 415
Dead Man 861
Deseret 851
Flaming Creatures 420
Heaven and Earth Magic 412
Hold Me While I'm Naked 455
Meshes of the Afternoon 191
Report 471
Scorpio Rising 430
Too Early, Too Late 681
Vinyl 442
Wavelength 479
Zu Fruh, Zu Spat 681


## FANTASY


Andalusian Dog, An 74
Batman 776
Brightness 745

Chinese Ghost Story, A 758
Empire Strikes Back, The 668
Eraserhead 634
Ghost and Mrs. Muir, The 232
Groundhog Day 828
Himmel über Berlin, Der 746-747
King Kong 115
Lord of the Rings: The Fellowship of the Ring, The 940
Matter of Life and Death, A 223
Orphée 255
Orpheus 255
Princess Bride, The 755
Purple Rose of Cairo, The 722
Return of the Jedi 697
Russian Ark 946
Russkij Kovcheg 946
Seventh Seal, The 338-339
Sinnui Yauman 758
Sjunde Inseglet, Det 338-339
Suspiria 639
Un chien andalou 74
Videodrome 696
Wings of Desire 756-747
Wizard of Oz, The 154-155
Yeelen 745


## FAMILY


Adventures of Robin Hood, The 146
Babe 852
Back to the Future 723
Big 767
Brave-Hearted Will Take the Bride, The 860
Bringing Up Baby 149
Christmas Story, A 695
Day the Earth Stood Still, The 270
Dilwale Dulhaniya le Jayenge 860
Duck Soup 112-113
Dumbo 178
E.T. the Extra-Terrestrial 682
Fantasia 166
Gold Rush, The 60
It's a Wonderful Life 228-229
Jungle Book, The 483
Kid Brother, The 71
Lion King, The 840
Muppet Movie, The 660
My Fair Lady 433
Night at the Opera, A 127
Our Hospitality 49
Pinocchio 169
Princess Bride, The 755
Sen To Chihiro No Kamikakushi 930-931
Seven Chances 56
Sherlock Jr. 54-55
Snow White and the Seven Dwarfs 143
Sound of Music, The 447
Spirited Away 930-931
Steamboat Bill, Jr. 76
Ten Commandments, The 336
Thief of Bagdad, The 50
Toy Story 853
Willy Wonka and the Chocolate Factory 538
Wizard of Oz, The 154-155


## FANTASY


Alice 776
Amélie 927
Artificial Intelligence: A.I. 944
Beauty and the Beast 221
Being John Malkovich 905
Big 767
Brazil 724-725
Cabinet of Dr. Caligari, The 36-37
Celine and Julie Go Boating 590
Céline et Julie Vont en Bateau 590
Crouching Tiger Hidden Dragon 920-921
Dawn of the Dead 646
Double Life of Veronique, The 816
Double Vie de Véronique, La 816
E.T. the Extra-Terrestrial 682
Edward Scissorhands 797
Evil Dead, The 686
Fabuleax Destin d'Amélie Poulain 927
Fantasia 166
Ghost Busters 713
Giulietta deglie Spiriti 451
India Song 604
It's a Wonderful Life 228-229
Juliet of the Spirits 451
Kabinett des Doktor Caligari, Das 36-37
La Belle et la Bête 221
Last Wave, The 625
Mononoke Hime 876
Monty Python and the Holy Grail 601
Naked Lunch 804
Neco z Alenky 776
Night of the Shooting Stars, The 693
Notte di San Lorenzo, La 693
Performance 531
Princess Mononoke 876
Rekopis Znaleziony w Saragossie 447
Saragossa Manuscript 447
Sen To Chihiro No Kamikakushi 930-931
Spirited Away 930-931
Star Wars 622-623
Toy Story 853
Who Framed Roger Rabbit 773
Willy Wonka and the Chocolate Factory 538
Wo Hu Cang Long 920-921


## HORROR


Alien 653
Aliens 737
American Werewolf in London 679

Audition, The 903
Bird with the Crystal Plumage, The 533
Birds, The 413
Black Cat, The 121
Blair Witch Project, The 898
Boucher, Le 519
Bram Stoker's Dracula 822
Bride of Frankenstein 129
Butcher, The 519
Cabinet of Dr. Caligari, The 36-37
Candyman 823
Carrie 613
Cat People 187
C'est arrivé près de chez vouz 825
Chinese Ghost Story, A 758
Cook, the Thief, His Wife, & Her Lover, The 779
Dawn of the Dead 646
Deliverance 555
Diaboliques, Les 298
Don't Look Now 574
Dr. Mabuse, der Spieler 43
Dr. Mabuse, Parts 1 and 2 43
Dracula 357
Dracula 92-93
Eraserhead 634
Evil Dead, The 686
Exorcist, The 576-577
Eyes Without a Face 365
Fly, The 736
Frankenstein 94
Freaks 106
Funny Games 881
Halloween 648-649
Haunting, The 426-427
Häxan 48
Henry: Portrait of a Serial Killer 798
Hills Have Eyes, The 636-637
Hour of the Wolf 500
I Walked with a Zombie 194
Invasion of the Body Snatchers 334
Jacob's Ladder 791
Jaws 612
Jurassic Park 830
Kabinett des Doktor Caligari, Das 36-37
King Kong 115
Kingdom, The 849
Man Bites Dog 825
Manhunter 732
Maschera del Demonio, La 388
Black Sunday 388
Masque of the Red Death, The 438
Midnight Song 139
Mulholland Dr. 938
Night of the Living Dead 502-503
Nightmare on Elm Street, A 711
Nosferatu, a Symphony of Terror 46-47
Nosferatu, eine Symphonie des Grauens 46-47
Nosferatu: Phantom der Nacht 663
Odishon 903
One Flew Over the Cuckoo's Nest 596
Onibaba 442
Peeping Tom 389
Phantom of the Opera, The 57
Poltergeist 683
Psycho 386-387
Repulsion 450
Riget 849
Ring 895
Rocky Horror Picture Show, The 598-599
Rosemary's Baby 492-493
Salò o le centoventi giornate di sodoma 606-607
Salo, or The 120 days of Sodom 606-607
Scream 872-873
Seventh Victim, The 194
Shining, The 666-667
Silence of the Lambs, The 809
Sinnui Yauman 758
Sixth Sense, The 910
Spoorloos 760-761
Suspiria 639
Terminator, The 708-709
Tetsuo 885
Texas Chainsaw Massacre, The 585
Thing, The 683
Uccello dalle Piume di Cristallo, L' 533
Unknown, The 67
Vampire, The 99
Vampires, Les 32-33
Vampyr 99
Vanishing, The 760-761
Vargtimmen 500
Videodrome 696
Vij 488
What Ever Happened to Baby Jane? 411
Wicker Man, The 572
Wolf Man, The 175
Ye Ban Ge Sheng 139
Yeux Sans Visage, Les 365
Young Frankenstein 587

## MUSICAL

42nd Street 108-109
All That Jazz 655
American In Paris, An 268
Artists and Models 310
Babes in Arms 152
Band Wagon, The 282
Cabaret 553
Carmen Jones 307
Chicago 949
Dancer in the Dark 925
Demoiselles de Rochefort, Les 474
Duck Soup 112-113
Dumbo 178
Fantasia 166
Footlight Parade 110
Gentlemen Prefer Blondes 289
Gigi 353
Gimme Shelter 532
Gold Diggers of 1933 110
Grease 644
Guys and Dolls 311
Hard Day's Night, A 436
High Society 336
Jungle Book, The 483
Lion King, The 840
Love Me Tonight 100
Meet Me in St. Louis 198-199
Moulin Rouge! 934-935
Muppet Movie, The 660
My Fair Lady 433
Nashville 608
Night at the Opera, A 127
On the Town 254
Parapluies de Cherbourg, Les 431
Producers, The 496
Rocky Horror Picture Show, The 598-599
Russian Ark 946
Russkij Kovcheg 946
Saturday Night Fever 631
Seven Brides for Seven Brothers 298
Singin' in the Rain 274-275
Snow White and the Seven Dwarfs 143
Sound of Music, The 447
Star is Born, A 302
Swing Time 132
Top Hat 130
Umbrellas of Cherbourg, The 431
West Side Story 402
Willy Wonka and the Chocolate Factory 538
Wizard of Oz, The 154-155
Woodstock 524-525
Yankee Doodle Dandy 190
Young Girls of Rochefort, The 474

## MYSTERY

12 Angry Men 337
Adventure, The 382-383
Alphaville 448
Alphaville, une Étrange Aventure de Lemmy Caution 448
American Friend, The 635
Amerikanische Freund, Der 635
Anatomy of a Murder 364
Année dernière à Marienbad, L' 393
Avventura, L' 382-383
Big Sleep, The 222
Bird with the Crystal Plumage, The 533
Blair Witch Project, The 898
Blowup 456-457
Blue Velvet 733
Chinatown 588-589
Chong Qing Sen Lin 845
Chungking Express 845
Citizen Kane 172-173
Conversation, The 584
Diaboliques, Les 298
Don't Look Now 574
Double Indemnity 204-205
Dr. Mabuse, der Spieler 43
Dr. Mabuse, Parts 1 and 2 43
Eyes Wide Shut 909
Gaslight 202
In a Lonely Place 263
In the Heat of the Night 461
Jacob's Ladder 791
JFK 810-811
Kingdom, The 849
Klute 541

L.A. Confidential 874
Last Wave, The 625
Last Year at Marienbad 393
Laura 201
Lone Star 870
Maltese Falcon, The 176-177
Memento 924
Mildred Pierce 208-209
Mulholland Dr. 938
Neuve Reinas 912
Nine Queens 912
Picnic at Hanging Rock 604
Rapture, The 805
Rashomon 256-257
Rear Window 300-301
Rebecca 165
Riget 849
Scream 872-873
Se7en 857
Seconds 461
Sixth Sense, The 910
Sleuth 554
Spellbound 207
Spider's Stratagem, The 526
Spoorloos 760-761
Stalker 652
Strange Days 853
Strategia del Ragno, La 526
The 39 Steps, The 128
Thin Man, The 124-125
Third Man, The 252-253
Uccello dalle Piume di Cristallo, L' 533
Usual Suspects, The 862
Vanishing, The 760-761
Vertigo 354-355
Wicker Man, The 572
Z 510

### NOIR

Angel Face 273
Asphalt Jungle, The 255
Big Carnival, The 263
Big Heat, The 290
Big Sleep, The 222
Detour 214
Double Indemnity 204-205
Farewell My Lovely 206
Fargo 864-865
Force of Evil 237
Gilda 230
Gun Crazy 248
High Sierra 179
I Am a Fugitive from a Chain Gang 101
In a Lonely Place 263
Killers, The 223
Kiss Me Deadly 319
Lady from Shanghai, The 240
Laura 201
M 96-97
Maltese Falcon, The 176-177
Mildred Pierce 208-209
Murder, My Sweet 206
Night of the Hunter, The 324-325
Notorious 226
Out of the Past 231
Phenix City Story, The 322
Pickup on South Street 288
Place in the Sun, A 269
Postman Always Rings Twice, The 217
Reckless Moment, The 251
Secret Beyond the Door 236
Shadow of a Doubt 196
Spellbound 207
Stranger, The 220
Strangers on a Train 265
Sunset Blvd. 260-261
Sweet Smell of Success 348
Third Man, The 252-253
Touch of Evil 350-351
White Heat 251
Wrong Man, The 335

### POLITICAL

1900 620
Conformist, The 511
Conformista, Il 511
Novecento 620

### POLITICAL THRILLER

All the President's Men 614
JFK 810-811
Manchurian Candidate, The 409
Z 510

### ROMANCE

42nd Street 108-109
Abre Los Ojos 883
Accidental Tourist, The 775
Actress, The 826
Adventure, The 382-383
Affair to Remember, An 340
African Queen, The 267
Age d'or, L' 84-85
Age of Gold, The 84-85
Ali: Fear Eats the Soul 594
All That Heaven Allows 332-333
Alphaville 448
Alphaville, une Étrange Aventure de Lemmy Caution 448
Amélie 927
American In Paris, An 268
American Werewolf in London 679
And Your Mother Too 928
Angst Essen Seele Auf 594
Année dernière à Marienbad, L' 393
Annie Hall 626-627
Apartment, The 390-391
Ariel 762
Artists and Models 310
Atalante, L' 120
Atlantic City 665
Avventura, L' 382-383
Awful Truth, The 144
Ba Wang Bie Ji 827
Band Wagon, The 282
Barry Lyndon 602
Beat the Devil 295
Ben-Hur 371
Best Years of Our Lives, The 215
Big Parade, The 61
Birds, The 413
Bram Stoker's Dracula 822
Braveheart 854
Brave-Hearted Will Take the Bride, The 860
Breakfast at Tiffany's 396
Breaking the Waves 867
Breathless 370
Brief Encounter 216
Brighter Summer Day, A 803
Bringing Up Baby 149
Broadcast News 754
Broken Blossoms 38
Bull Durham 762
Camille 135
Casablanca 184-185
Cat People 187
Children of Paradise, The 210
Chinese Ghost Story, A 758
Chong Qing Sen Lin 845
Chungking Express 845
Cinema Paradiso 765
City Lights 95
Clueless 855
Cook, the Thief, His Wife, & Her Lover, The 779
Cranes are Flying, The 347
Crouching Tiger Hidden Dragon 920-921
Crying Game, The 824
Dangerous Liaisons 768
Day in the Country, A 130
Delicatessen 802
Dilwale Dulhaniya le Jayenge 860
Dodsworth 136
Dr. Zhivago 444
Dut Yeung Nin Wa 913
Edward Scissorhands 797
Enfants du Paradis, Les 210
English Patient, The 868
Fabuleax Destin d'Amélie Poulain 927
Far from Heaven 948
Farewell My Concubine 827
Fatal Attraction 758
Four Weddings and a Funeral 839
From Here to Eternity 284
General, The 66
Ghost and Mrs. Muir, The 232
Giulietta deglie Spiriti 451
Gone with the Wind 158-159
Graduate, The 468-469
Groundhog Day 828
Guling Jie Shaonian Sha Ren Shijian 803
Hable con ella 944
Hannah and Her Sisters 734
Hard Day's Night, A 436
Harold and Maude 542-543
Heiress, The 246
Himmel über Berlin, Der 746-747
Hiroshima mon amour 374
His Girl Friday 164
How Green Was My Valley 182
Hsi Yen 834
I Know Where I'm Going! 214
In a Lonely Place 263
In the Mood for Love 913
India Song 604
It Happened One Night 122-123
It's a Wonderful Life 228-229
Juliet of the Spirits 451
Kid Brother, The 71
Lady Eve, The 174
Last Tango in Paris 553
Last Year at Marienbad 393
Laura 201
Letjat Zhuravli 347
Life and Death of Colonel Blimp, The 193

Lolita 409
Man of the West 349
Manhattan 661
Marketa Lazarová 483
Marty 316
Matter of Life and Death, A 223
Me and My Gal 107
Mildred Pierce 208-209
Monsoon Wedding 936
Moonstruck 756
Moulin Rouge! 934-935
Mulholland Dr. 938
My Brilliant Career 651
My Fair Lady 433
Natural Born Killers 842
Night at the Opera, A 127
Ninotchka 161
North By Northwest 361
Notorious 226
Now, Voyager 183
Nuovo Cinema Paradiso 765
On the Waterfront 296-297
Open Your Eyes 883
Out of Africa 721
Parapluies de Cherbourg, Les 431
Partie de Campagne, Une 130
Pépé le Moko 145
Philadelphia Story, The 167
Piano, The 833
Pillow Book, The 863
Place in the Sun, A 269
Pretty Woman 794
Princess Bride, The 755
Prizzi's Honor 728
Producers, The 496
Purple Rose of Cairo, The 722
Queen Christina 114
Quiet Man, The 271
Rebecca 165
Red Shoes, The 242-243
Rio Bravo 375
Rio Grande 258
Roman Holiday 286
Room with a View, A 739
Rushmore 890
Russian Ark 946
Russkij Kovcheg 946
Saturday Night Fever 631
Say Anything 787
Seven Brides for Seven Brothers 298
She's Gotta Have It 735
Shoot the Piano Player 381
Singin' in the Rain 274-275
Sinnui Yauman 758
Smiles of a Summer Night 322
Some Like it Hot 362-363
Sommarnattens Leede 322
Spellbound 207
Stagecoach 150-151
Steamboat Bill, Jr. 76
Strictly Ballroom 816
Sullivan's Travels 180-181
Sunrise 64-65
Swing Time 132
Tabu 91
Talk to Her 944
There's Something About Mary 896
Tirez sur le pianiste 381
Titanic 884
Tootsie 686
Top Hat 130
Trouble in Paradise 102-103
Ultimo Tango a Parigi 553
Umbrellas of Cherbourg, The 431
Unknown, The 67
Way Down East 39
Wedding Banquet, The 834
West Side Story 402
When Harry Met Sally 777
Wings of Desire 756-747
Wo Hu Cang Long 920-921
Y tu mama tambien 928
Yuen Ling-yuk 826


## SCI-FI


2001 498-499
Abre Los Ojos 883
Akira 764
Alien 653
Aliens 737
Alphaville 448
Alphaville, une Étrange Aventure de Lemmy Caution 448
Artificial Intelligence: A.I. 941
Back to the Future 723
Blade Runner 684-685
Brazil 724-725
Bride of Frankenstein 129
Clockwork Orange, A 536-537
Close Encounters of the Third Kind 624
Dawn of the Dead 646
Day the Earth Stood Still, The 270
Delicatessen 802
Dernier Combat, Le 698
Dr. Strangelove 434-435
E.T. the Extra-Terrestrial 682
Empire Strikes Back, The 668
Fantastic Planet 579
Fly, The 736
Forbidden Planet 326
Frankenstein 94
Ghost Busters 713
Incredible Shrinking Man, The 343
Independence Day 866
Invasion of the Body Snatchers 334
Jetée, La 394
Jurassic Park 830
Last Battle, The 698
Mad Max 662
Man Who Fell to Earth, The 621
Matrix, The 911
Metropolis 62-63
Naked Lunch 804
Night of the Living Dead 502-503
Open Your Eyes 883
Pi 890
Pier, The 394
Planet of the Apes 490
Planète Sauvage, La 579
Quiet Earth, The 727
Return of the Jedi 697
Rocky Horror Picture Show, The 598-599
Seconds 461
Sleeper 575
Solaris 556-557
Solyaris 556-557
Stalker 652
Star Wars 622-623
Strange Days 853
Terminator 2: Judgment Day 808
Terminator, The 708-709
Tetsuo 885
Thing, The 683
Things to Come 137
Total Recall 799
Trip to the Moon, A 26-27
Videodrome 696
Voyage dans la Lune, Le 26-27
War Game, The 445


## SHORT


Andalusian Dog, An 74
Battle of San Pietro, The 207
Blonde Cobra 415
Day in the Country, A 130

Dog Star Man 404
Great Train Robbery, The 28-29
Hold Me While I'm Naked 455
House is Black, The 425
Hurdes, Las 114
Jetée, La 394
Khaneh Siah Ast 425
Land Without Bread 114
Mad Masters, The 315
Maîtres fous, Les 315
Meshes of the Afternoon 191
Night and Fog 323
Nuit et Brouillard 323
Partie de Campagne, Une 130
Pier, The 394
Report 471
Scorpio Rising 430
Sherlock Jr. 54-55
Trip to the Moon, A 26-27
Un chien andalou 74
Voyage dans la Lune, Le 26-27
Zéro de conduite 107
Zero for Conduct 107

**THRILLER**

12 Angry Men 337
Abre Los Ojos 883
Akira 764
Alien 653
Aliens 737
All the President's Men 614
Alphaville 448
Alphaville, une Étrange Aventure de Lemmy Caution 448
American Friend, The 635
Amerikanische Freund, Der 635
Amores Perros 918
Audition, The 903
Bad Day at Black Rock 314
Badlands 566-567
Batman 776
Big Heat, The 290
Bird with the Crystal Plumage, The 533
Birds, The 413
Blackmail 77
Blair Witch Project, The 898
Blowup 456-457
Blue Velvet 733
Body Heat 677
Boucher, Le 519
Bram Stoker's Dracula 822
Butcher, The 519
Candyman 823
Cat People 187
Chinatown 588-589
Conversation, The 584
Crying Game, The 824
Dawn of the Dead 646
Day the Earth Stood Still, The 270
Daybreak 160
Deliverance 555
Diaboliques, Les 298
Die Hard 771
Die Xue Shuang Xiong 781
Dirty Harry 547
Don't Look Now 574
Dr. Mabuse, der Spieler 43
Dr. Mabuse, Parts 1 and 2 43
Evil Dead, The 686
Eyes Wide Shut 909
Eyes Without a Face 365
Farewell My Lovely 206
Fargo 864-865
Fatal Attraction 758
Fight Club 904
Fourth Man, The 702
French Connection, The 545
Frenzy 562
Funny Games 881
Gaslight 202
Get Carter 544
Godfather, Part II, The 592-593
Godson, The 475
Goldfinger 429
Halloween 648-649
Haunting, The 426-427
Heat 856
Henry: Portrait of a Serial Killer 798
High Noon 279
High Sierra 179
Hole, The 376
Invasion of the Body Snatchers 334
Jacob's Ladder 791
Jaws 612
JFK 810-811
Jour se lève, Le 160
Jurassic Park 830
Killer, The 781
King Kong 115
Kiss Me Deadly 319
Klute 541
L.A. Confidential 874
Last Seduction, The 842
Last Wave, The 625
Lock, Stock, and Two Smoking Barrels 888
Lola Rennt 889
M 96-97
Man Who Knew Too Much, The 331
Manchurian Candidate, The 409
Manhunter 732
Marnie 432
Matrix, The 911
Memento 924
Mulholland Dr. 938
Murder, My Sweet 206
Night of the Hunter, The 324-325
Night of the Living Dead 502-503
Nightmare on Elm Street, A 711
North By Northwest 361
Notorious 226
Odd Man Out 232
Odishon 903
Once Upon a Time in America 705
Open Your Eyes 883
Out of the Past 231
Peeping Tom 389
Pi 890
Player, The 817
Point Blank 478
Poltergeist 683
Postman Always Rings Twice, The 217
Psycho 386-387
Pulp Fiction 843
Rear Window 300-301

Rebecca 165
Repulsion 450
Resevoir Dogs 818
Rope 239
Rosemary's Baby 492-493
Run Lola Run 889
Sabotage 135
Safe 854
Salaire De La Peur, La 287
Salvador 742
Samouraï, Le 475
Scream 872-873
Se7en 857
Seconds 461
Shadow of a Doubt 196
Shining, The 666-667
Shoot the Piano Player 381
Silence of the Lambs, The 809
Sixth Sense, The 910
Sleuth 554
Soldaat Van Oranje 638
Soldier of Orange 638
Spellbound 207
Spoorloos 760-761
Stranger, The 220
Strangers on a Train 265
Straw Dogs 550
Suspiria 639
Targets 501
Taxi Driver 616-617
Terminator 2: Judgment Day 808
Terminator, The 708-709
Texas Chainsaw Massacre, The 585
The 39 Steps, The 128
Thing, The 683
Third Man, The 252-253
Tirez sur le pianiste 381
To Have and Have Not 200
Total Recall 799
Touch of Evil 350-351
Trou, Le 376
Uccello dalle Piume di Cristallo, L' 533
Usual Suspects, The 862
Vanishing, The 760-761
Vertigo 354-355
Videodrome 696
Vierde Man, De 702
Wages of Fear 287
What Ever Happened to Baby Jane? 411
Who Framed Roger Rabbit 773
Wicker Man, The 572
Yeux Sans Visage, Les 365
Z 510

**WAR**

African Queen, The 267
All Quiet on the Western Front 89
Andrei Rublev 518
Andrei Rublyov 518
Apocalypse Now 658-659
Ascent, The 619
Ashes and Diamonds 356
Barry Lyndon 602
Battaglia di Algeri, La 446
Battle of Algiers, The 446
Battle of San Pietro, The 207
Battleship Potemkin 58-59
Best Years of Our Lives, The 215
Big Parade, The 61
Big Red One, The 670
Biruma No Tategoto 327
Boat, The 675
Boot, Das 675
Braveheart 854
Bridge on the River Kwai, The 345
Bronenosets Potyomkin 58-59
Burmese Harp, The 327
Cabaret 553
Campanadas a Medianoche 449
Chagrin et la Pitié, Le 538
Chimes at Midnight 449
Come and See 720
Cranes are Flying, The 347
Csillagosok, Katonák 482
Dawn of the Dead 646
Deer Hunter, The 642-643
Dr. Strangelove 434-435
Dr. Zhivago 444
English Patient, The 868
Europa Europa 793
Forbidden Games 272
From Here to Eternity 284
Full Metal Jacket 750-751
Gallipoli 676
Gattopardo, Il 422-423
General, The 66
Glory 784
Gone with the Wind 158-159
Good Morning Vietnam 752
Grand Illusion 140
Grande Illusion, La 140
Grave of the Fireflies 768
Great Escape, The 421
Gunga Din 161
Henry V 202
Hill 24 Doesn't Answer 315
Hiroshima mon amour 374
Hitlerjunge Salomon 793
Hong Gao Liang 757
Hotaru No Haka 768
I Know Where I'm Going! 214
Idi I Smotri 720
Jeux interdits 272
Killing Fields, The 716
Kippur 916
Kumonosu Jo 343
Lawrence of Arabia 406-407
Leopard, The 422-423
Letjat Zhuravli 347
Life and Death of Colonel Blimp, The 193
M*A*S*H* 530
Napoléon 71
Night of the Shooting Stars, The 693
No Man's Land 933
Notte di San Lorenzo, La 693
Open City 211
Paisà 217
Paisan 217
Paths of Glory 348
Patton 530
Pianist, The 943
Platoon 740
Popiól I Diament 356
Potomok Chingis-Khana 76
Ran 718-719
Red and the White, The 482
Red Sorghum 757
Roma, Città Aperta 211
Salvador 742
Saving Private Ryan 886-887
Schindler's List 832
Senso 306
Sergeant York 178
Shame 497
Sherman's March 744
Shoah 730
Skammen 497
Soldaat Van Oranje 638
Soldier of Orange 638
Sorrow and the Pity, The 538
Storm over Asia 76
Thin Red Line, The 892-893
Three Kings 902
Throne of Blood 343
To Be or Not to Be 186
To Have and Have Not 200
Underground 860
Voskhozhdenie 619
War Game, The 445

**WESTERN**

Big Sky, The 279
Blazing Saddles 591
Buono, Il Brutto, Il Cattivo, Il 458-459
Butch Cassidy and the Sundance Kid 506
C'era Una Volta il West 489
Dances with Wolves 792
Dead Man 861
Destry Rides Again 156
El Topo 523
Good, the Bad, and the Ugly, The 458-459
Great Train Robbery, The 28-29
Gunfight at the OK Corral 345
High Noon 279
High Plains Drifter 554
Hombre 471
Hud 419
Johnny Guitar 295
Little Big Man 527
Man From Laramie, The 319
Man of the West 349
Man Who Shot Liberty Valance, The 410
McCabe and Mrs. Miller 539
My Darling Clementine 218-219
Naked Spur, The 288
Once Upon a Time in the West 489
One-Eyed Jacks 395
Outlaw Josey Wales, The 614
Ox-Bow Incident, The 195
Paleface, The 241
Pat Garrett and Billy the Kid 582
Red River 238
Ride Lonesome 366
Rio Bravo 375
Rio Grande 258
Searchers, The 328-329
Seven Brides for Seven Brothers 298
Shane 294
Silver Lode 307
Stagecoach 150-151
Unforgiven 820-821
Wild Bunch, The 516-517
Winchester '73 258

**France** (Star) 14m Silent BW
**Director:** Georges Méliès
**Producer:** Georges Méliès
**Screenplay:** Georges Méliès, from the novel *Le Voyage dans la Lune* by Jules Verne
**Photography:** Michaut, Lucien Tainguy
**Cast:** Victor André, Bleuette Bernon, Brunnet, Jeanne d'Alcy, Henri Delannoy, Depierre, Farjaut, Kelm, Georges Méliès

# LE VOYAGE DANS LA LUNE (1902)
## A TRIP TO THE MOON

When thinking about *A Trip to the Moon*, one's mind is quickly captured by the original and mythic idea of early filmmaking as an art whose "rules" were established in the very process of its production. This French movie was released in 1902 and represents a revolution for the time, given its length (approximately 14 minutes), as compared to the more common two-minute short films produced at the beginning of last century.

*A Trip to the Moon* directly reflects the histrionic personality of its director, Georges Méliès, whose past as a theater actor and magician influences the making of the movie. The film boldly experiments with some of the most famous cinematic techniques, such as superimpositions, dissolves, and editing practices that would be widely used later on. Despite the simplicity of its special effects, the film is generally considered the first example of science-fiction cinema. It offers many elements characteristic of the genre—a spaceship, the discovery of a new frontier—and establishes most of its conventions.

The movie opens with a Scientific Congress in which Professor Barbenfouillis (played by Méliès himself) tries to convince his colleagues to take part in a trip to explore the moon. Once his plan is accepted, the expedition is organized and the scientists are sent to the moon on a space ship. The missile-like ship lands right in the eye of the moon, which is represented as an anthropomorphic being. Once on the surface, the scientists soon meet the hostile inhabitants, the Selenites, who take them to their King. After discovering that the enemies easily disappear in a cloud of smoke with the simple touch of an umbrella, the French men manage to escape and return to earth. They fall into the ocean and explore the abyss until they are finally rescued and honored in Paris as heroes.

Méliès here creates a movie that deserves a legitimate place among the milestones in world cinema history. Despite its surreal look, *A Trip to the Moon* is an entertaining and groundbreaking film able to combine the tricks of the theater with the infinite possibilities of the cinematic medium. Méliès, the magician, was an orchestrator more than a director; he also contributed to the movie as a writer, actor, producer, set and costume designer, and cinematographer, creating special effects that were considered spectacular at the time. The first true science-fiction film cannot be missed by a spectator looking for the origin of those conventions that would later influence the entire genre and its most famous entries.

In a more general sense, *A Trip to the Moon* can also be regarded as the movie that establishes the major difference between cinematic fiction and nonfiction. During a time when filmmaking mostly portrayed daily life (such as in the films of the Lumière brothers at the end of the 19th century), Méliès was able to offer a fantasy constructed for pure entertainment. He opened the doors to future film artists by visually expressing his creativity in a way utterly uncommon to movies of the time. **CFe**

**U.S.** (Edison) 12m Silent BW (hand-colored)

**Director:** Edwin S. Porter

**Screenplay:** Scott Marble, Edwin S. Porter

**Photography:** Edwin S. Porter, Blair Smith

**Cast:** A.C. Abadie, Gilbert M. "Bronco Billy" Anderson, George Barnes, Walter Cameron, Frank Hanaway, Morgan Jones, Tom London, Marie Murray, Mary Snow

# THE GREAT TRAIN ROBBERY (1903)

Most histories regard *The Great Train Robbery* as the first Western, initiating a genre that was in a few short years to become the most popular in American cinema. Made by the Edison Company in November 1903, *The Great Train Robbery* was the most commercially successful film of the pre-Griffith period of American cinema and spawned a host of imitations.

What is exceptional about Edwin S. Porter's film is the degree of narrative sophistication, given the early date. There are over a dozen separate scenes, each further developing the story. In the opening scene two masked robbers force a telegraph operator to send a false message so that the train will make an unscheduled stop. In the next scene bandits board the train. The robbers enter the mail car, and after a fight, open the safe. In the next scene two robbers overpower the driver and fireman of the train and throw one of them off. Next the robbers stop the train and hold up the passengers. One runs away and is shot. Then the robbers escape aboard the engine, and in the subsequent scene we see them mount horses and ride off. Meanwhile the telegraph operator on the train sends a message calling for assistance. In a saloon a newcomer is being forced to dance at gunpoint, but when the message arrives everyone grabs their rifles and exits. Cut to the robbers pursued by a posse. There is a shoot-out, and the robbers are killed.

There's one extra shot, the best known in the film, showing one of the robbers firing point blank out of the screen. This was, it seems, sometimes shown at the start of the film, sometimes at the end. Either way, it gave the spectator a sense of being directly in the line of fire.

One actor in *The Great Train Robbery* was G.M. Anderson (real name Max Aronson). Among other parts, he played the passenger who is shot. Anderson was shortly to become the first star of Westerns, appearing as Bronco Billy in over a hundred films beginning in 1907.

In later years some have challenged the claim of *The Great Train Robbery* to be regarded as the first Western, on the grounds either that it is not the first or that it is not a Western. It is certainly true that there are earlier films with a Western theme, such as Thomas Edison's *Cripple Creek Bar-Room Scene* (1899), but they do not have the fully developed narrative of Porter's film. It's also true that it has its roots both in stage plays incorporating spectacular railroad scenes, and in other films of daring robberies that weren't Westerns. Nor can its claim to being a true Western be based on authentic locations, because *The Great Train Robbery* was shot on the Delaware and Lackawanna Railroad in New Jersey. But train robberies had since the days of Jesse James been part of Western lore, and other iconic elements such as six-shooters, cowboy hats, and horses all serve to give the film a genuine Western feel. **EB**

**U.S.** (D.W. Griffith & Epoch) 190m Silent BW

**Director:** D.W. Griffith

**Producer:** D.W. Griffith

**Screenplay:** Frank E. Woods, D.W. Griffith, from the novel *The Clansman: An Historical Romance of the Ku Klux Klan*, the novel *The Leopard's Spots*, and the play *The Clansman* by Thomas F. Dixon Jr.

**Photography:** G.W. Bitzer

**Music:** Joseph Carl Breil, D.W. Griffith

**Cast:** Lillian Gish, Mae Marsh, Henry B. Walthall, Miriam Cooper, Mary Alden, Ralph Lewis, George Siegmann, Walter Long, Robert Harron, Wallace Reid, Joseph Henabery, Elmer Clifton, Josephine Crowell, Spottiswoode Aitken, George Beranger

# THE BIRTH OF A NATION (1915)

Simultaneously one of the most revered and reviled films ever made, D.W. Griffith's *The Birth of a Nation* is important for the very reasons that prompt both of those divergent reactions. In fact, rarely has a film so equally deserved such praise and scorn, which in many ways raises the film's estimation not just in the annals of cinema but as an essential historic artifact (some might say relic).

Though it was based on Thomas Dixon's explicitly racist play *The Clansman: An Historical Romance of the Ku Klux Klan*, by many accounts Griffith was indifferent to the racist bent of the subject matter. Just how complicit that makes him in delivering its ugly message has been cause for almost a century of debate. However, there has been no debate concerning the film's technical and artistic merits. Griffith was as usual more interested in the possibilities of the medium than the message, and in this regard he set the standards for modern Hollywood.

Most overtly, *The Birth of a Nation* was the first real historical epic, proving that even in the silent era audiences were willing to sit through a nearly three-hour drama. But with countless artistic innovations, Griffith essentially created contemporary film language, and although elements of *The Birth of a Nation* may seem quaint or dated by contemporary standards, virtually every film is beholden to it in one way, shape, or form. Griffith introduced the use of dramatic close-ups, tracking shots, and other expressive camera movements; parallel action sequences, crosscutting, and other editing techniques; and even the first orchestral score. It's a shame all these groundbreaking elements were attached to a story of such dubious value.

The first half of the film begins before the Civil War, explaining the introduction of slavery to America before jumping into battle. Two families, the northern Stonemans and the southern Camerons, are introduced. The story is told through these two families and often their servants, epitomizing the worst

racial stereotypes. As the nation is torn apart by war, the slaves and their abolitionist supporters are seen as the destructive force behind it all.

The film's racism grows even worse in its second half, set during Reconstruction and featuring the rise of the Ku Klux Klan, introduced as the picture's would-be heroes. The fact that Griffith jammed a love story in the midst of his recreated race war is absolutely audacious. It's thrilling and disturbing, often at the same time.

*The Birth of a Nation* is no doubt a powerful piece of propaganda, albeit one with a stomach-churning political message. Only the puritanical Ku Klux Klan can maintain the unity of the nation, it seems to be saying, so is it any wonder that even at the time the film was met with outrage? It was protested by the National Association for the Advancement of Colored People (NAACP), sparked riots, and later forced Griffith himself to answer criticisms with his even more ambitious *Intolerance* (1916). Still, the fact that *The Birth of a Nation* remains respected and studied to this day—despite its subject matter—reveals its lasting importance. **JKl**

**France** (Gaumont) 440m Silent BW

**Director:** Louis Feuillade

**Screenplay:** Louis Feuillade

**Music:** Robert Israel

**Cast:** Musidora, Edouard Mathé, Marcel Lévesque, Jean Aymé, Fernand Herrmann, Stacia Napierkowska

# LES VAMPIRES (1915)

Louis Feuillade's legendary opus has been cited as a landmark movie serial, a precursor of the deep-focus aesthetic later advanced by Jean Renoir and Orson Welles, and a close cousin to the surrealist movement, but its strongest relationship is to the development of the movie thriller. Segmented into ten loosely connected parts that lack cliffhanger endings, vary widely in length, and were released at irregular intervals, *Les Vampires* falls somewhere between a film series and a film serial. The convoluted, often inconsistent plot centers on a flamboyant gang of Parisian criminals, the Vampires, and their dauntless opponent, the reporter Philippe Guérande (Edouard Mathé).

The Vampires, masters of disguise who often dress in black hoods and leotards while carrying out their crimes, are led by four successive "Grand Vampires," each killed off in turn, each faithfully served by the vampish Irma Vep (her name an anagram of Vampire), who constitutes the heart and soul not only of the Vampires but also of *Les Vampires* itself. Portrayed with voluptuous vitality by Musidora, who became a star as a result, Irma is the film's most attractive character, clearly surpassing the pallid hero Guérande and his hammy comic sidekick Mazamette (Marcel Lévesque). Her charisma undercuts the film's good-versus-evil theme and contributes to its somewhat amoral tone, reinforced by the way the good guys and the bad guys often use the same duplicitous methods and by the disturbingly ferocious slaughter of the Vampires at the end.

Much like the detective story and the haunted-house thriller, *Les Vampires* creates a sturdy-looking world of bourgeois order while also undermining it. The thick floors and walls of each château and hotel become porous with trap doors and secret panels. Massive fireplaces serve as thoroughfares for assassins and thieves, who scurry over Paris rooftops and shimmy up and down drainpipes like monkeys. Taxicabs bristle with stowaways on their roofs and disclose false floors to eject fugitives into convenient manholes. At one point, the hero unsuspectingly sticks his head out the window of his upper-story apartment, only to be looped around the neck by a wire snare wielded from below; he is yanked down to the street, bundled into a large basket, and whisked off by a taxi in less time than it takes to say "Irma Vep!" In another scene, a wall with a fireplace opens up to disgorge a large cannon, which slides to the window and lobs shells into a nearby cabaret.

Reinforcing this atmosphere of capricious stability, the plot is built around a series of tour de force reversals, involving deceptive appearances on both sides of the law: "dead" characters come to life, pillars of society (a priest, a judge, a policeman) turn out to be Vampires, and Vampires are revealed to be law enforcers operating in disguise. It is Feuillade's ability to create, on an extensive and imaginative scale, a double world—at once weighty and dreamlike, recognizably familiar and excitingly strange—that is of central importance to the evolution of the movie thriller and marks him as a major pioneer of the form. **MR**

**U.S.** (Triangle & Wark) 163m Silent BW

**Director:** D.W. Griffith

**Producer:** D.W. Griffith

**Screenplay:** Tod Browning, D.W. Griffith

**Photography:** G.W. Bitzer, Karl Brown

**Music:** Joseph Carl Breil, Carl Davis, D.W. Griffith

**Cast:** Spottiswoode Aitken, Mary Alden, Frank Bennett, Barney Bernard, Monte Blue, Lucille Browne, Tod Browning, William H. Brown, Edmund Burns, William E. Cassidy, Elmer Clifton, Miriam Cooper, Jack Cosgrave, Josephine Crowell, Dore Davidson, Sam De Grasse, Edward Dillon, Pearl Elmore, Lillian Gish, Ruth Handforth, Robert Harron, Joseph Henabery, Chandler House, Lloyd Ingraham, W.E. Lawrence, Ralph Lewis, Vera Lewis, Elmo Lincoln, Walter Long, Mrs. Arthur Mackley, Tully Marshall, Mae Marsh, Marguerite Marsh, John P. McCarthy, A.W. McClure, Seena Owen, Alfred Paget, Eugene Pallette, Georgia Pearce, Billy Quirk, Wallace Reid, Allan Sears, George Siegmann, Maxfield Stanley, Carl Stockdale, Madame Sul-Te-Wan, Constance Talmadge, F.A. Turner, W.S. Van Dyke, Guenther von Ritzau, Erich von Stroheim, George Walsh, Eleanor Washington, Margery Wilson, Tom Wilson

# INTOLERANCE (1916)

Perhaps in part a retort to those who found fault with the racial politics in *The Birth of a Nation* (1915), D.W. Griffith was equally concerned to argue against film censorship. This was addressed more directly in the pamphlet issued at the time of *Intolerance*'s exhibition, *The Rise and Fall of Free Speech in America*. Griffith's design for this film, which he finalized in the weeks following the release of his earlier epic production, is to juxtapose four stories from different periods of history that illustrate "Love's struggle throughout the ages." These include a selection of events from the life of Jesus; a tale from ancient Babylon, whose king is betrayed by those who resent his rejection of religious sectarianism; the story of the St. Bartholomew's Day Massacre of French Protestants by King Charles IX of France on the perfidious advice of his mother; and a modern story in which a young boy, wrongly convicted of the murder of a companion, is rescued from execution at the last minute by the intervention of his beloved, who gains a pardon from the governor. These stories are not presented in series. Instead, Griffith cuts from one to another and often introduces suspenseful crosscutting within the stories as well. This revolutionary structure proved too difficult for most filmgoers at the time, who may also have been put off by *Intolerance*'s length (more than three hours). Griffith may have invested as much as $2 million in the project, but the film never came close to making back its costs, even when recut and released as two separate features, *The Fall of Babylon* and *The Mother and the Law*.

No expenses were spared in the impressive historical recreations. The enormous sets for the Babylon story, which long afterward remained a Hollywood landmark, were dressed with 3,000 extras. These production values were equaled by the sumptuous costumes and elaborate crowd scenes of the French story. Though others wrote some title cards, Griffith himself was responsible for the complicated script, which he continued to work on as production progressed. His stock company of actors performed admirably in the various roles. Constance Talmadge is particularly effective as the "Mountain Girl" in love with the ill-fated Prince Belshazzar (Alfred Paget) in the Babylon story, as are Mae Marsh and Bobby Harron as the reunited lovers in the modern story.

As in *The Birth of a Nation*, Griffith uses the structures of Victorian melodrama to make his political points. Intolerance is examined through the lens of tragic love, which lends emotional energy and pathos to the narratives. In the Babylonian story, Belshazzar and his beloved Attarea (Seena Owen) commit suicide rather than fall into the hands of the victorious Cyrus the Persian (George Siegmann), and in the French story a young couple, he Catholic and she Protestant, are unable to escape the massacre.

*Intolerance* is a monument to Griffith's talent for screenwriting, directing actors, designing shots, and editing—a one of a kind masterpiece on a scope and scale that has never been equaled. Meant to persuade, this film exerted more influence on the Soviet revolutionary cinema of Sergei Eisenstein and others than on Griffith's American contemporaries. **RBP**

**Germany** (Decla-Bioscop) 71m Silent BW (tinted)

**Director:** Robert Wiene

**Producer:** Rudolf Meinert, Erich Pommer

**Screenplay:** Hans Janowitz, Carl Mayer

**Photography:** Willy Hameister

**Music:** Alfredo Antonini, Giuseppe Becce, Timothy Brock, Richard Marriott, Peter Schirmann, Rainer Viertlböck

**Cast:** Werner Krauss, Conrad Veidt, Friedrich Feher, Lil Dagover, Hans Heinrich von Twardowski, Rudolf Lettinger, Rudolf Klein-Rogge

# DAS KABINETT DES DOKTOR CALIGARI (1919)

## THE CABINET OF DR. CALIGARI

*The Cabinet of Dr. Caligari* is the keystone of a strain of bizarre, fantastical cinema that flourished in Germany in the 1920s and was linked, somewhat spuriously, with the Expressionist art movement. If much of the development of the movies in the medium's first two decades was directed toward the Lumière-style "window on the world," with fictional or documentary stories presented in an emotionally stirring manner designed to make audiences forget they were watching a film, *Caligari* returns to the mode of Georges Méliès by constantly presenting stylized, magical, theatrical effects that exaggerate or caricature reality. In this film, officials perch on ridiculously high stools, shadows are painted on walls and faces, jagged cutout shapes predominate in all the sets, exteriors are obviously painted, and unrealistic backdrops and performances are stylized to the point of hysteria.

Writers Carl Mayer and Hans Janowitz conceived the film as taking place in its own out-of-joint world, and director Robert Weine and set designers Hermann Warm, Walter Roehrig, and Walter Reimann put a twist on every scene and even intertitle to insist on this. Controversially, Fritz Lang—at an early stage attached as director—suggested that the radical style of *Caligari* would be too much for audiences to take without some "explanation." Lang devised a frame story in which hero Francis (Friedrich Feher) recounts the story—of sinister mesmerist charlatan Dr. Caligari (Werner Krauss), his zombie-like somnambulist slave Cesare (Conrad Veidt), and a series of murders in the rickety small town of Holstenwall—and is finally revealed to be an asylum inmate who, in *The Wizard of Oz* style, has imagined a narrative that incorporates various people in his daily life. This undercuts the antiauthoritarian tone of the film as Dr. Caligari, in the main story an asylum director who has become demented, is revealed to be a genuinely decent man out to help the hero. However, the asylum set in the frame story is exactly the same "unreal" one seen in the flashback, making the whole film and not just Francis's bracketed story

somehow unreliable. Indeed, by revealing its expressionist vision to be that of a madman, the film could even appeal to conservatives who deemed all modernist art as demented.

Weine, less innovative than most of his collaborators, makes surprisingly little use of cinematic technique, with the exception of the flashback-within-a-flashback as Krauss is driven mad by superimposed instructions that he "must become Caligari." The film relies entirely on theatrical devices, the camera fixed center stage as the sets are displayed and the actors (especially Veidt) providing any movement or impact. Lang's input did serve to make the movie a strange species of amphibian: It plays as an art movie to the high-class crowds who appreciate its innovations, but it's also a horror movie with a gimmick. With its sideshow ambience, hypnotic mad scientist villain, and leotard-clad, heroine-abducting monster, *The Cabinet of Dr. Caligari* is a major early entry in the horror genre, introducing images, themes, characters, and expressions that became fundamental to the likes of Tod Browning's *Dracula* and James Whale's *Frankenstein* (both 1931). **KN**

# BROKEN BLOSSOMS (1919)

**U.S.** (D.W. Griffith) 6,013ft Silent BW (tinted screen)

**Director:** D.W. Griffith

**Producer:** D.W. Griffith

**Screenplay:** Thomas Burke, D.W. Griffith

**Photography:** G.W. Bitzer

**Music:** D.W. Griffith

**Cast:** Lillian Gish, Richard Barthelmess, Donald Crisp, Arthur Howard, Edward Peil Sr., George Beranger, Norman Selby

D.W. Griffith's reputation in film studies is, if slightly overstated, nevertheless entirely unimpeachable. American (and world) cinema would surely be a different beast without his many contributions. *The Birth of a Nation* and *Intolerance* are, rightly, his most renowned films, remembered for their remarkable manipulations of story and editing. But another of his films, 1919's *Broken Blossoms*, has always stood out as among his very best, and it is surely his most beautiful.

Along with William Beaudine's glorious Mary Pickford vehicle *Sparrows*, *Broken Blossoms* exemplifies what was known in Hollywood as the "soft style." This was the ultimate in glamor photography: cinematographers used every available device—powder makeup, specialized lighting instruments, oil smeared on the lens, even immense sheets of diaphanous gauze hung from the studio ceiling—to soften, highlight, and otherwise accentuate the beauty of their stars. In *Broken Blossoms*, the face of the immortal Lillian Gish literally glows with a lovely, unearthly luminescence, outshining all other elements on the screen.

The beauty of *Broken Blossoms* must be experienced, for it is truly stunning. Gish and her costar, the excellent Richard Barthelmess, glide hauntedly through a London landscape defined by fog, eerie alleyway lights, and arcane, "Orientalist" sets. The film's simple story of forbidden love is complemented perfectly by the gorgeous, mysterious production design, created by Joseph Stringer. No other film looks like *Broken Blossoms*.

The collaboration between Gish and Griffith is one of American cinema's most fruitful: the two also worked together on *Intolerance*, *The Birth of a Nation*, *Orphans of the Storm*, and *Way Down East*, in addition to dozens of shorts. Surely this director-actor collaboration ranks with Scorsese–De Niro, Kurosawa–Mifune, and Leone–Eastwood, to name a few; indeed, it is the standard by which all others should be judged.

Griffith finds a perfect balance between the story's mundanity and the production's seedy lavishness (much of the film takes place in opium dens and dockside dives). It takes a skilled and confident director to handle a form/function split like this one; this is Griffith at the top of his abilities. It is the tension between the everyday and the extraordinary that drives on *Broken Blossoms*, securing its place in film history. **EdeS**

# WAY DOWN EAST (1920)

U.S. (D.W. Griffith) 100m Silent BW

**Director:** D.W. Griffith

**Screenplay:** Anthony Paul Kelly, Joseph R. Grismer, D.W. Griffith, from the play *Way Down East* by Joseph R. Grismer, William A. Brady and the play *Annie Laurie* by Lottie Blair Parker

**Cast:** Lillian Gish, Richard Barthelmess, Lowell Sherman, Burr McIntosh, Kate Bruce, Mary Hay, Creighton Hale, Emily Fitzroy, Porter Strong, George Neville, Edgar Nelson

Soon after *The Birth of a Nation* (1915), one of the most profitable films ever made, D.W. Griffith saw his career go into decline, mostly as a result of his inability to adapt to the changing desires of the filmgoing public. Griffith had specialized in bringing Victorian melodrama, with its tales of threatened female innocence, to the screen. By 1920, however, audiences had begun to show less interest in virtue rescued or preserved. It was therefore a surprise that Griffith decided to adapt for the screen the 1890s stage melodrama *Way Down East*, not to mention that he was able to breathe new life into the story and make it into a very successful film.

Anna Moore (Lillian Gish) leaves her small New England village to live with wealthier relatives in Boston. There she comes under the spell of an attractive young man named Sanderson (Lowell Sherman), who tricks her into sleeping with him by staging a phony marriage. He then sends her back to New England, with a command to keep silent about their nuptials. Upon discovering she is pregnant, Anna contacts him, only to learn the bitter truth. Nothing but disaster follows. Her mother dies. So does her child. She is driven away from the rooming house where she has taken shelter because the landlady suspects she isn't married. Luckily, she finds a new position at a nearby farm owned by Squire Barlett (Burr McIntosh), but Sanderson lives not far away. At the farm, Anna meets the squire's son David (Richard Barthelmess), and the two soon fall in love.

But Anna's past catches up with her. Dismissed from the squire's employ, she wanders off into a terrible snowstorm and finds herself on a frozen river. Floating away on an ice floe toward huge falls, Anna is rescued at the last minute by David. Sanderson's villainy is exposed, and Anna reconciles with the repentant squire. The film ends with their wedding. The dramatic parts of *Way Down East* are kept lively by Griffith's pacing of the narrative and the affecting performances of an able cast. The film's action conclusion, however, shows the director at his finest, both in the shooting of the sequence (parts were filmed on a frozen Vermont river) and in the editing, which is fast paced and thrilling. **RBP**

**U.S.** (Micheaux) 79m Silent BW

**Director:** Oscar Micheaux

**Producer:** Oscar Micheaux

**Screenplay:** Oscar Micheaux, Gene DeAnna

**Music:** Philip Carli

**Cast:** Evelyn Preer, Flo Clements, James D. Ruffin, Jack Chenault, William Smith, Charles D. Lucas, Bernice Ladd, Mrs. Evelyn, William Stark, Mattie Edwards, Ralph Johnson, E.G. Tatum, Grant Edwards, Grant Gorman, Leigh Whipper

# WITHIN OUR GATES (1920)

Successful author, publisher, homesteader, and filmmaker, Oscar Micheaux is widely considered the father of African American cinema; only his second effort, *Within Our Gates* is one of 40 films Micheaux wrote, directed, and independently produced between 1919 and 1948. Besides its gripping narrative and artistic merits, *Within Our Gates* has immense historical value as the earliest surviving feature by an African American director. Powerful, controversial, and still haunting in its depiction of the atrocities committed by white Americans against blacks during this era, the film remains, in the words of one critic, "a powerful and enlightening cultural document [that] is no less relevant today than it was in 1920."

Made just five years after D.W. Griffith's racist masterpiece *The Birth of a Nation* (1915), *Within Our Gates* follows the struggle of Sylvia Landry (Evelyn Preer), a Southern black teacher who travels north in an effort to raise money for her school. But this is only one of several stories that Micheaux (who also wrote the screenplay) weaves together in his gripping look at the physical, psychological, and economic repression of African Americans.

Few people saw *Within Our Gates* as Micheaux intended it; the film was repeatedly edited by the censors, who found the rape and lynching scenes too provocative after the 1919 Chicago race riots. Lost for 70 years, *Within Our Gates* was rediscovered at the Filmoteca Española in Madrid and restored soon after. **SJS**

# KÖRKARLEN (1921)
## THE PHANTOM CARRIAGE

A celebrated world success in its initial release, *The Phantom Carriage* not only cemented director-screenwriter-actor Victor Sjöström and the Swedish silent cinema's fame but also had a well-documented, artistic influence on many great directors and producers. The most well-known element of the film is undoubtedly the representation of the spiritual world as a tormented limbo between heaven and earth. The scene in which the protagonist—the hateful and self-destructive alcoholic David Holm (Sjöström)—wakes up at the chime of midnight on New Year's night only to stare at his own corpse, knowing that he is condemned to hell, is one of the most quoted scenes in cinema history.

Made in a simple but time-consuming and meticulously staged series of double exposures, the filmmaker, his photographer, and a lab manager created a three-dimensional illusion of a ghostly world that went beyond anything previously seen at the cinema. More important perhaps was the film's complex but readily accessible narration via a series of flashbacks—and even flashbacks-within-flashbacks—that elevated this gritty tale of poverty and degradation to poetic excellence.

Looking back at Sjöström's career, *The Phantom Carriage* is a theological and philosophical extension of the social themes introduced in his controversial breakthrough *Ingeborg Holm* (1913). Both films depict the step-by-step destruction of human dignity in a cold and heartless society, driving its victims into brutality and insanity. The connection is stressed by the presence of Hilda Borgström, unforgettable as Ingeborg Holm and now in the role of a tortured wife—another desperate Mrs. Holm. She is yet again playing a compassionate but poor mother on her way to suicide or a life in the mental asylum.

The religious naïveté at the heart of Selma Lagerlöf's faithfully adapted novel might draw occasional laughter from a secular audience some 80 years later, but the subdued, "realist" acting and the dark fate of the main characters, which almost comes to its logical conclusion, save for a melodramatic finale, never fails to impress. **MT**

**Sweden** (Svensk) AB) 93m Silent BW

**Director:** Victor Sjöström

**Producer:** Charles Magnusson,

**Screenplay:** Victor Sjöström, from novel by Selma Lagerlöf

**Photography:** Julius Jaenzon

**Cast:** Victor Sjöström, Hilda Borgström, Tore Svennberg, Astrid Holm, Concordia Selander, Lisa Lundholm, Tor Weijden, Einar Axelsson, Olof Ås, Nils Ahrén, Simon Lindstrand, Nils Elffors, Algot Gunnarsson, Hildur Lithman, John Ekman

## ORPHANS OF THE STORM (1921)

**U.S.** (D.W. Griffith) 150m Silent BW

**Director:** D.W. Griffith

**Producer:** D.W. Griffith

**Screenplay:** D.W. Griffith, from the play *The Two Orphans* by Eugène Cormon and Adolphe d'Ennery

**Photography:** Paul H. Allen, G.W. Bitzer, Hendrik Sartov

**Music:** Louis F. Gottschalk, William F. Peters

**Cast:** Lillian Gish, Dorothy Gish, Joseph Schildkraut, Frank Losee, Katherine Emmet, Morgan Wallace, Lucille La Verne, Sheldon Lewis, Frank Puglia, Creighton Hale, Leslie King, Monte Blue, Sidney Herbert, Lee Kohlmar, Marcia Harris

The last of D.W. Griffith's sweeping historical melodramas, *Orphans of the Storm* tells the story of two young girls caught in the turmoil of the French Revolution. Lillian and Dorothy Gish are Henriette and Louise Girard, two babies who become "sisters" when Henriette's impoverished father, thinking to abandon his daughter in a church, finds Louise and, moved by pity, brings both girls home to raise. Unfortunately, they are left orphaned at an early age when their parents die of the plague. Louise is left blind by the disease, and so the girls make their way to Paris in search of her cure. There they are separated. Henriette, kidnapped by the henchmen of an evil aristocrat, is befriended by a handsome nobleman, Vaudrey (Joseph Schildkraut). Louise is rescued by a kind young man after she falls into the River Seine but, brought to his house, she is put to work by the man's cruel brother. Adventures follow, including imprisonment in the Bastille, being condemned to death during the Reign of Terror, and saved from the guillotine by the politician Danton (Monte Blue), whose speech advocating the end of such bloodshed is one of the film's most impassioned moments.

Although based on a play that had been successful in the preceding decade, Griffith wrote the script during shooting. Despite resulting complications, *Orphans of the Storm* is a masterpiece of beautiful staging and acting, with the Gish sisters turning in what are perhaps the finest performances of their careers. **RBP**

## LA SOURIANTE MADAME BEUDET (1922)
### THE SMILING MADAME BEUDET

**France** 54m Silent BW

**Director:** Germaine Dulac

**Screenplay:** Denys Amiel, André Obey

**Photography:** Maurice Forster, Paul Parguel

**Cast:** Alexandre Arquillière, Germaine Dermoz, Jean d'Yd, Madeleine Guitty

Germaine Dulac's celebrated film is known as one of the earliest examples of both feminist and experimental cinema. The plot depicts the life of a bored provincial housewife trapped in a stifling bourgeois marriage. The most captivating aspect of *The Smiling Madame Beudet*, however, is composed of elaborate dream-sequences in which the eponymous housewife (Germaine Dermoz) fantasizes a life outside the confines of her monotonous existence. Using radical special effects and editing techniques, Dulac incorporates some of the early avant-garde aesthetics of the times to offset the rich, vivid feminine power of Madame Beudet's imaginary life to the dullness of the one she shares with her husband (Alexandre Arquillière). When the complex visual elaboration of her potential liberation through fantasy—the only thing that can put a smile on her face—is cut short by the appearance of her husband within her daydreams, she is left with only one possible solution: kill him.

Sadly, Madame Beudet's missed attempt on her husband's life at the end of the film is yet again misunderstood, as she is not even rewarded with Monsieur Beudet's acknowledgment of her protest against him. Ultimately, Dulac not only explicitly addresses the oppressive alienation of women within patriarchy, but more importantly, uses the still-new medium of film to offer her viewers a radical and subjective female perspective. This led to her picture's inclusion in the first Festival of Women's Films in New York in 1972. **CO**

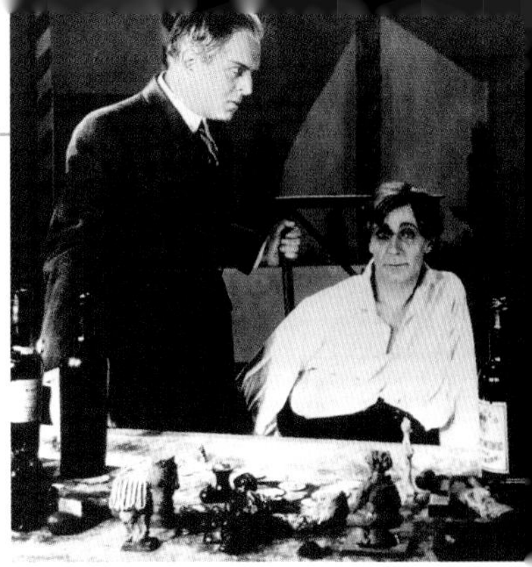

# DR. MABUSE, DER SPIELER (1922)
## DR. MABUSE, PARTS 1 AND 2

This two-part epic was a major commercial success in Germany in 1922, doubtless because of its everything-including-the-kitchen-sink approach, scrambling thrills, horrors, politics, satire, sex (including nude scenes!), magic, psychology, art, violence, low comedy, and special effects. Whereas the escapades of Fantômas (and even Fu Manchu) belong to that netherworld between the surreal and the pulpy, *Dr. Mabuse* was intended from the outset not merely as flamboyant thriller but as pointed editorial, using the figure of the master-of-disguise supercriminal to embody the real evils of its era.

The subtitles of each of the film's two parts, harping on about "our time," underline the point made obvious in the opening act, in which Mabuse's gang steals a Swiss-Dutch trade agreement—not to make use of the secret information, but to create a momentary stock market panic which affords Mabuse (Rudolf Klein-Rogge), in disguise as a cartoon plutocrat with top hat and fur coat, to make a fast fortune. He also employs a band of blind men as forgers, contributing to the sense German audiences at the time felt that money was worthless (Mabuse sees this coming and orders his men to switch over to forging U.S. currency since even real marks aren't worth as much as counterfeit dollars).

The film's eponymous villain shuffles photographs as if they were a deck of cards, selecting his identity for the day from various disguises, but it is nearly two hours before his "real" name is confirmed—by which time, we have seen Mabuse in several other guises, from respected psychiatrist to degenerate gambler to hotel manager. In Part 2, he appears as a one-armed stage illusionist, and finally loses his grip on the fragile core of his identity to become a ranting madman, tormented by the hollow-cheeked specters of those he has killed and, in a moment which still startles, by the creaking-to-life of vast, grotesque statues and bits of machinery in his final lair. Director Fritz Lang, and others, would return to Mabuse, still embodying the ills of the age—notably in the early talkie *Das Testament von Dr. Mabuse* and the 1961 hi-tech surveillance melodrama *The Thousand Eyes of Dr. Mabuse.* **KN**

**Germany** Uco-Film/ Ullstein/ Universum 95m (part 1) 100m (part 2), U.S. Silent BW

**Director:** Fritz Lang

**Producer:** Erich Pommer

**Screenplay:** Norbert Jacques, Fritz Lang, Thea von Harbou

**Photography:** Carl Hoffmann

**Music:** Konrad Elfers

**Cast:** Rudolf Klein-Rogge, Alfred Abel, Aud Egede Nissen, Gertrude Welcker, Bernhard Goetzke, Robert Forster-Larrinaga, Paul Richterll, Hans Adalbert Schlettow, Georg John, Grete Berger, Julius Falkenstein, Lydia Potechina, Anita Berber, Paul Biensfeldt, Karl Platen

**U.S.** (Les Frères Revillon, Pathé) 79m Silent BW

**Director:** Robert J. Flaherty

**Producer:** Robert J. Flaherty

**Screenplay:** Robert J. Flaherty

**Photography:** Robert J. Flaherty

**Music:** Stanley Silverman

**Cast:** Nanook, Nyla, Cunayou, Allee, Allegoo, Berry Kroeger (narrator—1939 re-release)

# NANOOK OF THE NORTH (1922)

The history of "documentary" filmmaking—an approach generally thought to involve a filmmaker's recording of an unmediated reality—begins really with the invention of the cinema itself, but for better or worse the nickname "father of the documentary" has generally been bestowed on Robert J. Flaherty. Raised near the U.S.-Canadian border, Flaherty loved exploring the far-off wilderness from an early age, and after his studies went to work as a mineral prospector in Canada's Far North. Before one of his trips, someone suggested he bring along a movie camera; over the next few years, Flaherty would film hours of material of both the land and its inhabitants, which in 1916 he began showing in private screenings in Toronto. The response was enthusiastic, but just as he was about to ship his footage to the United States, he dropped a cigarette ash and his entire negative—30,000 feet—burst into flames. Flaherty took years to raise enough money to go back north and shoot again; when he finally succeeded (thanks to Revillon Frères, a French furrier), he decided to focus his efforts on filming one Nanook, a celebrated Inuit hunter. Based on his memory of the best of what he had shot before, Flaherty fashioned the events to be included in the new film, including things Nanook commonly did, some things he never did, and some things he used to do but hadn't done in a while. The result was the deeply influential, but endlessly debated, *Nanook of the North*.

A series of vignettes that detail the life of Nanook and his family over a few weeks, Flaherty's film is a kind of romantic ode to human courage and fortitude in the face of an overwhelming and essentially hostile Nature. Despite Nanook getting pride of place in the title, many audiences are left with the memory of the arbitrary fury of the arctic landscape. Indeed, the film received a powerful (if tragic) publicity boost when it was revealed that Nanook and his family had indeed perished in a raging snowstorm not long after the film was completed, giving *Nanook of the North*'s extraordinary and already powerful final sequence—in which the family looks for shelter from a storm—a terrible poignancy.

Many contemporary film students are critical of the picture because so much of it seems staged for the camera—several times you can practically hear Flaherty barking out directions to Nanook and the others—but the film's many defenders over the years, such as André Bazin, wisely pointed out that Flaherty's most remarkable achievement here is the way he seemed to capture the texture of their daily lives. The details of the walrus hunt, such as whether or when a gun was used, seem less important than Flaherty's decision to simply follow in long shot Nanook's slow crawl toward his prey; if Nanook's beaming face as he warms his son's hands is part of an act, then he was simply one of the great screen performers in history. Call it what you will—documentary, fiction, or some hybrid—*Nanook of the North* remains one of the few films that completely deserves its description as a classic. **RP**

**Germany** (Jofa-Atelier Berlin-Johannisthal, Prana-Film) 94m Silent BW

**Director:** F.W. Murnau

**Screenplay:** Henrik Galeen

**Photography:** Günther Krampf, Fritz Arno Wagner

**Music:** James Bernard (restored version)

**Cast:** Max Schreck, Alexander Granach, Gustav von Wangenheim, Greta Schröder, Georg H. Schnell, Ruth Landshoff, John Gottowt, Gustav Botz, Max Nemetz, Wolfgang Heinz, Guido Herzfeld, Albert Venohr, Hardy von Francois

# NOSFERATU, EINE SYMPHONIE DES GRAUENS (1922)
## NOSFERATU, A SYMPHONY OF TERROR

Bram Stoker's *Dracula* inspired one of the most impressive of all silent features. The source material and the medium seem almost eerily meant for each other. Stoker's novel, largely written in the form of a series of letters, is light on traditional dialogue and heavy on description, perfect for the primarily visual storytelling of silent films. It is fitting that a story of the eternal conflict between light and darkness should be matched to a format consisting almost entirely of the interplay of light and darkness.

Director F.W. Murnau had already established himself as a star of the German Expressionist movement when he decided to adapt the Stoker novel, renamed *Nosferatu* after legal threats from Stoker's estate. In fact, the finished film barely evaded a court order that all copies be destroyed, but in the end little of Stoker's novel was ultimately altered, save the names of the characters, and indeed the success of *Nosferatu* led to dozens of subsequent (and mostly officially sanctioned) *Dracula* adaptations.

Yet *Nosferatu*, even so many years later, stands apart from most *Dracula* films. One key difference is the striking presence of star Max Schreck, whose last name in translation means "fear." Schreck plays the eponymous vampire with an almost-savage simplicity. His creature of the night is little different from the rats at his command, lurching instinctively toward any sight of blood with barely disguised lust.

This explains the terror of Hutter (Gustav von Wangenheim), who has traveled to the isolated castle of Count Orlok (Schreck) high in the Carpathian Mountains to help the strange man settle some legal matters. The mere mention of Orlok silences the townsfolk with fear, and Hutter's suspicions deepen when he discovers that the stagecoach taking him to the castle has no driver. Orlok himself offers little solace. He keeps odd hours and leaves Hutter locked in a tower. Fearing for his life—and specifically the bloodlust of his captor—he escapes and returns to Bremen, Germany. But Orlock follows, setting his sights not on Hutter but on his innocent wife, Ellen (Greta Schröder): "Your wife has a beautiful neck," comments Orlok to Hutter. Just as her connection with Hutter helps rescue him from Orlok's clutches, Ellen discovers that it is also up to her to lure the demonic creature to his (permanent) demise: to be vaporized by the rays of the morning sun.

With *Nosferatu* Murnau created some of cinema's most lasting and haunting imagery: Count Orlok creeping through his castle, striking creepy shadows while he's stalking Hutter; Orlock rising stiffly from his coffin; the Count, caught in a beam of sunlight, cringing in terror before fading from view. He also introduced several vampire myths that fill not just other *Dracula* films but permeate popular culture as well. **JKl**

**Denmark / Sweden** (Aljosha, Svensk) 87m Silent BW

**Director:** Benjamin Christensen

**Screenplay:** Benjamin Christensen from the novel *McTeague* by Frank Norris

**Photography:** Johan Ankerstjerne

**Music:** Launy Grøndahl (1922), Emil Reesen (1941 version)

**Cast:** Elisabeth Christensen, Astrid Holm, Karen Winther, Maren Pedersen, Ella La Cour, Emmy Schønfeld, Kate Fabian, Oscar Stribolt, Clara Pontoppidan, Else Vermehren, Alice O'Fredericks, Johannes Andersen, Elith Pio, Aage Hertel, Ib Schønberg

# HÄXAN (1923)

Pioneering Danish filmmaker Benjamin Christensen's notorious 1922 "documentary" *Häxan* is a bizarre silent-film oddity that explores the nature of witchcraft and diabolism from ancient Persia through then-modern times using various cinematic approaches, from still images to models to vivid, dramatic reenactments. It is a hard film to pin down, and it defies any boundaries of genre, especially those of the documentary film, which in the early 1920s was still amorphous and undefined. Part earnest academic exercise in correlating ancient fears with misunderstandings about mental illness and part salacious horror movie, *Häxan* is a truly unique work that still holds the power to unnerve even in today's jaded era.

To visualize his subject matter, Christensen fills the frames with every frightening image he can conjure out of the historical records, often freely blending fact and fantasy. We see a haggard old witch pull a severed, decomposing hand out of a bundle of sticks. There are shocking moments in which we witness a woman giving birth to two enormous demons, see a witches' sabbath, and endure tortures by inquisition judges. We watch an endless parade of demons of all shapes and sizes, some of whom look more or less human, whereas others are almost fully animal—pigs, twisted birds, cats, and the like.

Christensen was certainly a cinematic visionary, and he had a keen notion of the powerful effects of mise en scène. Although *Häxan* is often cited as a key forerunner of such modern devil-possession films as *The Exorcist* (1973), it also brings to mind Tobe Hooper's effective use of props and background detail in *The Texas Chain Saw Massacre* (1974) to create an enveloping atmosphere of potential violence. *Häxan* is a film that needs to be viewed more than once to gain a full appreciation of the set design and decoration—the eerie use of props, claustrophobic sets, and chiaroscuro lighting to set the tone. It is no surprise that the surrealists were so fond of the film and that its life was extended in the late 1960s, when it was reissued as a midnight movie with narration by none other than William S. Burroughs. **JKe**

## FOOLISH WIVES (1922)

Although *Greed* is Erich von Stroheim's most famous film, *Foolish Wives* is his masterpiece. Like *Greed*, it was heavily reedited, but what remains (especially after a major 1972 restoration) is a more accomplished and consistent work. Stroheim himself stars as the unscrupulous Count Karamzin, a Monte Carlo–based pseudoaristocrat who sets out to seduce the neglected wife of an American diplomat.

This witty, ruthlessly objective film confirms its director as the cinema's first great ironist. The antihero Karamzin is skewered with sardonic relish—absurdly foolish, brazenly insincere, thoroughly indiscriminate in his taste in women, and, when the chips are down, contemptibly cowardly—but he and his decadent colleagues are so much more entertaining than the virtuous American hubby and his commonplace spouse. The film's tone of cool, lively detachment is enhanced by its exhaustive elaboration of the world around the characters, articulating space through visual strategies (such as layered depth, peripheral motions, and multiple setups) that make us intensely aware of the entire 360-degree field of each scene. Stroheim stacks the deck by placing his dull, flat Americans in dull, flat spaces; otherwise, there's hardly a shot that doesn't dazzle the eye with rich, shimmering interplay of detail, lighting, gesture, and movement. **MR**

**U.S.** (Universal) 85m Silent BW

**Director:** Erich von Stroheim

**Screenplay:** Marian Ainslee, Walter Anthony, Erich von Stroheim

**Photography:** William H. Daniels, Ben F. Reynolds

**Music:** Sigmund Romberg

**Cast:** Rudolph Christians, Miss DuPont, Maude George, Mae Busch, Erich von Stroheim, Dale Fuller, Al Edmundsen, Cesare Gravina, Malvina Polo, Louis K. Webb, Mrs. Kent, C.J. Allen, Edward Reinach

## OUR HOSPITALITY (1923)

Arguably as great a film as the better-known *The General* (1927), *Our Hospitality*—Buster Keaton's masterly satire of traditional Southern manners—kicks off with a beautifully staged dramatic prologue that establishes the absurdly murderous parameters of the age-old feud between two families. By the time the main story takes over, Buster's Willie McKay is a twenty-something innocent, raised in New York but returning (thanks to a wondrously funny odyssey involving a primitive train) to his familial town, where his courtship of a girl met en route—the daughter, as it happens, of the clan still sworn to spilling his blood—places him in deadly peril, even though Southern hospitality dictates his enemies treat him properly as long as he's in their home.

Much of the humor thereafter derives from a darkly ironic situation whereby Willie determines to remain a guest of his would-be killers while they smilingly try to ensure his departure. Keaton's wit relies not on individual gags but on a firm grasp of character, predicament, period, place, and camera framing (see how he keeps the camera moving after he's fallen off the ludicrous bicycle it has been tracking alongside); the result is not only very funny, but also dramatically substantial and suspenseful—nowhere more so than the justly celebrated sequence when Willie saves his beloved from plunging over a waterfall. Never was Keaton's sense of timing so miraculous, his ability to elicit laughter and excitement simultaneously so gloriously evident. **GA**

**U.S.** (Joseph M. Schenck ) 74m Silent BW

**Director:** John G. Blystone, Buster Keaton

**Producer:** Joseph M. Schenck

**Screenplay:** Clyde Bruckman, Jean C. Havez

**Photography:** Gordon Jennings, Elgin Lessley

**Cast:** Joe Roberts, Ralph Bushman, Craig Ward, Monte Collins, Joe Keaton, Kitty Bradbury, Natalie Talmadge, Buster Keaton Jr., Buster Keaton

France (Abel Gance) Silent BW

**Director:** Abel Gance

**Producer:** Abel Gance, Charles Pathé

**Screenplay:** Abel Gance

**Photography:** Gaston Brun, Marc Bujard, Léonce-Henri Burel, Maurice Duverger

**Music:** Arthur Honegger

**Cast:** Severin-Mars, Ivy Close, Gabriel de Gravone, Pierre Magnier, Gil Clary, Max Maxudian, Georges Térof

# LA ROUE (1923)
## THE WHEEL

Visionary French filmmaker Abel Gance's *The Wheel* opens with a spectacular fast-cut train crash, as revolutionary to spectators in 1922 as the Lumières's train arriving in a station in 1895. Railwayman Sisif (Severin-Mars) saves Norma (Ivy Close) from the crash and brings her up as his daughter. Both he and his son Elie (Gabriel de Gravone) fall in love with her, so Sisif marries her off to a rich man. She and Elie eventually fall in love; both her husband and Elie die after a struggle. Sisif goes blind and dies, after being tended by Norma.

Then as now, opinions on what was originally a sprawling nine-hour film are divided. *The Wheel*'s melodramatic plot was combined with wide-ranging literary references, including Greek tragedy, as is suggested by Sisif's name (Sisyphus) and his blindness associated with incestuous desire (Oedipus). These "pretensions" were seen by intellectuals to conflict with the film's extraordinary cinematographic techniques (such as the accelerating montage sequences based on musical rhythms), which related the film to avant-garde preoccupations with a "pure" cinema and Cubist concerns with machines as the emblem of modernity. The film's contradictions are admirably brought together in the central metaphor of the title: the wheel of fate (Sisif/Sisyphus ends up driving the funicular railway up and down Mont Blanc), the wheel of desire, the wheel of the film itself with its many cyclical patterns. **PP**

**U.S.** (Douglas Fairbanks) 155m Silent BW (tinted)

**Director:** Raoul Walsh

**Producer:** Douglas Fairbanks

**Screenplay:** Douglas Fairbanks, Lotta Woods

**Photography:** Arthur Edeson

**Music:** Mortimer Wilson

**Cast:** Douglas Fairbanks, Snitz Edwards, Charles Belcher, Julanne Johnston, Sojin, Anna May Wong, Brandon Hurst, Tote Du Crow, Noble Johnson

# THE THIEF OF BAGDAD (1924)

*The Thief of Bagdad* marked the culmination of Douglas Fairbanks's career as the ultimate hero of swashbuckling costume spectacles. It is also one of the most visually breathtaking movies ever made, a unique and integral conception by a genius of film design, William Cameron Menzies. Building his mythical Bagdad on a six-and-a-half-acre site (the biggest in Hollywood history), Menzies created a shimmering, magical world, as insubstantial yet as real and haunting as a dream, with its reflective floors, soaring minarets, flying carpets, ferocious dragons, and winged horses.

As Ahmed the Thief in quest of his Princess, Fairbanks—bare chested and with clinging silken garments—explored a new sensuous eroticism in his screen persona, and found an appropriate costar in Anna May Wong, as the Mongol slave girl. Although the nominal director was the gifted and able Raoul Walsh, the overall concept for *The Thief of Bagdad* was Fairbanks's own, as producer, writer, star, stuntman, and showman of unbounded ambition. (Side note: the uncredited Persian Prince in the film is played by a woman, Mathilde Comont.) **DR**

# STACHKA (1924)
## STRIKE

U.S.S.R. (Goskino, Proletkult) 82m Silent BW

**Director:** Sergei M. Eisenstein

**Producer:** Boris Mikhin

**Screenplay:** Grigori Aleksandrov, Sergei M. Eisenstein

**Photography:** Vasili Khvatov, Vladimir Popov, Eduard Tisse

**Cast:** Grigori Aleksandrov, Aleksandr Antonov, Yudif Glizer, Mikhail Gomorov, I. Ivanov, Ivan Klyukvin, Anatoli Kuznetsov, M. Mamin, Maksim Shtraukh, Vladimir Uralsky, Vera Yanukova, Boris Yurtsev

Sergei M. Eisenstein was a revolutionary in every sense, forging a radically new breed of montage-based cinema from an unprecedented merger of Marxist philosophy, Constructivist aesthetics, and his own fascination with the visual contrasts, conflicts, and contradictions built into the dynamics of film itself.

*Strike*, his first feature, was intended as one installment in a series of works about the rise of Marxist-Leninist rule. Censorship by the new Soviet government thwarted many of Eisenstein's dreams in ensuing years, and this series never got beyond its initial production. Nonetheless, the feverishly energetic *Strike* stands on its own as a tour de force of expressive propaganda and the laboratory in which seminal ideas for his later silent masterpieces—*The Battleship Potemkin* (1925), *October* (1927), and *Old and New* (1928)—were first tested and refined.

*Strike* depicts a labor uprising in a Russian factory, where workers are goaded toward rebellion by the owners' greed and dishonesty. We see simmering unrest among the laborers, an act of treachery that pushes them into action, the excitement of their mutiny followed by the hardships of prolonged unemployment, and finally the counterstrike of the factory owners, abetted by troops who engage in wholesale slaughter of the workers. The film ends with an electrifying example of what Eisenstein called "intellectual montage," intercutting the massacre of strikers with images of animals being slain in a slaughterhouse.

The acting in *Strike* is as unconventional as its editing techniques, mixing naturalistic portrayals of the workers with stylized portrayals of the owners and their spies. The film illustrates Soviet theories of "typage," calling for actors who physically resemble the character types they play, and the "collective hero," whereby a story's protagonist is not a single individual but rather all the people standing on the correct side of history.

The political imperatives of *Strike* have dated since its premiere in 1925, but its visual power has not waned. "I don't believe in the kino-eye," Eisenstein once remarked, referring to a catchword of Dziga Vertov, his colleague and rival. "I believe in the kino-fist." That hard-hitting philosophy galvanizes every sequence of this unique film. **DS**

**U.S.** (MGM) 140m Silent BW
**Director:** Erich von Stroheim
**Producer:** Louis B. Mayer
**Screenplay:** Joseph Farnham, June Mathis
**Photography:** William H. Daniels, Ben F. Reynolds
**Cast:** Zasu Pitts, Gibson Gowland, Jean Hersholt, Dale Fuller, Tempe Pigott, Sylvia Ashton, Chester Conklin, Frank Hayes, Joan Standing

# GREED (1924)

The first movie ever shot entirely on location, *Greed* is notorious as much for the story behind its making as for its considerable artistic power. Director Erich von Stroheim wanted to make the most realistic movie possible with his adaptation of Frank Norris's novel *McTeague*, about the rise and violently murderous fall of working-class San Francisco dentist John "Mac" McTeague. But his creation, originally commissioned by the director-friendly Goldwyn Company, was destroyed when the studio became Metro-Goldwyn-Mayer (MGM), with von Stroheim's nemesis Irving Thalberg as the new General Manager.

MGM wanted a commercial film, and von Stroheim wanted to create an experiment in cinematic realism worthy of the 1990s Dogma school. During the two-year shoot, he rented a flat on Laguna Street in San Francisco which became the set for Mac's (Gibson Gowland) dental parlors. Many of the scenes there were shot entirely with natural light. Von Stroheim also insisted that his actors live in the flat to help them get into character. One of the fascinations in watching *Greed* is seeing all the historic San Francisco locations as they were in the early 1920s. When it came time to shoot the film's final climactic moments in Death Valley, von Stroheim shipped his whole crew out to the 120°F desert location, where the cameras became so overheated they had to be wrapped with iced towels.

The director's first cut was nearly nine hours long. It was a painstaking reenactment of Norris's novel, which itself was a re-creation of an actual crime that took place during the early 1880s. After a quack doctor helps Mac escape the Northern California mining town of his childhood, he becomes a dentist in San Francisco. There he meets Trina (Zasu Pitts), with whom he falls in love during a memorably creepy tooth-drilling scene. His best friend and rival for Trina's affections is Marcus (Jean Hersholt), who grants Mac permission to marry Trina but changes his mind after she wins a lottery. Using his connections in local government, Marcus manages to put Mac out of business

and send his former friend into a free fall of back-breaking day labor, drunkenness, and wife beating.

Trina turns to her lottery winnings as a source of satisfaction, hoarding her thousands in gold coins while she and Mac starve. One of *Greed's* most famous scenes has Trina climbing into bed with her money, caressing it, and rolling around with erotic abandon. Shortly thereafter Mac murders her, steals the money, and heads out to Death Valley where his life comes to a bitter end when Marcus hunts him down.

Only a small handful of people ever saw the original nine-hour version of *Greed*. After von Stroheim's friend helped him cut the picture down to 18 reels, or about four hours, the studios took it away from him and handed it over to a low-ranking editor who reduced it to 140 minutes. This version of the film, which von Stroheim called "a mutilation of my sincere work at the hands of the MGM executives," is nevertheless stark, captivating, and genuinely disturbing.

In 1999, film restorer Rick Schmidlin released a four-hour version of *Greed* reconstructed from original production stills and von Stroheim's shooting script. **AN**

# SHERLOCK, JR. (1924)

**U.S.** (Buster Keaton) 44m Silent BW
**Director:** Roscoe "Fatty" Arbuckle, Buster Keaton
**Producer:** Joseph M. Schenck, Buster Keaton
**Screenplay:** Clyde Bruckman, Jean C. Havez
**Photography:** Byron Houck Elgin Lessley
**Music:** Myles Boisen, Sheldon Brown, Beth Custer, Steve Kirk, Nik Phelps
**Cast:** Buster Keaton, Kathryn McGuire, Joe Keaton, Erwin Connelly, Ward Crane

*Sherlock, Jr.* is Buster Keaton's shortest feature film, yet it is a remarkable achievement, possessing a tightly integrated plot, stunning athleticism (Keaton did all his own stunts, unknowingly breaking his neck during one of them), artistic virtuosity, and an avant-garde exploration of the perennial dichotomy of reality versus illusion. Keaton here plays a projectionist and detective wannabe falsely accused of stealing from his girlfriend's father. Framed by a rival suitor (Ward Crane), the young man is banished from the girl's home. Dejected, he falls asleep on the job. In his dream state, he transcends into the screen (in a brilliant sequence of optical effects), where he is the dapper protagonist Sherlock, Jr.—the world's second greatest detective.

Unbelievable stunts and complicated gags move this 44-minute film along at a fever pitch. At first, the cinematic reality refuses to accept this new protagonist and the tension between the two worlds is magnificently presented via a montage of spatial shifts that land our bewildered hero in a lion's den, amid roaring waves, and in a snowdrift. Gradually, he assimilates fully into the film world. In the mise-en-abyme storyline, the villain (also played by Ward Crane) is trying to kill the hero in vain, before Sherlock, Jr. solves the mystery of the stolen pearls.

*Sherlock, Jr.* not only features the incredible stunts for which Keaton is famous, but also poses a number of issues. From a social perspective, it is a commentary on the fantasies about upward mobility in American society. On a psychological plane, it introduces the motif of the double striving for fulfillment in imaginary spaces, as the protagonist is unable to achieve it in ordinary, tangible reality. Above all, the film is a reflection on the nature of art, a theme that resurfaces again in *The Cameraman* (1928), when Keaton's focus shifts from medium to spectator.

Keaton's films remain interesting today, in part due to the director-star's almost otherworldly stoicism (compared to Chaplin's pathos), and in part due to their occasionally surreal nature (admired by Luis Buñuel and Federico García Lorca) and their delving into the nature of cinema and existence itself. Chuck Jones, Woody Allen, Wes Craven, Jackie Chan, and Steven Spielberg are among the filmmakers to pay homage to Keaton's irresistible mischief, and his films remain perhaps the most accessible of all silent movies. **RDe**

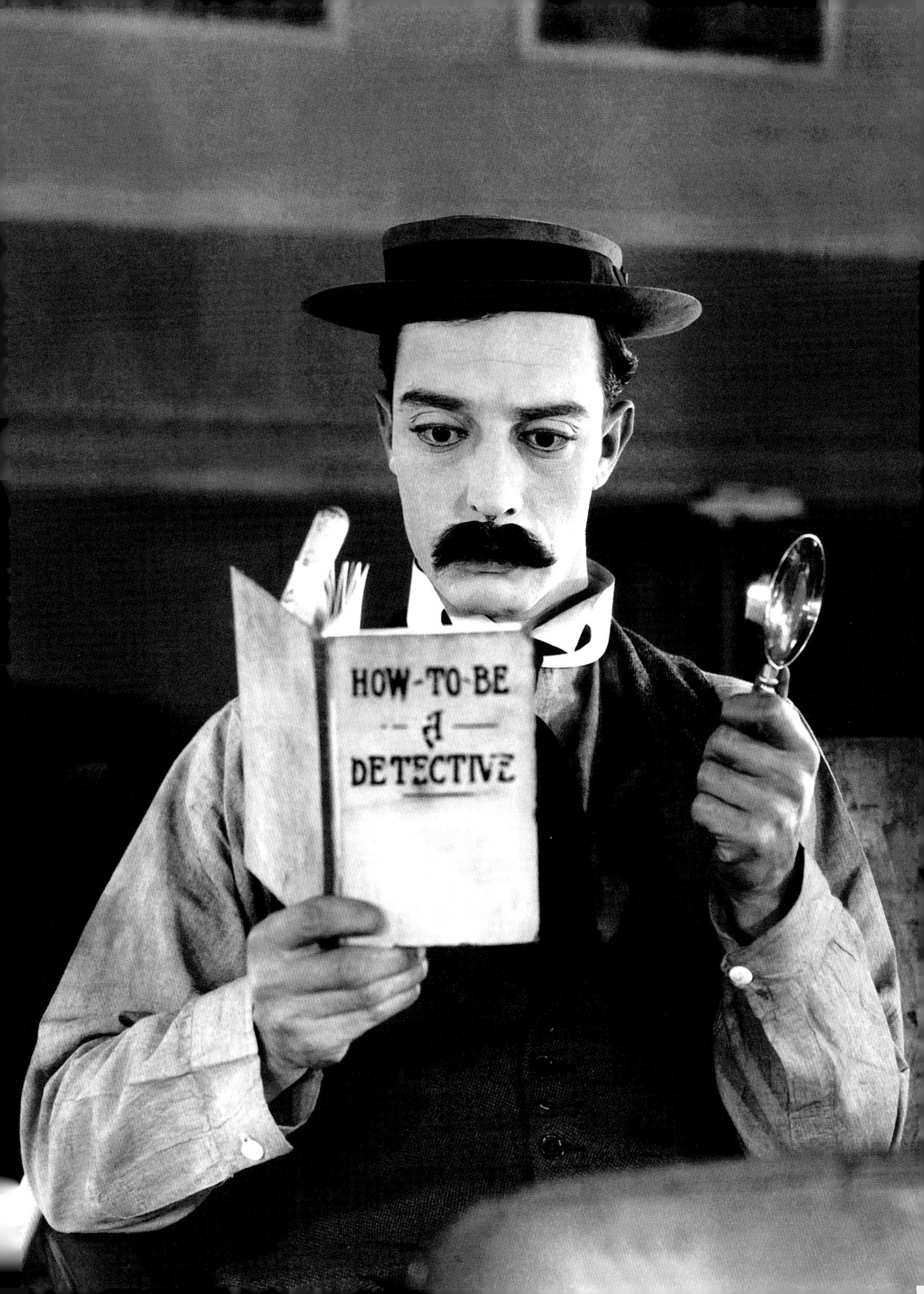
HOW-TO-BE
A
DETECTIVE

## DER LETZTE MANN (1924)
### THE LAST LAUGH

**Germany** (Universum, UFA) 77m Silent BW

**Director:** F.W. Murnau

**Producer:** Erich Pommer

**Screenplay:** Carl Mayer

**Photography:** Robert Baberske, Karl Freund

**Music:** Giuseppe Becce, Timothy Brock, Peter Schirmann

**Cast:** Emil Jannings, Maly Delschaft, Max Hiller, Emilie Kurz, Hans Unterkircher, Olaf Storm, Hermann Vallentin, Georg John, Emmy Wyda

Despite a ludicrously unconvincing happy ending grafted on at the insistence of UFA, F.W. Murnau's *The Last Laugh* remains a very impressive attempt to tell a story without the use of intertitles. The plot itself is nothing special—a hotel commissionaire, humiliated by his loss in status when he is demoted to lavatory attendant because of his advancing years, sinks so low that he is tempted to steal back his beloved uniform (the symbol of his professional pride.) In some respects the film is merely a vehicle for one of Emil Janning's typically grandstand performances.

Above and beyond this somewhat pathetic parable, however, exists one of Murnau's typically eloquent explorations of cinematic space: the camera prowls around with astonishing fluidity, articulating the protagonist's relationship with the world as it follows him around the hotel, the city streets, and his home in the slum tenements. Some of the camera work is "subjective," as when his drunken perceptions are rendered by optical distortion; at other times, it is the camera's mobility that is evocative, as when it passes through the revolving doors that serve as a symbol of destiny. The dazzling technique on display may, in fact, be rather too grand for the simple story of one old man, yet there is no denying the virtuosity either of Murnau's mise en scène or of Karl Freund's camera work. **GA**

## SEVEN CHANCES (1925)

**U.S.** (Buster Keaton) 60m BW/ Technicolor

**Director:** Buster Keaton

**Producer:** Joseph M. Schenck, Buster Keaton

**Screenplay:** Clyde Bruckman, Jean C. Havez, Joseph A. Mitchell

**Photography:** Byron Houck, Elgin Lessley

**Cast:** Buster Keaton, T. Roy Barnes, Snitz Edwards, Ruth Dwyer, Frances Raymond, Erwin Connelly, Jules Cowles

Every kind of cinematic gag gets worked out in *Seven Chances*, engineering laughter from an astonishing interplay of time, space, and physicality. Take the famous camera angle inside a church—Buster asleep in the front pew, invisible to the hundreds of grotesque women who completely fill the space behind him. (This is really all that remains in the film's woeful 1999 remake, *The Bachelor*.)

The serene nuttiness of Keaton's gag concepts buoyed the hearts of the surrealists who were his contemporaries: the plot's irrational fixation on the number seven (seven chances for Buster to be married on his 27th birthday by seven o'clock); or the wondrous gags that make complete nonsense of any fixed human identity—as in the sequence where a bunch of supposedly white, all-American, adult women turn out to be (respectively) a little girl, Jewish, black, and male.

Keaton's best and most extended gag sequences are dynamic and transformative. The whole world seems to unshape and reshape itself before our eyes. In the climactic chase sequence, Buster is pursued by an enormous pack of vengeful women. After he trips on a few rocks, suddenly the whole world is after him, in the form of a huge avalanche. **AM**

# THE PHANTOM OF THE OPERA (1925)

This 1925 silent remains the closest adaption of Gaston Leroux's trash masterpiece, a novel that has a terrific setting and a great central figure but a plot that creaks at every turn. The film is a strange combination of plodding direction (mostly from Rupert Julian, though other hands intervened) and incredible Universal Pictures set design, so that stick-figure characters—weedy hero Norman Kerry is especially annoying—pose in front of incredibly impressive tableaux.

*The Phantom of the Opera* delivers a series of masterly moments that cover up its rickety structure: the masked ball (a brief technicolor sequence), where the Phantom shows up dressed as Edgar Allen Poe's Red Death; the chandelier-dropping where the Phantom lets the audience know what he thinks of the current diva; various trips into the magical underworld beneath the Paris Opera House; and—best of all—the unmasking in which the tragic villain's disfigured skullface is first seen (so shocking that even the camera is terrified, going briefly out of focus).

The reason this is a classic is that it enshrines one of the greatest bits of melodramatic acting in the silent cinema, Lon Chaney's impeccably dressed, lovelorn, violent ghoul-genius. Favorite intertitle: "You are dancing on the tombs of tortured men!" **KN**

**U.S.** (Universal Pictures) 93m Silent BW/Color (2-strip Technicolor)

**Director:** Rupert Julian, Lon Chaney

**Producer:** Carl Laemmle

**Screenplay:** Gaston Leroux

**Photography:** Milton Bridenbecker, Virgil Miller, Charles Van Enger

**Music:** Gustav Hinrichs (1925 version), David Broekman, Sam Perry, William Schiller (1929 version)

**Cast:** Lon Chaney, Mary Philbin, Norman Kerry, Arthur Edmund Carewe, Gibson Gowland, John St. Polis, Snitz Edwards

**U.S.S.R.** (Goskino, Mosfilm) 75m Silent BW

**Director:** Grigori Aleksandrov, Sergei M. Eisenstein

**Producer:** Jacob Bliokh

**Screenplay:** Nina Agadzhanova, Sergei M. Eisenstein

**Photography:** Vladimir Popov, Eduard Tisse

**Music:** Nikolai Kryukov, Edmund Meisel, Dmitri Shostakovich

**Cast:** Aleksandr Antonov, Vladimir Barsky, Grigori Aleksandrov, Mikhail Gomorov, Ivan Bobrov, Beatrice Vitoldi, N. Poltavseva, Julia Eisenstein

# BRONENOSETS POTYOMKIN (1925)
## THE BATTLESHIP POTEMKIN

*The Battleship Potemkin*—such a famous film! Sergei Eisenstein's second feature was to become not just a point of ideological conflict between the East and the West, the Left and the Right, but a must-see film for every cinema lover on the planet. Decades of censorship and militant support, countless words analyzing its structure, its symbolism, its sources and effects, and thousands of visual quotations have all served to make it very difficult for us to see the story behind the film. Eisensteins's *Battleship Potemkin* may not be historically accurate, but his legendary vision of oppression and rebellion, individual and collective action, and its artistic ambition to work simultaneously with bodies, light, trivial objects, symbols, faces, movement, geometrical forms... is a unique keyboard. As a true artist of film, he manages to elaborate a magnificent and touching myth.

It should be kept in mind, however, that this aesthetic sensibility was endowed with political significance as well: the "changing of the world by conscious men" that had been dreamt of in those times and was known by the term "Revolution." But even without an awareness of what it meant, or—better—without a precise awareness of what it eventually turned into, the wind of an epic adventure still blows on the screen here, and makes it move. Whatever else one chooses to call it, this adventure is the unique impulse which drives the

people of Odessa toward liberty, the sailors of the eponymous battleship to battle against hunger and humiliation, and the filmmaker himself to invent new cinematic forms and rhythms.

*The Battleship Potemkin* has been seen too often in excerpted form, or on the basis of its most famous scenes and sequences. It may come as something of a surprise to find how powerful it is to see the film in its entirety—that is to say, as a dramatic and touching story—rather than treating it as a priceless jewelry box from which to remove individual pieces on occasion.

Such a renewed, innocent approach to the film will bring back a real sense of being to those icons that have become familiar to us all: the baby carriage on the steps; the face of the dead sailor under the tent at the end of the pier; the worms in the meat; the leather boots; the iron guns pointed toward bodies and faces; the glasses of a blind political, military, and religious power waiting in the void. Then, before it all becomes ideological interpretation, the stone lion coming alive to roar with anger and a desire for life will become a metaphor for the film itself, and for the high and daring idea of cinema it was bearing, escaping from its monumental status to be found, alive and fresh once again, by every new pair of eyes that looks upon it. **J-MF**

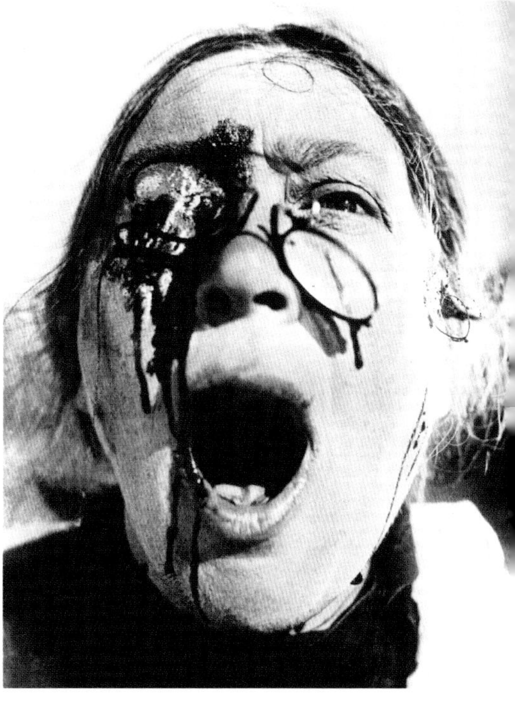

## THE GOLD RUSH (1925)

*The Gold Rush* affirmed Charles Chaplin's belief that tragedy and comedy are never far apart. His unlikely dual inspiration came from viewing some stereoscope slides of the privations of prospectors in the Klondyke Gold Rush of 1896–98, and reading a book about the Donner Party Disaster of 1846, when a party of immigrants, snowbound in the Sierra Nevada, were reduced to eating their own moccasins and the corpses of their dead comrades. Out of these grim and unlikely themes, Chaplin created high comedy. The familiar Little Tramp becomes a gold prospector, joining the mass of brave optimists to face all the hazards of cold, starvation, solitude, and the occasional incursion of a grizzly bear.

The film was in every respect the most elaborate undertaking of Chaplin's career. For two weeks the unit shot on location at Truckee in the snow country of the Sierra Nevada. Here Chaplin faithfully recreated the historic image of the prospectors struggling up the Chilkoot Pass. Some 600 extras, many drawn from the vagrants and derelicts of Sacramento, were brought by train to clamber up the 2,300-foot pass dug through the mountain snow. For the main shooting the unit returned to the Hollywood studio, where a remarkably convincing miniature mountain range was created out of timber, chicken wire, burlap, plaster, salt, and flour. In addition, the studio technicians devised exquisite models to produce the special effects which Chaplin required, like the miners' hut, which is blown by the tempest to teeter on the edge of a precipice, for one of the cinema's most sustained sequences of comic suspense. Often it is impossible to detect the shifts in the film from model to full-size set.

**U.S.** (Charles Chaplin) 72m Silent BW
**Director:** Charles Chaplin
**Producer:** Charles Chaplin
**Screenplay:** Charles Chaplin
**Photography:** Roland Totheroh
**Music:** Max Terr (1942 version)
**Cast:** Charles Chaplin, Mack Swain, Tom Murray, Henry Bergman, Malcolm Waite, Georgia Hale

*The Gold Rush* abounds with now-classic comedy scenes. The historic horrors of the starving 19th-century pioneers inspired the sequence in which Charlie and his partner Big Jim (Mack Swain) are snowbound and ravenous. Charlie cooks his boot, with all the airs of a gourmet. In the eyes of the delirious Big Jim, he is intermittently transformed into an oven-worthy chicken—a triumph both for the cameramen, who had to effect the elaborate trick work entirely in the camera, and for Chaplin, who magically assumes the characteristics of a bird.

The lone prospector's dream of hosting a New Year's dinner for the beautiful dance-hall girl (Georgia Hale, who replaced 16-year-old Lita Grey when Lita became pregnant and married Chaplin) provides the opportunity for another famous Chaplin set piece: the dance of the rolls. The gag had been seen in films before, but Chaplin gives unique personality to the dancing legs created out of forks and rolls.

Today, *The Gold Rush* appears as one of Chaplin's most perfectly accomplished films. Though his affections for his own work changed over time, to the end of his life he would frequently declare that this film was the one by which he would most wish to be remembered. **DR**

# THE BIG PARADE (1925)

Based on a story by Laurence Stallings, who wrote the Broadway smash *What Price Glory?*, King Vidor's epic film about the American experience of World War I traces the adventures of three soldiers from different backgrounds who find themselves in France. Rich boy Jim (John Gilbert), whose fiancée had encouraged him to join up, meets a beautiful French woman (Renée Adorée) in the village where their unit has been assigned lodging. In one of *The Big Parade*'s most tender scenes, she clutches the boot he has left with her as the soldiers make their way to the front. Once they arrive at the trenches, the battle of Belleau Wood commences. Attacking a machine gun nest, Jim's two buddies are killed and he is wounded. Seeking refuge in a shell hole, he discovers a dying German soldier already occupying it and the two share a cigarette. Eventually, he is found and then taken to a field hospital. His attempts to reach the farmhouse fail as he falls unconscious.

Back in America, Jim is reunited with his family, but is bitterly unhappy because he has lost a leg. His fiancée, in any case, has now fallen in love with his brother. Finally, Jim accepts his mother's advice and returns to France, where in the film's most moving scene he locates his lost love as she is helping her mother plow the fields. With its expert mixture of physical comedy (particularly in the French farmhouse scenes) and well-staged action, *The Big Parade* proved an immense success—a testimony to producer Irving Thalberg's oversight of the project—and counts as one of the triumphs of the late silent era.

Gilbert turns in a fine performance as Jim, showing the box-office appeal that made him one of the era's biggest stars, and Adorée is appropriately appealing as his love interest. Because it shows the horrors of war, *The Big Parade* has often been thought a pacifist tract, but in truth its politics are muted. As Thalberg wanted, the film is much more of a comedy romance, with the war serving as the means through which Jim becomes a man and discovers the kind of life he really wants to live. **RBP**

**U.S.** (MGM) 141m Silent BW (tinted sequences)

**Director:** King Vidor

**Producer:** Irving Thalberg

**Screenplay:** Harry Behn, Joseph Farnham

**Photography:** John Arnold

**Music:** William Axt, Maurice Baron, David Mendoza

**Cast:** John Gilbert, Renée Adorée, Hobart Bosworth, Claire McDowell, Claire Adams, Robert Ober, Tom O'Brien, Karl Dane, Rosita Marstini, George Beranger, Frank Currier

**Germany** (Universum/UFA) 120m Silent BW

**Director:** Fritz Lang

**Producer:** Erich Pommer

**Screenplay:** Fritz Lang, Thea von Harbou

**Photography:** Karl Freund, Günther Rittau

**Music:** Gottfried Huppertz

**Cast:** Alfred Abel, Gustav Fröhlich, Brigitte Helm, Rudolf Klein-Rogge, Fritz Rasp, Theodor Loos, Heinrich George

# METROPOLIS (1927)

Originally clocking at over two hours, Fritz Lang's *Metropolis* is the first science-fiction epic, with huge sets, thousands of extras, then-state-of-the-art special effects, lots of sex and violence, a heavy-handed moral, big acting, a streak of Germanic gothicism, and groundbreaking fantasy sequences. Bankrolled by UFA, Germany's giant film studio, it was controversial in its day and proved a box-office disaster that nearly ruined the studio.

The plot is almost as simplistic as a fairy tale, with Freder Fredersen (Gustav Frölich), pampered son of the Master of Metropolis (Alfred Abel), learning of the wretched lives of the multitude of workers who keep the gleaming supercity going. Freder comes to understand the way things work by the saintly Maria (Brigitte Helm), a pacifist who constantly preaches mediation in industrial disputes, as well as by secretly working on a hellish ten-hour shift at one of the grinding machines. The Master consults with mad engineer Rotwang (Rudolf Klein-Rogge), who has created a feminoid robot he reshapes to be an evil double of Maria and unleashes on the city. The robotrix goes from dancing naked in a decadent nightspot to inciting a destructive riot, which allows Lang to get the most value out of the huge factory sets by blowing them up and/or flooding them, but Freder and the real Maria save the day by rescuing the city's children from a flood. Society is reunited when Maria decrees that the heart (Freder) must mediate between the brain (the Master) and the hands (the workers).

Shortly after its premiere, the expensive film was pulled from distribution and reedited against Lang's wishes: this truncated, simplified form remained best-known, even in the colorized Giorgio Moroder remix of the 1980s, until the 21st century, when a partial restoration—with tactful linking titles to fill in the scenes that remain irretrievably missing—made it much closer to Lang's original vision. This version not only adds many scenes that went unseen for decades, but also restores their order in the original version and puts in the proper intertitles. Up to that point rated as a spectacular but simplistic science-fiction film, this new-old version reveals that the futuristic setting isn't intended as prophetic but mythical, with elements of 1920s architecture, industry, design, and politics mingled with the medieval and the Biblical to produce images of striking strangeness: a futuristic robot burned at the stake, a steel-handed mad scientist who is also a 15th-century alchemist, the trudging workers of a vast factory plodding into the jaws of a machine that is also the ancient god Moloch. Frölich's performance as the hero who represents the heart is still wildly overdone, but Klein-Rogge's engineer Rotwang, Abel's Master of Metropolis, and, especially, Helm in the dual role of saintly savior and metal femme fatale are astonishing. By restoring a great deal of story delving into the mixed motivations of the characters, the wild plot now makes more sense, and we can see it is as much a twisted family drama as an epic of repression, revolution, and reconciliation. **KN**

U.S. (Fox) 97m Silent BW
**Director:** F.W. Murnau
**Producer:** William Fox
**Screenplay:** Hermann Sudermann, Carl Mayer
**Photography:** Charles Rosher, Karl Struss
**Music:** Timothy Brock, Hugo Riesenfeld
**Cast:** George O'Brien, Janet Gaynor, Margaret Livingston, Bodil Rosing, J. Farrell MacDonald, Ralph Sipperly, Jane Winton, Arthur Housman, Eddie Boland, Barry Norton
**Oscar:** William Fox (unique and artistic picture), Janet Gaynor (actress), Charles Rosher, Karl Struss (photography)
**Oscar nomination:** Rochus Gliese (art direction)

# SUNRISE (1927)

Trivia buffs might note that although many history books often cite *Wings* as the first Best Picture recipient at the Academy Awards, the honor actually went to two films: William Wellman's *Wings*, for "production," and F.W. Murnau's *Sunrise*, for "unique and artistic production." If the latter category sounds more impressive than the former, that explains in part at least why *Sunrise*, and not *Wings*, remains one of the most revered films of all time. William Fox initially drew Murnau to America with the promise of a big budget and total creative freedom, and the fact that Murnau made the most of it with this stunning masterpiece ratified his peerless reputation as a cinematic genius.

*Sunrise* itself is deceptively simple. Subtitled somewhat enigmatically *A Song of Two Humans*, the film focuses on a country-dwelling married couple whose lives are disrupted by a temptress from the city. But Murnau draws waves of emotion from what could have been a rote melodrama, further enhanced by a bevy of groundbreaking filmmaking techniques. Most notable is the use of sound effects, pushing silent cinema one step closer to the talkie era—an achievement unfairly overshadowed by *The Jazz Singer*, released later in 1927. Murnau also creatively manipulates the use and effect of title cards (three years earlier, he had directed the title-free *The Last Laugh*).

The most striking aspect of *Sunrise* is its camera work. Working with a pair of cinematographers, Charles Rosher and Karl Struss, Murnau borrowed from his own experience in the German Expressionist movement as well as from the pastoral portraits of the Dutch masters, particularly Jan Vermeer. Linked with graceful and inventive camera movements and accented with in-camera tricks (such as multiple-exposures), each scene of *Sunrise* looks like a masterful still photograph.

As magical as the imagery may be, the very simplicity of the story lends *Sunrise* a formidable dramatic weight. George O'Brien, pondering the murder of his innocent wife Janet Gaynor, is wracked with guilt, and his wife responds with appropriate terror once his intentions become obvious. The boat trip leading to her intended demise is fraught with both suspense and an odd sense of sadness, as the good O'Brien struggles to bring his monstrous thoughts to their fruition. Margaret Livingston, as the urban seductress, in many ways seems like the feminine equivalent of Murnau's vampire Count Orlok (from the 1922 film *Nosferatu*), relentlessly preying on poor O'Brien's soul. In one scene he's even beset by spectral images of her, surrounding him, clutching at him, and provoking him with her murderous desires.

Alas, the film turned out to be a box-office flop, and Murnau died in a car accident a few years later. But *Sunrise* remains a benchmark by which all other films—silent or not—should be measured, a pinnacle of craft in a more primitive age whose sophistication belies the resources at the time. Its shadow looms over several subsequent great works, from Orson Welles's *Citizen Kane* (1941) to Jean Cocteau's *Beauty and the Beast* (1946), yet at the same time its own brilliance is inimitable. **JKl**

U.S. (Buster Keaton, United Artists)
75m Silent BW (Sepiatone)

**Director:** Clyde Bruckman, Buster Keaton

**Producer:** Buster Keaton, Joseph M. Schenck

**Screenplay:** Al Boasberg, Clyde Bruckman

**Photography:** Bert Haines, Devereaux Jennings

**Music:** Robert Israel, William P. Perry

**Cast:** Marion Mack, Charles Smith, Richard Allen, Glen Cavender, Jim Farley, Frederick Vroom, Joe Keaton, Mike Donlin, Tom Nawn, Buster Keaton

# THE GENERAL (1927)

Keaton made several films—*Our Hospitality* (1923), *Sherlock, Jr.* (1924), *Steamboat Bill Jr.* (1928)—that may be counted among the finest (and funniest) in cinema's entire comic output, but none is as strong a contender to the title of the greatest comedy ever made as this timeless masterpiece. It isn't merely the constant stream of great gags, nor the way they derive wholly from situation and character rather than existing in isolation from the film's drama. Rather, what makes *The General* so extraordinary is that it is superlative on every level: in terms of its humor, suspense, historical reconstruction, character study, visual beauty, and technical precision. One might even argue that it comes as close to flawless perfection as any feature ever made, comic or otherwise.

Much of the pleasure derives from the narrative itself, inspired by a book about the real-life exploits of a group of Northern soldiers who during the Civil War disguised themselves as Southerners to steal a train, which they drove north to rejoin their Unionist comrades until they were caught and executed. Keaton, understandably given that he was making a comedy, dropped the executions and changed the heroic perspective to that of a Southerner, Johnny Gray, a railway-driver who stoically if somewhat absurdly goes in solo pursuit of Unionist spies when they steal both his engine—"The General"—and, inside it, Annabelle Lee (Marion Mack), the other love of his life. The film's first half follows Johnny's rejection by the army with his chase after the train, which he recaptures behind enemy lines; the second half depicts his flight (with Annabelle) from the Union troops to his hometown where—after handing over the Girl, The General, and a real Northern army general inadvertently brought along for the ride—he is acclaimed as a hero.

This elegant symmetrical story line is both formally pleasing and the source of suspense and gags; but the voyage also lends the film an epic tone which, combined with Keaton's customarily meticulous historical detail, transforms it into perhaps the finest Civil War movie ever made. Then, finally, there is Buster's Johnny: unsmiling yet beautiful in his brave, faintly ridiculous determination—the epitome of this serio-comic masterpiece, and as deeply human a hero as the cinema has given us. **GA**

## THE UNKNOWN (1927)

**U.S.** (MGM) 65m Silent BW
**Director:** Tod Browning
**Screenplay:** Tod Browning, Waldemar Young
**Photography:** Merritt B. Gerstad
**Cast:** Lon Chaney, Norman Kerry, Joan Crawford, Nick De Ruiz, John George, Frank Lanning, Polly Moran

Best known for directing Bela Lugosi in the 1931 Universal horror classic *Dracula* (1931), and most notorious for his 1932 oddity *Freaks*, circus performer-turned-filmmaker Tod Browning's all-around greatest film is *The Unknown*. The film is an under-appreciated silent-era gem starring the writer/director's favorite (and most famous) actor, the so-called "Man of a Thousand Faces," Lon Chaney.

Wellknown and greatly admired for the physical pain he would regularly endure playing physically disabled antagonists or antiheroes, Chaney here outdoes himself as Alonzo, a criminal with an extra thumb on one hand who seeks to avoid capture by pretending to be an armless knife-thrower in a gypsy-run circus. The armless gig at first has an additional benefit, as Alonzo's beautiful assistant Nanon (Joan Crawford in one of her earliest leads), daughter of the circus owner, can't stand being embraced by men—in particular the chief competition with Alonzo for her affections, weight-lifting strongman Malabar the Mighty (Norman Kerry).

After Nanon's father accidentally sees his arms, Alonzo murders him in order to keep the secret from getting out. Nanon, meanwhile, catches a glimpse of the killer's double thumb without seeing his face. Obsessed with Nanon, distraught over the possibility that she will eventually discover his true identity, Alonzo dismisses the objections of his dwarf assistant Cojo (John George) and has his arms surgically amputated. But in one of *The Unknown*'s most delicious and disturbing ironies, when Alonzo returns to the circus after a lengthy convalescence he finds that Nanon has gotten over her phobia of being held, and has fallen head over heels for Malabar.

Seeking poetic justice (or just garden-variety revenge) for this ultra-cruel twist of fate, the now truly armless Alonzo attempts to rig Malabar's latest circus act—in which the strongman ties his arms to a pair of horses, each one pulling in the opposite direction—so that his rival will end up armless as well. However his scheme is foiled at the last second, and Alonzo himself gets killed saving Nanon from being trampled by one of the horses.

Drawing a remarkable and haunting performance from Chaney, filling the plot with striking twists and unforgettable characters, Browning here creates a chilling masterpiece of psychological (and psychosexual) drama. As Michael Koller writes, "*The Unknown* is a truly horrifying film that takes us into the darkest recesses of the human psyche." **SJS**

# OKTYABR (1927)
## OCTOBER

**U.S.S.R.** (Sovkino) 95m Silent BW
**Director:** Grigori Aleksandrov, Sergei M. Eisenstein
**Screenplay:** Grigori Aleksandrov, Sergei M. Eisenstein
**Photography:** Vladimir Nilsen, Vladimir Popov, Eduard Tisse
**Music:** Alfredo Antonini, Edmund Meisel
**Cast:** Vladimir Popov, Vasili Nikandrov, Layaschenko, Chibisov, Boris Livanov, Mikholyev, N. Podvoisky, Smelsky, Eduard Tisse

In 1926, Sergei M. Eisenstein went to Germany to present his new film *The Battleship Potemkin*. He left a promising young filmmaker, but he came back an international cultural superstar. A series of major film productions was being planned to commemorate the tenth anniversary of the Bolshevik victory. Eisenstein eagerly accepted the challenge of presenting on screen the revolutionary process in Russia—literally, how the country went from Aleksandr Kerensky's "Provisional Government," installed after the Czar's abdication, to the first victories of Lenin and his followers.

No expense was spared. Massive crowd scenes were organized, and city traffic was diverted so Eisenstein could shoot in the very sites where the depicted incident occurred. Contrary to popular belief the film contains not one meter of documentary footage. Every shot was a re-creation. Working feverishly, Eisenstein finished just in time for the anniversary celebrations, but the reactions, official and otherwise, were less than enthusiastic. Many found the film confusing and difficult to follow. Others wondered why the role of Lenin was so greatly reduced (the actor playing him, Vasili Nikandrov, appears only a handful of times on screen.) Several critics who had supported *Potemkin* suggested that Eisenstein go back to the editing room and keep working.

There is no denying that *October* is some sort of masterpiece, but figuring out what kind is a real challenge. As a didactic tool, a means of "explaining" the revolution to the masses at home and abroad, the film is simply ineffective. For many audiences sitting through it is a real chore. The characterizations are all paper thin, and anyone with even a smattering of historical knowledge can see right through its crude propaganda. Yet what is perhaps most powerful and touching about *October* is simply its level of ambition. Sergei M. Eisenstein was surely the cinema's most remarkable personality for the first 50 years of its existence, impossibly erudite, with an unlimited belief in cinema's potential. At his most delirious, Eisenstein imagined that cinema could represent "visual thinking"—not just arguments, but the process by which the mind constructs arguments. Photographic images, the raw material of cinema, had to be "neutralized" into sensations and stimuli so that a film could reveal concepts and not just people or things. The real engine that would drive the cinema machine as Eisenstein saw it was montage, editing: the "mystical" interaction that occurs when two separate pieces of film are joined together.

*October* is the purest, most cogent example of Eisenstein's theory and practice of cinema. There are several absolutely breathtaking sequences: the toppling of the Czar's statue, the raising of the bridge, and especially the frequently cited "For God and Country" sequence. Evidence of the cold engineer that Eisenstein originally trained to be, might be found in the cathedral-like intricacy of its editing. However, scratch just below the film's surface and you can feel the exhilaration—and the touch of madness—of an artist standing on the threshold of what he believes will be a brave new world. **RP**

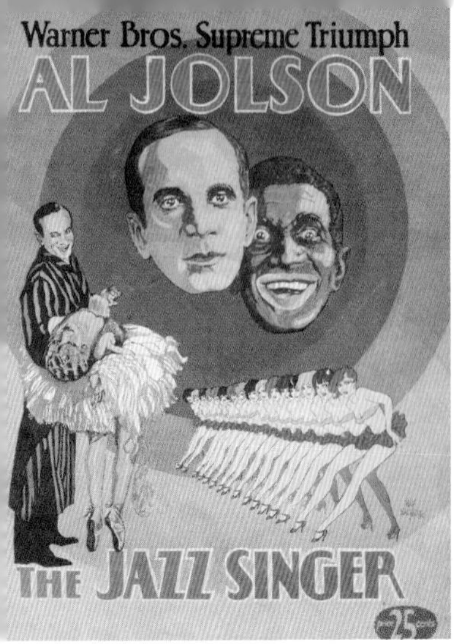


U.S. (Warner Bros.) 88m BW
**Director:** Alan Crosland
**Screenplay:** Alfred A. Cohn, Jack Jarmuth
**Photography:** Hal Mohr
**Music:** Ernie Erdman, James V. Monaco, Louis Silvers, Irving Berlin
**Cast:** Al Jolson, May McAvoy, Warner Oland, Eugenie Besserer, Otto Lederer, Bobby Gordon, Richard Tucker, Cantor Josef Rosenblatt
**Oscar:** Alfred A. Cohn, Jack Jarmuth (honorary award for pioneering talking pictures)
**Oscar nomination:** Alfred A. Cohn (screenplay)

# THE JAZZ SINGER (1927)

Throughout film history, certain movies have been the center of special attention, if not for their aesthetics, definitely for their role in the development of cinema as we know it. Alan Crosland's *The Jazz Singer* is undoubtedly one of the films that has marked the path of motion pictures as both an art form and a profitable industry. Released in 1927 by Warner Brothers and starring Al Jolson, one of the best-known vocal artists at the time, *The Jazz Singer* is unanimously considered the first feature-length sound movie. Although limited to musical performances and a few dialogues following and preceding such performances, the use of sound introduced innovative changes in the industry, destined to revolutionize Hollywood as hardly any other movie has done.

In its blend of vaudeville and melodrama, the plot is relatively simple. Jakie (Jolson) is the only teenage son of the devoted Cantor Rabinowitz (Warner Oland), who encourages his child to follow the same path of generations of Cantors in the family. Although profoundly influenced by his Jewish roots, Jakie's passion is jazz and he dreams about an audience inspired by his voice. After a family friend confesses to Cantor Rabinowitz to having seen Jakie singing in a café, the furious father punishes his son, causing him to run away from the family house and from his heartbroken mother Sara (Eugenie Besserer). Years later Jakie, aka Jack Robin, comes back as an affirmed jazz singer looking for reconciliation. Finding his father still harsh and now sick, Jack is forced to make a decision between his career as a blackface entertainer and his Jewish identity.

A milestone in film history representing a decisive step toward a new type of cinema and a new type of entertainment, *The Jazz Singer* is more than just the first "talkie." As Michael Rogin, the famed political scientist, has argued, *The Jazz Singer* can be cited as a typical example of Jewish transformation in U.S. society: the racial assimilation into white America, the religious conversion to less strict spiritual dogma, and the entrepreneurial integration into the American motion picture industry during the time of the coming of sound. **CFe**

## NAPOLÉON (1927)

At 333 minutes in its longest extant version, Abel Gance's 1927 biopic is an epic on a scale to satisfy its subject. Although it follows Bonaparte from his schooldays in 1780—marshalling snowball fights—through to his triumphant Italian campaign of 1796, by contemporary standards the film lacks depth. For Gance, Napoléon (played by the appropriately named Albert Dieudonné) was a "man of destiny," not pyschology. His paean to the French Emperor has something in common with Sergei Eisenstein's *Alexander Nevsky* (1938), both thrilling pieces of cinema in the service of nationalist propaganda.

If Gance is more of an innovator than an artist, it's a measure of his brilliance that *Napoléon* still brims with energy and invention today. None of his contemporaries—not even Murnau—used the camera with such inspiration. Gance thought nothing of strapping cameramen to horses; he even mounted a camera on the guillotine. In one brilliant sequence, he captures the revolutionary spirit of a rousing (silent) rendition of "La Marseilles" by swinging the camera above the set as if it were on a trapeze. His most spectacular coup, though, is "Polyvision," a split-screen effect which called for three projectors to create a triptych—nearly three decades before the advent of Cinerama. **TCh**

**France / Italy / Germany / Spain / Sweden / Czechoslovakia** (Gance, Soc. générale) 378m (original) Silent BW (some color)

**Director:** Abel Gance

**Producer:** Robert A. Harris

**Screenplay:** Abel Gance

**Photography:** Jules Kruger, Joseph-Louis Mundwiller, Torpkoff

**Music:** Arthur Honegger

**Cast:** Albert Dieudonné, Vladimir Roudenko, Edmond Van Daële, Alexandre Koubitzky, Antonin Artaud, Abel Gance, Gina Manès, Suzanne Bianchetti, Marguerite Gance, Yvette Dieudonné, Philippe Hériat, Pierre Batcheff, Eugénie Buffet, Acho Chakatouny, Nicolas Koline

## THE KID BROTHER (1927)

Harold Lloyd is often regarded as the "third genius" of silent American comedy, his 1920s' work often considerably more successful with the public than that of Buster Keaton, and even Charlie Chaplin. Often directly associated with the Zeitgeist of the Jazz Age, Lloyd's screen persona is routinely noted for its "speedy," can-do optimism and his films singled-out for the audacious, often dangerous stunts and acrobatic feats that they contain. In many of his films the wonders of modernity and their embodiment in the teeming city itself are chief preoccupations. *The Kid Brother*, Lloyd's second feature for Paramount, is often considered to be the bespectacled comic's best and most holistic film. In many ways it deliberately turns its back on the 1920s, returning somewhat to the rural "idyll" of the 1922 film *Grandma's Boy*.

The film's two most startling sequences provide a kind of essay in contrast, illustrating the combination of both a delicate and somewhat more rugged athleticism that marks Lloyd's best work. In the first sequence, Lloyd is shown climbing a tall tree to attain a slightly longer look at the woman he has just met (and fallen for). This sequence illustrates the often meticulous and technically adventurous aspects of Lloyd's cinema—an elevator was built to accommodate the ascending camera—and the ways these are intricately connected to elements of character and situation (also demonstrating Lloyd's masterly use of props). The second extended sequence features a fight between Lloyd and his chief antagonist, and is remarkable for its sustained ferocity and precise staging. Both sequences show Lloyd's character transcending his seeming limitations, moving beyond appearances, and traveling that common trajectory from mama's boy to triumphant "average" American. **AD**

**U.S.** (Paramount, Harold Lloyd) 84m Silent BW

**Director:** J.A. Howe, Ted Wilde

**Producer:** Jesse L. Lasky, Harold Lloyd, Adolph Zukor

**Screenplay:** Thomas J. Crizer, Howard J. Green, John Grey, Lex Neal, Ted Wilde

**Photography:** Walter Lundin

**Cast:** Harold Lloyd, Jobyna Ralston, Walter James, Leo Willis, Olin Francis, Constantine Romanoff, Eddie Boland, Frank Lanning, Ralph Yearsley

**U.S.** (MGM) 104m Silent BW
**Director:** King Vidor
**Producer:** Irving Thalberg
**Screenplay:** King Vidor & John V.A. Weaver
**Photography:** Henry Sharp
**Cast:** Eleanor Boardman, James Murray, Bert Roach, Estelle Clark, Daniel G. Tomlinson, Dell Henderson, Lucy Beaumont, Freddie Burke Frederick, Alice Mildred Puter
**Oscar nomination:** Irving Thalberg (best picture—unique and artistic picture), King Vidor (director)

# THE CROWD (1928)

"You've got to be good in that town if you want to beat the crowd." So says young John on his first sight of New York City, the thrilling metropolis where he's sure his special qualities will raise him high above the common herd.

Things work out differently for the hero of *The Crowd*, who shouldn't really be called a hero, because director King Vidor's intention was to portray a man so painfully ordinary that he could seem a randomly selected sample from the movie's eponymous urban multitude. He begins the story as a newborn baby indistinguishable from any other, and ends it as a New York bourgeois man indistinguishable from any other. In between, he undergoes experiences so humdrum that only a studio as adventurous as MGM under Irving G. Thalberg's regime would have considered it the stuff of Hollywood drama at all.

Nor would it have been if Vidor hadn't given it such stunningly imaginative treatment. From the stylized scene where John learns of his father's untimely death—filmed in a stairwell with forced perspective, borrowing from German film expressionism—to the closing shot of John and his wife Mary, the generically named protagonists of this generically titled film, engulfed in an unthinking throng of moviegoers who mirror their herdlike selves, as unerringly and relentlessly as they mirror our own.

Vidor was riding high in Hollywood when he made *The Crowd*, fresh from the success of his World War I epic *The Big Parade* two years earlier. To play Mary he chose the attractive star Eleanor Boardman, who also happened to be his wife; but for John he took a chance on the little-tested James Murray, whose erratic career ended in suicide less than a decade later.

Although both are brilliant, Murray shines brightest under Vidor's expert guidance; for evidence see the sequence when an unthinkable tragedy strikes the couple before their horrified eyes, uniting inspired acting with split-second editing and absolutely perfect camera work to produce one of the most unforgettable moments in all of silent cinema. It's a scene that stands leagues above the crowd in a movie that does the same from start to finish. **DS**

# THE DOCKS OF NEW YORK (1928)

U.S. (Famous Players-Lasky, Paramount) Silent BW

**Director:** Josef von Sternberg

**Producer:** J.G. Bachmann

**Screenplay:** Jules Furthman, from the story *The Dock Walloper* by John Monk Saunders

**Photography:** Harold Rosson

**Cast:** George Bancroft, Betty Compson, Olga Baclanova, Clyde Cook, Mitchell Lewis, Gustav von Seyffertitz, Guy Oliver, May Foster, Lillian Worth

1928, the last full year of Hollywood's silent era, produced some of its greatest masterpieces, marking the final maturation of a form that was soon to be extinct: *The Cameraman*, *The Crowd*, *Street Angel*, *The Wedding March*, *The Wind*. Like these others, Josef von Sternberg's *The Docks of New York* is a film of consummate economy and refinement. The plot is minimal and the characters few, leaving more room for the film's maximal elaboration of atmosphere and gesture.

The characters of *The Docks of New York* seem to have stepped out of the fatalistic naturalism of a Eugene O'Neill play and into the archetypal dreamscape of a fairy tale: Anna Christie and The Hairy Ape meet Beauty and the Beast. Sternberg's waterfront romance contains two main sections: night and morning. Night is a luminous shadowland of mist, smoke, pools of light, and rippling reflections. In this enchanted realm, hulking stoker Bill (George Bancroft) fishes suicidal tramp Mae (Betty Compson) out of the drink. The couple end up at a rowdy saloon where they talk each other into a spur-of-the-moment marriage that might be sincere or just the pretext for a one-night stand. The cold, clear light of morning brings desertion, disillusion, and a change of heart, as Bill impulsively jumps ship and returns to take the rap for a stolen dress he had given to Mae.

The restraint and precision of the performances—Bancroft's guarded nonchalance, the deliberate grace with which he moves his massive body, and Compson's languid weariness and the delicate balance between hurt and hope in her upturned eyes—maintain a constantly rippling veil of speculation over the main characters' inner thoughts and feelings. How much are Bill and Mae bluffing each other, how much are they deceived by each other, and how much are they deceiving themselves? Sternberg, by all accounts (including his own) was the iciest of directors, yet he created several of the cinema's most moving testaments to the power of love to make fools of us all. *The Docks of New York* is one of them, made all the more convincing by the self-deprecating reticence with which it reveals its foolish heart. **MR**

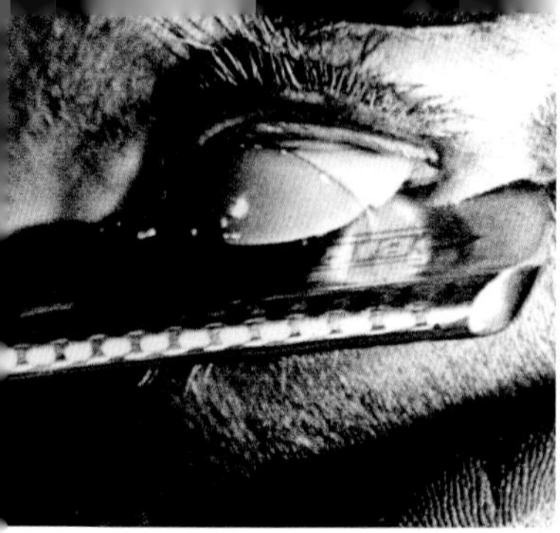

# UN CHIEN ANDALOU (1928)
## AN ANDALUSIAN DOG

**France** 16m silent BW
**Director:** Luis Buñuel
**Producer:** Luis Buñuel
**Screenplay:** Luis Buñuel, Salvador Dalí
**Photography:** Albert Duverger
**Cast:** Pierre Batcheff, Simone Mareuil, Luis Buñuel, Salvador Dalí

The directorial debut of Luis Buñuel, collaborating with artist Salvador Dalí, is etched into our consciousness of film history because of one image above all: a razor slicing open an eyeball. What is this: shock tactic, symbol of a modernist "vision," male aggression toward woman? For Jean Vigo—who hailed *An Andalusian Dog* for its "social consciousness"—Buñuel's associative montage raised a philosophical query: "Is it more dreadful than the spectacle of a cloud veiling a full moon?" One thing is certain: The image kicks off a classic surrealist parable of Eros ever denied, ever frustrated by institutions and mores.

Too often—because of its heavy influence on rock video—*An Andalusian Dog* has been reduced to, and recycled as, a collection of disconnected, striking, incongruous images: dead horse on a piano, ants in a hand. But this overlooks what gives the work its cohering force, the fact that, in many ways, Buñuel scrupulously respects certain conventions of classical continuity and linkage, creating a certain, disquieting narrative sense among these fragments from the unconscious. This is a dialectic of surface rationality versus deep, churning, forces from the Id that Buñuel would continue exploring to the very end of his career. **AM**

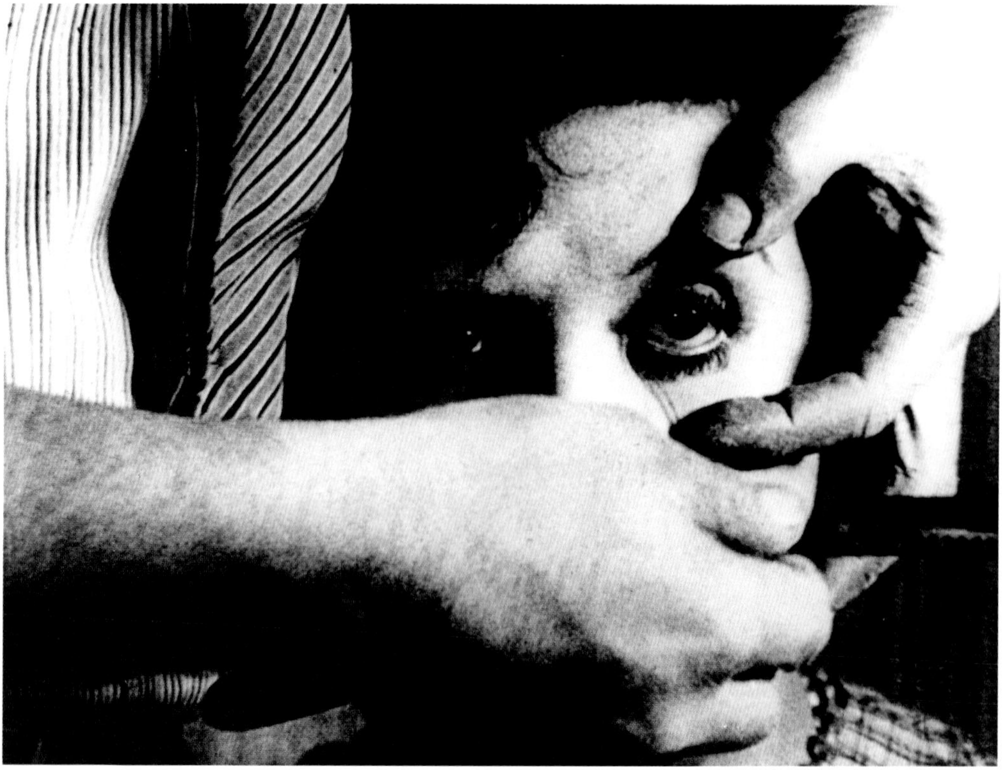

# LA PASSION DE JEANNE D'ARC (1928)
## THE PASSION OF JOAN OF ARC

**France** (Société générale) 110m Silent BW

**Director:** Carl Theodor Dreyer

**Screenplay:** Joseph Delteil, Carl Theodor Dreyer

**Photography:** Rudolph Maté

**Cast:** Eugene Silvain, André Berley, Maurice Schutz, Antonin Artaud, Michel Simon, Jean d'Yd, Louis Ravet, Armand Lurville, Jacques Arnna, Alexandre Mihalesco, Léon Larive

Carl Dreyer's 1928 masterpiece—his last silent film, and the greatest of all Joan of Arc films—is the work of his that brought him worldwide fame, although, like most of his later pictures, it was strictly a *succès d'estime* and fared poorly at the box office. A print of the original version—lost for half a century—was rediscovered in a Norwegian mental asylum in the 1980s. Other prints had perished in a warehouse fire, and the two versions subsequently circulated consisted of outtakes.

All of Dreyer's films were based on works of fiction or plays, with the exception of *The Passion of Joan of Arc*, which was essentially based on the official transcripts of the proceedings of Joan's trial—albeit highly selective and radically compressed portions of that trial. It was made only eight years after Joan was canonized in France and ten years after the end of World War I, both of which were central to Dreyer's interpretation. The helmets worn by the occupying British in 1431 resemble those in the recent war, and 1928 audiences saw the film as a historical "documentary" rather like the later films of Peter Watkins.

Joan is played by Renée Falconetti, a stage actress Dreyer discovered in a boulevard comedy, and following his instructions, she played the part without makeup. She and her interlocutors are filmed almost exclusively in close-ups. Though hers is one of the key performances in the history of movies, she never made another film. Antonin Artaud also appears in his most memorable screen role, as the sympathetic brother Jean Massieu.

Dreyer's radical approach to constructing space and the slow intensity of his mobile camera style make this a "difficult" film in the sense that, like all great films, it reinvents the world from the ground up. *The Passion of Joan of Arc* is also painful in a way that all Dreyer's tragedies are, but it will continue to live long after most commercial movies have vanished from memory. **JRos**

**U.S.** (Buster Keaton) 71m Silent BW

**Director:** Charles Reisner, Buster Keaton

**Producer:** Joseph M. Schenck

**Screenplay:** Carl Harbaugh

**Photography:** Bert Haines, Devereaux Jennings

**Cast:** Buster Keaton, Tom McGuire, Ernest Torrence, Tom Lewis, Marion Byron

# STEAMBOAT BILL, JR. (1928)

Even more than the formally experimental *Sherlock, Jr.* (1924), this film, along with *Our Hospitality* (1923) and *The General* (1927), reveals over and above his considerable talents as a comedian, just how great a director Keaton was. In *Steamboat Bill, Jr.*, by means of his customarily unintrusive but always expert placing of the camera, we get a real feeling for the small Mississippi riverside town where city slicker and college graduate Buster turns up to see his beleaguered steamboat-proprietor father. Dad, a rough-and-ready type, is dismayed by his son's somewhat foppish ways and is even less happy when the boy falls for the daughter of a wealthy rival determined to blow Bill, Sr., out of the water.

Needless to say, Buster finally gets to prove his mettle during a climactic typhoon that destroys the town in an extended sequence of virtuoso stunts, meticulously staged action sequences, and superbly paced suspense, but not before much fun has been had with notions of acceptable/unacceptable masculine behavior. One scene in particular, in which father and son shop for hats (played straight to camera as if it were a mirror), is not only hilarious but a prime example of Keaton's very "modern" and playful awareness of his comic persona. Magic. **GA**

**U.S.S.R.** (Mezhrabpomfilm) 93m Silent BW

**Director:** Vsevolod Pudovkin

**Screenplay:** Osip Brik, I. Novokshenov

**Photography:** Anatoli Golovnya

**Cast:** Valéry Inkijinoff, I. Dedintsev, Aleksandr Chistyakov, Viktor Tsoppi, F. Ivanov, V. Pro, Boris Barnet, K. Gurnyak, I. Inkishanov, L. Belinskaya, Anel Sudakevich

# POTOMOK CHINGIS-KHANA (1928)
## STORM OVER ASIA

Within a month of completing *1927: The End of St. Petersburg*, Vsevolod Pudovkin was at work on this epic fable, apparently inspired both by I. Novokshonov's original story of a herdsman who will rise to become a great leader, and by the prospect of shooting in virgin territory, exotic Outer Mongolia. Pudovkin's State Film School classmate Valeri Inkizhinov plays the unnamed hero, a Mongol who learns to distrust capitalists when a Western fur trader cheats him out of a rare silver fox pelt. The year is 1918, and the Mongol falls in with Socialist partisans fighting against the imperialist British occupying army. Captured, he is condemned to be shot (for recognizing the word "Moscow"), but his life is saved when an ancient talisman is found on his person, a document which proclaims the bearer to be a direct descendant of Genghis Khan. The British install him as a puppet king, but he escapes to lead his people to a fantastic victory.

A curious mix of rip-roaring adventure filmmaking, Soviet socialist propaganda, and ethnographic documentary, *Storm over Asia* is never less than entertaining. It is distinguished by Pudovkin's epic compositional sense, evident in the cavalry column fanning out to fill the horizon, and some striking, cubist-like montage sequences—as well as for its sardonic satire of Buddhist ritual and Western betrayal of faith. **TCh**

# BLACKMAIL (1929)

G.B. (BIP, Gainsborough) 96m BW
**Director:** Alfred Hitchcock
**Producer:** John Maxwell
**Screenplay:** Alfred Hitchcock, from play by Charles Bennett
**Photography:** Jack E. Cox
**Music:** James Campbell, Reg Connelly
**Cast:** Anny Ondra, Sara Allgood, Charles Paton, John Longden, Donald Calthrop, Cyril Ritchard, Hannah Jones, Harvey Braban, Ex-Detective Sergeant Bishop

Though Alfred Hitchcock laid down many of the themes he would return to throughout his career and staked his claim as master of the suspense genre with the silent *The Lodger* (1927), this 1929 picture really sealed his reputation and set him on the road to a remarkable career. *Blackmail* went into production as a silent movie but was rethought in midshoot as Britain's first all-talkie; that this decision was made shows how ambitious Hitchcock was even at this stage of his career, but also that his talents were obvious enough for paymaster producers to fund technical innovations. One of Hitchcock's greatest tricks was to be both avant-garde and commercial at the same time: here he uses new-fangled technology of the sort many still suspected would be short-lived in the service of a melodrama that may be psychologically acute but still succeeds in delivering thrills (and titillation).

Alice White (Anny Ondra) quarrels with her policeman boyfriend Frank (John Longden) and impulsively accompanies a lecherous artist (Cyril Ritchard) to his flat. When the heel tries to rape her, she stabs him in self-defense and gets away, though a breakfast-table conversation with her family becomes a reminder of the trauma as the word "knife" keeps stabbing at her and the sight of a bread knife nearly sends her into hysterics. Whereas other directors converting to talkies were working hard to ensure that every line of dialogue was recorded as if for an elocution demonstration, Hitchcock monkeys around with the soundtrack in this scene so that most of the conversation becomes an inaudible babble—the better to highlight the crystal-clear key word. This may be the moment when the talkies stopped just talking and singing and the real potential of sound as an addition to the director's arsenal became apparent.

Stuck with an already-cast Czech actress whose English wasn't up to standard, Hitchcock also experimented with dubbing, having Joan Barry off-camera reading the lines as Ondra mouthed them, an unusual (and rarely repeated) approach that allows for a successful synthesis of performance. Ondra, among the first of Hitchcock's bedeviled blondes, is a remarkably fresh, engaging presence and turns the trick of making her innocent killer sympathetic while the slimy creep who blackmails her is painted as the real villain. **KN**

**U.S.S.R.** (VUFKU) 80m Silent BW
**Director:** Dziga Vertov
**Screenplay:** Dziga Vertov
**Photography:** Dziga Vertov

# CHELOVEK S KINOAPPARATOM (1929)
## THE MAN WITH THE MOVIE CAMERA

Dziga Vertov (Denis Kaufman) began his career with newsreels, filming the Red Army as it fought during the Russian Civil War (1918–21) and screening the footage for audiences in villages and towns who boarded the "agit-trains." The experience helped Vertov formulate his ideas about cinema, ideas shared by a group of like-minded young filmmakers who called themselves Kino-glaz (Cine-Eye). The group's principles—the "honesty" of documentary as compared with fiction film, the "perfection" of the cinematic eye compared with the human eye—inform Vertov's most extraordinary picture, the dazzling *The Man with a Movie Camera*.

In this film Vertov combines radical politics with revolutionary aesthetics to exhilarating, even giddy effect. The two components of filmmaking—camera and editing—function as equal (and gendered) partners. Vertov's male cameraman (his brother Mikhail Kaufman) records a day in the life of the modern city—what Vertov called "life caught unawares"—while his female editor (wife Elizaveta Svilova) cuts and splices the footage, thus reformulating that life. By the end Vertov has exploited every available device of filming and editing—slow motion, animation, multiple images, split-screen, zooms and reverse zooms, blurring focus, and freeze-frames—to create a textbook of film technique as well as a hymn to the new Soviet state.

The camera begins to roll as the city gradually awakens, its buses and trams emerging from their night-hangars and its empty streets gradually filling, and continues by tracking denizens of the city (mostly Moscow but with extensive footage shot in Kiev, Yalta, and Odessa) through their routines of work and play. A lifetime is compressed into that day, as the camera peers between a woman's legs to watch a baby emerge, espies children entranced by a street conjuror, tracks an ambulance carrying an accident victim. New rituals supplant old as couples marry, separate, and divorce in a registry office instead of a church.

Vertov gives visual form to Marxist principles in a stunning montage that follows the transformation of hand-work into mechanized labor (women progress from sewing by hand to sewing by machine, from abacus to cash register) and that lauds the speed, efficiency, indeed the joy of assembly-line labor. Workers use their new-found leisure to socialize in state-subsidized clubs and beer-halls, to play music and chess, to swim and sunbathe, pole-vault and kick soccer balls. Moscow's "ordinary people" become stars of their own lives as they see themselves on screen. By the time Vertov bids an explosive farewell to the old by splitting the Bolshoi Theater in half, he has made his case for the revolutionary potential of cinema.

Ultimately, Vertov could not accommodate to Socialist Realism, and his career faltered. With *The Man with a Movie Camera*, however, he achieved his goal: a non-linear narrative form for cinema, a glorious tribute to everything that movie making can be. **JW**

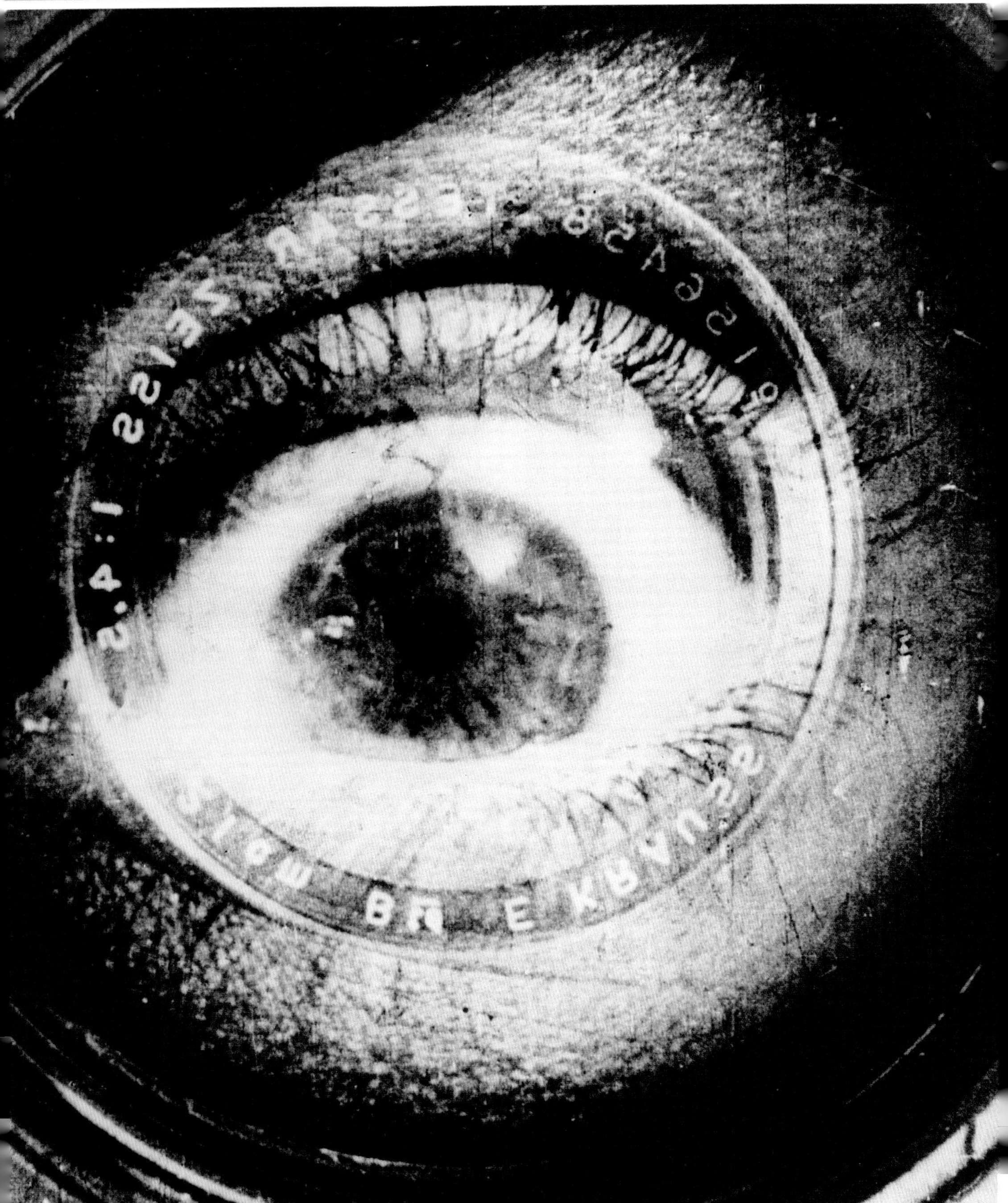

Germany (Nero-Film) 97m Silent BW

**Director:** Georg Wilhelm Pabst

**Producer:** Seymour Nebenzal

**Screenplay:** Joseph Fleisler, Georg Wilhelm Pabst, from the plays *Erdgeist* and *Die Büchse der Pandora* by Frank Wedekind

**Photography:** Günther Krampf

**Cast:** Louise Brooks, Fritz Kortner, Francis Lederer, Carl Goetz, Krafft-Raschig, Alice Roberts, Gustav Diessl

# DIE BÜCHSE DER PANDORA (1929)
## PANDORA'S BOX

A lasting masterpiece from G.W. Pabst, adapted from Frank Wedekind's "Lulu plays," *Pandora's Box* is remembered for the creation of an archetypal character in Lulu (Louise Brooks), an innocent temptress whose forthright sexuality somehow winds up ruining the lives of everyone around her. Though Pabst was criticized at the time for casting a foreigner in a role that was considered emblematically German, the main reason the film is remembered is the performance of American star Brooks. So powerful and sexual a presence that she never managed to make a transition from silent flapper parts to the talkie roles she deserved in a Hollywood dominated by Shirley Temple, Brooks is the definitive gamine vamp, modeling a sharp-banged bobbed haircut known as a "Louise Brooks" or "Lulu" to this day.

Presented in distinct theatrical "acts," the story picks up Lulu in a bourgeois Berlin drawing room, where she is the adored mistress of widowed newspaper publisher Peter Schön (Fritz Kortner), friendly with her lover's grown-up son Alwa (Franz Lederer) and even with the gnomish pimp Schigolch (Carl Goetz), who is either her father or her first lover. When Schön announces that he is remarrying, Lulu seems to be passed on to a nightclub strongman (Krafft-Raschig) but, provoked when Schön tells his son that "one does not marry" a woman like her, sets up an incident backstage at the music hall where she is dancing that breaks off the editor's engagement and prompts her lover to marry her, though he knows that it will be the death of him.

Though her husband in effect commits suicide, Lulu winds up convicted of his murder. On the run with Alwa, Schigolch, and her lesbian admirer Countess Geschwitz (Alice Roberts), she makes it to an opium-hazed gambling boat on the Seine—where she is almost sold to an Egyptian brothel and Alwa is humiliatingly caught cheating—then finally to a Christmassy London where she is stalked by Jack the Ripper (Gustav Diessl). Pabst surrounds Brooks with startling secondary characters and dizzying settings (the spectacle in the thronged wings of the cabaret eclipses anything taking place on stage), but it is the actress's vibrant, erotic, scary, and heartbreaking personality that resonates with modern audiences. Brooks's mix of image and attitude is so strong and fresh that she makes Madonna look like Phyllis Diller, and her acting style is strikingly unmannered for the silent era, unmediated by the trickery of mime or expressionist makeup. Her performance is also remarkably honest: never playing for easy sentiment, the audience is forced to recognize how destructive Lulu is even as we fall under her spell.

Though the original plays are set in 1888, the year of the Ripper murders, Pabst imagines a fantastical but contemporary setting, which seems to begin with the 1920s modernity of Berlin and then travels back in time to a foggy London for a death scene that is the cinema's first great insight into the mindset of a serial killer. Lulu, turned streetwalker so that Schigolch can afford a last Christmas pudding, charms the reticent Jack, who throws aside his knife and genuinely tries not to kill again but is overwhelmed by the urge to stab. **KN**

**Germany** (Universum Film A.G.–UFA) 99m BW

**Language:** German / English

**Director:** Josef von Sternberg

**Producer:** Erich Pommerr

**Screenplay:** Carl Zuckmayer, from the novel *Professor Unrat* by Heinrich Mann

**Music:** Frederick Hollander

**Photography:** Günther Rittau

**Cast:** Emil Jannings, Marlene Dietrich, Kurt Gerron, Rosa Valetti, Hans Albers, Reinhold Bernt, Eduard von Winterstein, Hans Roth, Rolf Müller, Roland Varno, Carl Balhaus, Robert Klein-Lörk, Charles Puffy, Wilhelm Diegelmann, Gerhard Bienert

# DER BLAUE ENGEL (1930)

## THE BLUE ANGEL

How appropriate that the film which launched Marlene Dietrich's stardom (although it was far from her first role) should begin with a woman cleaning a window behind which is Dietrich's poster as Lola Lola—and then measuring herself up against this idealized image. In this equation, it is the unglamorous reality of the street (or later, the stage) which is more on the mind of director Josef von Sternberg than that illusory ideal—setting the pattern for the pitiless logic of *The Blue Angel*.

The films Sternberg would go on to make with Dietrich in Hollywood are lush, baroque, often camp affairs. *The Blue Angel*—filmed simultaneously in somewhat different English- and German-language versions—shows the director still in his expressionist phase, tailoring a dark, heavy style to emphasize Emil Jannings's powerful histrionics. Jannings plays Professor Immanuel Rath, a respected schoolteacher who falls under the spell of Lola after he goes into the den of iniquity known as "The Blue Angel" to investigate the unhealthy obsession of his male students.

It is a tale, taken from Heinrich Mann's novel, of decline, of "downward mobility." In the course of the story, Rath will be reduced to a barely human clown—echoing the previous clown who functions as one of several ironic doubles for the doomed hero. Sternberg stresses, with exemplary and systematic rigor, the verticality of the film's spatial relations: Rath is always in a low position looking up at the image of Lola (as when she throws her underpants down on his head), unless—in a parody of his authoritative position—he is put on display in the Gods by the theater's sinister manager.

Lola is a classic femme fatale in so far as she lures men and then moves on when she tires of them—and, along the way, enjoys treating them like slaves. Yet there is also, for a time, a tender, loyal side in her relationship with Rath; when she reprises the famous "Falling in Love Again" we can almost accept her passive acceptance of her vagabond romantic destiny ("I know I'm not to blame"). **AM**

**France** (Corinth) 60m BW
**Language:** French
**Director:** Luis Buñuel
**Producer:** Le Vicomte de Noailles
**Photography:** Albert Duverger
**Screenplay:** Luis Buñuel, Salvador Dalí
**Music:** Georges Van Parys
**Cast:** Gaston Modot, Lya Lys, Caridad de Laberdesque, Max Ernst, Josep Llorens Artigas, Lionel Salem, Germaine Noizet, Duchange, Ibanez

# L'ÂGE D'OR (1930)
## THE AGE OF GOLD

In 1928, two young Spaniards in Paris—28-year-old Luis Buñuel and 24-year-old Salvador Dalí—conceived an authentically surrealist short film, *Un Chien Andalou*. Shot in two weeks, the film shocked, startled, and delighted the intelligentsia; and it encouraged the Vicomte de Noailles to give them the money to finance a feature film. Dali, however, quickly left the project (though his name remains on the credit titles), and the resulting film, *L'Âge d'Or*, must be assumed to be Buñuel's alone. In the director's own words, "The sexual instinct and the sense of death form the substance of the film. It is a romantic film performed in full Surrealist frenzy."

*L'Âge d'Or* is driven by the surrealist notion of *l'amour fou*, and—somewhat denying Surrealist principles—has its own episodic story progression. It opens with a documentary on scorpions—actually a 1912 film to which Buñuel has added a scientific commentary. A group of starving bandits struggle out of their hut while four bishops perform strange rituals on a beach. A fade returns to the bishops now reduced to skeletons. Boats bring a crowd of distinguished individuals evidently to honor the bishops' memory, but their ceremonial is interrupted by sexual cries from a man and woman. The man is arrested and dragged through the streets. Subsequent sequences are set in the home of the woman and at an elegant party in the grounds of a villa, where their amours are resumed but variously interrupted. Scenes of surrealist frenzy lead into the final sequence as De Sade's libertines depart from their orgies at the Château de Sellini. Their leader is clearly portrayed as Jesus.

Not surprisingly, the film aroused ferocious emotions and polemics between the surrealists and right-wing organizations, the League of Patriots, and the Anti-Jewish League organized demonstrations that resulted in serious damage to the theater, police prohibition of further shows, and violent political and critical polemics. Notably, Henry Miller wrote extensively on the film and its creator: "Either you are made like the rest of civilized humanity, or you are proud and whole like Buñuel. And if you are whole and proud, then you are an anarchist, and throw bombs."

Following surrealist tenets of "not making art," Buñuel demanded from his gifted cameraman Albert Duverger plain, simply lit visuals. He also rejected De Noailles's request that Stravinsky should compose the music, instead creating mischievous juxtapositions of his scabrous images, romantic symphonies (Wagner, Schubert, Debussy), and the harsh ceremonial drums of his native Calanda, Spain.

*L'Âge d'Or* has bequeathed some of the cinema's most unforgettable images—the mummified bishops; the painter Max Ernst as a frail, dying bandit; the cow on the bed of an elegant haute bourgeois villa; Lya Lys sucking the toe of a statue; the manic face of Gaston Modot; the angelic Jesus and his gleefully exhausted fellow libertines on the castle drawbridge. It is a film that exists out of time, retaining its power to stir and shock into the 21st century and beyond. **DRob**

**U.S.S.R.** (Wufku) 75m Silent BW
**Director:** Aleksandr Dovzhenko
**Screenplay:** Aleksandr Dovzhenko
**Photography:** Daniil Demutsky
**Music:** Lev Revutsky (restored version)
**Cast:** Stepan Shkurat, Semyon Svashenko, Yuliya Solntseva, Yelena Maksimova, Nikolai Nademsky, I. Franko, Arkhip, Pyotr Masokha, V. Mikhajlov, Pavel Petrik, P. Umanets, E. Bondina, L. Lyashenko, M. Matsyutsia, Nikolai Mikhajlov

# ZEMLYA (1930)
## EARTH

Arguably, Aleksandr Dovzhenko's *Earth* is the single greatest achievement of the ever-more-impressive Soviet silent cinema. A modernist who drew deep inspiration from folk art—not unlike his contemporaries Marc Chagall and Sholem Aleichem—Dovzhenko's ode to the beginning of collectivization in the Ukraine is a riot of delirious imagery of swaying wheat fields, ripening fruits, and stampeding horses. The arrival of a tractor is greeted with joy by the peasants, who begin to imagine new lives for themselves, but surviving *kulaks* (landowners) conspire to assassinate the inspiring young head of the Party's village committee. His death, though, only makes the villagers stronger in their resolve; in a mind-boggling finale Dovzhenko brings together themes of birth, death, harvest, progress, and solidarity as the dead man is reunited with the land he loved so well.

No summary, however, can really do justice to the extraordinary sensuality of the film, a quality not much appreciated by the Soviet censors. Among the choice bits removed from earlier released versions are a scene in which in a symbol of communion the village men urinate in the tractor's radiator, and a shot in which men draw strength and comfort by putting their hands inside the blouses of the women at their sides. Anyone looking for the origins of Andrei Tarkovsky's cinema must start with *Earth*. **RP**

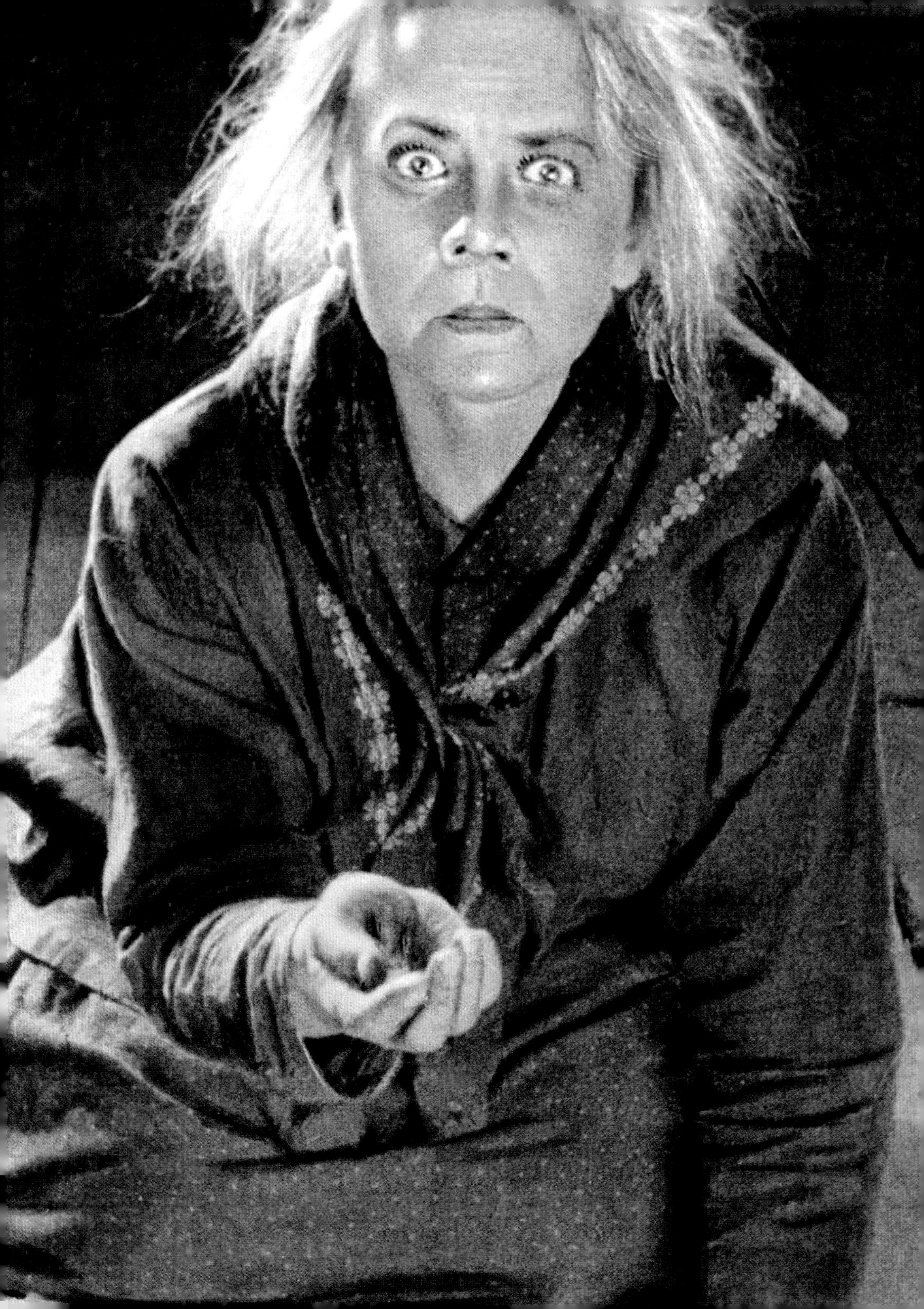

## LITTLE CAESAR (1930)

Genre can be used to read history and interpret moments in time. Accordingly, Mervyn LeRoy's *Little Caesar* helped to define the gangster movie while serving as an allegory of production circumstances because it was produced during the Great Depression. Within the film is inscribed a wholesale paranoia about individual achievement in the face of economic devastation. Leavening this theme alongside the demands of social conformity during the early 1930s means that LeRoy's screen classic is far more than the simple sum of its parts.

Caesar "Rico" Bandello (Edward G. Robinson) is a small-stakes thief with a partner named Joe (Douglas Fairbanks Jr.). Recognizing a dead-end future, he moves to the heart of Chicago where Joe becomes an entertainer and falls in love with a dancer named Olga (Glenda Farrell). In contrast, Rico gets a taste of the "life" and enjoys it. Possessing a psychotic ruthlessness, he gradually looms as the new power on-scene before finally succumbing to an ill-tempered ego and the syndicate-breaking police. Gut shot and dying beneath an ad for Joe and Olga's dinner act, Rico sputters some final words of self-determination, underlining how he won't ever be caught because he lived according to the terms of his own ambition.

For audiences, Rico's killer was undoubtedly a clear call of recent tensions about the state of the world at the time. Limited by the feature film's structure, but not dulled by censorial practice in the days before the Production Code Administration, *Little Caesar* offers a scornful look at free enterprise taken to an extreme. Seen through the long view of history and the focus on ill-gotten gains, it's a perfect corollary for Wall Street's collapse, itself the result of poor regulation, mass speculation, and hysteria manipulated to benefit the few at the expense of the many.

Acting out to get a bigger piece of the pie, Rico expresses the wish for acceptance and the drive toward success in an otherwise indifferent world. Simultaneously terrorizing innocents and devastating the society he desires to control, he ends up illuminating the demands of power with homicidal shadows in this, a seminal film of the early sound era. **GC-Q**

**U.S.** (First National) 79m BW

**Director:** Mervyn LeRoy

**Producer:** Hal B. Wallis, Darryl F. Zanuck

**Screenplay:** Francis Edward Faragoh, Robert N. Lee, from novel by W.R. Burnett

**Photography:** Tony Gaudio

**Music:** Erno Rapee

**Cast:** Edward G. Robinson, Douglas Fairbanks Jr., Glenda Farrell, William Collier Jr., Sidney Blackmer, Ralph Ince, Thomas E. Jackson, Stanley Fields, Maurice Black, George E. Stone, Armand Kaliz, Nicholas Bela

**Oscar nomination:** Francis Edward Faragoh, Robert N. Lee (screenplay)

## ALL QUIET ON THE WESTERN FRONT
(1930)

**U.S.** (Universal Pictures) 131m BW

**Language:** English / French

**Director:** Lewis Milestone

**Producer:** Carl Laemmle Jr.

**Screenplay:** Erich Maria Remarque, Maxwell Anderson

**Photography:** Arthur Edeson, Karl Freund

**Music:** David Broekman, Sam Perry, Heinz Roemheld

**Cast:** Louis Wolheim, Lew Ayres, John Wray, Arnold Lucy, Ben Alexander, Scott Kolk, Owen Davis Jr., Walter Rogers, William Bakewell, Russell Gleason, Richard Alexander, Harold Goodwin, Slim Summerville, G. Pat Collins, Beryl Mercer

**Oscar:** Carl Laemmle Jr. (best picture), Lewis Milestone (director)

**Oscar nomination:** George Abbott , Maxwell Anderson, Del Andrews (screenplay), Arthur Edeson (photography)

Undiminished by time (and restored in 1998), this classic antiwar film, adapted from Erich Maria Remarque's novel, is a landmark for its vivid depiction of the Great War's tragedy from a German soldier's point of view, for its technically inventive, spectacular battle scenes (at the dawn of sound in film), and for its prescient denunciation of fanatic nationalism and militarism. Lew Ayres, only 21 years-old, became an international star for his beautifully natural performance as the schoolboy eager to serve but disillusioned by the futility and horror of war. The final shot—a close-up of his hand reaching out to a butterfly, quivering as a gunshot cracks and falling still in death—is an amazingly poignant image.

*All Quiet on the Western Front* was only the third film to win the Academy Award for Best Picture, and war veteran Lewis Milestone received his second Oscar for direction. Interestingly, German censors passed the film despite violent protests by Nazi groups. In a cruel irony, Ayers's career was all but ruined by public condemnation of his stand as a conscientious objector in World War II, despite his heroic service as a medic rather than a combatant. A 1979 TV remake was strong, if far less remarkable than the original. **AE**

## À NOUS LA LIBERTÉ (1931)
### FREEDOM FOR US

**France** (Sonores Tobis) 104m BW

**Language:** French

**Director:** René Clair

**Producer:** Frank Clifford

**Screenplay:** René Clair

**Photography:** Georges Périnal

**Music:** Georges Auric

**Cast:** Raymond Cordy, Henri Marchand, Paul Ollivier, André Michaud, Rolla France, Germaine Aussey, Léon Lorin, William Burke, Vincent Hyspa, Jacques Shelly

Two con-men, Louis (Raymond Cordy) and Emile (Henri Marchand), plan their escape from prison. Upon breaking out Emile is recaptured but Louis runs free and builds an empire on the assembly-line principle. Eventually Emile is paroled and heads to Louis's factory. Within its walls he becomes smitten with a secretary named Jeanne (Rolla France) and asks his old friend for help. According to the rules of comeuppance, Louis is then threatened with discovery as an escaped felon, after which the two men earn lasting freedom as hobos on the road.

Unlike Charlie Chaplin's *Modern Times*, a film later sued for plagiarism by Tobis, the production company of *À Nous la Liberté*, Rene Clair's film is an exaltation of industrial society. Opening on an assembly line and closing in a mechanized factory, the fears often associated with modernization are wholly absent here. Instead these are substituted with values of loyalty and the comedy of circumstance.

Interestingly, much of the humor in *À Nous la Liberté* stems from carefully manipulated screen space and sequence. First the assembly line hiccups. Then a worker forgets his place, disrupts another worker, angers his boss, etc. It's a formula freed from dialogue and adopted directly from the silent cinema as a transitional vehicle into the talkies. **GC-Q**

# LE MILLION (1931)
## THE MILLION

René Clair's *The Million* opens on a Parisian rooftop. Two lovers flirt and retire to their respective apartments, after which the camera dollies along the skyline in a one-shot sequence using forced perspective, miniatures, and matte paintings. Such a tricky sequence demonstrates a profoundly advanced cinematic style while also revealing how Clair's film is no throwaway musical comedy.

A poor artist named Michel (René Lefèvre) owes money to various creditors. Engaged to the pure-hearted Beatrice (Annabella), he disregards her to chase after the floozy Wanda (Vanda Gréville) and otherwise keeps up with his friend Prosper (Louis Allibert). When the gangster Grandpa Tulip (Paul Ollivier) races into the apartment building to avoid the police, Beatrice gives him an old jacket of Michel's out of spite. Afterwards, Michel and Prosper realize that a lottery ticket they purchased is a millionaire's prize—but the ticket is in the jacket Beatrice gave Grandpa Tulip, who in turn pawned it to the tenor Sopranelli (Constantin Siroesco), who will soon travel to America. Thus the caper comedy of *The Million* is set in motion. Mix-ups, misidentification, disguises, upsets, reconciliation, and musical numbers follow, all of it to bring Michel and Beatrice together and restore the lottery ticket to its rightful owner. Along the way a thug in tuxedo tails cries for a love song, a race for the jacket is scored to the sounds of a rugby match, and the opportunistic demands of Michel's creditors and neighbors weigh in on his perceived riches.

Perhaps most remarkable among its virtues is the film's integration of synch-sound recording. Expository dialogue is offered to still camera setups whereas lesser remarks, often viewed as whispers between characters, are left in silence. To cover these gaps in the spoken record, ambient music stitches together each set piece with occasional bursts of song. More fluid and visually dynamic than many early sound films, *The Million* is also more entertaining than many subsequent talkies. In large part this is a credit to Clair's screenplay and deft direction, but it is also due to a willing cast carrying through the demands of a gentle fantasy. **GC-Q**

**France** (Sonores Tobis) 89m BW
**Language:** French
**Director:** René Clair
**Screenplay:** René Clair, from play by Georges Berr and Marcel Guillemaud
**Photography:** Georges Périnal, Georges Raulet
**Music:** Armand Bernard, Philippe Parès, Georges Van Parys
**Cast:** Jean-Louis Allibert, Annabella, Raymond Cordy, Vanda Gréville, René Lefèvre, Paul Ollivier, Constantin Siroesco, Odette Talazac

# TABU (1931)

U.S. (Murnau-Flaherty, Paramount)
84m Silent BW

**Director:** F.W. Murnau

**Producer:** F.W. Murnau

**Screenplay:** Robert J. Flaherty, F.W. Murnau

**Photography:** Floyd Crosby

**Nonoriginal music:** Hugo Riesenfeld, W. Franke Harling, Milan Roder, Chopin, Smetana

**Cast:** Reri, Matahi, Hitu, Jean, Jules, Ah Kong, Anne Chevalier

**Oscar:** Floyd Crosby (photography)

*Tabu* is the last film of F.W. Murnau, who was probably the greatest of all silent directors. He didn't live long enough to make sound films, dying in an auto accident a few days after work on the musical score for this masterpiece was completed and a week before the film's New York premiere. Filmed entirely in the South Seas in 1929 with a nonprofessional cast and gorgeous cinematography by Floyd Crosby, *Tabu* began as a collaboration with the great documentarist Robert Flaherty, who still rightly shares credit for the story. Clearly, though, the German romanticism of Murnau predominates, above all in the heroic poses of the islanders and the fateful diagonals in the compositions. As we now know, Flaherty was ultimately squeezed out of the project because Murnau, who had all the financial control, wasn't temperamentally suited to sharing directorial credit. This unfortunately hasn't prevented many commentators from continuing to miscredit Flaherty as a codirector.

Part of Murnau's greatness was his capacity to encompass studio artifice—in such large productions as *The Last Laugh* (1924), *Faust* (1926), and *Sunrise* (1927)—as well as documentary naturalism in *Burning Soil* (1922), *Nosferatu* (1922), and *Tabu*. This versatility bridges both his German and American work. *Tabu*, shot in natural locations and strictly speaking neither German nor American, exhibits facets of both of these talents. The simple plot—the two "chapters" of the film are titled "Paradise" and "Paradise Lost"—is an erotic love story involving a young woman who becomes sexually taboo when she is selected by an elder, one of Murnau's most chilling harbingers of doom, to replace a sacred maiden who has just died. An additional theme is the corrupting power of "civilization"—money in particular—on the innocent hedonism of the islanders. Murnau himself was in flight from the Hollywood studios when he made the picture, although Paramount wound up releasing it in 1931. However dated some of *Tabu*'s ethnographic idealism may seem today, the film's breathtaking beauty and artistry make it indispensable viewing, and the exquisite tragic ending—conceived musically and rhythmically as a gradually decelerating diminuendo—is one of the pinnacles of silent cinema. **JRos**

**U.S.** (Universal) 75m BW

**Language:** English / Hungarian

**Director:** Tod Browning

**Producer:** E.M. Asher, Tod Browning, Carl Laemmle Jr.

**Screenplay:** Garrett Fort, from play by John L. Balderston and Hamilton Deane

**Photography:** Karl Freund

**Nonoriginal music:** Schubert, Tchaikovsky, Wagner

**Cast:** Bela Lugosi, Helen Chandler, David Manners, Dwight Frye, Edward Van Sloan, Herbert Bunston, Frances Dade, Joan Standing, Charles K. Gerrard, Tod Browning, Michael Visaroff

# DRACULA (1931)

Though Bram Stoker's seminal 1897 vampire novel had been filmed by F. W. Murnau in 1922 as *Nosferatu* and director Tod Browning had cast Lon Chaney as a bogus vampire in the silent *London After Midnight*, this early talkie—shot in late 1930, released on Valentine's Day 1931—was the true beginning of the horror film as a distinct genre and the vampire movie as its most popular subgenre.

Cinematographer Karl Freund had a solid grounding in German Expressionist shadowmaking whereas Browning was the carny barker king of American grotesquerie, so the film represents a synthesis of the two major strains of silent chills. Like such major American horror properties as *The Cat and the Canary* and *The Bat*, this Dracula comes to the screen not from the pages of classic gothic literature but direct from the stage: the primary sources of the screenplay are a pair of theatrical takes on Stoker's novel, from Hamilton Deane and John L. Balderston. The break-out star of the new genre is Bela Lugosi, who had played Dracula on Broadway and was finally cast in the film after the early death of Browning's favored star, Chaney. It may be that the loss of Chaney took some of the spark out of Browning's direction, which is actually less inspired than George Melford's work on the simultaneously-shot (on the same sets, no less) Spanish version—though the latter suffers from the lack of an iconic Dracula and the fact that it represents exactly the shooting script, whereas the English-language *Dracula* was considerably tightened by an edit that took out 20 minutes of flab.

Prehistoric in cinema technique and stuck with a drawing-room-centered script, Browning's film nevertheless retains much of its creaky, sinister power, spotlighting (literally, via tiny pinlights aimed at his evil eyes) Lugosi's star-making turn as the vampire, squeezing Hungarian menace out of every syllable of phrases such as "Cheeldren of the naight, leesten to thaim" or "I nevair dreenk vine!" The film opens magnificently, with a snatch of *Swan Lake* and a rickety stagecoach taking us and estate agent Renfield (Dwight Frye) to Lugosi's cobwebbed and vermin-haunted castle (an armadillo nestles in a Transylvanian crypt). Dracula strides through a curtain of cobwebs, the vampire twitching with bloodlust as his guest cuts his finger while carving bread, and three soulless vampire brides descend upon the unwary visitor.

Once the story hops disappointingly over a dangerous sea voyage (snippets of stock footage) and the Count relocates to London, Lugosi calms down. But Edward Van Sloan is staunch as the vampire-killing Professor Abraham Van Helsing, the forgotten Helen Chandler is frailly charming as the bled-dry and semi-vampirized heroine Mina, and Frye steals every scene that isn't nailed down when Renfield transforms into a fly-eating, giggling maniac. Castle Dracula, with its five-story gothic windows, is the art direction highlight, but the London scenes offer an impressive staircase and catacombs for Dracula's English lair. Browning falters at the last, however, with a weak climax in which the Count is defeated far too easily, his death conveyed by an offscreen groan as he is impaled. **KN**

DRACULA
The BLOODY TERROR of TRANSYLVANIA
as the 'Count,' BELA LUGOSI
HELEN CHANDLER
From a novel by
ABRAHAM STOKER
Directed by
TOD BROWNING

# FRANKENSTEIN (1931)

U.S. (Universal) 71m BW

**Director:** James Whale

**Producer:** E.M. Asher, Carl Laemmle Jr.

**Screenplay:** John L. Balderston, Francis Edward Faragoh, Garrett Fort, from play by Peggy Webling and novel by Mary Shelley

**Photography:** Arthur Edeson, Paul Ivano

**Music:** Bernhard Kaun

**Cast:** Colin Clive, Mae Clarke, John Boles, Boris Karloff, Edward Van Sloan, Frederick Kerr, Dwight Frye, Lionel Belmore, Marilyn Harris

The single most important horror film ever made. James Whale hacked out of Mary Shelley's unwieldy novel a fable of an overreaching scientist and his abused, childlike outcast of a monster. Though Colin Clive's neurotic Frankenstein and Dwight Frye's hunchbacked dwarf assistant are definitive, the career break-out of the film is William Henry Pratt, a 42-year-old Englishman who turned his back on a privileged upbringing and emigrated to become a truck driver in Canada and a jobbing bit-player in the States.

Universal's makeup genius Jack Pierce devised the flattop, the neck terminals, the heavy eyelids, and the elongated, scarred hands, while Whale outfitted the creature with a shabby suit like those worn by the ex-soldier hoboes then riding the rails and added the clumping asphalt-spreader's boots. But it was Pratt who turned the Monster from a snarling bogeyman into a yearning, sympathetic, classic character whose misdeeds are accidental (drowning a little girl) or justified (hanging the dwarf who has tortured him with fire). In the opening credits, the Monster is billed as being played by "?"; only at the end of the film were audiences told it was a fellow by the name of Boris Karloff—Pratt's stage handle—who had terrified, moved, and inspired them.

*Frankenstein* claims a number of wondrous theatrical set pieces: the "creation," with lightning crackling around the tower and the Monster raised to the angry heavens on an operating table; the Monster's first appearance (seen from behind, he turns to show us his face and the camera stutters toward him); the heart-breaking sequence with the little girl who doesn't float; the primal attack on the heroine in her boudoir on her wedding day (a rare bit taken from the book); and the pursuit of the Monster by a mob of peasants with flaming torches, winding up in the old mill where creator and creation confront each other in one of the earliest horror movie inferno finales. The Universal horror cycle runs the gamut from perfection through pastiche and pulp to parody, but *Frankenstein* remains chilly and invigorating, the cornerstone of its entire genre. **KN**

## CITY LIGHTS (1931)

U.S. (Charles Chaplin) 87m Silent BW
**Director:** Charles Chaplin
**Producer:** Charles Chaplin
**Screenplay:** Charles Chaplin
**Photography:** Gordon Pollock, Roland Totheroh, Mark Marklatt
**Music:** Charles Chaplin, José Padilla
**Cast:** Virginia Cherrill, Florence Lee, Harry Myers, Al Ernest Garcia, Hank Mann, Charles Chaplin

Convinced that speech would mar the beauty of cinema, its greatest mime exponent, Charlie Chaplin, agonized over the introduction of sound technology and determined to ignore it, against all advice. Presented as "a comedy romance in pantomime," his defiantly silent 1931 film *City Lights* was in every way a triumph, its heartrending melodrama and hilarity withstanding audiences' craving for talkies. Although later, after the shooting of the film, Chaplin incorporated sound effects and composed and conducted his own score, as he would continue to do in his later pictures.

The Little Tramp is touched by a blind flower seller (graceful Virginia Cherrill) and saves an eccentric millionaire from suicide. His gentle wooing of the girl and his determination to restore her sight propel him into a variety of jobs that go awry—like the memorable "fixed" boxing bout—while his on-off relationship with the drunken, unpredictable tycoon provides a parallel string of zany situations. As ever in Chaplin's silent films, there is a deftly choreographed comedic eating scene—here a party streamer entwined in the oblivious Charlie's spaghetti—and a slapstick misadventure with the law. Beautifully acted, this quite perfect balancing act between laughter and eloquent pathos culminates in a deeply moving finish. One of the real, landmark greats. **AE**

## THE PUBLIC ENEMY (1931)

U.S. (Warner Bros.) 83m BW
**Director:** William A. Wellman
**Producer:** Darryl F. Zanuck
**Screenplay:** Harvey F. Thew, from story by John Bright & Kubec Glasmon
**Photography:** Devereaux Jennings
**Music:** David Mendoza
**Cast:** James Cagney, Edward Woods, Jean Harlow, Joan Blondell, Beryl Mercer, Donald Cook, Mae Clarke, Mia Marvin, Leslie Fenton, Robert Emmett O'Connor, Murray Kinnell, Snitz Edwards, Rita Flynn, Frank Coghlan Jr., Frankie Darro
**Oscar nominations:** John Bright, Kubec Glasmon (screenplay)

William Wellman's melodramatic chronicle of the rise and fall of gangster Tom Powers (James Cagney) is the greatest of the early 1930s gangster films. The genre's sometime sympathetic portrayal of ruthless criminals eager for the American dream of success at the deliberate and unlawful cost of others prompted the institution of the Production Code Administration to supervise the dubious moral value in Hollywood films. Raised in Chicago slums, Powers turns at an early age to crime, graduating as a young man to armed robbery and the murder of a policeman. Later, he becomes involved in bootlegging, making real money for the first time. Though his brother and mother plead with him to go straight, Tom rises in the gang, but after being badly wounded in a battle with rivals, he agrees to rejoin his family. He is taken from the hospital and murdered, his body dumped on the doorstep of his family home.

With its simplistic moralism, the plot of *The Public Enemy* has dated poorly. But Cagney remains powerful and energetic as Powers, dominating the screen in every scene and setting the pattern for all gangster films to come, including *The Godfather* series. Wellman directs the film with a strong visual sense, designing memorable scenes such as one in which Powers, in a sudden fit of anger, shoves a grapefruit into girlfriend Kitty's face. **RBP**

# M (1931)

**Germany** (Nero-Film AG) 117m BW
**Director:** Fritz Lang
**Producer:** Seymour Nebenzal
**Screenplay:** Egon Jacobson, Fritz Lang
**Photography:** Fritz Arno Wagner
**Nonoriginal music:** Grieg
**Cast:** Peter Lorre, Ellen Widmann, Inge Landgut, Otto Wernicke, Theodor Loos, Gustaf Gründgens, Friedrich Gnaß, Fritz Odemar, Paul Kemp, Theo Lingen, Rudolf Blümner, Georg John, Franz Stein, Ernst Stahl-Nachbaur, Gerhard Bienert

In the early 1930s, MGM's production genius Irving Thalberg assembled all his writers and directors for a screening of Fritz Lang's German thriller *M*, then criticized them en masse for not making films as innovative, exciting, profound, and commercial as this. Of course, Thalberg admitted, if anyone had pitched the studio a story about a serial killer of children who is ultimately a tragic victim and accuses all strata of society of a corruption deeper than his psychosis, they would have been kicked off the lot immediately.

Whereas Hollywood first saw sound pictures as best suited to all-singing musicals and all-talking drawing room theatrical adaptations, a generation of European filmmakers understood the new medium's potential for thrills and psychological effects. Inspired perhaps by the theme of Alfred Hitchcock's 1927 silent *The Lodger* and the techniques of his 1929 talkie *Blackmail*, Lang—who had ended his silent film career with *Metropolis* (1927) and *Woman in the Moon* (1929), both considered costly flops before their achievements were recognized—set out to reestablish himself as a popular artist. Nevertheless, *M* is an unusual piece of storytelling, presenting a series of montage-like scenes (often with voice-over narration, a new device) that add up to a portrait of a German city in terror. The cause of the uproar is Franz Becker (Peter Lorre), a pudgy young man who compulsively whistles an air from Edvard Grieg's "Hall of the Mountain King" as he approaches the children he murders (and, it is implied, molests). His crimes are conveyed by striking, pathetic images like a lost balloon floating against telephone wires or an abandoned ball. Establishing conventions still being used by serial-killer movies, Lang and scenarist Thea von Harbou intercut the pathetic life of the murderer with the frenzy of the police investigation into the outrageous crimes, and pay attention to such side issues as press coverage of the killings, vigilante action as an innocent asked the time by children is suddenly surrounded by an angry mob, and the political pressure that comes down from the politicians and hinders as much as encourages the police. In a cynical touch, the police crack down on all criminal activities in order to catch the killer, prompting the shadow society of professional crooks to track him down like an animal themselves.

In the powerful finale, Becker is put on trial by the underworld and pleads his case on the surprisingly moving grounds that his accusers have only chosen to commit crimes whereas he is compelled to commit them. Though the film establishes Inspector Karl "Fatty" Lohmann (Otto Wernicke)—who would return to take on Lang's eponymous archfiend (Rudolf Klein-Rogge) in *The Testament of Dr. Mabuse* (1933)—and black-gloved criminal kingpin Schranker (Gustaf Gründgens) as traditional cop-and-crook antagonists, Lorre's desperate, clear-eyed, animal-like impulse murderer is the final voice of *M*, forcing his persecutors (and us) to look into ourselves for the seeds of a psychosis that equals his own. Creatively emphasizing the technological developments in film sound, Lang has the killer heard before he is seen (allegedly, the director dubbed Lorre's whistling) and identified by a blind witness. **KN**

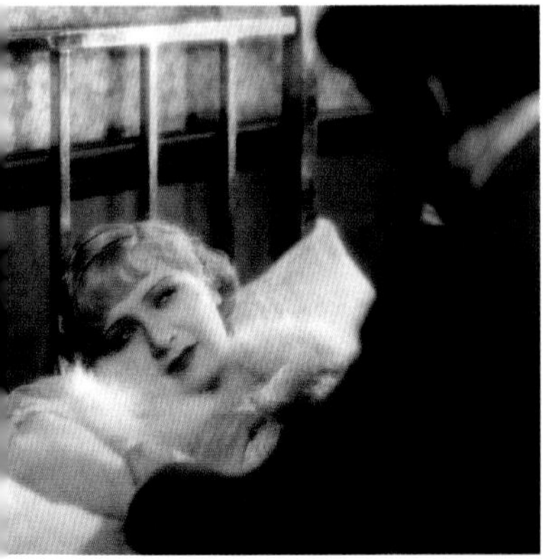

**France** (Jean Renoir, Braunberger-Richebé) 91m BW
**Director:** Jean Renoir
**Producer:** Charles David, Roger Richebé
**Screenplay:** André Girard, from novel by Georges de La Fouchardière
**Photography:** Theodor Sparkuhl
**Music:** Eugénie Buffet
**Cast:** Michel Simon, Janie Marèze, Georges Flamant, Roger Gaillard, Romain Bouquet, Pierre Desty, Mlle Doryans, Lucien Mancini, Jane Pierson, Argentin, Max Dalban, Jean Gehret, Magdeleine Bérubet

# LA CHIENNE (1931)
## THE BITCH

The first significant film of Jean Renoir's career, *La Chienne* inaugurated the run of masterpieces he directed in the 1930s, his finest decade. It also gave that most gloriously idiosyncratic of all French actors, Michel Simon, his first major role. Adapted from a novel by Georges de la Fouchardière, the film would later be remade by Fritz Lang as *Scarlet Street* (1945). But where Lang's film is mesmerizing for its aloof detachment and laid-out tensions of a psychological case study, Renoir plunges us into the gamy tumult and vitality of his native Montmartre.

Simon plays a middle-aged bank clerk, Maurice Legrand, despised at work, oppressed by a shrewish wife, who finds solace in his amateur passion for painting. Along the way he becomes obsessed with a young prostitute, Lulu (Janie Marèze), who exploits him at the urging of her pimp Dédé (Georges Flamant). Lulu milks him for cash and passes off his paintings as her own. But when Legrand catches her with Dédé and murders her in a jealous rage, the pimp is executed for the crime. Legrand becomes a tramp, his stolen paintings selling for large sums.

Shrugging off the limitations of early sound techniques, Renoir shot his exteriors on location in Montmartre, lending the film a rich visual and aural texture. As always with Renoir at his best, we get a powerful sense of off-screen space—of life going on, complex and abundant, around and between the events of the story. As Lulu, Marèze gives a performance of unabashed sensuality, feral and languid, that makes her early death all the more regrettable—she died in a car crash two weeks after shooting was completed.

Still, it is Michel Simon, avidly seizing his opportunity, who walks off with the film. Hankering after Lulu, his jowls quivering with resignation, Legrand is at once ludicrous and pitiable. Yet he brings to his scenes with Lulu the animal urgency of a man grasping a late, unlooked-for chance at sexual abandon. The pathos of his performance, and the warmth of Renoir's sympathetic gaze, lifts *La Chienne* out of the realm of petty melodrama, turning the banal story into something moving and universal. **PK**

# VAMPYR (1932)
## THE VAMPIRE

The greatness of Carl Theodor Dreyer's first sound film derives partly from its handling of the vampire theme in terms of sexuality and eroticism and partly from its highly distinctive, dreamy look, but it also has something to do with the director's radical recasting of narrative form. Synopsizing the film not only betrays but also misrepresents it: While never less than mesmerizing, it confounds conventions for establishing point of view and continuity, and inventing a narrative language all its own. Some of the moods and images conveyed by this language are truly uncanny: the long voyage of a coffin from the apparent viewpoint of the corpse inside; a dance of ghostly shadows inside a barn; a female vampire's expression of carnal desire for her fragile sister; an evil doctor's mysterious death by suffocation in a flour mill; and a protracted dream sequence that manages to dovetail eerily into the narrative proper.

Financed and produced by a Dutch cinephile, Baron Nicolas de Gunzburg—who was cast in the leading role of David Gray under the pseudonym of Julian West—*Vampyr* was freely adapted from a short story by Sheridan Le Fanu, "Carmilla," that appeared in his collection *Through a Glass Darkly* (not a novel, as stated erroneously in the film's credits). Like most of Dreyer's other sound features, it flopped commercially when it came out, then went on to become something of a horror and fantasy (as well as art movie) staple, despite never fitting snugly or unambiguously in any of these generic categories.

The remarkable sound track, created entirely in a studio, in contrast to the images, which were all filmed on location, is an essential part of the film's voluptuous and haunting otherworldliness. *Vampyr* was originally released by Dreyer in four separate versions—French, English, German, and Danish. Most circulating prints now contain portions of two or three of these versions, although the dialogue is pretty sparse. If you've never seen a Dreyer film and wonder why many critics regard him as possibly the greatest of all filmmakers, this chilling horror fantasy is the perfect place to begin to understand. **JRos**

**Germany** (Tobis Klangfilm) 83m BW
**Director:** Carl Theodor Dreyer
**Producer:** Carl Theodor Dreyer, Julian West
**Screenplay:** Carl Theodor Dreyer, Christen Jul, from the short story *Carmilla* by Sheridan Le Fanu
**Photography:** Rudolph Maté, Louis Née
**Music:** Wolfgang Zeller
**Cast:** Julian West, Maurice Schutz, Rena Mandel, Sybille Schmitz, Jan Hieronimko, Henriette Gérard, Albert Bras, N. Babanini, Jane Mora

# LOVE ME TONIGHT (1932)

As with so many of the sadly underrated Rouben Mamoulian's finest films, the delightful thing about this masterly variation on the romantic Ruritanian musical is the way the director manages to debunk, through an idiosyncratic combination of irreverent humor and technical innovation, the traditions of the very genre he is simultaneously helping to establish and expand. Here he contrives to outstrip the achievements of the then-widely-acclaimed masters of the form—Ernst Lubitsch and René Clair —without even seeming to make an effort, he makes the whole thing feel so wonderfully relaxed, good natured, and somehow...well, perfect. True, he's helped no end by having Richard Rodgers and Lorenz Hart's supremely witty yet hummably melodious songs to work with; but it's the unforced sense of sophisticated fun coexisting with real cinematic invention that reveal the Mamoulian touch, considerably lighter than that in most Lubitsch movies.

Jeannette MacDonald and Maurice Chevalier must also take credit for playing their respective romantic leads—the haughty but bored (and, let it be said, sexually frustrated) princess holed up in a fusty chateau, and the visiting tailor ("the best in Paris") sufficiently aroused by her to forget his lowly status—with emotional commitment and an engagingly delicate parodic irony. The supporting cast is top-notch, too: Myrna Loy, Charles Ruggles, Charles Butterworth, and the inimitable Sir C. Aubrey Smith (the last three especially delightful when improbably enlisted to sing, solo, verses of "Mimi") are merely the most memorable. But what is really impressive about *Love Me Tonight* is how music, dance, dialogue, performance, decor, lighting, camera work, editing, and special effects are all combined to create a cogent comic/dramatic whole in which each element serves narrative, characterization, and theme. The "Isn't It Romantic?" sequence, for example, which starts with Chevalier and a client in Paris, and proceeds with the song being passed via various minor characters (including, at one point, a whole platoon of soldiers!) to arrive finally at the lonely MacDonald's boudoir—the first link between the future lovers, who have yet to meet—is impressive, as is the final, climactic chase sequence (as exhilaratingly constructed as anything by the Soviets and with far more wit). In short, an enormously entertaining masterpiece. **GA**

**U.S.** (Paramount) 104m BW
**Director:** Rouben Mamoulian
**Producer:** Rouben Mamoulian
**Screenplay:** Samuel Hoffenstein, Waldemar Young, George Marion Jr. from the play *Tailor in the Château* by Paul Armont and Lepold Marchand
**Photography:** Victor Milner
**Music:** Richard Rodgers, John Leipold
**Cast:** Maurice Chevalier, Jeanette MacDonald, Charles Ruggles, Charles Butterworth, Myrna Loy, C. Aubrey Smith, Elizabeth Patterson, Ethel Griffies, Blanche Frederici, Joseph Cawthorn, Robert Greig, Bert Roach

# BOUDU SAUVÉ DES EAUX (1932)
## BOUDU SAVED FROM DROWNING

**France** (Pathé, Sirius) 90m BW
**Language:** French
**Director:** Jean Renoir
**Producer:** Jean Gehret, Michel Simon
**Screenplay:** Jean Renoir, Albert Valentin, from the play *Boudu sauvé des eaux* by René Fauchois
**Photography:** Léonce-Henri Burel, Marcel Lucien
**Music:** Léo Daniderff, Raphael, Johann Strauss
**Cast:** Michel Simon, Charles Granval, Marcelle Hainia, Severine Lerczinska, Jean Gehret, Max Dalban, Jean Dasté, Jane Pierson, Georges D'Arnoux, Régine Lutèce, Jacques Becker

With *Boudu Saved from Drowning*, Renoir had already made eleven films before being selected by Simon, who had decided to produce this adaptation of a stage play by René Fauchois. The pair had worked together three times previously, they were both the same age as the birth of cinema, and they were both rising personalities with a sense of freedom and a desire to explore unknown territories.

So, like a monstrous Aphrodite, Simon's Boudu the tramp was reborn from the water, brought back to a life he wanted to leave by the kindness of the Lestingois family, its generosity, and its wealth. Of course, comparisons with Charlie Chaplin's character in a similar situation come to mind here, and the two tramps do have a lot in common—the survivor's sense of life, the amoral relationship with society's rules, the focus on rich versus poor, and the urge for sex. But it is the differences between the two that reveal the power of the recipe above, about the film's connection and rupture with vaudeville (the rules of bourgeois theater), and about the body and diction of Simon.

In the character of Boudu, voice and physical presence work together as an eruption of carnality, a dissonant yet mesmerizing cello disturbing the happy quartet of the nice home filled with nice people wishing the world keeps spinning 'round. Boudu's ultimate return to the archaic spring is not only the smiling twist of an epicurean tale but also a troubling assessment of the hypothesis of a continuity between the oldest past and a future toward which the river flows. **J-MF**

# I AM A FUGITIVE FROM A CHAIN GANG (1932)

**U.S.** (Vitaphone, Warner Bros.) 93m BW
**Director:** Mervyn LeRoy
**Producer:** Hal B. Wallis
**Screenplay:** Howard J. Green, from memoir by Robert E. Burns
**Photography:** Sol Polito
**Music:** Leo F. Forbstein, Bernhard Kaun
**Cast:** Paul Muni, Glenda Farrell, Helen Vinson, Noel Francis, Preston Foster, Allen Jenkins, Berton Churchill, Edward Ellis, David Landau, Hale Hamilton, Sally Blane, Louise Carter, Willard Robertson, Robert McWade, Robert Warwick
**Oscar nomination:** Hal B. Wallis (best picture), Paul Muni (actor), Nathan Levinson (sound)

The grandpappy of prison movies, Mervyn LeRoy's searing indictment of penal practices common in its day was, with its titanic performance from Paul Muni (in a neat reversal from his thuggish role as Scarface the same year), arguably the finest of the hard-hitting social-protest dramas Warner Brothers specialized in during the 1930s.

Based on an autobiographical story by Robert E. Burns, *I Am a Fugitive from a Chain Gang* vividly depicts an innocent man brutalized and criminalized as a down-on-his-luck World War I veteran is railroaded into shackles and hard labor in the Deep South. Having broken out once to make a decent new life, he is betrayed, escapes again, and is condemned to life as a broken fugitive. Rock splitting, sadistic guards, escapes (including the seminal pursuit by baying bloodhounds through a swamp), solitary confinement—the vocabulary of the behind-bars genre was laid down here. Worth seeing just to appreciate how often it has been referenced (most recently in the Coens' *O Brother, Where Art Thou?*), it is dated but still powerfully disturbing down to the famously haunting last line. As Muni's fugitive Jim slips away into the night, his lover plaintively calls out "How do you live?" From the darkness comes the tragically ironic whisper, "I steal." **AE**

**U.S.** (Paramount) 83m BW
**Director:** Ernst Lubitsch
**Producer:** Ernst Lubitsch
**Screenplay:** Grover Jones, from the play *The Honest Finder* by Aladar Laszlo
**Photography:** Victor Milner
**Music:** W. Franke Harling
**Cast:** Miriam Hopkins, Kay Francis, Herbert Marshall, Charles Ruggles, Edward Everett Horton, C. Aubrey Smith, Robert Greig

# TROUBLE IN PARADISE (1932)

After his emigration from Europe and arrival in Hollywood at the tail end of the silent era, Ernst Lubitsch quickly established himself as a master of the technical with an ear for comedic pacing. Admirers called his particular talents the "Lubitsch Touch," but Lubitsch didn't work with any set formula or system. Rather, he brought from Europe a sophisticated sensibility that sent gentle shock waves through Hollywood, changing the tone of American comedies and leading to the rise of the "screwball" antics of Howard Hawks and Billy Wilder, both of whom revered him.

But that same sophistication kept Lubitsch from veering precipitously toward slapstick or more overt physical humor. That famed "Lubitsch Touch" indicated his deft method of delivering sexual politics with a barely discernable wink, and that meant a clever way with words and stories to subvert, surmount, or gently prod the relatively prudish (though still pre-Hays Code) American standards.

The most carnal and clever aspects of the "Lubitsch Touch" are firmly on display from the first frame of *Trouble in Paradise*, one of the director's first sound features. The title appears initially only in parts, so that for a moment the words "Trouble in..." linger over a shot of a bed. By the time the word "...Paradise" finally pops up, Lubitsch has already made clear what he meant by "Trouble in Paradise": The film may as well be titled "Trouble in Bed." Of course, *Trouble in Paradise* is only indirectly about sex, but that is typically the case with romantic comedies, of which Lubitsch was a significant pioneer.

Herbert Marshall and Miriam Hopkins are a match made in heaven. Both are expert thieves and con artists, and their courtship consists of robbing each other blind one fateful night in Venice. Over dinner they trade tentative praise, revealing stolen personal items in lieu of more traditional flirtation. Theirs is a romance built on deception, an ironic aphrodisiac, and they don't think anything of the other's chosen profession. "Baron, you are a crook," asserts Hopkins, "May I have the salt?". Life is good until the pair set their eyes on heiress Kay Francis. Hopkins sees a big bank account, but Marshall may see more. He tries to seduce his way into her safe, but finds his feelings for the heiress keep getting in the way.

The film's plot machinations are needed to toss the characters together, but *Trouble in Paradise* is less concerned with the big con than it is with companionship. Marshall initially wants Francis's money, but all the lonely Francis wants is Marshall, and soon the two become lovers, much to the chagrin of Hopkins. But *Trouble in Paradise* is nowhere near as predictable as it seems. Love is something that can't be stolen or bought, which explains the quandary of Lubitsch's compulsively criminal lead characters. As much as Marshall and Hopkins covet the acquisition of Francis's fortune, even at the cost of their relationship, they realize their uniquely larcenous dispositions make them particularly well-suited for one another. **JKl**

# SCARFACE: THE SHAME OF A NATION
(1932)

U.S. (Caddo, United Artists) 99m BW
**Director:** Howard Hawks
**Producer:** Howard Hawks, Howard Hughes
**Screenplay:** Ben Hecht, Fred Pasley, Seton I. Miller, John Lee Mahin, W.R. Burnett, Seton I. Miller, from novel by Armitage Trail
**Music:** Shelton Brooks, W.C. Handy
**Photography:** Lee Garmes, L. William O'Connell
**Cast:** Paul Muni, Ann Dvorak, Karen Morley, Osgood Perkins, C. Henry Gordon, George Raft, Vince Barnett, Boris Karloff, Purnell Pratt, Tully Marshall, Inez Palange, Edwin Maxwell

Introducing one of cinema history's most notorious, Machiavellian monsters in the perverted Horatio Alger myth that lies at the heart of every gangster film, *Scarface: The Shame of a Nation* stands as the peak of its genre. And it's a telling sign that Brian De Palma's 1983 version of the film, despite all the accolades accorded it, does nothing to diminish the power of Howard Hawks's original. On the contrary, like Shakespeare at his best (*Macbeth* might be the most obvious reference here), the film's seductive combination of fascination and revulsion with its corrupted protagonist and his equally corrupted world makes up the very fabric of the drama.

Completed before Hollywood's conservative Production Code became more rigidly enforced in 1934, ex-journalist Ben Hecht's screenplay uses the Al Capone legend as source material—staging recreations of the St. Valentine's Day Massacre and the murder of Big Jim Colosimo—to show Prohibition-era Chicago as a modern-day Sodom and Gomorrah. Amorality is rampant: Cops are brutal and on the take, journalists are cynical muckrakers. In contrast, the Capone-like protagonist Tony "Scarface" Camonte (Paul Muni) is at least frank in his greedy quest for power and the almighty dollar.

The ultimate irony of *Scarface* is that everything goes well as long as Tony treats his killing spree as purely business. The moment his emotions come into play, he's doomed. Much can be made of the strange twist in the plot when Tony starts losing control because of his violent jealousy concerning the love affair between his sister Cesca (Ann Dvorak) and his best friend Guino Rinaldo (George Raft). This could stem from incestuous feelings for his sister, or indicate a repressed homosexual bond with his friend. Hawks effectively underlines Tony's road to ruin with heavy symbolism, achieved via expressive lighting and street signs. The gangster is initially seen as a Nosferatu-like silhouette on the wall as he commits his first murder. At the end, his final showdown is marked by cross-shaped shadows and his dead body lying in the gutter under a travel sign that reads, ironically, "The world is yours." **MT**

# SHANGHAI EXPRESS (1932)

In the seven films he made with her, Josef von Sternberg took his obsession with Marlene Dietrich to ever more extreme lengths of intensity and stylization, until both star and story were all but subsumed in a welter of spectacle and design. Coming at the midpoint of the cycle, *Shanghai Express* holds the elements in near-perfect balance.

Sternberg loved to treat his films as controlled experiments in the play of light and shadow, so a plot whose action is largely confined to the eponymous train suited him perfectly. The *story*, such as it is, concerns a train journey from Peking to Shanghai, interrupted by a bandit attack. But the *subject* of the film is Dietrich's face, on which it plays an endless series of variations: veiled, shadowed, wreathed with smoke, nestling in furs or feathers, framed in intricate patterns of black on white. Dietrich herself, as the "notorious China coaster," Shanghai Lily, remains enigmatic, her eyes hooded and watchful, as Sternberg—and his regular cinematographer, Lee Garmes—use her face as an exquisite screen on which to project the appropriate emotions.

The setting of *Shanghai Express*, constructed in the studio artifice that Sternberg always preferred, is an elaborately conceived and utterly fictitious China, embodied in the film's opening sequence: a huge, dazzlingly white locomotive steams out of Peking Station and straight down the middle of a narrow street seething with lampshade-hatted coolies, stallholders, children, and animals. Years later, Sternberg visited China for the first time and was gratified to discover that the reality differed completely.

Clive Brook as Lily's ex-lover, a British army captain, plays the kind of staunchly traditional Englishman beside whose stiff upper lip steel-reinforced concrete would seem flabby, and Anna May Wong is no less enjoyably cartoonish as the embodiment of feline oriental guile. But the film belongs to Sternberg and Dietrich, and the strange fetishistic chemistry between them. Together they created something deliriously unique in cinema; apart they could never quite recapture the same magic. **PK**

**U.S.** (Paramount) 84m BW
**Languages:** English / French / Cantonese / German
**Director:** Josef von Sternberg
**Screenplay:** Jules Furthman
**Photography:** Lee Garmes
**Music:** W. Franke Harling
**Cast:** Marlene Dietrich, Clive Brook, Anna May Wong, Warner Oland, Eugene Pallette, Lawrence Grant, Louise Closser Hale, Gustav von Seyffertitz, Emile Chautard
**Oscar:** Lee Garmes (photography)
**Oscar nomination:** (best picture), Josef von Sternberg (director)

# FREAKS (1932)

From its original conception as a horror movie exceeding all expectations, something more disturbing than anything seen before (via Dwain Esper's exploitation of it under such dubious and misleading titles as *Forbidden Love*, *Monster Show*, and *Nature's Mistakes*), to its revival as an avant-garde film in the tradition of Luis Buñuel and Alain Robbe-Grillet, Tod Browning's *Freaks* has covered the range of horror, art-house, and documentary. This last—documentary—because of its realism as expressed in the movie's use of "real freaks." Nevertheless, despite its originality of conception and design, and its startling ability to both move and frighten audiences, *Freaks* has remained to this day an underappreciated film.

**U.S.** (MGM) 64m BW
**Director:** Tod Browning
**Producer:** Tod Browning
**Screenplay:** Clarence Aaron "Tod" Robbins, from his novel *Spurs*
**Photography:** Merritt B. Gerstad
**Cast:** Wallace Ford, Leila Hyams, Olga Baclanova, Roscoe Ates, Henry Victor, Harry Earles, Daisy Earles, Rose Dione, Daisy Hilton, Violet Hilton, Schlitze, Josephine Joseph, Johnny Eck, Frances O'Connor, Peter Robinson

*Freaks* opens with a carnival barker addressing some curious spectators. After the crowd catches sight of the female sideshow freak nearby, several women scream and the barker starts telling her story. Cleopatra (Olga Baclanova), a beautiful trapeze artist with the carnival, is adored by a midget named Hans (Harry Earles). But Cleopatra is having an affair with Hercules (Henry Victor), the Strong Man, and the couple devise a plot to get their hands on Hans's recently-inherited fortune: Cleopatra will marry the midget she despises and then poison him. During an unforgettable wedding ceremony-cum-initiation ritual, Cleopatra rebuffs the assembled freaks (when casting the film, Browning had the largest conglomeration of professional freaks ever assembled trying out for roles), teasing them mercilessly and calling them "dirty" and "slimy." Back in her wagon she poisons Hans's drink, but her plan is foiled and she is attacked by the freaks, who have banded together to exact a brutal revenge. Finally returning to the carnival barker in the present, we now see the result of the freaks' attack on Cleopatra: she has been turned into a legless, half-blind stump—a squawking chicken woman. A final scene, tacked on later as the studio insisted on a happy ending, shows Hans living like a millionaire in an elegant house; reconciled with his midget ex-girlfriend Frieda (Daisy Earles).

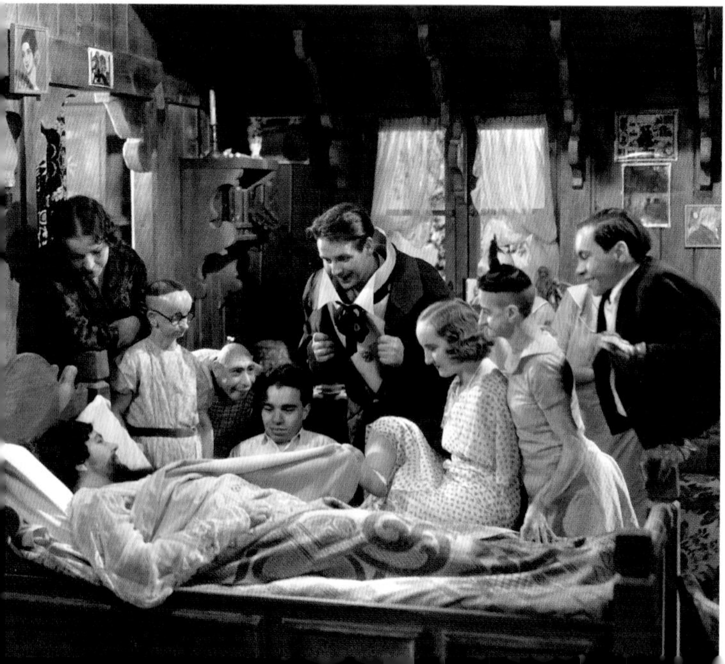

But no mere plot summary can do justice to this alarming yet profound movie, which must truly be seen to be "believed." A supreme oddity (freak?) of world cinema considered by many the most remarkable film in the career of a director whose credits include the original version of *Dracula* (1931). **BH**

# ME AND MY GAL (1932)

Set in Manhattan, the story has to do with a soft-hearted, none-too-brainy cop (Spencer Tracy) who romances a chowder-house waitress (Joan Bennett) and, through dumb luck, catches a notorious gangster who has conveniently chosen her sister's attic to hole up in. Raoul Walsh and his writers apparently took this rickety premise as their cue to do whatever the hell they wanted. The result is a delightful, unpretentious, often completely crazy film.

The populism of *Me and My Gal* rings true; although the film's portrait of Irish-American life in Depression-era New York is doubtless idealized, the real optimism, tenderness, warmth, and depth of shared experience behind the idealization are unmistakable. In this film made before the repeal of Prohibition, not only is there a running comic motif involving a belligerent little drunk (the eccentric Will Stanton), but there's also a wedding scene that riotously celebrates drinking, with the father of the bride (J. Farrell MacDonald) walking into close-up and shooting a jaunty invitation into the camera lens: "Who'd like a drink, huh?"

With all the comedy in *Me and My Girl*, it is neither surprising nor regrettable that the serious side of the plot gets shortchanged. Walsh's casual audacity with space, his fondness for the hard-boiled and the good-hearted, and his mastery of every nuance of his material are evident throughout the film, which, miraculously, at no moment lapses into the merely conventional. **CFu**

**U.S.** (Fox) 79m BW

**Director:** Raoul Walsh

**Screenplay:** Philip Klein, Barry Conners, Arthur Kober

**Photography:** Arthur C. Miller

**Music:** James F. Hanley

**Cast:** Spencer Tracy, Joan Bennett, Marion Burns, George Walsh, J. Farrell MacDonald, Noel Madison, Henry B. Walthall, Bert Hanlon, Adrian Morris, George Chandler

# ZÉRO DE CONDUITE (1933)
## ZERO FOR CONDUCT

"Young Devils at College": The secondary title of *Zero for Conduct* suggests a mild romp in the *Carry On* vein, but Jean Vigo's classic short film means business. At stake in this vignette of childhood rebellion against an oppressive school institution is nothing less than a veritable surrealist manifesto—one whose cosmic dimension is assured by the final shot in which its young devils, triumphant on a rooftop, appear ready to take flight.

This is a terrific movie to spring on students unprepared for what they will see: full frontal nudity, scatological and body-obsessed humor, antireligious blasphemy, insistent homoeroticism. But it transcends the simple duality of youth versus authority (unlike its loose remake, the 1968 film *If...*) via its vision of inescapable, polymorphous perversity: Even the stuffiest teachers here are twisted, secretly wild at heart.

The hearty provocation happens as much on the level of form as content: the experiments with slow-motion, animation, and trick photography are prodigious and wondrous. Vigo had absorbed the avant-gardism of Luis Buñuel and René Clair, but he also invented a unique aesthetic form: the "aquarium shot," a claustrophobic space in which strange apparitions are produced from every available corner and pocket—cinema as a magic act. **AM**

**France** (Argui-Film) 41m BW

**Language:** French

**Director:** Jean Vigo

**Producer:** Jacques-Louis Nounez, Jean Vigo

**Screenplay:** Jean Vigo

**Photography:** Boris Kaufman

**Music:** Maurice Jaubert

**Cast:** Jean Dasté, Robert le Flon, Du Verron, Delphin, Léon Larive, Mme. Emile, Louis De Gonzague-Frick, Raphaël Diligent, Louis Lefebvre, Gilbert Pruchon, Coco Golstein, Gérard de Bédarieux

U.S. (Warner Bros.) 89m BW

**Director:** Lloyd Bacon

**Producer:** Hal B. Wallis, Darryl F. Zanuck

**Screenplay:** Rian James, James Seymour, from novel by Bradford Ropes

**Photography:** Sol Polito

**Music:** Harry Warren

**Cast:** Warner Baxter, Bebe Daniels, George Brent, Ruby Keeler, Guy Kibbee, Una Merkel, Ginger Rogers, Ned Sparks, Dick Powell, Allen Jenkins, Edward J. Nugent, Robert McWade, George E. Stone

**Oscar nomination:** Hal B. Wallis, Darryl F. Zanuck (best picture), Nathan Levinson (sound)

# 42ND STREET (1933)

"Sawyer, you're going out a youngster, but you've *got* to come back a star!" The grandmother of backstage musicals is still a tuneful charmer (verified by its adaptation into a Broadway hit fifty years later), but it also occupies a special place in film history, for several appealing reasons.

*42nd Street*'s plot became one of the best-loved bores of showbiz lore. Fresh-faced dancer Peggy Sawyer (Ruby Keeler), newly arrived in New York during the Depression, lands a job in the chorus of a musical called *Pretty Lady*. The show's temperamental star Dorothy Brock (Bebe Daniels) injures her ankle the night before the show opens, so "real little trouper" Peggy steps into the lead, is drilled to exhaustion, and, with the fate of the company riding on her, bravely goes out there and wows 'em. Seventy years on, the script is a cherishable and disarming mix of naïvety, smart toughness, and sassy repartee.

Fleshing out the drama is a cast of characters who became archetypes: the stressed and ailing director (Warner Baxter, whose bullying and pep talks to his company are classic); the harassed dance director (George E. Stone); the saucy, wisecracking chorus girls (Una Merkel and Ginger Rogers); the puppyish juvenile (Dick Powell); and the well-heeled, lecherous backer (Guy Kibbee) with designs on the leading lady, who strings him along while conducting a clandestine romance with a down-on-his-luck vaudevillian (George Brent). The winning cast is a remarkable ensemble. The wonderful Baxter had won the Best Actor Oscar for *In Old Arizona*'s dashing *bandito* hero The Cisco Kid. Daniels was a top star of silent pictures who could also sing. Brent was another established romantic lead. Billed beneath them, half a dozen actors were already popular faces, including Rogers, soon to be teamed with Fred Astaire. Dick Powell, baby-faced and peppy, was among those whose careers were launched by *42nd Street*. The big discovery in her film debut was Ruby Keeler, Broadway darling and wife of Al Jolson. She wasn't much of a singer but was adorable, sweetly vivacious, and a tap-dancing treat.

Generally Warner Brothers films were renowned for realism. But to boost their musical fortunes, Mervyn LeRoy (who developed this project before illness made him defer directing to Lloyd Bacon) brought in songwriters Al Dubin and Harry Warren, who became chief tunesmiths for Warner Brothers. LeRoy also insisted on inventive dance director Busby Berkeley, who had enlivened several musical comedies for Sam Goldwyn. He made much out of the snappy songs, including "Shuffle off to Buffalo," "Young and Healthy," "You're Beginning to be a Habit with Me." For the show-stopping title song finale, Berkeley created an immortal production number in which Ruby dancing atop a taxi, swaying Manhattan skyscrapers, and scantily clad beauties arranged in geometric patterns shot from high overhead form a sensational rhythmic kaleidoscope. After seeing what he was up to, Warner Brothers contracted Berkeley and gave him carte blanche, initiating a long run of dazzling dance confections that brightened the decade and remain a highlight in screen musicals. **AE**

**U.S.** (Warner Bros.) 104m BW
**Director:** Lloyd Bacon
**Producer:** Robert Lord
**Screenplay:** Manuel Seff, James Seymour
**Photography:** George Barnes
**Music:** Al Dubin, Sammy Fain, Irving Kahal, Harry Warren, Walter Donaldson, Gus Kahn
**Cast:** James Cagney, Joan Blondell, Ruby Keeler, Dick Powell, Frank McHugh, Ruth Donnelly, Guy Kibbee, Hugh Herbert, Claire Dodd, Gordon Westcott, Arthur Hohl, Renee Whitney, Barbara Rogers, Paul Porcasi, Philip Faversham

# FOOTLIGHT PARADE (1933)

The greatest of all Depression-era musicals, *Footlight Parade* is really two films in one. The first is a fast, funny backstage story about frantic efforts to stage live musical interludes at movie houses, with James Cagney in top form as a hard-driving producer too preoccupied to appreciate his adoring secretary (Joan Blondell). The second is a climactic juggernaut of three consecutive Busby Berkeley spectacles, the rigor of whose design is matched by their uninhibited imagery.

I will pass too quickly over "Honeymoon Hotel," which takes a wholesomely naughty tour through an establishment devoted to conjugal bliss, and "Shanghai Lil," which transforms rakish oriental decadence into rousing New Deal morale boosting, in order to concentrate on "By a Waterfall." This aquatic rhapsody, featuring the glistening bodies and geometric group-formations displayed by a bevy of water nymphs, pushes its central tension between form and flesh further and further until it reaches an abstract outer space where depth collapses. The distinction between air and water dissolves and human bodies mutate into elemental cell-like units. You can have the "Star Gate" climax of *2001: A Space Odyssey*; when it comes to consciousness-expanding cinematic trips, I'll take a plunge into Berkeley's "Waterfall." **MR**

**U.S.** (Warner Bros.) 96m BW
**Director:** Mervyn LeRoy
**Producer:** Robert Lord, Jack L. Warner, Raymond Griffith
**Screenplay:** David Boehm, Erwin S. Gelsey
**Photography:** Sol Polito
**Music:** Harry Warren
**Cast:** Warren William, Joan Blondell, Aline MacMahon, Ruby Keeler, Dick Powell, Guy Kibbee, Ned Sparks, Ginger Rogers
**Oscar nomination:** Nathan Levinson (sound)

# GOLD DIGGERS OF 1933 (1933)

Of the series of classic early 1930s Warner Brothers musicals featuring numbers by Busby Berkeley, *Gold Diggers of 1933* is the one that most strongly evokes the Great Depression. The bawdy, wisecracking screenplay centers on struggling Broadway showgirls who do what's necessary—including the use of "gold digging" techniques on rich suckers—to keep the wolf from the door. The film's latter stages are dominated by three spectacular Berkeley numbers: the racy "Pettin' in the Park," elegant "Shadow Waltz," and topical "Remember My Forgotten Man."

An ironic disparity between onstage opulence and offstage economic crisis is established in the "We're in the Money" curtain-raiser, when a peppy paean to prosperity being rehearsed by coin-covered chorines is broken up by the show's creditors. The opening number's correlation of sex and money foreshadows the climactic "Remember My Forgotten Man," in which a streetwalker (Joan Blondell) laments the common man's closely-linked losses of earning power and sexual virility, in poignant contrast to his forgotten World War I military glory. With its partisan references to the controversial 1932 Bonus March of jobless veterans and its vivid tableaux connecting war, emasculation, and unemployment, "Remember My Forgotten Man" is one of Hollywood's hardest-hitting political statements of the 1930s. **MR**

# SHE DONE HIM WRONG (1933)

**U.S.** (Paramount) 66m BW

**Director:** Lowell Sherman

**Producer:** William LeBaron

**Screenplay:** Mae West, Harry Thew, John Bright, from the play *Diamond Lil* by Mae West

**Photography:** Charles Lang

**Music:** Ralph Rainger, Shelton Brooks, John Leipold, Stephan Pasternacki

**Cast:** Mae West, Cary Grant, Owen Moore, Gilbert Roland, Noah Beery, David Landau, Rafaela Ottiano, Dewey Robinson, Rochelle Hudson, Tammany Young, Fuzzy Knight, Grace La Rue, Robert Homans, Louise Beavers

**Oscar nomination:** William LeBaron (best picture)

In the early 1930s, Hollywood—beset with financial difficulties and production problems related to the conversion to sound cinema—turned to stage performers of proven popularity to lure customers back to the theaters. Among the most notable of these was Mae West, whose play *Diamond Lil* (which she wrote as a kind of showcase of her several talents) was immensely successful on Broadway and elsewhere. West proved a happy choice for Paramount, because her unique brand of sophisticated if bawdy humor easily translated on screen; her first film, *Night After Night* (1932), was a big hit with audiences. West's antics, especially her famous double entendres and sleazy style, offended religious conservatives of the time and hastened the foundation of the Breen Office in 1934 to enforce the Production Code (promulgated, but widely ignored, in the early 1930s). West's post-1934 films, although interesting, never recaptured the appeal of her earlier work, of which *She Done Him Wrong*—the screen adaptation of *Diamond Lil*—is the most notable example, even garnering an Academy Award nomination.

West plays a "saloon keeper" in New York's Bowery who is involved with various criminals in the neighborhood. As Lady Lou, West is pursued by two local entrepreneurs and her fiancé is just released from jail, but she is hardly in need of a man as she inhabits lavish quarters above her establishment, replete with servants and an impressive collection of diamond jewelry. Lou, however, is smitten by her new neighbor, the head of the Salvation Army mission (Cary Grant). Her initial appraisal of the younger man's attractiveness is part of Hollywood legend. To Grant she utters the famous line "Why don't you come up sometime, see me." As a demonstration of her affection (and power), she uses some of her considerable hoard of diamonds to purchase his mission and make him a present of it. In the end, Grant is revealed as a detective who promptly takes all the crooks into custody, but "imprisons" Lou quite differently—with a wedding ring. A classic Hollywood comedy, full of naughtiness and good humor. **RBP**

**U.S.** (Paramount) 70m BW
**Director:** Leo McCarey
**Producer:** Herman J. Mankiewicz
**Screenplay:** Bert Kalmar, Harry Ruby
**Photography:** Henry Sharp
**Music:** Bert Kalmar, John Leipold, Harry Ruby
**Cast:** Groucho Marx, Harpo Marx, Chico Marx, Zeppo Marx, Margaret Dumont, Raquel Torres, Louis Calhern, Edmund Breese, Leonid Kinskey, Charles Middleton, Edgar Kennedy

# DUCK SOUP (1933)

Released in 1933, this madcap comedy is the crowning glory of the comic team of the Marx Brothers, a New York phenomenon who honed their performing skills through vaudeville and went on to take Broadway with a series of comedies including *The Cocoanuts* and *Animal Crackers*. More than original performers, their timing was perfect in more ways than one: sound technology was taking over films just as they peaked on the stages of New York and looked for new audiences to conquer.

Among the five films made in Paramount's New York studios by the brothers—Groucho, Harpo, Chico, and Zeppo—*Duck Soup* is the last to feature all of them (Zeppo, the youngest brother and the group's straight man, went on to be an agent and inventor). It's crammed with visual and verbal gags, most of which are as fresh and funny today as they were in 1933. As with so many classics, *Duck Soup* enjoyed less-than-vigorous box-office traffic. It did so badly, in fact, that Paramount cancelled the Marx Brothers' contract soon afterward, causing them to head west to Hollywood and MGM, where *A Night at the Opera* and *A Day at the Races* were made.

*Duck Soup* is only 70 minutes long, but it packs in a seemingly endless string of virtually anything that might get a laugh, from jabs at Paul Revere and snide asides about then-current musicals to unexpected use of stock footage and astonishingly inventive physical sketches like the "three-hat routine," perfected by the brothers on stage over the years, and the famous mirror sequence. This routine—imitated by comics ever since—features Groucho, dressed in nightgown, nightcap, moustache, and cigar, meeting "himself' (Harpo as an identical image) in a doorway.

The plot, as such, involves Groucho as the dictator of the state of Freedonia. Named Rufus T. Firefly, his patron is the wealthy Mrs. Teasdale, played with ineffable dignity and grace under pressure by Margaret Dumont, again the perfect outrageous foil and the subject of most of Groucho's forcefully memorable putdowns. If the physical gags and Groucho's inimitable dialogue style were their own, the scripts had expert input from many great comedy writers, among them S.J. Perelman. More than a great physical comedy act, the Marx Brothers were comedians lucky enough to have witty dialogue and keen observation, another reason why *Duck Soup* has survived whereas the films of, say, the Ritz Brothers remain unrevered.

Sylvanian Ambassador Trintino (Louis Calhern) wants Freedonia for his own and so pays Harpo and Chico to be his intelligence agents. This slender plot line is strong enough to support some of the best comedy sequences ever filmed, and offensive enough to some to count as surrealist satire. Benito Mussolini banned the film in Italy because he took Groucho's role as a personal attack; nothing could have pleased the brothers more. Again, before the film's release, a small city in New York called Fredonia complained about the use of its name as well as the additional "e"; the response from the Marx Brothers camp was reassuringly predictable: "Change the name of your town, it's hurting our picture." **KK**

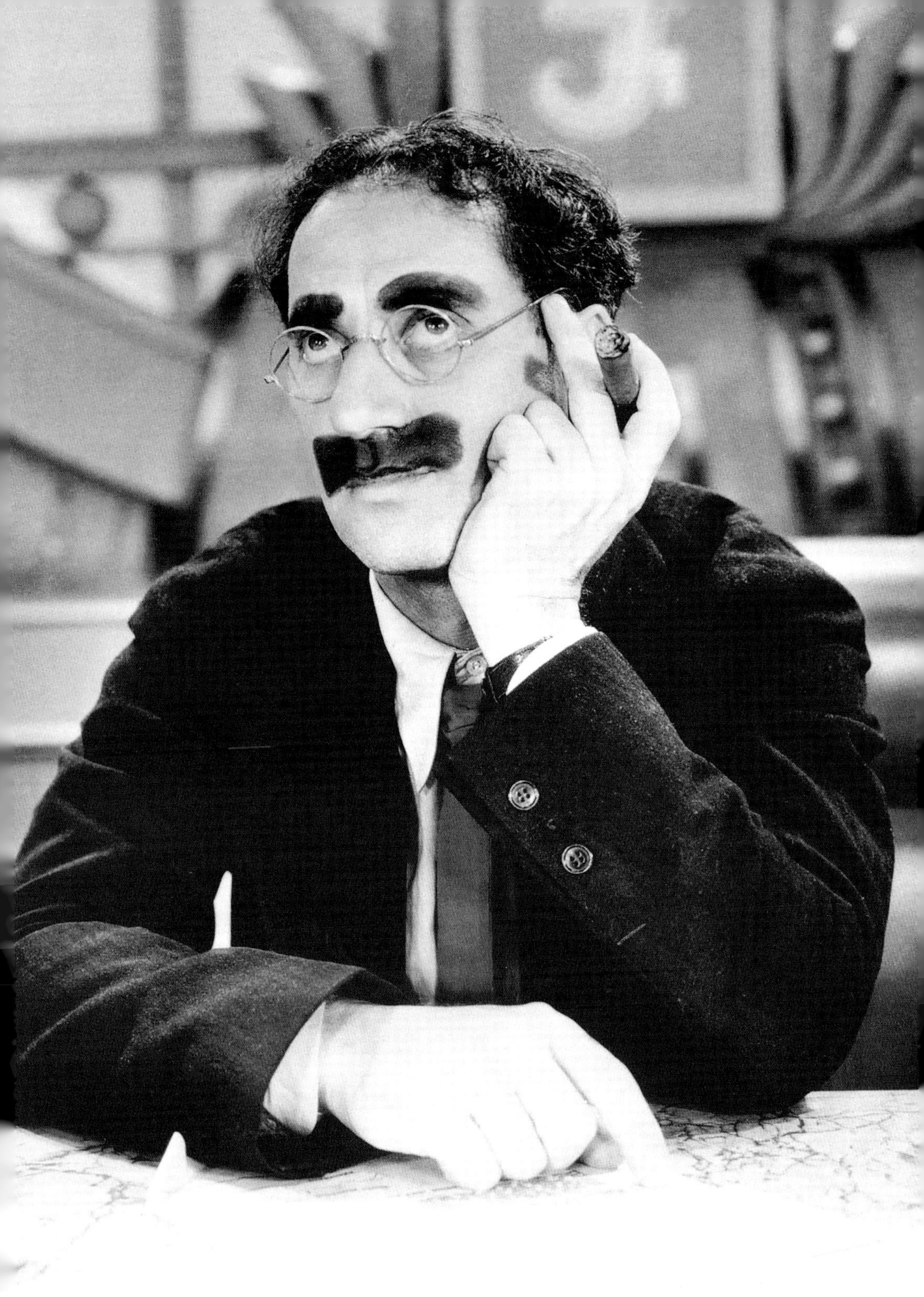

# QUEEN CHRISTINA (1933)

**U.S.** (MGM) 97m BW
**Director:** Rouben Mamoulian
**Producer:** Walter Wanger
**Screenplay:** S.N. Behrman, H.M. Harwood
**Photography:** William H. Daniels
**Music:** Herbert Stothart
**Cast:** Greta Garbo, John Gilbert, Ian Keith, Lewis Stone, Elizabeth Young, C. Aubrey Smith, Reginald Owen, Georges Renavent, David Torrence, Gustav von Seyffertitz, Ferdinand Munier
**Venice Film Festival:** Rouben Mamoulian nomination (Mussolini Cup)

Rouben Mamoulian's re-creation of the 17th-century Swedish court provides Greta Garbo with a perfect vehicle to dominate the screen. The historical Christina, daughter of Gustavus Adolphus, was a reclusive aesthete who eventually abdicated in order to have a life of her own and change her Lutheranism for Catholicism. Garbo's version, by way of contrast, is an alluring mixture of masculine and feminine qualities. Learned, resolute, she is also sexually experienced, even aggressive, yet committed to her independence.

The plot (which seems to have borrowed a good deal from screen versions of England's Elizabeth I) centers on her counselors' demand that she marry Charles of France, which angers her and her "consort," the burly Count Magnus (Ian Keith). Fleeing the court—and the restrictions placed on her as a woman—Christina dresses like a man and encounters, by chance, the Spanish ambassador, Antonio (John Gilbert, whom Garbo was romancing at the time). What follows are comic scenes of sexual disguise, as Christina begins to fall deeply in love with Antonio, and deep eroticism. When Antonio is killed protecting her honor, Christina abdicates, achieving the solitude that, because of her rank and personal qualities, seems her fate from the beginning. Garbo's performance in the role is inspired, helped by the glamorizing touch of Mamoulian's camera. Well-conceived art design, editing, and music make *Queen Christina* sensational viewing. **RBP**

# LAS HURDES (1933)
## LAND WITHOUT BREAD

**Spain** (Ramón Acín) 27m BW
**Language:** Spanish
**Director:** Luis Buñuel
**Producer:** Ramón Acín, Luis Buñuel
**Screenplay:** Luis Buñuel, Rafael Sánchez Ventura
**Photography:** Eli Lotar
**Nonoriginal music:** Brahms
**Cast:** Abel Jacquin (voice)

An extraordinarily powerful yet wholly unsentimental account of poverty, disease, malnutrition, and ignorance allowed to exist in a supposedly civilized Christian nation, Luis Buñuel's documentary *Land Without Bread* was shot in the remote mountainous region of Las Hurdes—a small area just north of Extremadura, less than 100 kilometers south of the glories of the university city of Salamanca—in 1932. Physical, psychic, and social ills are all calmly observed by a dispassionate camera, Buñuel realizing that the images would speak volumes for themselves. Nonetheless, he juxtaposed shots of the riches to be found in Catholic churches and, it was learned later, was not above shooting a goat or smearing an ailing ass with honey (to attract a lethal swarm of bees) to emphasize his argument.

But what has all this to do with a surrealist? The horrors are not only on view but they're also the stuff of nightmare; Buñuel also seems all-too-aware that the only true release from the Hurdanos's cruel sufferings (unless State and Church intervene, at least) is death itself, and certainly many of the actions taken to alleviate their hunger and pain seem informed by a perverse desire for extinction. Cruel, cool, strangely beautiful, and as pungent as sulfur. **GA**

# KING KONG (1933)

The undisputed champ of all monster movies—and an early Hollywood high-water mark for special-effects work—*King Kong* remains one of the most lasting and beloved motion-picture masterpieces. Essentially a simian take on the *Beauty and the Beast* fable, told without the transformative happy ending and on a gargantuan scale, Merian C. Cooper and Ernest B. Schoedsack's film fuses groundbreaking model work and emotional resonance to a degree rarely replicated by the literally hundreds of imitators that inevitably followed in its wake.

The story essentially plays out like that age-old conflict between city and nature. An expedition team arrives on the ominously named Skull Island, attracted by the promise that a giant prehistoric gorilla, feared and worshipped by the natives, might be brought home to New York and exploited as a must-see attraction. But mighty Kong doesn't take well to being caged and escapes on a destructive spree through the Big Apple.

The scenes set on Skull Island remain impressive even to this day, from Kong's magnificent first appearance to the number of other prehistoric creatures he and the expedition face in protecting or seeking, respectively, the abducted Ann Darrow (Faye Wray). Indeed, Kong is intimidated by Ann's beauty, and when he inevitably flees captivity and roams through New York City, the first thing he does is capture the young woman and retain her as his prisoner of love. Straddling the Empire State Building and swatting away pesky airplanes, King would ultimately rather sacrifice his own life than hurt Ann, which gives the film its famous, touching sign-off: "'Twas beauty killed the beast."

That the giant ape shifts from feared antagonist to sympathetic protagonist, with the former of course the perspective of his pursuers, shows the success of Willis O'Brian's intricate and expressive stop-animation work (future stop-animation savant Ray Harryhausen worked as his assistant). Although it is a B-movie at heart, *King Kong* set Hollywood's special-effects fetish on fast forward, and a case could be made that thanks to *Kong* many of today's films focus far more on flash than story. But unlike contemporary special-effects exercises, the majesty of *Kong* is destined to endure, thanks in no small part to the "performance" of its giant lead. **JKl**

**U.S.** (RKO) 100m BW

**Director:** Merian C. Cooper, Ernest B. Schoedsack

**Producer:** Merian C. Cooper, Ernest B. Schoedsack, David O. Selznick

**Screenplay:** James Ashmore Creelman, Ruth Rose, Edgar Wallace

**Photography:** Edward Linden, J.O. Taylor, Vernon L. Walker, Kenneth Peach

**Music:** Max Steiner

**Cast:** Fay Wray, Robert Armstrong, Bruce Cabot, Frank Reicher, Sam Hardy, Noble Johnson, Steve Clemente, James Flavin

## THE BITTER TEA OF GENERAL YEN (1933)

**U.S.** (Columbia ) 88m BW
**Language:** English / Mandarin / French
**Director:** Frank Capra
**Producer:** Walter Wanger
**Screenplay:** Edward E. Paramore Jr., Grace Zaring Stone
**Photography:** Joseph Walker
**Music:** W. Franke Harling
**Cast:** Barbara Stanwyck, Nils Asther, Toshia Mori, Walter Connolly, Gavin Gordon, Lucien Littlefield, Richard Loo, Helen Jerome Eddy, Emmett Corrigan

Frank Capra's atypical melodrama concerns an American missionary (Barbara Stanwyck) in Shanghai—a prim New England type named Megan Davis, engaged to another missionary, her childhood sweetheart. During an outbreak of civil war, she's taken prisoner by a Chinese warlord named Yen (Nils Asther). The unlikely love story that ensues is not only Capra's unsung masterpiece but also one of the great Hollywood love stories of the 1930s: subtle, delicate, moody, mystical, and passionate. Joseph Walker shot it through filters and with textured shadows that suggest the work of Josef von Sternberg; Edward Paramore wrote the script, adapted from a story by Grace Zaring Stone. Oddly enough, this perverse and beautiful film was chosen to open Radio City Music Hall in 1933. It was not one of Capra's commercial successes, but it arguably beats the rest of his films by miles, and both Stanwyck and Asther are extraordinary.

Among the film's highlights is a remarkable dream sequence in which Megan's bedroom is broken into by a Yellow Peril monster whom one assumes is Yen, and then Megan is saved by a masked man in western clothes, whom one assumes is her fiancé. But when she removes the mask, it turns out to be Yen, who is standing beside her when she wakes. No less memorable is the exquisite final sequence—which might be interpreted as a Hollywood brand of pop Buddhism, though it's rendered with sweetness and delicacy. **JRos**

## SONS OF THE DESERT (1933)

**U.S.** (Hal Roach, MGM) 68m BW
**Director:** William A. Seiter
**Producer:** Hal Roach
**Screenplay:** Frank Craven
**Photography:** Kenneth Peach
**Music:** William Axt, George M. Cohan, Marvin Hatley, Paul Marquardt, O'Donnell-Heath, Leroy Shield
**Cast:** Stan Laurel, Oliver Hardy, Charley Chase, Mae Busch, Dorothy Christy, Lucien Littlefield, John Elliott, William Gillespie, John Merton

Essentially a remake of the duo's 1930 film *Be Big*, this full-length Stan Laurel and Oliver Hardy comedy was their fourth feature, and arguably their best. Although other Laurel and Hardy films are, subjectively at least, equal to this one, they tend to inhabit atypical worlds—the fairyland of *Babes in the Wood*, for example, or the western fantasy of *Way Out West*. Although *Sons of the Desert* may be one of Laurel and Hardy's most conventional comedies, it best represents the strange domestic hell that the duo inhabit in their finest work, an oddly childlike world full of domineering wives, clandestine fun sessions, and illicit smoking and drinking.

Centering around a trip to Hawaii with the Freemason-like fraternity of the title and Stan and Ollie's attempts to conceal this jaunt from their wives, *Sons of the Desert* takes a basic farce plot and turns it into a vehicle for motion picture comedy's greatest double act. Superb supporting performances, most notably from Mae Busch as Mrs. Hardy and comedian-director Charlie Chase as a drunken version of himself, along with capable direction from William A. Seiter (whose other notable comedy was the Marx Brothers' workmanlike *Room Service* in 1938), also make *Sons of the Desert*—unusually for a 70-year-old film comedy—utterly watchable today. **KK**

# IT'S A GIFT (1934)

Undoubtedly the finest of all W.C. Fields's comedies, *It's a Gift* may not offer the inspired insanity of such waywardly surreal gems as *Never Give a Sucker an Even Break* (1941) or the unforgettable short *The Fatal Glass of Beer* (1933), but it is certainly the most coherent and most consistently funny of his features.

Despite having been cobbled together from old revue sketches and scenes from earlier movies like *It's the Old Army Game* (1926), Norman Z. McLeod's *It's a Gift* actually provides something resembling a proper story. Harold Bissonette (Fields) is so tired of the constant pressures of family life and running a general store that he secretly buys with his hard-earned savings the Californian orange grove of his dreams, and sets off with his family (all vocally horrified by what he's done, naturally), only to discover that their purchase is nothing like the palace pictured in the advertisement. That said, of course, this "plot" is simply an excuse for another of Fields' marvelously misanthropic essays on the perils and pitfalls of parenthood, marriage, neighbors, Prohibition, allowing him free rein to court our sympathy for an old curmudgeon who feels himself maltreated by virtually the entire world.

It is uncommonly difficult to select highlights from such a supremely even series of set pieces, but the catastrophically destructive visit to Fields's shop paid by the feeble, deaf, blind, and uncommonly belligerent Mr. Muckle (Charles Sellon) must rank as some kind of peak in politically incorrect hilarity. The protagonist's forlorn attempt to sleep on the porch—despite noisy neighbors, a nagging wife (the inimitable Kathleen Howard), a murderous screwdriver wielded by Baby LeRoy, a rolling coconut, a broken hammock, a rifle, and a quite crazily cheery insurance salesman in search of one Karl LaFong ("Capital K, small A, small R")—is quite simply as brilliant and nightmarish a portrait of ordinary life as deadpan Hollywood comedy ever got. Mind you, the shaving sequence is pretty great, too. Oh, and then there's the dinner with the family. And then, sheer genius. **GA**

**U.S.** (Paramount) 73m BW
**Director:** Norman Z. McLeod
**Producer:** William LeBaron
**Screenplay:** Jack Cunningham, W.C. Fields
**Photography:** Henry Sharp
**Music:** Lew Brown, Buddy G. DeSylva, Ray Henderson, Al Jolson, John Leipold
**Cast:** W.C. Fields, Kathleen Howard, Jean Rouverol, Julian Madison, Tommy Bupp, Baby LeRoy, Tammany Young, Morgan Wallace, Charles Sellon, Josephine Whittell, T. Roy Barnes, Diana Lewis, Spencer Charters, Guy Usher, Dell Henderson

**Germany** (Leni Riefenstahl, NSDAP-Reichsleitung) 114m BW
**Language:** German
**Director:** Leni Riefenstahl
**Producer:** Leni Riefenstahl
**Screenplay:** Leni Riefenstahl, Walter Ruttmann
**Photography:** Sepp Allgeier, Karl Attenberger, Werner Bohne, Walter Frentz, Willy Zielke
**Music:** Herbert Windt
**Cast:** Adolf Hitler, Max Amann, Martin Bormann, Walter Buch, Walter Darré, Otto Dietrich, Sepp Dietrich, Hans Frank, Josef Goebbels, Hermann Göring, Jakob Grimminger, Rudolf Hess, Reinhard Heydrich, Konstantin Hierl, Heinrich Himmler, Robert Ley, Viktor Lutze, Erich Raeder, Fritz Reinhardt, Alfred Rosenberg, Hjalmar Schacht, Franz Xaver Schwarz, Julius Streicher, Fritz Todt, Werner von Blomberg, Hans Georg von Friedeburg, Gerd von Rundstedt, Baldur von Schirach, Adolf Wagner

# TRIUMPH DES WILLENS (1934)
## TRIUMPH OF THE WILL

It was Adolf Hitler himself who commissioned dancer and actress turned filmmaker Leni Riefenstahl to make a grand, celebratory record of the sixth Nazi Party Congress held in September 1934 at Nuremberg—the medieval Bavarian showplace where, with deliberate irony, a court of Allied victors would convene in 1945–46 to judge war criminals of the Third Reich. Hitler also gave her the film's title. Riefenstahl was a careerist as well as a creative talent and, her postwar protestations to the contrary, there is evidence (not only here but in her photo-journalistic coverage of the invasion of Poland and in her later use of concentration camp inmates as "extras") that her enthusiasm for fascism was crafty if, debatably, naïve. But any discussion of motivation cannot diminish the devastating impact of *Triumph of the Will*. This is an awesome spectacle, vulgar, but mythic and technically an overwhelming, assured accomplishment.

She had all the resources a documentarian could desire. Nuremberg was as carefully prepared as if it were a massive soundstage housing a series of elaborate sets. Riefenstahl ordered new bridges and accesses constructed in the city center, and lighting towers and camera tracks built, all of which was carried out to her exact specifications. Deploying 30 cameras and 120 technicians, Riefenstahl brilliantly fulfilled her Nuremberg brief—to glorify the might of the Nazi state and tighten its grip on the hearts and minds of Germany—with breathtaking imagery on a spectacularly sinister, epic scale, creating an infamous masterpiece still regarded as the most powerful propaganda film ever made.

The documentary—which after six months' editing into a carefully selected two hours represents about three percent of the footage shot—opens with Hitler's arrival by plane, his descent from the clouds given the character of a Wagnerian hero's entrance, with his head in a halo of sunlight. The Führer's acclamation and adulation by saluting multitudes is central to this presentation of his political philosophy as world theater, lending him a disturbing charisma despite the posturing and the stridency so familiar from news archives, historical drama, and masterly parody, like Charlie Chaplin's in *The Great Dictator* (1940). Setting him off are a kaleidoscope of astonishing images: vigorous young men disporting, torchlit processions, swastika-brandishing ritual, militaristic display, thousands of well-drilled children pledging themselves to the Movement, and a continuous folkloric parade concluding with the Nazi anthem, the Horst Wessel Song.

*Triumph of the Will* is an unsubtle but innovative demonstration of technique, from ingenious camera angles and striking composition to the relentless pace of its canny editing. This is an enduringly fascinating, chilling testament to the power of film to impose a false spiritual aesthetic on the overtly political. After World War II, Riefenstahl was imprisoned for four years by the Americans and the French for her role in the Nazi propaganda machine over her insistence that she made "pure historical film, film vérité." Repeated attempts to revive her career were unsuccessful. Later she discovered underwater photography and demonstrated she still had the eye of an artist. **AE**

„Triumph des Willens" Foto: Reichsparteitagfilm

**France** (Gaumont-Franco Film-Aubert) 89m BW
**Language:** French
**Director:** Jean Vigo
**Producer:** Jacques-Louis Nounez
**Screenplay:** Jean Guinée, Albert Riéra
**Photography:** Jean-Paul Alphen, Louis Berger, Boris Kaufman
**Music:** Maurice Jaubert
**Cast:** Michel Simon, Dita Parlo, Jean Dasté, Gilles Margaritis, Louis Lefebvre, Maurice Gilles, Raphaël Diligent

# L'ATALANTE (1934)

Heretical as it may be to say in these enlightened times of gender politics, but Jean Vigo's masterpiece *L'Atalante* is the cinema's greatest ode to heterosexual passion. One simply cannot enter into its rapturous poetry without surrendering to the romantic series of oppositions between the sexes, comparisons rigorously installed at every possible level—spiritual, physical, erotic, and emotional. It is only this thrill of absolute "otherness" that can allow both the agony of nonalignment between lovers, and the sublimity of their eventual fusion.

This is far removed from the typical romance of the time. As Vigo once memorably complained, it takes "two pairs of lips and three thousand metres of film to come together, and almost as many to come unstuck again." Like Stanley Kubrick's *Eyes Wide Shut* (1999), *L'Atalante* casts the immortal love story within an adventure tale: man (Jean Dasté as Jean) the seafaring adventurer, woman (Dita Parlo as Juliette) the city-craving settler. The seductive temptations and drifts that temporarily split them up are forecast in a charged moment of almost metaphysical agony: In thick fog, Jean stumbles blindly over the boat's barge until he finds his bride and envelops her in an embrace at once angry and relieved, inspiring them instantly to head below deck to make love...

Between these poles of man and woman, however, there is Père Jules (Michel Simon), master of the boat. It is surely the mark of Vigo's greatness as an artist that his imagination could project itself fully into both the heterosexual ideal and the fluid identity of this inspired madman. Jules is a multiple being, man and woman, child and adult, friend and lover, without boundaries—at one point even visually doubled as he wrestles himself. He is a living text covered with extravagant tattoos; he is the cinematic apparatus itself, able to produce sound from records with his magically electrified finger. Jules is Vigo's surrealist sensibility incarnated by Simon, an astonishingly anarchic, instinctual performer.

Vigo develops and deepens the formal explorations of his previous film *Zero for Conduct* (1933). From silent, burlesque cinema and René Clair he borrows a parade gag for his prologue: stuff-shirts at the couple's funeral filing past the camera, gradually becoming faster until they are an unruly, disheveled mob. Aboard the boat, Vigo finds his beloved "aquarium spaces"—enclosed rooms filled with cats, oddities, and wonders, as in Jules's cabin devoted to exotic bric-a-brac—on deck, he uses ghostly, nocturnal lighting. Unifying the film is a superb rhythmic and expressive tone, at times bringing *L'Atalante* close to becoming a musical.

Vigo's death at the age of 29 was a tragic loss. But *L'Atalante* crowns his legacy—and is there any scene in cinema sexier than the magnificent, Eisensteinian montage of Jean's and Juliette's bodies, far apart, matched in postures of mutual arousal, an act of love made possible only through the soulful language of the movies? **AM**

## THE BLACK CAT (1934)

**U.S.** (Universal) 65m BW
**Director:** Edgar G. Ulmer
**Producer:** Carl Laemmle Jr.
**Screenplay:** Edgar G. Ulmer, from the story *House of Doom* by Edgar Allan Poe
**Photography:** John J. Mescall
**Music:** James Huntley, Heinz Roemheld
**Nonoriginal music:** Tchaikovsky, Liszt
**Cast:** Boris Karloff, Bela Lugosi, David Manners, Julie Bishop, Lucille Lund, Egon Brecher, Harry Cording, Henry Armetta, Albert Conti

The first screen teaming of the 1930s' great monster stars Boris Karloff (top-billed simply as "KARLOFF") and Bela Lugosi, *The Black Cat* is at once the most perverse and the artiest of the original run of Universal horror pictures, informed by the strange sensibilities of director Edgar G. Ulmer—beginning to seesaw between high art and poverty row—and poetic pulp screenwriter Peter Ruric.

Based on Edgar Allan Poe's story only in concept, it feels like the last German Expressionist horror film, with a tale of diabolism, revenge, necrophilia, betrayal, and bad manners set in a modernist castle (a rare instance of up-to-date gothic) built by widow's-peaked Satanist-cum-architect Hjalmar Poelzig (Karloff) atop the mass grave of the soldiers he betrayed to the enemy during World War I. Horror-style honeymooners David Manners and Jacqueline Wells are almost comically out of their depth, the templates for Brad and Janet in *The Rocky Horror Picture Show* (1975), as unwilling houseguests caught between Poelzig, who has his mistresses preserved like waxworks in cases in the cellar, and the vengeance-obsessed Vitus Werdegast (Lugosi), who winds up the odd chessgame plot by skinning the villain alive before the castle is blown up. Deliberately outrageous but also a tease, Karloff's elegantly delivered rituals are all commonplace clichés ("cum granulo salis") delivered in a lisping Latin. **KN**

## JUDGE PRIEST (1934)

**U.S.** (Fox) 80m BW
**Director:** John Ford
**Producer:** Sol M. Wurtzel
**Screenplay:** Irvin S. Cobb, Dudley Nichols
**Photography:** George Schneiderman
**Music:** Cyril J. Mockridge, Emil Gerstenberger, Samuel Kaylin
**Cast:** Will Rogers, Tom Brown, Anita Louise, Henry B. Walthall, David Landau, Rochelle Hudson, Roger Imhof, Frank Melton, Charley Grapewin, Berton Churchill, Brenda Fowler, Francis Ford, Hattie McDaniel, Stepin Fetchit

John Ford won his first Oscar for the prestigious and ponderous *The Informer* (1935), but this lesser-known work, released the previous year, has dated much better, despite its rambling structure, thick sentimentality, and flagrant lack of political correctness. Billy Priest (Will Rogers), magistrate of an 1890 Kentucky town, helps his nephew marry the right girl and foils an unjust legal action against a secretive blacksmith. The plot is secondary to a series of skits (many involving the discredited but brilliant black comedian Stepin Fetchit), songs, running gags, muttered asides, and incidental characters that evoke an idealized Old South community where pomposity is deflated, intolerance is kept in check, and blacks and whites coexist in sun-dappled harmony.

There are several inside references and general parallels that link *Judge Priest*'s director with its eponymous hero, who brings the audience to order in the precredits shot, allows digression rather than procedure to rule his courtroom, and shamelessly manipulates the spectators' emotions by arranging for a band to play "Dixie" at a crucial point in the trial. *Judge Priest* is one of the loveliest visions of innocence ever put on the American screen, and Judge Ford judiciously reminds us just how much artifice is necessary to make legend prevail over fact. **MR**

U.S. (Columbia) 105m BW

**Director:** Frank Capra

**Producer:** Frank Capra, Harry Cohn

**Screenplay:** Samuel Hopkins Adams, Robert Riskin

**Photography:** Joseph Walker

**Music:** Howard Jackson, Louis Silvers

**Cast:** Clark Gable, Claudette Colbert, Walter Connolly, Roscoe Karns, Jameson Thomas, Alan Hale, Arthur Hoyt, Blanche Frederici, Charles C. Wilson

**Oscar:** Frank Capra, Harry Cohn (best picture), Frank Capra (director), Robert Riskin (screenplay), Clark Gable (actor), Claudette Colbert (actress)

**Venice Film Festival:** Frank Capra nomination (Mussolini Cup)

# IT HAPPENED ONE NIGHT (1934)

Peter (Clark Gable) is a tough-talking journalist; Ellie (Claudette Colbert) is a "dizzy dame" on the run from home and her father. The two meet while on the road and are forced, reluctantly, to collaborate. He's the salt of the earth, she's a rich kid, and each exploits the other—for him, she means a big newspaper story, for her, he's a way to help her get to New York and a forbidden fiancé. In the course of the story, they move from antagonism to love. It could be one of a hundred routine, American romantic comedies of the 1930s or '40s.

But, make no mistake, Frank Capra's *It Happened One Night* is movie magic. This has something to do with how it conjures an entire milieu: a "people's America" filled with unlikely rogues and soft-hearted citizens, always ready to share a story and a song, or simply exhibit their lovable eccentricities. But the film is also careful to explore exceptions to its basic rule: Ellie's father, Andrews (Walter Connolly), turns out to be a pretty swell chap, just as the talkative bus passenger Shapeley (Roscoe Karns) ends up a weasel.

Capra was expert at cleverly weaving a story from altogether familiar and ordinary motifs: eating, verbal slang ("ah, nuts"), snoring, washing, dressing and undressing. True to the romantic comedy formula, identities are momentarily dissolved whenever a masquerade is necessary or able to be exploited for secret entertainment—although, whenever Peter and Ellie pretend to be husband and wife, more serious possibilities and destinies do suggest themselves...

*It Happened One Night* is a distant predecessor of today's "trash comedies," such as those by the Farrelly Brothers. Ass jokes abound ("That upon which you sit is mine"); the pretensions and privileges of the wealthy are mercilessly mocked (even their names are funny: King Westley!); Colbert's famous, bare legs stop traffic. And then there is the sexual tension angle: Working patiently through four nights of Peter and Ellie together, the entire film hinges on the symbolism of the "walls of Jericho" finally toppling—the ridding of the blanket that stands, weakly and tremblingly, as the barrier to the consummation of their growing love.

Critics cannot rhapsodize over Capra's powers of montage or mise en scène; style was a functional, conventional business for him. But what he did have was an impeccable sense of script (in both overall structure and small details), and a brilliant rapport with his charismatic actors. Gable and Colbert help to truly equalize this one-upmanship battle of the sexes, diluting that ideological thrust of the script which suggests that proletarian guys should teach spoiled gals a thing or two about real life. In the infectious interplay of these stars—in their mutual willingness to play, to laugh, to be vulnerable, to take a joke as good they give it—we encounter an ideal that has been well and truly lost in contemporary, mainstream cinema: fighting reciprocity between the sexes. **AM**

U.S. (Cosmopolitan, MGM) 93m BW
**Director:** W.S. Van Dyke
**Producer:** Hunt Stromberg
**Photography:** James Wong Howe
**Screenplay:** Albert Hackett, from novel by Dashiell Hammett
**Music:** William Axt
**Cast:** William Powell, Myrna Loy, Maureen O'Sullivan, Nat Pendleton, Minna Gombell, Porter Hall, Henry Wadsworth, William Henry, Harold Huber, Cesar Romero, Natalie Moorhead, Edward Brophy, Edward Ellis, Cyril Thornton
**Oscar nomination:** Hunt Stromberg (best picture), W.S. Van Dyke (director), Frances Goodrich, (screenplay), Albert Hackett (screenplay), William Powell (actor)

# THE THIN MAN (1934)

The chemistry between Myrna Loy and William Powell was so potent in the 1934 film *Manhattan Melodrama* that its director, W.S. Van Dyke, cast the two again in the same year. As Nick and Nora Charles, they are unique in the history of cinema. The first popular husband-and-wife detective team, they not only love each other, they like each other too without being insipid, disrespectful, or dull.

*The Thin Man*'s plot is a messy one. Nick Charles is officially a retired detective but he takes a personal interest in the disappearance of a crotchety inventor—the "thin man" of the title—whose daughter (Maureen O'Sullivan) is Nick's long-time acquaintance. The inventor's safety is thrown further into doubt when complications arise involving his suspicious mistress, grasping ex-wife, and her money-hungry husband (Cesar Romero). With the addition of multifarious mobsters, cops, and molls, it seems the whole criminal world turns up at the Charles's luxurious hotel suite at one time or another.

Trying to make sense of the story gets in the way of what is genuinely important—the snappy banter full of covetable lines between the rich, sophisticated Nora and her sharp lush of a husband. Disarming an unwanted guest one night, the incident is reported in the morning news. "I was shot twice in the *Tribune*," says Nick. "I read you were shot five times in the tabloids," says Nora. "It's not true. He didn't come anywhere near my tabloids." Said with cast-off ease, the lines are funny without jumping out as such. Nick may seem like an alcoholic, but he springs back and forth from relaxed giddiness to active sobriety in the wink of an eye. The couple's prodigious boozing seems to have little effect on their actions; it's more of an elegant prop—a vital element for a country just coming out of the Great Depression.

Taken from a novel written in the same year by Dashiell Hammett, Nick and Nora were supposedly modeled on Hammett's relationship with playwright Lillian Hellman. Shot in 14 days, this sparkling screwball detective story earned over $2 million and was nominated for four Academy Awards. Not surprisingly, popularity spawned four more movies as well as a radio and television series, and was the inspiration behind TV shows such as *McMillian & Wife* and *Hart to Hart*. **KK**

**U.S.** (Cosmopolitan, First National,Warner Bros. ) 119m BW

**Language:** English / French

**Director:** Michael Curtiz

**Producer:** Harry Joe Brown, Gordon Hollingshead, Hal B. Wallis

**Screenplay:** Casey Robinson, from novel by Rafael Sabatini

**Photography:** Ernest Haller, Hal Mohr

**Music:** Erich Wolfgang Korngold, Liszt

**Cast:** Errol Flynn, Olivia de Havilland, Lionel Atwill, Basil Rathbone, Ross Alexander, Guy Kibbee, Henry Stephenson, Robert Barrat, Hobart Cavanaugh, Donald Meek, Jessie Ralph, Forrester Harvey, Frank McGlynn Sr., Holmes Herbert, David Torrence

**Oscar nomination:** Erich Wolfgang Korngold (best picture—not awarded), Michael Curtiz (director), Casey Robinson (screenplay), Leo F. Forbstein (music), Nathan Levinson (sound)

# CAPTAIN BLOOD (1935)

A quintessential swashbuckling adventure directed by expert Michael Curtiz, *Captain Blood* made divinely attractive Australian Errol Flynn a star overnight. His animal magnetism hugely impressed Jack Warner, who handed him this break when Robert Donat disdained the role. The film marks the first pairing in a string of winning romantic costume pictures of Flynn with Olivia de Havilland, whose genteel prettiness was a charming foil for his exuberance and athletic sex appeal.

Flynn plays an honorable 17th-century Irish doctor, Peter Blood, unjustly sentenced to deportation to and slavery in the Caribbean, where he aims insolent barbs and suggestive glances at dainty mistress de Havilland. Leading an escape he turns pirate, the vengeful scourge of the bounding main, and forms an uneasy alliance with dastardly French buccaneer Basil Rathbone. Relations become strained when they fall out over booty and the captive beauty, de Havilland, resulting in a duel to the death in the first of their famously thrilling screen sword fights. *Captain Blood* has everything you could want in a swashbuckler—sea battles and flashing blades, a dashing hero, an imperiled but plucky heroine, cutthroats, plumed hats, wrongs righted, fellows swinging like gymnasts from masts, and a rousing score by Erich Wolfgang Korngold. It's super fun. **AE**

**U.S.** (MGM) 132m BW

**Director:** Frank Lloyd

**Producer:** Albert Lewin, Irving Thalberg

**Screenplay:** Talbot Jennings, Jules Furthman, from book by Charles Nordhoff & James Hall

**Photography:** Arthur Edeson

**Music:** Herbert Stothart, Walter Jurmann, Gus Kahn, Bronislau

**Cast:** Charles Laughton, Clark Gable, Franchot Tone, Herbert Mundin, Eddie Quillan, Dudley Digges, Donald Crisp, Henry Stephenson, Francis Lister, Spring Byington, Movita, Mamo Clark, Byron Russell, Percy Waram, David Torrence

**Oscar:** Albert Lewin, Irving Thalberg (best picture)

**Oscar nomination:** Frank Lloyd (director), Jules Furthman, Talbot Jennings, Carey Wilson (screenplay), Clark Gable, Franchot Tone, Charles Laughton (actor ), Margaret Booth (editing), Nat W. Finston (music)

# MUTINY ON THE BOUNTY (1935)

Epitomizing the classic Hollywood spirit, Frank Lloyd's *Mutiny on the Bounty* is a masterwork of studio moviemaking. The film's spare-no-expense canvas, travelogue quality, and moral center result in an adventure tale of remarkable beauty. Of course this overlooks an acting style long since left behind. Then there's an American cast imbuing this British cautionary tale with Depression-era optimism. Still, these minor criticisms serve to support how well produced the film is when considering MGM's house style that simultaneously emphasized profits, escapism, and the broadest possible entertainment.

Set in the late 18th century when the British Empire crested across the decks of its navy, the crew of the ship Bounty mutinies after months of mistreatment. Led by Fletcher Christian (Clark Gable), they put their cruel captain, Captain Bligh (Charles Laughton), to sea, only for him to find his way back to port in an effort nothing short of amazing. Into his wake sails the Bounty for the South Pacific, beset by various complications.

Gable appears without his moustache, and Laughton's bee-stung lips flutter with harsh discipline. In between are a number of nominal subplots, though in the end the film is perhaps most memorable as an early high-water mark for the art of production design. **GC-Q**

# A NIGHT AT THE OPERA (1935)

**U.S.** (MGM) 96m BW

**Language:** English / Italian

**Director:** Sam Wood

**Producer:** Irving Thalberg

**Screenplay:** James Kevin McGuinness, George S. Kaufman

**Photography:** Merritt B. Gerstad

**Music:** Nacio Herb Brown, Walter Jurmann, Bronislau Kaper, Herbert Stothart

**Cast:** Groucho Marx, Chico Marx, Harpo Marx, Kitty Carlisle, Allan Jones, Walter Woolf King, Sig Ruman, Margaret Dumont, Edward Keane, Robert Emmett O'Connor

I was very young, not much more than ten years old, when I walked into a cinema in France to watch *A Night at The Opera*—or, more precisely, was sent there by some adult who knew as little as I did about the Marx Brothers. At my age, reading the subtitles was still rather difficult, especially when this jumping character with a moustache and a cigar was shouting words to the audience like a crazy machine gun. But I had very little time to worry about this problem: I was lying on the floor, laughing so hard, so irrepressibly, and, if I may say, so *absolutely* that I spent most of the movie on the ground between the seats. Since then I have had the pleasure of seeing *A Night at the Opera* again, several times, along with the rest of the Marx Brothers' work. I am aware of both the continuity and the variations in their movies, and have been amazed by the brilliance of their performances. But I still feel—deep inside as well as on my skin—the incredible power of invention and transgression conveyed by this particular film.

More than the central scenes, like the crowd gathering in the ship cabin, *A Night at the Opera* remains such a strong and dazzling comedy thanks to its most elementary moments—a single word or gesture performed with an incredible sense of rhythm. There is much to say about the way the transgressive weapons of the three brothers initiate a crisis in the spectacle of an opera. The fourth brother, straight-man Zeppo, is useless in this process. Groucho's overflow of words and distortion of his body, Harpo's unnatural silence and child-like power of destruction, Chico's virtuosity and "foreign ethos"—all serve to disturb an opera based on a loathing of art, greed, and corruption. These elements do exist, and they are definitely interesting, but they come after this more obvious characteristic. *A Night at the Opera* was, and remains, a damn funny film. **J-MF**

G.B. (Gaumont British) 86m BW
**Director:** Alfred Hitchcock
**Producer:** Michael Balcon, Ivor Montagu
**Screenplay:** Charles Bennett, from novel by John Buchan
**Photography:** Bernard Knowles
**Music:** Jack Beaver, Hubert Bath
**Cast:** Robert Donat, Madeleine Carroll, Lucie Mannheim, Godfrey Tearle, Peggy Ashcroft, John Laurie, Helen Haye, Frank Cellier, Wylie Watson, Gus McNaughton, Jerry Verno, Peggy Simpson

# THE 39 STEPS (1935)

After several tentative early steps and a few small breakthroughs, *The 39 Steps* was the first clear creative peak in Alfred Hitchcock's British period and arguably marked the first fully successful film in the director's rapidly deepening oeuvre—starting at the end of the silent era, by the time of *The 39 Steps* he had already directed 18 films. After the picture's financial and critical success, Hitchcock further solidified his reputation as a master filmmaker by embarking on a nearly unparalleled streak of compelling and entertaining thrillers that would stretch for several decades. And indeed, many of his most popular films—*North by Northwest* (1959), for one—clearly have their roots in this early highlight.

Among its many noteworthy achievements, *The 39 Steps* introduced one key Hitchcock first: the notion of the wrong man, the innocent bystander accused, pursued, or punished for a crime he didn't commit. (The wrong-man theme was one the director would return to again and again, most overtly in his 1956 film *The Wrong Man*.) Richard Hannay (Robert Donat), a Canadian on holiday in England, meets a woman who is later murdered under mysterious circumstances. It seems he has stumbled into a spy plot involving something called "the 39 Steps," and he feels that with this knowledge only he can save the day. Handcuffed to an unwilling female accomplice (Madeleine Carroll), Hannay must simultaneously evade capture by the police and an archvillain with a missing finger in hot pursuit and reveal the titular mystery before it's too late.

In traditional Hitchcock fashion, the revelation of what "the 39 Steps" actually are, and indeed the entire spy plot—is almost peripheral to the flirtatious interplay between the two leads. Literally chained to one another in a teasing mockery of marriage, Donat and Carroll pack their quarrelsome exchanges with little innuendoes—when the chase leaves time for a breather, of course—morphing the espionage thriller into the unlikeliest of love stories. The film, like their relationship, plays out in a rush, a nonstop string of action sequences and chase scenes punctuated by witty dialogue and riveting suspense. **JKl**

# BRIDE OF FRANKENSTEIN (1935)

U.S. (Universal) 75m BW
**Director:** James Whale
**Producer:** Carl Laemmle Jr., James Whale
**Screenplay:** William Hurlbut, John L. Balderston
**Photography:** John J. Mescall
**Music:** Franz Waxman
**Cast:** Boris Karloff, Colin Clive, Valerie Hobson, Elsa Lanchester, Ernest Thesiger, Gavin Gordon, Douglas Walton, Una O'Connor, E.E. Clive, Lucien Prival, O.P. Heggie, Dwight Frye, Reginald Barlow, Mary Gordon, Anne Darling
**Oscar nomination:** Gilbert Kurland (sound)

Universal Studios had to wait nearly four years before James Whale finally accepted the offer to direct the follow-up to his 1931 box-office success, *Frankenstein*. But it turned out to be well worth the wait: under the director's nearly complete control (the producer, Carl Laemmle Jr., was vacationing in Europe during most of the production), *Bride of Frankenstein* is a surprising mix of terror and comedy that turned out to be in many ways superior to the original film.

Despite Boris Karloff's reluctance, it was decided that the Monster should now be able to pronounce a few chosen words. His humanization here makes him more complete and faithful to Mary Shelley's novel, and his desperate search for a friendly companion could hardly be more touching. Though it was of course played down at the censors' request, the Monster is mostly depicted in *Bride of Frankenstein* as a Christ-like figure who is led to kill because of his circumstances and the fear he inspires in society. Even the monstrous mate intended just for him is repulsed at first glance by his physical aspect. Without a doubt, Elsa Lanchester's bride remains to this day one of the most astonishing creatures ever seen on screen: her appearance—in a sort of grotesque version of a marriage ceremony—is still a highlight of the horror genre, what with her mummified body, her swan-like hissing, and her weird black-and-white-streaked Egyptian hairdo.

*Bride of Frankenstein*'s plot relies heavily on sharp contrasts that make the spectator jump from terror to pathos or comedy. Whale's particular sense of humor, which has often been described as camp, is mainly brought out by Minnie (Una O'Connor), the household maid, along with the outrageously effeminate acting of Ernest Thesiger, who plays the devilish figure Dr. Pretorius.

The immense interest in *Bride of Frankenstein* also stems from its portrayal of sexual relations, a portrayal that is considered by many to be at least potentially transgressive. The introduction of a second mad scientist (Pretorius) who forces Colin Clive's Henry Frankenstein to give life again, emphasizes one of the fundamental and disturbing implications of Shelley's myth: (pro-)creation as something achieved by men alone. Four years later, Whale's masterpiece itself gave birth to a "son," but the father of the bride would have nothing to do with it. **FL**

**U.S.** (RKO) 101m BW
**Director:** Mark Sandrich
**Producer:** Pandro S. Berman
**Screenplay:** Allan Scott, Dwight Taylor
**Photography:** David Abel
**Music:** Irving Berlin, Max Steiner
**Cast:** Fred Astaire, Ginger Rogers, Edward Everett Horton, Erik Rhodes, Eric Blore, Helen Broderick
**Oscar nomination:** Pandro S. Berman (best picture), Carroll Clark, Van Nest Polglase (art direction), Irving Berlin (music), Hermes Pan (dance)

# TOP HAT (1935)

There is no clear-cut classic among the Fred Astaire–Ginger Rogers musicals of the mid-1930s—all are mostly marvelous with crucial flaws—but *Top Hat* probably comes the closest. Its plot follows the series' basic formula: Fred instantly falls for Ginger, but a silly misunderstanding (here, she mistakes him for his married friend) stokes her hostility until the final moments.

The director is the underrated Mark Sandrich, whose impeccably superficial touch maximizes the swanky, syncopated slickness so essential to the series. The film's most famous number is "Top Hat," featuring fancy canework among Fred and a chorus of top-hatted gents, but the heart of *Top Hat* is its two great romantic duets, "Isn't It a Lovely Day" and "Cheek to Cheek," the first set on a London bandstand during a thunderstorm, the second beside the sparkling canals of RKO's goofily glossy Art Deco version of Venice. Such dances, with their progression from resistance to surrender, are Fred's main weapon in winning over Ginger, but it would be a mistake to read this process as simple sexual conquest. As Ginger's suppressed amusement makes clear, the two characters approach their respective roles of hot-to-trot and hard-to-get with playful irony, collaborating to prolong and intensify a deliciously elegant erotic game. **MR**

**France** (Pantheon) 40m BW
**Language:** French
**Director:** Jean Renoir
**Producer:** Pierre Braunberger
**Screenplay:** Jean Renoir, from story by Guy de Maupassant
**Photography:** Jean Bourgoin, Claude Renoir
**Music:** Joseph Kosma
**Cast:** Sylvia Bataille, Georges St. Saens, Jane Marken, André Gabriello, Jacques B. Brunius, Paul Temps, Gabrielle Fontan, Jean Renoir, Marguerite Renoir

# UNE PARTIE DE CAMPAGNE (1936)
## A DAY IN THE COUNTRY

One of the most powerful and unsettling devices in film fiction is the "years later" epilogue—which usually takes us, with wistful sadness, from the concentrated time of a story in which everything was briefly possible, to the singular destiny that ensued. At the end of Jean Renoir's *A Day in the Country*, Henriette (Sylvia Bataille) is seen unhappily married to the man with whom she was betrothed at the start, the gormless clerk Anatole (Paul Temps). But, in between these points, nothing is so fixed or certain.

Adapted from a story by Guy de Maupassant, the film was unfinished in the form originally envisaged by Renoir. It stands, however, as a self-sufficient gem. Its central action is devoted to the illicit pairing off of two local adventurers, Rodolphe (Jacques Borel) and Henri (Georges D'Arnoux), with Henriette and her mother, Juliette (Jeanne Marken). Renoir constructs a superb diagram of contrasts between these characters: Rodolphe and Juliette are lusty, frivolous; while Henri and Henriette are overwhelmed by grave emotion. So what started, in Henriette's words, as "a sort of vague desire" that calls forth both the beauty and harshness of nature, ends badly, as the "years pass, with Sundays as melancholy as Mondays." **AM**

# MODERN TIMES (1936)

*Modern Times* was the last film in which Charles Chaplin portrayed the character of the Little Tramp, which he had created in 1914 and which had brought him universal fame and affection. In the years between, the world had changed. When the Little Tramp was born, the 19th century was still close. In 1936, in the aftermath of the Great Depression, he confronted anxieties that are not so different from those of the 21st century—poverty, unemployment, strikes and strike breakers, political intolerance, economic inequalities, the tyranny of the machine, and narcotics.

These were problems with which Chaplin had become acutely preoccupied in the course of an 18-month world tour in 1931–32, when he had observed the rise of nationalism and the social effects of the Depression, unemployment, and automation. In 1931 he declared to a newspaper interviewer, "Unemployment is the vital question.... Machinery should benefit mankind. It should not spell tragedy and throw it out of work."

Exposing these problems to the searchlight of comedy, Chaplin transforms the Little Tramp into one of the millions working in factories throughout the world. He is first seen as a worker driven crazy by his monotonous, inhuman job on a conveyor belt and being used as a guinea pig to test a machine to feed workers as they perform their tasks. Exceptionally, the Little Tramp finds a companion in his battle with this new world—a young girl (Paulette Goddard) whose father has been killed in a strike and who joins forces with Chaplin. The couple are neither rebels nor victims, wrote Chaplin, but "the only two live spirits in a world of automatons."

By the time *Modern Times* was released, talking pictures had been established for almost a decade. Chaplin considered using dialogue and even prepared a script, but he finally recognized that the Little Tramp depended on silent pantomime. At one moment, though, his voice is heard, when, hired as a singing waiter, he improvises the song in a wonderful, mock-Italian gibberish.

Conceived in four "acts," each one equivalent to one of his old two-reel comedies, *Modern Times* shows Chaplin still at his unrivaled peak as a creator of visual comedy. The film survives no less as a commentary on human survival in the industrial, economic, and social circumstances of the 20th—and perhaps the 21st—century. **DR**

**U.S.** (Charles Chaplin, United Artists) 87m BW

**Director:** Charles Chaplin

**Producer:** Charles Chaplin

**Screenplay:** Charles Chaplin

**Photography:** Ira H. Morgan, Roland Totheroh

**Music:** Charles Chaplin

**Cast:** Charles Chaplin, Paulette Goddard, Henry Bergman, Tiny Sandford, Chester Conklin, Hank Mann, Stanley Blystone, Al Ernest Garcia, Richard Alexander, Cecil Reynolds, Mira McKinney, Murdock MacQuarrie, Wilfred Lucas, Edward LeSaint, Fred Malatesta

**U.S.** (RKO) 103m BW

**Director:** George Stevens

**Producer:** Pandro S. Berman

**Screenplay:** Erwin Gelsey, Howard Lindsay, Allan Scott, from the story *Portrait of John Garnett* by Elwin Gelsey

**Photography:** David Abel

**Music:** Jerome Kern, Dorothy Fields

**Cast:** Fred Astaire, Ginger Rogers, Victor Moore, Helen Broderick, Eric Blore, Betty Furness, Georges Metaxa

**Oscar:** Jerome Kern, Dorothy Fields (music)

**Oscar nomination:** Hermes Pan (dance)

# SWING TIME (1936)

A song-and-dance fantasia, George Stevens's *Swing Time* is an audiovisual spectacle organized around a backstage musical. Certainly a high-water mark for the mid-1930s, the film is equally a tease of things to come in the combination of Fred Astaire and Ginger Rogers.

Assembled by legendary RKO producer Pandro S. Berman, *Swing Time* is the story of Lucky Garnett (Fred Astaire), a well-regarded hoofer engaged to the pleasant, though uninspiring, Margaret Watson (Betty Furness). When he's forced to secure a large dowry to continue with his betrothal, their matrimonial plans are put on hold so he can seek his fortune in New York City. Once there, he meets Penny (Ginger Rogers), his true love, and thereafter the film more or less works through various disturbances before allowing them to fall into one another's arms.

Naturally, there are several scenes of mistaken intent, a few nontragic plot turns, and a happy ending, despite brief periods of sorrow and hand wringing. Yet the purpose of the film is undeniably the presentation of its musical numbers, several of which form part of the generic canon. Jerome Kern wrote the music with most of the lyrics provided by Dorothy Fields. Their combined efforts form the soundtrack's foundation, although the sheer energy, verve, and happy distraction of Astaire and Rogers is what makes every number shine with the addition of movement and tap shoes.

Highlights include Lucky's two solos in "The Way You Look Tonight," a nightclub standard, and "Never Gonna Dance," a sorrowfully ironic song given the actor's well-recognized talent for walking on air. Two duets expand the big-screen canvas in "Waltz in Swing Time" with Astaire and Rogers and, of course, their famous performance of "A Fine Romance." But the showstopper of the picture may well be "Bojangles of Harlem." Here, Lucky begins his performance from within an accompanying chorus while dressed in blackface. Definitely a nod to his training and heritage, if also an antiquated, possibly offensive bit of cultural history, the number builds to a climax of Astaire dancing in triplicate with rear-projection versions of himself. **GC-Q**

# MY MAN GODFREY (1936)

As one of the masters of sophisticated salon comedies, Gregory La Cava might not have had the most aching social consciousness in 1930s Hollywood. But he had a knack for satire with a social and political edge that is clearly visible in films such as *Gabriel over the White House* (1933), *She Married Her Boss* (1935), and especially *My Man Godfrey*, his most memorable work. Made at the end of the Depression era, this screwball classic deals with poor bum Godfrey (William Powell) being hired as a butler as part of a high-society party game on Park Avenue. Some hundred snappy lines later he has taken complete control over the rich people's house, charmed the beautiful Irene (Carole Lombard), exposed her birdbrained mother's boy toy (well, he is called "protégé" because of the Production Code) as a con man, and helped her grumpy father avoid bankruptcy and prison for fraud.

Not surprisingly, it is revealed that Godfrey himself had only been slumming as a hobo when the rich party found him, and so he can marry the socialite of his dreams. However, by then the upper class have been paraded in front of the camera as a bunch of narcissistic, infantile idiots. No doubt this was one reason for the film's great success with a mass audience in those days. *My Man Godfrey* loses some of its bite in the second half, when the fairy-tale ingredient takes over and ends the film on a silly note: that money is not everything! But even then it manages to captivate its audience by the sheer intelligence of its witty screenplay penned by novelist Eric Hatch and Morrie Ryskind. It has the true mark of a great film by not having a single bad line or weak character. La Cava's pacing is sometimes strikingly fast, delivering machine-gun tongue dueling in virtually every scene and applying a narrative economy so effortless that the film could serve as a prototype for classic Hollywood cinema. Though it premiered nearly seventy years ago, *My Man Godfrey* still holds up in a remarkable way and could easily be remade for any audience. **MT**

**U.S.** (Universal) 94m BW

**Director:** Gregory La Cava

**Producer:** Gregory La Cava, Charles R. Rogers

**Screenplay:** Eric Hatch, Morrie Ryskind, from novel by Eric Hatch

**Photography:** Ted Tetzlaff

**Music:** Charles Previn, Rudy Schrager

**Cast:** William Powell, Carole Lombard, Alice Brady, Gail Patrick, Eugene Pallette, Alan Mowbray, Jean Dixon, Molly, Mischa Auer, Carlo, Robert Light, Pat Flaherty

**Oscar nomination:** Gregory La Cava (director), Eric Hatch, Morrie Ryskind (screenplay), William Powell (actor), Mischa Auer (actor in support role), Carole Lombard (actress), Alice Brady (actress in support role)

**U.S.** (Columbia) 115m BW

**Director:** Frank Capra

**Producer:** Frank Capra

**Screenplay:** Clarence Budington Kelland, Robert Riskin

**Photography:** Joseph Walker

**Music:** Howard Jackson

**Cast:** Gary Cooper, Jean Arthur, George Bancroft, Lionel Stander, Douglass Dumbrille, Raymond Walburn, H.B. Warner, Ruth Donnelly, Walter Catlett, John Wray

**Oscar:** Frank Capra (director)

**Oscar nomination:** Frank Capra (best picture), Robert Riskin (screenplay), Gary Cooper (actor), John P. Livadary (sound)

# MR. DEEDS GOES TO TOWN (1936)

The film that invented the screwball comedy and solidified director Frank Capra's vision of American life, with a support of small-town, traditional values against self-serving city sophistication.

Longfellow Deeds (Gary Cooper) is a poet from rural Vermont whose life changes, and not for the better, when he suddenly inherits the estate of his multimillionaire uncle, whose New York lawyers (used to skimming funds for their own use) try to convince him to keep them on the payroll. But after several misadventures and a trip to Manhattan, Deeds is convinced that the money will do him no good and tries to give it away, intending to endow a rural commune for displaced farmers. The lawyers immediately take him to court, claiming he is insane, for no one in their right mind would give away so much money. Crucial to Deeds's eventual deliverance is Babe Bennett (Jean Arthur), a wisecracking reporter who first exploits the hick's naiveté in order to write scathing exclusives about the "Cinderella Man." Babe is transformed by Deeds's idealism, however, and her testimony sways the court in the poor man's favor.

Filled with bright comic moments (Deeds playing the tuba to clear his mind, feeding donuts to horses), *Mr. Deeds Goes to Town* is a hymn to antimaterialism and the simple country life in the best manner of Henry David Thoreau. **RBP**

## CAMILLE (1936)

George Cukor's *Camille* is one of the triumphs of early sound cinema, a showcase of superb acting from principals Greta Garbo and Robert Taylor, with able support from studio stalwarts Lionel Barrymore and Henry Daniell. Cukor evokes just enough of mid-19th-century Paris to render affecting the melodramatic stylization of what is perhaps the most famous popular play ever written, adapted for the stage by Alexandre Dumas, *fils*, from his sensational novel. With its witty and suggestive dialogue, the script makes the novelist's characters come alive for an American audience of another era.

Marguerite Gautier (Garbo), called Camille because of her love for the camellia, is a "courtesan" who falls in love with her "companion," Armand Duval (Taylor), scion of an influential family. Their relationship, which can never be legitimized because of her dubious background, must come to an end and does in two famous scenes that actresses have always relished. First, Armand's father persuades Camille that she must give him up so that he can pursue a diplomatic career. Heartbroken, she dismisses Armand with the lie that he no longer interests her. Armand returns later to find her on her deathbed, where she expires while he weeps uncontrollably. The Breen Office, charged with the task of enforcing the industry's then-reactionary production code, must also have been moved by this story of prohibited and tragic love, requiring only a scene in which the romantic pair, technically "illicit," vow their undying love to one another. **RBP**

**U.S.** (MGM) 109m

**Director:** George Cukor

**Producer:** David Lewis, Bernard H. Hyman

**Screenplay:** Zoe Akins, from the novel and play *La Dame aux camélias* by Alexandre Dumas fils

**Photography:** William H. Daniels, Karl Freund

**Music:** Herbert Stothart, Edward Ward

**Cast:** Greta Garbo, Robert Taylor, Lionel Barrymore, Elizabeth Allan, Jessie Ralph, Henry Daniell, Lenore Ulric, Laura Hope Crews, Rex O'Malley

**Oscar nomination:** Greta Garbo (actress)

## SABOTAGE (1936)

Alfred Hitchcock had just made a film entitled *Secret Agent*, based on stories by W. Somerset Maugham, and so his next project, based on Joseph Conrad's novel *The Secret Agent*, had to be retitled *Sabotage*. Oscar Homulka is Mr. Verloc, a sinister agent for a shadowy foreign power who carries out acts of sabotage. In a departure from the original novel, Verloc and his wife (Sylvia Sydney) manage a small cinema, which allows Hitchcock to have fun connecting events in the narrative to the films playing on the screen.

*Sabotage* has two memorable set pieces. In the first, Stevie (Desmond Tester), the young brother of Mrs. Verloc, is sent by her husband to deliver a can of film. Unknown to Stevie, it contains a bomb timed to go off at 1:45 P.M. As we track Stevie across London he is delayed by a series of holdups, and eventually the bomb explodes while he is sitting on a bus. Hitchcock later regretted this, judging that it violated the director's contract with the audience, not to harm someone they had been encouraged to sympathize with—though he wound up doing exactly the same in *Psycho* (1960). In any case, the death of Stevie sets up the second bravura scene, the revengeful murder of Verloc by his wife. **EB**

**G.B.** (Gaumont British) 76m BW

**Director:** Alfred Hitchcock

**Producer:** Michael Balcon, Ivor Montagu

**Screenplay:** Charles Bennett, Ian Hay, Helen Simpson, E.V.H. Emmett, from the novel *The Secret Agent* by Joseph Conrad

**Photography:** Bernard Knowles

**Music:** Louis Levy

**Cast:** Sylvia Sidney, Oskar Homolka, John Loder, Desmond Tester, Joyce Barbour, Matthew Boulton, S.J. Warmington, William Dewhurst

# DODSWORTH (1936)

William Wyler's compelling adaptation of Sinclair Lewis's novel about the dissolution of a wealthy American couple's marriage represents the height of intelligent Hollywood filmmaking. Walter Huston plays the title character, an automobile mogul, who, after selling his business, must face the challenges of an opulent retirement and decides to take a grand tour of Europe with his wife, Fran (Ruth Chatterton). They leave the United States to discover continental culture and refinement. In Europe the couple discovers that each wants something different from life, though in their own ways both want to stave off old age. Fran becomes involved in flirtations with playboys who roam the periphery of the rich and fashionable set. She becomes increasingly impatient with Dodsworth's stubbornly American, provincial ways. Dodsworth cannot reconcile with Fran and desperately fears becoming useless. On the journey they meet Edith Cortright (Mary Astor), an American expatriate who has found a new way to live and remain vibrant, and who can offer Dodsworth a solution.

The most remarkable aspects of the film are its moral complexity and its bittersweet tone. Wyler takes care not to portray Fran wholly as the villain. We are made to understand and sympathize with both husband and wife. Some of the most poignant moments of *Dodsworth* take place when Fran sees the illusory life that she has been trying to create fall apart around her. Huston, who was nominated for Best Actor at the Academy Awards, is pitch perfect in this wide-ranging role. His character transforms from a confident self-made tycoon to a dejected, more thoughtful, older man. Huston registers these changes in an introspective, heart-wrenching performance. Astor, an extremely young and dashing David Niven, and Maria Ouspenskaya are all marvelous in supporting roles. At a time when mainstream American filmmaking all seems to be aimed at the tastes of 14-year-old boys, *Dodsworth* is a welcome reminder that Hollywood once made films for adults. **RH**

**U.S.** (Samuel Goldwyn) 101m BW

**Director:** William Wyler

**Producer:** Samuel Goldwyn, Merritt Hulburd

**Screenplay:** Sidney Howard, from novel by Sinclair Lewis

**Photography:** Rudolph Maté

**Cast:** Walter Huston, Ruth Chatterton, Paul Lukas, Mary Astor, David Niven, Gregory Gaye, Maria Ouspenskaya, Odette Myrtil, Spring Byington, Harlan Briggs, Kathryn Marlowe, John Payne

**Oscar:** Richard Day (art direction)

**Oscar nomination:** Samuel Goldwyn, Merritt Hulburd (best picture), William Wyler (director), Sidney Howard (screenplay), Walter Huston (actor), Maria Ouspenskaya (actress in support role), Oscar Lagerstrom (sound)

# THINGS TO COME (1936)

G.B. (London) 100m BW
**Director:** William Cameron Menzies
**Producer:** Alexander Korda
**Screenplay:** H.G. Wells from his novel *The Shape of Things to Come*
**Photography:** Georges Périnal
**Music:** Arthur Bliss
**Cast:** Raymond Massey, Edward Chapman, Ralph Richardson, Margaretta Scott, Cedric Hardwicke, Maurice Braddell, Sophie Stewart, Derrick De Marney, Ann Todd, Pearl Argyle, Kenneth Villiers, Ivan Brandt, Anne McLaren, Patricia Hilliard, Charles Carson

William Cameron Menzies' screen version of H.G. Wells's speculations about the world's future after a disastrous Second World War destroys European civilization is perhaps the first true science-fiction film. Only Fritz Lang's *Metropolis* (1926) anticipates its envisioning of the future as a result of technological change and resulting political evolution, but Lang's film doesn't offer a similarly detailed analysis of the new course history might take. In fact, few science-fiction movies are as concerned as is *Things to Come* with a rigorously historical approach to fictionalized prophecy, and this is perhaps because Wells himself penned the screenplay, based on ideas found in his popular tome *The Outline of History*.

Neither Wells nor Menzies took much interest in character-driven narrative (the main characters all represent important ideas), and so the film has seemed distant and uninvolving to many, an effect exacerbated by the fact that the story covers a full century of history. The second European war lasts 25 years and manages to destroy most of the world, which regresses to something like the cutthroat feudalism of the early Middle Ages. But human progress is inevitable, thanks to the fact that the intellectual and rational element in man always proves superior to the innate human urge toward self-destruction. *Things to Come* thus offers a more optimistic twist on Freud's understanding of the perennial conflict between Eros and Thanatos, love and death, in human affairs. Like many utopian writers, Wells sees the future as marked significantly by an increased human control over the environment. The film's later sequences, like *Metropolis*, are dominated by a vision of the city of the future. It was in his handling of these architectural and art-design aspects of the film that Menzies made his most significant and telling contribution. Despite its episodic narrative, *Things to Come* is visually spectacular, a predecessor of other science-fiction films that imagine the urban future, including Ridley Scott's *Blade Runner* (1982).

Despite the presence of well-known actors (including Raymond Massey, Cedric Hardwicke, and Ralph Richardson), what is most memorable about this unusual film is its engagement with a philosophy of history and of human nature. It captures the anxieties and hopes of 1930s Britain perfectly, chillingly forecasting the blitz that would descend upon London only four years after its release. **RBP**

France (Cinéas) 85m BW

**Language:** French

**Director:** Sacha Guitry

**Producer:** Serge Sandberg

**Screenplay:** Sacha Guitry

**Photography:** Marcel Lucien

**Music:** Adolphe Borchard

**Cast:** Sacha Guitry, Marguerite Moreno, Jacqueline Delubac, Roger Duchesne, Rosine Deréan, Elmire Vautier, Serge Grave, Pauline Carton, Fréhel, Pierre Labry, Pierre Assy, Henri Pfeifer, Gaston Dupray

# LE ROMAN D'UN TRICHEUR (1936)

## THE STORY OF A CHEAT

Widely regarded as Sacha Guitry's masterpiece (though it has competition in 1937's *Pearls of the Crown*), this 1936 tour de force can be regarded as a kind of concerto for the writer-director-performer's special brand of brittle cleverness. After a credits sequence that introduces us to the film's cast and crew, *The Story of a Cheat* settles into a flashback account of how the title hero (played by Guitry himself) learned to benefit from cheating over the course of his life.

A notoriously anticinematic moviemaker whose first love was theater, Guitry nevertheless had a flair for cinematic antics when it came to adapting his plays (or in this case his novel *Memoires d'un Tricheur*) to film. *The Story of a Cheat* registers as a rather lively and stylishly inventive silent movie, with Guitry's character serving as offscreen lecturer. François Truffaut was sufficiently impressed to dub Guitry a French brother of Ernst Lubitsch, though Guitry clearly differs from this master of continental romance in the way his own personality invariably overwhelms that of his characters. **JS**

**U.S.** (MGM) 115m BW

**Director:** Victor Fleming

**Producer:** Louis D. Lighton

**Screenplay:** Marc Connelly, John Lee Mahin, Dale Van Every, from novel by Rudyard Kipling

**Photography:** Harold Rosson

**Music:** Franz Waxman

**Cast:** Freddie Bartholomew, Spencer Tracy, Lionel Barrymore, Melvyn Douglas, Charley Grapewin, Mickey Rooney, John Carradine, Oscar O'Shea, Jack La Rue, Walter Kingsford, Donald Briggs, Sam McDaniel, Bill Burrud

**Oscar:** Spencer Tracy (actor)

**Oscar nomination:** Louis D. Lighton (best picture), Marc Connelly, John Lee Mahin, Dale Van Every (screenplay), Elmo Veron (editing)

# CAPTAINS COURAGEOUS (1937)

Rudyard Kipling, who died in 1936, did not live long enough to see three of his books adapted for the screen the following year, including Victor Fleming's rousing childhood epic *Captains Courageous*. Freddie Bartholomew stars as Harvey Cheyne, a spoiled rich kid who, after drinking six ice cream sodas, falls off the ocean liner on which he and his father (Melvyn Douglas) are traveling. He has the good fortune to be picked up by a fishing boat out of Gloucester, whose crew, including the good-natured Manuel Fidello (Spencer Tracy), is unimpressed by his wealth and "position." Humiliated, Harvey is left to his own resources, but under Manuel's careful tutelage he learns the value of hard work and real accomplishment. Before they can return to port, however, Manuel dies in an accident. In port, Harvey is met by his father but wants to stay with the fishermen. After a moving memorial for his dead friend, however, father and son are reconciled.

Child star Bartholomew is excellent in a role that requires him to be both obnoxious and irresistible. And Spencer Tracy, his hair curled and face brown with makeup, does an excellent imitation of a Portuguese sailor. With humor, pathos, and an interesting moral, this is one of the best children's movies Hollywood ever produced. **RBP**

# YE BAN GE SHENG (1937)
## MIDNIGHT SONG

**China** (Xinhua) 123m BW
**Language:** Mandarin
**Director:** Ma-Xu Weibang
**Producer:** Shankun Zhang
**Screenplay:** Weibang Ma-Xu
**Photography:** Boqing Xue, Xingsan Yu
**Music:** Xinghai Xian (song)
**Cast:** Menghe Gu, Ping Hu, Shan Jin, Chao Shi

Gaston Leroux's 1919 novel *The Phantom of the Opera* has inspired a score of films. Ma-Xu Weibang's *Midnight Song*, made in Shanghai in 1936, is unarguably one of the most inspired. Ma-Xu (1905-1961) entered filmmaking as a title designer, graduating in turn to production design, acting, and direction. By the end of the silent period he had six films. *Midnight Song* was his second sound picture.

*Midnight Song* establishes its dark and eerie mood from the start, with the arrival of a touring opera company at a dilapidated theater, which they learn has been empty and crumbling since the apparent death there of the great opera star Song Danping, ten years before. The company's young star is rehearsing alone in the theater, when he hears a beautiful voice, which coaches him through his song. It is, of course, the fugitive Song Danping, now dreadfully disfigured, who reveals himself and relates his tragic story, shown in flashback. His physical state was inflicted on him on the orders of an evil feudal lord, angry at Song's love for his daughter. Since then he has hidden in the theater, awaiting a singer who can assume his mantle and perform his great operatic creation. The young singer is chosen for this role, and also made envoy to Song's lost love, Li Xiaoxia, whose mind has broken from sorrow.

The revolutionary difference from Western versions of Leroux is that the Phantom, instead of being a lurking menace, becomes a sympathetic and benevolent protagonist. In all other adaptations, the Phantom's protégée is a female singer, and the Phantom is motivated by sexual jealousy of her fiancé. Changing the sex to a protégé, Ma-Xu develops more complex and ambiguous relationships. Song sees the young man as a surrogate for himself in the affections of Li Xiaoxia, and suffers jealousy on her behalf when he discovers the young man has himself a girlfriend.

All this is staged in richly atmospheric settings, with a masterly use of light and shadow clearly inspired by German Expressionist cinema. An important element in the film's immense popularity were the songs, which have remained popular standards in China. In 1941, Ma-Xu was obliged to make a sequel, *Midnight Song II*, and the film has also inspired two Hong Kong remakes, *Mid-Nightmare* (1962) and *The Phantom Lover* (1995). **DR**

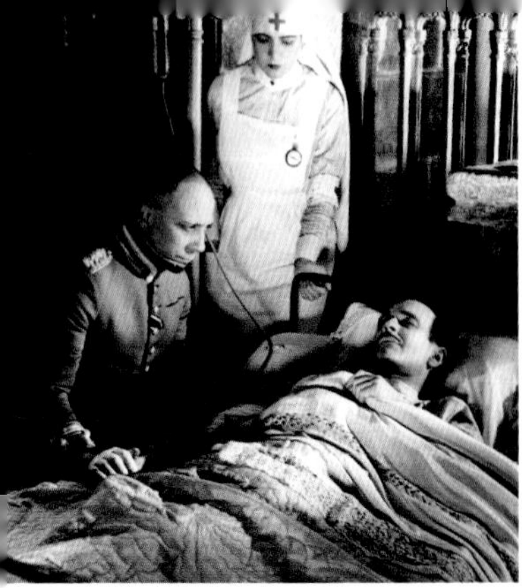

## LA GRANDE ILLUSION (1937)
### GRAND ILLUSION

**France** (R.A.C.) 114m BW
**Language:** French / German / English
**Director:** Jean Renoir
**Producer:** Albert Pinkovitch, Frank Rollmer
**Screenplay:** Jean Renoir, Charles Spaak
**Photography:** Christian Matras
**Music:** Joseph Kosma
**Cast:** Jean Gabin, Dita Parlo, Pierre Fresnay, Erich von Stroheim, Julien Carette, Georges Péclet, Werner Florian, Jean Dasté, Sylvain Itkine, Gaston Modot, Marcel Dalio
**Oscar nomination:** Frank Rollmer, Albert Pinkovitch (best picture)
**Venice Film Festival:** Jean Renoir (overall artistic contribution), Jean Renoir nomination (Mussolini Cup)

Sometimes it takes the horrors of war to reveal the things we all have in common. That humanistic irony is the central conceit of Jean Renoir's masterpiece *La Grand Illusion*, a film set during World War I that finds levity and fraternity in a German POW camp. Lieutenant Maréchal (Jean Gabin) and Captain de Boeldieu (Pierre Fresnay) are two French officers making the best of their situation with their men, under the watchful eye of the polite German commandant von Rauffenstein (Erich von Stroheim). They've developed a mirror image of aristocratic society based on honor and order, a system of mutual respect and protocol based on years of tradition.

But it's only an oasis—or, more specifically, a mirage—in the midst of devastating conflict, hence the title of the film: the grand illusion is that somehow class and upbringing sets these officers above the commonness of war, when in fact bullets don't know one bloodline from another. They tirelessly dig an escape tunnel without considering that once they return to freedom, the false camaraderie encouraged by incarceration will once again revert to the harsh realities of life.

One of the most poignant aspects of *La Grand Illusion* is the feeling that the central characters understand this truth all too well, yet subconsciously wish things could be different. You can sense that von Stroheim's melancholy commandant really wishes he were socializing with the French officers under different, less severe circumstances. In the POW camp, Rosenthal (Marcel Dalio) is one of the guys. On the outside, he's just a Jew, a jarring reminder of the imminent evils of World War II. In fact, the Germans later banned *La Grand Illusion* during their eventual occupation of France, so effective was its ever timely humanistic vision. That Renoir's remarkable film, with all its memorable characters, thought-provoking themes, and engaging dialogue, could have been lost forever because of its political viewpoint is a pointed reminder of the power of cinema and the ability of fiction to convey the kind of profound truths and moral guidelines that we use and need to direct our lives. **JKl**

## STELLA DALLAS (1937)

U.S. (Samuel Goldwyn) 105m BW
**Director:** King Vidor
**Producer:** Samuel Goldwyn, Merritt Hulburd
**Screenplay:** Joe Bigelow, Harry Wagstaff Gribble, Sarah Y. Mason, Gertrude Purcell, Victor Heerman, from novel by Olive Higgins Prouty
**Photography:** Rudolph Maté
**Music:** Alfred Newman
**Cast:** Barbara Stanwyck, John Boles, Anne Shirley, Barbara O'Neil, Alan Hale, Marjorie Main, George Walcott, Ann Shoemaker, Tim Holt, Nella Walker, Bruce Satterlee, Jimmy Butler, Jack Egger, Dickie Jones
**Oscar:** Barbara Stanwyck (actress), Anne Shirley (actress in support role)

King Vidor's *Stella Dallas* offers a lively and moving portrait of a working-class woman strong enough to sacrifice herself for the sake of her daughter's advancement in society. Olive Higgins Prouty's famous novel had already been filmed successfully in 1925. But unlike Henry King's silent version, Vidor's has the advantage of Barbara Stanwyck in the title role.

Stanwyck plays Stella as a resilient, glamorous, intelligent woman. It's easy to understand why well-to-do Stephen Dallas (John Boles) finds her attractive when he decides to abandon his family and strike out on his own. Not long after the birth of their daughter Laurel (Anne Shirley), however, Stephen wants to return to his former girlfriend. Stella raises Laurel on her own, devoting her life to the girl's happiness, but as a teenager Laurel finds herself attracted to her father's more affluent lifestyle and wants to live with him. Stella initially resists the move, but eventually relents, forcing her daughter to leave by pretending to be drunk and no longer interested in the young woman's company. Laurel decamps to her father's house and is soon married to a socialite at a huge wedding that her mother glimpses, tears streaming down her face, through a window from the street outside.

Stella will continue on, but never again will she cross the social divide separating her from Laurel. A moving and heartfelt story, under Vidor's able direction *Stella Dallas* never descends into mawkish sentimentality. **RBP**

## THE LIFE OF EMILE ZOLA (1937)

US (Warner Bros.) 116m BW
**Director:** William Dieterle
**Producer:** Henry Blanke
**Screenplay:** Norman Reilly Raine, Heinz Herald, Geza Herczeg, from book by Matthew Josephson
**Photography:** Tony Gaudio
**Music:** Max Steiner
**Cast:** Paul Muni, Gale Sondergaard, Joseph Schildkraut, Gloria Holden, Donald Crisp, Erin O'Brien-Moore, John Litel, Henry O'Neill, Morris Carnovsky, Louis Calhern, Ralph Morgan, Robert Barrat
**Oscar:** Henry Blanke (best picture), Heinz Herald, Geza Herczeg, Norman Reilly Raine (screenplay), Joseph Schildkraut (actor in support role)
**Oscar nomination:** William Dieterle (director), Heinz Herald, Geza Herczeg (screenplay), Paul Muni (actor), Anton Grot (art direction), Russell Saunders (assistant director), Max Steiner (music), Nathan Levinson (sound)

William Dieterle's *The Life of Emile Zola* was a follow-up to his highly successful biopic *The Story of Louis Pasteur* (1935), with actor Paul Muni in another story about a Frenchman of principle and enlightenment overcoming prejudice. At the beginning Zola struggles to establish himself as a writer, until the publication of *Nana*, his sensational novel about a prostitute. Success follows success, and Zola is set to enjoy a prosperous old age when he is visited by the wife of Alfred Dreyfus, a French army officer falsely accused of spying for the Germans and sent to Devil's Island. Zola's conscience is pricked and, in a big set piece tailor-made for Muni, he reads out his famous article "*J'Accuse*" to a newspaper editor. In a typical Warner Brothers's montage sequence, the newspaper staff gather around to listen, presses spew out the article, and people rush to buy the paper.

The film won the Oscar for best picture and its underlying seriousness is impressive. Yet though Dreyfus was the victim of antisemitic prejudice, not once in *The Life of Emile Zola* is the word "Jew" uttered. Evidently, Warner Brothers feared that in 1937, with the rising tide of antisemitism in Europe, pictures about anti-Jewish feeling would inflame the very prejudices they were designed to expose. **EB**

U.S. (Paramount) 91m BW
**Director:** Leo McCarey
**Producer:** Leo McCarey, Adolph Zukor
**Screenplay:** Viña Delmar, from the novel *The Years Are So Long* by Josephine Lawrence
**Photography:** William C. Mellor
**Music:** George Antheil, Victor Young, Sam Coslow, Leo Robin, Jean Schwartz
**Cast:** Victor Moore, Beulah Bondi, Fay Bainter, Thomas Mitchell, Porter Hall, Barbara Read, Maurice Moscovitch, Elisabeth Risdon, Minna Gombell, Ray Mayer, Ralph Remley, Louise Beavers, Louis Jean Heydt, Gene Morgan

# MAKE WAY FOR TOMORROW (1937)

In this one-of-a-kind masterpiece by one of the greatest American directors, Victor Moore and Beulah Bondi play Bark and Lucy Cooper, an elderly couple faced with financial disaster and forced to throw themselves on the mercy of their middle-aged children. The children's first step is to separate the two of them so that the inconvenience of hosting them can be divided. Gradually, the old people's self-confidence and dignity are eroded, until they submit to an arrangement whereby one of them will stay in a nursing home in New York, and the other will go to California.

Leo McCarey's direction in *Make Way for Tomorrow* is beyond praise. All of the actors are expansive and natural, and the generosity McCarey shows toward his characters is unstinting. He demonstrates an exquisite sense of when to cut from his central couple to reveal the attitudes of others, without suggesting either that their compassion is condescending or that their indifference is wicked, and without forcing our tears or rage (which would be a way of forfeiting them). There is nothing contrived about McCarey's handling of the story, and thus no escaping its poignancy.

Two examples will suffice to indicate the film's extraordinary discretion. During the painful sequence in which Lucy's presence inadvertently interferes with her daughter-in-law's attempt to host a bridge party, Lucy receives a phone call from Bark. Because she talks loudly on the phone—one of several annoying traits that McCarey and screenwriter Viña Delmar don't hesitate to give the elderly couple—the guests pause in their games to listen. Their reactions (not emphasized, but merely shown) mix annoyance, discomfort, and sorrow.

The last section of the film, dealing with the couple's brief reuniting and impromptu last idyll in Manhattan, is sublime. McCarey keeps us aware of the sympathy of outsiders (a car salesman, a coat-check girl, a hotel manager, a bandleader), but never imposes their reactions on us through superfluous reverse shots. Meanwhile, Lucy and Bark are constantly shown together in the same compositions. In its passionate commitment to their private universe, *Make Way for Tomorrow* is truly, deeply moving. **CFu**

# SNOW WHITE AND THE SEVEN DWARVES (1937)

*Snow White and the Seven Dwarves* begins with a slow zoom to a huge castle, where the wicked Queen queries her magic mirror with the immortal words, "Mirror mirror, on the wall, who's the fairest one of all?" The answer, of course, is her virginal rival Snow White, soon to be the target of her vanity. Like the classic Brothers Grimm story *Snow White* is based on, you're instantly pulled into this magical and sometime scary world. Yet at the time Hollywood considered Walt Disney's first foray into full-length feature animation something of a folly. Who would sit through a 90-minute animated film?

Needless to say, *Snow White* answered that rhetorical question by becoming one of the biggest hits in the history of cinema, solidifying Disney's claim as the world's foremost animation studio. In fact, advancing the stake was one of Walt Disney's own stated goals for the film. He had already broken the cartoon sound barrier with *Steamboat Willy*, and a few years later brought animation into vivid color. *Snow White* was merely the next step forward both artistically as well as financially: feature films meant more box-office sales.

Using the Brothers Grimm story as loose inspiration, Disney unleashed his team of animators on the material, giving them a great deal of freedom in the development of such a creative breakthrough. The film is peppered with gags but also filled with emotion, comprising a soaring combination of beautiful images and strong and enduring songs like "Whistle While You Work" and "Some Day My Prince Will Come," the latter virtually a standard. *Snow White*, incidentally, also marked the first commercially released soundtrack.

There is no way to overestimate the effect of *Snow White*. It not only permanently established Disney as one of the foremost studios in the world but also advanced the state of animation to such a degree that it wasn't really until the advent of computer animation that anyone arguably pushed the form further. A creative triumph, *Snow White* inspired hundreds of imitators, gave birth to an empire, and remains to this day the default template for nearly all animated features. **JKl**

**U.S.** (Walt Disney) 83m Technicolor
**Producer:** Walt Disney
**Screenplay:** Ted Sears, Richard Creedon
**Photography:** Maxwell Morgan
**Music:** Frank Churchill, Leigh Harline, Paul J. Smith
**Cast:** Roy Atwell, Stuart Buchanan, Adriana Caselotti, Eddie Collins, Pinto Colvig, Marion Darlington, Billy Gilbert, Otis Harlan, Lucille La Verne, James MacDonald, Scotty Mattraw, Moroni Olsen, Harry Stockwell
**Oscar:** (honorary award—one statuette, seven miniature statuettes)
**Oscar nomination:** Frank Churchill, Leigh Harline, Paul J. Smith (music)

**U.S.** (Columbia) 91m BW
**Director:** Leo McCarey
**Producer:** Leo McCarey, Everett Riskin
**Screenplay:** Viña Delmar, from play by Arthur Richman
**Photography:** Joseph Walker
**Music:** Ben Oakland, George Parrish
**Cast:** Irene Dunne, Cary Grant, Ralph Bellamy, Alexander D'Arcy, Cecil Cunningham, Molly Lamont, Esther Dale, Joyce Compton, Robert Allen, Robert Warwick, Mary Forbes
**Oscar:** Leo McCarey (director)
**Oscar nomination:** Leo McCarey, Everett Riskin (best picture), Viña Delmar (screenplay), Irene Dunne (actress), Ralph Bellamy (actor in support role), Al Clark (editing)

# THE AWFUL TRUTH (1937)

The legend of Leo McCarey's *The Awful Truth* is that it was largely improvised from day to day. This legend is perfectly in tune with the ethos of the film itself, in which spontaneity, playfulness, the ability to laugh at one's own "act" (as well as to see it with the eye of the person who is seeing right through you at that moment) are so central to its glorious, warm sense of humor as well as its exploration of how to make marriage work.

But the script structure, however it was arrived at, is satisfying. It starts with a rupture: Jerry (Cary Grant) and Lucy (Irene Dunne), believing they have caught each other in infidelieites, lies, and—worst of all—a lack of trust, decide to divorce. It takes half the film, covering Lucy's flirtation with Dan (Ralph Bellamy), for her to realize she still loves Jerry. But then it's his turn to hook up with someone, a "madcap heiress." Once all these bets are off, the story becomes a road-movie leading to a cabin in the woods—with two beds, and 30 minutes left before the divorce decree becomes final.

McCarey perfects every ingredient of the romantic comedy here, from the opposition of New Yorkers and Southerners, to the role of games, songs, and dances as ways of sorting out the characters' affections and allegiances. Full of splendid minor characters and inspired bits of business, *The Awful Truth* also has a heartbreakingly serious moment when Jerry and Lucy remember their unofficial marriage vow ("This comes from the heart, I'll always adore you").

Of all the great movies, this may be the one that most resists description in words. This has much to do with its small jokes of subtle verbal delivery, where ordinary phrases are transformed by timing, rhythm, and tone: from Lucy's defensively repeated "had better go" and Jerry's stumbling on "Tulsa" to Dan's exasperated "Mom!" via the black servant's reaction to Jerry's fake tan: "You're looking weellll..." Above all, the film is a monument to the sheer, magical lovability of its stars. **AM**

## PÉPÉ LE MOKO (1937)

**France** (Paris) 90m BW

**Language:** French

**Director:** Julien Duvivier

**Producer:** Raymond Hakim, Robert Hakim

**Screenplay:** Jacques Constant, Julien Duvivier

**Photography:** Marc Fossard, Jules Kruger

**Music:** Vincent Scotto, Mohamed Ygerbuchen

**Cast:** Jean Gabin, Mireille Balin, Gabriel Gabrio, Lucas Gridoux, Gilbert Gil, Line Noro, Saturnin Fabre, Fernand Charpin, Marcel Dalio, Charles Granval, Gaston Modot, René Bergeron, Paul Escoffier, Roger Legris, Jean Témerson

*Pépé le Moko* was the film that consolidated Jean Gabin's stardom and defined his on-screen persona as a tough, streetwise character, outwardly cynical but with an underlying romantic streak that will cause his downfall. As Pépé, an expatriate French hood who has become top dog in the Casbah (the Arab quarter of Algiers), he relishes his power but yearns nostalgically for Paris. When a beautiful French tourist (Mireille Balin), embodiment of his longed-for homeland, catches his eye, the temptation becomes too great. But once outside the Casbah he's vulnerable, because there a tireless policeman (Lucas Gridoux) lies in wait.

Director Julien Duvivier's skill at evoking atmosphere creates a vivid (if romanticized) vision of the Casbah, an exotic labyrinth of twisting alleyways full of pungent detail. Borrowing motifs from the classic Hollywood gangster movies but seasoning them with doomy Gallic romanticism, *Pépé le Moko* prefigures film noir. Images of bars, grilles, and fences recur throughout the film, underlining Pépé's entrapment within his little fiefdom. The movie is pervaded by a mood of longing, of lost youthful dreams, and of desires that can never be fulfilled. This fatalism led to its being banned during the war by the Vichy regime, but its warm reception after this temporary absence only confirmed its status as a classic. **PK**

## JEZEBEL (1938)

**U.S.** (First National, Warner Bros.) 103m BW

**Director:** William Wyler

**Producer:** Henry Blanke, Hal B. Wallis, William Wyler

**Screenplay:** Clements Ripley, Abem Finkel, John Huston, Robert Buckner, from play by Owen Davis

**Photography:** Ernest Haller

**Music:** Al Dubin, Max Steiner, Harry Warren

**Cast:** Bette Davis, Henry Fonda, George Brent, Margaret Lindsay, Donald Crisp, Fay Bainter, Richard Cromwell, Henry O'Neill, Spring Byington, John Litel, Gordon Oliver, Janet Shaw, Theresa Harris, Margaret Early, Irving Pichel

**Oscar:** Bette Davis (actress)

**Oscar nomination:** Hal B. Wallis, Henry Blanke (best picture), Fay Bainter (actress), Ernest Haller (photography), Max Steiner (music)

Hollywood's second most famous portrayal of a spoiled Southern belle, *Jezebel* offered Bette Davis the perfect vehicle to display her acting talents in a breakthrough role. Davis plays Julie Marsden, who is the most sought-after debutante in 1850s New Orleans, a society ruled by rigid codes of behavior that the young woman finds confining. Engaged to Preston Dillard (Henry Fonda), a Northerner, Julie does not sever her relationship to Buck Cantrell (George Brent), an honorable Southern gentleman and the story's most sympathetic figure. Soon after, Preston leaves New Orleans to return north; when he comes back to the city, he is married to another woman. In her petulance, Julie causes a duel in which Buck is killed, and she becomes a pariah, even to her own family. But then she redeems herself through heroic self-sacrifice during a yellow fever outbreak, when she accompanies the desperately ill Preston to the miserable island where victims of the disease are confined.

William Wyler makes use of a lavish budget and meticulous art design in this intriguing evocation of the period. Much more of a character study than *Gone with the Wind* (1939), *Jezebel* also avoids the "plantation myth" so prominent in that film. Its New Orleans is a decadent place with no dancing darkies, ruled by a planter class intent on its jealous sense of honor. **RBP**

**U.S.** (First National, Warner Bros.) 102m Technicolor

**Director:** Michael Curtiz, William Keighley

**Producer:** Henry Blanke, Hal B. Wallis

**Screenplay:** Norman Reilly Raine, Seton I. Miller

**Photography:** Tony Gaudio, Sol Polito

**Music:** Erich Wolfgang Korngold

**Cast:** Errol Flynn, Olivia de Havilland, Basil Rathbone, Claude Rains, Patric Knowles, Eugene Pallette, Alan Hale, Melville Cooper, Ian Hunter, Una O'Connor, Herbert Mundin, Montagu Love, Leonard Willey, Robert Noble, Kenneth Hunter

**Oscar:** Carl Jules Weyl (art direction), Ralph Dawson (editing), Erich Wolfgang Korngold (music)

**Oscar nomination:** Hal B. Wallis, Henry Blanke (best picture)

# THE ADVENTURES OF ROBIN HOOD (1938)

Whether considered as a swashbuckler, a costume romance, or a mockery of history, *The Adventures of Robin Hood* is simply the best production of its kind ever made. With King Richard on the Crusades, the kingdom is ruled by his rotten brother John, played by Claude Rains as a waspish tyrant who overhears groans from a torture chamber and muses "Ah, more complaints about the new taxes from our Saxon friends." John's less amusing but more deadly sidekick, Sir Guy of Gisbourne, is incarnated with razor-profiled malice by the unmatchably ruthless Basil Rathbone.

The fairest lady in the land is Marian, an impossibly lovely Olivia de Havilland in Technicolor flesh tones. But it's dispossessed outlaw Robin of Locksley who brings life to this court of intrigue, with Errol Flynn's jaunty goatee and Tasmanian twinkle making Robin a rare hero who can be a light-hearted trickster one moment but spin on a knife-point to become a determined rebel ("It's injustice I hate, not Normandy!") and a balcony-climbing romantic.

It is truly amazing how fast-paced and jam-packed this movie is: the story is as complicated as a Shakespearean comedy; there's a real delight in the sword-clashing and arrow-shooting battles, and it ends as all stories should—with good triumphant and lovers united. **KN**

**U.S.** (First National) 97m BW

**Director:** Michael Curtiz

**Producer:** Samuel Bischoff

**Screenplay:** Rowland Brown, John Wexley, Warren Duff

**Photography:** Sol Polito

**Music:** Max Steiner

**Cast:** James Cagney, Pat O'Brien, Humphrey Bogart, Ann Sheridan, George Bancroft, Billy Halop, Bobby Jordan, Leo Gorcey, Gabriel Dell, Huntz Hall, Bernard Punsly, Joe Downing, Edward Pawley, Adrian Morris, Frankie Burke

**Oscar nomination:** Michael Curtiz (director), Rowland Brown (screenplay), James Cagney (actor)

# ANGELS WITH DIRTY FACES (1938)

Michael Curtiz's films preach social responsibility, and *Angels with Dirty Faces* is his most powerful sermon. Rocky and Jerry, two pals from a tough New York neighborhood, grow up to be a notorious gangster (James Cagney) and crusading priest (Pat O'Brien), respectively. A gang of teenagers idolize Rocky, until Father Jerry urges his condemned friend to "go yellow" at his execution. In keeping with its didactic mission, the film's visual and performing styles are emphatic and crisp to the point of caricature. In fact, Cagney's performance here, all cocky swagger and hitched-up shoulders, provided the primary model for impressionists such as Frank Gorshin and Rich Little.

Curtiz may be a moralizer, but he is not a facile one. Rocky's final capitulation is a tough pill to swallow, and the director does not sugarcoat it. Rocky is a charismatic rebel, and Father Jerry is a sanctimonious nag, but the film leaves little doubt which choice serves the greater good. The harrowing climax, a nightmare of gruesome details and expressionist shadows as Rocky is dragged whimpering to the electric chair, still has the power to enrage viewers who do not share the film's stern moral viewpoint, but, for Father Mike, such attitudes are sentimental at best and irresponsible at worst. Amen. **MR**

# OLYMPIA (1938)
# OLYMPIA 1. TEIL - FEST DER VÖLKER
### PART 1: FESTIVAL OF THE NATIONS
# OLYMPIA 2. TEIL - FEST DER SCHÖNHEIT
### PART 2: FESTIVAL OF BEAUTY

Leni Riefenstahl's epic documentary of the 1936 Olympic games held in Berlin is sometimes criticized for its politics. Sponsored by Hitler, the film does contain some sequences that seem to support the notion of "Aryan" superiority. Still, the filmmaker did receive a gold medal for her efforts from the Olympic Committee in 1948, long after Hitler's dream of a 1,000-year Reich had disintegrated. This is not to deny that *Olympia* is a piece of propaganda; Riefenstahl would never have received the incredible funding and support needed if the result had not been politically useful. In many ways, though, *Olympia* transcends politics. Overall, it is more a hymn of praise to athletic prowess and to the poetry of the human body in motion.

Few filmmakers have shown Riefenstahl's aesthetic interest in physical form and motion, and her feat in making this documentary has never been duplicated. Filming the games and supervising the immense task of postproduction would take a Herculean effort today. In the late 1930s, the job was done with primitive equipment. Despite its overtly political message (the opening traces the carrying of the Olympic torch from Greece to Germany as a kind of holy quest), the film is an artistic triumph, evidence not only of Riefenstahl's personal talent and vision, but also of the energies and expertise of her team of assistants, who numbered several hundred.

Huge preparation was necessary. Steel camera towers were constructed in the stadium, platforms built for tracking shots, and Germany scoured for the best talent. Nearly 250 hours of film was shot, and the task of editing (including the addition of sound effects and music) was personally supervised by Riefenstahl. The final edited version, in the best tradition of German documentary cinema, is masterfully paced, with exquisite matched cuts and just enough variation in repetitive events (such as the featured track and field) to sustain visual interest. Riefenstahl's protestations of political innocence may be unconvincing, but *Olympia* does have another and more enduring side. Simply put, it is the most moving cinematic record of human sport and physical competition ever produced. **RBP**

**Germany** (IOC, Olympia Film, Tobis) 118 m and 107m BW

**Language:** German

**Director:** Leni Riefenstahl

**Producer:** Leni Riefenstahl

**Screenplay:** Leni Riefenstahl

**Photography:** Wilfried Basse, Werner Bundhausen, Leo De Lafrue, Walter Frentz, Hans Karl Gottschalk, Willy Hameister, Walter Hege, Carl Junghans, Albert Kling, Ernst Kunstmann, Guzzi Lantschner, Otto Lantschner, Kurt Neubert, Erich Nitzschmann, Hans Scheib, Hugo O. Schulze, Károly Vass, Willy Zielke, Andor von Barsy, Franz von Friedl, Heinz von Jaworsky, Hugo von Kaweczynski, Alexander von Lagorio

**Music:** Herbert Windt, Walter Gronostay

**Cast:** David Albritton, Jack Beresford, Henri de Baillet-Latour, Philip Edwards, Donald Finlay, Wilhelm Frick, Josef Goebbels, Hermann Göring, Ernest Harper, Rudolf Hess, Adolf Hitler, Cornelius Johnson, Theodor Lewald, Luz Long, John Lovelock, Ralph Metcalfe, Seung-yong Nam, Henri Nannen, Dorothy Odam, Martinus Osendarp, Jesse Owens, Leni Riefenstahl, Julius Schaub, Fritz Schilgen, Kee-chung Sohn, Julius Streicher, Forrest Towns, Werner von Blomberg, August von Mackensen, Glenn Morris, Conrad von Wangenheim

**Venice Film Festival:** Leni Riefenstahl (Mussolini Cup—best film)

# LA FEMME DU BOULANGER (1938)
## THE BAKER'S WIFE

**France** (Marcel Pagnol) 133m BW
**Language:** French
**Director:** Marcel Pagnol
**Producer:** Leon Bourrely, Charles Pons
**Screenplay:** Marcel Pagnol, from the novel *Jean le Bleu* by Jean Giono
**Photography:** Georges Benoît
**Music:** Vincent Scotto
**Cast:** Raimu, Ginette Leclerc, Robert Vattier, Robert Bassac, Fernand Charpin, Edouard Delmont, Charles Blavette, Marcel Maupi, Maximilienne, Alida Rouffe, Odette Roger, Charles Moulin, Yvette Fournier, Charblay, Julien Maffre

Orson Welles thought that Raimu was one of the greatest actors of his time; *The Baker's Wife* proves him right. Directed by Marcel Pagnol from a short story by Jean Giono, this is the tale of Aimable Castanier, a middle-aged baker (Raimu) in a small Provençal village. When his young wife Aurélie (Ginette Leclerc) deserts him for a handsome shepherd, the distraught baker stops baking and without bread the village comes to a halt. Catholic priest, left-wing teacher, lord of the manor, and all the villagers forget their old feuds and gang up to bring back the errant wife. Life resumes happily.

From such simple material Pagnol fashioned a comic gem and a humanist masterpiece. With his regular troupe of actors—Raimu, Fernand Charpin, Robert Vattier, and others—Pagnol animates a galaxy of characters that is both funny and touching. His light touch and the actors' talents transcend the crude stereotypes (womanizing aristocrat, pedantic teacher, cantankerous old maid, cuckolded husband), creating a world in which each has his or her own clearly-defined role. Giono and Pagnol's Provence is conservative and patriarchal (the wife does not have much of a say), but it is a world in which shared fundamental values—here represented by bread, both a Christian and pagan symbol—cement social cohesiveness.

Raimu's towering performance effortlessly alternates comic theatricality with minimalist realism, turning his comic cuckold into a tragic hero. Raimu, from the South of France himself, was a superlative stage actor, at ease with the florid language and emphatic delivery of the Marseilles vernacular. His filmic modernity however, came from his ability to switch within seconds to understated moments, giving them extraordinary emotional impact, as illustrated by the film's most famous scene. As the repentant wife returns, Raimu welcomes her back as if nothing had happened and instead takes it out on a surrogate, the straying female cat "Pomponnette," in the most vivid and affecting terms. In this moment of contrived high comedy I defy anyone to remain dry-eyed. It may be called *The Baker's Wife*, but it is definitely Raimu's film. **GV**

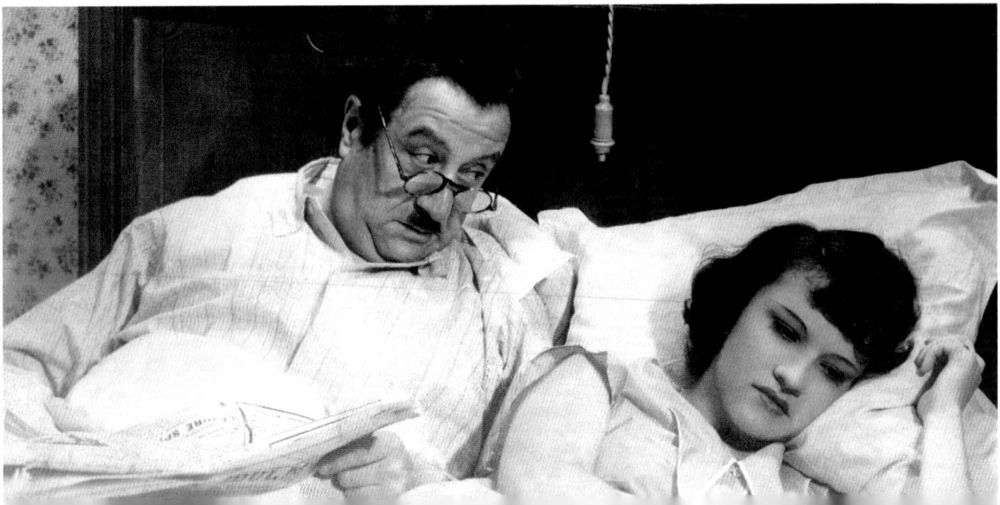

# BRINGING UP BABY (1938)

U.S. (RKO) 102m BW
**Director:** Howard Hawks
**Producer:** Howard Hawks, Cliff Reid
**Screenplay:** Hagar Wilde, Dudley Nichols
**Photography:** Russell Metty
**Music:** Roy Webb
**Cast:** Katharine Hepburn, Cary Grant, Charles Ruggles, Walter Catlett, Barry Fitzgerald, May Robson, Fritz Feld, Leona Roberts, George Irving, Tala Birell, Virginia Walker, John Kelly

*Bringing Up Baby*, the definitive screwball comedy, was the first film Howard Hawks made in a six-picture contract with RKO in 1937. Unpromisingly based on a short story about a young couple and their tamed leopard, the shoot went forty days over schedule and over budget. It earned so little upon its release in 1938 that Hawks was fired from RKO and Katherine Hepburn had to buy herself out of her own contract. Ahead of its time, its amazing breakneck pace and disarmingly witty dialogue set new standards for all such comedies thereafter.

At his whimsical best, Cary Grant is Dr. David Huxley, a handsome and easily distracted paleontologist who spends his days piecing together a brontosaurus skeleton while he is taken apart by his henpecking fiancée. With one more bone to go before the four-year museum project will be complete, Huxley manages to bumble an important meeting on the golf course with a wealthy potential patron. There, Huxley meets Susan Vance (Hepburn). As beautiful and scatterbrained as he is, she steals his golf ball; after that, Huxley's world never snaps back into place. Trying anything to keep him from marrying another girl, Vance uses Baby, the house-trained pet leopard sent to her by her brother in South America, as a worthy Huxley diversion. By the time the family dog buries Huxley's precious dinosaur bone, the couple are headed to jail.

The laughs in *Bringing Up Baby* are real, almost completely disguising its deft analyses of 1930s-style gender expectations, sex, and marriage. So suspicious was the censor of the script's deeper and possibly sexual meanings that Huxley's quest to find his "lost bone" was queried as a reference to lost masculinity. The scene where Huxley dons Vance's feathery feminine bathrobe didn't help dissuade that notion, containing as it does one of the first popular appearances of the word "gay" being used to mean something other than "extremely happy." The critics may have hated it, the audiences may have stayed away, and Oscar didn't smile upon it at the time, but *Bringing Up Baby* has had the last laugh on all its detractors. It remains one of the true masterpieces of celluloid wit. **KK**

**U.S.** (Walter Wanger) 96m BW

**Director:** John Ford

**Producer:** Walter Wanger, John Ford

**Screenplay:** Ernest Haycox, Dudley Nichols

**Photography:** Bert Glennon

**Music:** Louis Gruenberg, Richard Hageman, Franke Harling, John Leipold, Leo Shuken

**Cast:** Claire Trevor, John Wayne, Andy Devine, John Carradine, Thomas Mitchell, Louise Platt, George Bancroft, Donald Meek, Berton Churchill, Tim Holt, Tom Tyler

**Oscar:** Thomas Mitchell (actor in support role)

**Oscar nomination:** Walter Wanger (best picture), John Ford (director), Bert Glennon (photography), Alexander Toluboff (art direction), Otho Lovering, Dorothy Spencer (editing), Richard Hageman, W. Franke Harling, John Leipold, Leo Shuken (music)

# STAGECOACH (1939)

The 1930s wasn't a great decade for the Western. After a few expensive flops such as *The Big Trail* (1930) and *Cimarron* (1931), the major studios largely abandoned the genre to Poverty Row producers making cheap B movies. John Ford hadn't made a Western for a dozen years when he cast John Wayne and Claire Trevor in a story about a stagecoach ride through dangerous Indian territory. In trying to sell it to producer David O. Sleznick, Ford described *Stagecoach* as a "classic Western," a cut above the B westerns which Wayne himself had been making. One thing this meant was giving it more appeal to women in the audience. So Ford and screenwriter Dudley Nichols added to the original story by Ernest Haycox a more developed love story and the birth of a baby. But this wasn't enough for Selznick, who looked down his nose and passed on the project.

Not that *Stagecoach* stints on the genre's more traditional satisfactions. The last part of the film packs in plenty of action, including a gunfight between Wayne and the Plummer gang and a stirring Indian attack as the stagecoach careers across the flat desert. The sequence was enriched by some superlative stuntwork by Yakima Canutt, who, playing one of the Apache attackers, leaps onto one of the stage's horses, is then shot, and has to fall between the horses' hooves and under the wheels.

This was Wayne's second chance at major stardom after the failure of *The Big Trail*, and he took it with both hands. From his first entrance, standing in the desert waving down the stage, he cuts an impressive figure as the Ringo Kid, who has busted out of jail in order to be revenged on the Plummers, killers of his father and brother. But Wayne's appearance is delayed while Ford explores the characters of the other travelers on the coach. Each is deftly and memorably sketched in: Dallas (Claire Trevor), the girl who is no better than she should be, and who is run out of town together with drunken Doc Boone (Thomas Mitchell) by the puritanical ladies of the Law and Order League; Peacock (Donald Meek), a timid whiskey salesman; Hatfield (John Carradine), a southern gambler; Mrs. Mallory (Louise Platt), the pregnant wife of a cavalry officer; and Gatewood (Berton Churchill), a banker who is making off with the assets. On the outside of the coach are Buck (Andy Devine), the portly driver, and Curly (George Bancroft), the local sheriff. The interaction between this oddly assorted group allows Ford to explore a cherished theme, the superior moral qualities of those whom "respectable" society disdains.

*Stagecoach* was the first film Ford shot in Monument Valley, a landscape of towering sandstone buttes on the border between Utah and Arizona. As the tiny coach makes its way through the vastness of the desert, the frailty of its occupants is doubly emphasized as the camera tracks toward a group of Indians observing its progress. Ford makes no attempt to present the Indians as individuals; they are merely a force of nature.

The film's healthy performance at the box office helped reestablish the Western genre. **EB**

**Japan** (Shochiku) 143m BW

**Language:** Japanese

**Director:** Kenji Mizoguchi

**Screenplay:** Matsutarô Kawaguchi, Yoshikata Yoda, from novel by Shôfû Muramatsu

**Photography:** Yozô Fuji, Minoru Miki

**Music:** Shirô Fukai, Senji Itô

**Cast:** Shôtarô Hanayagi, Kôkichi Takada, Gonjurô Kawarazaki, Kakuko Mori, Tokusaburo Arashi, Yôko Umemura

# ZANGIKU MONOGATARI (1939)
## THE STORY OF THE LATE CHRYSANTHEMUMS

In the 19th century, a lazy and untalented Kabuki actor born into a famous family falls in love with his brother's wet nurse. Opposed to their match, his family casts her out of the house. He follows her, and she devotes her life to helping him improve his art, ruining her health in the process. In the end, she dies at home while he, having at last achieved recognition as an actor, leads his troupe on a triumphal boat procession through Osaka.

*The Story of the Late Chrysanthemums* is one of the essential Kenji Mizoguchi films, a work of dazzling elegance and formal rigor and a powerful attack on the social structures that impose the roles of sacrificial victims upon women. Mizoguchi's long takes move the narrative slowly, enfolding the inexorable logic of events within larger and more complex structures. The film allows time for reflection and interiorization, as the characters, recognizing their places in the patterns of power, react with fear, horror, sadness, or revolt to events. The narrative, with its emphasis on metaphorical journeys—the migrations of the acting troupe and the hero's path to artistic excellence—allows Mizoguchi to create a double metaphorical filter. For him, cinema and theater are machines for the distillation of beauty and the achievement of tragic understanding. **CFu**

**U.S.** (MGM) 93m BW

**Director:** Busby Berkeley

**Producer:** Arthur Freed

**Screenplay:** Jack McGowan, Kay Van Riper

**Photography:** Ray June

**Music (song):** Harold Arlen, Nacio Herb Brown, Richard Rodgers

**Cast:** Mickey Rooney, Judy Garland, Charles Winninger, Guy Kibbee, June Preisser, Grace Hayes, Betty Jaynes, Douglas McPhail, Rand Brooks, Leni Lynn, Henry Hull, Barnett Parker, Ann Shoemaker, Margaret Hamilton, Joseph Crehan

**Oscar nomination:** Mickey Rooney (actor), Roger Edens, George E. Stoll (music—score)

# BABES IN ARMS (1939)

Busby Berkeley, key contributor to the waning spectacle-oriented musical at Warner Brothers, made *Babes in Arms* shortly after his move to book-oriented MGM, and its success spawned three similar follow-ups re-teaming Berkeley with adolescent icons Mickey Rooney and Judy Garland.

The film centers on the generation gap, MGM/1939-style. To close that gap, it moves in two directions—a nostalgic recollection of the dying entertainment tradition (minstrel show, vaudeville) practiced by the kids' parents, and the kids' demand to claim their place in the spotlight over their parents' objections. This impatience erupts in the film's most impressive number "Babes in Arms." Rooney leads a defiant mob of torch-toting juveniles ("They call us babes in arms,/But we are babes in armor!") through winding back alleys to a playground where nursery rhymes counterpoint the main song and a raging bonfire signifies the immolation of childish things. Those oh-so-earnest kids tend to get a little soppy at times, so *Babes in Arms* benefits from the drier presence of June Preisser, as an amiably arrogant ex-child star, and Margaret Hamilton, at her Wicked-Witch best, as a biddy who wants to toss all the stage brats into a state work school. **MR**

# MR. SMITH GOES TO WASHINGTON (1939)

Frank Capra's hymn of praise to the American system of government was considered so incisive in its indictment of special-interest corruption that some in Washington thought *Mr. Smith Goes to Washington* should not be released into a world on the verge of war. To show that the system works, however, Capra must demonstrate how it can correct itself. Republicanism (not democracy) is saved in the film by the heroic efforts of a stubborn idealist, who, in the best tradition of the Jeffersonian individualism for which he is named, refuses to go along with party bosses, who plot his ruin. Ashamed, the smooth-talking machine politician assigned to discredit him publicly confesses the plot.

Jimmy Stewart is perfect as Jefferson Smith, whose chief qualification is that he is hopelessly unsophisticated, a man who spends all his time mentoring a troop of young "rangers." But this rube is neither stupid nor lacking in courage. Smith first convinces the cynical woman (Jean Arthur) charged with looking after him of his virtue and his keen sense. And then, after unintentionally creating trouble by proposing a national boys' camp on the precise site that the "machine" hopes to use for its pork barrel project, he defends himself against false charges in a filibuster that goes on for many hours and leaves him barely able to speak or stand. Crucial in Smith's passage from irrelevance through disgrace to vindication is the part played by Senator Joseph Paine (Claude Rains). As opposed to the crudely venal political boss Jim Taylor (Edward Arnold), Paine is a man who believes in the American system but who has been seduced by a politics of compromise and deal making. Smith can only be rescued by Paine's conversion. Smith's deliverance is also made possible by the peculiarly American institution of the filibuster, which permits the individual—symbolically enough, not the group—unlimited free speech according to established rules. Smith can thereby exert a power against the group that would condemn him, insuring his vindication.

An impressive bit of Americana, Capra's film is full of memorable moments, the most moving of which is the montage sequence tracing the newly arrived senator's tour of Washington monuments, including the Lincoln memorial. **RBP**

**U.S.** (Columbia) 125m BW

**Director:** Frank Capra

**Producer:** Frank Capra

**Screenplay:** Lewis R. Foster, Sidney Buchman

**Photography:** Joseph Walker

**Music:** Dimitri Tiomkin

**Cast:** Jean Arthur, James Stewart, Claude Rains, Edward Arnold, Guy Kibbee, Thomas Mitchell, Eugene Pallette, Beulah Bondi, H.B. Warner, Harry Carey, Astrid Allwyn, Ruth Donnelly, Grant Mitchell, Porter Hall, Pierre Watkin

**Oscar:** Lewis R. Foster (screenplay)

**Oscar nomination:** Frank Capra (best picture), Frank Capra (director), Sidney Buchman (screenplay), James Stewart (actor), Claude Rains (actor in support role), Harry Carey (actor in support role), Lionel Banks (art direction), Gene Havlick, Al Clark (editing), Dimitri Tiomkin (music), John P. Livadary (sound)

# THE WIZARD OF OZ (1939)

**U.S.** (MGM) 101m BW
**Director:** Victor Fleming
**Producer:** Mervyn LeRoy, Arthur Freed
**Screenplay:** Noel Langley, Florence Ryerson, Edgar Allan Woolf, from the novel *The Wonderful Wizard of Oz* by L. Frank Baum
**Photography:** Harold Rosson
**Music:** Harold Arlen, E.Y. Harburg, George Bassman, George E. Stoll, Herbert Stothart
**Cast:** Judy Garland, Frank Morgan, Ray Bolger, Bert Lahr, Jack Haley, Billie Burke, Margaret Hamilton, Charley Grapewin, Pat Walshe, Clara Blandick, Terry the dog, The Singer Midgets
**Oscar:** Herbert Stothart (music), Harold Arlen, E.Y. Harburg (song)
**Oscar nomination:** Mervyn LeRoy (best picture), Harold Rosson (photography), Cedric Gibbons, William A. Horning (art direction), A. Arnold Gillespie (special visual effects), Douglas Shearer (special sound effects)
**Cannes Film Festival:** Victor Fleming nomination (Golden Palm)

Based on *The Wonderful Wizard of Oz*, the turn-of-the-century children's novel by L. Frank Baum, this evergreen classic is one of the great film fairy tales, also a first-rate musical and the vehicle that turned Judy Garland from a talented child performer into a lasting and iconic movie star. Not hugely profitable on its first release, perhaps because it was such an expensive production, *The Wizard of Oz* has become beloved by successive generations. Like *It's a Wonderful Life* (1946), its popularity was boosted in the 1950s by annual Christmas television screenings, which established it as among the most beloved of all movies.

Along with her little dog Toto, Garland's Dorothy Gale (breasts strapped down to make her seem younger) is whisked out of a sepia Kansas by a tornado and dumped in the ravishing Technicolor Land of Oz, where she squashes a witch under her house, is gifted by Glinda the Good (Billie Burke) with the dead hag's magic ruby slippers, and takes off down the Yellow Brick Road to the Emerald City in order to find her way back to the farm from which she once wished she could escape. The "no-place-like-home" theme, a screenwriter's convenience to keep all the characters focused on their quests, has always seemed like a slight cop-out (why would anyone want to leave the wonders of Oz and go back to Kansas?). It never quite squares with the spoilsport interpretation of the whole film as a delirious dream in which Dorothy has recast everyone she knows as her Land of Oz friends and enemies.

The film has many splendors: a superb Harold Arlen–E.Y. Harburg score (ranging from the wistful "Over the Rainbow" through the infectious jollity of "Off to See the Wizard" and "Ding-Dong, the Witch Is Dead" to the classic comedy of "If I Only Had a Brain"), incredible MGM set design, hundreds of squeaky Munchkins and flying monkeys, the "horse of a different color" gag, and perfect performances all round. There are also a number of unforgettable stand-out moments: Ray Bolger's Scarecrow being dismembered while Jack Haley's Tin Man laments "Well, that's you all over"; Bert Lahr's Cowardly Lion trying to be threatening ("I'll fight you with one paw tied behind my back"); Wicked Witch Margaret Hamilton's fate under a bucket of water ("I'm melting, I'm melting!"), Frank Morgan emerging from behind the curtain ("I'm a very good man, it's just that I'm a very bad wizard").

Like its 1939 MGM stablemate *Gone with the Wind*, *The Wizard of Oz* bears a director's credit for solid pro Victor Fleming but is actually a triumph of the producer's art, with Mervyn LeRoy pulling together all the diverse elements of a hardly smooth shoot. Buddy Ebsen was cast as the Scarecrow then switched to playing the Tin Man until he turned out to be allergic to the makeup; a whole "Jitterbug" number was dropped and hidden until it showed up in *That's Entertainment!* (1974); and the midgets cast as the Munchkins reputedly ran riot. Best line: "Hearts will never be practical until they can be made unbreakable." **KN**

**U.S.** (Universal) 94m BW
**Director:** George Marshall
**Producer:** Islin Auster, Joe Pasternak
**Screenplay:** Felix Jackson, from novel by Max Brand
**Photography:** Hal Mohr
**Music:** Frederick Hollander, Frank Skinner, Ralph Freed
**Cast:** Marlene Dietrich, James Stewart, Mischa Auer, Charles Winninger, Brian Donlevy, Allen Jenkins, Warren Hymer, Irene Hervey, Una Merkel, Billy Gilbert, Samuel S. Hinds, Jack Carson, Tom Fadden, Virginia Brissac, Edmund MacDonald

# DESTRY RIDES AGAIN (1939)

Like most comedy Westerns, George Marshall's *Destry Rides Again* is a satire on the conventions of manly heroism. Destry (played by James Stewart in his best "aw, shucks" manner), sheriff of the unruly town of Bottleneck, prefers milk to whiskey and refuses to carry a gun. This gives him a special appeal for saloon girl Frenchy, with Marlene Dietrich belatedly reprising the role that made her famous in *The Blue Angel*. Dietrich sings a couple of rousing numbers in the Last Chance Saloon, including the celebrated "See What the Boys in the Back Room Will Have." In another reversal of stereotype, the usual "fight in the saloon" scene takes place between two women, as Frenchy and Lily Belle (Una Merkel) engage in an unladylike wrestling match.

Frenchy transfers her affections from gambler Kent (Brian Donlevy) to Destry, then leads the women of the town in a final rout of the bad guys, before throwing herself in front of Destry to take a bullet meant to kill him. It's an amusing tale handled with a deft touch, very different in spirit from the original novel by Max Brand, the most prolific of all Western fiction writers, which was first filmed in 1932 with Tom Mix in the title role, and then again in 1954 with Audie Murphy. **EB**

# ONLY ANGELS HAVE WINGS (1939)

**U.S.** (Columbia) 121m BW
**Director:** Howard Hawks
**Producer:** Howard Hawks
**Screenplay:** Jules Furthman, Howard Hawks
**Photography:** Joseph Walker
**Music:** Dimitri Tiomkin, Manuel Álvarez Maciste
**Cast:** Cary Grant, Jean Arthur, Richard Barthelmess, Rita Hayworth, Thomas Mitchell, Allyn Joslyn, Sig Ruman, Victor Kilian, John Carroll, Don "Red" Barry, Noah Beery Jr., Manuel Maciste, Milisa Sierra, Lucio Villegas, Pat Flaherty
**Oscar nomination:** Joseph Walker (photography), Roy Davidson, Roy Davidson (special visual effects), Edwin C. Hahn (special sound effects)

Though Howard Hawks turned his attention to the manly cameraderie of dangerous professions (especially aviation) in such early 1930s action pictures as *The Dawn Patrol*, *The Crowd Roars*, and *Ceiling Zero*, this 1939 drama marks a transformation of his style, imprinting a personal stamp on a melodramatic genre to set the heroic-comic-romantic tone he would later pursue in *To Have and Have Not*, *Rio Bravo*, and *El Dorado*—note the community sing-alongs, the in-group banter, the shared domestic chores, the nicknames and gossip, the wryly amusing streak of prissiness among tough guys, and the veneer of cynicism that masks honest sentiment.

There are remarkable, exciting, stunt-heavy flying sequences in *Only Angels Have Wings*, especially a very dangerous landing and takeoff on a high Andean plateau, but the meat of the film is on the ground, observing the cohesion of a disparate group who cluster around white hat hero Geoff Carter (Cary Grant). Striding a head taller than his crew and looking every inch the star, Geoff runs an air-mail service in South America, inspiring a group of traumatized veterans, fresh kids, and deadbeats to hop over the Andes in outmoded aeroplanes. Showgirl Bonnie Lee (Jean Arthur) is stranded at the airfield: at first appalled by the ostensibly macho attitudes of the pilots when one of their number is killed in a needless accident, she gradually comes to understand their sensitive side, eventually joining Geoff in a spirited rendition of "The Peanut Vendor."

At heart a tough soap opera, the film has a group of "damaged" people showing their worth in crises and cuts between funny, sassy, sexy dialogue exchanges on the ground and still-effective aerial action scenes. It also has a great supporting cast of familiar faces—Richard Barthelmess (trying to live down a reputation for cowardice because he bailed out of a crashing plane and left his engineer behind), Thomas Mitchell (an aging sidekick covering up his increasing blindness), Noah Beery Jr., Sig Rumann, and Rita Hayworth (as the sort of woman men shouldn't mess with but usually do). Catch-phrases include "Calling Barranca" and "Who's Joe?" **KN**

U.S. (Selznick) 222m Technicolor

**Director:** Victor Fleming, George Cukor

**Producer:** David O. Selznick

**Screenplay:** Sidney Howard, from novel by Margaret Mitchell

**Photography:** Ernest Haller, Ray Rennahan, Lee Garmes

**Music:** Max Steiner

**Cast:** Clark Gable, Vivien Leigh, Leslie Howard, Olivia de Havilland, Thomas Mitchell, Barbara O'Neil, Evelyn Keyes, Ann Rutherford, George Reeves, Fred Crane, Hattie McDaniel, Oscar Polk, Butterfly McQueen, Victor Jory, Everett Brown

**Oscar:** William Cameron Menzies (honorary award—use of color), David O. Selznick (best picture), Victor Fleming (director), Sidney Howard (screenplay), Vivien Leigh (actress), Hattie McDaniel (actress in support role), Lyle R. Wheeler (art direction), Ernest Haller Ray Rennahan (photography), Hal C. Kern, James E. Newcom (editing), Don Musgrave (technical achievement award)

**Oscar nomination:** Clark Gable (actor), Olivia de Havilland (actress in support role), Max Steiner (music), Thomas T. Moulton (sound), Jack Cosgrove, Fred Albin, Arthur Johns (special effects)

# GONE WITH THE WIND (1939)

Margaret Mitchell's Civil War bestseller was snapped up by megalomaniac producer David O. Selznick, who resisted Mitchell's suggestion that he cast Basil Rathbone as Rhett Butler in favor of the fans' only choice, Clark Gable. After a nationwide talent search and a Hollywood catfight involving every potential leading lady in town, Selznick hired British Vivien Leigh to play Southern belle Scarlett O'Hara. Insistent from the first that every detail be sumptuous, Selznick then wore out at least three directors (Sam Wood, George Cukor, and Victor Fleming), set fire to the surviving *King Kong* sets to stage the burning of Atlanta, hired enough extras to refight the Civil War, and sat back to watch the Oscars and acclaim roll in.

Conceived from the outset as the ultimate Hollywood movie, *Gone with the Wind* became the benchmark for popular epic cinema for decades to come. Though the film is monumental enough to be beyond criticism, most of its really great scenes come in the first half, which was substantially directed by Cukor, who brought his skilled touch with character and nuance to the material with a great epic sweep. Fleming, meanwhile, best known for directing macho action, somehow wound up handling the soapier stretches as the leads' marriage falters through postbellum ups and downs far less compelling than the war-torn cross-purposes romance that got them together.

The motor of the plot is the vacillating heart of Scarlett, whom Leigh plays first as flighty then flinty: she is so infatuated with gentlemanly Ashley Wilkes (Leslie Howard) that she marries several lesser (and doomed) milksops when he opts for the more conventionally feminine (and doomed) Melanie (Olivia de Havilland). Rhett Butler, a pragmatist rather than an idealist, enters the picture and she is drawn to him as the war overturns the Southern way of life, marrying him after she has sworn never to go hungry again and to do anything it takes to keep Tara, her father's plantation, going despite the depradations of Yankees and carpetbaggers. Only when Rhett rejects her does she realize she truly loves him, prompting the classic have-it-both-ways ending in which he walks out ("Frankly my dear, I don't give a damn") and she swears to win him back ("Tomorrow is another day").

Like *The Birth of a Nation* (1915), *Gone with the Wind* tidies up a lot of complex history, showing only happy devoted slaves and depicting Ashley's postwar involvement in a hooded Klan organization as a genuinely heroic (if doomed) endeavor. But the sweep of the movie is near irresistible, and Selznick's set pieces are among the most emblematic in cinema history: the pullback from Scarlett as she ministers to the wounded to fill the screen with injured soldiers in gray, the dash through the blazes as Atlanta burns, Gable carrying Leigh upstairs into sexual shadows. Dressed up with gorgeous 1939 Technicolor, pastel-pretty for the dresses and blazing red for the passions, and a thunderous Max Steiner score, this still has a fair claim to be considered the last word in Hollywood filmmaking. **KN**

**France** (Sigma, Vauban) 93m BW

**Language:** French

**Director:** Marcel Carné

**Screenplay:** Jacques Prévert, Jacques Viot

**Photography:** Philippe Agostini, André Bac, Albert Viguier, Curt Courant

**Music:** Maurice Jaubert

**Cast:** Jean Gabin, Jules Berry, Arletty, Mady Berry, René Génin, Arthur Devère, René Bergeron, Bernard Blier, Marcel Pérès, Germaine Lix, Gabrielle Fontan, Jacques Baumer, Jacqueline Laurent

**Venice Film Festival:** Marcel Carné nomination (Mussolini Cup—best film)

# LE JOUR SE LÈVE (1939)
## DAYBREAK

Although it was not the first film to use dissolves to signal flashbacks, Marcel Carné's *Daybreak* was deemed so innovative in 1939 that the producers insisted on a pretitle card to dispel any confusion: "A man has committed murder. Locked, trapped in a room, he recalls how he became a murderer."

The murderer is François (Jean Gabin), a common factory worker who has been lured into murder by the victim, an amoral and manipulative vaudeville entertainer by the name of Valentin (Jules Berry). Their fate is bound up with two women: the earthy, sensual Clara (Arletty), who leaves Valentin to take up with François, and the pure, idealized Françoise (Jacqueline Laurent), whom François loves, but who has been corrupted by her association with the other man.

Among the remarkable series of classic films to spring from the collaboration between Carné and screenwriter Jacques Prévert (the others include *Port of Shadows* [1938], *The Devil's Envoys* [1942], and, preeminently, *Children of Paradise* [1945]), *Daybreak* is arguably the most influential. Certainly it rehearses themes the team would return to in *Children of Paradise.* Although it wears its allegorical themes lightly, François clearly stands for the French working man, and *Daybreak* gives voice to the despair that overtook the supporters of the Popular Front in the late 1930s as the state swept aside progressive socialist reforms and the specter of fascism loomed. When one friend yells from the crowd gathered outside his building that there's still hope, François retorts "It's over, there isn't a François anymore... There isn't anything anymore."

The film's doom-laden sense of existential alienation and austere, claustrophobic atmosphere clearly anticipated the mood and form of American *film noir.* In fact RKO remade the film with Henry Fonda and Vincent Price as *The Long Night* in 1946 (the studio attempted to destroy all prints of the original, but mercifully failed, and it's *The Long Night* that has virtually disappeared from view). Similarly, Gabin's rough-hewn romantic predates American counterparts like John Garfield and Humphrey Bogart as an iconic working-class hero. *Daybreak* stands as probably the masterpiece of French poetic realism. **TCh**

## GUNGA DIN (1939)

Classic Hollywood's purest adventure story derives, strangely enough, from a Rudyard Kipling poem, which furnished writers Ben Hecht and Charles MacArthur with only atmosphere and the minor character of its title.

The most famous entry in a series of 1930s productions that praise British shouldering of the white man's burden, *Gunga Din* tells the story of three professional soldiers (Cary Grant, Douglas Fairbanks Jr., and Victor McLaglen) in the "Imperial Lancers." At first the trio seem about to break up, with one man on the verge of marriage—a fate worse than death in this world of exclusive male values. Fortunately, a terrible threat to the community soon arises in the form of a fanatic sect of ritual murderers, the Thuggees. Two set-piece battles follow, expertly staged by Stevens. At the film's climax, the three sergeants are locked in a standoff with the Thuggees, whose evil leader has used them to lure the regiment into a trap. But Gunga Din (Sam Jaffe) rises as if from the dead to sound his bugle and warn the troop, who then slaughter the fanatics. The trio are reunited with their regiment to celebrate the heroism of their fallen companion.

Made on what was a huge budget for the time, *Gunga Din* is a spectacular visual treat, one of the most impressive action films ever made– the buddy film to end all buddy films. **RBP**

**U.S.** (RKO) 117m BW

**Director:** George Stevens

**Producer:** George Stevens

**Screenplay:** Ben Hecht, from poem by Rudyard Kipling

**Photography:** Joseph H. August

**Music:** Alfred Newman

**Cast:** Cary Grant, Victor McLaglen, Douglas Fairbanks Jr., Sam Jaffe, Eduardo Ciannelli, Joan Fontaine, Montagu Love, Robert Coote, Abner Biberman, Lumsden Hare

**Oscar nomination:** Joseph H. August (photography)

## NINOTCHKA (1939)

Ernst Lubitsch's most charming and humorous comedy of European manners features Greta Garbo in a rare comic role. Set in Paris during the 1920s, *Ninotchka*'s plot revolves around the attempt of the Soviet government to recover priceless jewels from the exiled Grand Duchess Swana (Ina Claire). Three bumbling bureaucrats fail at this mission and find themselves seduced by the luxuries and freedoms of Western society. So it is up to Ninotchka (Garbo) to regain the treasure by dealing with the lover of the Grand Duchess, the smooth and handsome Leon (Melvyn Douglas).

In the end, Ninotchka is able to get the jewels only by returning to Moscow and breaking with Leon, who soon follows her to Russia. Though they are in love, she refuses to betray her country, and Leon must use subterfuge to have her travel to Istanbul, where he meets her and they decide to marry. The film's political themes are hardly serious but serve as the background for one comic shtick after another, most memorably perhaps Ninotchka's attempt—in a fancy Paris nightclub—to get the ladies room attendants to go on strike. Douglas is perfect as the enamored and self-indulgent Leon, but this is Garbo's picture and her last great screen role. **RBP**

**U.S.** (Loew's, MGM) 110m BW

**Director:** Ernst Lubitsch

**Producer:** Ernst Lubitsch

**Screenplay:** Melchior Lengyel, Charles Brackett

**Photography:** William H. Daniels

**Music:** Werner R. Heymann

**Cast:** Greta Garbo, Melvyn Douglas, Ina Claire, Bela Lugosi, Sig Ruman, Felix Bressart, Alexander Granach, Gregory Gaye, Rolfe Sedan, Edwin Maxwell, Richard Carle

**Oscar nomination:** Sidney Franklin (best picture), Melchior Lengyel, Charles Brackett, Walter Reisch, Billy Wilder (screenplay), Greta Garbo (actress)

France (Les Nouvelles Editions Françaises) 110m BW

**Language:** French

**Director:** Jean Renoir

**Producer:** Claude Renoir

**Screenplay:** Carl Koch, Jean Renoir

**Photography:** Jean-Paul Alphen, Jean Bachelet, Jacques Lemare, Alain Renoir

**Music:** Roger Désormières

**Cast:** Nora Gregor, Paulette Dubost, Mila Parély, Odette Talazac, Claire Gérard, Anne Mayen, Lise Elina, Marcel Dalio, Julien Carette, Roland Toutain, Gaston Modot, Jean Renoir, Pierre Magnier, Eddy Debray, Pierre Nay

# LA RÈGLE DU JEU (1939)
## THE RULES OF THE GAME

After the great success of *The Grand Illusion* (1937) and *La Bête Humaine* (1938), Jean Renoir together with his brother Claude and three friends founded his own production company, Les Nouvelles Editions Françaises. The NEF's first announced project was an adaptation and updating of Pierre de Marivaux's *Les Caprices de Marianne*; asked to describe what his film would be like, Renoir answered "An exact description of the bourgeoisie of our time." This is the film that was eventually titled *The Rules of the Game*.

After completing a trans-Atlantic flight in record time, aviator André Jurieux (Roland Toutain) announces over the radio his disappointment that a certain someone isn't at the airport to greet him. That "someone" is Christine (Nora Gregor), an Austrian married to mechanical bird collector Robert de la Cheyniest (Marcel Dalio). Octave (played by Renoir himself), friend and confidant of both André and Christine, convinces Robert to invite André out to a hunting party at his lavish estate La Colinière as a way of saving face; for his part, Robert hopes having André around might distract Christine while he settles accounts with his longtime mistress Geneviève (Mila Parély). That's what's happening among the "masters." Turning to the "servants," there's Lisette (Paulette Dubost), maid to Christine and married to Schumacher (Gaston Modot), groundskeeper at La Colinière, who catches the eye of Marceau (Julien Carette), a poacher who gets hired by Robert as a house servant. Renoir's screenplay will bring the various amorous adventures of the masters and servants together, heading finally to the "accidental" shooting of André, sacrificed so that a corrupt social order can remain intact.

A cinematic style favoring deep spaces and a highly mobile camera here reaches its perfection, as Renoir underlines the theatrical atmosphere that dominates both on and off-stage. Most of the performances are flawless: Dalio as Robert, Carette as Marceau, Dubost as Lisette, Modot as Schumacher. Reviewers over the years have quibbled over Gregor's performance as Christine, wondering why so many men in the film are smitten with her—but perhaps that's precisely the point. Boldly, Renoir cast himself as Octave, a devastating portrait of a man who fills in the emptiness of his own life by serving as the intermediary for the affairs of others.

A commercial disaster when first released in the summer of 1939, *The Rules of the Game* was cut and recut but to no avail; soon after the war began that Fall it was banned as a danger to public morale. In the late 1940s and 1950s, the film's legend was kept alive by André Bazin and his disciples at *Cahiers du Cinéma*, who claimed that alongside *Citizen Kane* (1941) *Rules* had been the harbinger of modern cinema, yet it was known only in a radically shortened version (88 minutes). In 1956, it was reconstructed to almost its complete original length (113 minutes, but it's still missing one scene), presented at the Venice Film Festival in 1959, and the rest is film history, with *The Rules of the Game* finally celebrated internationally as the masterpiece it is. **RP**

**U.S.** (Samuel Goldwyn) 103m BW
**Director:** William Wyler
**Producer:** Samuel Goldwyn
**Screenplay:** Charles MacArthur, from novel by Emily Brontë
**Photography:** Gregg Toland
**Music:** Alfred Newman
**Cast:** Merle Oberon, Laurence Olivier, David Niven, Flora Robson, Donald Crisp, Geraldine Fitzgerald, Hugh Williams, Leo G. Carroll, Miles Mander, Cecil Kellaway, Cecil Humphreys, Sarita Wooton, Rex Downing, Douglas Scott
**Oscar:** Gregg Toland (photography)
**Oscar nomination:** Samuel Goldwyn (best picture), William Wyler (director), Ben Hecht, Charles MacArthur (screenplay), Laurence Olivier (actor), Geraldine Fitzgerald (actress in support role), Alfred Newman (music), James Basevi (art direction)

# WUTHERING HEIGHTS (1939)

William Wyler's film version of Emily Brontë's *Wuthering Heights* is unsurpassed as a gothic tale of inextinguishable passion, thwarted by social circumstance and mischance. A lonely traveler, Dr. Kenneth (Donald Crisp), making his way across the moors of Northern England, spends the night at Wuthering Heights, where an aged servant tells him the tragic story of Heathcliff (Laurence Olivier), the house's current owner. A gypsy waif, he had been adopted by the Earnshaws and raised with their own two children. Heathcliff is the constant companion of young Cathy (Merle Oberon), whose snobbish brother Hindley (Hugh Williams) scorns him. Wealthy neighbor Edgar Linton (David Niven) falls in love with Cathy, and she dismisses Heathcliff, who goes to America. Cathy forgets him and ends up marrying Edgar. Heathcliff returns to England a rich man but, furious at Cathy's betrayal, marries Edgar's sister (Geraldine Fitzgerald), mistreating the poor woman as a means of getting revenge. Cathy is miserable with Edgar and falls ill, but before she dies the former lovers are briefly united.

Heathcliff's speech about the life they will live together is one of the most poignant moments in any Hollywood film. It is the acting of Olivier and Oberon as the doomed lovers, framed against the forbidding wildness of the studio-crafted moors, that makes the film most memorable. **RBP**

**U.S.** (Columbia) 92m BW
**Director:** Howard Hawks
**Producer:** Howard Hawks
**Screenplay:** Ben Hecht, Charles MacArthur
**Photography:** Joseph Walker
**Music:** Sidney Cutner, Felix Mills
**Cast:** Cary Grant, Rosalind Russell, Ralph Bellamy, Gene Lockhart, Porter Hall, Ernest Truex, Cliff Edwards, Clarence Kolb, Roscoe Karns, Frank Jenks, Regis Toomey, Abner Biberman, Frank Orth, Helen Mack, John Qualen

# HIS GIRL FRIDAY (1940)

Ben Hecht's and Charles MacArthur's classic newspaper play *The Front Page* had been filmed successfully before and would be again after this sparkling 1939 version, scripted by Hecht and Charles Lederer. But astute and witty director Howard Hawks delights in the simple twist that was a stroke of genius—turning ace reporter Hildy Johnson into a woman. Voila, *His Girl Friday* became the fastest-talking battle of the sexes in the history of romantic screwball comedy.

Scintillating Rosalind Russell is the wisecracking star reporter her editor and ex-husband (Cary Grant as the unscrupulous and aggressively charming Walter Burns) can't lose in the middle of a hot murder story. When she announces that she's quitting to marry a meek square (Ralph Bellamy), Walter's incredulity and dismay launch him into conniving overdrive. As wily Walter calculates, Hildy can't resist a last big story and is shortly up to her absurd hat in a jailhouse break and corruption exposé. Grant and Russell engage in dizzying verbal play of machine-gun speed in a plot that reaches farcical heights, with a great character ensemble of gum-chewing, smoke-wreathed, poker-playing hacks acting as their cynical chorus. Theatrical and stylish, *His Girl Friday* is unrivaled for comic timing and snappy repartee. **AE**

# REBECCA (1940)

It is somewhat surprising that despite his long, fruitful career, and despite several subsequent nominations, only *Rebecca*, his first American film, earned Alfred Hitchcock an Academy Award for Best Picture. Then again, that may say more about the persuasive power of producer David O. Selznick. Hot from the success of the 1939 film *Gone with the Wind*, Selznick seized the opportunity to work with Hitchcock, pairing the director with Daphne Du Maurier's gothic ghost story.

Working with a big budget, Hitchcock transformed the Manderley mansion into a character unto itself—later the inspiration for the imposing Xanadu in *Citizen Kane*. The palatial seaside estate is the atmospheric setting for the strained romance between Joan Fontaine and Laurence Olivier. He's a wealthy widower wooing the innocent Fontaine, and she never questions her good fortune in finding such a loving man. They marry after a whirlwind romance, but as their relationship deepens, Fontaine is haunted more and more by the spirit of his dead wife—Rebecca. Is the haunting merely a figment of her imagination, or the fruits of paranoia, or is a more nefarious force at work? And what, if anything, does the suspicious servant Mrs. Danvers (Judith Anderson), who always seems to be hovering near the nerve-wracked Fontaine, have to do with the strange goings-on?

*Rebecca* marked Hitchcock's auspicious arrival in America. In fact, at the Oscars the film ironically beat out Hitchcock's final British picture, *Foreign Correspondent*. All his artistic traits were used to full effect: there's the murky, mysterious earlier history, the barely contained suspicions, the fairy-tale romance doomed by the encroaching past, and, of course, the looming specter of foul play. *Rebecca* does lack some of Hitchcock's trademark playfulness, and the sense of humor is missed; the absence of levity is due in no small part to the unremittingly gloomy, gothic nature of Du Maurier's melodramatic novel. Innocent Fontaine is nearly driven to madness by the lingering secrets of Manderley, but Hitchcock is more than happy to let the tension build and build toward the haunting conclusion. **JKl**

**U.S.** (Selznick) 130m BW

**Director:** Alfred Hitchcock

**Producer:** David O. Selznick

**Screenplay:** Philip MacDonald, from novel by Daphne Du Maurier

**Photography:** George Barnes

**Music:** Franz Waxman

**Cast:** Laurence Olivier, Joan Fontaine, George Sanders, Judith Anderson, Gladys Cooper, Nigel Bruce, Reginald Denny, C. Aubrey Smith, Melville Cooper, Florence Bates, Leonard Carey, Leo G. Carroll, Edward Fielding, Lumsden Hare, Forrester Harvey

**Oscar:** David O. Selznick (best picture), George Barnes (photography)

**Oscar nomination:** Alfred Hitchcock (director), Robert E. Sherwood, Joan Harrison (screenplay), Laurence Olivier (actor), Joan Fontaine (actress), Judith Anderson (actress in support role), Lyle R. Wheeler (art direction), Hal C. Kern (editing), Jack Cosgrove, Arthur Johns (special effects), Franz Waxman (music)

**U.S.** (Walt Disney) 120m Technicolor

**Director:** Ben Sharpsteen (supervisor)

**Producer:** Walt Disney, Ben Sharpsteen

**Screenplay:** Joe Grant, Dick Huemer

**Photography:** James Wong Howe, Maxwell Morgan

**Nonoriginal music:** Bach, Beethoven, Dukas, Mussorgsky, Schubert, Stravinsky, Tchaikovsky

**Cast:** Leopold Stokowski (conductor, The Philadelphia Orchestra), Deems Taylor (narrator), Julietta Novis (soloist)

**Oscar:** Walt Disney, William E. Garity, J.N.A. Hawkins (honorary award), Leopold Stokowski & associates (honorary award)

# FANTASIA (1940)

Although now commonplace, creating images to interpret music was revolutionary when this audacious milestone in animation and stereophonic audio recording was conceived and executed by the Walt Disney studio to universal acclaim and astonishment. Graced by the eminent symphonic star Leopold Stokowski conducting the Philadelphia Orchestra, *Fantasia*'s eight wide-ranging sequences comprise a concert with ambitious, amusing, portentous, and experimental cartoons accompanying pieces by Tchaikovsky, Mussorgsky, Schubert, and others.

Even on IMAX screens, the exhibition scene of choice for the most recent of Disney's several anniversary restorations, rerecordings, and rereleases of their prized 1940 animation landmark (revamped with reasonable success with five new segments in their updated production *Fantasia 2000*), can be disappointing because it is still a remorselessly kitsch experience, however impressive and groundbreaking an achievement. Baby Boomers who enjoyed it on hallucinogenics in their youths are probably the audience fondest of it now. But there are some magical sequences that endure, as befits a film made by sixty animators working under no less than eleven directors (under the supervision of Ben Sharpsteen).

Most watchable are the abstractions ahead of their time to Bach, in which the multichannel sound is perfectly synchronized to the drawings and seems to soar out of the screen. Mickey Mouse, never more delightful than as the Sorcerer's Apprentice desperately trying to halt the self-replicating brooms he has conjured up to do his chores, the dancing Chinese mushrooms, a darling chorus line of eyelash-batting pachyderms, the hippos in ballet tutus cavorting daintily and fleeing caped alligators to "The Dance of the Hours"—all still a hoot. Together these make for a sweet hour of greatness. In between are sequences that have not aged as well. The capering fairies who are nude but tastefully free from sexual organs, the seemingly interminable decline of the dinosaurs to Stravinsky's "Rite Of Spring," and the vulgar absurdity to which Beethoven's Pastorale has been subjected (centaurs flirtatiously pursuing coy, suspiciously pubescent-looking centaurettes who are uniformly coiffed in the style of Joan Crawford) all take some beating for incredulity value. **AE**

# THE PHILADELPHIA STORY (1940)

George Cukor's 1940 adaptation of Philip Barry's theatrical farce is the uncontested classic of all sophisticated slapstick comedies. Katharine Hepburn had starred in the play on Broadway and it is said that playwright Phillip Barry based the leading female character on her reputation at the time. Having left RKO on less than ideal terms, the public saw Hepburn as bossy and unfeminine, certainly not the womanly ideal for the late 1930s.

In the opening scene, now famous for its virtually dialogue-free fury, heiress Tracy Lord (Hepburn) watches her recently divorced playboy husband Dexter Haven (Cary Grant) put a few of his belongings in the car, snapping a golf club over her thigh in anger. Trying to prove that she is not impossible to love, Tracy plans to marry a respectable if colorless man at the family mansion when Dexter returns with two reporters in tow, Mike Connor (James Stewart) and Liz Imbrie (Ruth Hussey), specifically to ruin the wedding. Never more luminous, Hepburn outdoes herself in a role which demands impeccable comic timing as well as true vulnerability. Her scenes with Stewart in the garden the night before her fateful wedding capture the essence of impetuous attraction.

Hepburn was responsible for the making of *The Philadelphia Story* as it stands. She owned the rights to the project, which she then wisely sold to MGM on condition that she recap her leading role as well as choose the director and cast. She wanted Clark Gable as Dexter and Spencer Tracy as Mike, but because of scheduling clashes neither were available. Instead Grant, her on-screen partner on three previous occasions, and Stewart were cast. Director George Cukor managed to make Hepburn's negative public image work for her through her character, eliciting feelings of sorrow for a beautiful woman so misunderstood. The film was an enormous success, with an award-winning screenplay that matched comedy with social commentary. In 1956, the play, with additional musical numbers, was remade into *High Society*. **KK**

**U.S.** (MGM) 112m BW

**Director:** George Cukor

**Producer:** Joseph L. Mankiewicz

**Screenplay:** Donald Ogden Stewart, from play by Philip Barry

**Photography:** Joseph Ruttenberg

**Music:** Franz Waxman

**Cast:** Cary Grant, Katharine Hepburn, James Stewart, Ruth Hussey, John Howard, Roland Young, John Halliday, Mary Nash, Virginia Weidler, Henry Daniell, Lionel Pape, Rex Evans

**Oscar:** Donald Ogden Stewart (screenplay), James Stewart (actor)

**Oscar nomination:** Joseph L. Mankiewicz (best picture), George Cukor (director), Katharine Hepburn (actress), Ruth Hussey (actress in support role)

U.S. (Fox) 128m BW

**Director:** John Ford

**Producer:** Nunnally Johnson, Darryl F. Zanuck

**Screenplay:** Nunnally Johnson, from novel by John Steinbeck

**Photography:** Gregg Toland

**Cast:** Henry Fonda, Jane Darwell, John Carradine, Charley Grapewin, Dorris Bowdon, Russell Simpson, O.Z. Whitehead, John Qualen, Eddie Quillan, Zeffie Tilbury, Frank Sully, Frank Darien, Darryl Hickman, Shirley Mills, Roger Imhof

**Oscar:** John Ford (director), Jane Darwell (actress in support role)

**Oscar nomination:** Darryl F. Zanuck, Nunnally Johnson (best picture), Nunnally Johnson (screenplay), Henry Fonda (actor), Robert L. Simpson (editing), Edmund H. Hansen (sound)

# THE GRAPES OF WRATH (1940)

Few American pictures in the 1930s got to grips with the suffering and dislocation of the Great Depression. Hollywood largely left it to other media such as the theater, novels, and photography to document the national disaster. John Steinbeck's novel *The Grapes of Wrath*, first published in 1939, was based on solid research, following dispossessed farming families from Oklahoma as they journeyed to the orchards of California in search of casual labor.

Despite objections from the conservative financiers who controlled the studio, Darryl Zanuck bought the book for 20th-Century Fox. He knew that John Ford was the right man to direct it, with his feeling for the American people and their history. Ford also identified what was most heartbreaking about the plight of the Joad family—not their acute poverty, but the psychological trauma of being uprooted from their home, of being cast out on the road, rootless. In a memorable scene Ma Joad (Jane Darwell) burns the possessions she can't take with her the night before they must abandon their farm.

For his hero, Tom Joad, Ford cast Henry Fonda, who had just appeared in Ford's *Young Mr. Lincoln* (1939) and *Drums Along the Mohawk* (1939), two other pieces of Americana. Members of the unofficial John Ford Stock Company to appear included Russell Simpson as Pa Joad, John Qualen as their friend Muley, and John Carradine as an itinerant preacher. And for his cameraman Ford made an inspired choice. Gregg Toland captured brilliantly the documentary look of the pictures that had been taken of the dustbowl tragedy by government-employed photographers such as Dorothea Lange. Nowhere is this better seen than in a sequence where the Joads drive into a squatters camp, the camera dwelling on the grim faces of the occupants and on the run-down shacks where they live.

Though *The Grapes of Wrath* does not shirk from showing the full enormity of its subjects' plight, there is a significant departure from the novel. In Steinbeck's book the Joads first find easier conditions in a government-run camp, but by the end are reduced to starvation wages. In the film, they find the government camp later on, thus making their progress an upward curve, marked by Ma's final speech: "We're the people.... We'll go on forever." **EB**

## DANCE, GIRL, DANCE (1940)

Those who are only familiar with Lucille Ball from her popular 1950s television series should examine her work here in Dorothy Arzner's camp classic *Dance, Girl, Dance*. As "Bubbles"/"Tiger" Lily White, Ball all but steals the film from Maureen O'Hara's dedicated ballet dancer who is forced into burlesque or starve.

*Dance* is the oft-told tale of life in the sordid world of burlesque as seen through the eyes of Judy O'Brian (O'Hara), an aspiring ballet dancer given hope by her mentor Madame Basilova (the always camp Maria Ouspenskaya), who unfortunately is run over by a truck before her protégé can reveal her talent. Bubbles offers Judy a spot in her burlesque act to appear as her stooge. Before long, Judy can take no more and in a fiery speech to her all-male audience she screams at them to "Go ahead and look, get your fifty cents worth!" Many have taken this to be Arzner's feminist stance light years before it was fashionable. Nevertheless, it is Ball that Arzner gets the most fun out of, and no one will forget Lucy when she does the hula or belts out the Jitterbug bite.

If backstage cat fights and a bit of women-as-spectacle amuse you, then check out *Dance, Girl, Dance*. As Bubbles would say, "Listen kid, I don't fall into gutters—I pick my spots." Ironically, Ball would one day own the very studio that made this film: RKO! **DDV**

**U.S.** (RKO) 90m BW

**Director:** Dorothy Arzner

**Producer:** Harry E. Edington, Erich Pommer

**Screenplay:** Tess Slesinger, Frank Davis, from story by Vicki Baum

**Photography:** Russell Metty, Joseph H. August

**Music:** Chet Forrest, Edward Ward, Bob Wright

**Cast:** Maureen O'Hara, Louis Hayward, Lucille Ball, Virginia Field, Ralph Bellamy, Maria Ouspenskaya, Mary Carlisle, Katharine Alexander, Edward Brophy, Walter Abel, Harold Huber, Ernest Truex, Chester Clute, Lorraine Krueger, Lola Jensen

## PINOCCHIO (1940)

Some of the darker elements of Carlo Collodi's original Italian fable were, of course, discarded once Disney had the story. But only some. The lasting appeal of the animated *Pinocchio* shows that not all of the alterations the studio made to the story of a wooden puppet brought to life were necessarily for the worse, and several of the story's most frightening details remain prominent. The classic still features plenty of horror as Pinocchio faces the perils of peer pressure that distract him from his goal of becoming a real boy. Guided (but not always led) by his insect "conscience" Jiminy Cricket, Pinocchio must learn not just responsibility but also courage and love during his innocently roguish quest for life.

As Disney's second feature (after *Snow White*), *Pinocchio* showed the then-uncharted world of animation to be rife with possibility, resulting in such enchanting and ethereal creations as the luminous Blue Fairy, and such amazing sequences as the escape from cursed Pleasure Island and the thrilling encounter with the fittingly named Monstro the Whale. Add to these such now standard songs as "When You Wish Upon A Star," and is it any wonder *Pinocchio* has remained a towering standard by which so many animated films are judged? **JKl**

**U.S.** (Walt Disney) 88m Technicolor

**Director:** Hamilton Luske, Ben Sharpsteen

**Producer:** Walt Disney

**Screenplay:** Aurelius Battaglia, from novel by Carlo Collodi

**Music:** Leigh Harline, Paul J. Smith, Ned Washington

**Cast:** (voices) Dickie Jones, Don Brodie, Walter Catlett, Frankie Darro, Cliff Edwards, Charles Judels, Christian Rub, Evelyn Venable

**Oscar:** Leigh Harline, Paul J. Smith, Ned Washington (music), Leigh Harline, Ned Washington (song)

U.S. (Loew's, MGM) 100m BW

**Director:** Frank Borzage

**Producer:** Frank Borzage

**Screenplay:** George Froeschel, Hans Rameau, Claudine West, from novel by Phyllis Bottome

**Photography:** William H. Daniels

**Music:** Bronislau Kaper, Eugene Zador

**Cast:** Margaret Sullavan, James Stewart, Robert Young, Frank Morgan, Robert Stack, Bonita Granville, Irene Rich, William T. Orr, Maria Ouspenskaya, Gene Reynolds, Russell Hicks, William Edmunds, Esther Dale, Dan Dailey, Granville Bates

# THE MORTAL STORM (1940)

One of the few anti-Nazi films Hollywood made before Pearl Harbor—detailed and passionate in its condemnation of Nazism—Frank Borzage's *The Mortal Storm* opens on the day Adolf Hitler becomes Chancellor of Germany. The day also happens to be the 60th birthday of Professor Viktor Roth (Frank Morgan), a beloved science professor at a university in southern Germany. The film shows the consolidation of Nazi Germany through the destruction of the "non-Aryan" Roth and his family: his wife, his two Aryan stepsons, who become rabid Nazis, and his actual daughter, Freya (Margaret Sullavan).

Borzage portrays Nazism as a form of insanity, to which many men—only one woman, that we see—succumb as if by contagion or by natural predisposition—the film makes no analysis of the socioeconomic roots of Nazism—but with which, in some individuals, a residual humanity comes into conflict. The magnificent final scene locates this conflict within the character played by Robert Stack. Alone in his stepfather's house, he walks through its empty rooms. The camera tracks past him, exploring the shadowy space, the soundtrack filled with dialogue from earlier scenes; we hear the young man's footsteps as he goes out of the house.

The *Mortal Storm* is one of American cinema's great love stories. Borzage's poignant and subtle handling of the relationship between Freya and Martin (James Stewart) is in keeping with the director's career-long commitment to the transcendent power of love—an idealism to which the admirable performances of Sullavan and Stewart are uncompromisingly faithful. Just before the lovers' trek to the mountainous pass across the Austrian border, Martin's mother (Maria Ouspenskaya) has them celebrate their union by drinking from a ceremonial wine cup. This scene is one of the most luminous in all Borzage's work.

Uncredited coproducer Victor Saville said he directed much of the film, a claim that has been widely repeated but contradicted by several key cast and crew members. There can be no doubt that *The Mortal Storm* is fully representative of the style, philosophy, and concerns of Frank Borzage. **CFu**

# THE BANK DICK (1940)

U.S. (Matty Fox, Universal) 74m BW
**Director:** Edward F. Cline
**Producer:** Jack J. Gross
**Screenplay:** W.C. Fields
**Photography:** Milton R. Krasner
**Music:** Charles Previn
**Cast:** W.C. Fields, Cora Witherspoon, Una Merkel, Evelyn Del Rio, Jessie Ralph, Franklin Pangborn, Shemp Howard, Dick Purcell, Grady Sutton, Russell Hicks, Pierre Watkin, Al Hill, George Moran, Bill Wolfe, Jack Norton

Written by W.C. Fields under the name "Mahatma Kane Jeeves," which suggests something of his ambitions, and directed by amiable traffic cop Eddie Cline, whose job was to clear the way so Fields could cut loose with all his multiple idiosyncracies, *The Bank Dick* finds the star as usual cast as a mild-mannered but resentful bumbler who wants only to be left in peace, but is nagged by an unreasonable world into making the effort to respond to various impolite intruders into his happy doze.

Egbert Sousè, a put-upon bumbler who would like nothing more than to spend his life in bars getting quietly drunk, is constantly harrassed by his frightful wife (Cora Witherspoon), ghastly mother-in-law (Jessie Relph), obnoxious teenage daughter (Una Merkel), her chinless boob fiancee (Grady Sutton), and his own bratty younger child into making something of himself. When he accidentally foils a bank robbery by blundering into the crook, he is given the job of uniformed security guard and allowed to cause trouble in a succession of absolutely perfect routines that pit him against snooty officials (Franklin Pangborn as a bank inspector driven to distraction), hard-bitten crooks (one would-be robber is dragged off on a hilarious road chase sequence on a par with any silent slapstick), and offensive customers.

Like all the best Fields films (*It's a Gift* [1934], *Never Give a Sucker an Even Break* [1941]), the premise here is just an excuse for a succession of vaudeville-like sketches in which he is pitted against a partner too eccentric to be classed as a straight man but also too vicious to be a victim. Some of the routines in *The Bank Dick* (a bit in which Sousè somehow finds himself in the director's chair while a movie is being shot) stray far afield from the bank, but the marbled, pompous halls of commerce and capital, with gladhanding moneybags who receive their come-uppance as Sousè somehow becomes rich and "reformed," are an ideal setting for mischief and anarchy. Fields was a rare comedian who could be funny while strangling a small child, and this 75-minute gem is among his masterpieces. **KN**

# CITIZEN KANE (1941)

**U.S.** (Mercury, RKO) 119m BW
**Director:** Orson Welles
**Producer:** Orson Welles, Richard Baer, George Schaefer
**Screenplay:** Herman J. Mankiewicz, Orson Welles
**Photography:** Gregg Toland
**Music:** Bernard Herrmann, Charlie Barnet, Pepe Guízar
**Cast:** Orson Welles, Joseph Cotten, Dorothy Comingore, Agnes Moorehead, Ruth Warrick, Ray Collins, Erskine Sanford, Everett Sloane, William Alland, Paul Stewart, George Coulouris, Fortunio Bonanova, Gus Schilling, Philip Van Zandt, Georgia Backus, Harry Shannon
**Oscar:** Herman J. Mankiewicz, Orson Welles (screenplay)
**Oscar nomination:** Orson Welles (best picture), Orson Welles (director), Orson Welles (actor), Perry Ferguson, Van Nest Polglase, A. Roland Fields, Darrell Silvera (art direction), Gregg Toland (photography), Robert Wise (editing), Bernard Herrmann (music), John Aalberg (sound)

Since 1962, *Sight & Sound* magazine's oft-cited critics' poll of the greatest films ever made has placed *Citizen Kane*, Orson Welles's remarkable debut film, at the top of the list. By 1998, the American Film Institute called it the greatest movie of all time. It also garnered Best Picture awards from the New York Film Critics Circle and the National Board of Review, and won an Oscar for its screenplay. The legend of *Citizen Kane* has partly been fueled by the fact that Welles was only 24 when he made the film, but also from the obvious comparisons between the titular character and newspaper magnate William Randolph Hearst, who moved heaven and earth to stop the picture from being made and then, when not stopped from being distributed, he tried to discredit it. But beyond the ridiculous hype of any single film being "the greatest movie of all time," *Citizen Kane* is of tremendous interest and importance, for a number of reasons.

The film tells a great story: Charles Foster Kane (played brilliantly by Welles himself) is born poor, but strikes it rich through a gold mine bequeathed to his mother. As a young man he begins to assemble a populist newspaper and radio empire, eventually marrying the niece of an American president and running for governor. But any ambition he has for real power is stymied. As Kane becomes alienated from his power, he becomes increasingly abusive to the women in his life, first his wife, then his mistress. He dies, almost alone, in his reconstructed but unfinished castle, longing for the simplicity of his childhood. Firmly within the traditions of New Deal populism, *Citizen Kane* extols the very American perspective that money cannot buy happiness, but in a highly prosaic, almost Dickensian way.

More significantly, *Citizen Kane* begins with Kane's death, and the enigmatic final word he utters: "Rosebud". A group of intrepid newsreel reporters try to discover the meaning of this last word and interview several of Kane's acquaintances. Not only is the film told in flashback, but each character only knows the man from a certain perspective, which is presented in due course. The film's narrative complexity, without ever violating Classical Hollywood narrative continuity and causality, is a remarkable tour de force, responsible in large part for critic Pauline Kael's accusation that the film's true genius lay not in the hands of wunderkind Welles, but in those of screenwriter Herman J. Mankiewicz.

The film's real power, though, lies in its cinematography: Gregg Toland developed a technique for deep-focus photography, wherein the extreme foreground, central middle-ground, and background were all in focus at the same time, allowing the eye to focus on any part of the image. This technique was criticized at the time for calling attention to itself, in direct violation of the codes of Classical Hollywood cinematography, wherein good photography was assumed to be invisible. Even by today's different standards, *Citizen Kane's* cinematography is striking and unforgettable. **MK**

ANE

U.S. (Paramount) 97m BW

**Director:** Preston Sturges

**Producer:** Paul Jones

**Screenplay:** Monckton Hoffe, Preston Sturges

**Photography:** Victor Milner

**Music:** Clara Edwards, Sigmund Krumgold

**Cast:** Barbara Stanwyck, Henry Fonda, Charles Coburn, Eugene Pallette, William Demarest, Eric Blore, Melville Cooper, Martha O'Driscoll, Janet Beecher, Robert Greig, Dora Clement, Luis Alberni

**Oscar nomination:** Monckton Hoffe (screenplay)

# THE LADY EVE (1941)

*The Lady Eve* is a classic screwball comedy and a quintessential Preston Sturges film, reflecting the writer-director's view of romance as the greatest con game of all. The script abounds in superb lines, the dialogue is fast-paced and witty, and the plot offers a clever variation on the familiar battle-of-the-sexes motif.

The film begins on a cruise ship, where the resourceful and sophisticated temptress Jean Harrington (Barbara Stanwyck) tries to seduce the guileless snake-lover Charles "Hopsie" Pike (Henry Fonda) in order to con him out of his fortune built on "Pike's Ale." In a highly implausible but nevertheless delightful plot twist, the action then shifts to Hopsie's Connecticut mansion where Jean reappears as an English heiress, Lady Eve Sidwich. She seduces Hopsie again, and makes him marry her with the intention of dumping him afterward as retribution for having deserted her earlier. In the end, however, her scheming backfires when she truly falls in love with him.

Despite the existing censorship restrictions, Sturges somehow manages to get away with quite a lot in *The Lady Eve*. Weaving in numerous references to the biblical story of the Fall, he emphasizes sexuality in a way that few filmmakers at the time would have even dared. *The Lady Eve* was remade in 1956 as (the considerably inferior) *The Birds and the Bees*, starring Mitzi Gaynor and David Niven. **RDe**

# THE WOLF MAN (1941)

U.S. (Universal) 70m BW
**Director:** George Waggner
**Producer:** Jack J. Gross, George Waggner
**Screenplay:** Curt Siodmak
**Photography:** Joseph A. Valentine
**Music:** Charles Previn, Hans J. Salter, Frank Skinner
**Cast:** Claude Rains, Warren William, Ralph Bellamy, Patric Knowles, Bela Lugosi, Maria Ouspenskaya, Evelyn Ankers, J.M. Kerrigan, Fay Helm, Lon Chaney Jr., Forrester Harvey

The figure of the wolf man—that bipedal, cinematic version of the werewolf archetype, dramatically embodying the Jekyll/Hyde (superego/Id) dichotomy present in us all—first took center stage in Universal's *Werewolf of London* (1935), starring Henry Hull in a role reprised decades later by Jack Nicholson in *Wolf* (1994). Shortly thereafter, Curt Siodmak finished the screenplay for what was to be Universal Pictures' latest horror classic—following *Dracula* (1931), *Frankenstein* (1931), and *The Mummy* (1932)—*The Wolf Man*, directed by George Waggner. In what still remains the most recognizable and cherished version of the myth, Lon Chaney Jr. stars as Lawrence Talbot, an American-educated Welshman who wants nothing more than to be cured of his irrepressible (when the moon is full) lycanthropy.

Makeup king Jack Pierce devised an elaborate yak-hair costume for Chaney that would come to serve as the template for countless Halloween masks. What distinguishes Siodmark's story from previous werewolf tales was the coded emphasis on repressed sexual energy as the motivating force behind Talbot's full-moon transformations. As the gypsy-woman Maleva (Maria Ouspenskaya) explains, "Even a man that is pure in heart, and says his prayers by night, may become a wolf when the wolfbane blooms and the autumn moon is bright."

The success of Waggner's picture led to four more Chaney-driven Wolf Man films in the 1940s alone. Dozens of imitators, updates, take-offs, spoofs have since followed. **SJS**

# THE MALTESE FALCON (1941)

**U.S.** (First National, Warner Bros.) 101m BW
**Director:** John Huston
**Producer:** Henry Blanke, Hal B. Wallis
**Screenplay:** John Huston, from novel by Dashiell Hammett
**Photography:** Arthur Edeson
**Music:** Adolph Deutsch
**Cast:** Humphrey Bogart, Mary Astor, Gladys George, Peter Lorre, Barton MacLane, Lee Patrick, Sydney Greenstreet, Ward Bond, Jerome Cowan, Elisha Cook Jr., James Burke, Murray Alper, John Hamilton
**Oscar nomination:** Hal B. Wallis (best picture), John Huston (screenplay), Sydney Greenstreet (actor in support role)

By 1941, Dashiell Hammett's great private eye novel had been acceptably filmed twice, under its own title in 1931 with Ricardo Cortez as Sam Spade and as *Satan Met a Lady* in 1935 with Warren William as the Spade character (and the falcon McGuffin turned into the Horn of Roland). John Huston, having served an apprenticeship as a writer, selected the book from Warner Brothers' catalogue of properties and was so confident in the strength of his material that his script consists essentially of a transcription of Hammett's dialogue. He was fortunate enough to have a letter-perfect cast down to the smallest bit parts, and the restraint not to go over the top. This debut feature has little of the razzle-dazzle of the same year's *Citizen Kane*, announcing the arrival not of an enfant terrible but of a consummate professional.

Often considered a cornerstone of film noir, *The Maltese Falcon* is sparing in its use of symbolic shadows—which are withheld until the elevator door casts jail-bar shapes across the face of the duplicitous heroine at the end—and takes place almost entirely in anonymously tidy hotel rooms and offices worlds away from the seedy glamor of *The Big Sleep* (1946) or *Murder, My Sweet* (1944). Humphrey Bogart, graduating from bad-guy roles to tough romantic heroes, is San Francisco private eye Sam Spade. A sharp-suited businessman who is out to bring in the murderer of his partner and thwart a group of treacherous adventurers who have become so caught up in the search for the fabulous jeweled bird of the title that they make the fatal mistake of assuming everyone is as corrupt and greedy as they are. Mary Astor might at first glance seem a little matronly for a femme fatale, but her strange primness in tight suits and tighter hairstyle is weirdly apt for a woman who always has a backup lie in place. Sydney Greenstreet's talkative, obese, self-delighted Kaspar Gutman and Peter Lorre's polite, sad, scented, whiny Joel Cairo are screen immortals, a Bing and Bob or Laurel and Hardy of crime, with perennial loser/fall guy Elisha Cook Jr. as the angry little gunman Wilmer who is doomed always to be on the outside of the deal.

Hammett's reputation rests on his addition of a certain social realism to the American mystery story, with private eyes who are solid professionals rather than supersleuths. He was also addicted to plots as twisted and bizarre as Jacobean drama—*The Maltese Falcon* climaxes not only with the hysterical punchline that the black bird everyone has been scheming and killing to possess is actually a fraud but also the classic moment as the detective admits that he loves the murderess but is still going to let her get hauled off to jail. Whereas other great Hollywood directors pursue their own visions, Huston continued to be at his best—from *The Treasure of the Sierra Madre* (1948) through to *The Asphalt Jungle* (1950), *Fat City* (1972) *Wise Blood* (1979), and *The Dead* (1987)—when making faithful adaptations of minor classic novels. **KN**

U.S. (Warner Bros.) 134m BW

**Director:** Howard Hawks

**Producer:** Howard Hawks, Jesse L. Lasky, Hal B. Wallis

**Screenplay:** Harry Chandlee, Abem Finkel

**Photography:** Sol Polito

**Music:** Max Steiner

**Cast:** Gary Cooper, Walter Brennan, Joan Leslie, George Tobias, Stanley Ridges, Margaret Wycherly, Ward Bond, Noah Beery Jr., June Lockhart

**Oscar:** Gary Cooper (actor), William Holmes (editing)

**Oscar nomination:** Jesse L. Lasky, Hal B. Wallis (best picture), Howard Hawks (director), Harry Chandlee, Abem Finkel, John Huston, Howard Koch (screenplay), Walter Brennan (actor in support role), Margaret Wycherly (actress in support role), Sol Polito (photography), John Hughes, Fred M. MacLean (art direction), Max Steiner (music), Nathan Levinson (sound)

# SERGEANT YORK (1941)

Howard Hawks's *Sergeant York* celebrates the good fight of World War I just as the United States was preparing for World War II. A bellicose subtext is everywhere apparent, yet it is easily assimilated into the moral framework of the film's eponymous lead.

Alvin York, as characterized by Gary Cooper, speaks with a down-home slang, the country bumpkin. His transformation from a spirited Tennessee farmer into a Christian Pacifist and finally into a doughboy hero celebrates an array of Hollywood conventions, including sacred mothers and fair-minded leaders. Hackneyed? Yes. But this gem's importance rests in making Cooper a star, if not also for fairly depicting trench warfare only a few months before Pearl Harbor.

That no greater context for World War I is offered here is precisely the point. *Sergeant York* is narrowly concerned with courage and sacrifice. Anything more would undermine its portrait positing the defense of freedom as an ultimate goal. Simultaneously loving Biblical virtue and skilled gunplay, the movie revels in camaraderie, chaste romance, and dueling fisticuffs. In short, it's a Hawksian world here perfectly transposed into a biopic long on small-town values and short on the violent conflict that made the real-life Alvin York famous. **GC-Q**

**U.S.** (Walt Disney) 64m Technicolor

**Director:** Ben Sharpsteen

**Producer:** Walt Disney

**Screenplay:** Otto Englander, from book by Helen Aberson

**Music:** Frank Churchill, Oliver Wallace

**Cast voices:** Herman Bing, Billy Bletcher, Edward Brophy, Jim Carmichael, Hall Johnson Choir, Cliff Edwards, Verna Felton, Noreen Gammill, Sterling Holloway, Malcolm Hutton, Harold Manley, John McLeish, Tony Neil, Dorothy Scott, Sarah Selby, Billy Sheets, Charles Stubbs, Margaret Wright

**Oscar:** Frank Churchill, Oliver Wallace (music)

**Oscar nomination:** Frank Churchill, Ned Washington (song)

**Cannes Film Festival:** Walt Disney (Prix du meilleur dessin animé—best animation design)

# DUMBO (1941)

Even today, Walt Disney's animation mills regularly turn to traditional fairy tales and familiar folk favorites for inspiration. But Disney's fourth animated feature, *Dumbo*, like the immediately subsequent *Bambi*, was derived from a relatively low-profile book, which apparently freed the animators from more standard-issue prince-rescues-princess romanticism.

*Dumbo* is still awash in sentimentality, but the anthropomorphized leads—Dumbo, the outcast baby circus elephant whose giant ears and clumsiness make him the object of ridicule, and Timothy, his worldly rodent companion—lend themselves to some joyfully chaotic action as well as some creatively rendered circus sequences. Yet two scenes during Dumbo's quest for self-worth stick out above all the rest: the protopsychedelic pink elephant hallucination and the tender, wrenching meeting between Dumbo and his wrongfully "jailed" mother. Animation has rarely been as inventive, moving, and alive as in these two segments, which are paired with equally memorable songs. Dumbo's eventual triumph over adversity, as well as his reunion with his mother, may be telegraphed from the start, but the film's emotional arc is so carefully constructed that the jump-through-the-hoops challenges faced by the put-upon elephant only enhance the heart-warming conclusion. **JKl**

# HIGH SIERRA (1941)

*High Sierra* is a landmark of the gangster genre, a career turning point for Humphrey Bogart, and a model of action-film existentialism by Raoul Walsh. Like Walsh's earlier *The Roaring Twenties* (1939), *High Sierra* is an elegiac gangster film, unusual in this Code-ruled period for its sympathetic portrayal of the gangster as an outdated outcast. Old-timer Roy Earle (Bogart), the nobly named hero, towers above the punks and hypocrites he encounters on both sides of the law as he leads an ill-fated hotel heist, foolishly pursues a respectable girl (Joan Leslie), and briefly finds more suitable companionship with a fellow outcast (Ida Lupino).

In contrast to such contemporaries as John Ford, Howard Hawks, Frank Capra, and Michael Curtiz who stress the value of the community or group, Walsh in this period gave more weight to his heroes' egotism, nonconformity, and antisocial qualities. *High Sierra*'s view of straight-and-narrow society is remarkably scathing, reaching a peak in the scene in which Roy is humiliatingly rejected by his vapid middle-class princess in favor of her smug conformist boyfriend.

After a decade of playing squares and punks, Bogart got his most substantial role yet in *High Sierra*. In *The Maltese Falcon*, his other important film of 1941, Bogart is expansive, smart-alecky, domineering. In the Walshian universe of *High Sierra*, Bogart's subtler performance creates a distinctively different persona: moody, withdrawn, and tense, with his shoulders hunched and his gestures cramped to emphasize the character's insular nature. Even in Roy's intimate scenes with his soulmate Marie (Lupino), Walsh places objects and barriers between the lovers to underline their essential isolation.

*High Sierra* begins and ends with the lofty peak of Mount Whitney, which appears throughout the film, its siren presence beckoning the hero to his lonely destiny. Another underworld character says to Roy, "You remember what Johnny Dillinger said about guys like you and him? He said you were just rushing toward death. Yeah, that's it: just rushing toward death!" The great car-chase scene in which the cops pursue Roy up the fatal mountain—a spectacular payoff of the entire film's tight, kinetic style —translates those words into the dynamic visual language of action cinema at its height. **MR**

**U.S.** (Warner Bros.) 100m BW
**Director:** Raoul Walsh
**Producer:** Mark Hellinger, Hal B. Wallis
**Screenplay:** John Huston, from novel by W.R. Burnett
**Photography:** Tony Gaudio
**Music:** Adolph Deutsch
**Cast:** Ida Lupino, Humphrey Bogart, Alan Curtis, Arthur Kennedy, Joan Leslie, Henry Hull, Henry Travers, Jerome Cowan, Minna Gombell, Barton MacLane, Elisabeth Risdon, Cornel Wilde, Donald MacBride, Paul Harvey, Isabel Jewell

# SULLIVAN'S TRAVELS (1941)

**U.S.** (Paramount) 90m BW
**Director:** Preston Sturges
**Producer:** Paul Jones, Buddy G. DeSylva, Preston Sturges
**Screenplay:** Preston Sturges
**Photography:** John F. Seitz
**Music:** Charles Bradshaw, Leo Shuken
**Cast:** Joel McCrea, Veronica Lake, Robert Warwick, William Demarest, Franklin Pangborn, Porter Hall, Byron Foulger, Margaret Hayes, Robert Greig, Eric Blore, Torben Meyer, Victor Potel, Richard Webb, Charles R. Moore, Almira Sessions

As one of American cinema's earliest auteurs and cutting a distinctly modern figure (his mother's best friend was Isadora Duncan; he spent his youth criss-crossing the Atlantic; a "kiss-proof" lipstick and ticker-tape machine were among his patented inventions), Preston Sturges was responsible for an explosion of now-classic films in the 1940s. These films are known for their sophisticated verbal wit, uproarious physical comedy, and their affectionate portrayal of eccentric, scene-stealing supporting characters. But Sturges's work is also consistent in its exploration of the possibilities and prospects of upward—and occasionally downward—mobility. In what may be his finest, most complex film, *Sullivan's Travels* (1942), Sturges brilliantly mixes broad humor with sharp-edged cultural commentary, once again—as in *The Great McGinty* (1940), *Christmas in July* (1940), and *The Lady Eve* (1941)—revealing social identity to be a highly unstable proposition, capable of hyperbolic transformation through such prosaic means as disguise, confusion, and self-deception.

John L. Sullivan (Joel McCrea) is a can't-miss Hollywood director who specializes in lightweight entertainment, exemplified by broad comedies such as the 1939 film *Ants in Your Pants*. Naïve and sheltered by a solicitous staff who have no interest in seeing their meal ticket change genres or become overly ambitious in his cinematic pursuits, Sully nonetheless sets his sights on directing an epic social commentary picture about tough times in depression-era America, to be entitled *O Brother, Where Art Thou?* (a fictional title eventually used by the Coen Brothers for their own 2000 film, in clever tribute to Sturges). To research his topic, which involves such unpleasantries as suffering, deprivation, and racial inequality Sully insists on disguising himself as a hobo and making his way across the country to experience "real life" firsthand.

Once on the road, assorted adventures, meetings (notably with Veronica Lake's down-on-her-luck ingenue), and mishaps—some hilarious, others surprisingly poignant—transpire before Sully eventually comes to terms with his true calling as a lowbrow moviemaker with a gift for making people laugh. The lesson here is that strained seriousness and forced profundity have far less benefit for the masses than good old-fashioned humor, with its power to help people forget their troubles, if only for a while.

That *Sullivan's Travels* possesses an autobiographical dimension is impossible to deny, with Sturges affirming the value of what he himself did best—making smart comedies with the power to lift viewers' spirits—while ripping the pretentiousness of Hollywood's more sober and "socially committed" filmmakers. Personal statements aside, however, the tour de force script brings together a remarkable range of genres, including slapstick, action, melodrama, social documentary, romance, musical, and prison movie. Though it failed to garner a single Oscar nomination, *Sullivan's Travels* is the most remarkable film in the career of one of America's greatest filmmakers. **SJS**

# HOW GREEN WAS MY VALLEY (1941)

Though John Ford was most famous, of course, for making Westerns, he also had a fondness for all things Irish. Not that this Oscar-winning version of Richard Llewellyn's novel was transported across the Irish Sea from its setting in the Welsh coal-mining valleys; rather, the film is imbued with the same kind of fulsome nostalgia for the eccentric satisfactions of family life in the old country that distinguished the 1952 film *The Quiet Man*. Ford's Wales, in fact, is just as much a country of the mind as was his beloved Ireland (at least in terms of how it was depicted on screen or invoked in words). This explains why Richard Day's beautifully designed mining village, for all the painstaking detail applied to its construction on the Fox backlot, feels like a dream of archetypal Welshness rather than any real village.

That, however, is wholly appropriate to the mood of nostalgia that fuels *How Green Was My Valley* from start to finish. The story is narrated by a man reflecting on his now-distant childhood, when as the youngest son (Roddy McDowall) of the Morgan family, he would see his father (Donald Crisp) and four brothers traipse daily up the hill on the way to the pit. What he recalls are not just the hardships—the perilous working conditions, the threat of poverty, cold, and hunger—and the tragic deaths but also the warm, loving sense of community that reigned in the lives both of the family and of the village as a whole. But that happy togetherness was forever lost when wage cuts brought strikes and conflict between the kindly but traditional patriarch and the (marginally) more militant sons: a conflict that resulted in the boys going off to find better-paid work in the Promised Land of—where else?—America.

The entire film is colored by bittersweet remembrance: by the loss of family, childhood innocence, one's country, and a stern but fair father. It's true Ford idealizes the world he depicts, but that is what makes it so effective. Yes, the film is a tearjerker, it is clichéd (the miners never seem to stop singing), and the accents are an odd mix from all around the United Kingdom and Ireland—but aren't dreams ever thus? **GA**

**U.S.** (Fox) 118 min BW

**Director:** John Ford

**Producer:** Darryl F. Zanuck

**Screenplay:** Philip Dunne, from novel by Richard Llewellyn

**Photography:** Arthur C. Miller

**Music:** Alfred Newman

**Cast:** Walter Pidgeon, Maureen O'Hara, Anna Lee, Donald Crisp, Roddy McDowall, John Loder, Sara Allgood, Barry Fitzgerald, Patric Knowles, Morton Lowry, Arthur Shields, Ann E. Todd, Frederick Worlock, Richard Fraser, Evan S. Evans

**Oscar:** Darryl F. Zanuck (best picture), John Ford (director), Donald Crisp (actor in support role), Richard Day, Nathan Juran, Thomas Little (art direction), Arthur C. Miller (photography)

**Oscar nomination:** Philip Dunne (screenplay), Sara Allgood (actress in support role), James B. Clark (editing), Alfred Newman (music), Edmund H. Hansen (sound)

## THE PALM BEACH STORY (1942)

Rudy Vallee turns in his all-time best performance as a gentle, puny millionaire named John D. Hackensacker III in this brilliant, simultaneously tender and scalding 1942 screwball comedy. Claudette Colbert, married to an ambitious but penniless architectural engineer (Joel McCrea), takes off for Florida and winds up being wooed by Hackensacker. When McCrea shows up she persuades him to pose as her brother. Also on hand are such indelible Sturges creations as the Weenie King (Robert Dudley), the madly destructive Ale and Quail Club, Hackensacker's acerbic sister (Mary Astor), her European boyfriend of obscure national origins, and many Sturges regulars.

The Hackensacker character may be the closest thing to a parodic self-portrait in the Sturges canon, but *The Palm Beach Story* is informed with such wry wisdom and humor that it transcends its personal nature. The part was written for Vallee after Sturges saw him in a film musical, noticed that the audience laughed every time he opened his mouth, and concluded that the man was hilarious without even knowing it. This unawareness played a major role in Sturges's conception of comedy, extending to the gullibility of viewers as well as characters. The frantic opening sequence "gives away" the plot's surprise ending before the audience can even begin to grasp what's going on. As critic James Harvey aptly noted, "In this movie, whenever reality becomes a problem—on the way to Penn Station, for example, when a cab driver played by Frank Faylen agrees to take Colbert there for nothing—it's simply revoked." **JRos**

**U.S.** (Paramount) 88m BW

**Director:** Preston Sturges

**Producer:** Paul Jones

**Screenplay:** Preston Sturges

**Photography:** Victor Milner

**Music:** Victor Young

**Cast:** Claudette Colbert, Joel McCrea, Mary Astor, Rudy Vallee, Sig Arno, Robert Warwick, Arthur Stuart Hull, Torben Meyer, Jimmy Conlin, Victor Potel, William Demarest, Jack Norton, Robert Greig, Roscoe Ates, Dewey Robinson

## NOW, VOYAGER (1942)

The enduring popularity of Irving Rapper's *Now, Voyager* derives from the film's unembarrassed emotional crescendos, its star power, and particularly the pleasure—however perverse—we get from seeing Bette Davis's transformation from ugly duckling to swan (she was nominated for an Academy Award for her performance).

One of the classic American melodramas and the model "makeover" movie, *Now, Voyager* tells the elaborate story of spinster Charlotte Vale (Davis), the impossibly frumpy daughter (her heavy eyebrows and glasses tell it all) of an oppressive Boston matriarch. Psychiatrist Dr. Jaquith (Claude Rains) rescues Charlotte by sending her to a sanitarium, where her cure is signaled by the doctor's dramatic breaking of her eyeglasses (what "normal" woman needs them?) and her reemergence (set to a dramatic Max Steiner score) as movie star Bette Davis: gorgeous from plucked brows to two-toned pumps. This newly hatched butterfly goes on a cruise and falls in love with Jerry Durrance (Paul Henreid), a married man; their romance is told largely through the expressive use of cigarettes, which imply the sex that is not seen on screen. The plot spirals wonderfully out from there, ending with the decision not to pursue more than friendship with Charlotte's famous, if cryptic, lines: "Oh, Jerry, don't let's ask for the moon. We have the stars." **MO**

**U.S.** (Warner Bros.) 117m BW

**Director:** Irving Rapper

**Producer:** Hal B. Wallis

**Screenplay:** Casey Robinson, from novel by Olive Higgins Prouty

**Photography:** Sol Polito

**Music:** Max Steiner

**Cast:** Bette Davis, Paul Henreid, Claude Rains, Gladys Cooper, Bonita Granville, John Loder, Ilka Chase, Lee Patrick, Franklin Pangborn, Katharine Alexander, James Rennie, Mary Wickes

**Oscar:** Max Steiner (music)

**Oscar nomination:** Bette Davis (actress), Gladys Cooper (actress in support role)

## CASABLANCA (1942)

U.S. (Warner Bros.) 102m BW
**Language:** English / French / German
**Director:** Michael Curtiz
**Producer:** Hal B. Wallis, Jack L. Warner
**Screenplay:** Murray Burnett, Joan Alison
**Photography:** Arthur Edeson
**Music:** M.K. Jerome, Jack Scholl, Max Steiner
**Cast:** Humphrey Bogart, Ingrid Bergman, Paul Henreid, Claude Rains, Conrad Veidt, Sydney Greenstreet, Peter Lorre, S.Z. Sakall, Madeleine LeBeau, Dooley Wilson, Joy Page, John Qualen, Leonid Kinskey, Curt Bois
**Oscar:** Hal B. Wallis (best picture), Michael Curtiz (director), Julius J. Epstein, Philip G. Epstein, Howard Koch (screenplay)
**Oscar nomination:** Humphrey Bogart (actor), Claude Rains (actor in support role), Arthur Edeson (photography), Owen Marks (editing), Max Steiner (music)

The most beloved Academy Award Best Picture winner of all, this romantic war melodrama epitomizes the 1940s craze for studio-bound exotica, with the Warners lot transformed into a fantastical North Africa that has far more resonance than any mere real place possibly could. *Casablanca* also offers more cult performers, quotable lines, instant clichés, and Hollywood chutzpah than any other film of the movies' golden age.

Humphrey Bogart's Rick ("of all the gin joints..."), in white dinner jacket or belted trenchcoat, and Ingrid Bergman's Ilsa ("I know that I'll never have the strength to leave you again"), a vision in creations more suited to a studio floor than a desert city, moon over each other in a café-casino as that haunting tune ("As Time Goes By") tinkles in the background, transporting them back to a simpler life before the war soured everything. But the best performance comes from Claude Rains as the cynical but romantic police chief Renault ("round up the usual suspects"), a wry observer of life's absurdities who is at once an opportunist survivor and the film's truest romantic—fully deserving of the famous final moments ("this could be the start of a beautiful friendship") that show it is he not Ilsa who is the fitting partner for Rick's newly-dedicated-to-freedom hero.

Also memorable in an enormous supporting cast: Paul Henried's Czech patriot Victor Laszlo, leading the scum of the continent in a rousing rendition of "La Marseilleise" that drowns out the Nazi sing-along and restores even the most ardent collaborationists and parasites to patriotic fervor; Peter Lorre's hustler Ugarte, shyly admitting that he trusts Rick because the man despises him; Conrad Veidt's heel-clicking Nazi villain Major Strasser, reaching to make a phone call he'll never complete; Dooley Wilson's loyal Sam, stroking the piano and exchanging looks with the leads; S. Z. Sakall's blubbery majordomo Carl, a displaced Austro-Hungarian sweating despite the ceiling fan; and Sydney Greenstreet's unlikely Arab-Italian entrepreneur Ferrari, squatting befezzed on what looks like a magic carpet. Even the extras are brilliantly cast, adding to the lively, seductive, populated feel of a movie that, more than any other, its fans have wanted to inhabit—an impulse that fuels Woody Allen's charming homage in *Play It Again Sam*.

Curtiz tells a complicated, gimmicky story, weighted down with exposition and structured around a midpoint Paris flashback that breaks most of the screenwriting rules, with so little fuss and so much confidence that the whole assembly seems seamless even though it was apparently rewritten from day to day so that Bergman did not know until the shooting of the final scene whether she would fly off with Henreid or stick around with Bogey. Lasting cult greatness came about through its attitude, but also its rare sense of the incomplete—made before the war was over, it dares to leave its characters literally up in the air or out in the desert, leaving its original audiences and the many who have discovered the film over the years to wonder what happened to these people (whose petty problems don't amount to "a hill of beans") during the next few turbulent years. **KN**

# TO BE OR NOT TO BE (1942)

**U.S.** (Romaine) 99m BW

**Director:** Ernst Lubitsch

**Producer:** Alexander Korda, Ernst Lubitsch

**Screenplay:** Melchior Lengyel, Edwin Justus Mayer

**Photography:** Rudolph Maté

**Music:** Werner R. Heymann, Miklós Rózsa

**Cast:** Carole Lombard, Jack Benny, Robert Stack, Felix Bressart, Lionel Atwill, Stanley Ridges, Sig Ruman, Tom Dugan, Charles Halton, George Lynn, Henry Victor, Maude Eburne, Halliwell Hobbes, Miles Mander

**Oscar nomination:** Werner R. Heymann (music)

"What he did to Shakespeare, we are now doing to Poland," jokes a German colonel about a hammy thespian in Ernst Lubitsch's outrageous wartime black comedy. In an age when nothing is too sacred or serious to be lampooned, it is difficult to imagine the controversy that originally surrounded Lubitsch's sparklingly witty, screamingly funny screwball anti-Nazi farce.

Lubitsch was a German Jew who settled in the United States in the 1920s and made a string of smashing, inimitably stylish comedies. Even so, he was dubious when Melchior Lengyel, who conceived Lubitsch's *Ninotchka* (1939), pitched his concept about an acting troupe who impersonate members of the Gestapo to save Polish resistants. But eventually the director felt—and hoped—that Americans would be more concerned about Poland if he could arouse their sympathy through laughter by applying the celebrated Lubitsch Touch (with a sophisticated screenplay by Edwin Justus Mayer) to the Nazis and their adversaries.

Comic Jack Benny in his finest hour plays Josef Tura, vain actor-manager of a theater company, forever at odds with his flirtatious wife and leading lady Maria, played by delicious Carole Lombard (who took the part over the misgivings of husband Clark Gable and was tragically killed before the film's release). After a battle of the sexes setup, the Turas have bigger things to worry about—like the invasion of Poland—and they become embroiled in espionage. The tone shifts with a betrayal and shifts again when Tura's bickering troupe put aside their differences and devise an audacious masquerade to extract Maria and her Resistance hero admirer (Robert Stack) from Gestapo headquarters.

It has often been remarked that this is Lubitsch's funniest film because it is his most serious—proven by Mel Brooks's 1983 remake, which featured amusing mugging but missed the urgency of desperate deeds in a dangerous time. Sardonic laughs (like Tom Dugan's fiendish Hitler impersonation) do not obscure the substance of the satire, the film's insight into the evil ordinary men are capable of when they get a taste of power, or its engaging message that even egotistical actors can do something swell when they act like human beings. **AE**

# CAT PEOPLE (1942)

The Val Lewton/RKO–produced horror films of the 1940s are a high point of the horror genre, films renowned for a subtle aura of dread rather than gross special effects. *Cat People*, directed by Jacques Tourneur, presents the tragic tale of Irena the cat-woman, who fears she will destroy those she loves most.

Ollie Reed (Kent Smith) spots sweet and sexy Irena Dubrovna (Simone Simon) sketching the black panther at the zoo. Their whirlwind romance leads to marriage, but signs of trouble show up early. Irena seems obsessed with the big cats and listens to their cries ("like a woman") in the night. But when Ollie takes a cute kitten home to her, it hisses and spits. "Strange," the pet store owner tells Ollie, "cats can always tell if there's something not right about a person."

What's wrong with Irena remains fundamentally ambiguous, and that is a strength of this film. Is she a repressed young woman afraid to consummate her marriage, as her psychiatrist (Tom Conway) implies, or heir to the evil Satan-worshipping witches of her home village back in Serbia? Irena fears that strong passions of lust, jealousy, or anger will unleash the murderous panther within her. These passions do run amok: in one scene she destroys her amorous shrink, and in other scary sequences she stalks her rival Alice (Jane Randolph), who works with Ollie and also loves him.

*Cat People* will not scare the pants off you, but neither does it overdo the sexual angle as did the ludicrous Paul Schrader remake of 1982, with its bondage scenes and graphic violence. It is creepily effective, particularly in its use of light and shadows. In a justly famous scene, Irena follows Alice to a basement swimming pool, forcing her to tread water in panic while mysterious sounds erupt and shadows flicker across reflections of watery light.

Though somewhat dated, *Cat People* features sharp dialogue. Alice is likeable as "the new kind of other woman"—smart, independent, decent, and caring. Ollie is probably too bland to merit the love of such wonderful women. It is Irena who remains central and lingers in the viewer's mind, one of horror's most sympathetic monsters (like Boris Karloff as the Frankenstein creature). Simon is charming—a bit "off" with her catlike visage, sweet, sad, and unwillingly dangerous. **CFr**

**U.S.** (RKO) 73m BW

**Director:** Jacques Tourneur

**Producer:** Val Lewton, Lou L. Ostrow

**Screenplay:** DeWitt Bodeen

**Photography:** Nicholas Musuraca

**Music:** Roy Webb

**Cast:** Simone Simon, Kent Smith, Tom Conway, Jane Randolph, Jack Holt

**U.S.** (Mercury, RKO) 88m BW

**Director:** Orson Welles, Fred Fleck

**Producer:** Jack Moss, George Schaefer, Orson Welles

**Screenplay:** Orson Welles, from novel by Booth Tarkington

**Photography:** Stanley Cortez

**Music:** Bernard Herrmann, Roy Webb

**Cast:** Joseph Cotten, Dolores Costello, Anne Baxter, Tim Holt, Agnes Moorehead, Ray Collins, Erskine Sanford, Richard Bennett, Orson Welles (narrator)

**Oscar nomination:** Orson Welles (best picture), Agnes Moorehead (actress in support role), Stanley Cortez (photography), Albert S. D'Agostino, A. Roland Fields, Darrell Silvera (art direction)

# THE MAGNIFICENT AMBERSONS (1942)

The unprecedented deal with RKO Pictures that Orson Welles signed in 1940 for two films allowed total creative freedom but within strict budgets. *The Magnificent Ambersons* is the too-often-overlooked second movie made under that contract. It was undertaken after the completion of *Citizen Kane* (1941) but before the wrath of William Randolph Hearst and his own unreliable genius "wrecked" Welles's career as a Hollywood filmmaker. Welles's desire to bring Booth Tarkington's novel *The Ambersons* (he also wrote *Alice Adams, Monsieur Beaucaire,* and the Penrod stories—all film staples) to the big screen was obviously a more personal project for him than *Kane*. He had already completed an adaptation of the novel with the Mercury Theatre, which was presented on the Air on radio.

Rooted in the turn-of-the-century haut bourgeois world he remembered from his own childhood, *The Magnificent Ambersons* is the story of George Amberson Minafer (Tim Holt), the talented but unlikable offspring of an aristocratic family who receives the comeuppance everyone wants for him. Apart from all the other parallels, Welles's suppressed first name was George. As this must have seemed not only autobiographical but, at the stage the film was being made, horribly prophetic, it is to Welles's credit that his ego let him cast Holt, a juvenile cowboy taking a rare serious role (as he would again only in 1948's *The Treasure of the Sierra Madre*), as the lead.

The first 70 minutes are a revelation of creative genius, more than equalling *Kane*. The film opens with a charming but pointed lecture on male fashions, narrated by Welles and displayed by Joseph Cotten, then recreates precisely the cluttered, stuffy, lively, strange world of the Ambersons that is gradually torn apart by the 20th-century—symbolized, presciently, by the motor car—and its own hidden weaknesses. Working with cinematographer Stanley Cortez rather than Gregg Toland, Welles crafts a film that is as visually striking as *Kane*, but which also manages a warmer, melancholy nostalgia for sleigh rides and *cartes de visite* even as it shows how the iniquities of a class-bound society constrain decent folk to lifelong misery. Enterprising Eugene (Cotten) loses his wellborn love Isabel (Costello) to a clod from a prominent family but is unable to separate himself from the magnificence of the Ambersons even as the march of time reduces it to pathetic shreds.

Although *Citizen Kane* is all set pieces, *The Magnificent Ambersons* is seamless: typical is a ballroom sequence as the camera whirls through the dancers, picking up snatches of plot and dialogue, following a large cast, surrendering to music and history. It's a tragedy that Welles's original cut was taken away—admittedly, while he was in Brazil having a good time and not returning phone calls—and cut down. In the last ten minutes, the cast adopt fixed expressions as they struggle through a happy ending stuck on by someone else (probably editor Robert Wise). It's like a Groucho moustache daubed onto the Mona Lisa, though Alfonso Arau's 2002 remake, which sticks to Welles's original scripted ending, found little favor: the magic was obviously unrepeatable. **KN**

U.S. (Warner Bros.) 126m BW

**Director:** Michael Curtiz

**Producer:** William Cagney, Hal B. Wallis, Jack L. Warner

**Screenplay:** Robert Buckner, Edmund Joseph

**Photography:** James Wong Howe

**Music:** George M. Cohan, Ray Heindorf, Heinz Roemheld

**Cast:** James Cagney, Joan Leslie, Walter Huston, Richard Whorf, Irene Manning, George Tobias, Rosemary DeCamp, Jeanne Cagney, Frances Langford, George Barbier, S.Z. Sakall, Walter Catlett, Douglas Croft, Eddie Foy Jr., Minor Watson

**Oscar:** James Cagney (actor), Ray Heindorf, Heinz Roemheld (music), Nathan Levinson (sound)

**Oscar nomination:** Jack L. Warner, Hal B. Wallis, William Cagney (best picture), Michael Curtiz (director), Robert Buckner (screenplay), Walter Huston (actor in support role), George Amy (editing)

# YANKEE DOODLE DANDY (1942)

How terribly easy it would be from a postmodern, politically correct, and sophisticated perspective to regard *Yankee Doodle Dandy* as jingoistic propaganda. Indeed, this flag-waving musical extravaganza biopic, detailing the life of patriotic Irish American song-and-dance man George M. Cohan (the first performer to be awarded the Congressional Medal of Honor), gushes with sentimental, simplistic musical numbers invariably characterized by Cohan's trademark stiff-kneed, effervescent, brash dancing style and championing through their lyrics the most stolid American institutions: "Grand Old Flag," "Give My Regards to Broadway," "Over There," and the title song, to name a few. The film is a flashback—told by a modest Cohan to FDR—that ends with a self-conscious advertisement for intervention: "I wouldn't worry about this country if I were you. We've got this thing licked. Where else in the world could a plain guy like me come in and talk things over with the head man?"

But such a cynical reading would fail grossly to miss something surprising and touching and grand that runs through *Yankee Doodle Dandy* like a clear river, and that is James Cagney's magnificent sincerity in the title role. This is evident in his way of embarrassedly smiling to punctuate his thoughts, in his soft and civilized speaking voice; in the astonishing virtuosity of his dancing which is persuasive and original in style, unrelentingly athletic while also being childish, playful, and beautifully meaningless; and in something we rarely see onscreen anymore since alienated distance has overtaken Hollywood performance, and that is Cagney's complete and loving belief in everything he does. Michael Curtiz's direction never overplays him, James Wong Howe's lush black-and-white cinematography never fails to show every nuance of his posture and expression in articulate light. And when his hoofer father (Walter Huston) is falling away into death, with Georgie at his bedside, Cagney gives in to a rush of honest feeling that carries him into tears. So much, in fact, do we care for this man we forget we are watching a performance. Cagney has become Cohan. Even more, he has become the optimistic spirit of the screen. **MP**

# MESHES OF THE AFTERNOON (1943)

**U.S.** 18m Silent BW

**Director:** Maya Deren, Alexander Hammid

**Screenplay:** Maya Deren

**Photography:** Alexander Hammid

**Music:** Teiji Ito (added 1952)

**Cast:** Maya Deren, Alexander Hammid

A famous image from the avant-garde classic *Meshes of the Afternoon* shows its auteur and star, Maya Deren, at a window, tree leaves reflected lyrically in the glass; she looks out wistfully, hands on the pane. This image has metamorphosed many times—into Anna Karina at a futuristic motel window (*Alphaville* [1965]); into Annette Bening in a padded cell (*In Dreams* [1998]); into Caroline Dulcey in her gleaming, white apartment (*Romance* [1999]). Whatever its mutation, the image remains a vivid, dreamy, terrifying picture of women's confinement.

*Meshes* comes from that branch of the American avant-garde taken with a special kind of storytelling, the surrealist journey of a figure through an ever-changing dreamscape. Deren, working from her own fantasies and shooting in her own home, made an intuitive leap that has given the film its lasting resonance. Her vision of Los Angeles links this mythopoetic impulse with an atmosphere that is proto-film noir in its use of architecture and interior design, not to mention its atmosphere of dread and menace.

This was one of the first films to make the indelible link between a woman's gothic experience of coming unglued—splintered into multiple personalities, plagued by visions, slipping between alternate realities—and the sunny spaces of home, whose every tiny facet, from the slope of the lounge room staircase to the kitchen table's bread knife, is heightened. For Deren, it is the domestic everyday that lays the meshes that ensnare and traumatize women.

Among the many arts in which Deren involved herself, dance was prominent. Her extraordinary body language in *Meshes* marries choreography to ordinary rituals, another combination that influenced women's cinema for decades. Deren used her movements as a way to trigger montage, to suggest rhythmic forms and create pictorial shapes: In this flux of dream projections, she is the only anchor.

Yet, for all her movement, the last shot of *Meshes* reveals that this modern heroine has probably not even moved from her lounge chair. But what she has imagined manages to destroy her; this is the tale of a death drive, of a dream that kills. **AM**

**G.B.** (Crown) 80m BW
**Director:** Humphrey Jennings
**Producer:** Ian Dalrymple
**Photography:** C.M. Pennington-Richards
**Music:** William Alwyn
**Cast:** Philip Dickson, George Gravett, Fred Griffiths, Johnny Houghton, Loris Rey

# FIRES WERE STARTED (1943)

Humphrey Jennings's wartime classic was previewed in a longer version with a more attention-grabbing title, *I Was a Fireman*, which was oddly unsuitable for its resolutely collectivist vision of blitzed Britain. In 1942, *Fires Were Started* was considered a "documentary" and set against the commercial tradition of filmmaking, hailed as more authentic than an Ealing fiction film on the same subject, *The Bells Go Down*. Now, its use of nonprofessional actors who happened to be real firemen playing fictionally named characters in an archetypal story of a day on shift and a fire at night under a full moon ("a bomber's moon") looks far more like neorealism or even straight off-Hollywood filmmaking. There is some newsreel stock footage, but the fire station is a set and the fire consists of physical effects. It has a rough credibility that is sometimes helped by the awkwardness of a few players—though the reactions to the tragic death of the most lovably cockney of the team feel forced ("Jacko's copped it") and the moral ("snap out of it") misses the "who's Joe?" from *Only Angels Have Wings* (1939).

Among the cast are Fred Griffiths, who went pro and became a familiar character actor, and—in the role of the ad exec newbie who is shown the ropes—William Sansom, who became a writer of interestingly creepy short fiction. It's the epitome of Angus Calder's "Myth of the Blitz," with a cross-class, even multicultural (we see an East End Chinaman) group knuckling down to get the job done, and no sign of any pompous stuffed shirts among the well-spoken bureaucrats or telephone operators whose jobs are just as vital to fire fighting as the hose wielders (a much-parodied moment has the telephone operator apologize for the interruption after diving under her desk when a bomb hits).

The fiery finale, in which a blaze is controlled before it sets light to a munitions ship, delivers action and suspense. But Jennings seems less stirred by it than the acutely observed buildup in which he catches the men singing round the piano, playing pool, training, doing menial work-related tasks, and generally acting like real people. **KN**

## THE MAN IN GREY (1943)

English cinema is perhaps best known for realist dramas, but an important second tradition is the costume melodrama, of which *The Man in Grey* is probably the finest example and one of the more popular films Gainsborough Studios ever made. The plot is fairly forgettable, involving two young women whose lives interestingly intersect. Clarissa (Phyllis Calvert) marries the cruelly indifferent Marquis of Rohan (James Mason), but her friend Hesther (Margaret Lockwood) introduces her to another rogue, the bold and immoral Rokeby (Stewart Granger). Soon the pair have switched partners, but all ends badly as Clarissa dies miserably and the crazed Marquis beats Hesther to death.

The plot, however, derived from a subliterary novel by Lady Eleanor Smith, is not the main focus of director Leslie Arliss's efforts. Calvert and Lockwood turn in suitably intense performances as the contrasting blonde- and dark-haired leads, and Mason is effectively reptilian as the Marquis. The real star of the film, however, is its art design. Regency period England is faithfully resurrected with its elaborate interior decor and European furniture, and its elaborate and elegant dress for actors and actresses alike. The sumptuous look of *The Man in Grey* provides a perfect contrast to its exploration of the dark underside of aristocratic life, with the story's gothic elements eliciting a suitable frisson from the absorbed viewer. **RBP**

**G.B.** (Gainsborough) 116m BW

**Director:** Leslie Arliss

**Producer:** Edward Black

**Screenplay:** Leslie Arliss, Margaret Kennedy

**Photography:** Arthur Crabtree

**Music:** Cedric Mallabey

**Cast:** Margaret Lockwood, James Mason, Phyllis Calvert, Stewart Granger, Helen Haye, Raymond Lovell, Nora Swinburne, Martita Hunt, Jane Gill-Davis, Amy Veness, Stuart Lindsell, Diana King, Beatrice Varley

## THE LIFE AND DEATH OF COLONEL BLIMP (1943)

Clive Wynne-Candy (Roger Livesey) is a veteran of both the Boer War and World War I, twice retired, who believes that all of life's conflicts can be met with honor and decorum. He doesn't realize that the world has changed around him, and that his old-fashioned dictums of behavior may no longer apply in the World War II arena, yet with the stubbornness of a good soldier he holds firm to his beliefs and hurtles forward.

Michael Powell and Emeric Pressburger made *The Life and Death of Colonel Blimp* at the height of World War II, when London was being bombed nightly by the Germans. A comedy of manners may not appear the best way to address current events, but the Powell/Pressburger team once again comes through, delicately revealing the horrible truth of modern warfare with grace and humor. It doesn't hurt that they tell the story through three romances, as Livesey woos the ever-luminous Deborah Kerr (in three different roles) over the years. It all adds up to one of the most ambitious and impressive achievements of not just Powell and Pressburger but in all of British cinema. **JKl**

**G.B.** (Independent, Archers) 163 m Technicolor

**Director:** Michael Powell, Emeric Pressburger

**Producer:** Michael Powell, Emeric Pressburger, Richard Vernon

**Screenplay:** Michael Powell, Emeric Pressburger

**Photography:** Georges Périnal

**Music:** Allan Gray

**Cast:** James McKechnie, Neville Mapp, Vincent Holman, Roger Livesey, David Hutcheson, Spencer Trevor, Roland Culver, James Knight, Deborah Kerr, Dennis Arundell, David Ward, Jan Van Loewen, Valentine Dyall, Carl Jaffe, Albert Lieven

**U.S.** (RKO) 69m BW

**Director:** Jacques Tourneur

**Producer:** Val Lewton

**Screenplay:** Inez Wallace, Curt Siodmak

**Photography:** J. Roy Hunt

**Music:** Roy Webb

**Cast:** James Ellison, Frances Dee, Tom Conway, Edith Barrett, James Bell, Christine Gordon, Theresa Harris, Sir Lancelot, Darby Jones, Jeni Le Gon

# I WALKED WITH A ZOMBIE (1943)

The second Val Lewton–Jacques Tourneur horror film, *I Walked with a Zombie*, transposes the plot of *Jane Eyre* into the West Indies, with a young nurse (Frances Dee) discovering that her employer's apparently catatonic wife (Christine Gordon) has been transformed by voodoo into one of the walking dead. Framed by a calypso which fills in the plot background ("Shame and Sorrow in the Family"), this is a remarkably eerie picture.

Heroine Betsy Connell (Dee) succumbs to an exquisitely-conjured atmosphere of the supernatural, yet works hard to understand the culture of natives other films would dismiss as superstitious. Here, though, they turn out to be far more tuned in to what is happening than any of the supposedly civilized white characters. As in many of Lewton's films, the most memorable sequence is a night-time walk, with Dee leading the blonde zombie through the cane fields, coming up against an unforgettable bug-eyed island creature (Darby Jones). *I Walked With a Zombie* uses Caribbean folklore and weird religious imagery (a figurehead of St. Sebastian) to spice up a romantic tangle, one that ends with nobody happy and the villain lured into the waves after his zombie beloved. About as far from Bela Lugosi in *The Corpse Vanishes* as could possibly be imagined. **KN**

**U.S.** (RKO) 71m BW

**Director:** Mark Robson

**Producer:** Val Lewton

**Screenplay:** DeWitt Bodeen, Charles O'Neal

**Photography:** Nicholas Musuraca

**Music:** Roy Webb

**Cast:** Tom Conway, Jean Brooks, Isabel Jewell, Kim Hunter, Evelyn Brent, Erford Gage, Ben Bard, Hugh Beaumont, Chef Milani, Marguerita Sylva

# THE SEVENTH VICTIM (1943)

Perhaps the best of the run of terrific RKO horror films produced by Val Lewton in the 1940s, *The Seventh Victim* is a strikingly modern, poetically doom-laden picture. Naïve orphan Mary Gibson (Kim Hunter) comes to Manhattan in search of her strange elder sister Jacqueline (Jean Brooks, with a memorable Cleopatra wig) and learns she was mixed up with a sect of chic diabolists who now want to drive her to suicide for betraying their cult.

Director Mark Robson stages several remarkable suspense sequences—two Satanists trying to get rid of a corpse in a crowded subway train, Brooks's pursuit through the city by sinister figures and her own neuroses—and indulges in weirdly arty touches that take the horror film away from traditional witchcraft toward something very like existential angst. *The Seventh Victim* is full of things that must have been startling in 1943 and are still unusual now: a gaggle of varied lesbian characters (not all unsympathetic), a heroine who comes to seem as calculating as the villains, and a desperate finish which contrasts a dying woman (Elizabeth Russell) dressed up to go out on the town for the last time with the end-of-her-tether Jacqueline as she shuts herself up in a grim rented room to hang herself. **KN**

# THE OX-BOW INCIDENT (1943)

A key film in the history of the Western, one of many made in the 1940s which showed that the Western—previously a genre with low cultural prestige—could take on important issues. In a small Nevada town in 1885, a rumor spreads that a local rancher has been killed by rustlers. While the sheriff is out of town a lynch mob is formed and captures three passing strangers. Despite their protestations of innocence, the men are hanged, only for the perpetrators to discover the rancher is not dead and the real rustlers have been apprehended.

This concise little film (only 75 minutes long) packs a good deal of star power. Henry Fonda is a local cowboy, shown initially as a thoughtless saloon brawler, who eventually stands up against the mob. The three victims are played by Dana Andrews, a patently innocent family man; Anthony Quinn, a Mexican drifter; and Francis Ford, brother of the more illustrious John, a senile old man. Frank Conroy is excellent as a blustering ex-Confederate major who bullies his son into helping with the hanging, and Jane Darwell, notable as Ma Joad in John Ford's *The Grapes of Wrath* three years earlier, is a merciless old cattlewoman.

*The Ox-Bow Incident* makes a powerful plea for the rule of law as the basis of civilization. Besides Fonda, the only townspeople who resist the mob hysteria are a storekeeper (Harry Davenport) and a black preacher (Leigh Whipper), who has more reason than most to protest, having seen his own brother lynched. At the end, when the truth has sunk in, Fonda shames the mob by reading out a letter written by Andrews's character to his wife.

Darryl Zanuck, head of 20th-Century Fox at the time, insisted the film be cheaply shot on studio sets; in fact, the confined spaces give *The Ox-Bow Incident* a greater intensity than it might have derived from expansive Western landscapes. The script is based on a highly accomplished first novel by Walter Van Tilburg Clark, a Nevadan whose later novel, *Track of the Cat*, was also filmed by William Wellman. **EB**

**U.S.** (Fox) 75m BW

**Director:** William A. Wellman

**Producer:** Lamar Trotti

**Screenplay:** Lamar Trotti, from novel by Walter Van Tilburg Clark

**Photography:** Arthur C. Miller

**Music:** Cyril J. Mockridge

**Cast:** Henry Fonda, Dana Andrews, Mary Beth Hughes, Anthony Quinn, William Eythe, Harry Morgan, Jane Darwell, Matt Briggs, Harry Davenport, Frank Conroy, Marc Lawrence, Paul Hurst, Victor Kilian, Chris-Pin Martin, Willard Robertson

**Oscar nomination:** Lamar Trotti (best picture)

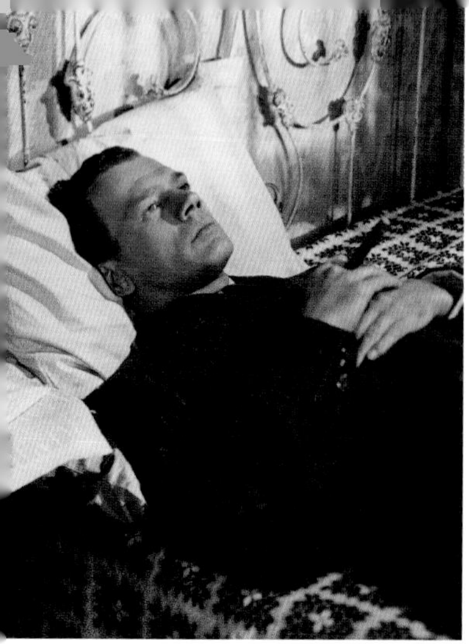

# SHADOW OF A DOUBT (1943)

When interviewed by admirer and famous acolyte François Truffaut, Alfred Hitchcock referred to *Shadow of a Doubt* as his favorite film. Tellingly, it's also one of his least flashy works, a quiet character study set in the heart of suburbia. Although the heart of his suburbia is still rotten with murder and deceit, Hitchcock emphasizes traditional suspense beats over intricate set pieces, stocking the story with just as much uneasy humor as suspense.

Charlie (Teresa Wright) is elated when her uncle and namesake Charlie (played to smarmy perfection by Joseph Cotton) comes to visit her and her sick mother. She soon suspects her revered Uncle Charlie is actually a serial killer, "the Merry Widow Murderer," on the run from his latest killing. Once on to her suspicions, her Uncle Charlie doesn't seem interested in leaving behind any loose ends, but the younger Charlie doesn't know how to reconcile her affection for her uncle with her fears.

Hitchcock actually shot *Shadow of a Doubt* on location, in the small town of Santa Rosa, California, the better to tear apart the flimsy façade and expose the bland, safe suburbs for the hotbed of secrets it no doubt is. The script, written by Thornton Wilder with input from Hitchcock's wife Alma Reville, takes perverse glee in destroying preconceived notions of quiet, small town life. The film is also peppered with numerous references to twins and the duality of good and evil, paralleling the trustful and innocent Charlie with her dangerous and deceitful uncle.

Dimitri Tiomkin's score keeps the suspense ratcheted up, particularly his "Merry Widow" waltz—the signifier of Uncle Charlie's guilt and the haunting motif that represents the horrific inclinations he can barely disguise or suppress. A pair of nosey neighbors also offer a running commentary, discussing the various means and methods by which a murder might be committed and then covered up. That a real murder lurks right next door provides dollops of ironic humor. The neighbors continue to ruminate on various homicidal scenarios as Charlie races to settle her conflicted feelings for her Uncle Charlie before he permanently does it for her. **JKl**

**U.S.** (Skirball, Universal) 108m BW
**Director:** Alfred Hitchcock
**Producer:** Jack H. Skirball
**Screenplay:** Gordon McDonell, Thornton Wilder
**Photography:** Joseph A. Valentine
**Music:** Dimitri Tiomkin
**Cast:** Teresa Wright, Joseph Cotten, Macdonald Carey, Henry Travers, Patricia Collinge, Hume Cronyn, Wallace Ford, Edna May Wonacott, Charles Bates, Irving Bacon, Clarence Muse, Janet Shaw, Estelle Jewell
**Oscar nomination:** Gordon McDonell (screenplay)

Italy (ICI) 142m BW
**Language:** Italian
**Director:** Luchino Visconti
**Producer:** Libero Solaroli
**Screenplay:** Luchino Visconti, Mario Alicata
**Photography:** Domenico Scala, Aldo Tonti
**Music:** Giuseppe Rosati
**Cast:** Clara Calamai, Massimo Girotti, Dhia Cristiani, Elio Marcuzzo, Vittorio Duse, Michele Riccardini, Juan de Landa

# OSSESSIONE (1943)

One of the great speculative games one can play with cinema history centers on Luchino Visconti's *Ossessione*: what if this had been the picture that heralded the arrival of an exciting new film movement from Italy, and not Roberto Rossellini's *Open City* in 1945? It would have indeed been interesting, but alas we'll never know; because Visconti's screenplay was clearly lifted from James M. Cain's *The Postman Always Rings Twice*, Cain and his publishers kept it off American screens until 1976, when it had its much belated premiere at the New York Film Festival. Cain had just died, and probably never saw it—a pity, because he would have discovered the best cinematic adaptation of his work.

Massimo Girotti is Gino Costa, a sweaty, T-shirt-clad drifter who lands a job in a roadside café run by portly opera buff Bragana (Juan de Landa). Bragana has a wife, Giovanna (the luminous Clara Calamai, Rossellini's first choice for the Anna Magnani role in *Open City*), and it isn't long before Gino and Giovanna are in each others arms, making plans to get away. Adhering closely to Cain's storyline, Visconti is immensely aided by the sheer physical chemistry between Calamai and Girotti; all of Cain's descriptions of burning flesh and animal lust are rendered in *Ossessione* with an almost frightening intensity. Consequently, the whole economic imperative for the eventual murder takes somewhat of a backseat here. Visconti also doesn't avoid the obviously homoerotic overtones of Gino's relationship with "lo Spagnolo" (Elio Marcuzzo) a Spanish street performer with whom he goes on the road for a while, rather remarkable when one considers the film was made under the fascist regime.

One scene that surely would have delighted Cain, himself the son of an opera singer, is the local opera competition in which Bragana performs. A gruff and somewhat unapproachable figure—a far cry from Cecil Kellaway's bumbling fool in Tay Garnett's 1946 Hollywood version of the novel—he suddenly comes alive as he bursts into an aria, with a final flourish that brings the assembled listeners to their feet. *Ossessione* could have been the great example of the union of American film noir and Italian neorealism; instead it remains something like the ancestral missing link for both movements. **RP**

# MEET ME IN ST. LOUIS (1944)

**U.S.** (MGM) 113m Technicolor

**Director:** Vincente Minnelli

**Producer:** Roger Edens, Arthur Freed

**Screenplay:** Irving Brecher, Fred F. Finklehoffe, from novel by Sally Benson

**Photography:** George J. Folsey

**Music:** Ralph Blane, Hugh Martin, Nacio Herb Brown, Arthur Freed, George E. Stoll

**Cast:** Judy Garland, Margaret O'Brien, Mary Astor, Lucille Bremer, Leon Ames, Tom Drake, Marjorie Main, Harry Davenport, June Lockhart, Henry H. Daniels Jr., Joan Carroll, Hugh Marlowe, Robert Sully, Chill Wills, Gary Gray, Dorothy Raye

**Oscar nomination:** Irving Brecher, Fred F. Finklehoffe (screenplay), George J. Folsey (photography), George E. Stoll (music), Ralph Blane, Hugh Martin (song)

A little girl named Tootie (Margaret O'Brien), crying and angry, breaks domestic rank and runs out to the snow. Once there, she sets to destroying her beloved snowmen—a symbol of everything that is stable and reassuring in her familial existence—with a vigor and venom that is extremely disquieting. Who would ever have thought that Judy Garland singing "Have Yourself a Merry Little Christmas" could have such a devastating effect on a child's delicate psyche—or, indeed, on ours?

Vincente Minnelli's *Meet Me in St. Louis* is one of the most unusual and highly-charged musicals in Hollywood history. It blends the two genres at which Minnelli was most adept—musical and melodrama—and even, in its darkest moments (such as a sequence devoted to Halloween terrors), edges toward being a horror movie. It is also a film that, then as now, offers itself up to be read in starkly contrasting ways: either as a perfectly innocent and naïve celebration of traditional family values, or else a brooding meditation on everything that tears the family unit apart from within. Put another way: Is it comforting, "safety valve" entertainment that admits to just enough that is problematic in order to smooth out and reinforce the status quo, or is it—almost despite itself—a subversive gesture at the heart of the Hollywood system, a howl of unrepressed rage like Tootie's slaughter of imaginary snow people?

Yes, I am talking about the same film in which Garland moons and croons "The Boy Next Door" and—in a showstopping highlight—sways with a pack of colorful passengers as she belts out "The Trolley Song" ("Zing, zing, zing went my heartstrings..."). Minnelli's project is quietly ambitious: not merely to tell the story of a lovably "average" family—and the challenges it stoically faces—but to also sketch the history of a bold new 20th-century society defined by events such as the World's Fair.

Minnelli's artistic sensibility—his sexuality is either an open question or an open secret, depending on which Hollywood history you consult—responded well to female yearning and male anxiety, and an excess of both makes this musical unfailingly melodramatic. Patriarchy comes in the cuddly, grumpy form of Leon Ames, valiantly trying to assert his authority in the face of an overwhelmingly female household. The parade of boyfriends for the girls have, likewise, to be prodded, manipulated, and informed of their rightful, mating destiny.

As for the aesthetic challenges of the musical, Minnelli and his collaborators went a long way toward integrating singing and dancing into a whimsical, fairy tale flow of incidents. Songs begin as throwaway phrases, spoken or hummed out in the street or at the door; they suddenly die away as a plot intrigue kicks in.

Beneath the elegant display of filmic style, and the civilized veneer of manners, it is only Tootie who can express emotions that are savage and untamed—as her "exotica" duet with Judy, "Under the Bamboo Tree," jovially indicates. **AM**

U.S. (Warner Bros.) 100m BW

**Director:** Howard Hawks

**Producer:** Howard Hawks, Jack L. Warner

**Screenplay:** Jules Furthman, from novel by Ernest Hemingway

**Photography:** Sidney Hickox

**Music:** Hoagy Carmichael, William Lava, Franz Waxman

**Cast:** Humphrey Bogart, Walter Brennan, Lauren Bacall, Dolores Moran, Hoagy Carmichael, Sheldon Leonard, Walter Szurovy, Marcel Dalio, Walter Sande, Dan Seymour, Aldo Nadi

# TO HAVE AND HAVE NOT (1944)

Coscripted by two Nobel prizewinners, Ernest Hemingway and William Faulkner, allegedly from Hemingway's book of the same title, *To Have and Have Not* was mainly improvised by director Howard Hawks and his peerless cast. One of a run of films made after Humphrey Bogart's triumph in *Casablanca* (1942), this even more romantic picture offers a central love affair that threatens to edge World War II offscreen. Hawks, who discovered Lauren Bacall before Bogart did, eventually felt betrayed by his stars' marriage, but he also in great part created the characters the couple wound up playing in real life.

Set in Vichy, Martinique, as opposed to the novel's Cuba, *To Have and Have Not* once again has Bogart's Yankee ex-pat caught up with the Free French and finally committing to the allied cause. The real-life electricity sparking between Bogie and a debuting Bacall, as the girl who drifts into his life and takes over, leads to a sassy, upbeat ending that sends you home with a greater glow even than the wistful resignation of *Casablanca*. Unlike Rick (Bogart) and Ilsa (Ingrid Bergman) in the earlier film, who choose the greater good over love, Harry and Slim rescue each other from isolationism and are able to maintain their relationship because they are willing to work together to win the war. Hawks would have no patience with a woman who saw her job solely in terms of making a happy home life for the hero and so makes Bacall's Slim as intrepid and daring as Bogart's Harry—not just a love interest, but a partner.

Hawks packs every scene in *To Have and Have Not* with relishable business: hilarious but sexy love talk between the stars ("You do know how to whistle?"), comedy relief sidekick Walter Brennan asking "Was you ever stung by a dead bee?", Hoagy Carmichael singing "Hong Kong Blues" and accompanying a husky Bacall (or is it Andy Williams's voice?) on "How Little We Know?", and Bogie snarling at various petty officials and nasty fascists with the genuine voice of a democratic wiseguy who won't put up with any totalitarian nonsense. When John Huston didn't have an ending for his 1948 Bogart–Bacall thriller *Key Largo*, Hawks gave him the shootout-on-a-boat finish of Hemingway's novel that he had never got around to including in this film. **KN**

# LAURA (1944)

Men adore her. Women admire her. Yet alluring young designer Laura Hunt (Gene Tierney) doesn't take center stage *Laura*, any more than her chilly socialite friend Ann (Judith Anderson); her duplicitous suitor Shelby (Vincent Price); or hard-boiled detective Mark McPherson (Dana Andrews), who, searching for her murderer, falls in love with her ghost. But viciously smarmy author/broadcaster Waldo Lydecker (Clifton Webb) utterly fascinates, adopting Laura as his protégée, making her famous, then fixating upon her life like a spider who has her in its web.

If Otto Preminger's *Laura* intrigues in its jarring mélange of styles—noir psychodrama, melodrama, and crime thriller—then in brief moments of portraiture it becomes monumental. Particularly notable scene: Ann explaining to Laura why it should be she who has Shelby ("We're both losers"); or the romantic tryst at the police station when, turning off the glaring third-degree lights, Mark sees Laura's true radiance. But paramount is Lydecker's poisonous poise when he regales Laura with Shelby's faults. "I'll call him," she says anxiously; "He's not there," Waldo acidly retorts, "He's dining with Ann, didn't you know?" More than doting upon her life he is inhabiting it, perhaps narrative cinema's first example of a man who wishes he were a woman. **MP**

**U.S.** (Fox) 88m BW

**Director:** Otto Preminger, Rouben Mamoulian

**Producer:** Otto Preminger

**Screenplay:** Jay Dratler, Samuel Hoffenstein, Elizabeth Reinhardt, from novel by Vera Caspary

**Photography:** Joseph LaShelle, Lucien Ballard

**Music:** David Raksin

**Cast:** Gene Tierney, Dana Andrews, Clifton Webb, Vincent Price, Judith Anderson, Cy Kendall, Grant Mitchell

**Oscar:** Joseph LaShelle (photography)

**Oscar nomination:** Clifton Webb (actor in support role), Otto Preminger (director), Jay Dratler, Samuel Hoffenstein, Elizabeth Reinhardt (screenplay), Lyle R. Wheeler, Leland Fuller, Thomas Little (art direction)

**U.S.** (MGM) 114m BW
**Director:** George Cukor
**Producer:** Arthur Hornblow Jr.
**Screenplay:** John Van Druten, Walter Reisch, John L. Balderston, from the play *Angel Street* by Patrick Hamilton
**Photography:** Joseph Ruttenberg
**Music:** Bronislau Kaper
**Cast:** Charles Boyer, Ingrid Bergman, Joseph Cotten, Dame May Whitty, Angela Lansbury, Barbara Everest, Emil Rameau, Edmund Breon, Halliwell Hobbes, Tom Stevenson, Heather Thatcher, Lawrence Grossmith
**Oscar:** Ingrid Bergman (actress), Cedric Gibbons, William Ferrari, Edwin B. Willis, Paul Huldschinsky (art direction)
**Oscar nomination:** Arthur Hornblow Jr. (best picture), John L. Balderston, Walter Reisch, John Van Druten (screenplay), Charles Boyer (actor), Angela Lansbury (actress in support role), Joseph Ruttenberg (photography)

# GASLIGHT (1944)

George Cukor's Hollywood version of an earlier British gothic romance is heavy on threatening atmosphere, with a spine-chilling thriller plot. Paula Alquist (Ingrid Bergman) finds herself wooed by the attractive, if strangely possessive, Gregory Anton (Charles Boyer), who seems more interested in the London house Paula owns than in the rather timid woman herself. It turns out that Anton is a clever thief who, some ten years before, had killed Paula's aunt in a failed attempt to steal her fabulously valuable jewels. As he systematically ransacks Paula's house by night, he does his best to convince her, and others, that she is losing her mind. His intention is to put her entirely under his power so that he can have a free hand searching the house. Anton's plot, however, is discovered by Brian Cameron (Joseph Cotten), who, falling in love with the woman he sees mistreated and threatened, intervenes just in time to save her from worse.

While *Gaslight*'s plot is somewhat thin, Cukor draws fine performances from an ensemble cast, including newcomer Angela Lansbury as a saucy servant who, like everything and everyone else in the house, seems to be plotting against its ostensible mistress. With its evocation of persecution and paranoia, *Gaslight* makes an elegant period-piece companion to the film noir series then featured by Hollywood. **RBP**

**G.B.** (Two Cities) 135m Technicolor
**Language:** English / French
**Director:** Laurence Olivier
**Producer:** Dallas Bower, Filippo Del Giudice, Laurence Olivier
**Screenplay:** Dallas Bower, Alan Dent, from play by William Shakespeare
**Photography:** Jack Hildyard, Robert Krasker
**Music:** William Walton
**Cast:** Felix Aylmer, Leslie Banks, Robert Helpmann, Vernon Greeves, Gerald Case, Griffith Jones, Morland Graham, Nicholas Hannen, Michael Warre, Laurence Olivier, Ralph Truman, Ernest Thesiger, Roy Emerton, Robert Newton, Freda Jackson
**Oscar:** Laurence Olivier (honorary award)
**Oscar nomination:** Laurence Olivier (best picture), Laurence Olivier (actor), Paul Sheriff, Carmen Dillon (art direction), William Walton (music)

# HENRY V (1944)

*Henry V* was regarded by the British government as ideal patriotic wartime propaganda, and Laurence Olivier, serving in the Fleet Air Arm, was released to star in it and—after William Wyler had turned it down—to direct it as well. Aiming to preserve both Shakespeare's innately theatrical artifice and the soaring, protocinematic sweep of his imagination, Olivier hit on the device of framing the film within a production in the Globe Theatre itself. As *Henry V* opens, the camera soars over a superbly detailed miniature of Elizabethan London, down into the bustle and bawdy of the Globe audience and into a high-flown stage performance—only to expand exhilaratingly into cinematic space as the action moves toward France.

Throughout, the film plays with different levels of stylization, from the scenes at the French court—which borrow the exquisite colors and naïve perspectives of medieval miniature paintings—to the realism of the battle scenes, inspired in their exuberant dynamism by Sergei Eisenstein's *Aleksandr Nevsky* (1938). The rhythm of Shakespeare's text, discreetly trimmed to fit the war effort—the three English traitors are dropped, for a start—is buoyed up by the vigor of Olivier's barnstorming performance and William Walton's sweeping score. *Henry V* is the first Shakespeare film that succeeds in being at once truly Shakespearean and wholly cinematic. **PK**

# IVAN THE TERRIBLE, PARTS ONE AND TWO (1944)

## IVAN GROZNYJ I i II

**U.S.S.R.** (Alma Ata) 100m BW
**Language:** Russian
**Director:** Sergei M. Eisenstein
**Producer:** Sergei M. Eisenstein
**Screenplay:** Sergei M. Eisenstein
**Photography:** Andrei Moskvin, Eduard Tisse
**Music:** Sergei Prokofiev
**Cast:** Nikolai Cherkasov, Lyudmila Tselikovskaya, Serafima Birman, Mikhail Nazvanov, Mikhail Zharov, Amvrosi Buchma, Mikhail Kuznetsov, Pavel Kadochnikov, Andrei Abrikosov, Aleksandr Mgebrov, Maksim Mikhajlov, Vsevolod Pudovkin

Sergei Eisenstein is one of those names that inevitably appear when studying film theory and aesthetics. Particularly famous for his dramatic sequence of the Odessa steps in *The Battleship Potemkin* (1925), the Russian director offers further proof of his immense talent with *Ivan the Terrible*. This epic movie narrates the life of the despotic Czar and was originally conceived as a trilogy, the filming for which began in the early 1940s upon Stalin's request. Eisenstein could only complete parts I and II, however, because of his premature death. Part I came out in 1945, whereas Part II underwent governmental censorship. Stalin saw in *Ivan the Terrible* a critique of his own despotism and banned the movie as a result. Part II was finally released in 1958 after both Eisenstein's and Stalin's deaths.

*Ivan the Terrible* recounts the rise and fall of one of Russia's most famous Czars, Ivan IV, responsible for the unification of the country in the late Middle Ages. The first film opens with Ivan's (Nikolai Cherkasov) coronation and his intention to defeat the Boyars. Part I focuses on Ivan's establishment of power and shows the favor of the peasants. Part II narrates the machinations of the Boyars in their attempt to assassinate Ivan and reveals the progressive cruelty of the Czar, who creates his own police to keep the country under control. Ivan discovers the plots against him and defeats his enemies by killing them. The acting is particularly staged: Eisenstein makes strong use of extreme close-ups and seems more interested with the characters' reaction to the events than with the events themselves. In Part II, a curiosity can be found in the use of two color scenes in a movie that is mostly black and white.

*Alexander Nevsky* (1938) and *Ivan the Terrible* are Eisenstein's only non-silent films. If one compares the latter to the silent movies he directed in the 1920s, not only can a change in style be detected, due primarily to the coming of sound, but also a change in the very themes narrated. Eisenstein here renounces the depiction of the proletarian struggles at the heart of his previous films, turning instead to an epic story, one connected to a "safe" past that does not involve manifest critiques of contemporary political events. **CFe**

U.S. (Paramount) 107m BW

**Director:** Billy Wilder

**Producer:** Joseph Sistrom

**Screenplay:** Billy Wilder, Raymond Chandler, from the novel *Double Indemnity in Three of a Kind* by James M. Cain

**Photography:** John F. Seitz

**Music:** Miklós Rózsa

**Cast:** Fred MacMurray, Barbara Stanwyck, Edward G. Robinson, Porter Hall, Jean Heather, Tom Powers, Byron Barr, Richard Gaines, Fortunio Bonanova, John Philliber

**Oscar nomination:** Joseph Sistrom (best picture), Billy Wilder (director), Raymond Chandler, Billy Wilder (screenplay), Barbara Stanwyck (actress), John F. Seitz (photography), Miklós Rózsa (music), Loren L. Ryder (sound)

# DOUBLE INDEMNITY (1944)

Adapted by director Billy Wilder and author Raymond Chandler from the hard-boiled novel by James M. Cain, *Double Indemnity* is the archetypal film noir, the tale of a desperate dame and a greedy man, of murder for sordid profit and sudden, violent betrayal. Yet it has a weird, evocative romanticism ("How could I have known that murder can sometimes smell like honeysuckle?") and pays off, extraordinarily for 1944, with a confession not only of murder but also of love between two men. The last line, addressed by dying Fred MacMurray to heartbroken Edward G. Robinson is "I love you, too."

A wounded man staggers by night into a Los Angeles insurance company office, and settles down at his desk to dictate confessional notes on "the Dietrichson claim." He introduces himself as "Walter Neff, insurance salesman, 35 years old, unmarried, no visible scars—until a while ago, that is." MacMurray spent his whole career, first at Paramount then at Disney and finally in sitcoms, as a genial nice guy, always smiling, always folksy; twice (his other change-of-pace, also for Wilder, is *The Apartment*) he crawled behind his smile and marvelously played a complete heel, his cleft chin sweaty and in need of a shave, his smooth salesman's talk a cover for lechery, larceny, and murderous intent. The bait that tempts this average nobody off the straight-and-narrow comes fresh from a sunbath, barely wrapped in a towel, flashing an ankle bracelet. Calling at a fake Spanish mansion on Los Feliz Boulevard about an auto policy renewal, Neff encounters Mrs. Phyllis Dietrichson (Barbara Stanwyck) and can't resist putting verbal moves on her. Neff backs off when she innocently asks if it's possible to insure her older husband (Tom Powers) against accidental death without him knowing about it. Neff mulls it over and, after an embrace in his apartment, agrees to pitch in with the murder plan.

The couple trick Mr. D into signing up for a policy that pays off double if death occurs on a train, then arrange it so his broken-necked corpse is found on the railroad tracks. Enter Barton Keyes (Robinson), a claims investigator of Columbo-like tenacity whose only blind spot is his devotion to Neff. Keyes fusses around the case, ruling out suicide in a brilliant speech about the unlikeliness of suicide by jumping from a train and homing in on the gamey blonde as a murderess and rooting around for her partner in crime. Keyes doesn't even have to do much work, because postkilling pressures are already splitting Neff and Phyllis apart, as they try not to panic during meets in a local supermarket and come to suspect each other of additional double crosses. In that stifling, shadowed mansion, with "Tangerine" on the radio and honeysuckle in the air, the lovers riddle each other with bullets, and Neff staggers away to confess. Keyes joins him in the office and sadly catches the end of the story. Neff asks for four hours so he can head for Mexico, but Keyes knows, "You'll never make the border. You'll never even make the elevator." **KN**

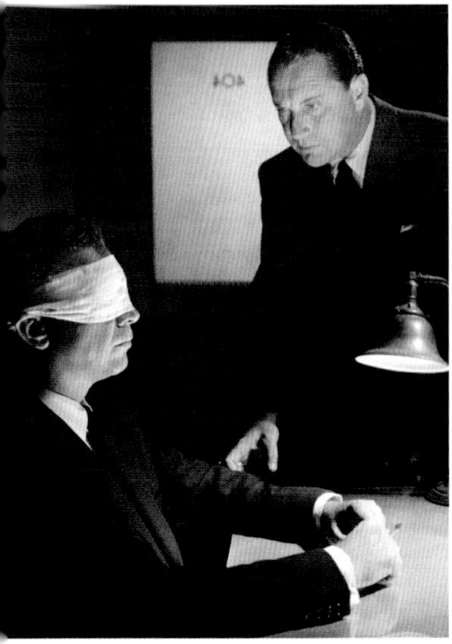

# MURDER, MY SWEET (1944)
## FAREWELL MY LOVELY

The first screen adaptation of Raymond Chandler's second novel *Farewell My Lovely* was *The Falcon Takes Over*, a 1942 quickie in which Chandler's private eye Philip Marlowe was replaced by George Sanders's gentleman sleuth. When Chandler's reputation rose, RKO found they no longer had to pay for the film rights to mount this more faithful adaptation, in which ex-crooner Dick Powell surprised audiences with his wry toughness and bruised romanticism as the first proper screen incarnation of Marlowe. The title change came about because it was assumed that audiences would mistake it for a schmaltzy wartime romance, though the novel's title was retained in Britain where Chandler was already a respected figure.

The book was one of several Marlowe novels Chandler wrought by cannibalizing several earlier, cruder novellas, which explains why it has several plot threads that turn out to intersect via the odd, unlikely coincidence. *Murder, My Sweet* opens with Marlowe blinded and interrogated by the cops, allowing for the retention of much of Chandler's first-person commentary, as flashbacks take the hero through a puzzle that begins with ex-con "Moose" Malloy (Mike Mazurki) hiring Marlowe to track down the ex-girlfriend who sold him out but with whom he is still smitten. The story takes a left turn when he is also retained by slinky society vamp Helen Grayle (Claire Trevor) to get back some stolen jade and see off a blackmailing "psychic consultant" (Otto Kruger).

No other film so perfectly encapsulates the pleasures of film noir, as director Edward Dmytryk deploys shadows, rain, drug-induced hallucinations ("a black pool opened up"), and sudden bursts of violence within a cobweb of plot traps, slimy master crooks, worthless femmes fatales, gorilla-brained thugs, weary cops, and quack doctors. Powell's Marlowe, striking a match on Cupid's marble bottom and playing hopscotch on the tiled floor of a millionaire's mansion, is closer to Chandler's tone of boyish insolence than better-known readings of the role by Humphrey Bogart or Robert Mitchum. As always with Chandler, the villain turns out to be the strongest woman in the plot—as Moose's tarty Velma and the silken murderess Helen are revealed to be the same person. **KN**

**U.S.** (RKO) 95m BW

**Director:** Edward Dmytryk

**Producer:** Sid Rogell, Adrian Scott

**Screenplay:** John Paxton, from the novel *Farewell, My Lovely* by Raymond Chandler

**Photography:** Harry J. Wild

**Music:** Roy Webb

**Cast:** Dick Powell, Claire Trevor, Anne Shirley, Otto Kruger, Mike Mazurki, Miles Mander, Douglas Walton, Donald Douglas, Ralf Harolde, Esther Howard

## THE BATTLE OF SAN PIETRO (1945)

Made for the Army as a propaganda film, John Huston's *The Battle of San Pietro* remains the best war documentary ever made, despite changes made to remove some material thought too disturbing for civilian viewers. The picture details the taking of an Italian hill town from tenacious and well-entrenched German defenders, a battle that cost American units more than a thousand casualties.

While the inconclusiveness of the struggle implicitly indicts a flawed American strategy (despite the director's flag-waving voice-over), Huston's main purpose was to portray the experience of war seen from the viewpoint of those who fight it and have no concern about larger calculations of loss or gain. Huston's crew captures the horror and confusion of combat: the wounding of American soldiers: the pain and suffering of civilians; the boredom and campaigning for troops far from home; the inevitable cost of "victory," measured in the huge number of body bags loaded onto trucks; and the rows and rows of temporary graves dug to accommodate them.

The film was eventually released to the American public only after final victory in Europe, too late to play any role in influencing opinion about the war. *The Battle of San Pietro* is Huston's tribute to the brave men he lived among, as well as a poignant, graphic treatment of battle and its consequences, with some stock footage and staged scenes not detracting from the overall effect of authenticity and objectivity. **RBP**

**U.S.** (U.S. Army) 33m BW
**Director:** John Huston
**Producer:** Frank Capra
**Screenplay:** John Huston
**Photography:** Jules Buck
**Music:** Dimitri Tiomkin
**Cast:** John Huston (narrator)

## SPELLBOUND (1945)

Alfred Hitchcock's *Spellbound* presents an intriguing and promising puzzle box of a plot. Amnesiac Gregory Peck, realizing he's not who thinks he is, enlists Dr. Constance Peterson (Ingrid Bergman) to help discover his actual identity, as well as the fate of the person he's apparently impersonating. But fascinated by the novelty of psychoanalysis, *Spellbound* spends a little too much time focusing on the subconscious and not quite enough time focusing on actual suspense. It's one of Hitchcock's more interesting "failures," notable for its acting, production design, and music but not especially for the central mystery.

Regardless, a savvy Hitchcock smartly (and with more than a little modest deference) enlisted surrealist artist Salvador Dali to design the film's famous dream sequences, envisioned by Peck while under hypnosis, and those haunting, hallucinatory visions of card games, eyes, and strange landscapes remain justly lauded as mini works of art in and of themselves. Equally pioneering was Miklós Rózsa's Oscar-winning score, the first to incorporate the electronic hum of the Theremin, whose eerie, wavering tone became a keystone of many genre films. Even if Ben Hecht's screenplay indulges in a little too much meandering psychobabble, *Spellbound* did serve to introduce Hitchcock's increasingly literal interest in the subconscious. **JKl**

**U.S.** (Selznick) 111m BW
**Director:** Alfred Hitchcock
**Producer:** David O. Selznick
**Screenplay:** Angus MacPhail, Ben Hecht
**Photography:** George Barnes
**Music:** Miklós Rózsa
**Cast:** Ingrid Bergman, Gregory Peck, Michael Chekhov, Leo G. Carroll, John Emery, Steven Geray, Paul Harvey, Donald Curtis, Rhonda Fleming, Norman Lloyd, Wallace Ford, Bill Goodwin, Art Baker, Regis Toomey, Irving Bacon
**Oscar:** Miklós Rózsa (music)
**Oscar nomination:** David O. Selznick (best picture), Alfred Hitchcock (director), Michael Chekhov (actor in support role), George Barnes (photography), Jack Cosgrove (special effects)

# MILDRED PIERCE (1945)

Gunshots crack in the night and a dying man gasps "Mildred!" In a flashback classic that goes back to the genesis of obsession and murder, the mink-clad confessor Mildred Pierce (Joan Crawford in the Oscar-winning role that revived the 41-year-old fading star's stalled career) explains in a police interrogation how she toiled her way from housewife, waitress, and pie baker to prosperous restaurateur in order to fulfill her daughter Veda's (Ann Blyth) demands for the finer things. When they are both fatefully drawn in by a smooth, duplicitous cad (Zachary Scott), the possessive Mildred's smothering, neurotic indulgence and the ungrateful Veda's precocious appetites inevitably boil over in sexual betrayal and rage.

A definitive 1940s women's picture and a seething domestic soap opera, Michael Curtiz's film, adapted by Ranald MacDougall from a breathtakingly perverse novel by James M. Cain (of *Double Indemnity* and *The Postman Always Rings Twice* fame), is also a superbly nasty noir, one that plays havoc with the era's ideals of maternal devotion and mom's apple pie. Mildred is admirable for her hard work and self-sacrifice. She is smart, ambitious, and driven, qualities respected and rewarded in the American ethic. But gradually, as she detaches from her decent but unsuccessful husband (Bruce Bennett), and as she favors the insolent Veda over her sweeter younger daughter, putting the child's death behind her with no evident afterthought, we begin to sense an unhealthy, even pathological, aspect to Mildred's compulsion.

Throbbing melodrama doesn't come with more conviction. Even to those usually turned off by the tough, square-shouldered Crawford, her intense, no-holds-barred performance as Mildred is tragically twisted and compelling. Blyth, only 17, is sneeringly sensational as the disdainful femme fatale. A director who imposed his personality on films in every genre, Curtiz's masterly deployment of his actors (sterling support players such as Eve Arden, Jack Carson, and Lee Patrick) and the disparate technical elements—*Gone with the Wind*'s Oscar-winning cinematographer Ernest Haller's expressive shifts from sunny suburbia to shadowy nightmare, and Max Steiner's dramatic score—are intoxicating. **AE**

**U.S.** (Warner Bros.) 111m BW
**Director:** Michael Curtiz
**Producer:** Jerry Wald, Jack L. Warner
**Screenplay:** Ranald MacDougall, from novel by James M. Cain
**Photography:** Ernest Haller
**Music:** Max Steiner
**Cast:** Joan Crawford, Jack Carson, Zachary Scott, Eve Arden, Ann Blyth, Bruce Bennett, Lee Patrick, Moroni Olsen, Veda Ann Borg, Jo Ann Marlowe
**Oscar:** Joan Crawford (actress)
**Oscar nomination:** Jerry Wald (best picture), Ranald MacDougall (screenplay), Eve Arden (actress in support role), Ann Blyth (actress in support role), Ernest Haller (photography)

# LES ENFANTS DU PARADIS (1945)
## THE CHILDREN OF PARADISE

**France** (Pathé) 190m BW
**Language:** French
**Director:** Marcel Carné
**Producer:** Raymond Borderie, Fred Orain
**Screenplay:** Jacques Prévert
**Photography:** Marc Fossard, Roger Hubert
**Music:** Joseph Kosma, Maurice Thiriet
**Cast:** Arletty, Jean-Louis Barrault, Pierre Brasseur, Pierre Renoir, María Casares, Gaston Modot, Fabien Loris, Marcel Pérès, Palau, Etienne Decroux, Jane Marken, Marcelle Monthil, Louis Florencie, Habib Benglia, Rognoni
**Oscar nomination:** Jacques Prévert (screenplay)

Ever since its triumphant premiere in the newly liberated France of 1945, *The Children of Paradise* has maintained its place as one of the greatest French films of all time. It represents the high point of the genre often called "poetic realism" (though "pessimistic romanticism" might be a more apt term) and also of the partnership that perfected that genre—that of screenwriter Jacques Prévert and director Marcel Carné. They made an oddly assorted couple: Prévert gregarious, passionate, highly committed politically, one of the finest popular French poets of the century; Carné remote, fastidious, withdrawn, a cool perfectionist. Yet together they created cinematic magic that neither man could equal after they parted. *The Children of Paradise* was their last great success.

The film was some 18 months in production and involved building the largest studio set in the history of French cinema—the quarter-mile of street frontage, reproduced in scrupulous detail, representing the "Boulevard du Crime," the theater district of Paris in the 1830s and 40s. This would have been a daunting enterprise at the best of times; in wartime France, under the conditions of the Occupation, it was little short of heroic. Transport, materials, costumes, and film stock were all scarce. The Italian coproducers pulled out when Italy capitulated. The original French producer had to withdraw when he came under investigation by the Nazis. One lead actor, a prominent pro-Nazi, fled to Germany after D-Day and had to be replaced at the last minute. Alexandre Trauner, the brilliant set designer, and the composer Joseph Kosma, who were both Jewish, were obliged to work in hiding and transmit their ideas through intermediaries.

Despite all this, *Children* is a consummate achievement with all the richness and complexity of a great 19th-century novel. The crowd scenes set in the bustling, gaudy boulevard deploy their 1,500 extras in riotous profusion, cramming every corner of the screen with lively detail. A defiant affirmation of French theatrical culture at a time when the nation was conquered and occupied, the film offers a multilayered meditation on the nature of masquerade, fantasy, and representation. All dialogue is heightened, all actions masterfully staged. The three lead male characters are all performers—Lemaître the great romantic actor (Pierre Brasseur); Debureau, the supreme mime artiste (Jean-Louis Barrault); and Lacenaire, the failed playwright turned dandyish master criminal (Marcel Herrand). All are real historical personages. The woman they all love, the *grande horizontale* Garance (Arletty in her greatest screen role), is fiction—less a real woman than an icon of the eternal feminine, elusive and infinitely desirable.

Though it runs over three hours, *Children* never seems a minute too long. A celebration of theater as the great popular art of the 19th century (as cinema was of the 20th), it mixes farce, romance, melodrama, and tragedy in an overwhelming narrative sweep. Carné was above all a supreme director of actors, and the film offers a feast of great French screen acting, along with wit, grace, passion, and an all-pervading sense of transience—the melancholy that underlies all Romantic art. **PK**

# ROMA, CITTÀ APERTA (1945)
## OPEN CITY

Considered the initiator of an aesthetic revolution in film, Roberto Rossellini's *Open City* was the first major work of Italian neorealism, and it managed to explode the conventions of the Mussolinian "cinema of white telephones" that was fashionable in Italy at the beginning of the 1940s. Rossellini's film about the Italian Resistance was scripted in the days of the underground battle against the Nazis. Recalling Sergei Eisenstein's formula of the "choral film," it tells of a group of patriots hiding in the apartment of a lithographer named Francesco (Francesco Grandjaquet). The communist who leads the group, Manfredi (Marcello Pagliero), is chased by the Gestapo, and is finally captured and executed. Francesco's wife Pina (Anna Magnani) and a sympathetic priest, Don Pietro (Aldo Fabrizi), die too, trying to help Manfredi escape. But it is the solidarity of Rome as a city that anticipates a final victory against the invaders.

The scarcity of technical and financial resources available to Rossellini proved to be a virtue of *Open City*, which was shot in a documentary style. Showing real people in real locations, the film brought some fresh air to the existing Western cinema. The freedom of the camera movements and the authenticity of the characters, allied to a new way of storytelling, were among the qualities that made *Open City* the revelation of the 1946 Cannes Film Festival, where it was awarded the *Palme d'Or*. Neorealism quickly became an aesthetic model for directors interested in a vivid description of history and society.

One of the most amazing things about *Open City* is the approach Rossellini takes to each character's drama. Some of the film's heroes will forever remain in the hearts of viewers. Who can forget the sight of a pregnant Pina running through bullets or the kind priest shot before the frightened eyes of the children? Although it may veer toward the melodramatic, the story is just as moving today as it was then. And it should come as no surprise to learn that, after this role, Magnani became one of the greatest actresses of the Italian screen. **DD**

**Italy** (Excelsa, Minerva) 100m BW

**Language:** Italian / German

**Director:** Roberto Rossellini

**Producer:** Giuseppe Amato, Ferruccio De Martino, Roberto Rossellini

**Photography:** Ubaldo Arata

**Screenplay:** Sergio Amidei, Federico Fellini

**Music:** Renzo Rossellini

**Cast:** Aldo Fabrizi, Anna Magnani, Marcello Pagliero, Maria Michi, Harry Feist

**Oscar nomination:** Sergio Amidei, Federico Fellini (screenplay)

**Cannes Film Festival:** Roberto Rossellini (Grand Prize of the Festival)

U.S. (Paramount) 101m BW

**Director:** Billy Wilder

**Producer:** Charles Brackett

**Screenplay:** Charles Brackett, Billy Wilder, from novel by Charles R. Jackson

**Photography:** John F. Seitz

**Music:** Miklós Rózsa

**Cast:** Ray Milland, Jane Wyman, Phillip Terry, Howard Da Silva, Doris Dowling, Frank Faylen, Mary Young, Anita Sharp-Bolster, Lillian Fontaine, Frank Orth, Lewis L. Russell, Clarence Muse

**Oscar:** Charles Brackett (best picture), Billy Wilder (director), Charles Brackett, Billy Wilder (screenplay), Ray Milland (actor)

**Oscar nomination:** John F. Seitz (photography), Doane Harrison (editing), Miklós Rózsa (music)

**Cannes Film Festival:** Billy Wilder (Grand Prize of the Festival), Ray Milland (actor)

# THE LOST WEEKEND (1945)

Before *The Lost Weekend*, drunkards in Hollywood movies were mostly figures of fun, indeed of farce—lovable buffoons reeling around uttering slurred witticisms and making hopeless passes at pretty girls. Billy Wilder and his regular coscreenwriter, Charles Brackett, dared to do something different, creating American cinema's first adult, intelligent, unsparing look at the grim degradation of alcoholism. Even today, some of the scenes are almost too painful to watch.

Ray Milland, in a career-defining role that netted him his first Oscar, plays a New York writer, Don Birnam, struggling with and finally succumbing to his craving over the space of one long, parched summer weekend in the city. Just as he had done with Fred MacMurray in *Double Indemnity* (1944), Wilder ferrets out and avidly exploits the insecurity behind Milland's bland screen persona. Rather than letting us stand back and judge in detached compassion, Wilder pulls us along with Birnam on his downward trajectory. We're obliged to accompany him as he sheds all his remaining moral scruples, showing himself ready to lie, cheat, and steal to get money for drink, until with awful inevitability he ends up in the hell of a public hospital's alcoholics ward, screaming in horror at the hallucinations of delirium tremens.

Parts of the film were shot on Manhattan locations, and Wilder makes the most of the dry, sun-bleached streets, shot by his director of photography John F. Seitz to look bleak and tawdry, as if through Birnam's bleary, self-loathing gaze. In one unforgettable sequence the writer, reduced to trying to hock his typewriter to raise funds for booze, traipses the dusty length of 3rd Avenue dragging the heavy machine—only to realize that it's Yom Kippur and all the pawnshops are closed. Even more harrowing is the scene in a smart nightclub where Birman succumbs to temptation and tries to filch money from a woman's handbag—only to be caught and humiliatingly thrown out while the club pianist leads the clientele in a chorus of "Somebody stole her purse" (to the tune of "Somebody Stole My Gal"). And Miklós Rózsa's score makes masterly use of the theremin, that early electronic instrument whose eerie, swooping tone perfectly conjures up Birnam's woozy, out-of-control vision of the world.

The strictures of the Hays Code imposed a happy ending, though Wilder and Brackett managed to sidestep anything too mindlessly reassuring. Even so, Paramount was convinced the movie was doomed to failure, with an alarmed liquor industry offering the studio $5 million to bury the film altogether. Prohibitionists, on the other hand, were up in arms, claiming the film would encourage drinking. In any event, *The Lost Weekend* was a major critical and commercial hit. "It was after this picture," Wilder noted, "that people started taking me seriously." No subsequent film on alcoholism, or any other form of addiction, has been able to avoid a nod to *The Lost Weekend*. **PK**

U.S. (PRC) 67m BW

**Director:** Edgar G. Ulmer

**Producer:** Leon Fromkess, Martin Mooney

**Screenplay:** Martin Goldsmith, from his novel

**Photography:** Benjam H. Kline

**Music:** Leo Erdody, Clarence Gaskill, Jimmy McHugh

**Cast:** Tom Neal, Ann Savage, Claudia Drake, Edmund MacDonald, Tim Ryan, Esther Howard, Pat Gleason

# DETOUR (1945)

"Fate or some mysterious force can put the finger on you or me for no good reason at all." One of the greatest of all B movies, *Detour* makes no attempt to rise above its budget and brief shooting schedule, instead reveling in its cheapness, presenting a world somewhere between pulp fiction and existentialism where life has low production values and a short running time.

A grubby jazz musician (Tom Neal) hitchhikes across country, descending into an on-the-road Hell as a driver drops dead, incriminating him. He hooks up with a trampy woman (Ann Savage) who leads him to degradation and murder, climaxing in an unforgettable tussle in a tawdry motel room in which a telephone cord gets tangled up around Savage's neck.

Edgar G. Ulmer, a German Expressionist toiling along Poverty Row, was a more pretentious filmmaker than his admirers will admit, but this is the one genuine masterpiece from his time in the Z-trenches. The unknown stars (real-life loser Neal later did time for murder) are resolutely unglamorous, and the studio sets, anonymous roadsides, and back-projected landscapes conjure up a world spiraling out of control—one where the coincidence-driven plotting of a thrown-together B picture script can suggest the malign hand of merciless destiny. **KN**

G.B. (Rank, The Archers) 92m BW

**Language:** English / Gaelic

**Director:** Michael Powell & Emeric Pressburger

**Producer:** George R. Busby, Michael Powell, Emeric Pressburger

**Screenplay:** Michael Powell & Emeric Pressburger

**Photography:** Erwin Hillier

**Music:** Allan Gray

**Cast:** Wendy Hiller, Roger Livesey, George Carney, Pamela Brown, Walter Hudd, Captain Duncan MacKenzie, Ian Sadler, Finlay Currie, Murdo Morrison, Margot Fitzsimmons, Captain C.W.R. Knight, Donald Strachan, John Rae, Duncan McIntyre, Jean Cadell

# I KNOW WHERE I'M GOING! (1945)

*I Know Where I'm Going!* stands tall as one of the most perfect of the run of delirious masterpieces made by the team of Michael Powell and Emeric Pressburger in the 1940s. Joan Webster (Wendy Hiller), very sexy in smart suits, is the practical post-war English miss who travels to the Hebrides to marry a millionaire old enough to be her father. But she finds her determined gold-digging sidetracked by an island-load of strange Scots who arrange for her to be diverted into the arms of her predestined lover Torquil MacNeil (Roger Livesey), the local penniless squire and war hero.

Aside from being the only filmmakers who could get away with naming a romantic hero "Torquil," Powell and Pressburger go against the cynical vision of conniving, drunken Scots islanders found in Ealing Studio's 1949 *Whisky Galore!*, presenting a crew who are just as devious but working for good ends. Joan's urban toughness is quickly overwhelmed with lots of Celtic legendry involving the local whirlpool, which represents the Gods and allows for an exciting rescue-at-sea finale. In a large supporting cast, Pamela Brown is especially memorable as the spookily alluring local girl, Catriona Potts. **KN**

# THE BEST YEARS OF OUR LIVES (1946)

This domestic epic about three World War II veterans returning to civilian life, 172 minutes long and winner of nine Oscars, isn't considered hip nowadays. Critics as sharp as Manny Farber and Robert Warshow were pretty contemptuous of it when it came out—although seemingly from opposite political viewpoints. Farber saw it as liberal hogwash from a conservative angle whereas Warshow skewered it more from a Marxist perspective. Its director, William Wyler, and the literary source, MacKinlay Kantor's novel, are far from fashionable today. The veteran in the cast, Harold Russell, who lost his hands in the war, occasioned outraged reflections from Warshow about challenged masculinity and even sick jokes from humorist Terry Southern many years later. For all that, I would call this the best American movie about returning soldiers that I've ever seen—the most moving and the most deeply felt. It bears witness to its times and contemporaries like few other Hollywood features, and Gregg Toland's deep-focus cinematography is one of the best things he ever did.

Part of what is so unusual about *The Best Years of Our Lives* as a Hollywood picture is its sense of class distinctions—the way that the separate fates and careers of veterans who are well-to-do (March), middle-class (Russell), and working-class (Andrews) are juxtaposed. Admittedly, the fact that they all meet one another at a bar presided over by Hoagy Carmichael is something of a sentimental contrivance, yet the relative blurring of class lines in the armed services that carries over briefly into civilian life has its plausible side as well. Similarly, the limitations of Russell as an actor have been held against the picture, yet the fact that we accept him as the real disabled veteran that he was seems far more important, documentary truth in this case superseding the interests of fiction. The scenes between him and his (fictional) fiancée, as they both struggle to adjust to their reconfigured relationship, are wrenching in their tenderness as well as their honesty, with few passages in American cinema to equal them. **JRos**

**U.S.** (Samuel Goldwyn) 172m BW
**Director:** William Wyler
**Producer:** Samuel Goldwyn
**Screenplay:** Robert E. Sherwood, from the novel *Glory for Me* by MacKinlay Kantor
**Photography:** Gregg Toland
**Music:** Hugo Friedhofer
**Cast:** Myrna Loy, Fredric March, Dana Andrews, Teresa Wright, Virginia Mayo, Cathy O'Donnell, Hoagy Carmichael, Harold Russell, Gladys George, Roman Bohnen, Ray Collins, Minna Gombell, Walter Baldwin, Steve Cochran, Dorothy Adams
**Oscar:** Harold Russell (honorary award), Samuel Goldwyn (best picture), William Wyler (director), Robert E. Sherwood (screenplay), Fredric March (actor ), Harold Russell (actor), Daniel Mandell (editing), Hugo Friedhofer (music)
**Oscar nomination:** Gordon Sawyer (sound)

# BRIEF ENCOUNTER (1946)

The imposing epics of David Lean's later years sometimes threaten to overshadow the director's relatively modest early works, but to focus too much on the sheer spectacle of *Lawrence of Arabia* or *Doctor Zhivago* would be to overlook some of Lean's greatest accomplishments. After all, only a filmmaker of the highest order could direct *Lawrence of Arabia*, and that same mastery of the form is on display in Lean's formative films, albeit on a much smaller scale.

Lean had already directed three adaptations of Noel Coward's work when he began *Brief Encounter*, based on Coward's one-act play *Still Life*. But the play's brevity forced Lean to expand the material, and in the process he expanded his own film vocabulary as well. Told in flashback, *Brief Encounter* follows the platonic love affair between housewife Laura (Celia Johnson) and doctor Alec (Trevor Howard), who meet fortuitously in a train station. There's obviously a connection between the two, but they know their romance can't proceed further than a few furtive lunch meetings.

In crafting one of the most effective tearjerkers in cinema history, Lean made a number of formal advances that quickly established him as more than just someone riding the coattails of Noel Coward. For starters, Lean took the story out of the train station, adding more details to the doomed affair. And he exploited all the cinematic tools at his disposal; the lighting, for example, approaches the severe look of Lean's subsequent Dickens adaptations, making the symbolic most of the dark, smoky station. He also makes good use of sound effects (particularly that of a speeding train), as well as music, incorporating Rachmaninoff's Piano Concerto No. 2 as the film's running theme.

But most importantly, Lean includes frequent closeups of Johnson's eyes, which tell a better story than most scripts. She and Howard are superlative in this saddest of stories, their every movement steeped in meaning and the sterling dialogue laced with deep emotions. A passing glance, the brush of a finger across a hand, and a shared laugh are virtually all these illfated lovers are allowed, and Johnson and Howard beautifully convey this sad realization. **JKl**

**G.B.** (Cineguild, Rank) 86m BW

**Director:** David Lean

**Producer:** Noel Coward, Anthony Havelock-Allan, Ronald Neame

**Screenplay:** Anthony Havelock-Allan, David Lean, from the play *Still Life* by Noel Coward

**Photography:** Robert Krasker

**Nonoriginal music:** Rachmaninov

**Cast:** Celia Johnson, Trevor Howard, Stanley Holloway, Joyce Carey, Cyril Raymond, Everley Gregg, Marjorie Mars

**Oscar nomination:** David Lean (director), Anthony Havelock-Allan, David Lean, Ronald Neame (screenplay), Celia Johnson (actress )

**Cannes Film Festival:** David Lean (Grand Prize of the Festival)

# PAISÀ (1946)
## PAISAN

Anyone approaching *Paisà* without foreknowledge of its status as a neorealist masterpiece could be forgiven for giving up early on: stock footage of the American campaign in Italy, Hollywood-style music, bad actors barking military commands. It is only by the end of the first of six self-contained episodes that Roberto Rossellini's off-hand style has begun to weave its stark magic—soon after a bullet abruptly kills of a soldier telling his life story, we see the corpse of his companion, killed by the Germans and dismissed, unknowingly, by the surviving Americans as a "dirty Iti."

Rossellini's chronicle of 1943–46 is marked by devastation, brutality, and incomprehension at all levels. An American does not realize that a prostitute is the woman he loved six months earlier; a street-urchin befriends a drunken, black soldier and steals his shoes the instant he falls asleep; the film's final image—unforgettably bleak—shows the merciless execution of a line of partisans.

Rossellini develops a structure to match this succession of events, based on startling plot ellipses, cross-purpose dialogues in multiple languages, and a rigorously unsentimental presentation of horrors. *Paisà* locates the telling traces of personal life within the nightmare of war's history. **AM**

**Italy** (Foreign Film, OFI) 120m BW

**Language:** Italian / English / German

**Director:** Roberto Rossellini

**Producer:** Mario Conti, Rod E. Geiger, Roberto Rossellini

**Screenplay:** Sergio Amidei, Federico Fellini

**Photography:** Otello Martelli

**Music:** Renzo Rossellini

**Cast:** Carmela Sazio, Robert Van Loon, Benjam Emmanuel, Harold Wagner, Merlin Berth, Dots Johnson, Alfonsino Pasca, Maria Michi, Gar Moore, Harriet Medin, Renzo Avanzo, William Tubbs, Dale Edmonds, Cigolani, Allen Dan

**Oscar nomination:** Alfred Hayes, Federico Fellini, Sergio Amidei, Marcello Pagliero, Roberto Rossellini (screenplay)

# THE POSTMAN ALWAYS RINGS TWICE (1946)

Lana Turner was never more attractive than in her role as Cora Smith, who marries an unattractive older man (Cecil Kellaway) as an escape from poverty but, deeply dissatisfied, gives in to her attraction for a young drifter, Frank Chambers (John Garfield). As in many films noir, the doomed couple's affair hinges on a crime, the murder of Cora's husband. Aided by a shyster lawyer, the pair are exonerated. Yet they fail to find happiness as Cora is killed in a car accident and Frank is executed for this "crime."

Director Tay Garnett's tight framing emphasizes the imprisonment of the fatal lovers, and the film's gloomy and forbidding mise en scène is the perfect setting for their grim story. With white costuming and glamorizing lighting, Turner becomes the visual center of the story, which was based on the James M. Cain novel published a decade earlier. Cora is no ordinary femme fatale. Her feelings for Frank are genuine, not artful manipulation.

*The Postman Always Rings Twice* reflects the Depression culture of the 1930s, with most of the scenes played in a barely respectable roadside diner, a potent image of rootlessness and limited opportunity. The flashback narrative suits the omnipresent pessimism of the noir series, of which this is one of the most justly celebrated examples. **RBP**

**U.S.** (MGM) 113m BW

**Director:** Tay Garnett

**Producer:** Carey Wilson

**Screenplay:** Harry Ruskin, from novel by James M. Cain

**Photography:** Sidney Wagner

**Music:** George Bassman

**Cast:** Lana Turner, John Garfield, Cecil Kellaway, Hume Cronyn, Leon Ames, Audrey Totter, Alan Reed, Jeff York

U.S. (Fox) 97m BW

**Director:** John Ford

**Producer:** Samuel G. Engel, Darryl F. Zanuck

**Photography:** Joseph MacDonald

**Screenplay:** Samuel G. Engel, Sam Hellman

**Music:** Cyril J. Mockridge

**Cast:** Henry Fonda, Linda Darnell, Victor Mature, Cathy Downs, Walter Brennan, Tim Holt, Ward Bond, Alan Mowbray, John Ireland, Roy Roberts, Jane Darwell, Grant Withers, J. Farrell MacDonald, Russell Simpson

# MY DARLING CLEMENTINE (1946)

Though *Gunfight at the OK Corral*, *Hour of the Gun*, *Doc*, *Tombstone*, and *Wyatt Earp* are all more "historically accurate" (for what that's worth), John Ford's romantic, balladlike take on the old, old story remains *the* Wyatt Earp–Doc Holliday–OK Corral movie.

Peaceable cattleman Wyatt (Henry Fonda) rides into the nightmarish helltown of Tombstone and turns down the job of Marshal even though he's the only man who dares intervene to end the rampage of a drunken Indian. When rustlers murder one of his brothers, he holds a Fordian conversation with the youth's gravestone before facing up to responsibilities and pinning on the badge. In cleaning up the wide-open town, Earp makes the community safe for the ordinary church-going, square-dancing folks who have been hiding in the shadows while the place was overrun by the fiendish Old Man Clanton (Walter Brennan) and his gang of killer sons. However, for all the splendors of Monument Valley (the familiar landscape augmented by picturesque cactus) and Fonda's tight-lipped moral integrity, there is a downside to a crusade won only at the cost of the life of Doc Holliday (Victor Mature), a noble outlaw washed away along with the bad elements by bullets and consumption. This dark theme will later resurface in *The Man Who Shot Liberty Valance* (1962), Ford's disillusioned revision of the town-taming Western.

Mature has a reputation for woodenness, but his turn here as the consumptive surgeon-gunman is heart wrenching and a bitterly witty turn. Fonda's hero unbends slowly, emerging with stick insect-like grace in one of Ford's trademark community dance scenes and memorably depicted in perfect balance on the porch, chair on two legs, one boot against a post. As always with the Fordian West, the action thrills represented by the elaborate last-reel gunfight are leavened by comic elements: a Shakespearean drunk who needs to be prompted by Doc in the middle of "To Be or Not to Be" and romantic complications with the luminous Chihuaha (Linda Darnell) and the schoolmarm Clementine (Cathy Downs). However, the tone is as often wistful or awestruck by the beauties of the landscape as it is cheer-along shoot-'em-up Saturday matinee material. **KN**

U.S. (Haig, International, RKO) 95m
**Director:** Orson Welles
**Producer:** Sam Spiegel
**Screenplay:** Anthony Veiller, Victor Trivas, Decia Dunning
**Photography:** Russell Metty
**Music:** Bronislau Kaper
**Cast:** Edward G. Robinson, Loretta Young, Orson Welles, Philip Merivale, Richard Long, Konstantin Shayne, Byron Keith, Billy House, Martha Wentworth
**Oscar nomination:** Victor Trivas (screenplay)
**Venice Film Festival:** nomination Orson Welles (Golden Lion)

# THE STRANGER (1946)

Orson Welles's least-known film as a director, *The Stranger* was a medium-budget project he took from producer Sam Spiegel to prove that he could make a "proper, commercial film." One of a run of immediate postwar thrillers about tracking down Nazi war criminals (others include *Cornered* [1945] and *Notorious* [1946]), it hearkens back to the antifascist credentials Welles established with his famous stage *Julius Caesar* and even has echoes of a novel he considered filming before settling on *Citizen Kane* (1941) as his debut project—Nicholas Blake's prewar mystery about British fascism, *The Smiler With a Knife*.

Anonymously named government investigator Wilson (Edward G. Robinson) tracks down charismatic Nazi Franz Kindler—who is supposed to have invented the extermination camp—to a small college town in Connecticut. Kindler is posing as history professor Charles Rankin and has just married Mary (Loretta Young), the daughter of a Supreme Court Justice. Less complicated than the love-political triangle of *Notorious*, the film works on a similar theme as Wilson persuades Mary to help expose her evil husband, before turning into a variant on those popular 1940s thrillers (*Gaslight* [1944], and *The Two Mrs. Carrolls* [1947]) in which evil husbands plot to murder their innocent wives.

Welles makes a convincing *übermensch* villain, giving himself away in conversation by stating that "Marx wasn't a German, he was a Jew," his rottenness seeping into the petty world of the picturesque small town as he pursues his obsessive hobby by restoring an ancient clock. *The Stranger* still has the Welles visual pizzazz, but by 1946 film noir had caught up with his love for shadows and grotesqueries, so it does indeed blend in with other pictures of its type.

The film becomes especially melodramatic in the finale, which takes place at the top of a rickety sabotaged ladder in the clock tower, with Kindler cornered like King Kong and killed, a mechanical clockwork figure impaling him on an outthrust sword—the sort of explicit violence justifiable in a 1946 Hollywood movie if the villain was an unrepentant Nazi. Prefiguring David Lynch by decades, Welles establishes a folksy small-town atmosphere and subverts it, with drugstore philosophers who cheat at checkers and prom queens who marry fascists. **KN**

# LA BELLE ET LA BÊTE (1946)
## BEAUTY AND THE BEAST

**France** (DisCina) 96m BW
**Language:** French
**Director:** Jean Cocteau
**Producer:** André Paulvé
**Screenplay:** Jean Cocteau, Jeanne-Marie Leprince de Beaumont
**Photography:** Henri Alekan
**Music:** Georges Auric
**Cast:** Jean Marais, Josette Day, Mila Parély, Nane Germon, Michel Auclair, Raoul Marco, Marcel André

Jean Cocteau never called himself a filmmaker, per se. He considered himself a poet; film was just one of the many art forms he delved into throughout his career. Yet even if Cocteau thought himself a poet rather than a "mere" filmmaker, his brilliant, visionary rendition of this classic folktale certainly proved the two titles were not mutually exclusive. Moreover, the fact that of all his projects the dreamlike *Beauty and the Beast* remains his most beloved work reveals not only both his immense versatility and talent, but also the endurance and mass acceptance of film over all his other preferred formats.

Indeed, Cocteau approached *Beauty and the Beast*—only his second feature film—fully cognizant of the medium's broad reach and fueled by an agenda. On the one hand, his peers were looking to him to put French filmmaking back on the map after the massive cultural setback of the German occupation; *Beauty and the Beast* was to be a de facto national statement of purpose from France's artistic community. On the other hand, Cocteau was also being egged on by the critics, who accused the artist of elitism and of being out of touch with the public's tastes. Could he ever produce a mainstream work that would be embraced by the people?

With both challenges in mind, Cocteau approached the centuries-old "Beauty and the Beast" fable as an outlet for even his most outlandish and fantastic creative impulses. In fact, the relatively straightforward framework of the original story encouraged such experimentation. When her father is held captive by a seemingly monstrous beast (Jean Marais) in a remote castle, daughter Beauty (Josette Day) volunteers to take his place. But the Beast's bargain is more than it seems: he tells Beauty he wants to marry her, and Beauty must look past the appearance and to the good heart of her hairy suitor before making her decision.

Cocteau sets their courtship in a magical castle—the proving ground for a number of beautiful effects. Beauty doesn't just walk through the halls; she glides. Candles are lodged not in traditional holders but grasped by humanoid arms affixed to the walls. Mirrors are transformed to liquid portals, flames flicker and extinguish with a mind of their own, and statues come to life. The castle works both as a metaphor for the creative process personified as well as an excuse for numerous Freudian images. Because Beauty can't really consummate her relationship with the Beast until he is transformed, Cocteau has her fondling knives and traveling down long corridors as a means of revealing her subconscious desires.

But Cocteau's greatest achievement was making the monstrous Beast convincing as well as appealing. With Marais buried under elaborate makeup, the Beast's goodness must be conveyed through his actions and deeds, thus revealing the humanity both literally and figuratively beneath the fur and fangs. In fact, so successful is Marais's portrayal that at the film's premiere, when the Beast is finally transformed into a blandly handsome Prince and he and Beauty live happily ever after, actress Marlene Dietrich famously exclaimed "Where is my beautiful beast?" **JKl**

**U.S.** (First National, Warner) 114m BW
**Director:** Howard Hawks
**Producer:** Howard Hawks, Jack L. Warner
**Screenplay:** William Faulkner, from novel by Raymond Chandler
**Photography:** Sidney Hickox
**Music:** Max Steiner
**Cast:** Humphrey Bogart, Lauren Bacall, John Ridgely, Martha Vickers, Dorothy Malone, Peggy Knudsen, Regis Toomey, Charles Waldron, Charles D. Brown, Bob Steele, Elisha Cook Jr., Louis Jean Heydt

# THE BIG SLEEP (1946)

Supposedly when director Howard Hawks asked novelist Raymond Chandler to explain the numerous double crosses, twists, and surprises revealed throughout his book *The Big Sleep*, the writer famously and honestly replied "I have no idea." That isn't to say the various twists and turns are not important to *The Big Sleep*, or even that their presence in the book is just arbitrary confusion. Rather, Chandler's notoriously muddled "whodunit" merely complicates an already complicated tale of Los Angeles corruption, further tainting a nearly endless list of seedy characters.

It should therefore come as no surprise that Hawks gently shifted the focus of his adaptation from sleuthing to the sleuth, in his case Humphrey Bogart as hard-boiled private investigator Philip Marlowe. Taking advantage of the success of the 1944 film *To Have and Have Not*, Hawks reunited Bogart with Lauren Bacall and played up their palpable chemistry. When they're on the screen together, the detective story fades to the background (they were married six months after shooting ended). Hawks exploited that sexual tension, adding extra scenes with the two actors and stressing the innuendo-laced dialogue, particularly racy (especially an exchange about horses and saddles) in light of the era's production code.

And what of the whodunit? Thankfully, the central investigation, confusing though it may be, is still a joy to watch. Marlowe acts as our Virgil-like guide as he descends into Hollywood's darkest and dirtiest corners, unraveling a murder/blackmail plot that involves pornographers, nymphomaniacs, and a bevy of hired hoods who barely have time to reveal more plot points (and red herrings) before getting plugged.

*The Big Sleep* is a reference to death, and indeed death pervades the movie. This is a film noir masterpiece missing several standard film noir tenets. There are numerous femme fatales, but no flashbacks; chiaroscuro lighting, but no voiceover. More important, Bogart's Marlowe seems not lost in a world of lies and deception but utterly confident and in control at all times. He's a droll antihero, cool in the face of cruelty, unfazed in the face of wanton sleaze, and always appreciative of a pretty face. **JKl**

# THE KILLERS (1946)

The first ten minutes of Robert Siodmak's classic film noir reproduces Hemingway's brief 1927 story almost verbatim: two hit men barge into a sleepy burg to gun down the unresisting recluse Swede (Burt Lancaster). Extrapolating imaginatively, screenwriters Anthony Veiller and John Huston invent Riordan (Edmond O'Brien), a zealous insurance investigator who uncovers Swede's past: an ex-pug mixed up with a shady dame (Ava Gardner), a payroll heist, and a double cross.

*Citizen Kane* fractured its narrative into flashbacks related by different narrators; *The Killers* takes the idea a step further by scrambling the flashbacks' temporal order. The process of piecing together this jigsaw reinforces a reciprocal link between the spectator and Riordan. As he delves into Swede's past, the restless company-man Riordan gets the thrill of vicariously living a film noir life without paying the usual consequences. The relationship between Riordan and Swede's illicit world becomes analogous to that between the spectator and the film—a concept crystallized when, just before the showdown, Riordan sits silhouetted in the foreground as if he were in the front row of a movie theater. *The Killers* is not only a superior film noir but also a commentary on why we enjoy films noir, as an escape from humdrum security into danger and doom, but only at a safe distance. **MR**

**U.S.** (Mark Hellinger, Universal) 105m BW

**Director:** Robert Siodmak

**Producer:** Mark Hellinger

**Screenplay:** Anthony Veiller, from story by Ernest Hemgway

**Photography:** Elwood Bredell

**Music:** Miklós Rózsa

**Cast:** Burt Lancaster, Ava Gardner, Edmond O'Brien, Albert Dekker, Sam Levene, Vince Barnett, Virginia Christine, Jack Lambert, Charles D. Brown, Donald MacBride, Charles McGraw, William Conrad

**Oscar nomination:** Robert Siodmak (director), Anthony Veiller (screenplay), Arthur Hilton (editing), Miklós Rózsa (music)

# A MATTER OF LIFE AND DEATH (1946)

Michael Powell and Emeric Pressburger's 1946 fantasy, *A Matter of Life and Death* (renamed *Stairway To Heaven* for the U.S. market), was intended as a propaganda film to ameliorate strained relations between Britain and America. The movie outstrips its original purpose, however, ending up a lasting tale of romance and human goodness that is both visually exciting and verbally amusing.

Ready to jump from his burning airplane to certain death, a World War II pilot (David Niven) falls in love with the voice of an American radio operator (Kim Hunter). He awakes on a beach, believing he is in heaven. Finding that he is alive, he seizes the opportunity to fall in love with the American girl in person. But the powers above have made an error, and Heavenly Conductor 71 (Marius Goring) is sent to tell him the truth and take him to heaven where he belongs. The outstanding set design by Alfred Junge raises this film above its already impressive sentiments and nimble script, which switches with ease between earth (filmed in Technicolor) and the ethereal black and white of Heaven. Along with its use of freeze-frames and breathtaking set décor in the great beyond, the camera includes a behind-the-eyeball shot of which Salvador Dali would approve. **KK**

**G.B.** (The Archers, Independent, Rank) 104m BW & Technicolor

**Director:** Michael Powell & Emeric Pressburger

**Producer:** George R. Busby, Michael Powell, Emeric Pressburger

**Screenplay:** Michael Powell & Emeric Pressburger

**Photography:** Jack Cardiff

**Music:** Allan Gray

**Cast:** David Niven, Kim Hunter, Robert Coote, Kathleen Byron, Richard Attenborough, Bonar Colleano, Joan Maude, Marius Goring, Roger Livesey, Robert Atkins, Bob Roberts, Edwin Max, Betty Potter, Abraham Sofaer, Raymond Massey

# GREAT EXPECTATIONS (1946)

**G.B.** (Cineguild, Rank) 118m BW
**Director:** David Lean
**Producer:** Anthony Havelock-Allan, Ronald Neame
**Screenplay:** Anthony Havelock-Allan, David Lean, Ronald Neame, from novel by Charles Dickens
**Photography:** Guy Green
**Music:** Walter Goehr, Kenneth Pakeman
**Cast:** John Mills, Anthony Wager, Valerie Hobson, Jean Simmons, Bernard Miles, Francis L. Sullivan, Finlay Currie, Martita Hunt, Alec Guinness, Ivor Barnard, Freda Jackson, Eileen Erskine, George Hayes, Hay Petrie, John Forrest
**Oscar:** John Bryan, Wilfred Shingleton (art direction), Guy Green (photography)
**Oscar nomination:** Ronald Neame (best picture), David Lean (director), David Lean, Ronald Neame, Anthony Havelock-Allan (screenplay)

Filmed in 1946 in the wake of the successes *Brief Encounter* and *Blithe Spirit*, this was David Lean's first adaptation of Charles Dickens's novels; *Oliver Twist* was to follow in 1948. Taking on the literary masterpiece as a cinematic task in every sense of the word, Lean explores and exploits the broad emotional horizon of the story and makes it a sweeping, mesmeric visual journey as well. The result is the finest literary adaptation ever filmed, as well as one of the best British films ever made.

*Great Expectations* shares elements with many horror films, opening on a broad marsh, which leads to a lonely neglected cemetery. This opening scene was so vital that Lean, who had exact ideas about how the film should look, replaced the original cinematographer Robert Krasker with Guy Green. Here, the young hero Pip is threatened by a fierce and desperate escaped convict named Magwitch (Finlay Currie) who demands food and a file with which to remove his chains. Later, Pip is brought to the decrepit mansion of the equally decrepit and embittered Miss Havisham (Martita Hunt). Jilted at her wedding breakfast many years before, Miss Havisham still wears the remnants of her bridal gown and lingers around the dusty, rotting, and rodent-infested remains of that fateful dinner. Her macabre plan revolves around making her ward, the young and beautiful Estella (Jean Simmons), into a one-woman avenger against all men. This includes Pip, who has fallen in love with her. His situation changes when a mysterious benefactor finances Pip's move to London and his becoming a gentleman of means. Sharing a flat with Herbert Pocket (Alec Guinness in his first important role), the adult Pip (John Mills) becomes a snob, believing that Miss Havisham is his benefactor and that Estella is destined to be his wife. Any reader accustomed to Dickens knows better.

Some have argued that Mills at 38 was far too old to play a character who is 20 going on 21, as dictated by the novel. However, the fact is Pip needs only to be a witness to the drama played out around him rather than an active participant in his own destiny. Lean, who spent seven years as a film editor before directing his first feature, knew this well and so surrounds Mills with a solid yet colorful supporting cast. Some scenes are pure delight, such as Pip's visit to the house of Wemmick (Ivor Barnard), his lawyer's assistant, where our hero meets Wemmick's elderly and slightly senile father called "Aged P," shorthand for "aged parent" and a term still used by some to refer to their own. Although not essential for the plot, the scene is memorably heartwarming and amusing, bringing with it a great dollop of Dickensian appeal.

Despite its age, *Great Expectations* has not lost any of its grandeur or poignancy. Rated number five on the British Film Institute's list of all-time greatest British movies, it earned Academy Awards for Best Art Direction and Best Black-and-White Cinematography, and was nominated for Best Director, Best Picture, and Best Adapted Screenplay. In scope, vision, and coherence, this remains the supreme film based on Dickens's work. **KK**

U.S. (RKO, Vanguard) 101m BW
**Language:** English / French
**Director:** Alfred Hitchcock
**Producer:** Alfred Hitchcock
**Screenplay:** Ben Hecht
**Photography:** Ted Tetzlaff
**Music:** Roy Webb
**Cast:** Cary Grant, Ingrid Bergman, Claude Rains, Louis Calhern, Leopoldine Konstantin, Reinhold Schünzel, Moroni Olsen, Ivan Triesault, Alex Minotis
**Oscar nomination:** Ben Hecht (screenplay), Claude Rains (actor in support role)

# NOTORIOUS (1946)

Though producer David O. Selznick reunited the winning team of director Alfred Hitchcock, star Ingrid Bergman, and writer Ben Hecht from Hitchcock's psychoanalytical drama *Spellbound* (1945), and oversaw (with his customary blizzard of memos) the development of this classy, romantic spy story, he eventually sold the whole package to RKO and let Hitchcock produce it himself. Even David Thomson, Selznick's biographer, admits that the film is as good as it is because Selznick wasn't there to ruin it.

Toward the end of World War II, suave spymaster T. R. Devlin (Cary Grant) recruits loose-living Alicia Huberman (Bergman), the estranged daughter of a convicted traitor, to infiltrate a group of Nazi exiles in Argentina. Having fallen for the man who has rescued her from a life of trampy uselessness, Alicia is agonized when she feels Devlin is pimping her for the cause, and she is driven to take her mission to extremes by marrying the almost-fatherly fascist Alexander Sebastian (Claude Rains). Inside Sebastian's chilly, luxurious mansion, Alicia earns the hatred of the true power among the evil exiles, Sebastian's smothering monster mother (Madame Konstantin), who is the sort of creature Mrs. Bates might have been if left alive. At a party, with a classic suspense mechanism in the dwindling supply of champagne that will eventually lead to a servant venturing into the wine cellar where the angelic Alicia and the devilish Devlin are snooping, Hitchcock produces his most elegant and yet topical detail: wine bottles full of uranium being used to create a Nazi A-bomb. The payoff is an agonizing moment of discovery when Sebastian is duped into believing that his wife is only unfaithful as opposed to a spy.

*Notorious*'s intense triangle drama constantly forces you to change your feelings about the three leads, with Rains even showing a bizarre heroism in the finale. The film is also a sumptuous romance, with Grant and Bergman sharing what was, at that point, the screen's longest close-up kiss. Gorgeously shot by Ted Tetzlaff in luminous monochrome, with the stars looking (and acting) their best, this last reel was extremely unnerving as the monstrous mother supervises Alicia's slow poisoning. **KN**

# BLACK NARCISSUS (1946)

G.B. (Independent, Rank, The Archers) 100m Technicolor

**Director:** Michael Powell, Emeric Pressburger

**Producer:** George R. Busby, Michael Powell, Emeric Pressburger

**Screenplay:** Michael Powell, Emeric Pressburger, from novel by Rumer Godden

**Photography:** Jack Cardiff

**Music:** Brian Easdale

**Cast:** Deborah Kerr, Sabu, David Farrar, Flora Robson, Esmond Knight, Jean Simmons, Kathleen Byron, Jenny Laird, Judith Furse, May Hallatt, Eddie Whaley Jr., Shaun Noble, Nancy Roberts, Ley On

**Oscar:** Alfred Junge (art direction), Jack Cardiff (photography)

David Thomson probably understates the case when he refers to *Black Narcissus* as "that rare thing, an erotic English film about the fantasies of nuns." Based very closely on Rumer Godden's 1939 novel, the picture follows a small group of sisters who are gifted with a building high up in the Himalayas that they attempt to turn into a convent school-cum-hospital. The drafty building was once a harem and is still adorned with explicit murals, while a cackling ayah left over from the times of licentiousness gleefully predicts that the sisters will succumb to the place's atmosphere.

On one level, *Black Narcissus* is a matter-of-fact account of the failings of empire: these sensible Christians arrive with good intentions but are in an absurd situation, teaching only pupils who are paid by the local maharajah to attend lessons which mean nothing to them, and doctoring only minor cases—since if they should try and fail to save a patient, the hospital will be abandoned as if cursed. Directors Powell and Pressburger see the humor in the nuns' frustrations, observing a culture clash without dismissing either the rational or primitive point of view, relishing the irony that it is the most religious characters who are the most sensible here (when they should be prone to all manner of unfounded beliefs), and the godless ones who are most inclined to superstition.

Sister Clodagh (Deborah Kerr), promoted too young, tries to keep the mission together like an inexperienced officer in a war movie, thrown together with the smoldering, disreputable Mr. Dean (David Farrar) and thus exciting the eventually homicidal jealousy of the most repressed of the nuns, Sister Ruth (Kathleen Byron). As the obsessions begin to bite, the film becomes more surreal, with the studio-bound exotica glowing under Jack Cardiff's vivid Technicolor cinematography and Kerr and Byron trembling under their wimples as the passionate nuns. Among the most startling moments in British cinema is the "revelation" of Sister Ruth stripped of her habit, in a mail-order dress and blood-red lipstick, transformed into a harpie who tries to push Clodagh over a precipice as she sounds the convent bell. With a nearly grown-up Sabu (Mowgli in the 1942 *Jungle Book*) and a young Jean Simmons (with a jeweled snail on her nose) as the sensual innocents who set a bad example. **KN**

# IT'S A WONDERFUL LIFE (1946)

**U.S.** (Liberty, RKO) 130m BW

**Director:** Frank Capra

**Screenplay:** Philip Van Doren Stern, Frances Goodrich

**Cast:** James Stewart, Donna Reed, Lionel Barrymore, Thomas Mitchell, Henry Travers, Beulah Bondi, Frank Faylen, Ward Bond, Gloria Grahame, H.B. Warner, Frank Albertson, Todd Karns, Samuel S. Hinds, Mary Treen, Virginia Patton

**Oscar nomination:** Frank Capra (best picture), Frank Capra (director), James Stewart (actor), William Hornbeck (editing), John Aalberg (sound)

After celebrating the common man in such 1930s classics as *It Happened One Night*, *Mr. Deeds Goes to Town*, and *You Can't Take It with You*, Frank Capra's first postwar film revels unashamedly in the goodness of ordinary folks as well as the value of humble dreams, even if they don't come true. Based on *The Greatest Gift*, a short story written on a Christmas card by Philip Van Doren Stern, the film's vital leading role of a young man saddled by responsibility was almost turned down by war-weary James Stewart. Released in 1946 to mixed reviews, the film was nevertheless nominated for five Academy Awards (including Best Picture and Best Actor), but it didn't win in any category. Whether it was a film that required frequent viewing to be fully appreciated or that simply had been made at the wrong time is now a moot point. By the 1960s, the film's copyright expired which opened the floodgates for a "public domain" version to be circulated for cheap and frequent television broadcast. Repeated heavily around the holiday season, it became a mainstay of wholesome family viewing. As an emotional touchstone for several generations, public broadcasting stations in the 1970s cemented the film's reputation of quality by scheduling it against the commercial networks' crass and materialistic holiday fare.

Gangling, good-hearted George Bailey (Stewart) grows up in tiny Bedford Falls, Connecticut but dreams of traveling the world. Duty, though, steps in again and again to crush George's dream. The loss of his freedom is only softened by George's marriage to local beauty Mary (Donna Reed) and later by his young family and his own sense of homey philanthropy in helping the working people of Bedford Falls afford their own homes. Finally, forced to take over the family savings and loan, which is threatened with foreclosure by the greedy town banker Mr. Potter (Lionel Barrymore was rarely more disagreeable), George becomes so overburdened that he attempts suicide by jumping off the local bridge. But a miracle happens: an angel named Clarence (Henry Travers) is sent from heaven to show George what the town would have become if George had had his wish and hadn't lived at all. If and only if George is convinced of his own value will his suicide be undone, the town be returned to normal, and Clarence, a second-class angel, get his wings.

Almost sixty years later, *It's a Wonderful Life* remains a holiday favorite for its uplifting message tempered by a foreboding notion of "what if." Viewed on a big screen without holiday distractions, the film is actually more of a delightfully shrewd screwball comedy packed with fast, incisive observations on love, sex, and society. The high quality of the banter especially points to uncredited script input from Dorothy Parker, Dalton Trumbo, and Clifford Odets. The movie was a favorite of Capra and Stewart, both of whom expressed extreme dismay when it became an early victim of the colorization craze. **KK**

## GILDA (1946)

U.S. (Columbia) 110m BW
**Director:** Charles Vidor
**Producer:** Virginia Van Upp
**Screenplay:** Jo Eisinger, E.A. Ellington
**Photography:** Rudolph Maté
**Music:** Doris Fisher, Allan Roberts, Hugo Friedhofer
**Cast:** Rita Hayworth, Glenn Ford, George Macready, Joseph Calleia, Steven Geray, Joe Sawyer, Gerald Mohr, Robert E. Scott, Ludwig Donath, Donald Douglas

"Statistics show there are more women in the world than anything else," snaps cynical hero Johnny Farrell (Glenn Ford), adding, with peculiar loathing, "except insects!" And yet this misogyny coexists in director Charles Vidor's film with the exquisite Gilda (Rita Hayworth) herself. A character who is at once a total blank and a masterful ironist, whose signature tune "Put the Blame on Mame"—to which she performs a supremely exotic striptease involving only the removal of her elbow-length velvet gloves—is a pointed exposé of the way women are made to seem responsible for the havoc wreaked by men who become obsessed with them.

Johnny, a hardboiled gambler who looks suavely uncomfortable in his dinner jacket, becomes manager of a casino in Buenos Aires, working for Ballin Mundson (George Macready), a frozen-faced mastermind who wields a sword cane, enjoys spying on his customers and associates from a control room in the gambling joint, and forms the apex of a three-way love triangle that triggers the plot. Ford and Hayworth, limited but engaging and photogenic actors, have definitive performances drawn out of them like teeth, and Macready has the time of his life as the complex villain. As the posters claim, "there never was a woman like Gilda!" **KN**

## MONSIEUR VERDOUX (1947)

U.S. (Charles Chaplin, United Artists) 124m BW
**Director:** Charles Chaplin
**Producer:** Charles Chaplin
**Screenplay:** Charles Chaplin
**Photography:** Roland Totheroh
**Music:** Charles Chaplin
**Cast:** Charles Chaplin, Mady Correll, Allison Roddan, Robert Lewis, Audrey Betz, Martha Raye, Ada May, Isobel Elsom, Marjorie Bennett, Helene Heigh, Margaret Hoffman, Marilyn Nash, Irving Bacon, Edwin Mills, Virginia Brissac
**Oscar nomination:** Charles Chaplin (screenplay)

Charles Chaplin bought the idea for his blackest comedy (for $5,000) from Orson Welles, who had originally planned a dramatized documentary about the legendary French serial wife killer Henri Desiré Landru. Chaplin gave the story a new and acute sociosatirical edge, in response to the then-growing political paranoia of the Cold War years. Verdoux (Chaplin), the suave and charming little bourgeois, only adopts his lucrative profession of marrying and murdering rich widows when economic depression removes the possibility of his earning an honest living as a bank clerk. Finally brought to justice, his defense is that although private murder is condemned, public killing—in the form of war—is glorified: "One murder makes a villain—millions a hero. Numbers sanctify." These were not popular sentiments in 1946 America, and Chaplin found himself more and more the target of the political right—a witch-hunt that led to his permanent departure from the United States in 1952.

Verdoux, accompanied by his jaunty little theme tune (Chaplin as usual was his own composer), is a rich and vivid character. The tight economies of the postwar period obliged Chaplin to work more quickly and with much more planning than on any previous films. The result is one of his most tightly constructed narratives, which he unselfconsciously considered "the cleverest and most brilliant film of my career." **DR**

# OUT OF THE PAST (1947)

On an Acapulco beach, with the sea shimmering through a fisherman's nets, gumshoe Jeff Markham (Robert Mitchum) kisses Kathy Moffat (Jane Greer), the woman he has been hired to find for gangster Whit Sterling (Kirk Douglas), her former boyfriend. Kathy sits alongside Jeff and reveals she knows he been sent to find her. She confesses to shooting Whit but denies taking his $40,000. She asks Jeff to believe her. Leaning forward to kiss her, Jeff nearly whispers, "Baby, I don't care."

Jacques Tourneur's *Out of the Past*, adapted from Daniel Mainwaring's novel *Build My Gallows High*, may be the masterpiece of film noir. All the elements are there: the woman who lies, but is so beautiful that one could forgive almost anything, or at least die at her side. The bitter past that rises up again and destroys the main character. The private eye, a man of wit and know-how who makes the mistake of giving in to his passion—more than once. Mitchum perfectly embodies this figure. Like Humphrey Bogart, he possesses a calm interiority that expresses independence and confidence. As one character says of him, "he just sits and stays inside himself." But unlike the cautious Bogart, Mitchum literally slouches into his role as Jeff, his heavy relaxation making his vulnerability not only believable but tragic.

Is Kathy's passion for Jeff real? In spite of her inability to endure difficulties for his sake and her fatalistic attitude about love, does she really love him? For that matter, is Jeff's ardor for her sincere? Although he phones the police to convert their final getaway into an ambush, is he surrendering to her allure once again? This is the question that Jeff's small-town girlfriend Ann (Virginia Huston) asks The Kid (Dickie Moore), Jeff's deaf-mute companion, at the film's end. The Kid nods yes. Is he telling the truth? We feel that this gesture will free Ann from any future entanglement with Jeff's fatal world. But does that mean it's a lie? *Out of the Past*, like film noir generally, leaves us with the enigmas of fatal desires, the ambiguities of loves laced with fear. **TG**

**U.S.** (RKO) 97m BW

**Director:** Jacques Tourneur

**Producer:** Warren Duff

**Screenplay:** Daniel Mainwaring, from his novel *Build My Gallows High*

**Photography :** Nicholas Musuraca

**Music:** Roy Webb

**Cast:** Robert Mitchum, Jane Greer, Kirk Douglas, Rhonda Fleming, Richard Webb, Steve Brodie, Virginia Huston, Paul Valentine, Dickie Moore, Ken Niles

U.S. (Fox) 104m BW

**Director:** Joseph L. Mankiewicz

**Producer:** Fred Kohlmar

**Screenplay:** R.A. Dick, Philip Dunne, from novel by R.A. Dick

**Photography:** Charles Lang

**Music:** Bernard Herrmann

**Cast:** Gene Tierney, Rex Harrison, George Sanders, Edna Best, Vanessa Brown, Anna Lee, Robert Coote, Natalie Wood, Isobel Elsom, Victoria Horne

**Oscar nomination:** Charles Lang (photography)

# THE GHOST AND MRS. MUIR (1947)

A romantic, gentle, and wholly unscary ghost story, *The Ghost and Mrs. Muir* playfully toys with notions of souls meeting across time and the liberating power of the imagination. Gene Tierney, her wistful beauty for once well used, plays a pretty young widow who rents a haunted cliff-top cottage. Rex Harrison, one of director Joseph L. Mankiewicz's favorite actors, plays the ghostly sea captain who becomes her guide and mentor—and whose ghosted, as it were, memoirs he encourages her to publish under her own name. Their relationship, warm but—for obvious reasons—unconsummated, sustains the film's featherlight charm and adds a touch of poignancy. Harrison's gruff performance, and a portrayal of suave caddishness from George Sanders as Tierney's would-be suitor, prevents the fantasy from sliding into whimsy and keeps sentimentality at bay.

Despite the strictures of the prevailing censorship, Philip Dunne's urbane script does an ingenious job of suggesting the captain's salty vocabulary. *The Ghost and Mrs. Muir* also benefits from Charles Lang's translucent cinematography, and one of Bernard Herrmann's gentlest and most lyrical scores. The film was fondly enough remembered to give rise to a successful television series in the late 1960s. **PK**

**G.B.** (Two Cities) 116m BW

**Director:** Carol Reed

**Producer:** Carol Reed, Phil C. Samuel

**Screenplay:** R.C. Sherriff, from novel by F.L. Green

**Photography:** Robert Krasker

**Music:** William Alwyn

**Cast:** James Mason, Robert Newton, Cyril Cusack, Peter Judge, William Hartnell, Fay Compton, Denis O'Dea, W.G. Fay, Maureen Delaney, Elwyn Brook-Jones, Robert Beatty, Dan O'Herlihy, Kitty Kirwan, Beryl Measor, Roy Irving

**Oscar nomination:** Fergus McDonnell (editing)

# ODD MAN OUT (1947)

Carol Reed's chronicle of an Irish republican soldier plays like an expressionist fever dream. James Mason, as Johnny McQueen, plays the leader of an anti-British group that plans a robbery that will help to fund their cause. On the night of the crime, Johnny kills a man and is shot himself, and must run from the authorities who set up a dragnet across the city to catch him and his associates. The entire film takes place during the rest of this night as Johnny seeks refuge and his girlfriend Kathleen (Kathleen Ryan) tries to find him.

Johnny discovers that people he trusted or thought were sympathetic to his cause will not stick their necks out for him. He is forced to keep moving and is passed along from one person to the next; each has a reason not to help him or to use him for their own aims. As his wound worsens, Johnny becomes deliriously philosophical and begins to understand that he is fundamentally alone in the world. The film's score and shadowy black-and-white photography add to the overall sense of moral uncertainty. The way in which *Odd Man Out* bursts the seams of the political thriller genre and becomes a moving, thoughtful, and powerful meditation on social existence will continue to astonish moviegoers for all time. **RH**

# LADRI DI BICICLETTE (1948)
## THE BICYCLE THIEF

Antonio Ricci (Lamberto Maggiorani), an unemployed worker in postwar Rome, finds a job putting up movie posters after his wife pawns the family's bedsheets to get his bicycle out of hock. But right after he starts work the bike is stolen, and with his little boy Bruno (Enzo Staiola) in tow he crisscrosses the city trying to recover it, encountering various aspects of Roman society, including some of the more acute class differences, in the process.

This masterpiece—the Italian title translates as "bicycle thieves"—is generally and correctly known as one of the key works of Italian neorealism. French critic André Bazin also recognized it as one of the great communist films. The fact that it received the 1949 Oscar for best foreign film suggests that it wasn't perceived that way in the United States at the time. Ironically, the only thing American censors cared about was a scene in which the little boy urinates on the street. For some followers of auteur theory the film lost some of its power because it didn't derive from a single creative intelligence. A collaboration between screenwriter Cesare Zavattini, director Vittorio De Sica, nonprofessional actors, and many others, the production is so charged with a common purpose that there is little point in even trying to separate achievements.

*The Bicycle Thief* contains what is possibly the greatest depiction of a relationship between a father and son in the history of cinema, full of subtle fluctuations and evolving gradations between the two characters in terms of respect and trust, and it's an awesome heartbreaker. It also has its moments of Chaplinesque comedy—the contrasting behavior of two little boys having lunch at the same restaurant. Set alongside a film like *Life Is Beautiful* (1997), provides some notion of how much of mainstream world cinema and its relation to reality has been infantilized over the past half century. **JRos**

**Italy** (De Sica) 93m BW

**Language:** Italian

**Director:** Vittorio De Sica

**Producer:** Giuseppe Amato, Vittorio De Sica

**Screenplay:** Cesare Zavattini, Oreste Biancoli, Suso d'Amico, Vittorio De Sica, Adolfo Franci, Gerardo Guerrieri, from the novel *Ladri di biciclette* by Luigi Bartolini

**Photography:** Carlo Montuori

**Music:** Alessandro Cicognini

**Cast:** Lamberto Maggiorani, Enzo Staiola, Lianella Carell, Gino Saltamerenda, Vittorio Antonucci, Giulio Chiari, Elena Altieri, Carlo Jachino, Michele Sakara, Emma Druetti, Fausto Guerzoni

**Oscar:** Giuseppe Amato, Vittorio De Sica (honorary award—best foreign language film)

**Oscar nomination:** Cesare Zavattini (screenplay)

U.S. (Rampart, Universal) 86m BW
**Director:** Max Ophüls
**Producer:** John Houseman
**Screenplay:** Howard Koch, Stefan Zweig, from the novel *Brief einer Unbekannten* by Stefan Zweig
**Photography:** Franz Planer
**Music:** Daniele Amfitheatrof
**Cast:** Joan Fontaine, Louis Jourdan, Mady Christians, Marcel Journet, Art Smith, Carol Yorke, Howard Freeman, John Good, Leo B. Pessin, Erskine Sanford, Otto Waldis, Sonja Bryden

# LETTER FROM AN UNKNOWN WOMAN
## (1948)

Stefan Brand (Louis Jourdan), a concert pianist and gentleman dandy in turn-of-the-century Vienna, arrives home after yet another evening of dissipation. His mute servant hands him a letter. It is from a woman, and its first words well and truly halt him in his tracks: "By the time you read this, I will be dead..."

What unfolds from this extraordinary opening has more than a fair claim to being not only the best film of director Max Ophüls, and a supreme achievement in the often unfairly maligned genre of melodrama, but also one of the greatest films in world cinema history. It is, in its own terms, one of the few movies that deserve to be rated as perfect, right down to the smallest detail.

Superbly adapted from Stefan Zweig's novella by Howard Koch, this is the apotheosis of "doomed love" fiction. Flashing back to trace the hopeless infatuation of young Lisa Berndl (Joan Fontaine) for Stefan, Ophüls gives us a vivid, heartbreaking portrait of a love that should never have been: Her naïve romanticization of artistic men mismatched with his indifferent objectification of available women adds up to gloomy tragedy. Ophüls's intuitive grasp of the inequity of gender roles in 20th-century Western society is breathtaking.

Ophüls constructs a most exquisitely poised work. While encouraging us to identify with Lisa's longing, and the dreams of a whole society fed by its popular culture (a mobile scenic backdrop standing in for a later era's movies), *Letter from an Unknown Woman* at the same time provides a trenchant and devastating critique of the myth and ideology of romantic love. Our understanding of the tale hinges on its delicate shifts in mood and viewpoint.

Relentlessly and hypnotically, Ophüls's mise en scène strips away the veils of illusion that envelop Lisa. Either the staging reveals the banal conditions of reality that underwrite these flights of fantasy, or the camera suggests—in subtle positionings and movements slightly detached from the story's world—a knowing perspective that eludes the characters.

The film is a triumph not just of meaningful, expressive style, but of purposive narrative structure. With poignant voiceover narration from Lisa, decades are bridged and key years artfully skipped thanks to a patterning of significant details arranged as motifs, concentrated in repeated gestures (such as the giving of a flower), lines of dialogue (references to passing time are ubiquitous), and key objects (the staircase leading to Stefan's apartment). By the time Ophüls reaches a Hollywood staple—the ghost-like apparition of young Lisa at last conjured in Stefan's memory—the cliché is gloriously transcended, and tears overcome even those modern viewers who resist such old-fashioned "soaps."

*Letter from an Unknown Woman* is an inexhaustibly rich film, one that has drawn myriad film-lovers to try to unravel its themes, patterns, suggestions, and ironies. But no amount of close analysis can ever extinguish the rich, tearing emotion that this masterpiece elicits. **AM**

**U.S.** (Diana) 99m BW
**Director:** Fritz Lang
**Producer:** Fritz Lang, Walter Wanger
**Screenplay:** Rufus King, Silvia Richards
**Photography:** Stanley Cortez
**Music:** Miklós Rózsa
**Cast:** Joan Bennett, Michael Redgrave, Anne Revere, Barbara O'Neil, Natalie Schafer, Anabel Shaw, Rosa Rey, James Seay, Mark Dennis, Paul Cavanagh

# SECRET BEYOND THE DOOR (1948)

Fritz Lang fans often divide on whether they prefer the certified, highbrow classics like *M* (1931), *Metropolis* (1926), and *The Big Heat* (1953), or the stranger, more cryptic and perverse films in his oeuvre that plumb less reputable areas of pop culture, such as *Rancho Notorious* (1952) and *Moonfleet* (1955). *Secret Beyond the Door* scrapes by in some accounts as a respectable film noir, but it is the beguiling mixture of many genres—women's melodrama, Freudian case study, serial killer mystery, and allegory of the artistic/creative process—that makes it such a special and haunting oddity in the director's career.

The film partakes of Hollywood's "Female Gothic" cycle, exploring the fraught attachment of a woman (here, Joan Bennett) to a man (Michael Redgrave) who is all at once enigmatic, seductive, and (as the plot unravels) potentially life threatening. As in Hitchcock's *Rebecca* (1940), which inspired Lang, the heroine enters a home of strangers, brimming with past, unspoken traumas, and sick, subterranean relationships.

Lang fixes the frankly sadomasochistic ambiguities of this plot (What is the true nature of the male beast, sensitivity or aggression? What does the woman really want from him, anyway, love or death?) into a startlingly novel context: Redgrave is a tormented-genius architect who has built a house of "felicitous rooms," each the reconstructed scene of a grisly, patently psychosexual murder.

*Secret Beyond the Door* joins a special group of 1940s films, including Jean Renoir's *The Woman on the Beach* (1947) and the Val Lewton production *The Seventh Victim* (1943), whose potent, dreamlike aura is virtually guaranteed by their B movie sparseness and free-association plotting—as well as, here, a voiceover narration that disorientatingly shifts from Bennett to Redgrave and back again. Heretical it may be for a card-carrying auteurist to suggest, but the cuts imposed by Universal on Lang's initial edit probably enhanced this dreamlike quality. The end result may be short on rational links and explanations, but *Secret Beyond the Door* is one of the precious occasions when Lang—aided immeasurably by Stanley Cortez's baroque cinematography and Miklós Rózsa's lush score—managed to add a richly poetic dimension to his familiar fatalism. **AM**

# FORCE OF EVIL (1948)

Like *The Night of the Hunter*, *Force of Evil* is a unique event in the history of American cinema. Its director, Abraham Polonsky, made two subsequent movies much later and scripted others, but this is the sole film in which the full extent of his promising brilliance shined, before being snuffed out by the McCarthy-era blacklist.

*Force of Evil* sits uncomfortably within the film noir genre, despite the presence of a star (John Garfield) associated with hard-boiled, streetwise movies. It is above all a film of poetry, carried by a "blank verse" voiceover and a highly stylized singsong dialogue, which are among the most astounding and radical innovations of 1940s cinema, anticipating Malick's *Badlands* (1973).

This is a story of amorality, guilt, and redemption, dramatized through the near-Biblical device of betrayal between brothers. Polonsky breaks up the fatalistic gloom of the piece (its final image of a descent to a corpse among garbage is chilling) with a touching and very modern love story between Garfield and Beatrice Pearson.

The film is stylized down to the smallest detail in line with its poetic ambition: to liberate sound, image, and performance and have all three interact in an intoxicating polyphony. **AM**

**U.S.** (Enterprise, MGM) 78m BW

**Director:** Abraham Polonsky

**Producer:** Bob Roberts

**Screenplay:** Abraham Polonsky, Ira Wolfert, from the novel *Tucker's People* by Ira Wolfert

**Photography:** George Barnes

**Music:** David Raksin

**Cast:** John Garfield, Thomas Gomez, Marie Windsor, Howland Chamberlain, Roy Roberts, Paul Fix, Stanley Prager, Barry Kelley, Paul McVey, Beatrice Pearson, Fred O. Sommers

# XIAO CHENG ZHI CHUN (1948)
## SPRING IN A SMALL TOWN

If one mark of a great film is its ability to introduce characters in an economical way, Fei Mu's *Spring in a Small City* projects its greatness instantly. Deftly and poignantly, the film unveils to us five figures: "The Wife" (Wei Wei), lonely and weary of daily chores; "The Husband" (Shi Yu), a sickly melancholic; "The Sister" (Zhang Hongmei), youthfully vivacious; Lao Huang, "The Servant" (Cui Chaoming), ever watchful; and "The Visitor" (Li Wei), strolling into this city (and out of the past) to become the catalyst for change.

Sparingly, the film builds its postwar drama: the desires, hopes, dreams, and hurts that play among these characters caught in the arrangement of bodies in the frame, a choreography of furtive looks, and sudden gestures of resistance or resignation. But there is also a modernist element: The wife's voiceover narration, which poetically reiterates what is plainly visible, covers events she has not witnessed, and puts sad realities into brutal words.

This masterpiece of Chinese cinema has only recently received the worldwide recognition it deserves, influencing Wong Kar-Wai's *In the Mood for Love* (2001) and occasioning a respectful remake (2002). *Spring in a Small City* stands among cinema's finest, richest, and most moving melodramas. **AM**

**China** 85m BW

**Language:** Mandarin

**Director:** Fei Mu

**Screenplay:** Li Tianji

**Photography:** Li Shengwei

**Music:** Huang Yijun

**Cast:** Cui Chaoming, Li Wei, Shi Yu, Wei Wei, Zhang Hongmei

**U.S.** (Charles K. Feldman, Monterey) 133m BW

**Director:** Howard Hawks, Arthur Rosson

**Producer:** Charles K. Feldman, Howard Hawks

**Screenplay:** Borden Chase, Charles Schnee

**Photography:** Russell Harlan

**Music:** Dimitri Tiomkin

**Cast:** John Wayne, Montgomery Clift, Joanne Dru, Walter Brennan, Coleen Gray, Harry Carey, John Ireland, Noah Beery Jr., Harry Carey Jr., Chief Yowlachie, Paul Fix, Hank Worden, Mickey Kuhn, Ray Hyke, Wally Wales

**Oscar nomination:** Borden Chase (screenplay), Christian Nyby (editing)

# RED RIVER (1948)

A Western remake of *Mutiny on the Bounty* (1935), this is a considerably deeper film than its source, presenting the Bligh/Christian relationship in terms of a father-son conflict. Star John Wayne—one of the most beautiful male leads of the 1930s, playing older than his real age with authentic and prescient crustiness—is interestingly matched by Hawks against the photogenic Montgomery Clift, epitome of a kind of sensitive, manly neurosis that would come in fashion in the next decade.

After a long prologue set during the aftermath of an 1851 Indian attack, in which we see how bereft Tom Dunson (Wayne) and orphaned Matthew Garth (Clift) combine their herds to form a cattle empire, we pick up the Red River D in a post-Civil War economic depression. Leading a cattle drive up into Missouri, the inflexible Dunson becomes more and more tyrannical, prompting Matt to rebel and steer the herd West by a safer route to Abilene. Dunson admires the kid's guts, but nevertheless swears to track him down and shoot him dead, leading to one of the most emotional climaxes in the genre as the men who love each other face off among milling cattle in the Abilene streets.

Hawks, the great film chronicler of macho pursuits, here stages the definitive cow opera, putting all other cattle drive Westerns in the shade, with beautiful, lyrical, exciting sequences of stampeding, rough weather, cowboying, and Indian skirmishes. The leads are at their best, with Wayne astonishingly matching Clift for subtlety, and you get sterling support from Walter Brennan as the toothless coot, John Ireland as a lanky gunslinger, and Joanne Dru as a pioneer gal who can take an arrow in the shoulder without hardly flinching. Though known for his Westerns, Hawks made surprisingly few films in the genre. This seems like an affectionate tribute to John Ford, mixed in with a certain I-can-do-that-too attitude, as Hawks casts several members of his peer's stock company: Harry Carey Senior and Junior, Hank Worden, even Wayne himself. Hawks uses a Fordian approach to the dangerous splendors of the Western landscape along with a Ford-like folk song-based score from Dimitri Tiomkin. **KN**

# ROPE (1948)

Though he owed his fame to showmanship and thrills, Alfred Hitchcock was always among the most experimental of commercial filmmakers. With a strong source in a play by Patrick Hamilton (of *Gaslight* fame) based on the Leopold and Loeb case, more conventionally dramatized in the 1959 film *Compulsion*, *Rope* calls attention to its theatrical one-set setting by consisting of reel-long takes spliced together almost invisibly so that the film appears to unspool unedited. Given that, in 1948, many film audiences had barely registered that movies consisted of brief snippets cut together for dramatic effect—most films about filmmaking even now seem to suggest that scenes are shot as if they were happening in live theater—it may well be that Hitchcock was most interested in addressing his fellow professionals, demonstrating an alternate manner of telling a film story in much the way that the later Dogme95 movement or *The Blair Witch Project* (1999) set out to do.

Apart from the technical challenges of having the camera follow characters around a large New York apartment, telling a story in "real time," *Rope* has quite a bit of intrinsic interest as two cohabiting bachelors (John Dall and Farley Granger) try to get away with a casual murder to prove an obscure point. At once an intense psychological drama and a black comedy in the vein of *Arsenic and Old Lace* (1944), the film delivers cat-and-mouse conflict as the killers invite professorial Jimmy Stewart around to impress him with their cleverness, flirting in more than one way with revelation.

The technique is less of a distraction than it might be, allowing Stewart and Dall to face off in a great battle of murderous camp and moral rectitude; it may be that all the attention paid to the long takes made the censors overlook the unusually frank depiction of a quasi-gay relationship between the murderers—it's never addressed in the dialogue but there is only one bedroom in the apartment they share. Granger's shakiness isn't helped by the merciless length of the takes, but Dall and Stewart rise to the occasion, challenged to deliver sustained, theater-style performances in the more intimate medium of film. **KN**

**U.S.** (Transatlantic, Warner Bros.)
80m Technicolor

**Director:** Alfred Hitchcock

**Producer:** Sidney Bernstein

**Screenplay:** Hume Cronyn, Arthur Laurents, from the play *Rope's End* by Patrick Hamilton

**Photography:** William V. Skall, Joseph A. Valentine

**Music:** David Buttolph

**Cast:** James Stewart, John Dall, Farley Granger, Cedric Hardwicke, Constance Collier, Douglas Dick, Edith Evanson, Dick Hogan, Joan Chandler

U.S. (Fox) 108m BW

**Director:** Anatole Litvak

**Producer:** Robert Bassler, Anatole Litvak, Darryl F. Zanuck

**Screenplay:** Millen Brand, Frank Partos, from novel by Mary Jane Ward

**Photography:** Leo Tover

**Music:** Alfred Newman

**Cast:** Olivia de Havilland, Mark Stevens, Leo Genn, Celeste Holm, Glenn Langan, Helen Craig, Leif Erickson, Beulah Bondi, Lee Patrick, Howard Freeman, Natalie Schafer, Ruth Donnelly, Katherine Locke, Frank Conroy, Minna Gombell

**Oscar nomination:** Robert Bassler, Anatole Litvak (best picture), Anatole Litvak (director), Frank Partos, Millen Brand (screenplay), Olivia de Havilland (actress), Alfred Newman (music)

# THE SNAKE PIT (1948)

Among the more impressive products of Hollywood's postwar turn toward greater realism is Anatole Litvak's brutally honest treatment of mental illness and its cure in the modern sanitarium, whose horrors include the overcrowded ward where the incurables are warehoused—the "snake pit" of the film's title. *The Snake Pit* offers a more balanced view of mental disturbance than many more recent films, including the often praised *One Flew over the Cuckoo's Nest* (1976).

Virginia Cunningham (Olivia de Havilland) seems at first a hopeless psychotic, but with treatment from a sympathetic doctor, Mark Kick (Leo Genn), she is able to undergo a "talking cure." Flashbacks show a childhood in which she is denied not only her mother's love but also attention from her father, who died when Virginia was very young. Virginia also suffers the death of the man she loves, for which she believes she is responsible. Under Dr. Kick's care, she graduates to the "best" ward, only to be bullied there by a tyrannical nurse. Virginia's subsequent misbehavior lands her in the "snake pit," but this horrifying experience proves strangely therapeutic. Finally she wins release, at last understanding how her feelings of guilt are irrational.

Memorable is how the film shows the terror that Virginia's illness makes her suffer. *The Snake Pit*'s optimistic realism contrasts with the pseudo-Freudian solutions of other movies of the period, including Hitchcock's *Spellbound* (1945). **RBP**

**U.S.** (Columbia, Mercury) 87m BW

**Language:** English / Cantonese

**Director:** Orson Welles

**Producer:** William Castle, Orson Welles, Richard Wilson

**Screenplay:** Orson Welles, from the novel *If I Die Before I Wake* by Sherwood King

**Photography:** Charles Lawton Jr.

**Music:** Doris Fisher, Allan Roberts, Heinz Roemheld

**Cast:** Rita Hayworth, Orson Welles, Everett Sloane, Glenn Anders, Ted de Corsia, Erskine Sanford, Gus Schilling, Carl Frank, Louis Merrill, Evelyn Ellis, Harry Shannon

# THE LADY FROM SHANGHAI (1948)

Having proved with *The Stranger* (1946) that he could make a "regular" film if he wanted to, Orson Welles here returns to the film noir genre, picking up almost at random a pulp novel (Sherwood King's *If I Die Before I Wake*) and delivering something so rich and strange it was guaranteed to irk Columbia head Harry Cohn. Simply by shearing Rita Hayworth's trademarked long hair and dying her crop blonde, Welles deliberately devalued a studio asset who happened to be his ex-wife, and that was even before it emerged that she was playing not the sympathetic bombshell of *Gilda* (1946) but a villainness so nasty that even her undoubted sex appeal becomes repulsive.

With a variable Irish accent, Welles is a seaman hired by a crippled lawyer (Everett Sloane, lizardy and scary) to crew his yacht and perhaps also (as in the anecdote preserved by Welles as *The Immortal Story* [1968]) to service his beautiful wife. A murder takes place, followed by a trial in which everyone acts unethically at best, and the crazy kaleidoscope is shattered by a finale involving a shoot-out in a hall of mirrors. *The Lady from Shanghai* is a broken mirror of a film, with shards of genius that can never be put together into anything that makes sense. **KN**

# THE PALEFACE (1948)

Jane Russell plays Calamity Jane, recruited by the U.S. government to help track down a gang of renegade whites who are selling guns to the Indians. In order to pose as an emigrant on a wagon train going West she marries Painless Peter Potter, an incompetent and cowardly dentist she encounters in a bathhouse—one doesn't look for plausibility in such material! As Painless, Bob Hope has a wonderful time, letting forth a fusillade of jokes on the principle that if you don't like this one there will be another one along in a minute. Much of the humor in *The Paleface* is along predictable lines, with Indians inhaling the dentist's laughing gas and Hope performing all manner of unheroics, leading to his being mistaken for a courageous Indian fighter. Hope is of course madly attracted to the curvaceous Russell—"You've got just the kind of mouth I like to work on." There's a running joke about the endlessly postponed consummation of the marriage as Russell gets on with the job of defeating the bad guys.

Painless and Calamity are captured and taken to an Indian camp, where Indians are played both by Chief Yowlachie (a genuine Native American) and by Iron Eyes Cody (an Italian-American who passed as a Native American). The comedy at their expense, though hardly politically correct, is too silly to give serious offense.

Hope gives a pleasing rendition of the song "Buttons and Bows," written by Victor Young, which won an Oscar. It's a plea for girls to go back East and wear pretty clothes, but Russell looks equally fetching in satin dresses and buckskin pants. Four years later "Buttons and Bows" was repeated in a sequel, titled *Son of Paleface* (directed by the writer of *The Paleface*, Frank Tashlin). Hope and Russell are reunited, this time supported by Roy Rogers and his horse Trigger, who gets a song of his own, "A Four-Legged Friend." **EB**

**U.S.** (Paramount) 91m Technicolor

**Director:** Norman Z. McLeod

**Producer:** Robert L. Welch

**Screenplay:** Edmund L. Hartmann, Frank Tashlin

**Photography:** Ray Rennahan

**Music:** Ray Evans, Jay Livingston, Victor Young

**Cast:** Bob Hope, Jane Russell, Robert Armstrong, Iris Adrian, Bobby Watson, Jackie Searl, Joseph Vitale, Charles Trowbridge, Clem Bevans, Jeff York, Stanley Andrews, Wade Crosby, Chief Yowlachie, Iron Eyes Cody, John Maxwell

**Oscar:** Jay Livingston, Ray Evans (song)

**G.B.** (Independent, Rank, The Archers) 133m Technicolor

**Director:** Michael Powell, Emeric Pressburger

**Producer:** George R. Busby, Michael Powell, Emeric Pressburger

**Screenplay:** Emeric Pressburger, Michael Powell, Keith Winter, from story by Hans Christian Andersen

**Photography:** Jack Cardiff

**Music:** Brian Easdale

**Cast:** Anton Walbrook, Marius Goring, Moira Shearer, Robert Helpmann, Léonide Massine, Albert Bassermann, Ludmilla Tchérina, Esmond Knight

**Oscar:** Hein Heckroth, Arthur Lawson (art direction), Brian Easdale (music)

**Oscar nomination:** Michael Powell, Emeric Pressburger (best picture), Emeric Pressburger (screenplay), Reginald Mills (editing)

# THE RED SHOES (1948)

The 1948 Michael Powell–Emeric Pressberger production has been beloved by generations of girls who want to grow up to be ballerinas, though its message to them is decidedly double-edged. In a dazzling twist on the old showbiz star-is-born story, winsome, willful, talented debutante-cum-dancer Victoria Page (Moira Shearer) falls under the spell of Svengali-cum-Rasputin-cum-Diaghilev impresario Boris Lermontov (Anton Walbrook). She neglects her private life (a romance with composer Marius Goring) in favor of a passionate and almost unhealthy devotion to Art, with a beautifully choreographed tragic ending in the offing. After the departure of prima ballerina Boronskaja (Ludmilla Tchérina), whom Lermontov drops when she wants to get married, Vicky makes her starring debut in an especially created ballet version of the Hans Christian Andersen story of the girl whose shoes keep her dancing until she drops dead. This spurs the filmmakers—augmented by choreographer-dancer Robert Helpmann, costar Leonide Massine, and conductor Sir Thomas Beecham—to a 20-minute fantasy dance sequence that set a trend (see *An American in Paris*, *On the Town*, *Oklahoma!*) for such stylized high-culture interludes in musicals but manages far better than any of the imitators to retell in miniature the larger story of the film while still playing credibly as a performance piece in its own right.

Of course, Vicky's off-stage life sadly follows that of Andersen's heroine, climaxing in a balletic leap in front of a train and the unforgettable tribute performance in which her devastated costars dance the Red Shoes ballet again with only the shoes to stand in for the star. Shearer, tiny and astonishing in her screen debut, is a powerhouse presence who can stand up to the full force of Walbrook's overwhelming performance, convincing both as the ingenue dancing in a cramped hall with a third-rate company and as the great star adored by the whole world. The heroine is surrounded with weird fairy-tale backdrops for the daringly lush ballet, but production designer Hein Heckroth, art director Arthur Lawson, and cinematographer Jack Cardiff work as hard to make the supposedly normal off-stage scenes as rich and strange as the theatrical highlights.

Walbrook, eyes glowing when not hiding behind beetle black dark glasses, coos and hisses Mephistophelean lines with a self-delight that's impossible not to share, manipulating all about him with ease but still tragically alone in his monklike devotion to the ballet. *The Red Shoes* is a rare musical to capture the magic of theatrical performance without neglecting the sweaty, agonizing effort necessary to create such transports of delight. Its gossipy insider feel went a great way toward making ballet accessible outside its supposed high-class audience, contrasting the eager expectation of the musical students crowded into the highest (cheapest) seats with the offhand take-it-for-granted patronage of the well-dressed swine in the stalls before whom the artistic pearls are cast. Wrapped up with gorgeous sparkly color, off-the-beaten-track classical music selections, and a sinister edge that perfectly catches the ambiguity of traditional as opposed to Disney fairy tales, this is a luminous masterpiece. **KN**

**U.S.** (Warner Bros.) 126m BW
**Director:** John Huston
**Producer:** Henry Blanke, Jack L. Warner
**Screenplay:** John Huston, B. Traven, from novel by B. Traven
**Photography:** Ted D. McCord
**Music:** Buddy Kaye, Max Steiner
**Cast:** Humphrey Bogart, Walter Huston, Tim Holt, Bruce Bennett, Barton MacLane, Alfonso Bedoya, Arturo Soto Rangel, Manuel Dondé, José Torvay, Margarito Luna
**Oscar:** John Huston (director) (screenplay), Walter Huston (actor in support role)
**Oscar nomination:** Henry Blanke (best picture)

# THE TREASURE OF THE SIERRA MADRE
(1948)

The failed quest, fueled by ambition and frustrated by greed and internal dissension, was John Huston's favorite plot, appealing to the mixture of romantic and cynic that made up his character. From *The Maltese Falcon* (1941) to *The Man Who Would Be King* (1975) he played repeated variations on this theme—but *The Treasure of the Sierra Madre* presents it in something close to its archetypal form. Three ill-assorted American drifters in Mexico join forces to prospect for gold, find it, and—inevitably—in the end, snatch defeat from the jaws of victory and lose it again. Huston, always a great adaptor of literature for the screen, drew his story from a novel by the mysterious and reclusive writer B. Traven and, as ever, treated his source material with respect and affection, preserving much of Traven's laconic dialogue and sardonic outlook.

Despite the studio's opposition—because location filming, at least for A-list Hollywood productions, was rare in those days—Huston insisted on shooting almost entirely on location in Mexico, near an isolated village some 140 miles north of the capital. His intransigence paid off. The film's texture exudes the dusty aridity of the Mexican landscape, so that watching it you can almost taste the grit between your teeth; and the actors, exiled from the comfortable environment of the studio and having to contend with the elements, were pushed into giving taut, edgy performances. This fitted *Treasure*'s theme: how people react under pressure. Whereas the old prospector (played by the director's father Walter Huston) and the naïve youngster (cowboy-movie actor Tim Holt) hang on to their principles in the face of adversity and the temptation of gold, the paranoid Fred C. Dobbs (Humphrey Bogart in one of his most memorably unsettling roles) cracks up and succumbs.

Huston's determination to shoot *Treasure* the way he wanted paid off for the studio too. Jack Warner initially detested the film, but it brought Warner Brothers not only a box-office smash hit but triumphs at the Academy Awards. Huston won Oscars for Best Director and Best Screenplay, while his father picked up the Best Supporting Actor Oscar. It was the first and—so far—only time a father-and-son team had won at the Awards. **PK**

# LOUISIANA STORY (1948)

For his last film, *Louisiana Story*, the great documentarist Robert J. Flaherty accepted sponsorship from Standard Oil to make a movie about oil prospecting in the Louisiana bayous. The funding came without strings, but even so Flaherty maybe soft-pedaled his depiction of the oil company a little, showing it as a benign force causing no damage to the unspoiled wilderness. But a hint of naïvete isn't entirely out of place; events in the bayou, and the arrival of the oilmen, are shown us through the eyes of a 12-year-old boy (Joseph Boudreaux). The haunted, waterlogged landscape becomes a magical place, full of dark foliage and exotic wildlife, where an oil derrick gliding majestically up a waterway seems as mythical and unfathomable as the werewolves and mermaids the boy believes in.

Dialogue is minimal—partly because the director, as usual, was working with local people, not professional actors—and Flaherty relies mainly on his charged, lyrical images and Virgil Thomson's score to carry the narrative. Thomson's music, drawing ingeniously on original Cajun themes, was awarded a Pulitzer Prize—the first film score to win this honor. In *Louisiana Story*, as in all his finest work, Flaherty celebrates the beauty, danger, and fascination of the wild places of the earth. **PK**

**U.S.** (Robert Flaherty) 78m BW

**Language:** English / French

**Director:** Robert J. Flaherty

**Producer:** Robert J. Flaherty

**Screenplay:** Frances H. Flaherty, Robert J. Flaherty

**Photography:** Richard Leacock

**Music:** Virgil Thomson

**Cast:** Joseph Boudreaux, Lionel Le Blanc, E. Bienvenu, Frank Hardy, C.P. Guedry

**Oscar nomination:** Frances H. Flaherty, Robert J. Flaherty (screenplay)

**U.S.** (Paramount) 115m BW

**Director:** William Wyler

**Producer:** Lester Koenig, Robert Wyler, William Wyler

**Screenplay:** Augustus Goetz, Ruth Goetz, from the novel *Washington Square* by Henry James

**Photography:** Leo Tover

**Music:** Aaron Copland

**Cast:** Olivia de Havilland, Montgomery Clift, Ralph Richardson, Miriam Hopkins, Vanessa Brown, Betty Linley, Ray Collins, Mona Freeman, Selena Royle, Paul Lees, Harry Antrim, Russ Conway, David Thursby

**Oscar:** William Wyler (best picture), William Wyler (director), Olivia de Havilland (actress), John Meehan, Harry Horner, Emile Kuri (art direction), Edith Head, Gile Steele (costume ), Aaron Copland (music)

**Oscar nomination:** Ralph Richardson (actor in support role), Leo Tover (photography)

# THE HEIRESS (1949)

"How can you be so cruel?" "I have been taught by masters." William Wyler's unforgettable adaptation of Henry James's novel *Washington Square* (pointlessly remade in 1997) revolves around indelible performances, intensified by the director's trademark demanding long takes and meticulous mastery of mood, lighting, and camera technique. Olivia de Havilland, who received her second Academy Award, is heart stopping as the dreadfully plain, painfully gauche girl marked as a spinster despite the fortune she will inherit from the cold, caustic father (Ralph Richardson), who regards her as an embarrassment.

Then beautiful, fortune-hunting wastrel Montgomery Clift courts her, as insincere as he is irresistible. Over the insulting objections of her father and with the connivance of her foolishly romantic aunt (Miriam Hopkins), Catherine plots an elopement; when her lover decides to take his chances elsewhere she undergoes a steely transformation. When the naïve Catherine realizes that she has been jilted, de Havilland's slow, exhausted ascent up the stairs is forever haunting. Her final ascent upstairs, in bitter triumph as her returned suitor pounds desperately at the door, is no less affecting. The class of the entire production is underlined by Aaron Copland's evocative original score, also an Oscar winner. **AE**

# KIND HEARTS AND CORONETS (1949)

Among the earliest of the Ealing Comedies produced by Sir Michael Balcon's West London hothouse of comedic creativity, and a prime example of their distinctively British humor, *Kind Hearts and Coronets* is without equal for grace and *savoir faire* in black comedy. It is sophisticated, deliciously sly, and resolved with another Ealing trademark, the smart sting in the tale.

Eight members of the snobbish, wealthy, and aristocratic D'Ascoyne family stand between their bitter, coolly self-possessed poor relation Louis Mazzini (suave Dennis Price) and a dukedom, provoking him to mass murder in Robert Hamer's audaciously elegant black comedy of class. The film was adapted by Hamer and John Dighton from a pungent novel of society decadence, *Israel Rank* by Roy Horniman, but also, arguably, it was influenced by Charlie Chaplin's more controversial *Monsieur Verdoux* (1947). In his inexorable, unscrupulous rise, Price's Machievellian Mazzini becomes fatefully entangled with two different women: Edith D'Ascoyne (Valerie Hobson, wife of John Profumo, notorious principal of the 1963 sex scandal that brought down the British government), the touchingly gracious widow of one of his victims, and Sibella, the fabulously eccentric, dangerously feline sex kitten played by Ealing favorite Joan Greenwood.

All eight of the clearly inbred, dotty D'Ascoynes—including the hatchet-faced suffragette Lady Agatha who is shot down in a balloon, the bluff general condemned to short-lived enjoyment of an explosive pot of caviar, and the insane admiral who does Mazzini's job for him by going down with his ship—are famously played by Ealing's man of a thousand faces, unrecognizable from one film to the next (and in this case from one scene to the next), the delightful Alec Guinness.

Hamer's all-too-brief directorial heyday peaked with *Kind Hearts and Coronets*. He had come to the film with a valuable background as an editor and found a balance between the smart dialogue and pithy, satiric visual vignettes. The slick black-and-white work of wartime news cameraman-turned-cinematographer Douglas Slocombe led to a much longer and prolific career: he shot many classic British films of the 1960s and, later, such international hits as the *Indiana Jones* trilogy. **AE**

**G.B.** (Ealing studios) 106m BW

**Director:** Robert Hamer

**Producer:** Michael Balcon, Michael Relph

**Screenplay:** Robert Hamer, Roy Horniman, John Dighton, from the novel *Israel Rank* by Roy Horniman

**Photography:** Douglas Slocombe

**Music:** Ernest Irving

**Cast:** Dennis Price, Valerie Hobson, Joan Greenwood, Alec Guinness, Audrey Fildes, Miles Malleson, Clive Morton, John Penrose, Cecil Ramage, Hugh Griffith, John Salew, Eric Messiter, Lyn Evans, Barbara Leake, Peggy Ann Clifford

**Venice Film Festival:** Robert Hamer nomination (Golden Lion)

**U.S.** (King, Pioneer) 86m BW
**Director:** Joseph H. Lewis
**Producer:** Frank King, Maurice King
**Screenplay:** MacKinlay Kantor, Millard Kaufman
**Photography:** Russell Harlan
**Music:** Victor Young
**Cast:** Peggy Cummins, John Dall, Berry Kroeger, Morris Carnovsky, Anabel Shaw, Harry Lewis, Nedrick Young, Russ Tamblyn, Ross Elliott

# GUN CRAZY (1949)

Joseph H. Lewis's cult gem *Gun Crazy* (a.k.a. *Deadly Is the Female*) is something of a test case in contemporary debates on the meaning of the critically disputed term film noir. Based loosely on the story of infamous 1930s bandits Bonnie Parker and Clyde Barrow (the screenplay was developed by MacKinlay Kantor and blacklisted writer Dalton Trumbo, the latter here credited as Millard Kaufman to conceal the fact that he was one of the Hollywood Ten), this tale of rural love-on-the-run appears to have little in common with the hard-boiled nocturnal urban underworld that more often defines the noir tradition. But set alongside the similar story of star-crossed lovers in *They Live By Night* (1948), as well as films that featured down-on-their-luck honest laborers—*Desperate* (1947), *Thieves' Highway* (1949), and *The Sound of Fury* (1951)—*Gun Crazy* shares the noir theme of the rootless, marginal man (prevalent during the Depression and a continuing source of anxiety in the years following World War II), which also characterizes canonical noirs such as *The Postman Always Rings Twice* (1946) and *Detour* (1945), both fatalistic tales of drifters.

From an early age, Bart Tare (John Dall) has been obsessed with firearms. After leaving the army, he meets and instantly falls in love with the stunningly beautiful Annie Laurie Starr (Peggy Cummins), who shares his gun fetishism, having been the sharp-shooting main attraction in a traveling tent show. They set out on a series of robberies that, before their death at the law's hands, culminates in the holdup of the pay department in a meatpacking plant.

At the formal level, claims for *Gun Crazy*'s exceptional status amongst the plethora of B movies are more than justified in virtue of the film's aesthetic innovations within low-budget restraints—the long single-shot scene of a bank robbery, the chase through the abattoir—and in Cummins's peerless characterization of a psychotic femme fatale. This timeless tale of amour fou (mad love) was a major influence on Jean-Luc Godard's French New Wave classic *Breathless* (1960). **PS**

# ADAM'S RIB (1949)

"We all have our tricks." This choice battle-of-the-sexes comedy has been an inspiration for countless other films and television series about combative but sexually combustible couples. Of the nine movies legendary partners Spencer Tracy and Katharine Hepburn made together between 1942 and 1967, *Adam's Rib* is arguably the best, still crackling with witty dialogue, spirited discussion of double standards and sexual stereotypes, and wonderful performances. The screenplay was written by Tracy and Hepburn's great pals, the married team of Ruth Gordon (the actress who won an Oscar in *Rosemary's Baby*) and Garson Kanin. The true story that sparked the project was that of husband-and-wife lawyers William and Dorothy Whitney, who represented Mr. and Mrs. Raymond Massey in their divorce, then divorced each other and married their respective clients.

It doesn't quite come to that in *Adam's Rib*. When sweet, ditsy blonde Doris Attinger—played by sensationally funny Judy Holliday making her debut in the role that launched her meteoric career—is charged with the attempted murder of her two-timing husband Warren (Tom Ewell), proto-feminist attorney Amanda "Pinkie" Bonner (Hepburn) agrees to defend her. But Amanda's husband, Adam "Pinky" Bonner (Tracy), is the prosecuting attorney, and their courtroom battle quickly extends into the bedroom, hostilities aggravated by the attentions shown Amanda by smitten songwriter Kip (David Wayne), who composes "Farewell, Amanda" in her honor (a song written by Cole Porter).

Director George Cukor, recognizing the inherent theatricality of courtroom situations, deliberately keeps the proceedings stagy after the comedy-suspense opening sequence of Doris tailing Warren from work to the tryst with his floozy mistress, Beryl (Jean Hagen), and the inept shooting. The film's long single takes give Hepburn free rein for her outrageously crafty showboating in court and allow Tracy to work up his indignation at her tactics and principles. Highlights include brainy Amanda's early questioning of dimwitted Doris, and the spectacle of Adam tearfully getting in touch with his feminine side to get back into his wife's good graces. Although some of the arguments may seem quaint today, the sophistication is undiminished. **AE**

**U.S.** (MGM) 101m BW

**Director:** George Cukor

**Producer:** Lawrence Weingarten

**Screenplay:** Ruth Gordon, Garson Kanin

**Photography:** George J. Folsey

**Music:** Cole Porter, Miklós Rózsa

**Cast:** Spencer Tracy, Katharine Hepburn, Judy Holliday, Tom Ewell, Francis Attinger, David Wayne, Jean Hagen, Hope Emerson, Eve March, Clarence Kolb, Emerson Treacy, Polly Moran, Will Wright, Elizabeth Flournoy

**Oscar nomination:** Ruth Gordon, Garson Kanin (screenplay)

**G.B.** (Ealing Studios, Rank) 82m BW

**Language:** English / Gaelic

**Director:** Alexander Mackendrick

**Producer:** Michael Balcon, Monja Danischewsky

**Screenplay:** Angus MacPhail & Compton MacKenzie, from novel by Compton Mackenzie

**Photography:** Gerald Gibbs

**Music:** Ernest Irving

**Cast:** Basil Radford, Catherine Lacey, Bruce Seton, Joan Greenwood, Wylie Watson, Gabrielle Blunt, Gordon Jackson, Jean Cadell, James Robertson Justice, Morland Graham, John Gregson, James Woodburn, James Anderson, Jameson Clark, Duncan Macrae

# WHISKY GALORE! (1949)

Along with *Passport to Pimlico* and *Kind Hearts and Coronets*, *Whisky Galore!* was in the first, miraculous vintage of celebrated postwar comedies from Britain's Ealing Studios under paternal producer Sir Michael Balcon. Universally admired, the film was key in establishing the distinctive, self-deprecating, and understated satiric tone of those following, as well as the common thread of defiant little people triumphing over those more powerful.

Alexander "Sandy" Mackendrick's influential culture clash comedy, shot beautifully on location on Barra in the Outer Hebrides, in the style of a mock documentary, sees the sanctimonious, English, by-the-book and teetotaling Home Guard captain Basil Radford's hunt for a foundered ship's "salvaged" cargo of malt whisky, intended for America but seized by thirsty islanders deprived by war-time, well and truly foiled by the wily natives of Todday, who run rings around him and the Excise men. The story, immortalized by writer Compton MacKenzie, was inspired by the true "disappearance" of 50,000 cases of whisky after a cargo ship was wrecked off the Isle of Eriskay. Novelist-screenwriter MacKenzie appears in the film as the S.S. Cabinet Minister's captain.

*Whisky Galore!* is more dated than some of the other Ealing comedies, though the quaint charm is countered by the film's hectic hilarity, the affectionate and astute social observation, the authenticity of Hebridean life, and the delightful performances. Ealing's leading English enchantress Joan Greenwood is superb as the canny publican Macroon's (Wylie Watson) flirtatious daughter, as are the mainly genuine Scots players like James Robertson Justice, Gordon Jackson, and the droll narrator, Finlay Currie. The universal appeal of the film's antiauthoritarian humor lies in its idealization of a remote, isolated village world full of eccentrics, cards, pretty lasses, and gutsy, commonsensical folk pricking the balloons of the pompous and bureaucratic types opposing them.

The Scottish (though American-born) Mackendrick, director of three of Ealing's most sparkling gems (the other two being *The Man in the White Suit*, 1951 and *The Ladykillers*, 1955) would prove equally impressive directing drama later in his career, notably, after his move to America, with the 1957 film *Sweet Smell of Success*. **AE**

## WHITE HEAT (1949)

"Do you know what to do?" barks Cody (James Cagney) at his sidekick at the start of a daring train robbery; when the guy starts replying, Cody cuts him off: "Just do it, stop gabbing!" This headlong, action-only attitude sums up the drive of Raoul Walsh's films, which (as Peter Lloyd once remarked) "take the pulse of an individual energy" and embed it within a "demented trajectory out of which is born the construction of a rhythm." Few films are as taut, sustained, and economical in their telling as *White Heat*.

Walsh is a relentlessly linear, forward-moving director whose work harkens back to silent cinema—as in that exciting car-meets-train opener. But he also explores the intriguing, complicating possibilities of 20th-century psychology. On the job, Cody kills ruthlessly. Once holed up like a caged animal with his gang—as he will later be imprisoned—his psychopathology begins to emerge: indifference to others' suffering, fixation on a tough mom, and searing migraines that send him berserk.

Cody, as immortalized in Cagney's powerhouse performance, embodies the ultimate contradiction that brings down movie gangsters: fantastic egotism and dreams of invincibility ("Look, Ma, top of the world!") undermined by all-too-human dependencies and vulnerabilities. **AM**

**U.S.** (Warner Bros.) 114m BW

**Director:** Raoul Walsh

**Producer:** Louis F. Edelman

**Screenplay:** Virginia Kellogg, Ivan Goff, Ben Roberts

**Photography:** Sidney Hickox

**Music:** Max Steiner

**Cast:** James Cagney, Virginia Mayo, Edmond O'Brien, Margaret Wycherly, Steve Cochran, John Archer, Wally Cassell, Fred Clark

**Oscar nomination:** Virginia Kellogg (screenplay)

## THE RECKLESS MOMENT (1949)

*The Reckless Moment* is an unusual film noir in that it reverses the sexes in a replay of the familiar story (as in *Double Indemnity* and *Scarlet Street*) of an innocent who gets involved with a seductive no-good and is embroiled in crime. Here, class and respectability assume the status usually accorded sex and money as housewife Lucia Harper (Joan Bennett) loses her grip on suburbia when the sleazy specimen (Shepperd Strudwick) who has been seeing her daughter (Geraldine Brooks) is semiaccidentally killed under suspicious circumstances and she moves his corpse to make things look better.

Lucia's nemesis is played by James Mason, oddly but effectively cast as an Irish lowlife, who starts out blackmailing her but begins, disturbingly, to make sincere romantic overtures. The focus of the film then changes as the criminal is driven to make a sacrifice which will restore the heroine's life but also suggests that Bennett—who, after all, was the tramp in *Scarlet Street* (1945)—may have unwittingly been manipulating him to her advantage all along. Viennese director Max Ophüls is more interested in irony and emotion than crime and drama, which gives this a uniquely nerve-fraying feel, and he nudges the lead actors into revelatory, unusual performances. **KN**

**U.S.** (Columbia) 82m BW

**Director:** Max Ophüls

**Producer:** Walter Wanger

**Screenplay:** Mel Dinelli, Henry Garson

**Photography:** Burnett Guffey

**Music:** Hans J. Salter

**Cast:** James Mason, Joan Bennett, Geraldine Brooks, Henry O'Neill, Shepperd Strudwick, David Blair, Roy Roberts

# THE THIRD MAN (1949)

**G.B.** (British Lion, London) 104m BW
**Language:** English / German
**Director:** Carol Reed
**Producer:** Hugh Perceval, Carol Reed
**Screenplay:** Graham Greene, Alexander Korda
**Photography:** Robert Krasker
**Music:** Henry Love, Anton Karas
**Cast:** Joseph Cotten, Alida Valli, Orson Welles, Trevor Howard, Paul Hörbiger, Ernst Deutsch, Erich Ponto, Siegfried Breuer, Hedwig Bleibtreu, Bernard Lee, Wilfrid Hyde-White
**Oscar:** Robert Krasker (photography)
**Oscar nomination:** Carol Reed (director), Oswald Hafenrichter (editing)

Written for the screen by Graham Greene—the still-in-print book is actually a novelization!—Carol Reed's *The Third Man* effectively transfers the urban nightmare world of Hollywood film noir of the 1940s to a European setting. Picking up the messy aftermath of the war and providing a five-years-on follow-up to the works of British thriller writers and European exile filmmakers, it shows the postwar consequences of movements expressed in early Hitchcock films like *The Lady Vanishes* (1938) and *Secret Agent* (1936), midperiod Fritz Lang-like the Greene-derived *Ministry of Fear* (1944) or the Geoffrey Household-inspired *Man Hunt* (1941), and Eric Ambler adaptations like *Journey into Fear* (1942) and *The Mask of Dimitrios* (1944). Occupied Vienna, divided between four military powers and plagued by black-marketing scoundrels, is as fantastical a setting as any devised for studio exoticism, but Reed and his crew were able to shoot on location, amid rubble and glitz, capturing a world of fear that was all too real.

Into this devastated world of corruption comes American innocent Holly Martins (Joseph Cotten). A writer of pulp Westerns, he was somehow asked to deliver a serious literary lecture to a stuffy cultural group. Only the military police sergeant (Bernard Lee) at the back of the hall has ever read any of his work. Holly is shocked to learn that his boyhood friend Harry Lime (Orson Welles) has recently met a mysterious death and is suspected of involvement in an especially dastardly racket. Holly gets mixed up with one of Harry's girlfriends (Alida Valli) and a succession of sinister eccentrics, in search of the "third man" who was seen carrying Lime's body away. Harry, as everyone except Holly knows, turns out to have faked his own death to get away from policeman Calloway (Trevor Howard).

After all these years, it isn't exactly a surprise, but the moment of revelation as Welles's Harry is caught by the beam of a streetlight as a cat nuzzles his shoes is still magic. Anton Karras's haunting and unforgettable zither theme "plung-ka-plungs" on the soundtrack, and Welles spins a virtual cameo into one of the screen's greatest charming villains. *The Third Man*'s most famous speech—the "cuckoo clock" anecdote, delivered up above the "little dots" on the Vienna Ferris Wheel—was written by Welles on the spur of the moment as an addition to Greene's script, filling out the character and perhaps securing the picture's lasting greatness.

A rare British film that is as accomplished technically as the best of classic Hollywood—Reed never did anything as masterly again—*The Third Man* is an outstanding mix of political thriller, weird romance, gothic mystery, and black-and-white romantic agony. Welles, who is truly brilliant for five minutes, has hogged all the press, but it's a perfectly acted film, with wonderful work from Cotten as the bewildered and disappointed hero—his "literary lecture" is priceless—and the luminous beauty of Italian star Valli as the heroine-by-default. It's a film that constantly shimmers, in its nocturnal cityscapes, its glowing haunted faces, and the gushing waters of the sewers in which Lime is finally flushed away. **KN**

U.S. (MGM) 98m Technicolor
**Director:** Stanley Donen, Gene Kelly
**Producer:** Roger Edens, Arthur Freed
**Screenplay:** Adolph Green & Betty Comden, from their play
**Photography:** Harold Rosson
**Music:** Leonard Bernstein, Saul Chaplin, Roger Edens
**Cast:** Gene Kelly, Frank Sinatra, Betty Garrett, Ann Miller, Jules Munshin, Vera-Ellen, Florence Bates, Alice Pearce, George Meader, Judy Holliday
**Oscar:** Roger Edens, Lennie Hayton (music)

# ON THE TOWN (1949)

Two sailors, Gabey (Gene Kelly) and Chip (Frank Sinatra), in the company of cab driver Brunhilde (Betty Garrett), burst into an art school's life-modeling session. They gasp at the sight of a naked woman, glimpsed from the back. The model turns: She is merely wearing a backless dress. Then our trio rushes out through the swinging doors they entered through: revealed are a third sailor, Ozzie (Jules Munshin), and his anthropologist girlfriend Claire (Ann Miller), furtively kissing.

The lightly subversive fun of *On the Town* is contained in this elaborate gag. It is basically about a hunt for casual sex: Three sailors, on a 24-hour leave, want to get laid. Of course, on the surface, the film attempts to disavow this base impulse—there is, after all, Gabey's love for the sweet, innocent "Miss Turnstiles," Ivy (Vera-Ellen)—but the proof is everywhere: in cultural references (surrealist art; a museum devoted to "homo erectus"), double entendres (Brunhilde: "He wanted to see the sights, and I showed him plenty"), and above all in the high energy of the song-and-dance numbers, into which all eroticism is artfully sublimated—although there's nothing particularly hidden in Miller's bravura performance of "Prehistoric Man!"

*On the Town* hangs many, varied delights on its simple but driving "lifetime in a day" premise, codirectors Kelly and Stanley Donen still some years away from their ideal of the dramatically integrated musical. Once the sailors split up, the film becomes especially busy, ranging from low burlesque ("You Can Count On Me") to high ballet, the latter via the Sinatra–Garret duet "Come Up to My Place," a highlight of Leonard Bernstein's jazzy score. Proceedings make room for all manner of reveries (Gabey's zany imagining of Ivy as a gal for all seasons), digressions, and gags.

The left-wing aspect of Kelly's life and career is often overlooked. *On the Town* has, lurking under its surface alongside that sex drive, a political aspiration: This "city symphony" (taking advantage of some terrific location photography) is truly an ode to the joys and woes of ordinary workers, cramming experiences into the cracks of a punishing schedule. **AM**

# ORPHÉE (1949)
## ORPHEUS

"It is the privilege of legends to be be timeless," notes the narrator at the outset. And so it has proved for Jean Cocteau's fantasy film *Orpheus*, an infinitely strange and beguiling allegory which is also a kind of coded autobiography. Orphée (played by Cocteau's lover, Jean Marais) is an acclaimed poet who has fallen out of fashion. After a despised rival is knocked over by two uniformed motorcyclists, he becomes fascinated with the Princess Death (María Casarès), but when his neglected wife Eurydice (Marie Déa) dies, Orphée follows into the underworld to reclaim her.

Looked at simply as a special-effects movie, this is still a landmark film for Cocteau's ingenious use of reverse motion and back projection. Mirrors are the doors to the other side ("Look at a mirror for a lifetime you will see Death at work"), although only poets can move through them at will. Purgatory is a slow-motion limbo where the laws of physics are suspended. Although the enigmatic narrative is occasionally confusing (it doesn't help that Orphée and Cocteau alike seem more taken with Death than with Eurydice), the film's poetic imagination is spellbinding. **TCh**

**France** (Andre Paulve, Palais Royal) 112m BW

**Language:** French

**Director:** Jean Cocteau

**Producer:** André Paulvé

**Screenplay:** Jean Cocteau

**Photography:** Nicolas Hayer

**Music:** Georges Auric

**Cast:** Jean Marais, François Périer, María Casarès, Marie Déa, Henri Crémieux, Juliette Gréco, Roger Blin, Edouard Dermithe, Maurice Carnege, René Worms, Raymond Faure, Pierre Bertin, Jacques Varennes, Claude Mauriac

# THE ASPHALT JUNGLE (1950)

Perhaps the most finely detailed "caper" film Hollywood ever produced, John Huston's study of a jewelry store robbery shows the business relationships between career criminals of different kinds—from a mastermind plotter to the "box man" who breaks into the safe, to the "muscle" needed to handle the guards. Such crime is merely "a left-handed form of endeavor," suggests the "respectable" businessman who is to fence the proceeds.

*The Asphalt Jungle* concentrates not only on the robbery but also on the personal lives of the gang members, who are individualized with notable touches of dialogue and visual style. Huston expertly handles a fine ensemble of actors, including Marilyn Monroe—who plays an old man's dizzy-headed mistress in one of her most important early roles. As in most Huston films, the thematic emphasis is on the joys and sorrows of male bonding, with the criminals' inevitable defeat by the law—and their own weaknesses—rendered almost heroic. The gang leader Doc Riedenschneider (Sam Jaffe) is captured because he lingers in a café watching a beautiful young girl dance, and tough guy Dix (Sterling Hayden) bleeds to death as he tries to return to the country and the horses he loves. Such melodramatic elements contrast interestingly with the film's otherwise grim portrayal of alienation, betrayal, and sociopathy. **RBP**

**U.S.** (MGM) 112m BW

**Director:** John Huston

**Producer:** Arthur Hornblow Jr.

**Screenplay:** W.R. Burnett, Ben Maddow, John Huston, from novel by W.R. Burnett

**Photography:** Harold Rosson

**Music:** Miklós Rózsa

**Cast:** Sterling Hayden, Louis Calhern, Jean Hagen, James Whitmore, Sam Jaffe, John McIntire, Commissioner Hardy, Marc Lawrence, Barry Kelley, Anthony Caruso, Teresa Celli, Marilyn Monroe, William "Wee Willie" Davis, Dorothy Tree, Brad Dexter, John Maxwell

**Oscar nomination:** John Huston (director), Ben Maddow, John Huston (screenplay), Sam Jaffe (actor in support role), Harold Rosson (photography)

**Japan** (Daiei) 88m BW

**Language:** Japanese

**Director:** Akira Kurosawa

**Producer:** Minoru Jingo, Masaichi Nagata

**Screenplay:** Ryunosuke Akutagawa, Akira Kurosawa, Shinobu Hashimoto, from the stories *Rashomon* and *In a Grove* by Ryunosuke Akutagawa

Photography: Kazuo Miyagawa

Music: Fumio Hayasaka

**Cast:** Toshirô Mifune, Machiko Kyô, Masayuki Mori, Takashi Shimura, Minoru Chiaki, Kichijiro Ueda, Fumiko Honma, Daisuke Katô

**Oscar:** Akira Kurosawa (honorary award)

**Oscar nomination:** So Matsuyama, H. Motsumoto (art direction)

**Venice Film Festival:** Akira Kurosawa (Golden Lion), Akira Kurosawa (Italian film critics award)

# RASHOMON (1950)

Three travelers collect under a ruined temple during a storm. Woodcutter (Takashi Shimura), Priest (Minoru Chiaki), and Commoner (Kichijiro Ueda) build a fire and wonder about a troubling story. So begins the story-within a-story about a married couple and bandit who meet on a forest road. Woodcutter later finds the husband's corpse and testifies before a police commission investigating what happened. The explanation so horrifies Priest and entertains Commoner it occupies them through the storm with four depictions of a crime.

Plotted with competing points-of-view in flashback style, framed with a fluid, moving camera, and shot under a canopy of dappled light, *Rashomon* details unreliable perspectives. The veracity of on-screen characters and depicted actions are therefore rendered false and misleading. Facts are submitted into evidence but immediately questioned. Disagreement among the overlapping stories of husband, wife, and bandit complicate straightforward reportage. In short, every narrator is untrustworthy, along with the overall film.

Nothing less than an epistemological nightmare, Akira Kurosawa's Oscar winner still concludes with an infusion of moral goodness. Although *Rashomon* implicitly explores the lost possibility of renewal and redemption, its central theme about discovering truth as a distinction between good and evil is upheld through simple acts of kindness and sacrifice.

As the forest road is explored from the perspective of the bandit Tajomaru (Toshirô Mifune), he is characterized as a hellion. After seeing Masako (Machiko Kyô), he ravishes her into willing submission before cutting loose her samurai husband Takehiro (Masayuki Mori) so the two men can fight until the latter is killed. From Masako's point of view, she is raped, shamed, then rebuffed by her husband, and submitting to hysterical rage she kills him. Agreeing only that he was killed, Takehiro speaks through a medium (Fumiko Honma) explaining how his wife equalled Tajomaru's passion before demanding his death at the hands of the bandit. Seeing no good result in murder, Tajomaru flees, as does Masako, leaving Takehiro behind to commit suicide.

Each story is told in a self-serving way. Tajomaru is therefore a ruthless criminal, Masako a set-upon innocent, and Takehiro a proud warrior. All true, it seems, until Woodcutter explains what he saw from the shadows. His perspective affirms the wife's shallowness, the bandit's false bravado, and the husband's cowardice. It also conceals his own complicity in the crime until Commoner draws this out, dismissing the search for truth.

Kurosawa ends the bleak tale on a positive note. An abandoned baby is discovered beneath the temple ruin. Woodcutter intoduces the idea of human goodness by taking it upon himself in redemption to care for the orphan. A consistent conclusion, given *Rashomon*'s formal schizophrenia in a brilliant narrative structure—Kurosawa's first masterwork. **GC-Q**

## WINCHESTER '73 (1950)

U.S. (Universal) 92m BW

**Director:** Anthony Mann

**Producer:** Aaron Rosenberg

**Screenplay:** Borden Chase, Stuart N. Lake, Robert L. Richards, from story by Stuart N. Lake

**Photography:** William H. Daniels

**Music:** Walter Scharf

**Cast:** James Stewart, Shelley Winters, Dan Duryea, Stephen McNally, Millard Mitchell, Charles Drake, John McIntire, Will Geer, Jay C. Flippen, Rock Hudson, John Alexander, Steve Brodie, James Millican, Abner Biberman, Tony Curtis

The first of eight collaborations between director Anthony Mann and actor James Stewart, *Winchester '73* sets the tone for this legendary partnership. The Westerns these two men made together are unusually bitter and starkly beautiful, with fascinating overtones of moral uncertainty.

*Winchester '73* revolves around a high-powered rifle that changes hands repeatedly. Each man who comes into possession of it is changed in some way—sometimes for good, sometimes for bad. It all comes to a head in a shooting contest, for which the prize is the titular rifle itself.

The cast is extremely strong. Shelley Winters is excellent, and the supporting players include such versatile character actors as Millard Mitchell, Stephen McNally, Will Geer, and the incomparable Dan Duryea. (See if you can spot a young Tony Curtis, and Rock Hudson as an Indian brave!)

Now regarded as an actor of unusual versatility, Stewart was, at the time of the film's production, concerned about perceptions regarding his limited breadth. His character, Lin McAdam, is an unusual hero—somewhat tentative, even if he is the film's moral center. Stewart's performances for Mann would get increasingly complex and cynical in films like *The Man from Laramie* and *The Naked Spur*, proving beyond a doubt that this master of the craft could adeptly handle any role that came his way. **EdeS**

## RIO GRANDE (1950)

U.S. (Argosy, Republic) 105m BW

**Director:** John Ford

**Producer:** Merian C. Cooper, John Ford, Herbert J. Yates

**Screenplay:** James Warner Bellah, James Kevin McGuinness, from the story *Mission With No Record* by James Warner Bellah

**Photography:** Bert Glennon

**Music:** Dale Evans, Stan Jones, Tex Owens, Victor Young

**Cast:** John Wayne, Maureen O'Hara, Ben Johnson, Claude Jarman Jr., Harry Carey Jr., Chill Wills, J. Carrol Naish, Victor McLaglen, Grant Withers, Peter Ortiz, Steve Pendleton, Karolyn Grimes, Alberto Morin, Stan Jones, Fred Kennedy

The last installment of John Ford's "Cavalry Trilogy"—*Fort Apache* (1948) and *She Wore a Yellow Ribbon* (1949), being the other two—*Rio Grande* is a minor work, albeit a key one, allegedly undertaken to secure financing for the director's personal project, *The Quiet Man* (1952). It's less revisionary, mythmaking, or elegiac than the previous Cavalry films, offering a mix of soapsuds, barracks larking, and hard-riding action.

Crusty Yankee Captain Kirby York (John Wayne, not quite recreating his Kirby York of *Fort Apache*) reconciles with estranged southern wife Kathleen (Maureen O'Hara)—whose mansion he burned down during the Civil War—in order to share the raising of their raw recruit son (Claude Jarman, Jr.). The son becomes a man under his father's influence without losing his mother's sensitivity. York leads his men in pursuit of Indian raiders who have snuck up from Mexico with kidnap in mind, suggesting the embryo of Ford and Wayne's masterpiece, *The Searchers* (1956). This is a less neurotic, more action-oriented quest and a rare Ford movie that unquestioningly adopts a goodies versus baddies view of the Indian wars.

Ben Johnson shows off his rodeo skills and great riding stunt work, and the Sons of the Pioneers add to the folkloric feel with appropriate ballads, though "Bold Fenian Men" is an unlikely favorite out West in the 1870s. **KN**

# ALL ABOUT EVE (1950)

Considered one of the sharpest and darkest films ever made about show business, Joseph L. Mankiewicz's 1950 drama was taken from a 1946 *Cosmopolitan* magazine short story called "The Wisdom of Eve," which was also made into a radio production. Avoided by other studios for four years, the combination of Mankiewicz's cynical, witty screenplay, and a high-caliber cast transformed the story into an enormous cinematic success. Nominated for a then record fourteen Academy Awards, *All About Eve* won six, including Best Picture and Best Supporting Actor (for George Sanders), as well as Best Director and Best Screenplay awards for Mankiewicz. Nominations went to Bette Davis, Anne Baxter, Celeste Holm, and Thelma Ritter, thus holding the record for most female acting nominations in a single film.

Opening with an acceptance speech given by gracious young actress Eve Harrington (Anne Baxter), the film pans over the audience. Addison DeWitt (Sanders) begins a narration which goes back in time to the real tale of how such success was achieved. Bette Davis is Margo Channing, an aging, 40-year-old Broadway actress who befriends Eve, a young fan plagued by a hard life. Margo's dresser Birdie (Ritter) is the first to see through Eve's sob story, saying, "What a story! Everything but the bloodhounds snappin' at her rear end." Eve repays Margo's trust by worming into her idol's professional and personal life with more than a few lies. Eve goes on to deceive Margo's best friend (Holm), beguile her loyal but devious critic (Sanders), and vainly attempt to steal away her fiancé Bill (Gary Merrill, Davis's real-life husband). In a brief but dazzling cameo, Marilyn Monroe appears on the arm of DeWitt at Margo's party, the same party where Margo utters the now famous line, "Fasten your seat belts. It's going to be a bumpy night."

Having also won an Oscar in 1949 for *A Letter to Three Wives*, some see Mankiewicz's victory in *All About Eve* as final vindication of his talent in comparison to brother Herman, who won the Best Original Screenplay Oscar for *Citizen Kane*. That debate aside, *All About Eve* is widely considered to be the crowning achievement in Davis's lengthy career; its only flaw is Baxter, who seems to be nothing but pure ambition in womanly form. **KK**

**U.S.** (Fox) 138m BW

**Director:** Joseph L. Mankiewicz

**Producer:** Darryl F. Zanuck

**Screenplay:** Joseph L. Mankiewicz, from the story *The Wisdom of Eve* by Mary Orr

**Photography:** Milton R. Krasner

**Music:** Alfred Newman

**Cast:** Bette Davis, Anne Baxter, George Sanders, Celeste Holm, Gary Merrill, Hugh Marlowe, Gregory Ratoff, Barbara Bates, Marilyn Monroe, Thelma Ritter, Walter Hampden, Randy Stuart, Craig Hill, Leland Harris, Barbara White

**Oscar:** Darryl F. Zanuck (best picture), Joseph L. Mankiewicz (director), Joseph L. Mankiewicz (screenplay), George Sanders (actor in support role), Edith Head, Charles Le Maire (costume)

**Oscar nomination:** Anne Baxter, Bette Davis (actress), Celeste Holm, Thelma Ritter (actress in support role), Lyle R. Wheeler, George W. Davis, Thomas Little, Walter M. Scott (art direction), Milton R. Krasner (photography), Barbara McLean (editing), Alfred Newman (music)

**Cannes Film Festival:** Joseph L. Mankiewicz (special jury prize), Bette Davis (actress)

**U.S.** (Paramount) 110m BW

**Director:** Billy Wilder

**Producer:** Charles Brackett

**Screenplay:** Charles Brackett, Billy Wilder, D.M. Marshman Jr, from the story *A Can of Beans* by Charles Brackett and Billy Wilder

**Photography:** John F. Seitz

**Music:** Jay Livingston, Franz Waxman

**Cast:** William Holden, Gloria Swanson, Erich von Stroheim, Nancy Olson, Fred Clark, Lloyd Gough, Jack Webb, Franklyn Farnum, Larry J. Blake, Charles Dayton, Cecil B. DeMille, Hedda Hopper, Buster Keaton, Anna Q. Nilsson, H.B. Warner

**Oscar:** Charles Brackett, Billy Wilder, D.M. Marshman Jr (screenplay), Hans Dreier, John Meehan, Sam Comer, Ray Moyer (art direction), Franz Waxman (music)

**Oscar nomination:** Charles Brackett (best picture), Billy Wilder (director), William Holden (actor), Gloria Swanson (actress), Erich von Stroheim (actor in support role), Nancy Olson (actress in support role), John F. Seitz (photography), Doane Harrison, Arthur P. Schmidt (editing)

# SUNSET BLVD. (1950)

Unemployed screenwriter Joe Gillis (William Holden), floating dead in a swimming pool, recounts his doomed personal and professional involvement with megalomaniac silent movie queen Norma Desmond (Gloria Swanson). A flapper vampire, whose attempts to stay youthful into her fifties paradoxically make her seem a thousand years old, Norma lives in a decaying mansion on Sunset Boulevard, holding a midnight funeral for her pet monkey ("he must have been a very important chimp," muses Joe), scrawling an unproducable script, and dreaming of an impossible comeback ("I hate that word! This will be a return!") as Salome. In attendance is a sinister butler (Erich von Stroheim) who used to be her favored director and, incidentally, her first husband.

Usually not a filmmaker given to ostentatious visuals, Wilder is encouraged by this scenario to create compositions that evoke the lair of the Phantom of the Opera and Kane's Xanadu, a huge close-up of white-gloved hands playing a wheezy pipe organ as the trapped gigolo flutters in the background. Wilder's acidic, yet nostalgic, traipse through the film industry's haunted house is a picture that can be endlessly rewatched, even after its influence has seeped into the horror genre (Robert Aldrich's *Whatever Happened to Baby Jane?*) and spun off an Andrew Lloyd Webber stage adaptation—combining strange affection for has-been Norma and never-was Joe with a somewhat sadistic use of such ravaged and frozen silent faces as Buster Keaton, H. B. Warner, and Anna Q. Nilsson.

One of *Sunset Blvd.'s* unstressed ironies is that although Norma can't get away with her insanity ("nobody walks out on a star!"), the industry allows and indeed encourages everyone else to act like a monster: Cecil B. DeMille (playing himself) gently reminds Norma that the picture business has changed, but Wilder concludes his scene by having the camera note his polished riding boots

and absurdly outdated on-set strut. Though they recognized their chances for one last blaze of glory, Swanson (who took the role after Mary Pickford turned it down) and von Stroheim (who is forced to watch an extract from *Queen Kelly*, an unfinished 1920s disaster he directed Swanson in) understood the cruelty of Wilder's vision and the way he made monsters of all of them. It's a hard and cynical film, which struggles with its doomed but sweet "normal" love affair: in the end, Norma is as terrified that Joe is writing a script ("Untitled Love Story") with D girl Nancy Olson as she is that he will leave her for a younger rival. Swanson ("I am big, it's the pictures that got small") is vibrant in her madness, climaxing with a moment of unforgettable horror-glamor as she vamps toward a newsreel cameraman during her arrest for murder and declares that she is ready for her close-up, even as Wilder pulls back to frame her in a long shot that emphasizes her isolation in insanity as the big carnival of a celebrity murder scandal begins. This points the way to Wilder's *Ace in the Hole* (1951) and a culture of media-exploited crime that remains horribly alive more than half a century on. **KN**

# LOS OLVIDADOS (1950)
## THE YOUNG AND THE DAMNED

**Mexico** (Ultramar) 85m BW
**Language:** Spanish
**Director:** Luis Buñuel
**Producer:** Óscar Dancigers, Sergio Kogan, Jaime A. Menasce
**Screenplay:** Luis Alcoriza, Luis Buñuel
**Photography:** Gabriel Figueroa
**Music:** Rodolfo Halffter, Gustavo Pittaluga
**Cast:** Alfonso Mejía, Estela Inda, Miguel Inclán, Roberto Cobo, Alma Delia Fuentes, Francisco Jambrina, Jesús Navarro, Efraín Arauz, Sergio Villarreal, Jorge Pérez, Javier Amézcua, Mário Ramírez
**Cannes Film Festival:** Luis Buñuel (director)

Although *Los Olvidados* invokes many conventions of social-problem films, it goes far beyond them. Set in the slums of Mexico City, Luis Buñuel's scathing masterpiece centers on two doomed boys: Pedro (Alfonso Mejía), who struggles to be good, and the older, incorrigible Jaibo (Roberto Cobo), who keeps popping up like a demon brother to lead Pedro astray. Critical of Italian neorealism, Buñuel demanded that the concept of realism be expanded to include such essentials as dream, poetry, and irrationality—represented by Pedro's nightmare, in which tangled threads of guilt and wish-fulfillment resolve into the sensational image of a slab of raw meat offered by the hungry boy's mother, and by Jaibo's dying vision, in which the angel of death appears as a mangy dog leading him down a long, dark road.

Other lost souls in Buñuel's city of the damned include the nasty blind beggar Carmelo (Miguel Inclán); the abandoned boy Ojitos (Mário Ramírez), enslaved by Carmelo; the nymphet Meche (Alma Delia Fuentes), whose bare thighs are splashed with *leche* in one of the film's many provocative images; and the virtuous Julián (Javier Amézcua), quickly slaughtered by Jaibo. Borrowing a tag line from *Nashville*, one could say that the final essential character is you, the hypocrite spectator. A crucial factor that elevates *Los Olvidados* above other social-problem films is its aggressive discomfiting of the viewer—most startlingly when Pedro, sulking in a reform school, hurls an egg at the camera.

In less spectacular but still striking ways, *Los Olvidados* discourages the spectator from settling into the position of noble sensitivity commonly cultivated by liberal message films. For one thing, the tone is too caustic, distancing, contradictory—as when the pathetic spectacle of blind Carmelo beaten by Jaibo's gang is capped with a derisive shot of a gawking chicken. In addition, Buñuel neatly sidesteps a veritable catalog of message-film cop-outs, including the use of a surrogate figure to guide our feelings and the concentration on special cases to ameliorate the larger problem. *Los Olvidados* has been criticized for callousness and a lack of constructive solutions, but Buñuel is an artist, not a legislator, and the compassion of this remarkably honest film might be difficult to recognize only because it isn't cushioned with sentimentality. **MR**

## IN A LONELY PLACE (1950)

*In a Lonely Place* qualifies as a masterpiece on many grounds: as the single best film of cult director Nicholas Ray; as a uniquely romantic and doom-haunted noir drama; as a showcase for personal best performances by Humphrey Bogart and Gloria Grahame; and as one of the most insightful films about Hollywood.

Short-fused screenwriter Dix Steele (Bogart) is suspected of an especially vicious murder, but his next-door-neighbor Laurel Gray (Grahame) can give him an alibi. This leads the pair into a passionate affair that is undermined as Laurel becomes terrified by Dix's violent streak, coming to wonder if he really did commit the murder. After years of playing romantic tough guys, Bogart here gets deeper inside his own persona, revealing the neurotic edge that might have made Sam Spade or Rick Blaine unstable and becoming absolutely terrifying in the sequences where he explodes in fist-frenzy at the deserving and undeserving alike.

The film's downbeat subject matter is rendered exhilarating by Ray's dark visuals and a streak of almost surrealist poetry. Dorothy B. Hughes's fine novel is interestingly adapted: in the book, Steele really does turn out to be the murderer, but the screenplay is actually bleaker in that finally what matters isn't that he's innocent but that he easily could not be. **KN**

**U.S.** (Columbia, Santana) 94m BW

**Director:** Nicholas Ray

**Producer:** Henry S. Kesler, Robert Lord

**Screenplay:** Dorothy B. Hughes, Edmund H. North, Andrew Solt, from novel by Dorothy B. Hughes

**Photography:** Burnett Guffey

**Music:** George Antheil

**Cast:** Humphrey Bogart, Gloria Grahame, Frank Lovejoy, Carl Benton Reid, Art Smith, Jeff Donnell, Martha Stewart, Robert Warwick, Morris Ankrum, William Ching, Steven Geray, Hadda Brooks

## THE BIG CARNIVAL (1951)

*The Big Carnival* is noted for two things: it's the only collaboration between Kirk Douglas and Billy Wilder, and it's one of the angriest and most bitter films ever to come out of the Hollywood studio system.

Douglas plays Chuck Tatum, a cynical, arrogant reporter exiled to a small-town newspaper in New Mexico after getting fired from several big-city papers. When he goes out to cover a story about a prospector (Richard Benedict) trapped under a rockslide, he sees his chance to make it back to the big time. He manipulates the sheriff into delaying the rescue efforts with the promise of luring tourists, thrill seekers, and onlookers coming to be a part of this stirring human interest story. Tatum whips up the media frenzy, positions himself as the sole reporter with the scoop, and escalates the event into a carnival. Even the hapless prospector's wife (Jan Sterling), a self-serving poster child for High Maintenance, is drawn into Tatum's spin as she proves his match in venal self-interest. And everything goes as you would expect, which is horribly, horribly badly.

The anger lingers far beyond the story's end, and Wilder's trademark verbal zingers barely sugar-coat the story's bitter core, which indicts us all. Poignant and thoughtful. **AT**

**U.S.** (Paramount) 111 m BW

**Language:** English / Latin

**Director:** Billy Wilder

**Producer:** William Schorr, Billy Wilder

**Screenplay:** Walter Newman, Lesser Samuels, Billy Wilder

**Photography:** Charles Lang

**Music:** Hugo Friedhofer

**Cast:** Kirk Douglas, Jan Sterling, Robert Arthur, Porter Hall, Frank Cady, Richard Benedict, Ray Teal, Frank Jaquet

**Oscar nomination:** Billy Wilder, Lesser Samuels, Walter Newman (screenplay)

**Venice Film Festival:** Billy Wilder (international award), nomination (Golden Lion)

**U.S.** (Charles K. Feldman, Warner Bros.) 122 min BW

**Director:** Elia Kazan

**Producer:** Charles K. Feldman

**Screenplay:** Tennessee Williams, Oscar Saul, from play by Tennessee Williams

**Photography:** Harry Stradling Sr.

**Music:** Alex North

**Cast:** Vivien Leigh, Marlon Brando, Kim Hunter, Karl Malden, Rudy Bond, Nick Dennis, Peg Hillias, Wright King, Richard Garrick, Ann Dere, Edna Thomas, Mickey Kuhn

**Oscar:** Vivien Leigh (actress), Karl Malden (actor in support role), Kim Hunter (actress in support role), Richard Day, George James Hopkins (art direction)

**Oscar nomination:** Charles K. Feldman (best picture), Elia Kazan (director), Tennessee Williams (screenplay), Marlon Brando (actor), Harry Stradling Sr. (photography), Lucinda Ballard (costume), Alex North (music), Nathan Levinson (sound)

# A STREETCAR NAMED DESIRE (1951)

"I have always depended on the kindness of strangers." Although Tennessee Williams's play was meant to be all about the desperate, poetic heroism of Blanche DuBois, Marlon Brando's uncouth, sweaty animal magnetism opposite Vivien Leigh's frail, faded belle commanded the screen. Just as it had electrified Broadway theatergoers opposite Jessica Tandy's Blanche four years earlier (a production also directed by Elia Kazan). Brando's brooding naturalism, his earthy sexuality, and his howls of "Stell-ahhhh!" remain a nearly impossible act to follow for the actors who have subsequently assayed the brutish Stanley Kowalski.

Ironically, Kazan's screen version—also scripted by Williams but subjected to censorship of some frank content—won three of the four acting Oscars for Leigh, who had also played Blanche in London's West End production, directed by her husband Sir Laurence Olivier. Oscars were also won by supporting actors Kim Hunter and Karl Malden, but Brando was beaten at the post by Humphrey Bogart (for *The African Queen*). Nevertheless, Brando's impact in *Streetcar* placed him at the forefront of modern screen actors, the most famous and influential of the Actors Studio's "Method" exponents.

Having lost the long-in-decline family estate to back taxes and her reputation while seeking oblivion or solace, Blanche arrives in New Orleans to stay with her pregnant sister Stella and churlish brother-in-law Stanley in their cramped, sweltering apartment. Stanley, convinced that Blanche is holding out on a mythical inheritance, is driven wild by the neurotic woman, pathetically clinging to her refinement and delusions. Under Stanley's resentful bullying, Blanche's last hopes are brutally destroyed, and she retreats into a psychotic state.

Although it was Kazan's seventh feature film, *Streetcar* is theatrical rather than cinematic. Its power emanates from the performances, particularly the absorbing duel between the poignant, ethereal, classic (one might say determined), stagey Leigh and the explosive, instinctive Brando, who are as different in their acting approaches as Blanche and Stanley are in personality. Kazan, who was a cofounder of the Actors Studio in 1947 and still a force in American theater at the time, was showing little interest in the visual possibilities of the medium, but his way with actors is amply apparent here. **AE**

# STRANGERS ON A TRAIN (1951)

**U.S.** (Warner Bros) 101m BW
**Director:** Alfred Hitchcock
**Producer:** Alfred Hitchcock
**Screenplay:** Raymond Chandler, Whitfield Cook, Czenzi Ormonde, from novel by Patricia Highsmith
**Photography:** Robert Burks
**Music:** Dimitri Tiomkin
**Cast:** Farley Granger, Ruth Roman, Robert Walker, Leo G. Carroll, Patricia Hitchcock, Kasey Rogers, Marion Lorne, Jonathan Hale, Howard St. John, John Brown, Norma Varden, Robert Gist
**Oscar nomination:** Robert Burks (photography)

Is there any wonder why Alfred Hitchcock was drawn to author Patricia Highsmith's *Strangers on a Train?* Her first novel, *Strangers* includes elements found in virtually all of Hitchcock's films, a fascination with murder, mix-ups, and barely suppressed homosexual urges. Needless to say, it didn't take long for the director to purchase the rights and get to work, and with a great screenplay from Raymond Chandler—with a touch-up by Ben Hecht, among others—the film turned out to be one of Hitchcock's most effective.

*Strangers on a Train* begins innocently enough. Guy Haines (Farley Granger), a successful tennis player, literally bumps into fellow train passenger Bruno Anthony (Robert Walker), an eccentric and excitable stranger. Both have someone in their lives they'd rather be without. Guy wants his wife out of the picture and Bruno his domineering father, so Bruno devises the "perfect" murder to solve both men's problems: they'll simply swap victims. Guy brushes the crazy idea off, but soon Bruno is blackmailing him into fulfilling his part of the bargain.

Almost a black comedy, *Strangers on a Train* also works as a bizarre courtship ritual, where Granger plays the straight man to Walker's flamboyant lunatic. As usual, Hitchcock takes particular glee in exploiting the plight of his protagonist. The dialogue sparkles as Walker tightens the screws around Granger, leading to what could be the most suspenseful tennis game in movie history. But this being Hitchcock, the thrilling conclusion takes place on a moving carousel, with Granger and Walker wrestling as the out-of-control ride spins faster and faster.

It's a jarring finale to what is largely an internalized film about madness, blackmail, and guilt, yet Hitchcock pulls it off brilliantly. As the campy charm of Walker leads to more overtly murderous impulses, his stature as a villain grows, and he can only be dispatched in a manner that does justice to his larger-than-life personality. Indeed, Walker (in his last role) dominates the film. He's the ego unleashed, the flashy flip side to the more repressed insanity Hitchcock would explore nine years later in *Psycho.* **JKl**

# THE LAVENDER HILL MOB (1951)

**G.B.** (Ealing, Rank) 78m BW
**Director:** Charles Crichton
**Producer:** Michael Balcon, Michael Truman
**Screenplay:** T.E.B. Clarke
**Photography:** Douglas Slocombe
**Music:** Georges Auric
**Cast:** Alec Guinness, Stanley Holloway, Sid James, Alfie Bass, Marjorie Fielding, Edie Martin, John Salew, Ronald Adam, Arthur Hambling, Gibb McLaughlin, John Gregson, Clive Morton, Sydney Tafler, Marie Burke, Audrey Hepburn
**Oscar:** T.E.B. Clarke (screenplay)
**Oscar nomination:** Alec Guinness (actor)

Along with 1955 film *The Ladykillers*, also a stickup caper, *The Lavender Hill Mob* is the laugh-out-loud funniest of the celebrated Ealing Comedies produced by Sir Michael Balcon and internationally beloved for their irreverent, ironic, inimitably British humor. Peerless Alec Guinness plays the bespectacled, insignificant bank clerk who has it in mind to finance a high-living retirement as recompense for a career being taken for granted. He plans a daring gold bullion robbery with souvenir maker Stanley Holloway and inept career burglars Sid James and Alfie Bass in one-time policeman T.E.B. "Tibby" Clarke's Oscar-winning screenplay.

The film is a master class in neat plotting and incident, served superbly by Charles Crichton's exhilarating direction, particularly of the loot snafu at the Eiffel Tower (Guinness and Holloway hurtling down the spiral stairs in vain pursuit of the English schoolgirls who have innocently purchased erroneously switched, solid gold models of the Parisian landmark) and the riotous chase climax (in which, at one point, a singing Welsh policeman grabs a ride on the running board of the aghast fleeing duo's car). Check out young Audrey Hepburn in the opening scene in Rio, where a benevolent, dapper Guinness tells his story to an interested party. **AE**

# PANDORA AND THE FLYING DUTCHMAN (1951)

**G.B.** (Dorkay, Romulus) 122 m Technicolor
**Language:** English / Spanish
**Director:** Albert Lewin
**Producer:** Joseph Kaufman, Albert Lewin
**Screenplay:** Albert Lewin
**Photography:** Jack Cardiff
**Music:** Alan Rawsthorne
**Cast:** James Mason, Ava Gardner, Nigel Patrick, Sheila Sim, Harold Warrender, Mario Cabré, Marius Goring, John Laurie, Pamela Mason, Patricia Raine, Margarita D'Alvarez, La Pillina, Abraham Sofaer, Francisco Igual, Guillermo Beltrán

Once dismissed as pretentious and preposterous, the reputation of this magical romantic fantasy has steadily grown over the years. Set in the early 1930s in a town called Esperanza ("Hope") on "the Mediterranean coast of Spain," where idle rich exiles mingle with working fisherfolk, *Pandora and the Flying Dutchman* begins with the discovery of two drowned corpses, hands locked together. In flashback, Pandora Reynolds (Ava Gardner), an American singer who specializes in driving men to death and distraction, meets her predestined match in Hendrick Van Der Zee (James Mason), captain and sole crew of a luxury yacht which turns out to be the Flying Dutchman, cursed to sail the seas until he finds a woman willing to die for him.

Producer, director, and writer Albert Lewin, one of Hollywood's few open intellectuals, was a man of ostentatious literary leanings (his films are littered with quoted poetry, to the point that Pandora makes an off-hand remark about how everything people say to her sounds like a quotation) and fantastical romanticism (all his pictures are about impossible loves that find perfect moments between curses). Shot in dark-hued but ravishing Technicolor by Jack Cardiff, the film is a tribute to the beauty of Ava Gardner, with footnotes about the brooding intensity of James Mason. **KN**

# THE AFRICAN QUEEN (1951)

**G.B.** (Horizon, Romulus) 105 m Technicolor

**Language:** English / German / Swahili

**Director:** John Huston

**Screenplay:** James Agee, John Huston, from novel by C.S. Forester

**Cast:** Humphrey Bogart, Katharine Hepburn, Robert Morley, Peter Bull, Theodore Bikel, Walter Gotell, Peter Swanwick, Richard Marner

**Oscar:** Humphrey Bogart (actor)

**Oscar nomination:** John Huston (director), James Agee, John Huston (screenplay), Katharine Hepburn (actress)

John Huston's 1951 classic is one of Hollywood's most impressive, entertaining, and compelling adventure stories. Based on C.S. Forester's 1935 novel of the same name, *The African Queen* narrates the unlikely love affair between tramp steamer captain Charlie Allnut (Humphrey Bogart) and puritanical missionary spinster Rose Sayer (Katharine Hepburn). Rose can barely tolerate Charlie, but fate throws them together. Caught amid the violence of the impending World War I, Rose must escape downriver with Charlie in his battered tugboat. A German warship, however, blocks their exit route, and Rose launches a plan to rig Charlie's cargo with explosive materials so as to thwart the Germans and make their escape.

The adventure tale, however, is secondary to the rocky relationship between Charlie and Rose, and despite the overt political content of the war narrative, *The African Queen's* more interesting allegory plays out in their love story. Rose's prim, repressed British spinster is seduced by Charlie's unshaven, gin-swigging American masculinity. Though set in 1914, the film's post-World War II subtext of the United States' emergence as a primary international player as the influence of traditional colonial powers waned, is unmistakable.

Hepburn and Bogart are tremendously enjoyable as the leads. Both veteran, grizzled stars using their trademark gestures and tics to full effect, they suffuse the film with a light, comic air that does not diminish the action. The chemistry between them is perfect, and the movement from polar opposites to comrades and lovers plays out effortlessly and convincingly, although they are at their most entertaining when they are at each other's throats. The color photography and truly astounding location shots of the jungle all add to *The African Queen*'s tremendous appeal. Bogart won his only Oscar for the film and Huston (for direction and writing), Hepburn, and screenwriter James Agee were also nominated. This description and the many subsequent accolades that the film has received cannot capture all its magic, somehow. After many viewings it never fails to leave me smiling and in a good mood, and of the many wonderful films summarized in this book, it truly is a must-see. **RH**

**France** (UGC) 110 m BW

**Language:** French

**Director:** Robert Bresson

**Screenplay:** Robert Bresson, from novel by Georges Bernanos

**Producer:** Léon Carré, Robert Sussfeld

**Photography:** Léonce-Henri Burel

**Music:** Jean-Jacques Grünenwald

**Cast:** Claude Laydu, Léon Arvel, Antoine Balpêtré, Jean Danet, Jeanne Étiévant, André Guibert, Bernard Hubrenne, Nicole Ladmiral, Martine Lemaire, Nicole Maurey, Louise (Mme. Louise) Martial Morange, Jean Riveyre, Gaston Séverin, Gilberte Terbois, Marie-Monique Arkell

**Venice Film Festival:** Robert Bresson (international award), (Italian film critics award), (OCIC award), nomination (Golden Lion)

# JOURNAL D'UN CURE DE CAMPAGNE (1951)

## DIARY OF A COUNTRY PRIEST

One of the cinema's greatest artists was searching for inspiration and he found it in the *Diary of a Country Priest*. With imagination, courage, and rigor, Robert Bresson discovered that filmmaking did not require big budgets, stars, or special effects. The cinema could tell any story, provoke any emotion, open itself to all the material and immaterial, private and collective themes through the most elementary uses of its true nature.

Georges Bernanos's novel tells the tale of a young priest living in the countryside dealing with the difficulties of everyday life and the interrogation of his actions and his faith. Bernanos refuses to leave either believers or atheists in peace, opening up chasms in the concrete world. Bresson's adaptation of the *Diary of a Country Priest* is a humble achievement, one that shows what the Christian message is based on—a message that the cinema is designed to translate into images and sounds: the word made into flesh.

Cinema is the concrete and communal accomplishment of the Mystery of Incarnation. Bresson's film demonstrates that everything can become possible: joking with death, writing on the screen, playing with desire, watching the insights of the psyche, generating fascination for life in rural France in the mid-20th century, and confronting religious questions. **J-MF**

**U.S.** (MGM) 113 m Technicolor

**Language:** English / French

**Director:** Vincente Minnelli

**Producer:** Roger Edens, Arthur Freed

**Screenplay:** Alan Jay Lerner

**Photography:** John Alton, Alfred Gilks

**Music:** Saul Chaplin

**Cast:** Gene Kelly, Jerry Mulligan, Leslie Caron, Lise Bouvier, Oscar Levant, Adam Cook, Georges Guétary, Henri Baurel, Nina Foch, Milo Roberts

**Oscar:** Arthur Freed (best picture), Alan Jay Lerner (screenplay), Cedric Gibbons, E. Preston Ames, Edwin B. Willis, F. Keogh Gleason (art direction), Alfred Gilks, John Alton (photography), Orry-Kelly, Walter Plunkett, Irene Sharaff (costume), Johnny Green, Saul Chaplin (music)

**Oscar nomination:** Vincente Minnelli (director), Adrienne Fazan (editing)

# AN AMERICAN IN PARIS (1951)

Winner of six Academy Awards—including Best Picture (over supposed favorites *A Streetcar Named Desire* and *A Place in the Sun*)—as well as a special citation for choreographer-star Gene Kelly and the Thalberg Memorial award for MGM producer Alan Freed. Vincente Minnelli's joyous musical, *An American in Paris*, was an original for the screen, conceived by Freed as a vehicle for Kelly and constructed around a clutch of George Gershwin's most popular songs ("I Got Rhythm," "'S Wonderful").

Penniless artist Kelly brings his athletic exuberance to a sanitized Montmartre, tap dances with urchins, falls for gamine muse Leslie Caron, and vies for her with suave French singer Georges Guétary. Meanwhile jealous patron Nina Foch seethes, all dryly observed by the composer pal played by pianist and Gershwin exponent Oscar Levant. Sending up the penchant of Lost Generation Americans to immerse themselves in a little culture Française, Minnelli fills the film with vitality, romance, and a riot of color. The sensational, innovative highlight is Kelly's original 18-minute ballet to the title music, staged through sets in the style of French artists, notably Toulouse Lautrec, and the blissfully romantic Kelly–Caron "Our Love Is Here To Stay" dance number on the banks of the river Seine. **AE**

# A PLACE IN THE SUN (1951)

In adapting Theodore Dreiser's *An American Tragedy* for the screen, director George Stevens was faced with the difficulty of making the novelist's grimly naturalist tale of class warfare interesting to a 1950s audience more eager for entertainment than political instruction. His solution was brilliantly effective: to emphasize the erotic longings of George Eastman (Montgomery Clift) for the beautiful Angela Vickers (Elizabeth Taylor). A poor relation of a rich industrialist, George is sent to the man by his mother so that he can make good. But George, dominated by feelings of deprivation and exclusion, shows neither the drive nor the initiative to work his way up from the bottom. In fact, he is so weak that he has barely begun work at the factory when he violates one of its cardinal rules. Dating a fellow employee, he ends up impregnating the poor, desperate woman, in whom he has already lost interest.

Played as a kind of pathetic naïf by Clift, George's principal asset becomes his beauty and gentleness. *A Place in the Sun* thus became one of classic Hollywood's most touching and tragic romances, a result of Stevens's careful coaching of the principals (who were told to emphasize body language rather than dialogue) and his artful manipulation of two contrasting styles. George's fairy-tale encounter with the innocent Angela is dominated by intimate camerawork, especially carefully juxtaposed close-ups composed in soft focus. Scenes in the factory, with his first girlfriend Alice (Shelley Winters), and later in the courtroom, however, are photographed in a film noir style, emphasizing chiaroscuro lighting and unbalanced compositions that nicely express the threat circumstances pose to George's desire for his "place in the sun."

Pregnant, Alice threatens to expose George to his family if he doesn't marry her; he is saved from this fate only because the town hall is closed for a holiday when the couple arrives. George suggests a lake outing in a small boat; his intention is that there should be an "accident" and that Alice will drown. He cannot go through with the murder, but then Alice, frightened, tips over the boat. She drowns because he doesn't try to save her, and George pays with his life for his indifference. Stevens, however, makes him more memorable as a tragic lover than as a socio-political object lesson. **BP**

**U.S.** (Paramount) 122 min BW

**Director:** George Stevens

**Producer:** Ivan Moffat, George Stevens

**Screenplay:** Harry Brown, Theodore Dreiser, Patrick Kearney, Michael Wilson, from the novel *An American Tragedy* by Theodore Dreiser and the play *A Place in the Sun* by Patrick Kearney

**Photography:** William C. Mellor

**Music:** Franz Waxman

**Cast:** Montgomery Clift, Elizabeth Taylor, Shelley Winters, Anne Revere, Keefe Brasselle, Fred Clark, Raymond Burr, Herbert Heyes, Shepperd Strudwick, Frieda Inescort, Kathryn Givney, Walter Sande, Ted de Corsia, John Ridgely, Lois Chartrand

**Oscar:** George Stevens (director), Michael Wilson, Harry Brown (screenplay), William C. Mellor (cinematography BW), Edith Head (costume), William Hornbeck (editing), Franz Waxman (music)

**Oscar nomination:** George Stevens (best picture), Montgomery Clift (actor), Shelley Winters (actress)

**U.S.** (Fox) 92m BW

**Director:** Robert Wise

**Producer:** Julian Blaustein

**Screenplay:** Harry Bates, Edmund H. North, from the story *Farewell to the Master* by Harry Bates

**Photography:** Leo Tover

**Music:** Bernard Herrmann

**Cast:** Michael Rennie, Patricia Neal, Hugh Marlowe, Sam Jaffe, Billy Gray, Frances Bavier, Lock Martin

# THE DAY THE EARTH STOOD STILL (1951)

Robert Wise's 1951 science-fiction drama based on *Farewell to the Master*, a short story by Harry Bates, hit a nerve with nuclear-war weary and politician-wary audiences of the time. Beginning in an almost documentary style, it spreads a chilling antiwar message via spectacular special effects and memorable characterizations. More than a B movie, it is the first popular adult science-fiction film to send out a real message about humanity.

An interstellar emissary called Klaatu (Michael Rennie) lands in Washington, D.C., to deliver the message that war on earth must stop. His spacecraft surrounded by guns and tanks, Klaatu is accidentally injured and whisked away to a military hospital, leaving only Gort (Lock Martin), a 7-foot-tall robot, to guard the craft. Faceless, speechless, and possessing a deadly laserlike ray, Gort is invincible. The only way to get him to stop defending the spacecraft is by uttering, "Gort, Klaatu barada niktoh," a sentence learned by heart by virtually every child who has seen the film.

Klaatu escapes from the hospital and meets Helen (Patricia Neal), a beautiful woman of exceptional intelligence, and her son Bobby (Billy Gray), and it is Helen who must disarm the deadly Gort. To prove his power and lend weight to his message of peace, Klaatu devises a plan to stop all mechanical movement in the world (with the exception of airplanes and hospitals).

The role of Klaatu was originally intended for Claude Rains but a scheduling conflict opened the part for Rennie, whose angular face and calm demeanor lend a remote, gentle superiority to the character. Neal, a symbol of feminine bravery, sums up the best of what humanity has to offer. Gort was played by Martin, a 7'7" usher at Los Angeles' Graumann's Chinese Theater. Burdened by the heavy suit, Martin needed extra help to hold Neal in his arms, and in some scenes assisting wires are easily seen. To make the spacecraft appear seamless, the door crevice was puttied in and painted with silver. The putty tore open, allowing the door to suddenly appear without visual warning. Never bettered, *The Day the Earth Stood Still* is a classic on many fronts, not the least for its antiwar message and clever visual effects as well as Bernard Herrmann's haunting use of the theremin, an early electronic instrument. **KK**

# THE QUIET MAN (1952)

Director John Ford is most famous for his celebrations of American history and culture, but he also made a number of films that explored his Celtic, and especially Irish, roots, of which *The Quiet Man* is perhaps the most successful. An interesting mixture of drama and comedy, the film traces the homecoming of Irish-American Sean Thornton (John Wayne) to the "old sod," where he begins a passionate and stormy relationship with Mary Kate Danaher (Maureen O'Hara). Filmed in County Galway (from which Ford's family had emigrated to the United States), *The Quiet Man* features plenty of action in the Ford style, with the fitting, epic climax being ex-boxer Sean's fistfight with Mary's brother Will Danaher (Victor McLaglen) over his refusal to grant the American Mary's hand.

The battle ends with both men getting too drunk (during pauses in the action) to continue; they end as friends and, ultimately, family after Will agrees to the marriage. Yet the film is not really about masculine values. Mary is much more than the simple object of their contention. Though she wants Sean, Mary refuses to go against her brother to marry him. Marrying Sean under these circumstances would be an insult to her. At first Sean—who had killed a man in the ring—will not fight, and Mary thinks he does not love her enough to risk the struggle with her brother. A plot is hatched by others in the village to trick Danaher into granting his permission, and the couple is married. But the brother soon discovers the deceit and withholds her dowry. Mary refuses to sleep with Sean before the dowry, which represents her independent worth, is paid. The concluding boxing match settles both questions, however, and the couple is thereby reconciled.

Under Ford's astute direction, *The Quiet Man* plays off the conventional quaintness of the village against the beautiful natural scenery, resulting in a film that is serious enough to be affecting, but enough of a fantasy to be uproariously funny. **BP**

**U.S.** (Argosy, Republic) 129m Technicolor

**Language:** English / Gaelic

**Director:** John Ford

**Producer:** Merian C. Cooper, G.B. Forbes, John Ford, L.T. Rosso

**Screenplay:** Frank S. Nugent, Maurice Walsh, from the story *Green Rushes* by Maurice Walsh

**Photography:** Winton C. Hoch

**Music:** Victor Young

**Cast:** John Wayne, Maureen O'Hara, Barry Fitzgerald, Ward Bond, Victor McLaglen, Mildred Natwick, Francis Ford, Eileen Crowe, May Craig, Arthur Shields, Charles B. Fitzsimons, James Lilburn, Sean McClory, Jack MacGowran, Joseph O'Dea

**Oscar:** John Ford (director), Winton C. Hoch, Archie Stout (photography)

**Oscar nomination:** John Ford, Merian C. Cooper (best picture), Frank S. Nugent (screenplay), Victor McLaglen (actor in support role), Frank Hotaling, John McCarthy Jr., Charles S. Thompson (art direction), Daniel J. Bloomberg (sound)

**Venice Film Festival:** John Ford (international award), (OCIC award), nomination (Golden Lion)

## JEUX INTERDITS (1952)
### FORBIDDEN GAMES

A good many films have heightened the absurdities and cruelties of human life by depicting them through the eyes of children; but few more effectively, or more poignantly, than René Clément's finest film, *Forbidden Games*. The setting, as with much of Clément's best work, is World War II: a five-year-old girl, Paulette (Brigitte Fossey), is orphaned when her parents, fleeing from Paris, are killed in an aerial attack. Grudgingly taken in by a peasant family, she forms a bond with the younger son, 11-year-old Michel (Georges Poujouly), and the two create a secret world that reflects the death they see all around them. Collecting the corpses of animals and insects, they perform solemn rites over them and bury them in a disused barn, muttering half-understood phrases from the Catholic burial service. These, the "forbidden games" of the title, outrage the adults who discover them, and the children—distressed and bewildered—are torn apart.

Clément made his name with a dramatized documentary, *The Battle of the Rails* (1946), about the operations of the Resistance on the French rail network, and the opening of *Forbidden Games* carries a powerfully realistic charge as German fighter planes bomb and machine-gun a straggling column of refugees. The sequence of the attack is all the more horrifying for relying entirely on natural sound effects, with no added music, and for taking place amid the soft summer warmth of the French countryside. But after this the film grows more stylized. On the one hand is the adult world of the peasants, seen through the puzzled, fascinated eyes of the children—the petty feuds and bickering are caricatured, with lip service paid to religion while lives are ruled by greed and malice. By contrast, the children are observed with tenderness and sympathy as they construct their hidden fantasy world, and their final enforced separation is heartrending.

From his lead child actors, Clément draws remarkably expressive and convincing performances, refreshingly free from cuteness; there's an instinctive grace in the boy's gentleness toward his young friend. Narciso Yepes contributes a lyrical solo guitar score, expressive in its simplicity. **PK**

**France** (Silver) 102 m BW

**Language:** French

**Director:** René Clément

**Producer:** Robert Dorfmann

**Screenplay:** François Boyer, Jean Aurenche, Pierre Bost, René Clément, from the novel *Les Jeux Inconnus* by François Boyer

**Photography:** Robert Juillard

**Music:** Narciso Yepes

**Cast:** Georges Poujouly, Brigitte Fossey, Amédée, Laurence Badie, Madeleine Barbulée, Suzanne Courtal, Lucien Hubert, Jacques Marin, Pierre Merovée, Violette Monnier, Denise Péronne, Fernande Roy, Louis Saintève, André Wasle

**Oscar:** France (honorary award—best foreign language film)

**Oscar nomination:** François Boyer (screenplay)

**Venice Film Festival:** René Clément (Golden Lion)

# ANGEL FACE (1952)

U.S. (RKO) 91m BW

**Director:** Otto Preminger

**Producer:** Otto Preminger, Howard Hughes

**Screenplay:** Chester Erskine, Oscar Millard, Frank S. Nugent

**Photography:** Harry Stradling Sr.

**Music:** Dimitri Tiomkin

**Cast:** Robert Mitchum, Jean Simmons, Mona Freeman, Herbert Marshall, Leon Ames, Barbara O'Neil, Kenneth Tobey, Raymond Greenleaf, Griff Barnett, Robert Gist, Morgan Farley, Jim Backus

The American film noir movement is dominated by doomed romances and powerfully manipulative femmes fatales, who lure gullible men to their destruction. Otto Preminger's *Angel Face* appears late in the series and obviously owes much to earlier films such as Jacques Tourneur's *Out of the Past* (1947). This features Robert Mitchum in a similar role as a private investigator who discovers, but cannot escape from, the machinations of the amoral woman he loves.

*Angel Face*, however, is more cynical and sardonic than its predecessors. It traces the obsession of a working-class man, Frank Jessup (Mitchum), for a beautiful rich woman who involves him in a plot to murder her stepmother. Earlier, Diane Tremayne (Jean Simmons, cast effectively against type) had deliberately broken up Frank's engagement to Mary (Mona Freeman), the "good" woman who represents a normal life that is no longer enough for Frank once he meets Diane and develops a taste for rich living. The murder plot succeeds, but only at the additional and unexpected cost of the life of Diane's father. Diane, however, never feels a twinge of guilt, and nothing derails her plans. The couple are indicted for what is soon suspected to be a crime, but, in the tradition of *The Postman Always Rings Twice*, they are acquitted because of the shyster lawyer she hires to defend them. Though seemingly destined for a life together, Frank finally has an attack of conscience. He attempts to break with Diane after the trial and resume his previous life. In a gesture that dooms him (again recalling Mitchum's role in *Out of the Past*), Frank allows Diane to drive him to the bus station. But she would rather die than give him up. Diane backs the car over a cliff, killing them both, in a gesture that recalls the "accident" she plotted earlier.

*Angel Face* features impressive performances from Mitchum and Simmons, which Preminger's direction subtly reinforces through an artful manipulation of mise en scène stage setting—classic film noir. **BP**

# SINGIN' IN THE RAIN
(1952)

Some films are held in high esteem for their famous firsts—impressive artistic breakthroughs or stunning acting debuts. Other films are revered simply for being the best of a kind. *Singin' in the Rain* falls into this latter category. It isn't a pioneer in any real sense of the word, nor does it greatly advance the language of film, but few other pictures have so effortlessly and wonderfully encapsulated everything good about the movies: the joyous highs, the pitiful lows, and the perfect, perpetual seesaw between those two poles.

**U.S.** (MGM) 103m Technicolor
**Director:** Stanley Donen, Gene Kelly
**Producer:** Arthur Freed
**Screenplay:** Betty Comden, Adolph Green
**Photography:** Harold Rosson
**Music:** Nacio Herb Brown, Lennie Hayton
**Cast:** Gene Kelly, Donald O'Connor, Debbie Reynolds, Jean Hagen, Millard Mitchell, Cyd Charisse, Douglas Fowley, Rita Moreno
**Oscar nomination:** Jean Hagen (actress in support role), Lennie Hayton (music)

It is wholly appropriate that the greatest of all Hollywood musicals should be in essence about sound itself. Or at least the arrival of sound. The year is 1927, and Don Lockwood (Gene Kelly) is a celebrated silent film star. In the middle of shooting another swashbuckler with his on-screen partner Lina Lamont (Jean Hagan), the studio learns of the imminent debut of *The Jazz Singer* and shuts the production down. The only way for the film to compete is to transform it into a musical, but there are two problems: Don can barely stand his leading lady Lina, and her thick New York accent will never work in the new era of sound films. The solution? Dub Lamont's horrible singing voice with ingénue Kathy (Debbie Reynolds) and hope the public never finds out. But that stop-gap measure leads to yet another problem: Don has fallen in love with Kathy, which throws off his working relationship with Lina.

Codirected by Kelly and Stanley Donen, *Singin' in the Rain* features several great song-and-dance numbers, particularly Donald O'Connor's "Make 'Em Laugh" routine and Kelly's famous solo turn during the title song. Kelly, in a yellow rain slicker, swings from a light pole and stomps ecstatically in puddles, so enamored is he of the new love in his life. Oddly enough, several of the songs from *Singin' in the Rain* were actually recycled from MGM's music vaults, but Kelly and crew breathe such new life into them that they're now inextricably linked to *Singin'*. The screenplay, by Adolph Green and Betty Comden, is fleet and funny, parodying the rocky transition from silent films to talkies with the rapid wit only a generation of writing for the latter could foster.

In an irony worthy of the film itself, *Singin' in the Rain* was initially met with relative indifference and went mostly unnoticed at the Academy Awards. But as time went on its joyful sequences and charismatic stars became too strong to resist. Thank the repertoire circuit in part for crowning *Singin' in the Rain* as king of all musicals, thank numerous film critics and groups for placing it on the top ten list, but most of all thank Donen and Kelly for making it. The world of movies and beyond is a better place with *Singin' in the Rain* in it. **JKl**

# IKIRU (1952)
## TO LIVE

Though best known for his samurai epics (*The Seven Samurai*, *Yojimbo*), Akira Kurosawa was not, in the end, principally concerned with blood and guts—though, arguably, no other director has so thoroughly explored the potential of violent imagery on screen. Kurosawa was cinema's greatest humanist, and nowhere is this more evident than in *Ikiru*.

The film centers on Kenji Watanabe (Kurosawa regular Takashi Shimura), a *sarariman* ("salary man," or mid-level bureaucrat) whose daily life is dull and unfulfilling. His greatest achievement—one he takes quite seriously—is that he hasn't missed a day of work at the Citizen's Section of the Municipal Office in 30 years. It is not that he regrets the mundanity of his life; it's just that he knows no other option.

This all changes when he learns that he has cancer, and has but a short time still to live. In the last months of his life, Watanabe reconsiders his achievements (none) and his priorities (none), and decides that it is not too late for him to change the world for the better. He devotes all his energies to the construction of a public park—a small gesture that nevertheless takes on great significance for Watanabe, as well as for Kurosawa.

Shimura gives the performance of his life in *Ikiru*. After Watanabe learns of his illness, the actor's face tells us all we need to know: from inexpressibility to humility, it's all there in Shimura's features. Moving through the film with the look of a man who has been truly harrowed, it is impossible not to feel Watanabe's pain.

Though full of sadness, *Ikiru* is ultimately a movie of no small spiritual uplift. And this was Kurosawa's point—that to achieve anything like satisfaction or happiness, one must suffer. But suffering, too, is a part of life, and it can be used for good. *Ikiru* is immensely life-affirming, even if it is about death and sorrow. Kurosawa's gift was to show how these moods are not contradictory, but united as part of the cycle of life. His sincere belief that small things make a difference is both refreshing and touching, especially in today's irony-soaked global village. **EdeS**

**Japan** (Toho) 143m BW
**Language:** Japanese
**Director:** Akira Kurosawa
**Producer:** Sojiro Motoki
**Screenplay:** Shinobu Hashimoto, Akira Kurosawa, Hideo Oguni
**Photography:** Asakazu Nakai
**Music:** Fumio Hayasaka
**Cast:** Takashi Shimura, Shinichi Himori, Haruo Tanaka, Minoru Chiaki, Miki Odagiri, Bokuzen Hidari, Minosuke Yamada, Kamatari Fujiwara, Makoto Kobori, Nobuo Kaneko, Nobuo Nakamura, Atsushi Watanabe, Isao Kimura, Masao Shimizu, Yunosuke Ito
**Berlin International Film Festival:** Akira Kurosawa (special prize of the senate of Berlin)

# EUROPA '51 (1952)

Roberto Rossellini's *Europa '51* contains the most unpredictable mixture of ingredients one can think of, a stew you might not be so sure you want to taste—one that includes a Scandinavian actress-turned-Hollywood movie star; the father of Italian neorealism; a statement on the social conditions of cities in postwar Europe; a metaphysical meditation about the nature of good and evil and about the inalienable right to self-determination; the opposition of bourgeoisie and popular classes on every level; the death of a child; the betrayal and redemption of a mother... *mamma mia!* And then, you sit in the dark, the screen lights up, the movie begins. It's simple, it's obvious. Elegant, deeply moving, incredibly alive.

One year earlier, in *Stromboli*, Rossellini had turned a willing Ingrid Bergman into an extraordinary puppet simultaneously submitted to the hand of God and the hand of her director (and lover). No such thing this time, only the daring invention—by the same filmmaker and star—of a previously unknown fusion of the melodrama as a popular genre and the auteur film with its ethical and social concerns. Each situation in *Europa '51* is composed of conventional stuff, and every scene comes as unexpected, filled with a disturbing sense of reality, of secret connections with real life, though it seems to deal only with the usual references, both on the Romanesque side and on the thematic side. And it all takes places without any overly dramatic effect, without any kind of boasting, but, on the contrary, with an incredible modesty (by a director and an actress who were anything but humble) in the way the story is told, the way it is shot, and the way it is acted.

*Europa '51* slips beyond all the frames it would appear to belong to, reaching a level of essential humanism rarely achieved in the cinema—and never by using heavy means. As Bergman's character, Irene Girard, walks through all the obstacles on her way to being called a saint by the people, the film itself walks its way through, escaping from all the sins it seems to have had to endure. A "saintly" film? Why not? **J-MF**

**Italy** (Ponti-De Laurentiis) 113m BW

**Language:** Italian

**Director:** Roberto Rossellini

**Producer:** Dino De Laurentiis, Roberto Rossellini

**Screenplay:** Sandro De Feo, Mario Pannunzio, Ivo Perilli, Brunello Rondi, Roberto Rossellini

**Photography:** Aldo Tonti

**Music:** Renzo Rossellini

**Cast:** Ingrid Bergman, Alexander Knox, Ettore Giannini, Giulietta Masina, Teresa Pellati, Sandro Franchina, William Tubbs, Alfred Brown

**Venice Film Festival:** Roberto Rossellini (international award), nomination (Golden Lion)

**U.S.** (Loew's, MGM) 118m BW

**Director:** Vincente Minnelli

**Producer:** John Houseman

**Screenplay:** George Bradshaw, Charles Schnee

**Photography:** Robert Surtees

**Music:** David Raksin

**Cast:** Lana Turner, Kirk Douglas, Walter Pidgeon, Dick Powell, Barry Sullivan, Gloria Grahame, Gilbert Roland, Leo G. Carroll, Vanessa Brown, Paul Stewart, Sammy White, Elaine Stewart, Ivan Triesault

**Oscar:** Charles Schnee (screenplay), Gloria Grahame (actress in support role), Cedric Gibbons, Edward C. Carfagno, Edwin B. Willis, F. Keogh Gleason (art direction), Robert Surtees (photography), Helen Rose (costume)

**Oscar nomination:** Kirk Douglas (actor)

# THE BAD AND THE BEAUTIFUL (1952)

Still the best Hollywood-on-Hollywood movie, *The Bad and the Beautiful* is loosely based on the career of David O. Selznick, detouring to take in a few insider anecdotes about Val Lewton, Orson Welles, Raymond Chandler, Diana Barrymore, Alfred Hitchcock, and Irving Thalberg. Also note the British director's (played by Hitchcock's regular Leo G. Carroll) silent but influential wife.

Three people with good cause to hate producer Jonathan Shields (Kirk Douglas) are gathered to take a phone call from Paris in which the washed-up Shields will pitch a new project. In flashbacks, they cover his up-from-Poverty Row career, remembering why they loathe him so much. Director Fred Amiel (Barry Sullivan) is an early partner who is inspired by Shields to make something of a cheap monster picture called *The Doom of the Cat Man* (think *Cat People*), but is then shut out of his dream project, a hilariously "significant" Mexican project called *The Faraway Mountain*. Georgia Lorrison (Lana Turner), drunken trampy daughter of a John Barrymore-style hellraising star, is hauled out of the gutter and turned into a second generation movie goddess through personal attention and then dumped for an available slut (the wonderfully wry Elaine Stewart) on the night of the premiere. Least likely to forgive is professorial screenwriter James Lee Bartlow (Dick Powell), whose flighty, flirty distraction of a wife (Academy Award winner Gloria Grahame) Shields passes on to "Latin lover" Victor "Gaucho" Ribera (Gilbert Roland), who gets her killed in a plane crash.

No one can match Douglas as an ambitious megalomaniac, and this teeth-clenched, dimple-thrusting portrait is among his best work. The gossipy screenplay (another Oscar winner, Charles Schnee) is served wonderfully by director Vincente Minnelli's lush melodramatics and David Raksin's seductive score. In 50 years, the film has taken on more tragic-comic resonance as Selznick's reputation has taken a nosedive—Shields's conviction that he is making great art (shared by his accountant!) worth sacrificing other people's lives for, is all the more unsettling in that Minnelli allows glimpses of exactly the sort of bloated, huge self-important spectacle that now plays less well than more modest efforts. In the Shields filmography, you know you'd rather see *The Doom of the Cat Man* than *The Faraway Mountain*. **KN**

## THE BIG SKY (1952)

In Howard Hawks's *The Big Sky*, Kirk Douglas and Dewey Martin are fur traders in the 1830s, journeying up the Missouri river into Blackfoot country on a keelboat. The film is based on an excellent novel by A.B. Guthrie Jr., who also wrote the script for *Shane* (1953), and whose novels *These Thousand Hills* and *The Way West* were also made into Western movies. On the way, Douglas and Martin meet hazards both natural and human, and forge their crew into a Hawksian professional elite. This camaraderie is threatened when they capture an Indian girl, Teal Eye (Elizabeth Threatt) as a hostage to guarantee their safety. Both men fall for her, but eventually it's resolved.

Shot in black-and-white, with some impressive scenery, Hawks's film is ultimately less interested in the epic possibilities of the story than in the rich gallery of characters, including Hank Worden as a crazed old Indian, Arthur Hunnicutt as a feisty old-timer, and Steven Geray as Frenchy, the captain of the boat. There are also characteristic touches of Hawksian black humor, notably when Douglas has to have his finger amputated, a scene that was originally intended to be performed by John Wayne in *Red River* (1948). **EB**

**U.S.** (Winchester) 140m BW

**Director:** Howard Hawks

**Producer:** Howard Hawks, Edward Lasker

**Screenplay:** A.B. Guthrie Jr, Dudley Nichols, from novel by A.B. Guthrie Jr.

**Photography:** Russell Harlan

**Music:** Dimitri Tiomkin

**Cast:** Kirk Douglas, Dewey Martin, Elizabeth Threatt, Arthur Hunnicutt, Buddy Baer, Steven Geray, Henri Letondal, Hank Worden, Jim Davis

**Oscar nomination:** Arthur Hunnicutt (actor in support role), Russell Harlan (photography)

## HIGH NOON (1952)

One Sunday morning in the tamed Western town of Hadleyville, New Mexico, as Marshal Will Kane (Gary Cooper) is about to marry a peace-loving Quaker (Grace Kelly), news arrives that Frank Miller (Ian MacDonald)—the psycho Kane previously put away—has been pardoned and is due in on the 12 P.M. train. As Miller's most vicious accomplices (including a harmonica-sucking Lee Van Cleef) loiter at the station, the Marshal appeals for help. But the townspeople (colleagues, friends, dignitaries) refuse to risk their lives and stand by him against the outlaw who wants not only revenge but to run Hadleyville again.

Various clocks reveal that it's getting near noontime; everyone urges Kane to leave town, but the Cooper-style hero must face his responsibilities. *High Noon* plays out in real time, the deadline ticking closer and closer as the ballad theme song ("Do Not Forsake Me Oh My Darling") insists on the situation, with those the Marshal assumes will help him falling like ninepins. In a finale that remains potent even in these days of one-man-against-an-army action movies, he is left almost alone against four villains. Fred Zinneman's film is at once a great suspense Western and a stark allegory of the climate of fear and suspicion prevailing during the McCarthy era. **KN**

**U.S.** (Stanley Kramer) 85m BW

**Director:** Fred Zinnemann

**Producer:** Carl Foreman, Stanley Kramer

**Screenplay:** John W. Cunningham, Carl Foreman, from the story *The Tin Star* by John W. Cunningham

**Photography:** Floyd Crosby

**Music:** Dimitri Tiomkin

**Cast:** Gary Cooper, Thomas Mitchell, Lloyd Bridges, Katy Jurado, Grace Kelly, Otto Kruger, Lon Chaney Jr., Harry Morgan, Ian MacDonald, Eve McVeagh, Morgan Farley, Harry Shannon, Lee Van Cleef, Robert J. Wilke, Sheb Wooley

**Oscar:** Gary Cooper (actor), Elmo Williams, Harry W. Gerstad (editing), Dimitri Tiomkin (music), Dimitri Tiomkin, Ned Washington (song)

**Oscar nomination:** Stanley Kramer (best picture), Fred Zinnemann (director), Carl Foreman (screenplay)

**Italy** (Amato, De Sica, Rizzoli) 91m BW

**Language:** Italian

**Director:** Vittorio De Sica

**Producer:** Giuseppe Amato, Vittorio De Sica, Angelo Rizzoli

**Screenplay:** Cesare Zavattini

**Photography:** Aldo Graziati

**Music:** Alessandro Cicognini

**Cast:** Carlo Battisti, Maria-Pia Casilio, Lina Gennari, Ileana Simova, Elena Rea, Memmo Carotenuto

**Oscar nomination:** Cesare Zavattini (screenplay)

# UMBERTO D (1952)

This heart-wrenching film of a retired bureaucrat (Carlo Battisti) and his dog, Flike, will stay with you forever. After having made the neorealist classic *The Bicycle Thief* in 1948, director Vittorio De Sica and screenwriter Cesare Zavattini return to similar subject matter and method in *Umberto D*. Their technique is to structure the film around an emotionally charged and compelling personal story that reveals, in its telling, the general social conditions in which the story is set.

*Umberto D* is shot on the streets of Rome and the major parts are played by nonprofessional actors, adding to the film's immediacy and authenticity. One major criticism of neorealism is that the melodramatic treatment of the small story dilutes the larger social message and claim to realism made by the film in question. With its unapologetic tragic story of an old man's despair and love for his pet, and its pointed observations of social injustice, *Umberto D* provides the perfect opportunity for the viewer to consider this question about one of the most influential movements in the history of cinema.

Battisti, a retired professor, plays the title character with an understated sense of both dignity and resignation concerning his situation. Living on an insufficient pension, Umberto can barely afford his rented room, where he is at the mercy of his callous landlady, who wants to get rid of him. He shares the food he gets at a local charity with his dog, who is his sole companion and source of solace. As things get worse and worse for Umberto, he is on several occasions forced to choose between his own life and that of Flike. In one of the film's central sequences, Flike gets lost and Umberto fears that he will be destroyed at the city pound. As in *The Bicycle Thief*, the suspense built up around the ever-more-desperate search rivals a Hitchcock thriller. A pet who gives joy to a joyless existence (or a bicycle that will provide work in a time of great want), is shown to be capable of generating the same interest and excitement as a set of blueprints for a secret weapon or a cache of stolen jewels in a more fantastic scenario. Here, De Sica leaves us wondering whether Umberto's love for his dog, who depends on him alone, is redemptory or futile. **RH**

# LE CARROSSE D'OR (1952)
## THE GOLDEN COACH

The first in Jean Renoir's loose "theater" trilogy (the other two, *French Cancan* in 1955 and *Elena and Her Men* the following year), this Italian/French co-production features an Anglo-Italian cast led by the indefatigable Anna Magnani. In the English-language version, she laments the impossibility of acting in a foreign language in her inimitably thick Italian accent. She plays Camilla, Columbine in a *commedia dell'arte* troupe that arrives in 18th-century Peru. Instead of streets paved with gold, they find no pavement at all—they even have to build the theater for which they've been engaged.

"What do they make of the new world?"

"It'll be nice when they finish it."

Despite Camilla's first impressions, she is soon being courted by three eligible suitors, one of them the Spanish viceroy (Duncan Lamont), who presents her with the golden coach of the title. Alas, for an actor, sincerity in life is no guarantee of a happy ending. The movie's surface frivolity and farcical plotting camouflage a mature, even melancholy film about the fraught relations between love, art, and life. François Truffaut called it "the noblest and most refined film ever made . . . It is all breeding and politeness, grace and freshness . . . a film about theatre in the theatre." Antonio Vivaldi provides the soundtrack and Renoir's brother Claude the exquisite color cinematography. **TCh**

**Italy / France** (Hoche, Panaria) 103m Technicolor

**Director:** Jean Renoir

**Producer:** Francesco Alliata, Renzo Avanzo

**Screenplay:** Renzo Avanzo, Jack Kirkland, Ginette Doynel, Giulio Macchi, Jean Renoir, from the play *Le Carrosse du Saint-Sacrement* by Prosper Mérimée

**Photography:** Claude Renoir

**Nonoriginal music:** Antonio Vivaldi

**Cast:** Anna Magnani, Odoardo Spadaro, Nada Fiorelli, Dante, Duncan Lamont, George Higgins, Ralph Truman, Gisella Mathews, Raf De La Torre, Elena Altieri, Paul Campbell, Riccardo Rioli, William Tubbs, Jean Debucourt

# THE BIGAMIST (1953)

This haunting film is one of several out-of-nowhere masterpieces directed during a too-brief period by Ida Lupino, considered "the poor man's Bette Davis," when she was a hard-boiled Warner Brothers star in the 1940s. Edmond O'Brien stars as Harry Graham, a refrigerator salesman who, from shambling clumsily through life, ends up with two wives, Eve (Joan Fontaine) and Phyllis (Lupino), each unaware of the other's existence. Lupino's understated direction enfolds the characters with discreet, helpless pity.

Such drama as there is in *The Bigamist* is born from the sadness of three people: Harry's loneliness, Eve's sorrow over her father's death and her inability to conceive a child, and Phyllis's reluctance to have Harry acknowledge her because she doesn't want to be a burden to him. The whole film is the crystallization of this collective sadness in terms of environment (San Francisco and Los Angeles as the settings of Harry's dual life), deportment (Harry's numbed, pained passivity; Phyllis's hard-bitten isolation; Eve's desperate and pathetic attempt to be both the perfect wife and the perfect business partner), and, above all, the looks shared or half-avoided between people. In the shattering final courtroom scene, the orchestration of these looks achieves a combination of ambiguity and intensity that recalls both Carl Dreyer and Nicholas Ray. **CFu**

**U.S.** (Filmmakers) 80m BW

**Director:** Ida Lupino

**Producer:** Collier Young

**Screenplay:** Larry Marcus, Lou Schor, Collier Young

**Photography:** George E. Diskant

**Music:** Leith Stevens

**Cast:** Joan Fontaine, Edmund Gwenn, Ida Lupino, Edmond O'Brien, Kenneth Tobey, Jane Darwell, Peggy Maley

**U.S.** (MGM) 111m Technicolor

**Director:** Vincente Minnelli

**Producer:** Arthur Freed

**Screenplay:** Betty Comden, Adolph Green

**Photography:** Harry Jackson

**Music:** Arthur Schwartz (songs)

**Cast:** Fred Astaire, Cyd Charisse, Oscar Levant, Nanette Fabray, Jack Buchanan, James Mitchell, Robert Gist

**Oscar nomination:** Betty Comden, Adolph Green (screenplay), Mary Ann Nyberg (costume), Adolph Deutsch (music)

# THE BAND WAGON (1953)

Like *Singin' in the Rain* released the previous year, Vincente Minnelli's *The Band Wagon* is a musical that affectionately reflects upon the history of its genre—in order to pioneer a new, "integrated" style based on character and plot while simultaneously enjoying the benefits of the old, "revue" style. It cleverly does so by making the Fred Astaire of *Top Hat* (1935) a dinosaur in a modern, showbiz milieu, and by giving him a trial wherein he must grapple with the overbearing vision of an Orson Welles-like director (Jack Buchanan), and ultimately affirm his worth as an old-fashioned but adaptable "hoofer" in a dynamic, hit show.

Like most musicals, *The Band Wagon* is about compromise, the marriage of antagonistic tendencies. The characters symbolize the extremes of lowbrow and highbrow culture: Tony Hunter (Astaire) versus his reluctant leading lady Gabrielle Gerard (Cyd Charisse) from ballet. But when push comes to shove, such cultural divisions break down easily: Tony turns out to be a fine art connoisseur, and Gaby will belt out "I See a New Sun" on stage like a song-and-dance trouper. This aesthetic melding is also a literal romance, clinched by the immortal pas de deux in Central Park, "Dancing in the Dark."

Mainly, however, *The Band Wagon* is a delightfully colorful "montage of attractions"—starting with the high-energy comedic contributions of Nanette Fabray and Oscar Levant, alter egos for the writers Betty Comden and Adolph Green. Minnelli gets to show off many kinds of mise en scène: playing on décor and architecture in the scene where Buchanan pitches his "Faust" while characters in three adjoining rooms eavesdrop; fluidly moving a group of performers through switches in mood in the indelible "That's Entertainment"; enjoying the purely theatrical novelty of the kooky number "Triplets."

But the ultimate spectacle is the extraordinary, 11-minute "Girl Hunt: A Murder Mystery in Jazz," a film noir parody (in vibrant color), in which Michael Kidd's dance choreography explodes in stylized arabesques of familiar gestures (shooting, smoking, fighting) and the stars turn on their glamor, whether in erotic display (Charisse) or the simple joy of walking (Astaire). **AM**

# MADAME DE... (1953)

Few films establish so much, on so many levels, with such stunning economy, as Max Ophüls's sublime *Madame de . . .* Louise (Danielle Darrieux) is "Madame de..." because she is anonymous, typical of her privileged class; it is only the earrings we see in the opening frames—about to be pawned—that precipitate her into a drama. As those earrings are moved the camera moves with them, finally revealing Louise in a mirror, amidst her material possessions. From that moment on, Ophüls will never let us overlook the underpinnings of this wealthy world: the flows of money and debt, the ubiquitous servants on call, the etiquette of preparation before public appearances. Even the journey from bedroom to front door becomes an elegant sociological exposé.

After home and the pawnshop, there is the church (site of bourgeois hypocrisy) and the opera, where all is show; there we will meet Louise's husband, André (Charles Boyer), "debonair" as long as he can control the affairs (both his own and hers) that define this "sophisticated" marriage. By the time the earrings come back into André's hands a third time—and Louise has fallen dangerously in love with Donati (Vittorio De Sica)—what could have easily been a cute conceit (the earrings linking all characters, reminiscent of Ophüls's earlier *La Ronde* [1950]) ultimately comes to articulate all the fine, crucial distinctions of plot and theme. For Louise, who lives in a state of denial about the conditions that enable her supposed freedom, the earrings are a token of her love with Donati; for André, they are a sign of possession, of the patriarchal, military, and aristocratic power he wields over other people's destinies.

*Madame de...* is, by turns, brittle, brutal, compassionate, and moving. Ophüls delineates this world with Brechtian precision, yet he never discounts the strength or significance of stifled, individual yearnings. Even as the characters writhe in their metaphoric prisons or shut these traps on each other, their passions touch us: supremely, when André closes the windows on Louise like a jailer as he declares, half whispering in secret: "I love you." **AM**

**France/Italy** (Franco London, Indus, Rizzoli) 105m BW

**Language:** French

**Director:** Max Ophüls

**Producer:** Ralph Baum

**Screenplay:** Marcel Achard, Max Ophüls, Annette Wademant, from the novel *Madame de* by Louise de Vilmorin

**Photography:** Christian Matras

**Music:** Oscar Straus, Georges Van Parys

**Cast:** Charles Boyer, Danielle Darrieux, Vittorio De Sica, Jean Debucourt, Jean Galland, Mireille Perrey, Paul Azaïs, Josselin Hubert Noël, Lia Di Leo

**Oscar nomination:** Georges Annenkov, Rosine Delamare (costume )

## FROM HERE TO ETERNITY (1953)

U.S. (Columbia) 118m BW

**Director:** Fred Zinnemann

**Producer:** Buddy Adler

**Screenplay:** James Jones, Daniel Taradash, from novel by James Jones

**Photography:** Burnett Guffey

**Music:** George Duning, James Jones, Fred Karger, Robert Wells

**Cast:** Burt Lancaster, Montgomery Clift, Deborah Kerr, Donna Reed, Frank Sinatra, Philip Ober, Mickey Shaughnessy, Harry Bellaver, Ernest Borgnine, Jack Warden, John Dennis, Merle Travis, Tim Ryan, Arthur Keegan, Barbara Morrison

**Oscar:** Buddy Adler (best picture), Fred Zinnemann (director), Daniel Taradash (screenplay), Frank Sinatra (actor in support role), Donna Reed (actress in support role), Burnett Guffey (photography), William A. Lyon (editing), John P. Livadary (sound)

**Oscar nomination:** Montgomery Clift (actor), Burt Lancaster (actor), Deborah Kerr (actress), Jean Louis (costume design, BW), Morris Stoloff, George Duning (music)

Notwithstanding the famously iconic scene of Burt Lancaster and Deborah Kerr rolling and smooching in the Hawaiian surf, Fred Zinnemann's version of James Jones's best seller about life on an U.S. army base in 1941 immediately prior to the Japanese attack on Pearl Harbor is a somewhat modified affair. Although the language, the sex, and the violence may have been toned down, the focus on adultery, prostitution, corruption, and sadistic bullying ensured that *From Here to Eternity* was welcomed as an unusually adult Hollywood movie worthy of eight Oscars. With the passing of time, the film's sensationalist elements have come to feel less daring, and it's the vivid performances of its starry cast that now stick in the memory. Lancaster is the principled but pragmatic Sergeant Warden. Montgomery Clift is Prewitt, the bugler new to the barracks (whose conscientious refusal to box for his platoon's team provokes prejudicial treatment by the officers), and Frank Sinatra is his friend Maggio, picked on by obnoxious stockade sergeant Fatso (a memorable Ernest Borgnine). Inevitably, perhaps, in this deeply "masculine" study of rugged courage and individual honor in conflict with the conformist expectations of the community at large, the actresses fare less well. English rose Kerr is just slightly self-conscious as a sultry American adulteress, and Donna Reed plays a dancehall whore passed off as a hostess.

Zinnemann probably wasn't quite right to direct such fare. A rather meticulous craftsman who progressed from modest but reasonably efficient fillers to rather self-consciously "significant" films, he was here at what would prove a turning point in his career. The Oscars meant he could go on to more conspicuous "quality" films, but this movie might have benefited from a less cautiously "realistic" touch. After all, it's really a melodrama, and a touch of lurid expressionism would not have gone amiss. That said, the film is good on the dynamics of bullying, on officers conveniently turning a blind eye to misdemeanors, and on the prejudices that infect any closed group. Plus he did get those sturdy performances out of his actors. And after that roll in the surf barracks life would never seem the same again. **GA**

# TOKYO STORY (1953)

"Isn't life disappointing?" asks a teenage girl of her widowed sister-in-law at her mother's funeral; "Yes," comes the answer—with a smile. This brief exchange, near the close of Yasujiro Ozu's masterpiece *Tokyo Story*, typifies the unsentimental mood of becalmed acceptance that distinguishes his work. The performances, setting—the middle-class home the girl has shared with, until now, both of her elderly parents—and dialogue are wholly naturalistic in tone, and never for a moment seem as if they've been arranged as part of some grand climax, yet by the time the words are uttered, they carry enormous emotional and philosophical weight. Ozu's films were marvelously understated, deceptively simple affairs, mostly depicting the everyday domestic and professional rituals of middle-class Japanese life with an idiosyncratic lack of emphasis (dramatic or stylistic) that might mislead the inattentive into believing them banal. Here, all that happens is that the old folks leave their youngest daughter at home in the provinces to visit their other children in Tokyo; they've never been to the capital, but make the effort in the knowledge that time is running short. But the kids have their own families now, and shunt their parents around, barely disguising their need to get on with their busy lives in postwar Japan. Only their daughter-in-law, who lost her husband in the war, seems to have enough time for them. Not that they'd complain, any more than she would.

All this is observed, as was Ozu's custom, with a static camera placed a couple of feet off the ground; there is only one shot in the film that moves—and even then it tracks with inconspicuous slowness, albeit at the very moment when the old folks decide to go home. So how does Ozu hold our attention, when what we see or hear is so uninflected by what most viewers consider dramatic or unusual? It all comes down to the contemplative quality of his gaze, implying that any human activity, however "unimportant," is worthy of our attention. In contrast to his own particular (and particularly illuminating) cinematic style, his characters' experiences, emotions, and thoughts are as "universal" as anything in the movies—a paradox that has rightly enshrined this film's reputation as one of the greatest ever made. **GA**

**Japan** (Shochiku) 136m BW
**Language:** Japanese
**Director:** Yasujiro Ozu
**Producer:** Takeshi Yamamoto
**Screenplay:** Kôgo Noda, Yasujiro Ozu
**Photography:** Yuharu Atsuta
**Music:** Kojun Saitô
**Cast:** Chishu Ryu, Chieko Higashiyama, Setsuko Hara, Haruko Sugimura, Sô Yamamura, Kuniko Miyake, Kyôko Kagawa, Eijirô Tono, Nobuo Nakamura, Shirô Osaka, Hisao Toake, Teruko Nagaoka, Mutsuko Sakura, Toyoko Takahashi, Toru Abe

# ROMAN HOLIDAY (1953)

If the filmmakers knew exactly what they had on their hands at the time, they might have retitled *Roman Holiday* as *A Star Is Born*. Audrey Hepburn had only appeared in a few European roles and in a Broadway production of *Gigi* when she was cast as a princess in William Wyler's film. Needless to say, the role fit, *Roman Holiday* was a hit, and Hepburn was catapulted to the top of Tinseltown royalty. She was the Cinderella story made real by the magic of Hollywood.

*Roman Holiday* itself actually presents the flip side to the Cinderella fable. Hepburn's Princess Ann is tired of the pomp and circumstance of her official duties. One night she slips out from under her handlers' control and, under the guise of an everyday girl, encounters American journalist Joe Bradley (Gregory Peck). He recognizes the princess as the possible scoop of his career, but as he gets to know her better he feels terrible about taking advantage of her innocence. As the two tour the city, they realize they're falling in love, but the realities of their respective situations may make such a relationship impossible. So they enjoy the city and all its charms, knowing that this short time they spend together may be the last.

Peck and Hepburn are excellent as the two mismatched lovers, and Eddie Albert is perfect as Peck's eager tagalong cameraman. Wyler, one of Hollywood's most reliable directors, shot the film on location in Rome, and the city's landmarks help enhance the already magical story. Just as essential is the enjoyable script, which proved controversial because it was penned by blacklisted writer Dalton Trumbo. It was literally decades before Trumbo finally got the credit he deserved for helping to craft such a wonderful film.

The rest of the crew didn't need to wait nearly as long—*Roman Holiday* earned a whopping ten Academy Award nominations, including a win for the relatively unknown Hepburn. She'd be cast as the ingenue many more times over in her career, but it was this film that officially and auspiciously marked her arrival. **JKl**

**U.S.** (Paramount) 118m BW

**Director:** William Wyler

**Producer:** Robert Wyler, William Wyler

**Screenplay:** Ian McLellan Hunter, John Dighton

**Music:** Georges Auric

**Photography:** Henri Alekan, Franz Planer

**Cast:** Gregory Peck, Audrey Hepburn, Eddie Albert, Hartley Power, Harcourt Williams, Margaret Rawlings, Tullio Carminati, Paolo Carlini, Claudio Ermelli, Paola Borboni, Alfredo Rizzo, Laura Solari, Gorella Gori, Heinz Hindrich, John Horne

**Oscar:** Audrey Hepburn (actress), Edith Head (costume), Ian McLellan Hunter (Dalton Trumbo) (screenplay - story)

**Oscar nomination:** William Wyler (best picture), William Wyler (director), Ian McLellan Hunter (Dalton Trumbo), John Dighton (screenplay, writing), Eddie Albert (actor in support role), Hal Pereira, Walter H. Tyler (art direction), Franz Planer, Henri Alekan (photography), Robert Swink (editing)

# LE SALAIRE DE LA PEUR (1953)
## WAGES OF FEAR

A withering depiction of greed and the corrupting influence of capitalism disguised as an adventure film, Henri Georges-Clouzot's *Wages of Fear* justifiably stands as possibly the most tension-filled movie ever made. Set in South America, two teams compete to complete a relatively straightforward task: transport a truckload of nitroglycerin along a three-hundred mile mountain pass to the site of an oil refinery fire so that the oil company can then blow the pipeline and put out the blaze. The catch? Notoriously unstable and sensitive, the nitro cargo will blow the drivers to bits if they're not exceedingly careful.

With sadistic invention Clouzot throws as many obstacles in the way of the two trucks as they race (at a snail's pace) through the bumpy mountain pass. Hairpin turns and rickety bridges would pose their own innate problems were the trucks not primed to blow, and each pothole or falling rock brings with it the possibility of instant doom. It isn't the promise of glory that sets each pair of drivers on such a dangerous task, either, but the promise of cash, and as the film proceeds you begin to wonder how far they will go to get their hands on the money.

Vitally, Clouzot precedes the death-defying action with a long segment—at one point cut for its political sentiment set in a slum of a South American crossroads where wanderers and vagabonds end up after they have nowhere else to go, and where we learn that the rogues willing to risk their lives for money are in many ways almost not worth knowing. Their suicidal actions are driven by selfishness and desperation, traits to be exploited by the opportunistic corporation that cynically holds out the carrot on the stick for these de facto mules. Indeed, full of distrust and dislike, the motley crew of mercenaries act with a primal, feral quality, posing as much of a threat to one another as the truckloads of explosives do to them all. It's a lose-lose situation, as the finish line promises financial reward at the cost of spiritual ruin. **JKl**

**France / Italy** (CICC, Filmsonor, Fono, Vera) 141m BW

**Language:** French / English / Spanish / German

**Director:** Henri-Georges Clouzot

**Producer:** Raymond Borderie, Henri-Georges Clouzot, Louis Wipf

**Screenplay:** Henri-Georges Clouzot, Jérôme Géronimi, from novel by Georges Arnaud

**Photography:** Armand Thirard

**Music:** Georges Auric

**Cast:** Yves Montand, Charles Vanel, Peter van Eyck, Antonio Centa, Darling Légitimus, Luis De Lima, Jo Dest, Darío Moreno, Faustini, Seguna, William Tubbs, Véra Clouzot, Folco Lulli, Jeronimo Mitchell

**Berlin International Film Festival:** Henri-Georges Clouzot (Golden Bear)

**Cannes Film Festival:** Henri-Georges Clouzot (grand prize of the festival), Charles Vanel (special mention—acting)

U.S. (Loew's, MGM) 91m Technicolor
**Director:** Anthony Mann
**Producer:** William H. Wright
**Screenplay:** Sam Rolfe, Harold Jack Bloom
**Photography:** William C. Mellor
**Music:** Bronislau Kaper
**Cast:** James Stewart, Janet Leigh, Robert Ryan, Ralph Meeker, Millard Mitchell
**Oscar nomination:** Sam Rolfe, Harold Jack Bloom (screenplay)

# THE NAKED SPUR (1953)

The third of the remarkable series of Westerns director Anthony Mann made with James Stewart in the 1950s, *The Naked Spur* has Stewart as Howard Kemp, an embittered bounty hunter trying to earn money to buy back the ranch he lost when his wife was unfaithful to him during the Civil War. Along the trail he falls in with Jesse (Millard Mitchell), an elderly prospector, and Anderson (Ralph Meeker), a renegade army officer. Eventually Stewart gets his man, a sardonic killer named Ben (Robert Ryan), but Kemp's troubles are just beginning. The arduous journey through the wilderness to bring Ben to justice tests Kemp to the limits.

What makes this an exceptional film is, first, the tautly scripted and finely acted exploration of the tensions between the characters, as Kemp and Ben each strive to gain psychological supremacy, with Ben using his girlfriend Lina (Janet Leigh) as bait, as he senses Kemp's vulnerability beneath the tough exterior. James Stewart gives a brilliant portrayal of a man on the edge of hysteria. Second, Mann has a wonderful way with mountain scenery, using the arduous nature of the terrain as a physical counterpoint to the characters' inner turmoil. Virtually the entire film was shot on location. **EB**

**U.S.** (Fox) 80m BW
**Director:** Samuel Fuller
**Producer:** Jules Schermer
**Screenplay:** Samuel Fuller, from story by Dwight Taylor
**Photography:** Joseph MacDonald
**Music:** Leigh Harline
**Cast:** Richard Widmark, Jean Peters, Thelma Ritter, Murvyn Vye, Richard Kiley, Willis Bouchey, Jerry O'Sullivan, Harry Carter, George E. Stone, George Eldredge, Stuart Randall, Frank Kumagai, Victor Perry, Emmett Lynn, Parley Baer
**Oscar nomination:** Thelma Ritter (actress in support role)
**Venice Film Festival:** Samuel Fuller nomination (Golden Lion)

# PICKUP ON SOUTH STREET (1953)

A minor phenomenon of the early Cold War, the cycle of anticommunist spy film genre produced one masterpiece, *Pickup on South Street.* A pickpocket must choose between patriotism and profit after he swipes a top secret microfilm. *Pickup* transcends its subgenre through its dynamic style and vivid depiction of New York lowlife. Samuel Fuller displays a prodigious range of stylistic invention, finding fresh visual concepts for nearly every scene. The key ingredient is the close-up, with the camera shoved in the actors' faces so aggressively you can almost see their breath fogging the lens. These copious close-ups signal the film's placement of the intimate over the ideological, its endorsement of actions motivated not by abstractions but by love, loyalty, and guilt on the closest personal level.

The main actors never did better work: cocky cynic Richard Widmark, bighearted bimbo Jean Peters, sweaty rat Richard Kiley, and, especially, unapologetic stoolie Thelma Ritter. The most powerful scene depicts a weary Ritter facing obliteration by gunman Kiley. In a film so devoted to the personal, it is fitting that her greatest fear is not death itself but an unmarked grave. As she says in one of the script's many punchy lines, "If I was to be buried in Potter's Field, it would just about kill me!" **MR**

# GENTLEMEN PREFER BLONDES (1953)

It is not the most famous number in *Gentlemen Prefer Blondes*, but the song "When Love Goes Wrong" captures what is most infectious about this garish, hilariously camp musical. Dorothy (Jane Russell) and Lorelei (Marilyn Monroe) mope at an outdoors Parisian café about the difficulty of sustaining romances with men. As a crowd gathers, the two women warm to the increasingly expansive rhythm of their lament, which soon has them out of their seats, striding and strutting with bystanders in the style of choreographer Jack Cole. And then the commotion winds down: the music thins, the crowd disperses, and our heroines are gliding away in a cab—from banality to ecstasy and back again, beautifully.

Typical of the 1950s, *Gentlemen Prefer Blondes* is an acerbic comedy about gold digging, unafraid to mix sentimental dreams with brittle sarcasm, glamorous magic with a materialist sense of what a girl must do to get by—a set of merry contradictions immortalized in Monroe's oft-imitated "Diamonds are a Girl's best Friend." As Jonathan Rosenbaum wrote, the film is "an impossible object—a CinemaScope of the mind, a capitalist Potemkin."

The film is (as theorists say) a palimpsest, picking up and discarding at whim bits of Anita Loos's novel, its Broadway adaptation, songs by the teams of Leo Robin/Jule Styne and Hoagy Carmichael/Harold Adamson, and, above all, the possibilities accruing to its two powerhouse stars. Russell's persona brings together raunchiness and practicality; Monroe is a potent mixture of slinky eroticism and childlike guilelessness, laced with a hint of savvy manipulation. The comic highpoint comes when the roles swap for Dorothy's brash courtroom imitation of Lorelei.

Howard Hawks is generally regarded as a very classical, restrained director, but here he veers toward the crazy, spectacularly vulgar comedies of Frank Tashlin—a connection clinched by the presence of that wonderfully grotesque child, George Winslow. The excess and oddity of certain set pieces (such as Russell's deathless serenade addressed to indifferent musclemen, "Ain't There Anyone Here for Love?"), and their frequently tangential relation to the nominal plot, are all part of what makes the film so enjoyable to a contemporary audience. **AM**

**U.S.** (Fox) 91m Technicolor

**Director:** Howard Hawks

**Producer:** Sol C. Siegel

**Screenplay:** Charles Lederer, from novel by Anita Loos and play by Joseph Fields and Anita Loos

**Photography:** Harry J. Wild

**Music:** Harold Adamson, Hoagy Carmichael, Leo Robin, Jule Styne

**Cast:** Jane Russell, Marilyn Monroe, Charles Coburn, Elliott Reid, Tommy Noonan, George Winslow, Marcel Dalio, Taylor Holmes, Norma Varden, Howard Wendell, Steven Geray, Henri Letondal, Leo Mostovoy, Alex Frazer, George Davis

## THE BIG HEAT (1953)

Like Fritz Lang's 1952 Western *Rancho Notorious*, *The Big Heat* is a ballad of "hate, murder, and revenge": it opens with a close-up of a gun about to be used by corrupt cop Tom Duncan to commit suicide, and proceeds rapidly through jolting horrors that malform the characters. Cop Dave Bannion (Glenn Ford) turns from family man to obsessive when his wife (Jocelyn Brando) is blown up by a car bomb meant for him. Moll Debby (Gloria Grahame) is embittered when her thug boyfriend Vince (Lee Marvin) disfigures her with a faceful of hot coffee and takes up Bannion's quest. In a crucial development, the embittered hero still can't commit cold-blooded murder, and so a double has to step in to pull the last thread that allows justice to be done: the big heat that brings down crime boss Lagana (Alexander Scourby) is precipitated when Debby confronts and murders her "sister under the mink," the crooked cop's grasping widow.

Grounded more in political reality than most of Lang's noirs, thanks to the hard-hitting detail of William P. McGivern's novel and Sydney Boehm's script, *The Big Heat* is one of a 1950s cycle of syndicate-runs-the-town crime exposés—others include *The Phenix City Story* (1955) and *The Captive City* (1952). Lang's direction is still indebted to expressionism here, with sets that reflect the characters' overriding personality traits: the cold luxury of the Duncan house, bought with dirty money; the tasteless wealth of Lagana's mansion, with its hideous portrait of the mobster's sainted mother and jiving teenage party; the penthouse moderne of Vince and Debby, where the police commissioner plays cards with killers; the cramped, poor-but-honest apartment of the Bannion family; and the hotel room where Bannion ends up, his life pared down to the need for vengeance. The finale is hardly comforting: after the fall of the crime syndicate, the hero returns to his desk in the Homicide Department. The welcome of workmates—expressed, of course, by an offer of coffee—is curtailed, and the end title appears over Bannion putting on his hat and coat to go out and deal with "a hit and run over on South Street." **KN**

**U.S.** (Columbia) 89m BW

**Director:** Fritz Lang

**Producer:** Robert Arthur

**Screenplay:** Sydney Boehm, from novel by William P. McGivern

**Photography:** Charles Lang

**Music:** Daniele Amfitheatrof, Arthur Morton

**Cast:** Glenn Ford, Gloria Grahame, Jocelyn Brando, Alexander Scourby, Lee Marvin, Jeanette Nolan, Peter Whitney, Willis Bouchey, Robert Burton, Adam Williams, Howard Wendell, Chris Alcaide, Michael Granger, Dorothy Green, Carolyn Jones

# LES VACANCES DE M. HULOT (1953)
## M. HULOT'S HOLIDAY

**France** (Cady Films, Specta Films)
114m BW

**Language:** French

**Director:** Jacques Tati

**Producer:** Fred Orain

**Screenplay:** Jacques Tati, Henri Marquet, Pierre Aubert, Jacques Lagrange

**Photography:** Jacques Mercanton, Jean Mousselle

**Music:** Alain Romans

**Cast:** Nathalie Pascaud, Michèle Rolla, Raymond Carl, Lucien Frégis, Valentine Camax

**Oscar nomination:** Jacques Tati, Henri Marquet (screenplay)

This enduring and endearing classic of French cinema revealed Jacques Tati, in only his second feature as a director, to be one of the medium's most inventive and original stylists. A virtually plotless and wordless succession of incidents occurring at a beachside resort, the film milks laughter from the most seemingly banal minutiae of everyday life. Alongside the elaborately staged events—such as a pack of travelers racing from one train platform to the next as incomprehensibly distorted loudspeaker messages blare—there are many droll, lovely moments where nothing much is happening at all. People just sit, eat, read, and stare, determined to be in holiday mode at all times. The stoic silliness of it all is extremely infectious.

Tati understood as finely as Alfred Hitchcock that mise en scène is not something to be imposed by filmmakers but discovered within the rituals of everyday life: how close people sit to each other in a dining room; the codes governing when people are allowed to look at one another; all the rules of etiquette and public deportment in play during the free-but-structured time of the French holiday period—Tati found the inspiration for his comedy in such acute observation.

The film rigorously controls the comic timing, spatial set-ups, and post-synchronized sounds of its brilliantly conceived gags—even the oft-repeated noise of a spring door is funny, due to the way Tati "musicalizes" it. He takes familiar gag forms—like the Keatonesque manner in which the hero berserkly imitates the movements of an exercise-freak—and then makes them strange through the way he shoots and cuts the action, often quickly switching attention to another gag beginning nearby.

Although in his later films Tati deliberately restricted his own on-screen appearances, here the gangly, awkward figure of his eponymous Hulot is a major source of charm and hilarity—and there is even the poignant trace of a tentative but missed love intrigue. Forever hesitating before entering any space, forever apologizing and politely greeting everyone present once he does, Hulot cannot fail to trigger some calamity with his over-anxious body movements—culminating in the cinema's most inspired display of fireworks.
**AM**

France / Italy (Titanus, Italia, Junior, Ariane, S.F.C., SCG, Sveva) 100m BW

**Director:** Roberto Rossellini

**Screenplay:** Vitaliano Brancati, Roberto Rossellini

**Photography:** Enzo Serafin

**Music:** Renzo Rossellini

**Cast:** Ingrid Bergman, George Sanders, Leslie Daniels, Natalia Ray, Maria Mauban, Anna Proclemer, Jackie Frost, Paul Müller

# VIAGGIO IN ITALIA (1953)

## VOYAGE IN ITALY

Jacques Rivette once wrote that Roberto Rossellini's *Voyage in Italy* "opens a breach [which] all cinema, on pain of death, must pass through." This is evident from the first shots, sudden and raw—a shaky, forward driving view down a road into Naples; a glimpse of the landscape going by; and finally two stars, Ingrid Bergman and George Sanders, shipwrecked far from Hollywood in a plotless, not-quite-picaresque road-movie cruise in which they express the deepest levels of character through terse banalities and simple, mundane gestures.

Nowadays, critics talk about the "comedy of remarriage," a genre in which couples put their union to the test and, after many complications, reaffirm it. *Voyage in Italy* is that rarer thing: a drama of remarriage, where the spark of revitalization must be found within the undramatic flow of daily togetherness. The Joyces, Alex (Sanders) and Katherine (Bergman), bored and resentful of each other, are in a state of suspension. Being "on holiday" leaves them disquieted, sometimes distressed by the foreign culture that surrounds them. The food is different, sleep beckons at odd hours under the sun, there are encounters with strangers who offer distraction or temptation.

And then there is the landscape, the cities of Naples, Capri, and Pompei. *Voyage in Italy* typifies the radical turn in Rossellini's work of the 1950s: no longer "social issue" neorealism, but an inner, emotional realism, prefiguring Michelangelo Antonioni and especially the Jean-Luc Godard of *Contempt* (1963). But there is still a sense of documentary reality in the views Katherine sees from her car, in the churches, catacombs, mud pools, archaeological excavations . . . . This insistent environment adds context, history, and even mythology to the personal, marital story. It brings the past to bear upon the present, prompting the characters to endlessly recall formative moments. And it places this one, small crisis into a great, cosmic cycle of birth, death, and rebirth.

Little is explained in *Voyage in Italy*, but everything is felt: This is a film that can proudly end—just before yet another shot of a passing, ordinary crowd—with a sweeping crane shot and the age-old declaration: "I love you." **AM**

# UGETSU MONOGATARI (1953)

## TALES OF UGETSU

In the mid-1950s, when the international circuit of film festivals got underway, the cineastes of the West finally discovered what their Japanese counterparts had known for years: This Kenji Mizoguchi fellow was really something special. *Ugetsu monogatari* (literally, *The Story of Ugetsu*; commonly known simply as *Ugetsu*) was the film on which the international gaze focused. Though it is not necessarily Mizoguchi's best (that honor could just as easily go to the profoundly moving 1939 *The Story of the Late Chrysanthemums*), it is the one for which he is still best known in Europe and America, and surely one of the great masterpieces of world cinema.

Mizoguchi had been writing and directing films since the 1920s, but we have no one, really, to blame for the fact that his work went largely unseen in the West, because Japan's was an insular film market. But when *Ugetsu* did hit Western shores, it hit hard: critics from Europe and the United States alike praised it vigorously, heralding it as the bellwether of an entirely new way of filmmaking. They may have been correct. But what is it that makes *Ugetsu* so remarkable?

Key to the film is the mixing of the real and the supernatural, a theme that infiltrates Mizoguchi's framing and his actors' performances at every turn. The master pulls us from one realm of existence into the other—sometimes with warning, sometimes without. Mizoguchi's control over his film's tone is precise: the aura of unearthliness and unholiness never quite dissipates.

But this is no ordinary ghost story. *Ugetsu* uses the real/supernatural split to explore issues of love, honor, responsibility, and family; each one of these themes is touched in some way by the ghost world Mizoguchi carefully maps atop the familiar world, and not one of them emerges unchanged. The foolish men and the long-suffering women of *Ugetsu* all go through wrenching transformations brought about by the interaction of the supernatural with the real.

*Ugetsu* is troubling, perplexing, and beautiful. Mostly, though, it is beautiful, and truly humbling: To watch it is to be in the presence of greatness. **EdeS**

**Japan** (Daiei) 94m BW

**Language:** Japanese

**Director:** Kenji Mizoguchi

**Producer:** Masaichi Nagata

**Screenplay:** Matsutarô Kawaguchi, Akinari Ueda, Yoshikata Yoda, from stories *Asaji Ga Yado* and *Jasei No In* by Akinari Ueda

**Photography:** Kazuo Miyagawa

**Music:** Fumio Hayasaka, Tamekichi Mochizuki, Ichirô Saitô

**Cast:** Masayuki Mori, Machiko Kyô, Kinuyo Tanaka, Eitarô Ozawa, Ikio Sawamura, Mitsuko Mito, Kikue Môri, Ryosuke Kagawa, Eigoro Onoe, Saburo Date, Sugisaku Aoyama, Reiko Kondo Shozo Nanbu, Kozabuno Ramon, Ichirô Amano

**Oscar nomination:** Kusune Kainosho (costume)

**Venice Film Festival:** Kenji Mizoguchi (Silver Lion), nomination (Golden Lion)

**U.S.** (Paramount) 118m Technicolor
**Director:** George Stevens
**Producer:** Ivan Moffat, George Stevens
**Screenplay:** A.B. Guthrie Jr., from story by Jack Schaefer
**Photography:** Loyal Griggs
**Music:** Victor Young
**Cast:** Alan Ladd, Jean Arthur, Van Heflin, Brandon De Wilde, Jack Palance, Ben Johnson, Edgar Buchanan, Emile Meyer, Elisha Cook Jr., Douglas Spencer, John Dierkes, Ellen Corby, Paul McVey, John Miller, Edith Evanson
**Oscar:** Loyal Griggs (photography)
**Oscar nomination:** George Stevens (best picture), George Stevens (director), A.B. Guthrie Jr. (screenplay), Brandon De Wilde (actor in support role), Jack Palance (actor in support role)

# SHANE (1953)

*Shane* is not the most glorious Western—for me, that is *El Dorado* (1967)—or the most masculine—that is *Red River* (1948)—or the most authentic—*McCabe & Mrs. Miller* (1971)—the strangest—*Johnny Guitar* (1954)—or the most dramatic—*Stagecoach* (1939). But it is surely the most iconic, the Western that burns itself into our memory, the Western no one who sees it will ever forget. Everything in the film, in fact, is a pure image: the hero in white buckskin who happens to ride into town (Alan Ladd); the conniving rancher (Emile Meyer) with his mangy, ill-mannered cowboys; the humble homesteader (Van Heflin) with his doting, dutiful, domesticating wife (Jean Arthur) and twinkle-eyed son (Brandon De Wilde); the taciturn, cautious, aging barkeep and owner of the general store (Paul McVey); the timid Swedish settler (Douglas Spencer); the dark, sinuous, slimy, personification of Evil Incarnate, Wilson the hired gun (Jack Palance, dressed in black from head to toe). Indeed, the characters alone are the story.

The rancher wants the homesteader's land. Shane settles in with the homesteader to help him protect it, in the process charming the tidy wife—perhaps a little too much—and the goggle-eyed boy completely out of his childhood. Wilson is imported to clean out the settlers, and but for the intervention of Shane—gun to gun, eye to eye, nobility vs. evil—he would surely succeed. But Good triumphs, so very deeply, indeed, that Shane comes to see his own effect on this charming little family, mounts his obedient steed, and rides away at film's end into a sunset that outshines all sunsets. After him runs little Joey, crying out "Shane! I love you, Shane!"

Shot at Jackson Hole, and before the days of widescreen and Dolby Stereo, Shane is studded with iconic visions. The purple Grand Tetons in the background, a deer grazing in a mirroring pool while the boy takes pot shots at it with his toy rifle, the filthy sneer on the rancher's face when Starrett (Heflin) refuses to give up his land, the look in Palance's eyes when he guns the gunless Frank "Stonewall" Torrey (Elisha Cook Jr.) down in the mud. Director George Stevens makes the mud tactile, like melted chocolate.

For two images alone this film is worth seeing again and again. They testify, if not to history, then to cinema. When Wilson struts onto the wooden sidewalk with his spurred boots ringing, the town dog is shown up close, creeping away with its tail between its legs. And after Shane has met the Starretts and accepted their invitation to dinner, he feasts on an apple pie. This is the apple pie to end apple pies (the pie that taught Martha Stewart): steaming, golden, latticed, voluminous, lifted out of the oven by a pretty gal in blue gingham and served up with good black coffee. It is apple pie like this that made the American West, we may well think; not guns, not cattle, not the dreamy far sighted gaze toward the next horizon **MP**

## BEAT THE DEVIL (1953)

**G.B. / U.S. / Italy** (Rizzoli-Haggiag, Romulus, Santana) 100m BW
**Director:** John Huston
**Producer:** Jack Clayton
**Screenplay:** Truman Capote, John Huston, from novel by James Helvick
**Photography:** Oswald Morris
**Music:** Franco Mannino
**Cast:** Humphrey Bogart, Jennifer Jones, Gina Lollobrigida, Robert Morley, Peter Lorre, Edward Underdown, Ivor Barnard, Marco Tulli, Bernard Lee, Mario Perrone, Giulio Donnini, Saro Urzì, Aldo Silvani, Juan de Landa

Easily one of the most irreverent, tongue-in-cheek movies made under Hollywood auspices, *Beat the Devil* stands out for many reasons. First, the amount and level of talent involved here is truly extraordinary. John Huston directs from a witty, bitter script on which he collaborated with none other than Truman Capote; cinematographer Oswald Morris was assisted by future cinematographic giant Freddie Francis; even a young Stephen Sondheim made his way onto the set as the clapper boy!

Then there's the cast. Humphrey Bogart served as one of the producers, and it was his clout that enabled the film to be made in the first place. Onscreen, he's joined by Gina Lollobrigida and Jennifer Jones, along with two of the all-time-great character actors, Peter Lorre and Robert Morley. This is a production where you can sense the actors had a tremendous amount of fun on the set.

The story has something to do with uranium rights in Africa, but it's not really that important. Traditional rules of cause and effect are loosened here, thanks partly to the fact that the film was an independent, international coproduction. This led to increased creative freedom and financial autonomy, and the talents behind *Beat the Devil* plainly took advantage here. This is a one-of-a-kind movie that slipped through the cracks. **EdeS**

## JOHNNY GUITAR (1954)

**U.S.** (Republic) 110m Trucolor
**Director:** Nicholas Ray
**Producer:** Herbert J. Yates
**Screenplay:** Philip Yordan, from novel by Roy Chanslor
**Photography:** Harry Stradling Sr.
**Music:** Victor Young
**Cast:** Joan Crawford, Sterling Hayden, Mercedes McCambridge, Scott Brady, Ward Bond, Ben Cooper, Ernest Borgnine, John Carradine, Royal Dano, Frank Ferguson, Paul Fix, Rhys Williams, Ian MacDonald

The melodrama of *Johnny Guitar* is so over-the-top that some will find it laughable. Others will fall under the spell of its hypnotic power. Joan Crawford plays Vienna, the owner of a saloon that stands on land valued by the railroad. Mercedes McCambridge is Emma Small, the black-clad spinster daughter of a big landowner who lusts after the Dancing Kid (Scott Brady), who in turn wants Vienna, who has another man in her past: Johnny Guitar, played by Sterling Hayden. Driven crazy by frustrated desire, Emma leads a lynch mob to burn down Vienna's saloon and hang the Kid. But Vienna stands firm. At the end there's a shoot-out between Emma and Vienna, the kind of reversal of convention that has led some critics to claim the film for feminism. It's also been read as an anti-McCarthy allegory, against mob hysteria and for those who make a stand on principle.

Whatever its ultimate meaning, the film, financed by the minor studio Republic, is boldly baroque in its use of strong colors, its bravura acting style (with Crawford in particular outstanding), and in the haunting beauty of its theme song, sung by the great Peggy Lee. If you can't take this much artifice, perhaps you'd be safer watching documentaries. **EB**

**U.S.** (Columbia, Horizon) 108m BW

**Director:** Elia Kazan

**Producer:** Sam Spiegel

**Screenplay:** Malcolm Johnson, Budd Schulberg, from articles by Malcolm Johnson

**Photography:** Boris Kaufman

**Music:** Leonard Bernstein

**Cast:** Marlon Brando, Karl Malden, Lee J. Cobb, Rod Steiger, Pat Henning, Leif Erickson, James Westerfield, Tony Galento, Tami Mauriello, John F. Hamilton, John Heldabrand, Rudy Bond, Don Blackman, Arthur Keegan, Abe Simon

**Oscar:** Sam Spiegel (best picture), Elia Kazan (director), Budd Schulberg (screenplay), Marlon Brando (actor), Eva Marie Saint (actress in support role), Richard Day (art direction), Boris Kaufman (photography), Gene Milford (editing)

**Oscar nomination:** Lee J. Cobb (actor in support role), Karl Malden (actor in support role), Rod Steiger (actor in support role), Leonard Bernstein (music)

**Venice Film Festival:** Elia Kazan (OCIC award), (Silver Lion), (Italian film critics award), nomination (Golden Lion)

# ON THE WATERFRONT (1954)

"I coulda had class. I coulda been a contender. I coulda been somebody, instead of a bum, which is what I am, let's face it." One of the all-time great American films, *On the Waterfront* exploded on a country shaken by the betrayals and paranoia of the anticommunist scare. Searing and tender, it ushered into Hollywood a new kind of hard-hitting social realism, not least because it was filled with indelible performances from a number of New York theater's hot postwar generation of naturalistic and Method actors.

Slow-witted but sensitive Terry Malloy (Marlon Brando, never more beautiful), a failed boxer turned longshoreman and errand boy for corrupt union boss Johnny Friendly (Lee J. Cobb), is disturbed by his unwitting role in the murder of a disaffected docker. His guilt is exacerbated when he falls in love with the dead man's sister, Edie Doyle (Eva Marie Saint in her film debut), but his illuminating crisis is his realization that he, too, has been sold out—most heartbreakingly by his older, smarter brother Charley (Rod Steiger), who is Friendly's sharp lawyer and right-hand man. After Edie shames the initially ineffectual parish priest (Karl Malden) into leading the crusade against harbor union racketeering, Friendly's intimidation turns more deadly. Terry painfully defies the code of silence and testifies at a congressional commission. Despite doing the right thing, Terry is ostracized for "ratting" by the waterfront community and is beaten to a pulp in the dockyard before his fearful comrades fall in behind him, breaking Friendly's hold on their lives and labor.

The film was most visibly inspired by "Crime on the Waterfront," a series of newspaper articles by Malcolm Johnson exposing racketeering in the New York/New Jersey dockyards. Playwright Arthur Miller began working on a screenplay at the behest of director Elia Kazan. But when Kazan testified before the House Un-American Activities Committee, Miller broke with him. Kazan turned to a fellow "friendly witness," writer Budd Schulberg. Both men's reputations suffered permanent damage and *On the Waterfront* is frequently labeled their apology or defense. Kazan admitted he identified with Terry Malloy's conflict of loyalties. Wherever one's sympathies lie, the painful real-life background invested the film with a gut-wrenching, truthful emotional center for the realism of its subject and setting and for the naturalism of its performances (complimented by Leonard Bernstein's evocative score).

Terry confronting Charley in the back of a cab is the most often cited classic scene, but there are many other unforgettable moments: Brando fiddling with Saint's little glove, putting it on his own hand; Terry discovering that all his lovingly cared for pigeons have been killed by the neighborhood boy who admired him; Terry beating down Edie's door and forcing an admission of love as they slide down to the floor in a desperate kiss.

Fifty years on it endures as an unflinching contemplation of betrayal. **AE**

**U.S.** (MGM) 102m Anscocolor

**Director:** Stanley Donen

**Producer:** Jack Cummings

**Screenplay:** Albert Hackett, Frances Goodrich, Dorothy Kingsley, from the story *The Sobbin' Women* by Stephen Vincent Benet

**Photography:** George J. Folsey

**Music:** Adolph Deutsch, Saul Chaplin, Johnny Mercer, Gene de Paul

**Cast:** Jane Powell, Howard Keel, Jeff Richards, Russ Tamblyn, Tommy Rall, Marc Platt, Matt Mattox, Jacques d'Amboise, Julie Newmar, Nancy Kilgas, Betty Carr, Virginia Gibson, Ruta Lee, Norma Doggett, Ian Wolfe

**Oscar:** Adolph Deutsch, Saul Chaplin (music)

**Oscar nomination:** Jack Cummings (best picture), Albert Hackett, Frances Goodrich, Dorothy Kingsley (screenplay), George J. Folsey (photography), Ralph E. Winters (editing)

# SEVEN BRIDES FOR SEVEN BROTHERS (1954)

*Seven Brides for Seven Brothers* is a profoundly sexist and eminently hummable 1954 musical—supposedly set in the great outdoors, but mainly filmed on soundstages—with some terrific athletic Michael Kidd choreography and better-than-average direction by Stanley Donen. Based on a story by Stephen Vincent Benet, who took his plot from the rape of the Sabine women, it concerns six mangy fur-trapping brothers who go to town to find wives after big brother Adam (Howard Keel) marries Milly (Jane Powell). They wind up following their frontiersmen instincts by kidnapping the women, but then have to mope through the winter until their impromptu mates get around to forgiving them in the spring.

A fascinating glimpse at the kind of patriarchal rape fantasies that were considered good-natured and even "cute" at the time, performed to the catchy music of Johnny Mercer and Gene DePaul, *Seven Brides for Seven Brothers* includes Russ Tamblyn, Virginia Gibson, and Tommy Rall. Among the most memorable tunes, some of whose titles accurately pinpoint the movie's sexual politics, are "Bless Your Beautiful Hide," "Sobbin' Women," "Goin' Courtin'," "I'm a Lonesome Polecat," and "Spring, Spring, Spring." **JRos**

**France** (Filmsonor,Vera) 114m BW

**Language:** French

**Director:** Henri-Georges Clouzot

**Producer:** Henri-Georges Clouzot

**Screenplay:** Henri-Georges Clouzot, Jérôme Géronimi, Frédéric Grendel, René Masson from the novel *Celle qui n'était plus* by Pierre Boileau & Thomas Narcejac

**Photography:** Armand Thirard

**Music:** Georges Van Parys

**Cast:** Simone Signoret, Véra Clouzot, Paul Meurisse, Charles Vanel, Jean Brochard, Pierre Larquey, Michel Serrault, Thérèse Dorny, Noël Roquevert, Yves-Marie Maurin, Georges Poujouly, Georges Chamarat, Jacques Varennes, Robert Dalban, Jean Lefebvre

# LES DIABOLIQUES (1954)

In a run-down, provincial public school, murderous passions seethe just below the surface. The put-upon, weak-hearted wife (Véra Clouzot) and mysteriously sensual girlfriend (Simone Signoret) of a sadistic headmaster (Paul Meurisse) murder him, dumping the corpse in the weeded-over swimming pool. When the pool is drained, the body is missing and the women start to lose their minds, especially when a pupil claims to have seen a ghost. Soon, the women too are seeing things, and something ghastly shows up in the bath.

A major international hit in 1954, *Les Diaboliques* has lost little of its power to disturb, though dozens of films (e.g., *Deathtrap*, *Hush...Hush, Sweet Charlotte*) have borrowed its tricky storyline and made familiar the most shocking moments. Henri-Georges Clouzot directs with a gray cruelty that combines a nastily tangled storyline worthy of Hitchcock (the Master is rumored to have made *Psycho* to reclaim the King of Suspense crown he lost briefly to Clouzot) with three strong central performances and a marvelously seedy setting. The film has scenes of physical horror (one trick with contact lenses is unforgettably creepy), but Clouzot also sets the flesh creeping with incidences of ordinary nastiness, as when Meurisse forces his wife to eat a disgusting school dinner. **KN**

# ANIMAL FARM (1954)

*Animal Farm* was the first-ever feature-length British animated film (if you ignore a 1945 wartime instructional, *Handling Ships*). It was directed by the husband-and-wife team of Halas-Batchelor (the Hungarian-born John Halas and the English Joy Batchelor) and based on George Orwell's mordant political fable of 1945.

At the time the film was produced, full-length animation was dominated by Disney. Determined to get away from Uncle Walt's style of cutesy, cuddly animals, Halas-Batchelor eagerly accepted a commission from the American producer Louis De Rochement (best known for the *March of Time* newsreel series) to make the first seriously intended adult animated feature outside the Communist bloc. Until its final reel, *Animal Farm* sticks closely to the original novel, written by Orwell as a satire of the betrayal of the ideals of the Russian Revolution. On Manor Farm the animals revolt against their drunken, decadent owner and set up a democratic community, free from humans, in which "All Animals Are Equal." But gradually the pigs, the most intelligent animals, engineer a totalitarian state under the dictatorship of the pig Napoleon, where "All Animals Are Equal–But Some Animals Are More Equal Than Others." The mass of the animals, oppressed and terrorized, have just swapped one Czar for another.

To make the film, Halas-Batchelor's company was expanded to become the largest animation unit in Western Europe. The animation strikes a shrewd balance between stylization and naturalism—the animals are not anthropomorphized, and the farm backgrounds are rendered realistically. Real farmyard noises were recorded for the soundtrack. The classical composer Matyas Seiber (like Halas, a Hungarian-born Briton) contributes a powerful, emotive score that blends folk elements with modernism, and all the animals are voiced—with astounding versatility—by the actor Maurice Denham.

*Animal Farm* faithfully preserves the anger, compassion, and sardonic humor of Orwell's novel. The cruelty of certain incidents isn't muted—to the alarm of parents at the time, who had taken their children along expecting Disneyesque sentimentality. Only the ending is modified to something more optimistic. De Rochemont and Halas-Batchelor agreed that the bleak despair of the original was more than audiences could take. The change can claim some historical justification, too; Stalin died while the film was in production. **PK**

**G.B.** (Halas and Batchelor) 72m Technicolor

**Director:** Joy Batchelor, John Halas

**Producer:** Louis De Rochemont, John Halas

**Screenplay:** Joy Batchelor, John Halas, Borden Mace, Philip Stapp, Lothar Wolff, from novel by George Orwell

**Photography:** S.G. Griffiths, J. Gurr, W. Traylor, R. Turk

**Music:** Matyas Seiber

**Cast:** Gordon Heath (narrator), Maurice Denham (all animals)

U.S. (Paramount, Patron) 112m Technicolor

**Director:** Alfred Hitchcock

**Producer:** Alfred Hitchcock

**Screenplay:** John Michael Hayes, from the story *It had to be Murder* by Cornell Woolrich

**Photography:** Robert Burks

**Music:** Franz Waxman

**Cast:** James Stewart, Grace Kelly, Wendell Corey, Thelma Ritter, Raymond Burr, Judith Evelyn, Ross Bagdasarian, Georgine Darcy, Sara Berner, Frank Cady, Jesslyn Fax, Rand Harper, Irene Winston, Havis Davenport

**Oscar nomination:** Alfred Hitchcock (director), John Michael Hayes (screenplay), Robert Burks (photography), Loren L. Ryder (sound)

# REAR WINDOW (1954)

The apotheosis of all his simmering and barely suppressed psychosexual fixations, Alfred Hitchcock's *Rear Window* is also probably (with the possible exception of the 1958 film *Vertigo*) the most successful merger of entertainment, intrigue, and psychology of the director's remarkable career. A fascinating study of obsession and voyeurism—*Rear Window* combines a perfect cast, a perfect screenplay, and particularly a perfect set for a movie—that's even better than the sum of its parts.

For maximum freedom, Hitchcock constructed an intricate replication of a crowded and constantly bustling New York City tenement building and its equally busy courtyard. Each window offers a glimpse into another life and in effect tells another story. In one unit, a composer hunches over his piano struggling with his latest work. In another, a dancer practices compulsively. One apartment houses a lonely woman, unlucky in love, and another an amorous newlywed couple.

L. B. "Jeff" Jeffries (James Stewart) is a successful photojournalist sidelined with a broken leg. Stuck in a wheelchair all day, he has nothing better to do than spy on his neighbors. Or at least that's what he claims, because his fashion model girlfriend (and would-be wife) Lisa (played by a surprisingly carnal Grace Kelly in one of her final roles before retiring) and his cranky caretaker Stella (Thelma Ritter) perceptively observe that he's merely addicted to the thrill of voyeurism.

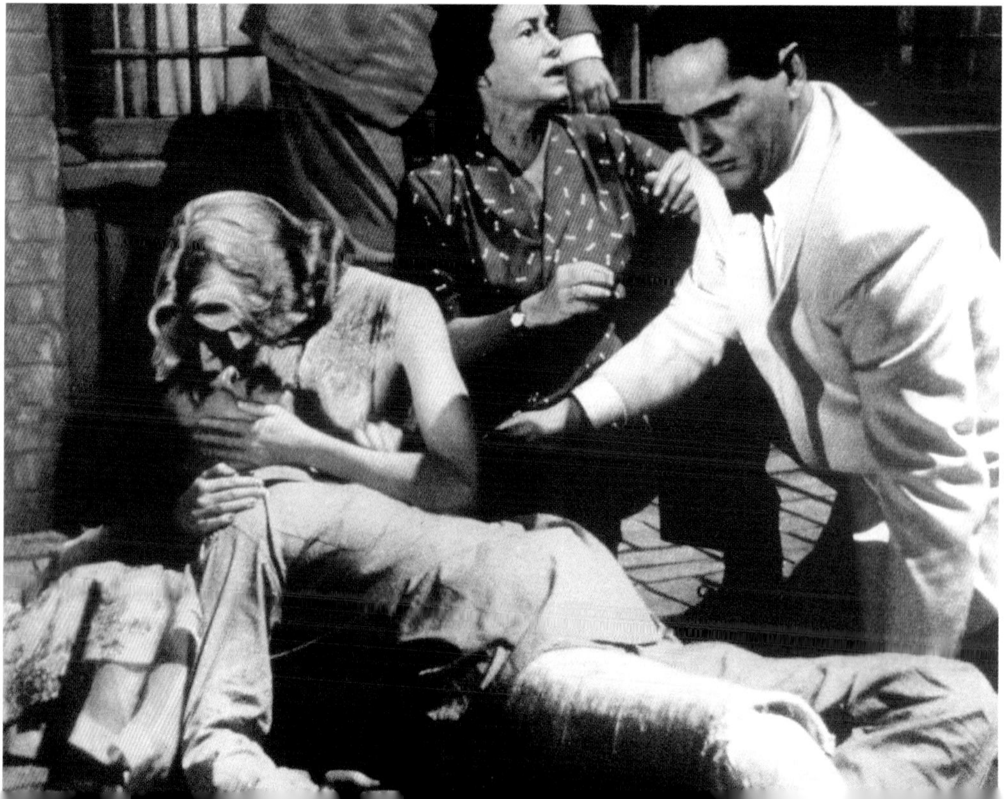

The notion of anyone able to keep their eyes off a character as beautiful and luminous as Lisa is hard to believe, until Jeff begins to suspect one of his neighbors (a glowering Raymond Burr) of murdering his wife. Soon enough, Jeff has dragged Lisa and Stella into the mystery, obsessively studying Burr's character's behavior for signs of his guilt. But as Jeff's furtive investigation advances, so do the ongoing stories of all of his other neighbors, oblivious to the nefarious plot possibly unfolding literally right next door.

*Rear Window*, the film, is constructed every bit as thoroughly as its elaborate set. Watching it is like watching a living, breathing ecosystem, with the added thrill of a murder mystery thrown in for good measure. Hitchcock relishes the film's particularly postmodern scenario: we, the viewers, are entranced by the actions of these characters, who are in turn entranced by the actions of still other characters. It's a vicious circle of obsession laced with black humor and a dash of sexiness.

Indeed, although the nosey Jeff may discover a murder in his urban hamlet, it's the numerous romances transpiring in the other units that first draw his attention to the courtyard peep show. It's wholly ironic that his obsessions with the love lives of his neighbors prevent him from acknowledging the romantic interest of Lisa. In fact, the bachelor in Jeff looks to his neighbors as an excuse to ward off her advances. It is only when his actions put her in danger that he finally understands that what he has in front of him is better than anything he can see out the window. **JKl**

## A STAR IS BORN (1954)

**U.S.** (Transcona, Warner Bros.) 181m Technicolor

**Director:** George Cukor

**Producer:** Vern Alves, Sidney Luft

**Screenplay:** Moss Hart, from the 1937 screenplay by Alan Campbell and Dorothy Parker, story by William A.Wellman

**Photography:** Sam Leavitt

**Music:** Harold Arlen, Ray Heindorf

**Cast:** Judy Garland, James Mason, Jack Carson, Charles Bickford, Tommy Noonan, Lucy Marlow, Amanda Blake, Irving Bacon, Hazel Shermet

**Oscar nomination:** James Mason (actor), Judy Garland (actress), Malcolm C. Bert, Gene Allen, Irene Sharaff, George James Hopkins (art direction), Jean Louis Mary, Ann Nyberg, Irene Sharaff (costume), Ray Heindorf (music), Harold Arlen, Ira Gershwin (song)

The third is the very best of four films (and the second directed by George Cukor) about a marriage doomed by the meteoric rise to stardom of the younger wife and the self-destruction of the falling idol/mentor she loves. William Wellman's 1937 movie starring Fredric March and Janet Gaynor is still a moving drama; the 1976 rock version with Barbra Streisand and Kris Kristofferson is memorable only for her singing. But Cukor's musical, with Judy Garland (in a triumphant comeback) and James Mason both terrific, broke new ground in the musical genre by propelling dramatic narrative with songs—signally in Garland's tortured "The Man That Got Away" and the show-stopping production number "Born In A Trunk." Not to be outdone, Mason's Norman Maine is spellbinding in his drunken display at the Academy Awards.

Part Hollywood satire—amusingly in the studio transformation of plain Esther Blodgett into glamorous Vicky Lester, acidly in the publicity machine entrapping Esther and Norman—the film is a beautiful blend of music, wit, and romantic tragedy, done with compelling conviction. In 1983, more than twenty minutes of previously cut footage was restored, including two numbers written for Garland by Harold Arlen and Ira Gershwin. **AE**

## THE BAREFOOT CONTESSA (1954)

**U.S. / Italy** (Figaro, Rizzoli-Haggiag) 128m Technicolor

**Director:** Joseph L. Mankiewicz

**Producer:** Franco Magli

**Screenplay:** Joseph L. Mankiewicz

**Photography:** Jack Cardiff

**Music:** Mario Nascimbene

**Cast:** Humphrey Bogart, Ava Gardner, Edmond O'Brien, Marius Goring, Valentina Cortese, Rossano Brazzi, Elizabeth Sellars, Warren Stevens, Franco Interlenghi, Mari Aldon, Alberto Rabagliati, Enzo Staiola, Maria Zanoli, Renato Chiantoni, Bill Fraser

**Oscar:** Edmond O'Brien (actor in support role)

**Oscar nomination:** Joseph L. Mankiewicz (screenplay)

The surface appeal of Joseph Mankiewicz's *The Barefoot Contessa* is obvious—Ava Gardner at her most glamorous as the rags-to-riches star Maria Vargas alongside Humphrey Bogart at his most acerbic yet tender as filmmaker Harry Dawes; the flood of quotable quotes in the dialogue ("It's never too late to develop character"); and the intriguing allusions to real-life celebrities, including Rita Hayward and Howard Hughes. But there is much more going on.

The film owes much to *Citizen Kane* (1941), especially the mosaic structure which offers various points of view on a character—ultimately affirming only that person's inscrutability. From the initial "springboard" situation of Maria's funeral, eight flashbacks proceed from four narrators. Long before *Pulp Fiction* (1994), Mankiewicz contrives a sequence which shows Maria's transition from Bravano (Marius Goring) to Vincenzo (Rossano Brazzi) from two viewpoints.

Even more intricate is the film's journey through three social worlds—Hollywood show business, the French leisure set, and Italian aristocracy—that register as uncanny variations on each other, each one enclosed, decadent, and dying. Significantly, this suite of decay echoes the presentation of the theater world in Mankiewicz's 1950 classic, *All About Eve*. While his films are sometimes justly criticized as stagey and word-bound, the richness and coherence of *The Barefoot Contessa* come from its metaphor of theatrical spectacle. Mankiewicz's signature touch is the "frieze," where the plot stops and a narrator fills us in on the character and background of each "player" at a table. **AM**

# LA STRADA (1954)
## THE ROAD

*La Strada* is Federico Fellini's fourth film, and it is the one that made his international reputation. Starring Anthony Quinn as Zampano the Strongman and the director's wife, Giulietta Masina, as the waif Gelsomina, it is a story of love and jealousy set in the circus, a milieu to which Fellini returns time and again. Zampano does a hackneyed routine of bursting out of chains wrapped around his chest. He needs an assistant, and so he buys Gelsomina from her mother to accompany him on the road. She acts as a clown, and her gestures are reminiscent of Charlie Chaplin. When they join a traveling circus, Gelsomina is temporarily fascinated by an acrobat, the Fool, played by Richard Baseheart. Although he treats her badly, Zampano becomes jealous of the Fool and his actions lead the film to its powerful conclusion.

*La Strada* is told in a fabulist style that begins to move away from the postwar neorealism of much of Italian cinema, a movement with which Fellini was intimately involved as a screenwriter. Although it is shot on location, it could take place in the present day or it could be 100 years ago. Zampano and Gelsomina are archetypes, simple characters driven by the most elemental emotions and desires. The action of the film plays out as though it is predetermined and these characters must act as they do, which makes the story tragic. Masina's moving portrayal of the abused but plucky Gelsomina would define her screen persona in several later Fellini films, and in much of her other work as an actress. Quinn is equally unforgettable as the brutish strongman, incapable of understanding his own feelings toward Gelsomina. Both actors highlight the disjuncture between their characters' performances and the realities of their lives.

Throughout his work, Fellini was fascinated by the tension between a character's theatrical facade and his or her unexplored, messy interior life. *La Strada* won the Academy Award for best foreign film and is probably the director's most accessible and well-loved picture. Snobs and sophisticates should not hold that against this complex and moving film, however, which continues to provide new insights and ideas on each subsequent viewing. **RH**

**Italy** (Ponti-De Laurentiis) 94m BW

**Language:** Italian

**Director:** Federico Fellini

**Producer:** Dino De Laurentiis, Carlo Ponti

**Screenplay:** Federico Fellini, Tullio Pinelli

**Photography:** Otello Martelli, Carlo Carlini

**Music:** Nino Rota

**Cast:** Anthony Quinn, Giulietta Masina, Richard Basehart, Aldo Silvani, Marcella Rovere, Livia Venturini

**Oscar:** Italy (best foreign language film)

**Oscar nomination:** Federico Fellini, Tullio Pinelli (screenplay)

**Venice Film Festival:** Federico Fellini (Silver Lion), nomination (Golden Lion)

**Japan** (Toho) 155m BW
**Language:** Japanese
**Director:** Akira Kurosawa
**Producer:** Sojiro Motoki
**Screenplay:** Shinobu Hashimoto, Akira Kurosawa, Hideo Oguni
**Photography:** Asakazu Nakai
**Music:** Fumio Hayasaka
**Cast:** Takashi Shimura, Toshirô Mifune, Yoshio Inaba, Seiji Miyaguchi, Minoru Chiaki, Daisuke Katô, Isao Kimura, Keiko Tsushima, Yukiko Shimazaki, Kamatari Fujiwara, Yoshio Kosugi, Bokuzen Hidari, Yoshio Tsuchiya, Kokuten Kodo, Jiro Kumagai
**Oscar nomination:** So Matsuyama (art direction), Kôhei Ezaki (costume)
**Venice Film Festival:** Akira Kurosawa (Silver Lion), nomination (Golden Lion)

# SHICHININ NO SAMURAI (1954)
## THE SEVEN SAMURAI

Akira Kurosawa is the Japanese director best known around the world. His thrilling, compellingly humane epic *The Seven Samurai* is his most enduringly popular, most widely seen masterpiece. Its rousing, if less profound, gunslinging Hollywood remake, *The Magnificent Seven* (1960), is the most successful of the several Western pictures modeled on Kurosawa's work—including the 1964 film *The Outrage*, a reworking of *Rashomon* (1950), and the landmark spaghetti Western *A Fistful of Dollars* (1964), lifted wholesale by Sergio Leone from *Yojimbo* (1961). The entertaining cultural crossover is delightful testimony to cinema's universal vocabulary and appeal. Kurosawa was inspired by the Westerns of John Ford and made a bold departure from the limited traditions of the typical Japanese *jidai-geki*, historical costume pictures with the emphasis on swordfights in a medieval Japan depicted as a fantasy land. *The Seven Samurai* is packed with a blur of astounding action, comic incident, misadventure, social drama, beautiful character development, and the conflict between duty and desire, all treated with immaculate care for realism.

A poor village of farmers, at the mercy of bandits who return every year to rape, kill, and steal, take the radical decision to fight back by hiring *ronin* (itinerant, masterless samurai) to save them. Because they are able to offer only meager portions of rice in payment, the nervous emissaries who set out in search of swords for hire are lucky to encounter Kambei (Takashi Shimura), an honorable, compassionate man resigned to doing what a man's gotta do, despite knowing he will gain nothing from doing it. Very much the hero figure, he recruits five other wanderers willing to fight for food or fun, including a good-natured old friend, a dewy-eyed young disciple, and a master swordsman of few words. Hot-headed, impulsive, clownish young Kikuchiyo (Toshiro Mifune) is rejected by the seasoned men, but the peasant masquerading as a samurai tags along anyway, frantic to prove himself and impress Kambei. The villagers treat them with mistrust but gradually bonds form, a love affair blossoms, the children are drawn to their heroes, and Kambei organizes a spirited resistance that astonishes, enrages, and ultimately overcomes the invaders.

The film is tireless, fast moving, and economical, eliminating unnecessary exposition. It evokes mystery and sustains a sense of apprehension—with quick shots and short cuts making up the peasants' search for potential protectors and putting their case to Kambei. There are many scenes of overwhelming visual and emotional power—a dying woman drags herself from a burning mill and hands her baby to Kikuchiyo, who sits down in the stream in shock, sobbing and crying "This baby, it's me. The same thing happened to me," the mill wheel, aflame, turning behind him. But the greatest moment of the film is the resolution: the three survivors survey their comrades' graves as the forgetful villagers below turn all their attention to their joyful rice-planting ritual. **AE**

**Italy** (Lux) 117m Technicolor

**Language:** English / Italian

**Director:** Luchino Visconti

**Producer:** Domenico Forges Davanzati

**Screenplay:** Carlo Alianello, Giorgio Bassani, Paul Bowles, Suso Cecchi d'Amico, Giorgio Prosperi, Luchino Visconti, Tennessee Williams, from novella by Camillo Boito

**Photography:** Aldo Graziati, Robert Krasker

**Music:** Anton Bruckner

**Cast:** Alida Valli, Farley Granger, Heinz Moog, Rina Morelli, Christian Marquand, Sergio Fantoni, Tino Bianchi, Ernst Nadherny, Tonio Selwart, Marcella Mariani, Massimo Girotti

**Venice Film Festival:** Luchino Visconti nomination (Golden Lion)

# SENSO (1954)
## THE WANTON COUNTESS

*Senso* was Count Luchino Visconti's third film, and his first in color. Set in Venice and Verona in the 1860s, on the verge of Giuseppe Garibaldi's expulsion of the Austrians and the creation of the modern Italian state, it marked a complete departure from the working-class milieu of the director's earlier films, *Ossessione* (1942) and *La Terra Trema* (1948). Nevertheless, *Senso*'s overt theatricality is not so different from the extravagant passions of *Ossessione*, and it is no less "authentic" for its sumptuous aristocratic setting (the director apparently insisted on daily fresh cut flowers for every room on the set, whether or not they would be filming there).

Alida Valli is the Countess Livia Sepieri, a Garibaldi supporter who intercedes on her cousin's behalf when he suicidally challenges an Austrian officer to a duel. Lt. Franz Mahler (Farley Granger) characteristically ducks out of the fight. A handsome, unprincipled charmer, Mahler seduces the Countess, who will recklessly betray her husband, her honor, and even her country for his love.

With screenplay credits for both Tennessee Williams and Paul Bowles—among six writers in total—*Senso* is a distinctly high-class melodrama. An actress who was past her prime, eyes flashing, teeth bared, Valli seems barely able to credit her own actions as she flings caution to the wind and stakes everything on a feckless character who makes no bones about his own cowardice. (The film was actually retitled *The Wanton Countess* for its belated U.S release.) Farley Granger is even better, especially in the big climactic scene where he lets rip with his self-loathing. Similarly unbalanced, sadomasochistic relationships recur in Visconti's later films, especially *The Damned* (1969) and *Death in Venice* (1971), but neither quite matched the ferocity displayed here.

*Senso* begins at the opera, and Anton Bruckner's score punctuates every dramatic turning point with an operatic thundercrack. "I like opera very much, but not when it happens off-stage," the Countess remarks, as she tries to dissuade Mahler from taking up her cousin's challenge. Italy's most renowned director of operas, Visconti clearly believed otherwise. **TCh**

## SILVER LODE (1954)

In this gripping Western, John Payne stars as Dan Ballard, a respected and well-liked rancher in the small town where he has lived for the past two years. During the town's Fourth of July celebration, four strangers ride into town, led by a belligerent and unpleasant thug (Dan Duryea) who claims to be a U.S. Marshal with a warrant for Ballard's arrest for murder. Over the course of the action (which is equivalent in span to the film's running time), the townspeople turn against Ballard, eventually forming a mob to hunt him down as he labors to prove his innocence.

*Silver Lode* is the Allan Dwan film par excellence: concise, plain, inventive, fluid, ironic, unspectacular-but-beautiful. No Western, probably, has more shots through windows (Dwan likes to stage scenes in depth and to emphasize situations in which characters observe each other), and few make such splendid use of the familiar architecture and decor of the Hollywood Western town. In a single stunning shot, Dwan's camera tracks with Payne as he runs four blocks across town. Thanks to the director's visual assurance (and the lighting genius of John Alton), *Silver Lode* is one of the best of the American cinema's many underrated Westerns. **CFu**

**U.S.** (Pinecrest) 81m Technicolor

**Director:** Allan Dwan

**Producer:** Benedict Bogeaus

**Screenplay:** Karen DeWolf

**Photography:** John Alton

**Music:** Louis Forbes

**Cast:** John Payne, Lizabeth Scott, Dan Duryea, Dolores Moran, Emile Meyer, Robert Warwick, John Hudson, Harry Carey Jr., Alan Hale Jr.

## CARMEN JONES (1954)

The legendarily beautiful and troubled African-American actress Dorothy Dandridge, like so many sex symbols, was a martyr to her beauty in life, while in death she lies buried beneath her own mythology. *Carmen Jones* is the substance behind the hype, a potent explanation of her appeal and hold on the imagination so long after her death.

Based on Bizet's opera *Carmen*, *Carmen Jones* is the story of a hungry, ambitious young woman (Dandridge) whose narcissism and greed lead to the destruction of Joe (Harry Belafonte), a good man who loves her dearly. Filled with classic songs (the music and book are by the legendary Oscar Hammerstein) and a first-rate supporting cast that includes Pearl Bailey and a young Diahann Carroll, the film is packed with sensational musical numbers (mostly shot in single takes by director Otto Preminger) that are integral to the film. But as impeccable as craft, crew, and supporting cast are, this is Dandridge's vehicle all the way. Her Carmen is one of the fieriest, most viscerally devastating sex goddesses ever caught on film—her cool feline strut, curvaceous body, blazing eyes, and mixture of lust and contempt for the men caught in her snare add up to a creature that's otherworldly. It's a powerhouse performance that elevates an excellent film into the realm of classic. **EH**

**U.S.** (Fox, Carlyle) 105m Color

**Director:** Otto Preminger

**Producer:** Otto Preminger

**Screenplay:** Harry Kleiner, from the novel *Carmen* by Prosper Mérimée

**Photography:** Sam Leavitt

**Music:** Georges Bizet, Oscar Hammerstein

**Cast:** Harry Belafonte, Dorothy Dandridge, Pearl Bailey, Olga James, Joe Adams, Brock Peters, Roy Glenn, Nick Stewart, Diahann Carroll, LeVern Hutcherson, Marilyn Horne, Marvin Hayes

**Oscar nomination:** Dorothy Dandridge (actress), Herschel Burke Gilbert (music)

**Berlin International Film Festival:** Otto Preminger (Bronze Bear)

**Japan** (Daiei) 120m BW

**Language:** Japanese

**Director:** Kenji Mizoguchi

**Producer:** Masaichi Nagata

**Screenplay:** Yahiro Fuji, Ogai Mori, Yoshikata Yoda, from story by Ogai Mori

**Photography:** Kazuo Miyagawa

**Music:** Fumio Hayasaka, Tamekichi Mochizuki, Kanahichi Odera

**Cast:** Kinuyo Tanaka, Yoshiaki Hanayagi, Kyôko Kagawa, Eitarô Shindô, Akitake Kôno, Masao Shimizu, Ken Mitsuda, Kazukimi Okuni, Yôko Kosono, Noriko Tachibana, Ichirô Sugai, Teruko Omi, Masahiko Kato, Keiko Enami, Bontarô Akemi

**Venice Film Festival:** Kenji Mizoguchi (Silver Lion), nomination (Golden Lion)

# SANSHÔ DAYÛ (1954)
## SANSHO THE BALIFF

"Without compassion, a man is no longer human." So states Taira (Masao Shimizu), a governor in medieval Japan being sent into exile because of his liberal policies, to his young son Zushiô. Together with his mother Tamaki (the great Kinuyo Tanaka) and his sister Anju, Zushiô flees from his family's estate; betrayed by a priestess, Zushiô and Anju are sent off to the enormous slave-labor compound run by the notoriously cruel Sanshô (Eitarô Shindô), while their mother is kidnapped into prostitution on a distant island. Thus begins one of the great emotional and philosophical journeys ever made for the cinema. Possibly the high point in an unbroken string of masterpieces made by Kenji Mizoguchi shortly before his death, *Sanshô the Baliff* features the perfection of a signature visual style, made up predominantly by long, complexly staged shots paced by gliding camera movements, that Mizoguchi had already begun to develop in the 1930s.

After this harrowing opening, the story jumps ahead several years. The adult Zushiô (Yoshiaki Hanayagi), strong but emotionally dead, has become one of Sanshô's most reliable henchman; with unblinking cruelty, he carries out orders to torture and maim. One day Zushiô is ordered to leave an old, ailing woman outside the compound's walls to die; Anju (Kyôko Kagawa) follows him ostensibly to help, but then a minor accident—the two fall down when trying to break off a tree branch—conjures up a childhood memory of their time together before being enslaved. Suddenly Zushiô realizes how horrible he has become; he and Anju decide to run away, but fearing they'll be caught if they stay together, Anju sacrifices herself so her brother may escape.

Zushiô does escape, and eventually is able to reclaim his family's noble standing. He returns, now as an official, to Sanshô's compound; dismissing Sanshô, he turns the compound over to its inmates, who burn it down in a remarkable scene of orgiastic frenzy. Abandoning his official post, Zushiô goes off to find his mother. Years before, he and Anju had heard a story about an old, lame prostitute on an island who constantly sang a lament about her lost children; he goes to the island and, on a lonely stretch of beach, is reunited with his mother. He breaks down, asking forgiveness for all the evil he's done; on the contrary, his mother assures him, his father would have been proud that his son lived so faithfully by his teachings.

If at this point you're not a sobbing mass, there's simply a hole in your soul. Mizoguchi's worldview is pitch black: violence, betrayal, and wanton cruelty are simply the order of the day. Yet although one can't change this, one can protest by simply staying true to an ideal. The battle between good and evil is finally a battle within oneself, and in the film's magnificent final sequence, as mother and son huddle together sobbing, one feels that the love between them is the most powerful force in the universe; even if that love can't conquer the world, it can transcend it. **RP**

# SALT OF THE EARTH (1954)

**U.S.** (Independent, Intl Union of Mine, Mill & Smelter Workers) 94m BW

**Director:** Herbert J. Biberman

**Producer:** Adolfo Barela, Sonja Dahl Biberman, Paul Jarrico

**Screenplay:** Michael Biberman, Michael Wilson

**Photography:** Stanley Meredith, Leonard Stark

**Music:** Sol Kaplan

**Cast:** Rosaura Revueltas, Will Geer, David Wolfe, Mervin Williams, David Sarvis, Juan Chacón, Henrietta Williams, Ernesto Velázquez, Ángela Sánchez, Joe T. Morales, Clorinda Alderette, Charles Coleman, Virginia Jencks, Clinton Jencks, Víctor Torres

This rarely screened classic is the only major American independent feature made by communists. A fictional story about the Mexican-American zinc miners in New Mexico then striking against their Anglo management, *Salt of the Earth* was informed by feminist attitudes that are quite uncharacteristic of the period. The film was inspired by the blacklisting of director Herbert Biberman, screenwriter Michael Wilson, producer and former screenwriter Paul Jarrico, and composer Sol Kaplan. As Jarrico later reasoned, because they'd been drummed out of Hollywood for being subversives, they'd commit a "crime to fit the punishment" by making a subversive film. The results are leftist propaganda of a high order, powerful and intelligent even when the film registers in spots as naïve or dated.

Basically kept out of American theaters until 1965, it was widely shown and honored in Europe, but it's never received the recognition it deserves Stateside. Regrettably, its best-known critical discussion in the United States is a Pauline Kael broadside in which the film is ridiculed as "propaganda." As accurate as Kael is about some of *Salt of the Earth*'s left-wing clichés, she indiscriminately takes some of her examples from the original script rather than the film itself, and gives no hint as to why it could remain so vital half a century later. **JRos**

# ARTISTS AND MODELS (1955)

**U.S.** (Paramount) 109m Technicolor

**Director:** Frank Tashlin

**Producer:** Paul Nathan, Hal B. Wallis

**Screenplay:** Don McGuire, Frank Tashlin, from the story *Rock-A-Bye Baby* by Michael Davidson and Norman Lessine

**Photography:** Daniel L. Fapp

**Music:** Harry Warren

**Cast:** Dean Martin, Jerry Lewis, Shirley MacLaine, Dorothy Malone, Eddie Mayehoff, Eva Gabor, Anita Ekberg, George Winslow, Jack Elam, Herbert Rudley, Richard Shannon, Richard Webb, Alan Lee, Otto Waldis

Like Douglas Sirk's melodramas, Frank Tashlin's crazy comedies exaggerate to the point of subversion the popular values of the American 1950s. Tashlin's terrain was the media-sphere of advertising, TV, movies, and showbiz: By gleefully embracing and slyly satirizing this "plastic" arena of clichés and stereotypes, he anticipated Pop Art.

*Artists and Models*, which provided the Dean Martin–Jerry Lewis duo with its finest screen hour, is a dizzily self-reflexive play on movie illusion. Eugene Fullstack (Lewis) is a comic book addict whose colorful dreams are transcribed—and secretly sold—by Rick Todd (Martin). They are mirrored by two women, sultry graphic artist Abby (Dorothy Malone) and ditzy Bessie (Shirley MacLaine). Tashlin's endlessly inventive game of permutation and combination between these four characters builds to a great piece of burlesque mayhem: Eugene and Bessie's delirious *détournement* of the kitsch romantic ballad "Inamorata."

With a plot that launches without warning into an international espionage intrigue (enter Eva Gabor), and a splendid musical demonstration of image-and-sound artifice ("When You Pretend"), it is only fitting that the strategies of *Artists and Models* are echoed in the merry modernisms of Jacques Rivette (*Celine and Julie Go Boating*), P. T. Anderson (*Punch-Drunk Love*), and Australia's Yahoo Serious (*Mr. Accident*). **AM**

# GUYS AND DOLLS (1955)

Hollywood's stereotyping of national cultures regularly gives offense, but who can resist the glimpse of Havana, Cuba, in a central scene of *Guys and Dolls*? Suave gambler Sky Masterson (Marlon Brando) has talked prim, Salvation Army member Sarah Brown (Jean Simmons) into taking a plane and dining with him. As she gets drunk and succumbs to her reckless impulses, she is enflamed by the primal, Latin American drama unfolding around her: her instant rival, an exotic dancer, trying to seduce Sky. Soon the whole room is swept up in a hilarious dance of drunken passions.

The scene offers a magnificent example of Michael Kidd's revolutionary choreography for film. Normal, everyday gestures, such as walking or pointing, are by degrees stylized, made angular and rhythmic, until the point of full-blown dance. The actions of individuals are woven into group patterns. And, above all, the staging incorporates movements that are deliberately ungainly, awkward, seemingly amateur—such as Sarah's drunken lunges and swings.

*Guys and Dolls* is really two films in one, divided up for its dual male stars—and indeed, there is an over-the-table dialogue between Brando and Frank Sinatra that anticipates the Al Pacino–Robert De Niro encounter 40 years later in *Heat* (1995). The Nathan Detroit (Sinatra) half is more indebted to writer-director Joseph Mankiewicz's source, Damon Runyan's tales of lovable, streetwise crooks (every "ethnic" tic of New York speech and behavior lovingly exaggerated). Nathan has a long-suffering dame, Adelaide (Vivian Blaine), which leads to amusing material about their fraught path to the altar, such as "Adelaide's Lament" in Frank Loesser's colorful score.

But—although the more conventionally polished, show-stopping group numbers like "Luck Be a Lady" and "Sit Down, You're Rockin' the Boat" are the ones Broadway devotees remember best—it is in the more romantic, Sky–Sarah half that the film really soars, Mankiewicz for once overcoming his screen talkiness. The songs "If I Were a Bell" and "I'll Know When My Love Comes Along" are glorious swellings of amorous emotion, and Mankiewicz surrounds them with a wonderful mise en scène of comings and goings, attractions and repulsions between these two admirable bodies. **AM**

**U.S.** (Samuel Goldwyn) 150m Eastmancolor

**Director:** Joseph L. Mankiewicz

**Producer:** Samuel Goldwyn

**Screenplay:** Joseph L. Mankiewicz from play by Jo Swerling and Abe Burrows and the story *The Idyll of Miss Sarah Brown* by Damon Runyon

**Photography:** Harry Stradling Sr.

**Music:** Jay Blackton, Frank Loesser

**Cast:** Marlon Brando, Jean Simmons, Frank Sinatra, Vivian Blaine, Robert Keith, Stubby Kaye, B.S. Pulley, Johnny Silver, Sheldon Leonard, Danny Dayton, George E. Stone, Regis Toomey, Kathryn Givney, Veda Ann Borg, Mary Alan Hokanson

**Oscar nomination:** Oliver Smith, Joseph C. Wright, Howard Bristol (art direction), Harry Stradling Sr. (photography), Irene Sharaff (costume), Jay Blackton, Cyril J. Mockridge (music)

# PATHER PANCHALI (1955)

**India** (Government of West Bengal)
115m BW

**Language:** Bengali

**Director:** Satyajit Ray

**Screenplay:** Satyajit Ray, from novel by Bibhutibhushan Bandyopadhyay

**Photography:** Subrata Mitra

**Music:** Ravi Shankar

**Cast:** Kanu Bannerjee, Karuna Bannerjee, Subir Bannerjee, Uma Das Gupta, Chunibala Devi, Runki Banerjee, Reba Devi, Aparna Devi, Haren Banerjee, Tulsi Chakraborty, Nibhanani Devi, Roma Ganguli, Binoy Mukherjee, Harimohan Nag, Kshirod Roy, Rama Gangopadhaya

**Cannes Film Festival:** Satyajit Ray (human document award), (OCIC award—special mention)

Based on a classic novel by the Bengali writer Bibhutibhusan Bandyopadhyay, *Pather Panchali*, Satyajit Ray's first film, was eventually to form part of a trilogy together with *Aparajito* (1957) and *The World of Apu* (1959). Ray, who was working in a Calcutta advertising agency at the time, had great difficulty in raising the money to make his film. Eventually he borrowed enough to begin shooting, in the hopes that the footage would persuade backers to help him complete it. Though filming initially began in October 1952, it was not until early in 1955 that *Pather Panchali* was at last finished.

Apu (Subir Bannerjee) is a little boy growing up in a remote country village in Bengal. His parents are poor and can hardly provide food enough for Apu and his older sister Durga (Uma Das Gupta), let alone the aged woman known as Auntie (Chunibala Devi) who lives with them. In an early scene Durga has stolen some mangoes, which she gives to Auntie, but the children's mother, Sarbajaya (Karuna Bannerjee), scolds her. Later, Durga is accused by a more wealthy neighbor of stealing a necklace. Sarbajaya, shamed by the allegation, throws Durga out of the house. We see not only the distress of mother and daughter but Apu's response too, as he implicitly sides with his sister.

These minor moments of drama are punctuated by greater tragedies. One of the best-known scenes in the film comes when the children quarrel and Durga has once more been scolded by her mother. She runs away across the fields, with Apu following. We see black smoke rising and then a train. Apu and Durga run toward it, excited by this vision of something from the wide world beyond their village. On the way back, chattering together, their quarrel made up, they encounter Auntie sitting in a bamboo grove. When Durga touches her, she keels over. She is dying.

The father, Harihar (Kanu Bannerjee), leaves for the city to try and make some money. While he is away, Durga catches pneumonia and dies. Unaware, the father returns, flushed with success and carrying gifts for his family, including a sari for Durga. Sarbajaya breaks down and weeps. Harihar collapses in grief. We observe Apu listening to his father's cries.

Eventually Harihar decides to take the remainder of his family back to the city. In a telling moment, while helping clear the house Apu finds a necklace hidden in a bowl. So Durga did steal it after all; the knowledge makes Apu's grief more poignant. Apu throws the necklace into a pond, where the weeds close over it.

Ray's mise en scène has great delicacy, capable of expressing both strong emotion and lyrical delight. Few will forget the sequence in which Apu and Durga hear the sound of the traveling sweets seller. Though they have no money to buy, they trot along behind him, followed in turn by a curious dog; the little procession is reflected in a pool of water.

Helped by Ravi Shankar's marvelous music, *Pather Panchali* achieved worldwide success, earning Ray recognition at the 1956 Cannes Film Festival. **EB**

U.S. (MGM) 81m Eastmancolor

**Director:** John Sturges

**Producer:** Herman Hoffman, Dore Schary

**Screenplay:** Howard Breslin, Don McGuire, Millard Kaufman, from the story *Bad Day at Hondo* by Howard Breslin

**Photography:** William C. Mellor

**Music:** André Previn

**Cast:** Spencer Tracy, Robert Ryan, Anne Francis, Dean Jagger, Walter Brennan, John Ericson, Ernest Borgnine, Lee Marvin, Russell Collins, Walter Sande

**Oscar nominations:** John Sturges (director), Millard Kaufman (screenplay), Spencer Tracy (actor)

**Venice Film Festival:** Spencer Tracy (actor), tied with cast of *Bolshaya semya*

# BAD DAY AT BLACK ROCK (1955)

It's 1945, just after World War II, and Spencer Tracy is a one-armed ex-army man who steps off the train in Black Rock, a remote California desert town. We don't know what he's come for, nor do the inhabitants. But they are hostile, and it soon becomes clear that they are hiding something. Director John Sturges slowly tightens the tension as Tracy digs deeper into the town's secret, while the inhabitants cut the phone wires and disable a car in which he tries to leave.

Set in an arid western landscape, to which the film's CinemaScope ratio gives full value, and shot in color, mostly in blinding sunlight, *Bad Day at Black Rock* is sandwiched between a number of notable Sturges Westerns, including *Escape from Fort Bravo* and *Gunfight at the OK Corral*. Yet despite its look, *Black Rock* is really more of a *film noir*, with its story of dark secrets in the past. There's little physical action and hardly any gunplay, though one scene is memorable, when Tracy is finally provoked to fight by the brutish Ernest Borgnine. The one-armed man reveals a repertoire of karate chops and punches that fell his opponent like a slaughtered ox.

Tracy faces an impressive line-up of heavies here, including ringleader Robert Ryan, whose hysteria is never far below the surface, and Lee Marvin in one of his most menacing roles. Tracy has to rely for help on the community's weaker members: the reclusive Doc (Walter Brennan) and the drunken, cowardly sheriff (Dean Jagger). Eventually Tracy manages to invest them with a little of his courage and they help him make a break, but ultimately he is forced to rely on his own ingenuity.

The town's dirty secret proves to be the murder of a Japanese-American in the days following Pearl Harbor. The film was produced by Dore Schary, who tried to stand up to blacklisting and whose regime at MGM was marked by a number of liberal productions. *Bad Day at Black Rock* is a good example, a taut, expertly acted and directed thriller that pushes a fairly straightforward message about racial tolerance. But whatever its good intentions, it's Tracy that we remember most. Few actors could project basic goodness so well, without a trace of sanctimoniousness. **EB**

## LES MAÎTRES FOUS (1955)
### THE MAD MASTERS

In 1954, ethnographic filmmaker Jean Rouch was invited by a small group of Hauka in the West African city of Accra to document their yearly religious ritual. Over the course of this ceremony, the Hauka went into a trance-like state and were possessed by spirits representing the Western colonialists (the engineer, the wife of the doctor, the governor-general, the cruel major, etc.)

Though only 36 minutes long, the imagery in *Les Maîtres Fous* (a.k.a. *The Mad Masters*) is striking and frequently alarming: possessed men, their eyes rolling, foaming at the mouth, burning their bodies with torches. Indeed, Peter Brook's 1966 film *Marat/Sade* would reference the histrionics and made-up language here captured on camera by Rouch.

But as the director himself has noted, for the Hauka possession by spirits was truth, not art. While the film never fully explains the meaning behind the ritual, Rouch's narration hints that participation in this religious ceremony results in a kind of catharsis, one that gives the Hauka—mostly rural migrant laborers—the strength needed to maintain their self-respect and continue working under harsh and oppressive conditions. As one scholar observes, the most intriguing issue raised by *Les Maîtres Fous*—a film in which "the oppressed become, for a day, the possessed and the powerful"—concerns the complex relation of the Hauka sect to their experience of colonialism. One of the masterpieces of ethnographic cinema. **SJS**

**France** (Pléïade) 36m
**Language:** French
**Director:** Jean Rouch
**Photography:** Jean Rouch
**Cast:** Jean Rouch (narrator)

## HILL 24 DOESN'T ANSWER (1955)

Made by British director Thorold Dickinson, who had come to Israel to make a documentary on the army (*The Red Background*), *Hill 24 Doesn't Answer* was the first film of the national period to achieve an international success. Dickinson, who was influenced by the documentary/fiction films made in Britain during World War II, uses time-tested techniques of that genre (explanatory maps, an authoritative voice-over) to tell the story of a small Israeli unit defending a strategic hill position near Jerusalem against Arab attack in the 1948 war.

In the manner of David Lean's *In Which We Serve*, Dickinson spends little time on the action itself, which becomes the framework for telling the stories of the four main characters: an American Jew, an Irishman, a native-born Israeli, and a Sephardic Jew. All die in the successful defense of the position, which is thereby assured, after the visit of a U.N. observer, as belonging to Israeli. Flashbacks detail the reasons why each soldier has chosen to fight. The film is fervently pro-Zionist, with Druse and British characters presented sympathetically and the Arabs as an anonymous, hostile, destructive force, whose reasons for attack are never made clear. Despite the obvious propaganda, Dickinson's film is a small-scale masterpiece, an intriguing examination of motivation and heroism in the midst of deadly ideological struggle. **BP**

**Israel** (Israel Motion Picture, Sik'or) 101m BW
**Language:** English / Hebrew
**Director:** Thorold Dickinson
**Producer:** Thorold Dickinson, Peter Frye, Zvi Kolitz, Jack Padwa
**Screenplay:** Peter Frye, Zvi Kolitz
**Photography:** Gerald Gibbs
**Music:** Paul Ben Chayim
**Cast:** Edward Mulhare, Michael Wager, Margalit Oved, Arik Lavi, Michael Shillo, Haya Harareet, Eric Greene, Stanley Preston, Haim Eynav, Zalman Lebiush, Azaria Rapaport

**G.B.** (Ealing, Rank) 97m Technicolor
**Director:** Alexander Mackendrick
**Producer:** Michael Balcon, Seth Holt
**Screenplay:** William Rose
**Photography:** Otto Heller
**Music:** Tristram Cary
**Cast:** Alec Guinness, Cecil Parker, Herbert Lom, Peter Sellers, Danny Green, Jack Warner, Katie Johnson, Philip Stainton, Frankie Howerd
**Oscar nomination:** William Rose (screenplay)

# THE LADYKILLERS (1955)

Alexander Mackendrick's final Ealing film (and also his darkest), made before he went to Hollywood and gave us the memorably bilious *Sweet Smell of Success* (1957), is a deliciously black comedy of English manners. A gang of thieves, hiding out disguised as a music quintet in the genteel Edwardian home of innocent and very, very proper little old lady Katie Johnson, decide they must murder her after she finds out about their recent robbery and insists they return the loot. The trouble is, the honor among these particular thieves is skewed, and although they can't quite bring themselves to kill off the sweet old thing, they have no such reservations with regard to one another.

Essentially, then, *The Ladykillers* is a farcical variation on the classic heist-gone-wrong theme, fascinating both for its deft characterizations (the gang comprise a devious mastermind, a bluff military type, an Italianate hit man, a spivvish "Teddy boy," and an intellectually challenged muscle man) and for its suggestion that postwar Britain, overly reverential toward an earlier age, was so divided as to be unable to move forward into the modern era. Otto Heller's color camera work and Jim Morahan's production design serve to reinforce the sense of a society trapped in the past. **GA**

**U.S.** (Hecht, Hill & Lancaster, Steven) 91m BW
**Director:** Delbert Mann
**Producer:** Harold Hecht
**Screenplay:** Paddy Chayefsky
**Photography:** Joseph LaShelle
**Music:** George Bassman, Harry Warren, Roy Webb
**Cast:** Ernest Borgnine, Betsy Blair, Esther Minciotti, Augusta Ciolli, Joe Mantell, Karen Steele, Jerry Paris
**Oscar:** Harold Hecht (best picture), Delbert Mann (director), Paddy Chayefsky (screenplay), Ernest Borgnine (actor)
**Oscar nomination:** Joe Mantell (actor in support role), Betsy Blair (actress in support role), Ted Haworth, Walter M. Simonds, Robert Priestley (art direction), Joseph LaShelle (photography)
**Cannes Film Festival:** Delbert Mann (Golden Palm) and (OCIC award)

# MARTY (1955)

During the Golden Age of Television, Paddy Chayefsky wrote the teleplay *Marty*. It was notable for its focus on the ordinary life of an unmarried butcher. Chayefsky then translated the script for the big screen with Ernest Borgnine as the star. Thereafter Marty Pilletti became a *cause célèbre* for seizing happiness outside the mold of mid-1950s conformity and consensus.

Tagged "It's the love story of an unsung hero!", *Marty* thrilled audiences in its tale of a man who lives at home with his mother, the classic Italian matriarch. Trolling singles spots with his best friend Angie (Joe Mantell), he meets Clara (Betsy Blair) and they begin a ritual courtship. Angie quickly becomes jealous, Mrs. Pilletti (Esther Minciotti) confounds matters with nightmares of abandonment, but Marty finally pursues Clara because he likes her.

Described thusly, *Marty* suggests a yawn fest. But as a portrait of the times, especially of postwar neuroses about domestic tranquility, the film is rich with sociological value. Current cultural politics aside, the struggle for lonely people to find acceptance and love is without doubt a powerful theme. Giving the film buoyancy, this motive also sings the praises of the everyday and the beautiful, one and the same. **GC-Q**

## ORDET (1955)

An extraordinary work, and arguably the finest achievement of this great filmmaker, Carl Theodor Dreyer's adaptation of Kaj Munk's play is a cinematic rarity in that, with the simplest of means and no special effects whatsoever, it manages to persuade the viewer that a miracle can happen.

*Ordet* concerns the Borgens, a farming family, loving and close but also beset by tensions arising from a number of disagreements and misfortunes—notably the wayward behavior of one of the grown-up brothers, seemingly insane due to excessive travails while studying religious thought. Not everyone thinks Johannes (Preben Lerdorff Rye) mad, however, and when Inger (Birgitte Federspiel), another brother's wife, dies, her child asks him to bring her mother back—which, at the end of the film, he appears to do. In fact, Dreyer leaves it to the spectator to decide whether her revival is a matter of mere scientific inability to understand the improbable or of strength of faith, but the scene is remarkably powerful, precisely because he refuses both to explain and to rev up the film's dramatic engines; the scene convinces thanks to its own air of tranquility and that of everything preceding it.

Indeed, this is in many respects the most "realistic" or "naturalistic" of films dealing with the power of faith, love (in every sense), and the supernatural; Dreyer eschews any kind of trickery. Though Henning Bendtsen's pared-down yet outstandingly beautiful black-and-white images do endow the Borgens's cottage and pastures with a lustrous quality, Dreyer's quiet rhythms, long takes, and deceptively simple mise en scène may suggest that the movie is a straightforward chamber drama about ordinary farming folk. Only Johannes's wheedling voice appears at all unusual, and he, after all, is not quite right in the head. Wherein lies *Ordet*'s greatness: by the time the "miracle" occurs, the film has earned our respect for its integrity—we understand the people on screen, because their actions, emotions, thoughts, and doubts are like our own. And when Inger opens her eyes once more, we probably feel much as they do: astonishment, happiness, and genuine wonder. For even if *Ordet* fails to convert us to religious belief, we have, at least, witnessed cinematic art of the highest order. **GA**

**Denmark** (Palladium) 126m BW

**Language:** Danish

**Director:** Carl Theodor Dreyer

**Producer:** Carl Theodor Dreyer, Erik Nielsen, Tage Nielsen

**Screenplay:** Kaj Munk, from his play

**Photography:** Henning Bendtsen

**Music:** Poul Schierbeck, Sylvia Schierbeck

**Cast:** Hanne Agesen, Kirsten Andreasen, Sylvia Eckhausen, Birgitte Federspiel, Ejner Federspiel, Emil Hass Christensen, Cay Kristiansen, Preben Lerdorff Rye, Henrik Malberg, Gerda Nielsen, Ann Elisabeth Rud, Ove Rud, Susanne Rud, Henry Skjær, Edith Trane

**Venice Film Festival:** Carl Theodor Dreyer (Golden Lion)

# BOB LE FLAMBEUR
## BOB THE GAMBLER (1955)

**France** (OGC, Play Art, Cyme) 98m BW

**Language:** French

**Director:** Jean-Pierre Melville

**Producer:** Jean-Pierre Melville

**Screenplay:** Auguste Le Breton, Jean-Pierre Melville

**Photography:** Henri Decaë

**Music:** Eddie Barclay

**Cast:** Isabelle Corey, Daniel Cauchy, Roger Duchesne, Guy Decomble, André Garet, Gérard Buhr, Claude Cerval, Colette Fleury, René Havard, Simone Paris, Howard Vernon, Henry Allaume, Germaine Amiel, Yvette Amirante, Dominique Antoine

*Bob the Gambler*, Jean-Pierre Melville's fourth feature, belongs to a very specific moment in history, and in the history of cinema. It is the milestone of a subtle turning point, and it maintains the flavor of this moment. Previously there was European cinema and American cinema. There was classic cinema and modern cinema. There were gangster films and comedies and daily chronicles. There was a guy, still rather young for a director, who at age 39, with one or two lives already behind him, had made a ghostly war film of incredible intensity (*The Silence of the Sea*), an adaptation from a Jean Cocteau novel (*Les Enfants Terribles*), and a lame melodrama (*When You Read This Letter*). Later, he would become the Uncle of the New Wave, the French master of films noirs, the director who paved the road for Sergio Leone, John Woo, and many others, the owner of a studio (quickly ruined), and the ultimate dandy of European filmmaking. But at the moment in question, Melville was working out the modernity of the second half of the twentieth century using the tools of the first half. *Bob the Gambler* is nostalgic and burlesque, yet filled with compassion and an accurate and respectful attention to places, objects, words, and the dreams everyone is entitled to live with.

Casino attacks, large-shouldered gangsters, macho talk, cars running fast in the dark, betrayal...sure! The film is a matter of human material, an inflection of voices, a remembrance of golden ages that never existed. It is often said that great films are universal and for all time. But *Bob the Gambler* is great for precisely the opposite reason: it belongs to its time and place, more or less consciously elaborating from that toward a completely different future. Although its ironic plot is important, the film's essence lies in its beauty and melancholy. Certainly, the world has gone on since *Bob the Gambler*. But something was captured in this film, like in a glass snowglobe, for us to look back on and remember. And there is nothing sad in that. **J-MF**

## KISS ME DEADLY (1955)

*Kiss Me Deadly* is a thick-ear masterpiece, wrenched by director Robert Aldrich and screenwriter A.I. Bezzerides from Mickey Spillane's trash novel, shot through with poetry ("Remember Me" by Christina Rosetti), unspeakable violence (the kicking naked legs of a woman tortured vaginally with a pair of pliers), hopped-up street talk ("3D-Pow! Va-va-voom!"), strange characters, and fringe-fantastical elements.

After credits that roll the wrong way and a nighttime drive, the desperate Cloris Leachman, naked under a trenchcoat, flags down thuggish private eye Mike Hammer (Ralph Meeker) and drags him into a plot involving spies, hoodlums, cops, a mastermind so erudite that he can only speak in metaphors when warning a dim-bulb blonde not to tamper with something deadly enough to kill everyone in range, codeword-dropping secret agents ("Los Alamos… Trinity… Manhattan Project") and a suitcase containing "the big whatsit" (a box of fissionable treasure that might be either pure plutonium or the head of Medusa). Meeker's nasty hero (note his smile as he tortures innocent witnesses by breaking irreplaceable opera records or slamming hands in drawers) sucker punches his way through a cast of perverts and sluts, then (at least in some prints) goes up with a mushroom cloud that rises from a beach house at the 1950s apocalypse of a finish. **KN**

**U.S.** (Parklane) 106m BW

**Director:** Robert Aldrich

**Producer:** Robert Aldrich

**Screenplay:** Mickey Spillane, A.I. Bezzerides, from novel by Mickey Spillane

**Photography:** Ernest Laszlo

**Music:** Frank De Vol

**Cast:** Ralph Meeker, Albert Dekker, Paul Stewart, Juano Hernandez, Wesley Addy, Marian Carr, Marjorie Bennett, Maxine Cooper, Fortunio Bonanova, Cloris Leachman, Gaby Rodgers, Robert Cornthwaite, Nick Dennis, Jack Lambert, Jack Elam

## THE MAN FROM LARAMIE (1955)

The last of a run of outstanding Westerns made by Anthony Mann, shortly to graduate to bigger (perhaps less interesting) projects like *El Cid* (1961), and James Stewart, whose angst-driven cowboys of the 1950s run parallel with his self-doubting Hitchcock heroes. The plot hook is almost noirish, prefiguring 1971's *Get Carter*, as Will Lockhart (Stewart) investigates his brother's death and gets embroiled in the Lear-like family struggle of a blind cattle baron (Donald Crisp) whose beloved son (Alex Nicol) is a sadistic weakling. Audiences in 1955 were shocked by the scene in which Nicol has his minions hold down Stewart and repays him for a wound by shooting the hero's hand at point-blank range.

Trail-boss Vic Hansbro (Arthur Kennedy) is—as in Mann's earlier Western *Bend of the River* (1952)— the hero's near-equal in manliness, but turns out to be his demonic counterpart, driven by resentment of the family whose ranch he runs but will never inherit to a dirty deal involving selling guns to renegade Apaches. *The Man from Laramie* is a taut, tragic tale with a memorable hit theme song ("The West will never see a man with so many notches on his gun") and Mann's trademarked sense of the way desperate and obsessed men relate to each other and the dangerous landscape that emphasizes their extreme psychological states. **KN**

**U.S.** (Columbia) 104m Technicolor

**Director:** Anthony Mann

**Producer:** William Goetz

**Screenplay:** Philip Yordan, Frank Burt, from story by Thomas T. Flynn

**Photography:** Charles Lang

**Music:** George Duning

**Cast:** James Stewart, Arthur Kennedy, Donald Crisp, Cathy O'Donnell, Alex Nicol, Aline MacMahon, Wallace Ford, Jack Elam, John War Eagle, James Millican, Gregg Barton, Boyd Stockman, Frank DeKova

# REBEL WITHOUT A CAUSE (1955)

Too often, this acknowledged classic is unwittingly damned with faint praise as being the finest of the three features in which James Dean starred during his tragically short life. *Rebel* remains by far the best 1950s film dealing with the then-new phenomenon of teenage delinquency. It is also a key work from Nicholas Ray, an enormously talented and distinctive director who, sadly, remains as underrated now as he was when he worked in Hollywood.

"You're tearing me apart!" screams Dean's Jim Stark at his bickering parents, giving voice to the agonizing confusion and alienation felt by so many of Ray's protagonists. From his first film, *They Live By Night* (1949), the director had repeatedly treated the lonely predicament of America's outsiders, showing himself especially sympathetic to the vulnerable young who looked for guidance from an older generation no wiser or happier than themselves. Jim feels let down by his family, his teachers, the cops, and most of his peers. The constant quest for kicks is as irresponsible (albeit less culpable, given their youth) as the adults' refusal to confront moral dilemmas. Together with other lost souls, Judy (Natalie Wood) and Plato (Sal Mineo), Jim tries to establish his own alternative family, one based on mutual understanding. Small wonder that the trio, brought together by the absurd, unnecessary death of a friend driven by boredom to test his worth in a clifftop "chickee run," and united by idealistic notions of "sincerity," lives in a derelict dreamhouse in the Los Angeles hills, well away from other people.

Ray's response to the question of how to depict his young dreamers' romantic idealism is admirably and exhilaratingly physical. The film was originally slated for black-and-white, but Ray persuaded Warners to let him shoot in color. The often luridly expressionist hues and Ray's typically fraught CinemaScope compositions evoke the feverish nature of adolescent experience. Similarly, Ray uses architecture and setting, particularly the difference between public and private space, to heighten our understanding of the characters' emotions. The darkness inside a planetarium becomes a space to indulge in private jokes, refuge, and reverie, even contemplation of the individual's place in the cosmos. The terrace outside is later transformed by a lofty camera position into a sunlit arena where a bullfight-like knife fight is played out with appropriately histrionic gestures. Ray understands how, especially when young, we view our lives as drama. His immaculate sense of color, composition, cutting, lighting, and performance enhances the importance of the action.

One reason why he and Dean were made for each other; it wasn't just the actor's style but his whole body that gave dramatic life to the turmoil within. Seeing Dean's Jim is witnessing a character being born, growing from moment to moment before our eyes. That, of course, is fitting for *Rebel*'s subject matter, but it also complements Ray's direction in terms of how its acute physicality expresses the tormented vitality within. How sad, then, that the projects Ray and Dean planned to work on together never came to fruition. One great film had to suffice. **GA**

**U.S.** (Warner Bros.) 111m Warnercolor

**Director:** Nicholas Ray

**Producer:** David Weisbart

**Screenplay:** Nicholas Ray, Irving Shulman, Stewart Stern

**Music:** Leonard Rosenman

**Cast:** James Dean, Natalie Wood, Sal Mineo, Jim Backus, Ann Doran, Corey Allen, William Hopper, Rochelle Hudson, Dennis Hopper, Edward Platt, Steffi Sidney, Marietta Canty, Virginia Brissac, Beverly Long, Ian Wolfe

**Oscar nomination:** Nicholas Ray (screenplay), Sal Mineo (actor in support role), Natalie Wood (actress in support role)

**U.S.** (Allied Artists) 100m BW

**Director:** Phil Karlson

**Producer:** Samuel Bischoff, David Diamond

**Screenplay:** Daniel Mainwaring, Crane Wilbur

**Photography:** Harry Neumann

**Music:** Harry Sukman

**Cast:** John McIntire, Richard Kiley, Kathryn Grant, Edward Andrews, Lenka Peterson, Biff McGuire, Truman Smith, Jean Carson, Kathy Marlowe, John Larch, Allen Nourse, Helen Martin, Otto Hulett, George Mitchell, Ma Beachie

# THE PHENIX CITY STORY (1955)

Decent citizens fight a bloody war to drive out the vice racket that has earned their Alabama town the title of "Sin City, U.S.A." Based on fact and shot on location, Phil Karlson's *The Phenix City Story* relates to such postwar trends as the semidocumentary, the corrupt city exposé, and the syndicate gangster movie, but none of these labels accounts for the film's extraordinary visceral power.

Although its graphic violence was virtually unprecedented in Hollywood, what makes this low-budget shocker truly innovative is its recognition that new content calls for new form. *The Phenix City Story* is a purposefully ugly movie, full of ugly rednecks, ugly juke joints, ugly camera angles (in the sense that they flout the conventions of "good" composition), and ugly, unaestheticized violence. A little girl's glassy-eyed corpse is heaved onto a suburban lawn, a crippled old man is shot point-blank in the mouth, the townspeople are bloodied and blasted with battlefield-like regularity. The atrocities are either shoved abruptly in our faces or kept at a bewildering distance, as if they were overwhelming the picture's capacity to represent them properly. Many movies since have portrayed more explicit and elaborate violence, but few have conveyed violence's chaotic force with such intelligent crudeness. **MR**

**Sweden** (Svensk) 108m BW

**Language:** Swedish

**Director:** Ingmar Bergman

**Producer:** Allan Ekelund

**Screenplay:** Ingmar Bergman

**Photography:** Gunnar Fischer

**Music:** Erik Nordgren

**Cast:** Ulla Jacobsson, Eva Dahlbeck, Harriet Andersson, Margit Carlqvist, Gunnar Björnstrand, Jarl Kulle, Åke Fridell, Björn Bjelfvenstam, Naima Wifstrand, Jullan Kindahl, Gull Natorp, Birgitta Valberg, Bibi Andersson

**Cannes Film Festival:** Ingmar Bergman (poetic humor award)

# SOMMARNATTENS LEENDE (1955)
## SMILES OF A SUMMER NIGHT

This first international success by Ingmar Bergman might in retrospect look like an anomaly in his career. In interviews Bergman often claims to have no talent for comedy, and his later work in the genre—*The Devil's Eye* (1960) and *All These Women* (1964)—would seem to confirm this sentiment. However, with *Waiting Women* (1952) and especially *A Lesson in Love* (1954), he found a successful formula for witty, sophisticated comedies featuring the two excellent actors Gunnar Björnstrand and Eva Dahlbeck (lovingly referred to by the director as "The Battleship Femininity") as a middle-aged couple playfully tormenting each other.

*Smiles of a Summer Night* is a variation of this formula, transposed into a 19th-century moral comedy and with a theatrical plot heavily influenced by Shakespeare's *A Midsummer Night's Dream*. Here the Björnstrand character is a middle-aged philistine and Dahlbeck's an aging actress. Both are vain and self-important, living in separate relationships that have proved to be even more frustrating than their own former liaison. Egged on by an aphrodisiac wine and the magical twilight of a midsummer night, their—and their spouses'—true feelings are revealed. Everybody finds his/her true mate. But this new equilibrium of bourgeois complacency was later to be disrupted by Bergman with a vengeance in his hellish visions of marriage and midlife crisis in *Scenes from a Marriage* (1973) and *From the Life of the Marionettes* (1980). **MT**

# NUIT ET BROUILLARD (1955)
## NIGHT AND FOG

Documentation of man's inhumanity to man is as old as history itself. Even so, little prepared the world for the specific atrocities of the Holocaust, a concerted series of events so horrific that it still boggles the mind. Aware how the passage of time has a way of diluting memories, however powerful, filmmaker Alain Resnais (who later rose to greater prominence as the director of such features as *Hiroshima, mon amour* and *Last Year at Marienbad*) decided to capture the Nazi atrocities on camera, if not for posterity then certainly as a lasting reminder of what we are capable of doing to one another.

The first film to truly address the Holocaust at a time when World War II still produced raw feelings, especially in Europe, *Night and Fog* juxtaposed black-and-white archival footage of concentration camps and their victims with pastoral color footage of the buildings and locations ten years later. Revealing the depths of distrust and denial that existed even a decade after the fall of the Third Reich, Resnais used footage from France, Belgium, and Poland, but conspicuously not from Germany. He showed that many of the people involved in the death camps either didn't know how to deal with their own guilt and complicity or didn't want to.

Denial is the driving point of *Night and Fog*. Resnais includes footage of the dead being bulldozed into mass graves, corpses hung on barbed wire fences, emaciated faces frozen in fear, skeletal nude bodies being paraded out for humiliation, and anonymous trains and trucks shipping who knows what to who knows where. He documents the gas chambers and crematoriums, as well as the Nazi's gruesome attempts to find a use for the discarded possessions, bones, skin, and bodies of their victims.

Resnais, in his own footage, notes that these death camps existed not in isolated outposts but frequently nearby major cities, hinting that everything that transpired happened with at least some degree of complicity on the part of civilians. Yet even the Nazis in charge of the camps deny culpability. One after the other, each claims "I am not responsible." But if not them, asks the film, then who?

*Night and Fog* is more concerned with attributing collective blame than with pointing fingers at any specific figure. Even so soon after the war, Resnais realized that the fleeting nature of memory risked erasure of the Nazi horrors. "A crematorium may look as pretty as a picture postcard," notes the narrator. "Today tourists are photographed standing in front of them." Working from a script by Holocaust survivor Jean Cayrol and enlisting an oddly meandering score by Hanns Eisler (a Marxist and German exile who was also deported from America during Hollywood's own communist purge), Resnais lets the accumulated images of death and terror serve as a vivid rebuttal to any who would ever again turn their backs on such atrocities. If the brief but powerful *Night and Fog* does ultimately parallel the pithy form of a postcard, it is a postcard offering a perpetually valid message—evil can always resurface. **JKl**

**France** (Argos) 32m BW/ Color
**Language:** French
**Director:** Alain Resnais
**Producer:** Anatole Dauman, Samy Halfon, Philippe Lifchitz
**Screenplay:** Jean Cayrol
**Photography:** Ghislain Cloquet, Sacha Vierny
**Music:** Hanns Eisler
**Cast:** Michel Bouquet, Reinhard Heydrich, Heinrich Himmler, Adolf Hitler, Julius Streicher

**U.S.** (Paul Gregory, United Artists) 93m BW

**Director:** Charles Laughton

**Producer:** Paul Gregory

**Screenplay:** James Agee, from novel by Davis Grubb

**Photography:** Stanley Cortez

**Music:** Walter Schumann

**Cast:** Robert Mitchum, Shelley Winters, Lillian Gish, James Gleason, Evelyn Varden, Peter Graves, Don Beddoe, Billy Chapin, Sally Jane Bruce, Gloria Castillo

# THE NIGHT OF THE HUNTER (1955)

Based on a slim, stark novel by Davis Grubb, Charles Laughton's sole film as a director is a Depression-set fable of psychosis and faith, strikingly sinister and yet deeply humane. Told mostly from the point of view of children, the story is like a fairy tale in its simplicity, and yet seethes with adult complications. The trigger is a stash of money stolen by hard-up bandit Ben Harper (Peter Graves) and entrusted to his children John (Billy Chapin) and Pearl (Sally Jane Bruce), which makes Ben's desperate widow Willa (Shelley Winters) an object of attraction for one of the screen's most unforgettable villains. "Reverend" Harry Powell (Robert Mitchum), in black-and-white clerical garb with a puritan flat hat that curls into a set of demonic-looking horns, is associated with the Bible and a switchblade; with the words "love" and "hate" tattooed on his knuckles, his sermon consists of an allegorical talk about these forces locked in conflict illustrated as he arm wrestles with himself. Powell's wooing of Willa is high-pressure, fooling the woman (who ends up serenely drowned) but not the children, who flee after the murder, the money stashed in the little girl's doll.

Mitchum, usually associated with cynical heroes, here plays a sincerely committed villain, moonlighting as a serial killer of loose women but sexually obsessed with the money he feels he needs to fund his bloody crusade. The nocturnal escape down river, shot in expressionist monochrome, is a magical sequence, with close-ups of strange-looking swampland flora and fauna. With Evil/Hate so powerfully conveyed, *The Night of the Hunter* needs an equally strong force to represent Good/Love. Laughton managed to get silent star Lillian Gish to come out of semiretirement to play Rachel, a kindly woman whose farm is open to the many underage runaways who come down the path. Like the snake in Eden, Powell threatens Rachel's idyll, working his seamy charm on one of the older girls to find a way onto the farm. In a remarkable siege finale, Mitchum's menacing drone of an edited hymn ("Leanin' ") is joined and completed by Gish, who knows the full lyric ("Lean on Jesus") and adds her voice to his, banishing his darkness aurally before he is actually defeated. **KN**

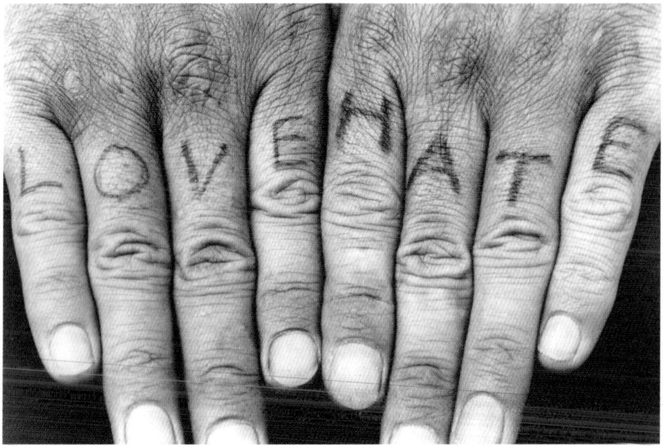

LOVE

France / West Germany (Florida, Gamma, Oska-Film) 110m Eastmancolor

**Language:** French / English / German

**Director:** Max Ophüls

**Producer:** Albert Caraco

**Screenplay:** Max Ophüls, Annette Wademant, Jacques Natanson, from the novel *La Vie Extraordinaire de Lola Montès* by Cécil Saint-Laurent

**Photography:** Christian Matras

**Music:** Georges Auric

**Cast:** Martine Carol, Peter Ustinov, Anton Walbrook, Henri Guisol, Lise Delamare, Paulette Dubost, Oskar Werner, Jean Galland, Will Quadflieg, Héléna Manson, Germaine Delbat, Carl Esmond, Jacques Fayet, Friedrich Domin, Werner Finck

# LOLA MONTÈS (1955)

## THE SINS OF LOLA MONTES

German-born, naturalized French, Viennese by lifelong sensibility, Max Ophüls was ideally suited to film the life of Lola Montès, one of the great cosmopolitan femmes fatales. Montès, dancer and courtesan extraordinaire, cut a swathe of scandal through Europe in the mid-19th century, numbering among her many lovers Franz Liszt and the King of Bavaria.

Ophüls's film, his last (and his only one in color) is no conventional biopic. Instead, he mounts a lavish baroque extravaganza, part circus, part pageant, packed with flashbacks, and sends his famously mobile camera scaling around the elaborate decor. In the title role, Martine Carol gives a sullen, emotionally glazed performance, and Anton Walbrook's pensive king all but steals the movie. But for all her limitations, Carol fits Ophüls's conception. As always, his concern is the gulf between the ideal of love and its flawed, disenchanted reality. His Lola is merely a passive blank onto which men project their fantasies; her final destiny, as a circus sideshow attraction selling kisses for a dollar, reduces her profession to its most brutal logic. *The Sins of Lola Montes*, a classic *film maudit*, was butchered by its distributors and long available only in a truncated version, but a recent restoration allows us to appreciate Ophüls's swan song in its full poignant splendor. **PK**

**U.S.** (MGM) 98m Eastmancolor

**Director:** Fred M. Wilcox

**Producer:** Nicholas Nayfack

**Screenplay:** Irving Block, Allen Adler, Cyril Hume

**Photography:** George J. Folsey

**Music:** Bebe Barron, Louis Barron

**Cast:** Walter Pidgeon, Anne Francis, Leslie Nielsen, Robby the Robot, Warren Stevens, Jack Kelly, Richard Anderson, Earl Holliman, George Wallace, Robert Dix, Jimmy Thompson, James Drury, Harry Harvey Jr., Roger McGee, Peter Miller

**Oscar nomination:** A. Arnold Gillespie, Irving G. Ries, Wesley C. Miller (special effects)

# FORBIDDEN PLANET (1956)

This superior 1950s sci-fi gem by director Fred M. Wilcox, ambitiously shot in widescreen CinemaScope, owes nothing to the period's paranoid McCarthyite preoccupation with hostile invaders from outer space but a great deal to the plot of William Shakespeare's *The Tempest* and the sophisticated psychological premise that the most dangerous monsters are those lurking in the primitive impulses of the subconscious mind.

A mission led by Commander John J. Adams (Leslie Nielsen) to the planet Altair 4, to discover what became of an expedition from Earth of whom nothing has been heard for decades, finds the only survivors of the colony are brilliant, arrogant scientist Edward Morbius (Walter Pidgeon) and his seductively miniskirted, child-of-nature daughter Altaira (Anne Francis), attended by one of the best-loved metallic characters of the screen, versatile and obliging Robby the Robot. Doctor Morbius has found the awesome remains of the ancient, annihilated Krell civilization, and dabbling with its technological wonders brings destruction down upon them all. Outstanding effects (including the unleashed "monsters from the id"), the awesome Krell underground complex, and an eerie, groundbreaking score of electronic tones are among the treats in a much-referenced picture that inspired many later speculative fictions of technology running away with its users. **AE**

# BIRUMA NO TATEGOTO (1956)
## THE BURMESE HARP

Although Akira Kurosawa may be the most famous Japanese filmmaker in the West, his contemporary Kon Ichikawa has displayed equal artistry in literally dozens of films, among them *The Burmese Harp*, his elegy for lost innocence. Opening at the end of World War II, Captain Inouye (Rentaro Mikuni) leads his platoon into Burma with a healthy mix of discipline and musical instruction. Having trained his soldiers to fight, but also to sing, they are an odd assortment of conscripts who eventually collide with Armistice Day.

Held in a British internment camp awaiting repatriation, they hear rumors about an isolated group of Japanese refusing to surrender. As Inouye's harp player and the center of his platoon's spiritual life, Mizushima (Shôji Yasui) volunteers to talk down the soldiers rather than let them die in an artillery barrage. Unimpressed with his entreaties, the entrenched force is killed and Mizushima assumed lost but for the rumors his platoon clings to about his survival.

What follows is a touching journey as Mizushima awakens from the attack, injured and afraid. Aided by peasants, he begins making his way back to Inouye but gradually realizes a higher purpose. Garbed as a Buddhist monk he sets about burying the war dead strewn across Southeast Asia without funerary attention or final messages home. He recognizes the need to mourn, but also how the peace will be based on mutual care and personal loyalty, and so forsakes his old life to walk the earth bringing small labors to bear where they're needed. He subsequently crosses paths with Inouye on several occasions but finally explains his cause as a lasting tribute to the dead, both innocent and guilty, good and evil because it's upon their backs the future will rise.

A breath of warm sentiment inserted over a macabre scenario, *The Burmese Harp* retains every bit of dignity associated with gentility and kindness. Burma itself becomes a passive supporting character but the idea of a spiritual renewal, presented without dogma or propagandistic impulses, proves a likable epilogue to the horrors of World War II in this, Ichikawa's early masterpiece. **GC-Q**

**Japan** (Nikkatsu) 116m BW

**Language:** Japanese

**Director:** Kon Ichikawa

**Producer:** Masayuki Takaki

**Screenplay:** Natto Wada, from novel by Michio Takeyama

**Photography:** Minoru Yokoyama

**Music:** Akira Ifukube

**Cast:** Rentaro Mikuni, Shôji Yasui, Jun Hamamura, Taketoshi Naitô, Ko Nishimura, Hiroshi Tsuchikata, Sanpei Mine, Yoshiaki Kato, Sojiro Amano, Yôji Nagahama, Eiji Nakamura, Shojiro Ogasawara, Tomoko Tonai, Tatsuya Mihashi, Yunosuke Ito

**Oscar nomination:** Japan (best foreign language film)

**Venice Film Festival:** Kon Ichikawa (OCIC award—honorable mention)

Nomination: Kon Ichikawa (Golden Lion)

**U.S.** (Whitney, Warner Bros.) 120m Technicolor

**Director:** John Ford

**Producer:** Merian C. Cooper, Patrick Ford, C.V. Whitney

**Screenplay:** Frank S. Nugent, from novel by Alan Le May

**Photography:** Winton C. Hoch

**Music:** Stan Jones, Max Steiner

**Cast:** John Wayne, Jeffrey Hunter, Vera Miles, Ward Bond, Natalie Wood, John Qualen, Olive Carey, Henry Brandon, Ken Curtis, Harry Carey Jr., Antonio Moreno, Hank Worden, Beulah Archuletta, Walter Coy, Dorothy Jordan

# THE SEARCHERS (1956)

*The Searchers* opens on a shot of a desert landscape seen from inside a house. Someone is approaching on horseback. It is Ethan Edwards (John Wayne), returned from the Civil War to his brother's ranch in Texas. From a series of looks and gestures we realize that Ethan is in love with his brother's wife, Martha (Dorothy Jordan). Next day he departs with a party of Texas Rangers in pursuit of Indians who have stolen some cattle. While he's away Comanches attack the ranch, killing Ethan's brother and sister-in-law and capturing their two daughters. For the remainder of the film, in actions set over a period of five years, Ethan and his part-Indian companion Martin (Jeffrey Hunter) crisscross the West in search of the girls.

How did John Ford turn this simple story into one of the greatest of all Westerns? First, there's the setting. Ford shot many Westerns in Monument Valley, an isolated region on the border between Utah and Arizona. The eroded red sandstone rocks are an awesome spectacle, and Ford's unerring eye for composition invests them with a special aura. The sheer size of the landscape makes the human figures seem especially vulnerable, and the life of the Texan settlers precarious. How could anyone scratch a living in such a barren wilderness?

At the heart of the story, though, is the figure of Ethan Edwards. As played by Wayne, Ethan is a colossus, overwhelming and indomitable. But he has a tragic flaw. Ethan is eaten up with hatred of the Indians, and it becomes clear that his quest is driven by an implacable racism. His intention, as Martin discerns, is not to rescue Debbie (Natalie Wood), his surviving niece, but to murder her. In Ethan's view she has become irredeemably contaminated through contact with her Comanche captors. Slowly we realize that the Comanche chief Scar (Henry Brandon) functions as a kind of mirror image of Ethan. In raping Martha before he kills her, Scar has performed a horrific travesty of the act that Ethan secretly dreamed of committing. Ethan's urge to kill both Scar and Debbie thus arises from his need to obliterate his own illegitimate desires.

The true genius of *The Searchers* is in its being able to keep the audience's sympathy for Ethan, despite the evident fact that he is a murderous racist. In doing so, it elicits a far more complex and productive response than that of more obviously liberal films in this vein, such as *Broken Arrow* (1950). Instead of preaching a message, Ford leads us into the complexities of the American experience of racial difference.

Along the way there are many other pleasures, including a marvelous score by Max Steiner and plenty of comedy from stalwarts of the John Ford Stock Company such as Harry Carey Jr., Ken Curtis, Hank Worden, and Ward Bond. Vera Miles is excellent as Marty's girlfriend Laurie, whose mother is played by Olive Carey, widow of Ford's first Western star, Harry Carey.

In 1992, *The Searchers* was voted the fifth greatest movie of all time in a poll of international film critics held by *Sight & Sound* magazine. That's quite an accolade, but Ford's picture lives up to it. **EB**

France (Gaumont, Nouvelles Éditions) 99m BW

**Language:** French

**Director:** Robert Bresson

**Producer:** Alain Poiré, Jean Thuillier

**Screenplay:** Robert Bresson, from memoir by André Devigny

**Photography:** Léonce-Henri Burel

**Nonoriginal music:** Wolfgang Amadeus Mozart

**Cast:** François Leterrier, Charles Le Clainche, Maurice Beerblock, Roland Monod, Jacques Ertaud, Jean Paul Delhumeau, Roger Treherne, Jean Philippe Delamarre, César Gattegno, Jacques Oerlemans, Klaus Detlef Grevenhorst, Leonhard Schmidt

**Cannes Film Festival:** Robert Bresson (director)

# UN CONDAMNÉ À MORT S'EST ÉCHAPPÉ OU LE VENT SOUFFLE OÙ IL VEUT (1956)

## A MAN ESCAPED

If anyone needs to be won over to the joys and rewards of minimalism in cinema, *A Man Escaped* is the best place to start. Much of it shows Fontaine (François Leterrier) alone in his cell, making contact with fellow prisoners and slowly chipping his way to freedom.

Like all Bresson's films, this one illustrates his long-developed theories of the "cinematograph": nonprofessionals giving strictly de-dramatized performances; enormous emphasis on off-screen sound and the information it carries; music held off until a final, glorious moment. And like the other great prison films of French cinema, Jacques Becker's *The Hole* (1960) and Jean Genet's *A Song of Love* (1950), *A Man Escaped* offers a remarkably potent allegory of human suffering and the drive to liberation. At the same time, it delivers an attenuated, taut form of suspense to rival the best of Alfred Hitchcock.

For many years, *A Man Escaped* was appreciated for its existential and spiritual dimensions: man's solitude, the fragility of communication with others, the gift of God's grace. More recently, its political dimension has been foregrounded, as a reflection of Bresson's experience in the Resistance—thus giving his entire career, with its themes of subjection and "souls in torment," a socially grounded urgency. **AM**

**U.S.** (Universal) 99m Technicolor

**Director:** Douglas Sirk

**Producer:** Albert Zugsmith

**Screenplay:** George Zuckerman, from novel by Robert Wilder

**Photography:** Russell Metty

**Music:** Frank Skinner, Victor Young

**Cast:** Rock Hudson, Lauren Bacall, Robert Stack, Dorothy Malone, Robert Keith, Grant Williams, Robert J. Wilke, Edward Platt, Harry Shannon, John Larch, Joseph Granby, Roy Glenn, Sam, Maidie Norman, William Schallert, Joanne Jordan

**Oscar:** Dorothy Malone (actress in support role)

**Oscar nomination:** Robert Stack (actor in support role), Victor Young, Sammy Cahn (song)

# WRITTEN ON THE WIND (1956)

Robert Stack, in a drunken rage, smashes a bottle of booze against the wall. Lauren Bacall, at her bedroom curtain, faints. Gunshots, death, tears. And on the soundtrack, a male chorus begins singing: "Our night of stolen bliss was written on the wind." From its first moments, this is the Hollywood melodrama that contains all others, in an electric, condensed, powerfully lyrical fashion.

*Written on the Wind* is about the twisted, fatal connections between sex, power, and money. Characters are arranged into inverted mirror images of each other, good facing evil—but everyone, ultimately, inhabits a complex, contradictory position in the impossible scheme of things. Dorothy Malone, marvelous as the quintessential bad girl who drinks, smokes, loves jazz, picks up guys at oil derricks, and sends her father plummeting down the stairs, is particularly riveting.

Few films are at once as visceral and insightful as *Written on the Wind*—a soap opera with passion, seriousness, and intelligence. Director Douglas Sirk specialized in films that were once dismissed by highbrows and lowbrows alike as "women's weepies." When they were finally rediscovered in the early 1970s at film festivals around the world, the audaciousness and true subversiveness of his work were appreciated for the first time. **AM**

## THE MAN WHO KNEW TOO MUCH (1956)

Hitchcock's only remake of one of his own films raises the issue of the superiority of his American work to his British productions. Though the original 1934 version is witty, the remake is more lavish and expert, with some of Hitchcock's most powerful scenes. James Stewart plays an American doctor on holiday in Morocco with his family who accidentally learns of a political assassination to take place in the near future. A friendly English couple are in fact spies in on the plot, and they kidnap Stewart's son to ensure his silence. So he must prevent the killing without putting his son in harm's way.

As in most Hitchcock films, the international intrigue is less important than the odyssey of the hero. Stewart indeed "knows too much," not valuing his wife's (Doris Day) capabilities. As the plot unfolds, however, her assistance proves essential, despite his fears of her emotional collapse (he even drugs her before telling her of the kidnapping). The film climaxes in the Albert Hall, one of Hitchcock's best-ever set pieces. *The Man Who Knew Too Much* features excellent performances by Stewart and Day, and by Bernard Miles and Brenda De Banzie as the British agents. The score by Bernard Herrmann, who appears in the film directing the orchestra, is one of his best. **BP**

**U.S.** (Paramount) 120m Technicolor

**Director:** Alfred Hitchcock

**Producer:** Herbert Coleman

**Screenplay:** Charles Bennett, D.B. Wyndham-Lewis, John Michael Hayes

**Photography:** Robert Burks

**Music:** Bernard Herrmann

**Cast:** James Stewart, Doris Day, Brenda De Banzie, Bernard Miles, Ralph Truman, Daniel Gélin, Mogens Wieth, Alan Mowbray, Hillary Brooke, Christopher Olsen, Reggie Nalder, Richard Wattis, Noel Willman, Alix Talton, Yves Brainville

**Oscar:** Jay Livingston, Ray Evans (song)

## GIANT (1956)

Edna Ferber specialized in writing sprawling family sagas, several of them set in the West. Her 1930 novel *Cimarron* was twice filmed by Hollywood, as was the 1926 film *Show Boat*, set in the Deep South. In *Giant*, written in 1950, Bick Benedict (Rock Hudson) is a Texas cattle baron who marries a spirited Maryland belle, Leslie (Elizabeth Taylor). Bick's sister has left some of the property to Jett Rink (James Dean), a former employee. Rink discovers oil and becomes immensely rich, but his personal life is a disappointment (he carries a torch for Leslie) and he declines into alcoholism. As Bick and Leslie grow older, they are concerned with who will run the ranch after they've gone. Their daughter, (Carroll Baker) wants to take over, but Leslie doesn't approve. To Bick's disappointment, their son (Dennis Hopper) has married a Latina woman and become a doctor. Eventually Bick and Leslie come to terms with life.

At well over three hours, *Giant* certainly lives up to its title. But the performances are outstanding, not least James Dean's, who was tragically killed in a car crash shortly after completing his part. Director George Stevens does justice to the immensity of the Texas landscape, and unusually for the time the film deals interestingly with both racial and class differences. **EB**

**U.S.** (Giant, Warner Bros) 197m Warnercolor

**Language:** English / Spanish

**Director:** George Stevens

**Producer:** Henry Ginsberg, George Stevens

**Screenplay:** Fred Guiol, Ivan Moffat, from novel by Edna Ferber

**Photography:** William C. Mellor

**Music:** Dimitri Tiomkin

**Cast:** Elizabeth Taylor, Rock Hudson, James Dean, Carroll Baker, Jane Withers, Chill Wills, Mercedes McCambridge, Dennis Hopper, Sal Mineo, Rod Taylor, Judith Evelyn, Earl Holliman, Robert Nichols, Paul Fix

**Oscar:** George Stevens (director)

**Oscar nomination:** George Stevens, Henry Ginsberg (best picture), Fred Guiol, Ivan Moffat (screenplay), James Dean (actor), Rock Hudson (actor), Mercedes McCambridge (actress in support role), Boris Leven, Ralph S. Hurst (art direction), Moss Mabry, Marjorie Best (costume), William Hornbeck, Philip W. Anderson, Fred Bohanan (editing), Dimitri Tiomkin (music)

**U.S.** (Universal) 89m Technicolor
**Director:** Douglas Sirk
**Producer:** Ross Hunter
**Screenplay:** Peg Fenwick, Edna L. Lee, Harry Lee, from story by Edna L. Lee
**Photography:** Russell Metty
**Music:** Frank Skinner
**Cast:** Jane Wyman, Rock Hudson, Agnes Moorehead, Conrad Nagel, Virginia Grey, Gloria Talbott, William Reynolds, Charles Drake, Hayden Rorke, Jacqueline deWit, Leigh Snowden, Donald Curtis, Alex Gerry, Nestor Paiva, Forrest Lewis

# ALL THAT HEAVEN ALLOWS (1956)

On one level, Douglas Sirk's *All That Heaven Allows* is like a fabulous, ironic piece of performance art, the relic of a specifically mid-20th-century genre that degenerated into television soap opera. But the core emotional experiences of the film's distant lives are timelessly compelling. This is arguably the finest example of the plush 1950s Technicolor melodramas, and the most classic one made at Universal by Danish-born Sirk (formerly Detlef Sierck), a leftist theater-director-turned-filmmaker of some stature who fled with his Jewish wife from Nazi Germany to Hollywood. Back to square one as an unknown émigré, he applied distinctive taste to seemingly undemanding and trite assignments. His European sophistication and formal visual style elevated absurd and maudlin stories into deliriously entertaining heightened reality and multiple-hanky domestic dramas, including *Magnificent Obsession* (1954), *Written on the Wind* (1956), *The Tarnished Angels* (1958), and *Imitation of Life* (1959).

In *All That Heaven Allows*, pleasant middle-class widow Cary Scott (Jane Wyman), suffering estrangement from her selfish grown children and facing social ostracism from her shallow country club set, falls in love with the much younger gardener and nurseryman Ron Kirby (Rock Hudson)—Hudson was a favorite of Sirk's and also appears as Wyman's leading man in *Magnificent Obsession*. Her distant son Ned (William Reynolds) is preoccupied with his career and spoiled college-girl daughter Kay (Gloria Talbott) is embarrassed her mother is a woman with needs. Their idea of a great gift to fill mom's time is a TV set. Love wins out, but only after being tested by cruel gossip, tearful sacrificial separation, and a life-threatening crisis. These are all traditional staples of vintage women's pictures, but Sirk presents them with an eye for darker impulses beneath the sunny suburban wholesomeness idealized in 1950s America, and with a subtle handling of its repressed insecurities.

Along with *Imitation of Life*, *All That Heaven Allows* was a touchstone for Todd Haynes's bold, sumptuous homage melodrama *Far From Heaven* (2002). It also provided the source of Rainer Werner Fassbinder's racially charged reworking further down the socioeconomic scale. *Ali: Fear Eats the Soul* (1974), featuring a poor German widow who is exposed to prejudice and derision when she falls in love with the much younger Ali, a kind, equally lonely North African immigrant. Costume design from *All That Heaven Allows* even found its way into the period homage French farce *Eight Women* (2002), with Catherine Deneuve's daughter arriving home for the holidays in a replica of Gloria Talbott's beanie hat and ensemble.

Hunky Hudson, who did much of his best work with Sirk, is perfectly sincere as the rugged but sensitive young outdoorsman in whom Wyman's soulful homemaker finds liberating warmth and empathy. The picture looks good enough to eat, with wonderful color, compositions, lighting, art direction, costumes, and cinematography. But the style serves the content superbly, observation of human nature with high gloss making heavenly romantic melodrama. **AE**

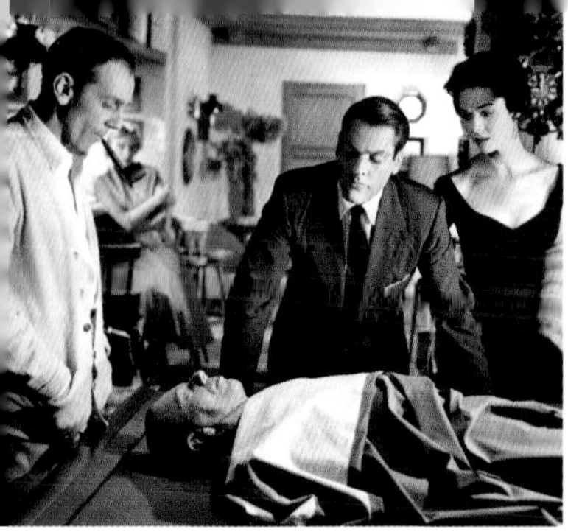

# INVASION OF THE BODY SNATCHERS
(1956)

**U.S.** (Allied Artists, Walter Wanger) 80m BW

**Director:** Don Siegel

**Producer:** Walter Wanger

**Screenplay:** Daniel Mainwaring, from the novel *The Body Snatchers* by Jack Finney

**Photography:** Ellsworth Fredericks

**Music:** Carmen Dragon

**Cast:** Kevin McCarthy, Dana Wynter, Larry Gates, King Donovan, Carolyn Jones, Jean Willes, Ralph Dumke, Virginia Christine, Tom Fadden, Kenneth Patterson, Guy Way, Eileen Stevens, Beatrice Maude, Jean Andren, Bobby Clark

One of the most popular and paranoid films from the Golden Age of American science-fiction cinema, Don Siegel's *Invasion of the Body Snatchers* simultaneously stands as ambiguous/ambivalent Cold War allegory and extra-terrestrial terror tale.

Despite its B movie feel, Siegel's film—based on the novel by Jack Finney—is less concerned with subscribing to generic sci-fi convention than with dramatizing the dangers of social conformity and the threat of invasion coming both from outside and inside one's own community. But the absence of any manifest monsters—partly due to economic considerations, the theme of "body snatching" plants and doppelganger drones served as a creative cost-cutting tactic—is more than made up for by the uncanny depiction of "ordinary life" that may no longer be so ordinary. As Kim Newman writes, "Rather than rubbery claws, animated dinosaurs and alien death rays, the film finds horror in an uncle mowing the lawn, an abandoned roadside vegetable stall, a bar all but empty of patrons, a mother putting a plant in baby's playpen, or a crowd purposefully gathering in a town square at 7:45 on a Saturday morning."

When Dr. Miles Bennell (Kevin McCarthy) returns home to his small California town of Santa Mira from a medical convention, he is confronted by strange reports from several of his patients, who insist that their seemingly benign relatives are in fact imposters. After some initial skepticism, Miles is convinced when, during a barbecue with some friends, he discovers two huge seed pods that burst open to release a bubbly fluid and two incomplete human replicas, one of which is well on its way to looking just like Miles himself. Speculating that a bizarre alien invasion is underway, Miles and his love interest Becky (Dana Wynter) attempt a getaway as the entire town falls sway to the pods' dehumanizing effects.

A cinematic nightmare concerning the potential communist threat or an anti-McCarthyist "message" movie wrapped in the protective garb of sci-fi fantasy? *Invasion of the Body Snatchers* offers evidence to support either interpretation. And the film's open, pessimistic ending, as Miles wanders onto a highway and shouts "You're next!" directly to the camera, will make you wonder who you're really sleeping next to at night. **SJS**

## THE WRONG MAN (1956)

*The Wrong Man* is one of the bleakest pictures Hitchcock ever made. Henry Fonda plays Manny Balestrero, a jazz musician who is mistakenly identified as the man who held up an insurance office. Though he's released on bail, the worry and disgrace begin to affect his wife Rose (Vera Miles). They try to find the people who can confirm Manny's alibi, but they fail. Rose has a breakdown before the trial and is confined to an asylum. Eventually, quite by chance, the real hold-up man is discovered, but this has little effect on her state of mind.

Shot in black-and-white, with an almost documentary-style realism, *The Wrong Man* is based on an actual case, as stated by Hitchcock himself in a short prologue. It explores one of Hitchcock's perennial themes, that of the man accused of a crime he did not commit (Hitchcock's 1959 film *North By Northwest* has a similar situation). The director brilliantly conveys how readily the procedures of indictment and incarceration conspire to impart a sensation of guilt even in the innocent. In a masterly sequence making use of a subjective camera, we see Manny suffer the humiliation of being booked, searched, and fingerprinted, the dirty ink on his hands seeming like a confirmation of his guilt. **EB**

**U.S.** (First National, Warner Bros.) 105m BW

**Director:** Alfred Hitchcock

**Producer:** Herbert Coleman, Alfred Hitchcock

**Screenplay:** Angus MacPhail, Maxwell Anderson, the from the novel *The True Story of Christopher Emmanuel Balestrero* by Maxwell Anderson

**Photography:** Robert Burks

**Music:** Bernard Herrmann

**Cast:** Henry Fonda, Vera Miles, Anthony Quayle, Harold Stone, John Heldabrand, Doreen Lang, Norma Connolly, Lola D'Annunzio, Robert Essen, Dayton Lummis, Charles Cooper, Esther Minciotti, Laurinda Barrett, Nehemiah Persoff, Kippy Campbell

## BIGGER THAN LIFE (1956)

The very finest of Nicholas Ray's films is a brilliant expressionist melodrama that used the then-topical controversy over the discovery and deployment of the "wonder-drug" cortisone (a type of steroid) to mount a devastating critique on the materialistic, middle-class conformism that defined the American Dream during the postwar era.

The brooding James Mason (who also produced) is perfectly cast as a small-town teacher beset by worries about money and middle age who, having been prescribed steroids, becomes addicted to the sense of well-being it brings. This turns him into an irascibly neurotic, megalomaniac tyrant to his wife, son, and everyone around him. The drug, of course, is merely the catalyst that ignites the loathing he feels for himself and the staid, complacently unquestioning world in which he is trapped. Indeed, his despair goes so deep that when, finally, he decides he must save his son from the depravities of humanity by killing him, and his wife (Barbara Rush) reminds him that God stopped Abraham from killing Isaac, Mason simply responds: "God was wrong."

A profoundly radical Hollywood movie, then, distinguished not only by its distaste for suburban notions of "normality" but by the beautifully nightmarish clarity of its intensely colored 'Scope imagery. A masterpiece. **GA**

**U.S.** (Fox) 95m DeLuxe

**Director:** Nicholas Ray

**Producer:** James Mason

**Screenplay:** Cyril Hume, Richard Maibaum, from article by Burton Roueche

**Photography:** Joseph MacDonald

**Music:** David Raksin

**Cast:** James Mason, Barbara Rush, Walter Matthau, Robert F. Simon, Christopher Olsen, Roland Winters, Rusty Lane, Rachel Stephens, Kipp Hamilton

**Venice Film Festival nomination:** Nicholas Ray (Golden Lion)

U.S. (Bing Crosby, MGM, Sol C. Siegel) 107m Technicolor

**Director:** Charles Walters

**Producer:** Sol C. Siegel

**Screenplay:** John Patrick, from the play *The Philadelphia Story* by Philip Barry

**Photography:** Paul Vogel

**Music:** Saul Chaplin, Cole Porter

**Cast:** Bing Crosby, Grace Kelly, Frank Sinatra, Celeste Holm, John Lund, Louis Calhern, Sidney Blackmer, Louis Armstrong, Margalo Gillmore

**Oscar nomination:** Edward Bernds, Elwood Ullman (screenplay)*, Johnny Green, Saul Chaplin (music), Cole Porter (song)

* nomination declined when the Academy realized it had confused Bernds and Ullman's *High Society* with Sol Siegel's production

# HIGH SOCIETY (1956)

A musical update of George Cukor's upper-class romantic farce *The Philadelphia Story*, *High Society* unites the unbeatable melodic talents of Bing Crosby, Frank Sinatra, and Louis Armstrong with the beauty of Grace Kelly in her final film role before she left Hollywood to become Princess Grace of Monaco.

Icy, spoiled Tracy (Kelly) is due to marry dull, dependable beau George (John Lund), but on the eve of her nuptials, her ex-husband Dexter (Crosby) returns to try and put a stop to the wedding. On hand to report on the shenanigans behind the social event of the year are journalists Liz (Celeste Holm) and Mike (Sinatra), with jazz-great Armstrong (appearing as himself) providing something of a Greek chorus, bringing the audience up to speed with Dexter and Tracy's complicated entanglements.

Following endless Hollywood musicals of the 1940s and early 1950s that were packed with elaborate song and dance numbers, director Charles Walters seamlessly fits nine simple renditions of Cole Porter songs into the proceedings, rather than have them take over the film. Armstrong begins by singing the plot-explaining "High Society" from the back of a cramped limousine shared with his band, while the classic "Who Wants to be a Millionaire?" is spiritedly sung by Sinatra and Holm alone in a room filled with Tracy's many extravagant wedding gifts. A light, frothy, and timeless piece of musical comedy. **JB**

U.S. (Cecil B. DeMille, Paramount) 220m Technicolor

**Director:** Cecil B. DeMille

**Producer:** Cecil B. DeMille, Henry Wilcoxon

**Screenplay:** Æneas MacKenzie, Jesse Lasky Jr., Jack Gariss, Fredric M. Frank, From the novels, *Pillar of Fire* by J.H. Ingraham, *On Eagle's Wing* by A.E. Southon, *Prince of Egypt* by Dorothy Clarke Wilson

**Photography:** Loyal Griggs

**Music:** Elmer Bernstein

**Cast:** Charlton Heston, Yul Brynner, Anne Baxter, Edward G. Robinson, Yvonne De Carlo, Debra Paget, John Derek, Cedric Hardwicke, Nina Foch

**Oscar:** John P. Fulton (special effects)

**Oscar nomination:** Cecil B. DeMille (best picture), Hal Pereira, Walter H. Tyler, Albert Nozaki, Sam Comer, Ray Moyer (art direction), Loyal Griggs (photography), Edith Head, Ralph Jester, John Jensen, Dorothy Jeakins, Arnold Friberg (costume), Anne Bauchens (editing), Loren L. Ryder (sound recording)

# THE TEN COMMANDMENTS (1956)

With a running time of nearly four hours, Cecil B. De Mille's last feature and most extravagant blockbuster is full of absurdities and vulgarities, but the color is ravishing, and De Mille's form of showmanship, which includes his own narration, never falters. Charlton Heston might be said to achieve his apotheosis as Moses—unless one decides that it's Moses who's achieving his apotheosis as Heston—and most of the others in the cast are comparably mythic.

Simultaneously ludicrous and splendid, this epic is driven by the sort of personal conviction one almost never finds in subsequent Hollywood monoliths. To read it properly, one has to see it as an ideological, spiritual manifesto relating specifically to how De Mille viewed the Cold War world in 1956. Thus, when he appears in front of a gold-tasseled curtain to introduce the film, his main point isn't simply his use of ancient sources such as Philo and Josephus to recount the 30 years of Moses's life omitted in the Bible, but also to declare that "The theme of this picture is whether man should be ruled by God's laws or...by the whims of a dictator like Ramses." By "dictator," he's clearly thinking of a Mao Tse-tung figure, which the orientalism suggested by Yul Brynner as Ramses makes clear.

The film has sometimes been rereleased—most recently, in 1990—in a stretched, anamorphic widescreen format, which means that the top and bottom of every frame is cropped. There may be some form of divine retribution at work here; De Mille was a notorious foot fetishist, and thanks to this studio trick, many of De Mille's foreground players have now been deprived of their feet. **JRos**

# 12 ANGRY MEN (1957)

Sidney Lumet's courtroom drama enjoys enduring popularity because it is a hothouse for smart performances, sudden twists, and impassioned monologues. Uniquely, the brilliantly economical and riveting drama of *12 Angry Men* does not actually take place in the courtroom—except for a brief prologue as the jury is sent out with the judge's instructions—but during a single, sweltering afternoon in the jury room.

Henry Fonda plays Juror Number 8, the holdout whose reasonable doubt and well-reasoned resistance gradually bring eleven other jury members around from their first swift verdict of guilty in the case of a youth prosecuted for the murder of his father. Fonda was impressed by the power in Reginald Rose's ingeniously contrived teleplay, broadcast live on CBS in 1954 (and believed lost until 2003, when a tape was discovered). Recognizing a role that perfectly suited his calm sincerity and seeing the opportunity for a gripping feature he put his own money into producing the film. He gave the assignment to Lumet, a dynamic veteran of live TV drama whose expertise enabled him and director of photography Boris Kaufman—another expert at working in restricted spaces and in black-and-white—to mine the mounting tension from Rose's tightly structured script and to wrap the film in under twenty days.

Lumet's much loved, engrossing debut film makes no apologies for its theatricality but makes a virtue of its claustrophobic, sweaty intensity. And each actor makes his mark in this showcase of superb characterizations and ensemble dynamics, from Martin Balsam's insecure foreman to a leonine Lee J. Cobb's belligerent, embittered Juror No. 3. Interestingly, two of the men, Joseph Sweeney as elderly, insightful Juror No. 9 and George Voskovec as methodically minded Juror No. 11, had been in the original television production. Class and ethnic prejudices, private assumptions, and personalities all come out in a colossal struggle for unclouded judgment. The film won the Golden Bear at the Berlin Film Festival but its greatest accolade is that after seeing this picture no one ever enters into jury duty without fantasizing about becoming a dogged champion of justice à la Fonda, whatever the case at hand. **AE**

**U.S.** (Orion-Nova) 96m BW
**Director:** Sidney Lumet
**Screenplay:** Reginald Rose
**Photography:** Boris Kaufman
**Music:** Kenyon Hopkins
**Cast:** Henry Fonda, Lee J. Cobb, Ed Begley, E.G. Marshall, Jack Warden, Martin Balsam, John Fiedler, Jack Klugman, Ed Binns, Joseph Sweeney, George Voskovec, Robert Webber
**Oscar nomination:** Henry Fonda, Reginald Rose (best picture), Sidney Lumet (director), Reginald Rose (screenplay)
**Berlin International Film Festival:** Sidney Lumet (Golden Bear), Sidney Lumet (OCIC Award)

**Sweden** (Svensk) 96m BW

**Language:** Swedish

**Director:** Ingmar Bergman

**Producer:** Allan Ekelund

**Screenplay:** Ingmar Bergman, from the play *Trämålning* by Ingmar Bergman

**Photography:** Gunnar Fischer

**Music:** Erik Nordgren

**Cast:** Gunnar Björnstrand, Bengt Ekerot, Nils Poppe, Max von Sydow, Bibi Andersson, Inga Gill, Maud Hansson, Inga Landgré, Gunnel Lindblom, Bertil Anderberg, Anders Ek, Åke Fridell, Gunnar Olsson, Erik Strandmark

**Cannes Film Festival:** Ingmar Bergman, tied with *Kanal* (special jury prize)

# DET SJUNDE INSEGLET (1957)

## THE SEVENTH SEAL

The image of a black-robed, white-faced Death (Bengt Ekerot) playing chess on the beach with a weary, questioning crusader (Max von Sydow) is as deeply-ingrained in the collective memory of moviegoers as King Kong atop the Empire State Building, Humphrey Bogart spurning Ingrid Bergman at the airport, Janet Leigh stabbed in the shower, or the Imperial Cruiser passing over the camera. This one scene from the Swedish arthouse release *The Seventh Seal* epitomizes the momentousness, the excitement, and the impact new types of cinema had at a point when Hollywood certainties were in recession: How else to explain the parodies or references that recur in films as varied as Roger Corman's *Masque of the Red Death* (1964), Woody Allen's *Love and Death*, John McTiernan's *Last Action Hero* (1993), and Peter Hewitt's *Bill & Ted's Bogus Journey* (1991), in the last of which Death plays twister?

This scene has been spoofed frequently and it's a shame that it has come to represent the whole of the film in popular imagination. There's an unfair sense that writer-director Ingmar Bergman was being overly solemn, setting out to make something that could stand as an archetype of seriousness or artiness. Actually, *The Seventh Seal*, although rooted in the big themes of Bergman's great period, is a very playful, frequently comic picture, a medieval fable influenced by Bergman's enthusiasm for the samurai movies of Akira Kurosawa and as concerned with celebrating simple pleasures as indicting complicated torments.

Antonius Block (Sydow), returning after ten years on a bloody crusade that was started by a con man who now makes a living robbing corpses, feels that his faith in God is a disease that mankind should root out. With his squire (Gunnar Björnstrand), as much a debating partner as sidekick, Block encounters death in the form of a plague-ridden corpse before he meets the literal Grim Reaper. The game of chess played throughout the film between Death and the knight is not merely for the crusader's life but for his feelings about God, religion, and

humanity. In the end, hope comes from an alternative Holy Family—a jolly juggler (Nils Poppe), his earthy sensual wife (Gunnel Lindblom), and their lively, innocent toddler—whom Block saves from the plague by willingly joining the dance of death that claims more venal, corrupted characters.

If the knight, who is constantly tormented by curiosities about God and the void (he even visits an accused witch on the point of being burned to ask her what the Devil knows about God), represents one side of Bergman and the simple showman gently upbraided by his practical wife ("You and your dreams and visions," she says in the film's closing line) another, seeking redemption through honest entertainment, and appalled when his innocent show is upstaged by the horrible, Church-approved spectacle of a crowd of penitents being lashed and tortured. Bergman is always angry and saddened by human evils, especially when sanctioned by supposed religion, but the film also celebrates physical and spiritual love, communal artistic expression, food and drink, and natural beauty. **KN**

**U.S.** (Fox) 119m DeLuxe

**Director:** Leo McCarey

**Producer:** Leo McCarey, Jerry Wald

**Screenplay:** Leo McCarey, Mildred Cram, Delmer Daves, Donald Ogden Stewart

**Photography:** Milton R. Krasner

**Music:** Hugo Friedhofer, Harry Warren

**Cast:** Cary Grant, Deborah Kerr, Richard Denning, Neva Patterson, Cathleen Nesbitt, Robert Q. Lewis, Charles Watts, Fortunio Bonanova, George Winslow

**Oscar nomination:** Milton R. Krasner (photography), Charles Le Maire (costume), Hugo Friedhofer (music), Harry Warren, Harold Adamson, Leo McCarey (song)

# AN AFFAIR TO REMEMBER (1957)

"Darling if you can paint, I can walk again!" For years Cary Grant's and Deborah Kerr's thorny path in *An Affair to Remember* was almost illicitly adored. Then it was outed, by its prominent part in the 1993 film *Sleepless in Seattle*, as one of the definitive chicks'-night-in flicks, ideally viewed with abundant chocolate and a box of tissues at hand. The film—a remake of his own 1939 comedy-drama starring Irene Dunne and Charles Boyer, *Love Affair*—reflects two competing sides of producer/writer/director Leo McCarey. In his prime, the comedy mastermind teamed Laurel with Hardy, directed the Marx Brothers in *Duck Soup*, and won his first Oscar directing Grant in the 1930s screwball classic *The Awful Truth*. But McCarey also had a shameless sentimentality that oozed in his 40s favorite *Going My Way* (for which he won Academy Awards for Best Picture, Director, and Writer).

Grant's witty playboy Nickie Ferrante, a failed artist, and Kerr's wary nightclub singer Terry McKay (her vocals dubbed by premiere studio singer Marnie Nixon, who also voiced Kerr in *The King and I*) meet aboard a luxury liner and surrender—amid much worldly good humor—to their attraction. Unfortunately, both are encumbered with fiancés and pasts. They make a romantic pact. In six months, if they have turned their lives around they will meet atop the Empire State Building and live happily ever after. In due course, the reformed Grant puts his paintbrushes away and happily paces the skyscraper's observation deck, but Kerr, running excitedly to him, is hit by a car.

What follows is almost inconceivable to the mobile phone generation but, believing he's been stood up, Grant succumbs to embittered cynicism, unaware Kerr is bravely coming to terms with paralysis, too proud to let him know her situation. Comedy is abandoned in the hanky-wringing second half of the film, as the audience is kept in a deliciously protracted will-they-or-won't-they agony. McCarey overdoes it with songs, but even Kerr coaching a choir of overly cute urchins can't spoil the reunion, revelation, big-clinch climax. **AE**

# SMULTRONSTÄLLET (1957)
## WILD STRAWBERRIES

Arguably the warmest of Ingmar Bergman's masterpieces, *Wild Strawberries* charts the geographical and spiritual odyssey traveled by the elderly Professor Isak Borg—his name in Swedish more or less means "icy fortress"— (played by Victor Sjöström). Borg drives, in the company of his daughter-in-law Marianne (Ingrid Thulin), from Stockholm to the University of Lund to receive an honorary degree. En route he gives a ride to three young hitchhikers—including the vivacious Sara (Bibi Andersson), who in name and nature reminds him of the love of his life—and a middle-aged couple. He visits his now-ancient mother, before finally trying to have a heart-to-heart talk with his son Evald (Gunnar Björnstrand), a cynical misanthrope whom Marianne has been planning to leave. The conversation Borg has with Evald is crucial, not only because it might save his son's marriage but because it shows that the professor's journey has brought him a degree of self-knowledge. He has become properly aware not only of his mortality but of his own emotional reticence—inherited from his parents, consolidated by life's disappointments and his immersion in work. He has almost unwittingly passed it on, like a virus, to Evald.

The strength of Bergman's account of this day in the life—or, rather, a life in the day, the long day's journey bringing back all manner of telling memories—is the assured manner in which he combines the objective and subjective realities of Borg's life. The inner and external details progressively throw more light upon the man. It is not only his dreams and memories that illuminate our understanding of him (and his understanding of himself) but also his various encounters and conversations. Marianne, although tactful and affectionate, is comparatively explicit in alluding to Borg's failings. Sara reminds him of his more passionate youth. The arguing couple call to mind both his own grouchiness and the future Marianne may face with Evald.

Borg's redemptive acquisition of self-knowledge affects those around him too, and the miracle of *Wild Strawberries* is that Bergman never inflects this conclusion with sentimentality. Blessed with a radiant yet courageously uningratiating performance from Sjöström—himself Sweden's greatest filmmaker before Bergman—in this remarkable, much-imitated film, *Wild Strawberries* has an emotional honesty entirely in keeping with the voyage undergone by its protagonist. **GA**

**Sweden** (Svensk) 91m BW

**Language:** Swedish / Latin

**Director:** Ingmar Bergman

**Producer:** Allan Ekelund

**Screenplay:** Ingmar Bergman

**Photography:** Gunnar Fischer

**Music:** Erik Nordgren

**Cast:** Victor Sjöström, Bibi Andersson, Ingrid Thulin, Gunnar Björnstrand, Jullan Kindahl, Folke Sundquist, Björn Bjelfvenstam, Naima Wifstrand, Gunnel Broström, Gertrud Fridh, Sif Ruud, Gunnar Sjöberg, Max von Sydow, Åke Fridell, Yngve Nordwall

**Oscar nomination:** Ingmar Bergman (screenplay)

**Berlin International Film Festival:** Victor Sjöström (FIPRESCI award), Ingmar Bergman (Golden Bear)

**Venice Film Festival:** Ingmar Bergman (Italian film critics award)

**Italy / France** (De Laurentiis, Marceau) 110m BW

**Language:** Italian

**Director:** Federico Fellini

**Screenplay:** Federico Fellini, Ennio Flaiano, Tullio Pinelli, Pier Paolo Pasolini

**Cast:** Giulietta Masina, François Périer, Amedeo Nazzari, Aldo Silvani, Franca Marzi, Dorian Gray, Mario Passante, Pina Gualandri, Polidor, Ennio Girolami, Christian Tassou, Jean Mollier, Riccardo Fellini, María Luisa Rolando, Amedeo Girardi

**Oscar:** Italy (best foreign language film)

**Cannes Film Festival:** Giulietta Masina (best actress), Federico Fellini (OCIC award—special mention)

# LE NOTTI DI CABIRIA (1957)
## THE NIGHTS OF CABIRIA

The Cabiria of the title in Federico Fellini's 1957 classic is played by the filmmaker's wife, Giulietta Masina, who justifiably won the best actress award at Cannes for her portrayal of a naïve prostitute. Shamed by her profession, the feisty Cabiria hopelessly searches for a wealthy sugar daddy to take her away, but deep down what she's actually looking for is lasting love.

After its premiere, a controversial segment involving a good Samaritan with a sack full of good will was excised following the protest of the Catholic Church. Apparently spontaneous generosity is a provincial trait, but fortunately the footage was eventually returned. Indeed, the issue of goodness is paramount in Fellini's film, where beneath a worldly facade Cabiria just wishes to be happy, like anybody else. Yet Cabiria is the ultimate hooker with a heart of gold, never so glum that a good mambo or a street fair can't raise her spirits.

Cabiria can't help but to spread her kindness, but it often sets her up for disappointment or, even worse, humiliation. A chance encounter with a carnival hypnotist (Aldo Silvani) who draws out her inner desires is quite moving but particularly cruel, as it underlines the prospect that her dreams and fantasies of a better life may actually come true. Her openness even leads an onlooker to exploit her emotional weakness. The equally cruel attentions of a philandering movie star (Alberto Lazzari) also set her up with false hopes, even if Cabiria is ultimately (and literally) treated no better than a dog.

Cabiria's dreams never do come true, and in fact frequently result in casual violence as predators prey on her plucky innocence. Still, Fellini doesn't exploit Cabiria's story for easy sympathy. She's a strong, proud woman who gets into fights, responding to every setback by picking herself up, brushing herself off, and starting her march to a new, better life all over again. *The Nights of Cabiria* is, like Fellini's *La Dolce Vita* (1960), told from the perspective of the underclass, a glimpse at the proverbial other half gilded with optimistic joy but ultimately steeped in sadness. **JKI**

# KUMONOSU JO (1957)
## THRONE OF BLOOD

Quite rightly, Akira Kurosawa's artfully chilling, formal, and extremely close adaptation of *Macbeth* is widely regarded as one of the most breathtaking screen versions of Shakespeare's play. The plot and psychology translate beautifully to feudal Japan, where valorous samurai warrior General Washizu (Toshiro Mifune) and his fiendish wife Lady Asaji (Isuzu Yamada), driven by ruthless ambition and inspired by a witch's prophecy, murder their warlord, seize a kingdom, and damn themselves to an inescapable, ritual finality of bloodshed, paranoia, madness, and ruin.

The wonderful Mifune—Kurosawa's favorite leading man in a long-running collaboration (more than sixteen films) as notable as that of Martin Scorsese's with Robert De Niro—furthered his reputation as Japan's preeminent international star with this performance, and his brilliantly staged death scene, transfixed in a hail of arrows, is one of the great iconic images of world cinema. Elements of Noh theater, traditional Japanese battle art, historical realism, and contemporary thinking on the nature of good and evil are fused here in a confined, mist-shrouded world of sinister and magical portents in forest and castle (set in locations high up Mount Fuji, where the castle was built with the brawny assistance of a U.S. Marine battalion stationed nearby). **AE**

**Japan** (Toho) 105m BW

**Language:** Japanese

**Director:** Akira Kurosawa

**Producer:** Akira Kurosawa, Sojiro Motoki

**Screenplay:** Shinobu Hashimoto, Ryuzo Kikushima, Akira Kurosawa, Hideo Oguni, from the play *Macbeth* by William Shakespeare

**Photography:** Asakazu Nakai

**Music:** Masaru Satô

**Cast:** Toshirô Mifune, Isuzu Yamada, Takashi Shimura, Akira Kubo, Hiroshi Tachikawa, Minoru Chiaki, Takamaru Sasaki, Kokuten Kodo, Kichijiro Ueda, Eiko Miyoshi, Chieko Naniwa, Nakajiro Tomita, Yu Fujiki, Sachio Sakai, Shin Otomo

**Venice Film Festival:** Akira Kurosawa nomination (Golden Lion)

# THE INCREDIBLE SHRINKING MAN (1957)

Exposed to a mysterious, probably radioactive cloud while on a cruise, Scott Carey (Grant Williams) finds himself gradually shrinking. Director Jack Arnold's visual flatness is perfectly suited to the absurdity and ambiguity of the premise of Richard Matheson's story. The first half of *The Incredible Shrinking Man*—portraying the hero's predicament as alternately a medical, a domestic, and a socioeconomic problem—is a worthy companion piece to Nicholas Ray's *Bigger Than Life* (1956) and Douglas Sirk's *Written on the Wind* (1956), in its ironic and terrifying depiction of American middle-class life turned inside out. But it's in the second half of the film— Scott, now smaller than the heel of a shoe, is marooned in his basement and must cope with various natural threats—that *The Incredible Shrinking Man* really takes off, becoming a gripping and poetic science-fiction adventure. The inspirational conclusion—"to God, there is no zero"—is a rare example of popular cinema explicitly dealing with metaphysics.

Much of the force of the film comes from its psychological incisiveness and from its vivid and precise use of objects—its architecture of stairs, crates, matchboxes, and paint cans. For Matheson and Arnold, Scott Carey is an atomic-age Everyman: his adventure is an object lesson in the hostility of the built-up environment and in the indestructible propensity of humankind to make itself the measure of all things. **CFu**

**U.S.** (Universal) 81m BW

**Director:** Jack Arnold

**Producer:** Albert Zugsmith

**Screenplay:** Richard Matheson, Richard Alan Simmons, from the novel *The Shrinking Man* by Richard Matheson

**Photography:** Ellis W. Carter

**Music:** Foster Carling, Earl E. Lawrence

**Cast:** Grant Williams, Randy Stuart, April Kent, Paul Langton, Raymond Bailey, William Schallert, Frank J. Scannell, Helene Marshall, Diana Darrin, Billy Curtis

**India** (Epic) 127m BW
**Language:** Bengali
**Director:** Satyajit Ray
**Producer:** Satyajit Ray
**Screenplay:** Satyajit Ray, from novel by Bibhutibhushan Bandyopadhyay
**Photography:** Subrata Mitra
**Music:** Ravi Shankar
**Cast:** Kanu Bannerjee, Karuna Bannerjee, Pinaki Sengupta, Smaran Ghosal, Santi Gupta, Ramani Sengupta, Ranibala, Sudipta Roy, Ajay Mitra, Charuprakash Ghosh, Subodh Ganguli, Mani Srimani, Hemanta Chatterjee, Kali Bannerjee, Kalicharan Roy
**Venice Film Festival:** Satyajit Ray (Golden Lion)

# APARAJITO (1957)
## THE UNVANQUISHED

*Aparajito* is the second film in Satjyajit Ray's great *Apu* trilogy. Following the death of his sister in *Pather Panchali*, the young Apu (Pinaki Sengupta) and his parents have moved to Benares. While his father Harihar (Kanu Bannerjee) earns his priestly living on the banks of the Ganges, the boy roams the city, fascinated and delighted by the rich ferment of sights and sounds it affords. But Harihar contracts a fever and dies, and Apu's mother Sarbojaya (Karuna Bannerjee), unable to survive on her own, takes her son back to the country to her father-in-law's household. Apu, having tasted the great wide world, is no longer satisfied with the simple village life he grew up with, and the local schoolmaster encourages the lad in his ambition and curiosity. At sixteen he wins a scholarship to study in Calcutta. Caught up in the excitement of the teeming city, Apu (now played by Smaran Ghosal) returns home rarely and reluctantly. Sarbojaya, lonely and desperately sick, refuses to appeal to her son's sympathy for fear of hampering his education. Finally a letter from Apu's uncle brings him home—a day too late. After the funeral, refusing to follow his father into the priesthood, he leaves again for Calcutta.

As befits its midway status, *Aparajito* forms the essential bridge in Ray's trilogy. It opens up the timeless, self-contained life of *Pather Panchali*'s Bengali village to the disruptive influence of the city, showing Ray's young hero torn between the two worlds, gradually and inevitably growing away from his parents. As always, Ray doesn't load the dice in favor of one character or another. We can understand why Apu feels compelled to seek the wider world; we share his delight in learning, his sense of personal achievement. At the same time, however, we see Sarbojaya's pain; she's lost her daughter to an early death, now she's losing her son. In the film's most poignant moment Sarbojaya, near death, waits at night for the train that she hopes will bring Apu back to her one last time. In the distance a train arrives; she stumbles eagerly to her feet, gazing into the darkness. Nothing—only silence and the dance of the fireflies. **PK**

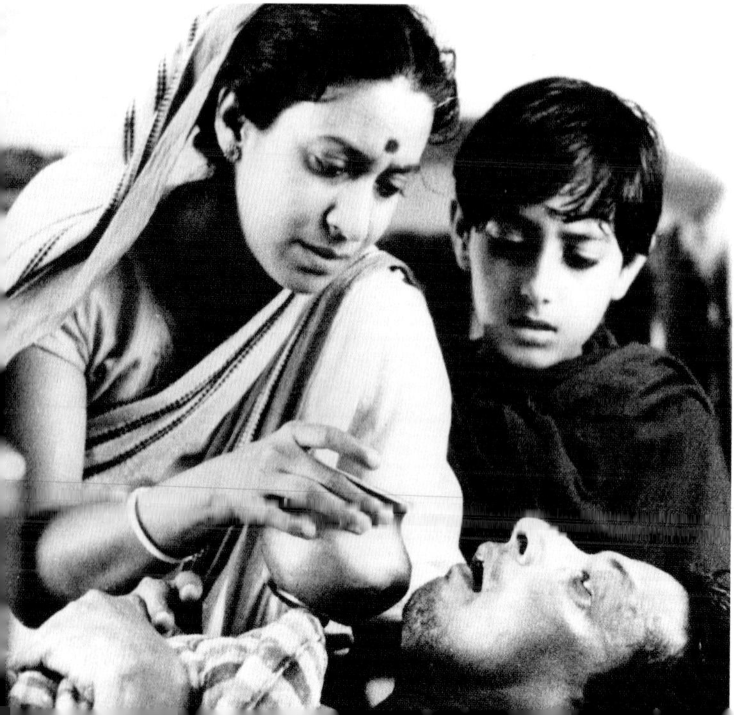

## GUNFIGHT AT THE OK CORRAL (1957)

**U.S.** (Paramount) 122m Technicolor
**Director:** John Sturges
**Producer:** Joseph H. Hazen, Paul Nathan, Hal B. Wallis
**Screenplay:** George Scullin, Leon Uris, from the article *The Killer* by George Scullin
**Photography:** Charles Lang
**Music:** Dimitri Tiomkin
**Cast:** Burt Lancaster, Kirk Douglas, Rhonda Fleming, Jo Van Fleet, John Ireland, Lyle Bettger, Frank Faylen, Earl Holliman, Ted de Corsia, Dennis Hopper, Whit Bissell, George Mathews, John Hudson, DeForest Kelley, Martin Milner
**Oscar nomination:** Warren Low (editing), George Dutton (sound)

John Sturges's staging of the famous battle between Wyatt Earp and the Clanton gang in Tombstone, Arizona on October 26, 1881, was not the first film version. But Sturges's film is a little more accurate than John Ford's *My Darling Clementine* (1946). Ford, for example, has Earp's associate Doc Holliday killed in the battle; in fact he survived six more years. *Gunfight at the OK Corral* is a slick production, technically excellent and with a big budget, and it benefits from a fine cast. Burt Lancaster is full of authority as Earp, at times chilling in his determination. By contrast, Kirk Douglas has great fun with the consumptive Holliday, flashing a ready smile but deadly as a snake. There is also strong support from Jo Van Fleet as "Big Nose" Kate, Doc's put-upon woman, and John Ireland as gunslinger Johnny Ringo.

The melodious score, by Dimitri Tiomkin, who also did the music for other town-taming Westerns such as *High Noon* and *Rio Bravo*, made a considerable contribution, and Frankie Laine's theme song was a big hit. However, those wanting a more realistically down-beat treatment of the Wyatt Earp story should watch Sturges's 1967 sequel, *Hour of the Gun*, in which the incident at the OK Corral is just the start. **EB**

## THE BRIDGE ON THE RIVER KWAI (1957)

**G.B.** (Columbia, Horizon) 161m Technicolor
**Language:** English / Japanese / Thai
**Director:** David Lean
**Producer:** Sam Spiegel
**Screenplay:** Carl Foreman, Michael Wilson, from the novel *Le pont de la rivière Kwai* by Pierre Boulle
**Photography:** Jack Hildyard
**Music:** Malcolm Arnold
**Cast:** William Holden, Alec Guinness, Jack Hawkins, Sessue Hayakawa, James Donald, Geoffrey Horne, André Morell, Peter Williams, John Boxer, Percy Herbert, Harold Goodwin, Ann Sears, Heihachiro Okawa, Keiichiro Katsumoto, M.R.B. Chakrabandhu
**Oscar:** Sam Spiegel (best picture), David Lean (director), Pierre Boulle, Carl Foreman, Michael Wilson (screenplay)*, Alec Guinness (actor), Jack Hildyard (photography), Peter Taylor (editing), Malcolm Arnold (music) * Blacklisted writers Carl Foreman and Michael Wilson posthumously awarded Oscars in 1984
**Oscar nomination:** Sessue Hayakawa (actor in support role)

There may be no honor among thieves, but wartime enemies are a different matter. At least that's the belief of Alec Guinness's Colonel Nicholson in *The Bridge on the River Kwai*, who insists that the Japanese overseers of their sweltering Burmese prison camp treat his men and him with decency. But as this consummate commander and paragon of English pragmatism organizes the construction of an enemy railroad bridge, a team of Americans led by escaped POW Major Shears (William Holden) is on its way to blow it to bits.

Director David Lean plays the looming conflict for maximum irony, setting Guinness up as the tragic counterpart to Holden's unsentimental Yank. As usual, Lean loads his film with tons of details, filling the widescreen image with elaborate action and immaculately constructed sets. But holding this epic World War II film together are the performances of its three iconic leads, the stiff and traditional Guinness, the loose and cynical Holden, and Sessue Hayakawa as the Japanese colonel unknowingly stuck in the middle of a battle of cross-Atlantic wills. Where the final scenes of destruction are justly lauded for their stunt work, choreography, and editing, one of the most memorable elements of *Kwai* remains Malcolm Arnold's whimsical, whistled "The Colonel Bogey March." **JKl**

## BHARAT MATA (1957)
### MOTHER INDIA

**India** (Mehboob ) 172m Technicolor
**Language:** Hindi
**Director:** Mehboob Khan
**Producer:** Mehboob Khan
**Screenplay:** Mehboob Khan, Wajahat Mirza, S. Ali Raza
**Photography:** Faredoon A. Irani
**Music:** Naushad
**Cast:** Nargis, Sunil Dutt, Raaj Kumar, Rajendra Kumar, Kanhaiyalal, Kumkum, Master Sajid, Sitara Devi, Mukri, Sajid Khan, Azra, Chanchal, Kanan Kaushal, Sheela Naik
**Oscar nomination:** India (best foreign language film)

Mehboob Khan's *Mother India* remains the quintessential Indian film even almost fifty years after its release. The picture depicts the struggle of a woman, Radha (Nargis), to reconcile traditional values and village life with a promised modern utopia. An international success with audiences across much of Asia and Africa—who regarded India as a role model in the struggle for decolonization. *Mother India* also gained recognition in Europe and America as one of the few Indian films ever nominated for an Oscar.

Mehboob Khan, one of the first directors in India to use color to great effect, had worked on an epic scale in his historical films, and he brought these skills to bear in this study of village life, in the process forging a national epic, a new story for a new nation. *Mother India* has a powerful storyline, following the heroine from marriage to old age, and is dense in mythological references, as characters' names associate them with key figures in the Hindu pantheon.

The film features the top stars of its day, notably Nargis, Raj Kumar, and Sunil Dutt. A frisson occurred when Nargis, who had been romantically linked to the legendary Raj Kapoor, married Sunil Dutt after the film's completion, not least because he played her son on screen. *Mother India*'s perennially popular music is by Naushad Ali, a blend of folk tunes and classical ragas (melodies) orchestrated in a Western style with the hundred-piece orchestra, a byword of Hindi film style, which Ali is said to have introduced. *Mother India* also has spectacular visuals; its shots of the heroine dragging a plow like a beast of burden, and the happy faces of Radha with her sons after the harvest, looking out to a bright future in the style of Soviet realism, have become iconic.

The complexities of *Mother India* and the host of different readings it has generated make this film one of the few that can still draw audiences to the theater whenever it is screened. It is the first Indian movie to which anyone with an interest in world cinema should turn. **RDw**

# LETJAT ZHURAVLI (1957)
## THE CRANES ARE FLYING

**U.S.S.R.** (Mosfilm) 97m BW
**Language:** Russian
**Director:** Mikheil Kalatozishvili
**Producer:** Mikheil Kalatozishvili
**Screenplay:** Viktor Rozov, from his play *Letjat zhuravli*
**Photography:** Sergei Urusevsky
**Music:** Moisej Vajnberg
**Cast:** Tatyana Samojlova, Aleksei Batalov, Vasili Merkuryev, Aleksandr Shvorin, Svetlana Kharitonova, Konstantin Nikitin, Valentin Zubkov, Antonina Bogdanova, Boris Kokovkin, Yekaterina Kupriyanova
**Cannes Film Festival:** Mikheil Kalatozishvili (Golden Palm), Tatyana Samojlova (special mention)

In the last years of Stalin and Stalinism, Soviet cinema practically disappeared. The continuing economic devastation wrought by the war, as well as the pervasive fear that defined everyday life, caused the once-thriving Soviet studios to practically close shop. After Stalin's death in 1953, a reborn Soviet cinema slowly began to emerge, and the film which came to symbolize that rebirth was Mikhail Kalatozov's *The Cranes Are Flying*. Ostensibly a wartime romance about lovers, Boris (Aleksei Batalov) and Veronika (Tatiana Samoilova), who are separated soon after the start of the conflict, the film boldly defied just about every cliché of the genre. Rather than celebrating the glorious victories of the Red Army, *Cranes* focuses on some of the war's darkest moments, when the highly efficient and terrifying German war machine was easily routing the poorly organized and equipped (if heroic) Russian army.

On the home front there is little but despair and a sense that one has to look out for number one. Admirably, Soviet audiences heartily embraced this reflection of their wartime experiences; tired perhaps of propaganda, they knew only too well that the war had in truth produced few heroes of any sort. As the young lovers, Batalov and Samoilova are wonderfully affecting, sexy, and endearing, yet the true star of the film is cinematographer Sergei Urusevsky's voluptuous camera work. With his breathtaking crane shots, sweeping pans, and vibrant handheld work, Urusevsky (who had worked with Dovzhenko on the brilliant wartime documentary *The Battle for the Soviet Ukraine*) makes the sense of a world that has lost its moorings or even any fixed point of reference—moral, political, or otherwise—practically tangible. Urusevsky would go on to make with Kalatozov the infamous if much admired *I Am Cuba* (1964), yet although that film for some seems eventually overwhelmed by its baroque stylization, *Cranes* never indulges in visual effects for their own sake. *Cranes* also became the first Cold War-era Soviet film to receive wide distribution (by Warner Brothers) in the United States. **RP**

U.S. (Bryna, Harris-Kubrick) 87m BW

**Language:** English / German

**Director:** Stanley Kubrick

**Producer:** Kirk Douglas, James B. Harris, Stanley Kubrick

**Screenplay:** Stanley Kubrick, Calder Willingham, Jim Thompson, from novel by Humphrey Cobb

**Photography:** Georg Krause

**Music:** Gerald Fried

**Cast:** Kirk Douglas, Ralph Meeker, Adolphe Menjou, George Macready, Wayne Morris, Richard Anderson, Joe Turkel, Christiane Kubrick, Jerry Hausner, Peter Capell, Emile Meyer, Bert Freed, Kem Dibbs, Timothy Carey, Fred Bell

# PATHS OF GLORY (1957)

Stanley Kubrick kept returning to the theme of war. Humphrey Cobb's novel, about an actual, dreadful incident which took place in the French army in World War I, was adapted (by Kubrick, Jim Thompson, and Calder Willingham) into a powerful film—one that is all the more effective for the director's matter-of-fact coolness in dealing with the unthinkably horrible.

A pair of ruthless but inept generals (Adolphe Menjou, George Macready) order their men to hurl themselves suicidally at the German positions; when a few survivors limp back after being practically wiped out, the regiment is accused of cowardice, and a randomly selected trio of foot soldiers are put on trial. Committed Colonel Dax (Kirk Douglas) mounts a defense, but politics decree that the three humble, innocent soldiers—absolutely the bravest imaginable—go to the wall. Grim, intelligent, and wonderfully acted, this is the best type of war movie: It makes its audience angry. It also climaxes, after the executions, with the most emotional scene Kubrick ever directed, in which a roomful of jeering soldiers force a captured German girl (Susanne Christian, later Christiane Kubrick) to entertain them by singing a song, only to be moved to silence by her awkward, sincere, melancholy performance. **KN**

U.S. (Hecht, Hill & Lancaster, Norma-Curtleigh) 96m BW

**Director:** Alexander Mackendrick

**Producer:** Tony Curtis, Harold Hecht, James Hill, Burt Lancaster

**Screenplay:** Clifford Odets, Ernest Lehman, Alexander Mackendrick, from novella by Ernest Lehman

**Photography:** James Wong Howe

**Music:** Elmer Bernstein

**Cast:** Burt Lancaster, Tony Curtis, Susan Harrison, Martin Milner, Sam Levene, Barbara Nichols, Jeff Donnell, Sally, Joe Frisco, Emile Meyer, Edith Atwater, Chico Hamilton

# SWEET SMELL OF SUCCESS (1957)

A wonderfully bitter satire on the celebrity biz, with smarmy press agent Sidney Falco (Tony Curtis) toadying to monstrous newspaper columnist J.J. Hunsecker (Burt Lancaster), but clearly on the road to wrecking his own life through his devotion to getting ahead. *Sweet Smell of Success* has a great smoky jazz score from Chico Hamilton and reeks of New York *circa* 1957, taking us through the buzzing night spots where the desperate pay court to the demented and souls are sold for column inches, to the rainswept streets where brutally crooked cops plant dope on jazz musicians or beat J.J.'s enemies half to death.

Director Alexander Mackendrick more than makes the transfer from Ealing comedy whimsy to ferocious frenzy, picking up on the cynical, observational attitude of Ernest Lehmann's hardboiled newsprint script and adding gothic shadows. The monumental Lancaster, lit like the Frankenstein Monster, is amazingly hateful ("match me, Sidney"), and Curtis does his best screen work as the quivering minion, eating himself up from the inside as he tries to do J.J. a favor—one that rebounds dreadfully by breaking up the romance between a square-john jazzman (Marty Milner) and the fragile little sister (the sadly unprolific Susan Harrison) that J.J. is smothering with a palpably incestuous love. **KN**

# MAN OF THE WEST (1958)

**U.S.** (Ashton) 100m Color
**Director:** Anthony Mann
**Producer:** Walter Mirisch
**Screenplay:** Reginald Rose, from the novel *The Border Jumpers* by Will C. Brown
**Photography:** Ernest Haller
**Music:** Leigh Harline
**Cast:** Gary Cooper, Julie London, Lee J. Cobb, Arthur O'Connell, Jack Lord, John Dehner, Royal Dano, Robert J. Wilke

After making a series of exemplary Westerns starring James Stewart during the 1950s, Anthony Mann cast an aging Gary Cooper as a man forced to confront a past which he thought he had left behind him. As is usual in Mann's Westerns, personal history exerts a grip on the characters that only death can loosen. Cooper plays Link Jones, an apparently respectable citizen on his way to hire a schoolteacher for his town. After the train he's traveling on is robbed, Link finds himself marooned in the middle of nowhere with a saloon girl named Billie (Julie London), and in desperation he decides to seek help from some former associates nearby. But Link is revealed to have a criminal past, and his one-time friends are a gang of menacing grotesques, played by Western stalwarts Royal Dano, Robert Wilke, and John Dehner. It soon becomes evident that there are scores to be settled, and the gang tries to force Link to help them with a robbery, threatening Billie with rape. Their behavior in turn calls up a murderous rage in the hitherto mild-mannered Link, who hands out a brutal beating to one of the gang.

The leader of the gang is Dock Tobin (a barn-storming performance by Lee J. Cobb). In Mann's Westerns, family ties always prove stronger than any sense of the wider community, and Tobin's gang functions as a monstrous parody of kith and kin. Dock indeed regards Link as a surrogate son. In the final confrontation, beautifully staged by Mann in an old ghost town, Dock, having finally raped Billie as a direct provocation, incites Link into what amounts to an act of parricide. In finally laying to rest the threat of his menacing "father," however, Link reveals in himself a savage violence only barely under control.

Unusually for a Mann Western, a lot of the action takes place in dark and gloomy interiors, as the tensions between Link and the gang play out. But Mann's camerawork is as assured as ever. Make sure you see this film in the full CinemaScope ratio! **EB**

**U.S.** (Universal) 95m BW

**Director:** Orson Welles

**Producer:** Albert Zugsmith

**Screenplay:** Orson Welles, from the novel *Badge of Evil* by Whit Masterson

**Photography:** Russell Metty

**Music:** Henry Mancini

**Cast:** Charlton Heston, Janet Leigh, Orson Welles, Joseph Calleia, Akim Tamiroff, Joanna Cook Moore, Ray Collins, Dennis Weaver, Valentin de Vargas, Mort Mills, Victor Millan, Lalo Rios, Risto, Michael Sargent, Phil Harvey, Joi Lansing

# TOUCH OF EVIL (1958)

"He was some kind of a man." For decades, filmmakers have paid homage to Orson Welles's potent 1950s noir *Touch of Evil*. It's a lurid tale of corruption and conscience, played out in the strip joints and motels of a sleazy border town, with honorable Mexican narcotics official Charlton Heston and degenerate American cop Welles at odds over a murder whose jurisdiction is in dispute while Janet Leigh becomes a terrorized pawn in their battle of wills.

Heston strong-armed Universal into hiring Hollywood pariah Welles to direct as well as play the role of Hank Quinlan. Welles immediately threw away the script and wrote his own free adaptation of Whit Masterson's pulp novel *Badge of Evil*, transforming a cheap little thriller into great art. Steeped in sinister atmosphere, the film is still celebrated for its remarkable single tracking-shot opening, a dazzling three minutes in which the camera crane swoops through the busy night scene as Miguel "Mike" Vargas (Heston) and his pert blonde American bride Susan (Leigh) stroll across into the United States for an ice-cream soda. An unidentifiable man plants a bomb in a convertible, pedestrians scurry around, the driver's floozy companion complains she's "got this ticking noise in my head," the newlyweds and a border patrol guard exchange enough small talk to establish their back story, and ka-boom, the honeymoon is over.

Police chief Quinlan arrives from the American side of the border to control the investigation while Susan is waylaid by the Mexican drug dealers Vargas has been working to shut down. Within minutes the cards have been dealt in a malevolent, deeply perverse game. To prevent Vargas from exposing him as a criminal, Quinlan will have Susan abducted and drugged (by Mercedes McCambridge's lesbian in leather and her reefer-maddened thugs). Quinlan is one of the giant noir psychopaths, a bloated figure whose abuse of power has turned him into a monster (the already hefty Welles expanded with padding and false nose), momentarily unrecognized by Marlene Dietrich's enigmatic whore as her one-time intimate. Heston as a Mexican seems a preposterous idea, but his performance is interesting, his confidence in a sophisticated role sufficient to prevent the satiric Welles from crushing him. But the most affecting character is the tragic, belatedly ennobled figure of Quinlan's adoring lackey, Pete Menzies (Joseph Calleia).

Rivaling the opening are a series of bold, complex set pieces that have given *Touch of Evil* its reputation as film noir's epitaph, Welles theatrically exaggerating stylistic elements while achieving a hyperrealism with Russell Means's sharp black-and-white cinematography and Henry Mancini's Latino/jazz/rock-'n'-roll score. The end chase is a delirium of flamboyant visuals, experimental sound effects, and pervasive doom.

Welles disliked Universal's editing, and in 1998 a restoration meticulously made from his notes was released. A few minutes longer, its most satisfying alterations are the removal of credits over the famous opening sequence and more intricate cutting between Susan's motel ordeal and Vargas's disturbing journey with Quinlan. Whether the Before or After version, *Touch of Evil* endures as a superbly kinky masterpiece of technique, imagination, and audacity. **AE**

**Egypt** (Gabriel Talhami) 95m BW
**Language:** Arabic
**Director:** Youssef Chahine
**Producer:** Gabriel Talhami
**Screenplay:** Mohamed Abu Youssef, Abdel Hay Adib
**Photography:** Alevise Orfanelli
**Music:** Fouad El-Zahry
**Cast:** Farid Shawqi, Hind Rostom, Youssef Chahine, Hassan el Baroudi, Abdel Aziz Khalil, Naima Wasfy, Said Khalil, Abdel Ghani Nagdi, Loutfi El Hakim, Abdel Hamid Bodaoha, F. El Demerdache, Said El Araby, Ahmed Abaza, Hana Abdel Fattah, Safia Sarwat

# BAB EL HADID (1958)
## CAIRO STATION

First, there was nothing. This view was wrong and stupid, of course, as there were plenty of films being made in Egypt, in Arab countries, in Africa; plenty of stories being told, images being composed. But none of these stories, images, or films were being seen outside their places of origin—they were hardly known. Then there was an anticolonialist surge, an awakening of the nations of the South, Nasser, Suez, and—at the same moment—the arrival of singing comedies and sugary dramas, with (more or less) veiled and rather carnal beauties, young men with burning eyes and voices. These films were nice, exotic, sometimes quite remarkably made—if you ever got a chance to see one, you could appreciate it with some condescension.

Then came *Cairo Station*. And it was as if cinema having reached adolescence is suddenly thrust back into infancy in a hitherto unknown part of its world. This new cinema had learned from Hollywood and Italian neorealism to build a form of its own. It is filled with humor, wisdom, and anguish; pays attention to the minute details of everyday life of the city; portrays the primal powers of lust and desire; and delves into classical and oriental iconography—all presented in a mix of fantasy and reality. *Cairo Station* is vivid and moving, precise in its portrayals, original both as the creation of a single individual and as the embodiment of a secular culture, one that is so close and yet so different to that of the West.

And who is responsible for it? Youssef Chahine, a "crazy" little guy filled with longing and despair. Bringing disturbing revelations about himself and life to the screen, he plays a crippled newspaper vendor named Kenaoui who bears an unrequited desire for a voluptuous lemonade seller (Hind Rostom). Although the plot components are simple enough, the world depicted here is both dangerous and complex. The way events turn out opens up dark abysses in the city's life, made the more unexpected by the initial friendly codes the film uses. Panned by Egyptian viewers upon its initial release, *Cairo Station* has justly been hailed as a masterpiece on its rediscovery some two decades later. **J-MF**

## GIGI (1958)

Finally breaking the record number of Academy Awards won by *Gone with the Wind*, Vincente Minnelli's scrumptious MGM musical took home nine Oscars, including Best Picture and Director. Based on Colette's short story of a petite Parisienne groomed by her grandmother and great aunt to be a courtesan in the family tradition, *Gigi* was created for the screen with a witty songbook commissioned from Alan Jay Lerner and Frederick Loewe. Favorites include "Thank Heaven for Little Girls" and "I'm Glad I'm Not Young Anymore" (both sung by the ultimate boulevardier, Maurice Chevalier, in a career rebirth), and the droll Chevalier–Hermione Gingold duet shakily recollecting a long-ago liaison, "I Remember it Well."

Leslie Caron is a perfect delight as the coltish child, suffering lessons in etiquette, coquetry, seduction, and gem valuation before her sudden, inevitable transformation into a poised and desirable young woman. Louis Jordan is just divine as the bored man-about-town tunefully perplexed by the depth of his feelings for her. Fin-de-siècle Paris never looked lovelier (authentic locations include the Bois de Boulogne, the Tuileries, and swank mecca Maxim's), and Cecil Beaton's costumes rival his work on Lerner and Loewe's *My Fair Lady*. *Gigi* is forever charming. **AE**

**U.S.** (MGM) 119m Metrocolor

**Director:** Vincente Minnelli

**Producer:** Arthur Freed

**Screenplay:** Alan Jay Lerner, Anita Loos, from novel by Colette

**Photography:** Joseph Ruttenberg

**Music:** Frederick Loewe

**Cast:** Leslie Caron, Maurice Chevalier, Louis Jourdan, Hermione Gingold, Eva Gabor, Jacques Bergerac, Isabel Jeans, John Abbott

**Oscar:** Arthur Freed (best picture), Vincente Minnelli (director), Alan Jay Lerner (screenplay), William A. Horning, E. Preston Ames, Henry Grace, F. Keogh Gleason (art direction), Joseph Ruttenberg (photography), Cecil Beaton (costume), Adrienne Fazan (editing), André Previn (music), Frederick Loewe, Alan Jay Lerner (song)

## THE DEFIANT ONES (1958)

A self-avowed "message" picture, Stanley Kramer's *The Defiant Ones* deploys a potent symbol of American race relations: two convicts, one white and one black (Tony Curtis and Sidney Poitier), are chained together when the truck taking them to prison turns over. Both men harbor racist feelings, and at first they want only to separate—but, appropriately enough in this allegory of American history, they cannot. Their unavoidable closeness makes them reach beyond stereotypes and angry words to get to know each other as individuals.

A robbery to get food goes wrong, and the pair, much to the white man's chagrin, are pursued by a mob eager to lynch them both. Arriving at a farmhouse presided over by a lonely white woman, they finally get the means to break the chain. Yet they do not then go their own ways, even though the white woman tries to separate them. A final dash for freedom through a swamp and then onto a freight train fails, and the men are recaptured.

Fine acting from both Curtis and Poitier gives life and intellectual force to the narrative, which could easily have descended into ineffective melodrama. *The Defiant Ones* is perhaps the film that best captures the agenda of "realist" liberals in the 1950s, as American society attempted to come to terms with the fact of the African-American presence. **BP**

**U.S.** (Curtleigh, Lomitas) 97m BW

**Director:** Stanley Kramer

**Producer:** Stanley Kramer

**Screenplay:** Nedrick Young, Harold Jacob Smith

**Photography:** Sam Leavitt

**Music:** Ernest Gold

**Cast:** Tony Curtis, Sidney Poitier, Theodore Bikel, Charles McGraw, Lon Chaney Jr., King Donovan, Claude Akins, Lawrence Dobkin, Whit Bissell, Carl "Alfalfa" Switzer, Kevin Coughlin, Cara Williams

**Oscar:** Nedrick Young, Harold Jacob Smith (screenplay), Sam Leavitt (photography)

**Oscar nomination:** Stanley Kramer (best picture), Stanley Kramer (director), Tony Curtis (actor), Sidney Poitier (actor), Theodore Bikel (actor in support role), Cara Williams (actress in support role), Frederic Knudtson (editing)

**Berlin International Film Festival:** Sidney Poitier (Silver Bear)

**U.S.** (Alfred J. Hitchcock, Paramount) 128m Technicolor

**Director:** Alfred Hitchcock

**Producer:** Alfred Hitchcock

**Screenplay:** Samuel A. Taylor, Alec Coppel, from the novel *d'Entre les Morts* by Pierre Boileau and Thomas Narcejac

**Photography:** Robert Burks

**Music:** Bernard Herrmann

**Cast:** James Stewart, Kim Novak, Barbara Bel Geddes, Tom Helmore, Henry Jones, Raymond Bailey, Ellen Corby, Konstantin Shayne, Lee Patrick

**Oscar nomination:** Hal Pereira, Henry Bumstead, Sam Comer, Frank R. McKelvy (art direction), George Dutton (sound)

# VERTIGO (1958)

Though director Alfred Hitchcock was then at the height of his critical success and commercial fame, *Vertigo* was not a well-liked film at the time of its release. Most criticism focused on the [illegible] and unlikely plot dependent on a fiendishly implausible murder scheme on the part of a thinly characterized villain, whose exposure is about as much of a surprise as the ending of your average *Scooby-Doo* episode. The climax is so concerned with something else that the killer seems to get away with it—though Hitchcock shot an unnecessary tag, in the spirit of his TV narrations, to reveal that he was brought to justice. Closer to the mark, there was a genuine feeling of discomfort at the nasty little relationship between Jimmy Stewart and Kim Novak around which the film turns. But during a lengthy period in which *Vertigo* was unavailable for copyright reasons, the film was critically reassessed. Now it is held to be one of the Master's greatest works.

John "Scottie" Ferguson (Stewart) is a San Francisco cop who quits the force after a prologue in which his fear of heights prevents him saving the life of a colleague. Working casually as a private eye, he is hired by old friend Gavin Elster (Tom Elmore) to tail his wife Madeleine (Novak), an icy blonde in a severe suit who is apparently obsessed with a look-alike ancestress who drowned in the 19th century. The first half of the film is almost a ghost story, as Scottie is drawn to the neurotic Madeleine, with the suggestion that her reincarnation is ironically going to lead to her death. Here, you get the Hitchcock who was a master of atmosphere as well as suspense, and a genuine evocation of the unearthly. After Madeleine's fatal plunge from a bell tower, the film changes tack and becomes more intense, with Scottie going even further beyond Stewart's aw-shucks mannerisms into mania as he comes across Judy Barton (Novak again), a brassy, brunette shopgirl who resembles the lost Madeleine, and enters into a relationship with her. Few mainstream Hollywood movies dare to be as unsettling as *Vertigo* is in the scenes where Scottie tries to force a new reincarnation of his lost love by manipulating the new girl as she is transformed by a new hairstyle and wardrobe into the elusive Madeleine. For many, the scene in which Judy is finally transformed and embraces Scottie with a vampirish hunger is as emotionally devastating as the shower scene in *Psycho* is physically shocking.

Like several other Hitchcock greats (*Rear Window*, *North by Northwest*, *Psycho*), *Vertigo* has been endlessly imitated, homaged, and reworked. Movies like Brian De Palma's *Obsession* are feature-length footnotes to the original. Technical tricks—the simultaneous zoom-in and track-back used to convey Stewart's vertigo—have been added to the repertoire (Steven Spielberg used it in *Jaws*). Clips from the film have even been used to add mood to other movies (such as Terry Gilliam's *Twelve Monkeys*). In all, *Vertigo* is a gorgeous, disturbing, icily romantic film. With steel gray Technicolor images, evocative moments of close-up surrealism, and an insistent, probing Bernard Herrmann score. **KN**

# POPIÓL I DIAMENT (1958)
## ASHES AND DIAMONDS

For a few years at the end the 1950s, after Italian neorealism waned and before the French New Wave rolled in, Polish cinema was the art cinema. With their complex, often ambiguous tales of wartime solidarity, sacrifice, and commitment, the Poles offered the most cogent example yet of socialism with a human face. Films by Aleksandr Ford, Andrzej Munk, Jerzy Kawalerowicz, and others won a slew of festival prizes and attracted international audiences. Perhaps the finest of all the Polish films of this era, the one that came to stand for an emerging generation of East European artists and intellectuals, was Andrzej Wajda's *Ashes and Diamonds*.

Based on the controversial novel by Jerzy Andrzejewski, Wajda's masterpiece unspools on the last day of World War II. The enemy has surrendered, but the winners aren't sure what they've won: both Communists and Nationalists can already sense that their fragile wartime alliance is unraveling. Enter Maciek (Zbigniew Cybulski), a young hothead attached to the Nationalist underground in a provincial town; assigned to kill the recently arrived Communist district leader, he holes up in a hotel for the night. But this is just about the first night of peace that Maciek has known in his adult life, and he's eager to see what else life might offer. He meets and falls for a pretty young woman, and his attention to her threatens to get in the way of his mission.

Throughout *Ashes and Diamonds*, Wajda employs a looming deep focus, so that disparate characters as well as opposing political agendas take on equal weight in the frame. Yet the real show is Wajda's revelation of Polish actor Cybulski as Maciek. With his eyes perpetually hidden behind shades and his slightly gawky but endearing manner, Cybulski was hailed as the "James Dean of the East," the symbol for a generation that wanted to look past political labels to focus on an individual's human qualities. Within the space of a few shots, he can go from dementia to helplessness to anger; his final "death dance," with his chilling laughter as he staggers through a field after being fatally shot, is surely one of the most powerful—and often quoted—endings in film history. **RP**

**Poland** (Polski, ZRF) 105m BW
**Language:** Polish
**Director:** Andrzej Wajda
**Producer:** Stanislaw Adler
**Screenplay:** Jerzy Andrzejewski, Andrzej Wajda, from the novel *Popiól i diament* by Jerzy Andrzejewski
**Photography:** Jerzy Wójcik
**Music:** Jan Krenz, Filip Nowak
**Cast:** Zbigniew Cybulski, Ewa Krzyzewska, Waclaw Zastrzezynski, Adam Pawlikowski, Bogumil Kobiela, Jan Ciecierski, Stanislaw Milski, Artur Mlodnicki, Halina Kwiatkowska, Ignacy Machowski, Zbigniew Skowronski, Barbara Krafftówna, Aleksander Sewruk, Zofia Czerwinska, Wiktor Grotowicz
**Venice Film Festival:** Andrzej Wajda (FIPRESCI award)

# DRACULA (1958)

Hammer Films's revision of Bram Stoker's famous novel is one of the great horror films. Director Terence Fisher, who combines a cutter's eye for bold contrast with a delight in the logical unfolding of space, demonstrates a complete mastery of melodramatic modes. He's aided by Jack Asher's vibrant cinematography, James Bernard's unabashedly lurid and exciting score, and two career-defining performances: Peter Cushing's intellectual, refined, and athletic Van Helsing and Christopher Lee's icy, imperious, handsome Count.

Like Hammer's previous film *The Curse of Frankenstein*, *Dracula* came as quite a shock to its first viewers and reviewers, and as late as the early 1970s, Hammer's emphasis on the physical aspects of horror was generally recognized both as a turning point in genre history and as the trademark of a legendary production company. Even today, sensitive viewers can appreciate the boldness with which *Dracula* oversteps the boundaries defined by earlier cinematic horrors. This is seen most clearly in Dracula's feral eyes and fangs, the blood welling up from the hearts of staked vampire women, and the unmistakable sexuality of the relationship between the vampire and his victims. At one point, Dracula enters his victim's bedroom and shuts the door on the camera, positioned in the corridor. The tactful and expected approach would have been to end the scene there, but Fisher cuts directly inside the room, as Dracula backs the young woman toward her bed. The cut itself conveys inexorability, violation, and dread. **CFu**

**G.B.** (Hammer) 82m Technicolor

**Director:** Terence Fisher

**Producer:** Michael Carreras, Anthony Hinds, Anthony Nelson Keys

**Screenplay:** Jimmy Sangster, from novel by Bram Stoker

**Photography:** Jack Asher

**Music:** James Bernard

**Cast:** Peter Cushing, Christopher Lee, Michael Gough, Melissa Stribling, Carol Marsh, Olga Dickie, John Van Eyssen, Valerie Gaunt, Janina Faye, Barbara Archer, Charles Lloyd Pack, George Merritt, George Woodbridge, George Benson, Miles Malleson

# MON ONCLE (1958)
## MY UNCLE

In his first two features, *The Big Day* (1948) and *Mr. Hulot's Holiday* (1953), Jacques Tati lovingly celebrated the charms of the provincial, random, and dilapidated. In *My Uncle*, he directs his satire against the mania for mechanization that threatens those easygoing old ways of life.

Tati's perennial screen persona, the gangling, near-wordless Monsieur Hulot, lives in a rickety old *quartier* of Paris. Not far away live the Arpels, his sister and brother-in-law (Adrienne Servantie and Jean-Pierre Zola), in a trendily ultramodern house packed with gadgets. Inevitably, most of these gadgets malfunction—especially when the well-meaning Hulot is around.

As always with Tati, the humor is almost entirely visual—and aural. Few comedians have made such creative use of the soundtrack, and the clickings, buzzings, hissings, and sputterings of the Arpels's assorted gizmos and of the machinery in the factory where Arpel ill-advisedly gives his brother-in-law a job, often reach a pitch of controlled lunacy. Tati takes mischievous delight in showing how automation, supposedly designed to improve the quality of life, works against comfort, relaxation, and pleasure. But the human element, represented by the walking disaster area that is Hulot, can never be excluded. There is a melancholy undertow to *My Uncle*—pneumatic drills rattle ominously over the credits—but a wistful optimism too. **PK**

**France / Italy** (Alter, Centauro, Gray, Specta) 110m Eastmancolor

**Language:** French

**Director:** Jacques Tati

**Producer:** Louis Dolivet, Jacques Tati, Alain Terouanne

**Screenplay:** Jacques Lagrange, Jean L'Hôte, Jacques Tati

**Photography:** Jean Bourgoin

**Music:** Franck Barcellini, Alain Romans

**Cast:** Jean-Pierre Zola, Adrienne Servantie, Lucien Frégis, Betty Schneider, Jean-François Martial, Dominique Marie, Yvonne Arnaud, Adelaide Danieli, Alain Bécourt, Régis Fontenay, Claude Badolle, Max Martel, Nicolas Bataille, Jacques Tati

**Oscar:** France (best foreign language film)

**Cannes Film Festival:** Jacques Tati (special jury prize)

India (Aurora) 100 m BW

**Language:** Bengali

**Director:** Satyajit Ray

**Producer:** Satyajit Ray

**Screenplay:** Satyajit Ray, from novel by Tarashankar Banerjee

**Photography:** Subrata Mitra

**Music:** Ustad Vilayat Khan, Asis Kumar, Robin Majumder, Dakhin Mohan Takhur

**Cast:** Chhabi Biswas, Padma Devi, Pinaki Sen Gupta, Gangapada Basu, Tulsi Lahiri, Kali Sarkar, Waheed Khan, Roshan Kumari, Sardar Akhtar, Tulsi Chakraborty, Bismillah Khan, Salamat Ali Khan

# JALSAGHAR (1958)
## THE MUSIC ROOM

Satyajit Ray is best known for his "Apu" trilogy, a set of three films that together chronicle the life of a poor Bengali villager from childhood through adulthood. These films introduced Indian art cinema to a world that was familiar only with the fantasy and spectacle of the Bollywood musical. Ray revealed a different India, the life of a traditional village, the ravages of famine and drought, and of poverty. Greatly influenced by Italian neorealism, Ray's beautiful and moving pictures sought to explore moral and social injustices. Beautifully shot in the countryside, they made every attempt to be authentic documents of Indian life. In *The Music Room*, however, Ray's style and intentions change. This moody, atmospheric, and elegiac film will be a great surprise to those expecting the Ray of the Apu trilogy and *Distant Thunder* (1973). With this tour de force, Ray transcends our typical notions of national cinema, particularly in the Third World context.

*The Music Room* tells the Chekhovian story of a fading lord, Huzur Roy, in the 1920s. The character is played with a sad-eyed gravity and impressive nobility by one of Ray's most beloved actors, Chhabi Biswas. Roy's power and fortune have slowly faded away to nothing, his palace is crumbling, his staff of servants has dwindled down, and he spends his days sitting on his roof in silent reveries of past glory. He sits looking out on a barren landscape. Mahim Ganguly (Gangapada Basu) is a money lender, one whose crass manners do not betray his rising power and status. Ganguly represents all that Roy has lost and threatens his very existence. When Ganguly announces that he is going to hold a concert, Roy decides that he will hold a concert on the same night, pitting the old and the new against one another for a final confrontation. Roy's opulent music room is his great love, and the film flashes back to earlier concerts held in the room in better times. This last concert will be his final grand gesture, although it will wipe out Roy's treasury completely. It is his chance to live as he was once accustomed to doing, and to keep his inevitable end at bay for one last night of music and beauty.

The film's atmosphere of decay and melancholy is almost intoxicating. We feel the end of Roy's world viscerally and yet, like him, wish impossibly that it will not end. The close observation and careful evocation of a time and place that characterized Ray's neorealist films work well in this picture, but to more expressionist ends. We see that the two remaining servants are losing their battle with the elements as plants and insects are taking over the palace. The bare plains over which Roy looks out mirror his creeping demise. Satyajit Ray is exploring new ideas and techniques in this film, and it is fascinating to watch his style expand. *The Music Room* is a sensual delight and an essential masterpiece of World cinema. **RH**

**France** (Carrosse, Sédif) 94m BW
**Language:** French
**Director:** François Truffaut
**Producer:** François Truffaut
**Screenplay:** François Truffaut
**Photography:** Henri Decaë
**Music:** Jean Constantin
**Cast:** Jean-Pierre Léaud, Claire Maurier, Albert Rémy, Guy Decomble, Georges Flamant, Patrick Auffray, Daniel Couturier, François Nocher, Richard Kanayan, Renaud Fontanarosa, Michel Girard, Henry Moati, Bernard Abbou, Jean-François Bergouignan, Michel Lesignor
**Oscar nomination:** François Truffaut, Marcel Moussy (screenplay)
**Cannes Film Festival:** François Truffaut (director) (OCIC award)

# LES QUATRE CENTS COUPS (1959)
## THE 400 BLOWS

François Truffaut's debut feature, *The 400 Blows* earned the prize for best director at the Cannes International Film Festival in 1959. In an instant its young maker was on the map of international film culture—and smoothing the way for such New Wave colleagues as Jean-Luc Godard and Eric Rohmer, already immersed in cutting-edge projects of their own.

Like the other New Wave filmmakers, Truffaut cultivated his key ideas writing articles for *Cahiers de Cinéma*, the literate film magazine edited by André Bazin, who encouraged his critics to pursue their convictions often far from his own distinctive blend of aesthetic and philosophical concerns. Truffaut was the most aggressive writer of the group, fiercely criticizing French cinema's "tradition of quality" while formulating the *politique des auteurs* that saw strongly creative directors as the primary authors of their films.

*The 400 Blows* abounds with the spirit of personal filmmaking that Truffaut had celebrated as a critic. The hero, Antoine Doinel (Jean-Pierre Léaud), is a thinly fictionalized version of the *auteur* himself, and Truffaut later revealed that he boosted the intensity of the 15-year-old actor's performance by joining him in a private conspiracy against the rest of the cast and crew. Master cinematographer Henri Decaë shot the picture in real Paris locations, and Truffaut never hesitated to stray from the story for moments of poignantly conveyed emotional detail. One such sequence comes when Antoine rides in an amusement-park centrifuge, twisting his body into wry contortions that express his rather weak impulse to rebel against society's constricting norms. Another comes at the end of the film, when Truffaut's camera escapes from a detention camp with Antoine, tracking on and on as he runs breathlessly toward nowhere, then zooming toward his face to capture a freeze-frame portrait of existential angst that is arguably the most powerful single moment in New Wave cinema.

Truffaut and Léaud continued Antoine's adventures in four more films, ending the series with *Love on the Run* in 1979, four years before Truffaut's untimely death. While these sequels have their charm, *The 400 Blows* remains unsurpassed as a distillation of the New Wave's most exuberant creative instincts. **DS**

# NORTH BY NORTHWEST (1959)

Shortly after Cary Grant's character Roger O. Thornhill, an advertising executive, introduces himself, a woman asks him what the "O" stands for. Grant's famous reply? "Nothing." On one hand it's a sly dig at former Hitchcock producer David O. Selznick. But the "O," like many elements in Alfred Hitchcock's most entertaining film *North by Northwest*, is also just another extraneous detail ancillary to the action.

In fact, *North by Northwest* sometimes seems like one big extraneous detail in its entirety, which oddly accounts for much of the movie's considerable appeal. The film is pure funhouse: mistaken for a spy and suspected for the murder of a U.N. diplomat, Thornhill (armed only with vast stores of charm and witty rejoinders) flees across the country, pursued by villains (led by James Mason and a creepy Martin Landau) and shadowed by government agents. Somewhere in between is the stunningly beautiful and shamelessly sensual Eve Kendall (Eva Marie Saint), whose allegiances wobble warily between the twin poles of good guys and bad guys.

Will Grant elude his would-be assassins? Does he discover the truth behind his mistaken identity quandary? Does it really matter? Working from one of the all-time great scripts by Ernest Lehman, and featuring several of cinema's greatest action sequences—the crop duster attack, the chase across the face(s) of Mount Rushmore—Hitchcock ended his golden period on the highest of notes with *North by Northwest*. Even the title sequences, designed by Saul Bass, are memorable, and Bernard Herrmann's score is equal to his iconic themes from *Psycho* (1960) and *Vertigo* (1958).

Far from Kim Novak's icy blonde in *Vertigo*, which preceded *North by Northwest*, Saint is one of Hitchcock's more vulnerable female leads, and from their first encounter it is clear that she and Grant are meant for each other. It's the perennial bachelor's ultimate trial by fire on the way to wedded bliss. Therefore, the question becomes not whether but how the pair ends up together. Grant is made to surmount various threats not just for his life but implicitly for his and Saint's future life together, and Hitchcock—ever the romantic sadist—has a hoot putting up the roadblocks. **JKl**

**U.S.** (MGM) 136m Technicolor
**Director:** Alfred Hitchcock
**Screenplay:** Ernest Lehman
**Photography:** Robert Burks
**Music:** Bernard Herrmann
**Cast:** Cary Grant, Eva Marie Saint, James Mason, Jessie Royce Landis, Leo G. Carroll, Josephine Hutchinson, Philip Ober, Martin Landau, Adam Williams, Edward Platt, Robert Ellenstein, Les Tremayne, Philip Coolidge, Patrick McVey, Ed Binns
**Oscar nomination:** Ernest Lehman (screenplay), William A. Horning, Robert F. Boyle, Merrill Pye, Henry Grace, Frank R. McKelvy (art direction), George Tomasini (editing)

# SOME LIKE IT HOT (1959)

Down-on-their-luck jazz musicians Joe (Tony Curtis) and Jerry (Jack Lemmon) witness the 1929 St. Valentine's Day Massacre and flee Chicago with an all girl band bound for Miami, posing as "Josephine" and "Daphne." Both are taken with Sugar Kane Kowalczyk (Marilyn Monroe), a vulnerable, boozy singer. But Daphne attracts the persistent attentions of lecherous playboy Osgood Fielding III (Joe E. Brown), and things get even more complicated when the very gangsters the boys want to avoid, Chicago mob boss Spats Columbo (George Raft) and his henchmen, arrive at the Florida hotel for a gangland summit.

This legendary drag comedy is sensationally funny, fizzing from start to finish with great situations, cleverly crafted gags, breakneck timing, and terrific performances. The 1950s top sex goddess at her most enchanting, Monroe's forlorn-funny turn, maddening though it was for her costars and director to capture, is mythic. Curtis's self-consciousness in drag gave him an aloof control that is in superb contrast to the uninhibited, priceless Lemmon.

*Some Like It Hot* was independently produced and directed by Billy Wilder in his second screenwriting collaboration with I.A.L. "Iz" Diamond, and was sparked by the German farce *Fanfaren der Liebe* (1951), in which two unemployed musicians join an all-girl band, take a train journey, and go in for some quick-change romancing with the band's singer. Wilder didn't want his two heroes to be camp; they had to be heatedly heterosexual so that their escapade aboard the train surrounded by temptation was comically excruciating. Therefore, they had to have a desperately good reason to masquerade as women. Running for their lives from ruthless killers provided strong motivation. And although the gangsters have their own good jokes, they are effectively played straight for a note of delicious menace, with Wilder's neat noir touch of shooting Raft's key entrances from his distinctive footwear up.

The film's famous last line was written the night before shooting finished by Diamond, who insisted to the dubious Wilder that it was funny because it's so unexpected; the last reaction the audience expects to Jerry's revelation "I'm a MAN!" is Osgood's philosophical shrug, "Nobody's perfect." The other most fondly recalled moment is Daphne's engagement announcement. Lemmon shaking his maracas in absurd ecstasy is a masterpiece of comic timing, Wilder insisting on joyous fits of gourd rattling to leave space for audience laughter between lines. He also overrode objections to filming in black-and-white, not only to enhance the period setting but, shrewdly, to mute the men's makeup. Their transformation is startlingly amusing, but imagined in Technicolor it would be too grotesque. Industry mavens predicted the film would be a disaster because it broke several traditional rules of film comedy (the story springs from a grisly mass murder, the script was only half-written when shooting began, and the picture runs two hours, to cite a few), but audiences went crazy and still do, long after *Some Like It Hot* was selected by the American Film Institute as the Best Comedy of All Time. **AE**

**U.S.** (Ashton, Mirisch) 120m BW

**Director:** Billy Wilder

**Producer:** I.A.L. Diamond, Doane Harrison, Billy Wilder

**Screenplay:** I.A.L. Diamond, Billy Wilder

**Photography:** Charles Lang

**Music:** Adolph Deutsch, Gus Kahn, Bert Kalmar, Leo Wood

**Cast:** Marilyn Monroe, Tony Curtis, Jack Lemmon, George Raft, Pat O'Brien, Joe E. Brown, Nehemiah Persoff, Joan Shawlee, Billy Gray, George E. Stone, Dave Barry, Mike Mazurki, Harry Wilson, Beverly Wills, Barbara Drew

**Oscar:** Orry-Kelly (costume)

**Oscar nomination:** Billy Wilder (director), I.A.L. Diamond, Billy Wilder (screenplay), Jack Lemmon (actor), Ted Haworth, Edward G. Boyle (art direction), Charles Lang (photography)

Last year's No. 1 best-seller...This year's No. 1 motion picture.
OTTO PREMINGER'S
ANATOMY OF A MURDER
JAMES STEWART
LEE REMICK
BEN GAZZARA
ARTHUR O'CONNELL
EVE ARDEN
KATHRYN GRANT


# ANATOMY OF A MURDER (1959)

Otto Preminger's 1959 film of the 1957 novel by Rober Traver (a pen name for Michigan Supreme Court Justice John D. Voelker) was controversial in its day—making frank onscreen use of then-unheard words like "panties," "rape," and "spermatogenesis"—and remains a trenchant, bitter, tough, witty dissection of the American legal system.

From its striking Saul Bass title design (featured also on the poster) and jazzy Duke Ellington score, *Anatomy of a Murder* takes a sophisticated approach unusual for a Hollywood film of its vintage. Most radically, it refuses to show the murder or any of the private scenes recounted in court, leaving it up to us to decide along with the jury whether the grumpy and unconcerned Lieutenant Frederick Manion (Ben Gazzara) was or was not subject to an "irresistible impulse" tantamount to insanity when he shot dead Barney Quill, the bear-like bar owner alleged to have raped Manion's teasing trailer-trash wife Laura (Lee Remick in unfeasably tight trousers). Manion snags as his defense counsel Paul "Polly" Biegler (James Stewart), a former district attorney keen to get back into court to clash with the political dullard who replaced him in office, and Biegler calls on the skills of his snide secretary (Eve Arden) and boozy-but-brilliant research partner (Arthur O'Connell). For the prosecution, the befuddled local DA hauls in Claude Dancer (George C. Scott), a prissy legal eagle from the local big city whose sharp-suited, sly elegance makes an interesting clash with Biegler's aw-shucks "jimmystewartian" conniving. On the bench is a real-life courtroom giant: playing the judge is Joseph Welch, the attorney whose quiet persistence ("have you no shame?") literally put an end to the career of Senator Joseph McCarthy.

Simply the best trial movie ever made, far less contrived than the brilliant but stagey *12 Angry Men*, with a real understanding on the part of Stewart and Scott (both among the film's Oscar nominees) of the way lawyers have to be not only great actors but stars, assuming personalities that exaggerate their inner selves and weighing every outburst and objection for the effect it has on the poor saps in the jury box. **KN**

**U.S.** (Carlyle, Columbia) 160m BW

**Director:** Otto Preminger

**Producer:** Otto Preminger

**Screenplay:** Wendell Mayes, from novel by John D. Voelker

**Photography:** Sam Leavitt

**Music:** Duke Ellington

**Cast:** James Stewart, Lee Remick, Ben Gazzara, Arthur O'Connell, Eve Arden, Kathryn Grant, George C. Scott, Orson Bean, Russ Brown, Murray Hamilton, Brooks West, Ken Lynch, John Qualen, Howard McNear, Alexander Campbell

**Oscar nomination:** Otto Preminger (best picture), Wendell Mayes (screenplay), James Stewart (actor), Arthur O'Connell (actor in support role), George C. Scott (actor in support role), Sam Leavitt (photography), Louis R. Loeffler (editing)

**Venice Film Festival:** James Stewart (Volpi cup—actor)

**Venice Film Festival:** Otto Preminger nomination (Golden Lion)

# LES YEUX SANS VISAGE (1959)
## EYES WITHOUT A FACE

Much has been written about Georges Franju's *Eyes Without a Face*—the only foray into the horror genre by the cofounder of the Paris Cinémathèque. While the film is justifiably celebrated as a masterpiece, connections are frequently made between its pulp fiction plot and the poetry of its cinematography—Jean Cocteau filming Edgar Allen Poe. The brilliant Doctor Génessier (Pierre Brasseur), experimenting with overcoming transplanted organ rejection, is dedicated to finding a young woman with a face to replace that of his daughter Christiane (Edith Scob), which was disfigured in a car accident he was responsible for.

Franju brings a sensitivity and complexity to the stock characters of the mad scientist and his assistant (here played by Alida Valli), not to mention his "monster"; he magnificently situates audience identification with the faceless Christiane early in the film. The first shot, of two headlights cutting through the dark French countryside, seen from within the car, creates a mask-like image echoing Christiane's expressionless mask, only from within. Our first encounter with the film is from within that mask, and when we finally see Christiane's face it is neither the plastic visage of her own mask nor (when it comes off) the out-of-focus exposed muscle which grabs our attention, but the young woman's eyes—which we've already seen through in that echoing first shot. This is what gives the film its meaning: we are the "monster" for whom Doctor Génessier commits his horrible crimes.

*Eyes Without a Face* can be seen as Grand Guignol theater on the big screen: the film operates to give us an ever-increasing series of grotesque spectacles, beginning with Christiane's mask, a face being lifted from one young victim (amidst other medical horrors), the glimpses of Christiane's missing face, and finally to Doctor Génessier being torn apart by his own dogs. Franju here gives us a conflation of high and low cultural tastes, wherein we are shown beauty and poetry from inside the horror due to the director's refusal to exploit or turn away from the graphic images. If indeed we are the monster, the film seems to say, we would not necessarily see the events portrayed as horrific. **MK**

**France / Italy** (Champs-Élysées, Lux) 88m BW

**Language:** French

**Director:** Georges Franju

**Producer:** Jules Borkon

**Screenplay:** Pierre Boileau, Claude Sautet, Pierre Gascar, Thomas Narcejac, from novel by Jean Redon

**Photography:** Eugen Schüfftan

**Music:** Maurice Jarre

**Cast:** Pierre Brasseur, Edith Scob, Alida Valli, François Guérin, Alexandre Rignault, Béatrice Altariba, Juliette Mayniel, Charles Blavette, Claude Brasseur, Michel Etcheverry, Yvette Etiévant, René Génin, Lucien Hubert, Marcel Pérès

## RIDE LONESOME (1959)

**U.S.** (Columbia) 73m Eastmancolor
**Director:** Budd Boetticher
**Producer:** Budd Boetticher, Harry Joe Brown
**Screenplay:** Burt Kennedy
**Photography:** Charles Lawton Jr.
**Music:** Heinz Roemheld
**Cast:** Randolph Scott, Karen Steele, Pernell Roberts, James Best, Lee Van Cleef, James Coburn

The seven Westerns Budd Boetticher made with leading man Randolph Scott are notable for Scott's wry, laconic, weather-beaten virtuousness; colorful secondary characters; visual gracefulness; stark, abstract landscapes; and a muted but aching sense of tragedy. If *Ride Lonesome* stands out in the series, it's because of the optimism of its ending, the easygoing interplay between Pernell Roberts and James Coburn as Boetticher's two most likable villains, and the perfection of Burt Kennedy's script.

Scott plays a bounty hunter with the fabulous name of Ben Brigade, who, after capturing a notorious killer—a memorably infantile James Best—in the film's first scene, takes him across open country to collect his reward. During his trek, Brigade acquires, against his will, three companions: a station master's sexy wife (Karen Steele) and the aforementioned pair of good badmen, who plan on robbing Brigade of his captive. The latter's outlaw brother (Lee Van Cleef), meanwhile, is in hot pursuit of the group.

The characters are locked in a pattern of competing or complementary goals—no one can make a move without someone else making a countermove—and all are aware that they are headed together toward a fatal showdown. Boetticher, shooting in CinemaScope, does full justice both to the elegance of this scenario and to his protagonist's mythic solitude. **CFu**

## ORFEU NEGRO (1959)
### BLACK ORPHEUS

**Brazil / France / Italy** (Dispat, Gemma, Tupan Filmes) 100m Eastmancolor
**Language:** Portuguese
**Director:** Marcel Camus
**Producer:** Sacha Gordine
**Screenplay:** Vinicius De Moraes, Marcel Camus, Jacques Viot, from the play *Orfeu do Carnaval* by Vinicius De Moraes
**Photography:** Jean Bourgoin
**Music:** Luiz Bonfá, Antonio Carlos Jobim
**Cast:** Breno Mello, Marpessa Dawn, Lourdes de Oliveira, Léa Garcia, Ademar Da Silva, Alexandro Constantino, Waldemar De Souza, Jorge Dos Santos, Aurino Cassiano
**Oscar:** France (best foreign language film)
**Cannes Film Festival:** Marcel Camus (Golden Palm)

Marcel Camus's restaging of the myth of Orpheus in Rio de Janeiro during Carnival was the surprise winner of the *Palme d'Or* at Cannes and later of the Academy Award for best foreign picture. Filmed using neorealist techniques—an amateur cast and extensive location shooting in the teeming streets—it was highly praised for its vibrant depiction of Brazilian life and folklore. *Black Orpheus* was also championed as revolutionary for being one of the first international art films to have an entirely black cast. Adding to this acclaim and sense of authenticity is one of the movie's enduring charms: its glorious soundtrack composed by Luiz Bonfá and Antonio Carlos Jobim, two of the greatest composers of Afro-Brazilian sambas (Jobim wrote 1967 song "The Girl from Ipanema").

Ironically, in Brazil the film is perennially criticized for exoticizing the country as an all-night dance party, populated by hot-blooded Latin caricatures. Although it is difficult to argue with these criticisms, which highlight many contemporary debates about visibility politics, the film is best appreciated on its own terms. Self-consciously a fable, *Black Orpheus* is beautifully shot and wonderfully played by Marpessa Dawn and Breno Mello. Camus's depiction of the River Styx and the ferryman Charon as a night watchman at a government building, standing in a hallway with fluttering bits of paper blowing past his feet, is unforgettable. **RH**

## SHADOWS (1959)

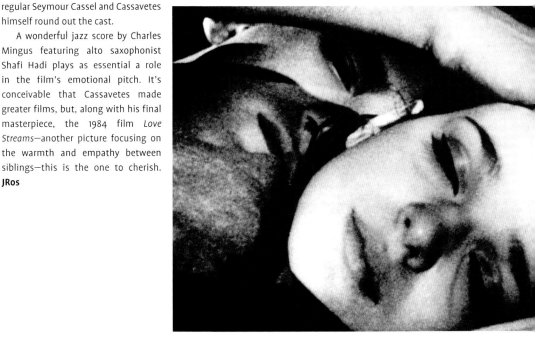

John Cassavetes's exquisite and poignant first feature, shot in 16mm and subsequently blown up to 35mm, centers on two brothers and a sister living together in Manhattan. The oldest, a third-rate nightclub singer (Hugh Hurd), is visibly black, whereas the other two (Ben Carruthers and Lelia Goldoni) are sufficiently light skinned to pass for white. This is the only Cassavetes film made without a script in the usual sense of that term, although Cassavetes scholar Ray Carney has demonstrated at length how the closing title, announcing that the film you have just seen is an "improvisation," is closer to being a sales pitch than an objective description. In fact Cassavetes and Robert Alan Aurthur wrote most of *Shadows*, basing their work on a workshop improvisation that was carried out under Cassavetes's supervision. An earlier and shorter version of the film, reportedly less bound by narrative, is apparently lost.

*Shadows* is also the only one of Cassavetes' films that focuses mainly on young people, with the actors using their own first names to increase the feeling of intimacy. Rarely has so much warmth, delicacy, subtlety, and raw feeling emerged so naturally and beautifully from performances in an American film. This movie is contemporaneous with early masterpieces of the French New Wave such as *Breathless* and *The 400 Blows*, and deserves to be ranked alongside them for the freshness and freedom of its vision. In its portrait of a now-vanished Manhattan during the beat period, it also serves as a poignant time capsule. Tony Ray (the son of director Nicholas Ray), Rupert Crosse, Dennis Sallas, Tom Allen, Davey Jones, and cameos by subsequent Cassavetes regular Seymour Cassel and Cassavetes himself round out the cast.

A wonderful jazz score by Charles Mingus featuring alto saxophonist Shafi Hadi plays as essential a role in the film's emotional pitch. It's conceivable that Cassavetes made greater films, but, along with his final masterpiece, the 1984 film *Love Streams*—another picture focusing on the warmth and empathy between siblings—this is the one to cherish. **JRos**

**U.S.** (Lion) 81m BW

**Director:** John Cassavetes

**Prooducer:** Seymour Cassel, Maurice McEndree

**Screenplay:** John Cassavetes

**Photography:** Erich Kollmar

**Music:** Shifi Hadi

**Cast:** Ben Carruthers, Lelia Goldoni, Hugh Hurd, Anthony Ray, Dennis Sallas, Tom Allen, David Pokitillow, Rupert Crosse, David Jones, Pir Marini, Victoria Vargas, Jack Ackerman, Jacqueline Walcott, Cliff Carnell, Jay Crecco

**India** (Satyajit Ray) 117m BW

**Language:** Bengali

**Direction:** Satyajit Ray

**Producer:** Satyajit Ray

**Screenplay:** Satyajit Ray, from the novel *Aparajita* by Bibhutibhushan Bandyopadhyay

**Photography:** Subrata Mitra

**Music:** Ravi Shankar

**Cast:** Soumitra Chatterjee, Sharmila Tagore, Alok Chakravarty, Swapan Mukherjee, Dhiresh Majumdar, Sefallka Devi, Dhiren Ghosh, Belarani, Shanti Bhattacherjee, Abhijit Chatterjee

# APUR SANSAR (1959)

## THE WORLD OF APU

*The World of Apu* completes the *Apu* trilogy that made Satyajit Ray's name and introduced Indian cinema to the world. With both his parents now dead, the adult Apu (Soumitra Chatterjee) is living in shabby lodgings in Calcutta, beside the railway tracks, trying to make his name as a writer. His friend Pulu (Swapan Mukherjee) invites him to his sister's wedding in a small Bengali village. But the festivities are blighted; the intended bridegroom proves to be mentally deficient. If the bride doesn't marry at the appointed hour she will be utterly disgraced. Apu, protesting and bewildered, is pressed into service and takes his teenage bride back to his urban hovel. Against all the odds the marriage is a joyful success. After a year of happiness, Aparna (Sharmila Tagore) returns home to have her child. A message comes; she has died in childbirth. Shattered, Apu refuses even to see his son. Five years later Pulu finds him working in a remote coal mine and persuades him to come and take charge of the child, who has grown up wild and intractable. At first the boy savagely rejects this stranger posing as his father, but gradually a wary trust grows between them until Apu, his son riding on his shoulders, can start back for the city and the world.

This conclusion—Apu has symbolically returned to his native village and confronted his own childhood self—gives the whole trilogy the satisfying cyclical form of a myth. Each of the Apu films is structured around two deaths, although in *The World of Apu* the second death is that of Apu himself. He dies spiritually after losing Aparna, and only a chance event saves him from suicide; not until he reclaims his son is he reborn. The chosen instrument of his attempted suicide is a train; here, as throughout the trilogy, trains stand for the irresistible, impersonal forces that bring change, separation, and death.

At the heart of *The World of Apu* lies the brief marriage of Apu and Aparna. It is brief too in terms of screen time, running barely half an hour, yet it carries a powerful emotional and erotic impact. Not that Ray features any overt sexual contact; even had he wanted to, Indian moral conventions would have forbidden it. But he conveys a wealth of erotic revelation in moments like the one where Apu, waking in his formerly solitary bed and listening to Aparna cheerfully preparing breakfast, wonderingly discovers a hairpin on the pillow beside him. Ray draws from Chatterjee and Tagore, making their screen debuts, acting of astonishing depth and conviction; no wonder that both went on to become major stars of Indian cinema, as well as regular players in Ray's films. Tagore, enchantingly pretty as Aparna, was only fourteen at the time. Thanks to their performances, and the encompassing warmth and subtlety of Ray's direction, this rates as one of the most touching and intimate depictions of married love in all cinema. *The World of Apu* not only rounds off Ray's masterly trilogy, but encompasses a heartrending tale of love and loss. **PK**

**France** (Impéria, Georges de Beauregard, SNC) 87m BW

**Language:** French

**Director:** Jean-Luc Godard

**Producer:** Georges de Beauregard

**Screenplay:** Jean-Luc Godard, François Truffaut

**Photography:** Raoul Coutard

**Music:** Martial Solal

**Cast:** Jean-Paul Belmondo, Jean Seberg, Daniel Boulanger, Jean-Pierre Melville, Henri-Jacques Huet, Van Doude, Claude Mansard, Jean-Luc Godard, Richard Balducci, Roger Hanin, Jean-Louis Richard, Liliane David, Jean Domarchi, Jean Douchet, Raymond Huntley, André S. Labarthe, François Moreuil, Liliane Robin

**Berlin International Film Festival:** Jean-Luc Godard (Silver Bear), nomination (Golden Bear)

# A BOUT DE SOUFFLE (1959)
## BREATHLESS

What remains of *Breathless* today, what speaks to a contemporary, young audience—when jump cuts figure in every [illegible] commercial, when its stars are long dead (Jean Seberg) or in their twilight career phase (Jean-Paul Belmondo), when “comedies of manners” pitting Americans against Europeans are commonplace, and when the mixture of a loose gangster-crime plot, a smart attitude, and a hip array of high and low culture citations are more likely to be attributed to Quentin Tarantino than his genuine predecessor, Jean-Luc Godard?

Surprisingly, from an artistic iconoclast whose evolution was so rapid and ambitious, *Breathless* is a modest debut by Godard. There is the semblance of a thriller plot, complete with a betrayal, tailing cops, and a final shootout. There is a lovely but conventional film noir jazz score by Martial Solal. There is an insolent, mildly outrageous rap pouring from Belmondo’s punk motormouth, but even that scarcely contradicts the Chandler–Hammet–Spillane tradition of hard-boiled talk.

But the subtle, formal pleasures of *Breathless* have yet to be fully appreciated. Whether through accident or design, Godard’s low-budget, on-the-fly shooting style produced remarkable innovations. Eschewing direct sound recording and using total postsynchronization not only led to an Orson Welles-style speed and inventiveness in the dialogue delivery but also paved the way for a radical sound mix in which one can no longer spot the difference between “real” sound happening within the story and sound imposed by the filmmaker. Likewise, filming indoors in close quarters led to a new form of cinematic contemplation: the “visual study,” in which a sequence of just slightly different views offers a cubist mosaic of the many moods and aspects of these extraordinary star presences.

But it is as a modern love story that *Breathless* retains its immense appeal for members of Generation X and beyond. The children of existentialist reflection, postwar affluence, Beat culture cool, and pop culture flip, these antiheroes treat love as a game, and their own identities as makeshift masks. They are stranded between traditional values that they reject, and a future way of loving that has not yet materialized. Sound familiar? **AM**

# BEN-HUR (1959)

Based on a 19th-century novel by Civil War general Lew Wallace, William Wyler's *Ben-Hur* is the third and most famous version of a legendary tale of Christian forgiveness amid violent Roman times. Legendary for its exciting, action-packed, and myth-ridden chariot race which cost one million dollars alone to devise, the film featured 350 speaking roles with over 50,000 extras. Nominated for twelve Oscars, it set a record by winning every nomination but one, a feat only equaled 40 years later by *Titanic*. The production's overt excesses incited some intellectual dismissiveness, such as Mort Sahl's four-word review, "Loved him, hated *Hur*." This was perhaps a comment on the commercialism of "Ben-His" and "Ben-Hers" towels available at the time of the film's release—one of the earliest instances of movie merchandising.

Ostensibly a film about Jesus Christ, the story actively centers on the friendship between Messala (Stephen Boyd) and Judah Ben-Hur (Charlton Heston), a young man whose life becomes a quest for revenge after being framed for an attempt on the life of a Roman governor. Condemned to the life of a galley slave, his wife and sister abducted, Ben-Hur seeks the death of Messala, who is by then an officer in the Roman legions. They have their duel in the infamous and truly dangerous chariot race where Ben-Hur wreaks vengeance on his old friend. In the end there were over forty different versions of the script; one of its many screenwriters was Gore Vidal, who insisted upon a homosexual element between Messala and Ben-Hur. This can be seen in Boyd's performance if one looks for it; apparently the actor was told that Messala's relationship with Ben-Hur was mainly motivated by man-to-man love.

If *Ben-Hur's* movie message was love, its aim was money: its studio, MGM, was in dire straits financially. Despite the film's gargantuan production problems (some of them simple oversights such as not agreeing what the hippodrome should look like or that a camera was too big for a ship), the film's enormous appeal guaranteed box-office success. This saved the studio from bankruptcy, making a matinee idol of Heston in the process. **KK**

**U.S.** (MGM) 212m Technicolor

**Director:** William Wyler

**Producer:** Sam Zimbalist

**Screenplay:** Karl Tunberg, from novel by Lew Wallace

**Photography:** Robert Surtees

**Music:** Miklós Rózsa

**Cast:** Charlton Heston, Jack Hawkins, Haya Harareet, Stephen Boyd, Hugh Griffith, Martha Scott, Cathy O'Donnell, Sam Jaffe, Finlay Currie, Frank Thring, Terence Longdon, George Relph, André Morell

**Oscar:** Sam Zimbalist (best picture), William Wyler (director), Charlton Heston (actor), Hugh Griffith (actor in support role), William A. Horning, Edward C. Carfagno, Hugh Hunt (art direction), Robert Surtees (photography), Elizabeth Haffenden (costume), A. Arnold Gillespie, Robert MacDonald, Milo B. Lory (special effects), Ralph E. Winters, John D. Dunning (editing), Miklós Rózsa (music), Franklin Milton (sound)

**Oscar nomination:** Karl Tunberg (screenplay)

France (Lux) 75m BW

**Language:** French

**Director:** Robert Bresson

**Producer:** Agnès Delahaie

**Screenplay:** Robert Bresson

**Photography:** Léonce-Henri Burel

**Music:** Jean-Baptiste Lully

**Cast:** Martin LaSalle, Marika Green, Jean Pélégri, Dolly Scal, Pierre Leymarie, Kassagi, Pierre Étaix, César Gattegno

**Berlin International Film Festival:** Robert Bresson nomination (Golden Bear)

# PICKPOCKET (1959)

Robert Bresson uses film to express the spiritual inferiority of life in a uniquely paradoxical way: by revealing the indescribable through an intense concentration on concrete images and sounds. Every detail and every nuance of the physical world is exposed by Bresson's intently focused camera. Eschewing traditional dramatization in the form of emoting actors, melodramatic situations, or intricate plots, Bresson allows the action to tell the story. Deadpan voice-over is used to nominally explain the motivations and feelings of characters. Bresson often used nonprofessional actors, whom he tellingly called "models," and directed them to strenuously avoid any theatricality and to simply move through his films. He uses music sparingly as well, allowing it be heard only during key moments of the story, to express something that cannot be verbally articulated. His films are pared down to their essential elements. This simplicity and lack of manipulation allow the audience a great deal of freedom to interpret the actions on screen, so viewer and character alike are involved in the same process of questioning and trying to understand the dilemmas posed by the picture in question.

*Pickpocket* is among the most perfect examples of Bresson's style. It tells the story of Michel (Martin LaSalle), a disaffected young intellectual who becomes obsessed with picking pockets. At first he sees it simply as a means to further his own ends, but he soon comes to view it as an end in itself and as a creative act. After an amateurish attempt at the crime, which gets him caught almost immediately, he apprentices himself to a professional thief to really learn the craft. The scenes of pickpocketing are breathtaking and rival any in cinema for their excitement and sheer cinematic virtuosity. Although Michel has contact with his sick mother and is involved with a girlfriend, Jeanne (Marika Green), the pickpocketing provides him with his most emotionally and sensually satisfying human connections. This becomes more and more obvious as Michel no longer steals for financial gain. He even seems indifferent about being caught by the end.

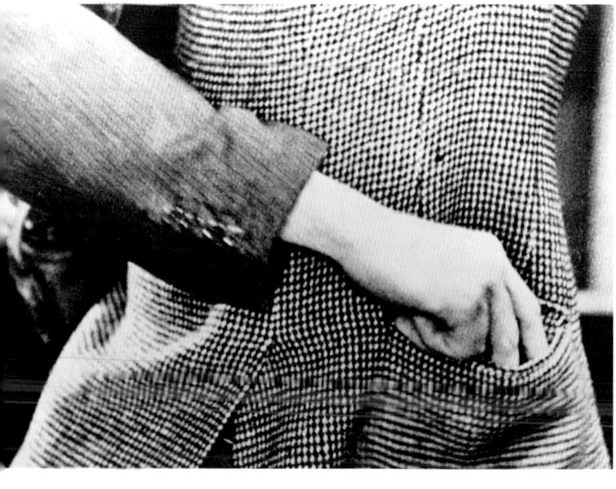

Although Bresson avoids the typical tools of drama, *Pickpocket* is completely engrossing and Michel's moral questioning and sense of displacement are deeply affecting. This is one of those pictures that compltely changes one's understanding of what cinema is or can be. Bresson is one of the most novelistic of filmmakers, in that he is able to depict the inner world of characters and abstract philosophical concepts that are more easily expressed in language. His achievement here is all the more ingenious because he uses the literal quality of the cinema to achieve his ends, using and shaping the very specific material of the real world. *Pickpocket* expands the vocabulary of the movies. Watching a Bresson film is a demanding but extremely satisfying and enjoyable experience. **RH**

# HIROSHIMA MON AMOUR (1959)

**France / Japan** (Argos, Como, Daiei, Pathé) 90m BW

**Language:** French / Japanese / English

**Director:** Alain Resnais

**Producer:** Anatole Dauman, Samy Halfon, Sacha Kamenka, Takeo Shirakawa

**Screenplay:** Marguerite Duras

**Photography:** Michio Takahashi, Sacha Vierny

**Music:** Georges Delerue, Giovanni Fusco

**Cast:** Emmanuelle Riva, Eiji Okada, Stella Dassas, Pierre Barbaud, Bernard Fresson

**Oscar nomination:** Marguerite Duras (screenplay)

In his first feature, Alain Resnais draws on the experience of his documentary short films. A Frenchwoman (Emmanuelle Riva) is having an affair with a Japanese architect (Eiji Okada) in Hiroshima, where she has come to shoot a film. Resnais uses documentary footage of the 1945 nuclear attack on the city together with shots of the museum and the rebuilt city. (In fact the film began as a documentary about Hiroshima and the bomb, which Resnais then decided to turn into a feature.) These are interspersed with lyrical scenes of the couple's love affair. The juxtaposition of the tenderness of love and the horrors of war cause the woman to remember her own past in the French town of Nevers. During the war she had an affair with a German soldier and was planning to leave the town with him when, on the last day of fighting, he was killed. Sweet and painful memories of this episode in her life rise up with increasing intensity as her brief affair with the Japanese man takes its course. At the end of *Hiroshima Mon Amour* this affair will be concluded, each returning to their marriages.

The film was specially written for the screen by Marguerite Duras, who was an important influence on French cinema, later to become a director herself, and whose work shows a preoccupation with the idea of memory and the influence of the past on the present. Memory too is a constant theme in Resnais's work; one of his documentaries, about the French National Library, is entitled *The Whole Memory of the World* (1956). In *Hiroshima Mon Amour*, Resnais employs a complex flashback structure, which gradually reveals more and more of the past as it intrudes on the present. This structure is held together by the haunting score of Giovanni Fusco and Georges Delerue, and is given a powerful emotional charge by the acting, particularly of Riva, whose face registers the complex emotions of her character down to the tiniest nuance. Our identities, the film seems to say, depend on our memories, but ultimately these will fade. **EB**

# RIO BRAVO (1959)

Fred Zinnemann's *High Noon* (1952) famously depicted one man's courageous stand against adversity in the name of the law. Howard Hawks's *Rio Bravo*, a response of sorts to *High Noon*, concerns another brave stand, also in the name of the law, but this time small Texas town sheriff John T. Chance (John Wayne) isn't alone. He's aided by the local drunk (Dean Martin), a gun-slinging young singing cowboy (Ricky Nelson), and a crippled old deputy nicknamed Stumpy (Walter Brennan). Together they must fend off a band of desperados who have laid siege to the town, intent on springing the villain's brother from jail.

Hawks was always one of Hollywood's most reliable and versatile directors, but after *Gentlemen Prefer Blondes* (1953) he left America for a disappointing stint in Europe. *Rio Bravo* marked a rousing return to America and to form, with Hawks offering a genre-smashing collision of everything he knows best. There's a musical number—with Martin and Nelson in the film, how could there not be?— moments of comedy, a touch of romance, thanks to stranded traveler Angie Dickenson, and plenty of action, all unified by yet another casually iconic Wayne performance as the pragmatic hero bound by a sense of duty.

The siege-scenario Hawks sets up—a motley crew of mismatched characters hole up in one place for one last stand—has become a genre-film standby, borrowed repeatedly by such Hawks worshippers as John Carpenter and George Romero. Both recognized how the limited setting of *Rio Bravo* could be applied to their own low-budget films. The Hawks touch is that the siege itself isn't as important as the interaction of the characters under siege. By sticking them all together in one place, Hawks has fun letting them play off of one another, revealing colorful little character traits as they fight back against insurmountable odds. Coming not long after John Ford's eulogy to the Western with his haunting *The Searchers* (1956), *Rio Bravo* also stands as one of the last of its kind, an old-fashioned and fun romp of a Western where the line between good guys and bad guys couldn't be more clear. **JKl**

**U.S.** (Armada) 141m Technicolor

**Director:** Howard Hawks

**Producer:** Howard Hawks

**Screenplay:** Leigh Brackett, Jules Furthman, from story by B.H. McCampbell

**Photography:** Russell Harlan

**Music:** Dimitri Tiomkin

**Cast:** John Wayne, Dean Martin, Ricky Nelson, Angie Dickinson, Walter Brennan, Ward Bond, John Russell, Pedro Gonzales-Gonzales, Estelita Rodriguez, Claude Akins, Malcolm Atterbury

**France / Italy** (Filmsonor, Play Art, Titanus ) 109m BW

**Language:** French

**Director:** Jacques Becker

**Producer:** Serge Silberman

**Screenplay:** Jean Aurel, Jacques Becker, José Giovanni, from novel by José Giovanni

**Photography:** Ghislain Cloquet

**Music:** Philippe Arthuys

**Cast:** Michel Constantin, Jean Keraudy, Philippe Leroy, Raymond Meunier, Marc Michel, André Bervil, Jean-Paul Coquelin, Eddy Rasimi, Gérard Hernandez, Paul Pavel, Catherine Spaak, Dominique Zardi

# LE TROU (1959)

## THE HOLE

The last film by the great and too-little known director Jacques Becker, *The Hole* is based on a novel by José Giovanni, which recounts the true story of an attempted prison escape in which the author took part in 1947. Becker wrote the script with Giovanni and cast the film with nonprofessional actors, one of whom, Jean Keraudy, played the same role in real life that he plays in the film.

Becker's use of nonprofessionals is one of several elements that heighten this extraordinary film's sense of absolute authenticity. Also crucial to our experience of *The Hole* is Becker's control of film time. The scene in which the five cell mates smash through the stone floor of their cell is done in an unbroken take of almost four minutes, making us aware that we're watching people expend the exact amount of effort required to produce the effects on the stone that we see. By making us share a collective duration with the heroes, Becker involves us more intensely in their collective struggle.

Our involvement is heightened by our also sharing, uneasily and never completely, the point of view of Gaspard (Marc Michel), a prisoner who, transferred from another cell, lands unexpectedly among the original plotters. His arrival forces the others to decide whether to give up their plan or take him into their confidence. Although they choose the latter course, Gaspard is never fully integrated into the group: He's excluded not just by his education and manners, but, subtly, by the fact that we are given the details of his case only. The tension his presence creates provides *The Hole's* main psychological interest and, in the film's stunning conclusion, allows it to achieve a tragic dimension.

Becker uses Gaspard's isolation as a device to help us perceive and value the others' comradeship. The bonds between the original members of the team are proved and celebrated in appreciative looks and smiles at each step of the journey to freedom. In one of the rare moments when Gaspard seems at one with the group, he shares his rice cake with them. Long after most directors would fade out, Becker holds the camera on the wordless scene: a fine example of his career-long insistence on showing his characters existing outside the framework created by the direct concerns of the plot.

Inevitably, *The Hole* has been compared with Robert Bresson's *A Man Escaped* (1956) and Jean Renoir's *The Grand Illusion* (1937), but Becker is less concerned than Bresson with transcendence or Renoir's critique of social differences. The virtues proved by the prisoners—meticulousness, inventiveness, and the ability to form a collective—become the highest values of *The Hole*. Perhaps Becker is, of all directors, including even Howard Hawks, the one who has embodied and articulated these values most firmly.

Becker was in ill health throughout the production and editing of the film, and died leaving the sound mixing unfinished. *The Hole* was completed according to the director's wishes, but after its initial release in a 140-minute version, producer Serge Silberman had it reduced by about 24 minutes to enhance its commercial possibilities. The missing footage remains lost, but as it stands, *The Hole* is still a masterpiece. **CFu**

# UKIGUSA (1959)
## FLOATING WEEDS

Yasujiro Ozu's second color film, exquisitely shot by Kenji Mizoguchi's favored cinematographer, Kazuo Miyagawa, is a beautifully composed and staged late work, demonstrating the director's growing mastery of an expanded tonal palette. One of a series of explicit remakes Ozu undertook around this time, it concentrates on the activities of an itinerant acting troupe ("floating weeds") while maintaining the director's characteristic fascination with familial and generational interaction. In contrast to Ozu's 1934 film *A Story of Floating Weeds*, which was more comic and dramatic, this one has a decidedly autumnal, nostalgic, and philosophical air, a quality illustrated by many of its serenely staged compositions and "distilled" combinations of image and sound.

Although Ozu's films generally contain a surprisingly large number of shots and routinely experiment with the construction of cinematic space, the predominant impression one takes from *Floating Weeds* is of a series of interlocking still lifes, and a rhythm matched to the lulling repetition of everyday life. The film's opening shot—contrasting and comparing the volume, shape, and color of a bottle and lighthouse—suggests no further movement, the chugging beat of a boat's motor on the soundtrack reinforcing the "completeness" or "fullness" of the image on display. In these moments the film achieves, a kind of stillness, a resigned, gestalt serenity which accompanies even Ozu's most tragic work, such as 1953's *Tokyo Story*. **AD**

**Japan** (Daiei) 119m Eastmancolor

**Language:** Japanese

**Director:** Yasujiro Ozu

**Producer:** Masaichi Nagata

**Screenplay:** Kôgo Noda, Yasujiro Ozu

**Photography:** Kazuo Miyagawa

**Music:** Kojun Saitô

**Cast:** Ganjiro Nakamura, Machiko Kyô, Ayako Wakao, Hiroshi Kawaguchi, Haruko Sugimura, Hikaru Hoshi, Yosuke Irie, Hideo Mitsui, Hitomi Nozoe, Chishu Ryu, Masahiko Shimazu, Haruo Tanaka, Kumeko Urabe, Mantarô Ushio

# ROCCO E I SUOI FRATELLI (1960)
## ROCCO AND HIS BROTHERS

A key transitional film in Luchino Visconti's shift away from his initial adherence to the principles of neorealism (admittedly already diluted by an interest in tragedy verging on the melodramatic) toward the decoratively operatic excesses of much of his later work, *Rocco and His Brothers* also remains one of his best. Giuseppe Rotunno's black-and-white camera work is tantalizingly pitched between grim, documentary-style neorealism and the stylization of film noir, with Nino Rota's score eloquently reflecting the emotional dynamics of the story about a family newly arrived in Milan from Sicily and falling apart as the influences of money, rootlessness, and sex work their destructive magic.

It is difficult, perhaps, to be convinced by the astonishingly beautiful Alain Delon as a boxer of such saintliness that he sacrifices his happiness in the forlorn hope of keeping the family united, and Katina Paxinou's clichéd histrionics as the long-suffering matriarch are a little hard to take; however, Renato Salvatori is convincing as the brutish and irresponsible elder brother ruined by greed and obsessive jealousy, and Annie Girardot is both sexy and remarkably persuasive as the emotionally complex girl who comes between Salvatori and Delon. The final moments of her martyrlike death may be over the top, but they are nevertheless effectively cathartic. **GA**

**France / Italy** (Marceau-Cocinor, Titanus) 175m BW

**Language:** Italian

**Director:** Luchino Visconti

**Producer:** Goffredo Lombardo

**Screenplay:** Luchino Visconti, Suso Cecchi d'Amico, Vasco Pratolini, Pasquale Festa Campanile, Massimo Franciosa, Enrico Medioli, from the novel *Il Ponte della Ghisolfa* by Giovanni Testori

**Photography:** Giuseppe Rotunno

**Music:** Nino Rota

**Cast:** Alain Delon, Renato Salvatori, Annie Girardot, Katina Paxinou, Alessandra Panaro, Spiros Focás, Max Cartier, Corrado Pani, Rocco Vidolazzi, Claudia Mori, Adriana Asti, Enzo Fiermonte, Nino Castelnuovo, Rosario Borelli, Renato Terra

**Venice Film Festival:** Luchino Visconti (FIPRESCI award), (special prize), nomination (Golden Lion)

**Italy / France** (Pathé, Riama) 167m BW
**Language:** Italian / English
**Director:** Federico Fellini
**Producer:** Giuseppe Amato, Franco Magli, Angelo Rizzoli
**Screenplay:** Federico Fellini, Ennio Flaiano, Tullio Pinelli, Brunello Rondi
**Music:** Nino Rota
**Photography:** Otello Martelli
**Cast:** Marcello Mastroianni, Anita Ekberg, Anouk Aimée, Yvonne Furneaux, Magali Noël, Alain Cuny, Annibale Ninchi, Walter Santesso, Valeria Ciangottini, Riccardo Garrone, Ida Galli, Audrey McDonald, Polidor, Alain Dijon, Enzo Cerusico
**Oscar:** Piero Gherardi (costume)
**Oscar nomination:** Federico Fellini (director), Federico Fellini, Tullio Pinelli, Ennio Flaiano, Brunello Rondi (screenplay), Piero Gherardi (art direction)
**Cannes Film Festival:** Federico Fellini (Golden Palm)

# LA DOLCE VITA (1960)

An epic about triviality, Federico Fellini's portrait of a place and time captures perfectly the style and attitudes of Rome's fashionable party folk during the summer of 1959, all the while condemning them for being such gorgeous parasites. The enduring strength of *La Dolce Vita* comes from the tension between viciously attacking a world whose excesses are beyond satire and the fascination it can't help but feel for the mad parade of modern decadents.

Like *A Clockwork Orange*, *Apocalypse Now*, and *Wall Street*, this is a film that paradoxically set as many fashion styles as it set out to demolish, encouraging people to sit about cafés on the Via Veneto in an unironic attempt to emulate the sweet life. The expression *paparazzi* comes from the film character of Paparazzo, who epitomizes the swarm of insect-like photojournalists found around every passing celebrity, snapping away and jostling for the best place and the most exploitable shot. The same camera horde who press around Marilyn Monroe-like American superstar Sylvia (Anita Ekberg) later, more disturbingly, snap away at an innocent housewife returning home. She is briefly flattered that they might think she is "some actress," only to learn that they are interested in her because her philospher husband Steiner (Alain Cuny) has shot their two children and himself.

Marcello Mastroianni, defining a generation of cool in his beetle-black sunglasses, is the character whose fall from at least potential grace we follow. Once he was a serious writer, but now he's a sleazy journalist who dances attendance on the pointlessly famous and gets no thrill at all from his various escapades and is always being humiliated as a hanger-on. *La Dolce Vita* is well remembered for the glorious image of Ekberg in the Trevi Fountain, but the scene is about the embarrassment, discomfort, and ultimate pain of Mastroianni's Marcello Rubini. He had scorned the star as "like a big doll" but becomes hopelessly smitten with her, despatched on an impossible errand (finding milk for a stray kitten at dead of night), which she has forgotten by the time he fulfills it, then joining her in the fountain against his better judgment to coo a wonderful Italian come-on speech ("you are the first woman on the first day of creation"). She doesn't understand, and his night ends getting sucker-punched by Sylvia's drunken actor lover (Lex Barker). Marcello's slide, which ends after the philosopher's shocking murder-suicide as he abandons all pretense at writing to become (shudder) a press agent, is prompted by ridiculous media farces. Like a bogus miracle in the rain incited by cannily corrupt children, a ghost hunt at a haunted mansion (where Nico wears a mediaeval helmet), an attempted orgy that fizzles in unsettling references to Tod Browning's *Freaks* as a pinhead-like dancer wheels about while Marcello cruelly abuses and feathers a drunken girl singled out at random, and the ultimate dragging of a shark-ray monster from the seas. "By 1965, there'll be total depravity," muses a bystander, and the innocent smiling girl who represents a possible hope for Marcello can't make herself heard over the useless noise, leaving him sadly to join the doomed throng. **KN**

**G.B.** (Bryanston, Woodfall) 89m BW
**Director:** Karel Reisz
**Producer:** Tony Richardson, Harry Saltzman
**Screenplay:** Alan Sillitoe, from his novel
**Photography:** Freddie Francis
**Music:** John Dankworth
**Cast:** Albert Finney, Shirley Anne Field, Rachel Roberts, Hylda Baker, Norman Rossington, Bryan Pringle, Robert Cawdron, Edna Morris, Elsie Wagstaff, Frank Pettitt, Avis Bunnage, Colin Blakely, Irene Richmond, Louise Dunn, Anne Blake

# SATURDAY NIGHT AND SUNDAY MORNING (1960)

In the late 1950s and early 1960s, British cinema turned to social realism, usually dealing with stirrings of rebelliousness or aspirations of betterment among clever, articulate, embittered working-class youngsters. Almost all of these films were taken from works by "angry young man" playwrights and novelists like John Osborne (*Look Back in Anger*), John Braine (*Room at the Top*), and Stan Barstow (*A Kind of Loving*). Alan Sillitoe's book *Saturday Night and Sunday Morning* became the best of these films, though the direction of Karel Reisz isn't free from a sort of sentimental inclination to the picturesque that often came about when Cambridge-educated filmmakers trekked to the North to make slag-heaps look like alien landscapes and to spy on the strange behavior of pub-going factory workers in Nottingham.

The strength of the film is in Sillitoe's voice ("What I'm out for is a good time—all the rest is propaganda") and the delivery of his dialogue by Albert Finney, making a terrific first impression as Arthur Seaton, the grumbling, virile hedonist who bristles with indignation in the workplace and cuts loose in his off hours. The title implies the process of taming that has traditionally ground down Arthur's class, with the high-living of drunkenness and sexual excess on Saturday night paid for on Sunday morning with being coffined into a respectable marriage and a new home.

The film shows how Arthur's father (Frank Pettitt) has been reduced to staring at the television and that most of his slightly older friends (notably the mate he cuckolds) are on their way to being trapped. Although Arthur comes out of a relationship with a married woman (Rachel Roberts) by being lured into an engagement with a pretty but conventional girl (Shirley Anne Field), he is still resolving to keep throwing stones and breaking windows. Though, like many films in this cycle, *Saturday Night and Sunday Morning* tends to indulge in a species of proletarian machismo that verges on misogyny (for Arthur, all women are traps), Roberts—in a role similar to that taken by Simone Signoret in *Room at the Top* (1959)—expresses a real pain that provides an alternative reading of Arthur's rebellion. **KN**

# TIREZ SUR LE PIANISTE (1960)
## SHOOT THE PIANO PLAYER

**France** (Pléïade) 85m BW

**Language:** French

**Director:** François Truffaut

**Producer:** Pierre Braunberger

**Screenplay:** Marcel Moussy, François Truffaut, from the novel *Down There* by David Goodis

**Photography:** Raoul Coutard

**Music:** Georges Delerue, Boby Lapointe, Félix Leclerc, Lucienne Vernay

**Cast:** Charles Aznavour, Marie Dubois, Nicole Berger, Michèle Mercier, Albert Rémy, Serge Davri, Claude Mansard, Richard Kanayan, Jean-Jacques Aslanian, Daniel Boulanger, Claude Heymann, Alex Joffé, Boby Lapointe, Catherine Lutz

With his second feature, *Shoot the Piano Player*, François Truffaut deliberately set out to make a film as different as possible from his acclaimed debut, *The 400 Blows*. Where *Blows* was sensitive, realistic, and strongly autobiographical in content, *Piano Player* is zany, irreverent, and set in a lovingly pastiched B movie world of doom-laden losers and thick-eared hoods. "I wanted to break with linear narrative," Truffaut later explained, "and make a film where all the scenes would please me. I shot without any other criteria."

The plot, freely adapted from a pulp crime novel by David Goodis, is classic *noir*. The hero, a once-famous concert pianist (played with sad-eyed doggy charm by singer Charles Aznavour), abandoned his career on discovering how his wife had betrayed him and now plays piano in a tawdry Paris bar. Thanks to his roughneck brothers, he gets involved in a gangland feud and finds himself, and the waitress he loves, caught up in a farcically lethal affair of kidnappings and gunplay.

Because no funding was forthcoming for a studio production, Truffaut and his crew shot on the streets, often making up the script as they went along and deciding the ending on the basis of who was still available for the final showdown. This blithely haphazard approach paid off in unpredictable mood-switches and incongruous dialogue riffs, many of which anticipate Quentin Tarantino's *Reservoir Dogs* (1992). The heavies are played as comic-strip figures, and the hero's siblings bear names recalling the Marx Brothers: Chico, Momo, and Fido. Truffaut takes mischievous delight in playing all kinds of cinematic games: when a crook swears he's telling the truth "on my mother's life," we get a quick cut to an elderly lady keeling over with a heart attack, and a nonsense song sung in the bar punctuates the action (*"Avanie et framboise sont les mamelles de la vie"*—"Affront and raspberry are the breasts of life").

*Piano Player* scored a hit in cinephile circles, but the general public was baffled by the mix of genres and the picture was a commercial disaster. Shaken, Truffaut retreated back to more conventional narrative styles; never again would he let himself have quite so much fun with a film. **PK**

**Italy / France** (Cino Del Duca, Cinematografiche Europee, R. & R. Hakim, Lyre) 145m BW

**Language:** Italian

**Director:** Michelangelo Antonioni

**Producer:** Amato Pennasilico

**Screenplay:** Michelangelo Antonioni, Elio Bartolini, Tonino Guerra

**Photography:** Aldo Scavarda

**Music:** Giovanni Fusco

**Cast:** Gabriele Ferzetti, Monica Vitti, Lea Massari, Dominique Blanchar, Renzo Ricci, James Addams, Dorothy De Poliolo, Lelio Luttazzi, Giovanni Petrucci, Esmeralda Ruspoli, Jack O'Connell, Angela Tommasi Di Lampedusa, Franco Cimino, Prof. Cucco, Giovanni Danesi

**Cannes Film Festival:** Michelangelo Antonioni (jury prize), tied with *Kagi*

# L'AVVENTURA (1960)
## THE ADVENTURE

At its premiere at the Cannes Film Festival in 1960, *L'Avventura* was jeered at and booed by a predominantly hostile audience, though a large number of influential critics and filmmakers took the unprecedented step of signing a statement rejecting this reaction and hailing it as the most important film ever shown at the festival. Within two years, *L'Avventura* was reckoned by the international critics' poll conducted by Britain's *Sight & Sound* magazine as the second greatest movie ever made. Though writer/director Michelangelo Antonioni had been making documentaries and features for nearly 20 years, this epic-length film was his major artistic and commercial breakthrough. Not least because it was his first proper collaboration with Monica Vitti, the actress who is the human and humane channel through which a listless, jaded, dehumanized society is viewed and who would become the focus of his subsequent films *La Notte*, *L'Eclisse*, and *Il Deserto Rosso*.

*L'Avventura*'s premise is disarmingly simple, yet deeply unsettling: a small party of monied Roman characters take a cruise from Sicily and stop off at a desolate, rocky island to pass an idle afternoon that stretches into an ordeal when Anna (Lea Massari) disappears. The slightly vain, uncommitted girl has indicated to her more sensible friend Claudia (Vitti), that she knows something is not right between her and her architectural consultant lover Sandro (Gabriele Ferzetti) and has attracted attention by pretending to sight a shark while swimming. Watching the film for the second time, knowing that this major character will disappear after 26 minutes, we might notice that there really was a shark and that a small, never-mentioned boat can be glimpsed passing the island a short fade after our last look at Anna.

A major cause of initial audience befuddlement and fury with *L'Avventura* is that Antonioni never reveals what has happened to Anna. Claudia and Sandro are drawn together as they search, but none of the other characters even seem that interested in the girl's fate, and the main emotional impact comes from Claudia's feelings of guilt as she gets together romantically with Sandro rather than her desire to find her friend. The plot, presumably by coincidence, rather parallels Hitchcock's *Psycho* (1960), with the jarring absence of the character we assumed to be the heroine in the second part of the film and an uneasy, not-quite-relationship growing between the missing woman's lover and a woman with an equal interest in her welfare. The subject matter also parallels the same year's *La Dolce Vita*. Anita Ekberg's starlet has an equivalent in *L'Avventura*'s flighty star-writer-whore (Dorothy De Poliolo), who is mobbed by "fans" early on when she (deliberately?) rips her tight skirt in public and pops up not so much to wreck the central couple's new relationship as to reveal it as a sham—but there is none of the ambiguous glamor of Fellini's film here. Like Marcello Mastroianni's writer-slid-to-PR man, Ferzetti's architect-turned-rich-man's-flunky epitomizes the failed promise of a direction, and Antonioni can only find a trace of hope in an eternal feminine who ultimately stands apart from the corruption of new money or too-easy sex. **KN**

**U.S. / Mexico** (Olmeca) 95m BW
**Language:** English / Spanish
**Director:** Luis Buñuel
**Producer:** George P. Werker
**Screenplay:** Hugo Butler and Luis Buñuel, from the story *Travellin' Man* by Peter Matthiessen
**Photography:** Gabriel Figueroa
**Cast:** Zachary Scott, Bernie Hamilton, Key Meersman, Crahan Denton, Claudio Brook
**Cannes Film Festival:** Luis Buñuel (special mention)

# LA JOVEN (1960)
## THE YOUNG ONE

Luis Buñuel's two English-language films, this one and the 1952 film *The Adventures of Robinson Crusoe*, are among the most neglected of his middle-period Mexican films—made between his early surrealist masterpieces (*Un Chien Andalou*, *L'Âge d'Or*, *Land without Bread*) and the late European features (*Viridiana*, *That Obscure Object of Desire*) that revived his world reputation. *The Young One* is a taut comedy-thriller set on a game-preserve island off the Carolina coast, though shot, surprisingly, in Mexico. A northern black jazz musician (Bernie Hamilton), fleeing a trumped-up rape charge involving a white woman, arrives on the island and is briefly befriended by a young teenage orphan (Key Meersman), the granddaughter of a handyman who's just died. An unfriendly game warden (Zachary Scott) who's taken a shine to the girl tries to kill the musician; eventually a local preacher (Claudio Brook) and the game warden's boatman (Crahan Denton) also turn up.

A satiric look at both racism and sexual hypocrisy that refuses to take sides, this dark, sensual comedy of manners, adapted quite freely from a Peter Matthiessen story by the gifted blacklisted screenwriter Hugo Butler (under a pseudonym) along with Buñuel, is full of poetic asides and unexpected developments, revealing the filmmaker's dark, philosophical wit at its most personal. **JRos**

**India** (Chitrakalpa) 134m BW
**Language:** Bengali
**Director:** Ritwik Ghatak
**Screenplay:** Ritwik Ghatak, from novel by Shaktipada Rajguru
**Photography:** Dinen Gupta
**Music:** Jyotirindra Moitra, Rabindranath Tagore
**Cast:** Supriya Choudhury, Anil Chatterjee, Niranjan Ray, Gita Ghatak, Bijon Bhattacharya, Gita De, Dwiju Bhawal, Gyanesh Mukherjee, Ranen Ray Choudhury

# MEGHE DHAKA TARA (1960)
## THE CLOUD-CAPPED STAR

"Those who suffer for others, suffer forever," remarks a character in this, Ritwik Ghatak's most famous film, a melodrama that comes close to tragedy. Its heroine's tragic flaw, the sin of omission: She fails to protest at injustice, injustice to herself and her dreams, and at the hands of those she loves most dearly. Nita (Supriya Choudhury) works night and day to keep her refugee Bengali family solvent. Her father is a teacher but earns a pittance. Her elder brother wants to be a singer, and claims the artist's right to time the rest of them can ill afford. Meanwhile her mother hopes the science student who is Nita's intended may transfer his affections to her sister.

*The Cloud-Capped Star* is a searing piece of work, resonant and beautifully composed—and it proved a rare commercial success for its director in India. For all its implicit criticism of the harsh social conditions the refugees live under, the film is less overtly political than Ghatak's subsequent work, notably *Subarnarekha* (1965) and *A River Named Titash* (1973). "I accuse—no one" says the old man, limply, in a key late scene. See it for the grace of Ghatak's mise en scène, his expressionist sound design, and the enormous sense of loss. **TCh**

## HAYNO (1960)
## THE HOUSEMAID

**South Korea** (Kuk Dong, Seki) 90m BW
**Language:** Korean
**Director:** Kim Ki-young
**Screenplay:** Kim Ki-young
**Photography:** Kim Deok-jin
**Music:** Han Sang-gi
**Cast:** Lee Eun-shim, Ju Jeung-nyeo, Kim Jin Kyu

From the point of view of a Westerner, the discovery of a film like *The Housemaid*, more than 40 years after it was made, is a marvelous feeling—marvelous not just because one finds in writer-director Kim Ki-young a truly extraordinary image maker, but in his film such an utterly unpredictable work. So Luis Buñuel had a Korean brother! This filmmaker is capable of probing deep into the human mind, its desires and impulses, while paying sarcastic attention to the details, the bad taste of contemporary colors as secret codes of one's state of being.

What makes *The Housemaid* so shocking is the intensity of the passion that the music composer and his maid experience; the fully self-conscious mechanics of the love triangle existing between the husband, his wife, and his mistress; and the way this triangle can, at any moment, be disturbed, even exploded, by the unusual length of one of the director's shots, by his pop-art use of everyday objects, or by the invading presence of the human (feminine) body. But the shocking nature of the film is both disturbing and pleasurable, as the use of seemingly trivial musical notes and the surprising mixture of sentimentality and cruelty opens the door to new sensations for the viewer, all the more amazing coming from such an unexpected source. Moreoever, Kim Ki-young's depiction of the interior soul of his characters was also a passionate and accusatory statement regarding the inhuman development of South Korean society after the Civil War, a commentary on what the change of spirit and greed for material comforts was doing to its people.

*The Housemaid* was only the first major achievement by a filmmaker running wild through obsessions and rebellion, his compassion for the despised women of his culture revealed again and again in movies with such titles as *The Insect Woman* (1972), *Promise of the Flesh* (1975), *Fire Woman* (1970), *Beasts of Prey* (1985), and *Water Lady* (1979). But the diversity of styles and references present in Kim Ki-young's films—ranging from melodrama to burlesque, from classical tragedy to horror fantasy—makes the matrix that is *The Housemaid* all the more impressive, for this is the picture that opens a still-too-secret door into the history of cinema. **J-MF**

**U.S.** (Shamley, Alfred Hitchcock) 109m BW

**Director:** Alfred Hitchcock

**Producer:** Alfred Hitchcock

**Screenplay:** Joseph Stefano, from novel by Robert Bloch

**Photography:** John L. Russell

**Music:** Bernard Herrmann

**Cast:** Anthony Perkins, Vera Miles, John Gavin, Martin Balsam, John McIntire, Simon Oakland, Vaughn Taylor, Frank Albertson, Lurene Tuttle, Patricia Hitchcock, John Anderson, Mort Mills, Janet Leigh

**Oscar nomination:** Alfred Hitchcock (director), Janet Leigh (actress in support role), Joseph Hurley, Robert Clatworthy, George Milo (art direction), John L. Russell (photography)

# PSYCHO (1960)

One of the most famous movies of all time, and quite possibly the most influential horror film in history, Alfred Hitchcock's *Psycho* traded the supernatural beings of the genre's past—vampires, werewolves, zombies, and the like—for an all-too-human monster. The film made "Norman Bates" a household name and permanently guaranteed its director's status as the master of suspense.

Adapted by Joseph Stefano from a creepy but forgettable novel by Robert Bloch, who based the character of Norman on a real-life Wisconsin serial killer, Ed Gein, *Psycho* tells the story of Marion Crane, an attractive young woman who steals $40,000 from her place of work. She leaves town without a plan, except a vague desire to shack up with her married boyfriend. Driving all night in the rain, she finally stops at a roadside motel, where the manager is an awkward but nice-enough young man named Norman (played to quirky perfection by Anthony Perkins). In a shocking twist that had audiences at the time literally screaming in the aisles, Marion is stabbed to death while taking a shower that evening by what looks like an old lady with a foot-long carving knife. Shrieking violins on the soundtrack (composed by Hitchcock regular Bernard Herrmann) punctuate the terrifying attack. Never before had the central character of a commercial movie been killed off so brutally less than halfway through the film! After an insurance detective assigned to the case, Milton Arbogast (Martin Balsam), gets snuffed out as well, Marion's sister Lila (Vera Miles) and boyfriend Sam Loomis (John Gavin) track her to the Bates family home up the road from the motel. They discover that the killer is actually Norman, a homicidal, cross-dressing schizophrenic who makes himself up just like his dead mother whenever sexual or threatening feelings arise. Although a police-employed psychologist (Simon Oakland) "explains" the cause of Norman's illness at the film's end, there can be little doubt that whatever truly motivates him lies beyond the ability of rational minds to comprehend.

When *Psycho* first opened, it received mostly lukewarm reviews from critics—though better by a mile than the venom that greeted Michael Powell's eerily similar *Peeping Tom*, also released in 1960. Public reaction to the film was staggering, however, with people lining up around the block for tickets. Generating additional buzz was Hitchcock's newly initiated "special policy" of not allowing anyone to enter the theater after *Psycho*'s opening credits had run. Clearly, this British-born filmmaker had found a way of tapping directly into America's collective psyche: By making his monster so very normal, and by uniting sex, madness, and murder in one spooky and sordid tale, he effectively predicted the headlines of many of the coming decades' top news stories. The success of *Psycho* led to three forgettable "sequels," including one directed by Perkins himself in 1986, a short-lived television series, 1987's "Bates Motel," and Gus Van Sant's notorious "shot-for-shot" remake in 1998—a colorized experiment which nonetheless paled in comparison to Hitchcock's black-and-white original. **SJS**

**Italy** (Galatea, Jolly) 87m BW

**Language:** Italian

**Director:** Mario Bava, Lee Kresel

**Producer:** Samuel Z. Arkoff, Massimo De Rita

**Screenplay:** Mario Bava, Ennio De Concini, Mario Serandrei, from story by Nikolai Gogol

**Photography:** Mario Bava

**Music:** Robert Nicolosi

**Cast:** Barbara Steele, John Richardson, Andrea Checchi, Ivo Garrani, Arturo Dominici, Enrico Olivieri, Antonio Pierfederici, Tino Bianchi, Clara Bindi, Mario Passante, Renato Terra, Germana Dominici

# LA MASCHERA DEL DEMONIO (1960)
## REVENGE OF THE VAMPIRE / BLACK SUNDAY

Filmed in Italy as *La Maschera Del Demonio*, this was prepared for English-language release as *The Mask of Satan* but wound up being released in a different form (with Robert Nicolosi's subtle score replaced by Les Baxter's jazzy bombast) in America as *Black Sunday* and, after a ban of some years and severe cuts, in the United Kingdom as *Revenge of the Vampire*.

Cinematographer Mario Bava had several times stepped in to complete the direction of films he was photographing, taking over both *I Vampiri* (1957) and *Caltiki, the Immortal Monster* (1959) from Riccardo Freda and doing major second-unit work on the enormously successful Steve Reeves Hercules films. Having won a shot at making his own picture, Bava turned to a Russian folk legend preserved in "The Vij," a story by Nikolai Gogol, and extrapolated a beguiling fairy tale about a young doctor (John Richardson) who finds himself stranded in a haunted Moldavian community in the 19th century and falls for heiress Katja Vajda (Barbara Steele), whose body becomes possessed by executed-for-witchcraft ancestress Asa (Steele again).

The plot is the usual mix of secret passages, family curses, and sudden deaths, but Bava crams every frame with fascinating, horrid detail. It opens with a marvelously grotesque execution as spiked demon masks are hammered onto the skulls of witches, and features many unforgettably eerie images as the vampires crawl from their graves to persecute the living. Beside the lavish monochrome images, the eerie music, and the touches of blood-spurting goo, *The Mask of Satan* is also your best chance to savor the unique screen presence of Steele, the most strangely sexual actress ever to star in a horror film. An unlikely graduate of the genteel Rank Charm School, a mix of finishing school and dramatic academy, the dark, huge-eyed Steele had found few roles suited to her startling looks in the British cinema and had to venture abroad. She soon became the reigning queen of 1960s Italian horror films before finding a niche battling Sophia Loren for Federico Fellini in *8½* (1963). Under any of its titles, this is the greatest gothic horror movie ever made in Italy. **KN**

## PEEPING TOM (1960)

G.B. (Anglo-Amalgamated, Michael Powell) 101m Eastmancolor

**Director:** Michael Powell

**Producer:** Michael Powell

**Screenplay:** Leo Marks

**Photography:** Otto Heller

**Music:** Brian Easdale, Angela Morley, Freddie Phillips

**Cast:** Karlheinz Böhm, Moira Shearer, Anna Massey, Maxine Audley, Brenda Bruce, Miles Malleson, Esmond Knight, Martin Miller, Bartlett Mullins, Michael Goodliffe, Nigel Davenport, Jack Watson, Shirley Anne Field, Pamela Green, Brian Wallace

The invasiveness of the camera is given a disturbing twist in Michael Powell's infamous, career-destroying *Peeping Tom*. A young man named Mark Lewis (Carl Boehm) introduces himself to women as a documentary filmmaker. But attached to his camera is a metal spike with which he kills his subject as his films them. We learn this from the opening moments of *Peeping Tom*, as we witness a harrowing murder captured in the virtual crosshairs of a viewfinder.

No question Mark is a monster, but Powell reveals bits and pieces of a troubled childhood that at least make him more sympathetic. His sadistic father tormented the boy while filming him for psychoanalytic experiments, shining lights in his eyes to rouse him from sleep, and dropping lizards into his bed. Later we see him posed with his dead mother, a film he combines with footage of his father's remarriage. For Mark, sex, death, love, and hate all bleed into one, and the camera is the one thing capable of capturing all those fleeting emotions. Only through the literal fusion of these feelings with his equipment is Mark able to reconcile the violent and conflicted impulses of his subconscious.

Perhaps it was its subject's ambiguous motives that turned off audiences, or maybe it was the fact that a director as beloved as Powell had turned his sights on such dark and surprising subject matter. But it just as easily could have been the film's subtle implication that the viewer, a fellow voyeur, is somehow complicit in Mark's murderous deeds, riveted by his perverse atrocities and to a degree enabling them.

Vitally, Powell presents this twisted tale with all the skill and craft he brought to his other more innocent movies. The colors of *Peeping Tom* are vibrant, often most so at the moments you wish they weren't. Even compared to the black-and-white of Alfred Hitchcock's somewhat likeminded shocker *Psycho* (also 1960), the vivid *Peeping Tom* comes across as more immediate and ultimately more frightening. We're shoved deep down into the recesses of a madman's brain, and Powell doesn't give us an easy way out. **JKl**

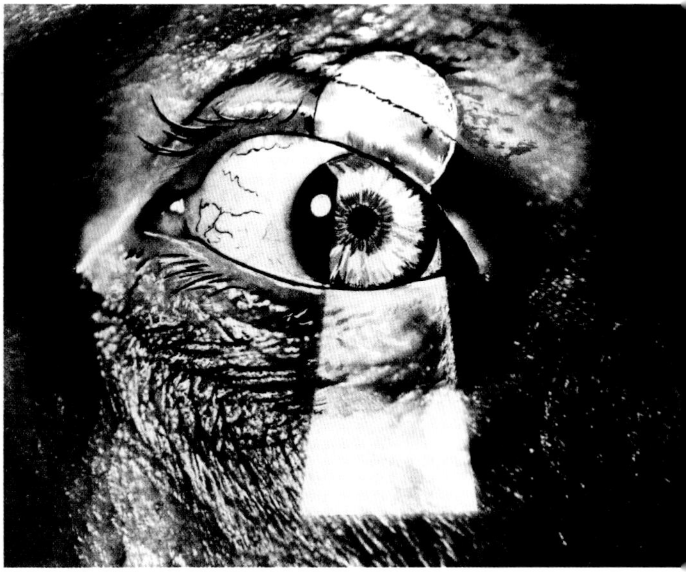

**U.S.** (Mirisch) 125m BW

**Director:** Billy Wilder

**Producer:** I.A.L. Diamond, Duane Harrison, Billy Wilder

**Screenplay:** Billy Wilder and I.A.L. Diamond

**Photography:** Joseph LaShelle

**Music:** Adolph Deutsch

**Cast:** Jack Lemmon, Shirley MacLaine, Fred MacMurray, Ray Walston, Jack Kruschen, David Lewis, Hope Holiday, Joan Shawlee, Naomi Stevens, Johnny Seven, Joyce Jameson, Willard Waterman, David White, Edie Adams

**Oscar:** Billy Wilder (best picture), Billy Wilder (director), Billy Wilder, I.A.L. Diamond (screenplay), Alexandre Trauner, Edward G. Boyle (art direction), Daniel Mandell (editing)

**Oscar nomination:** Jack Lemmon (actor), Shirley MacLaine (actress), Jack Kruschen (actor in support role), Joseph LaShelle (photography), Gordon Sawyer (sound)

**Venice Film Festival:** Shirley MacLaine (Volpi cup—actress), Billy Wilder nomination (Golden Lion)

# THE APARTMENT (1960)

Billy Wilder used to scratch American society where it itches. Inspired by David Lean's *Brief Encounter* (1945), he had to wait ten years for the necessary slackening of censorship before being able to tell the story of the "third" man, the one who lends his apartment to the adulterous couple. Surprisingly, despite its sensitive subject matter, *The Apartment* won no fewer than five Academy Awards (including Best Picture, Director, and Screenplay), and is now considered by many to be the last truly "realist" film made by its director.

Some have criticized the amorality of Jack Lemmon's character C.C. Baxter, who gets promoted quickly only because he helps some of the executives at the big insurance company where he works in their efforts to cheat on their wives. But Lemmon—who used to play Wilder's Everyman characters—brings to the role here a solid touch of humanity, and Baxter finally appears as nothing more than a slavish clerk unwillingly trapped in a situation that already exists at the beginning of the film and is beyond his control. Despite its humor, *The Apartment* is indeed a severe social critique, as well as an examination of contemporary American life and sexual mores. It is also a strong attack on the basic corruption of the capitalist system, in which anyone with a little influence is capable of feeding off someone else.

*The Apartment* skillfully blends various genres, but, by and large, it begins as a satiric comedy, transforms into a powerful drama, and finishes as a romantic comedy. Meticulously constructed, the disillusioned screenplay by Wilder and I.A.L. Diamond can in some ways be considered a kind of bitter follow-up to *The Seven Year Itch* (1955)—one that was beautifully shot in a rather gloomy black-and-white CinemaScope. After their summer vacations, when men had affairs in their wives' absence, they quickly quit their mistresses. Fran Kubelik (Shirley MacLaine) is one of these unfortunate girls, and she believes that love affairs are not just another species of consumer good. In the end, the bureaucrat is finally redeemed by love for this other lonely heart, although the film manages to avoid any syrupy feeling. Although Wilder apparently didn't think that MacLaine and Lemmon formed a great couple, viewers can legitimately hold the opposite opinion. **FL**

**U.S.** (Bryna) 196m Technicolor

**Director:** Stanley Kubrick

**Producer:** Kirk Douglas, Edward Lewis

**Screenplay:** Dalton Trumbo, from novel by Howard Fast

**Photography:** Russell Metty, Clifford Stine

**Music:** Alex North

**Cast:** Kirk Douglas, Laurence Olivier, Jean Simmons, Charles Laughton, Peter Ustinov, John Gavin, Nina Foch, John Ireland, Herbert Lom, John Dall, Charles McGraw, Joanna Barnes, Harold Stone, Woody Strode, Peter Brocco

**Oscar:** Peter Ustinov (actor in support role), Alexander Golitzen, Eric Orbom, Russell A. Gausman, Julia Heron (art direction), Russell Metty (photography), Valles, Bill Thomas (costume)

**Oscar nomination:** Robert Lawrence (editing), Alex North (music)

# SPARTACUS (1960)

This epic's first director, Anthony Mann, was fired by star Kirk Douglas not long after shooting began, although some early scenes he shot in the desert remain in the final film. It fell to a pre-*2001: A Space Odyssey* Stanley Kubrick to bring Howard Fast's tale of a slave revolt in Ancient Rome to life, and he rose to the task brilliantly, mixing scenes of the power struggle in the senate with ones of brotherhood between the slaves.

Spartacus (Douglas) is the slave at the center of the action, who inspires many like him to rise up against their oppressors, including young Antoninus (Tony Curtis), a favorite of Roman Marcus Crassus (Laurence Olivier) who is none too pleased when his pretty boy goes AWOL. When the film was restored three decades after it was made, a bath scene explaining more of the relationship between the master and slave, cut in 1960 because of its homosexual references, was edited in, with Anthony Hopkins rerecording the late Olivier's lost dialogue.

Kubrick stages the slave revolt and battle sequences brilliantly, but the biggest surprise from the director not known for his emotional scenes is the way he films the final, heart-wrenching moments as Spartacus's love Varinia (Jean Simmons) holds up their child for him to see as he dies, crucified alongside the men who followed him. Superb. **JB**

**U.S.** (NBI, Newton, Warner Bros.) 124m Technicolor

**Director:** Elia Kazan

**Screenplay:** William Inge

**Producer:** William Inge, Elia Kazan, Charles H. Maguire

**Photography:** Boris Kaufman

**Music:** David Amram

**Cast:** Natalie Wood, Pat Hingle, Audrey Christie, Barbara Loden, Zohra Lampert, Warren Beatty, Fred Stewart, Joanna Roos, John McGovern, Jan Norris, Martine Bartlett, Gary Lockwood, Sandy Dennis, Crystal Field, Marla Adams

**Oscar:** William Inge (screenplay)

**Oscar nomination:** Natalie Wood (actress)

# SPLENDOR IN THE GRASS (1961)

From the first notes of David Amram's intense score and the opening image of Bud (first-timer Warren Beatty) and Deanie (Natalie Wood) kissing in a car by a raging waterfall, *Splendor in the Grass* sums up the appeal of Hollywood melodrama at its finest. The passions repressed by society (the setting is Kansas 1928) find a displaced expression in every explosive burst of color, sound, and gesture.

Repression is everywhere in this movie, a force that twists people in monstrous, dysfunctional directions. Men are obliged to be successful and macho, while women must choose between virginity and whorishness—as is the case for Bud's unconventional "flapper" sister, Ginny, indelibly incarnated by Barbara Loden.

Director Elia Kazan worked at the intersection of studio-nurtured classical narrative and the innovative, dynamic forms introduced by Method acting and the French New Wave. Here, collaborating with the dramatist William Inge, he achieved a sublime synthesis of both approaches. The film offers a lucid, concentrated analysis of the social contradictions determined by class, wealth, industry, church, and family. At the same time, *Splendor in the Grass* is a film in which the characters register as authentic individuals, acting and reacting in a register that is far from the Hollywood cliché. **AM**

# L'ANNÉE DERNIÈRE À MARIENBAD (1961)
## LAST YEAR AT MARIENBAD

*Last Year at Marienbad* is a touchstone of modernist cinema in general, and of postwar French film in particular.

It was instantly clear in 1961 that Alain Resnais's second feature—like his first, *Hiroshima Mon Amour*, released in 1959—marked a radical departure from movies shaped by the long-dominant "tradition of quality," a dismissive phrase coined by Resnais's somewhat younger French New Wave colleagues. It wasn't just offbeat or eccentric. It mounted a full-blooded assault on ingrained assumptions of narrative film, interrogating and subverting every aspect of "correct" moviemaking from temporal structure to photographic composition to character development.

*Marienbad* is not the brainchild of Resnais alone. Its greatness grows organically from the dreamish poetry of Alain Robbe-Grillet's exquisitely crafted screenplay—much more witty and whimsical than even admirers tend to notice—and from Sacha Vierney's majestic widescreen cinematography, in itself a towering achievement. Looking deeper still, one should credit the insights of the *Cahiers du Cinéma* film critics, developments in modernist painting, the Existentialist and Bergsonian strains of European philosophy, and other invigorating theoretical/cultural/sociopolitical innovations of this hugely fertile period in French culture.

And then there's the extraordinary cast, with legendary Delphine Seyrig as the woman called A, inimitable Giorgio Albertazzi as the inscrutable stranger called X, and subtly expressive Sacha Pitoëff as M, the perplexed husband of the tale. They portray the enigmatic characters of this ultimately inscrutable fable with a sense of quietly restrained passion that suits its elegant atmospherics to perfection.

Still, to see *Marienbad* as fundamentally a Resnais movie is both to acknowledge its kinship with his other masterpieces—the extraordinary *Muriel ou le Temps d'un Retour* (1963), *Providence* (1977), and *Mon Oncle d'Amérique* (1980), among them—and to recognize his overwhelming importance to progressive cinema. With characteristic modesty, he once called *Marienbad* a "crude and primitive . . . attempt" to capture "the complexity of thought and its mechanisms." He was wrong in his choice of adjectives, but right about everything else connected with this strange and stirring film. Nowhere else in cinema have the labyrinthine workings of consciousness and memory been evoked more forcefully or explored more resonantly. **DS**

**France / Italy** (Argos, Cineriz, Cinétel, Como, Cormoran, Tamara, Precitel, Silver, Soc. Nouvelle, Terra) 94m BW

**Language:** French

**Director:** Alain Resnais

**Producer:** Pierre Courau, Raymond Froment

**Screenplay:** Alain Robbe-Grillet, from the novel *The Invention of Morel* by Adolfo Bioy Casares

**Photography:** Sacha Vierny

**Music:** Francis Seyrig

**Cast:** Delphine Seyrig, Giorgio Albertazzi, Sacha Pitoëff, Françoise Bertin, Luce Garcia-Ville, Héléna Kornel, François Spira, Karin Toche-Mittler, Pierre Barbaud, Wilhelm von Deek, Jean Lanier, Gérard Lorin, Davide Montemuri, Gilles Quéant, Gabriel Werner

**Oscar nomination:** Alain Robbe-Grillet (screenplay)

**Venice Film Festival:** Alain Resnais (Golden Lion)

**France** (Argos) 28m BW

**Language:** French

**Director:** Chris Marker

**Producer:** Anatole Dauman

**Screenplay:** Chris Marker

**Photography:** Jean Chiabaut, Chris Marker

**Music:** Trevor Duncan

**Cast:** Jean Négroni, Hélène Chatelain, Davos Hanich, Jacques Ledoux, André Heinrich, Jacques Branchu, Pierre Joffroy, Étienne Becker, Philbert von Lifchitz, Ligia Branice, Janine Klein, William Klein, Germano Faccetti

# LA JETÉE (1961)

## THE PIER

An experimental film couched in the trappings of science fiction ("remade" by Terry Gilliam in 1995 as *Twelve Monkeys*), Chris Marker's short work *La Jetée* is the kind of deceptively simple project that grows in resonance and complexity as time goes on. Though the film is composed almost entirely of black-and-white still photos, Marker nonetheless infuses it with a thought-provoking narrative thrust, showing once and for all that moving pictures need not always actually move to move us.

Set in the near future after a nuclear apocalypse has sent any survivors scurrying underground for safety, *La Jetée* is narrated by a man sent back in time to both discover and avert the cause of the devastating war. During his trips into the past he becomes obsessed with a violent image he recalls from his childhood—a man being shot—as well as a mysterious, beautiful woman. By the time he realizes the connection between the two it is too late, and history is doomed to repeat itself.

Marker's use of still images and spare bits of narration forces him to focus on sound design. The chatter of voices and strange noises replicates the hazy mechanics of time travel, here presented as a sort of metaphysical manipulation of memory and space. As the narrator's trips back through time progress, they also grow more lucid, leading to one of the film's most affecting moments. Picturing the beautiful woman asleep, Marker films her eyes flickering open, the one scene of *La Jetée* that shows moving images.

This brief moment helps to illustrate the connection between the narrator and the woman, revealing why he would want to deviate from his compulsory mission and also setting the stage for the mind-bending (or is that time-bending?) twist at the film's conclusion. *La Jetée* is short at 25 minutes, but Marker still manages to generate more of an impact than many films three times as long. That his intentionally cold montage achieves any sort of emotional resonance validates his creativity and ingenuity, and helps explain why such an unconventional cinematic work is revered as an influential science-fiction masterpiece. **JKl**

# ONE-EYED JACKS (1961)

Of course Marlon Brando can act. The bigger question raised by *One-Eyed Jacks*, his directorial debut, is: Can he direct?

As the man who first popularized the Stanislavsky Method for American cinema in the early 1950s, Brando epitomizes his unique style in the film's opening scene. As he slowly relishes a banana, the camera dollies backward, emphasizing his calm in what is revealed to be a bank robbery where his character, Rio, is the ringleader. He smiles, and the camera stops in an establishing shot. He swallows the last bite of fruit before taking a female customer's ring.

A wonderful scene, it also reveals Rio's partner, the rough and tumble Dad Longworth (Karl Malden), along with the easy pace of the Western. Thereafter Brando's debut turns into a revenge fantasy stretching from Northern Mexico to Monterey. Though reputedly a troubled production, *One-Eyed Jacks* sports excellent design elements, the brilliance of casting Malden against type as a villain, and otherwise delivers a spectacle of remarkably determined moral ambivalence, visual beauty, and believable character motivation.

To sketch the rest of the plot, Dad ends up double-crossing Rio and leaving him in a Mexican jail where a lifelong grudge is commenced. Five years pass before Rio breaks out of prison. Hell-bent on reaping his revenge, he falls in with a band of outlaws led by Bob Amory (Ben Johnson) and the group rides north along the California coast looking for action. In Monterey they finally catch up with Dad, now the local sheriff with a Chicana wife, Maria (Katy Jurado), and a teenage stepdaughter, Louisa (Pina Pellicer). Rio pretends friendship, Dad lies about his past, Bob plans a bank robbery, and Louisa falls under the swaggering outlaw's sway. Needless to say, Rio earns his rightful comeuppance as all the other men die in pursuit of their varied vices.

A fine addition to Brando's filmography and important in connecting Western classics of the 1950s with the genre experimentation of the 1970s, *One-Eyed Jacks* deftly explores the two sides of a man, realizing the theme suggested by its title and remaining a little-seen treasure. **GC-Q**

**U.S.** (Paramount, Pennebaker) 141m Technicolor

**Director:** Marlon Brando

**Producer:** Frank P. Rosenberg

**Screenplay:** Guy Trosper, Calder Willingham, from the novel *The Authentic Death of Hendry Jones* by Charles Neider

**Photography:** Charles Lang

**Music:** Hugo Friedhofer

**Cast:** Marlon Brando, Karl Malden, Katy Jurado, Pina Pellicer, Ben Johnson, Slim Pickens, Larry Duran, Sam Gilman, Timothy Carey, Miriam Colon, Elisha Cook Jr., Rodolfo Acosta, Joan Petrone, Tom Webb, Ray Teal

**Oscar nomination:** Charles Lang (photography)

**France / Italy** (EIA, Rome-Paris) 90m BW

**Language:** French

**Director:** Jacques Demy

**Producer:** Carlo Ponti, Georges de Beauregard

**Screenplay:** Jacques Demy

**Photography:** Raoul Coutard

**Music:** Michel Legrand

**Cast:** Anouk Aimée, Marc Michel, Jacques Harden, Alan Scott, Elina Labourdette, Margo Lion, Annie Duperoux, Catherine Lutz, Corinne Marchand, Yvette Anziani, Dorothée Blank, Isabelle Lunghini, Annick Noël, Ginette Valton, Anne Zamire

# LOLA (1961)

Jacques Demy's magical first feature anticipates his two later masterpieces, *The Umbrellas of Cherbourg* and *The Young Ladies of Rochefort*, not merely in its efforts to introduce an air of fairy-tale romance into the banal world of an Atlantic port (in this case his native Nantes) but also in its use of music and dance. While the latter elements aren't yet constant in this film, they still inform plot, characterization, and mood, right from the opening sequence's use of Beethoven and Michel Legrand's jazz to accompany a white Cadillac's mysterious glide into town.

It would be wrong to write off as trivial the romantic roundelay that unrolls around alluring but enigmatic cabaret-dancer and single mom Lola (Anouk Aimée), delaying a decision between several suitors while she awaits her long-gone true love's return from abroad. For all the breezy byplay, Raoul Coutard's elegantly circling camerawork (the film is a delicious tribute to Max Ophüls), jaunty melodies, and far-fetched coincidences, *Lola* is imbued with a poignant awareness of the transience of happiness and the difficulties and unlikelihood of love. Formally too, the film is more complex than it first appears, with most of the minor characters legible as telling variations on the central couple. Oh, and Anouk is unforgettable. **GA**

**U.S.** (Jurow-Shepherd, Paramount) 115m Technicolor

**Director:** Blake Edwards

**Producer:** Martin Jurow, Richard Shepherd

**Screenplay:** George Axelrod, from novel by Truman Capote

**Photography:** Franz Planer

**Music:** Henry Mancini

**Cast:** Audrey Hepburn, George Peppard, Patricia Neal, Buddy Ebsen, Martin Balsam, José Luis de Villalonga, John McGiver, Alan Reed, Dorothy Whitney, Beverly Powers, Stanley Adams, Claude Stroud, Elvia Allman, Mickey Rooney

**Oscar:** Henry Mancini (music), Henry Mancini, Johnny Mercer (song)

**Oscar nomination:** George Axelrod (screenplay), Audrey Hepburn (actress), Hal Pereira, Roland Anderson, Sam Comer, Ray Moyer (art direction)

# BREAKFAST AT TIFFANY'S (1961)

Truman Capote, on whose novella *Breakfast at Tiffany's* is based, originally imagined Marilyn Monroe in the lead role of good-time girl Holly Golightly, but it's now hard to imagine anyone that could have suited the part better than Audrey Hepburn. Standing outside famous Manhattan jewelry store Tiffany's in the film's memorable opening scene, the actress never looked more beautifully luminous or enchanting.

In Capote's novel Holly is clearly a call girl, but since Blake Edwards's movie version was made in 1961 when such matters gave censors nightmares, Hepburn's Holly is depicted as a bohemian gal living off the gifts of gentlemen. Sharing the same apartment building is struggling writer Paul (George Peppard), who himself is a kept man thanks to a wealthy benefactor (Patricia Neal) with whom he is having an affair. The delicate balance of both his and Holly's relationships are placed under threat, however, when Paul falls in love with his beautiful, if sometimes maddening, neighbor.

Audrey Hepburn, her hair swept back, dressed in a chic black dress, and carrying her elegant cigarette holder, provides an unforgettable image that hasn't faded over time. Add Henry Mancini's haunting score and classic cinematic moments (Hepburn singing "Moon River," or searching for her beloved Cat in the pouring New York rain) and you have one of Hollywood's most delightful and unforgettable romantic dramas. **JB**

# LA NOTTE (1961)
## THE NIGHT

**Italy / France** (Nepi, Silver, Sofitedip) 122m BW

**Language:** Italian

**Director:** Michelangelo Antonioni

**Screenplay:** Michelangelo Antonioni, Ennio Flaiano, Tonino Guerra

**Photography:** Gianni di Venanzo

**Music:** Giorgio Gaslini

**Cast:** Marcello Mastroianni, Jeanne Moreau, Monica Vitti, Bernhard Wicki, Rosy Mazzacurati, Maria Pia Luzi, Guido A. Marsan, Vittorio Bertolini, Vincenzo Corbella, Ugo Fortunati, Gitt Magrini, Giorgio Negro, Roberta Speroni

**Berlin International Film Festival:** Michelangelo Antonioni (Golden Bear)

Michelangelo Antonioni's follow-up to his groundbreaking *L'Avventura* (1960) is the middle feature in a loose trilogy ending with *L'Eclisse* (1962) that was made at the height of his intellectual prestige in the international film scene. Repeating many of the melancholic themes and stylistic moves of its predecessor, with particular emphasis on the boredom and atrophied emotions of the rich, *La Notte* ends with the kind of regretful recollection of former sexual desire that characterizes the final scene of James Joyce's short story "The Dead." For better and for worse, the mainstream clichés that would circulate throughout the 1960s about Antonioni as a highbrow director making boring films about the bored rich stem largely from the excesses of this feature—despite the fact that it also showcases some of the filmmaker's most subtle and modulated work.

*La Notte*'s success as a structured and shapely narrative is somewhat more mixed than that of either *L'Avventura* or *L'Eclisse*, and the performances are generally better than those of the former and not as good as those in the latter. The minimal plot, restricted to less than 24 hours, involves the death of passion between a successful novelist, Giovanni Pontano (Marcello Mastroianni), and his frustrated wife Lidia (Jeanne Moreau). The best parts of this film tend to cluster around the beginning and end, and include the novelist's brief encounter with a nymphomaniac patient at a hospital while visiting a dying friend (Bernhard Wicki) and his much longer encounter with the daughter (Monica Vitti) of an industrialist at a party, both of which foreground his shifting impulses and moods. Both these sequences show Antonioni's mise en scène at its most intricately plotted and emotionally subtle. By contrast, probably the weakest section is an extended walk taken by the wife around Milan, full of symbolic details meant to suggest her mental state, which arguably shows some of the ill effects that Ingmar Bergman had on certain filmmakers during the early 60s. Yet whatever one's occasional misgivings, this feature comes from what is widely and justifiably considered to be Antonioni's richest period, and evidence of his stunning mastery is readily apparent throughout. **JRos**

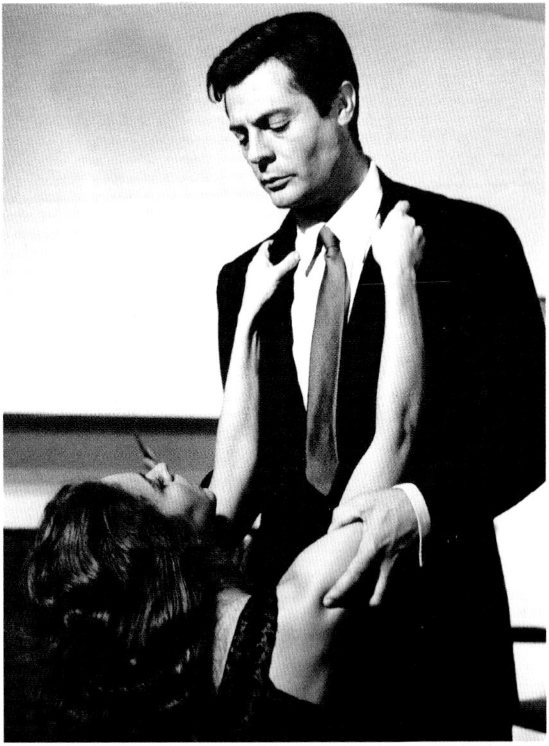

France (Carrosse, Sédif) 100m BW

**Language:** French

**Director:** François Truffaut

**Producer:** Marcel Berbert

**Screenplay:** Jean Gruault, François Truffaut, from novel by Henri-Pierre Roché,

**Photography:** Raoul Coutard

**Music:** Georges Delerue

**Cast:** Jeanne Moreau, Oskar Werner, Henri Serre, Vanna Urbino, Boris Bassiak, Anny Nelsen, Sabine Haudepin, Marie Dubois, Christiane Wagner, Michel Subor

# JULES ET JIM (1962)
## JULES AND JIM

She wore rings on every finger. She sang the song. She wore a mustache and a thug cap, and she loved two men—one French, the other German—as the war was coming. She would love many more men, before, after, and during that time, and bicycles were running fast on the curved roads of happiness. In the end there was death. Mr. Jules (Oskar Werner) and Mr. Jim (Henri Serre) opened the door to the magical summer of cinema's modernity, but they came from the summer of another modernity, one that occurred way back at the beginning of the 20th century—when Henri-Pierre Roché lived this story and then wrote it as a diary. They opened the door, and Catherine (Jeanne Moreau) ran right through it, shining with grace and strength and faith in being human. She would win all the races on the bridge—even the one where the bridge ends in the middle. It would be a tragedy, but it was shown as slapstick.

Never see *Jules and Jim* in a dubbed version, François Truffaut's voice-over is the sound of a wind that caresses and makes one world disappear, another world appear. The beauty of the black-and-white CinemaScope is hardly large enough, delicate and nuanced enough, rooted in the origin and contemporary enough, contrasted enough to convey the vivid and subtle energy the film is made out of. Look at Moreau! Look how beautiful she is! Truffaut was in love with her (how could he not be?). *Jules and Jim* was created from this love—it would have been impossible to make this movie without the obvious happiness of the director filming his actress, the strength they gave to each other. A shadow of sadness can be felt each time she leaves the frame, a thrill of joy and desire each time she enters it again.

Cinema is the art of recording, not only the recording of objects but also visual forms and sounds. It is also the recording of that distorted reality produced by powerful emotions. *Jules and Jim* records just such a distorted reality, to an extraordinary extent. War was to come, as was delusion, and death. The film knew it, its black and white were also the colors of mourning. It was also Truffaut's third film, still made in the original impulse of the New Wave. And yet, after the autobiographical and child-centered *The 400 Blows* (1959) and the avant-garde, virtuoso game of *Shoot the Piano Player* (1960), *Jules and Jim* signaled a more adult and middle-of-the-road effort without losing any of the young and disruptive energy of the revolution he and his accomplices had just launched in world cinema. And, at least during this brief moment, that is exactly what happened. Truffaut's third film kept alive a moment of turbulence that would never come again—a jump into the future, with love. **J-MF**

## VIRIDIANA (1961)

In 1960 the new generation of Spanish filmmakers persuaded Luis Buñuel to work in his native Spain for the first time since his departure in 1936. The project he devised was an ironic drama. Viridiana (Silvia Pinal), on the eve of taking her final vows and entering a convent, visits her uncle (Fernando Rey), a rich landowner. Excited by her resemblance to his dead wife, he plots to rape her, but repents at the last moment. In his remorse he kills himself, leaving Viridiana as coheir to his estates with his cynical natural son. Zealous in her efforts to better the world around her, Viridiana adopts a monstrous group of thieves, beggars, and whores. Inevitably her charity leads to disaster and her own undoing.

The Spanish authorities approved the script with few changes but had no opportunity to see the finished film before its competition in the 1961 Cannes Film Festival. Despite its award of the Cannes Grand Prix, *Viridiana* was instantly (and for several years) banned in Spain: Having enhanced the script in his realization, Buñuel had evidently lost none of his ability to shock and offend bigots. Full of moments of surreal observation, the film remains one of Buñuel's most perfect expositions of the irredeemable follies of human nature and the irrepressible comedy of life. **DR**

**Spain / Mexico** (59, Gustavo Alatriste, UNINCI) 90m BW

**Language:** Spanish

**Director:** Luis Buñuel

**Producer:** Gustavo Alatriste, Ricardo Muñoz Suay, Pedro Portabella

**Screenplay:** Julio Alejandro, Luis Buñuel

**Photography:** José F. Aguayo

**Music:** Gustavo Pittaluga

**Cast:** Silvia Pinal, Francisco Rabal, Fernando Rey, José Calvo, Margarita Lozano, José Manuel Martín, Victoria Zinny, Luis Heredia, Joaquín Roa, Lola Gaos, María Isbert, Teresa Rabal

**Cannes Film Festival:** Luis Buñuel (Golden Palm), tied with Henri Colpi's *Une Aussi Longue Absence*

## THE LADIES MAN (1961)

Jerry Lewis has never been one to be ignored. It may finally be time to admit that our movie-loving French friends know what they're talking about. Already one of the three or four most influential American screen comedians, Jerry's immense popularity as an actor did not adequately prepare the world for his talent as a director, or for the many glories of *The Ladies Man*.

In *The Ladies Man*, Lewis demonstrates a mastery of mise en scène that has rarely been rivaled. Very few could arrange the elements of a film frame with such skill and pitch-perfect comic timing. The proof is in, most famously, the incredible scene in which the many denizens of the women-only rooming house wake up and perform their morning rituals. In one remarkable shot, we see young women in different rooms combing their hair, exercising, and playing the French horn (!)—all while the camera cranes through the famous cutaway "dollhouse" set. Their movements are syncopated to the music, and perfectly integrated into the lavish setting. The result is a cavalcade of comic 1960s femininity that unfolds in vivid colors and psychosexual madness.

Add to this the fact that Jerry gives one of his wildest and weirdest performances, and that, as a director, he is willing to gleefully suspend reality at the drop of a hat—as in the famously bizarre "Spider Lady" sequence. *The Ladies Man* also features what is, for my money, cinema's finest "slow burn." The film is a high point not only in Jerry Lewis's comic style, but in the use of mise en scène in American motion pictures. **EdeS**

**U.S.** (Paramount) Color

**Director:** Jerry Lewis

**Producer:** Ernest D. Glucksman, Jerry Lewis

**Screenplay:** Jerry Lewis, Bill Richmond

**Photography:** W. Wallace Kelley

**Music:** Jack Brooks, Walter Scharf, Harry Warren

**Cast:** Jerry Lewis, Helen Traubel, Kathleen Freeman, Hope Holiday, Lynn Ross, Gretchen Houser, Lillian Briggs, Mary LaRoche, Madlyn Rhue, Alex Gerry, Jack Kruschen, Vicki Benet, Pat Stanley, Dee Arlen, Francesca Bellini

**Sweden** (Svensk) 89m BW
**Language:** Swedish
**Director:** Ingmar Bergman
**Producer:** Allan Ekelund
**Screenplay:** Ingmar Bergman
**Photography:** Sven Nykvist
**Nonoriginal music:** Johann Sebastian Bach
**Cast:** Harriet Andersson, Gunnar Björnstrand, Max von Sydow, Lars Passgård
**Oscar:** Sweden (best foreign language film)
**Oscar nomination:** Ingmar Bergman (screenplay)
**Berlin International Film Festival:** Ingmar Bergman (OCIC award), nomination (Golden Bear)

# SÅSOM I EN SPEGEL (1961)
## THROUGH A GLASS DARKLY

The first film in what later became known as Bergman's chamber-trilogy on the silence of God (though the director himself has here and there advised against any such formal approach to the films in question), *Through a Glass Darkly* begins somewhat misleadingly with four people—Kårin (Harriet Andersson), her husband Martin (Max von Sydow), her father David (Gunnar Björnstrand), and her teenage brother Minus (Lars Passgård)—emerging from the sea, as if out of nowhere, in peals of laughter suggestive of happiness and a sense of togetherness. They are on holiday—indeed this is the first of Bergman's films to be set on the island of Faro, which he later made his home—and as the sun sets the mood is one of relaxed enjoyment; only gradually do we learn of the despair, doubts, and divisions within the family, as the film advances inexorably toward its dark conclusion, exactly a day later.

In that time, Kårin will learn that the mental illness she has believed she was getting over has been found to be incurable; Martin will discover that all the love he feels for her cannot prevent her hallucinations; David will confess that he has tended to put his work (he's a successful writer) before his family, and that for all his efforts he cannot change; Minus, already in teenage turmoil, will be sucked in by Karin's spiraling madness; and she, hoping that God will show himself and help them in their need, breaks down when He reveals his cold, stony face as that of a spider. This terrifying scene (we don't see the spider, only her distraught reaction to His imagined visitation) constitutes both the dramatic climax and the logical thematic conclusion of an immaculately wrought drama virtually unmatched even by Bergman's other films for its sheer intensity.

Influenced by Strindberg, *Through a Glass Darkly*—with its handful of characters, isolated setting, brief time span, and uncluttered visuals (apart from the characters, all we seem to see are their house, the sea, sky, rocky shore, and a wrecked boat in which Karin first experiences her breakdown)—allows nothing to dilute the force of its emotional and philosophical thrust; no wonder Bergman saw it as the first of his films to pave the way toward the masterpiece that was *Persona* (1966).
**GA**

# CHRONIQUE D'UN ÉTÉ (1961)
## CHRONICLE OF A SUMMER

**France** (Argos) 85m BW
**Language:** French
**Director:** Edgar Morin, Jean Rouch
**Photography:** Raoul Coutard, Roger Morillière, Jean-Jacques Tarbès
**Cast:** Marceline Loridan Ivens, Marilù Parolini, Jean Rouch

Anthropologist Jean Rouch and sociologist Edgar Morin's *Chronicle of a Summer* is one of the most significant and quoted of all documentary films. Drawing on the traditions and techniques of several pioneers of the form—Dziga Vertov and Robert Flaherty—Rouch and Morin document the patterns and performances of everyday life in early 1960s Paris. Capitalizing on some of the key changes in 16 mm filmmaking equipment and technique occurring at the time, the film demonstrates the nascent possibilities of an increasingly mobile and "objective" medium.

Although in some ways *Chronicle of a Summer* can be said to be observational in style, it constantly insists on interrogating its methodological and ethical approach. In this respect, the film extends Flaherty's practice—he insisted on showing his rushes to the Inuit subjects of *Nanook of the North* (1922)—by including a screening and critical discussion of the "finished" film within the film itself. And though *Chronicle of a Summer* "shows" us moments in the lives of its characters—sometimes talking to Morin, at others just "being" for the camera—it also self-consciously stamps itself as an ethnographic or anthropological experiment incorporating the interactive responses of its subjects.

Perhaps the most remarkable aspect of *Chronicle of a Summer* is less its ability to capture unmediated moments of reality, than its capacity to critically examine the mixture of reality and performance (and performance as reality) insisted upon by the presence of the camera. Unlike the documentaries of Frederick Wiseman, which painstakingly attempt to efface both the camera and the filmmaker, the presence of both in Rouch and Morin's film is constantly insisted upon. Thus, rather than being constructed as observers of everyday life, the camera and filmmaker are implicated in both its unfolding and its construction. Nevertheless, in the walk of concentration camp survivor Marcelline through the streets of Paris—accompanied by her explicitly "personal" commentary—one can glimpse the approaching "freedom" of the *cinéma vérité* form. This is a visionary work, both formative and already a critical exploration of the powers and techniques of "direct" cinema. **AD**

**U.S.** (Fox) 134m BW

**Director:** Robert Rossen

**Producer:** Robert Rossen

**Screenplay:** Sidney Carroll, Robert Rossen, from novel by Walter Tevis

**Photography:** Eugen Schüfftan

**Music:** Kenyon Hopkins

**Cast:** Paul Newman, Jackie Gleason, Piper Laurie, George C. Scott, Myron McCormick, Murray Hamilton, Michael Constantine, Stefan Gierasch, Clifford A. Pellow, Jake LaMotta, Gordon B. Clarke, Alexander Rose

**Oscar:** Harry Horner, Gene Callahan (art direction), Eugen Schüfftan (photography)

**Oscar nomination:** Robert Rossen (best picture), Robert Rossen (director), Sidney Carroll, Robert Rossen (screenplay), Paul Newman (actor), George C. Scott (actor in support role), refused nomination, Jackie Gleason (actor in support role), Piper Laurie (actress)

# THE HUSTLER (1961)

In *The Hustler*, Paul Newman plays "Fast Eddie" Felson, a cocky pool shark who spends his time shuttling from pool hall to pool hall searching for a few suckers to scam. The vulture-like middleman George C. Scott sees promise in Eddie and tries to teach him how keeping your cool is the key to winning, but Newman discovers the hard way that keeping your cool also means excluding everything and everybody from your life save the pool table and the man you're trying to beat.

The spectacular black-and-white widescreen shots of smoky pool halls aside, *The Hustler* is a movie about people, and as such it features an array of impressive acting. Along with Newman and Scott is a laconic Jackie Gleason and a sad-sack Piper Laurie, who plays Newman's doomed, alcoholic love interest (though love may be too strong a word to describe what they share). Robert Rossen's film remains one of the most remarkably bitter and cynical portrayals of human nature ever made, a cold-blooded depiction of a world where loyalty only lasts as long as a winning streak, and a victory isn't always distinguishable from a loss. **JKl**

**U.S.** (Mirisch, Seven Arts) 151m Technicolor

**Language:** English / Spanish

**Director:** Jerome Robbins, Robert Wise

**Producer:** Robert Wise,

**Screenplay:** Jerome Robbins, Ernest Lehman, from play by Arthur Laurents

**Photography:** Daniel L. Fapp

**Music:** Leonard Bernstein, Saul Chaplin

**Cast:** Natalie Wood, Richard Beymer, Russ Tamblyn, Rita Moreno, George Chakiris, Simon Oakland

**Oscar:** Robert Wise (best picture), Robert Wise, Jerome Robbins (director), George Chakiris (actor in support role), Rita Moreno (actress in support role), Boris Leven, Victor A. Gangelin (art direction), Daniel L. Fapp (photography), Irene Sharaff (costume), Thomas Stanford (editing), Saul Chaplin, Johnny Green, Sid Ram, Irwin Kostal (music), Fred Hynes, Gordon Sawyer (sound)

**Oscar nomination:** Ernest Lehman (screenplay)

# WEST SIDE STORY (1961)

An early instance of the Shakespearean approach to teen drama, getting in on the act decades before it was trendy, this Oscar-winning filming of the Broadway musical hit relocates the story of *Romeo and Juliet* among New York street gangs, with the Capulets and the Montagues morphed into the Puerto Rican Sharks and the Polish Jets. Stolid director Robert Wise holds the fort in the nonmusical scenes, but the film really takes off in the musical numbers by allowing the unrestrained Jerome Robbins to choreograph dances like fights and fights like dances on mostly real locations.

*West Side Story* stumbles by casting charisma-free Richard Beymer in the lead (the Colonel wouldn't let Elvis play Tony) and can't exactly pass the winning Natalie Wood off as Puerto Rican, but the supporting cast are perfect: Russ Tamblyn as the leader of the Jets ("Little boy you're a man, little man you're a king"), George Chakiris as his Shark opposite number, and a show-stopping Rita Moreno as the best friend who takes the lead in "I Like to Be in America." Each and every Leonard Bernstein–Stephen Sondheim number is a classic belter: "I Feel Pretty," "When You're a Jet," "Tonight," "Gee Officer Krupke," "Maria," "Stay Cool, Boy," "There's a Place for Us." **KN**

# MONDO CANE (1962)
## A DOG'S LIFE

An immensely popular documentary that problematizes the boundaries separating fiction from nonfiction filmmaking practices, *Mondo Cane* initiated its own subgenre of "mondo films" (or "Shockumentaries"). It also begat a wave of imitators and has proven formative for such diverse pop and pseudodocumentary traditions as mockumentaries, "snuff" films, hardcore pornography, execution videos, and reality television.

Purporting to subscribe to the adage that "truth can be stranger than fiction," all the while betraying its own principles by presenting often misleading voice-over commentary and manipulated (if not wholly faked) footage, Gualtiero Jacopetti's sensationalist travelogue-cum-nature film set out to shock viewers with its exposé of bizarre cultural behavior, which fluctuated "from the exotic to the erotic to the undeniably repellant."

A one-time journalist and war correspondent, Jacopetti was hired to write the voice-over narration for two celebratory compilation films of popular nightclub acts. This gave him the initial idea for *Mondo Cane*; only *his* documentary would showcase all that was lurid and sensational by contemporary Western standards. Jacopetti traveled across Europe, Asia, North America, and Africa with his associates, collecting assorted footage of tribal ceremonies, extreme cruelty to animals, religious rituals involving cross-dressing and self-flagellation, and environmental catastrophes. This more-or-less random material was then assembled into a 105-minute episodic whole, the various segments connected by the thinnest of associative links.

Along with its bloated orchestral score (the theme song, "More," won a Grammy Award, as well as an Oscar nomination), the film's pretentious and heavily ironized voice-over became a key ingredient of the mondo cycle to follow. The privileged opening words of *Mondo Cane* were both spoken and appeared as text on the screen: "All the scenes you will see in this film are true and are taken only from life. If often they are shocking, it is because there are many shocking things in this world. Besides, the duty of the chronicler is not to sweeten the truth but to report it objectively." Even if the scenes then presented were "true," in the sense of being detached and unbiased recordings of actual events—which they clearly are not; the only question concerns precisely which footage is real, which is reconstructed, and which is completely staged—*Mondo Cane* still breaks its promise, as the film's reportage is anything but "objective." Besides dishing out the occasional piece of gross misinformation, Stefano Sibaldi's voice-over is haughty and condescending, and sometimes even takes on racist overtones.

Complicating any straightforwardly xenophobic (fear of anything strange or foreign) reading of the film, are its segments ridiculing Western cultural practices, like the one where we tour with a gaggle of American senior citizens eager to waste their retirement savings on a Hawaiian vacation package. In this respect, *Mondo Cane*'s creators come across as equal-opportunity exploiters. By the end, and as the film's alternative title declares, it does seem like we are watching "a dog's life" ("mondo cane" translates as "world of dogs"). **SJS**

**Italy** (Cineriz) 105m Technicolor
**Language:** Italian
**Director:** Paolo Cavara, Gualtiero Jacopetti, Franco E. Prosperi
**Screenplay:** Paolo Cavara, Gualtiero Jacopetti
**Photography:** Antonio Climati, Benito Frattari
**Music:** Nino Oliviero, Riz Ortolani
**Cast:** Rossano Brazzi, Stefano Sibaldi
**Oscar nomination:** Riz Ortolan, Nino Oliviero, Norman Newell (song)

France / Italy (Rome-Paris) 90m BW/ Color

**Language:** French

**Director:** Agnès Varda

**Producer:** Georges de Beauregard

**Screenplay:** Agnès Varda

**Photography:** Jean Rabier

**Music:** Michel Legrand

**Cast:** Corinne Marchand, Antoine Bourseiller, Dominique Davray, Dorothée Blank, Michel Legrand, José Luis de Villalonga, Loye Payen, Renée Duchateau, Lucienne Le Marchand, Serge Korber, Robert Postee

# CLÉO DE 5 À 7 (1962)
## CLEO FROM 5 TO 7

Precursor of the French New Wave with her debut feature *La Pointe Courte* (1956), writer-director Agnès Varda focuses in *Cleo from 5 to 7* on a French singer (Corinne Marchand) awaiting the results of a vital medical examination. As the film's title indicates, Varda has chosen to show Cléo's anguish virtually in real time, thereby taking into account the emergence and development of the techniques of "direct cinema." The casualness of the narrative allows fiction to merge with documentary as the young woman wanders through the left bank of Paris, mostly around Montparnasse Station, followed by dazzling tracking shots. But Varda's realism is also capable of generating powerful emotion, showing in a crescendo the slow breakdown of her lead character's face.

To a certain extent, *Cleo from 5 to 7* reflects the sociopolitical tensions of its time, with Cléo witnessing the aftermath of an attack in a bar and encountering a soldier on leave who is just about to go back to Algeria—in a way, he too can be seen as condemned. On the anecdotal side, movie buffs will appreciate the combination of a short silent film-within-the-film featuring Jean-Luc Godard with various famous actors, including Eddie Constantine, Anna Karina, and Yves Robert. **FL**

**U.S.** (Canyon Cinema) 30m Color

**Director:** Stan Brakhage

**Producer:** Stan Brakhage

**Screenplay:** Stan Brakhage

**Photography:** Jane Brakhage, Stan Brakhage

**Cast:** Jane Brakhage, Stan Brakhage

# DOG STAR MAN (1962)

Arguably the most prolific and influential figure in all of American avant-garde cinema, Stan Brakhage made films so profoundly personal that viewing them is like plunging into the tumultuous processes of thought itself. His lifelong project was to rediscover the purity and intensity of perception that people possess until education and acculturation force our unfettered mental energies into a narrow range of socially approved patterns.

*Dog Star Man* is exemplary Brakhage in every way, from its revolutionary aesthetic strategies to its philosophical vision of an existential hero questing for the infinite possibilities of being through a physical, psychological, and spiritual journey into inner and outer space. The narrative line is minimal: a man (Brakhage) trudges up a mountainside with his dog. By contrast, the film's structure grows ever more complex, as five discrete sections weave an escalating number of superimposed images into a rapid-fire visual tapestry so intricate that an alternate, "unraveled" version, *The Art of Vision*, runs about four-and-a-half hours.

The title *Dog Star Man* can be taken as a nickname for the protagonist, or as an invocation of archetypal entities—the biological, the cosmological, the human—that intertwine as inextricably in this extraordinary film as in the innermost recesses of consciousness and unconsciousness themselves. **DS**

## SANMA NO AJI (1962)
### AN AUTUMN AFTERNOON

**Japan** (Shochiku) 112m Agfacolor
**Language:** Japanese
**Director:** Yasujiro Ozu
**Producer:** Shizuo Yamanouchi
**Screenplay:** Kôgo Noda, Yasujiro Ozu
**Photography:** Yûshun Atsuta
**Music:** Kojun Saitô
**Cast:** Chishu Ryu, Shima Iwashita, Shinichirô Mikami, Keiji Sada, Mariko Okada, Nobuo Nakamura, Kuniko Miyake, Ryuji Kita, Eijirô Tono, Teruo Yoshida, Daisuke Katô, Miseyo Tamaki, Haruko Sugimura, Kyôko Kishida, Noriko Maki

Yasujiro Ozu's final film and only his second one in color (the other being *Good Morning*), *An Autumn Afternoon* is a marvelous testament to a career notable both for its idiosyncratic stylistic uniformity (after a few early movies, he stuck resolutely to quiet domestic dramas and comedies shot almost exclusively with a static camera positioned two or three feet above floor level), and for the likewise extraordinary riches attained through such limited methods. He returned to the same themes—and, indeed, stories—again and again, and this exquisitely poignant film is to all intents and purposes a remake of the 1949 film *Late Spring*, in which the director's favorite actor, Chishu Ryu, also played a widower trying to persuade the grown-up daughter who lives with him that she should get married.

The pair's mutual awareness that such a change would leave him lonely is counterbalanced by their love of one another, creating a dilemma for each that is both banal in its everyday universality and hugely significant for the individuals involved. Ozu negotiates this precarious balancing act with his customary mastery, exercising his unerring eye for the telling detail, leavening the proceedings with gentle humor, and using the palette of colors to maintain a beautifully becalmed mood of understated melancholy. **GA**

## L'ECLISSE (1962)
### THE ECLIPSE

**Italy / France** (Cineriz, Interopa, Paris) 118m BW
**Language:** French / Italian
**Director:** Michelangelo Antonioni
**Producer:** Raymond Hakim, Robert Hakim, Danilo Marciani
**Screenplay:** Michelangelo Antonioni, Elio Bartolini, Tonino Guerra, Ottiero Ottieri
**Photography:** Gianni Di Venanzo
**Music:** Giovanni Fusco
**Cast:** Alain Delon, Monica Vitti, Francisco Rabal, Louis Seigner, Lilla Brignone, Rosanna Rory, Mirella Ricciardi
**Cannes Film Festival:** Michelangelo Antonioni (special jury prize), tied with *Procès de Jeanne d'Arc*

The conclusion of Michelangelo Antonioni's loose trilogy about modern life at midcentury (preceded by 1960's *L'Avventura* and *La Notte*), *The Eclipse* is conceivably the greatest film of his career, but perhaps significantly it has the least consequential plot. A sometime translator (Monica Vitti) recovering from an unhappy love affair briefly links up with a stockbroker (Alain Delon) in Rome, though the stunning final montage sequence—perhaps the most powerful thing Antonioni has ever done—does without these characters entirely. And because these two leads arguably give the most nuanced and charismatic performances of their careers here, the shock of losing them before the end of the picture is central to the film's devastating final effect.

Alternately an essay and a prose poem about the contemporary world in which the "love story" figures as one of many motifs, *The Eclipse* is remarkable both for its visual/atmospheric richness and its polyphonic and polyrhythmic mise en scène. Antonioni's handling of crowds at the Roman stock exchange is never less than amazing, recalling the choreographic use of deep focus used in the early features of Orson Welles, where foreground and background details are juggled together in brilliant juxtapositions. But it is probably the final sequence, which depends on editing rather than mise en scène, that best sums up the hope and despair of the filmmaker's vision. **JRos**

**G.B.** (Horizon) 216m Technicolor

**Director:** David Lean

**Producer:** Sam Spiegel

**Screenplay:** Robert Bolt, from memoir by T.E. Lawrence

**Photography:** Freddie Young

**Music:** Maurice Jarre

**Cast:** Peter O'Toole, Alec Guinness, Anthony Quinn, Jack Hawkins, Omar Sharif, José Ferrer, Anthony Quayle, Claude Rains, Arthur Kennedy, Donald Wolfit, I.S. Johar, Gamil Ratib, Michel Ray, John Dimech, Zia Mohyeddin

**Oscar:** Sam Spiegel (best picture), David Lean (director), John Box, John Stoll, Dario Simoni (art direction), Freddie Young (photography), Anne V. Coates (editing), Maurice Jarre (music), John Cox (best sound)

**Oscar nomination:** Robert Bolt (screenplay), Peter O'Toole (actor), Omar Sharif (actor in support role)

# LAWRENCE OF ARABIA (1962)

One of the greatest epics of all time, *Lawrence of Arabia* epitomizes all that motion pictures can be. Ambitious in every sense of the word, David Lean's Oscar grabbing masterpiece, based loosely on the life of the eccentric British officer T.E. Lawrence and his campaign against the Turks in World War I, makes most movies pale in comparison and has served as an inspiration for countless filmmakers, most notably technical masters like George Lucas and Steven Spielberg. The latter eventually helped restore *Lawrence* to its proper length and luster alongside fellow enthusiast Martin Scorsese. From Maurice Jarre's sweeping score to Robert Bolt's literary script to Freddie Young's gorgeous desert cinematography to the literal cast of thousands, the film deserves and demands to be seen and heard on the big screen.

Designed for 70mm projection, the format enhances the film's minute details, from star Peter O'Toole's piercing blue eyes to the sun beaming down on the constantly shifting sand. *Lawrence of Arabia*'s famous images and set pieces, such as Omar Sharif's appearance out of a desert mirage, the famed cut from a lit match to the sunrise, and the mind-boggling assault on Akaba, look spectacular and, indeed, unrepeatable. They were especially impressive for a picture made in the days before computer-generated special effects. Spielberg, for one, estimates the cost of making *Lawrence* today at around $285 million, and he would know, but the truth of the matter is that no filmmaker would dare attempt to outdo Lean, a superb director and storyteller at the top of his game.

That substance runs parallel to the spectacle only enhances the stature of *Lawrence of Arabia* and the reputation of Lean. The follies of colonialism and the hypocrisies of war are cast into stark relief, as Colonel Lawrence lets the success of his Arab-fought campaign against the Turks go to his head. Yet his larger-than-life persona is cut down to size once he realizes that bloodlust has replaced honor and arrogance has replaced courage. It's a sad fall from grace shown with subtley, literacy, and craft—a true epic with the scope and scale of great literature. **JKl**

U.S. (Pakula-Mulligan, Brentwood, Universal) 129m BW

**Director:** Robert Mulligan

**Producer:** Alan J. Pakula

**Screenplay:** Horton Foote, from novel by Harper Lee

**Photography:** Russell Harlan

**Music:** Elmer Bernstein, Mack David

**Cast:** Gregory Peck, Mary Badham, John Megna, Frank Overton, Rosemary Murphy, Ruth White, Brock Peters, Estelle Evans, Paul Fix, Collin Wilcox Paxton, James Anderson, Alice Ghostley, Robert Duvall, William Windom, Crahan Denton, Richard Hale

**Oscar:** Horton Foote (screenplay), Gregory Peck (actor), Alexander Golitzen, Henry Bumstead, Oliver Emert (art direction)

**Oscar nomination:** Alan J. Pakula (best picture), Robert Mulligan (director), Mary Badham (actress in support role), Russell Harlan (photography), Elmer Bernstein (music)

**Cannes Film Festival:** Robert Mulligan (Gary Cooper award)

# TO KILL A MOCKINGBIRD (1962)

Harper Lee's beloved, Pulitzer Prize–winning novel of childhood in the Deep South during the Depression received a rare, superlative translation to the screen by the new, independent, and socially conscious production partnership of Alan J. Pakula, who produced, and Robert Mulligan, who directed this first of six films they made together in the 1960s. The adaptation was written by playwright Horton Foote, who won his first Academy Award for a screenplay that typified his feel for authentic rural Americana and real people.

Although the story is seen through the eyes of a little girl (whose adult viewpoint as narrator is voiced by Method luminary Kim Stanley), the film has a strong center in the Oscar-winning performance of Gregory Peck as the *ne plus ultra* of all the decent men he embodied, Atticus Finch—the widowed, kindly Alabama lawyer whose passionate defense of a black man (Brock Peters) falsely accused of raping a white woman exposes Southern small-town bigotry at its worst and teaches his young children a painful lesson in moral courage. *To Kill a Mockingbird* is a model for literary adaptations, retaining seemingly inconsequential details along with major, heartbreaking, or deadly events—whether the children's games, a hungry farm boy drowning his dinner in syrup, Atticus shooting a rabid dog, the lynch mob outside the jailhouse shamed to their senses by a child, the black community tensely following the trial in the stifling balcony—Mulligan bringing his experience in live TV production to craft a discreetly atmospheric, intimate character drama.

In important roles the children are terrifically natural, particularly the ingenuous Scout Finch played by nine-year-old Alabaman Mary Badham (whose brother John, then at Yale, would go on to direct *Saturday Night Fever* [1977] and *WarGames* [1983]). *To Kill a Mockingbird* also boasts the feature debut of Robert Duvall as the children's elusive neighbor, bogeyman of their fantasies, and ultimately their savior, Boo Radley. Duvall would receive his own Academy Award 20 years later in another Oscar-winning screenplay by Foote, *Tender Mercies*. The melodious score by Elmer Bernstein is another asset in this tender, heartfelt film. **AE**

## THE MANCHURIAN CANDIDATE (1962)

One of the strangest and most mercurial movies ever made in Hollywood, adapted from a novel of the same name by Richard Condon, *The Manchurian Candidate* was originally released in 1962 and then unseen for years after its star, Frank Sinatra, purchased the rights in the 1970s and withdrew the film from circulation. A salad of mixed genres and emotional textures, this political thriller runs more than two hours and never flags for an instant. The film got the green light with the active encouragement of President John F. Kennedy, a fan of the novel and a friend of Sinatra.

It's conceivably the only commercial American film that deserves to be linked with the French New Wave. Early on, there's a virtuoso 360-degree pan moving around a lady's garden club meeting that gradually and inexplicably turns into a demonstration of brainwashing by Chinese communists—a literal Cold War nightmare worthy of Joseph McCarthy. The politically incorrect audacity only expands from there, eventually widening to include irreverent satire, ghoulish black humor, surrealist nonsense, and incest.

Angela Lansbury and Laurence Harvey, both brilliantly cast as evil mother and masochistically subservient son, have never been better and Sinatra and Janet Leigh have never been used as weirdly. The talented secondary cast—James Gregory, James Edwards, Leslie Parrish, John McGiver, and Khigh Dhiegh—is never less than effective. A powerful experience, alternately corrosive with dark parodic humor; suspenseful, moving, and terrifying. **JRos**

**U.S.** (M.C. Productions) 126m BW

**Director:** John Frankenheimer

**Producer:** George Axelrod, John Frankenheimer, Howard W. Koch

**Screenplay:** George Axelrod, from novel by Richard Condon

**Photography:** Lionel Lindon

**Music:** David Amram

**Cast:** Frank Sinatra, Laurence Harvey, Janet Leigh, Angela Lansbury, Henry Silva, James Gregory, Leslie Parrish, John McGiver, Khigh Dhiegh, James Edwards, Douglas Henderson, Albert Paulsen, Barry Kelley, Lloyd Corrigan, Madame Spivy

**Oscar nomination:** Angela Lansbury (actress in support role), Ferris Webster (editing)

## LOLITA (1962)

"How have they made a movie of *Lolita*?" asked a teasing trailer for Stanley Kubrick's 1962 film of Vladimir Nabokov's much-banned novel. Working from a Nabokov script, Kubrick slightly raised the age of Dolores "Lolita" Haze (Sue Lyon), from the book's twelve to somewhere around fourteen, but otherwise manages remarkably within the limits of censorship to deliver a picture exactly as erotic, absurd, obsessive, erudite, and low-comic as the book.

Shot in Britain, Kubrick's *Lolita* lacks the book's preroad movie feel for America's tacky motels and roadside attractions but homes in on the characters, with James Mason giving a remarkable performance as the middle-aged academic Humbert Humbert, as ridiculously lusted after by Lo's leopard-print-clad mama (Shelley Winters) as he is ridiculously smitten with the underage temptress herself. Opening with the aftermath of an orgy and Humbert's murder of his pedophile rival, "genius" Clare Quilty (Peter Sellers), the film stretches from slapstick (struggling with a folding bed in a motel room) to tragedy (Humbert's affecting sobs as he realizes how incidental he has been to the girl's life), with Mason's sly, careful, pointed presence matched by Sellers in a succession of personae as a shape-shifting Satan accompanied by Marianne Stone as his silent Morticia-like muse Vivian Darkbloom (an anagram). **KN**

**U.S. / G.B.** (Anya, Harris-Kubrick, Seven Arts, Transwood) 152m BW

**Director:** Stanley Kubrick

**Producer:** James B. Harris

**Screenplay:** Vladimir Nabokov, from his novel

**Photography:** Oswald Morris

**Music:** Bob Harris, Nelson Riddle

**Cast:** James Mason, Shelley Winters, Sue Lyon, Gary Cockrell, Jerry Stovin, Diana Decker, Lois Maxwell, Cec Linder, Bill Greene, Shirley Douglas, Marianne Stone, Marion Mathie, James Dyrenforth, Maxine Holden, John Harrison

**Oscar nomination:** Vladimir Nabokov (screenplay)

**Venice Film Festival:** Stanley Kubrick nomination (Golden Lion)

**Brazil / Portugal** (Cinedistri, Francisco de Castro) 98m BW

**Language:** Portuguese

**Director:** Anselmo Duarte

**Producer:** Francisco de Castro, Anselmo Duarte, Oswaldo Massaini

**Screenplay:** Anselmo Duarte, from play by Alfredo Dias Gomes

**Photography:** H.E. Fowle

**Music:** Gabriel Migliori

**Cast:** Leonardo Villar, Glória Menezes, Dionísio Azevedo, Norma Bengell, Geraldo Del Rey, Roberto Ferreira, Othon Bastos, Canjiquinha, Américo Coimbra, Walter da Silveira, Veveldo Diniz, João Di Sordi, Napoleao Lopes Filho, Milton Gaucho, Alair Liguori, Gilberto Marques, Garibaldo Matos, Jurema Penna, Antonio Pitanga, Cecília Rabelo, Conceição Senna, Irenio Simoes, Carlos Torres, Enoch Torres

**Oscar nomination:** Brazil (best foreign language film)

**Cannes Film Festival:** Anselmo Duarte (Golden Palm)

# O PAGADOR DE PROMESSAS (1962)
## KEEPER OF PROMISES

Based on the play by Brazilian playwright Alfredo Dias Gomes, *Keeper of Promises* is a parable about unconditional faith in the face of adversity. The plot revolves around Zé do Burro (Leonardo Villar), a simple-minded farmer trying to fulfill a promise to a spirit he believes saved the life of his donkey. Zé and his wife Rosa (Glória Menezes) live on a farm about 30 miles from Salvador. In the context of Brazilian spirtuality, Salvador symbolizes a religious space where Catholic and African pagan rituals blend together into a positive whole.

After the donkey's miraculous recovery, Zé sets out on the pilgrimage carrying a huge cross on his back, which he wants to place inside the church of Saint Barbara. His wish clashes with the imperviousness of priest Olavo (Dionísio Azevedo), who bans him from the church. Zé's naïveté is further exploited by unscrupulous characters. So cruel is the portrayal of the human race in the film that it is easy to understand why Zé's best friend is a donkey.

*Keeper of Promises* is an unequivocal indictment against the intolerance of the Catholic Church as compared with the religious open-mindedness defining Brazilian sensibility, and it has a tragic ending that is cruel, sad, and extremely beautiful. Nominated for Best Foreign Film at the Academy Awards, its highest achievement was the Palme d'Or at the 1962 Cannes International Film Festival. **RDe**

**U.S.** (John Ford, Paramount) 123m BW

**Director:** John Ford

**Producer:** Willis Goldbeck

**Screenplay:** James Warner Bellah, Willis Goldbeck, Dorothy M. Johnson

**Photography:** William H. Clothier

**Music:** Cyril J. Mockridge

**Cast:** John Wayne, James Stewart, Vera Miles, Lee Marvin, Edmond O'Brien, Andy Devine, Ken Murray, John Carradine, Jeanette Nolan, John Qualen, Willis Bouchey, Carleton Young, Woody Strode, Denver Pyle, Strother Martin

**Oscar nomination:** Edith Head (costume)

# THE MAN WHO SHOT LIBERTY VALANCE (1962)

As if explaining away the beautiful evasions and downright lies of his earlier Westerns, *The Man Who Shot Liberty Valance* finds John Ford concluding that if the legend is better than the truth, then you should "print the legend." Lawyer Ransom Stoddard (James Stewart) poaches the credit for ridding the territory of a subhuman outlaw (Lee Marvin) and riding on to political success in the 20th century while the real man who shot Liberty Valance (John Wayne) dies broke and drunk. There's further irony in that the ultimate Western hero is here a back shooter who plugs Liberty from the shadows while the supposedly unmanly politico stands suicidally out in the open playing it fair.

Shot in black and white on a soundstage to avoid the lyricism of Ford's Monument Valley epics, this revisits the cleaning-up-the-town theme of *My Darling Clementine* (1946) with a cynical insight into the whole process of civilizing the wilderness. Wayne, like Stewart too old for his role but nevertheless perfect, represents the cowboy heroism and integrity that Stewart's lawyer-teacher-congressman will whittle away as he comes to run the West. **KN**

# WHAT EVER HAPPENED TO BABY JANE?
(1962)

**U.S.** (Aldrich, Seven Arts, Warner Bros.) 134m BW

**Director:** Robert Aldrich

**Producer:** Robert Aldrich, Kenneth Hyman

**Screenplay:** Lukas Heller, from novel by Henry Farrell

**Photography:** Ernest Haller

**Music:** Frank De Vol

**Cast:** Bette Davis, Joan Crawford, Victor Buono, Wesley Addy, Julie Allred, Anne Barton, Marjorie Bennett, Bert Freed, Anna Lee, Maidie Norman, Dave Willock, William Aldrich, Ernest Anderson, Russ Conway, Maxine Cooper

**Oscar:** Norma Koch (costume)

**Oscar nomination:** Bette Davis (actress), Victor Buono (actor in support role), Ernest Haller (photography), Joseph D. Kelly (sound)

An epic slice of Hollywood Grand Guignol, which considerably ups the grotesquerie of *Sunset Boulevard.* (1950) as two aging *grandes dames* of the cinema tear each other to metaphoric shreds in a decaying movie-star mansion.

Based on a novel by Henry Farrell and directed with black glee by Robert Aldrich, *What Ever Happened to Baby Jane?* is a remarkable vehicle for Joan Crawford, as the wheelchair-bound ex-1930s superstar at the mercy of her mad sister, and Bette Davis, in the title role as a middle-aged child star who insists on dressing in her old stage outfit, singing her one hit song ("I've Written a Letter to Daddy"), and dreaming of a big comeback. The plot is wound around the long-ago accident that crippled Blanche (Crawford) at the height of her fame and hinges on some genuinely unexpected revelations, but the nasty fun comes from the spectacle of these two screen queens—who evidently hated each other—pouring venom on one another. The supporting cast has room for a marvelously slatternly Agnes Moorehead as the housekeeper and the enormously creepy Victor Buono as an opportunist who takes the job as piano player for Jane's act. Favorite moment: Bette serving Joan a cooked rat under a platter for dinner. **KN**

**France** (Pléïade, Pathé) 80m BW
**Language:** French
**Director:** Jean-Luc Godard
**Producer:** Pierre Braunberger
**Screenplay:** Jean-Luc Godard, from book by Marcel Sacotte
**Photography:** Raoul Coutard
**Music:** Michel Legrand
**Cast:** Anna Karina, Sady Rebbot, André S. Labarthe, Guylaine Schlumberger, Gérard Hoffman, Monique Messine, Paul Pavel, Dimitri Dineff, Peter Kassovitz, Eric Schlumberger, Brice Parain, Henri Attal, Gilles Quéant, Odile Geoffroy, Marcel Charton
**Venice Film Festival:** Jean-Luc Godard (Pasinetti award), (special jury prize), nominated (Golden Lion)

# VIVRE SA VIE: FILM EN DOUZE TABLEAUX (1962)

## MY LIFE TO LIVE

An episodic account of the short life of a young prostitute, *My Life To Live* is the first of Jean-Luc Godard's mature masterpieces. Like much of his best work, it is both supremely analytical and supremely sensuous, achieving an austere, wintry beauty—in contrast to the colorful summerscapes of *Contempt* (1963) and *Pierrot le fou* (1965). *My Life to Live*'s primary reference points are the rigorous spirituality of filmmakers Carl Theodor Dreyer and Robert Bresson, and the lost Eden of silent cinema. Both come together most strikingly when the heroine (Anna Karina) foresees her own martyrdom at a screening of Dreyer's silent classic, *The Passion of Joan of Arc*.

The Dreyer excerpt is one of several semiautonomous texts (including a jukebox ballad, a primer on prostitution, a discussion with philosopher Brice Parain, and Poe's "The Oval Portrait") punctuating the film, which additionally is divided into twelve chapters and a series of distinct formal units inscribed by the camera. Arranged into overlapping but incongruent patterns, these elements open up the narrative to juxtaposed commentaries on such topics as mainstream film style, the burden of language, and Godard's relationship with his leading lady, whose face—as riveting as those of the great silent stars—anchors *My Life to Live*'s diverse strands without subsuming them into static harmony. **MR**

**U.S.** 66m BW
**Director:** Harry Smith

# HEAVEN AND EARTH MAGIC (1962)

Harry Smith is perhaps the least known major figure of American avant-garde cinema. His films reflect a wide-ranging fascination with alchemy and the occult, as well as a technique of incorporating the rediscovery of the cultural debris of previous eras. On his death in 1991, Smith left behind an eclectic body of "work," the landmark *The Anthology of American Folk Music* and a small number of films, mostly incomplete. *Heaven and Earth Magic*, his magnum opus, was "completed," off-and-on, throughout the 1950s.

The film's narrative is deliberately oblique, arguably surrealist, and its mostly cut-out-based animation predominantly "abstract" or symbolist in form. *Heaven and Earth Magic* does have a story of sorts. The spectator can grasp onto the graphic and associational links that exist between the objects and shapes that dance across and within the frame. In preparing his film, Smith attempted to short-circuit the processes of logic and explicit linearity, entering into the realm of the subconscious, automatic, and symbolic.

Like Joseph Cornell, Smith is concerned with placing objects, images, and sounds in new contexts and associations. *Heaven and Earth Magic* resembles both the hypnotic, trancelike juxtaposition of image and sound in *Rose Hobart* (1936), and the intricate, hand-crafted, indirectly personal qualities of Cornell's display boxes. It is totally in keeping with Smith's own broader artistic practice. Incomplete, deeply idiosyncratic, rearranged from materials taken largely from an earlier period—a Victorian-era catalogue—it is explicitly "folk" in nature. **AD**

# THE BIRDS (1963)

*The Birds* stands out as an anomaly among Alfred Hitchcock's films for many reasons. For one, it's the closest the director ever came to a conventional horror movie. But it's also perhaps the most enigmatic of all his films. *The Birds* invites many interpretations, yet Hitchcock never tips his hand. If he intended any single specific meaning to be gleaned from it, he tantalizingly (and teasingly) presents few explanations for the terror that transpires.

Tippi Hedren (hand-picked by Hitchcock as the latest in a long line of blonde leads) arrives in the small, sleepy coastal town of Bodega Bay, where she bumps into Rod Taylor at a pet store. After she later decides to drop by at his house to surprise him, she's attacked by a seagull, foreshadowing the fate of the entire town: With little warning, Bodega Bay comes under attack by flocks of frenzied birds. No explanation is ever given for the onslaught, and no one is safe. All the characters can do is board themselves up inside and wait out the mysterious, deadly attack.

Hitchcock infamously nearly led Hedren to a nervous breakdown, his increasingly sadistic work ethic (perhaps misplaced aggression following the retirement of his favored star Grace Kelly) too intense for her to handle. In fact, coming after *Psycho* (1960), with its numerous references to "birds" (both the animal and the slang term for women), *The Birds* (Hitchcock's third film based on a Daphne Du Maurier work) may have been intended as a vaguely misogynistic sexual allegory, with Taylor the sole male amidst several women vying for his attention.

But again, the theme of the film remains oblique at best, with Hitchcock instead stressing the horror and horrific effects. *The Birds* features some pioneering uses of matte work which, combined with a few mechanical birds and several of the real thing, makes each attack a harrowing experience. The tension is increased with the groundbreaking electronic score (overseen by Bernard Herrmann), a mix of strange sounds that often blurs ominously with the sounds of the cooing birds and the menacing flap of their wings. **JKl**

**U.S.** (Alfred J. Hitchcock, Universal) 119m Technicolor
**Director:** Alfred Hitchcock
**Producer:** Alfred Hitchcock
**Screenplay:** Evan Hunter, from story by Daphne Du Maurier
**Photography:** Robert Burks
**Cast:** Tippi Hedren, Rod Taylor, Jessica Tandy, Suzanne Pleshette, Veronica Cartwright, Ethel Griffies, Charles McGraw, Ruth McDevitt, Lonny Chapman, Joe Mantell, Doodles Weaver, Malcolm Atterbury, John McGovern, Karl Swenson, Richard Deacon
**Oscar nomination:** Ub Iwerks (special visual effects)

**U.S.** (Jerry Lewis, Paramount) 107m Technicolor

**Director:** Jerry Lewis

**Producer:** Ernest D. Glucksman, Arthur P. Schmidt

**Screenplay:** Jerry Lewis and Bill Richmond

**Photography:** W. Wallace Kelley

**Music:** Louis Y. Brown, Walter Scharf

**Cast:** Jerry Lewis, Stella Stevens, Del Moore, Kathleen Freeman, Med Flory, Norman Alden, Howard Morris, Elvia Allman, Milton Frome, Buddy Lester, Marvin Kaplan, David Landfield, Skip Ward, Julie Parrish, Henry Gibson

# THE NUTTY PROFESSOR (1963)

A skit on *Dr. Jekyll and Mr Hyde, The Nutty Professor* (as Eddie Murphy later discovered) could only be made by someone who wasn't as secure in the affections of the audience as he had been in the previous decade. In 1963, it was read as a strange summation of the Martin-and-Lewis films, with infantile comic Jerry Lewis proving that he didn't need a smooth straight man because he could play both roles, and the Hyde figure of swinger "Buddy Love" seen as a nasty caricature of Dino. Actually, Buddy plays more like Dean Martin's Rat Pack padrone, Frank Sinatra, and what Lewis was really doing was presenting his own showbiz dark side, emerging from the cocoon of his sweet, child-pleasing but adult-irritating comic persona. The Jekyll equivalent, Julius Kelp, is buck-toothed in an ironic nod to Fredric March's 1932 Hyde makeup, and speaks with the strangled Lewis whine that makes nonfans want to kill him. Allowing for a near-masochist series of humiliations Kelp is picked on by the dean, football players, muscle men at a gym (Richard Kiel, another human cartoon, has a tiny cameo), and his students, exciting the sympathy only of lovely blonde student Stella Purdy (Stella Stevens).

Murphy's Buddy Love avenges wrongs done to his Sherman Klump, but Lewis's Buddy despises his alter ego and makes a play for Stella in such an unpleasant manner that he becomes the worst of the series of bullies who have picked on Kelp. From the wonderfully colored expressionist parody of the traditional Jekyll-and-Hyde transformation, in which Kelp turns into a series of evermore grotesque Hyde types before becoming the "swingingest" Buddy, through to Buddy's rise to power at the local happening place, the Purple Pit, *The Nutty Professor* is among the most uncomfortable of American comedies. Unlike Jekyll, Kelp learns his lesson, but not before he has had to accept that he has a monster inside him. The finale, in which Love transforms into Kelp in front of the whole campus, is dead serious, and as devastating as Cliff Robertson's regression to imbecility in the last reel of *Charly* (1968). **KN**

## BLONDE COBRA (1963)

U.S. 33m

**Director:** Ken Jacobs

**Cast:** Ken Jacobs, Jack Smith

Generally considered one of the masterpieces of the New York underground film scene, Ken Jacobs's *Blonde Cobra* is perhaps first and foremost a fascinating audio-visual testament to the tragicomic performance of the inimitable Jack Smith. Smith, who died of AIDS in 1989, was a photographer, writer, filmmaker, performer, and queer muse for the New York avant-garde arts scene in the 1960s and '70s. *Blonde Cobra*, which Jacobs edited from material Smith shot with collaborator Bob Fleischner, is comprised of sequences of Smith clowning around with coperformer Jerry Sims, juxtaposed with long stretches of black leader.

During the imageless black sequences, we are treated to the hilarious and perverse stories that Smith delivers in his characteristic nasal drone on the soundtrack. These at times confessional tales of a little boy's "frustrated longings" and an older Nun's dreams of lesbianism, for example, are interspersed with other Smithian ruminations ("Why shave . . . when I can't even think of a reason for living?"), as well as with bits from the radio, a German tango, and a Fred Astaire/Ginger Rogers song. Though perhaps a bit "heavy," as Smith described it, Jacobs's *Blonde Cobra* provides an alluring portrait of the improvisational talents of a great experimental performer. **MS**

## THE COOL WORLD (1963)

**U.S.** (Wiseman) 125m BW

**Director:** Shirley Clarke

**Producer:** Frederick Wiseman

**Screenplay:** Shirley Clarke, Carl Lee, Robert Rossen, from novel and play by Warren Miller

**Photography:** Baird Bryant

**Music:** Mal Waldron

**Cast:** Hampton Clanton, Yolanda Rodríguez, Bostic Felton, Gary Bolling, Carl Lee, Clarence Williams, Gloria Foster, Georgia Burke

"When I got to Hollywood, all the movie moguls claimed to be astounded by the reality of my films. How did I do it? And I'd say, 'Well, it wasn't hard to make Harlem look like Harlem.'" This was how writer and director Shirley Clarke described the response of mainstream Hollywood moviemakers to her independently-made "fictional documentary," *The Cool World*. A radical and rarely-screened classic of 1960s American experimental cinema, the film combines real locations, a loose narrative, naturalistic acting, and highly expressive editing and cinematography in a raw, unflinching look at the power struggles and casual violence of Harlem's street gangs.

Based on a play by Warren Miller and Robert Rossen (which was in turn adapted from Miller's best-selling novel), and produced by acclaimed documentary filmmaker Frederick Wiseman (four years before his own directorial debut, the 1967 film *Titticut Follies*), *The Cool World* also boasts a powerful jazz soundtrack by one-time Billie Holiday accompanist Mal Waldon. The starkness of the music serves to make the already depressed living conditions seem all the more rough and unkind. Along with the score, it is *The Cool World*'s unforgettable images that led film critic Judith Christ to describe it as a "loud, long and powerful cry of outrage at the world society has created for Harlem youngsters, and at the human condition in the slum ghetto." Find a copy somewhere, somehow—you won't regret it. **SJS**

**Italy / France** (Cineriz, Francinex)
145m BW

**Language:** Italian / English / French

**Director:** Federico Fellini

**Producer:** Angelo Rizzoli

**Screenplay:** Federico Fellini, Ennio Flaiano, Tullio Pinelli, Brunello Rondi

**Photography:** Gianni Di Venanzo

**Music:** Nino Rota

**Cast:** Marcello Mastroianni, Claudia Cardinale, Anouk Aimée, Sandra Milo, Rossella Falk, Barbara Steele, Madeleine LeBeau, Caterina Boratto, Eddra Gale, Guido Alberti, Mario Conocchia, Bruno Agostini, Cesarino Miceli Picardi, Jean Rougeul, Mario Pisu

**Oscar:** Piero Gherardi (costume), Italy (best foreign language film)

**Oscar nomination:** Federico Fellini (director), Federico Fellini, Ennio Flaiano, Tullio Pinelli, Brunello Rondi (screenplay), Piero Gherardi (art direction)

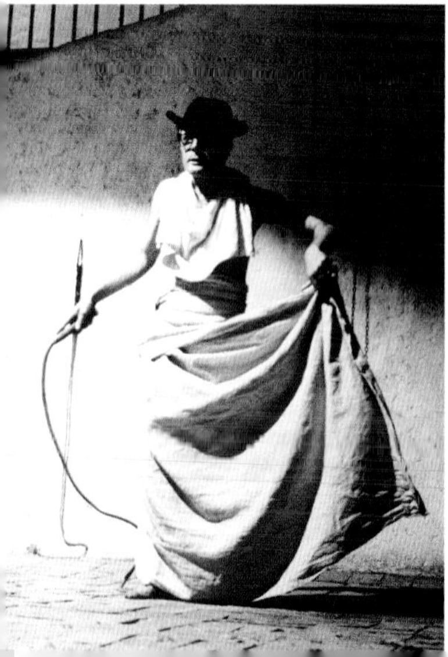

# 8 ½ (1963)

Marcello Mastroianni with hat and cigar in a bathtub . . . . Immemorial white walls and the black line of a whip . . . . Impressive women and fantasies . . . . The images of Federico Fellini's *8 ½* remain, and the sounds as well (a pity for those who have never heard the film in its original, though so artificial, Italian). The picture stands as a testimony to an icon of the European Baroque at the midpoint of the 20th century. It is also one of the most brilliant, imaginative, and funny movies of its time. But that's not all. A turning point in the career of one of the greatest filmmakers of his era, who succeeded in transforming a personal crisis into a work of art, Fellini here paved the road for such subsequent classics as *Amarcord*, *Roma*, *Satyricon*, *La Cita Delle Donne*, *Casanova*, and *E la Nave Va*.

After his eight first features, Fellini had received all the recognition a director could possibly wish for (including, beyond the success, awards, and critical acclaim, scandal and even excommunication for *La Dolce Vita*), paid tribute, and flew away from his masters (Rossellini, Visconti, De Sica, etc.). Somehow, though only 43 years old, he had managed to achieve a completeness in his work. *8 ½* stands as the bridge between this early period of fulfillment and a new adventure—one which, though probably his most original and creative, turns out to be only the second of three (there is also a third, and wonderful, period of Fellini's late works).

But there is even more to *8 ½*. The film represents a major step forward in cinema's march toward modernity, one of the most inventive constructions of a mirror reflection on the creative act itself. Its mental processes as well as its material, psychological, and libidinal obligations are enacted in a Pirandellian extravaganza to be cherished by anyone who cares about the exploration of artistic mechanisms and psychic labyrinths. But even this is not sufficient. Not beyond but *inside* all these good reasons to treasure *8 ½* lies the main one, which (it should be said) is also the most modest one.

This story about the anguish of a director having to make a film, about an artist having to make a work, about a man having to deal with women, about a human having to face life and death, is a very simple and touching tale. Through its inventive visions and disturbing situations, playing on the frontier between reality and dreams with humor and fear, it interrogates everyone's relationship with the world, with our parents, our children, the people we work with, the difficulties of getting old, or getting lost, or returning to childhood terrors. With its magnificent black and white look, its geometric and non-realistic framing, and its suggestive use of sounds and images, *8 ½* does not elaborate a thesis on the state of the art or engage in psychoanalytic investigation. Instead, it opens a window inside each and every one of us, artist or not, man or woman. **J-MF**

Poland (P.P., WFF) 62m BW

**Language:** Polish

**Director:** Witold Lesiewicz, Andrzej Munk

**Screenplay:** Andrzej Munk, Zofia Posmysz-Piasecka

**Photography:** Krzysztof Winiewicz

**Music:** Tadeusz Baird

**Nonoriginal music:** Johann Sebastian Bach

**Cast:** Aleksandra Slaska, Anna Ciepielewska, Jan Kreczmar, Marek Walczewski, Maria Koscialkowska, Irena Malkiewicz, Leon Pietraszkiewicz, Janusz Bylczynski, A. Golebiowska

**Cannes Film Festival:** Andrzej Munk (special mention)

**Venice Film Festival:** Andrzej Munk (Italian film critics award)

# PASAZERKA (1963)
## PASSENGER

Andrzej Munk's most famous film was also his last. The Polish director's death during the movie's production left *Passenger* unfinished; it was reconstructed in 1963 in the form of a speculation that compounds the questions Munk posed of his story and of his characters with questions about where he would have taken them had he survived. The interrogatory form proves apt for this stark and relentless work.

The central character, Liza (Aleksandra Slaska), recounts two versions of her past as an SS overseer at Auschwitz: in the first, sanitized version, which she gives her husband aboard a luxury liner on which she returns to Germany for the first time since the end of the war, Liza benevolently reunites two lovers among the prisoners but is powerless to intervene further in their destinies. In the second, more detailed version, which Liza remembers in solitude, her own motives are tangled and obscure, and her relationship with the female prisoner appears obsessive.

As much as for the psychological interest of this relationship, *Passenger* is extraordinary for its terrifying exactness of tone and for its indelible representation of brutalities enacted in the background, or on the periphery, of the main character's consciousness. This fragmentary film is no less painful and abrupt than Munk's short but brilliant career. **CFu**

**France / Italy** (Compagnia, Concordia, Rome-Paris) 103m Technicolor

**Language:** French / English / German / Italian

**Director:** Jean-Luc Godard

**Producer:** Carlo Ponti, Georges de Beauregard

**Screenplay:** Jean-Luc Godard, from the novel *Il Disprezzo* by Alberto Moravia

**Photography:** Raoul Coutard

**Music:** Georges Delerue

**Cast:** Brigitte Bardot, Michel Piccoli, Jack Palance, Giorgia Moll, Fritz Lang

# LE MÉPRIS (1963)
## CONTEMPT

The sixth feature to be directed by Jean-Luc Godard, most daring of the New Wave filmmakers of the 1960s, *Contempt* combines the portrait of a marriage with a story about making a film. Camille (Brigitte Bardot) is married to screenwriter Paul (Michel Piccoli). In the first sequence she makes an inventory of her naked body, asking him which bit he likes best. Then he takes her to meet Hollywood producer Jeremy Prokosch (Jack Palance). Prokosch is making a movie of Homer's *Odyssey*, to be directed by veteran German filmmaker Fritz Lang, playing himself. Palance plays his role to the hilt, intoning, "I like gods. I know exactly how they feel." Lang replies with some gnomic observations on cinema ("CinemaScope is fine for shooting snakes and coffins").

*Contempt* is packed with cinematic references to Chaplin and Griffith and to Hawks, Ray, Minnelli, and other heroes of the French film magazine *Cahiers du Cinéma*, for whom Godard was a critic. Paul's contribution is to remark that, show a woman a camera and she immediately bares her bottom—ironic given that Bardot's naked behind is frequently in view.

And contempt? It's what Camille has come to feel for her husband, whom she accuses of trying to pimp her to Prokosch and of selling out his principles for money. A clever, elegant film with a shocking ending. **EB**

# HUD (1963)

This modern Western directed by Martin Ritt is set in the featureless landscape of West Texas. Paul Newman is Hud Bannon, who cares for little in life besides drinking and chasing women. His view of life is undiluted cynicism: "You take the sinners away from the saints, you're lucky to end up with Abraham Lincoln." Yet Hud is looked up to by Lonnie (Brandon De Wilde), his dead brother's son who at seventeen admires his uncle's easy charm. There is bad blood between Hud and his father (Melvyn Douglas), a rancher of the old school. Hud wants to drill for oil, but his father refuses: "I don't want that kind of money." Their housekeeper is Alma (Patricia Neal), divorced and approaching middle age, but too much her own woman to accept Hud's advances.

When the father's precious herd of cattle is suspected of having foot-and-mouth disease, Hud proposes selling them before the disease is confirmed. The old man won't hear of it, but the slaughter of the herd removes his will to live. By the end, Lonnie and Alma have gone too, leaving Hud to nurse his beer. It's a brilliantly acted film that catches much of the feel for the dusty locale of Larry McMurtry's original novel, *Horseman Pass By*. **EB**

**U.S.** (Paramount, Salem-Dover) 112m BW

**Director:** Martin Ritt

**Producer:** Irving Ravetch, Martin Ritt

**Screenplay:** Harriet Frank Jr., Irving Ravetch, from the novel *Horseman Pass By* by Larry McMurtry

**Photography:** James Wong Howe

**Music:** Elmer Bernstein

**Cast:** Paul Newman, Melvyn Douglas, Patricia Neal, Brandon De Wilde, Whit Bissell, Crahan Denton, John Ashley, Val Avery, George Petrie, Curt Conway

**Oscar:** Patricia Neal (actress), Melvyn Douglas (actor in support role), James Wong Howe (photography)

**Oscar nomination:** Martin Ritt (director), Irving Ravetch, Harriet Frank Jr. (screenplay), Paul Newman (actor), Hal Pereira, Tambi Larsen, Sam Comer, Robert R. Benton (art direction)

**Venice Film Festival:** Martin Ritt (OCIC award), nomination (Golden Lion)

# NATTVARDSGÄSTERNA (1963)
## WINTER LIGHT

The second part of Ingmar Bergman's "Silence of God" trilogy—the other installments being the 1961 film *Through a Glass Darkly* and the 1963 film *The Silence*—centers on the pastor (Gunnar Björnstrand) of a small parish. Ever since his wife's death he has become increasingly anguished and embittered by his growing uncertainty as to God's existence. His faith is further put to the test by a teacher (Ingrid Thulin) who suffers from eczema and tries to persuade him to marry her, and by a depressive (Max von Sydow) who needs help in coping with his suicidal fears of nuclear conflict.

*Winter Light* is Bergman at his most intense. The narrative is pared down, terse, wholly to the point. The cast is shot largely in magnificently illuminating close-up by Sven Nykvist, affording performances of great restraint, subtlety, and power; the simple, chilly gray sets and locations add to the overall aura of rigorous austerity. The film lacks the leavening hints of hope, or at least of resigned acceptance, that arise in some of Bergman's later films, which means that it is not the most heartening account of human experience. That said, the sheer artistry on view is, in its own strange way, thrilling in itself. **GA**

**Sweden** (Svensk) 81m BW

**Language:** Swedish

**Director:** Ingmar Bergman

**Producer:** Allan Ekelund

**Screenplay:** Ingmar Bergman

**Photography:** Sven Nykvist

**Cast:** Ingrid Thulin, Gunnar Björnstrand, Gunnel Lindblom, Max von Sydow, Allan Edwall, Kolbjörn Knudsen, Olof Thunberg, Elsa Ebbesen

**U.S.** 45m BW

**Director:** Jack Smith

**Cast:** Joel Markman, Mario Montez

# FLAMING CREATURES (1963)

Originally intended as a comedy, Jack Smith's stunning 1963 film *Flaming Creatures* paradoxically became the greatest scandal of an increasingly notorious underground cinema scene. Throughout the 1960s and '70s, screenings of the film were frequently interrupted by riotous crowds and irritated cops. This unfortunate and violent reaction to Smith's beautiful, innovative picture speaks volumes for the prudery of state-enforced norms regarding gender and sexual representation.

Shot on outdated black-and-white film stock, *Flaming Creatures* is a gorgeous, flickering series of cloudy images, featuring Smith's friends in various forms of exotic, low-budget drag. Eschewing narrative continuity, the film instead presents a number of sequences and disconnected tableaux that recall the aesthetic indulgences of Josef von Sternberg and the exotic fantasy world of Smith's muse, the 1940s "Queen of Technicolor," Maria Montez. Beginning with a lengthy, teasing introduction to the creatures, the film moves on to a coy scene of flirtation and a hilarious and beautiful lipstick sequence. When the butch yet demure Francis Francine chases and begins to ravish the enticing Delicious Dolores (Sheila Bick), all the creatures join in and fall into an at times aggressively delirious rapture. Their orgiastic frenzy is interrupted by the falling plaster caused by a seeming earthquake, which calms or kills them until Our Lady of the Docks (a mesmerizing Joel Markman) emerges from a coffin, breathes life into the creatures, and arouses them into a final, joyous dance. The great underground drag superstar Mario Montez (credited here as Delores Flores) makes his appearance as The Spanish Girl, dancing and flapping her fan in the midst of the Busby Berkeleyesque finale. The film also boasts an eclectic soundtrack which includes Deanna Durbin, Béla Bartók, the Everly Brothers, and excerpts from various Sternberg and Montez films.

The distinctive beauty of *Flaming Creatures* is due largely to Smith's nimble use of the handheld camera. His unexpected framings yield dense images of fabrics, body parts, and heavily made-up faces. The open links between these images, and among the bodies, body parts, and genders flaunted on the screen, make *Flaming Creatures* a boundless practical resource for living one's life fabulously. **MS**

## THE GREAT ESCAPE (1963)

A terrific war film boasting an all-star cast from director John Sturges, *The Great Escape* remains as entertaining, moving, and thrilling now as when it was first released in 1963.

Nearly every scene is a classic, as the American and British prisoners of war plot to escape from their camp using three tunnels they have dug named Tom, Dick, and Harry. Among the potential escapees: Richard Attenborough and Gordon Jackson are two of the British stiff upper lips planning the getaway; Charles Bronson, the tunneler afraid of enclosed spaces; Donald Pleasance, the forger with diminishing eyesight; James Garner, the man who can scrounge just about anything from the guards and fellow prisoners; and, of course, Steve McQueen as Hilts, a seasoned escapee dubbed "the cooler king" following his solitary confinement every time his escape attempts fail and he is recaptured.

An epic much like Sturges's previous picture *The Magnificent Seven* (three of that film's cast also appear here: McQueen, Bronson, and James Coburn), this heroic adventure, based on the novel by Paul Brickhill, is backed by a memorable score by Elmer Bernstein that beautifully punctuates every fantastic moment. **JB**

**U.S.** (Mirisch) 172m Color DeLuxe

**Director:** John Sturges

**Producer:** John Sturges

**Screenplay:** James Clavell, W.R. Burnett, from book by Paul Brickhill

**Photography:** Daniel L. Fapp

**Music:** Elmer Bernstein

**Cast:** Steve McQueen, James Garner, Richard Attenborough, James Donald, Charles Bronson, Donald Pleasence, James Coburn, Hannes Messemer, David McCallum, Gordon Jackson, John Leyton, Angus Lennie, Nigel Stock, Robert Graf, Jud Taylor

**Oscar nomination:** Ferris Webster (editing)

## SHOCK CORRIDOR (1963)

Working in the world of exploitation films and B movies, with shoestring budgets and no studio expectations beyond profitability, Samuel Fuller ironically found a great deal more freedom to explore controversial ideas and new cinematic techniques than many of his higher-profile peers. *Shock Corridor* hinges on what has become a hoary cliché: A hotshot reporter has himself committed to an insane asylum to investigate a murder. He finds more than he bargained for, of course, and just the same Fuller offers more than a simple exploitation film.

*Shock Corridor*'s camerawork, by Stanley Cortez (*The Magnificent Ambersons*, *The Night of the Hunter*), is every bit as nuts as the colorful cast of characters populating the asylum, lurching, looming, and leaping from black and white into color. The acting is likewise all over the place, with the cast obviously encouraged to give voice to their inner psychotic. A fat man claims to be a famous opera singer, a pack of nymphomaniacs roam the ward like wild animals, and a black man preaches racism. Fuller doesn't always arrange the film like he knows exactly where it's going, and its inherent trashiness never belies its B-movie origins—but he does imbue *Shock Corridor* with a crazed energy more than befitting its striking name. **JKl**

**U.S.** (Allied Artists, F & F) 101m BW/ Technicolor

**Director:** Samuel Fuller

**Producer:** Sam Firks, Leon Fromkess, Samuel Fuller

**Screenplay:** Samuel Fuller

**Photography:** Stanley Cortez

**Music:** Paul Dunlap

**Cast:** Peter Breck, Constance Towers, Gene Evans, James Best, Hari Rhodes, Larry Tucker, Paul Dubov, Chuck Roberson, Neyle Morrow, John Matthews, Bill Zuckert, John Craig, Philip Ahn, Frank Gerstle, Rachel Romen

# IL GATTOPARDO (1963)
## THE LEOPARD

**Italy / France** (S.G.C, Nouvelle Pathé, Titanus) 205m Technicolor

**Language:** Italian / English

**Director:** Luchino Visconti

**Producer:** Goffredo Lombardo

**Screenplay:** Suso Cecchi d'Amico, Pasquale Festa Campanile, Massimo Franciosa, Enrico Medioli, Luchino Visconti, from novel by Giuseppe Tomasi Di Lampedusa

**Photography:** Giuseppe Rotunno

**Music:** Nino Rota, Vincenzo Bellini, Giuseppe Verdi

**Cast:** Burt Lancaster, Claudia Cardinale, Alain Delon, Paolo Stoppa, Rina Morelli, Romolo Valli, Terence Hill, Pierre Clémenti, Lucilla Morlacchi, Giuliano Gemma, Ida Galli, Ottavia Piccolo, Carlo Valenzano, Brook Fuller, Anna Maria Bottini

**Oscar nomination:** Piero Tosi (costume)

**Cannes Film Festival:** Luchino Visconti (Golden Palm)

A "cult classic," Luchino Visconti's adaptation from the novel of Giuseppe Tomasi Di Lampedusa, set in Sicily in the 1860s, is a sumptuous fresco of a world that's active at twilight. It accounts for the major social changes in Italy after the "Risorgimento" movement through the story of the prince Fabrizio di Salina (Burt Lancaster). Trying to avoid a confrontation with Garibaldi's army, the aristocrat has to move, together with his family, to their retreat at Donnafugata. One of the few of his caste to understand that the world is irreversibly changing, he is disposed to make a pact with the representatives of the bourgeoisie. Following his personal motto, "something has to change, to keep everything in place," he decides to marry his nephew, Tancredi Falconeri (Alain Delon), to the daughter of the local mayor. The alliance between "the Leopard" and "the Jackal" will be celebrated in the marriage scene, which covers the third part of the movie.

Brightly directed and photographed, this segment of the film is where the central metaphor comes to life. The amazing camera work of Giuseppe Rotunno provides an unforgettable sense of the palace's magnificence. Beyond the splendor of the settings and costumes, however, one can feel the imminence of extinction. Even the portraits bear symbolic connotations, as we can see, for instance, by looking at the pale faces of the members of the Salina family during the ceremony. By way of contrast, the camera's eye also makes us attend to the vitality and rudeness of the newly rich.

Tons of ink has been spilled analyzing the ideological and stylistic features of this masterpiece, one of the best adaptations in the history of cinema. Some critics have pointed out the autobiographical suggestions of *The Leopard*, as Visconti himself was an aristocrat who flirted with the Communist Party. The analogies between the author and main character can also be extended to a deeper, more psychological level; both men are obsessed with death and perceive its premonitory signs everywhere. Visconti would return to this theme in several of his subsequent pictures, including *The Damned* (1969), *Death in Venice* (1971), *Ludwig* (1972), and 1975's *Conversation Piece*, in which "the Leopard" Burt Lancaster again plays the director's alter-ego. No other filmmaker handled Lancaster the way Visconti did, making him look so aristocratic, so distinguished, but also so human. His wonderful performance made Prince Salina one of the emblematic noble characters in movie history, but one should not ignore the splendid roles played by Delon and Claudia Cardinale, whose beauty here is truly breathtaking.

The film's refined chromatic and visual style, based on Visconti's competence in the fine arts, became his signature. One of the most expensive and sumptuous movies ever produced in Europe, *The Leopard* was accused by some critics of being "a monumental production in the first person." Perhaps this charge is accurate, but that is hardly a bad thing. A film that mesmerizes huge audiences and is at the same time highly personal—a *film d'auteur*—must be the dream of directors everywhere. **DD**

**Brazil** (Sino) 103m BW

**Language:** Portuguese

**Director:** Nelson Pereira dos Santos

**Producer:** Luiz Carlos Barreto, Herbert Richers, Danilo Trelles.

**Screenplay:** Nelson Pereira dos Santos, from novel by Graciliano Ramos

**Photography:** Luiz Carlos Barreto, José Rosa

**Music:** Leonardo Alencar

**Cast:** Genivaldo, Gilvan, Átila Iório, Orlando Macedo, Maria Ribeiro, Jofre Soares

**Cannes Film Festival:** Nelson Pereira dos Santos (OCIC award), tied with *Les Parapluies de Cherbourg*

# VIDAS SECAS (1963)
## BARREN LIVES

It is hard to imagine just how enormous the impact of Italian neorealism was on world cinema; by the mid-1950s, long after the movement had ceased to exist in Italy, one could find neorealist advocates and practitioners on every continent. In Brazil, Alex Viany's 1953 film *A Needle in a Haystack*, a gentle comedy shot on real locations in Rio, was the clear precursor of neorealism there. Viany's chief assistant on that film, former law student Nelson Pereira dos Santos, would go on in 1955 to make *Rio, 40 Degrees*, a daring "group portrait" of Rio that follows a number of different storylines all happening on the same day. The harsh, strikingly unsentimental depiction of the Rio *favelas* (slums), as well as the vibrant, documentary-flavored camera work, made that film a kind of manifesto for a new cinema in Brazil.

This new cinema, or *Cinema Novo* as it became known, was finally acknowledged as a major cultural movement in 1963 with the release of dos Santos's fifth feature film, *Barren Lives*. An extraordinary adaptation of the homonymous novel by Graciliano Ramos, one of the unquestionable masterpieces of Brazilian literature, *Barren Lives* tells the story of a family of *retirantes*, migrant laborers in the drought-stricken northeast. Often compared to Faulkner, Ramos's novel, written in 1938, is divided into brief chapters, each one offering an intensely sensual, individual point of view of one of the family members over the course of two years. Dos Santos renders this literary device exquisitely, even giving us, in one of the film's most heart-breaking scenes, the "mind" of the family dog in its dying moments. A collection of incidents and encounters, rather than a clear narrative, *Barren Lives* ends as it began, with the family once again on the road. Dos Santos's film has an effect similar to that of Luis Buñuel's *Land Without Bread*: You feel that you've passed through "realism" to arrive at something else, something abstract but powerful nonetheless. A final conversation between husband and wife hints at the possibility of change, but by this point we've seen too much to dare imagine any easy solutions. **RP**

## MÉDITERRANÉE (1963)

**France** 45m
**Language:** French
**Director:** Jean-Daniel Pollet, Barbet Schroeder
**Screenplay:** Jean-Daniel Pollet, Philippe Sollers
**Photography:** Jean-Daniel Pollet
**Music:** Antoine Duhamel

Jean-Daniel Pollet's 43-minute *Méditerranée*, shot in 1963 and first shown publicly four years later, remains the most influential of his experimental films. Its impact on Jean-Luc Godard's 1963 film *Contempt* is especially striking, and one reason why it remains so impressive as a minimalist tour de force is that Pollet was able to spend so much time editing it. Accompanied by an evocative text written by Philippe Sollers and a haunting score by Antoine Duhamel, who also wrote the music for Godard's 1965 film *Pierrot le Fou*, the footage shot in various countries and of various subjects around the Mediterranean—a Sicilian garden, a Greek temple, a fisherman, a young girl on an operating table—reappears throughout the film, each time in a separate order and for different lengths of time.

*Méditerranée* inspired one of Godard's most poetic critical texts for the French film journal *Cahiers du Cinéma*, written in 1964 but published in 1967, in which he wrote, "In this banal series of 16mm images over which breathes the ineffable spirit of 70mm, it is up to us to discover the space which only the cinema can transform into lost time...or rather the contrary... [F]or here are smooth, round shots abandoned on the screen like pebbles on the beach." **JRos**

## KHANEH SIAH AST (1963)
### THE HOUSE IS BLACK

**Iran** (Golestan) 20m BW
**Language:** Farsi
**Director:** Forugh Farrokhzad
**Producer:** Ebrahim Golestan
**Screenplay:** Forugh Farrokhzad
**Photography:** Soleiman Minasian
**Cast (narration):** Ebrahim Golestan, Forugh Farrokhzad

Forugh Farrokhzad's 20-odd-minute black-and-white documentary about a leper colony in northern Iran is the most powerful Iranian film I've seen—the most poetic as well as the most radically humanist. Farrokhzad (1935–1967) is commonly regarded as the greatest Persian poet of the 20th century, and one of her poems can be heard recited by the hero in Abbas Kiarostami's *The Wind Will Carry Us* (1999), whose title is that of the poem. Her only film—which reflects the probable influence of silent Soviet cinema without being in any way obviously derivative of it—seamlessly adapts the techniques of poetry to its framing, editing, sound, and narration. The latter is split between two voices: The male voice, belonging to Ebrahim Golestan—the film's producer, Farrokhzad's lover, and a considerable filmmaker in his own right—is mainly objective and factual; the female voice is Farrokhzad's, offering a poetic and highly emotional reverie about her subject that incorporates passages from the Old Testament.

At once lyrical and extremely matter-of-fact, devoid of sentimentality or voyeurism yet profoundly humanist, *The House Is Black* offers a view of everyday life in the colony—people eating, various medical treatments, children at school and at play—that is spiritual, unflinching, and beautiful in ways that have no apparent Western counterparts; to my eyes and ears, it registers like a prayer. **JRos**

G.B. (Argyle, MGM) 112m BW

**Director:** Robert Wise

**Producer:** Denis Johnson, Robert Wise

**Screenplay:** Nelson Gidding, from novel by Shirley Jackson

**Photography:** Davis Boulton

**Music:** Humphrey Searle

**Cast:** Julie Harris, Claire Bloom, Richard Johnson, Russ Tamblyn, Fay Compton, Rosalie Crutchley, Lois Maxwell, Valentine Dyall, Diane Clare, Ronald Adam

# THE HAUNTING (1963)

In 1959, acclaimed American novelist Shirley Jackson published *The Haunting of Hill House*. Since then it has been widely praised as one of the most frightening tales ever committed to paper. Three years later, director Robert Wise chose this story as the one he would adapt for the big screen to honor the memory of his former mentor, Val Lewton. The result, *The Haunting*, is considered by a great many critics, aficionados, and casual fans of the horror genre to be one of the scariest films of all time—if not the scariest.

In an extremely creepy prologue we learn the troubled history of Hill House—built by a stern, heartless man named Hugh Crain 80 years earlier, the residence saw the mysterious deaths of no fewer than four women since that time. We then meet Eleanor Lance (Julie Harris), a lonely and repressed woman in her mid 30s who jumps at the chance to partake in a psychic experiment arranged by one Dr. John Markway (Richard Johnson), an anthropologist who seeks scientific evidence of paranormal activity. After arriving at Hill House, Eleanor meets Dr. Markway (to whom she is instantly attracted), Luke Sanderson (Russ Tamblyn), skeptical nephew of the current landlord, and Theodora—"just Theodora"(Claire Bloom)—an artist, psychic, and (it is strongly suggested) lesbian with an apparent interest getting her new roomate to open up.

Shortly thereafter, the house begins making its presence felt—strange banging noises in the middle of the night, inexplicable cold spots, and a famously frightening scene in which Eleanor discovers that she has been holding hands with no one. It becomes increasingly clear that Eleanor is the primary target of Hill House's attention—either that or she herself is somehow responsible for the haunting. When Dr. Markway's wife shows up unexpectedly, Eleanor's anticipated breakdown (chillingly conveyed through Harris's running internal monologue) becomes a reality. Sent away by the others, who fear her complete collapse, she loses control of her car to unseen forces and crashes headlong into a tree, where she dies in the same spot as Hugh Crain's first wife did years earlier.

Making brilliant use of canted frames, mirror reflections, fish-eye lenses, and uncanny sound and image editing, Wise succeeds both in bringing Hill House to life and in making ambiguous the true source of the threat. Do not watch this one alone! **SJS**

**Japan** (Daiei) 113m Eastmancolor

**Language:** Japanese

**Director:** Kon Ichikawa

**Producer:** Masaichi Nagata

**Screenplay:** Daisuke Itô, Teinosuke Kinugasa, Natto Wada, from novel by Otokichi Mikami

**Photography:** Setsuo Kobayashi

**Music:** Yasushi Akutagawa

**Cast:** Kazuo Hasegawa, Fujiko Yamamoto, Ayako Wakao, Eiji Funakoshi, Narutoshi Hayashi, Eijirô Yanagi, Chûsha Ichikawa, Ganjiro Nakamura, Saburo Date, Jun Hamamura, Kikue Môri, Masayoshi Kikuno, Raizô Ichikawa, Shintarô Katsu, Yutaka Nakayama

# YUKINOJO HENGE (1963)
## AN ACTOR'S REVENGE

*An Actor's Revenge* is one of the most outrageously entertaining Japanese films ever produced. At the time it was made, its director, Kon Ichikawa, was out of favor with his studio, as his last two films had lost money. By way of punishment he was assigned the task of making a film to mark the 300th screen role of legendary actor Kazuo Hasegawa. This was to be a remake of Hasegawa's most popular film, a creaky old melodrama called *The Revenge of Yukinojo*—and Hasegawa would reprise his double role as a transvestite *kabuki* actor who avenges the death of his parents, and as the thief who helps him. When Hasegawa first played this swashbuckling double role he was 27. Now he was 55.

Far from trying to tone down the project's absurdities and improbabilities, Ichikawa gleefully plays up everything artificial and theatrical about the story, unpredictably switching tone and idiom, drawing on his cartoonist's background to throw in thought bubbles, blatantly fake sets, anomalous music, and distorted visuals. The conventions of *kabuki* theater are affectionately parodied, with ultrastylized lighting and horizontal wipes across the 'Scope screen. And Ichikawa makes the most of the plot's rich opportunities for sexual ambiguity: at one point Hasegawa as a man watches himself as a man-playing-a-woman making love to a woman. **PK**

**G.B.** (Elstree, Sprinukok) 112m BW

**Director:** Joseph Losey

**Producer:** Joseph Losey, Norman Priggen

**Screenplay:** Harold Pinter, from novel by Robin Maugham

**Photography:** Douglas Slocombe

**Music:** John Dankworth

**Cast:** Dirk Bogarde, Sarah Miles, Wendy Craig, James Fox, Catherine Lacey, Richard Vernon, Anne Firbank, Doris Knox, Patrick Magee, Jill Melford, Alun Owen, Harold Pinter, Derek Tansley, Brian Phelan, Hazel Terry

**Venice Film Festival:** Joseph Losey nomination (Golden Lion)

# THE SERVANT (1963)

As an expatriate American in Britain, Joseph Losey had always brought a cool, disenchanted eye to bear on the customs of his adopted country. But in *The Servant*, the first of his three collaborations with Harold Pinter, his gaze came still more sharply into focus. Pinter's script, typically elliptical and oblique, and Losey's crisp, astringent direction offer a sardonic analysis of class, sex, and power relationships in 1960s London. An effete young upper-class bachelor, Tony (James Fox in his first starring role), hires a manservant, Barrett (Dirk Bogarde), who gradually takes over his employer's life, undermines, and destroys him.

Bogarde, at last casting off the matinee-idol image that so long dogged him, gives one of his finest performances, his flickering, contemptuous smile and insinuating, off-Cockney accent embodying a whole history of festering class resentment. But Losey and Pinter create a sense of entrapment that extends to both men. Their roles may be gradually reversed, but they're still bound together in mutual exploitation—a feeling abetted by Douglas Slocombe's camera as it sinuously explores the claustrophobic spaces of the terraced house, turning it into an elegantly appointed cage and observing its residents from unsettling angles. Funny, sinister, and unnerving, *The Servant* still retains the power of unease. **PK**

## GOLDFINGER (1964)

**G.B.** (Danjaq, Eon) 112m Technicolor
**Director:** Guy Hamilton
**Producer:** Albert R. Broccoli, Harry Saltzman
**Screenplay:** Richard Maibaum, Paul Dehn, from novel by Ian Fleming
**Photography:** Ted Moore
**Music:** John Barry, Monty Norman
**Cast:** Sean Connery, Honor Blackman, Gert Fröbe, Shirley Eaton, Tania Mallet, Harold Sakata, Bernard Lee, Martin Benson, Cec Linder, Austin Willis, Lois Maxwell, Bill Nagy, Michael Mellinger, Peter Cranwell, Nadja Regin
**Oscar:** Norman Wanstall (special sound effects)

If *Dr. No* was a sputnik-era Fu Manchu picture and *From Russia With Love* a Cold War Eric Ambler adventure, *Goldfinger*—the third entry in the Harry Saltzman–Albert Broccoli 007 series—marked the point when the James Bond films became their own genre. The rather brutal wit of the earlier movies is modified in the precredits sequence: Sean Connery's super-agent is first seen wearing a decoy duck on his head, then removes his wet-suit to reveal a perfect tuxedo and disposes of a villain through the old electric-heater-tossed-in-the-bath gambit, delivering another of his pointed epitaph epithets ("shocking").

With a megalomaniac millionaire, Auric Goldfinger (Gert Fröbe), as the chief villain rather than the Soviet SMERSH of the books or the communist-affiliated SPECTRE of the first films, *Goldfinger* spins away from geopolitical realities into a comic book world, albeit one where the Chinese will lend a nuclear weapon to a baddie in order to cripple the West's economy. Included in the mix are gold-plated murder victims, impeccably-dressed Korean wrestler minions (Harold Sakata as the bowler-throwing Oddjob), improbably-named heroines (Honor Blackman as Pussy Galore), hi-tech torture by laser-beam, and a scheme not to rob Fort Knox but to irradiate it for centuries—thus increasing the net value of the villain's own gold stocks. All of the vintage 007 ingredients are shaken not stirred here: A belting John Barry theme tune delivered by Shirley Bassey ("Go-o-o-o-ldfinger...he's the man, the man with the Midas touch, a spider's touch..."), the gadget-packed Aston Martin with its bulletproof shield and passenger-side ejector seat (inspiration for the first great bestselling movie tie-in toy), and the vast Ken Adam sets (note Goldfinger's lair with the model of Fort Knox under glass as a huge coffee table, and the poison gas vents—a big room designed to be used only once). In addition one finds the residual Ian Fleming suspicion that a person is contemptible if he has a foreign accent and cheats at golf, and the touchingly macho notion that a clinch in the hay with Sean Connery is enough to persuade Pussy to change not only sides but sexual orientation. Ever since, the series has been recycling. **KN**

U.S. (Puck) 30m Color
**Director:** Kenneth Anger
**Cast:** Bruce Byron

# SCORPIO RISING (1964)

One of the most influential of all "underground" films, this 29-minute epic spells out its title and director's name in studs on the back of a black leather biker jacket, then plays a jukebox-worth of pop hits from the late 1950s and early 1960s (such as Elvis Presley's "Devil in Disguise," the Angels' "My Boyfriend's Back," Ray Charles's "Hit the Road, Jack") over images mostly shot in a Brooklyn biker garage. Images of romantic fetishization fill the camera screen: black leather, hair and oil grease, naked torsos, gleaming chrome, toys and motorbikes, images from comic books and movies (stills of James Dean, TV snips of Marlon Brando in the 1953 film *The Wild One*), rings and insignia, and muscular Tom-of-Finland-look youths lolling pinup style in tight jeans and peaked caps.

Without *Scorpio Rising*, Martin Scorsese would not use pop music the way he does in *Mean Streets* (1973), David Lynch couldn't have found the disturbing undercurrents in Bobby Vinton's song "Blue Velvet" (which is also used here), and action movies wouldn't include homoerotic strapping-on-the-weapons montages. Most controversial, to the extent of prompting legal action, is the witty but deliberately provocative juxtaposition of the Crystals' "He's a Rebel" with found footage from some Sunday school version of *The Life of Christ* intercut, putting forward the heretical if not sacreligious notion of the Disciples as a strutting, gay-tinged youth gang out to overthrow the established order even as the lyrics provide a surprisingly sermonly reading ("that's no reason why I shouldn't give him all my love").

The passion play continues under The Ron-Dells' "Party Lights" as Christ's life is intercut with the sort of swastika-swathed biker *walpurgisnacht* later hymned by Roger Corman's *The Wild Angels* (1966). As with all of Kenneth Anger's films, the magical is never far away, with a purple-veiled skeleton representing Death.

However, this is a far less impervious piece than most of his works, oddly accessible on an MTV level in its demonstration that songs don't have to be performed on camera (as in the classical Hollywood musical) to work in the context of cinema. They can be illustrated, undercut, and lent greater depth by apt or even wildly inapt images. **KN**

# LES PARAPLUIES DE CHERBOURG (1964)
## THE UMBRELLAS OF CHERBOURG

Movie audiences have long turned to musicals as the ultimate form of escapism. Imagine, emotions so strong that mere words can't express them, inspiring characters to burst into song and dance. The characters of Jacques Demy's musical *The Umbrellas of Cherbourg* are no exception, but with this most rapturous of melodramas Demy incorporates song and dance in the service not of escape but of realism. The effect is as riveting as it is profoundly moving.

Yet *The Umbrellas of Cherbourg* further deviates from most musicals in the sense that all its dialogue is sung, matched to Michel Legrand's wall-to-wall score. The effect is both hypnotic and beautiful. The nonstop music draws us even deeper into the devastating story, and the incessant singing elicits wonderfully open and direct performances from the cast. Catherine Deneuve plays Geneviève Emery, a young girl in love with a mechanic named Guy (Nino Castelnuovo). They pledge their undying affection for one another. Then Guy heads off to war and Geneviève discovers she's pregnant. She is persuaded to accept the marriage proposal of a wealthy gem-dealer patron (Marc Michel) of her mother's shop, whose love for Geneviève is so strong he promises to raise the child as his own.

Geneviève's emotional dilemma is, of course, played for maximum pathos, and when she only hears back once from her true love Guy your heart breaks along with hers. Yet Demy never lets the film lapse into easy sentimentality. The final scene is immensely moving, but not manipulatively so, and although the music does its job, directing and reflecting the feelings of the characters, it never comes across as overly sentimental. The sad sense of inevitability that pervades *The Umbrellas of Cherbourg* at least partly accounts for its immense appeal. Demy, like most people, understood that in the real world not all stories have happy endings, and thanks to his great cast (especially the beautiful and extremely convincing Deneuve) he was deft enough to convey that realization with immense emotional honesty, magic, and maturity. **JKl**

**France / West Germany** (Beta, Madeleine, Parc) 87m Eastmancolor

**Language:** French

**Director:** Jacques Demy

**Producer:** Mag Bodard

**Screenplay:** Jacques Demy

**Photography:** Jean Rabier

**Music:** Michel Legrand

**Cast:** Catherine Deneuve, Nino Castelnuovo, Anne Vernon, Marc Michel, Ellen Farner, Mireille Perrey, Jean Champion, Pierre Caden, Jean-Pierre Dorat, Bernard Fradet, Michel Benoist, Philippe Dumat, Dorothée Blank, Jane Carat, Harald Wolff

**Oscar nomination:** France (best foreign language film), Jacques Demy (screenplay), Michel Legrand, Jacques Demy (music), Michel Legrand (music), Michel Legrand, Jacques Demy (song)

**Cannes Film Festival:** Jacques Demy (Golden Palm) and (OCIC award), tie with *Vidas secas*

# MARNIE (1964)

After her debut in the 1963 film *The Birds*, Hitchcock once again cast Tippi Hedren, this time as a beautiful kleptomaniac whom we first see striding down a railroad station platform. In a hotel she washes her hair, rinsing out the black dye to become blonde again. We discover that Marnie has recently robbed her employer, and gradually we realize something is deeply wrong with her. She gets hysterical attacks when she sees the color red, and a visit to her mother reveals an unloving relationship. Then Marnie is hired by handsome businessman Mark Rutland (Sean Connery). In a brilliantly suspenseful scene, Marnie robs his safe while a cleaning woman mops the floor. Marnie sees the woman before she can be discovered, and creeps past her in stockinged feet, only for a shoe to drop out of her pocket. But the cleaning woman doesn't turn round; at the end of the scene we discover she is deaf.

Mark soon tracks Marnie down and offers her a choice: marriage or the police. On their honeymoon cruise Marnie tells him she can't bear men touching her, but in an uncomfortable scene he forces himself upon her. Mark tries to psychoanalyze his bride, educating himself from a book entitled *Sexual Abberations of the Criminal Female*, but Marnie's response is to try and rob him again. This time Mark forces her to go with him on a visit to her mother, and there the secret of Marnie's condition is traced back to a childhood trauma.

Though full of deft and seductive Hitchcockian touches, *Marnie* is a strange and unsettling film, in part because of Mark's character. Though he professes love of Marnie and tries to help her overcome her neurosis, his conduct is full of barely suppressed sadism, treating her like a caged animal. As Marnie says, "I'm just something you caught." The scene in which he in effect rapes her on the honeymoon caused discord between Hitchcock and his writer, Evan Hunter, who wanted to drop it on the grounds that it made Mark unsympathetic. Hitchcock refused and the script was finished by Jay Presson Allen. **EB**

**U.S.** (Geoffrey-Stanley, Universal) 130m Technicolor

**Director:** Alfred Hitchcock

**Producer:** Alfred Hitchcock

**Screenplay:** Jay Presson Allen, from novel by Winston Graham

**Photography:** Robert Burks

**Music:** Bernard Herrmann

**Cast:** Tippi Hedren, Sean Connery, Diane Baker, Martin Gabel, Louise Latham, Bob Sweeney, Milton Selzer, Mariette Hartley, Alan Napier, Bruce Dern, Henry Beckman, S. John Launer, Edith Evanson, Meg Wyllie

# MY FAIR LADY (1964)

*My Fair Lady* is a lumbering, airy musical, a strange compromise between Broadway and Hollywood spectacle—and a true artifact of the mid 1960s, when the studio system and its veteran professionals were floundering in the face of a new world and new ways of making movies. Yet, for all its dead time and cavernous space—André Téchiné, then a young *Cahiers du Cinéma* modernist, admired its "astonishing vacuum"—the basic story (from George Bernard Shaw's *Pygmalion*) is so undeniably affecting as to constitute a veritable modern myth.

At its center is a hate-turned-to-love match that is hard to beat: Rex Harrison as the grumpy linguist Henry Higgins and Audrey Hepburn as Eliza Dolittle, the street urchin whom he picks for his "social experiment." We empathize with Eliza at every step of her trial—when she is a pauper resisting Higgins's brutal training, when she is a collaborator slowly falling in love, and finally when she has become a resplendent "lady" fighting off superficial suitors.

George Cukor's gay sensibility was attune to the unlikely alchemy of this star duo, as well as the reserves of glamor at his disposal (Cecil Beaton worked on costumes and art direction). And the songs are irresistible. **AM**

**U.S.** (Warner Bros.) 170m Technicolor

**Director:** George Cukor

**Producer:** Jack L. Warner

**Screenplay:** Alan Jay Lerner, from the play *Pygmalion* by George Bernard Shaw

**Photography:** Harry Stradling Sr.

**Music:** Frederick Loewe

**Cast:** Audrey Hepburn, Rex Harrison, Stanley Holloway, Wilfrid Hyde-White, Gladys Cooper, Jeremy Brett, Theodore Bikel, Mona Washbourne

**Oscar:** Jack L. Warner (best picture), George Cukor (director), Rex Harrison (actor), Gene Allen, Cecil Beaton, George James Hopkins (art direction), Harry Stradling Sr. (photography), Cecil Beaton (costume), André Previn (music), George Groves (sound)

**Oscar nomination:** Alan Jay Lerner (screenplay), Stanley Holloway (actor in support role), Gladys Cooper (actress in support role), William H. Ziegler (editing)

# SUNA NO ONNA (1964)
## WOMAN IN THE DUNES

Hiroshi Teshigahara's strange existential parable *Woman in the Dunes* strikes an unusual balance between realism and metaphor. An entomologist (Eiji Okada) gathering insects on the beach accepts an invitation of hospitality from a mysterious woman (Kyôko Kishida). But he quickly finds himself trapped like one of his collections in the woman's home, built at the bottom of a sandpit, where the incessantly creeping crystals of sand can only be slowed through constant shoveling.

Part neofeminist exercise, part political treatise, part survival tale, *Woman in the Dunes* adds up to both more and less than its premise. Okada can't escape the pit without inviting disaster, but why build a home in a sandpit in the first place? Kishida offers sexual rewards for Okada's labor, but how much of this is just her method of staving off loneliness? Does *Woman in the Dunes* mock domesticity, praise it, or depict it as a Sisiphisian horror? Teshigahara's film doesn't offer answers. It does, however, offer some remarkable sand photography. Like the film itself, the dunes captured by Hiroshi Segawa's cinematography frequently shift, slide, sink, and sift to where you least expect it. **JKl**

**Japan** (Teshigahara, Toho) 123m BW

**Language:** Japanese

**Director:** Hiroshi Teshigahara

**Producer:** Kiichi Ichikawa, Tadashi Oono

**Screenplay:** Kôbô Abe, from his novel

**Photography:** Hiroshi Segawa

**Music:** Tôru Takemitsu

**Cast:** Eiji Okada, Kyôko Kishida, Hiroko Ito, Koji Mitsui, Sen Yano, Kinzo Sekiguchi

**Oscar nomination:** Japan (best foreign language film), Hiroshi Teshigahara (director)

**Cannes Film Festival:** Hiroshi Teshigahara (special jury prize)

G.B. (Hawk) 93m BW

**Director:** Stanley Kubrick

**Producer:** Stanley Kubrick, Victor Lyndon

**Screenplay:** Terry Southern, Stanley Kubrick, from the novel *Red Alert* by Peter George

**Photography:** Gilbert Taylor

**Music:** Laurie Johnson

**Cast:** Peter Sellers, George C. Scott, Sterling Hayden, Keenan Wynn, Slim Pickens, Peter Bull, James Earl Jones, Tracy Reed, Jack Creley, Frank Berry, Robert O'Neil, Glenn Beck, Roy Stephens, Shane Rimmer, Hal Galili

**Oscar nomination:** Stanley Kubrick (director), Stanley Kubrick (best picture), Stanley Kubrick, Peter George, Terry Southern (screenplay) Peter Sellers (actor)

# DR. STRANGELOVE (1964)
## OR: HOW I LEARNED TO STOP WORRYING AND LOVE THE BOMB

"Gentlemen, you can't fight in here! This is the War Room!" *Dr. Strangelove* is a brilliant black comedy that works as political satire, suspense farce, and cautionary tale of technology running away with us. When a fanatical U.S. general launches a nuclear attack on the U.S.S.R. the President has his hands full recalling bombers and calming Russians while contending with his advisers and a twisted scientist. The thriller plot came from a serious novel by RAF officer Peter George, published in the United States as *Red Alert* and in the United Kingdom as *Two Hours to Doom*. Kubrick loved it but thought people were so overwhelmed by the threat of annihilation that they were in denial, apathetic to nuclear documentary or drama. So he would surprise audiences into reacting to the real prospect of global extermination with outrageously funny and provocative cartoon tactics.

Kubrick and cowriter Terry Southern created a cast of grotesques whose absurd fixations, by their incongruity, play up the realism against which they are set (and which is enhanced by Gilbert Taylor's outstanding black-and-white cinematography). The information about a doomsday device is factual, as are the Strategic Air Command operations and the B-52 crew's procedures. The computers that take the situation beyond human intervention have only become more capable. Be afraid. Be very afraid.

There are just three locations, each experiencing a failure to communicate. At Burpelson Air Force Base, maniacal General Jack D. Ripper (Sterling Hayden), obsessed with bodily fluids and commie conspiracy, circumvents Fail-Safe protocol and orders a bomber wing to nuke the "Russkies," taking appalled RAF officer Lionel Mandrake (Peter Sellers) captive. Aboard the B-52 code-named Leper Colony, dogged Major T.J. "King" Kong (Slim Pickens) and his crew (including James Earl Jones in his debut) suffer radio failure and are oblivious to frantic efforts to recall them. In the War Room at The Pentagon—an awesome set by production designer Ken Adam President Merkin Muffley (Sellers), rampant General Buck Turgidson (George C. Scott), Soviet Ambassador de Sadesky (Peter Bull), and demented Dr. Strangelove (Sellars again, in Kubrick's nod to *Metropolis*'s mad scientist Rotwang) are gathered in a futile attempt to stop Armageddon.

Sellers's sidesplitting three performances are legend but the entire ensemble gives a masterclass in exaggerated, perfectly timed posturing. Two images are unforgettable—Kong astride the H-bomb, yee-hawing all the way down, and demented Dr. Strangelove, unable to stop his mechanical arm from flying into the Nazi salute and throttling himself. Every viewing is a reminder the film is stuffed with hilarious dialogue, and President Muffley on the hot line to Moscow breaking it to the Soviet Premier that one of his base commanders "went and did a silly thing" remains a classic monologue. Kubrick would return to the potential menace of computer dependency in *2001: A Space Odyssey*, to institutional and political violence in *A Clockwork Orange*, and to the savage, surreal madness of war in *Full Metal Jacket*. But he never made us laugh this much in any other film. **AE**

G.B. (Proscenium) 87m BW

**Director:** Richard Lester

**Producer:** Walter Shenson

**Screenplay:** Alun Owen

**Photography:** Gilbert Taylor

**Music:** George Harrison, John Lennon, George Martin, Paul McCartney

**Cast:** John Lennon, Paul McCartney, George Harrison, Ringo Starr, Wilfrid Brambell, Norman Rossington, John Junkin, Victor Spinetti, Anna Quayle, Deryck Guyler, Richard Vernon, Edward Malin, Robin Ray, Lionel Blair, Alison Seebohm

**Oscar nomination:** Alun Owen (screenplay), George Martin (music)

# A HARD DAY'S NIGHT (1964)

Famously described by an over-excited *Village Voice* as "the *Citizen Kane* of jukebox movies," Richard Lester's 1964 comedy starring The Beatles and their music may not be quite that (although it is funnier), but it did change the shape of pop music films forever. With a witty, social-realist script by Liverpudlian playwright Alun Owen and traces of Lester's British surrealist influences (he had worked with The Beatles' 1950s comic idols, The Goons), *A Hard Day's Night* takes a day in the life of a hugely-successful teen group sensation and turns it into something thrilling. The camera follows The Beatles—who play a recognizable version of themselves—through a typical day of being chased by fans, hanging around, fielding idiotic press questions, and, at the end, actually playing. Lester gave the four members of the band just enough to do, most notably Ringo Starr, whose affecting scene on a canal towpath with a young boy was enhanced by the fact that Starr was monumentally hungover.

Lennon, McCartney, Harrison, and Starr come across as likeable, slightly rebellious, intelligent young men, who, in the tradition of realistic North-of-England dramas, are down-to-earth, unpretentious, and prone to seeing through the falseness of others ("I fought the War for the likes of you," says a derby-hatted old-timer to Starr, who replies, "I bet you're sorry you won"). This constant rejection of just about everything—TV producers, ad-men, authority in general—might have aged badly were it not contrasted with the astonishing force and glamor of the band's music. This combination acted exactly as it was intended, as a blast of propaganda for not only The Beatles, but also the then much-vaunted "younger generation." While *A Hard Day's Night* cannot be held directly responsible for inventing the counterculture, ousting old Hollywood, and ending the Vietnam War, it was seen, absorbed, and revered by a host of future artistic talent, particularly in the United States, where that younger generation found the movie genuinely liberating. The songs are great, too. **KK**

## IL DESERTO ROSSO (1964)
### THE RED DESERT

Michelangelo Antonioni's first feature in color remains a high-water mark for using color. To get the precise hues he wanted, Antonioni had entire fields painted. Restored prints make it clear why audiences were so excited by his innovations, not only for his expressive use of color, but also his striking editing. *Red Desert* comes at the tail end of Antonioni's most fertile period, immediately after his remarkable trilogy *The Adventure* (1960), *The Night* (1960), and *The Eclipse* (1962). Although *Red Desert* may fall somewhat short of the first and last of these earlier classics, the film's ecological concerns look a lot more prescient today than they seemed at the time of its initial release.

Monica Vitti plays a neurotic married woman (Giuliana) attracted to industrialist Richard Harris. Antonioni does eerie, memorable work with the industrial shapes and colors that surround her, shown alternately as threatening and beautiful as she walks through a science-fiction landscape. Like any self-respecting Antonioni heroine, she is looking for love and meaning—and finds sex. In one sequence a postcoital melancholy is strikingly conveyed via an expressionist use of color, following Giuliana's shifting moods.

The film's most spellbinding sequence depicts a pantheistic, utopian fantasy of innocence, which the heroine recounts to her ailing son, implicitly offering a beautiful girl and a beautiful sea as an alternative to the troubled woman and the industrial red desert of the title. **JRos**

**Italy / France** (Federiz, Duemila, Franco Riz) 120m Technicolor

**Language:** Italian

**Director:** Michelangelo Antonioni

**Producer:** Tonino Cervi, Angelo Rizzoli

**Screenplay:** Michelangelo Antonioni, Tonino Guerra

**Photography:** Carlo Di Palma

**Music:** Giovanni Fusco, Vittorio Gelmetti (electronic music)

**Cast:** Monica Vitti, Richard Harris, Carlo Chionetti, Xenia Valderi, Rita Renoir, Lili Rheims, Aldo Grotti, Valerio Bartoleschi, Emanuela Paola Carboni, Bruno Borghi, Beppe Conti, Julio Cotignoli, Giovanni Lolli, Hiram Mino Madonia, Giuliano Missirini

**Venice Film Festival:** Michelangelo Antonioni (FIPRESCI award), (Golden Lion)

## TINI ZABUTYKH PREDKIV (1964)
### SHADOWS OF FORGOTTEN ANCESTORS

Adapted from Ukrainian Mikhaylo Koysyubinskiy's novel, Sergei Paradjanov's extraordinary merging of myth, history, poetry, ethnography, dance, and ritual remains one of the supreme works of the Soviet sound cinema, and even subsequent Paradjanov features have failed to dim its intoxicating splendors.

Set in the harsh and beautiful Carpathian Mountains, the film tells of a doomed love between a couple belonging to feuding families, Ivan (Ivan Mikolajchuk) and Marichka (Larisa Kadochnikova), and of Ivan's life and marriage after Marichka's death. The plot is affecting, but it serves Paradjanov mainly as an armature to support the exhilarating rush of his lyrical camera movements (executed by master cinematographer Yuri Ilyenko), his innovative use of nature and interiors, his deft juggling of folklore and fancy in relation to pagan and Christian rituals, and his astonishing handling of color and music.

A film worthy of Aleksandr Dovzhenko, whose poetic vision of Ukrainian life is frequently alluded to, *Shadows of Our Forgotten Ancestors* also evokes fairy tales in general and even at times some of Walt Disney's animated representations of their settings, such as the cottage in *Snow White and the Seven Dwarfs* (1937). The visceral physicality of many other shots is no less unmistakable, exemplified by a startling one early on which places the camera on top of a just-chopped tree—taking the viewer with it on its vertiginous plunge toward the ground. **JRos**

**U.S.S.R.** (Dovzhenko) 97m Sovcolor

**Language:** Ukrainian

**Director:** Sergei Parajanov

**Screenplay:** Ivan Chendej, from story by Mikhaylo Mikhaylovich Koysyubinskiy

**Photography:** Viktor Bestayev, Yuri Ilyenko

**Music:** Miroslav Skorik

**Cast:** Ivan Mikolajchuk, Larisa Kadochnikova, Tatyana Bestayeva, Spartak Bagashvili, Nikolai Grinko, Leonid Yengibarov, Nina Alisova, Aleksandr Gaj, Neonila Gnepovskaya, A. Raydanov, I. Dzyura, V. Glyanko

**G.B.** (Alta Vista, AIP, Anglo-Amalgamated) 89m Pathécolor

**Director:** Roger Corman

**Producer:** Roger Corman

**Screenplay:** Charles Beaumont, R. Wright Campbell, from the stories *The Masque of the Red Death* and *Hop-Frog* by Edgar Allan Poe

**Photography:** Nicolas Roeg

**Music:** David Lee

**Cast:** Vincent Price, Hazel Court, Jane Asher, David Weston, Nigel Green, Patrick Magee, Paul Whitsun-Jones, Robert Brown, Julian Burton, David Davies, Skip Martin, Gaye Brown, Verina Greenlaw, Doreen Dawn, Brian Hewlett

# THE MASQUE OF THE RED DEATH (1964)

As Roger Corman's series of Vincent Price–starring, Edgar Allan Poe–based widescreen gothics advanced in America from *The Fall of the House of Usher* (1960) to *The Raven* (1963), each installment became more self-referential and comic in tone. However, when production of the series shifted in 1964 to Britain, the tone changed radically for two final masterpieces, the baroque *Masque of the Red Death* and the chilling *Tomb of Ligeia* (1965).

*Masque* casts Price ideally as Prince Prospero, an Italian Satanist who hosts a decadent masked ball as the plague ravages the countryside. There's a youth-themed plot about an innocent abducted girl (Jane Asher) and her revolutionary love interest, but here the emphasis is on corrupt luxury, with Price twitching his moustache and eyebrows with elegant, weary cynicism even as Death itself invades his ball and spreads the contagion in a Bergmanesque dance of death. Cinematographer Nicolas Roeg is encouraged to add his own flourishes, including long tracks through a succession of differently colored rooms (an image from the story), with the shock effects having a daring sensuality. Patrick Magee is dressed as an ape and burned alive by a dwarf jester (an import from Poe's *Hop-Frog*) and Hazel Court brands her swanny cleavage in tribute to Satan before being murdered by a swooping falcon. **KN**

**Italy** (Cineriz, Iride) 115m BW

**Language:** Italian

**Director:** Bernardo Bertolucci

**Screenplay:** Gianni Amico, Bernardo Bertolucci

**Photography:** Aldo Scavarda

**Music:** Ennio Morricone, Gino Paoli, Aldo Scavarda

**Nonoriginal music:** Giuseppe Verdi

**Cast:** Evelina Alpi, Gianni Amico, Adriana Asti, Cecrope Barilli, Francesco Barilli, Amelia Bordi, Salvatore Enrico, Guido Fanti, Iole Lunardi, Antonio Maghenzani, Allen Midgette, Morando Morandini, Goliardo Padova, Cristina Pariset, Ida Pellegri

# PRIMA DELLA RIVOLUZIONE (1964)
## BEFORE THE REVOLUTION

Bernardo Bertolucci's *Before the Revolution* is an astonishing film. When one realizes that the director was only 22 years old at the time it was made, it becomes miraculous. A transposition of Stendhal's *La Chartreuse de Parme* to the modern day, this is the story of a young man, Fabrizio (Francesco Barilli), and his hopeless love for his aunt Gina (Adriana Asti), who is ten years his senior.

This is not, as the title might lead you to expect, a militant story of heroic revolutionary struggle, but an elegy for those bourgois lives doomed because they take place before the revolution. The story is simple: Fabrizio, on the edge of adulthood, has a life mapped out according to the middle class norms of his city. Then the death by drowning of his friend Agostino (Allen Midgette) causes him to call his future into doubt as he starts a tempestuous affair with Gina. The final section of the film, which contrasts the future sketched by Fabrizio's Communist teacher and Gina's friend who is about to lose his hereditary estate, makes clear that Fabrizio himself can live neither in the future nor in the past, but only in an uneasy present. *Before the Revolution* is a perfect portrait of the generation who were to embrace revolt in the late 1960s, and a stunning portrait of Parma—Bertolucci's own city. **CM**

# GERTRUD (1964)

**Denmark** (Palladium) 119m BW
**Language:** Danish
**Director:** Carl Theodor Dreyer
**Producer:** Jørgen Nielsen
**Screenplay:** Carl Theodor Dreyer, from play by Hjalmar Söderberg
**Photography:** Henning Bendtsen
**Music:** Jørgen Jersild, Grethe Risbjerg Thomsens
**Cast:** Nina Pens Rode, Bendt Rothe, Ebbe Rode, Baard Owe, Axel Strøbye, Karl Gustav Ahlefeldt, Vera Gebuhr, Lars Knutzon, Anna Malberg, Edouard Mielche
**Cannes Film Festival:** Carl Theodor Dreyer (FIPRESCI award)

In *Gertrud*, his final film, Carl Dreyer brings to its logical culmination the process of fining down, of attenuation, that he had been pursuing for some 40 years. It's an old man's film in its sense of quiet renunciation, yet at the same time a very modern one. The film's ascetic simplicity, the introspective minimalism of its style, aligns it with the approaches that far younger directors like Michelangelo Antonioni and Miklós Jancsó were exploring during the same period. But Dreyer was never interested in following fashion; the 75-year-old director had arrived at the same point by his own wholly individual route.

*Gertrud* is adapted from a 1906 play by the Swedish playwright Hjalmar Söderberg, whose heroine is closely based on a woman with whom he'd had a passionate affair. Dreyer's adaptation purges the play of its more misogynistic elements (Söderberg's lover had just jilted him for a younger man) and presents Gertrud as an erotic idealist, a woman who will accept love only on her own exacting, single-minded terms. Three men—her husband, a poet, and a young musician—love her, but because none of them will put his love for her before everything else in his life, she rejects them all, preferring to live celibate in Paris and devote herself to the life of the mind. In an epilogue, grown old and still alone, she speaks her epitaph: "I have known love."

Dreyer shoots his film with mesmerizing restraint. Nearly two hours long, it consists of less than 90 shots. For long periods the camera remains motionless in medium shot, observing two people as they talk. The characters, though driven by strong passions, love, and despair, rarely raise their voices. There are few sets and only one exterior scene; decors are pared down to basics. Of major directors, perhaps only Ozu ever dared risk such austere stylistic economy. At its premiere in Paris, *Gertrud* was received with uncomprehending hostility by press and public alike. Since then, it has come to be recognized as the last lapidary statement of one of the most individual of filmmakers—a film, like its heroine, to be approached on its own terms. **PK**

**France / Italy** (Arco, Lux) 137 m BW

**Language:** Italian

**Director:** Pier Paolo Pasolini

**Producer:** Alfredo Bini

**Screenplay:** Pier Paolo Pasolini

**Photography:** Tonino Delli Colli

**Music:** Luis Enríquez Bacalov

**Cast:** Enrique Irazoqui, Margherita Caruso, Susanna Pasolini, Marcello Morante, Mario Socrate, Settimio Di Porto, Alfonso Gatto, Luigi Barbini, Giacomo Morante, Giorgio Agamben, Guido Cerretani, Rosario Migale, Ferruccio Nuzzo, Marcello Galdini, Elio Spaziani

**Oscar nomination:** Luigi Scaccianoce (art direction), Danilo Donati (costume), Luis Enríquez Bacalov (music)

**Venice Film Festival:** Pier Paolo Pasolini (OCIC award), (special jury prize), tied with Gamlet, nomination (Golden Lion)

# IL VANGELO SECONDO MATTEO (1964)

## THE GOSPEL ACCORDING TO ST. MATTHEW

This early work by Pier Paolo Pasolini, drawing freely from religious, Marxist, and neorealist traditions, will forever change your conception of a biblical epic. Pasolini was a film critic, writer, and political theorist before he started making movies, and many of his productions bear the weight of his intellectual ambitions. In this relatively straightforward film set in the landscape of southern Italy, Pasolini uses minimal sets and simple camera setups to create a convincing portrait of the biblical era. Pasolini cast nonprofessional actors—Enrique Irazoqui, who plays Jesus, was a student before getting the part—depicting the disciples as a group of socially committed young men, acting in a revolutionary cause. The youth and inexperience of the actors gives a sense of the tenuous nature of the fledgling Christian movement, as something unsure and as yet unformed; it is as though Pasolini wants to erase 2,000 years of dogma and tradition to examine the gospels anew.

Pasolini draws on other arts to elevate this simply told and acted story into a spiritual realm. Using little dialogue, he places his characters in iconic close-ups that recall medieval religious portraiture. Alternating with the close-ups are medium and long shots that recall the works of Peter Breugel, placing the story of Christ in a teeming, immediate context. Music, ranging from masses by Bach and Mozart to blues recordings, imparts extra meaning—a canny technique to handle the untried cast, who at times seem to be underemoting.

Pasolini succeeds in creating a moving and convincing film of the gospel as well as mounting a Marxist critique of Christianity. Without viscerally and intellectually assaulting the viewer as in his later films, *Gospel* contains many of the ideas of his later works and is a fine introduction to his work. **RH**

# DEUS E O DIABO NA TERRA DO SOL (1964)
## BLACK GOD, WHITE DEVIL

**Brazil** (New Cinema, Copacabana, Luiz Augusto Mendes) 110m BW
**Language:** Portuguese
**Director:** Glauber Rocha
**Producer:** Luiz Paulino Dos Santos, Luiz Augusto Mendes
**Screenplay:** Walter Lima Jr., Glauber Rocha, Paulo Gil Soares
**Photography:** Waldemar Lima
**Music:** Sérgio Ricardo, Glauber Rocha
**Cast:** Othon Bastos, Billy Davis, Geraldo Del Rey, Sonia Dos Humildes, Maurício do Valle, João Gama, Mário Gusmão, Yoná Magalhães, Marrom, Antonio Pinto, Maria Olívia Rebouças, Milton Rosa, Regina Rosenburgo, Roque Santos, Lidio Silva

After attending an early screening of Glauber Rocha's *Black God, White Devil*, one Brazilian film critic was overheard marveling "Oh my God, Eisenstein's been reborn...and he's Brazilian!" Born in Bahia, the northeastern Brazilian state known as ground zero for Afro-Brazilian culture, Glauber grew up fascinated by mysticism and American Westerns. In his early twenties, he moved to Rio de Janeiro, where he quickly fell in with a core of young cinephiles who would go on to found the influential *Cinema Novo* movement.

Drawn like so many of his generation to radical politics, Glauber in *Black God, White Devil* sought to explore the connections between historical change and violence. Brazilian history has been (mercifully) free from violent upheaval; all the major transitions—from colony to Empire, Empire to First Republic, and so on—have been relatively bloodless. Here, Rocha focuses on examples of popular rebellion in Brazil's backlands. After killing his abusive employer, Manoel (Geraldo Del Rey) flees with his wife Rosa (Yoná Magalhães) into the arid backlands known as the *sertao*. They first meet up with Sebastiao (Lidio Silva), a black mystic who preaches that a millennial upheaval is coming that will "turn the sea into the land and the land into the sea." Sebastiao is eventually killed by Rosa, and his followers are dispatched by the rifle of Antonio das Mortes (Maurício do Valle), a mysterious figure hired by the Church and large landowners. Next, Manoel and Rosa meet up with Corisco (Othon Bastos), the blond "devil" who's the last surviving *cangaceiro*, wildly dressed bandits who took on a certain Robin Hood aura in popular consciousness. Eventually, das Mortes catches up with him too, but Manoel and Rosa keep running, still rebellious but now aware that neither banditry nor mysticism can truly address their needs.

Shot in a harsh black-and-white that practically makes the screen glow from heat, *Black God, White Devil* alternates frenetic camera movements with dynamic montage sequences, while juxtaposing Villa Lobos with wind, screams, and gunshots. The ultimate effect is a feeling that the film, and the country it's depicting, is about to burst apart; perhaps not unexpectedly, between the completion of the film and its commercial release the Brazilian military staged a coup, establishing a dictatorship that would continue for over twenty years. **RP**

**Japan** (Kindai Eiga Kyokai, Toho, Tokyo Eiga) 103m BW

**Language:** Japanese

**Director:** Kaneto Shindô

**Producer:** Hisao Itoya, Tamotsu Minato, Setsuo Noto

**Screenplay:** Kaneto Shindô

**Photography:** Kiyomi Kuroda

**Music:** Hikaru Hayashi

**Cast:** Nobuko Otowa, Jitsuko Yoshimura, Kei Sato, Jukichi Uno, Taiji Tonoyama, Somesho Matsumoto, Kentaro Kaji, Hosui Araya

# ONIBABA (1964)
## THE DEMON

Kaneto Shindô's *Onibaba* portrays history as a tale of unmitigated horror from the perspective of its losers. In so doing, he makes a passionate allegorical statement about life amid both scarcity and class and gender antagonism; and also reveals the ideological impulses underlying the horror genre itself.

The plot centers on two peasants, a mother (Nobuko Otowa) and her daughter-in-law (Jitsuko Yoshimura), who survive a medieval war by killing lost and wandering samurai and selling the mens' armor for food. Then one day a samurai with a frightening mask enters the old woman's hut and asks her to show him the way through the surrounding reeds. Obsessed with the desire to see his face she kills him and in one of the film's most stunning moments, she removes the mask to see the face of a Japanese A-bomb victim (*hibakusha*).

The old woman begins to wear the mask herself, and in a terrifying scene finds it permanently affixed to her face. The younger woman reluctantly breaks open the mask with an axe and uncovers the bleeding, tortured face of an alive hibakusha, from whom she flees in revulsion. The film ends with three repeat shots of the old woman running behind the younger woman, crying "I am not a demon, I am a human being."

By transforming the demonic mask into a cover for the disfigured face of the hibakusha—a group of people who were stigmatized in Japan after World War II—Shindô brilliantly connects generic convention with the all-too-real horrors of his home country. **JKe**

**U.S.** (Andy Warhol) 70m

**Director:** Andy Warhol

**Screenplay:** Ronald Tavel, from the novel *A Clockwork Orange* by Anthony Burgess

**Photography:** Andy Warhol

**Cast:** Edie Sedgwick, Tosh Carillo, Gerard Malanga, J.D. McDermott, Ondine, Jacques Potin

# VINYL (1965)

Andy Warhol's 1965 film, consisting of two unedited 33-minute black-and-white reels, is a fascinating, sexy, pre-Stanley Kubrick rendering of Anthony Burgess's novel *A Clockwork Orange*. In *Vinyl* the homoerotics of sadomasochism take center stage, as the juvenile delinquent (or JD) Victor, played by a deliciously wooden Gerard Malanga, receives his "reeducation" at the hands of the police. The clever scenario by Warhol's frequent collaborator Ronald Tavel calls for Victor to rough up some guy, get roughed up by the police in return, watch some "flickers" of JD violence, wear an SM leather mask, sniff poppers, and dance wildly to The Supremes' song, "Nowhere to Run." This story of Victor's re-education is juxtaposed with a sadomasochism scene led by the Doc (a sexy Tosh Carillo in tight white jeans) who slowly taunts his willingly restrained, bare-chested accomplice.

*Vinyl's* brilliance is largely due to Warhol's framing of the action. His use of a static camera set-up condenses all the scenes into the cramped but dynamic space of the single frame: Victor's reeducation in the foreground; Doc's SM session in the background; the queeny Ondine in the middle; and, perhaps, most striking of all, a silent Edie Sedgwick sparkling at the right corner of the screen. **MS**

# OBCHOD NA KORZE (1965)
## THE SHOP ON MAIN STREET

**Czechoslovakia** (Barrandov) 128m BW

**Language:** Czech / Slovak

**Director:** Ján Kadár, Elmar Klos

**Screenplay:** Ladislav Grosman, Ján Kadár, Elmar Klos

**Cast:** Ida Kaminska, Jozef Kroner, Hana Slivková, Martin Holly, Adám Matejka, Frantisek Zvarík, Mikulas Ladizinsky, Martin Gregor, Alojz Kramar, Gita Misurova, Frantisek Papp, Helena Zvaríková, Tibor Vadas, Eugen Senaj, Luise Grossova

**Oscar:** Czechoslovakia (best foreign language film)

**Oscar nomination:** Ida Kaminska (actress)

**Cannes Film Festival:** Jozef Kroner, Ida Kaminska (special mention—acting)

Perhaps the most moving drama ever made about the Holocaust, Ján Kadár and Elmar Klos's *The Shop on Main Street* deals with individual morality and responsibility in the context of a "total" society, a theme whose provocation was not lost on official Czech censors. Though it addresses the irreducible human questions raised by the relationship between Jew and Gentile in German-occupied Czechoslovakia, the film discovers a utopian hope for collective happiness in the midst of profound despair. The protagonist, Tono (Jozef Kroner), is a carpenter in a small town whose worst problem is his nagging wife Evelyna (Hana Slivková), who is always pushing him to make more money by collaborating with the Germans like his reptilian brother-in-law Marcus (Frantisek Zvarík).

Finding such hopes of advancement a little appealing, Tono does eventually agree to be appointed the "Aryan controller" of a small Jewish shop presided over by a quite old and somewhat senile woman, Mrs. Lautmann (Ida Kaminska). Tono discovers that the shop makes no money and that the widow is supported by the other Jews of the town, who soon hire Tono to look after her. For the first time in his life, Tono must spend time with a Jew, and the odd couple soon become quite close. But then the order goes out for the Jews to pack their belongings for transport to a "labor" camp. At first, Tono tries to force the uncomprehending woman outside to join the other Jews. But she resists, and Tono, confused and panicked, decides to lock her into a closet until the deportation has ended, hoping in the end that they will both be saved. His rough handling of the old woman, however, has killed her. Discovering Mrs. Lautmann's lifeless body, Tono is overwhelmed by guilt. He puts a noose around his head and hangs himself.

Tono is a kind of Everyman who, uninterested in the play of ideologies around him, discovers that circumstances force him to both choose and act. As he acts, he assumes responsibility and, feeling guilt, also has a vision of a community beyond ideology and sectarianism. Beautifully acted and staged, *The Shop on Main Street* is one of the masterpieces of the Czech renaissance. **RBP**

# DOCTOR ZHIVAGO (1965)

Perhaps the greatest screen epic ever produced, David Lean's film of Boris Pasternak's novel chronicles the discontents of early 20th-century Russian society: the disastrous effects of World War I on the country, as well as the revolution that destroyed the old order, only to deliver Russia to the agonies of, first, a civil war and, then, continuing political turmoil and insecurity.

Robert Bolt's screenplay judiciously compresses *Doctor Zhivago*'s sprawling story, which is told in flashback from the perspective of the 1930s and a time of continuing economic and social transformation. Zhivago (Omar Sharif) is a well-born doctor whose avocation is poetry. He marries his childhood sweetheart Tonya (Geraldine Chaplin), before departing for service in the war. There he meets Lara (Julie Christie), the great love of his life, who is married to a prominent revolutionary. After the revolution, Zhivago's family suffers, and he is forced to work as the medical officer for a Bolshevik band in the civil war. Eventually, however, he escapes, only to learn his family has fled to Paris to avoid imprisonment or worse. Finding Lara, the two live together, during which time he writes his best poetry. But the two lovers must part, never to see one another again.

Though a poignant love story, with Christie and Sharif effective as an ill-starred couple, *Doctor Zhivago* is perhaps most memorable for its magnificent set pieces—the assault by sword-wielding Cossacks on a group of protestors, the interminable journey by train across the country endured by Zhivago's family, the wintry landscape through which Zhivago must trudge to rejoin Lara in a deserted country estate. Lean expertly handled the international ensemble of well-known actors, with the performances by Rod Steiger and Tom Courtenay in supporting character roles particularly effective. Freddie Young's cinematography evokes the expansiveness and raw beauty of the Russian landscape, and Maurice Jarré's score complements the story admirably.

*Dr. Zhivago* proved hugely profitable at the box office and has continued to draw many viewers in subsequent television exhibition, with its memorable characters, riveting action, and moving depiction of important historical events. **RBP**

**U.S.** (MGM, Sostar) 197m Metrocolor

**Director:** David Lean

**Producer:** Arvid Griffen, David Lean, Carlo Ponti

**Screenplay:** Robert Bolt, from novel by Boris Pasternak

**Photography:** Freddie Young

**Music:** Maurice Jarre

**Cast:** Omar Sharif, Julie Christie, Geraldine Chaplin, Rod Steiger, Alec Guinness, Tom Courtenay, Siobhan McKenna, Ralph Richardson, Rita Tushingham, Jeffrey Rockland, Tarek Sharif, Bernard Kay, Klaus Kinski, Gérard Tichy, Noel Willman

**Oscar:** Robert Bolt (screenplay), John Box, Terence Marsh, Dario Simoni (art direction), Freddie Young (photography), Phyllis Dalton (costume), Maurice Jarre (music)

**Oscar nomination:** Carlo Ponti (best picture), David Lean (director), Tom Courtenay (actor in support role), Norman Savage (editing), A.W. Watkins, Franklin Milton (sound)

**Cannes Film Festival:** David Lean, nomination (Golden Palm)

## THE WAR GAME (1965)

A hypothesis about the aftermath of a nuclear attack on England, *The War Game* was banned by BBC-TV, which produced it, ostensibly because (among other reasons stated or hinted at) "it was too horrific for the medium of broadcasting." *The War Game* fast became a cause célèbre and won an Oscar, and remains the most widely known of Peter Watkins's films.

The film mixes scenes seemingly shot by a newsreel crew with others filmed in a documentary style (handheld, single-camera, available-lit) in situations that contradict the presence of a camera. The offscreen narrator (using a bland BBC voice) sometimes speaks as if the events shown have already taken place, giving dates and times and using the past tense, and then switches without warning to an informational mode or to the what-if ("if evacuation plans were carried out, scenes like this would be inevitable"; "This could be the way the last two minutes of peace in Britain would look"). Watkins's free play with narrative strategies gives the film a surging restlessness that's as compelling as his imagery of devastation. *The War Game* is a tour de force that has lost none of its power to horrify since its initial release. **CFu**

**G.B.** (BBC) 48m BW
**Director:** Peter Watkins
**Screenplay:** Peter Watkins
**Photography:** Peter Bartlett
**Cast:** Michael Aspel, Peter Graham
**Oscar:** Peter Watkins (documentary)
**Venice Film Festival:** Peter Watkins (special prize)

## TOKYO ORIMPIKKU (1965)
### TOKYO OLYMPIAD

Kon Ichikawa's record of the 1964 Tokyo Olympiad raised the stakes of epic documentary and achieved a level of artistic reportage subsequent sports programming has been clamoring to mimic ever since. It begins with a rising sun and closes the same way with occasional amplification by Japanocentric flag ceremonies. In the mix are both famous and little-known events, with occasional asides to spy on riveted spectators or tour Tokyo's hot spots.

Putting action to image, however, is Ichikawa's strength. Bodies are synechdochally represented with feet, buttocks, or straining neck turning physical achievement into the very grace of existence. Purposefulness is found both in preparing and executing athletic achievements and, as is often the case in documentary, historicity itself remains indelible.

The now obsolete scissors-kick high-jump technique stings with an imprecise physics. A side-armed volleyball serve seems out of place, and the grunt-and-throw shot put, rather than a spin, defies modern excellence. Even so, the human element shows through in *Tokyo Olympiad*, perhaps most sensually during the women's 80-meter hurdles final when all ambient sound and accompanying music stops for slow-motion movement. Kneecaps scrape by. Faces grimace. Muscles loosen and pound. In short, it's the essence and root cause of sport transformed into movie magic. **GC-Q**

**Japan** (Organizing Committee for the XVIII Olympiad, Toho) 170m Eastmancolor
**Language:** Japanese
**Director:** Kon Ichikawa
**Producer:** Suketaru Taguchi
**Screenplay:** Kon Ichikawa, Yoshio Shirasaka, Shuntaro Tanikawa, Natto Wada
**Photography:** Shigeo Hayashida, Kazuo Miyagawa, Shigeichi Nagano, Kenichi Nakamura, Tadashi Tanaka
**Music:** Toshirô Mayuzumi
**Cast:** Abebe Bikila, Jack Douglas

# LA BATTAGLIA DI ALGERI (1965)
## THE BATTLE OF ALGIERS

A chemistry graduate turned journalist who became a youthful leader of the partisans' antifascist Resistance in Italy through World War II, Gillo Pontecorvo entered the world of cinema as a documentary filmmaker. He brought his intellect, fierce political beliefs, and personal experience to this seminal, electrifying, political thriller, which recounts the bloody Algerian struggle for independence from France. The action takes place between 1954 and 1962 in gritty, authentic drama-documentary style, cast largely with nonprofessional actors and shot and narrated in the manner of a newsreel. Winner of the prestigious Golden Lion at the Venice Film Festival, *The Battle of Algiers* was one of the most influential films to come out of Italy in the 1960s, and it has lost none of its passionate power.

The film begins as the most wanted man in Algeria, Ali La Point (Brahim Haggiag), and his closest supporters, including a woman and a child, are cornered in their hiding place by an overwhelming number of French troops—acting on a tip-off obtained by torture—and ordered to surrender or die. As the seconds of the ultimatum tick by, the narrative returns to Ali's origins as a petty thief, his recruitment to the cause of ousting the French, and his progress to living legend and heroic martyr. Meanwhile, the French authorities respond to the grassroots uprising that became a model for modern guerrilla revolt, employing a crack force of paratroopers under an iron-willed commander and tactician (Jean Martin).

Although Pontecorvo had financial assistance from the Algerian government—and the film wears its anticolonialist heart on its sleeve—horrifying and heartrending scenes of atrocities and reprisals are laudably evenhanded, depicting both sides of the conflict and its awful human cost. It is gripping from start to finish. A particularly uncompromising tour de force is a nail-biting sequence that follows women of the Algiers casbah slipping through checkpoints and planting primitive bombs—in an airport lounge, in a milk bar—where oblivious French teens are gyrating to pop songs, to an inevitably grievous aftermath. The really superb, emotive score was cocomposed by Pontecorvo himself and the great Ennio Morricone. **AE**

**Algeria / Italy** (Casbah, Igor) 117m BW
**Language:** French
**Director:** Gillo Pontecorvo
**Producer:** Antonio Musu, Yacef Saadi
**Screenplay:** Gillo Pontecorvo, Franco Solinas
**Photography:** Marcello Gatti
**Music:** Ennio Morricone, Gillo Pontecorvo
**Cast:** Jean Martin, Yacef Saadi, Brahim Haggiag, Samia Kerbash, Tommaso Neri, Michele Kerbash, Ugo Paletti, Fusia El Kader, Franco Morici
**Oscar nomination:** Italy (best foreign language film), Gillo Pontecorvo (director), Franco Solinas, Gillo Pontecorvo (screenplay)
**Venice Film Festival:** Gillo Pontecorvo (FIPRESCI award), nomination for (Golden Lion)

## THE SOUND OF MUSIC (1965)

It is all too easy to knock Robert Wise's enormously successful screen adaptation of Rodgers and Hammerstein's musical hit, what with singing nuns and a kind-of-cute clutch of seven kids coping with the double trouble of an absurdly disciplinarian widower father and the rise of the Nazi regime in 1930s Salzburg. But one should never underestimate the effectiveness of the lead performances—Julie Andrews as the eccentrically vivacious nun-turned-governess and Christopher Plummer as the strict, buttoned-up patriarch whose heart she melts. There is also the unsentimental precision of Ernest Lehman's script (he did, after all, also work on *Sweet Smell of Success* [1957] and *North by Northwest* [1959]), and the solid, unshowy expertise of Wise's direction, in which his editor's sensitivity to structure, rhythm, and rhyming juxtapositions is always evident.

That exhilarating opening helicopter shot across the mountaintops—finally alighting on Andrews running exuberantly as she bursts into "The hills are alive" may now seem hackneyed, but that's only because its efficiency in establishing mood (and, indeed, meaning, since *The Sound of Music* is a film in which music and the life force are inextricably linked) has meant that it's been much imitated. And let us not forget: like it or not, those tunes really are unforgettable. **GA**

**U.S.** (Fox, Argyle) 174m Color Deluxe
**Director:** Robert Wise
**Producer:** Robert Wise
**Screenplay:** Ernest Lehman, Richard Rodgers, Oscar Hammerstein (from stage musical) and from books by Howard Lindsay and Russel Crouse
**Music:** Richard Rodgers, Irwin Kostal
**Cast:** Julie Andrews, Christopher Plummer, Eleanor Parker, Richard Haydn, Peggy Wood, Charmian Carr, Heather Menzies, Nicholas Hammond, Duane Chase, Angela Cartwright
**Oscar:** Robert Wise (best picture), Robert Wise (director), William Reynolds (editing), Irwin Kostal (music), James Corcoran, Fred Hynes (sound)
**Oscar nomination:** Julie Andrews (actress), Peggy Wood (actress in support role), Boris Leven, Walter M. Scott, Ruby R. Levitt (art direction), Ted D. McCord (photography), Dorothy Jeakins (costume)

## REKOPIS ZNALEZIONY W SARAGOSSIE (1965)
### THE SARAGOSSA MANUSCRIPT

Jerry Garcia proclaimed this 1965 Polish feature his favorite movie, having seen a pared-down version in San Francisco's North Beach during the 1960s, and a few years back he, Martin Scorsese, and Francis Ford Coppola helped to restore it to its original three-hour length. It's easy to see how *The Saragossa Manuscript* became a cult film. Toward the end of the Spanish Inquisition a Napoleonic military officer—Zbigniew Cybulski, the Polish James Dean, though pudgier than usual here—is morally tested by two seductive Muslim princesses, incestuous sisters from Tunisia, and no less than nine interconnected flashbacks recounted by various characters figure in the labyrinthine plot, its tales within tales imparting some of the flavor of *The Arabian Nights* and occasional echoes of Kafka (mainly in the eroticism).

Krzysztof Penderecki's score runs the gamut from classical music to flamenco to modernist electronic noodling, and the stark, rocky settings are elegantly filmed in black-and-white 'Scope. The late Wojciech Has was a fine journeyman director, though a film of this kind really calls for someone more obsessive, like Roman Polanski. Adapted by Tadeusz Kwiatkowski from Jan Potocki's 1813 novel, it is certainly an intriguing fantasy and a haunting reflection on the processes of storytelling. **JRos**

**Poland** (Kamera) 124m BW
**Language:** Polish
**Director:** Wojciech Has
**Screenplay:** Tadeusz Kwiatkowski, from novel by Jan Potocki
**Photography:** Mieczyslaw Jahoda
**Music:** Krzysztof Penderecki
**Cast:** Zbigniew Cybulski, Kazimierz Opalinski, Iga Cembrzynska, Joanna Jedryka, Slawomir Lindner, Miroslawa Lombardo, Aleksander Fogiel, Franciszek Pieczka, Ludwik Benoit, Barbara Krafftówna, Pola Raksa, August Kowalczyk, Adam Pawlikowski, Beata Tyszkiewicz, Gustaw Holoubek

**France / Italy** (Athos, Chaumiane, Filmstudio) 99m BW

**Language:** French

**Director:** Jean-Luc Godard

**Producer:** André Michelin

**Screenplay:** Jean-Luc Godard, from the novel *La Capitale de la douleur* by Paul Éluard

**Photography:** Raoul Coutard

**Music:** Paul Misraki

**Cast:** Eddie Constantine, Anna Karina, Akim Tamiroff

**Berlin Film Festival:** Jean-Luc Godard (Golden Bear)

# ALPHAVILLE, UNE ÉTRANGE AVENTURE DE LEMMY CAUTION (1965)

## ALPHAVILLE

In the future, secret agent Lemmy Caution (Eddie Constantine) cruises into Alphaville, which is either a city or a planet, in his Ford Galaxie, which is either a car or a spaceship. His mission is to find and perhaps liquidate the missing Professor Von Braun (Howard Vernon). First, Caution runs into Henri Dickson (Akim Tamiroff), an agent who has gone native, and then the mad scientist's daughter Natacha (Anna Karina), who has never heard the words "love" or "conscience." Alphaville is run by a croaking super-computer that has made honest emotion a capital crime, insisting on mass executions carried out ceremonially in an eerie swimming pool. He-man hero Caution naturally sets out to destroy the computer (by feeding it poetry), and incidentally woos the fragile Natacha, awakening her dormant emotions.

Jean-Luc Godard, powerhouse of the French *nouvelle vague*, set out to create a science-fiction film without expensive sets or special effects. Shooting in cleverly-selected Paris locations, he discovers the seeds of a totalitarian future in contemporary hotel lobbies, neon signage, office buildings, and bureaucratic waiting rooms. *Alphaville*'s relationship with science fiction was initially parodic, as is Godard's affectionate borrowing of trench coat characters and gun-pulling poses from hard-boiled Franco-American pulp (Constantine had previously played author Peter Cheyney's Mike Hammer-ish sleuth Lemmy Caution in a run of thick-ear thrillers). However, considered as a product of the times—when Philip K. Dick was exploring similar themes in ever-more-ambitious novels—*Alphaville* now looks a lot like proper sci-fi, to the extent of influencing a run of adaptations (from François Truffaut's take on Ray Bradbury's *Fahrenheit 451* to Ridley Scott's Dick-derived *Blade Runner*).

Like many Godards, *Alphaville* deliberately runs out of plot after an hour and has two characters sit in a hotel room arguing for minutes. As in *Breathless* and *Contempt*, this free-ranging conversation, with Caution shaking Natacha out of zombiehood, ought to be a dead spot but is actually a highlight, confirming Godard as almost the equal of Joseph L. Mankiewicz in the cinema of conversation. The film shows a wry humor and a poetic seriousness (sometimes, silliness), and is a rare futurist vision that simply does not date. **KN**

# CHIMES AT MIDNIGHT (1965)
## CAMPANADAS A MEDIANOCHE

**Spain / Switzerland** (Alpine, Española) 113m BW

**Director:** Orson Welles

**Producer:** Ángel Escolano, Emiliano Piedra, Harry Saltzman, Alessandro Tasca

**Screenplay:** Orson Welles, from plays of William Shakespeare and book by Raphael Holinshed

**Photography:** Edmond Richard

**Music:** Angelo Francesco Lavagnino

**Cast:** Orson Welles, Jeanne Moreau, Margaret Rutherford, John Gielgud, Marina Vlady, Walter Chiari, Michael Aldridge, Julio Peña, Tony Beckley, Andrés Mejuto, Keith Pyott, Jeremy Rowe, Alan Webb, Fernando Rey, Keith Baxter

**Cannes Film Festival:** Orson Welles (20th anniversary prize), (grand technical prize), tied with *Skaterdater*, nomination (Golden Palm)

Orson Welles was always fascinated by Shakespeare and filmed both an *Othello* and a *Macbeth* as well as a television version of *The Merchant of Venice*. There is no doubt, however, that his greatest achievement in this vein is his adapatation of the *Henry IV* plays, *Chimes at Midnight*. But don't go looking for a faithful Shakespeare adapatation here. Scholarly opinion divides between those who think that the young Prince Hal is merely sowing his wild oats with the drunk reprobate Falstaff and is justified in abandoning him when he comes to the throne, and those who feel that the abandonment of the fat knight shows that Hal is a machiavellian prince with no human feeling. Welles does not bother to balance his opinions. This is *Henry IV* Parts 1 and 2 told from Falstaff's point of view. His drinking and thieving, his cowardice and his greed are not faults but foibles. Falstaff is fat and Welles glories in his physical embodiment of the corpulent knight. The comic scenes in Eastcheap, particularly after the failed robbery at Gadhill, are masterful.

Shakespeare's repartee has never been so gloriously performed as it is by Welles. But even more affecting are the battle scenes shot without nobility or honor, wretched fields on which men die to serve the crooked purpose of their masters. But the real triumph of *Chimes at Midnight* is the scenes from which the film takes its title, Falstaff's encounter with Justice Shallow (Alan Webb), the acquaintance of his riotous youth who has become a country magistrate. The pathos of these encounters, which go well beyond the Shakespearean play, are truly affecting—particularly as we are in no doubt of the tragic emotional fate that awaits Falstaff as he is banished by the love of his life, young Prince Hal now become King Henry V. The cast is magnificent, with John Gielgud as Henry IV, Norman Rodway as Hotspur, Keith Baxter as Hal, and even Jeanne Moreau showing up as Doll Tearsheet and Marina Vlady as Hotspur's wife. One warning: the postsynchronization of the dialogue is truly appalling—it has to be heard to be believed. Otherwise a masterpiece. **CM**

# REPULSION (1965)

**G.B.** (Compton) 104m BW

**Director:** Roman Polanski

**Producer:** Gene Gutowski, Michael Klinger, Robert Sterne, Tony Tenser, Sam Waynberg

**Screenplay:** Gérard Brach, Roman Polanski, David Stone

**Photography:** Gilbert Taylor

**Music:** Chico Hamilton

**Cast:** Catherine Deneuve, Ian Hendry, John Fraser, Yvonne Furneaux, Patrick Wymark, Renee Houston, Valerie Taylor, James Villiers, Helen Fraser, Hugh Futcher, Monica Merlin, Imogen Graham, Mike Pratt, Roman Polanski

**Berlin Film Festival:** Roman Polanski (FIPRESCI award), (Silver Bear—special jury prize), nomination (Golden Bear)

Roman Polanski's first film in English is still his scariest and most disturbing—not only for its evocations of sexual panic but also because his masterful use of sound puts the audience's imagination to work in numerous ways. It is also the most expressionistic of his early black-and-white features, using wide angles that become increasingly wider and deep focus, along with other visual strategies, to convey subjective states of mind in which dreams, imagination, and everyday reality are worked into the same continuum. One result of such an expressionist style is that the conventional apartment in which most of the action takes place gradually assumes the shape and form of a tortured consciousness.

Catherine Deneuve gives one of her most impressive performances here as Carole Ledoux, a quiet and quietly mad Belgian manicurist terrified of men and living with her older sister in London. When the sister and her boyfriend, whose lovemaking in an adjacent room already disturbs and frightens her, take off on a holiday, Carole's fears and isolation in the apartment fester along with the uncooked food—including a sinister-looking skinned rabbit. The results are increasingly violent and macabre, Carole's madness becoming more and more apparent.

As narrative the film works only part of the time, and as case study it may occasionally seem too obvious, but as subjective nightmare *Repulsion* is a stunning piece of filmmaking. Put together with expertly calibrated shocks and a gradually developing sense of dread, in many respects, this thriller became something of a template for many of Polanski's subsequent ventures into horror. His films are of isolation and claustrophobia and include such disparate works as *The Tenant* in 1976 (in which Polanski played the starring role) and *The Pianist* over a quarter of a century later. Yet ironically, in his 1984 autobiography, Polanski wrote that he and his cowriter Gérard Brach regarded *Repulsion* mainly as "a means to an end"—namely, a commercial success to enable them to finance *Cul-de-sac* (1966), a much more personal, if less commercial, film in English that would star Deneuve's sister Françoise Dorléac. **JRos**

# JULIET OF THE SPIRITS (1965)
## GIULIETTA DEGLI SPIRITI

**Italy / France / West Germany**
(Eichberg, Federiz, Francoriz, Rizzoli)
148m Technicolor
**Language:** Italian
**Director:** Federico Fellini
**Producer:** Angelo Rizzoli
**Screenplay:** Federico Fellini, Ennio Flaiano, Tullio Pinelli, Brunello Rondi
**Photography:** Gianni Di Venanzo
**Music:** Nino Rota
**Cast:** Giulietta Masina, Sandra Milo, Mario Pisu, Valentina Cortese, José Luis de Villalonga, Caterina Boratto, Sylva Koscina, Frederick Ledebur, Luisa Della Noce, Valeska Gert, Lou Gilbert, Silvana Jachino, Milena Vukotic, Fred Williams, Dany París
**Oscar nomination:** Piero Gherardi (art direction) and (costume)

Today, the excellence of color work in cinematography and film design is judged on the achievement of an overall, carefully modulated palette. In Federico Fellini's *Juliet of the Spirits*, color is the occasion to create an aesthetic riot between and within shots: A frame which is all red and green, for instance, intercut with one that is gleaming white.

In his first color film, Fellini explored the possibilities with glee. Conceived as a companion piece to *8 ½* (1963), it delves into the psyche of Juliet, played by Fellini's famous wife Giulietta Masina. Faced with an uncertain marriage and a philandering husband (the film is lightly autobiographical), Juliet strays into a highly eroticized world of spiritual mediums, high-class whores, and affluent acquaintances. Soon, the spirit-visions come, tormenting Juliet with the gap between her oppressive, religious upbringing and the liberation or contentment she seeks.

One of the most extraordinary aspects of this movie today is its absolute modernity. The faces, costumes, and attitudes do not seem dated. The film is uniquely prescient: Already, Fellini had absorbed, and lovingly exaggerated, the pop-mystical fads that were to explode in "New Age" culture, especially concerning "body and mind" philosophies—for this is truly a movie about body and mind as surrealistic "communicating vessels."

Although Fellini was reproached for using women as the ground for his narcissistic projections, Juliet is in fact his finest female character—Masina bringing to the outlandish proceedings both a childlike wonder and a down-to-earth hesitation and skepticism which make her a natural figure of identification for the viewer.

Stylistically, Fellini here began marrying his dream-fed visions with the technological bric-a-brac of the modern world (telephones, movie projectors, screens), thus simultaneously making sublime things mundane, and mundane things sublime. His camera is a roving eye, sometimes seemingly lost: The relentless entries and exits from the frame, the artful shuttling of multiple bodies, the sudden moments when an image is revealed as Juliet's point of view—all these devices, swinging to the rhythm of Nino Rota's rich, carnival-style score, evoke a heady plunge into the realm of the unconscious. **AM**

**France / Italy** (De Laurentiis, Rome Paris, SNC) 110m Eastmancolor
**Language:** French
**Director:** Jean-Luc Godard
**Producer:** Georges de Beauregard
**Screenplay:** Jean-Luc Godard
**Photography:** Raoul Coutard
**Music:** Antoine Duhamel
**Cast:** Jean-Paul Belmondo, Ferdinand Griffon, Anna Karina, Marianne Renoir
**Venice Film Festival:** Jean-Luc Godard nomination (Golden Lion)

# PIERROT LE FOU (1965)
## PIERROT GOES WILD

Jean-Luc Godard's masterpiece *Pierrot le Fou* is an important milestone in the director's long and brilliant career. A turning point of sorts, the film straddles the experimental *élan* of Godard works such as *Breathless* (1960) and *My Life to Live* (1962) and the highly politicized, cynical, and bitterly funny films like *Week End* (1967) and *Wind from the East* (1969). *Pierrot le Fou* contains elements of both, and is a rich viewing experience for this reason alone. But one thing the film also possesses, in spades, is a sense of true beauty. Critics tend to forget that Godard, for all his polemicism, made some exquisitely beautiful films. *Pierrot le Fou* must surely be considered alongside *Contempt* (1963) in this regard.

Godard always had a love-hate relationship with Hollywood. For him, American films are at once the most beautiful and honest, but also the most crass and ugly. As in many of his works, Godard uses American "low" culture and genre filmmaking as his launching pad: *Pierrot le Fou* is (extremely) loosely based on pulp novelist Lionel White's *Obsession*, and it features an extended cameo by underappreciated Hollywood maverick and Godard favorite Samuel Fuller. The very fact that the film was shot in Techniscope by the great Raoul Coutard is a comment on the manufactured grandeur of so many Hollywood prestige pictures of the 1950s and 60s. If you know Hollywood cinema from this era, watching *Pierrot le Fou* can be an immensely rewarding, if confounding, experience, for satire in Godard is never quite as plain as one might expect.

*Pierrot* is bitter, satirical, humorous, and beautiful—something that is clear on first viewing. But perhaps its most charming (and arresting) feature is its sheer outrageousness. Ferdinand/Pierrot and Marianne (Godard's regulars Jean-Paul Belmondo and Anna Karina) move deliriously from one ridiculous situation to another—be it the world's most insufferable party, a free-for-all with gas station attendants, or a bizarrely uplifting self-immolation. Almost anything is possible in this film, yet it still manages to surprise, even upon repeated viewings. The potency of Godard's imagery and satire has not diminished with age. If anything, it is even more relevant today. **EdeS**

## FASTER, PUSSYCAT! KILL! KILL! (1965)

What can you say about Russ Meyer? His movies are, to paraphrase a well-known saying about life itself, nasty, brutish, and short. Arguments have been made in favor of his occasional artistry and, sometimes, we are asked to reconsider the troublesome sexual politics of his films. And, although both arguments (and many of the films themselves) should be approached with caution, *Faster, Pussycat! Kill! Kill!* remains a favorite—and not just for John Waters, who likes to claim that it's the best movie ever made.

*Faster, Pussycat! Kill! Kill!* traces the exploits (an especially significant term in this context) of its three curvy and violent drag-racing female protagonists: Varla (Tura Satana), Rosie (Haji), and Billie (Lori Williams). After a racing-related murder, the crew hides out at a nearby ranch where they spend the rest of the picture scheming to liberate the rancher of his finances. The film enjoys its place at the top of many cult lists in part because of its several inherent delights—creative and flashy editing, smart black-and-white cinematography, a jazzy score, and plenty of innuendo—and in part because it is a fascinating barometer of the shifts occurring during the 1960s, especially with respect to cinema itself. **DO**

**U.S.** (Eve) 83m BW
**Director:** Russ Meyer
**Producer:** George Costello, Eve Meyer, Russ Meyer, Fred Owens
**Screenplay:** Russ Meyer, Jack Moran
**Photography:** Walter Schenk
**Music:** Paul Sawtell, Bert Shefter
**Cast:** Tura Satana, Haji, Rosie, Lori Williams, Sue Bernard, Stuart Lancaster, Paul Trinka, Dennis Busch, Ray Barlow, Michael Finn

**India** (J.J. Films) 143m BW

**Language:** Bengali

**Director:** Ritwik Ghatak

**Screenplay:** Ritwik Ghatak, from novel by Radheshyam Jhunjhunwala

**Photography:** Dilip Ranjan Mukhopadhyay

**Music:** Ustad Bahadur Khan, Nino Rota (from Fellini's *La Dolce Vita*)

**Cast:** Abhi Bhattacharya, Madhabi Mukherjee, Satindra Bhattacharya, Bijon Bhattacharya, Indrani Chakrabarty, Sriman Tarun, Jahar Ray, Pitambar, Sriman Ashok Bhattacharya, Sita Mukherjee, Radha Govinda Ghosh, Abinash Bannerjee, Gita De, Umanath Bhattacharya, Arun Chowdhury

# SUBARNAREKHA (1965)

## GOLDEN RIVER

Ritwik Ghatak is best known for *The Cloud-Capped Star* (1960), but *Subarnarekha* may be even stronger—indeed, for some it ranks among the greatest undiscovered masterpieces of cinema. A native of Dhaka, East Bengal (now Bangladesh), Ghatak was 22 years old at the time of the Partition, the trauma that defined him as an artist. *Subarnarekha* begins in a colony of impoverished Bengali refugees in Calcutta with news of Gandhi's assassination. Ishwar Chakraborty (Abhi Bhattacharya) is rearing a young daughter and also takes an abandoned boy under his wing—so when an affluent college friend offers him a post in a provincial factory, he accepts it to secure their future, even at the cost of his broader aspirations.

Years pass. When the boy, Abhiram (Satindra Bhattacharya), returns from college an aspiring writer, it emerges that he is in love with his half-sister Shita (Madhabi Mukherjee), and she with him. The declaration of love is a haunting example of Ghatak's innovative experiments with sound: The words are drawn out of the young man in a whisper that seems to bypass his mouth entirely—passion straight from the heart. Of course Ishwar opposes his children's union, though this is complicated by the revelation that Abhiram is of low caste, and thus unworthy of his daughter. A good man watches appalled as everything his life has stood for unravels before his eyes. Totally defeated, incapable even of suicide, he resolves to be "quits with the devil"—and Ghatak hereby elevates popular melodrama to the upper reaches of tragedy.

The American filmmaker has not been born who can match Ghatak for the cinematic expression of utter, unadulterated anguish. His dynamic compositional sense distills the power-plays operative in personal relationships, yet an insistent expressionist edge exposes a wider underlying powerlessness before social, ethnic, economic—and, perhaps, mythopoetic—forces. He is especially sensitive to the fate of the marginalized: Women, the young, the old, and the insane. From the ruins of these lives, Ghatak unearths a shimmering mirage of hope. However, *Subarnarekha* proved too harrowing for audiences, and received only limited distribution; the filmmaker himself succumbed to alcoholism. He died in 1976 at age 51. **TCh**

# DE MAN DIE ZIJN HAAR KORT LIET KNIPPEN (1965)
## THE MAN WHO HAD HIS HAIR CUT SHORT

**Belgium** (BRT, Ministerie van Nationale Opvoeding en Kultuur) 94m BW
**Language:** Dutch
**Director:** André Delvaux
**Producer:** Paul Louyet, Jos Op De Beeck
**Screenplay:** Anna De Pagter, from novel by Johan Daisne
**Photography:** Ghislain Cloquet
**Music:** Frédéric Devreese
**Cast:** Senne Rouffaer, Beata Tyszkiewicz, Hector Camerlynck, Hilde Uytterlinden, Annemarie Van Dijk, Hilda Van Roose, François Beukelaers, Arlette Emmery, Paul S'Jongers, Luc Philips, François Bernard, Vic Moeremans, Maurits Goossens

*The Man Who Had His Hair Cut Short* is the film through which Belgian cinema entered modernism. The feature debut of André Delvaux, it also marks the arrival of Belgium's own national cinematic style, magic realism—a unique blend of reality and eerie fantasy, addressing the surreal melancholy of everyday life.

Delvaux's film follows a curious narrative, from love story to mystery-thriller, over to an exploration of the thin line between sanity and madness. Govert Miereveld (Senne Roufaer) is a teacher who falls in love with a pupil who soon disappears, leaving us—and Govert—to wonder whether or not he has killed her. Much more than a mere detective tale, *The Man Who Had His Hair Cut Short* is a quest into the protagonist's identity crisis; together with Govert we gradually realize we can no longer trust what we see or hear, as reality itself becomes a dream. A crucial scene in the film is a countryside autopsy, mixing realism, revulsion, and dreamlike alienation.

Stylistically, *The Man Who Had His Hair Cut Short* is a very subtle movie. Minute details in the language, visuals, and behavior of the characters cast doubts upon the veracity of the very realistic settings in which Govert lives and travels, until, in the end, we give up looking for truth, settling, with Govert, for quiet contemplation—a surrender to strangeness. **EM**

# HOLD ME WHILE I'M NAKED (1966)

**U.S.** 17m Color
**Director:** George Kuchar
**Cast:** Donna Kerness, George Kuchar, Andrea Lunin, Hope Morris, Steve Packard

George Kuchar's first 16mm color film is a charming and melodramatic tour de force of underground invention. The most popular of the hundreds of films Kuchar has made since the late 1950s, this 1966 low-budget short tells the story of an endearing loser of a filmmaker (Kuchar) who battles bouts of depression and loneliness in his attempt to make a film. When his voluptuous starlet (the tantalizing Donna Kerness) finds passion in the shower, Kuchar's self-pity and alienation achieve even greater depths.

Like many of George and twin brother Mike's Bronx-made Hollywood epics, *Hold Me While I'm Naked* attains a level of emotional seriousness that makes it stand out among the camp and trash Hollywood parodies to which it is inevitably compared. This is due in large part to Kuchar's technical and creative skills: His stunning title and production design; his ingenious inventory of odd and unflattering camera angles; and his insatiable talent at adapting the glamorous concerns and emotional extremes of Hollywood flicks to the banal realities and human proportions of his neighborhood friends. A colorful example of Kuchar resourcefulness, *Hold Me While I'm Naked* has incited many a viewer—John Waters among them—to mobilize friends for their own glorious screen epics. **MS**

# BLOWUP (1966)

G.B. (Bridge) 111m Metrocolor
**Director:** Michelangelo Antonioni
**Producer:** Carlo Ponti, Pierre Rouve
**Screenplay:** Michelangelo Antonioni, Tonino Guerra, Edward Bond, from story by Julio Cortázar
**Photography:** Carlo Di Palma
**Music:** Herbie Hancock
**Cast:** David Hemmings, Vanessa Redgrave, Peter Bowles, Sarah Miles, John Castle, Jane Birkin, Gillian Hills, Veruschka von Lehndorff, Julian Chagrin, Claude Chagrin
**Oscar nomination:** Michelangelo Antonioni (director), Michelangelo Antonioni, Tonino Guerra, Edward Bond (screenplay)
**Cannes Film Festival:** Michelangelo Antonioni (Golden Palm)

After a run of masterpieces from *L'Avventura* to *Il Deserto Rosso*, revolving around jaded Italian upper-class ennui and Monica Vitti, Michelangelo Antonioni became an international filmmaker with this 1966 picture. Based on an anecdote-like short story by Julio Cortazar, *Blowup* follows *L'Avventura* in offering a mystery with no solution but goes even further by wondering after a great deal of obsessive investigation whether there even *was* a mystery outside the protagonist's mind. Turning his outsider's eye on a London that was just beginning to swing, Antonioni captures precisely a time and a place that seemed culturally significant. As with Fellini's *La Dolce Vita*, a film intended as a satirical attack on a certain type of modern sophistication and emptiness emerges almost as a celebration of the fashions, mores, music, sexuality, and strangeness of a world it would like to disapprove of.

The central character is Thomas (David Hemmings), a photographer who—perhaps like Antonioni—divides his time between assault-like sessions with vapidly lovely fashion models and verité work among down-and-outs. Snapping away in an eerily unpopulated park in the hopes of finding a peaceful image to conclude his latest book, Thomas gets some shots that seem to show an older man and a younger woman (Vanessa Redgrave) having an innocent, quiet moment. However, the woman pursues Thomas and demands he turn over the film, then turns up at his studio to press her case with a jittery, neurotic flirtatiousness that further piques the terminally cool Thomas's interest. He palms her off with the wrong film and develops his photographs: under extreme analysis, he seems to find a man with a gun lurking in the undergrowth catching the woman's panicky or complicit eye. Another photograph shows a vague form that might be a body, and another visit to the park turns up an actual corpse—but then all the evidence is taken away and Thomas loses his conviction that he has latched onto a murder and surrenders to the distractions that clutter his life.

Despite its thriller-style hook (often hommaged in straighter suspense films like Coppola's *The Conversation* or De Palma's *Blow Out*), this is less a mystery than a portrait of swinging alienation. In 1966, when nudity in English-language films wasn't commonplace, there was a real charge to Redgrave taking off her blouse and lounging around the studio with her arms crossed over her breasts, not to mention the notorious (and actually rather tactful) sequence in which Thomas grapples on the floor with a pair of gawky, giggling groupies. Most of all, this is a film about an alien world: The creepily unvisited park, a concert (featuring The Yardbirds) where the audience stand impassive until a guitar is smashed and they erupt into a feeding frenzy, a pot party where Thomas searches for someone he is then unable to explain anything to, and a game of tennis between student mimes that leads to an ambiguous finish as Thomas is drawn into the game by returning a lost "ball." **KN**

**Italy / Spain** (Arturo González, PEA)
161m Technicolor

**Language:** Italian

**Director:** Sergio Leone

**Producer:** Alberto Grimaldi

**Screenplay:** Luciano Vincenzoni, Sergio Leone, Agenore Incrocci, Furio Scarpelli

**Photography:** Tonino Delli Colli

**Music:** Ennio Morricone

**Cast:** Clint Eastwood, Lee Van Cleef, Eli Wallach, Aldo Giuffrè, Luigi Pistilli, Rada Rassimov, Enzo Petito, Claudio Scarchilli, John Bartha, Livio Lorenzon, Antonio Casale, Sandro Scarchilli, Benito Stefanelli, Angelo Novi, Antonio Casas

# IL BUONO, IL BRUTTO, IL CATTIVO (1966)
## THE GOOD, THE BAD, AND THE UGLY

By the mid 1960s, Hollywood had grown largely tired of the Western, which was increasingly viewed as a stodgy and hokey relic of another era. Sure, the films remained essential elements of movie history, but the times were changing and Westerns no longer appeared to have a firm place in popular culture. Sergio Leone thought differently. The Italian director sensed that the moribund genre was ripe for reinvention, and the enduring influence of his so-called Spaghetti Westerns (nicknamed for both the Italian location shoots as well as the copious blood) demonstrates that he was right.

Leone had worked on a handful of films before inviting then relative unknown Clint Eastwood over to Italy to remake Akira Kurosawa's *Yojimbo* (1961), itself based on Dashiell Hammett's novel *Red Harvest*, into the first of his iconic "man with no name" Westerns, *A Fistful of Dollars* (1964). Shot on a shoestring budget, the stylish, innovative film became a huge success, and Leone followed it with *For a Few Dollars More* (1965), which also starred Eastwood as another laconic and anonymous antihero.

But the third part of his "man with no name" trilogy, *The Good, the Bad, and the Ugly*, is what really confirmed Leone's reputation in cinematic legend. Set during the Civil War, the film follows three rogues who, although clearly identified as each of the title's categories, really blur the line between the three. Eastwood returns, this time as a crooked bounty hunter (ostensibly "the good") who repeatedly captures (and then releases) outlaw Eli Wallach ("the ugly") in order to drive up the price on his head. Following a sadistic falling out, the erstwhile partners team up again in search of stolen Confederate gold, but the opportunistic, amoral Lee Van Cleef (the "bad") complicates their quest.

Leone isn't terribly interested in plot—*The Good, the Bad, and the Ugly* embraces purely cinematic elements of filmmaking. He carefully composes each widescreen image like he's painting a great landscape, frequently indulging himself in extreme close-ups—often little more than a character's eyes. Leone propels the story forward with radical editing techniques, often cut to the rhythms of Ennio Morricone's famous score, pairing odd instrumentation and electric guitars to more traditional orchestration. Style drips from each frame like the sweat pouring down his stars' faces.

*The Good, the Bad, and the Ugly* literally comes down to the faces of Eastwood, Wallach, and Van Cleef, as the mutual antagonists perform a three-way duel in an old graveyard. The scene has since become one of the most imitated and parodied in motion picture history. Morricone's hypnotic score intensifies with quickening film cuts from face to face, capturing each set of squinting eyes, each hand reaching for a gun. Camp and kitsch and utterly entrancing, the work is of a master rewriting the rules of the Western to suit Leone's own unique vision. **JKl**

Czechoslovakia (Ceskoslovensky Státní, Barrandov) 74m Eastmancolor

**Language:** Czech

**Director:** Vera Chytilová

**Screenplay:** Vera Chytilová, Ester Krumbachová

**Photography:** Jaroslav Kucera

**Music:** Jirí Slitr, Jirí Sust

**Cast:** Julius Albert, Jitka Cerhová, Marie Cesková, Ivana Karbanová, Jan Klusák

# SEDMIKRASKY (1966)

## DAISIES

Surely one of the most exhilarating stylistic and psychedelic cinematic explosions of the 1960s, Vera Chytilová's *Daisies* is a madcap and aggressive feminist farce that explodes in any number of directions. Although many American and Western European filmmakers during this period prided themselves on their subversiveness, it is possible that the most radical film of the decade, ideologically as well as formally, came from the East—from the liberating ferment building toward the short-lived political reforms of 1968's Prague Spring in Czechoslovakia.

Featuring two uninhibited 17-year-olds named Marie (Jitka Cerhová and Ivana Karbanová)—whose various escapades, which add up less to a plot than to a string of outrageous set pieces, include several antiphallic gags (such as slicing up cucumbers and bananas), a penchant for exploiting dirty old men, and a free-for-all with fancy food (rivaling Laurel and Hardy) that got Chytilová in trouble with the authorities. This disturbing yet liberating tour de force shows what this talented director can do with freedom. A major influence on Jacques Rivette's *Celine and Julie Go Boating*, *Daisies* is chock-full of female giggling, which might be interpreted in context as what critic Ruby Rich has called the laughter of Medusa: Subversive, bracing, energizing, and rather off-putting (if challenging) to most male spectators. **JRos**

**Hong Kong** (Shaw Brothers) 95m Color

**Language:** Mandarin

**Director:** King Hu

**Producer:** Run Run Shaw

**Screenplay:** Ye Yang

**Cast:** Cheng Pei-pei, Hua Yueh, Chen Hung Lieh, Biao Yuen, Jackie Chan

# DA ZUI XIA (1966)

## COME DRINK WITH ME

Long before there was *Crouching Tiger, Hidden Dragon* there was the great King Hu, a master director who, beginning with his *Come Drink with Me*, helped revolutionize the martial arts costume drama: After a young official is kidnapped, the authorities send a magnificent but mysterious swordswoman named Golden Swallow (Cheng Pei-pei) to rescue him. Aided by Drunken Cat, a kung-fu master disguised as a beggar, Golden Swallow hatches a daring plan to assault the corrupt monastery where the official is being held.

The film is a visual tour de force, each sequence meticulously designed by King Hu into a feast of color, movement, and high-flying action. Yet despite its great charm, this is still early King Hu; his mastery of all aspects of the medium, especially his inimitable approach to editing, would only be perfected in later masterworks such as *A Touch of Zen*. Young star Cheng Pei-pei, who wields a sword like nobody before or perhaps after her, perfectly combines steely determination with a kind of touching fragility; despite her prowess, there's always a hint that each battle may be her last. She would go on to a successful career in Hong Kong cinema and would win great acclaim for her return to the screen as the evil Nanny in Ang Lee's *Crouching Tiger*. **RP**

## SECONDS (1966)

Thomas Wolfe once said "You can't go home again," and anyone familiar with John Frankenheimer's Faustian vision of alienation in suburban America would understand this only too well. Long ignored in mainstream criticism, *Seconds* has achieved the status of a cult classic.

Arthur Hamilton (John Randolph) is offered a chance to leave his middle-class emotional isolation for a new life, provided he undergoes radical surgery and lets go of his past. This miracle is offered by a sinister organization known simply as the company, populated by black-listed character actors who all but steal the film, including Will Greer as the old man with all the answers and especially Jeff Corey as the salesman from hell who zestfully explains how Hamilton will become the handsome and talented painter Tony Wilson (Rock Hudson). Once the transformation is effected, *Seconds* becomes a Kafkaesque nightmare as our reborn protagonist fails to adjust to the bohemian lifestyle provided by the company.

The real star here is seasoned cinematographer James Wong Howe, whose distorted lenses and offbeat camera angles earned him an Oscar nomination and made *Seconds* one of the great black-and-white films of the late 1960s. Jerry Goldsmith created one of the most unsettling scores ever used in a psychodrama, creating a surreal mood from the opening credits to the paranoid ending. **DDV**

**U.S.** (Joel, John Frankenheimer, Paramount ) 100m BW

**Director:** John Frankenheimer

**Producer:** John Frankenheimer, Edward Lewis

**Screenplay:** Lewis John Carlino, from novel by David Ely

**Photography:** James Wong Howe

**Music:** Jerry Goldsmith

**Cast:** Rock Hudson, Salome Jens, John Randolph, Will Geer, Jeff Corey, Richard Anderson, Murray Hamilton, Karl Swenson, Khigh Dhiegh, Frances Reid, Wesley Addy, John Lawrence, Elisabeth Fraser, Dodie Heath, Robert Brubaker

**Oscar nomination:** James Wong Howe (photography)

**Cannes Film Festival:** John Frankenheimer nomination (Golden Palm)

## IN THE HEAT OF THE NIGHT (1967)

"They call me *Mister* Tibbs." Racism was still underexplored on screen when independent producer Walter Mirisch and director Norman Jewison had John Ball's novel *In the Heat of the Night* adapted specifically for Sidney Poitier. The result was in the vanguard of new social crime thrillers elevating what earlier would have been B fare into important pictures.

Virgil Tibbs (Poitier) is arrested simply because he is a black man with money passing through segregated Sparta, Mississippi, the night of a Northern industrialist's murder. To the bigoted police chief's (Rod Steiger) chagrin, Tibbs is a Philadelphia homicide detective, and the inimical odd couple are forced to cooperate in the investigation. The crime element and atmosphere are strong (enhanced by a memorable Quincy Jones score), but the film's enduring impact results from the fascinating relationship developed between the men. Poitier commands his top billing with princely disdain for the white trash who beset him while he unravels a Chandleresque tangle, but Steiger's gum-snapping, hot-tempered, huge but subtle peformance claimed the Academy Award for Best Actor. The film also won Oscars for Best Picture, Screenplay (Stirling Silliphant), Sound, and Editing (Hal Ashby, who would direct some of the most interesting films of the 1970s). Poitier reprised the role of Tibbs in two sequels. **AE**

**U.S.** (Mirisch Company) 109m Color

**Director:** Norman Jewison

**Producer:** Walter Mirisch

**Screenplay:** Stirling Silliphant, from novel by John Ball

**Photography:** Haskell Wexler

**Music:** Quincy Jones

**Cast:** Sidney Poitier, Rod Steiger, Warren Oates, Lee Grant, Larry Gates, James Patterson, William Schallert, Beah Richards, Peter Whitney, Kermit Murdock, Larry D. Mann, Matt Clark, Arthur Malet, Fred Stewart, Quentin Dean

**Oscar:** Walter Mirisch (best picture), Stirling Silliphant (screenplay), Rod Steiger (actor), Hal Ashby (editing), (sound)

**Oscar nomination:** Norman Jewison (director), James Richard (special sound effects)

**U.S.** (Chenault, Warner Bros.) 134m BW

**Director:** Mike Nichols

**Producer:** Ernest Lehman

**Screenplay:** Ernest Lehman, from play by Edward Albee

**Photography:** Haskell Wexler

**Music:** Alex North

**Cast:** Elizabeth Taylor, Richard Burton, George Segal, Sandy Dennis, Frank Flanagan

**Oscar:** Elizabeth Taylor (actress), Sandy Dennis (actress in support role), Richard Sylbert, George James Hopkins (art direction), Haskell Wexler (photography), Irene Sharaff (costume)

**Oscar nomination:** Ernest Lehman (best picture), Mike Nichols (director), Ernest Lehman (screenplay), Richard Burton (actor), George Segal (actor in support role), Sam O'Steen (editing), Alex North (music), George Groves (sound)

# WHO'S AFRAID OF VIRGINIA WOOLF? (1966)

With its unremitting portrait of an older married couple who draw a young husband and wife into their destructive love/hate games, Edward Albee's Broadway smash of the early 1960s was at first considered too brutal in terms of language and theme to be brought to the screen because of Production Code restrictions. But by the middle of the decade, Hollywood was abandoning the code in favor of a ratings system that would permit the exhibition of more adult dramas, and Mike Nichols's adaptation of Albee's play was among the first to appear on screens (theater owners were asked not to admit anyone under 18, as the new ratings categories had not yet been finalized).

Nichols's version of *Who's Afraid of Virginia Woolf?* is an important part of another trend—the move, in part, away from traditional entertainment toward a greater seriousness that would characterize the Hollywood Renaissance of the late 1960s and 1970s. Filmed in black-and-white and based on a fine screenplay by Ernest Lehman that keeps much of the play's dialogue, Nichols, who came to Hollywood from stage directing, preserves the essence of Albee's original. The casting was an extraordinary coup, with the world's most tempestuous and passionate couple, Richard Burton and Elizabeth Taylor, cast as George and Martha, whose unremitting verbal and mental fencing constitutes the main action. George is a history professor at the local college and Martha the daughter of its president; they invite a younger faculty member (George Segal) and his wife (Sandy Dennis) for a late evening of mental games: First "Humiliate the Host," but then, more destructively, "Get the Guests." In this unequal contest, the young marrieds come off second best, with the less-than-honorable aspects of their marriage laid bare and the young man's confidence in himself severely shaken. Of the many attempts to use the Burtons effectively in a film, *Who's Afraid of Virginia Woolf?* is by far the most successful, as Nichols elicited the best performance of the actress's career and Burton is effective as a weak man possessed of enormous emotional strength and an inexhaustible capacity to love. The film richly deserved its five Academy Awards; it is certainly one of the finest adaptations of a stage play ever produced. **RBP**

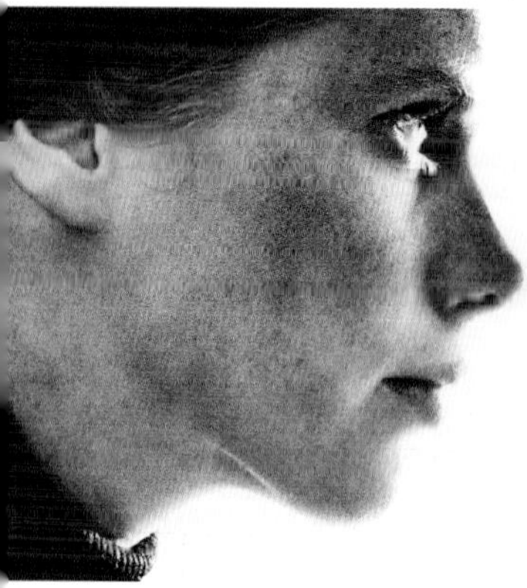

Sweden (Svensk) 85m BW

**Language:** Swedish

**Director:** Ingmar Bergman

**Producer:** Ingmar Bergman

**Screenplay:** Ingmar Bergman

**Photography:** Sven Nykvist

**Music:** Lars Johan Werle

**Cast:** Bibi Andersson, Liv Ullmann, Margaretha Krook, Gunnar Björnstrand

# PERSONA (1966)

As with other prominent examples of 1960s European art-cinema narration, much of the critical discussion of Ingmar Bergman's *Persona* has portrayed it as obscure and beyond words. True, the director wanted his film to be a visual poem, and he composed the famous opening credit sequence to underline this. However, even in this dense, associative montage, most of the images are recognizable as references to familiar Bergman motifs: The Spider-God (spider), the Christian legacy (crucifixion, lamb to slaughter), art/illusion as construction (the film's title, details of a film projector, the film-within-the-film from the 1949 film *Prison*), the cold womb (a morgue interior with the young boy from the 1964 film *The Silence* naked and reaching toward a cold and distant "mom"). This sequence functions as a prelude summing up Bergman's artistic profile, as if he wished to take stock and then clear the slate for a fresh artistic start. Indeed, the whole film can be seen as a journey to an existential and aesthetic dead end, one where identity, meaning, and language finally collapse, destroying Bergman's art itself as the film strip stops in its tracks, melts, and breaks before starting again.

Superficially the plot of *Persona* is constructed as a variation of the female power game in August Strindberg's chamber play *The Stronger*. Initially, the stronger of the two women in the film appears to be psychiatric nurse Alma (Bibi Andersson), especially because she appears certain of herself and does all the talking—thus taking control over her silent counterpart. But faced with this enigmatic patient, famous actress Elisabet Vogler (Liv Ullmann), in an isolated summer cottage on a remote island, Alma's own seemingly stable, down-to-earth world-view begins to crumble. Her therapeutic talks turn into confessions of her own hidden secrets and desires. Gradually she is stripped of her own persona, the mask of lies and self-deception that makes up her identity and provides her life with a sense of meaning.

*Persona*'s climax comes in the famous scene where the two women sit opposite each other dressed in identical black clothes. Alma begins to talk about Elisabet's rejection of motherhood and marriage, but soon finds herself talking about her own doubts concerning the family life she has previously envisioned with naïve enthusiasm. Realizing this, she struggles to regain control with new words of certainty, but even her construction of language breaks down and she can only utter incoherent phrases. It is at this point that Bergman uses the optical effect of fusing the two women's faces into one haunting image, a horrific vision of identity in a total state of decomposition.

The film logically ends with Alma doing the only thing she can to reconstruct her life and sense of self: She returns to the ordinary world that defines her and rejects Elisabet as the Other. In their final scene together we are back at the hospital from the opening scenes of the drama. Alma, now back in her old uniform and persona, forces Elisabet to repeat the word "nothing." Cut back to the boy at the morgue—Elisabet's unwanted child? Alma's aborted fetus?—and then the projector stops. Darkness. **MT**

France / Sweden (Anouchka, Argos Films, Sandrews, Svensk) 103m BW

**Language:** French / Swedish

**Director:** Jean-Luc Godard

**Producer:** Anatole Dauman

**Screenplay:** Jean-Luc Godard, from the stories *La Femme de Paul* and *Le Signe* by Guy de Maupassant

**Photography:** Willy Kurant

**Music:** Jean-Jacques Debout

**Cast:** Jean-Pierre Léaud, Chantal Goya, Marlène Jobert, Michel Debord, Catherine-Isabelle Duport, Eva-Britt Strandberg, Birger Malmsten

**Berlin International Film Festival:** Jean-Luc Godard (Interfilm award—honorable mention), (youth film award, best feature for young people), nomination (Golden Bear), Jean-Pierre Léaud (Silver Bear—actor)

# MASCULIN, FÉMININ (1966)
## MASCULINE-FEMININE

From the start of his career, there has been scarcely anything resembling conventional dialogue in the films of Jean-Luc Godard; back-and-forth banter between characters takes the form of interviews or inquisitions. By the time of *Masculine-Feminine*, this was a rigorous principle. What gives the film its bleakness is the sense that people cannot even talk to each other anymore except through pop-quizzes, aggressive interrogations, or "celebrity" profiling. And Godard's clean, reportage way of filming such exchanges—this is the least lyrical of his black-and-white works—increases the isolation of the characters in their existential cells.

Godard conceived this film—much to the chagrin of youth audiences then—as an unempathetic, sociological investigation. Its view of gender roles verges on the misanthropic: Girls are empty glamor-bunnies, would-be pop stars, pawns of a consumerist society; while boys are posturing, graceless, wannabe revolutionaries. All their stated ideals seem as empty and transient as their intimate relationships; here, Godard anticipated Jean Eustache's *The Mother and the Whore* (1973).

And yet there remains something affecting, the fleeting residue of Godardian poetry: Amid the public confusion there is private reverie, the melancholy of solitude, given immortal expression in the darting eyes of Jean-Pierre Léaud and his inner thoughts while transfixed at the movies. **AM**

**France / Sweden** (Argos, Athos, Parc, Svensk, Svenska) 95m BW

**Language:** French

**Director:** Robert Bresson

**Producer:** Mag Bodard

**Screenplay:** Robert Bresson

**Photography:** Ghislain Cloquet

**Music:** Jean Wiener

**Cast:** Anne Wiazemsky, François Lafarge, Philippe Asselin, Nathalie Joyaut, Walter Green, Jean-Claude Guilbert, Pierre Klossowski, François Sullerot, M.C. Fremont, Jean Rémignard

**Venice Film Festival:** Robert Bresson (OCIC award)

# AU HASARD BALTHAZAR (1966)
## BALTHAZAR

Robert Bresson's penultimate black-and-white film—a companion piece to the 1967 film *Mouchette*—is a study in saintliness, a powerful and poignant tale of wickedness and suffering, and a grim look at the innate cruelty and destructive impulses of man. By treating the eponymous donkey as a symbol of purity, virtue, and salvation, and by giving his picture a simple yet effective episodic structure, Bresson invests *Au hasard Balthazar* with a remarkable intensity that is only enhanced by the stark visual style.

Balthazar is an oft-exploited burro who gets passed from owner to owner, in the process experiencing and observing all manner of human good and evil. His harsh and sorrowful existence, in which he is frequently mistreated, is paralleled by that of Marie (Anne Wiazemsky), a reserved young woman who becomes involved with a cruel and sadistic man, Gerard (François Lafarge), who eventually rejects her. Toward the end of his difficult life, however, the former children's pet, circus attraction, and beast of burden becomes the property of a gentle old miller who views him as a reincarnated saint.

Bresson's film has been labeled by at least one critic "the zenith of purity in the cinema." But the highest praise of all comes from none other than Andrew Sarris. In his classic *Village Voice* review of the film, Sarris writes that *Au hasard Balthazar* "stands alone atop one of the loftiest pinnacles of artistically realized emotional experiences." **SJS**

# 2 OU 3 CHOSES QUE JE SAIS D'ELLE (1967)
## TWO OR THREE THINGS I KNOW ABOUT HER

**France** (Anouchka, Argos, Carrosse, Parc) 90m Eastmancolor
**Language:** French
**Director:** Jean-Luc Godard
**Producer:** Anatole Dauman, Raoul Lévy
**Screenplay:** Jean-Luc Godard, from letter by Catherine Vimenet
**Photography:** Raoul Coutard
**Music:** Ludwig van Beethoven
**Cast:** Joseph Gehrard, Marina Vlady, Anny Duperey, Roger Montsoret, Raoul Lévy, Jean Narboni

*Two or Three Things I Know About Her* is one of several Jean-Luc Godard films which take prostitution as a central metaphor for life in the modern capitalist state. For Godard, a woman selling herself for money provides a perfect image of how what is most personal and life-enhancing, the sexual act, becomes, like everything else, a commodity. In the process the human being becomes alienated from herself, a mere thing to be bought and sold.

*My Life to Live* (1962) had been an earlier essay on this theme by Godard, in which the heroine becomes a full-time prostitute, with tragic results. *Two or Three Things* was sparked off by some articles in a French magazine that investigated the phenomenon of suburban housewives who engage in part-time prostitution to make ends meet. The film begins by presenting a shot of a woman at the window of her flat. Godard's own voice on the soundtrack informs us that she is Marina Vlady. "She is an actress. She's wearing a sweater with yellow stripes. She is of Russian origin. She has got fair hair, or maybe light brown. I'm not quite sure." The sequence thus announces a number of characteristic motifs. First, the Brechtian technique of separating the actor from the role, to make the audience question the nature of the fiction being narrated. Godard repeats the shot from another angle, this time describing the character, not the actress. "She is Juliette Janson. She lives here. She is wearing a sweater . . . ." Second, direct address by the director is another Godardian technique for distancing the spectator from the action, preventing a too-close identification with the fiction. Third, the hesitancy ("I'm not sure . . .") raises a doubt about the accuracy of what we see. The film uses some of the techniques of the documentary, but constantly intervenes to create a gap between images and their meaning.

The sequence described above is not quite the opening of the film, which starts with several views of the city of Paris. It is Paris, not the central female character, who is the "Her" referred to in the title. Not for the first or last time, Godard investigates the nature of modern urban living. One of his targets is consumerism and the artificial stimulation of the desire for material goods, which produces the need for more and more money and hence leads to prostitution. Godard fills the screen with colorful images of objects (cups of coffee, cars, tins of food), rendering them at once alluring and absurd.

Overlaid on the brightly colored surface of the film, part documentary, part fiction, is another discourse, about world events. Juliette's husband (Roger Montsoret) is a radio ham, who sits at home listening to news of the Vietnam War, and her small son has a dream in which North and South Vietnam are united. Godard's revolutionary politics, at this stage marked by a kind of knee-jerk anti-Americanism (the other side of the coin to his fascination with Hollywood), would soon turn to fully fledged Maoism, but his intellectual playfulness and curiosity about the nature of cinema are what endow *Two or Three Things* with enduring appeal. **EB**

**U.S.** (Embassy, Lawrence Turman) 105m Technicolor

**Director:** Mike Nichols

**Producer:** Joseph E. Levine, Lawrence Turman

**Screenplay:** Buck Henry, Calder Willingham, from novel by Charles Webb

**Photography:** Robert Surtees

**Music:** Dave Grusin, Paul Simon

**Cast:** Anne Bancroft, Dustin Hoffman, Katharine Ross, William Daniels, Murray Hamilton, Elizabeth Wilson, Buck Henry, Brian Avery, Walter Brooke, Norman Fell, Alice Ghostley, Marion Lorne, Eddra Gale

**Oscar:** Mike Nichols (director)

**Oscar nomination:** Lawrence Turman (best picture), Calder Willingham, Buck Henry (screenplay), Dustin Hoffman (actor), Anne Bancroft (actress), Katharine Ross (actress in support role), Robert Surtees (photography)

# THE GRADUATE (1967)

As unlikely as it sounds today, *The Graduate* struck many moviegoers as daring, even a bit scandalous when it opened in 1967, a year when the decade's much-vaunted sexual revolution was still struggling to take hold. Never before had a high-profile Hollywood film taken such a candid look at sex in the suburbs or focused on a more unlikely romantic trio: A college grad with too much time on his hands, an alcoholic housewife who's determined to get into his pants, and her daughter, a quintessentially nice girl who has no idea her main sexual rival is her own predatory parent. If any mainstream movie hammered the last nail into the coffin of midcentury "momism," this was it. Neither motherhood, suburbia, nor the suffocating fog of postwar middle-class mores would ever seem quite the same.

The creative team behind *The Graduate* was as fresh as its subject and style. Mike Nichols had made a strong impression with his only previous picture, the screen adaptation of Edward Albee's play *Who's Afraid of Virginia Woolf?* (1966). *The Graduate* offered him an even better opportunity to fuse his eye for sardonic details with the ear for razor-sharp verbal wit that he'd honed with Elaine May in the innovative comedy act that had made them synonymous with urban hipness. One of his most original ideas was to supplement a small amount of newly composed Simon and Garfunkel music (most notably "Mrs. Robinson") with previously recorded songs by the duo ("The Sounds of Silence," "Scarborough Fair/Canticle") that were already loved by millions of teen and twenty-something fans. He used their popularity as an additional selling point and, equally important, a signal that this film would plug into youth-culture sensibilities more directly and sympathetically than any other of its time. The gambit worked aesthetically and commercially, influencing the music tracks of countless Hollywood pictures in years to come.

Dustin Hoffman became a star via his portrayal of Benjamin Braddock, the recently returned graduate stirred by a nebulous dread of his parents' empty-headed materialism. It's part of the movie's legend that Nichols instructed Hoffman to play the part without acting, and the unforced awkwardness of Ben's mannerisms is a key reason for the film's enduring emotional appeal. In a movie with many mythical moments, perhaps the one that has burrowed most deeply under America's pop-culture skin comes when Ben hears a family friend's one-word prescription for financial and professional happiness—"Plastics!"—and reacts with a blend of fear, loathing, and perplexity that's as understated as it is indelible.

The creatively chosen supporting cast includes Anne Bancroft as Mrs. Robinson, a less-impressive Katharine Ross as her daughter, Norman Fell as a landlord with a paranoid fear of what 1960s conservatives called "outside agitators," an uncredited Richard Dreyfuss as a roomer in his boarding house, and Buck Henry as a hotel clerk. Then a newcomer to feature films, Henry cowrote the screenplay with Calder Willingham, based on Charles Webb's novel. Nichols turned their script into a key achievement of '60s cinema. **DS**

**France / Italy** (Jolly, Specta) 155m Eastmancolor

**Language:** French / English / German

**Director:** Jacques Tati

**Producer:** René Silvera

**Screenplay:** Jacques Lagrange, Jacques Tati, Art Buchwald

**Photography:** Jean Badal, Andréas Winding

**Music:** Francis Lemarque , James Campbell

**Cast:** Jacques Tati, Barbara Dennek, Rita Maiden, France Rumilly, France Delahalle, Valérie Camille, Erika Dentzler, Nicole Ray, Yvette Ducreux, Nathalie Jem, Jacqueline Lecomte, Oliva Poli, Alice Field, Sophie Wennek, Evy Cavallaro

# PLAYTIME (1967)

*Playtime* is less a film than one man's successful attempt to encourage us to see with new eyes. Indeed, director Jacques Tati's timeless masterpiece is concerned, from start to finish, with imbuing the viewer with a totally new set of sensory experiences. Like no other movie, *Playtime* has the power to make us question our very faculties of eyes and ears.

Known for years as the bumbling Monsieur Hulot in such great works as *Mr. Hulot's Holiday* (1953) and *My Uncle* (1958), Tati was far more than a clown, though he played that role with aplomb. Tati's comic work is a bridge between silent and sound film, between vaudeville and the modern era. But it is for his visual sensibilities that he is best remembered. The gags in his films aren't really gags at all, but odd little moments that add up to an overall tone of a world being slightly askew. When there are enough such moments—and they are crammed into literally every corner of *Playtime*'s unbelievably dense mise en scène—we begin to realize that they are not there to make us laugh so much as to make us consider our roles as viewers.

*Playtime* takes place in a cold, clinical version of a futuristic city, and the fiercely rectilinear sets were built from the ground up, at great expense. *Playtime* was an immensely costly film—not least because it was shot in 70mm—and its box-office returns were minuscule, which kept Tati in hock for a decade after its release. "Tativille" is one of the great achievements of set design—or of megalomania, depending on your perspective. The set had its own roads, electrical systems, and one of the office buildings even had a working elevator. And not since the days of German Expressionism had a director achieved so much with forced perspective: Carefully building to scale in order to make something look much farther away than it is.

The world of Tativille is clinical, harsh, and sterile, but Hulot, who wanders through it all with bemused detachment, occasionally finds little patches of organic matter. He finds a flower vendor, for example, who brings a little color to this gray city; and Hulot alone is able to make sense of the bizarrely designed streetlights by likening their shape to that of a tiny bouquet. *Playtime* has much to say about clinical modernity impinging upon older, more earthy ways of life. On one level, the film is about how modern city living has the potential to crush any shred of individuality one may still possess.

*Playtime*'s elaborate visual jokes are far, far too numerous to recount here. Suffice it to say that almost every single object of modern existence—televisions, cars, supermarkets, airports, vacuum cleaners—is given new life and new form here as a comic object.

All the patterns in *Playtime* come to a head in the incredible restaurant scene, which lasts 45 minutes and which is so visually and sonically dense that repeated viewings are absolutely essential. But repeated viewings are simply more occasions for pleasure. No film offers so rich a viewing experience as *Playtime*. **EdeS**

## REPORT (1967)

U.S. (Canyon) BW 13min 16mm

**Director:** Bruce Conner

On the day that John F. Kennedy was shot, Bruce Conner started recording images of the assassination off his TV set onto Super 8. Four years of obsessive reworking and reediting of the found footage resulted in the 13-minute *Report*, an avant-garde classic.

On the soundtrack, we hear the television and radio commentaries of that day, relating the event with rising hysteria. On the image track, however, Conner withholds the violence. At the point of death we see a white screen and then a violent, flickering alternation of black and white frames. Representational images return—hundreds of them, from newsreels, ads, cartoons, and fiction films, montaged in a frantic free association.

It is as if Conner had instantly intuited, from that first TV moment, that henceforth our entire relation to this event would be through images and sounds recorded and disseminated by the mass media—and that our obsession with making sense of it would happen through an endless replay of that footage. *Report* correctly predicted two polarized responses to the Kennedy assassination: Either to be frustrated by the lack of anything to truthfully see in the audiovisual archive; or to see too much, imagining one conspiracy after another, Oliver Stone-style. **AM**

## HOMBRE (1967)

U.S. (20th Century Fox, Hombre Productions) 111m Color

**Director:** Martin Ritt

**Producer:** Irving Ravetch, Martin Ritt

**Screenplay:** Irving Ravetch, Elmore Leonard, Harriet Frank Jr., from the novel by Elmore Leonard

**Photography:** James Wong Howe

**Music:** David Rose

**Cast:** Paul Newman, Fredric March, Richard Boone, Diane Cilento, Cameron Mitchell, Barbara Rush, Peter Lazer, Margaret Blye, Martin Balsam, Skip Ward, Frank Silvera, David Canary, Val Avery, Larry Ward

Paul Newman is a white man kidnapped by the Apache as a child and brought up as one of their own. Having inherited property and reverted to white, he finds himself on a stagecoach in New Mexico along with an assorted group of travelers, who include Diane Cilento as a feisty widow, Fredric March as a corrupt Indian agent, and Martin Balsam as a Mexican stage driver. Halfway through their journey they are held up by a gang in league with another passenger, Richard Boone. Newman, demonstrating his Apache training, kills a couple of the gang, but sees no reason to offer further assistance to the travelers, some of whom have made clear their hatred of Indians.

Martin Ritt's *Hombre* displays much of the liberal sentiment that became commonplace in Westerns of the 1960s and after, but the preaching takes second place to the tightening tensions between the characters as the cat-and-mouse game between the gang and their quarry is played out. Newman is excellent as the icily controlled John Russell, whose dual ethnicity gives him a special insight into racial prejudice, and Richard Boone as his adversary jovially cuts through the hypocrisy of the more respectable citizens. **EB**

**France / Italy** (Five, Paris) 101m Eastmancolor

**Language:** French

**Director:** Luis Buñuel

**Producer:** Henri Baum, Raymond Hakim, Robert Hakim

**Screenplay:** Luis Buñuel, Jean-Claude Carrière, from novel by Joseph Kessel

**Photography:** Sacha Vierny

**Cast:** Catherine Deneuve, Jean Sorel, Michel Piccoli, Geneviève Page, Pierre Clémenti, Françoise Fabian, Macha Méril, Muni, Pallas, Maria Latour, Claude Cerval, Michel Charrel, Iska Khan, Bernard Musson, Marcel Charvey, François Maistre, Francisco Rabal, Georges Marchal, Francis Blanch

**Venice Film Festival:** Luis Buñuel (Golden Lion), (Pasinetti award—best film)

# BELLE DE JOUR (1967)

Luis Buñuel unfussily described *Belle de jour* as "pornographic," but added that it explored "chaste eroticism." Indeed, it is probably the last great sex film of the 1960s before the greater permissiveness and (temporarily) relaxed censorship regulations created a new graphicness in erotic representations.

*Belle de jour* is a prime Sixties artifact in another way too: Alongside such movies as *Breathless* and *La Dolce Vita* that have enjoyed worldwide re-releases since the 1990s, it captures a certain "style" of the era in its smallest details of speech, gesture, dress, and attitude.

*Belle de jour* is a sublimely fetishistic movie. Buñuel cares not for Catherine Deneuve's nakedness, but for the clothes and veils that cover it, and for her extraordinarily polished and glazed feminine surface. Although the film revolves around the goings-on at a high-class brothel, sex is never shown. Taking place behind closed doors, within secret nooks, and even in one hilarious scene under a coffin, the sexual perversions hinted at defy the wildest imagination.

Deneuve plays Séverine Serizy, a bourgeois wife who is frigid (perhaps even virginal) with her husband Pierre (Jean Sorel). She eventually assumes a double life on weekday afternoons as a prostitute. Here she feels safe, it seems, to explore her prodigious, masochistic sexual fantasies. However, the neatness of her system is overturned when a flamboyantly seedy gangster (Pierre Clementi) both wins her heart and intrudes into her respectable life.

Summarized like this, *Belle de jour* may seem a schematic, preposterous male fantasy. In fact, it is one of the most mysterious, poetic, complex, and beguiling films ever made. No character's psychology is ever rendered simply or clearly. Nor is the nature of the everyday world they inhabit.

Quietly but surely, Buñuel leads us into a strange territory poised perfectly between dream and reality. Hallucinatory effects that are both funny and disturbing fill the film—such as different characters referring ominously to "letting in the cats" that we hear but never see. Well before the extraordinary final scene, viewers who are open to this seductive, dream-like texture will no longer expect to know what is really happening—a sweet liberation indeed. **AM**

ROBERT et RAYMOND HAKIM présentent
CATHERINE DENEUVE
JEAN SOREL
MICHEL PICCOLI
dans un film de
Luis Bunuel
BELLE DE JOUR
d'après le roman de JOSEPH KESSEL de l'Académie Française
avec
GENEVIÈVE PAGE
PIERRE CLÉMENTI
FRANCISCO RABAL
FRANÇOISE FABIAN
MACHA MERIL
MARIA LATOUR-MUNI
et GEORGES MARCHAL
avec la participation de
FRANCIS BLANCHE
EASTMANCOLOR
MIJN NAAM IS
"BELLE DE JOUR"

**France** (Madeleine, Parc) 120m Eastmancolor

**Language:** English / French

**Director:** Jacques Demy, Agnès Varda

**Producer:** Mag Bodard, Gilbert de Goldschmidt

**Screenplay:** Jacques Demy

**Photography:** Ghislain Cloquet

**Music:** Michel Legrand

**Cast:** Catherine Deneuve, George Chakiris, Françoise Dorléac, Jacques Perrin, Michel Piccoli, Jacques Riberolles, Grover Dale, Véronique Duval, Geneviève Thénier, Henri Crémieux, Pamela Hart, Leslie North, Patrick Jeantet, Gene Kelly, Danielle Darrieux

**Oscar nomination:** Michel Legrand, Jacques Demy (music)

# LES DEMOISELLES DE ROCHEFORT (1967)

## THE YOUNG GIRLS OF ROCHEFORT

*The Young Girls of Rochefort*, Jacques Demy's companion piece to his marvelous *The Umbrellas of Cherbourg* (1964), accomplishes a goal that few other films have achieved, or even strived to attain. For its two hours, *The Young Girls of Rochefort* maintains a tone of unmitigated joy and exuberance—bordering, for true lovers of the film, on something close to rapture.

Everything in this movie connotes happiness, buoyancy, and a joie de vivre that is unmatched in cinema. Even *Umbrellas*, which has an almost unrivaled capacity to amaze and impress, has plenty of moments where the sadness of the story runs counter to the vivaciousness of the imagery. Here there is no such tension. The colors leap from the frame and head right for the pleasure centers of the brain—same for the costumes, the sets, and, especially, the performances and musical numbers. Working once again with music maestro Michel Legrand, Demy conjures up a magical land—referring specifically to the worlds created in MGM's musicals of the 1950s —where identically garbed sisters sing about the joys of being sisters—where a weekend-long local street fair becomes the apotheosis of love and happiness, where the mundane act of crossing a bridge inspires carefully choreographed displays of frivolity.

Put simply, *The Young Girls of Rochefort* will make you happier than almost any other film you can imagine. And this is no small achievement. **EdeS**

**France / Italy** (Ascot, Comacico, Copernic, Lira) 105m Eastmancolor

**Language:** French

**Director:** Jean-Luc Godard

**Screenplay:** Jean-Luc Godard

**Photography:** Raoul Coutard

**Music:** Antoine Duhamel, Guy Béart, Wolfgang Amadeus Mozart

**Cast:** Mireille Darc, Jean Yanne, Jean-Pierre Kalfon, Valérie Lagrange, Jean-Pierre Léaud, Yves Beneyton, Paul Gégauff, Daniel Pommereulle, Virginie Vignon, Yves Afonso, Blandine Jeanson, Ernest Menzer, Georges Staquet, Juliet Berto, Helen Scott

**Berlin International Film Festival:** Jean-Luc Godard nomination (Golden Bear)

# WEEK END (1967)

*Week End* might be the wildest and wooliest of all of Jean-Luc Godard's films—which is saying something. It's also one of his most audacious.

This is a film in which anything goes: A mundane phone conversation becomes an absurdly charming musical number, our heroes encounter fairy-tale characters in the woods, and main characters can meet grisly ends at, really, any time at all. Godard's decision to move from episode to bizarre episode was bold and highly influential. Radical filmmakers of all stripes and colors owe a great debt to *Week End*.

But "radical" is a somewhat unfortunate label for the film, for it connotes dire politicization and humorlessness. Rest assured that *Week End* suffers from neither of these problems. In fact, it's a deeply funny film, in part *because* of its political attitudes. The ability to blend the serious, the comic, the beautiful, and the absurd was but one of Godard's many gifts.

No discussion of *Week End* is complete without mention of its most famous shot—one of the most famous shots in cinema. Perhaps the film's centerpiece is the ten-minute or so tracking shot of the world's nastiest traffic jam—interrupted by Godard's irrepressible penchant for didactic, elliptical intertitles. This is no ordinary gridlock—Godard's nightmarish but hilarious version includes zoo animals, boats, the occasional picnic, and a hell of a lot of blood. But, as the director once famously said, it's nothing to worry about: It's really only red paint. **EdeS**

## LE SAMOURAÏ (1967)
## THE GODSON

France / Italy (CICC, Fida, Filmel, TC) 105m Eastmancolor

**Language:** French

**Director:** Jean-Pierre Melville

**Producer:** Raymond Borderie, Eugène Lépicier

**Screenplay:** Jean-Pierre Melville, Georges Pellegrin, from the novel *The Ronin* by Joan McLeod

**Photography:** Henri Decaë

**Music:** François de Roubaix

**Cast:** Alain Delon, François Périer, Nathalie Delon, Cathy Rosier, Jacques Leroy, Michel Boisrond, Robert Favart, Jean-Pierre Posier, Catherine Jourdan, Roger Fradet, Carlo Nell, Robert Rondo, André Salgues, André Thorent, Jacques Deschamps

Jean-Pierre Melville had the flair to invent a quotation from the "Bushido Book of the Samurai" as an on-screen preface: "There is no greater solitude than the samurai's, unless it is that of the tiger in the jungle . . . perhaps . . . ." No further allusion to Japanese culture is required: That's enough to give *Le Samouraï* an abstract, mythic, timeless air. It is a breathtaking work, stylized to the point of asphyxiation, in which the imaginary world of cinema beats reality hands down. No wonder filmmakers from John Woo to Paul Thomas Anderson via Quentin Tarantino and Walter Hill have plundered it as the veritable Bible of cool moves.

Jef Costello (Alain Delon) is a steely hit man for whom the adjective "hardboiled" is an understatement. Methodical, asexual, and apparently amoral in his willingness to kill on command, Jef finds himself set-up and pursued—like his namesake played by Robert Mitchum in *Out of the Past* (1947), he's "in a frame" and needs to go in and "look at the picture." His ultimate confrontation with the witness who could incriminate him exposes the enigma of his inner motivations throughout.

Melville's vision of Paris is filtered through his love of American film noir: jazz nightclubs with black singers, dark and rainy streets. The cops function as in a Fritz Lang film, mapping the city through intricate surveillance and tracking this elusive human blip. Yet the heady atmosphere of movie fantasy is balanced by Melville's legendary, maniacal attention to detail, which itself borders on the obsessiveness of a police procedural: The logistics of every gesture, of every movement around the city, are impeccably plotted and recorded.

It is hard to watch *Le Samourai*—largely without dialogue, in which every sound (such as the chirping bird in Jef's apartment, the roar of an car engine, or the clanking of a key ring) is isolated and heightened, in which actors pose like gorgeous mannequins (Delon here as porcelain as Catherine Deneuve in 1967's *Belle de jour*)—without remembering Robert Bresson. Melville rejected the comparison, but it's true: Jef is almost an ascetic priest, animated by an inner calling. **AM**

U.S. (Jalem, Warner Bros.) 126m Technicolor

**Director:** Stuart Rosenberg

**Producer:** Gordon Carroll, Carter De Haven Jr.

**Screenplay:** Donn Pearce and Frank Pierson, from novel by Donn Pearce

**Photography:** Conrad L. Hall

**Music:** Lalo Schifrin

**Cast:** Paul Newman, George Kennedy, J.D. Cannon, Lou Antonio, Robert Drivas, Strother Martin, Jo Van Fleet, Clifton James, Morgan Woodward, Luke Askew, Marc Cavell, Richard Davalos, Robert Donner, Warren Finnerty, Dennis Hopper, Harry Dean Stanton

**Oscar:** George Kennedy (actor)

**Oscar nomination:** Donn Pearce, Frank Pierson (screenplay), Paul Newman (actor), Lalo Schifrin (music)

# COOL HAND LUKE (1967)

There are stars and then there are actors like Paul Newman, whose iconic presence and piercing blue eyes regularly transcend even the best material in which he works. The cocky gait of *Cool Hand Luke* may wobble from time to time, but Newman's magnetic personality lends the film the weight its relatively simple story struggles nobly to support. Shot in stunning widescreen by Conrad Hall (all the better to capture the glint of the high noon sun and the glistening, shirtless prisoners of a chain gang), Stuart Rosenberg's film ambitiously vacillates from a straightforward antiauthoritarian story to a macho tall tale and winds up ultimately as a somewhat curious and incomplete Christ allegory.

That it falls awkwardly somewhere in between should surprise no one, but *Cool Hand Luke* remains thoroughly engaging all the same. Newman plays an enigmatically recalcitrant everyday guy, Lucas "Cool Hand" Jackson, thrown into prison for rebelliously cutting the tops off parking meters. Once incarcerated, he unsurprisingly butts against an even more stubborn system of rules, and as his trouble-making stoicism grows more disruptive, the punishments doled out to him grow more severe. Filled with quotable lines and memorable scenes, *Cool Hand Luke* exists as an iconic work in and of itself, deceptively light in meaning but definitely full of cultural (and countercultural) significance.

Indeed, several lines from the film have entered the cinema lexicon (the menacing understatement "What we have here is failure to communicate," for one), whereas scenes like the egg-eating bet and a prison yard fistfight are the stuff of movie legend. A great deal of *Cool Hand Luke*'s considerable charm stems from its colorful cast of supporting actors, a contingent of notable faces that include a young Dennis Hopper, Harry Dean Stanton, and George Kennedy as Newman's rival turned right-hand man.

Kennedy took home the Academy Award for Best Supporting Actor for his portrayal of the ultimately naïve tough guy Dragline. But at the heart of the film is Newman's quietly charismatic performance, which showcased the actor at the top of his game and propelled him toward the peak of his popularity. Compared to Jack Nicholson's scenery-chewing performance in the oddly similar *One Flew Over the Cuckoo's Nest*, Newman in *Cool Hand Luke* is all subtle, knowing smiles and beaming confidence. Short on soliloquies, Newman's Luke doesn't telegraph his every move or even clarify his motives. He seems almost to have sought out prison as an arbitrary challenge, inviting a conflict with the system just to see if he can win. In fact, it isn't until close to the film's conclusion that the toll imprisonment has taken on the free-spirited Luke becomes clearer. Unlike the rest of the prisoners, Luke steadfastly rejects the institutional conformity that comes with confinement, and his uncooperative stance ultimately leads to tragedy. If *Cool Hand Luke* is partly about how far one man can push the system, it's also about what happens when that same system pushes back. **JKl**

# POINT BLANK (1967)

**U.S.** (MGM) 92m Metrocolor
**Director:** John Boorman
**Producer:** Judd Bernard, Robert Chartoff
**Screenplay:** Alexander Jacobs, David Newhouse, Rafe Newhouse, from the novel *The Hunter* by Donald E. Westlake
**Photography:** Philip H. Lathrop
**Music:** Stu Gardner, Johnny Mandel
**Cast:** Lee Marvin, Angie Dickinson, Keenan Wynn, Carroll O'Connor, Lloyd Bochner, Michael Strong, John Vernon, Sharon Acker, James Sikking, Sandra Warner, Roberta Haynes, Kathleen Freeman, Victor Creatore, Lawrence Hauben, Susan Holloway

Based on Donald E. Westlake's 1964 novel *The Hunter*, John Boorman's thriller is as arrestingly and unselfconsciously stylish as the day it was released. Beginning with the trick of apparently killing off its main character, the two bullets that pierce Walker (Lee Marvin) set this masculine film—full of tough action and even tougher sexual circumstances—into action.

Walker is left for dead after being betrayed by his friend, gangster Mal Reese (the pock-marked John Vernon). Reese turns out to be the lover of Walker's wife. The bullet wounds healed, Walker wants the $93,000 Reese stole from him, as well as vengeance on his wife Lynne (Sharon Acker), Reese, and all his accomplices. Walker's scheme draws into its vortex Lynne's sister Chris (Angie Dickinson), who is bedded, abused, then abandoned. The long moment where she seduces Reese for Walker's revenge remains an agonizing and perversely sexual love scene, erotic yet gut-wrenchingly distasteful.

The perfect thriller in both form and vision, Boorman's use of widescreen to full effect—urban horizons appear bleak and wide; characters are thrown from one long end of the frame to another—means that *Point Blank* works as well on television as it does in the cinema. **KK**

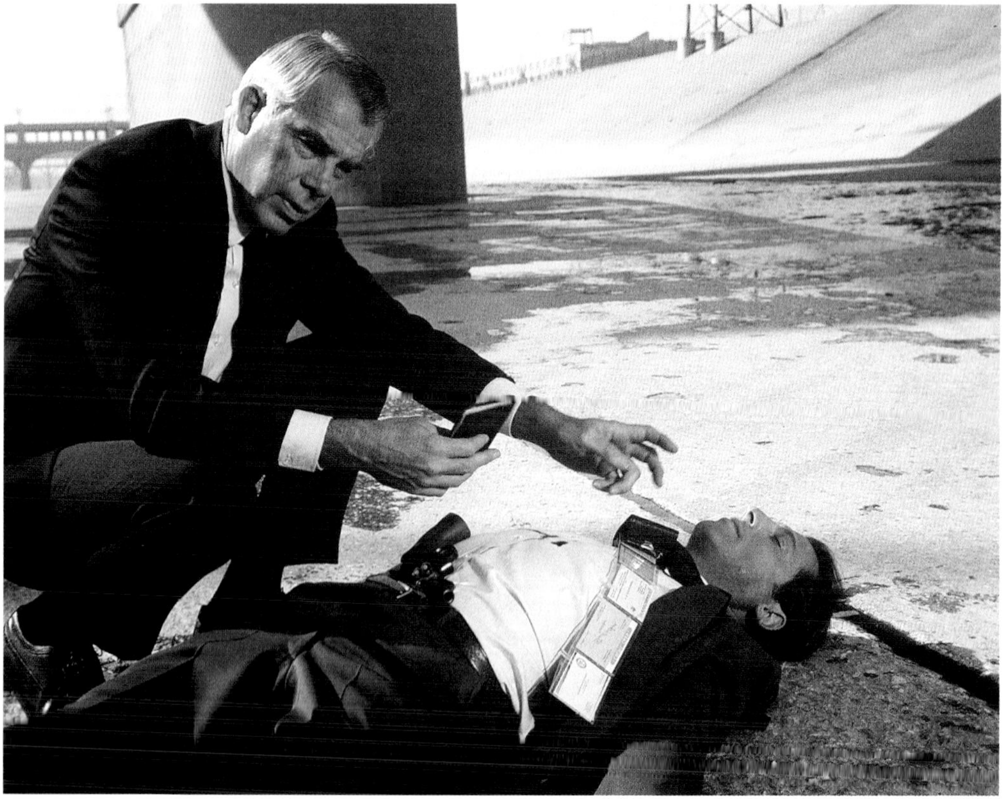

# WAVELENGTH (1967)

Ostensibly an archetype of minimalism, *Wavelength* is actually action-packed, not only in the sense of its formal and thematic content but even in the amount of story it manages to allude to as it plays a rigorous game with screen space and time. An experimental movie that acknowledges the conventions of mystery and narrative inherent in all cinema, this film was designed to change forever the relationship the viewer has with the screen, forcing audiences to think through processes and factors that most films take for granted.

Director Michael Snow presents the whole film in a single shot, a 45-minute tracking shot across a large urban room to focus on a detail of a photograph (of waves) fixed to the far wall. It's a relentless film, witty at its own expense as it forces you to deal with physical space and the intrusions of the tiniest elements of human narrative. There's even an apparent murder as a man (Hollis Frampton) walks on during a commotion and falls dead, with a woman later showing up to discover the corpse and make a phone call and police sirens indicating the ripples of this event spreading, but by the time this melodrama is in swing, the camera has tracked in so far that the big picture presented at the outset is no longer available. We are too close to the wall—and to entering into what might be another universe via the photograph—to be able to comprehend what has taken place.

Though *Wavelength* consists of a single shot, it is not a single take: On the voyage across the room, filmstock, color processes, and lighting change, taking into account apparently random and actually designed elements; meanwhile, a sine wave on the soundtrack progresses from its lowest note (50 cycles per second) to its highest (12,000 cycles) with ironic snatches of The Beatles ("Strawberry Fields Forever") mixed in along with the mini-melodrama. Like much underground and experimental cinema, *Wavelength* is easy to parody as pretentious or dismiss as intellectual indulgence, but it is still a vital, important, and necessary work. **KN**

**U.S. / Canada** (Canyon) 45m 16mm Color

**Director:** Michael Snow

**Producer:** Michael Snow

**Screenplay:** Michael Snow

**Photography:** Michael Snow

**Cast:** Hollis Frampton, Joyce Wieland, Amy Yadrin, Lyne Grossman, Maoto Nakagawa, Roswell Rudd

U.S. (Tatira-Hiller, Warner Bros/Seven Arts) 111m Technicolor
**Director:** Arthur Penn
**Producer:** Warren Beatty
**Screenplay:** David Newman, Robert Benton
**Photography:** Burnett Guffey
**Music:** Charles Strouse
**Cast:** Warren Beatty, Faye Dunaway, Michael J. Pollard, Gene Hackman, Estelle Parsons, Denver Pyle, Dub Taylor, Evans Evans, Gene Wilder
**Oscar:** Estelle Parsons (actress in support role), Burnett Guffey (photography)
**Oscar nomination:** Warren Beatty (best picture), Arthur Penn (director), David Newman, Robert Benton (screenplay), Warren Beatty (actor), Faye Dunaway (actress), Michael J. Pollard (actor in support role), Gene Hackman (actor in support role), Theadora Van Runkle (costume)

# BONNIE AND CLYDE (1967)

Arthur Penn's attempt to make an American "outlaw" film with French New Wave style and youthful exuberance proved an outstanding success with audiences, who appreciated its antiestablishment politics. Critics too eventually applauded the director's effort to infuse U.S. cinema with a new energy and seriousness. Upon its release, however, *Bonnie and Clyde* was roundly condemned for its graphic depiction of violence. Technological developments had made it possible to show gunshot wounds more realistically, and Penn's camera often lingers on the effects of bodies being torn apart and on the pain and suffering that results. Previous American films, of course, had often centered on violence, but *Bonnie and Clyde* was the first Hollywood picture to make the spectator strongly experience its horror and, even, mesmerizing beauty.

Initial reviews of the film were generally dismissive, even condemnatory, but the tide of critical opinion soon dramatically turned, prompting some magazines to publish revisionist reviews. Alternating effectively between scenes of terror, brutal realism, and almost slapstick comedy, *Bonnie and Clyde* is loosely biographical and has a very realistic feel due to meticulous art design and location shooting in northeast Texas, where the landscape of the dustbowl era is nicely reproduced. With some historical inaccuracies, it traces the exploits and eventual tragic end of the Depression era's most famous bank robbing duo, who in their own time were celebrated as folk heroes. Warren Beatty and Faye Dunaway are scintillating as the criminal couple, while terrific support is provided by Gene Hackman, Estelle Parsons, and Michael J. Pollard, who play other members of the gang. After a successful early spree, the gang is cornered by police in Iowa where Clyde's brother Buck (Hackman) is killed and his wife Blanche (Parsons) is blinded and captured. The other three elude police pursuit, but eventually Bonnie and Clyde are lured into an ambush where they are riddled with machine-gun bullets in a slow-motion ballet of death.

The film's frank treatment of sex, particularly the unusual relationship between the impotent Clyde and the aggressive Bonnie, also broke new ground. By the late 1960s, Hollywood had abandoned Production Code restrictions for a ratings system that permitted greater freedom in the portrayal of sex and violence. *Bonnie and Clyde* is among the first and most successful films made under this new system. It earned ten Academy Award nominations, and its immense drawing power at the box office helped pull American cinema out of the red and back into a newfound profitability.

*Bonnie and Clyde* is a powerfully ambiguous statement about the place of violence and the individual in American society. In movie history, however, its importance is much greater. The film's popular and critical success showed the Hollywood establishment, struggling to reconnect with its national audience, that pictures combining European stylization and seriousness with traditional American themes (mediated by conventional genres) could be successful, especially if they were fast paced and featured spectacular set-piece action sequences. *Bonnie and Clyde* paved the way for the "Hollywood Renaissance" of the 1970s, with masterpieces like Francis Ford Coppola's *The Godfather* paying Penn's film the sincere praise of close imitation. **RBP**

# CSILLAGOSOK, KATONÁK (1967)
## THE RED AND THE WHITE

This 1967 feature was one of the first by Hungarian filmmaker Miklós Jancsó to have some impact in the United States, and the stylistic virtuosity, ritualistic power, and sheer beauty of his work are already fully apparent here. In this black-and-white pageant, set during the aftermath of the Russian Revolution, the reds are the revolutionaries and the whites are the government forces ordered to crush them. Working in elaborately choreographed long takes with often spectacular vistas, Jancso invites us to study the mechanisms of power almost abstractly (as suggested by the Stendhalian ring of his title), with a cold eroticism that may glancingly suggest some of the subsequent work of Stanley Kubrick. But this shouldn't mislead one into concluding that Jancsó is any way detached from either politics or emotions.

For one thing, the markedly nationalistic elements in *The Red and the White* could be, and were, interpreted as anti-Russian, especially if one considers that the film was made less than a decade after the Soviet repression of the Hungarian Revolution, which left more than 7,000 Hungarians dead. And significantly, although the film was a Hungarian-Russian coproduction, the Russian authorities refused to show the film in the Soviet Union.

Jancsó's preference for long shots can't be translated into any sort of disdain for his actors. József Madaras, one of Jancsó's regular actors, has explained that "with him, the actor's *face* plays a subordinate role: He will formulate and express the psyche through the movements of human masses. That's what audiences, accustomed to conventional representations, may find strange. But he insists on fully creative collaboration from his actors—only in a manner departing from the conventional. He'll never psychologize, never analyze. He makes you move. And from the way he keeps you moving I can figure out what he wants me to do, how he visualizes a character. He thinks in terms of music and sees in terms of rhythm."

If you have never encountered Jancsó's work, this is an ideal place to start; *The Red and the White* was the first of his features that I saw, and it led me to many more. He may well be the key Hungarian filmmaker of the sound era, and certain later figures such as Béla Tarr would be inconceivable without him. **JRos**

**Hungary / U.S.S.R.** 90m BW
**Language:** Hungarian / Russian
**Director:** Miklós Jancsó
**Producer:** Jenoe Goetz, András Németh, Kirill Sirjajev
**Screenplay:** Gyula Hernádi, Miklós Jancsó, Luca Karall, Valeri Karen, Giorgi Mdivani
**Photography:** Tamás Somló
**Cast:** József Madaras, Tibor Molnár, András Kozák, Jácint Juhász, Anatoli Yabbarov, Sergei Nikonenko, Mikhail Kozakov, Bolot Bejshenaliyev, Tatyana Konyukhova, Krystyna Mikolajewska, Viktor Avdyushko, Gleb Strizhenov, Nikita Mikhalkov, Vladimir Prokofyev, Valentin Bryleyev

## MARKETA LAZAROVÁ (1967)

Czechoslovakia (Barrandov) 162m BW

**Language:** Czech

**Director:** Frantisek Vlácil

**Producer:** Josef Ouzky

**Screenplay:** Frantisek Pavlicek, Frantisek Vlácil, from novel by Vladislav Vancura

**Photography:** Bedrich Batka

**Music:** Zdenek Liska

**Cast:** Josef Kemr, Magda Vásáryová, Nada Hejna, Jaroslav Moucka, Frantisek Velecky, Karel Vasicek, Ivan Palúch, Martin Mrazek, Václav Sloup, Pavla Polaskova, Alena Pavlíková, Michal Kozuch, Zdenek Lipovcan, Harry Studt, Vlastimil Harapes

Set in the 13th-century Bohemian forests, Frantisek Vlácil's ambitious and multilayered medieval epic thematizes the transition from paganism to Christianity through the abduction and brutal rape by a fierce pagan warrior, Mikolás Kozlík (Frantisek Veleck), of the eponymous female lead (Magda Vásáryová), the innocent, convent-bound daughter of a clan leader.

Upon its initial release (after six years in the making), *Variety* magazine declared *Marketa Lazarová*, with its nearly three-hour length, elliptical narrative, and emphasis on symbol and metaphor, "a stunning work—unsuitable for general commercial release." Eventually given its due, this black-and-white Gothic masterpiece—based on a prewar avant-garde novel and visually evocative of Carl Theodor Dreyer, Akira Kurosawa, and Ingmar Bergman—was voted the best Czech film of all time by a panel of the country's critics and industry leaders in 1998.

Rather than reduce the story to an action-filled but superficial adventure, Vlácil—known for his poetic lyricism and historical films (his 1961 film *The Devil's Trap* was set during the counter-Reformation, and his 1967 film *Valley of the Bees* has its Czech hero brought up as a member of the Teutonic Knights)—here makes use of haunting cinematography and period details to delve into the psychological and spiritual state of his ancestral characters. As such, *Marketa Lazarová* stands as "an atavistic nightmare, a cinematic poem difficult to categorize in terms of genre or fear." **SJS**

## THE JUNGLE BOOK (1967)

U.S. (Walt Disney) 78m Technicolor

**Director:** Wolfgang Reitherman

**Producer:** Walt Disney

**Screenplay:** Larry Clemmons, Ralph Wright, Ken Anderson, Vance Gerry, from novel by Rudyard Kipling

**Music:** George Bruns, Terry Gilkyson, Richard M. Sherman

**Cast:** Phil Harris, Sebastian Cabot, Louis Prima, George Sanders, Sterling Holloway, J. Pat O'Malley, Bruce Reitherman, Verna Felton, Clint Howard, Chad Stuart, Lord Tim Hudson, John Abbott, Ben Wright, Darleen Carr

**Oscar nomination:** Terry Gilkyson (song)

Perhaps the best loved of all the Disney animated features, *The Jungle Book* kicks off from Rudyard Kipling's story of a boy raised in the jungle by wolves. Unlike the live-action versions by Zoltan Korda (1942) and Stephen Sommers (1994), which focus on the boy's experiences on returning to civilization, the cartoon is about Mowgli's last days in the wild; the return of the ferocious tiger Shere Khan means it's no longer safe for him here. Mowgli demurs, but like Pinocchio before him, he is easily led astray, and only saved from the clutches of Kaa (the snake)and King Louie (the ape), by his friends Bagheera (a panther), and Baloo (the bear).

Although it's a slight story and the animation is unexceptional, the characterization and score give the picture distinction. The last animated feature to be overseen by Walt Disney himself, *The Jungle Book* was the first to use stars for the voice talent: An unmistakeable George Sanders is the insidious Shere Khan, Louis Prima sings "I'm the King of the Swingers," and Phil Harris has a ball as the beatnik dropout, Baloo, with his signature song "The Bear Necessities." A belated sequel, *Jungle Book 2*, followed in 2003. **TCh**

**Czechoslovakia / Italy** (Carlo Ponti, Barrandov) 71m Eastmancolor
**Language:** Czech
**Director:** Milos Forman
**Producer:** Rudolf Hájek, Carlo Ponti
**Screenplay:** Milos Forman, Jaroslav Papousek, Ivan Passer, Václav Sasek
**Photography:** Miroslav Ondrícek
**Music:** Karel Mares
**Cast:** Jan Vostrcil, Josef Sebanek, Josef Valnoha, Frantisek Debelka, Josef Kolb, Jan Stöckl, Vratislav Cermák, Josef Rehorek, Václav Novotny, Frantisek Reinstein, Frantisek Paska, Stanislav Holubec, Josef Kutálek, Frantisek Svet, Ladislav Adam
**Oscar nomination:** Czechoslovakia (best foreign language film)

# HORÍ, MÁ PANENKO (1967)
## THE FIREMAN'S BALL

Although Milos Forman never aspired to produce an allegory his *The Fireman's Ball* is nevertheless a potent black comedy about the evils of a Soviet-style society. Also an award-winning movie and part of the reason why Forman defected to the West, the film was lambasted for its political subtext by coproducer Carlo Ponti despite being a smash hit that debuted precisely when tanks invaded Prague to extend the Iron Curtain.

Set in a small Czechoslovakian village, this film has several points of interest: The namesake party, a ceremony to honor the volunteer fire department's retired leader, a raffle for valuable foodstuffs, a beauty contest, and a fire that breaks out toward evening's end to tragicomic result.

Not compelling for its plot alone, *The Fireman's Ball* is a must-see title featuring a motley ensemble of laypeople discovered in the town where the film was shot. Episodic in structure, naturalistic in style, and interested in the broadest possible humor, including physical slapstick and the comedy of errors, the picture skillfully develops its careful observations about group behavior within confined circumstances.

Opening as the well-intentioned committee members of a volunteer fire department commission a trophy to honor their outgoing chief, the town's meeting hall holds fine goods for a raffle. As the hall fills with guests and the committee is consumed with an effort to find pretty young women for the "Miss" contest—an opportunity for members to ogle bared flesh—the raffle prizes are stolen, one by one. Everyone present is therefore suspect of burgling the goods because of the obvious scarcity that makes taking fine products like meat and expensive liquors extremely tempting for all.

The "Miss" contest subsequently spins out of control and then a fire breaks out across town. Despite all efforts by the now-drunken committee to tame the angry flames, an old man is left to watch his home burn down in the snow. By film's end the committee's members are left with a threefold failure to hold a raffle, promote a beauty contest, or put out a fire with but one remaining grace. Celebrating their retired leader, regardless of implicit cynicism about committees, comrades, and optimism for a better tomorrow—all core values of the predominant communist rhetoric—the bestowal of respect on one's elders appears as nothing more than empty pomp and circumstance.

Written by Forman, Jaroslav Papousek, and Ivan Passer, who were inspired by a real-life fireman's ball, the film demonstrates a critical awareness of Soviet society. Without overemphasizing that condition and the consequent want and deprivation everywhere part of Czechoslovakian life in 1967, *The Fireman's Ball* further suggests how moral fortitude fails in the face of corrupt leadership benefiting the few at the expense of the many. Of course this tendency stems from a lack of everyday staples like good food and water, but it easily extends to an overall breakdown in civilized behavior, which seems like the film's allegorical resonance no matter Forman's intentions. **GC-Q**

# TERRA EM TRANSE (1967)
## EARTH ENTRANCED

On April 1, 1964, a military coup took over Brazil, ushering in a 25-year-long dictatorship. For the very active and vocal Brazilian Left, the biggest shock of the takeover was not that it happened, but how quickly and bloodlessly the civilian government fell. This gnawing combination of rage, guilt, and depression curiously led to a number of remarkable cinematic meditations on politics, violence, and the role of intellectuals in both. Glauber Rocha's *Earth Entranced* was perhaps the finest example of this impressive crop.

In a land called Eldorado, the poet and filmmaker Paulo Martins (Jardel Filho) decides to abandon the patronage of the political patriarch Porfirio Diaz (Paulo Autran) to throw his support behind populist Felipe Vieira (José Lewgoy) for governor. Vieira is elected, but soon reneges on his campaign promises; Vieira brutally puts down a peasant revolt, causing Paulo to leave him and return to the wild, orgiastic life he knew so well. But led by Sara (Glauce Rocha), Paulo's former lover, a group of "radicals" who support Vieira convince Paulo it's his duty to use his connections to destroy his former patron Diaz. Paulo obliges, but the experience leaves him disgusted with all politics. Learning later that he's been betrayed, and that martial law has been declared, Paulo opts for armed, militant resistance, but he's gunned down by the police.

That's the story; what emerges while watching the film is something quite different. Told in flashback, Rocha's film is a wild mélange of grand opera and cinema vérité, Villa Lobos and Afro-Brazilian exorcisms. The personal and political turmoil personified by Paulo Martins is rendered viscerally by a visual style that alternates rapid-fire jump cuts with long, daredevil handheld camera sequences. Rocha creates a galaxy of archetypes that adroitly capture the spectrum of Latin American politics in the 1950s and 60s, experiences that by the early 1970s led to military dictatorship throughout the region. Few films were as insightful, nor as universally criticized. Attacked with equal vitriol by both the Left and the Right, the film was somewhat neglected in favor of Rocha's rural epics, *Black God, White Devil* (1964) and *Antonio das Mortes* (1969). Yet seen today it seems not only Rocha's masterpiece, but also that of the new Latin American cinema. **RP**

**Brazil** (Mapa) 106m BW

**Language:** Portuguese

**Director:** Glauber Rocha

**Producer:** Luiz Carlos Barreto, Carlos Diegues , Raymundo Wanderley Reis, Glauber Rocha, Zelito Viana

**Screenplay:** Glauber Rocha

**Photography:** Luiz Carlos Barreto

**Music:** Sérgio Ricardo

**Cast:** Jardel Filho, Paulo Autran, José Lewgoy, Glauce Rocha, Paulo Gracindo, Hugo Carvana, Danuza Leão, Jofre Soares, Modesto De Souza, Mário Lago, Flávio Migliaccio, Telma Reston, José Marinho, Francisco Milani, Paulo César Peréio

**Cannes Film Festival:** Glauber Rocha (FIPRESCI award), nomination (Golden Palm)

# OSTRE SLEDOVANÉ VLAKY (1967)

## CLOSELY WATCHED TRAINS

**Czechoslovakia** (Barrandov) 92m BW/ Color

**Language:** Czech / German

**Director:** Jirí Menzel

**Producer:** Zdenek Oves

**Screenplay:** Jirí Menzel, from novel by Bohumil Hrabal

**Photography:** Jaromír Sofr

**Music:** Jirí Pavlik, Jirí Sust

**Cast:** Václav Neckár, Josef Somr, Vlastimil Brodsky, Vladimír Valenta, Alois Vachek, Ferdinand Kruta, Jitka Bendová, Jitka Zelenohorská, Nada Urbánková, Libuse Havelková, Kveta Fialová, Pavla Marsálková, Milada Jezková, Zuzana Minichova, Václav Fiser

**Oscar:** Czechoslovakia (best foreign language film)

With its bittersweet humor, lovingly observed detail, and ruefully affectionate humanism, *Closely Watched Trains* stands as the epitome of the cinema of the Czech New Wave. It was Jirí Menzel's first full-length feature and, like much of his early work, was adapted from the writings of the Czech novelist Bohumil Hrabal. The relationship between the writer and the director, who collaborated together on the script, was exceptionally close and cordial; Menzel, accepting his Oscar for Best Foreign Film, attributed all the credit to the novelist, whereas Hrabal always maintained he preferred the film to the original.

*Trains* takes as its main narrative thread that perennial favorite, the sentimental education of a timid, sensitive adolescent lad. Milo, played by Václav Neckár, with a wide-eyed, wondering gaze that often recalls Buster Keaton, is touchingly proud of his new uniform as a station guard that will allow him "to stand on a platform and avoid hard work." Yearningly in love with a pretty conductress on a local train, he plunges into despair when nervousness causes his failure to consummate. His role model is his older colleague, the cynical and tirelessly randy Hubi-ka (Josef Somr), who divides his time between quietly undermining authority and pursuing every female who crosses his path.

This theme—though freshly and beguilingly observed—would be conventional enough were it not for the setting: A sleepy backwater railroad station during the last years of World War II. The war, ever present but at first largely disregarded, gradually comes to overshadow events, adding layers of complexity and tragedy to Milo's story. By approaching this period (generally depicted in earlier Czech cinema as an era of heroic struggle against the Occupation) from an oblique, ironic angle, Menzel's intention was to deconstruct the heroic myth of war, "because most films, whether they mean to or not, glamorize the war." *Trains* doesn't deal in heroes: Hubi-ka is far more concerned with his amorous adventures than with his contribution to the Resistance, for example, and Milo gets involved largely by accident.

Likewise, nobody is demonized: A group of German soldiers, wistfully eyeing a train-load of pretty nurses, are no strutting fascist beasts but lost, homesick youngsters, and the pro-Nazi Czech collaborator, Counselor Zednícek (Vlastimil Brodsky), is more fool than villain, accompanied by pompous music on the soundtrack that ridicules his Wagnerian pretensions. A side-glance at the Soviet domination of Czechoslovakia is never insisted upon, but would certainly have been picked up by domestic audiences at the time.

The spirit of the *Good Soldier Svejk*, embodiment of the Czech genius for smiling insubordination and dumb insolence, hovers over the film—never more so than in the station staff's straight-faced response to Zednícek's explanation of how the Wehrmacht's retreat on all fronts is in fact a brilliant tactic to ensure victory. Like Hasek's classic novel, *Closely Watched Trains* blends comedy, tragedy, and farce, eroticism and satire, naturalism and absurdity, into a highly idiosyncratic and beguiling mix. And, thanks to Hrabal, Menzel let himself be persuaded not to soften the novel's tragic ending. **PK**

## VIJ (1967)

**U.S.S.R.** (Mosfilm) 78m Color

**Language:** Russian

**Director:** Georgi Kropachyov, Konstantin Yershov

**Screenplay:** Georgi Kropachyov, Aleksandr Ptushko, Konstantin Yershov, from story by Nikolai Gogol

**Photography:** Viktor Pishchalnikov, Fyodor Provorov

**Music:** Karen Khachaturyan

**Cast:** Leonid Kuravlyov, Natalya Varley, Aleksei Glazyrin, Vadim Zakharchenko, Nikolai Kutuzov, Pyotr Vesklyarov, Dmitri Kapka, Stepan Shkurat, G. Sochevko, Nikolai Yakovchenko, Nikolai Panasyev, Vladimir Salnikov

Based on the same short story by famed 19th-century Russian author Nikolai Gogol that inspired Mario Bava's Italian horror classic *The Mask of Satan* (1960), Georgi Kropachyov and Konstantin Yershov's *Vij* is a colorful, entertaining, and genuinely frightening film of demons and witchcraft that boasts some remarkable special-effects work by Russia's master of cinematic fantasy, Aleksandr Ptushko (*The New Gulliver* [1935], *The Stone Flower* [1946], *Ruslan i Lyudmila* [1972]).

Ill-fated seminary student Khoma Brutus (Leonid Kuravlyov) gets lost in some fields while on holiday, and ends up staying the night in an old crone's barn. The woman soon reveals herself to be a witch, using Khoma as a living broomstick. After beating her unconscious, Khoma watches with a mix of guilt and awe as the hag transforms into a beautiful young lady. Following this, Khoma is summoned to a remote village, where he has been specially selected to preside over the wake of a young woman in an ancient church. This entails spending three nights alone with the eerily familiar-looking corpse, only his faltering faith to protect him.

It is here that the film truly amazes, as nightmarish creatures from Beyond begin a parade across the screen. The church scenes culminate with the appearance of the demon Vij, who, in the words of one reviewer, "makes his entrance against a backdrop of one of the finest collections of ghoulies, ghosties and long-leggity beasties" ever to appear in the movies. **SJS**

## GAAV (1968)
### THE COW

**Iran** (Iranian Ministry of Culture) 100m BW

**Language:** Farsi

**Director:** Dariush Mehrjui

**Producer:** Dariush Mehrjui

**Screenplay:** Dariush Mehrjui, from play by Gholam-Hossein Saedi

**Photography:** Fereduyn Ghovanlu

**Music:** Hormoz Farhat

**Cast:** Ezzatolah Entezami, Mahmoud Dowlatabadi, Parviz Fanizadeh, Jamshid Mashayekhi, Ali Nassirian, Esmat Safavi, Khosrow Shojazadeh, Jafar Vali

**Berlin International Film Festival:** Dariush Mehrjui (OCIC award—recommendation, forum of new film)

Rumor has it that after seeing *The Cow*, the Ayatollah Khomeini opined that perhaps there might be a place for filmmaking in the Islamic Republic, thus creating at least the theoretical possibility for the Iranian cinema of Abbas Kiarostami, Mohsen Makhmalbaf, Jafar Panahi, and others. The first Iranian feature film to attract significant international attention, *The Cow* was the second feature by the UCLA-educated Dariush Mehrjui, who returned to Iran determined to create a new kind of filmmaking comparable to the new Third World cinema then just emerging.

Based on a play by Gholam-Hossein Saedi, who also contributed to the screenplay, *The Cow* is the story of Masht Hassan (Ezzatolah Entezami), proud owner of the only cow in a poor village. One day, when he is away on business, the cow unexpectedly dies; rather than reveal the truth to him, the other villagers pretend the cow has merely strayed. With so much of his identity and status wrapped up in that cow, Hassan grows increasingly obsessed with finding it, to the point of madness. Financed largely by the Shah's government, the movie's image of Iranian backwardness and poverty so outraged its producers that they forced the filmmakers to tack on a disclaimer stating that the events depicted occurred long before the current regime. **RP**

# C'ERA UNA VOLTA IL WEST (1968)
## ONCE UPON A TIME IN THE WEST

Sergio Leone's Western masterpiece finds Charles Bronson stepping into the No Name role as the vengeance-seeking Harmonica and Henry Fonda trashing his Wyatt Earp image as the dead-faced, blue-eyed killer, Frank. The opening—Woody Strode, Al Mulock, and Jack Elam waiting for a train and bothered by a fly and dripping water—is masterful bravura, homing in on tiny details for a fascinating but eventless length of time before Bronson arrives for the shoot-out that gets the film going.

*Once Upon a Time in the West* is the first Leone film to place violence in a truly political context, indicting the corrupt (and crippled) railroad tycoon who "leaves two shiny, slimy tracks like a snail" as he bulldozes across the landscape, employing outlaw flunkeys to dispose of inconvenient settlers who won't unsettle easily. Rapacious civilization taints the wide open spaces as Harmonica quests to track down the sadist who hanged his brother, widow-whore-earth mother Claudia Cardinale tries to fulfill her murdered husband's dream of a real community out West, and bandido Jason Robards just wants to be left in a natural state of childish abandon. With striking widescreen compositions and epic running time, this is truly a Western that wins points for both length and width. **KN**

**U.S.** (Paramount, Rafran, San Marco) 165m Technicolor

**Language:** Italian

**Director:** Sergio Leone

**Producer:** Bino Cicogna, Fulvio Morsella

**Screenplay:** Dario Argento, Bernardo Bertolucci, Sergio Donati, Mickey Knox, Sergio Leone

**Photography:** Tonino Delli Colli

**Music:** Ennio Morricone

**Cast:** Henry Fonda, Claudia Cardinale, Jason Robards, Charles Bronson, Gabriele Ferzetti, Paolo Stoppa, Woody Strode, Jack Elam, Snaky, Keenan Wynn, Frank Wolff, Lionel Stander

U.S. (Fox, APJAC) 112m Color

**Director:** Franklin J. Schaffner

**Producer:** Mort Abrahams, Arthur P. Jacobs

**Screenplay:** Michael Wilson, Rod Serling, from the novel *La Planète des singes* by Pierre Boulle

**Photography:** Leon Shamroy

**Music:** Jerry Goldsmith

**Cast:** Charlton Heston, Roddy McDowall, Kim Hunter, Maurice Evans, James Whitmore, James Daly, Linda Harrison, Robert Gunner, Lou Wagner, Woodrow Parfrey, Jeff Burton, Buck Kartalian, Norman Burton, Wright King, Paul Lambert

**Oscar:** John Chambers (honorary award—makeup)

**Oscar nomination:** Morton Haack (costume), Jerry Goldsmith (music)

# PLANET OF THE APES (1968)

A classic science-fiction adventure that remains as powerful today as when it was first released, *Planet of the Apes* was a project that had the potential to go horribly wrong—the 2001 Tim Burton remake being an example of just how. Even if the $100 million budget was still two decades away, it was still a risky proposition to make a movie of Pierre Boulle's novel *La Planète des singes*. So many actors in ape suits was surely a recipe for audiences sniggering rather than cowering behind their hands.

Before the film went into production, makeup supremo John Chambers allayed the fears of studio bosses by shooting a test scene with Charlton Heston (playing the human character, Taylor) and Edward G. Robinson (as apeman Dr. Zaius). Once the ape makeup was proved convincing, Chambers was given $50,000 to develop the simian effects in the film—Robinson, fearing hours in makeup chair would threaten his already failing health, pulled out and was replaced by Maurice Evans.

It was money well spent. The apes that Taylor and his two fellow astronauts encounter when their spaceship crashes on a desolate planet are scary indeed, especially when we and Taylor realize that they rule and humans are the mute animals in this strange place. The casting is perfect—Heston, running around in little more than a leather handkerchief, is butch and gruff, and Roddy McDowall and Kim Hunter, as "friendly" apes Cornelius and Zira, manage to escape the confines of their impressive makeup to deliver heartfelt performances.

Punctuated by memorable set pieces—Taylor's first glimpse of this new planet, his capture, and, of course, the unforgettable ending, and Rod Serling and Michael Wilson's witty script packed with killer lines ("Get your stinking paws off me, you damned dirty ape!")—this classic piece of cinema was followed by three sequels, a TV series, the aforementioned disappointing remake, and even a hilarious spoof in an episode of *The Simpsons*. **JB**

# FACES (1968)

Laughter, because it is so hard to act, often comes across as phony when depicted onscreen. But in *Faces*, every kind of laughter—lunatic, lusty, nervous, hysterical, defensive—is rendered with absolute authenticity, even when prescripted or postsynchronized.

What was John Cassavetes's secret? His rapport with actors was so total, his work with them so intensely detailed, that he was able to capture lived reality like no other American director. After the experiment of *Shadows* (1959) and bad experiences within the Hollywood system, *Faces* confidently marked the beginning of the Cassavetes "signature." Filmed in his home, it records vivid scenes in the lives of people who are at once hopelessly yearning and furiously alienated—stranded, like all Cassavetes characters, between the difficult responsibilities of daily routine and the reckless intoxications of nightlife.

Cassavetes shows his brilliant ensemble cast—John Marley and Lynn Carlin are especially memorable—always *in media res*, their bodies off center in the frame, their words and gestures truncated by the editing. Each scene is based on an unpredictable and often terrifying "turn," a sudden change in a character's mood or manner toward another. *Faces* invents a new way of experiencing time in cinema, where sudden pauses register as (in Cassavetes's swords) "like stepping off a fast train."

Sometimes taken as the condemnation of a soulless, materialist middle class, the film is, rather, a painfully intimate and compassionate account of everyday suffering. Cassavetes stakes out the terrain he would often revisit—marital crisis, casual sex, hedonistic abandon, family ties—within a narrative that constantly shuffles and compares character's journey through a long night and its aftermath.

Is *Faces* the first film in cinema history where characters talk (indeed, laugh themselves stupid) about cunnilingus? Some 35 years later, directors including Neil LaBute and Lars von Trier are still trying to catch up to Cassavetes's astonishing ability to show the messy complexity of adult relationships. **AM**

**U.S.** (Castle Hill) 130m BW

**Director:** John Cassavetes

**Producer:** John Cassavetes, Maurice McEndree

**Screenplay:** John Cassavetes

**Photography:** Maurice McEndree, Al Ruban

**Music:** Jack Ackerman, Charlie Smalls

**Cast:** John Marley, Gena Rowlands, Lynn Carlin, Seymour Cassel, Fred Draper, Val Avery, Dorothy Gulliver, Jerry Howard, Carolyn Fleming, Don Kraatz, John Hale, Midge Ware, Kay Michaels, Laurie Mock, Christina Crawford

**Oscar nomination:** John Cassavetes (screenplay), Seymour Cassel (actor in support role), Lynn Carlin (actress in support role)

**Venice Film Festival:** John Marley (Volpi Cup - actor), John Cassavetes nomination (Golden Lion)

## ROSEMARY'S BABY (1968)

**U.S.** (Paramount) 136m Technicolor
**Director:** Roman Polanski
**Producer:** William Castle, Dona Holloway
**Screenplay:** Roman Polanski, from novel by Ira Levin
**Photography:** William A. Fraker
**Music:** Christopher Komeda
**Cast:** Mia Farrow, John Cassavetes, Ruth Gordon, Sidney Blackmer, Maurice Evans, Ralph Bellamy, Victoria Vetri, Patsy Kelly, Elisha Cook Jr., Emmaline Henry, Charles Grodin, Hanna Landy, Phil Leeds, D'Urville Martin, Hope Summers
**Oscar:** Ruth Gordon (actress in support role)
**Oscar nomination:** Roman Polanski (screenplay)

When a gaunt, hollow-eyed Rosemary Woodhouse (Mia Farrow) exclaims with relief, "It's alive," about a third of the way into the film, the baby growing in her womb finally kicking, her insides before that eerily still, her husband Guy (John Cassavetes) recoils in horror touching her belly. In her excitement, Rosemary doesn't notice his response. Even more important, she quells both her better instincts and her growing suspicion that her husband, their new apartment and neighbors, and even her pregnancy are all somehow mysteriously and darkly linked. In doing so, she stays the course for what is, arguably, one of the finest horror films ever made.

Crystallized in that one scene are many of the familiar and defining concerns of director Roman Polanski—betrayal, corruption, the boundaries of sanity, and the "mysteries" of woman. Polanski's magnificent weaving together of these elements elevates the mildly pulp source (Ira Levin's hugely successful novel) into a cinematic classic. Time has done nothing to diminish the film's taut, focused, building sense of dread, and familiarity with the movie only keeps one that much more in awe of Polanski's detail, his rhythm and pacing, his skill with his actors, and the fine script he adapted for the screen. Revisiting the film uncovers humor that is sly and intentional. The casting of the now-iconic Cassavetes—an ever-glowing symbol of the pure artist in life at the time—playing a man who has sold his soul to the devil for show-biz success. The humor that has been layered on over the years and after the fact; Mia Farrow's desperation to be a mother now inspires uneasy giggles in its own right, thanks to her midlife tabloid travails.

Scenes and characters from *Rosemary's Baby* are etched into memory: Farrow hunched over a kitchen sink, her mouth bloody as she gnaws raw animal flesh, catching herself in shock; the dreamscape rape/consummation of Rosemary far more unsettling for what is suggested than actually shown; Ruth Gordon's dithering senior citizen slowly evolving into something much more sinister; Rosemary, near the film's end, entering the gathering of the tribe with a knife, desperate to see the baby that she's been told is dead. Still, it isn't only the Satanic aspect of the film that makes your skin crawl. Predicated on the abuse of marital trust, on the idea that the security of family and friends might all be an illusion, a force to be used against rather than for you, *Rosemary's Baby* taps into visceral fears. We can't really know the people around us. We can't trust anyone, not even ourselves. There is no sure protection. Polanski's masterful manipulation of these existential fears gives the film its power. And who among viewers can help but feel that Rosemary is their proxy as she watches the good people around her fall dead or ill, all while discovering just how pervasive the evil is around her? **EH**

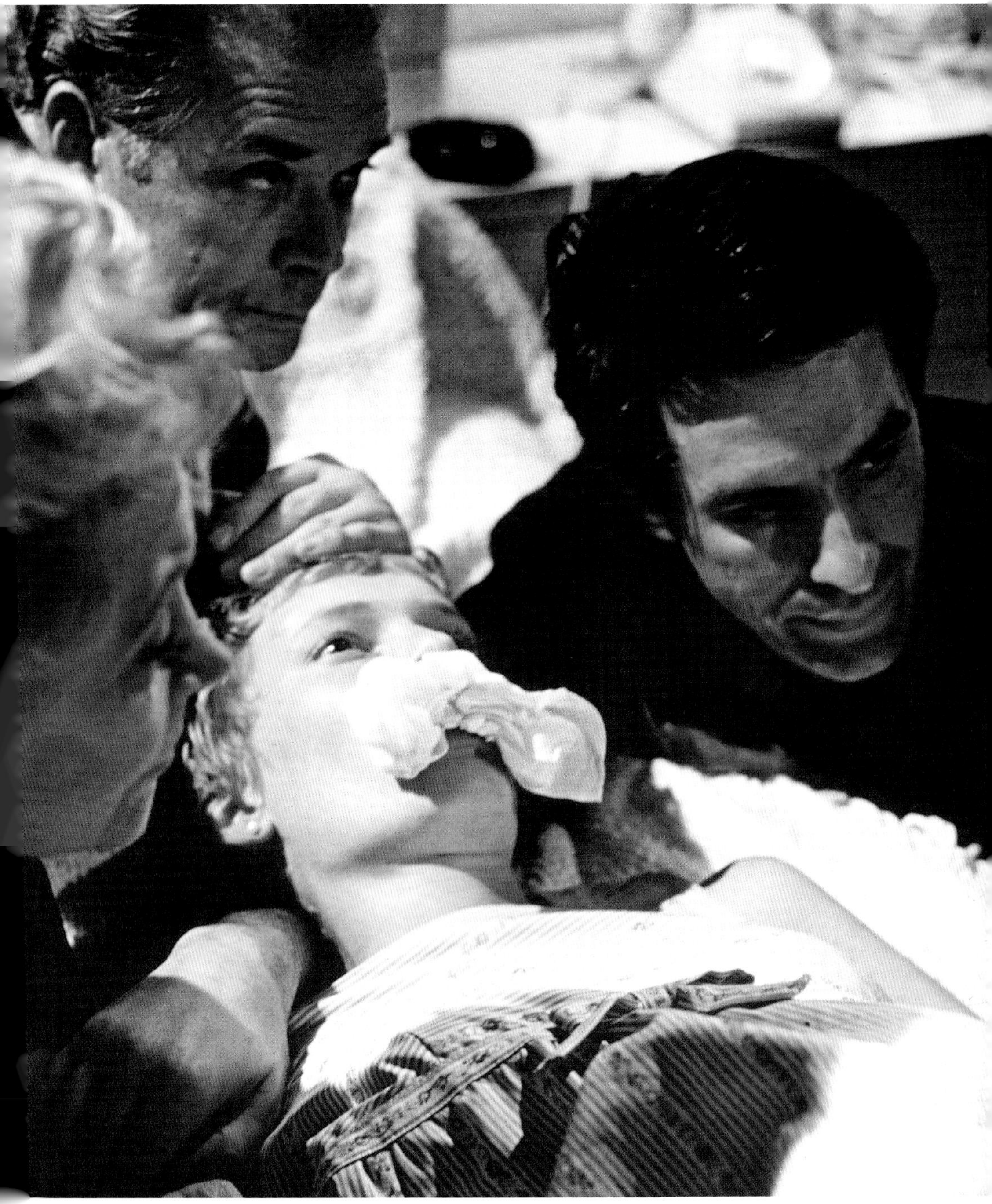

**G.B.** (Memorial) 111 mins BW / Eastmancolor

**Director:** Lindsay Anderson

**Producer:** Lindsay Anderson, Michael Medwin

**Screenplay:** David Sherwin, John Howlett

**Photography:** Miroslav Ondrícek

**Music:** Marc Wilkinson

**Cast:** Malcolm McDowell, David Wood, Richard Warwick, Christine Noonan, Rupert Webster, Robert Swann, Hugh Thomas, Michael Cadman, Peter Sproule, Peter Jeffrey, Anthony Nicholls, Arthur Lowe, Mona Washbourne, Mary MacLeod, Geoffrey Chater

**Cannes Film Festival:** Lindsay Anderson (Golden Palm)

# IF... (1968)

Modeled on Jean Vigo's brief hymn to schoolboy anarchy *Zéro de Conduite* (1933), Lindsay Anderson's follow up to his *This Sporting Life* (1963) gets away from the realism and working-class rebellion that characterized the "kitchen sink" cinema movement and embraces a satiric style that now seems like a link between the classic surrealists and the Monty Python troupe.

Whereas the earlier film required that Anderson, who came from a respectable upper-class background, make an ethnographic study of Northern rugby-playing louts, *If...* is also paradoxically a more genuinely realist film, in that it was made by someone who actually came from the public school system it so rigorously attacks. The opening section of the film follows 16-year-old Mick Travis (Malcolm McDowell) and his few equally "antisocial" friends as they are bored by masters and bullied by prefects, bristling against a system that imposes punishments at once farcical and cruel like floggings in the gym administered with all the ceremony of a 19th-century execution. Alternating between color and black-and-white film stock, allegedly not for any significant reason but because the budget for color ran out before the film was finished, *If...* breaks out of the rigid confines of the school, with its crusty character actors and licensed homosexual predation, as Mick begins a perhaps-imaginary affair with a voluptuous waitress (Christine Noonan). The sex scene, explicit for 1969, is unusual in the area of taboo-breaking in that it depicts not a rape or self-hating promiscuity with morality rammed home afterward but a couple enjoying physical love.

While Vigo overturned his school's shabby dignity with a pillow fight, Anderson—working after the student risings of 1968 and the growth of the protest movement—has Mick and his friends don guerilla chic outfits and stage an attack on the school's Speech Day, gunning down the patronizing headmaster (Peter Jeffrey) and other establishment figures. Though shot in a fantastical manner, with odd gags such as a speaking corpse in a filing cabinet, there is no return to "reality" to blunt the revolutionary wish-fulfillment fervor. Anderson, writer David Sherwin, and star McDowell brought the character of Mick Travis back for two further, wildly different satires, *O Lucky Man!* (1973) and *Britannia Hospital* (1982). **KN**

# MEMORIAS DEL SUBDESARROLLO (1968)
## MEMORIES OF UNDERDEVELOPMENT

**Cuba** (Cuban State Film, ICAIC) 97m BW

**Language:** Spanish

**Director:** Tomás Gutiérrez Alea

**Producer:** Miguel Mendoza

**Screenplay:** Edmundo Desnoes, Tomás Gutiérrez Alea, from the novel *Memorias del subdesarrollo* by Edmundo Desnoes

**Photography:** Ramón F. Suárez

**Music:** Leo Brouwer

**Cast:** Sergio Corrieri, Daisy Granados, Eslinda Núñez, Omar Valdés, René de la Cruz, Yolanda Farr, Ofelia González, Jose Gil Abad, Daniel Jordan, Luis López, Rafael Sosa

Part documentary, part feature film, Tomás Gutiérrez Alea's *Memories of Underdevelopment* portrays an important segment of Cuban life during the period 1961–62. Centered on Sergio (Sergio Corrieri), a wealthy former businessman-turned-aspiring-writer, the movie considers his relationship to the transformation of Havana into a communist dictatorship organized around a police state. Always his interactions with the people and landscapes of home are informed with the pallor of disbelief, sadness, and neglect, but also of optimism because Sergio is in touch with his disconnection while trying to make himself whole once again.

First seen sending his parents and ex-wife to a new life in Miami, he instead stays behind, hoping to find genuine reminders of what it is to be alive. So he begins typing a manuscript, including fantasies about his maid, recollections of his lost true love, and the beginning of a troublesome dalliance with the lovely Elena (Daisy Granados). Eventually accused and acquitted of rape after narrowly avoiding a shotgun wedding—a parable about individual freedom in a state-run justice system with corrupt values—Sergio finally resigns himself to waiting and seeing what may come of his country's revolutionary fervor.

Layered with voiceover narration, Alea peppers the account of Sergio's life with frequent discourses on various subjects. There is an illuminating monologue about the Marxist dialectic, curiosity about the struggles of aging in a tropical climate, the general theme of underdevelopment, and social inconsistency during the early days of Fidel Castro's reign.

Perhaps Cuba's most internationally famous film, and directed by one of the founders of the state-run film studio, the Instituto Cubano del Arte e Industrias Cinematográficos (ICAIC), *Memories of Underdevelopment* is a trenchant critique of capitalism and the Communist Revolution. Within its simple story of one man in crisis are elements of fantasy, rolls of newsreel footage, and poignant bits of situational drama to express simultaneous wonder and contempt at the upheaval of the Cold War. Elegant and powerful, it's a tribute to Cuban creative influence in a moment of acute cultural suppression as the mask for a better tomorrow. **GC-Q**

## THE PRODUCERS (1968)

**U.S.** (Crossbow, MGM, Springtime) 88m Pathécolor
**Director:** Mel Brooks
**Producer:** Sidney Glazier, Jack Grossberg
**Screenplay:** Mel Brooks
**Photography:** Joseph F. Coffey
**Music:** Norman Blagman, Mel Brooks, John Morris
**Cast:** Zero Mostel, Gene Wilder, Kenneth Mars, Estelle Winwood, Renée Taylor, Christopher Hewett, Lee Meredith, William Hickey, Andréas Voutsinas, David Patch, Dick Shawn, Barney Martin, Madelyn Cates, Shimen Ruskin, Frank Campanella
**Oscar:** Mel Brooks (screenplay)
**Oscar nomination:** Gene Wilder (actor in support role)

"Will the dancing Hitlers please wait in the wings!" The first feature by writer-director-producer Mel Brooks is his gem. Less vulgar and more dangerous than anything else in his ouevre, *The Producers* won the Oscar for his screenplay, a classic farce with gasp-inducing irony: A New York showbiz Jew, however deviously, staging a musical, however detestable, about Hitler.

The biggest joy of the film is incomparable Zero Mostel, a Broadway titan returning after blacklisting blighted his film career and finding immortality as irrepressible scoundrel Max Bialystock. His foil is uptight accountant Leo Bloom (Gene Wilder), who innocently observes that a dishonest man could make a fortune if he knew a show would fail. Raise a million dollars to produce it for a fraction of that amount, and when it closes no one expects their money back. Electrified, Max perpetrates the fraud with a surefire flop, *Springtime For Hitler*, authored by a demented Nazi (Kenneth Mars). Absurdly, the show is a smash, leading to an opening at Leavenworth for Max's penitentiary opus "Prisoners of Love."

The film's beloved production number "Springtime for Hitler" gives new meaning to the term "showstopper," with its Busby Berkeley homage of dancers in swastika formation. Beautifully acted and staged lunacy, *The Producers* gets better on each viewing. **AE**

## DAVID HOLZMAN'S DIARY (1968)

**U.S.** (Paradigm) 74m BW
**Director:** Jim McBride
**Producer:** Jim McBride
**Screenplay:** Jim McBride
**Photography:** Michael Wadleigh
**Cast:** L.M. Kit Carson, Eileen Dietz, Lorenzo Mans, Louise Levine, Fern McBride, Michel Lévine, Robert Lesser, Jack Baran

In his early 20s, on the staggeringly small budget of $2,500, Jim McBride began making *David Holzman's Diary* from three ideas: The image of a man filming himself in a mirror, the banality of daily life, and how the oppressiveness of New York affects people's perceptions and behavior.

David (screenwriter L.M. Kit Carson) is a schmuck. He decides to film the smallest details of his daily life to "find the truth." But his approach, by turns obsessive, voyeuristic, and paranoiac, swiftly alienates everyone around him. Far from a standard "mockumentary," McBride's recreation of the stages of this audiovisual diary is peppered with dramatic ellipses, emotional suspense, and a pleasing, always surprising set of variations. The result is remarkably prescient. The cinéma vérité obsessions of the 1960s targeted here were to reach their full flowering much later, in the eras of video and digital.

*David Holzman's Diary* has aged well. Not only has it been paid elaborate homage—in Roman Coppola's *CQ* (2001)—but its formal inventions, static long takes, black screen, fish-eye distortion, lateral traveling shots, single-frame pixillations, have prefigured many other experiments. McBride had already synthesized, and critiqued, the legacies of Godard, Mekas, and "direct cinema." **AM**

# SKAMMEN (1968)
## SHAME

Sweden (AB, Svensk) 103m BW
**Language:** Swedish
**Director:** Ingmar Bergman
**Producer:** Lars-Owe Carlberg
**Screenplay:** Ingmar Bergman
**Photography:** Sven Nykvist
**Cast:** Liv Ullmann, Max von Sydow, Sigge Fürst, Gunnar Björnstrand, Birgitta Valberg, Hans Alfredson, Ingvar Kjellson, Frank Sundström, Ulf Johansson, Vilgot Sjöman, Bengt Eklund, Gösta Prüzelius, Willy Peters, Barbro Hiort af Ornäs, Agda Helin

Of the films Ingmar Bergman made in the mid-to-late 1960s with Max von Sydow and Liv Ullmann on his beloved island of Faro, *Shame* is perhaps the greatest. Not that Bergman, reconsidering the film in his book *Images: My Life in Film*, was too happy with it. He felt that the script was uneven, resulting in a poor first half and a better second half. He also felt that he had perhaps taken on too much in attempting to depict war. Such an assessment seems far too harsh. This study of the devastating effects of war on a couple is one of the most persuasive accounts of a relationship transformed by forces over which it has little or no control. Bergman may not have had Hollywood's resources on hand to stage spectacular destruction and carnage, but he more than compensated for such material constraints with the boldness, assurance, and conviction of his drama and the acuity of his psychological, emotional, and social insights.

Ullmann and von Sydow play a couple, their love flawed by weakness and complacency but able to sustain itself. But when the war they have managed more or less to ignore finally turns up on their doorstep, it forces them to look at themselves, each other, and their relationship with a new, cruel honesty. The violence, death, and betrayals around them are both arbitrary and terrifying, but perhaps no more so than these more intimate and, indeed, more shocking revelations. All par for the course, perhaps, in Bergman's corrosive chamber dramas. But here they are lent added force by the wider context of a world in conflagration. Sven Nykvist's typically magnificent black-and-white cinematography, eloquent in its close-ups of faces as in its shots of trundling tanks, burning trees, and scarred landscapes, and the performances do ample justice to Bergman's magisterial conception. The two leads are memorable in the justly famous scene of a last, brief moment of sunny, domestic happiness just before the conflict arrives at their farm. But also is Gunnar Björnstrand, as a well-connected friend who helps them out, only to abuse his privileged position later on. Grim, hauntingly beautiful, and still, of course, scarily relevant. **GA**

# 2001: A SPACE ODYSSEY (1968)

**G.B.** (MGM, Polaris) 141m Metrocolor
**Language:** English / Russian
**Director:** Stanley Kubrick
**Producer:** Stanley Kubrick
**Screenplay:** Stanley Kubrick, Arthur C. Clarke, from the story *The Sentinel* by Arthur C. Clarke
**Photography:** Geoffrey Unsworth
**Music:** Aram Khachaturyan, György Ligeti, Richard Strauss, Johann Strauss
**Cast:** Keir Dullea, Gary Lockwood, William Sylvester, Daniel Richter, Leonard Rossiter, Margaret Tyzack, Robert Beatty, Sean Sullivan, Douglas Rain, Frank Miller, Bill Weston, Ed Bishop, Glenn Beck, Alan Gifford, Ann Gillis
**Oscar:** Stanley Kubrick (special visual effects)
**Oscar nomination:** Stanley Kubrick (director), Stanley Kubrick, Arthur C. Clarke (screenplay), Anthony Masters, Harry Lange, Ernest Archer (art direction)

An artifact of evidently extraterrestrial origin triggers and monitors key stages on man's journey from ape to star child. At the dawn of man a mysterious monolith is the catalyst for an evolutionary leap in primates, from scavenger and gatherer to tool-wielding hunter and killer. Many millennia later a monolith uncovered by a geological team stationed on the moon alarmingly emits a short radio signal toward Jupiter. A manned expedition to investigate (impassively shepherded by Keir Dullea and Gary Lockwood while mission specialists slumber in stasis) is sabotaged by the spaceship Discovery's psychologically disturbed computer HAL (voiced by Douglas Rain), but surviving astronaut Bowman's (Dullea) contact with another monolith in Jupiter's orbit hurtles him though a gateway "full of stars"—through time and space, to age, die, and be reborn into a new phase of existence. That's one summary of a film that has enjoyed an enduring reputation for unfathomability.

Influential but still unique, coolly detached, obsessional, pretentious, contentious, bewildering, forever fascinating—*2001* is all of these. Certainly it deviates from director Stanley Kubrick's stated intention to make the "proverbial good science-fiction movie" from his coscreenwriter Arthur C. Clarke's intriguing novella *The Sentinel*, as his film defies genre convention and is unlike any science-fiction movie before it. Visually, *2001* is undeniably awesome. Oscar-winning, ground-breaking special effects (designed by the fastidious Kubrick, supervised by pioneering Douglas Trumbull) are a dazzling mix of imagination and science. Meticulous mime work and 1960s' state-of-the-art prosthetics makeup in the first of the film's four distinct acts create the best ape impersonations by humans ever seen at the time (and still highly effective, though arguably topped by John Chambers's creations for 1968's *Planet Of The Apes*). And the movie is strewn with unforgettable images: The unexpected, stunning cut from a bone brandished by an ape-man and thrown aloft to a satellite; the magnificent alignment of sun and moon directly above the rim of the monolith; the orbital waltz of the space station and a docking shuttle; the circular crew habitat of the Discovery (made a reality, if considerably smaller, in NASA's space shuttle program).

The sound is equally rich, with its experimental choral music, the classical themes (Richard Strauss's "Thus Spoke Zarathustra," Johann Strauss's "Blue Danube Waltz") that forever bring the film to mind, and its snippets of minimalist dialogue ("Open the pod bay doors, Hal") which recur in wide-ranging homages and cultural references.

*2001* can be taken as a mysterious adventure, sermon, or vision, one that was understandably the ultimate trip for hippies on psychedelics, but even viewed simply as a haunting spectacle it is unsurpassed, demanding to be seen on a big screen to be fully appreciated. Its faults—its overblown abstraction and its sketchy narrative of scarcely articulated, unresolved speculation on the origins and destiny of human life—are more than compensated for by its gripping engagement between man and machine, its visual starkness and serenity, and, above all, its rhapsodic wonder at heaven and earth and the infinite beyond. **AE**

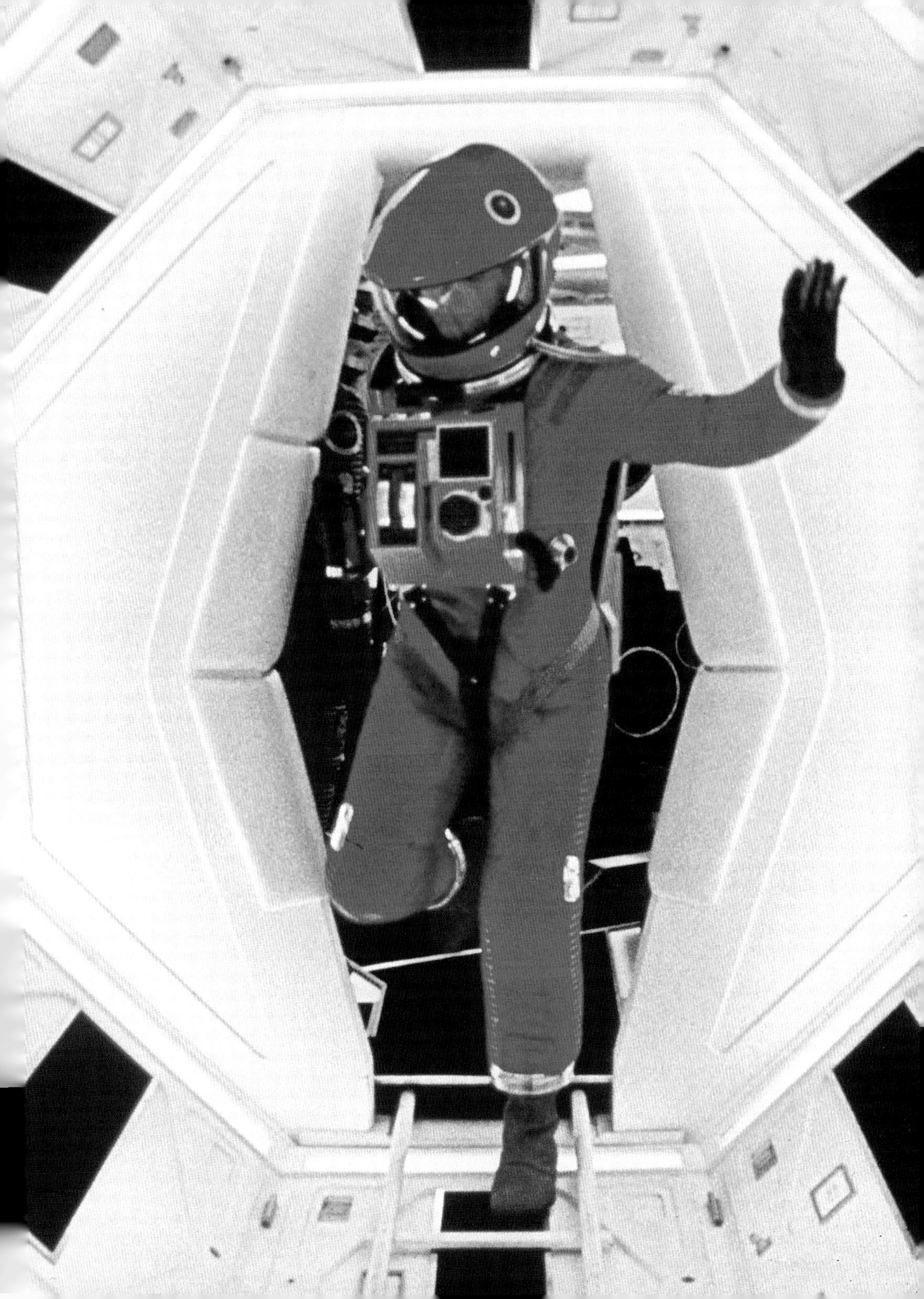

**Sweden** (Svensk) 90m BW
**Language:** Swedish
**Director:** Ingmar Bergman
**Producer:** Lars-Owe Carlberg
**Screenplay:** Ingmar Bergman
**Photography:** Sven Nykvist
**Music:** Lars Johan Werle
**Cast:** Max von Sydow, Liv Ullmann, Gertrud Fridh, Georg Rydeberg, Erland Josephson, Naima Wifstrand, Ulf Johansson, Gudrun Brost, Bertil Anderberg, Ingrid Thulin

# VARGTIMMEN (1968)
## HOUR OF THE WOLF

The original 1964 script was entitled *The Cannibals* and was conceived as an expensive, monumental film. But due to a serious bout of pneumonia and the decision upon hospital recovery to make the low-budget project *Persona* (1966), writer/director Ingmar Bergman reworked the scenario into a companion piece to the latter film on a much smaller scale than originally intended. In *Hour of the Wolf* the artist's spiritual torment is not witnessed as an enigma from the outside, as in *Persona*, but conveyed to us directly from the artist's own thoughts by way of the film's staging of texts from his diary. Clearly inspired by the uncanny writings of E.T.A. Hoffmann—even down to the names of characters—this is an all-out horror film about a sensitive (if not sympathetic) artist spiritually torn to pieces by his demonic critics and audience.

Reversing the vampire metaphor from *Persona*, in which nurse Alma (Bibi Andersson) dreams about actress Elisabet Vogler (Liv Ullmann) sucking her blood, painter Johan Borg (Max von Sydow) in *Hour of the Wolf* sees his feudal and bourgeois benefactors at Baron von Merkens's (Erland Josephson) castle as living-dead creatures of the night in vampiric need of an artist to prey on. For their sadistic amusement, they invite him to a party only to treat him like a court jester. His pretensions to artistic freedom are openly mocked as the tormentors adoringly present a toy theater version of Mozart's *The Magic Flute* (later to be staged and filmed by Bergman) and then praise it as a commodity, suggesting that its value stems from the fact that it was a commissioned piece. The ultimate humiliation comes in a scene where Johan finds himself wearing clown/female makeup and being teased by his mistress Veronica Vogler (Ingrid Thulin) while his tormentors laughingly watch in the dark.

However, Bergman also hints that Johan as a narrator is not to be trusted. His tormentors possess supernatural qualities and an uncanny insight into his psyche that ultimately reveal them as projections of destructive forces from within himself. This makes the film yet another variation of Bergman's recurring motif concerning the predatory relationship between the artist and his audience. **MT**

## TARGETS (1968)

U.S. (Saticoy) 90 m Pathécolor

**Director:** Peter Bogdanovich

**Producer:** Peter Bogdanovich, Daniel Selznick

**Screenplay:** Polly Platt, Peter Bogdanovich, Orson Welles

**Photography:** László Kovács

**Cast:** Tim O'Kelly, Boris Karloff, Arthur Peterson, Monte Landis, Nancy Hsueh, Peter Bogdanovich, Daniel Ades, Stafford Morgan, James Brown, Mary Jackson, Tanya Morgan, Timothy Burns, Warren White, Mark Dennis, Sandy Baron

The story goes that Peter Bogdanovich got his chance to direct when producer Roger Corman realized Boris Karloff owed him two shooting days. He also had about 20 minutes of unused footage from *The Terror* (1963), which he told Bogdanovich to use. But instead of the Edgar Allen Poe rip-off Corman had been expecting, Bogdanovich came up with a brilliant original scenario: Karloff in effect plays himself (his character is an old horror movie star called Byron Orlok), and Bogdanovich co-stars as the earnest young director trying to coax him into one last performance. This is cross-cut with a parallel story in which the apparently all-American "boy next door," Bobby Thompson (Tim O'Kelly), murders his wife and mother, then embarks on a random shooting spree, first from a water tower overlooking a highway, then from behind the screen at a drive-in cinema—where Orlok is making a personal guest appearance (and where Bogdanovich works in the footage from *The Terror*, including shots of a young Jack Nicholson).

*Targets* is an American counterpart to the French *nouvelle vague* films by directors like François Truffaut and Claude Chabrol. Like them, Bogdanovich was an auteurist film critic, and *Targets* features direct or coded references to Howard Hawks's *The Criminal Code* (1931—a film that starred Karloff), Orson Welles's *Touch of Evil* (1958), and Alfred Hitchcock's *Psycho* (1960). This postmodernist aesthetic extends to the film's self-reflexivity: "I'm an anachronism," says Orlok. "My kind of horror isn't horror any more." His point is chillingly underlined by Thompson's motiveless crimes. Obviously based on the Texas tower sniper Charles Whitman—the ex-marine who murdered his mother, then shot 14 strangers on August 1, 1966—Thomson is clean-cut, a "normal, healthy boy," who is nevertheless fascinated with guns . . . he carries a small arsenal around with him in the back of his car. The film plays on this same fixation, putting the camera behind Thomson's sight lines, asking us, like Harry Lime (Orson Welles) in *The Third Man* (1949), how much we really care about those dots in the distance. Coolly dissociative and intelligently mounted, *Targets* is a sharp snapshot of America falling to a new, violent age. **TCh**

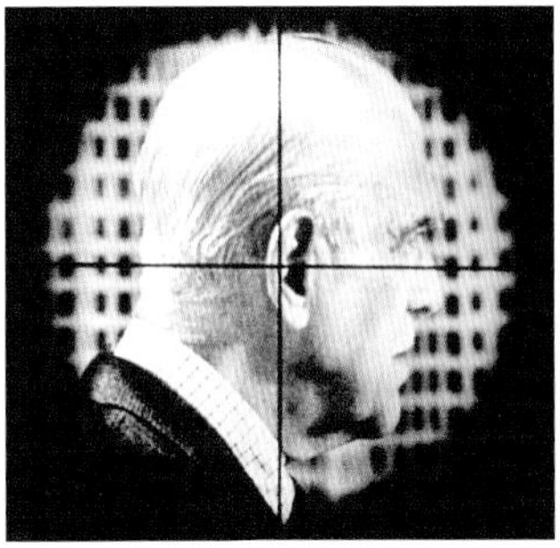

**U.S.** (Image Ten, Laurel, Market Square) 96m BW
**Director:** George A. Romero
**Producer:** Karl Hardman, Russell Streiner, Karen L. Wolf
**Screenplay:** George A. Romero, John A. Russo
**Photography:** George A. Romero
**Music:** Scott Vladimir Licina
**Cast:** Duane Jones, Judith O'Dea, Karl Hardman, Marilyn Eastman, Keith Wayne, Judith Ridley, Kyra Schon, Charles Craig, S. William Hinzman, George Kosana, Frank Doak, Bill Cardille, A.C. McDonald, Samuel R. Solito, Mark Ricci

# NIGHT OF THE LIVING DEAD (1968)

It looks cheaply-shot and starts out seeming like it might turn into a comedy: A brother and sister visit their mother's grave to pay their respects and the brother tries to scare his sibling by pretending to be a ghoul out to get her. Minutes later, however, he is killed and the young woman finds herself holed up in an abandoned farmhouse with an assortment of people as they are attacked by a mindless mob made up of the dead, newly risen, mindless, and craving the taste of human flesh.

Slowly, through emergency broadcasts on radio and television, the refugees begin to piece together what is happening. Corpses are getting up across the land, possibly even the world, and attacking the living in order to eat their flesh. Tensions arise among the heroes as they argue over what course of action to take. Should they try to escape or should they hold up and wait for help that may never arrive? Who should be taking the lead and giving the orders: the calm, rational black man or the impulsive family man? As the number of walking dead increases outside, the farmhouse may not hold for much longer, and drastic action will have to be taken. Before long, all bets are off. Every glimmer of hope and expectation you might have in a story is undercut by a wrong decision, bad luck, a cruel twist of fate, and all we are left with is the horror of despair.

This is the horror movie that raised the bar on the genre in the second half of the 20th century, dragging the stories away from the antiquated gothic conventions of yesteryear and into the cold, merciless light of the present. George Romero's *Night of the Living Dead*, with its matter-of-fact, almost documentary-style approach, touches upon the issues that preoccupied America in the late 1960s: civil unrest, racism, the breakdown of the nuclear family, fear of the mob, and Armageddon itself. Nothing can be taken for granted. Good does not always triumph. And for the first time, a horror movie reflected the sense of unease that permeated contemporary society with no offer of comfort or reassurance. **AT**

**France** (FFD, Pléïade, deux mondes, Carrosse, Losange, Guéville, Renn, Simar, SFP, Two World) 110m BW

**Language:** French

**Director:** Eric Rohmer

**Producer:** Pierre Cottrell, Barbet Schroeder

**Screenplay:** Eric Rohmer

**Photography:** Néstor Almendros

**Cast:** Jean-Louis Trintignant, Françoise Fabian, Marie-Christine Barrault, Antoine Vitez, Léonide Kogan, Guy Léger, Anne Dubot

**Oscar nomination:** France (best foreign language film), Eric Rohmer (screenplay)

**Cannes Film Festival:** Eric Rohmer nomination (Golden Palm)

# MA NUIT CHEZ MAUD (1969)

## MY NIGHT WITH MAUD

*My Night with Maud*, the third of Eric Rohmer's six "Moral Tales" and often considered the best, takes place over a few days one winter in the provincial city of Clermont, France. Jean-Louis Trintignant plays an engineer, a practicing Jesuit, who decides to marry a student, Françoise (Marie-Christine Barrault), whom he has seen at Mass but never met. By chance, he runs into an old school friend (Antoine Vitez) who takes him to the apartment of the witty, intelligent Maud (Françoise Fabian), a divorced doctor. Over the course of a long conversation that forms the centerpiece of the film, the hero and Maud discover an affinity for each other.

In no other filmmaker's work are place and season more important. In *My Night with Maud*, the falling snow cools the air in the long scene in Maud's apartment, provides a pretext for the hero's spending the night there, and later makes it possible for him to meet and spend the night with the student. The film's complexity and poignancy owe as much to Néstor Almendros's black-and-white cinematography, with its range of subtle tones, as it does to the vigorous and brilliant dialogue. An atmosphere of uneasy detente prevails, keyed emotionally to the hero's agreeable alienation. Despite Trintignant's great likeability (this is one of this best performances), the film is not, finally, on the hero's side, and it views his decisions with a sadness that lingers with the viewer long after the film is over. **CFu**

**Cuba** (ICAIC) 160m BW

**Language:** Spanish

**Director:** Humberto Solás

**Screenplay:** Julio García Espinosa, Nelson Rodríguez, Humberto Solás

**Photography:** Jorge Herrero

**Cast:** Raquel Revuelta, Eslinda Núñez, Adela Legrá, Eduardo Moure, Ramón Brito, Adolfo Llauradó, Idalia Anreus, Silvia Planas, Flora Lauten, Rogelio Blain, Maria Elena Molinet, Aramís Delgado, Teté Vergara, Flavio Calderín

# LUCÍA (1969)

Humerto Solás's *Lucía* is undoubtedly one of the landmark works of modern, postrevolutionary Cuban cinema. In many ways, it can be said to offer a kind of summation of many of the key tenets of the cinema of this decade. This exhilarating mix of styles and tones is partly accommodated by the film's three-part structure, following the fate—and love stories—of three characters named Lucía at pivotal moments in "modern" Cuban history.

From a contemporary perspective, the most remarkable aspect of *Lucía* is its ability to move dynamically between various modes of cinema and present eye-popping tableaux of equal beauty and horror. In this respect, the film's opening segment is probably the most commented upon and remembered. In particular, the battle sequences—featuring naked black riders slaughtering government troops—have a visceral ferocity akin to Orson Welles's *Chimes at Midnight* (1965). In its mixture of various styles of performance, its fatalistic staging of history, and its dynamic movement between proximity and distance, the extreme close-up and the long shot, it can also be said to resemble the equally operatic work of Sergio Leone. In its clashing of perspectives and approaches, *Lucía* explores the consciousness-raising possibilities of film as well as the link between postrevolutionary Cuban cinema and the new waves of Europe and South America. **AD**

# HSIA NU (1969)
## A TOUCH OF ZEN

The literal translation of this movie's Chinese title is "Warrior Woman," and it doesn't begin to do the story justice. There's a reason *A Touch of Zen* is considered a benchmark in Chinese cinema: it's like a Rosetta Stone of the *wuxia* or swords-and-sorcery genre. The story begins simply enough, centering on the life of a daydreaming scholar (Shih Chun) in a sleepy town outside Peking, whose mother despairs of his ever marrying and siring children to continue the family line. Then he becomes smitten with the mysterious woman (Feng Hsu) who has moved into the abandoned mansion, long rumored to be haunted, and the intimations of a ghost story come to the fore. And the revelation that she is in fact a princess fleeing from imperial enemies who slaughtered her family throws the story into even greater relief. Each plot twist opens the narrative up into something bigger, and before the end, mystical Buddhist monks with supernatural powers and metaphysical fantasy are added to the mix as well. Gender roles are reversed: the princess is no shrinking violet, but a highly trained swordswoman who can hold her own against a band of elite guards, while the scholar is a bookworm who doesn't know how to fight. At three hours, the pace is surprisingly brisk because this is a movie that's genuinely unpredictable you're just waiting for what's going to happen next since it could end up changing all your previous assumptions about the movie.

King Hu is rightly regarded as the pioneering director of the *wuxia* film, in spite of the genre's existence in film history since the silent era. Granted, *wuxia* novels may already have possessed a remarkable degree of richness and complexity, but it was Hu who succeeded in bringing these traits to the cinema, combining them with the acrobatics and pageantry of Peking Opera and the underpinnings of Zen Buddhism. Hu understood that films were experienced with the senses, and he fills the CinemaScope frame with a constant swirl of color and movement. Honing his craft on several previous *wuxia* films, *A Touch of Zen* stands as the zenith of Hu's career. **AT**

**Taiwan** (International, Lian Bang, Union) 200m Eastmancolor

**Director:** King Hu

**Producer:** Jung-Feng Sha, Shiqing Yang

**Screenplay:** King Hu, Songling Pu

**Photography:** Yeh-hsing Chou, Hui-ying Hua

**Music:** Tai Kong Ng, Dajiang Wu

**Cast:** Billy Chan, Ping-Yu Chang, Roy Chiao, Shih Chun, Hsue Han, Yin-Chieh Han, Feng Hsu, Ching-Ying Lam, Tien Miao, Hong Qiao, Peng Tien, Cien Tsao, Pai Ying

**Cannes Film Festival:** King Hu (grand technical prize), nomination (Golden Palm)

# BUTCH CASSIDY AND THE SUNDANCE KID (1969)

"What do you mean, you can't swim? The fall'll probably kill ya!" The iconic teaming of Paul Newman and Robert Redford was so magical—and so profitable, scoring the year's biggest hit—that this offbeat character study/action comedy in Western trappings and bathed in cinematographer Conrad Hall's Oscar-winning sepia hues has been a touchstone for bickering buddy pictures ever since.

Outlaws Butch (Newman) and The Kid (Redford, who subsequently named his Utah spread and film institute "Sundance") belong to the notorious Hole in the Wall Gang, but an over-the-top train robbery makes things too hot, with a tireless posse pursuit prompting the recurring question from Butch that became a catchphrase—"Who ARE those guys?"—and the decision to relaunch their career of crime abroad with the Kid's mistress Etta Place (Katharine Ross) in tow. The famous last act has its share of humor—memorably practicing "This is a robbery; back against the wall!" in Spanish to become the bandito scourge of Bolivia. But the film is immortal for its final image of the pair, freeze-framed as they run out into a shoot-'em-up with an army.

*Butch Cassidy and the Sundance Kid* is an utterly disarming combination of smart, original screenwriting, handsome visual treatment, and star power. With all the jokes and poses, there is still real interest in the well-defined, contrasting characters. Butch, the brains, is a smooth talker with vision, carried away by his enthusiasms, The Kid a golden boy with darkness within, cool and sardonic, ashamed to admit any weakness.

William Goldman's Oscar-winning screenplay is exciting, funny, and romantic, slyly satirizing and embracing Western legend (the real Butch and Sundance, naturally, were far from Newman's and Redford's charismatic charmers). It also has audacious nerve, as when The Kid accosts "teacher lady" Etta and orders her to undress at gunpoint. After the initial shock in a thus-far genial movie, it is an immense relief, a big laugh, and a turn-on when it becomes clear they are already well-acquainted. The Burt Bacharach song interlude, "Raindrops Keep Falling on My Head," is the only dated element. Movies just don't come more attractive and likeable than this one. **AE**

**U.S.** (Fox, Campanile) 110m BW (Sepiatone)/ Color

**Language:** English / Spanish

**Director:** George Roy Hill

**Producer:** John Foreman

**Screenplay:** William Goldman

**Photography:** Conrad L. Hall

**Music:** Burt Bacharach

**Cast:** Paul Newman, Robert Redford, Katharine Ross, Strother Martin, Henry Jones, Jeff Corey, George Furth, Cloris Leachman, Ted Cassidy, Kenneth Mars, Donnelly Rhodes, Jody Gilbert, Timothy Scott, Don Keefer, Charles Dierkop

**Oscar:** William Goldman (screenplay), Conrad L. Hall (photography), Burt Bacharach (music), Burt Bacharach, Hal David (song)

**Oscar nomination:** John Foreman (best picture), George Roy Hill (director), William E. Edmondson, David Dockendorf (sound)

# MIDNIGHT COWBOY (1969)

"I'm WALKIN' here!" Texan dishwasher Joe Buck (Jon Voight in a star-making performance) heads for New York City, to the infectious lament "Everybody's Talkin' At Me" sung by Harry Nilsson, believing wealthy women will be eager to pay a strapping stud for sex (the title is slang for a hustler). His tragicomic progress of the naïve newcomer is punctuated by sad, disturbing flashbacks, particularly a horrific assault on Joe and his girl Crazy Annie, played by the screenwriter Waldo Salt's daughter Jennifer. His "career path" in New York is a string of dispiriting encounters, unforgettably one with Sylvia Miles as a drab blond whose pitiful insistence she is "a gorgeous chick" sees the credulous Joe paying her.

Destitute and lonesome, Joe bonds with the crippled, consumptive con-man Enrico "Ratso" Rizzo (Dustin Hoffman, a compelling study of "street weasel"), who invites him to share his squat. Joe's hopes dim as his sordid failures mount, while as Ratso's chronic physical condition worsens his fantasies of a new life in Florida soar. Although the film is often called cynical and bleak, director John Schlesinger's view that it is ultimately a story of hope is justified by Joe's abandonment of his gigolo fantasy just when it seems attainable, for the sake of a real, human relationship. The British Schlesinger brought an acute eye to his American debut, finding a harsh vitality in the city that emphasized the characters' desperate isolation, and filming on location enhanced the seedy veirsimilitude.

Arguably the bravest choice ever made by Academy Award voters, *Midnight Cowboy* is the only X-rated movie to have won the Academy Award for Best Picture. The film also won Oscars for direction and Salt's adaptation of the James Leo Herlihy novel. The distinction prompted a rethink, and despite its then-thorny subject matter of homosexuality and prostitution the film's U.S. rating was changed to an R, its commercial success proving audiences were ready to embrace its maturity, frank realism, and the compassionate power of its performances. And despite the film's visual nods to 1960s fashion—most obviously in the Warhol circle's psychedelic loft party sequence—Schlesinger's focus on the relationship rather than style endures, and is always affecting. **AE**

**U.S.** (Florin, Jerome Hellman) 113m Color

**Director:** John Schlesinger

**Producer:** Jerome Hellman, Kenneth Utt

**Screenplay:** Waldo Salt, from novel by James Leo Herlihy

**Photography:** Adam Holender

**Music:** John Barry, Floyd Huddleston, Fred Neil

**Cast:** Dustin Hoffman, Jon Voight, Sylvia Miles, John McGiver, Brenda Vaccaro, Barnard Hughes, Ruth White, Jennifer Salt, Gilman Rankin, Gary Owens, T. Tom Marlow, George Eppersen, Al Scott, Linda Davis, J.T. Masters

**Oscar:** Jerome Hellman (best picture), John Schlesinger (director), Waldo Salt (screenplay)

**Oscar nomination:** Dustin Hoffman (actor), Jon Voight (actor), Sylvia Miles (actress in support role), Hugh A. Robertson (editing)

**Berlin International Film Festival:** John Schlesinger (OCIC award), nomination (Golden Bear)

**Italy / France** (PEA) 138m Technicolor

**Language:** Italian

**Director:** Federico Fellini

**Producer:** Alberto Grimaldi

**Screenplay:** Federico Fellini, Brunello Rondi, Bernardino Zapponi, from book by Petronius

**Photography:** Giuseppe Rotunno

**Music:** Tod Dockstader, Ilhan Mimaroglu, Nino Rota, Andrew Rudin

**Cast:** Martin Potter, Hiram Keller, Max Born, Salvo Randone, Mario Romagnoli, Magali Noël, Capucine, Alain Cuny, Fanfulla, Danica La Loggia, Giuseppe Sanvitale, Genius, Lucia Bosé, Joseph Wheeler, Hylette Adolphe

**Oscar nomination:** Federico Fellini (director)

# SATYRICON (1969)

The popularity of the European art film with American audiences began with the Italian neorealist films of the 1940s, and expanded with the engaged and visionary films of that movement's most influential successor, Federico Fellini. More famous, perhaps, for productions that examine the mores and difficulties of contemporary society, the director also, like many in the Italian film industry, showed an interest in historical reconstructions. *Satyricon* is an epic reimagining of Petronius's novella about life in the time of Nero. Fellini's sprawling film—the action ranges far and wide throughout the Roman world—was an immediate success with art-house audiences. Shocking scenes of debauchery, grotesquerie, and black comedy fully earned an R rating from the then recently installed ratings system, taking advantage of the new freedom of expression offered with the demise of the Production Code.

At once a quite faithful depiction of ancient Rome in the tradition of the Italian historical film and an evocation of the sexual revolution of the 1960s, *Satyricon* has much in common with the director's earlier films, particularly *La Dolce Vita* (1960). However, many reviewers felt it lacked the intellectual themes and meaningful stylizations of the director's earlier efforts. Certainly an emphasis on nudity and sex issued an appeal to certain segments within the "art cinema" audience of the period. Following his fragmentary source closely, Fellini offers a narrative of 25 distinct episodes, only loosely connected by the presence of the young and cynical Encolpio (Martin Potter). In the manner of Odysseus, Encolpio finds himself embarked on a continual series of adventures that threaten death and disaster, but from which he always manages to escape.

Encolpio's friendship with Ascilto (Hiram Keller), and their joint attraction to a handsome young slave boy (Max Born), is placed at the center of the film whose twists and turns are often difficult to follow. One thing is certain, however—Encolpio, much like the viewer, finds great difficulty understanding the morals and behavior of the many strange characters he encounters. The movie is filled with memorable sequences: a whorehouse filled with obese customers and prostitutes, animal sacrifices replete with rivers of blood, an earthquake that knocks down the building where Encolpio is staying, a nymphomaniac met in the desert whom Encolpio is called upon to satisfy, an encounter with a minotaur in the tradition of Theseus's famous adventure, and the startling richness of Trimalcione's (Mario Romagnoli) feast, whose guests, in the tradition of the nouveau riche, display an amazing vulgarity.

In the picaresque tradition, *Satyricon* ends not with some establishment of social stability, but with the hero's departure for even further adventures. A comment, perhaps (in the manner of Fellini's other works), on the hedonism and unrepentant materialism of modern society, the film is more memorable as a feast of surprising, even shocking images, with visual rhymes and repeated motifs imposing a kind of unity on the continuing flow. Released in 1972, Fellini's *Roma*, a kind of sequel, was unable to recapture the strange, compelling magic of the original. **RBP**

**Algeria / France** (Office National pour le Commerce et l'Industrie Cinématographique, Reggane, Valoria) 127m Eastmancolor

**Language:** French

**Director:** Costa-Gavras

**Producer:** Jacques Perrin, Ahmed Rachedi, Eric Schlumberger, Philippe d'Argila

**Screenplay:** Jorge Semprún, from novel by Vassilis Vassilikos

**Photography:** Raoul Coutard

**Music:** Mikis Theodorakis

**Cast:** Yves Montand, Irene Papas, Jean-Louis Trintignant, Jacques Perrin, Charles Denner, François Périer, Pierre Dux, Georges Géret, Bernard Fresson, Marcel Bozzuffi, Julien Guiomar, Magali Noël, Renato Salvatori, Habib Reda, Clotilde Joano

**Oscar:** Algeria (best foreign language film), Françoise Bonnot (editing)

**Oscar nomination:** Jacques Perrin, Ahmed Rachedi (best picture), Costa-Gavras (director), Jorge Semprún, Costa-Gavras (screenplay)

**Cannes Film Festival:** Jean-Louis Trintignant (actor), Costa-Gavras (jury prize), nomination (Golden Palm)

# Z (1969)

Costa-Gavras's fast-paced political drama confirmed its director's high standing in the international film community while bringing attention to the plight of Greek democratic rule, which was ousted following the shocking assassination of left-leaning professor and legislator Gregorios Lambrakis in Salonika in 1963.

Though *Z* is in French and stars mostly French actors, Costa-Gavras (a Greek émigré) is based on Vassili Vassilikos's fictionalized account of the Lambrakis affair. After a liberal politician (Yves Montand) is brutally murdered following a speech at a peace demonstration, the subsequent investigation brings to light a degree of corruption that threatens to bring down the entire military establishment. The sense of anxiety is heightened by the director's use of discontinuous, staccato editing techniques, balanced by the sharp cinematography of Raoul Coutard. In the words of Pauline Kael, "*Z* is almost intolerably exciting—a political thriller that builds up so much tension that you'll probably feel all knotted up by the time it's over." In addition to its stylistic accomplishments, the film boasts fine performances from Jean-Louis Trintignant as the examining magistrate and Irene Papas as Montand's wife. **SJS**

# IL CONFORMISTA (1969)
## THE CONFORMIST

**Italy / France / West Germany**
(Maran, Marianne, Mars) 115m
Technicolor
**Language:** Italian
**Director:** Bernardo Bertolucci
**Producer:** Giovanni Bertolucci, Maurizio Lodi-Fe
**Screenplay:** Bernardo Bertolucci, from novel by Alberto Moravia
**Photography:** Vittorio Storaro
**Music:** Georges Delerue
**Cast:** Jean-Louis Trintignant, Stefania Sandrelli, Gastone Moschin, Enzo Tarascio, Fosco Giachetti, José Quaglio, Dominique Sanda, Pierre Clémenti, Yvonne Sanson, Giuseppe Addobbati, Christian Aligny, Carlo Gaddi, Umberto Silvestri, Furio Pellerani
**Oscar nomination:** Bernardo Bertolucci (screenplay)
**Berlin International Film Festival:** Bernardo Bertolucci (interfilm award), (journalists' special award), nomination (Golden Bear)

The title of Bernardo Bertolucci's film refers to Marcello Clerici (Jean-Louis Trintignant), who readily embraces Mussolini's fascist government. He joins the secret police and is set up with a new life, including a new wife (Stefania Sandrelli), but his honeymoon has been linked with an ulterior motive. He is to assassinate an old college professor (Enzo Tarascio), a leader of the antifascist movement. However he begins to have doubts about the validity of his mission, provoked in part from repressed childhood memories.

Has there ever been a movie so utterly at odds with its title as *The Conformist*? Bertolucci's film couldn't be more conspicuously immodest in its audacious use of style; conformity appears to be the farthest element from its intent. The film features a nonlinear narrative, leaping back and forth across time with flashbacks to paint a more detailed portrait of Trintignant's complicated protagonist. Even more impressive is Vittorio Storaro's astounding cinematography. *The Conformist* makes such good use of color, camera placement, and design that the story often seems subservient to the images.

This is eye candy of the highest order, as undercover assassins and political intrigue have never looked so stylish. Yet the politics of Bertolucci's film never fade entirely to the background. *The Conformist* is, after all, a damning indictment of fascist collaborators. Trintignant is depicted as a weak-willed follower who ultimately pays the price for basing his life on the strong (and wrong) convictions of others.

Curiously, Bertolucci does cloud the story with a bit of dubious psychology. Trintignant's behavior, it seems, can be traced back to a sexual encounter in his childhood, a literal link between violence and sex at the root of his desire for order. It's as if his decision to join the fascist party will in some way keep his homosexuality in check. Like much of the film itself, the psychoanalysis is mostly surface and introduces little substance. But Bertolucci takes advantage of the muddy psychology by introducing copious symbolic references and images, some of them obvious, some of them oblique, but all never less than entrancing to watch. **JKl**

**U.S.** (BBS, Columbia, Pando, Raybert) 94m Technicolor

**Language:** English / Spanish

**Director:** Dennis Hopper

**Producer:** Peter Fonda, William Hayward, Bert Schneider

**Screenplay:** Peter Fonda, Dennis Hopper, Terry Southern

**Photography:** László Kovács

**Music:** Hoyt Axton, Mars Bonfire, Roger McGuinn, Jimi Hendrix

**Cast:** Peter Fonda, Dennis Hopper, Antonio Mendoza, Jack Nicholson, Phil Spector, Mac Mashourian, Warren Finnerty, Tita Colorado, Luke Askew, Luana Anders, Sabrina Scharf, Robert Walker Jr., Sandy Wyeth, Robert Ball, Carmen Phillips, Ellie Wood Walker

**Oscar nomination:** Peter Fonda, Dennis Hopper, Terry Southern (screenplay), Jack Nicholson (actor in support role)

**Cannes Film Festival:** Dennis Hopper (best first work), nomination (Golden Palm)

# EASY RIDER (1969)

*Easy Rider* is one of those movies whose importance goes far beyond its status as a work of art. The story is slight. Two young men, nicknamed Captain America (Peter Fonda) and Billy (Dennis Hopper), make a lot of money on some drugs that they buy South of the Border. Feeling rich, they decide to realize a long-standing ambition to visit New Orleans during Mardi Gras. They buy a couple of motorbikes and set off across country. On the way, they pass by some celebrated icons of the American West, including Monument Valley and Taos Pueblo. They drop in on a commune, run into an engaging small-town lawyer who helps them get out of jail, go on a drug trip with a couple of hookers in a New Orleans graveyard—all of which leads to the shock ending.

This seemingly inconsequential narrative proved to be one of the seminal films of the post-1968 generation in Hollywood, one of the first to put "the alternative society" on the screen. The two bikers are iconic figures, Hopper with his long hair, shades, and Indian necklace, Fonda with his stars and stripes helmet and bike. There is plentiful drug consumption (reputedly among cast and crew, as well as in the film itself). The two heroes go skinny-dipping with a couple of accommodating hippie girls and engage in marijuana-fueled campfire philosophizing with their lawyer friend George. Played by Jack Nicholson in his first big break, George is a rich man's son who rejects straight society, articulating most of what passes as the film's ideological position. In his view the country has gone to the dogs, terrified of the unconventional: "It's real hard to be free when you're bought and sold in the marketplace."

*Easy Rider* challenged much of the conventional Hollywood wisdom. It's a film by and for the young (Hopper was only 32 when he directed it), with music by such stalwarts of the counterculture as Steppenwolf, Jimi Hendrix, and Bob Dylan. None of the principals (Nicholson, Hopper, and Fonda) were big stars. The narrative is as freewheeling as the characters. There's no conventional love story, and the film has a brutally unhappy ending. Made for very little money, *Easy Rider* was a huge box-office success. It helped pave the way for works that challenged conventional Hollywood ideas, including further Jack Nicholson vehicles such as *Five Easy Pieces* and *The King of Marvin Gardens.*

Subsequently, there has been a lively disagreement as to who did exactly what on the film. Hopper has laid claim to being its "auteur," not only directing and starring but also in his view responsible for the script. Others see it differently, contending that the most articulate scenes in the film, as for example the conversations involving George, were carefully scripted in advance by Terry Southern, whose previous screen credits included Stanley Kubrick's *Dr. Strangelove, or How I Learned to Stop Worrying and Love the Bomb.* All agree on one thing, though—that the title was Southern's invention. **EB**

**U.S.** (Osti) 75m BW
**Director:** Frederick Wiseman
**Producer:** Frederick Wiseman
**Screenplay:** Frederick Wiseman
**Photography:** Richard Leiterman

# HIGH SCHOOL (1969)

Frederick Wiseman's second film is one of the most horrifying and ambiguous of his institutional studies. The film is a documentary view of Northeast High School in Philadelphia, apparently a public school serving a largely white, middle-class community. From the start, Wiseman makes it clear that his focus is on the authoritarianism of the teachers and administrators, the failure of the school to foster self-expression and critical thinking, and the emphasis on meaningless rituals and forms.

A Spanish teacher makes her students repeat the words "Jean-Paul Sartre" and "existentialista," with apparently no discussion of who Sartre is or what existential philosophy is about. An English teacher recites the poem "Casey at the Bat" to a room of 16-year-olds and is later heard to offer the inspirational wisdom, "The dictionary is the only place where success comes before work." A student protesting an imposed detention is told that unquestioning acceptance of punishment is a mark of maturity.

A college counselor advises one of her charges to prepare for the worst by applying to an inexpensive school with low academic standards. A gynecologist giving a sex-education lecture to an auditorium full of boys refers to the hymen as a "cherry" and reaps applause for joking that he gets paid to put his finger into vaginas. Female students must endure an inane calisthenics session in gym class (to the accompaniment of the 1910 Fruitgum Company's mind-numbing "Simon Says") and a fashion-show rehearsal in which a teacher (who must have graduated from the same modeling school as the millionaire's wife on *Gilligan's Island*) blithely describes a girl, in the latter's presence and in front of her peers, as having "a weight problem."

In the film's blood-freezing ending, a principal reads a letter she received from a recent graduate of the school, now serving in Vietnam, where he has volunteered for a dangerous mission. Thanking the school for the lessons he learned there, the student calls himself "only a body doing a job." In the last sounds heard in the film, the woman reading the letter claims that it proves that "we are very successful at Northeast High School." No filmmaker has ever cut to black with more stunning effect. Wiseman allows the principal's words, and the world view behind them, to stand out naked against the film's slatelike silence.

The portrait isn't entirely negative. Never a heavy-handed slagging of obvious problems, Wisemanian social criticism is based on a detailed and ironic exposition of situational and behavioral facts. Above all, Wiseman's filmmaking, sensitive to how his subjects reveal themselves, respects the humanity of even the most reprehensible among them. Thus he challenges the antipathies, no less than the complicities, of the viewer. Like Renoir, Wiseman reminds us that "everyone has his reasons"—a message that is no more reassuring in *High School* than it is in *La règle du jeu*. **CFu**

# IN THE YEAR OF THE PIG (1969)

**U.S.** (Pathé) 101m BW
**Director:** Emile de Antonio
**Producer:** Vincent Hanlon, Emile de Antonio
**Photography:** Jean-Jacques Rochut
**Cast:** Harry S. Ashmore, Daniel Berrigan, Joseph Buttinger, William R. Corson, Philippe Devillers, David Halberstam, Roger Hillsman, Jean Lacouture, Kenneth P. Landon, Thruston B. Morton, Paul Mus, Charlton Osburn, Harrison Salisbury, Ilya Todd, John Toller, David K. Tuck, David Werfel, John White
**Oscar nomination:** Emile de Antonio (documentary)

Argued through indirect means, Emile de Antonio's *In the Year of the Pig* mounts an impressive attack on American foreign policy and the war in Vietnam. One result is an extraordinarily provocative documentary. Another is a textbook example of flaws within the American sensibility that are most easily identified as simple arrogance.

Opening with images of protest, the film sketches a backdrop for American involvement in Southeast Asia, ostensibly to defend the world from communist infiltration, necessitating a digression into the history of colonialism. First up is China, then various European powers before France's expulsion at Dien Bien Phu in 1954. Throughout these sequences, interesting as they may be, de Antonio's film wastes precious little time getting to a point. Namely, that all Vietnam wars have been in no way inevitable, humane, or helpful in assisting the indigenous population form a sovereign nation when this much has always seemed to be their purpose.

Zeroing in on found footage or else relying on carefully edited interviews, the film manipulates talking heads into its argument without overtly stating its point. In this way, de Antonio and his production staff remain carefully off-screen even though their imprint is everywhere present. Thus the included historical figures produce discursive positions along the twin axes of fame and context.

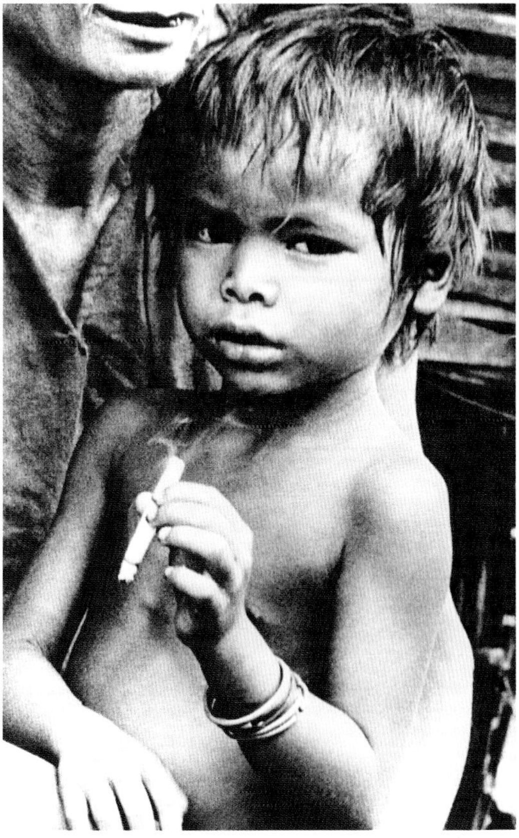

Expanding the former are a veritable "who's who" collection of important leaders, writers, and critics. Naturally certain of these are better known, including American presidents Dwight Eisenhower, John Kennedy, Lyndon Johnson, Richard Nixon, and Gerald Ford, Vietnamese hero Ho Chi Minh, red-baiter Joseph McCarthy, and war hawk Robert McNamara. Yet the weight of gold is supplied by those figures providing context rather than political drumbeats.

Among them David Halberstam, Jean de Lattre de Tassigny, Harry S. Ashmore, Hubert Humphrey, and even George S. Patton III enliven the morass from which American soldiers were dispatched to Vietnam. Of course, some of these figures have since become synonymous with establishment thinking. In 1969, however, their views formed the basis of this treatise and one of the more successful antiwar, if at moments anti-American, diatribes on the evils of political expediency. **GC-Q**

**U.S.** (Warner Bros./Seven Arts) 145m Technicolor
**Language:** English / Spanish
**Director:** Sam Peckinpah
**Producer:** Phil Feldman, Roy N. Sickner
**Screenplay:** Walon Green, Roy N. Sickner, Sam Peckinpah
**Photography:** Lucien Ballard
**Music:** Jerry Fielding
**Cast:** William Holden, Ernest Borgnine, Robert Ryan, Edmond O'Brien, Warren Oates, Jaime Sánchez, Ben Johnson, Emilio Fernández, Strother Martin, L.Q. Jones, Albert Dekker, Bo Hopkins, Dub Taylor, Paul Harper, Jorge Russek
**Oscar nomination:** Walon Green, Roy N. Sickner, Sam Peckinpah (screenplay), Jerry Fielding (music)

# THE WILD BUNCH (1969)

A Hemingwayesque answer to the Erich Segal-ish Western revisionism of *Butch Cassidy and the Sundance Kid* (1969), *The Wild Bunch* is at once disgusting and romantic, investigating the thesis that "even the worst of us" want to be children again—"perhaps the worst of us most of all." Director Sam Peckinpah, in his breakthrough picture, opens with innocent children pouring ants onto scorpions and setting fire to the nest as the Bunch ride into town disguised as the U.S. Army. Continually cutting away to kids watching the action, they imitate the grown-up bang-bang games and finally take part. Even the repulsive General Mapache (Emilio Fernandez) is hero-worshipped by a boy who picks up a gun to avenge his death. The opening bank raid is a complete botch as the corrupt railroad tycoon lures the Bunch into town with bags of washers disguised as payroll—"silver rings," gasps a hopeful idiot when the ruse is revealed. A shoot-out between the bandits and a crew of degenerate bounty hunters leads to the deaths of many innocents as a temperance parade marches into the gunfire—a scene that must have delighted the hard-drinking Peckinpah.

Violent but honorable badman Pike Bishop (William Holden) is pursued by his former friend Deke Thornton (Robert Ryan). Pike is admired by his sidekick Dutch (Ernest Borgnine) and tagalong Mexican (Jaime Sánchez), tolerated by the fractious, grumpy, childish Gorch brothers (Warren Oates, Ben Johnson), and looked over by father figure Freddy Sykes (Edmond O'Brien), though he abandoned the old man's crazy grandson (Bo Hopkins) during the initial raid. With the American frontier closing down, the Bunch find themselves appalled by the tyranny of pre-Revolutionary Mexico as Mapache, with his German advisors, represents a legitimate government but acts far worse than the most evil outlaws. In a classic "last stand," the grizzled heroes opt to take on Mapache's whole town in order to stick up for their fallen comrade. Peckinpah realized that the shots of four gunmen walking through the streets to the showdown are the necessary setup for the brilliantly edited, semi-slow-motion orgy of mass destruction that climaxes the picture as the Bunch die, taking an entire army with them, spurting blood like burst firehoses.

Set in 1913, at the end of the era of the Western outlaw, *The Wild Bunch* drags the cowboy movie myth into an age of mass-produced murder symbolized aptly by the Gatling gun and the Model-T Ford. Shot through with whiskery Western eccentricity, including a hilarious double act from L.Q. Jones and Strother Martin as human vultures ("This one's got gold in his teeth") and a great deal of picturesque dialogue ("Well, kiss my sister's black cat's ass"), this was the film that reclaimed the American tradition of the Western back from the Italians and proved that Peckinpah could pop more blood capsules than Sergio Leone. Famous at first for its gory violence, *The Wild Bunch* has lasted for its elegiac lyricism ("It ain't like it used to be, but it'll do"), strong performances, and sense of dead-end honor. **KN**

**U.S.S.R.** (Mosfilm) 181m BW / Color
**Language:** Russian / Italian
**Director:** Andrei Tarkovsky
**Producer:** Tamara Ogorodnikova
**Screenplay:** Andrei Konchalovsky, Andrei Tarkovsky
**Photography:** Vadim Yusov
**Music:** Vyacheslav Ovchinnikov
**Cast:** Anatoli Solonitsyn, Ivan Lapikov, Nikolai Grinko, Nikolai Sergeyev, Irma Raush, Nikolai Burlyayev, Yuri Nazarov, Yuri Nikulin, Rolan Bykov, Nikolai Grabbe, Mikhail Kononov, Stepan Krylov, Irina Miroshnichenko, Bolot Bejshenaliyev
**Cannes Film Festival:** Andrei Tarkovsky (FIPRESCI award)

# ANDREI RUBLYOV (1969)
## ANDREI RUBLEV

It's a mystery. Not a whispered mystery, but a mystery sung by the strong voice of gigantic bells, shouted by the storms, illuminated by the bonfires of war, of faith, of love. The origin of this powerful mystery is perfectly obvious: Andrei films Andrei. Evoking the similarities between Andrei Rublev (played here by Anatoli Solonitsyn), the 15th-century monk who became the master of icon painting, and Andrei Tarkovsky, the great 20th-century Soviet filmmaker, is not the goal. It is more like the huge caldron in which fear and hope, personal dedication (bordering on madness), and mass impulse can be heated up together.

Certainly, the film concerns the relationships between man and God, man and nature, the artist and the people, the artist and the art form, and the Russian and his land as a physical and mystical element. But as rich as *Andrei Rublev* might be on the thematic level (and rich it is, as much today as when it was made as a weapon against the Soviet regime), Tarkovsky's masterpiece fresco is not made out of ideas. It is made out of light and darkness, of noise and silence, of human faces and rough material. It is a telluric move and a magical stay, suspended above the void. Dark, sensual, and deeply moving, the film is a mystery, in the best sense of the word. **J-MF**

# LE BOUCHER (1969)
## THE BUTCHER

**France / Italy** (Euro International, La Boétie) 93m Eastmancolor
**Language:** French
**Director:** Claude Chabrol
**Producer:** André Génovès
**Screenplay:** Claude Chabrol
**Photography:** Jean Rabier
**Music:** Pierre Jansen
**Cast:** Stéphane Audran, Jean Yanne, Anthony Pass, Pascal Ferone, Mario Beccara, William Guérault, Roger Rudel

It is unusual for a single film to reshape the whole perception of the work of a major filmmaker. Claude Chabrol was seen as the cruel portraitist of the French bourgeoisie, drawing with dark ink and a ferocious sense of humor the complexities lying beyond the moral common law, the conformism of manners, the clichés of "good" and "bad" that mask the reality of impulses, the narrative conventions that destroy the possibility of apprehending the depths of human nature. And he certainly was all that, which is saying quite a lot. But he was not just that.

In 1969, during the boiling point of an ideological heating-up of the entire French society, when Chabrol seemed to be quite obviously in the grip of History, he took an incredible step back, to get a larger view, a broader comprehension of the world as a cosmic whole, beyond good and evil. The resulting film, *Le Boucher*, is a love story with a serial killer. This is what filmmaking can do: allow for the peaceful merging of two genres that seem to exclude one another, the murder story and the romance. Taking place in a remote portion of the Garden of Eden in southern France, Chabrol allows the intensity of his wonderful actors, Jean Yanne and Stéphane Audran, to burn slowly. The pair underplay their absurd parts—this absurdity is the flesh and bone of the terrestrial (not only human) condition—and let everything go to catastrophe.

He loved her, she was quite fond of him, and he killed young girls. The butcher Popaul (Yanne) is the flesh, the school headmistress (Audran) the mind. This is the state of things, water and blood and dark forces separate them, but that isn't a reason not to pay attention to each other, not to care for someone so different from yourself—quite the opposite, in fact. But Paradise is lost forever, and this too is what Chabrol's subtle cinema is about. Don't bother to question the director on this point: he is far too elegant and smart to admit it, and prefers instead to hide behind his social tales and genre games. Just enter the smooth sadness of *Le Boucher*. **J-MF**

**U.S.S.R. / Armenia** (Armenfilm) 73m Color

**Language:** Armenian

**Director:** Sergei Parajanov, Sergei Yutkevich

**Screenplay:** Sergei Parajanov, from the poetry of Sayat Nova

**Photography:** A. Samvelyan, Martyn Shakhbazyan, Suren Shakhbazyan

**Music:** Tigran Mansuryan

**Cast:** Sofiko Chiaureli, Melkon Aleksanyan, Vilen Galstyan, Giorgi Gegechkori, Spartak Bagashvili, Medea Djaparidze, Onik Minasyan

# SAYAT NOVA (1969)
## THE COLOR OF POMEGRANATES

Sergei Paradjanov's greatest film is also his most radical and obscure. It inaugurated the most serious difficulties he had with Russian authorities that culminated in his being sent to prison in 1973, for homosexuality and other charges—after having already been attacked as a formalist, a Ukrainian nationalist, and an ideological deviant. He was not able to make another film for more than a decade, and was only able to complete one further feature before he died of cancer in 1990. Born to an Armenian family in Georgia in 1924, Paradjanov suffered throughout much of his life for his celebration of non-Russian cultures as well as his defiance of bureaucracy, and this groundbreaking masterpiece remains the most extreme expression of his eccentric vision.

A mystical and historical mosaic about the life, work, and inner world of 18th-century Armenian poet Aruthin Sayadin, popularly known as Sayat Nova (the "King of Song"), *The Color of Pomegranates* was previously available only in an ethnically "dry-cleaned" Russian version. The superior original version, found in an Armenian studio in the early 1990s, can't be regarded as definitive, but it's certainly the finest available: some shots and sequences are new, some are positioned differently, and, of particular advantage to Western viewers, much more of the poetry is subtitled.

In both versions, the striking use of tableau-like framing recalls the shallow space of movies made roughly a century ago, whereas the gorgeous uses of color and the wild poetic and metaphoric conceits seem to derive from some utopian cinema of the future. The opening quotation from Sayadin can be read as the director's disclaimer: "My water is of a very special kind, / Not everyone can drink it. / My writing is of a very special kind, / Not everyone can read it. / My foundation's made not of sand, / But of solid granite." But we don't have to decode the images in any systematic way to experience their haunting power. The opening shots show three pomegranates oozing red juice on a white tablecloth, a bloodstained dagger, bare feet crushing grapes, a fish (which promptly becomes three fish) flopping between two pieces of driftwood, and water falling on books. At once "difficult" and immediate, cryptic and ravishing, the stark images throughout resemble Persian miniatures infused with ecstasy. **JRos**

## KES (1969)

**G.B.** (Kestrel, Woodfall) 110m
Technicolor

**Director:** Ken Loach

**Producer:** Tony Garnett

**Screenplay:** Tony Garnett, Ken Loach, from the novel *A Kestrel For A Knave* by Barry Hines

**Photography:** Chris Menges

**Music:** John Cameron

**Cast:** David Bradley, Freddie Fletcher, Lynne Perrie, Colin Welland, Brian Glover, Bob Bowes, Bernard Atha, Laurence Bould, Joey Kaye, Ted Carroll, Robert Naylor, Agnes Drumgoon, George Speed, Desmond Guthrie, Zoe Sutherland

With *Kes*, the director's first feature, Ken Loach essentially transferred the realist methodology he'd been using in his television work and proffered a statement of intent for his future films. Working with Barry Hines on an adaptation of the latter's novel, Loach depicts the brief opportunity of escape that opens up when a young Barnsley boy (David Bradley) finds and trains a kestrel (falcon). His growing interest in the art of falconry, coupled with his admiration for the bird's own hunting skills and proud independence, allows him at least to glimpse an alternative to the tediously oppressive present and uninvitingly constricted future of his life in the working-class English town.

Loach avoids the sentimental clichés of many earlier films set in Britain's industrial north by focusing not on grim, grimy streets and chimneys but on how human relationships and aspirations are stunted and twisted by a continuous diet of economic and cultural deprivation. Hence the emotional force of those scenes in which the lad's enthusiasm—long-neglected rather than nourished by family, friends, and all but one teacher—is betrayed and, finally, extinguished. And Chris Menges's typically fine camerawork catches the power of the falcon in flight, perfectly balancing the bird's very real agility with its value as a symbol of intuitive freedom. **GA**

## TRISTANA (1970)

**France / Italy / Spain** (Corona, Selenia, Talía, Época) 95m
Eastmancolor

**Language:** Spanish

**Director:** Luis Buñuel

**Producer:** Luis Buñuel, Robert Dorfmann

**Screenplay:** Julio Alejandro, Luis Buñuel, from novel by Benito Pérez Galdós

**Photography:** José F. Aguayo

**Nonoriginal music:** Frédéric Chopin

**Cast:** Catherine Deneuve, Fernando Rey, Franco Nero, Lola Gaos, Antonio Casas, Jesús Fernández, Vicente Solar, José Calvo, Fernando Cebrián, Antonio Ferrandis, José María Caffarel, Cándida Losada, Joaquín Pamplona, Mary Paz Pondal, Juanjo Menéndez

**Oscar nomination:** Spain (best foreign language film)

It is often said that the defining characteristic of classicists from John Ford to Clint Eastwood is the invisibility of their style. But even their films look ostentatious and contrived next to the late work of Luis Buñuel. What makes *Tristana* so disquieting is the seeming simplicity of its manner and the sense of it unfolding, with rigorous and brutal logic, into an inevitable tragedy.

Buñuel had nursed this adaptation of Benito Pérez Galdós's classic novel since 1963. It tackles one of his favorite topics: the seduction and corruption of an innocent, Tristana (Catherine Deneuve), by the much older Don Lope (Fernando Rey), a gentleman whose stated political ideals are far more radical than his treatment of women. Tristana survives this oppression, after the loss of one leg, by doubling its viciousness and spreading its effects—as in the disturbing scene where she exhibits her body to the young servant, Saturno (Jesús Fernández).

Is *Tristana* a surrealist film? Not obviously, but profoundly: A subterranean world of unconscious drives, a parallel dimension, seems to lurk just beneath the surface of everything Buñuel presents—peeking out only in the final glimpse of how this sad story could have headed in another direction altogether. **AM**

**U.S.** (BBS, Columbia, Raybert) 96m Technicolor

**Director:** Bob Rafelson

**Producer:** Bob Rafelson, Richard Wechsler

**Screenplay:** Carole Eastman, Bob Rafelson

**Photography:** László Kovács

**Music:** Bach, Chopin, Mozart

**Cast:** Jack Nicholson, Karen Black, Billy Green Bush, Fannie Flagg, Sally Struthers, Marlena MacGuire, Richard Stahl, Lois Smith, Helena Kallianiotes, Toni Basil, Lorna Thayer, Susan Anspach, Ralph Waite, William Challee, John P. Ryan

**Oscar nomination:** Bob Rafelson, Richard Wechsler (best picture), Bob Rafelson, Carole Eastman (screenplay), Jack Nicholson (actor), Karen Black (actress in support role)

# FIVE EASY PIECES (1970)

If for nothing else, Bob Rafelson's *Five Easy Pieces* is worth seeing for the pleasure of watching Jack Nicholson unable to get an order of toast. Nicholson's first star turn after gaining notoriety in his supporting role as the lawyer in *Easy Rider* (1969) is as Robert Dupea, an oil rigger living in a trailer park with his waitress girlfriend, Rayette (Karen Black). Robert decides to take a road trip up the West Coast to reconcile with his sick father. Structured around the road trip and Robert's return home, the film has a meandering, capricious style ideally suited to the revelation of character and savoring the actors' nuanced performances in a series of set pieces.

It is fascinating to see the beginnings of Nicholson's persona here, as a charismatic antihero with an edge of violence and vulnerability. Black is outstanding as a good-time girl, a little past her prime, who must slowly watch as she loses Robert to his past. The film is a thoughtful, meticulous character study that is ultimately extremely moving and surprising. *Five Easy Pieces* comes at the beginning of an innovative and fruitful period of American filmmaking, and is an excellent introduction to it. **RH**

# EL TOPO (1970)

During the 1960s and early 1970s, when the Western was splintering and mutating with Spaghetti Westerns introducing Marxist subtexts and odd attempts to meld comedy and the musical in films like *Cat Ballou* and *Paint Your Wagon*, *El Topo* stood out as the quintessential head-trip Western.

Taking his cue from Fellini, writer-director-star Alejandro Jodorowsky takes the deceptively simple story of a gunfighter who sets out to defeat the greatest gunslingers of the land and turns it into a allegory for man's quest for enlightenment. El Topo the gunslinger journeys across a desert filled with brutal gangs and grotesque, surreal warriors, who each symbolize a different stage in the hero's journey. There's an endless parade of biblical references, Freudian motifs, and Jungian symbols. Jodorowsky leaves nothing to chance. El Topo starts out vain and selfish, eager to attain power and glory, only to find himself bereft and empty once he achieves his goal. Realizing the futility of his mission, he renounces his worldly ambitions and need to satisfy his ego. He undergoes a symbolic death before returning from the desert a cleansed, empty vessel with the weight of the world's suffering on his shoulders, trying to protect a band of cripples and deformed, childlike freaks. Faced with a world as brutal and uncaring as the one he left, and a vengeful son he abandoned, he has no choice but to make one last sacrifice, an act of self-immolation that evokes the image of the monk who burned himself to death to protest against War and Destruction.

Unlike other Westerns, *El Topo* makes no pretense at naturalism or historical accuracy. The world depicted is a highly personal landscape, a setting for the cycle of Life, Death, and Rebirth. Granted, it could be said that Jodorowsky lays it on a bit thick, that his casting himself as the lead is the height of hubris and narcissism. But *El Topo* is fascinating for being a product of its time, a document of the lessons and philosophies people were then studying, and their fears, both conscious and unconscious. *El Topo* is still utterly unique in the history of film. **AT**

**Mexico** (Panicas) 125m Color
**Language:** Spanish
**Director:** Alejandro Jodorowsky
**Producer:** Juan López Moctezuma, Moshe Rosemberg, Roberto Viskin
**Screenplay:** Alejandro Jodorowsky
**Photography:** Rafael Corkidi
**Music:** Alejandro Jodorowsky, Nacho Méndez
**Cast:** Alejandro Jodorowsky, Brontis Jodorowsky, José Legarreta, Man Alfonso Arau, José Luis Fernández, Alf Junco, Gerardo Cepeda, René Barrera, René Alís, Federico Gonzáles, Pablo Leder, Giuliano Girini Sasseroli, Cristian Merkel, Aldo Grumelli, Mara Lorenzio

**U.S.** (Wadleigh-Maurice, Warner Bros.) 184m Technicolor

**Director:** Michael Wadleigh

**Producer:** Bob Maurice

**Photography:** Don Lenzer, David Myers, Richard Pearce, Michael Wadleigh, Al Wertheimer

**Music:** Sly Stone, Jimi Hendrix, John Lennon & Paul McCartney, Joni Mitchell, Alan Wilson

**Cast:** Richie Havens, Joan Baez, Roger Daltrey, John Entwistle, Keith Moon, Pete Townshend, Joe Cocker, Country Joe McDonald, Arlo Guthrie, David Crosby, Graham Nash, Stephen Stills, Alvin Lee, John Sebastian, Carlos Santana, Sly Stone, Jimi Hendrix, 10 Years After, Richard Alvarez, Lennie Baker, Jon Bauman, Canned Heat, Jack Casady, Chick Churchill, Johnny Contardo, Crosby Stills Nash & Young, Spencer Dryden, Lawrence Ferlinghetti, Jerry Garcia, Bill Graham, Frederick Greene, Bob Harvey, Bob Hite, Jefferson Airplane, Janis Joplin, Jorma Kaukonen, Michael Lang, Ric Lee, Leo Lyons, Jocko Marcellino, Hugh Romney, Sha-Na-Na, Group, Screamin Scott' Simon, Grace Slick, The Who, Johnny Winter, Max Yasgur, Donald York, Swami Satchidananda, Sidney Westerfield

**Oscar:** Bob Maurice (documentary)

**Oscar nomination:** Thelma Schoonmaker (editing), Dan Wallin, Larry Johnson (sound)

# WOODSTOCK (1970)

The 1960s generation crashed headlong into unchecked idealism and the pressures of practical reality when the last Baby Boomers reached majority age at the end of the decade. Thereafter the United States was increasingly embroiled in varied generational conflicts, not least of which centered on popular music and growing ambivalence about the overall American project.

Summer 1969 was therefore a turning point and a ripple in time. Although Boomers had already splintered into factions pursuing an array of cultural values from strictest patriotism to hallucinogenic drugs, what was needed was a milestone event to convey the fractured spirit of innocence on the cusp of experience. The three day Woodstock Music and Art Festival of Bethel, New York provided just such a punctuation mark and became a historical keynote. Its cultural currency has since been co-opted to sell soft drinks and new musical acts, although it continues to be the mirror through which the state of '60s youth is displayed in a flash of celebration and song.

As captured by documentarian Michael Wadleigh, who employed, among others, Martin Scorsese, George Lucas, and Thelma Schoonmaker on the picture, the best-laid plans of Woodstock's concert promoters are seen failing the realities of the event. Set in a paddock some distance from East Coast urban centers and with few approaching surface roads, a storm turns the Woodstock fields into a big mud puddle. Concert-goers show up in the thousands, way over estimates, to be serenaded by the best of R&B, rock, folk, and funk. Flooded and inconvenienced as they are, they become the most famous massed music audience for one of the greatest performance events ever staged.

That the concert was a money-loser is an interesting footnote. Regardless of this, subsequent generations see Woodstock as *the* iconic outdoor rock concert. The music, the atmosphere, the mythology, all of it together now symbolizes everything lost in the 1970s and the resulting Baby Boomlet. The point is made most forcefully in the brilliant, nearly four-hours long director's cut of Wadleigh's film, since mimicked by innumerable music-oriented movies and media spectacles. *Woodstock*'s split-screen techniques, stereophonic sound recording, simultaneous and multiple-coverage of events, and detached viewpoint fill the screen with absolutely accurate observations. The attitude of reportage further contributes to the film's value as a snapshot of the times without imposing too much of an authorial point of view, but still looking on with wonder now lost but once gloriously true.

Vignettes center on concert-goers dealing with festival discomforts and townies reacting to the waves of outsiders streaming into their village. Bad acid makes its way through the crowd. Marriage proposals are matched. Food is airlifted in to help relieve a state of emergency. People skinny dip, clean outhouses, smoke pot, smile, and sleep, all in the midst of many musical highlights, including an outstanding acoustic set by Crosby, Stills, and Nash, an appearance by Janis Joplin, the garage-band style of Canned Heat, and an improvised riff by Santana. **GC-Q**

**G.B. / Poland / West Germany**
(Bavaria Atelier, COKG, Kettledrum, Maran) 88m Eastmancolor
**Director:** Jerzy Skolimowski
**Producer:** Helmut Jedele
**Screenplay:** Jerzy Gruza, Jerzy Skolimowski, Boleslaw Sulik
**Photography:** Charly Steinberger
**Music:** The Can, Cat Stevens
**Cast:** Jane Asher, Sean Barry-Weske, Erica Beer, Will Danin, Diana Dors, Dieter Eppler, Cheryl Hall, Anne-Marie Kuster, Burt Kwouk, Karl Ludwig Lindt, Eduard Linkers, Anita Lochner, Louise Martini, Peter Martin, Ursula Mellin, John Moulder-Brown, Christina Paul, Gerald Rowland, Christopher Sandford, Jerzy Skolimowski, Uli Steigberg, Karl Michael Vogler, Erika Wackernagel

# DEEP END (1970)

Jerzy Skolimowski's first English-language film after writing Roman Polanski's *Knife in the Water* is a remarkable excursion into the mind of a sexually frustrated 15-year-old boy. *Deep End* functions as both a black sex comedy and a rite-of-passage tale with tragic consequences for all involved.

John Moulder-Brown plays the youth with a comedic sensitivity that darkens as the object of his desire rebuffs his advances, while Jane Asher plays the young woman who is his obsession with great insight, her performance as Susan semi-improvised to great effect. Both young people are trapped in the seedy world of the Newford Bathhouse, filled with unhappy people who live for sex and soccer. Susan uses her looks to make extra money with the clients and suggests the same to Brown. He is disgusted with her lifestyle and longs to take her away from it all.

Skolimowski shows an astute insight into the eccentricities of the British, and captures a side of the so-called swinging London that is both ugly and faded with a real sense of impending spiritual breakdown. The film attains a voyeuristic tone as Moulder-Brown searches though Soho's seedy strip joints until he steals a cardboard cutout of Susan for a final fantasy of his mental deep end. A date film to see before you die! **DDV**

**Italy** (RAI, Red Film) 100m Eastmancolor
**Language:** Italian
**Director:** Bernardo Bertolucci
**Producer:** Giovanni Bertolucci
**Screenplay:** Bernardo Bertolucci, Eduardo de Gregorio, Marilù Parolini, from the story *Theme of the Traitor and Hero* by Jorge Luis Borges
**Photography:** Franco Di Giacomo, Vittorio Storaro
**Nonoriginal Music:** Arnold Schönberg, Giuseppe Verdi
**Cast:** Giulio Brogi, Alida Valli, Pippo Campanini, Franco Giovanelli, Tino Scotti

# LA STRATEGIA DEL RAGNO (1970)
## THE SPIDER'S STRATAGEM

Bertolucci's *The Spider's Stratagem* is, for many, the definitive European art film. The narrative is fragmented, the characters behave inconsistently, it's nearly impossible to keep track of time and/or place, and viewers are left with an overall impression of uncertainty. All of this, of course, is there by design. Bertolucci, like Michelangelo Antonioni, Alain Resnais, and others, was interested in having us question even those elements of film comprehension which we normally take for granted: story, plot, time, space, action. This is the cinema of the anti-Hollywood.

But don't let this keep you away from the film. *The Spider's Stratagem* (a title that is never explained) is challenging, but few pictures encourage such delightful aesthetic consternation: if you go into it *not* expecting to have any questions answered, you will be richly rewarded.

The story concerns a man's (Giulio Brogi) journey to his father's hometown, where he intends to uncover the circumstances of his questionable political activities. But this simple quest soon takes over the protagonist's life, and, in fact, Bertolucci hints that he begins not only to fall in love with his father's former lover but also to become his own father. Through clever, innovative editing and framing, Bertolucci consistently toys with our narrative expectations. *The Spider's Stratagem* is a baffling film, to be sure, but we are being manipulated by the hands of a master. **EdeS**

# LITTLE BIG MAN (1970)

Thomas Berger's novel (published in 1964), on which Arthur Penn's *Little Big Man* is based, is one of the funniest and most original works of Western fiction. It relates the picaresque adventures of Jack Crabb, in the course of which he is several times captured by Indians, becomes a Western gunfighter, meets Wild Bill Hickok, and joins General Custer at the Battle of the Little Big Horn. In the movie, Jack is played by Dustin Hoffman, and is first encountered at the advanced age of 111 by an earnest researcher who swallows whole his unlikely tale.

What follows is a thoroughly entertaining debunking of the Western myth, showing Custer to be a vainglorious bully and Hickok an anxious neurotic. By contrast, the Cheyenne, who adopt Jack into the tribe, are a courteous and life-loving people, especially in the person of Old Lodge Skins, wonderfully played by Chief Dan George. The depiction of an attack on a Cheyenne camp by Custer's Seventh Cavalry (based on the 1868 Massacre of the Washita) hardly bothers to disguise its obvious reference to the Vietnam War, which was raging at the time the film was made, and in particular to the infamous My Lai Massacre. **EB**

**U.S.** (Cinema Center 100 Productions, Stockbridge-Hiller Productions) 147m Technicolor

**Director:** Arthur Penn

**Producer:** Gene Lasko, Stuart Millar

**Screenplay:** Calder Willingham, from novel by Thomas Berger

**Photography:** Harry Stradling Jr.

**Music:** John Hammond

**Cast:** Dustin Hoffman, Faye Dunaway, Chief Dan George, Martin Balsam, Richard Mulligan, Jeff Corey, Aimée Eccles, Kelly Jean Peters, Carole Androsky, Robert Little Star, Cal Bellini, Ruben Moreno, Steve Shemayne, William Hickey, James Anderson

**Oscar nomination:** Chief Dan George (actor in support role)

**Czechoslovakia** (Barrandov) 94m BW
**Language:** Czech
**Director:** Karel Kachyna
**Producer:** Karel Vejrík
**Screenplay:** Karel Kachyna, Jan Procházka, Ladislav Winkelhöfer
**Photography:** Josef Illig
**Music:** Svatopluk Havelka
**Cast:** Jirina Bohdalová, Radoslav Brzobohaty, Jirí Císler, Miroslav Holub, Borivoj Navrátil, Gustav Opocensky, Lubor Tokos
**Cannes Film Festival:** Karel Kachyna nomination (Golden Palm)

# UCHO (1970)
## THE EAR

Shot under the watchful eyes of the Soviet occupying forces, Karel Kachyna's daring political drama was withheld from circulation immediately upon completion. It wasn't until 1989 that the picture was first screened to art-house audiences. Although *The Ear*'s direct criticism of the rule of right wing party leader Gustave Husák distinguishes Kachyna from other former New Wave Czech directors, the film's back-to-basics look and hard-won insights into the not-so-private life of a passionate yet embittered married couple are the two main reasons for its enduring interest.

Ludvik (Radoslav Brzobohaty) is a senior official in the bureaucracy of Prague's ruling Communist Party. Anna (Jirina Bohdalova) is his alcoholic wife, daughter of a small town pub owner. The couple has a young son and lives in a comfortable home on a quiet street in a nice neighborhood. At first, the cruel insults, nasty looks, and open hostility they direct toward one another strike the viewer as little more than character development in the film—Ludvik and Anna coming across as the characteristically depoliticized citizens of Czech society at the time. Later we realize that their complex marital relationship is at the very center of *The Ear*'s concerns, at once allegorizing and distinguishing itself from the equally complex relationship between a ruthless, oppressive political regime and its justifiably paranoid populace.

The film's action takes place over the course of one long evening. Returning home from a casual political function, Ludvik and Anna find their front gate open and the spare set of house keys missing. Initially dismissing this as of no consequence, gradually other strange occurrences—including a power outage and dead phone lines—make them wonder whether they are not under surveillance by suspicious and unethical Communist authorities.

In his mind's eye, Ludvik replays scenes from earlier that night. What initially seemed innocuous now takes on the surreal quality of a nightmare, as every sentence spoken to Ludvik—"Sorry, the comrades are listening"; "All that counts is whether they accept socialist goals"; "Didn't they speak to you?"—seems now to signify that he is in great personal danger. Connecting the dots, Ludvik comes to believe that he is a target of the Communist Party and that his arrest is imminent.

Desperate to destroy any materials that could be cited as evidence against him, Ludvik burns his correspondence. Anna, meanwhile, needles him about the deteriorating state of their relationship and his utter lack of interest in her both sexually and emotionally. But as dawn approaches, a submerged dynamic in their relationship rises to the surface. Expressing great tenderness, protectiveness, and depth of feeling, the couple discuss how to proceed once the authorities come to take Ludvik away. Anna weeps hysterically. Ludvik tries to comfort her, the psychological warfare at an end as Big Brother closes in. The analogies established earlier between marriage and citizenship now diminish in importance. Instead we become sensitive to the dis-analogies: the limitless capacity of those in power to plot, conspire, use advanced technology, terrorize, manipulate, and control a population. **SJS**

Zacalo t

U.S. (Fox) 170m Color

**Director:** Franklin J. Schaffner

**Producer:** Frank McCarthy

**Screenplay:** Francis Ford Coppola, Edmund H. North

**Photography:** Fred J. Koenekamp

**Music:** Jerry Goldsmith

**Cast:** George C. Scott, Karl Malden, Stephen Young, Michael Strong, Carey Loftin, Albert Dumortier

**Oscar:** Frank McCarthy (best picture), Franklin J. Schaffner (director), Francis Ford Coppola, Edmund H. North (screenplay), George C. Scott (actor), Urie McCleary, Gil Parrondo, Antonio Mateos, Pierre-Louis Thévenet (art direction), Hugh S. Fowler (editing), Douglas O. Williams, Don J. Bassman (sound)

**Oscar nomination:** Fred J. Koenekamp (photography), Alex Weldon, (special effects), Jerry Goldsmith (music)

# PATTON (1970)

"Now I want you to remember that no bastard ever won a war by dying for his country. He won it by making the other poor dumb bastard die for his country." So begins the prologue of Franklin J. Schaffner's *Patton*.

After such a vivid monologue, the picture trails George C. Scott's eponymous lead in a race to fulfill his destiny. First up is Tunisia, then Sicily, some tongue-lashing for raucous insubordination, various real-life vignettes, much German preoccupation with his whereabouts, and a snowy race to the Battle of the Bulge. Concluding with Patton's demotion, the film's detail-rich canvas enlivens a fascinating personality during a moment of historic importance.

Scott's General is both nursemaid to dying men and terror to his foe. He's also conflicted about being a modern warrior put-upon by the political exigencies of his day. As a poet, trained killer, and acolyte of reincarnation, he is an enigma whose maverick sensibilities appealed to Vietnam War–era protestors and hawks alike.

His story consists of realistic battle sequences and was born from a Francis Ford Coppola cowritten script. Thus *Patton* valorizes a bureaucratic war machine while sanctifying individuality through the gravelly voice of a career soldier in what may well be the definitive biopic of the 1970s. **GC-Q**

**U.S.** (Fox, Aspen, Ingo Preminger) 116m Color

**Director:** Robert Altman

**Producer:** Leon Ericksen, Ingo Preminger

**Screenplay:** Ring Lardner Jr., from novel by Richard Hooker

**Photography:** Harold E. Stine

**Music:** Mike Altman, Ahmad Jamal, Johnny Mandel

**Cast:** Donald Sutherland, Elliott Gould, Tom Skerritt, Sally Kellerman, Robert Duvall, Roger Bowen, Rene Auberjonois, David Arkin

**Oscar:** Ring Lardner Jr. (screenplay)

**Oscar nomination:** Ingo Preminger (best picture), Robert Altman (director), Sally Kellerman (actress in support role), Danford B. Greene (editing)

**Cannes Film Festival:** Robert Altman (Golden Palm)

# M*A*S*H (1970)

It didn't take long before the innovations of Robert Altman's Korean War comedy *M*A*S*H* appeared almost quaint in their simplicity and obviousness, especially after Altman himself later compounded his achievements with the even more ambitious *Nashville*. Yet the use of chaotically overlapping dialogue within widescreen ensemble acting scenes proved as surprising and shocking, at the time of the film's release, as Altman's use of gory makeshift operating theaters as a vehicle for droll black comedy.

Altman's technique captured his actor's improvisations by zooming in from a distance, resulting in some playful thespian anarchy. The specter of the Vietnam War loomed large at the time. *M*A*S*H*'s antiestablishment streak in many ways reflected the mood of the antiwar movement, which increasingly viewed the folly of Vietnam as a black comedy itself. In fact, Altman created much of *M*A*S*H* on the sly, tricking the studio into thinking he was making a patriotic war film. The studio was ready to shelve the film until test audiences reacted favorably. Release led to a wave of acclaim cresting with a number of Academy Award nominations, and a successful television spin-off, immediately cementing Altman's reputation. **JKl**

# PERFORMANCE (1970)

Not so much a reflection of the 1960s counterculture as an outright affront to the Summer of Love, *Performance* (codirected by Donald Cammell and Nicolas Roeg) marked changing mores and attitudes with a confrontational and audacious sense of style. Although completed in 1967, the film sat on the shelf for two years as the studio scratched its head. What to do with such a unique and unusual film?

Yet the long wait actually worked to the film's advantage. By the time *Performance* appeared, hippie idealism was on the wane, and the utopia of Woodstock had given way to the hell of the Rolling Stone's Altamont debacle—captured in the 1970 concert film *Gimme Shelter*. *Performance* starring Stones singer Mick Jagger as a debauched aging rock star only heightened its cultural impact ("You'll look funny when you're forty," remarks James Fox's Chas to Jagger's Turner).

The story itself is relatively simple. Chas is a gangster (a "performer") who decides to give up his life of crime and goes on the lam. Searching for a place to secretly wait out his violent pursuers, he discovers a reclusive rock star, Turner, who lives a sex-and-drug-filled lifestyle in a fun house–like home. Chas realizes this is the last place anyone would ever look for him, so he rents a room and bunkers down with Turner and his two female housemates (Anita Pallenberg and Michèle Breton). But after changing his looks and lifestyle, and with Turner and his Sapphic crew as catalysts, Chas begins to change as well.

By the time the story plays out, nothing (and no one) we've seen is necessarily what we thought it was. Cammell's script and Roeg's camera keep everything off-kilter, not just through skewed drug logic but also through overtly and intentionally confusing editing, punctuated with startling bursts of violence. Frequent drug-fueled hallucinations drive *Performance* toward its mind-bending conclusion, when art and identity intersect and the line between fantasy and reality finally blurs into oblivion. **JKl**

**G.B.** (Goodtimes) 105m BW / Technicolor

**Director:** Donald Cammell, Nicolas Roeg

**Producer:** David Cammell, Sanford Lieberson

**Screenplay:** Donald Cammell

**Photography:** Nicolas Roeg

**Music:** Jack Nitzsche

**Cast:** James Fox, Mick Jagger, Anita Pallenberg, Michèle Breton, Ann Sidney, John Bindon, Stanley Meadows, Allan Cuthbertson, Anthony Morton, Johnny Shannon, Anthony Valentine, Kenneth Colley, John Sterland, Laraine Wickens

U.S. (Maysles Films) 91m Color

**Director:** Albert Maysles, David Maysles, Charlotte Zwerin

**Producer:** Ronald Schneider

**Photography:** Ron Dorfman, George Lucas, Albert Maysles, David Maysles, McKinney

**Music:** Mick Jagger, Keith Richards, The Rolling Stones

**Cast:** Mick Jagger, Keith Richards, Mick Taylor, Charlie Watts, Bill Wyman, Marty Balin, Melvin Belli, Dick Carter, Jerry Garcia, Meredith Hunter, Paul Kantner, Michael Lang, Phil Lesh, Ronald Schneider, Grace Slick, Ike Turner, Tina Turner, Bob Weir

# GIMME SHELTER (1970)

Rock documentaries are generally prosaic affairs, at best good extended promotional films for their subjects, at worst overlong pop videos with bad interviews. There are noble exceptions, the most famous being D.A. Pennebaker's Bob Dylan documentary *Don't Look Back*, but even that is only a heightened diary, a fly-on-the-wall character study. The most alarming and dramatically satisfying rock documentary must surely be the Maysles Brothers' *Gimme Shelter*, released in 1970, a film of the Rolling Stones's 1969 U.S. tour.

With its narrative structure—partially imposed rather than verité-style inherent—and its climax, the disastrous, tragic free concert at Altamont Speedway on December 6, 1969, *Gimme Shelter* is a harrowing, exciting social commentary and rock-'n'-roll all at the same time. The film begins conventionally enough, with the Stones performing at Madison Square Garden, but then cuts to an editing room, some months later, where the band are listening to a radio report on the aftermath of Altamont. This is a directed narrative, product of Albert and David Maysles's (and editor/codirector Charlotte Zwerin's) belief in Direct Cinema, which used techniques drawn from "fictional" movie-making and applied them to nonfiction works. Thus the Altamont concert is "reedited" to increase dramatic tension; sticklers for realism may carp at the fact that the murder of black concert-goer Meredith Hunter takes place during the wrong Stones song, but the Maysles were editing for dramatic effect, not for rock history books. *Gimme Shelter* ends with the Rolling Stones watching the murder (committed by one of the Hells Angels hired by the band for "security" purposes) in their editing suite. It's a unique moment, rock stars confronted by the consequences of their own actions.

The movie helped seal the image both of the Stones as rock devils and, more important, of Altamont as the Anti-Woodstock, as negative closure to the 1960s. It suggested that the counterculture was really a lot of drugged fools who thought murder was a "bummer" and that the '60s dream was well and truly over. That may be debatable, but the force and drama of this documentary are not. **KK**

## ZABRISKIE POINT (1970)

Though Michelangelo Antonioni's only American film was poorly received when it was released in 1969, time has in some ways been kinder to *Zabriskie Point* than to *La Notte*, made a decade earlier. The director's boldly nonrealistic and poetic approach to American counterculture myths, and his loose and deliberately slow approach to narrative, may still put some people off. He also cast two young unknowns as his romantic leads—a carpenter (Mark Frechette) and a college student (Daria Halprin), neither of whom has been seen since—along with a relatively wooden professional, Rod Taylor. Antonioni was at the height of his commercial prestige at the time, having just made his only international hit in England (*Blowup*), and expectations that he would bring off something similar in relation to countercultural America were undoubtedly overblown.

But his beautiful handling of widescreen compositions, Pop Art colors and subject matter (largely derived from southern California billboards), and wistful moods have many lingering aftereffects, and the grand and beautiful apocalyptic finale is downright spectacular. Some of Antonioni's other pictures—most notably, *Red Desert*, *Eclipse*, and *The Passenger*—end or almost end with passages of stylistic bravura that drastically recast as well as summarize everything in the pictures preceding them, and in this case, Antonioni doesn't disappoint. **JRos**

**U.S.** (MGM, Trianon) 110m Metrocolor
**Director:** Michelangelo Antonioni
**Producer:** Carlo Ponti, Harrison Starr
**Screenplay:** Michelangelo Antonioni, Franco Rossetti, Sam Shepard, Tonino Guerra, Clare Peploe
**Photography:** Alfio Contini
**Music:** Jerry Garcia, David Gilmour, Nick Mason, Roger Waters, Richard Wright, Roy Orbison
**Cast:** Mark Frechette, Daria Halprin, Paul Fix, G.D. Spradlin, Bill Garaway, Kathleen Cleaver, Rod Taylor

## L'UCCELLO DALLE PIUME DI CRISTALLO (1970)
### THE BIRD WITH THE CRYSTAL PLUMAGE

An unauthorized version of Fredric Brown's novel *The Screaming Mimi*—and far closer to the plot of the original than the "official" 1958 Gerd Oswald film—Dario Argento's *The Bird with the Crystal Plumage* took the guidelines for a particularly Italianate spin on the Hitchcockian thriller, laid down by Mario Bava in *The Evil Eye* (1963) and *Blood and Black Lace* (1964). In so doing, the director mapped out his own subgenre with this, his first feature.

Sam Dalmas (Tony Musante), an American writer in Rome, is walking late at night past a modern art gallery and is alerted by a struggle within. Trapped between two glass doors, he sees a man struggling with a woman and is helpless as the woman is stabbed. The victim survives and the hero is told that her attacker was a serial murderer at large in the city, but Musante becomes obsessed with the idea that he saw something during the incident that doesn't make sense. As his puzzled girlfriend (Suzy Kendall) inevitably catches the killer's interest and the cops follow up a bizarre audio clue connected with the title, Musante has a brush with the unforgettable skull-faced hit man (Reggie Nalder) from Hitchcock's *The Man Who Knew Too Much* (1956), and realizes in an ironic-horrific finale that he has always been The Man Who Didn't Realize What He Knew. **KN**

**Italy / West Germany** (CCC Filmkunst, Glazier, Seda Spettacoli) 98m Eastmancolor
**Language:** Italian
**Director:** Dario Argento
**Producer:** Salvatore Argento
**Screenplay:** Dario Argento, from the novel *The Screaming Mimi* by Fredric Brown
**Photography:** Vittorio Storaro
**Music:** Ennio Morricone
**Cast:** Tony Musante, Suzy Kendall, Enrico Maria Salerno, Eva Renzi, Umberto Raho, Renato Romano, Giuseppe Castellano, Mario Adorf, Pino Patti, Gildo Di Marco, Rosita Torosh, Omar Bonaro, Fulvio Mingozzi, Werner Peters, Karen Valenti

**Italy / West Germany** (CCC Filmkunst, Documento) 94m Eastmancolor
**Language:** Italian
**Director:** Vittorio De Sica
**Producer:** Artur Brauner, Arthur Cohn, Gianni Hecht Lucari
**Screenplay:** Vittorio Bonicelli, from novel by Giorgio Bassani
**Photography:** Ennio Guarnieri
**Music:** Bill Conti, Manuel De Sica
**Cast:** Lino Capolicchio, Dominique Sanda, Fabio Testi, Romolo Valli, Helmut Berger, Camillo Cesarei, Inna Alexeieff, Katina Morisani, Barbara Pilavin, Michael Berger, Ettore Geri
**Oscar:** Italy (best foreign language film)
**Oscar nomination:** Ugo Pirro, Vittorio Bonicelli (screenplay)
**Berlin International Film Festival:** Vittorio De Sica (Golden Bear), (Otto Dibelius film award)

# IL GIARDINO DEI FINZI-CONTINI (1970)
## THE GARDEN OF THE FINZI-CONTINIS

Vittorio De Sica's *The Garden of the Finzi-Continis* marked an international comeback for a director who had never stopped working, but whose star had fallen since the days of neorealist masterpieces like *Umberto D* (1952). Its story, derived from Giorgio Bassani's novel of Italian Jews slowly adapting to the coming fascist oppression, compellingly spoke to a 1970s audience appreciating the resurgence of such political-historical themes in art house cinema.

The story holds off its tragic punchline until the end, meanwhile intimating it as a dark shadow while the characters obliviously enjoy their last revelries. The beautiful young things who gather in their high-bourgeois paradise are caught in an agonizing daisy chain of mismatched desires—no one, straight or gay, is loved by the person they want.

Stylistically, the film is no masterpiece. But it comes alive in those moments when De Sica rivets his camera in close-up on his glamorous stars (Dominique Sanda and Helmut Berger especially), in order to observe the furtive darting of their soulfully expressive eyes.

*The Garden of Finzi-Continis* is a keen, touching parable about the interrelation of personal and political, private, and public drama. The encroaching social tragedy renders the romantic palpitations by turns petty, desperate, absurd, and poignant. **AM**

**U.S.** (Foundation for Filmakers) 102m Color
**Director:** Barbara Loden
**Producer:** Harry Shuster
**Screenplay:** Barbara Loden
**Photography:** Nicholas T. Proferes
**Cast:** Barbara Loden, Michael Higgins, Dorothy Shupenes, Peter Shupenes, Jerome Thier, Marian Thier, Anthony Rotell, M.L. Kennedy, Gerald Grippo, Milton Gittleman, Lila Gittleman, Arnold Kanig, Joe Dennis, Charles Dosinan, Jack Ford

# WANDA (1971)

The heartbreaking final image of *Wanda*—a freeze-frame snapshot of the eponymous character sadly drifting through a life of small-town bars and quiet misery—is given further tragic resonance through the knowledge that this masterpiece of American independent cinema remained the only film ever directed by its star, Barbara Loden, before she succumbed to cancer in 1980. The wife of Elia Kazan (and actress in Kazan's *Wild River* [1960] and *Splendor in the Grass* [1961]), Loden derived more inspiration from the improvisational vérité rhythms of the burgeoning independent film movement of the late '60s with this raw, naturalistic portrait of a destitute, uneducated young woman in a Pennsylvania steel town who abandons her husband and children with the same degree of apathy that guides her subsequent entanglement with a bullying bank robber (Michael Higgins).

Loden admirably refuses to transform her protagonist into a conveniently symbolic martyr for feminist causes, just as Loden also never shies from depicting Wanda's complicity in making poor choices that only contribute to her despair—and yet one can't help but retain great empathy for Wanda and her shattered self-esteem. Expertly coaxing authentic performances from a cast mixing professionals with local nonactors, Loden has chronicled a type of character rarely glimpsed in American film—and in the process, she also created one of the greatest "one-shot" directing achievements in this country's cinema. **TCr**

# W.R.: MISTERIJE ORGANIZMA (1971)
## W.R.: MYSTERIES OF THE ORGANISM

Yugoslavian filmmaker Dusan Makavejev's most critically acclaimed film, *W.R: Mysteries of the Organism*, is a magnificently obscene parody of Cold War politics and social mores. It also has a terrific soundtrack, featuring the song "Kill for Peace" by New York protest band The Fugs. A psychedelic collage of several plots, *W.R.* tells the story of three warring cultures in the late 1960s: old-fashioned Soviet-style communism, U.S. bourgeois militarism, and the sexual revolutionaries whose values put them at odds with both.

These cultures are explored through interlocked narratives whose juxtaposition is utterly silly and disturbing by turns. In one, a documentary look at the life of radical psychiatrist Wilhelm Reich, we are introduced to Reich's theory of the "orgone," a unit of erotic life energy that he believed could be captured in specially made boxes. After the Food and Drug Administration caught wind of Reich's unusual therapeutic practices—which included getting his clients together in large groups to moan, cry, and thrust their hips orgiastically—he was arrested and spent the rest of his life in jail.

Reich's story is intercut with a goofy fictional spoof of communist Yugoslavia, in which the sexually liberated, feminist-communist Milena tries to seduce an old-fashioned Russian "People's artist" with disastrous results—a homage to the 1962 cult classic *The Brain That Wouldn't Die*. Meanwhile, we follow The Fugs's singer Tuli Kupferberg around Manhattan while he dresses up like a soldier, goose-steps into random locations, and pretends to masturbate his rifle. Makavejev jams in footage of Stalin from a 1946 Soviet propaganda flick, followed by medical films of people getting electroshock therapy. Occasionally we are treated to interviews with American sexual subversives who managed to avoid Reich's fate: Transgender ingenue Jackie Curtis describes her first fumbling attempts to have sex as a man; activist Betty Dodson talks about teaching women to touch their own vaginas.

The cumulative effect of these story fragments is a growing sense that the world is in chaos because politics try—and fail—to constrain sexual desire. Makavejev is famous for saying that his collage-style filmmaking represents the true embodiment of Eisenstein's ideal of dialectical montage because Eisenstein himself just didn't have a good enough sense of humor to do it right. *W.R.* may be the only avant-garde slapstick communist documentary sex romp ever made. That alone makes it a must-see. **AN**

**Yugoslavia / West Germany**
(Neoplanta, Telepool) 85m BW

**Language:** Serbo-Croatian

**Director:** Dusan Makavejev

**Screenplay:** Dusan Makavejev

**Photography:** Aleksandar Petkovic, Predrag Popovic

**Music:** Bojana Marijan

**Cast:** Miodrag Andric, Jim Buckley, Jackie Curtis, Betty Dodson, Milena Dravic, Nancy Godfrey, Dragoljub Ivkov, Milan Jelic, Jagoda Kaloper, Tuli Kupferberg, Zivka Matic, Nikola Milic, Zoran Radmilovic, Wilhelm Reich, Ivica Vidovic

**Berlin International Film Festival:** Dusan Makavejev (FIPRESCI award—special mention), (Interfilm award—recommendation forum of new cinema)

# A CLOCKWORK ORANGE (1971)

**G.B.** (Hawk, Polaris, Warner Bros)
137m BW / Color
**Director:** Stanley Kubrick
**Producer:** Stanley Kubrick
**Screenplay:** Stanley Kubrick, from novel by Anthony Burgess
**Photography:** John Alcott
**Music:** Nacio Herb Brown, Walter Carlos, Rachel Elkind, Edward Elgar, Gioacchino Rossini, Ludwig van Beethoven, Henry Purcell, Nikolai Rimsky-Korsakov
**Cast:** Malcolm McDowell, Patrick Magee, Michael Bates, Warren Clarke, John Clive, Adrienne Corri, Carl Duering, Paul Farrell, Clive Francis, Michael Gover, Miriam Karlin, James Marcus, Aubrey Morris, Godfrey Quigley, Sheila Raynor
**Oscar nomination:** Stanley Kubrick (best picture), Stanley Kubrick (director), Stanley Kubrick (screenplay), William Butler (editing)

Stanley Kubrick's most controversial film, a social sci-fi fable made in 1971, was withdrawn in the United Kindom by the director himself for nearly 30 years despite its initial, phenomenally successful but heavily criticized release. It resurfaced, enveloped in mystique, not long after his death. *A Clockwork Orange* is still electrifying, a bold translation into cinematic terms of the dystopian Anthony Burgess novel that was itself published to a mixture of acclaim and notoriety in 1959 and was long believed unfilmable.

Delinquent but clever, smart-aleck youth Alex De Large (Malcolm McDowell) gets his kicks from pornography, Beethoven, and leading his bowler-hatted, white overall-clad gang of "Droogs" (including a baby-faced Warren Clark) on hectic vivid rampages of "ultra-violence" in which they speak a distinctive argot, a hybrid of Russian and London Cockney rhyming slang. The most disturbing scene in this first, twenty-minute section of the film is one that comes back to haunt Alex when he is helpless. After breaking into a futuristic luxury home, they cripple the husband (Patrick Magee) and rape the wife (Adrienne Corri) while Alex bellows "Singin' In The Rain," aiming vicious blows of his (recurring trendy) Doc Marten boots to the rhythm of the song. Although it is interesting that the rape looms large in memories as particularly nasty, Kubrick cuts away from the woman's ordeal just as Alex finishes cutting away her skin-tight red jumpsuit. Another thrill-seeking outing culminates in Alex bashing in a woman's brains with a giant phallic sculpture, the crime for which he is eventually apprehended.

But the institutionalized brutality that ensues in Alex's punishment and his "rehabilitation" into a craven, boot-licking victim is just as scary as the Droogs' misdeeds, and more thought provoking, in this scathing satire of society's hypocrisy, corruption, and sadism. Seeing a way out of prison, Alex cockily volunteers for a politically showcased, experimental aversion therapy and is subjected to dire behaviorist "cure"—strapped down, his eyes clamped wide open—that suppresses his violent tendencies but also robs him of his essential humanity. Stripped of his capacity to commit evil, he is an enfeebled individual. Back in the world, he doesn't enjoy his "freedom." Betrayed by former thug-comrades, who, ironically, have become policemen, he ultimately gets a hilariously unnerving comeuppance in an encounter with one of his damaged victims.

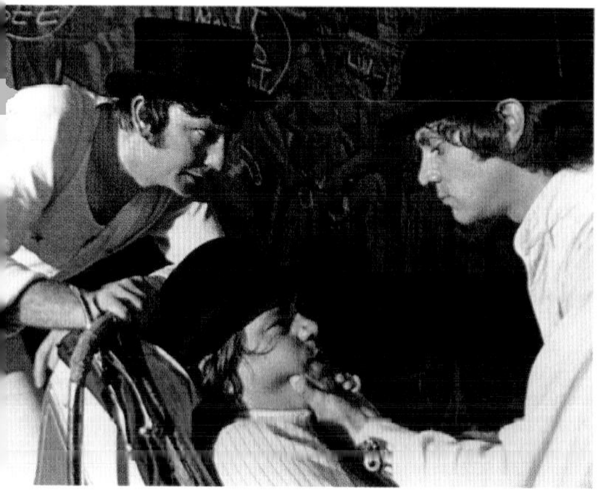

Kubrick's arresting vision of the not-too-distant future is amusingly dated in some details (vinyl records, Alex's IBM typewriter), and the violence for which it was so castigated on its release is discreet by contemporary visceral standards. But the picture of aimless louts alleviating their boredom in mindless viciousness is chillingly topical, as is the real issue at the picture's center—the fragility of individuality and personal rights when they do not conform to the desires of the state. Sensationally stylish and often startlingly funny, with a delirious soundtrack, *A Clockwork Orange* still packs far more punch than its many blatantly derivative descendants. **AE**

**France / West Germany / Switzerland** (NDR, Télévision Rencontre, TSR) 262m BW

**Language:** French / German / English

**Director:** Marcel Ophüls

**Producer:** André Harris, Alain de Sedouy

**Screenplay:** André Harris, Marcel Ophüls

**Photography:** André Gazut, Jürgen Thieme

**Cast:** Georges Bidault, Matheus Bleibinger, Charles Braun, Maurice Buckmaster, Emile Coulaudon, Emmanuel d'Astier de la Vigerie, René de Chambrun, Anthony Eden, Marcel Ophüls, Denis Rake, Henri Rochat, Paul Schmidt, Mme. Solange, Edward Spears, Helmut Tausend, Roger Tounze, Marcel Verdier

**Oscar nomination:** Marcel Ophüls (documentary)

# LE CHAGRIN ET LA PITIÉ (1971)

## THE SORROW AND THE PITY

For over two decades, French society seemed unwilling to examine the moral questions raised by the German Occupation, but the deep disturbances of May 1968 brought about a new openness. Marcel Ophüls's documentary *The Sorrow and the Pity* focuses on events in the town of Clermont-Ferrand. Though receiving initial support from French national television, Ophüls was not allowed to broadcast it. Instead, the film opened in art houses, quickly becoming the year's most controversial production. Worldwide distribution followed, and this four-hour recording of the reminiscences of survivors of the period, interspersed with archival footage, quickly became one of world cinema's most acclaimed documentaries.

Ophüls picked a town in the "free zone" of Vichy France so that he could explore the ways in which the collaborationist government operated. His informants ranged from members of the nobility to peasants to former German soldiers who are photographed wearing their medals. With a minimum of narration and distorting generalizations, *The Sorrow and the Pity* captures the ambiguities and contradictions of the period. The sense of the film, however, is the *chagrin* (sorrow, but also shame) of its title, established by the insistent questions of the interviewer and the lies or distortions that become obvious across the different forms of testimony and the unrehearsed reactions of the interviewees to difficult, embarrassing inquiries. **RBP**

**U.S.** (David L. Wolper, Quaker Oats, Warner Bros.) 100m Technicolor

**Director:** Mel Stuart

**Producer:** Stan Margulies, David L. Wolper

**Screenplay:** Roald Dahl, from his book *Charlie and the Chocolate Factory*

**Photography:** Arthur Ibbetson

**Music:** Leslie Bricusse, Anthony Newley

**Cast:** Gene Wilder, Jack Albertson, Peter Ostrum, Roy Kinnear, Julie Dawn Cole, Leonard Stone, Denise Nickerson, Nora Denney, Paris Themmen, Ursula Reit, Michael Bollner, Diana Sowle, Aubrey Woods, David Battley, Günter Meisner

**Oscar nomination:** Leslie Bricusse, Anthony Newley, Walter Scharf (music)

# WILLY WONKA AND THE CHOCOLATE FACTORY (1971)

Although most children's movies are saccharine, if not silly, Mel Stuart's adaptation of Roald Dahl's popular children's novel is a happy exception. *Willy Wonka and the Chocolate Factory* is a juvenile black comedy replete with flash visuals, engaging songs, and an over-the-top performance by Gene Wilder as the title character, whose claim to fame is being the world's greatest candy maker.

Wonka has hidden five golden tickets in his candy bars, and those who find them get to tour the factory and receive a lifetime supply of sweets. The factory offers a gallery of marvels, including a river of chocolate. The catch for the lucky winners is that they must obey Wonka's difficult and capricious rules. The point of the exercise, however, is to identify the one child who is truly honest (it turns out, of course, to be the most charming and irascible of the group). His reward is to be the inheritor of Wonka's factory; one day he will become the chocolate maker whose duty is not only to cater to children but also to provide the proper rite of passage into the adult world. Like *The Wizard of Oz* (1939), *Willy Wonka* is full of strange creatures, artificial sets, and lively song and dance numbers. A film to entertain the young and set their elders to thinking. **RBP**

# MCCABE AND MRS. MILLER (1971)

**U.S.** (Warner Bros.) 120m Technicolor

**Director:** Robert Altman

**Producer:** Mitchell Brower, Robert Eggenweiler, David Foster,

**Screenplay:** Robert Altman, Brian McKay, Edmund Naughton

**Photography:** Vilmos Zsigmond

**Music:** Leonard Cohen

**Cast:** Warren Beatty, Julie Christie, Rene Auberjonois, William Devane, John Schuck, Corey Fischer, Bert Remsen, Shelley Duvall, Keith Carradine, Michael Murphy, Antony Holland, Hugh Millais, Manfred Schulz, Jace Van Der Veen, Jackie Crossland

**Oscar nomination:** Julie Christie (actress)

At the peak of his 1970s powers director Robert Altman seemed capable of anything. Even so, *McCabe and Mrs. Miller*, arriving between *M*A*S*H* and *Nashville*, is something special, an elegiac tale of the Old West imbued with a sense of contemporary filmmaking adventure. Set in the Pacific Northwest in the early 1900s, the film stars a quiet Warren Beatty as the titular braggart, a cowardly but charismatic man who has lucked into a position of power. But the nature of the country is changing around him, and Beatty can't see the inevitable, violent consequences of progress for all his narcissistic pipe dreams.

Altman wanted his film to capture the feeling of an old photograph, so he instructed cinematographer Vilmos Zsigmond to flash-expose the film, resulting in a heavy haze that hangs over the image. Another brilliant decision was the use of Leonard Cohen for the film's anachronistic soundtrack, as the singer-songwriter's gloomy folk music perfectly suits the somber mood and darkly lit, snowy scenery. But best of all may be the casting of Julie Christie as an opium-addicted madam. She lends the role an ethereal quality at odds with Beatty's more natural performance as a bearded buffoon in a big fur coat, and hers is a ghostly presence that portends bad things to come.

*McCabe and Mrs. Miller* mourns the death of the Wild West even as it signals the fertile start of the '70s filmmaking renaissance. The picture is filled with striking widescreen imagery as well as Altman's usual roving camerawork, but the exercise exudes a palpable sadness here. *McCabe and Mrs. Miller*'s message seems to be that progress and capitalism go hand in hand, and not always for the better. The flourishing success of Beatty's frontier town initially draws workers, then well-wishers, but his hard work and vision mean nothing to the men who ultimately want to take it away. Altman's view of America as an experiment in Darwinism (accelerated with guns) might strike some as cynical, but the spectral visuals lend the film a palpable sadness that supplants any specific message. **JKl**

# WALKABOUT (1971)

Nicolas Roeg's second feature as director (and first solo effort) is deceptively simple: a bowler-hatted office worker (John Meillon) drives into the empty heart of Australia with his 16-year-old daughter (Jenny Agutter) and much younger son (Luc Roeg). The father sets fire to the car and shoots himself, stranding the siblings in the desert. At a dried-out waterhole, they meet an Aborigine youth (David Gulpilil) who is on his "walkabout," a time apart from the tribe when he must commune with nature. Of course, the city kids' spell in the wild also serves as a walkabout of their own, during which they learn something that is muted when they return to their lives, leaving behind a devastation that only the doomed Aborigine understands.

*Walkabout* is a deep film, but it's also elusive: constantly forcing you to think for yourself, or accept that some mysteries should never be solved. The story begins and ends with suicides that we don't have enough information to "understand." If the property (a novel by James Vance Marshall) were remade conventionally, the film would be full of exciting wilderness perils and go heavy on a *Blue Lagoon*-style love affair between the repressed miss and the nature boy, but Roeg takes a more elliptical, enigmatic approach. A drama of transformation and tragedy is played out through apparently throwaway dialogue. Flashes of cinematic trickery, footnote-like scenes, provide a "civilized" contrast with wilderness behavior—Gulpilil's spearing and bludgeoning of a kangaroo with a butcher knife impersonally chopping cuts of meat—combined with documentary footage of crawling lizards and swarming insects.

The normal skills associated with "acting" aren't required here, and Roeg cast two of the major roles with players who had never acted before, the Aborigine Gulpilil—later a fixture in Australian cinema from *The Last Wave* to *Crocodile Dundee*—and his own son Luc. *Walkabout* lives in the fantasies of a generation because Agutter, in and out of school uniform (she has a famous nude swim), emerged from her prim *Railway Children* television series image to be strikingly sensual as the girl who takes a "memory" of something that never happened back to the city. **KN**

**G.B.** (Fox, Litvinoff) 95m Eastmancolor

**Director:** Nicolas Roeg

**Producer:** Si Litvinoff, Max L. Raab

**Screenplay:** Edward Bond, from novel by James Vance Marshall

**Photography:** Nicolas Roeg

**Music:** John Barry, Warren Marley, Billy Mitchell, Rod Stewart, Karlheinz Stockhausen,

**Cast:** Jenny Agutter, Luc Roeg, David Gulpilil, John Meillon, Robert McDarra, Peter Carver, John Illingsworth, Hilary Bamberger, Barry Donnelly, Noeline Brown, Carlo Manchini

**Cannes Film Festival:** Nicolas Roeg nomination (Golden Palm)

# KLUTE (1971)

U.S. (Gus, Warner Bros.) 114m Technicolor
**Director:** Alan J. Pakula
**Producer:** C. Kenneth Deland, David Lange, Alan J. Pakula
**Screenplay:** Andy Lewis, Dave Lewis
**Photography:** Gordon Willis
**Music:** Michael Small
**Cast:** Jane Fonda, Donald Sutherland, Charles Cioffi, Roy Scheider, Dorothy Tristan, Rita Gam, Nathan George, Vivian Nathan, Morris Strassberg, Barry Snider, Betty Murray, Jane White, Shirley Stoler, Robert Milli, Anthony Holland
**Oscar:** Jane Fonda (actress)
**Oscar nomination:** Andy Lewis, David P. Lewis (screenplay)

The post-Vietnam/Watergate sensibilities of 1970s cinema were never more evident than in Alan Pakula's classic neonoir *Klute*. From the fetishized phone conversation of the opening credits, the director makes us aware of the surveillance age that would culminate so strikingly in Francis Coppola's *The Conversation*. *Klute* is an unconventional film that is both detective thriller and character-driven mood piece, one rife with subtexts of urban decay and a claustrophobic sense of helplessness.

Despite the title, this is Bree Daniels's (Jane Fonda) story, and its success relies on the complex inner life of Fonda's call girl, who is neither your typical tramp with a heart of gold nor a total bitch. Fonda's work here is the crowning achievement of her career. Bree wants to be an actress and model, and Pakula's depiction of New York makes it understandable that she would need to turn tricks to survive, as it is all just another acting assignment.

Enter John Klute (Donald Sutherland), a small-town detective out of his depth in the underbelly of New York vice and fraud, and an enigma for Bree as he seems beyond corruption. Sutherland's morally uptight investigator fascinates her enough to allow him into a world he could never hope to enter on his own. Much like Paul Schrader's *Hardcore* (1979), a small-town innocent is drawn into the shadowland of urban wickedness only to find it pathetic, and reaches out to a damaged soul in hopes of salvation, even if a relationship is out of the question.

As a mystery, *Klute* has no real suspense because the killer's identity is made known early on. The dynamic between the two leads is what keeps the film on target. The real joy is Fonda's acting virtuosity, and her ability to register so many edges and contradictions on camera. Pakula's aesthetic centers on the voyeuristic pleasure of watching Bree develop into a nonhero as fear envelopes her world and her tough veneer starts to crumble when she must trust a man, perhaps for the first time.

As for Pakula, his three masterworks (*Klute, The Parallax View*, and *All the President's Men*) more than justify his place among the great directors of the 1970s or any other decade. His style remained unique to the last. **DDV**

U.S. (Paramount) 91m Technicolor
**Director:** Hal Ashby
**Producer:** Colin Higgins, Mildred Lewis, Charles Mulvehill
**Screenplay:** Colin Higgins
**Photography:** John A. Alonzo
**Nonoriginal Music:** Cat Stevens, Johann Strauss, Tchaikovsky
**Cast:** Ruth Gordon, Bud Cort, Vivian Pickles, Cyril Cusack, Charles Tyner, Ellen Geer, Eric Christmas, G. Wood, Judy Engles, Shari Summers, Tom Skerritt, Susan Madigan, Ray K. Goman, Gordon Devol, Harvey Brumfield

# HAROLD AND MAUDE (1971)

The label of "cult film" is commonly used today as a marketing stunt for quasi-independent or mainstream films flirting with various subcultures. *Harold and Maude*, however, is the genuine thing, combining the directorial talents of former editor Hal Ashby with the oddball personas of main actors Bud Cort and Ruth Gordon. Cort, age 21, had just done his first leading part as a flight-obsessed kid in Robert Altman's *Brewster McCloud* (1970). Ex-screenwriter Gordon, age 76, had a string of memorable supporting roles behind her in the 1960s, the most well-known being her Academy Awarded Manhattan witch in Roman Polanski's *Rosemary's Baby* (1968). In *Harold and Maude* their peculiar chemistry made them an engaging, unforgettable romantic couple, challenging taboos of youth, aging, sex, death, and happiness.

Most interesting, perhaps, is that this challenge not only is a run-of-the-mill counterculture pose against traditional patriarchal society, but is even more aggressively directed against the contemporary youth-quake. This is primarily made by reversing the 1960s concept of youth as the vital, mold-breaking counterforce to the inevitable physical and spiritual deadness affecting everybody over age 30. Here the young and rich Harold is a living corpse because of his inability to break free from an oedipal fixation with his cold mother (Vivian Pickles), whose attention he tries to get in vain through a series of hilarious fake suicide attempts. It is only when he meets the old but vital and anarchic Maude that he comes to life. Thus Harold's fear of life is equated with a fear of growing up and aging. Maud, on the other hand, is not afraid of death, having survived the Nazi prison camps (implied by the number tattooed on her arm flashing by in a shot). Rather, we learn at the end of the film that she longs for it.

Ironically, this strange love story grows out of their obsessive habit of attending funerals, which—for different reasons, as we have seen—have a therapeutic value for them both. And it is to Ashby's credit that he doesn't turn this into a sentimental story of platonic friendship, in which the old and wise gives the young and reckless life lessons. Instead, Maud is the reckless one, impulsively acting out all her fantasies even to the point of stealing cars and seducing boys sixty years younger than herself. And it is their sexual liaison that is the key to this film, revolting as it seems to several of the characters and possibly to many in the audience—even to those who think of themselves as "liberated." The words of Eric Christmas's preaching priest that the thought of Harold's young body having intercourse with Maud's aging flesh "makes me want to puke," brings to mind acts of necromancy or a gothic horror film in which the old monster feeds on the young victim. Triumphantly, though, *Harold and Maude* rids us of all such cultural preconceptions. In the final scene, in which Maud prepares to die on her eightieth birthday, this bias toward youth is replaced with the existential insight that death is ultimately what gives life meaning. **MT**

**Hungary** (Mafilm) 88 min Eastmancolor

**Language:** Hungarian

**Director:** Miklós Jancsó

**Producer:** Ottó Föld

**Screenplay:** Yvette Biro, Gyula Hernádi

**Photography:** János Kende

**Music:** Tamás Cseh

**Cast:** Lajos Balázsovits, András Bálint, Gyöngyi Bürös, Erzsi Cserhalmi, Mari Csomós, László Csurka, Andrea Drahota, Zsuzsa Ferdinándy, Ilona Gurnik, Péter Haumann, Jácint Juhász, János Koltai, József Madaras, Tibor Molnár, Elemér Ragályi, Bertalan Solti, Éva Spányik, Frantisek Velecky, Márk Zala

**Cannes Film Festival:** Miklós Jancsó (director), nomination (Golden Palm)

# MÉG KÉR A NÉP (1971)

## RED PSALM

The 1997 documentary *East Side Story* assumes that communist-bloc directors were just itching to make Hollywood extravaganzas that invariably looked strained, square, and ill-equipped. But *Red Psalm*, Miklos Jancsó's dazzling, open-air revolutionary pageant, is a highly sensual communist musical that employs occasional nudity as lyrically as the singing, dancing, and nature; within its own idioms it swings as well as wails.

Set in the 19th century, when a group of peasants have demanded basic rights from a landowner and soldiers arrive on horseback, *Red Psalm* consists of only 26 shots, each one an intricate choreography of panning camera, landscape, and clustered bodies. Jancsó's awesome fusion of form with content, politics with poetry, equals the exciting innovations of the French New Wave. The music will play in your head for days, and the colors are ravishing.

The picture may well be the greatest Hungarian film of its time, summing up an entire strain in his work that lamentably has been forgotten in the United States. One of Jancsó's characteristic achievements is to create a striking continuum between past and present, a sense of immediacy about history found in few other period films. This suggests that the charge of formalism frequently leveled against him stems from an inability to fully comprehend his historical and political meanings—combined with an understandable effort to become intoxicated by the stylistic virtuosity and beauty. **JRos**

**G.B.** (MGM) 112m Metrocolor

**Director:** Mike Hodges

**Producer:** Michael Klinger

**Screenplay:** Mike Hodges, from the novel *Jack's Return Home* by Ted Lewis

**Photography:** Wolfgang Suschitzky

**Music:** Roy Budd

**Cast:** Michael Caine, Ian Hendry, Britt Ekland, John Osborne, Tony Beckley, George Sewell, Geraldine Moffat, Dorothy White, Rosemarie Dunham, Petra Markham, Alun Armstrong, Bryan Mosley, Glynn Edwards, Bernard Hepton, Terence Rigby

# GET CARTER (1971)

Gangster Jack Carter (Michael Caine), who works as strong-arm man for a London mob, returns to his Northern hometown of Newcastle to avenge the death of his brother. While there, he finds himself genocidally involved in a complicated series of faction fights between local crooks, and is set up to take a fall because he has unwisely been fooling around with his boss's girlfriend Anna (Britt Ekland).

Among *Get Carter*'s interestingly-cast provincial hoodlums are playwright John Osborne—surprisingly convincing as an effete gangland figure—and reliable hardhead Ian Hendry, memorably described as having eyes "like pissholes in the snow." Blunt and forceful, with effective use of underseen locations, Mike Hodges's film makes no concessions to morality and yet hardly condones the brutalities of its characters, with Caine getting a couple of shocks as he discovers that his niece (who might be his daughter) has starred in a credibly amateur porno movie, then coming to a bad end after he extracts rough justice on a deserted beach. Memorable scenes include a stark-naked Caine with a shotgun ejecting a couple of thugs from his bed-and-breakfast; the car going into the docks with an unnoticed passenger in the trunk; and a mob boss taking a dive from a multi-story parking garage. **KN**

# THE FRENCH CONNECTION (1971)

With *Bullitt* (1968) and *Dirty Harry* (1971), *The French Connection* spearheaded the cop-movie revival that took place around 1970. Loosely based on fact, it centers on the fanatical efforts of New York City police detective "Popeye" Doyle (Gene Hackman) to intercept a massive heroin shipment engineered by the urbane Marseilles entrepreneur Charnier (Fernando Rey). Although its view of the war on drugs as a class struggle waged by street cops against establishment fat cats now seems dated, *The French Connection* remains a tremendously exciting and powerful movie, primarily because of its vigorous editing style, epic vision of urban decay, and uncompromisingly pessimistic ending.

The editing—its rough-edged energy enhanced by jagged, truncated scene transitions—conveys both off-balance disorientation and reckless forward propulsion. The celebrated chase scene, in which Doyle's car hurtles down a busy avenue in pursuit of an elevated train, never seems an overblown set piece, because it simply extends the kinetic, careering, tunnel-vision effect sustained throughout the film.

*The French Connection*'s view of the embattled "drugopolis" goes beyond its impressively squalid locations to encompass a resonant interplay between different cityscapes. Gritty, grungy New York is at first ironically contrasted with spacious, gracious (but covertly vicious) Marseilles and then split into two of its boroughs: Manhattan, citadel of the rich and powerful, and Brooklyn, cockpit of junkies, smalltime hoods, and street cops. An added twist is provided by a brief scene in Washington, D.C.—shown as a lifeless White City, detached from the real urban battlegrounds.

Has there ever been a Best Picture Oscar winner with such a downbeat ending? After chasing Charnier into a hideously decayed building, Doyle not only loses his man but also gets swallowed up by his obsession. Too demented to acknowledge that he has just fragged an FBI agent, Doyle disappears in futile pursuit. The final scene can be read as an apocalyptic vision of the city's future, the ruined building as a relic of a lost civilization, the doorway through which Doyle vanishes as the gate of hell. The awesome bleakness of this conclusion is what finally lifts *The French Connection* above the level of middlebrow award winners and into the ranks of truly gripping films. **MR**

**U.S.** (Fox, D'Antoni, Schine-Moore) 104m Color

**Language:** English / French

**Director:** William Friedkin

**Producer:** Philip D'Antoni, G. David Schine, Kenneth Utt

**Screenplay:** Ernest Tidyman, from novel by Robin Moore

**Photography:** Owen Roizman

**Music:** Don Ellis

**Cast:** Gene Hackman, Fernando Rey, Roy Scheider, Tony Lo Bianco, Marcel Bozzuffi, Frédéric de Pasquale, Bill Hickman, Ann Rebbot, Harold Gary, Arlene Farber, Eddie Egan, André Ernotte, Sonny Grosso, Ben Marino, Patrick McDermott

**Oscar:** Philip D'Antoni (best picture), William Friedkin (director), Ernest Tidyman (screenplay), Gene Hackman (actor), Gerald B. Greenberg (editing)

**Oscar nomination:** Roy Scheider (actor in support role), Owen Roizman (photography), Theodore Soderberg, Christopher Newman (sound)

**U.S.** (MGM) 100m Metrocolor

**Director:** Gordon Parks

**Producer:** Joel Freeman, David Golden

**Screenplay:** Ernest Tidyman, John D.F. Black, from novel by Ernest Tidyman

**Photography:** Urs Furrer

**Music:** Isaac Hayes, J.J. Johnson

**Cast:** Richard Roundtree, Moses Gunn, Charles Cioffi, Christopher St. John, Gwenn Mitchell, Lawrence Pressman, Victor Arnold, Sherri Brewer, Rex Robbins, Camille Yarbrough, Margaret Warncke, Joseph Leon, Arnold Johnson, Dominic Barto, George Strus

**Oscar:** Isaac Hayes (song)

**Oscar nomination:** Isaac Hayes (music)

# SHAFT (1971)

"He's cool and tough. He's a black private dick who's a sex machine with all the chicks. He doesn't take orders from anybody, black or white, but he'd risk his neck for his brother man. I'm talkin' about Shaft. Can you dig it?" These lines, from Isaac Hayes's Oscar-winning theme, serves as the perfect introduction to Richard Roundtree's African-American hero/rebel/icon John Shaft, eponymous star of the wildly successful feature directed by Gordon Parks. *Shaft* followed directly on the heels of Melvin Van Peebles's *Sweet Sweetback's Baadasssss Song* (1971) and is widely acknowledged as the film that initiated the short-lived (but fondly remembered) blaxploitation cinema explosion of the 1970s.

The screenplay was written by Ernest Tidyman, author of a series of popular detective novels featuring the movie's protagonist. After the success of *Sweetback*, MGM gave Parks—an esteemed African-American photographer, writer, composer, and filmmaker—the go-ahead for a project that would hopefully capitalize on the fast-emerging black market. Parks wanted a fresh face to play the lead, and found exactly what he was looking for in Roundtree, a former Ebony model and occasional theater actor whose physical presence and acting chops provided just the right combination of machismo, virility, and confidence for the part.

The film's convoluted plot is fairly standard hard-boiled detective fare. After inadvertently causing the death of a gangster who shows up at his office, Shaft is coerced by a pair of white police inspectors to help them gather information about a gang war rumored to be taking place in Harlem. Meanwhile, a drug-dealing black godfather hires Shaft to save his daughter from the men who have recently kidnapped her. This turns out to be the Italian mafia, so with the help of a former comrade and his cadre of black nationalist followers, Shaft undertakes a dangerous but ultimately successful rescue mission. The mostly nonstop action is interrupted twice by romantic interludes. Shaft has no qualms about cheating on his girlfriend, and proves himself an equal-opportunity lover.

If ever there was a film in which the narrative is simply a vehicle for showcasing a particular character, *Shaft* is it. Together, Tidyman, Parks, and Roundtree create a strong black protagonist who—for the first time in Hollywood cinema—makes his own rules, listens to no one, *gives* the orders instead of taking them, and is not the least bit afraid of making jokes at the expense of white authority figures. Despite (perhaps because of) its subversive lead and militant undertones, *Shaft* did remarkable business among both black *and* white audiences, grossing over $23 million at U.S. box offices alone. Such broad-ranging success is partly explained by the fact that Shaft is perfectly comfortable in any situation, with people of every stripe (including a blatantly homosexual bartender, who feels compelled to pinch his butt), and that his magnetism and coolness under fire transcend mere color boundaries.

*Shaft* was followed by two sequels, *Shaft's Big Score!* (1972) and *Shaft in Africa (1973)*. In 2000, John Singleton directed a successful remake, with Samuel L. Jackson in the lead and with a supporting role for Roundtree. **SJS**

## DIRTY HARRY (1971)

One of the most influential and controversial police movies ever made, *Dirty Harry* is a canny mix of the simple and the sophisticated. The characters, notably supercop Harry Callahan (Clint Eastwood) and superpsycho Scorpio (Andy Robinson), are vivid, hyperbolic cartoons. They gain definition not through psychological depth and nuance but through their interaction with the film's intricate, richly articulated environments.

Brilliantly exploiting San Francisco locations, director Don Siegel gets a high-low motif going in the first shots, zooming back to reveal a woman swimming in a sky-blue pool on a high-rise roof while a sniper draws a bead on her from the top of another, taller building. From then on, the film soars and plunges in roller-coaster contours to delineate a multileveled metropolis where a precarious Sky City of helicopters, hilltops, rooftops, glass towers, and enveloping fog perches over a primitive underworld of burrows, tunnels, alleys, and quarries. No mere backdrop to the action, this formidable labyrinth molds and tests the characters as they twist and fight their way through it. This is vividly depicted in the tour de force sequence in which Scorpio runs Harry ragged from one end of town to the other as part of an evasive scheme to receive a bundle of ransom money. **MR**

**U.S.** (Malpaso, Warner Bros) 102m
**Director:** Don Siegel
**Producer:** Don Siegel
**Screenplay:** Harry Julian Fink, Rita M. Fink, Dean Riesner
**Photography:** Bruce Surtees
**Music:** Lalo Schifrin
**Cast:** Clint Eastwood, Harry Guardino, Reni Santoni, John Vernon, Andrew Robinson, John Larch, John Mitchum, Mae Mercer, Lyn Edgington, Ruth Kobart, Woodrow Parfrey, Josef Sommer, William Paterson, James Nolan, Maurice Argent

## LE SOUFFLE AU COEUR (1971)
### MURMUR OF THE HEART

Louis Malle liked to call *Murmur of the Heart* "my first film." In fact it was his eighth feature, but the first one he scripted on his own. It was also, he felt, his "first happy, optimistic film." Loosely based on Malle's own adolescent memories, it is set in a world seen entirely through the eyes of its hero, the 15-year-old Laurent Chevalier (Benoît Ferreux). The episodic plot springs few surprises: Laurent resents his father, adores his pretty young mother, veers unpredictably between childhood and adulthood, and is fascinated and disconcerted by his own rampant sexuality. The film's freshness lies in its evocative re-creation of French haut-bourgeois provincial society of the early '50s—and in the physical immediacy of family life, shown as a rich, lively mixture of jokes, rows, embarrassment, horseplay, feuds, and alliances.

The film's key moment—which ran it into major problems with the French government—is the act of incest between Laurent and his mother, filmed by Malle with great subtlety and discretion. Audaciously, he treats it not as a source of guilt and trauma, but as a loving, liberating event, to be recalled (as Laurent's mother tells him) "not with remorse, but with tenderness...as something beautiful." **PK**

**France / Italy / West Germany** (Franz Seitz, Marianne, NEF, Vides) 118m Eastmancolor
**Language:** French
**Director:** Louis Malle
**Producer:** Vincent Malle, Claude Nedjar
**Screenplay:** Louis Malle
**Photography:** Ricardo Aronovich
**Music:** Sidney Bechet, Gaston Frèche, Charlie Parker, Henri Renaud
**Cast:** Lea Massari, Benoît Ferreux, Daniel Géiln, Michael Lonsdale, Ave Ninchi, Gila von Weitershausen, Fabien Ferreux, Marc Winocourt, Micheline Bona, Henri Poirier, Liliane Sorval, Corinne Kersten, Eric Walter, François Werner, René Bouloc
**Oscar nomination:** Louis Malle (screenplay)
**Cannes Film Festival:** Louis Malle nomination (Golden Palm)

U.S. (Yeah) 97m Color

**Director:** Melvin Van Peebles

**Producer:** Jerry Gross, Melvin Van Peebles

**Screenplay:** Melvin Van Peebles

**Photography:** Robert Maxwell

**Music:** Earth Wind and Fire, Melvin Van Peebles

**Cast:** Simon Chuckster, Melvin Van Peebles, Hubert Scales, John Dullaghan, West Gale, Niva Rochelle, Rhetta Hughes, Nick Ferrari, Ed Rue, John Amos, Lavelle Roby, Ted Hayden, Mario Van Peebles, Sonja Dunson, Michael Agustus

# SWEET SWEETBACK'S BAADASSSSS SONG (1971)

"This film is dedicated to all the Brothers and Sisters who have had enough of the Man." With the $70,000 he earned from his 1970 race-reversal comedy *Watermelon Man*, plus additional funds (including a $50,000 loan from Bill Cosby), Melvin Van Peebles—one of the first African-American directors to work in Hollywood—financed his new project, *Sweet Sweetback's Baadasssss Song*. To keep costs down, he pretended to be making a porn flick, which enabled him to hire black and nonunion crew. Van Peebles wrote, directed, scored, and starred in the film, which not only was a sound economic decision but also ensured his creative control over every facet of production. Early in 1971, *Sweetback* opened in the only two theaters that would agree to show it on a first-run basis. By the end of the year the film had become the most profitable independent production in history. A sleeper hit across the nation, it ended up grossing over $15 million.

*Sweetback* is a film so original in both conception and realization that it defied all expectations, thereby satisfying the desire for a popular alternative to the dominant Hollywood paradigm. But it is also a film that borrows narrative threads and conventions from an assortment of different genres, including the chase film, the gangster movie, the biker flick, and the soft-core porno. Finally, *Sweetback* is a film whose staggering and unanticipated commercial success ensured its place at the head of an explosion in black-marketed, black-cast, and/or black-directed productions—an explosion that soon went by the ambivalent name of "Blaxploitation cinema."

The shocking first scene finds a preteen Sweetback (played by Melvin's son, Mario) working in a whorehouse, where a grateful call girl screams out his nickname during orgasm. We next observe the now grown-up Sweetback performing as a stud in a sex show in South Central Los Angeles. Watching as two white cops proceed to beat a young black activist (Hubert Scales) within an inch of his life, Sweetback jumps the officers and nearly kills them. The rest of the film tracks our hero's progress as he rides, runs, and hitches his way through decaying cityscapes in a desperate effort at avoiding capture. At one point, Sweetback has his life threatened by a motorcycle gang, and only manages to survive by winning a public sex duel with the female leader. And that's just the beginning—as one reviewer describes it. Sweetback "evades the police by raping a Black woman at knifepoint, spears a cop with a pool cue, kills a number of dogs tracking him, heals himself with his own urine, and bites off the head of a lizard before escaping across the Mexican border into the desert." The film concludes on an ominous note for white audiences, as the words "A Baadasssss nigger is coming to collect some dues" flash across the screen.

Whatever one makes of *Sweetback's* sociopolitical "message," the energy and innovativeness of Van Peeble's directorial style can hardly be denied. By making creative use of such techniques as montage, superimposition, freeze-frames, jump cuts, zoom ins, split-screen editing, stylized dialogue, multiply exposed scenes, and a soulful musical score, Van Peebles broke new ground and challenged viewers of all colors. **SJS**

# THE LAST PICTURE SHOW (1971)

An ardent formalist at a time when his early '70s peers were spending their time breaking rules, Peter Bogdanovich doggedly stuck to old-fashioned ideals and ideas when directing *The Last Picture Show*. In this sense, his adaptation of Larry McMurtry's novel stands as a eulogy for the previous generation of master filmmakers (like Howard Hawks or John Ford) as a new generation of youthful pioneers steered filmmaking in a looser, more visceral direction.

A coming-of-age story set in a small, dusty Texas town, *The Last Picture Show* bids adieu to the 1950s, capturing the nation's shifting mores and interests. A superb cast of newcomers (including Jeff Bridges, Cybill Sheppard, Randy Quaid, and Timothy Bottoms) plays against such veterans as Cloris Leachman and Ben Johnson as they all try to find their place in a changing world. Bogdanovich's vision is bleak but honest, and he captures (in stark but striking black and white) the awkward moments when innocence lurches into experience, without judgment and without pat nostalgia. The film is like a wake for an entire era, ripe with tragedy and exuding a heavy pall of unmistakable sadness. **JKl**

**U.S.** (BBS, Columbia) 118m BW

**Director:** Peter Bogdanovich

**Producer:** Stephen J. Friedman

**Screenplay:** Peter Bogdanovich, James Lee Barrett, from novel by Larry McMurtry

**Photography:** Robert Surtees

**Music:** Hank Williams, John Philip Sousa

**Cast:** Timothy Bottoms, Jeff Bridges, Cybill Shepherd, Ben Johnson, Cloris Leachman, Ellen Burstyn, Eileen Brennan, Clu Gulager, Sam Bottoms, Sharon Ullrick, Randy Quaid

**Oscar:** Ben Johnson (actor in support role), Cloris Leachman (actress in support role)

**Oscar nomination:** Stephen J. Friedman (best picture), Peter Bogdanovich (director), James Lee Barrett, Peter Bogdanovich (screenplay), Jeff Bridges (actor in support role), Ellen Burstyn (actress in support role), Robert Surtees (photography)

G.B. (ABC, Amerbroco, Talent) 118m Eastmancolor

**Director:** Sam Peckinpah

**Producer:** Daniel Melnick

**Screenplay:** David Zelag Goodman, Sam Peckinpah, from the novel *The Siege of Trencher's Farm* by Gordon M. Williams

**Photography:** John Coquillon

**Music:** Jerry Fielding

**Cast:** Dustin Hoffman, Susan George, Peter Vaughan, T.P. McKenna, Del Henney, Jim Norton, Donald Webster, Ken Hutchison, Len Jones, Sally Thomsett, Robert Keegan, Peter Arne, Cherina Schaer, Colin Welland

**Oscar nomination:** Jerry Fielding (music)

# STRAW DOGS (1971)

Sam Peckinpah was not a director known for his delicacy, and indeed *Straw Dogs* remains his most divisive and galvanizing film, especially following the more stylized Western violence of the 1969 film *The Wild Bunch*. Dustin Hoffman plays a timid mathematician who moves with his wife Susan George to her childhood village in the United Kingdom. There she flaunts her success and beauty before the insular townsfolk, who treat the arrival of Hoffman and her as an intrusion, and it's clear that their already rocky marriage may collapse under the strain. Hoffman, for his part, grows more and more uncomfortable, and the townsfolk more and more bold in their contempt for the couple—but it is only when his wife is raped that Hoffman explodes with violence.

More than just implicitly supporting vigilantism—the apparently inevitable outcome when one man is pushed too far—*Straw Dogs* proves equally ambiguous when it comes to George's character. She parades around in tight sweaters and flirts shamelessly with old flames, so when she is finally assaulted, Peckinpah initially makes it appear as if she'd invited the horrific invasion, both as an affront to her bookish husband and also as a provocative response to his inaction. But that ambiguity quickly passes as Peckinpah plays up the terror of the infamous rape scene, and by the time it's over the viewer is almost as shaken as George's character.

Given the brutal lead-up, Peckinpah hardly lets the audience off easy when it comes to *Straw Dogs*' wilfully barbaric conclusion. Having kept the film brilliantly off-balance with his disorienting editing and the steady, audacious ratcheting of intensity, Peckinpah further strains and exploits the viewer's emotions by stacking the deck against the brutish antagonists. But the disturbing, bloody outcome hardly results in any real catharsis or satisfaction. Rather, it leaves you feeling even more stunned and unsure of what you've seen than ever before. The uncertain morality of *Straw Dogs* sparked a great deal of controversy, which ironically validates Peckinpah's instincts. We may not like what we see, but we're compelled to watch it anyway. **JKl**

# TWO-LANE BLACKTOP (1971)

Monte Hellman's *Two-Lane Blacktop* is probably the best film to come out of the post-*Easy Rider* craze in Hollywood for greenlighting hippie-era road movies that studio executives and, sadly, most audiences, didn't understand.

Having made a pair of remarkable existentialist Westerns, *Ride in the Whirlwind* (1965) and *The Shooting* (1967), Hellman set out to strip away the longhaired glamor of *Easy Rider* (1969). *Blacktop* is a deliberately paced story about an absurd race between a pair of black car cultists in a '55 Chevrolet played by musicians (James Taylor, Dennis Wilson) and a fast-spieling, grinning neurotic in a yellow G.T.O. (Hellman regular Warren Oates), with glum tagalong chick Laurie Bird passed between them and pink slips put up as prize.

Whereas *Easy Rider* and *Vanishing Point* (1971) zoom down the highways toward apocalypse, *Two-Lane Blacktop* depicts a race with no end, the film burning up in the projector before any resolution has been reached. A depiction of a country in a profound state of bad faith, the film has a lot of on-the-road detail, with sharp little cameos from the likes of Harry Dean Stanton (as a gay hitchhiker), but presents a central set of relationships between uncommunicative folks who are as stuck in their cars and on their courses as toys on a boy's racing game. **KN**

**U.S.** (Michael Laughlin, Universal) 102m Technicolor

**Director:** Monte Hellman

**Producer:** Gary Kurtz, Michael Laughlin

**Screenplay:** Will Corry, Rudy Wurlitzer

**Photography:** Jack Deerson

**Music:** Billy James

**Cast:** James Taylor, Warren Oates, Laurie Bird, Dennis Wilson, David Drake, Richard Ruth, Rudy Wurlitzer, Jaclyn Hellman, Bill Keller, Harry Dean Stanton, Don Samuels, Charles Moore, Tom Green, W.H. Harrison, Alan Vint

# THE HEARTBREAK KID (1972)

Elaine May is the most underrated director in American cinema. *The Heartbreak Kid* is the closest she has yet come to mainstream success, but it stays true to her corrosive, uncompromising vision. While remaining essentially faithful to Neil Simon's script (with its echoes of the 1967 film *The Graduate*), May manages to slaughter the sentimental, feel-good aura of that writer's baleful contribution to popular movies. She does so by emphasizing the unpalatable facts of cruelty, humiliation, and embarrassment.

"Black comedy" here wears a mundane face. Lenny (Charles Grodin in his best role), a gormless salesman, is on his honeymoon to the nightmarish but good-hearted Lila (Jeannie Berlin—has ever a mother directed her daughter in such a brave, extreme part?). Feeling trapped and suffocated, Lenny's rather shallow fantasies turn to the all-American ideal, perky Kelly (Cybill Shepherd). Every consequence of this triangle is a disaster.

Few films plunge us so mercilessly into the tawdriness of romantic and sexual dreaming. May's focus on this material is pure John Cassavetes: an unflinching documentation of discomfort; real pain played out in real time. Our laughter—so brilliantly elicited by May's fractured mise en scène—turns hysterical in the psychoanalytic sense, a way of momentarily fleeing horror. **AM**

**U.S.** (Palomar) 106m

**Director:** Elaine May

**Producer:** Michael Hausman, Erik Lee Preminger, Edgar J. Scherick

**Screenplay:** Neil Simon, from the story *A Change of Plan* by Bruce Jay Friedman

**Photography:** Owen Roizman

**Music:** Cy Coleman, Sheldon Harnick, Garry Sherman

**Cast:** Charles Grodin, Cybill Shepherd, Jeannie Berlin, Audra Lindley, Eddie Albert, Mitchell Jason, William Prince, Augusta Dabney, Doris Roberts, Marilyn Putnam, Jack Hausman, Erik Lee Preminger, Art Metrano, Tim Browne, Jean Scoppa

**Oscar nomination:** Eddie Albert (actor in support role), Jeannie Berlin (actress in support role)

# AGUIRRE, DER ZORN GOTTES (1972)
## AGUIRRE, THE WRATH OF GOD

"I am the great traitor. I am the Wrath of God." Werner Herzog had a remarkable run of important films in the radical and exciting New German Cinema. But his epic adventures featuring his maniacal tormentor and impulsive, inspired interpreter, Klaus Kinski, are the best known. And *Aguirre: The Wrath of God*—the first of Herzog's features widely seen internationally—is the most spellbinding. The film, supposedly narrated from the diary of the Spanish monk Gaspar de Carvajal, is a disturbing parable that encapsulates Herzog's flair for allegory, metaphor, dark humor, and the grotesque, his interest in alienation, obsession, and social decay; and his sense of the landscape taking on awful, human aspects.

Don Lope de Aguirre (Kinski) is one of Pizarro's pillaging conquistadors cutting a swathe across 16th-century South America. Having overwhelmed the Incas, Pizarro's soldiers are greedy for conquest and gold, but the expedition reaches an impasse in difficult terrain. What is supposed to be a one-week foraging and scouting trip by a party sent up the Amazon basin by raft quickly begins to suffer disasters. Soldiers and slaves are picked off by Indians, disease, and hunger; Aguirre leads a revolt against his commander; and the desperate journey degenerates into a homicidal power trip driven on by Aguirre's increasingly demented obsession with reaching the fabled city of gold, El Dorado.

Shooting on remote locations in Peru on a tiny budget was sufficiently problematic and arduous, but Herzog's account (particularly vivid in his documentary *My Best Fiend*) of a frequently raving Kinski adds appalling and entertaining background to the film. Toward the end of shooting, Herzog prevented Kinski from walking out by threatening to shoot him. Clearly the real-life struggles enhanced the film's heated intensity, its tragic inevitability signaled by the murdered commander's graceful wife, carefully dressed in her (improbably clean) best, determinedly walking away into the jungle. By the end, a mad Aguirre rules a floating bier strewn with corpses and swarming with squealing monkeys. Kinski's fascinating presence may dominate the film, but it is Herzog's uncompromising vision and control that keeps it on its hallucinatory, hypnotic course. **AE**

**West Germany / Peru / Mexico**
(Werner Herzog) 100m Eastmancolor
**Language:** German
**Director:** Werner Herzog
**Producer:** Werner Herzog
**Screenplay:** Werner Herzog
**Photography:** Thomas Mauch
**Music:** Popol Vuh
**Cast:** Klaus Kinski, Daniel Ades, Peter Berling, Daniel Farfán, Justo González, Ruy Guerra, Julio E. Martínez, Del Negro, Armando Polanah, Alejandro Repulles, Cecilia Rivera, Helena Rojo, Edward Roland

## CABARET (1972)

What was just the second film of director, dancer, choreographer, and Broadway giant Bob Fosse took home eight Academy Awards, including Best Director over Francis Ford Coppola for *The Godfather*. *Cabaret* was the only truly great musical made in the 1970s, despite prophecies that it would be Fosse's "Springtime For Hitler" ("Who wants to see a musical with Nazis?").

The answer was anybody who cares to be dazzled. Fosse was a cynic, brought up in vaudeville, who came of age in burlesque and sleazy nightclubs. No one else could have taken the John Kander–Fred Ebb musical (based on John Van Druten's play *I Am A Camera*, itself based on Christopher Isherwood's *Goodbye To Berlin*) and cast such a cold, glittering eye on its sinful, soulless denizens of 1930s Berlin. The film's sharp, shiny musical numbers and incisive cuts between the cabaret and the world outside chillingly counterpoint the doom-laden tale of misconceived love and ambition amid the rise of Nazism, while Joel Grey's sinister club emcee is brilliant. But ultimately the film belongs to Liza Minnelli, who brought desperate-to-please nervous energy to sad, wild-eyed Sally Bowles with her feverish vitality and feigned depravity, giving warmth and frailty to a masterpiece of menace and show-stopping tunes. **AE**

**U.S.** (ABC) 124m Technicolor

**Director:** Bob Fosse

**Producer:** Cy Feuer

**Screenplay:** Jay Presson Allen, from the book *Berlin Stories* by Christopher Isherwood, from the play *I Am a Camera* by John Van Druten and musical by Joe Masteroff

**Photography:** Geoffrey Unsworth

**Music:** John Kander

**Cast:** Liza Minnelli, Michael York, Helmut Griem, Joel Grey, Fritz Wepper, Marisa Berenson, Elisabeth Neumann-Viertel, Helen Vita

**Oscar:** Bob Fosse (director), Liza Minnelli (actress), Joel Grey (actor in support role), Rolf Zehetbauer, Hans Jürgen Kiebach, Herbert Strabel (art direction), Geoffrey Unsworth (photography), David Bretherton (editing), Ralph Burns (music), Robert Knudson, David Hildyard (sound)

**Oscar nomination:** Cy Feuer (best picture), Jay Presson Allen (screenplay)

## ULTIMO TANGO A PARIGI (1972)
### LAST TANGO IN PARIS

Bernardo Bertolucci's *Last Tango in Paris* started a trend in arthouse erotica that has endured to this day—films including *Intimacy* (2001) continue its premise of a "no questions asked" sexual affair that gives way to difficult familiarity; while writer-director Catherine Breillat (*Romance* [1999]), who appears in it, updates its themes of Eros and Thanatos.

Would *Last Tango in Paris* have mattered without Brando? His remarkable performance alludes to many previous, iconic roles. His obscene, scatological monologues, replete with Bertolucci's allusions to theories of Reich and Bataille, still have the power to startle. And the emotions of this middle-aged, despairing man are palpable.

A casting coup set the relatively inexperienced Maria Schneider against Brando. Her scenes with Jean-Pierre Léaud are deliberately superficial, contrasting with the central, primal, relationship and its stripping away of illusions.

Yet *Last Tango in Paris* is more than the sum of its big ideas. Bertolucci's hyper-baroque style takes us into a subterranean, fractured, psychic space. Partitions, mirror reflections, incongruous props, and off-center framings multiply, disorienting the viewer at every turn, perfectly accompanied by Gato Barbieri's surging saxophone waltzes. A film of obstinate bloodstains and empty walls, inarticulate cries and bodily convulsions, *Last Tango in Paris* vigorously enacts its descent into the "womb of death." **AM**

**Italy / France** (Artistes Associés, PEA) 129m Technicolor

**Language:** English / French

**Director:** Bernardo Bertolucci

**Producer:** Alberto Grimaldi

**Screenplay:** Bernardo Bertolucci, Franco Arcalli, Agnès Varda

**Photography:** Vittorio Storaro

**Music:** Gato Barbieri

**Cast:** Marlon Brando, Maria Schneider, Maria Michi, Giovanna Galletti, Gitt Magrini, Catherine Allégret, Luce Marquand, Marie-Hélène Breillat, Catherine Breillat, Dan Diament, Catherine Sola, Mauro Marchetti, Jean-Pierre Léaud, Massimo Girotti

**Oscar nomination:** Bernardo Bertolucci (director), Marlon Brando (actor)

## HIGH PLAINS DRIFTER (1972)

**U.S.** (Malpaso) 105m Technicolor
**Director:** Clint Eastwood
**Producer:** Robert Daley
**Screenplay:** Ernest Tidyman
**Photography:** Bruce Surtees
**Music:** Dee Barton
**Cast:** Clint Eastwood, Verna Bloom, Marianna Hill, Mitch Ryan, Jack Ging, Stefan Gierasch, Ted Hartley, Billy Curtis, Geoffrey Lewis, Scott Walker, Walter Barnes, Paul Brinegar, Richard Bull, Alex Tinne, John Hillerman

Clint Eastwood's second film as director-star (after *Play Misty for Me*) relocates his Spaghetti Western persona into an American gothic morality tale. An unshaven saddle tramp rides out of a desert haze into Lago, where the townsfolk once stood by as a marshal was whipped to death. In a surreal rerun of *High Noon*, Eastwood—who might be the murdered man's ghost, or more prosaically his brother—is begged to stand up to three outlaws just released from territorial prison and on their way home for violent revenge.

The mystery man demonstrates his powers not only by meting out the kind of gunplay and abuse expected of a grungy cowboy antihero circa 1972, but also by forcing everyone to take part in a bizarre fiesta. The latter involves making a dwarf into the combined Sheriff and Mayor, literally painting the town red, and renaming it "Hell." Recalling the Vietnam slogan "we destroyed the village in order to save it," the stranger finally burns down the town. With at least as much borrowed from Luis Buñuel as Sergio Leone, this is a funny, brutal, scary movie, daringly weird in its mixture of Western and horror themes, and shot through with acid self-analysis. **KN**

## SLEUTH (1972)

**G.B.** (Palomar) 138m Color
**Director:** Joseph L. Mankiewicz
**Producer:** Morton Gottlieb
**Screenplay:** Anthony Shaffer, from his play
**Photography:** Oswald Morris
**Music:** John Addison, Cole Porter
**Cast:** Laurence Olivier, Michael Caine, Alec Cawthorne, John Matthews, Eve Channing, Teddy Martin
**Oscar nomination:** Joseph L. Mankiewicz (director), Michael Caine (actor), Laurence Olivier (actor), John Addison (music)

Given Joseph L. Mankiewicz's reputation as the most conversational of filmmakers, a man who always prized high-quality talk over visual flash, he was a perfect choice to direct the film version of Anthony Shaffer's long-running Broadway and West End stage hit, *Sleuth*. Though a few scenes "open out" the setting by venturing into the garden of mystery writer Andrew Wyke's prop-filled stately home, the piece remains essentially confined to the drawing room as two actors from different generations clash in style, temperament, and method.

Sir Laurence Olivier, reclaiming the status of movie star after more "serious" theater work, plays the role of Wyke, a mischievous sadist with a childish delight in nasty trickery ("that's a puzzle jug") and an addiction to complex games (an all-white jigsaw). Michael Caine is Milo Tindle, hairdresser and lover of Wyke's neglected wife. At first apparently outclassed in every way by his opponent, he reveals a surprising emotional range in the first act climax. He pulls a coup de théâtre in the second act that really works even if you see it coming—invited over to be ensnared in a plot that has many twists and turns before it ends unhappily but justly for all concerned. **KN**

# DELIVERANCE (1972)

Like Sam Peckinpah's *Straw Dogs* and Wes Craven's *Last House on the Left*, John Boorman's *Deliverance* deals with complacent, middle-class folk faced with unreasoning, disturbingly sexualized violence in the wilds away from civilization, only to discover in themselves that they are "natural-born killers." Ironically, while the American Peckinpah, who had considered making *Deliverance*, was in Britain filming *Straw Dogs*, British director Boorman was in Georgia, using the Chattooga River to sub for poet-novelist James Dickey's fictional Cahulawassee River, shooting his own journey into the heart of darkness.

The film opens with four contrasted suburban types—quiet Ed (Jon Voight), survivalist Lewis (Burt Reynolds), bluff Bobby (Ned Beatty), and sensitive Drew (Ronny Cox)—traveling into woodland about to be destroyed by a dam which will create a new lake, opting to take a canoe trip downriver rather than play golf. When Ed and Bobby are waylaid by a pair of frightening, irrational hillbillies, Bobby is stripped, made to "squeal like a pig," and raped while Ed is tethered to a tree with his own belt, absurdly hanging on to his pipe through the ordeal. Archer Lewis intervenes, killing the rapist (Bill McKinney), and the quartet, with deeply mixed feelings, opts to cover up the incident and get out of the region, pitted against the surviving hillbilly rifleman (Herbert Coward) and the hostile landscape.

Most other directors, especially with Burt Reynolds signed up as the most macho of the suburbanites, would have made a standard he-man adventure movie, but Boorman, working from Dickey's screenplay, goes for a more disturbing approach, always questioning what the characters' heroism really means. The film eventually concludes that Voight's sad-eyed Ed, finding in himself the bestiality to survive, has lost rather than won. Reynolds, given a chance to rethink his good ol' boy screen persona, gives as generously self-critical a performance as John Wayne's in *The Searchers*. Among the highlights: the unforgettable "feudin' banjos" scene as Drew plays a duet with a withered, porch-sitting manchild who turns out to be an amazing musician, and an oft-imitated last-minute horror twist (cf. *Carrie*), as Ed's sleep is troubled by dreams of a hand emerging from the waters of the new lake. **KN**

**U.S.** (Elmer, Warner Bros.) 109m Technicolor

**Director:** John Boorman

**Producer:** John Boorman

**Screenplay:** James Dickey, from his novel

**Photography:** Vilmos Zsigmond

**Music:** Eric Weissberg

**Cast:** Jon Voight, Burt Reynolds, Ned Beatty, Ronny Cox, Ed Ramey, Billy Redden, Seamon Glass, Randall Deal, Bill McKinney, Herbert Coward, Lewis Crone, Ken Keener, Johnny Popwell, John Fowler, Kathy Rickman

**Oscar nomination:** John Boorman (best picture), John Boorman (director), Tom Priestley (editing)

# SOLYARIS (1972)
## SOLARIS

**U.S.S.R.** (Creative Unit of Writers & Cinema Workers, Mosfilm, Unit Four) 165m BW / Sovcolor

**Language:** Russian

**Director:** Andrei Tarkovsky

**Producer:** Viacheslav Tarasov

**Screenplay:** Fridrikh Gorenshtein, Andrei Tarkovsky, from novel by Stanislaw Lem

**Photography:** Vadim Yusov

**Music:** Eduard Artemyev, Johann Sebastian Bach

**Cast:** Natalya Bondarchuk, Donatas Banionis, Jüri Järvet, Vladislav Dvorzhetsky, Nikolai Grinko, Anatoli Solonitsyn

**Cannes Film Festival:** Andrei Tarkovsky (FIPRESCI award), (grand prize of the jury), nomination (Golden Palm)

Adapted from the bestseller by Stanislaw Lem, Andrei Tarkovsky's *Solaris* meditates on an imaginary planet and Stanley Kubrick's *2001: A Space Odyssey* (1968). A sci-fi masterpiece, the film is equally an epic performed without a budget. Instead of offering innovative special effects or mind-blowing spectacle it's confined to the experience of a character through whom fantasy and everyday life merge into one.

When psychologist Kris Kelvin (Donatas Banionis) is asked to evaluate the usefulness of a space station orbiting Solaris, he is confronted with the unsettling story of astronaut Berton (Vladislav Dvorzhetsky). Some years earlier, when there was hope to unravel the secrets of the new world's swirling oceans of consciousness, all turned for the worse when Berton became the lone survivor of a mishap that killed several explorers. Intrigued, Kris visits the space station and meets Dr. Snauth (Jüri Järvet), Dr. Sartorius (Anatoli Solonitsyn), and the suicide case Dr. Gibaryan (Sos Sarkisyan). They advise him to take his time and adjust. Meanwhile strange sights and sounds assault him, including the appearance of his long-dead wife Khari (Natalya Bondarchuk). Thus he begins realizing the ability of Solaris to recreate the memories of visitors.

In fear of Khari's seeming reality, Kris destroys, or aids the destruction of, several different Kharis, only to discover other truths about Solaris. Namely, that its illusions are materially real, emotionally as needy as he is, and that he's the first person to form a lasting relationship with the planet's sentience. Finally unable to perform his duty, Kris joins with Khari and all she represents. Snauth and Sartorius recognize his fall and accept the burden of ending Solaris, although the film's final image is of the planet fashioning itself into Kris's imagined redemption.

A brilliant experience of duration and big ideas combined with ascetic production values, *Solaris* is an argument against the ambivalence of lived reality in favor of fantasy's all-inclusive satisfaction. Through Kris's journey from indifferent outsider to being literally the center of a world created just for him, we see the unmaking of a rational mind by sheer desire. As such, Tarkovsky's film uses the widescreen frame and lengthy takes to organize truly beautiful imagery. In this fashion, *Solaris* externalizes interior states to embody the mood of its protagonist.

Banionis's Kris Kelvin is a sad, middle-aged man. His shock of white hair on an otherwise brunette scalp suggests tragic experience and orients his first attempts to categorize Solaris before submitting to its dream logic. The irresolvable conflict of the planet—both soothing and all consuming—is then perfectly expressed in various sequences shot in circular patterns. While a stationary camera spins slowly on a central pivot, the actors and sets change to reveal new layers of possibility from what existed only moments before.

A mind game in the same way *2001* was a head film, *Solaris* was produced in the heart of Soviet pogroms against free expression, and certainly without benefit of a large budget. Least of all a philosophical drama, Tarkovsky's film is a touchstone of the cinematic impetus to unravel what it is to be alive. **GC-Q**

U.S. (Paramount) 175m Technicolor
**Language:** English / Italian
**Director:** Francis Ford Coppola
**Producer:** Albert S. Ruddy
**Screenplay:** Francis Ford Coppola, Mario Puzo, from novel by Mario Puzo
**Photography:** Gordon Willis
**Music:** Carmine Coppola, Nino Rota
**Cast:** Marlon Brando, Al Pacino, Diane Keaton, Richard S. Castellano, Robert Duvall, James Caan, Sterling Hayden, Talia Shire, John Marley, Richard Conte, Al Lettieri, Abe Vigoda, Gianni Russo, John Cazale, Rudy Bond
**Oscar:** Albert S. Ruddy (best picture), Mario Puzo, Francis Ford Coppola (screenplay), Marlon Brando (actor—refused award)
**Oscar nomination:** Francis Ford Coppola (director), James Caan (actor in support role), Al Pacino (actor in support role), Robert Duvall (actor in support role), Anna Hill Johnstone (costume), William Reynolds, Peter Zinner (editing), Nino Rota (music—ineligible because he reused Fortunella score), Charles Grenzbach, Richard Portman, Christopher Newman (sound)

# THE GODFATHER (1972)

"Make him an offer he can't refuse." The youngest son, Michael Corleone (Al Pacino), returns from World War II outside the family business, organized crime. When his father, Don Corleone (Marlon Brando) is gunned down, however, Michael is driven to commit a revenge murder, bound by blood and "honor" to a violent course (or curse) of underworld power and survival. Eventually Michael inherits the role as family head, closing the door on his uncomprehending WASP wife (Diane Keaton) as he receives the homage as the new "Godfather."

The dialogue and characters of *The Godfather* instantly entered the collective consciousness of filmgoers. It made stars of Pacino and James Caan (hot-headed elder brother Sonny), won Oscars for Picture, Screenplay, and Best Actor for Brando, in a triumphant comeback. It is one of the greatest American films, beloved by all, not only those who adore making Corleone impersonations but also businessmen who consider it the font of wisdom. Adapting Mario Puzo's bestseller, writer-director Francis Ford Coppola made a pulp fiction gangster opera, an epic of patriarchy, family, and of America itself. Original protests by Italian-Americans citing defamation were swept away in the film's staggering popularity. All descendants of immigrants viewed with nostalgic yearning the Corleone clan pounding the pasta, celebrating and sorrowing together. Anecdotes, footnotes, and postscripts are part of film folklore—Brando did not stuff his cheeks with cotton, but had resin blobs clipped to his back teeth. The baby baptized is Sofia Coppola. Brando sent a fake Indian "Satcheen Littlefeather" to the Academy Awards ceremony to reject his Oscar.

It is a masterly work, fully deserving of its reputation. Coppola laid much of the groundwork of 1970s cinema with his commanding technique. The audacious, visceral, and stately set pieces are legend—the horse's head in the bed, Sonny's slaughter, the intercutting of a sunny wedding party in the garden with Don Corleone's court indoors, and the dazzling finale of assassinations carried out during the christening of a new Corleone (in effect the sacramental rites for Michael as he assumes the role of Godfather). The film's finest qualities reveal Coppola's fluency in classics, pulp, noir, and social dramas, but an enduring criticism of *The Godfather* is that it glorifies the Mafia. Pacino's Michael is the film's hero, and Michael is not a good guy. But its mythic exploration of familial ties, be it one cursed in blood and ambition, still entices viewers with the idea that Family is better than no family at all. **AE**

# VISKINGAR OCH ROP (1972)
## CRIES AND WHISPERS

One of Ingmar Bergman's most exquisitely executed achievements, *Cries and Whispers* begins with early-morning shots of a country estate, Sven Nykvist's camerawork capturing the play of sunlight through trees and mist to ravishing effect. By the time we have entered the house itself, where antique clocks tick inexorably on as a woman is awakened from her slumbers by the agony of the cancer consuming her from within, it's clear we are witnessing a filmmaker at the peak of his artistry, so assured and seemingly effortless are the measured rhythms of his editing, the placement of the camera, and the telling use of sound and color. Indeed, it is perhaps color that sticks most vividly in the mind after a viewing of this autumnal masterpiece. The rich red so unnaturally predominant both in the furnishings and on the walls of most of the mansion's rooms, in sharp contrast to the graceful white gowns favored by the four women whose lives we glimpse therein.

Bergman explained that he'd imagined the human soul to be this shade of red; certainly, its brooding presence intensifies his study of death and its influence on the living. The four women are the mansion's dying owner (Harriet Andersson), her devoted maid (Kari Sylwan), and the two sisters (Ingrid Thulin and Liv Ullmann) who have come to tend to her during her final days. The former is emotionally and physically reticent thanks in part to a loveless marriage, the latter at least is superficially warmer but given to flightiness and insecurity. As the sisters and maid try first to comfort the sick woman and then to come to terms with her death, Bergman provides a glimpse into the inner life of each, tracing their fears, frustrations, anxieties, and regrets by means of memories and, at least for the maid, nightmarish fantasy. Such is his dramatic expertise that he blends the stuff of horror movies—vampirish kisses, the nightmarish prospect of a corpse returning to life—with chamber drama evocative of Chekhov or Strindberg, and makes it not only coherent and compelling but immediately recognizable as part of his own artistic universe. He's helped in this, of course, by extraordinary performances by actresses he'd worked with for many years, but then what a gift to them was his screenplay! **GA**

**Sweden** (Cinematograph AB, Svenska) 106m Eastmancolor

**Language:** Swedish

**Director:** Ingmar Bergman

**Producer:** Lars-Owe Carlberg

**Screenplay:** Ingmar Bergman

**Photography:** Sven Nykvist

**Nonoriginal music:** Johann Sebastian Bach, Frédéric Chopin

**Cast:** Harriet Andersson, Kari Sylwan, Ingrid Thulin, Liv Ullmann, Anders Ek, Inga Gill, Erland Josephson, Henning Moritzen, Georg Årlin, Fredrik

**Oscar:** Sven Nykvist (photography)

**Oscar nomination:** Ingmar Bergman (best picture), Ingmar Bergman (director), Ingmar Bergman (screenplay), Marik Vos-Lundh (costume)

**Cannes Film Festival:** Ingmar Bergman (grand technical prize)

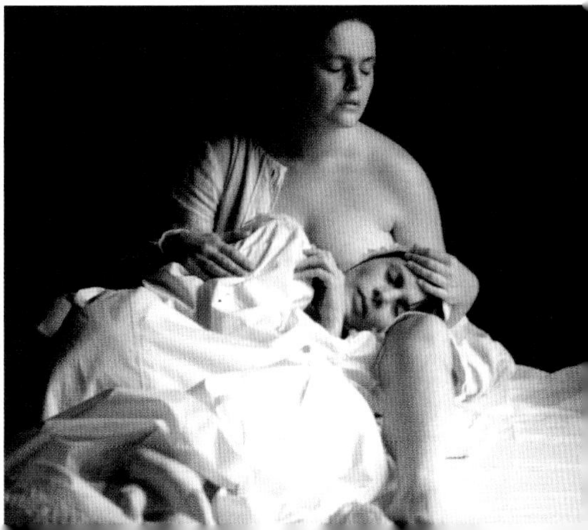

**U.S.** (Columbia, Rastar) 100 min Technicolor

**Director:** John Huston

**Producer:** John Huston, Ray Stark

**Screenplay:** Leonard Gardner, from his novel

**Photography:** Conrad L. Hall

**Music:** Kris Kristofferson

**Cast:** Stacy Keach, Jeff Bridges, Susan Tyrrell, Candy Clark, Nicholas Colasanto, Art Aragon, Curtis Cokes, Sixto Rodriguez, Billy Walker, Wayne Mahan, Ruben Navarro

**Oscar nomination:** Susan Tyrrell (actress in support role)

# FAT CITY (1972)

John Huston's most effective "small film," *Fat City* tells the story of an over-the-hill boxer (Stacy Keach) who, conforming to Hollywood stereotypes, launches a comeback that inevitably fails, even as his gritty determination in defeat offers him a kind of transcendence. Like most Hustonian heroes, Tully (Keach) has missed his main chance, but is tendered yet another opportunity by chance to reclaim his self-respect. He connects with a younger boxer named Ernie (Jeff Bridges), becoming his mentor and rival as the pair seek to "make it big." Ernie may be talented enough to make a success of boxing, but he too becomes trapped by circumstances, forced to marry his girlfriend and enter a life of unending responsibility. Paradoxically, perhaps, Tully's romantic interest, the psychotic and self-destructive Oma (Susan Tyrrell), abandons him for a former lover, a man who abuses and mistreats her.

At the end of the film, Tully is not so much "free" to live the life of masculine accomplishment, as he is confirmed in his isolation and failure. There is, Huston suggests, no easy path to the "fat city" that is the American dream. With its authentic boxing sequences, drab California locations, and fine, understated acting from a talented ensemble, *Fat City* offers a realistic, yet poetic portrait of the all-too-human obsession to realize unrealizable dreams of self-transformation and transcendence. **RBP**

**France / Italy / Spain** (Dean, Greenwich, Jet) 105m Eastmancolor

**Language:** French / Spanish

**Director:** Luis Buñuel

**Producer:** Serge Silberman

**Screenplay:** Luis Buñuel, Jean-Claude Carrière

**Photography:** Edmond Richard

**Cast:** Fernando Rey, Paul Frankeur, Delphine Seyrig, Bulle Ogier, Stéphane Audran, Jean-Pierre Cassel, Julien Bertheau, Milena Vukotic, Maria Gabriella Maione, Claude Piéplu, Muni, Pierre Maguelon, François Maistre, Michel Piccoli, Ellen Bahl

**Oscar:** France (best foreign language film)

**Oscar nomination:** Luis Buñuel, Jean-Claude Carrière (screenplay)

# LE CHARME DISCRET DE LA BOURGEOISIE (1972)

## THE DISCREET CHARM OF THE BOURGEOISIE

*The Discreet Charm of the Bourgeoisie*, Luis Buñuel's comic masterpiece, about three well-to-do couples who try, but fail, to sit down and have a meal together, is perhaps the most perfectly achieved and executed of all his late French films. The film proceeds with diverse interruptions, digressions, and interpolations that identify the characters, their class, and their seeming indestructibility with the very processes of narrative illusion and narrative continuity.

One thing that makes *The Discreet Charm of the Bourgeoisie* as charming as it is, despite its radicalism, and helped Buñuel to win his only Oscar, is the perfect cast, many of whom bring along nearly mythic associations acquired in previous films. Thus Delphine Seyrig makes us think of *Last Year at Marienbad* (1961), Stéphane Audran summons up the high bourgeoisie of Claude Chabrol's middle period, Bulle Ogier's neurotic is like a light-comic version of the mad character she played in *L'Amour Fou* (1969), and even Rey unmistakably calls to mind *The French Connection* (1971) when he brandishes some cocaine.

Shortly after this film was nominated for an Oscar, Buñuel was interviewed by reporters in a Mexican restaurant, and when they asked if he expected to win, his reply was immediate: "Of course. I've already paid the $25,000 they wanted. Americans may have their weaknesses, but they do keep their promises." **JRos**

# DIE BITTEREN TRÄNEN DER PETRA VON KANT (1972)

## THE BITTER TEARS OF PETRA VON KANT

For many prominent gay artists, George Cukor's *The Women* (1939) has proved an irresistible model for cinematic storytelling in a queer mode: a group of women stuck together in a house, their destinies nominally defined and dominated by off-screen males, but lived through the melodramatic intensity of same-sex exchanges.

*The Bitter Tears of Petra von Kant*—cheekily subtitled "a case history"—is Rainer Werner Fassbinder's lesbian variation on this model. Preserving and indeed exaggerating the claustrophobic theatricality of his play, Fassbinder offers a parade of chic women who visit Petra (Margit Carstensen), a fashion designer, and her mute and ever-obedient servant Marlene (Irm Hermann). Psychological domination and expert game playing are Petra's forte (she gives good phone) and, in her lair, transactions are a dance in and around her bed—while the seethingly jealous Marlene types and sketches forever in the background.

The possibilities that arise for camp humor are many, such as the ironically contrapuntal use of old pop hits, but Fassbinder keeps it cool. His film builds to a simple but valuable life lesson for those embroiled in emotionally sadomasochistic relations, which for Fassbinder means everyone: "The weaker" in any situation has one ultimate, devastating weapon—the power to walk away. **AM**

**West Germany** (Autoren, Tango)
124m Color

**Language:** German

**Director:** Rainer Werner Fassbinder

**Producer:** Rainer Werner Fassbinder, Michael Fengler

**Screenplay:** Rainer Werner Fassbinder, from his play

**Photography:** Michael Ballhaus

**Nonoriginal music:** Giuseppe Verdi

**Cast:** Margit Carstensen, Hanna Schygulla, Katrin Schaake, Eva Mattes, Gisela Fackeldey, Irm Hermann

**Berlin International Film Festival:** Rainer Werner Fassbinder nomination (Golden Bear)

**G.B.** (Universal) 116m Technicolor

**Director:** Alfred Hitchcock

**Producer:** William Hill, Alfred Hitchcock

**Screenplay:** Anthony Shaffer, from the novel *Goodbye Piccadilly, Farewell Leicester Square* by Arthur La Bern

**Photography:** Gilbert Taylor

**Music:** Ron Goodwin

**Cast:** Jon Finch, Alec McCowen, Barry Foster, Billie Whitelaw, Anna Massey, Barbara Leigh-Hunt, Bernard Cribbins, Vivien Merchant, Michael Bates, Jean Marsh, Clive Swift, John Boxer, Madge Ryan, George Tovey, Elsie Randolph

# FRENZY (1972)

Alfred Hitchcock returned to Britain in 1972 to collaborate with playwright Anthony Shaffer on a film version of Arthur La Bern's novel *Goodbye Piccadilly, Farewell Leicester Square*, which resurrects many of the conventions of the director's first hit, *The Lodger* (1926). Here again, London is plagued by a Jack the Ripper-like serial murderer, and the leading man does himself no favors by acting so suspiciously that he becomes the prime suspect.

Hitchcock evokes a precise mix of prurient fascination and genuine horror in the English attitude to murder that is also a great part of his own obsession. Embittered ex-RAF officer Richard Blaney (Jon Finch) is an alcoholic working as a bartender in a Covent Garden pub, reduced to sponging off his sensible ex-wife Brenda (Barbara Leigh-Hunt), who in an ironic stroke runs a successful matchmaking agency. In one of the creepiest, most explicit scenes the Master of Suspense ever directed, Brenda is visited by cheery cockney fruit-market trader Bob Rusk (Barry Foster), whose unstated but perverse special requirements she doesn't want to fulfill professionally; Rusk then reveals himself as the notorious Necktie Murderer by raping the woman and strangling her with his paisley tie.

*Frenzy* proceeds by cutting between the antisocial, unpleasant, degraded hero—who is reduced to bedding down in a homeless shelter at one point—and the charming, engaging, successful villain, who further inconveniences Blaney by murdering his sometime-girlfriend (Edith Massey), a chirrupy barmaid. As in *Psycho* and *Strangers on a Train*, Hitchcock manages a suspense sequence by enlisting our sympathies in a murderer's attempt to cover up his crime, showing Rusk fumbling about with a nude corpse in a potato sack in the back of a van to get back his incriminating tie clip. Hitchcock takes advantage of the period's more relaxed censorship regulations to be more explicit with the sex and violence, though he also knows when a long, slow pull-back away from a murder will convey more horror than another close-up of plunder and strangulation. There is a streak of Mike Leigh-style comedy of social embarrassment in the subplot of a police inspector (Alec McCowen) whose wife (Vivien Merchant) keeps confronting him with hideous gourmet meals. **KN**

# PINK FLAMINGOS (1972)

U.S. (Dreamland) 93m Color
**Director:** John Waters
**Producer:** John Waters
**Screenplay:** John Waters
**Photography:** John Waters
**Cast:** Divine, David Lochary, Mary Vivian Pearce, Mink Stole, Danny Mills, Edith Massey, Channing Wilroy, Cookie Mueller, Paul Swift, Susan Walsh, Pat Moran, Pat Lefaiver, Jack Walsh, Bob Skidmore, Jackie Sidel

Quite possibly the best worst movie ever made—certainly one of the most notorious and beloved (if that's the right word) pieces of trash cinema to come out of the American underground—John Waters's 1972 feature offers a virtual manual on the aesthetics of "pure" gross-out moviemaking.

Shot in and around Waters's beloved hometown of Baltimore, Maryland, *Pink Flamingos* traces the inevitable victory of the writer-director's transvestite diva Divine, who lives in a trailer with her equally eccentric family—including her retarded hippie son, Crackers (Danny Mills), and her obese, egg-obsessed, playpen-residing mama, Edie (Edith Massey, truly unforgettable). The battle is to outdo the self-consciously twisted and antisocial Marbles (Waters regulars Mink Stole and David Lochary) in disgusting and immoral behavior to become nothing less, or more, than "The Filthiest People Alive."

Whereas the Marbles pose a strong challenge by abducting and impregnating female hitchhikers, selling their babies to lesbian couples, and using the money to finance schoolyard heroin schemes, Divine's Babs Johnson is not to be denied in her mission to maintain her family's throne.

The gritty, home-movie feel of the *Pink Flamingos* (with its occasionally off-centered and out-of-focus cinematography, seemingly random zooms and cutaways, and uneven sound quality) only adds to the trash and cult movie-watching experience. After all, we're dealing here with a film that gives extended screen time to butthole lip-synching, bowel movements delivered by post, and sex with chickens—and that's just for starters. In the notorious epilogue, Divine stops on a street in downtown Baltimore to pick up the freshly laid turd of a small dog. She puts it in her mouth, chews for a moment, then gags a bit and gives what can only be called a shit-eating grin to the camera. Critic Justin Frank hardly exaggerates when he identifies this scene as "the most famous...in all underground cinema—the underground equivalent of the shower scene in *Psycho*." Although Waters would go on to make several other memorable exercises in bad taste, including *Female Trouble* (1974) and *Desperate Living* (1977), before turning somewhat kinder and gentler in the 1980s and '90s, none of his movies so perfectly combine humor and vulgarity as this one. **SJS**

**U.S.** (Superfly, Warner Bros.) 93m Technicolor

**Director:** Gordon Parks Jr.

**Producer:** Sig Shore

**Screenplay:** Phillip Fenty

**Photography:** James Signorelli

**Music:** Curtis Mayfield

**Cast:** Ron O'Neal, Carl Lee, Sheila Frazier, Julius Harris, Charles McGregor, Nate Adams, Polly Niles, Yvonne Delaine, Henry Shapiro, K.C., James G. Richardson, Make Bray, Al Kiggins, Bob Bonds, Fred Rolaf

# SUPERFLY (1972)

One of the most beloved and oft-quoted films of the Blaxploitation cycle, boasting a sizzling funk soundtrack by Curtis Mayfield, a macho, drug-dealing antihero, and pimpin' 1970s streetware, *Superfly* is simply unforgettable. Directed by Gordon Parks Jr., the hard-boiled action/crime drama was financed by a group of independent African-American businessmen (making it the first to achieve this honor), with a crew that was nearly all Black as well. It anticipated the infiltration of flashy clothes and deadly recreational drugs, notably cocaine, into mainstream American pop culture.

*Superfly* tells the saga of a hip Harlem drug pusher, Youngblood Priest (Ron O'Neal), who hopes to make one last deal, converting all his coke to cash before starting a new, crime-free life for himself. It makes a strong statement about the continuous supply of drugs to the ghetto begetting pain, suffering, and an endless cycle of violence. It also makes Priest the richest, and most admired dude in the 'hood, glamorizing the era's "machismo-cocaine consciousness," and rendering Black political consciousness inconsequential and ineffectual.

It's damn near impossible to criticize *Superfly* for its lack of a coherent, politically correct message. The dialogue is so crisp, the still-frame montage to the tune of "Pusherman" so unselfconsciously affecting, O'Neal's character so quietly charismatic, that audiences can hardly help feeling the rush that comes from watching the film unfold. Or as one review succinctly puts it, *Superfly* perfectly captures "the essence of that which is the life of a Playa." **SJS**

**U.S.** (Universal) 129m Technicolor

**Director:** George Roy Hill

**Producer:** Tony Bill, Robert L. Crawford, Julia Phillips, Michael Phillips

**Screenplay:** David S. Ward

**Photography:** Robert Surtees

**Nonoriginal music:** Scott Joplin

**Cast:** Paul Newman, Robert Redford, Robert Shaw, Charles Durning, Ray Walston, Eileen Brennan, Harold Gould, John Heffernan, Dana Elcar, Jack Kehoe, Dimitra Arliss

**Oscar:** Tony Bill, Michael Phillips, Julia Phillips (best picture), George Roy Hill (director), David S. Ward (screenplay), Henry Bumstead, James Payne (art direction), Edith Head (costume), William Reynolds (editing), Marvin Hamlisch (music)

**Oscar nomination:** Robert Redford (actor), Robert Surtees (photography), Ronald Pierce, Robert R. Bertrand (sound)

# THE STING (1973)

George Roy Hill first directed Paul Newman and Robert Redford in *Butch Cassidy and the Sundance Kid* (1969). The results were far-reaching inasmuch as the film affirmed viewers' interest in movie Westerns while demonstrating the commercial attraction of Newman and Redford. Assembled again four years later in the caper pic *The Sting*, Hill gave the actors more room to play, though this time without any tragic resonance.

Set in post-Depression Chicago, Henry Gondorff (Newman) and Johnny Hooker (Redford) are two con men with ambition. After mobster Doyle Lonnegan (Robert Shaw) kills one of their friends, they set out for revenge. The subsequent effort, built on smoke, mirrors, and a number of situational reversals, also depends on a dense network within Chicago's criminal underworld.

Sparkling wit abounds as a strong supporting cast of smart men pitch personal style to other smart men. The timelessness of Scott Joplin's rags ring throughout the soundtrack and, in the end, the long con defeats the most intimidating bad guy.

Perhaps not high art, *The Sting* is nonetheless a luscious meringue. Blue-eyed Newman and dusty-haired Redford look great, and into their friendship is entrenched the joy of screen masters jousting in a comic adventure centered on loyalty and deception. **GC-Q**

# LA MAMAN ET LA PUTAIN (1973)
## THE MOTHER AND THE WHORE

Everything about *The Mother and the Whore*—length, performances, dialogue—is a tour de force. In this autobiographical feature, Jean Eustache spends an epic 220 minutes depicting an intense ménage à trois: Alexandre (Jean-Pierre Léaud) lives with Marie (Bernadette Lafont) but falls in love with Veronika (Françoise Lebrun).

Shot in 16mm and black and white, *The Mother and the Whore* deploys the aesthetics of the New Wave to offer a trenchant portrait of post-May '68 disillusionment. The mobile camera work (by the distinguished Pierre Lhomme) charts a seductive Parisian cityscape: old apartments, boulevards, and cafés in which the characters conduct a dizzying flow of conversation. While Eustache's extraordinary dialogues merge high literature, slang, and obscenities, Lhomme's camera stretches duration in extreme long takes and real-time scenes.

Like many New Wave films, *The Mother and the Whore* inhabits a Parisian intellectual world in which real-life film critics and filmmakers appear as secondary characters, including Eustache himself. But most evocative of the New Wave, apart from Lafont, is Léaud, François Truffaut's alter ego. The boy wonder of *The 400 Blows* (1959) and whimsical young man of *Stolen Kisses* (1969) has grown into the manic, obsessive, exasperating, and yet spellbinding Alexandre. As he discusses the meaning of life, love, and art, Léaud/Alexandre merges the anomic New Wave male with the May '68 libertarian; *The Mother and the Whore* is at once narcissistic portrayal and scathing exposé of this figure, and thus deeply of its time.

What of the "mother" and the "whore" of the title? Like Alexandre, the film wavers between them and swaps the two female stereotypes in the process. Both women, who have jobs while he is idle, emerge as stronger than the immature Alexandre. Yet the film turns them into "tragic" but ultimately marginal figures, subservient to his (and the director's) existential angst, despite stunning performances by Lafont and newcomer Lebrun. In this respect too, *The Mother and the Whore* is of its time, a monument to the confused, "liberated," and yet still oppressively patriarchal sexual politics of 1970s France. Eustache (who committed suicide in 1981) had enough talent to make it also deeply moving. **GV**

**France** (Ciné Qua Non, Elite, Losange, Simar Films, V.M) 219m BW

**Language:** French

**Director:** Jean Eustache

**Producer:** Pierre Cottrell, Vincent Malle

**Screenplay:** Jean Eustache

**Photography:** Pierre Lhomme

**Nonoriginal music:** Mozart, Offenbach

**Cast:** Bernadette Lafont, Jean-Pierre Léaud, Françoise Lebrun, Isabelle Weingarten, Jacques Renard, Jean-Noël Picq, Jessa Darrieux, Geneviève Mnich, Marinka Matuszewski

U.S. (Badlands, Pressman-Williams) 95m Color

**Director:** Terrence Malick

**Producer:** Jill Jakes, Terrence Malick, Edward R. Pressman, Louis A. Stroller

**Screenplay:** Terrence Malick

**Photography:** Tak Fujimoto, Stevan Larner, Brian Probyn

**Music:** Gunild Keetman, James Taylor, George Aliceson Tipton, Carl Orff, Erik Satie

**Cast:** Martin Sheen, Sissy Spacek, Warren Oates, Ramon Bieri, Alan Vint, Gary Littlejohn, John Carter, Bryan Montgomery, Gail Threlkeld, Charles Fitzpatrick, Howard Ragsdale, John Womack Jr., Dona Baldwin, Ben Bravo

# BADLANDS (1973)

"I can't deny we've had fun . . . and that's more than some can say." Harvard graduate, Rhodes scholar, sometime journalist and philosophy teacher at MIT, Terrence Malick was a true artist, utterly indifferent to the conventions and commercialism of the American film industry. He wrote, produced, and directed only two films in the 1970s before withdrawing from the fray for a reclusive twenty years (when he returned to make his long-mooted World War II project *A Thin Red Line*), becoming both a revered legend and a terrible loss to American cinema in the process. The 1979 film *Days Of Heaven* derives its power from its exquisite beauty and evocation of mood. But it is *Badlands*, a disturbing, fatalistic study of a mindlessly violent odyssey, that is the more arresting and influential cult favorite. It is more stark and austere in its visual beauty, which seems less a designed artifice, and is also more naturalistic and energetic. Far from dating, the film has a timeless quality and has become increasingly relevant in an age with little innocence but a mass hankering for celebrity.

In the roles of Kit and Holly, *Badlands*' two about-to-be stars are extraordinary. In his early thirites but looking much younger, wild, and edgy, Martin Sheen is explosive as the aimless and alienated Midwestern misfit eager for notoriety, a garbage man who fancies himself a James Dean look-alike outlaw. Sissy Spacek, 24 but utterly believable as a 15-year-old, is unnerving as his blank, freckle-faced, passive nymphet moll. Inspired by the real, shocking 1950s case of the delinquent teenaged Bonnie and Clyde, Charles Starkweather and Carol Fugate, there is a horrible fascination in this narrative of a bad boy and his baton-twirling baby doll. The casual disposing of the girl's dour father (Warren Oates), the building of a tree house love-nest refuge in a cotton grove, and a cross-country killing spree and chase are all reminiscent of Bonnie and Clyde.

*Badlands* is cool, bleak, and scary in its awareness that the seemingly ordinary adolescent girl has thrown in her lot compliantly with a sociopath because she doesn't have any other ideas. It is also singularly literate, with Malick finding a dispassionate, humorless distance from the violent psychodrama through clever writing. A brilliant device has Spacek gauchely reading her character's romanticized but banal diary entries—in the style of the trashy '50s movie fan magazines she reads—for a voice-over that adds odd pathos to the duo's nihilistic progress. The details, using the iconography of the era, are both disarming (the couple, heedless of their situation, dancing outdoors like any carefree kids to Mickey and Sylvia's "Love Is Strange" or dreamily in the beam of their headlights to Nat King Cole) and eloquent (Kit checking his hair in the mirror during a car chase when the police are all but on top of him, or cheerfully tossing souvenirs to his captors). The contrasts—of the American heartland landscapes with their run-down dwellings, tedious lives, and tawdry dreams; of the bright, vibrant musical score with recurring images of death—are continually striking. And the echoes of Malick's majestically brooding, moody style continue to reverberate in the love-on-the-run genre to this day. **AE**

U.S. (Lucasfilm, Coppola, Universal)
110m Technicolor

**Director:** George Lucas

**Producer:** Francis Ford Coppola, Gary Kurtz

**Screenplay:** George Lucas, Gloria Katz, Willard Huyck

**Photography:** Jan D'Alquen, Ron Eveslage

**Nonoriginal music:** Sherman Edwards, Chuck Berry, Buddy Holly, Booker T. Jones

**Cast:** Richard Dreyfuss, Ron Howard, Paul Le Mat, Charles Martin Smith, Cindy Williams, Candy Clark, Mackenzie Phillips, Wolfman Jack, Bo Hopkins, Manuel Padilla Jr., Beau Gentry, Harrison Ford, Jim Bohan, Jana Bellan, Deby Celiz, Johnny Weissmuller Jr., Suzanne Somers

**Oscar nomination:** Francis Ford Coppola, Gary Kurtz (best picture), George Lucas (director), George Lucas, Gloria Katz, Willard Huyck (screenplay), Candy Clark (actress in support role), Verna Fields, Marcia Lucas (editing)

# AMERICAN GRAFFITI (1973)

Produced by Francis Ford Coppola and directed by his protégé and former assistant George Lucas, who also cowrote the autobiographically-flavored screenplay, this hugely entertaining, perceptive coming-of-age ensemble piece of high school graduates cruising through one eventful summer's night in 1962 was inspired by 1950s teen pics but set the style—often imitated, never surpassed in hilarity, penetration, or technical virtuosity—for a hundred and one rites of passage comedies played out in classic cars to a vintage rocking soundtrack. It was also the clear inspiration for such wholesome, nostalgic television sitcoms as *Happy Days* and *Laverne and Shirley*, featuring some of the same players and fancifully revisiting that supposedly more carefree youth era before Vietnam.

Marvel at that *Graffiti* ensemble: Richard Dreyfuss and Ron Howard when he was still Ronny as the college-bound boys, Paul "whatever happened to?" LeMat as the Brylcreemed bad boy, Cindy Williams, Candy Clark, Charles Martin Smith, legendary rock-'n'-roll disc jockey Wolfman Jack, and, in humbler roles, Joe Spano, Suzanne Somers, Kathy before she became Kathleen Quinlan, and a not-so-very-young hopeful named Harrison Ford as drag racer Bob Falfa. The confluence of young talents brought energy, comedy, insight, and craft, superbly captured by cinematographer Haskell Wexler, one of Lucas's early mentors. *American Graffiti* was shot on location in Modesto and San Rafael, California—where the time-honored tradition of "dragging the main" was long a strictly-observed ritual of mooning, foam spraying, flirtatious pursuit, and furtively-obtained liquor in paper bags, and where Lucas was to build the center of his filmmaking empire, the Skywalker Ranch complex.

In what was only his second feature, Lucas demonstrated a charm and warmth not found in his cool, futuristic debut, the Orwellian *THX 1138*. Shot in just 28 nights for well under a million dollars, *American Graffitti* not only became a box office smash, one of the most profitable pictures of all time, but received critical kudos and five Academy Award nominations, including Best Picture, Director, and Screenplay, a triumph that enabled Lucas to make an even more phenomenal mark with his next film, *Star Wars*. **AE**

## PAPILLON (1973)

Tagged, "Two men with nothing in common but a will to live and a place to die," Franklin J. Schaffner's *Papillon* is a male love-story-turned-adventure tale. It opens with Papillon (Steve McQueen) being sent to a French Guyana prison for a crime he didn't commit. There he meets Dega (Dustin Hoffman), another convict. Afterward the film concerns their respective misadventures trying to escape until Papillon finally succeeds.

Accompanying this eye candy, Jerry Goldsmith's score echoes off tropical backdrops to make *Papillon* less an action vehicle and more a confrontation between man and nature. McQueen is therefore the foil for exploring individual loyalty and pain—the long-suffering hero. Attentive viewers will be struck by how little dialogue is spoken. Instead, *Papillon*'s impact comes from bits of actor's business and the sheer force of imprisonment. Perhaps the finest example is the lead's solitary confinement; although he speaks nary a word, McQueen still comes across as a powerful screen presence and star.

Yet the point of the film shines through in a nightmare. "I accuse you of a wasted life," Papillon is told, but the movie becomes a counter-argument because his triumph is that of an insignificant man defeating a system designed to break him. **GC-Q**

**U.S. / France** (Allied Artists, Corona-General, Solar) 150m Technicolor

**Director:** Franklin J. Schaffner

**Producer:** Robert Dorfmann, Ted Richmond, Franklin J. Schaffner

**Screenplay:** Dalton Trumbo, Lorenzo Semple Jr., from the novel by Henri Charrière

**Photography:** Fred J. Koenekamp

**Music:** Jerry Goldsmith

**Cast:** Steve McQueen, Dustin Hoffman, Victor Jory, Don Gordon, Anthony Zerbe, Robert Deman, Woodrow Parfrey, Bill Mumy, George Coulouris, Ratna Assan, William Smithers, Val Avery, Gregory Sierra, Vic Tayback, Mills Watson, Ron Soble, Barbara Morrison, Don Hanmer, E.J. André, Richard Angarola, Jack Denbo, Len Lesser, John Quade, Fred Sadoff, Allen Jaffe, Liam Dunn

**Oscar nomination:** Jerry Goldsmith (music)

## ENTER THE DRAGON (1973)

Having established his action movie superstar credentials with rough-hewn Hong Kong vehicles like *Fist of Fury* and *The Big Boss*, former cha-cha champion and American TV sidekick Bruce Lee only had one shot at completing a movie with Hollywood production values. Lee, a martial artist whose physical skills have attained a spiritual level, infiltrates a master-baddie's island enclave (along with sidekicks John Saxon and Jim Kelly) and sees off hordes and hordes of junior villains (Jackie Chan gets a walk-on necksnap).

Director Robert Clouse has the style you'd expect of someone directing a Brock Landers adventure (lots of zooms and flares), and Lee, whose real-life Hong Kong English was heavily-accented but fluent and distinctive, is stuck with Charlie Chan dialogue consisting of enigmatically wise pronouncements. But the action still delivers nonstop astonishment as, without the aid of the wires or effects used in the likes of *Crouching Tiger Hidden Dragon*, Lee goes magnificently through the motions, twirling his signature nunchucks, flexing his oiled torso. Influential on an entire genre of subsequent martial arts movies and a template for every beat-'em-up computer game, *Enter the Dragon* wins its place in film history purely on the strength of Lee's charismatic presence and literally inimitable fighting moves. **KN**

**Hong Kong / U.S.** (Concord, Sequoia, Warner Bros.) 98m Technicolor

**Director:** Robert Clouse

**Producer:** Raymond Chow, Paul M. Heller, Bruce Lee, Fred Weintraub

**Screenplay:** Michael Allin

**Photography:** Gil Hubbs

**Music:** Lalo Schifrin

**Cast:** Bruce Lee, John Saxon, Kien Shih, Jim Kelly, Ahna Capri, Robert Wall, Angela Mao, Bolo Yeung, Betty Chung, Geoffrey Weeks, Peter Archer, Ho Lee Yan, Marlene Clark, Allan Kent, William Keller

# MEAN STREETS (1973)

**U.S.** (Taplin - Perry - Scorsese) 110m Technicolor

**Director:** Martin Scorsese

**Producer:** E. Lee Perry, Martin Scorsese, Jonathan T. Taplin

**Screenplay:** Martin Scorsese, Mardik Martin

**Photography:** Kent L. Wakeford

**Nonoriginal music:** Eric Clapton, Bert Holland, Mick Jagger and Keith Richards

**Cast:** Robert De Niro, Harvey Keitel, David Proval, Amy Robinson, Richard Romanus, Cesare Danova, Victor Argo, George Memmoli, Lenny Scaletta, Jeannie Bell, Murray Moston, David Carradine, Robert Carradine, Lois Walden, Harry Northup, Catherine Scorsese, Martin Scorsese

Martin Scorsese's breakthrough movie was an instant declaration of the themes he's been elaborating ever since and of his showy talent. Set in his home turf of New York City's Little Italy, though actually shot mostly in Los Angeles with some spliced-in footage of the San Gennaro religious festival, *Mean Streets* is about hustlers in the midlevel of organized crime. It explores the exhilaration and the destructiveness of extended adolescence and a peculiar search for redemption that has continued throughout his filmography.

A young, smooth Harvey Keitel stars as Charlie Cappa, Scorsese's semiautobiographical stand-in (the director actually uses his own voice for the character's narration), a minor mob hanger-on who believes "you pay for your sins on the street not in church" but is still willing to hold his hand to a votive candle to atone for his crimes. So concerned with presenting an impressive face to the world that he fetishistically grooms himself like a knight donning armor, Charlie believes it is possible to have an old-fashioned sense of honor and loyalty and still prosper in a business run by gentlemanly elders. However, his cousin-girlfriend (Amy Robinson) undercuts his man-of-integrity attitudes by reminding him "St. Francis didn't run numbers."

Charlie spends his time palling around with his friends in Little Italy, exchanging Hope-and-Crosby wisecracks with his dangerously irresponsible cousin Johnny Boy (Robert De Niro), going to the movies (cue cinephile clips from John Ford's *The Searchers* and Roger Corman's *Tomb of Ligeia*, to show you where Marty is coming from), running minor scams (the filmgoing is financed by ripping off some students on a drug deal), wondering which girl to settle with, and hoping to advance himself in the rackets. However, his sense of what he must be seen to be leads him to get out of a relationship with his epileptic cousin because he is worried that he'll be tainted as a flake, and then to duck out on a possible liaison with an obviously wonderful woman he has been flirting with just because she's black. Meanwhile, his loyalty to Johnny Boy is clearly dragging him toward disaster as the irresponsible rebel, who simply doesn't care what anyone thinks, ticks off a powerful local loan shark (Richard Romanus) by not only not paying him back but by making a point of being contemptuous of him in public.

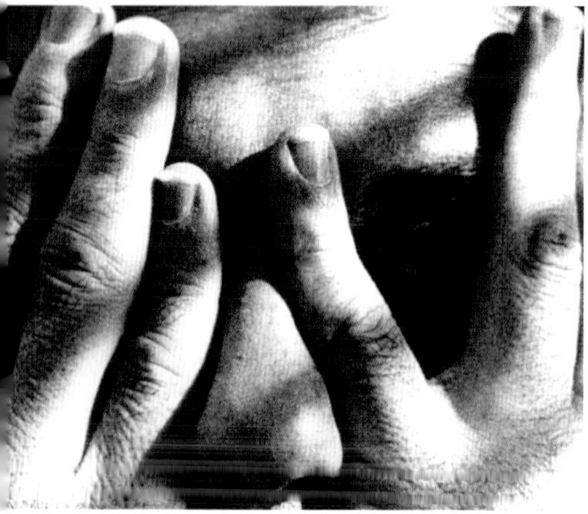

The intense, interior, earnest, considered Charlie and the explosive, free-associating, impulsive smart-ass Johnny Boy (first seen bombing a mailbox) are key characters in 1970s cinema, establishing personae the stars would explore in a run of outstanding work for Scorsese and others. It ends in a bloody apotheosis, a shoot-out-cum-car-crash that leaves some of the characters bleeding and others dead (though it isn't entirely clear which is which). Along the way, there is a joyous energy as Keitel struts into neon-lit bars in his sharp suits, the camera prowling along with him, while Scorsese's unparalleled record collection plays on the soundtrack. David Carradine, star of Scorsese's earlier *Boxcar Bertha* (1972), has a funny cameo as a drunken murder victim. **KN**

**U.S.** (E K Corp., Lions Gate) 112m Technicolor

**Director:** Robert Altman

**Producer:** Jerry Bick, Robert Eggenweiler

**Screenplay:** Leigh Brackett, from novel by Raymond Chandler

**Photography:** Vilmos Zsigmond

**Music:** John Williams

**Cast:** Elliott Gould, Nina Van Pallandt, Sterling Hayden, Mark Rydell, Henry Gibson, David Arkin, Jim Bouton, Warren Berlinger, Jo Ann Brody, Stephen Coit, Jack Knight, Pepe Callahan, Vincent Palmieri, Pancho Córdova, Enrique Lucero

# THE LONG GOODBYE (1973)

*The Long Goodbye*, Robert Altman's languid, free-form version of Raymond Chandler's last great novel, relocates the 1953 story to 1973, subtly critiquing the out of time values of Philip Marlowe. Elliott Gould's slobby, unshaven, chain-smoking private eye is an all-time loser, introduced in a brilliant sequence that has him try to pass off inferior pet food on his supercilious cat. Shambling through the remains of Chandler's plot, Gould tries to help an alcoholic Hemingwayesque writer (Sterling Hayden, who wrote his own scenes) and clear his only friend (Jim Bouton) of a murder rap.

John Williams's brilliant score plays endless variations on a title tune, and many sequences are astonishing: violent gangster Jark Rydell making a point by smashing a coke bottle in his mistress's face ("That's someone I love, you I don't even like"), Hayden's stumbling suicide on the beach, and an invigoratingly cynical punch line ("and I lost my cat") that turns Marlowe into some sort of winner after all. Arnold Schwarzenegger, no less, has an unbilled cameo as a minor thug. Altman makes sure a lot of the vital action happens almost unnoticed in the corners of the frame and loves highlighting tiny moments of visual and aural impact in a sun-struck tapestry of Los Angeles sleaze. **KN**

**G.B.** (British Lion) 102m Eastmancolor

**Director:** Robin Hardy

**Producer:** Peter Snell

**Screenplay:** Anthony Shaffer

**Photography:** Harry Waxman

**Music:** Paul Giovanni

**Cast:** Edward Woodward, Christopher Lee, Diane Cilento, Britt Ekland, Ingrid Pitt, Lindsay Kemp, Russell Waters, Aubrey Morris, Irene Sunters, Walter Carr, Ian Campbell, Leslie Blackater, Roy Boyd, Peter Brewis, Barbara Rafferty

# THE WICKER MAN (1973)

Repressed Scots policeman Howie (Edward Woodward), "a Christian copper," investigates the disappearance of a little girl on Summerisle, where the charming but fiendish local laird (Christopher Lee) is taking extreme measures to ensure the success of the next harvest. Written by Anthony Shaffer (*Sleuth*), *The Wicker Man* is a highly original combination of horror movie, murder mystery, pagan ethnography, and folk musical that stood as an auspicious debut for its sadly nonprolific director, Robin Hardy. It manages an audacious combination of the sexy and the sinister, leading to a shock ending that still has an impact, even though audiences coming fresh to the film tend now to know how things will turn out at the festival where a holy virgin fool is led to a giant man-shaped bonfire on the beach.

A bizarre cast includes a dubbed and body-doubled Britt Ekland as the landlord's seductive daughter, cult starlet Ingrid Pitt as the naked librarian, mime Lindsay Kemp as a slyly camp publican, and Diane Cilento as the headmistress-like high priestess. Though edited significantly for its original release, the version generally available now restores much (if not all) the trimmed footage—in some ways, the shorter cut plays a little better because the expanded version is a little heavy-handed in leading viewers to the final twist. **KN**

# LA NUIT AMÉRICAINE (1973)
## DAY FOR NIGHT

In a typical scene of *Day for Night*, the director Ferrand (played by François Truffaut) throws down a pile of his latest film-book acquisitions (on Bresson, Rossellini, Hitchcock), while Georges Delerue's musical theme is piped through a tinny telephone speaker. The mixture of everyday detail with an unexpected, carefully restrained surge of poetic lyricism is quintessential Truffaut.

*Day for Night* is Truffaut's valentine to the process of moviemaking. Controversially for the post-1968 period, he chose classical, studio-bound, generic cinema as his premise, not the nouvelle vague. The emphasis of the film is on filmmaking as craft rather than art (no one pretends that Ferrand's middlebrow diversion *Meet Pamela* is a masterpiece). And, ultimately, it is less about the "product" than the collective process leading to it. Truffaut paints an affectionate portrait of good-natured "family" relations among cast and crew in place of the vicious power plays usually presented, making *Day for Night* the polar opposite to Jean-Luc Godard's *Contempt* (1963) or Rainer Werner Fassbinder's *Beware of a Holy Whore* (1970).

Gentle, bittersweet wisdom is the keynote here, as a rich ensemble of performers (from smooth Jean-Pierre Aumont to firecracker Jean-Pierre Léaud) share fleeting lessons in life, love, and loss. The film deftly sketches a wide range of characters, cleverly compared on certain points: for example, their attitudes to casual sex (tragic and histrionic for Jacqueline Bisset's happily married character once Léaud makes their liaison public, flippant for Natalie Baye as a no-nonsense assistant director).

Truffaut stresses the transience, fragility, and unreality of life on a set—even allowing, in one surprising and hilarious scene, an outsider to finally explode and criticize these film people for their rampant immorality. *Day for Night* (as its title indicates) gently exposes the many illusions of the filmmaking process, but also maintains our awe over the magic of movies. Characteristically for Truffaut, the brisk montage scenes—devoted to the frenzy of the editing room, or an elaborate scene filmed in artificial snow—express a deep affection for, and appreciation of, the mundane practicalities of his trade.

As such strangely exhilarating montage scenes serve to show, Truffaut's cinema is essentially unspectacular. There is no melodramatic underlining in *Day for Night*, no ostentatious, point-making rhetoric in his mise en scène. Truffaut's obsession is with maintaining a lightness of tone, maximizing narrative flow, and conveying incidents with the utmost economy: In this he truly married the tautness of Hitchcock or Lang with the observational grace of Renoir or Becker. Those who dismiss *Day for Night* as inconsequential or lacking seriousness miss his unique achievement on this level.

Amid the whimsical succession of ordinary situations, the rare, strong moments of drama occur as sudden interruptions (such as Alexander's death) that switch the mood. The sadness of these "punctual" events enhances the keenness of the characters' fleeting pleasures: secret moments of intimacy or complicity, joyful epiphanies, chance eruptions of comedy, and stolen kisses. *Day for Night* contains some of Truffaut's loveliest vignettes of this kind. **AM**

**France / Italy** (Carrosse, PECF, PIC)
115m BW/Eastmancolor

**Language:** English / French

**Director:** François Truffaut

**Producer:** Marcel Berbert

**Screenplay:** Jean-Louis Richard, Suzanne Schiffman, François Truffaut

**Photography:** Pierre-William Glenn

**Music:** Georges Delerue

**Cast:** Jacqueline Bisset, Valentina Cortese, Dani, Alexandra Stewart, Jean-Pierre Aumont, Jean Champion, Jean-Pierre Léaud, François Truffaut, Nike Arrighi, Nathalie Baye, Maurice Seveno, David Markham, Bernard Menez, Gaston Joly, Zenaide Rossi

**Oscar:** France (best foreign language film)

**Oscar nomination:** François Truffaut (director), François Truffaut, Jean-Louis Richard, Suzanne Schiffman (screenplay), Valentina Cortese (actress in support role)

**G.B. / Italy** (Casey, Eldorado) 110m Technicolor

**Director:** Nicolas Roeg

**Producer:** Peter Katz, Frederick Muller, Anthony B. Unger

**Screenplay:** Allan Scott, Chris Bryant, from story by Daphne Du Maurier

**Photography:** Anthony B. Richmond

**Music:** Pino Donaggio (as Pino Donnagio)

**Cast:** Julie Christie, Donald Sutherland, Hilary Mason, Clelia Matania, Massimo Serato, Renato Scarpa, Giorgio Trestini, Leopoldo Trieste, David Tree, Ann Rye, Nicholas Salter, Sharon Williams, Bruno Cattaneo, Adelina Poerio

# DON'T LOOK NOW (1973)

Based on a short story by Daphne du Maurier, Nicholas Roeg's *Don't Look Now* showcases the British director's characteristically nonlinear style of storytelling, in which temporal ellipses and frenetic crosscuts serve to reflect and enhance the already palpable atmosphere of psychological disturbance and dread.

Shortly after their young daughter dies in a drowning accident, art restorer John Baxter (Donald Sutherland) and his wife Laura (Julie Christie) travel to Venice in the off-season to work on an old church and recover from their traumatic loss. Instead what they find is a creepy city filled with lonely canals and eccentric characters, including a pair of strange old sisters (Hilary Mason and Clelia Matania), one of them a blind psychic who insists that she can communicate with their late child and who warns them of impending danger. John is initially skeptical but starts to come around after catching random glimpses of his daughter darting through the streets wearing the same red raincoat she had on when she died.

In the film's unforgettable conclusion, John races through the Venice alleys at night in pursuit of the mysterious red-garbed figure—who he now believes is the ghost of his deceased child—only to catch up with her in a dark passageway, her back toward him. The figure then turns around, revealing an ambiguously gendered dwarf, and John can only stand there stunned as the little person (who is quite real, and quite deadly, having been on a killing spree in the city for some time) walks up to him and slashes his throat with a straight razor. It is no exaggeration to say that few scenes in the history of cinema have proven as effective at sending chills up the spines of viewers as this one.

But *Don't Look Now's* terrifying finale is not even the best-known scene in the film. That honor goes to the lengthy sex scene between John and Laura, mixed with quiet shots of the married couple impassively dressing for dinner. Rumor spread that the remarkable passion on display during this lovemaking session resulted from an off-screen affair between Christie and Sutherland. Whatever the case, it is this same passion that suffuses the entire picture. **SJS**

## SLEEPER (1973)

One of Woody Allen's self-described "early, funny films," this is a Bob Hope-style comedy vehicle for Allen's whiny neurotic Jewish character, set loose in a 1973 vision of the future informed by films like *2001: A Space Odyssey* (1968), *A Clockwork Orange* (1971), *THX 1138* (1971), and *Z.P.G.* (1972).

Miles Monroe (Allen), jazzman and proprietor of a Greenwich Village health food store, is defrosted 200 hundred years into the future after being cryofrozen in tinfoil when complications set in during a routine ulcer surgery. As in *Bananas* (1971) and *Love and Death* (1975), Allen's character is a foul-up who gets drawn into revolutionary activity that seems doomed to exchange one tyranny for another. There are some barbed philosophical bits about doomed romantic relationships, but the main focus of the picture is the comedy. It ranges from satiric jabs at contemporary mores seen from a skewed futurist perspective (it has been proved that fatty foods and cigarettes are better for you than health foods), through silent cinema-style slapstick (a giant banana naturally leads to a giant banana-skin gag), to left-field surrealism like a mental deprogramming session that kicks into a rerun of *A Streetcar Named Desire* (1951) with Diane Keaton and Allen doing Marlon Brando and Vivien Leigh. **KN**

**U.S.** (Rollins-Joffe Productions) 89m Color

**Director:** Woody Allen

**Producer:** Jack Grossberg

**Screenplay:** Woody Allen, Marshall Brickman

**Photography:** David M. Walsh

**Music:** Woody Allen

**Cast:** Woody Allen, Diane Keaton, John Beck, Mary Gregory, Don Keefer, John McLiam, Bartlett Robinson, Chris Forbes, Mews Small, Peter Hobbs, Susan Miller, Lou Picetti, Jessica Rains, Brian Avery, Spencer Milligan

## SERPICO (1973)

Maverick cops rooting out departmental corruption is now a familiar theme in many of TV's law enforcement drama series. In 1973, however, this was exciting cinematic territory fully exploited by director Sidney Lumet in *Serpico*, featuring a sizzling performance by Al Pacino. Based on Peter Maas's 1972 biography, this is the gripping story of New York cop Frank Serpico. The real-life Serpico refused to take paybacks, a decision which made him massively unpopular in the many departments he was transferred to. Receiving personal threats from fellow officers, he was mysteriously shot in the face on duty—yet lived to testify at an important police-corruption hearing.

Fresh off his groundbreaking role in the 1972 film *The Godfather*, Pacino's Serpico is a high-energy but low-key performance that won him the Golden Globe and the second of his many Oscar nominations. *Serpico* staves off being a mere cop cliché film because of its balanced view of the main character—a man in the right who becomes an embittered martyr. The only jarring element is Mikis Theodorakis's heavy-handed Mediterranean-themed soundtrack. Judd Hirsch and F. Murray Abraham appear in cameos. **KK**

**U.S. / Italy** (Paramount, De Laurentis) 129m Technicolor

**Director:** Sidney Lumet

**Producer:** Martin Bregman

**Screenplay:** Waldo Salt, Norman Wexler, from book by Peter Maas

**Photography:** Arthur J. Ornitz

**Music:** Mikis Theodorakis

**Cast:** Al Pacino, John Randolph, Jack Kehoe, Biff McGuire, Barbara Eda-Young, Cornelia Sharpe, Tony Roberts, John Medici, Allan Rich, Norman Ornellas, Edward Grover, Albert Henderson, Hank Garrett, Damien Leake, Joseph Bova

**Oscar nomination:** Waldo Salt, Norman Wexler (screenplay), Al Pacino (actor)

**U.S.** (Hoya Productions, Warner Bros.) 122m Metrocolor

**Language:** English / Latin / Greek / French / German / Arabic

**Director:** William Friedkin

**Producer:** William Peter Blatty

**Screenplay:** William Peter Blatty, from his novel

**Photography:** Owen Roizman, Billy Williams

**Music:** Jack Nitzsche, David Borden, George Crumb, Hans Werner Henze, Mike Oldfield, Krzysztof Penderecki, Anton Webern

**Cast:** Ellen Burstyn, Max von Sydow, Lee J. Cobb, Kitty Winn, Jack MacGowran, Jason Miller, Linda Blair, Reverend William O'Malley, Barton Heyman, Peter Masterson, Rudolf Schündler, Gina Petrushka, Robert Symonds, Arthur Storch, Reverend Thomas Bermingham

**Oscar:** William Peter Blatty (screenplay), Robert Knudson, Christopher Newman (sound)

**Oscar nomination:** William Peter Blatty (best picture), William Friedkin (director), Ellen Burstyn (actress), Jason Miller (actor in support role), Linda Blair (actress in support role), Bill Malley, Jerry Wunderlich (art direction), Owen Roizman (photography), John C. Broderick, Bud S. Smith, Evan A. Lottman, Norman Gay (editing)

# THE EXORCIST (1973)

The first major blockbuster in horror movie history, this film has exerted a powerful influence on the subsequent development of the genre. Never before had a horror film been the subject of so much prerelease hype, so much gossip about postproduction strife, so much speculation as to why people of all ages would stand in line for hours to watch something reputed to induce fits of vomiting, fainting, even temporary psychosis. The cultural impact of *The Exorcist* can hardly be overestimated. It challenged existing regulations specifying what was acceptable to show on the big screen. The film stole U.S. newspaper headlines away from the ongoing Watergate scandal, at least for a while, led to a detectable increase in the number of "real-life" spiritual possessions reported, and, as one critic wrote, "established . . . disgust as mass entertainment for a large audience."

Inspired by newspaper reports of a 13-year-old Maryland boy whose body was said to have been taken over by demonic forces, novelist William Peter Blatty made the possessee a girl. He sensationalized many details, adding heavy doses of philosophical-theological speculation on the nature of evil, and came out with the *The Exorcist* in 1971. Correctly anticipating a bestseller, Warner Brothers purchased the film rights and, after numerous rewrites of the original script, Blatty finally came up with a version of *The Exorcist* that managed to meet Friedkin's exacting demands.

After a lengthy prologue that is nearly incomprehensible to anyone who hasn't read the book, the first half of the film develops the essential character relationships and establishes the crisis situation. Regan MacNeil (Linda Blair) is the adorable, almost-pubescent daughter of divorcee and well-known movie

star Chris MacNeil (Ellen Burstyn). But when she prophesies the death of her mother's acquaintance and urinates in front of a roomful of dinner guests, Chris starts to wonder what has "gotten into" her daughter. More odd behavior, and a wildly shaking bed, lands Regan in the hospital, where she is subjected to a battery of extremely invasive procedures best described as medical pornography. A brain lesion is suspected, but the tests prove nothing. When Regan, supposedly under hypnosis, responds to the smug questions of a hospital shrink by grabbing his scrotum, it is recommended that Chris seek the Church's help. She does, pleading with doubt-ridden Jesuit priest Damien Karras (Jason Miller) to perform an exorcism. The film's second half culminates in an intense battle between Karras and Regan's demonic possessor, after the more experienced exorcist on the scene, Father Merrin (Max von Sydow) dies in the struggle. Karras finally saves Regan by accepting the demon into his own body, only to throw himself, or let himself be thrown, out of a window to his death.

In an era of student protest, experimental drug use, and general questioning of authority, *The Exorcist* allowed viewers to take pleasure in the terrible punishments inflicted on the rebellious Regan. But by making Regan-the-demon so fascinating to watch, so filled with nasty surprises, *The Exorcist* also allowed viewers to take pleasure in that rebelliousness. The film not only gave rise to a slew of lesser-quality sequels, imitations, and variants on the possession theme, it also made the child with malevolent powers a dominant motif in horror cinema. **SJS**

**Netherlands** (VNF) 112m Color

**Language:** Dutch

**Director:** Paul Verhoeven

**Producer:** Rob Houwer

**Screenplay:** Gerard Soeteman, from the novel *Turks Fruit* by Jan Wolkers

**Photography:** Jan de Bont

**Music:** Rogier van Otterloo

**Cast:** Monique van de Ven, Rutger Hauer, Tonny Huurdeman, Wim van den Brink, Hans Boskamp, Dolf de Vries, Manfred de Graaf, Dick Scheffer, Marjol Flore, Bert Dijkstra, Bert André, Jon Bluming, Paul Brandenburg, Suze Broks, David Conyers

**Oscar nomination:** Netherlands (best foreign language film)

# TURKS FRUIT (1973)

## TURKISH DELIGHT

*Turkish Delight* is Dutch director Paul Verhoeven's outrageous precursor to his cycle of big budget Hollywood movies probing human sexuality, such as *Basic Instinct* (1992), *Showgirls* (1995), and *Starship Troopers* (1997). Often criticized for his use of extreme violence and sexual explicitness, Verhoeven has always maintained that his films mirror life rather than influence it. *Turkish Delight* stars Rutger Hauer as Eric Vonk, a promiscuous sculptor who gets involved with the beautiful Olga (Monique van de Ven), whose sexual appetite matches his own. As the affair progresses, they decide to marry, but differences between Eric's and his in-laws' value systems bring about the end of their romance. Years later, Eric and Olga meet again and finally achieve some closure to their turbulent relationship. The film is constructed as a series of flashbacks through which Eric's inner world and sensibility are slowly revealed.

The film opens with Eric bludgeoning a man to death before putting a bullet between the eyes of a young woman. There is a panning shot of Eric's room until the camera freezes on him lying half-naked on his bed, with these fantasies still fresh in his mind. He then leafs through a box of photographs of the same woman, who we later learn is Olga. The next sequence then follows at a frenetic pace with Eric's seduction of a series of random women, and his obsessive collecting of sexual souvenirs. In an interesting narrative composition, halfway through *Turkish Delight* we are brought back to the present, and the latter section picks up from where the film started. The mood of the final third is vastly different from that of the beginning, almost as if it were another film. It is transformed into a moving tale of love and loss, of ecstasy and despair, and while there is a fair degree of erotic content, it is tempered with extreme doses of both fantasy and reality.

The free-spirited sexuality that drives Verhoeven's films is at the heart of *Turkish Delight*, here presented as the ultimate assault on bourgeois values. Sustained by the extreme behavior of the protagonist, this unconventional romance never fails to provoke, its effect enhanced by the explosive chemistry between Hauer and van de Ven. *Turkish Delight* was designated "Best Dutch Film of the Century" at the 1999 Nederlands Film Festival. **RDe**

# EL ESPÍRITU DE LA COLMENA (1973)
## THE SPIRIT OF THE BEEHIVE

**Spain** (Elías Querejeta) 97m
Eastmancolor
**Language:** Spanish
**Director:** Víctor Erice
**Producer:** Elías Querejeta
**Screenplay:** Víctor Erice, Ángel Fernández Santos, Francisco J. Querejeta
**Photography:** Luis Cuadrado
**Music:** Luis de Pablo
**Cast:** Fernando Fernán Gómez, Teresa Gimpera, Ana Torrent, Isabel Tellería, Ketty de la Cámara, Estanis González, José Villasante, Juan Francisco Margallo, Laly Soldevila, Miguel Picazo

Victor Erice's *The Spirit of the Beehive* takes almost 20 minutes to establish a few, basic facts—that there is a family comprising a father (Fernando Fernán Gómez), a mother (Teresa Gimpera), and two girls (Isabel Tellería as Isabel, Ana Torrent as Ana). Erice shows us the man with his bees, and in his study; the woman writing, riding, and passing a letter into a train; the girls in a crowd at a makeshift movie hall screening James Whale's *Frankenstein* (1931). These introductory portraits figure as studies in haunted solitude, the windows of the character's rooms resembling the cell-structures of the father's beehive.

This is a mysterious, unforgettable film, touching on many bases but refusing to congeal into any one genre or intention. As elsewhere in Erice's sadly unprolific career, the family unit is seen as the site of psychic trauma, and celebrated as the one place where intimate community seems possible.

Erice evokes with breathtaking delicacy the ambience of this small Castilian town. The characters dream of an elsewhere until reality comes crashing into an abandoned farmhouse—a political fugitive whom the impressionable, frightened but fascinated Ana takes to be the wandering "spirit" of the Frankenstein monster incarnated. This movie that begins as a fairytale ("Once upon a time...") ends with a stirring declaration addressed to the spirits of the wind: "I am Ana." **AM**

# LA PLANÈTE SAUVAGE (1973)
## FANTASTIC PLANET

**Czechoslovakia / France**
(Ceskoslovensky Filmexport, Krátky Film Praha, Les Films Armorial) 72m
Eastmancolor
**Language:** French
**Director:** René Laloux
**Producer:** Roger Corman, S. Damiani, Anatole Dauman, A. Valio-Cavaglione
**Screenplay:** Steve Hayes, René Laloux, Roland Topor, from the novel *Oms En Serie* by Stefan Wul
**Photography:** Boris Baromykin, Lubomir Rejthar
**Music:** Alain Goraguer
**Cannes Film Festival:** René Laloux (special award) and nomination (Golden Palm)

Animation became big business again in the late 1980s, and ever since then, it's become less and less likely that there will be another full-length animated feature quite as weird as René Laloux's underground French classic *Fantastic Planet*. Drawn with sharp details in warm pastel colors, the movie is just the kind of hippie allegory—and trippy visual experience—that many filmmakers of the 1960s produced.

Adapted from a novel by Stefan Wul, *Fantastic Planet* was inspired by the invasion of Czechoslovakia by the Russians in the late '60s. On the planet Ygam lives a race of giant, alien beings called Traags. These Traags keep the oddly humanlike Oms as pets, often treating them with the sadism and perverse maternalism humans frequently inflict upon their own pets. When one Om absconds with one of the Traags's knowledge devices, he uses the tool to foment a wild Om uprising. Laloux's film, which won the 1973 Cannes Grand Prix Prize, is a welcome respite from slick animated marketing vehicles and countless shoddy imitators.

Started in Prague but completed in Paris because of political pressure, *Fantastic Planet* uses an accessible medium to show the evils of propaganda and express the need for individuality. Laloux's vision of a Dalí-meets-Krazy Kat alien landscape populated by twisted creatures is quite striking, even if the film's psychedelic elements haven't exactly aged well. **JKl**

**Italy / France** (F.C., PECF) 127m Technicolor

**Language:** Italian

**Director:** Federico Fellini

**Producer:** Franco Cristaldi

**Screenplay:** Federico Fellini, Tonino Guerra

**Photography:** Giuseppe Rotunno

**Music:** Nino Rota

**Cast:** Pupella Maggio, Armando Brancia, Magali Noël, Ciccio Ingrassia, Nando Orfei, Luigi Rossi, Bruno Zanin, Gianfilippo Carcano, Josiane Tanzilli, Maria Antonietta Beluzzi, Giuseppe Ianigro, Ferruccio Brembilla, Antonino Faa Di Bruno, Mauro Misul, Ferdinando Villella, Antonio Spaccatini, Aristide Caporale, Gennaro Ombra, Domenico Pertica, Marcello Di Falco, Stefano Proietti, Alvaro Vitali, Bruno Scagnetti, Fernando De Felice, Bruno Lenzi, Gianfranco Marrocco, Francesco Vona, Donatella Gambini

**Oscar:** Italy (best foreign language film)

**Oscar nomination:** Federico Fellini (director), Federico Fellini, Tonino Guerra (screenplay)

# AMARCORD (1973)

Federico Fellini is at his gloomiest when dealing with individuals (as in 8 ½, 1963), and at his happiest when dealing with gangs, packs, and crowds. A magnificent scene in *Amarcord* is devoted to recording the diverse movements of every member of a community toward a beach. Propelled by Nino Rota's music, the entire world flows and sings in rhythmic fusion. And ultimately, Fellini will mark the end of a day and of a wedding ceremony—as well as the end of his reminiscence (and thus his film) and even the end of an era—by slowly emptying a long shot of its formerly teeming mass of humanity.

*Amarcord* ("I remember") is the least grandiose and most immediate of the maestro's later films and deserves to be rated among the finest screen memoirs of the 20th century. It offers an extraordinarily lyrical and vivid succession of vignettes, inside the most subtly rigorous narrative structure of Fellini's career.

It is the least obviously modernist of Fellini's films of the '60s and beyond, eschewing the sorts of self-reflexive games that fill *Roma* (1972) or *Ginger and Fred* (1986). Although the figure of the boy Titta is obviously his alter ego, Fellini builds a generously fractured mosaic that belongs to no one central character or even the on-screen narrator (the old, amateur historian who is a typically Felliniesque figure of fun)—a palpable influence on Scorsese's epic chronicles of criminal life, *Goodfellas* (1990) and *Casino* (1996). *Amarcord* uses certain time-honored, classical devices, such as a progression through the seasons, to great effect to wheel through a various modes, from the comic to the melancholic.

Like many autobiographical tales written or filmed, this one weaves the innocent, limited viewpoint of children into its wider social context, which here heralds the reign of fascism in Italy in the '30s. Poignant indeed is the gap, gradually revealed to the viewer, between the hints of violence and social exclusion to come (especially in relation to the Jewish population), and the life-affirming antics of youth. But children are not the only ones duped, for the politics of fascism comes to the adoring masses as showbiz—a giant head of Mussolini is paraded through the streets in an especially brilliant sequence poised between comedy and mordant social commentary—and mixed up with the glamorous images of the silver screen, as shown in a fantasy sequence imagined by town belle La Gradisca.

Fellini's comedy, refreshingly, goes to the outer limits of vulgarity in a number of hilarious scenes centered on urination, masturbation, and breast worship, revisiting the peculiarly Italian form of the "teen movie" genre, which he vigorously pioneered in *I Vitelloni* (1953).

Fellini's style, sometimes too baroque for its own good in works such as *Casanova* (1976), is streamlined here into a pure, exalted poetry of mist, flowing camera movements, pastel colors, and lightly artificial set design. A triumph of artistic form, its emotions are direct and affecting. **AM**

**Jamaica** (International) U.S. 120m Metrocolor
**Director:** Perry Henzell
**Producer:** Perry Henzell
**Screenplay:** Perry Henzell, Trevor D. Rhone
**Photography:** Peter Jessop, David McDonald, Franklyn St. Juste
**Music:** Jimmy Cliff, Desmond Dekker, The Slickers
**Cast:** Jimmy Cliff, Janet Barkley, Carl Bradshaw, Ras Daniel Hartman, Basil Keane, Bobby Charlton, Winston Stona, Lucia White, Volair Johnson, Beverly Anderson, Clover Lewis, Elijah Chambers, Prince Buster, Ed "Bum" Lewis, Bobby Loban

# THE HARDER THEY COME (1973)

A slice-of-life film set in Jamaica's slums, Perry Henzell's *The Harder They Come* features a pretty shopworn scenario: a country boy comes to the city and butts heads with local baddies. But as a low-budget homage to gangster films, *The Harder They Come* works great.

Thanks to the rough locations and unpolished acting, the film speeds along with a raw verisimilitude. Jimmy Cliff plays the naïve country boy who finds himself diving headfirst into a fight between corrupt cops and gangs that have infiltrated the reggae industry. Indeed, as impressive a mark as *The Harder They Come* may have made on the midnight movie circuit, its most lasting effect was the introduction of reggae to non-Jamaican ears. The soundtrack (a character in and of itself) features stellar work from the likes of Toots and the Maytals, and Cliff himself, whose "Many Rivers to Cross" remains one of the most soulful songs ever recorded. The soundtrack immediately set the stage for the ascent of superstar Bob Marley, but from the perspective of Jamaicans reggae was, of course, old news. They embraced the film as a vivid portrait of their meager everyday lives, a gritty postcard sent from the Caribbean to the world at large. **JKl**

**U.S.** (MGM) 122m Metrocolor
**Director:** Sam Peckinpah
**Producer:** Gordon Carroll
**Screenplay:** Rudy Wurlitzer
**Photography:** John Coquillon
**Music:** Bob Dylan
**Cast:** James Coburn, Kris Kristofferson, Richard Jaeckel, Katy Jurado, Chill Wills, Barry Sullivan, Jason Robards, Bob Dylan, R.G. Armstrong, Luke Askew, John Beck, Richard Bright, Matt Clark, Rita Coolidge, Jack Dodson

# PAT GARRETT AND BILLY THE KID (1973)

Truncated and neglected on its original release, Sam Peckinpah's final true Western has been restored to something like his original vision and can be hailed as one of the director's greatest films. It opens (in the restored version) with Pat Garrett (James Coburn, in the performance of his career) being shot dead and flashing back to the days when he gave up being an outlaw and pinned on a badge to hunt down his former friend Billy (Kris Kristofferson) because "this country's getting old, and I intend to get old with it." Along the way, Garrett loses every shred of integrity and Peckinpah shows us a West decaying in an almost gothic manner, as a succession of familiar genre faces crop up and mainly get bloodily shot.

On parade here are Slim Pickens, Katy Jurado, Jack Elam, Richard Jaeckel, L.Q. Jones, Harry Dean Stanton, Chill Wills, Matt Clark, Elisha Cook Jr., Denver Pyle, and Barry Sullivan. It would be hard to find a great Western that didn't include one of these players; collectively they provide a roll call of the form's greatness, and each cameo adds to the elegiac, melancholy, and wistful tapestry of Western and genre history, shot through with dollops of blood and poetry, plus original music by Bob Dylan. **KN**

## DERSU UZALA (1974)

A spectacular epic, made in screen-filling 70mm in the Soviet Union during a period when the great Japanese director Akira Kurosawa was surprisingly out of favor in his homeland. *Dersu Uzala*'s international success and Best Foreign Language Picture Oscar were factors in restoring the filmmaker's reputation, but its understated approach also served as a reminder that Kurosawa was a genuine master, not just a skilled maker of action-oriented samurai entertainments. This vast movie, dominated by awesomely empty landscapes, is also an intimate two-character piece built on tiny gestures and a simple evocation of deep love between apparent opposites.

Set in Siberia at the turn of the century and based on a story by Vladimir Arseniev, the film revolves around the relationship between an officer (Yuri Solomin) on a mapmaking expedition and Dersu (Maksim Munzuk), an elderly, bow-legged peasant woodsman recruited as a guide for the survey. Through minor brushes with bandits and a major struggle with the elements, Dersu shows his strength and knowledge of his environment. In the film's most tense sequence, a threatening storm gathers as the heroes use a theodolite and some grass to rig up life-saving shelter in the wilderness. It's about the vulnerability and hardiness of man in the vastness of creation, but it gets to its huge theme through a buildup of little details.

At first, the officer's associates think Dersu is a comical character, but it soon becomes apparent that his natural wisdom makes him far better suited than they are to endure in the amazingly harsh and unpredictably dangerous landscape. Five years after the initial expedition, the officer returns to Siberia to finish the job and rejoices in his reunion with Dersu, only to realize that the old man's health is failing—Dersu worries that he is going blind and that all the region's tigers are stalking him to avenge a big cat he has killed. In a poignant stretch, the well-intentioned mapmaker tries to take Dersu into his home back in more civilized regions but realizes that although the old man could help him survive in Siberia he can't repay the service by fitting Dersu into society. **KN**

**Japan / U.S.S.R.** (Atelier 41, Daiei Studios, Mosfilm, Satra) 137m Color

**Language:** Russian

**Director:** Akira Kurosawa

**Producer:** Yoichi Matsue, Nikolai Sizov

**Screenplay:** Akira Kurosawa, Yuri Nagibin, from journals by Vladimir Arseniev

**Photography:** Fyodor Dobronravov, Yuri Gantman, Asakazu Nakai

**Cast:** Yuri Solomin, Maksim Munzuk, Suimenkul Chokmorov, Svetlana Danilchenko, Dima Kortitschew, Vladimir Kremena, Aleksandr Pyatkov

**Oscar:** Soviet Union (best foreign language film)

**U.S.** (Zoetrope, Paramount, Coppola Co., Directors Co.) 113m Technicolor
**Director:** Francis Ford Coppola
**Producer:** Francis Ford Coppola
**Screenplay:** Francis Ford Coppola
**Photography:** Bill Butler
**Music:** David Shire
**Nonoriginal music:** Duke Ellington
**Cast:** Gene Hackman, John Cazale, Allen Garfield, Frederic Forrest, Cindy Williams, Michael Higgins, Elizabeth MacRae, Teri Garr, Harrison Ford, Mark Wheeler, Robert Shields, Phoebe Alexander
**Oscar nomination:** Francis Ford Coppola (best picture), Francis Ford Coppola (screenplay), Walter Murch, Art Rochester (sound)
**Cannes Film Festival:** Francis Ford Coppola (Golden Palm), (prize of the ecumenical jury—special mention)

# THE CONVERSATION (1974)

Riding a crest of creative energy, Francis Ford Coppola was always looking ahead to his next project even as he was still finishing the last. *The Conversation* appeared between the bookends of *Godfather I* and *Godfather II* (1972 and 1974), and it may seem small compared to those dual epics. But small does not mean slight, and *The Conversation* is every bit as provocative as the *Godfather* movies in its take on America's crumbling morals.

Gene Hackman, in a remarkably reserved and internalized performance, plays a surveillance expert who feels more at ease eavesdropping on strangers from hundreds of feet away than interacting with friends in the same room. He's a sad, shy, and inevitably lonely man of many secrets who prefers to sit in his Spartan apartment playing the saxophone, at least until a snippet of conversation gleaned from a jumble of static and noise he picked up piques his interest. Troubled by the distance professionalism imposes, Hackman personalizes the investigation. Sensing an imminent tragedy, he attempts to solve the mystery hidden in his scrambled surveillance tapes before time runs out only, to discover that the two things he trusts in the world—his eyes and ears—have deceived him.

As sad as it is cynical, *The Conversation* arrived shortly before the Watergate break-in and subsequent investigation, when surveillance and dishonesty rose to the fore of public consciousness, and in this way the film was eerily prescient. But Coppola also presents a postmodern study of voyeurism. As Hackman's Harry Caul uncovers more and more about his discovery, assembling some horrible truth out of bits and pieces of discussion fueled by his own imagination, we discover more and more about him. By the time Caul's obsessive investigation falls apart around him, he's left with virtually nothing: no friends, no belongings, no life, and no freedom in the face of rapidly encroaching and enveloping paranoia. Revered by his colleagues for his skills, we see Caul as something of a fraud, a broken shell of a man whose uncertainty about the world around him has effectively robbed him of any identity. **JKl**

# THE TEXAS CHAIN SAW MASSACRE (1974)

**U.S.** (Vortex) 83m Color
**Director:** Tobe Hooper
**Producer:** Tobe Hooper, Lou Peraino
**Screenplay:** Kim Henkel, Tobe Hooper
**Photography:** Daniel Pearl
**Music:** Wayne Bell, Tobe Hooper, John Lennon
**Cast:** Marilyn Burns, Allen Danziger, Paul A. Partain, William Vail, Teri McMinn, Edwin Neal, Jim Siedow, Gunnar Hansen, John Dugan, Robert Courtin, William Creamer, John Henry Faulk, Jerry Green, Ed Guinn, Joe Bill Hogan

Loosely inspired by the real-life story of Wisconsin serial killer Ed Gein—as was *Psycho* (1960) before it and *The Silence of the Lambs* (1991) after it—Tobe Hooper's ultra-low-budget shock-horror classic *The Texas Chain Saw Massacre* opened to a firestorm of controversy, and since then has continued to generate heated debate over its aesthetic merits and potentially damaging effects on viewers.

The film, which begins with some voiceover by a young (and then unknown) John Laroquette, follows five hippie-ish teenagers on a road trip through 1970s Texas who have the grave misfortune of bunking down next to an all-male clan of cannibalistic ex-slaughterhouse workers. The most memorable baddie is Leatherface (Gunnar Hansen in the role of a lifetime), he of the eponymous chain saw and gruesome mask made from the facial skin of several of his victims. After an unforgettable family dinner in which she is served as dessert to the ancient, vampiric patriarch who can barely move his lips enough to suck the blood from her finger, Sally Hardesty (Marilyn Burns)—the one teen still alive—manages an escape from this chamber of horrors by jumping through a second-story window. After a seemingly endless run through the woods at night, with Leatherface's motorized saw (which incredibly never runs out of gas) literally inches away from her back, Sally finally hops on the back of a conveniently situated pickup truck and drives away as Leatherface angrily waves his phallic weapon in the morning light.

Upon viewing this intense picture, with its relentless pace and quasi-documentary style, critic Rex Reed declared it one of the most frightening movies ever made. Shortly after its release, the Museum of Modern Art purchased a print for its permanent collection, and the film was honored in the "Directors' Fortnight" at Cannes. The accolades continued to pour in—the prestigious London Film Festival even went so far as to name it "Outstanding Film of the Year" in 1974. Eventually grossing close to $31 million at U.S. box offices alone, and spawning three sequels (plus a remake), Hooper's warped labor of love stood for a time as one of the most profitable independent films in motion picture history. **SJS**

**U.S.S.R.** (Mosfilm) 108m BW/ Color

**Language:** Russian / Spanish

**Director:** Andrei Tarkovsky

**Producer:** Erik Waisberg

**Screenplay:** Aleksandr Misharin, Andrei Tarkovsky

**Photography:** Georgi Rerberg

**Music:** Eduard Artemyev

**Cast:** Margarita Terekhova, Ignat Daniltsev, Larisa Tarkovskaya, Alla Demidova, Anatoli Solonitsyn, Tamara Ogorodnikova, Yuri Nazarov, Oleg Yankovsky, Filipp Yankovsky, S. Sventikov, Tamara Reshetnikova, Innokenti Smoktunovsky, Arseni Tarkovsky

# ZERKALO (1974)
## THE MIRROR

The great American avant-garde filmmaker Stan Brakhage once hailed Andrei Tarkovsky for cinematic achievement on three levels: telling the epic tales of the "tribes of the world"; keeping his work personal, and reaching his truth via that route; and "doing the dream-work to illuminate the borders of the unconscious." *Mirror* is a striking and haunting example of this threefold majesty.

It is a beguiling and remarkable film—hard to encapsulate, because it is so full of the pregnant mysteriousness of places, people, and gestures. This fugitive self-portrait by Tarkovsky is an intergenerational affair, in which the terse melancholy of his mother's situation—abandoned in the 1940s by her husband and left to raise a son—is mirrored by his own adult relationships (Margarita Terekhova plays both the mother in the past and the present-day wife). Men, largely absent from the story as from the image, appear as voices, and are poignantly identified with the making of art and poetry (the poems we periodically hear are by Tarkovsky's father).

Tarkovsky is a more radical and modernist figure than his Russian heir apparent, Alexandr Sokurov. *Mirror* is constructed as a collage, in which recreated vignettes that deliberately blur past and present are freely mingled with archival footage from several countries and disquietingly disconnected quotations from classical music (Bach, Pergolesi, Purcell). The ambience is dreamlike, secretive, elliptical. Yet there is also a beautiful simplicity in Tarkovsky, aligning him with Terrence Malick: the movement of natural elements (wind, fire, rain), the bottomless landscapes of the human face, and a sense of time passing, all conspire to give a sense of the world itself "breathing."

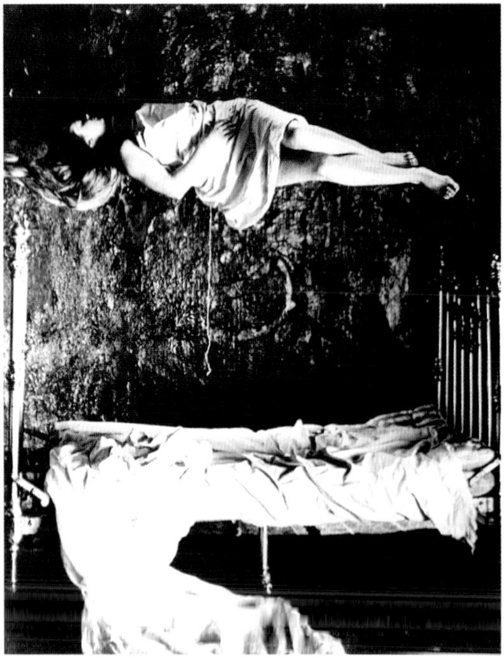

Tarkovsky, like Robert Bresson, is a master of the precisely chosen image and sound. The economy of his camera movements and the gradual revealing of the disparate parts of any scene create an aura and an effect that overflow the material reality of what we see and hear, opening a portal to another world. His is a cinema of texture, of aura, and the senses. *Mirror* is all at once an intimate confession, a summoning of history, and a cryptic poem. **AM**

## A WOMAN UNDER THE INFLUENCE (1974)

John Cassavetes and his wife Gena Rowlands collaborated on a number of challenging and risky projects, but it was Rowlands's exhausting portrayal of a housewife's impending nervous breakdown in *A Woman Under the Influence* that remains the apotheosis of their improvisation-fueled method. Full of ticks, strange noises, and unpredictable mannerisms, Rowlands's descent into madness eventually gives way to the realization that her frustrating behavior may not be as spontaneous or debilitating as it seems. Similarly, her rock of a husband (Peter Falk) may not be as sane as he initially appears to be, and the same could be said for his support network of friends and acquaintances.

Stuck in the middle are the couple's three children, a steady reminder that amidst the confusion is a surprisingly operational (if decidedly unconventional) nuclear family. In fact, *A Woman Under the Influence* may best be considered an unflinching depiction of what it sometimes takes to keep a family together, though Cassavetes never injects the film with such blatant moralizing. Rather, he prefers to leave the action ambiguous and relentless, united by Rowlands's unhinged and kinetic performance, and a strangely touching sentimentalism that achieves its emotional force honestly—mostly free from standard-issue plot conventions. **JKl**

**U.S.** (Faces) 155m Color
**Director:** John Cassavetes
**Producer:** Sam Shaw
**Screenplay:** John Cassavetes
**Photography:** Mitch Breit, Caleb Deschanel
**Music:** Bo Harwood
**Cast:** Peter Falk, Gena Rowlands, Fred Draper, Lady Rowlands, Katherine Cassavetes, Matthew Laborteaux, Matthew Cassel, Christina Grisanti, O.G. Dunn, Mario Gallo, Eddie Shaw, Angelo Grisanti, Charles Horvath, James Joyce, John Finnegan
**Oscar nomination:** Gena Rowlands (actress), John Cassavetes (director)

## YOUNG FRANKENSTEIN (1974)

Mel Brooks's 1974 black-and-white horror spoof of Mary Shelley's classic novel is the prolific director/writer's most balanced comedy in his overegged oeuvre. Having yet to come to terms with being the grandson of the famous Victor Frankenstein, Gene Wilder's modern young brain surgeon Dr. Frederick Frankenstein (pronounced, we are told, "Fronkunshteen") returns to the family castle in Transylvania. Assisted by trusty hunchback Igor (bulbous-eyed Marty Feldman), pretty village girl Inga (Teri Garr), and housekeeper Frau Bleucher (Cloris Leachman, so gloriously sinister that she went on to play similar roles in two more Brooks films), he sets out to recreate his grandfather's pioneering work in human reanimation. Who could predict the reaction between Frederick's overcoifed (and later oversexed) fiancée Elizabeth (Madeline Kahn) and the Monster (Peter Boyle)?

Gene Hackman has a show-stealing cameo as the lonely blind man who makes the mistake of offering hot soup and a cigar to the fire-shy untamed creature. Shot in the same castle and featuring lab equipment originally used in the 1931 James Whale classic, the film's overall reverential feel is marred (in a good way) by the singing and dancing "Puttin' on the Ritz" sequence featuring the monster and the doctor. A silly take and a serious homage, *Young Frankenstein* earned Academy Award nominations for Best Sound and Best Adapted Screenplay. **KK**

**U.S.** (Fox, Crossbow, Gruskoff/Venture, Jouer) 108m BW
**Language:** English / German
**Director:** Mel Brooks
**Producer:** Michael Gruskoff
**Screenplay:** Gene Wilder, Mel Brooks, from the novel *Frankenstein* by Mary Shelley
**Photography:** Gerald Hirschfeld
**Music:** John Morris
**Cast:** Gene Wilder, Peter Boyle, Marty Feldman, Madeline Kahn, Cloris Leachman, Teri Garr, Kenneth Mars, Richard Haydn, Liam Dunn, Danny Goldman, Oscar Beregi Jr., Arthur Malet, Richard A. Roth, Monte Landis, Rusty Blitz
**Oscar nomination:** Mel Brooks, Gene Wilder (screenplay), Richard Portman, Gene S. Cantamessa (sound)

# CHINATOWN (1974)

**U.S.** (Long Road, Paramount, Penthouse) 131m Technicolor
**Director:** Roman Polanski
**Producer:** Robert Evans
**Screenplay:** Robert Towne
**Photography:** John A. Alonzo
**Music:** Jerry Goldsmith
**Cast:** Jack Nicholson, Faye Dunaway, John Huston, Perry Lopez, John Hillerman, Darrell Zwerling, Diane Ladd, Roy Jenson, Roman Polanski, Richard Bakalyan, Joe Mantell, Bruce Glover, Nandu Hinds, James O'Rear, James Hong
**Oscar:** Robert Towne (screenplay)
**Oscar nomination:** Robert Evans (best picture), Roman Polanski (director), Jack Nicholson (actor), Faye Dunaway (actress), Richard Sylbert, W. Stewart Campbell, Ruby R. Levitt (art direction), John A. Alonzo (photography), Anthea Sylbert (costume), Sam O'Steen (editing), Jerry Goldsmith (music), Charles Grenzbach, Larry Jost (sound)

"It seems like half the city is trying to cover it all up, which is fine by me. But Mrs. Mulwray, I goddamn near lost my nose. And I like it. I like breathing through it." Robert Towne wrote *Chinatown* specifically for his friend Jack Nicholson and won the film's only Oscar in a year dominated by *The Godfather, Part II*. It is a conspiracy and a hard-boiled detective mystery in the Raymond Chandler/Dashiell Hammett line. It is also a highly sophisticated film that covered everyone involved in glory, including audiences who responded appreciatively to the compelling, complex puzzle and colossal performances.

Private eye Jake Gittes is more dapper, humorous, prosperous, and alienated than Chandler's Philip Marlowe or Hammett's Sam Spade. Jake is a former cop haunted by the past when his beat was Los Angeles's Chinatown. This is intriguingly alluded to, suggesting it represents failure and being out of his depth in something he doesn't understand, and hinting at the disaster he brings down back in Chinatown at the film's fateful climax. Jake is hired by a dolled-up broad (Diane Ladd) to spy on her allegedly philandering husband, prominent chief engineer for the city's water and power department. He gets the dirt but a rude awakening when the real and outraged Mrs. Mulwray (Faye Dunaway) appears. Jake, who doesn't like being made a fool of, persists in investigating further as intimidation and corpses mount. This leads him to bluff tycoon and chief villain Noah Cross (John Huston) into a catastrophe of greed, murder, and incest in the mean streets and orange groves of 1930s Los Angeles.

It was Roman Polanski's genius that made the film not merely an intelligent and intricate narrative but a great, disturbing vision. With his tragically intimate experience of evil, Polanski toughened up the script, most crucially by changing Towne's ending to the bitter but unforgettable conclusion which leaves Jake pole-axed. It was also Polanski who observed with humane and sharp perception the collected oddballs, victims, and miscreants (including the little weasel who slits Jake's nose, played by the director himself). That it is ultimately his film was verified by the unfathomable 1990 sequel *The Two Jakes*, scripted by Towne and directed by Nicholson revisiting his Gittes in 1948. It, too, is well acted, complicated, and polished-looking, but sadly lacking in unifying magic.

Faye Dunaway, whose neurasthenic quality has never been exploited to better advantage, is the cool, elegant Evelyn, whose birthmark—"a flaw in the iris"—represents the film's heart of darkness. She is presented as a high-class femme fatale and indeed her suspect motives enhance the menace and jeopardy until both her anxiousness and her glowing seduction scene are suddenly cast in a different light by the most shocking of *Chinatown*'s revelations. It is still Nicholson's show, though, his fatalistic glamor and presence as the cynical, wisecracking, impulsively decent snoop unspoiled by the ignominy of sporting a bandage over his nose for much of the film's running time. **AE**

**France** (Action, Christian Fechner, Le Films 7, Losange, Renn, Saga, Simar, V.M. Prod.) 193m Eastmancolor

**Language:** French

**Director:** Jacques Rivette

**Producer:** Barbet Schroeder

**Screenplay:** Juliet Berto, Eduardo de Gregorio, Dominique Labourier, Bulle Ogier, Marie-France Pisier, Jacques Rivette

**Photography:** Jacques Renard

**Music:** Jean-Marie Sénia

**Cast:** Juliet Berto, Dominique Labourier, Bulle Ogier, Marie-France Pisier, Barbet Schroeder, Nathalie Asnar, Marie-Thérèse Saussure, Philippe Clévenot, Anne Zamire, Jean Douchet, Adèle Taffetas, Monique Clément, Jérôme Richard, Michael Graham, Jean-Marie Sénia

# CÉLINE ET JULIE VONT EN BATEAU (1974)

## CELINE AND JULIE GO BOATING

English-speaking viewers will never taste the real flavor of this film. It starts with the title, which means nothing but, in its original version and for French-speaking people, opens wide the doors toward tales, jokes, and children's stories. *Celine and Julie Go Boating* is a password to a realm where sinuous roads travel the fringe between the exterior world and intimate dreams, between present and past, and between reality and fiction. When Alice followed the White Rabbit, she entered another world. When Julie (Dominique Labourier) entered the world of Celine (Juliet Berto), she seemed to do something similar—but not really. What was different? The obvious and crucial fact is that *Alice in Wonderland* is a book, and *Celine and Julie Go Boating* is a movie. A movie by one of the most demanding and delicate of film critics, Jacques Rivette, who turned into a remarkable explorer of the nature of cinema through the questioning of its relations with the real world and with other forms of art.

Rivette's magnificent work has always been made with a joyful taste for telling stories, watching pretty women, listening to songs and stories, sharing love and admiration for actors. Never, perhaps, was it designed in such a free and inventive way than at this moment, when he created the narrative labyrinths—infinite political, psychoanalytical, and aesthetic echoes—with the film's actresses. It was summer in Paris. They believed in utopias, feared nothing, and were ready for any adventure, particularly adventures of love. Along with writer Eduardo di Gregorio, Celine, Julie, Camille (Bulle Ogier), and Sophie (Marie-France Pisier) gave birth to this sunny inner travel, this diving into mirrors with a funny splash, a dance with specters so light. Ghosts and smiles followed the silent music, Jacques Rivette seemed to conduct without moving, and the world was spinning round—magic. **J-MF**

U.S. (Crossbow, Warner Bros.) 93m Technicolor

**Director:** Mel Brooks

**Producer:** Michael Hertzberg

**Screenplay:** Andrew Bergman Mel Brooks, Richard Pryor, Norman Steinberg, Alan Uger

**Photography:** Joseph F. Biroc

**Music:** Mel Brooks, Vernon Duke, John Morris

**Cast:** Cleavon Little, Gene Wilder, Slim Pickens, David Huddleston, Liam Dunn, Alex Karras, John Hillerman, George Furth, Jack Starrett, Mel Brooks, Harvey Korman, Carol DeLuise, Richard Collier, Charles McGregor

**Oscar nomination:** Madeline Kahn (actress in support role), John C. Howard, Danford B. Greene (editing), John Morris, Mel Brooks (song)

# BLAZING SADDLES (1974)

Though it may not be the peak of Mel Brooks's cinematic output—*The Producers* is still more shocking and pointed—with its mixture of surrealism, slapstick, and (then ground-breaking) vulgarity, *Blazing Saddles* is certainly his most influential film. Despite both its hackneyed setting—the old West—and its 1970s veneer—hip gags about race and sex—it stands as one of the more brilliant works in the career of a great 1950s comedy writer.

For all Brooks's much-publicized nods to the zany comedy of the Marx Brothers and the Three Stooges, *Blazing Saddles* owes a great deal to the deranged, parodic, reference-obsessed humor of early *Mad Magazine*. Brooks's film takes on that tradition—sight gags where Klansmen and Nazis wait in line to join an 1870s lynch mob, oxen with YES and NO painted on them, verbal references to other movies ("You'd do it for Randolph Scott!")—and puts it into the cinema for the first time. In doing so, it preempted and influenced the Zucker Brothers and their imitators, and hence invented a genre (there's also some Monty Python in the ending, which mirrors that of *Holy Grail*).

*Blazing Saddles* may, essentially, be an extended riff on *High Noon*, but its genius lies in being more than just a parody. While other, later Brooks movies waver by just being straight pastiches of one particular film, *Blazing Saddles* adds additional layers, most notable of which is the twist that the new sheriff is black. Cleavon Little (whose career sadly peaked with this film, and who died of colon cancer aged 53) beat Richard Pryor for the role of Sheriff Bart, largely because the studio believed that Pryor was an insane drug addict; and he is superbly supported by an almost restrained Gene Wilder. The movie is laced with the "n" word to an extent that anyone not familiar with modern rap records may find alarming, but is in fact constantly hilarious. While hardly a political film about color, *Blazing Saddles*' constant glee in using the word and mocking white prejudice makes the whole concept of racism seem absurd. **KK**

# THE GODFATHER: PART II (1974)

**U.S.** (Paramount, Coppola) 200m Technicolor

**Language:** English / Italian

**Director:** Francis Ford Coppola

**Producer:** Francis Ford Coppola, Gray Frederickson, Fred Roos

**Screenplay:** Francis Ford Coppola, Mario Puzo, from novel by Mario Puzo

**Photography:** Gordon Willis

**Music:** Carmine Coppola, C. Curet Alonso, Nino Rota

**Cast:** Al Pacino, Robert Duvall, Diane Keaton, Robert De Niro, John Cazale, Talia Shire, Lee Strasberg, Michael V. Gazzo, G.D. Spradlin, Richard Bright, Gastone Moschin, Tom Rosqui, Bruno Kirby, Frank Sivero, Francesca De Sapio

**Oscar:** Francis Ford Coppola, Gray Frederickson, Fred Roos (best picture), Francis Ford Coppola (director), Francis Ford Coppola, Mario Puzo (screenplay), Robert De Niro (actor in support role), Dean Tavoularis, Angelo P. Graham, George R. Nelson (art direction), Nino Rota, Carmine Coppola (music)

**Oscar nomination:** Al Pacino (actor), Michael V. Gazzo (actor in support role), Lee Strasberg (actor in support role), Talia Shire (actress in support role), Theadora Van Runkle (costume)

"Keep your friends close but your enemies closer." Time and two more pictures would highlight the despair and nihilism in *The Godfather* saga. This follow-up to the 1972 landmark original is an essential companion piece, "haunted," as writer director Francis Ford Coppola intended, by "the specter" of the first film. Ironically, considering that Coppola was nearly fired from the first movie—and was so worried about his financial situation that he was holed up in a hotel room scripting *The Great Gatsby* as *The Godfather* opened. After the film's enormous success Paramount wanted a sequel from him so badly they made him an offer he couldn't refuse. Besides receiving a hefty portion of the profits, he would also have complete artistic control.

*The Godfather: Part II* took six Oscars—including the only one for Best Picture ever awarded to a sequel—and is darker, more profound, and arguably even more compelling for its elaboration of power's corruption into complete moral decay. Scenes, patterns, and motifs deliberately mirror the original, but Part II is more elegiac and rueful and on a far grander scale, with its complex interweaving of time periods and its parallels and contrasts between the two Corleone dons, Vito (Robert De Niro) and Michael (Al Pacino). This time unequivocally down on the mob, Coppola explores two generations as Michael ascends in power and control as he descends into melancholy, ruthlessness, and betrayal. Family celebrations are again central to the cycle, the film opening in the 1950s on the overblown party at Michael's and Kay's (Diane Keaton) Lake Tahoe estate in honor of their son Anthony's confirmation. We learn that the master plan to legitimatize the Corleone family business is ongoing as Michael pursues his criminal interests from Nevada to Cuba. Michael is beset by problems at home, government scrutiny, and the threats posed by rivals and associates—including the highly influential Actors Studio director Lee Strasberg making his film debut, aged 71, as Hyman Roth—who take a dim view of Michael's expansionism.

Twinned with Michael's progress is the sepia-toned story of his father, born Vito Andolini in turn-of-the-century Corleone, Sicily, where a bloody vendetta makes him an orphan, a fugitive emigrant, and a bewildered detainee on Ellis Island. Years later, on New York's Lower East Side as a grocery clerk and family man, quiet Vito—De Niro, hot off Martin Scorcese's *Mean Streets* (1973), brilliantly reimagining Brando's characterization in the first film as a young man and winning his first Oscar—observes the power wielded by the feared local crime boss and stealthily, remorselessly, usurps it. Respected and prosperous, he returns to Corleone to settle old scores while nurturing a heritage for his sons.

Again the film is full of richly drawn characters and superb set pieces—the festa in Little Italy, the New Year's revolution in Havana. It is the last shot in *The Godfather: Part II* that continues to satisfy, however, with its chilling image of Michael, his sins accrued beyond redemption, alone. **AE**

West Germany (Autoren, Tango) 93m Eastmancolor

**Language:** German

**Director:** Rainer Werner Fassbinder

**Producer:** Christian Hohoff

**Screenplay:** Rainer Werner Fassbinder

**Photography:** Jürgen Jürges

**Music:** Rainer Werner Fassbinder

**Cast:** Brigitte Mira, El Hedi ben Salem, Barbara Valentin, Irm Hermann, Elma Karlowa, Anita Bucher, Gusti Kreissl, Doris Mattes, Margit Symo, Katharina Herberg, Lilo Pempeit, Peter Gauhe, Marquard Bohm, Walter Sedlmayr, Hannes Gromball

**Cannes Film Festival:** Rainer Werner Fassbinder (FIPRESCI award), (prize of the ecumenical jury), nomination (Golden Palm)

# ANGST ESSEN SEELE AUF (1974)

## ALI: FEAR EATS THE SOUL

Rainer Werner Fassbinder had the plot germ in mind for this film—the unlikely love affair between a 60-something German cleaning lady in Munich and a Moroccan guest worker 20 years her junior—at least since *The American Soldier* (1970), in which the chambermaid Margarethe von Trotta recounts the story of Emmi and her husband Ali. What he produced with it in 1974 combines poignant melodrama and occasionally over-the-top social satire. *Ali: Fear Eats the Soul* takes its visual style from Fassbinder's patient camera work, lingering on motionless faces or retreating through a doorway to a respectful distance. The film's texture is created from the details of working-class life, including the songs played on the local jukebox, and its heart from the acting of Brigitte Mira as Emmi and El Hedi ben Salem as Ali.

It starts out as a joke. Ali, challenged by a German girl in the bar he frequents to dance with the old lady sitting alone at the table. He finds a woman kind enough to invite him in for coffee, and actually interested in the man hidden behind the all-purpose "Ali"—with which Germans replace unpronounceable (and to them irrelevant) Arab names. Both are lonely: Ali shares a room with five other guest workers, dividing his time between work and bar; Emmi is widowed, her grown children indifferent to her, and her low-status job. The love affair blossoms against and despite a backdrop of near-universal mockery and hostility from neighbors and family. Emmi doesn't want to care, and pretends not to, but other people make up her world, and care she does.

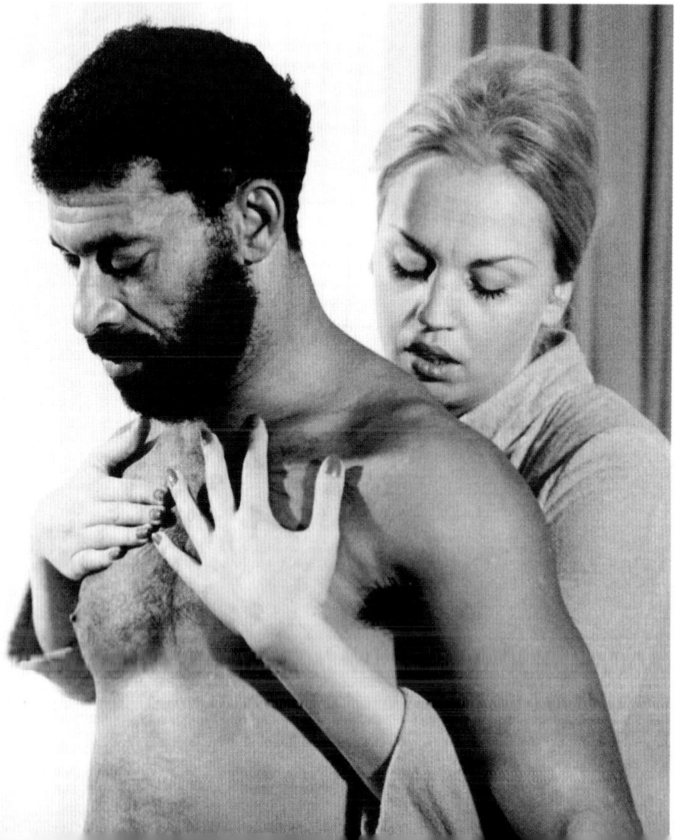

Gradually, though, external pressure lessens, not out of real acceptance but because everyone wants something from Emmi. Fassbinder falters when inner tensions mount in inverse proportion: the Emmi we have come to know would happily prepare couscous, not spurn it as foreign, and would never objectify Ali, showing off his muscles to her colleagues from work. But neither this nor the caricatured racist grocer and gossiping women (a homage to F.W. Murnau's great 1924 silent film *The Last Laugh*) detract from the indomitable and moving connection forged between these two people—and finding happiness with each other against all odds they are wise enough to know how lucky they are. **JW**

## BRING ME THE HEAD OF ALFREDO GARCIA (1974)

This is one of those rare films that divides audiences into those who rate it a five-star classic and those who see it as a one-star dog. Sam Peckinpah's most brutal, nihilistic vision follows seedy piano player Benny (Warren Oates) through a modern-day Mexico made as infernal as the nightmare Western world of the director's earlier classic, *The Wild Bunch*.

Because his daughter has been impregnated by the now-dead Alfredo, El Jefe (Emilio Fernandez, reincarnating his *Wild Bunch* evil patriarch) puts a bounty on the eponymous relic and Benny hopes to collect. Toting the fly-blown head across the desert in a sack, Oates tangles with mob hit-men and crazed bikers, hooks up with earth-mother whore Isela Vega, and arrives at the hacienda for one of the director's trademarked bullet-strewn apocalypse finales. *Bring Me the Head of Alfredo Garcia* is the quintessence of "cinema grunge," with an unshaven and weaselly antihero and a parade of amazingly corrupt supporting characters. Peckinpah goes out of his way to make the settings sleazy and repulsive, with a trace of blood-streaked pretension that suggests Ernest Hemingway at the point his brain exploded. Obviously the work of an alcoholic genius, with moments of affecting melancholy and beauty even during the rapes and gunfights. **KN**

**U.S. / Mexico** (Churubusco Azteca, Optimus) 112m Color
**Director:** Sam Peckinpah
**Producer:** Martin Baum, Helmut Dantine, Gordon T. Dawson
**Screenplay:** Gordon T. Dawson, Frank Kowalski, Sam Peckinpah
**Photography:** Álex Phillips Jr.
**Music:** Jerry Fielding
**Cast:** Warren Oates, Isela Vega, Robert Webber, Gig Young, Helmut Dantine, Emilio Fernández, Kris Kristofferson, Chano Urueta, Jorge Russek, Don Levy, Donnie Fritts, Chalo González, Enrique Lucero, Janine Maldonado, Tamara Garina

## DOG DAY AFTERNOON (1975)

Sidney Lumet's taut film of the true story of a bank robbery turned hostage crisis in Brooklyn is as quintessentially New York as anything by Woody Allen or Martin Scorsese. Al Pacino and John Cazale play hapless would-be bankrobbers (Sonny and Sal respectively), who are forced through circumstances into an impossible situation. Before the robbers can make their getaway, the bank is surrounded by police and Sonny decides to hold the bank employees and try to negotiate an escape. Abandoned before the robbery by their third accomplice, Sonny and Sal are outnumbered by the increasingly unruly employees. As the situation continues and Sonny's loud discussions with the police over a bullhorn are heard throughout the streets, a crowd gathers and begins to cheer Sonny on. For a few brief moments during the social unrest of the early 1970s, Sonny becomes a counterculture hero.

*Dog Day Afternoon* moves between moments of hyperbolic absurdity and scenes of real tragedy. Perhaps the most poignant character in the film is Cazale's Sal, whose limitations are revealed by his answer, "Ohio," when Sonny asks him what country he'd like to visit if they are able to get their demands met. The film captures the swirling passions of a moment in its characters' lives and in history, with a brilliant immediacy. **RH**

**U.S.** (Artists Entertainment Complex) 124m Technicolor
**Director:** Sidney Lumet
**Producer:** Martin Bregman, Martin Elfand
**Screenplay:** Frank Pierson, from article by P.F. Kluge and Thomas Moore
**Photography:** Victor J. Kemper
**Cast:** Penelope Allen, Al Pacino, Sully Boyar, John Cazale, Beulah Garrick, Carol Kane, Sandra Kazan, Marcia Jean Kurtz, Amy Levitt, John Marriott, Estelle Omens, Gary Springer, James Broderick, Charles Durning, Carmine Foresta
**Oscar:** Martin Bregman, Martin Elfand (best picture), Frank Pierson (screenplay)
**Oscar nomination:** Sidney Lumet (director), Al Pacino (actor), Chris Sarandon (actor in support role), Dede Allen (editing)

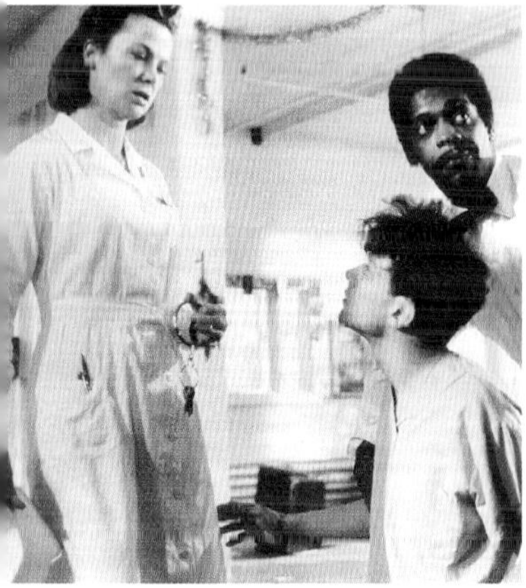

# ONE FLEW OVER THE CUCKOO'S NEST
## (1975)

A project of actor Kirk Douglas's for years (he owned the rights, but by the time the film made it to production he believed he was too old to star in it), *One Flew Over the Cuckoo's Nest* won his son Michael Douglas his first Oscar—not as an actor, but as the film's producer.

Based on Ken Kesey's best-selling novel, which he wrote after his experiences working in a California Veterans Hospital, the film is set in a state mental home where antiestablishment wiseguy Randle P. McMurphy (Jack Nicholson) is sent for rehabilitation. While there he falls under the watchful eye of the sadistic Nurse Ratched (Louise Fletcher, a role turned down by several top Hollywood actresses, including Jane Fonda, Anne Bancroft, Ellen Burstyn, and Faye Dunaway), and soon stirs up a rebellion against her with the help of some of the other patients.

A groundbreaking film that Kesey apparently never wanted to see—he was upset that the story isn't told from the perspective of Chief Bromden (Will Sampson), as in his book—*One Flew Over the Cuckoo's Nest* made Oscar-night history when it became only the second film to win five major awards. Each award was well deserved, with Czech director Forman (*The Loves of a Blonde*, *The Firemen's Ball*, and later *Amadeus* and *The People vs. Larry Flynt*) delivering a hypnotic and humanistic movie filled with eccentric characters (among the actors making their film debuts are Brad Dourif and Christopher Lloyd) and garnering a career-best performance from Fletcher. Nicholson, of course, is mesmerizing as the incarcerated but free-spirited McMurphy, and the scenes between him and Fletcher's contemptible Nurse Ratched are the most electric of this modern classic of American cinema. **JB**

**U.S.** (Fantasy, N.V. Zvaluw) 133m Color

**Director:** Milos Forman

**Producer:** Michael Douglas, Saul Zaentz

**Screenplay:** Bo Goldman, Lawrence Hauben, from novel by Ken Kesey

**Photography:** Haskell Wexler

**Music:** Jack Nitzsche

**Cast:** Jack Nicholson, Louise Fletcher, William Redfield, Michael Berryman, Peter Brocco, Dean R. Brooks, Alonzo Brown, Scatman Crothers, Mwako Cumbuka, Danny DeVito, William Duell, Josip Elic, Lan Fendors, Nathan George, Ken Kenny

**Oscar:** Saul Zaentz, Michael Douglas (best picture), Milos Forman (director), Lawrence Hauben, Bo Goldman (screenplay), Jack Nicholson (actor), Louise Fletcher (actress)

**Oscar nomination:** Brad Dourif (actor in support role), Haskell Wexler, Bill Butler (photography), Richard Chew, Lynzee Klingman, Sheldon Kahn (editing), Jack Nitzsche (music)

# JEANNE DIELMAN, 23 QUAI DU COMMERCE, 1080 BRUXELLES (1975)

**Belgium / France** (Paradise Unité Trois) 225m Color
**Language:** French
**Director:** Chantal Akerman
**Producer:** Corinne Jénart, Evelyne Paul
**Screenplay:** Chantal Akerman
**Photography:** Babette Mangolte
**Cast:** Chantal Akerman, Yves Bical, Jan Decorte, Jacques Doniol-Valcroze, Delphine Seyrig, Henri Storck

One of the key works of feminist filmmaking, not to mention one of the most important European films of the 1970s, Belgian director Chantal Akerman's minimalist masterwork *Jeanne Dielman* is admittedly demanding viewing, and this undoubtedly contributes to the film's marginalized status three decades later; it isn't available on home video, and even repertory screenings are now rare. The film offers a view of bourgeois ennui so spare and bleak that it makes *L'Avventura* (1960) look like a Frank Tashlin picture. With a degree of aesthetic rigor unusual even within that era's European auteur cinema, *Jeanne Dielman* is a 3-hour documentation of alienation, and the methodical precision of Akerman's approach inarguably defeats all but the most patient of filmgoers.

The film chronicles three days in the life of its eponymous protagonist, a widowed homemaker who supports the comfortable existence she shares with her adolescent son through occasional prostitution. The bulk of the picture simply observes Jeanne (Delphine Seyrig) in the minutiae of her daily life. Using static long shots, Akerman allows the monotonous domestic tasks to unfold in real time. However, the film is largely a bravura conceptual exercise ultimately defined by its final two shots. It concludes as Jeanne, after servicing one of her clients, calmly stabs him to death with a pair of scissors. Then she sits serenely alone in the darkness of the family dining room. Whereas the writer-director's other films are similarly meditative and deliberate in their style of pacing, they are largely also mesmerizing and hypnotic experiments in narrative, readily engaging the viewer through both emotional and formalist means. This film, however, is arguably Akerman's coldest, most difficult and remote work, and many will be left wondering if the film's expansive running time was truly necessary to relate the slim character study.

Although the film is taxing, its rewards are considerable and often inexorably linked to the work's length. For one, Akerman's feminist thesis is conveyed with a cogent urgency as a result of her decision to depict Jeanne's life in such unsparing detail. It isn't enough for Akerman to suggest the tedium of her protagonist's selfless existence, but rather, by explicitly presenting the drab banality of her routine in real time, Akerman expertly conveys the stifling emptiness that ultimately drives Jeanne to her tragic final act.

The film also triumphs as a study in performance. Seyrig's perfectly realized portrayal provides subtle glimpses into Jeanne's progressive psychological unraveling, with slight gradations of behavior that would likely be imperceptible if contained within a film of more compact structure and traditional dramatic emphasis. By the time the viewer arrives at the 3-hour mark, the microscopic tightening of facial muscles and increased brusqueness of gesture that accompany the boiling of coffee or the overcooking of potatoes assume the heft of epic melodrama. It may be the kind of picture that's better to contemplate in theory rather than as a vehicle for viewing pleasure, but for the spectator attuned to Akerman's austere approach, her film remains, in many respects, an unforgettable achievement. **TCr**

GB (Fox) 100m Eastmancolor

**Director:** Jim Sharman

**Producer:** Michael White

**Screenplay:** Jim Sharman, Richard O'Brien, from the play *The Rocky Horror Show* by Richard O'Brien

**Photography:** Peter Suschitzky, Richard O'Brien

**Cast:** Tim Curry, Susan Sarandon, Barry Bostwick, Richard O'Brien, Patricia Quinn, Nell Campbell, Jonathan Adams, Peter Hinwood, Meat Loaf, Charles Gray, Jeremy Newson, Hilary Labow, Perry Bedden, Christopher Biggins, Gaye Brown

# THE ROCKY HORROR PICTURE SHOW
(1975)

Richard O'Brien's unusual stage musical was translated onto the big screen in 1975, and on its initial release it flopped. However, when a New York cinema began to show it at midnight screenings word soon spread about the odd spoof sci fi/horror film. It became cult viewing and now holds the record for the longest theatrical run of any movie, having been shown in the same Munich, Germany cinema each week for more than 27 years.

A very young Susan Sarandon and Barry Bostwick star as Janet and Brad, an innocent couple whose car breaks down on a stormy night forcing them to seek refuge in a nearby castle, unaware that it belongs to stocking-and-suspender-clad transvestite Frank N Furter (Tim Curry, in a role he played on stage) and his Transylvanian pals, including sinister Riff Raff (Richard O'Brien) and Magenta (Patricia Quinn). Also living at the mansion are biker Eddie (Meat Loaf), a botched creation (think Frankenstein's monster) of Frank N Furter's, and Rocky (Peter Hinwood), his buff and tanned improvement/replacement.

Narrated by Dr. Everett Scott (Jonathan Adams), the film is a glam rock celebration of sexuality as Frank N Furter and his clan try to seduce the virginal Brad and Janet to the tune of memorable songs like "Touch-a Touch-a Touch Me," "Sweet Transvestite," and, of course, "Time Warp." The mixture of brazen sexuality, tongue-in-cheek humor, outrageous clothing, and double entendres are not quite like anything else ever committed to film. It is easy to see why the easy-to-remember songs and quotable dialogue have been such a hit with fans—the most devoted of whom dress up like the various characters, act out portions of the movie at screenings, and bring props for certain parts of the film (for example, they throw rice during the wedding scene). *The Rocky Horror Picture Show* may not be one to watch with Grandma, perhaps, but it's a terrific exercise in kitsch fun nonetheless. **JB**

# DEEWAAR (1975)
## THE WALL

**India** (Trimurti) 174m Color
**Language:** Hindi
**Director:** Yash Chopra
**Producer:** Gulshan Rai
**Screenplay:** Javed Akhtar, Salim Khan
**Music:** Rahul Dev Burman
**Cast:** Parveen Babi, Amitabh Bachchan, Iftekhar, Shashi Kapoor, Satyen Kappu, Yunus Parvez, Nirupa Roy, Neetu Singh

Yash Chopra had his own production house where he established his trademark style of romance among the wealthy urban bourgeoisie. But *Deewaar*, produced by Gulshan Rai's Trimurti Films, is more of an action movie, driven by one of the best scripts in Hindi film history, written by the major screenwriters of the 1970s, Salim Khan and Javed Akhtar. In many ways, *Deewaar* is an urban remake of Mehboob Khan's 1957 classic *Mother India*, although the emphasis is shifted from the mother to the wayward son, following his life from childhood to death.

India's greatest-ever superstar, Amitabh Bachchan, plays the role of Vijay Verma in what became one of the defining roles of his career—an innocent child whose family is wronged taking the law into his own hands in search of justice. *Deewaar* is unusual for its lack of songs, there being only a title number and a cabaret song, rather then the usual six to ten songs on which such films depended for their success and for which Yash Chopra is particularly famous. The picture manages without these great attractions by creating its own through iconic moments of image and dialogue.

Bombay provides a spectacular setting, with scenes shot in its docks, busy streets, and its glamorous hotels and mansions. These include Bachchan in his laborer's outfit of white flares and blue shirt, beating up a gang of villains in a warehouse, with stylized dialogues contributing to a new sense of "cool." One of the most famous dialogues in Hindi film history is the exchange between Vijay and his brother Ravi (Shashi Kapoor), who has become a policeman in his own search for justice. Vijay argues that he has riches and Ravi has nothing. Ravi's reply: "Mere paas maa hai" ("I have mummy"). Vijay's relationship with a call girl, shown in unusually explicit detail, is overshadowed by his devotion to his mother. At the end of the film, this avowed atheist dies in his mother's arms in a temple, saying he could never sleep away from her, in one of the most celebrated and symbolic death scenes in the history of Hindi film. **RDw**

# MONTY PYTHON AND THE HOLY GRAIL
(1975)

G.B. (Michael White, National Film Trustee, Python) 91m Technicolor

**Director:** Terry Gilliam, Terry Jones

**Producer:** Mark Forstater, Michael White

**Screenplay:** Graham Chapman, John Cleese, Eric Idle, Terry Gilliam, Terry Jones, Michael Palin

**Photography:** Terry Bedford

**Music:** De Wolfe, Neil Innes

**Cast:** Graham Chapman, John Cleese, Eric Idle, Terry Gilliam, Terry Jones, Michael Palin, Connie Booth, Carol Cleveland, Neil Innes, Bee Duffell, John Young, Rita Davies, Avril Stewart, Sally Kinghorn, Mark Zycon

It all started with a TV show called *Monty Python's Flying Circus*, featuring the verbal and visual antics of a comedy team comprising five British wits—John Cleese, Michael Palin, Eric Idle, Terry Jones, and Graham Chapman—and an American named Terry Gilliam, whose cutout animations stitched the program's flyaway episodes together.

Produced by the British Broadcasting Corporation, which seemed a tad surprised by the anarchic nature of the capers it had unleashed, the show ran more or less continuously from 1969 to 1974. A shot at wide-screen success seemed an obvious next step, especially because the compilation film *And Now for Something Completely Different* had been well received in 1971. These things combined led to the 1975 production of *Monty Python and the Holy Grail*, written by the whole Python crew and codirected by Gilliam and Jones.

The process of making the movie had aspects as darkly comical as a typical Monty Python sketch. For one thing, the two directors didn't make a compatible duo; they had different visions of the movie's style, and Gilliam resented Jones's tendency to reduce the grandeur of his set designs with cramped camera setups. For another, Chapman's alcoholism was in full flower, sometimes rendering the star of the production—in the key role of King Arthur—literally unable to enunciate his lines while the camera rolled.

But hey, you can't keep a good Python down. The troupe triumphed over these problems as readily as they overcame the production's dauntingly low funding. See how the knights skip along the ground on their feet, clicking coconuts to make the noise of horses' hooves? The inspiration for that morsel of surrealistic humor wasn't a stroke of comic genius—it was the need to get characters from one place to another with a budget so low that actual horses were out of the question!

Like much of Monty Python's best work, *Holy Grail* is a keen-minded parody with a political edge, debunking a foundational myth of Western power while playing Brechtian havoc with traditionalist ideas ranging from benevolent despotism to chivalric masculinity. And oh yes—it's a laugh riot, too. **DS**

**G.B.** (Hawk, Peregrine) 184m Eastmancolor

**Language:** English / German / French

**Director:** Stanley Kubrick

**Producer:** Stanley Kubrick, Bernard Williams

**Screenplay:** Stanley Kubrick, from novel by William Makepeace Thackeray

**Photography:** John Alcott

**Music:** Leonard Rosenman

**Nonoriginal music:** The Chieftains, Johann Sebastian Bach, Georg Friedrich Händel, Wolfgang Amadeus Mozart, Giovanni Paisiello, Franz Schubert, Frederick The Great, Antonio Vivaldi

**Cast:** Ryan O'Neal, Marisa Berenson, Patrick Magee, Hardy Krüger, Steven Berkoff, Gay Hamilton, Marie Kean, Belle, Diana Körner, Murray Melvin, Frank Middlemass, André Morell, Arthur O'Sullivan, Godfrey Quigley, Leonard Rossiter, Philip Stone

**Oscar:** Ken Adam, Roy Walker, Vernon Dixon (art direction), John Alcott (photography), Ulla-Britt Söderlund, Milena Canonero (costume), Leonard Rosenman (music)

**Oscar nomination:** Stanley Kubrick (best picture), Stanley Kubrick (director), Stanley Kubrick (screenplay)

# BARRY LYNDON (1975)

Perhaps Stanley Kubrick's most underrated film, *Barry Lyndon* adapted from William Makepeace Thackeray's 1844 picaresque novel *The Memoirs of Barry Lyndon, Esq, As Told By Himself*—inhabits the 18th century the way *A Clockwork Orange* and *2001: A Space Odyssey* inhabit the future, with perfect sets, costumes, and cinematography trapping characters whose rises and falls are at once deeply tragic and absurdly comical.

Narrated in avuncular form by Michael Hordern, who replaces Thackeray's ironically self-serving first-person hero with wise third-person melancholia, the film follows the fortunes of Redmond Barry (Ryan O'Neal), a handsome Irish youth forced to flee his hometown after a duel with a cowardly English officer (Leonard Rossiter). Stripped of his small fortune by a deferential highwayman, Barry joins the British army and fights in the Seven Years War, attempting a desertion that leads him into the Prussian army. A position as a spy on an exquisitely painted con man (Patrick Magee) leads to a life of gambling around the courts of Europe, and just before the intermission our hero achieves all he could want by marrying the wealthy, titled, beautiful widow Lady Lyndon (Marisa Berenson). A sign of Barry's willingness to humiliate himself for worldly advancement is that he takes his married name from his wife's titled first husband. However, Part Two reveals that Barry can no more be a clockwork orange than the protagonist of Kubrick's previous film, and his spendthrift ways, foolhardy pursuit of social advancement, and unwise treatment of his new family lead to several disasters, climaxing in another horrific (yet farcical) duel.

Shot by John Alcott almost entirely in the "magic hour," that point of the day when the light is mistily perfect, with innovative use of candlelight for interiors, *Barry Lyndon* looks ravishing, but the perfection of its images is matched by the inner turmoil of seemingly frozen characters. Kubrick is often accused of being unemotional, but his restraint here is all the more affecting, as when Barry is struck by the deaths of those close to him, his wife writhes into madness, or his stepson (Leon Vitali) vomits before he can stand his ground in a duel. **KN**

# FAUSTRECHT DER FREIHEIT (1975)
## FOX AND HIS FRIENDS

This Rainer Werner Fassbinder classic has often been portrayed as the bisexual director-writer-actor's study in homophobic self-hatred. However, the plot of *Fox and His Friends*—about gay, low-life crook Franz "Fox" Biberkopf's (Fassbinder) self-delusion of being elevated to the land of the rich and beautiful after he wins 500,000 marks in a lottery and suddenly becomes the love interest of handsome bourgeois Eugen Thiess (Peter Chatel)—is less about sexuality than it is about class. At first Fox, with his impulsive energy, insatiable libido, and cunning street smarts, seems to have the upper hand in the relationship, putting him in stark contrast to Eugen and his circle of friends' lifeless world of etiquette. Gradually, however, his brute force is worn down by Eugen's condescending treatment, transference of guilt, and manipulation. Fox might be a successful predator in the world of hoodlums and whores on the street, but in the salon world of capitalists (even small-time ones) he is no match for cold-hearted vampires like Eugen.

Fassbinder makes Fox's fateful journey all the more painful by inviting us to witness the telling signs of his doom early on, the first and most fateful one being his infatuation with and reverence of Eugen's lifestyle. The film poignantly dramatizes the ways in which the mass media has marketed desire for social status and wealth to the postwar working class through commercials, glossy magazines, and soap operas. The unforgettable final shot of Fox deprived by Eugen of all his money as well as his human dignity, collapsing or maybe dying of a broken heart in the subway only to be robbed of his last belongings by some boys, has been criticized as a melodramatic gimmick. But Fox's fate bears a connection to other men named Franz—mainly played by Fassbinder—for instance in his *Love Is Colder Than Death* (1969). However the most significant reference is, of course, to the tragic death of another Franz Biberkopf, the protagonist of the Alfred Döblin novel *Berlin Alexanderplatz* (adapted five years later for TV by the director)—one of the most powerful descriptions of death in a society where human value has a price tag. **MT**

**West Germany** (City, Tango) 123m Eastmancolor

**Language:** German

**Director:** Rainer Werner Fassbinder

**Producer:** Rainer Werner Fassbinder

**Screenplay:** Rainer Werner Fassbinder, Christian Hohoff

**Photography:** Michael Ballhaus

**Music:** Peer Raben

**Cast:** Peter Chatel, Rainer Werner Fassbinder, Adrian Hoven, Christiane Maybach, Hans Zander, Kurt Raab, Rudolf Lenz, Karl Scheydt, Peter Kern, Karl-Heinz Staudenmeyer, Walter Sedlmayr, Bruce Low, Brigitte Mira, Evelyn Künneke, Barbara Valentin

## INDIA SONG (1975)

**France** (Armorial, Sunchild) 120m Eastmancolor

**Language:** French

**Director:** Marguerite Duras

**Producer:** Stéphane Tchalgadjieff

**Screenplay:** Marguerite Duras

**Photography:** Bruno Nuytten

**Music:** Carlos d'Alessio

**Cast:** Delphine Seyrig, Michael Lonsdale, Claude Mann, Mathieu Carrière, Didier Flamand, Vernon Dobtcheff, Claude Juan, Satasinh Manila, Nicole Hiss, Monique Simonet, Viviane Forrester, Dionys Mascolo, Marguerite Duras, Françoise Lebrun, Benoît Jacquot

There is no room for middle ground when viewing the films of Marguerite Duras—one either finds the work to be hypnotically seductive or maddeningly pretentious, which is not to imply that those two reactions are mutually exclusive. Her films are largely an extension of her literature, and viewers attuned to experimental European filmmaking of the 1960s and 70s will likely recognize affinities with the cinema of directors Alain Resnais (a Duras collaborator) and Alain Robbe-Grillet, both thematically (explorations of the effects that time's passing has on the memory and identity of enigmatic characters) and formally (a languorous tone aided by slow tracking shots).

*India Song* is Duras's most renowned achievement, a trance-inducing evocation of 1937 Calcutta (filmed entirely near Paris), with Delphine Seyrig as the wealthy wife of a French diplomat, collapsing under the weight of boredom and mental distress. Duras has crafted an elliptical dream poem rather than a linear narrative, but *India Song* is most fascinating in its use of language and sound as a contrast to the images on display. She creates aural disorientation through jarring off-screen cries and shrieks, overlapping and discordant dialogue, and deceptively displaced narration, providing a jagged counterpoint to the somnolent visuals.

Duras's follow-up to this film, *Son Nom de Venise dans Calcutta Désert* (1976), uses *India Song's* complete soundtrack, accompanied by different visuals. *India Song* is demanding but fascinating viewing. **TCr**

## PICNIC AT HANGING ROCK (1975)

**Australia** (AFC, BEF, McElroy & McElroy, SAFC) 115m Eastmancolor

**Director:** Peter Weir

**Producer:** A. John Graves, Patricia Lovell, Hal McElroy, Jim McElroy

**Screenplay:** Cliff Green, from novel by Joan Lindsay

**Photography:** Russell Boyd

**Music:** Bruce Smeaton

**Nonoriginal music:** Bach, Mozart, Beethoven

**Cast:** Rachel Roberts, Vivean Gray, Helen Morse, Kirsty Child, Tony Llewellyn-Jones, Jacki Weaver, Frank Gunnell, Anne-Louise Lambert, Karen Robson, Jane Vallis, Christine Schuler, Margaret Nelson, Ingrid Mason, Jenny Lovell, Janet Murray

A ghost story without the ghosts, a puzzle without a solution, and a story of sexual repression without the sex, Peter Weir's enigmatic *Picnic at Hanging Rock* remains maddeningly elliptical.

The story itself is deceptively simple: a group of students from an all-girl Australian prep school go on a picnic in the Outback. But following a delirious hike to the top of the titular landmark, three girls and a teacher vanish, leaving behind no clues and the growing suspicion that something more dreadful than mere foul play was at work that day. With his sharp understanding that fear of the unknown often trumps the usual bogeymen, Weir bravely refuses to clarify the many lingering mysteries at the center of his brilliant film. When one student does show up, her mind is a complete blank.

As depicted, the excursion itself plays out like a fever dream or hallucination, a wobbly mirage provoked by the shimmering desert heat, and the remainder of the film drips with queasy menace even as Weir avoids enlisting overly familiar means of ratcheting up the suspense. One conspicuous exception is Bruce Smeaton's haunting, otherworldly electronic score, humming like a call from some other dimension. **JKl**

# MAYNILA: SA MGA KUKO NG LIWANAG
(1975)
## MANILA IN THE CLAWS OF BRIGHTNESS

**Philippines** 125m Color
**Director:** Lino Brocka
**Producer:** Severino Manotok
**Screenplay:** Clodualdo Del Mundo Jr.
**Photography:** Mike De Leon
**Music:** Max Jocson
**Cast:** Bembol Roco, Hilda Koronel, Lou Salvador, Princess Reymundo, Juling Bagabaldo

Lino Brocka's low-budget hit was a breakthrough for Filipino cinema and is still often regarded as the best Filipino film of all time. Julio (Bembol Roco), a poor fisherman from the country, comes to Manila to look for his lost love, Ligaya (Hilda Koronel). Working at a construction site, he encounters unfair labor practices, dangerous working conditions, and a range of attitudes and politics among his fellow workers. He also becomes involved with a male-prostitution ring. Finally, he finds that Ligaya has been recruited by a brothel. Julio's attempt to free her and himself from the hell of Manila ends in tragedy.

*Manila in the Claws of Brightness* captures the harshness of urban poverty through an assaulting soundtrack in which industrial noises, traffic sounds, and crowd hubbub are prominent, the crudeness of the recording and mixing contributing to an overwhelming tension, not lessened by the faux-Ennio Morricone songs and synthesizer music. The images of urban entrapment and pain are sharply contrasted with intermittent flashbacks to the lovers' coastal idyll in a direct manner that demonstrates Brocka's commitment to melodrama. The surprisingly strong quotient of homoeroticism—heightened by clips from Nicholas Ray's *King of Kings* (1961), which the hero and heroine view in a movie theater—anticipates Brocka's later *Macho Dancer* (1988). **CFu**

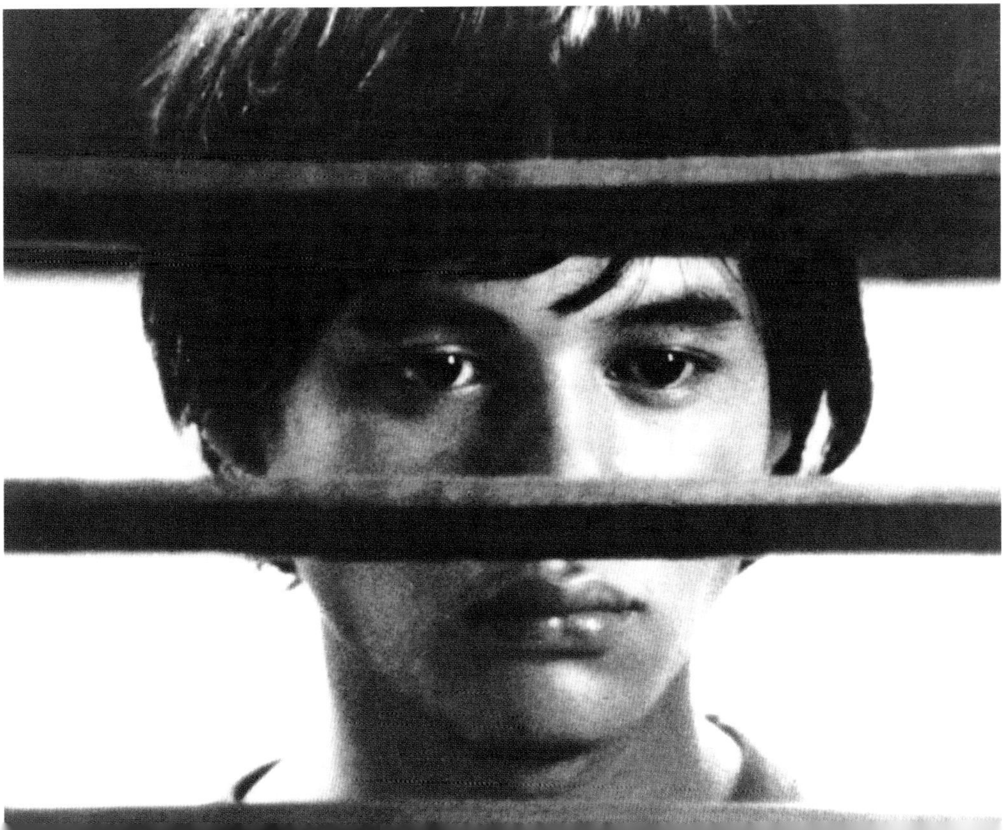

**Italy / France** (Artistes Associés, PEA)
117m Eastmancolor

**Language:** Italian

**Director:** Pier Paolo Pasolini

**Producer:** Alberto De Stefanis, Antonio Girasante, Alberto Grimaldi

**Screenplay:** Pier Paolo Pasolini, Roland Barthes, Maurice Blanchot, Sergio Citti, Pierre Klossowski, from the novel *Salo ou les 120 Journées de Sodome* by the Marquis de Sade

**Photography:** Tonino Delli Colli

**Music:** Ennio Morricone

**Cast:** Paolo Bonacelli, Giorgio Cataldi, Umberto Paolo Quintavalle, Aldo Valletti, Caterina Boratto, Hélène Surgère, Sonia Saviange, Elsa De Giorgi, Ines Pellegrini, Rinaldo Missaglia, Giuseppe Patruno, Guido Galletti, Efisio Etzi, Claudio Troccoli, Fabrizio Menichini

# SALÒ O LE CENTOVENTI GIORNATE DI SODOMA (1975)

## SALO, OR THE 120 DAYS OF SODOM

*Salo* is notionally based on *The 120 Days of Sodom*, a work by the Marquis de Sade, who gave his name to the form of sexual perversion that the film explores. Though the story makes many departures from de Sade's work, it retains much of the spirit of it. De Sade's project was in part political, one that satirized the established forces of the day, in particular the Catholic church. Pasolini too was fervently anticlerical, but relates *Salo* directly to Italian history.

The film is set in the short-lived republic of Salò, where Mussolini made a last stand at the end of World War II. Pasolini was caught up in these events, and his brother was killed in Salò. In Pasolini's fantasy of this wartime episode, four fascist libertines have total power over a group of attractive young captives of both sexes and subject them to a series of sexual tortures and humiliations. These are presented by the director in a series of bleakly formal scenes that are curiously devoid of erotic passion. There is scant attempt at characterization; even the libertines have little in the way of personality and seem to derive no real pleasure from their debaucheries, whereas their victims are largely anonymous, simply bodies to be abused and penetrated.

Pasolini's intent was to use the unbridled use of power, taken to the ultimate of sexual degradation, as a metaphor for fascism itself, seen as a philosophy that worships power for its own sake. But there are other messages. One libertine is identified as a bishop, and at one point two of the victims are put through a form of marriage ceremony, though the consummation is interrupted by the libertines, who interject their own bodies into the coupling of the newlyweds. And in a particularly notorious scene, a naked young woman is forced to eat excrement, which Pasolini maintained was a metaphor for consumer capitalism and its production of junk food.

The end of the film is an orgy of cruelty as victims are strangled and scalped, and have their tongues cut out and their nipples burned. All is set to the music of Carl Orff's *Carmina Burana*, which Pasolini considered fascist music, and a reading of the *Cantos* of Ezra Pound, the American poet who supported Mussolini. Yet though the obscenities the film presents have an undeniable power to shock, perhaps what is ultimately most disturbing is the sense that by this point in his career Pasolini had at best an ambiguous attitude toward the body and sexuality. If the object of pornography is to excite sexual desire, *Salo* would not fit the definition, because its effect, and presumably its purpose, is to arouse disgust.

Shortly after this powerful and disturbing film was completed, and before it was released, Pasolini was murdered. His film was prosecuted or banned in many countries and has only recently become generally available in Britain and the United States. **EB**

# NASHVILLE (1975)

Robert Altman's *Nashville* arrived at the intersection of two important periods in American history. It followed the combined scandals of Watergate and Vietnam, which diminished America's faith in its government and gave rise to a cynical national malaise, but preceded the country's bicentennial celebration, meant to honor the values and beliefs that gave birth to the United States. Altman recognized the hypocrisy of celebrating the roots of a faltering nation and in essence twisted the knife, setting his epic in the gaudy, populist heart of show business itself: Nashville, the home of country music.

With so much going on culturally, Altman tried to replicate that confusion cinematically. *Nashville* includes two dozen main characters and numerous storylines, all apparently colliding chaotically but actually controlled carefully by Altman's acute filmmaking instincts. Over the course of five days, a music festival and a political campaign cross paths (and cross fates), with Altman equating the folly of politics with the sleaze and dishonesty of the entertainment industry.

But populating Altman's mosaic is a wide and richly drawn variety of characters, some blindly ambitious but others barely holding on in a world caving in around them. It's these smaller characters that stick out from the vast cast and rambling story, and you root for their success and happiness. But these and all of *Nashville*'s characters bob up and down like buoys in a sea of failure and denial. This effect is heightened by Altman's famous overlapping dialogue, which constantly shifts your attention to the least expected corners of the wide-screen frame and to that barely familiar face in the crowd, who may or may not play an important role in the story (or what little obvious story exists).

Instead of a straight narrative, Altman works with various themes, but he never stresses one over the other. Instead, he uses country music (written and performed by his actors) as his Greek chorus, directing the flow of the film with their songs of banal populism and passivity. By the time the film is over it is unclear exactly what *Nashville* is about, but there's no question something has been conveyed by its colorful characters. The film is a portrait of life during wartime, a fight for national identity at a time when things like that seemed to matter the least. **JKl**

**U.S.** (ABC, Paramount) 159m Metrocolor

**Director:** Robert Altman

**Producer:** Robert Altman

**Screenplay:** Joan Tewkesbury

**Photography:** Paul Lohmann

**Music:** Arlene Barnett, Jonnie Barnett, Karen Black, Ronee Blakley, Gary Busey, Keith Carradine, Juan Grizzle, Allan F. Nicholls, Dave Peel, Joe Raposo

**Cast:** David Arkin, Barbara Baxley, Ned Beatty, Karen Black, Ronee Blakley, Timothy Brown, Keith Carradine, Geraldine Chaplin, Robert DoQui, Shelley Duvall, Allen Garfield, Henry Gibson, Scott Glenn, Jeff Goldblum, Barbara Harris

**Oscar:** Keith Carradine (song)

**Oscar nomination:** Robert Altman (best picture), Robert Altman (director), Ronee Blakley (actress in support role), Lily Tomlin (actress in support role)

# CRÍA CUERVOS (1975)
## CRIA!

"Raise ravens and they'll pluck out your eyes!" So goes the Spanish adage—equivalent perhaps to "you reap what you sow"—that gave Saura's best-loved film its title. Young Ana, played by the extraordinary Ana Torrent, awakes one night and goes downstairs; strange sounds seem to be emanating from her widowed father's bedroom. Suddenly a woman bursts out the door and flees the house. Her father, a Franco military man, is dead, and somehow Ana is sure she's to blame. After this haunting opening, *Cria!* becomes a chronicle of Ana and her two sisters as they negotiate the shoals of growing up, learning bit by bit what freedom might be.

Made literally as Franco lay dying, the film follows the metaphor of life under fascism as a kind of stunted childhood seen in several other Spanish movies of the period, yet handles it with a refreshing sensitivity and grace. Geraldine Chaplin, Saura's constant muse in these years, is wonderful in a dual role as Ana's cancer-stricken mother and the adult Ana reflecting back on all these events. Her assured presence as the adult Ana seems to imply that fascism is already a thing of the past, something painfully endured but in the end conquered. **RP**

**Spain** (Elías Querejeta, Querejeta y Gárate, Elías) 110m Eastmancolor

**Language:** Spanish

**Director:** Carlos Saura

**Producer:** Carlos Saura

**Screenplay:** Carlos Saura

**Photography:** Teodoro Escamilla

**Music:** Federico Mompou

**Cast:** Geraldine Chaplin, Mónica Randall, Florinda Chico, Ana Torrent, Héctor Alterio, Germán Cobos, Mirta Miller, Josefina Díaz, Conchita Pérez, Juan Sánchez Almendros, Mayte Sanchez

**Cannes Film Festival:** Carlos Saura (grand prize of the jury), tied with *Die Marquise von O*, nomination (Golden Palm)

**Greece** (Papalios) 230m Color
**Language:** Greek
**Director:** Theo Angelopoulos
**Producer:** Giorgis Samiotis
**Screenplay:** Theo Angelopoulos
**Photography:** Yorgos Arvanitis
**Music:** Loukianos Kilaidonis
**Cast:** Eva Kotamanidou, Aliki Georgouli, Stratos Pahis, Maria Vassiliou, Petros Zarkadis, Kiriakos Katrivanos, Yannis Firios, Nina Papazaphiropoulou, Alekos Boubis, Kosta Stiliaris, Greg Evaghelathos, Vangelis Kazan
**Berlin International Film Festival:** Theo Angelopoulos (Interfilm award, forum of new cinema)
**Cannes Film Festival:** Theo Angelopoulos (FIPRESCI award, parallel sections)

# O THIASSOS (1975)
## THE TRAVELLING PLAYERS

Since the early 1970s, Greek director Theo Angelopoulos has tirelessly explored a landscape that has largely remained unseen in cinema. His subject is Greece—not the sunny land of the travel brochures, but a northern wintry one, situated in a Balkan geography and bounded both by its classical and modern past and by geographic borders. Formerly a critic for a socialist newspaper, Angelopoulos claimed that the colonels' Junta provided his subject matter and made him want to understand the historic roots of dictatorship. He made *The Travelling Players* more or less surreptitiously, telling the authorities that he was working on a version of the Orestes myth, set in the time of the German Occupation. This is not inaccurate: in Angelopoulos's film, a troupe of traveling actors moves around Greece between 1939 and 1952, attempting to perform a 19th-century popular play, *Golfo the Shepherdess*. But they are always interrupted by history—from the German Occupation, through the Civil War, to the rise of the Papagos government—and their attempts at performing in front of a threadbare painted backdrop are invariably interrupted by gunfire, flight, or death.

The members of the troupe themselves reincarnate figures from the *Oresteia*—Aegisthus (Vangelis Kazan) is a Nazi collaborator, Orestes (Petros Zarkadis) a communist partisan, Agamemnon (Stratos Pachis) the troupe's betrayed leader. They are less characters, conventionally speaking, than archetypes or even ghosts. The troupe, with its dead members brought back to life, make a phantasmal reappearance in Angelopoulos's 1988 film, *Landscape in the Mist*. Time and space in the film have much the same uncertain quality that

character does. A single shot can drift seamlessly from one period to another, and the film begins with the players standing together in 1952, to end with an almost identical grouping in 1939.

Angelopoulos is one of cinema's great landscape artists, a specialist in those moments where space—a beach, a town square, a mountainside—turns into the stage for a vast dramatic panorama. But he is also a filmmaker of motion, who makes films about travel—on trains, cars, buses, on foot, and above all in the imagination. Claiming Orson Welles and Kenji Mizoguchi as his primary influences, Angelopoulos is known—together with his long-time cameraman Giorgos Arvanitis—as a specialist of flowing, precisely choreographed long takes. *The Travelling Players* is a prime example of that, a four-hour film containing only eighty shots. In the most distinctive of these, the camera and the actors move in such a way that time and space seem to turn inside out, to achieve a Möbius-strip elasticity.

Angelopoulos is a masterful director of crowd movements and set pieces: a characteristic shot that recurs throughout *The Travelling Players* has a group of figures walking through a town and emerging, as the camera tracks through the streets, in another year, perhaps crossing the path of another, larger grouping. His films suggest a theory of history as a sort of parade—at once funeral procession and political demonstration, continually crossing its own tracks, changing its direction and ideological colors. In *The Travelling Players*, movement itself becomes a formidably acute and supple tool for historical analysis. **JRom**

**U.S.** (Universal/Zanuck-Brown) 124m Technicolor

**Director:** Steven Spielberg

**Producer:** David Brown, Richard D. Zanuck

**Screenplay:** Carl Gottlieb, from the novel by Peter Benchley

**Photography:** Bill Butler

**Music:** John Williams

**Cast:** Roy Scheider, Robert Shaw, Richard Dreyfuss, Lorraine Gary, Murray Hamilton, Carl Gottlieb, Jeffrey Kramer, Susan Backlinie, Jonathan Filley, Ted Grossman, Chris Rebello, Jay Mello, Lee Fierro, Jeffrey Voorhees, Craig Kingsbury

**Oscar:** Verna Fields (editing), John Williams (music), Robert L. Hoyt, Roger Heman Jr., Earl Mabery, John R. Carter (sound)

**Oscar nomination:** Richard D. Zanuck, David Brown (best picture)

# JAWS (1975)

Throughout his career, be it with Michael Crichton's monster adventure *Jurassic Park* or Thomas Keneally's Holocaust drama *Schindler's List*, Steven Spielberg has been adept at translating novels onto the screen—and none with greater effect than his first hit movie, an adaptation of Peter Benchley's thriller *Jaws*.

Essentially a piece of pulp fiction about a killer shark terrorizing the East Coast resort of Amity Island, Spielberg (with the help of a lot of studio marketing money) created the first big summer "event" movie. Word of mouth was built up by advertising before the film was even released, and lines grew round the block once the movie came out and people saw it, told their friends, and then went to see it again.

One of the many joys of this adventure thriller is the cast. Roy Scheider is perfect as the Amity cop who first realizes that chewed torsos washing up on the local beach may be a good reason to keep bathers out of the water, but who fails to convince the mayor that there is anything to worry about. Luckily he has expert Matt Hooper (Richard Dreyfuss) and old sea dog Quint (the wonderful Robert Shaw) on his side, and soon it's three men against the aquatic munching machine, leading to a Captain Ahab/Moby Dick–style showdown that's just as tense the tenth time you watch it as the first.

It's Spielberg, of course, who deserves the credit for being the man who made a whole generation of people think twice before dipping their big toe in the sea. Playing on our fear of the unknown, he builds up the tension by slowly revealing the shark to the strains of John Williams's unforgettable score, partly to keep us on the edge of our seats and partly because he knew the rubber shark (named Bruce) used in the film looked more like the real thing the less we saw of it. His Hitchcockian sleights of hand clearly worked, as this cleverly scripted (by Benchley and Carl Gottlieb, while Shaw's infamous "Indianapolis" speech has been attributed to John Milius), tautly directed tale remains the scariest ocean-set movie ever made. **JB**

## THE KILLING OF A CHINESE BOOKIE (1976)

**U.S.** (John Cassavetes) 108m Color
**Director:** John Cassavetes
**Producer:** Al Ruban
**Screenplay:** John Cassavetes
**Photography:** Mitch Breit, Al Ruban
**Music:** Bo Harwood
**Cast:** Ben Gazzara, Timothy Carey, Seymour Cassel, Robert Phillips, Alice Friedland, Soto Joe Hugh, Al Ruban, Azizi Johari, Virginia Carrington, Meade Roberts

John Cassavetes's first crime thriller, a postnoir masterpiece, failed miserably at the box office when first released, and a recut, shorter version released two years later didn't fare much better. The first, longer, and in some ways better of the two versions is easier to follow, despite reports that—or maybe because—Cassavetes had less to do with the editing (though he certainly approved it). A personal, deeply felt character study rather than a routine action picture, *The Killing of a Chinese Bookie* follows Cosmo Vitelli (Ben Gazzara at his best), the charismatic owner of an Los Angeles strip joint—simultaneously a jerk and a saint—who recklessly gambles his way into debt and has to bump off a Chinese bookie to settle his accounts.

In many respects the film serves as a personal testament. What makes the tragicomic character of Cosmo so moving is its alter-ego relation to the filmmaker—the proud impresario and father figure of a tattered showbiz collective (read Cassavetes's actors and filmmaking crew) who must compromise his ethics to keep his little family afloat (read Cassavetes's career as a Hollywood actor). Peter Bogdanovich used Gazzara in a similar part in *Saint Jack* (1979), but as good as that film is, it doesn't catch the exquisite warmth and delicacy of feeling of Cassavetes's doom-ridden comedy-drama. **JRos**

## CARRIE (1976)

**U.S.** (Redbank) 98m Color
**Director:** Brian De Palma
**Producer:** Brian De Palma, Paul Monash,
**Screenplay:** Lawrence D. Cohen, from the novel by Stephen King
**Photography:** Mario Tosi
**Music:** Pino Donaggio
**Cast:** Sissy Spacek, Piper Laurie, Amy Irving, William Katt, Betty Buckley, Nancy Allen, John Travolta, P.J. Soles, Priscilla Pointer, Sydney Lassick, Stefan Gierasch, Michael Talbott, Doug Cox, Harry Gold, Noelle North
**Oscar nomination:** Sissy Spacek (actress), Piper Laurie (actress in support role)

By the mid 1970s, Brian De Palma had already spent over a decade honing his diverse influences, including Alfred Hitchcock, rock music, and political satire. But *Carrie* marked his breakthrough. It is an operatic horror-melodrama blending the family Gothic, supernaturalism, and teen movie. It remains the cinema's best adaptation of a Stephen King novel.

The film inaugurated De Palma's penchant for surprise switches between fantasy and reality, as in the opening, which segues from a soft-core porn fantasia of girls showering to the fact of Carrie's menstruation—the first sign of "otherness" that will set her apart as a monster from her small-minded community.

All the oppression that Carrie suffers both at home (with her religious fanatic mother played by Piper Laurie) and at school creates a smoldering tension which takes the form of telekinetic power. We watch with ambivalence as Carrie's revenge fantasies cross the line into uncontrolled mass murder in the climactic prom scene (a De Palma tour de force).

Sissy Spacek is astonishing in the title role. Her face and body contort like a living special effect to express the unbearable contradictions of Carrie's experience, as well as the character's startling passage from wallflower to Queen of Death. **AM**

U.S. (Malpaso) 135m Color

**Director:** Clint Eastwood

**Producer:** Robert Daley

**Screenplay:** Sonia Chernus, Philip Kaufman, from the novel *Gone to Texas* by Forrest Carter

**Photography:** Bruce Surtees

**Music:** Jerry Fielding

**Cast:** Clint Eastwood, Chief Dan George, Sondra Locke, Bill McKinney, John Vernon, Paula Trueman, Sam Bottoms, Geraldine Keams, Woodrow Parfrey, Joyce Jameson, Sheb Wooley, Royal Dano, Matt Clark, John Verros, Will Sampson

**Oscar nomination:** Jerry Fielding (music)

# THE OUTLAW JOSEY WALES (1976)

A truly great Western, and probably director-star Clint Eastwood's all round best picture. Josey Wales is the typical Eastwood character—a scarred, vengeance-crazed, super-skilled die-hard gunman who refuses to surrender after the Civil War is over and heads for Texas with hordes of scurvy bounty killers on his trail. Though the film racks up a genocidal body count as Josey guns down assorted human filth, it develops a surprising warm streak as the grim hero gradually loses his loner status by collecting a retinue of waifs and strays who finally form a community in the West that enables him to set aside his guns and settle down.

The most moving moment in *The Outlaw Josey Wales* comes when Josey faces an Indian chief (Will Sampson) set on massacring him, and—delivering the longest speech Eastwood has ever learned—makes a plea to set aside murder and get on with life. This speech not only constitutes a personal change on the part of Eastwood the star but also represents a major turning point in the Western genre as a whole. Chief Dan George is wonderful as the hero's wry Indian sidekick, and even the often irritating Sondra Locke is winning as a pioneer lass. *Unforgiven* (1992), in which a reformed Clint becomes a killer again, is a despairing thematic sequel. **KN**

U.S. (Warner Bros, Wildwood) 138m Technicolor

**Director:** Alan J. Pakula

**Producer:** Walter Coblenz

**Screenplay:** William Goldman, from book by Carl Bernstein and Bob Woodward

**Photography:** Gordon Willis

**Music:** David Shire

**Cast:** Dustin Hoffman, Robert Redford, Jack Warden, Martin Balsam, Hal Holbrook, Jason Robards, Jane Alexander, Meredith Baxter, Ned Beatty, Stephen Collins, Penny Fuller, John McMartin, Robert Walden, Frank Wills, F. Murray Abraham

**Oscar:** Walter Coblenz (best picture), Alan J. Pakula (director), William Goldman (screenplay), Jason Robards (actor in support role), George Jenkins, George Gaines (art direction), Arthur Piantadosi, Les Fresholtz, Rick Alexander, James E. Webb (sound)

**Oscar nomination:** Jane Alexander (actress in support role), Robert L. Wolfe (editing)

# ALL THE PRESIDENT'S MEN (1976)

The ultimate in investigative journalism pictures, the scoop of the century—as written by William Goldman and directed by Alan J. Pakula—continually pleases for the entertaining intelligence at work. It is among the most gripping, deft, and utterly compelling of thrillers, and this despite being based on well-known facts whose conclusion is never in doubt.

Following a break-in at the Watergate complex, *Washington Post* newspaper reporter Bob Woodward (Robert Redford) attends the low-key arraignment of the burglars and sniffs a mystery. Defying men in the corridors of power, with the support of editor Ben Bradlee (Jason Robards, winning the first of his two consecutive Oscars) and the melodramatic tipster Deep Throat (Hal Holbrook), Woodward and his thrusting colleague Carl Bernstein (Dustin Hoffman) doggedly get the goods on dirty tricks electioneering and its shameful cover-up conspiracy, ultimately leading them all the way to the White House and the ignominious resignation of President Richard Nixon. A satirist couldn't have concocted better villains than CREEP (The Committee to Re-Elect the President) and its schemers in this sorry story turned into a hopeful, heroic crusade, the real Woodward and Bernstein benefiting ever after from their identification with the decidedly more lustrous Redford and Hoffman. **AE**

# ROCKY (1976)

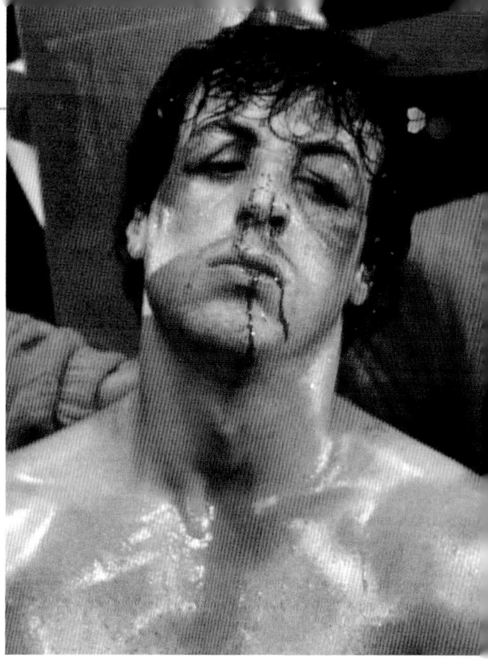

Short on brains, long on brawn—and heart. John G. Avildsen's *Rocky* catapulted the floundering career of Sylvester Stallone into the stratosphere. At the same time, it reaped unprecedented box-office sales, established a movie franchise, and landed a one-two punch of jock stereotypes as rich with caricature today as they were riveting performances in 1976.

The story centers on Rocky Balboa (Stallone), a boxer beyond his prime. He falls in love with Adrian (Talia Shire), the sister of his friend Paulie (Burt Young), and then works to earn the respect of his trainer Mickey (Burgess Meredith). On the receiving end of a publicity stunt, he eventually gets a chance to unseat Apollo Creed (Carl Weathers), the heavyweight boxing champion of the world.

Scored with Bill Conti's pulsing trumpet blasts and percussive rumble, *Rocky* is an immensely entertaining drama about struggling for satisfaction in an indifferent world. As the combined story work of former Mohammed Ali opponent Chuck Wepner and "Italian Stallion" Sylvester Stallone, the now famous actor/writer proved versatile and tenacious. Writing the script, he connected its sale to his participation in the lead role, despite being virtually unknown at the time. Desperate or inspired bid, he hit a grand slam and became one of Hollywood's biggest superstars.

The film is often overlooked as schmaltz, especially considering Stallone's subsequent career, yet *Rocky* lovingly details the white working class. Rocky, Paulie, Adrian, and Mickey respectively work as a debt collector, meat packer, pet store clerk, and gym proprietor; the only upward mobility each has are wishes and dreams. This "biopic" returns to a world of folklore where underdogs get their well-deserved chance after working hard.

Important in *Rocky* are the values of honor and courage, so often questioned in movies throughout the late 1960s and early 1970s. Such reassurance was well received, if gross receipts are any indication, and Avildsen's film walked off with Best Picture honors at the Academy Awards to make it one for the record books. **GC-Q**

**U.S.** (Chartoff-Winkler) 119m Technicolor

**Director:** John G. Avildsen

**Producer:** Robert Chartoff, Irwin Winkler

**Screenplay:** Sylvester Stallone

**Photography:** James Crabe

**Music:** Bill Conti

**Cast:** Sylvester Stallone, Talia Shire, Burt Young, Carl Weathers, Burgess Meredith, Thayer David, Joe Spinell, Jimmy Gambina, Bill Baldwin Sr., Al Silvani, George Memmoli, Jodi Letizia, Diana Lewis, George O'Hanlon, Larry Carroll

**Oscar:** Irwin Winkler, Robert Chartoff (best picture), John G. Avildsen (director), Richard Halsey, Scott Conrad (editing)

**Oscar nomination:** Sylvester Stallone (screenplay), Sylvester Stallone (actor), Burt Young (actor in support role), Burgess Meredith (actor in support role), Talia Shire (actress), Bill Conti, Carol Connors, Ayn Robbins (song), Harry W. Tetrick, William L. McCaughey, Lyle J. Burbridge, Bud Alper (sound)

# TAXI DRIVER (1976)

**U.S.** (Bill/Phillips, Columbia, Italo/Judeo) 113m Metrocolor

**Director:** Martin Scorsese

**Producer:** Julia Phillips, Michael Phillips

**Screenplay:** Paul Schrader

**Photography:** Michael Chapman

**Music:** Bernard Herrmann

**Cast:** Robert De Niro, Cybill Shepherd, Peter Boyle, Jodie Foster, Harvey Keitel, Leonard Harris, Albert Brooks, Diahnne Abbott, Frank Adu, Victor Argo, Gino Ardito, Garth Avery, Harry Cohn, Copper Cunningham, Brenda Dickson-Weinberg

**Oscar nomination:** Michael Phillips, Julia Phillips (best picture), Robert De Niro (actor), Jodie Foster (actress in support role), Bernard Herrmann (music)

**Cannes Film Festival:** Martin Scorsese (Golden Palm)

"Some day a real rain will come and wash all this scum off the street." So mutters tormented taxi driver malcontent Travis Bickle, played with maximum intensity by Robert De Niro in the first of his lauded lead turns for Martin Scorsese. Bickle's job shuttling back and forth across New York City—"anytime, anywhere," he boasts—provides him an insomniac's view of the city's underbelly, all those things on dark backstreets that most people never witness. But he's become so inured to the world around him that he feels numb, invisible, and ultimately impotent.

Yet Bickle is not so much outraged at the signs of social and physical decay around him as he is frustrated that he no longer knows anything else. He's also conflicted, attracted to the very things he purports to despise. Sick of himself and what he sees, he embarks on a final, desperate quest to reintegrate himself into society. "I don't believe that one should devote his life to morbid self-attention," he says, "I believe that one should become a person like other people." But in Paul Schrader's bleak, hell-on-earth script, there's no way out. Bickle is already too far gone.

Bickle's descent is at first painful to watch, then nerve-racking and ultimately pitiful. He begins by wooing beautiful campaign aid Betsy (Cybill Shepherd), and when his awkward romantic advances are inevitably rebuffed, his alienation grows more intense. After trying to rejoin society, Bickle's next goal is to destroy it, beginning with the planned assassination of a popular presidential candidate. When this plan also fails he then tries to redeem society, with the suicide-mission rescue of an underage prostitute (Jodie Foster) from her abusive pimp.

Portraits of urban malaise and anomie don't come any darker, bleaker, or more claustrophobic than *Taxi Driver*. The film has some noirish elements—Bickle's voiceover, Bernard Herrmann's haunting, jazzy score—but veers sharply when it comes to the actual storytelling. *Taxi Driver* proceeds like a film noir told from the perspective of an anonymous stranger standing at the corner of a murder scene, peering over the police tape at the shrouded body splayed out on the street. What's going through that person's head? How will he react when confronted with such a vivid display of violence?

Scorsese, Schrader, and De Niro seem to be asking that of us as well. For the film's duration we're stuck viewing the city from Bickle's relentlessly isolated perspective, with few peripheral glimmers of hope taking us out of his deranged head. He's Dostoyevsky's *Underground Man* surfacing with a gun and a death wish, a vigilante antihero with a hands-on approach to cleaning up the city. "Here is a man who would not take it anymore," he announces triumphantly. "A man who stood up against the scum, the cunts, the dogs, the filth, the shit. Here is a man who stood up."

But is this what we want? In an ironic ends-justifying-the-means twist, Bickle is ultimately praised as a crusading hero, and it's hard to say if Bickle's inadvertent triumph is actually a tragedy. Because the film has done such a successful job wobbling the moral compass, we're left desperately grappling for impossible answers. **JKl**

U.S. (MGM, United Artists) 120m
Metrocolor

**Director:** Sidney Lumet

**Producer:** Fred C. Caruso, Howard Gottfried

**Screenplay:** Paddy Chayefsky

**Photography:** Owen Roizman

**Music:** Elliot Lawrence

**Cast:** Faye Dunaway, William Holden, Peter Finch, Robert Duvall, Wesley Addy, Ned Beatty, Arthur Burghardt, Bill Burrows, John Carpenter, Jordan Charney, Kathy Cronkite, Ed Crowley, Jerome Dempsey, Conchata Ferrell, Gene Gross

**Oscar:** Paddy Chayefsky (screenplay), Peter Finch (actor), Faye Dunaway (actress), Beatrice Straight (actress in support role)

**Oscar nomination:** Howard Gottfried (best picture), Sidney Lumet (director), William Holden (actor), Ned Beatty (actor in support role), Owen Roizman (photography), Alan Heim (editing)

# NETWORK (1076)

Do television producers and executives bear any responsibility to the millions of people glued to the boob tube, or are they merely beholden to the bottom line? Sydney Lumet's cynical treatise on the moral and ethical decline of television hinges on the somewhat naïve belief that things were ever run differently. Even so, *Network* remains a biting satire of the lurid lengths television will go to appease its corporate overseers as well as the complicity of its vast, passive viewership.

In *Network*, ratings rule, and vice president of programming Diana Christensen (Faye Dunaway) will do anything to boost the numbers. That anything includes putting the messianic blathering of a suicidal Howard Beale (Peter Finch, subsequently the only posthumous recipient of an Academy Award for acting) on prime time, despite the delusional bent of his paranoid rants. His line, "I'm mad as hell and I'm not going to take it anymore," becomes his mantra and the mantra of his audience, yet Christensen doesn't see the danger of her runaway success. Max Schumacher (William Holden), head of the nightly news, does, and he grows increasingly disaffected when he sees what Christensen and fellow executive Frank Hackett (Robert Duvall) are doing to his cherished profession.

*Network* could have come across as hypocritical and patronizing had Sydney Lumet and writer Paddy Chayefsky not done such a sharp job of depicting the world of television as a particularly sleazy and destructive social parasite. They keep the bitter, desperate acts and darkly comic perversities coming at such a brisk clip that you barely realize the film is a damning portrayal of not just the television providers but *us*, the compulsive television viewers. It's enough to make you want to unplug your set and toss it out into the street, but one of the film's major points is that we can't. The sensationalism and tawdriness of TV is exactly what keeps us coming back to it: it's all about the numbers, which is what we are. **JKl**

# VOSKHOZHDENIE (1976)
## ASCENT

In 1942, Russian partisans and peasants run afoul of German invaders and Russian collaborators. The style Lariso Shepitko adopts for *Ascent* seems at first harsh, unadorned, and off-putting: flat lighting, shallow focus, jarring rhythms. Much of the action takes place in snowy landscapes in which the characters are relentlessly exposed and overlit. The visual flatness matches Shepitko's approach to the characters, who are less introduced than thrust before us. Although it attends to the details of faces and captures with special vividness the nervous expressiveness of eyes, the film avoids psychological depth in its characterizations. The three main characters exist less as fully realized individuals than as the starkly drawn symbolic figures of a morality play: the intellectual, self-sacrificing partisan Sotnikov (Boris Plotnikov); his frightened, wavering comrade (Vladimir Gostyukhin); their Satanic interrogator (played by Tarkovsky regular Anatoli Solonitsyn).

The intensity of Shepitko's film, which culminates in a feverish and protracted calvary, is heightened through elemental imagery (fire, snow, steam, wood, metal), Alfred Shnitke's shimmering, harrowing score, and Vladimir Chukhnov's lighting, which etherealizes an experience that would otherwise have been oppressive and hopeless. *Ascent* is one of the most powerful of all films that have war as their background. **CFu**

**U.S.S.R.** (Mosfilm) 111m BW
**Language:** Russian
**Director:** Larisa Shepitko
**Screenplay:** Yuri Klepikov, Larisa Shepitko, from the novel *Sotnikov* by Vasili Bykov
**Photography:** Vladimir Chukhnov, Pavel Lebeshev
**Music:** Alfred Shnitke
**Cast:** Boris Plotnikov, Vladimir Gostyukhin, Sergei Yakovlev, Lyudmila Polyakova, Viktoriya Goldentul, Anatoli Solonitsyn, Mariya Vinogradova, Nikolai Sektimenko
**Berlin International Film Festival:** Larisa Shepitko (FIPRESCI award), (Golden Bear), (Interfilm award—special mention), (OCIC award)

# AI NO CORRIDA (1976)
## IN THE REALM OF THE SENSES

Japan, 1936. A young prostitute, Sada (Eiko Matsuda), begins an affair with Kichi-zo (Tatsuya Fuji), the husband of the brothel madam. The relationship is intense and highly physical. They have sex in a series of explicit scenes, often watched by third parties: geishas, serving women, other prostitutes. They play sex games, Sada putting items of food in her vagina before feeding them to her lover, and encouraging Kichi-zo to have sex with other partners, including an old woman who comes to sing for them. But Sada eventually grows jealous of Kichi-zo's continuing sexual relations with his wife, and threatens to cut off his penis. They begin to play asphyxiation games during sexual intercourse, and at last, with his encouragement, Sada strangles her lover, then castrates him.

Oshima's film achieves an extraordinary level of erotic intimacy and physical frankness. For the first time in a picture not intended for the pornographic circuit there are frequent shots of the erect male penis and scenes of fellatio. But Oshima also manages to convince us that this story of crazy love, *l'amour fou,* is a true manifestation of passion, taken to the ultimate extreme. The elegance of the director's mise en scène is a cool counterpoint to the sexual frenzy of the lovers. **EB**

**Japan / France** (Argos, Oshima, Shibata) 105m Eastmancolor
**Language:** Japanese
**Director:** Nagisa Oshima
**Producer:** Anatole Dauman
**Screenplay:** Nagisa Oshima
**Photography:** Hideo Itoh
**Music:** Minoru Miki
**Cast:** Tatsuya Fuji, Eiko Matsuda, Aoi Nakajima, Yasuko Matsui, Meika Seri, Kanae Kobayashi, Taiji Tonoyama, Kyôji Kokonoe, Naomi Shiraishi, Shinkichi Noda, Komikichi Hori, Kikuhei Matsunoya, Akiko Koyama, Yuriko Azuma, Rei Minami

# NOVECENTO (1976)
## 1900

One of the first, and certainly one of the longest, political metaphor movies released in the 1970s, what was Bernardo Bertolucci's labor of love was made possible only after the astonishing success of his *Last Tango In Paris*. Spanning forty-five years of social history, this two part, five-hour film is not meant to be entertaining. A visually rewarding if heavy-handed polemic, *1900* assumes a basic knowledge of modern Italian history then pins the finer points of that social struggle onto the intertwining destinies of two men.

Beginning with bloody scenes in the Italian countryside at the end of World War II, the tale backtracks to the almost simultaneous birth of two important grandsons—that of the vineyard's owner (Burt Lancaster) and the other of his top worker (Sterling Hayden). The two become childhood friends, yet as grown men Alfredo (Robert De Niro) leads the vacuous, hedonistic life available to his aristocratic means while Olmo (Gerard Depardieu, here almost unrecognizable without his later girth) remains an angry working man. Set primarily on the estate and a nearby village, the limited locations add to the film's microcosmic feel: the men are Italy's divided social classes, the area they live in Italy itself. When Alfredo marries a sophisticate (Dominique Sanda) the workers hope their plight will end, but a brutal farm manager (Donald Sutherland) makes this impossible through his Black Shirt coercion.

No matter how lovingly filmed, these forty-five years of conflict between aristocrats and farm laborers rarely contain any happiness; reality always beats the stuffing out of any joy that accidentally raises its head. A viewer ignorant of Italian social history may hold on and hope to see if, by chance, things get better by the end. They don't, as the scrappy, violent attacks at the film's very beginning prove. It is the exceptional international cast of Italian, French, and American actors which now makes this politically tub-thumping experience a sensational cinematic experience. Bertolucci may have liked this film to be listed among the great political films, but its belabored message forces the viewer to seek pleasure elsewhere, particularly in the performances of De Niro and Depardieu. **KK**

**France / Italy / West Germany**
(Artémis, Artistes Associés, PEA)
320m Technicolor

**Language:** Italian

**Director:** Bernardo Bertolucci

**Producer:** Alberto Grimaldi

**Screenplay:** Franco Arcalli, Bernardo Bertolucci, Giuseppe Bertolucci

**Photography:** Vittorio Storaro

**Music:** Ennio Morricone

**Cast:** Robert De Niro, Gérard Depardieu, Dominique Sanda, Francesca Bertini, Laura Betti, Werner Bruhns, Stefania Casini, Sterling Hayden, Anna Henkel, Ellen Schwiers, Alida Valli, Romolo Valli, Bianca Magliacca, Giacomo Rizzo, Pippo Campanini

## THE MAN WHO FELL TO EARTH (1976)

An adaptation of the Walter Tevis novel of the same name, Nicholas Roeg's 1976 science-fiction story was and is often misunderstood. Directed in Roeg's trademark nervy style, *The Man Who Fell to Earth* is a visually challenging tale of an alien's doomed visit to our planet. Told in cross-edits with unexplained chronological and location jumps, this ultrasophisticated take on American culture, love, and homesickness was also a major technical achievement.

Early on, Peter O'Toole was considered for the role of the alien Thomas Jerome Newton, but the part ultimately went to David Bowie, an internationally renowned pop star with limited acting experience. Newton comes to earth seeking water for his dying world, and along the way becomes immensely wealthy by introducing lucrative new technologies to our world. Newton falls prey to human vices, alcohol in particular, and to human pursuers; his mission fails, the years roll away, and the vulnerable alien is milked for his advanced technical knowledge and then abandoned.

The recent successes of *Memento* (2000) and *Mulholland Dr.* (2001), two films that similarly displace time and place, show that *The Man Who Fell to Earth* was not only ahead of its time but also ahead of its audience. **KK**

**G.B.** (British Lion) 140m Color

**Director:** Nicolas Roeg

**Producer:** Michael Deeley, Barry Spikings

**Screenplay:** Paul Mayersberg, from the novel by Walter Tevis

**Photography:** Anthony B. Richmond

**Music:** John Phillips, Stomu Yamashta

**Cast:** David Bowie, Rip Torn, Candy Clark, Buck Henry, Bernie Casey, Jackson D. Kane, Rick Riccardo, Tony Mascia, Linda Hutton, Hilary Holland, Adrienne Larussa, Lilybelle Crawford, Richard Breeding, Albert Nelson, Peter Prouse

**Berlin International Film Festival:** Nicolas Roeg nomination (Golden Bear)

# STAR WARS (1977)

**U.S.** (Lucasfilm) 121m Technicolor
**Director:** George Lucas
**Producer:** Gary Kurtz, George Lucas
**Screenplay:** George Lucas
**Photography:** Gilbert Taylor
**Music:** John Williams
**Cast:** Mark Hamill, Harrison Ford, Carrie Fisher, Peter Cushing, Alec Guinness, Anthony Daniels, Kenny Baker, Peter Mayhew, David Prowse, James Earl Jones, Phil Brown, Shelagh Fraser, Jack Purvis, Alex McCrindle, Eddie Byrne
**Oscar:** John Barry, Norman Reynolds, Leslie Dilley, Roger Christian (art direction), John Mollo (costume), John Stears, John Dykstra, Richard Edlund, Grant McCune, Robert Blalack (special visual effects), Paul Hirsch, Marcia Lucas, Richard Chew (editing), John Williams (music), Don MacDougall, Ray West, Bob Minkler, Derek Ball (sound), Ben Burtt (special sound effects)
**Oscar nomination:** Gary Kurtz (best picture), George Lucas (director), George Lucas (screenplay), Alec Guinness (actor in support role)

Writer/director George Lucas's film was not expected to be a success. A "sci-fi western" with a virtually unknown principal cast (Harrison Ford, Mark Hamill, and Carrie Fisher), studio bosses were so convinced the movie would flop that they happily gave Lucas the merchandising rights to any *Star Wars* products for free. They obviously did not realize the film's huge potential, and never expected that it would lead to two sequels, three prequels, an Ewok spin-off, cartoons, computer games, toys, soundtracks, books, huge video and DVD sales, sweets, clothes, bed linen, and even food.

On paper, the movie that cost $11 million, and went on to make over $460 million, probably didn't sound like a potential blockbuster, let alone one of the most successful films ever made. After the death of the aunt and uncle who raised him, a headstrong young man, Luke Skywalker (Hamill), teams up with an old Jedi Knight, Ben "Obi-Wan" Kenobi (Alec Guinness), two creaky robots, a cocky spaceship pilot named Han Solo (a star-making performance from Ford), and Solo's furry Wookie pal Chewbacca (Peter Mayhew) to rescue a princess (Fisher) from an evil guy wearing robes and a big plastic helmet. *Star Wars* could have turned out a bit silly, especially considering that most people in the mid-1970s expected "sci-fi" to mean wobbly *Star Trek* sets or effects on a par with Ed Wood's hubcap-on-a-string from *Plan 9 from Outer Space* (1959).

But Lucas had much bigger ideas. A couple of decades before computer-generated images could be used to create fantastical worlds and distant

planets, Lucas, using incredibly detailed models, clever photography, and well-chosen locations—scenes featuring Luke's desertlike home planet of Tatooine, for example, were filmed on intricately built sets in Tunisia (reused in 1999 when Lucas filmed *Star Wars: Episode I—The Phantom Menace*)—tells the story of another universe, one in which the evil Empire led by Darth Vader (David Prowse, with voice supplied by James Earl Jones) rules, but where rebel forces are gathering to bring down the bad guys.

Lucas also created a mythology that has been embraced by young and old alike. As well as creating various creatures from his galaxy far, far away, his good-versus-evil storyline introduces us to people and objects that have since become part of the English language: the Millennium Falcon (Solo's spaceship, which Lucas originally imagined would look like a flying hamburger), light sabers (the swordlike weapon with its own recognizable "swoosh" sound), Imperial Stormtroopers, and, of course, the Jedi Knights (so much a part of our collective consciousness now that an internet campaign suggesting that people enter "Jedi" under the religion question of a United Kingdom census form proved hugely successful).

In giving the world *Star Wars*, Lucas succeeded in making much more than just a movie (one that would eventually get its own exhibit at the Smithsonian, no less); he made a world, a new style of cinema, and an unforgettable outer space opera that has been many times imitated but never bettered. And you never can see the strings. **JB**

U.S. (Columbia, EMI) 135m Metrocolor
**Language:** English / French
**Director:** Steven Spielberg
**Producer:** Julia Phillips, Michael Phillips
**Screenplay:** Steven Spielberg
**Photography:** Vilmos Zsigmond
**Music:** John Williams
**Cast:** Richard Dreyfuss, François Truffaut, Teri Garr, Melinda Dillon, Bob Balaban, J. Patrick McNamara, Warren J. Kemmerling, Roberts Blossom, Philip Dodds, Cary Guffey, Shawn Bishop, Adrienne Campbell, Justin Dreyfuss, Lance Henriksen, Merrill Connally
**Oscar:** Vilmos Zsigmond (photography), Frank Warner (special sound effects)
**Oscar nomination:** Steven Spielberg (director), Melinda Dillon (actress in support role), Joe Alves, Daniel A. Lomino, Phil Abramson (art direction), Roy Arbogast, Douglas Trumbull, Matthew Yuricich, Gregory Jein, Richard Yuricich (special visual effects), Michael Kahn (editing), John Williams (music), Robert Knudson, Robert J. Glass, Don MacDougall, Gene S. Cantamessa (sound)

# CLOSE ENCOUNTERS OF THE THIRD KIND (1977)

A terrific sci-fi mystery in which an Everyman's search for its meaning climaxes thrillingly in first contact with extraterrestrials, *Close Encounters* incorporates themes that recur throughout director Steven Spielberg's work. There are his staple characters (the individual on a quest, the sympathetic mother, the lost boy, the untrustworthy authorities), and a transforming experience. There are rescue, redemption, and affirmation of an individual's worth. Take away the spectacular special effects sound-and-light show, and what remains is a compassionate human story of an ordinary man in extraordinary circumstances.

Richard Dreyfuss's appealing Roy Neary is Joe Six-Pack having an epiphany. When his UFO encounter is dismissed he becomes obsessed with discovering what his experience means, alienating his family in the process. The only person who understands is Melinda Dillon's Jillian Guiler, driven by her own search for her son (Cary Guffey), who was taken in a terrifying visitation at her home. Eventually it becomes clear that they are among the "implantees" privileged with a shared connection. Paralleled with these intimate experiences of frustration and fear of the unknown, of courage and joy in confronting it (and finding something wonderful in the childlike aliens), are the globe-trotting efforts of François Truffaut's hopeful Claude Lacombe, head of the scientific project to investigate and respond to alien contact.

*Close Encounters* shows all the sensibilities of the suburban Baby Boomer nurtured on Disney and 1950s sci-fi, and was indeed an adult, professional rethink of Spielberg's adolescent, homemade epic, *Firelight*. While *E.T.* may be even more revealing of his psyche, *Close Encounters* is a definitive Spielberg film in both style and substance. It is also one he can't leave alone, reediting it into 1980's Special Edition (tightened middle section of Neary's crisis, extended alien climax) and 1997's Collector's Edition (digitally remastered, snippets reinstated, the unnecessary "afterthought" sequence inside the mothership deleted).

Released close to his friend George Lucas's *Star Wars*, *Close Encounters* was another instantly iconic event film. The five-tone greeting-cum-language musical motif by John Williams and the mashed potato mountain both directly entered popular culture, and the collective gasp of awe at the mothership coming over the mountain serves as yet another testimonial to Spielberg's gift for wonder. **AE**

# THE LAST WAVE (1977)

If *Picnic at Hanging Rock* (1975) appears to be about man's adversarial relationship with nature, then Peter Weir's enigmatic *The Last Wave* seems to be about man's symbiotic relationship with nature. Richard Chamberlain plays an attorney hired to defend an Aborigine accused of murder. The problem is, no one will talk about the murder, and Chamberlain begins to believe that something more mysterious (and maybe nefarious) is at work. The murder may have been an Aborigine ritual, strange weather formations are befalling Sydney, and Chamberlain is beset by frightening visions of an impending apocalypse. As his physical and spiritual journey takes him deeper into the realm of the mystical and the feeling of impending doom weighs heavier and heavier on his subconscious, Chamberlain begins to lose faith in reality.

Weir plays *The Last Wave* as a detective story steeped in the mythology of the Aborigines, whose profound (and perhaps supernatural) relationship with the land precedes and exceeds the flimsy laws and rules of the Anglo civilization around them. Increasing the tension with a hallucinatory intensity, Weir seems intent on leaving you as confused as his protagonist, leading up to a curious and utterly perplexing conclusion that may or may not belie everything we have been made to believe. **JKl**

**Australia** (Ayer, McElroy & McElroy) 106m Color

**Director:** Peter Weir

**Producer:** Hal McElroy, Jim McElroy

**Screenplay:** Peter Weir, Tony Morphett, Petru Popescu

**Photography:** Russell Boyd

**Music:** Charles Wain

**Cast:** Richard Chamberlain, Olivia Hamnett, David Gulpilil, Frederick Parslow, Vivean Gray, Nandjiwarra Amagula, Walter Amagula, Roy Bara, Cedrick Lalara, Morris Lalara, Peter Carroll, Athol Compton, Hedley Cullen, Michael Duffield, Wallas Eaton

# ANNIE HALL (1977)

**U.S.** (Rollins-Joffe) 93m Color
**Director:** Woody Allen
**Producer:** Charles H. Joffe, Jack Rollins
**Screenplay:** Woody Allen, Marshall Brickman
**Photography:** Gordon Willis
**Cast:** Woody Allen, Diane Keaton, Tony Roberts, Carol Kane, Paul Simon, Shelley Duvall, Janet Margolin, Colleen Dewhurst, Christopher Walken, Donald Symington, Helen Ludlam, Mordecai Lawner, Joan Neuman, Jonathan Munk, Ruth Volner
**Oscar:** Charles H. Joffe (best picture), Woody Allen (director), Woody Allen, Marshall Brickman (screenplay), Diane Keaton (actress)
**Oscar nomination:** Woody Allen (actor)

The most celebrated film of 1977 was originally designed as a modern take on the sophisticated 1930s comedies of Spencer Tracy and Kathryn Hepburn. Then Woody Allen and his cowriter Marshall Brickman instead embarked on a comedy set in Allen's mind, with flashbacks to the main male character's previous marriages and childhood crushes, and the addition of a murder mystery. Shortened and reshaped by editor Ralph Rosenbaum, alterations to the film included cuts to the opening monologue and the removal of scenes featuring a 13-year-old Brooke Shields. It was this streamlined version, now focused on the romance between Alvy, a neurotic, over-sexed comedian (played, inevitably, by Allen) and the eponymous Annie Hall (Diane Keaton, a one-time lover of Allen's), that captured the filmmaker's original intention—a modern screwball comedy colored with doubt, indecision, and not a little pop psychology.

Nominated for five Academy Awards, the film won four, including Best Picture of 1978, and was a critical and commercial hit. In fact, *Annie Hall*'s popularity was so great that parts of the dialogue lodged in the vernacular; some years had to pass before spiders were not typically described by ordinary people as being "the size of a Buick." *Annie Hall* was Allen's coming of age, a film that marked a turning point in his career as well as the way his talent was perceived. Until then, Allen's work comprised pure comedies like *Bananas* and *Sleeper*. While both are still extremely funny, neither has the emotional resonance or the zeitgeist-catching relevance of *Annie Hall*.

After a surreal, and severely-edited, opening monologue, *Annie Hall*'s story begins on a street in New York City, as Alvy and his friend Rob (Tony Roberts) reflect on the nature of life. Rob brought Annie into Alvy's life via a tennis match where Alvy's main concern was being allowed into the club because he was Jewish. (Although Allen insists that the character of Alvy is nonautobiographical, the similarities between Alvy and Allen are too many to be coincidental; as well as the fact that Keaton pretty much *is* Annie Hall, having been born Diane Hall and nicknamed Annie.) The film then becomes the story of Annie and Alvy's affair, weaving in elements of stand-up comedy, postmodern pieces to camera, Jewish humor, barbed observations about sex, love, and the differences between New York and Los Angeles, and a very funny scene with lobsters. Arguably Allen's most honest film, it is also (ironically, given its theme of emotional immaturity), his most emotionally mature one.

Originally titled *Anhedonia* (the incapacity for pleasure), *Annie Hall*'s was changed only three weeks before its first screening in 1977. While there was no sequel, major aspects of the film's original storyline and the pairing of Keaton and Allen were echoed in Allen's later *Manhattan Murder Mystery*. *Annie Hall* is also notable for some early acting appearances from Jeff Goldblum, Christopher Walken, Beverly D'Angelo, and (in a nonspeaking role at the movie's end) Sigourney Weaver. More bizarrely, both Truman Capote and Marshall MacLuhan make appearances; Capote plays "a Truman Capote look-alike," and MacLuhan was a last-minute (and reluctantly made) substitution for Federico Fellini. **KK**

**U.S.** 90m Color
**Director:** Jon Jost
**Screenplay:** Jon Jost
**Photography:** Jon Jost
**Cast:** Tom Blair, Wayne Crouse, Jessica St. John, Steve Voorheis

## LAST CHANTS FOR A SLOW DANCE (1977)

Long before American "indie" cinema made a fetish of serial killers, shattered masculinity, long takes, and songs-as-commentary, long before Paul Schrader's *Light Sleeper* (1991) or the oeuvres of Paul Thomas Anderson or Lodge Kerrigan, there was *Last Chants for a Slow Dance*, handmade on a ridiculously small amount of money, culminating in an endless shot of a murderer driving down a highway as we hear the haunting country ballad, "Fixing to Die."

The images, the cuts, even the song and its performance, come directly from one person: Jon Jost. *Last Chants* inaugurated what became known as the "Tom Blair Trilogy" (named after the astonishing lead actor), and together with *Sure Fire* (1990) and *The Bed You Sleep In* (1993), this body of work constitutes the least-known milestone of contemporary American cinema.

*Last Chants*, like its neighbors in the trilogy, is a despairing but ferociously lucid document of social breakdown and contradiction. Its antihero wanders through the landscape raving, screwing, killing; Jost weaves an avant-garde structure around his actions, which renders them both fascinating and horrifying. The film eschews easy spectacle but still goes to extremes—the slaughter of an animal, for instance, standing in for the killer's equally indifferent disposal of human life. This is a work that strategically displaces its violence from the content to the form, à la mid-1960s Godard: its shake up of the spectator is a rude but necessary gesture of art and political conscience combined.

Loosely inspired by the Gary Gilmore case, the film takes pride of place—alongside John McNaughton's *Henry: Portrait of a Serial Killer* (1990)—among cinema's most intelligent explorations of a difficult subject. Its distancing effects—color filters, words printed on-screen, stretched-out durations—push us not to judge but to understand this "deep dish" American culture nurtured on aggression, violence, and the hateful exclusion of anyone "other." The best index of its ambivalent sensitivity to the real world it traverses are its constant songs, simultaneously soulful and ironic tunes ("Hank Williams wrote it long ago," runs one chorus) that take us far deeper than the smarmy musical pastiches in Robert Altman's *Nashville* (1975). **AM**

# STROSZEK (1977)

In 1974, German director Werner Herzog made *The Enigma of Kaspar Hauser*, based on the 19th-century case of a man suddenly thrust into the world after years living in a cell. In the lead he cast Bruno S., a street musician and real-life social outsider who—with his strange tics and oddly histrionic speech rhythms—proved an inspired choice for the part. If *Kaspar Hauser* felt like an indirect portrait of Bruno S., that is even more true of *Stroszek*, in which he plays a street musician and drinker newly released from prison. Finding German life unmanageably brutal, he teams up with a prostitute (Eva Mattes) and a borderline-crazy father figure (Clemens Scheitz). Together they set out for a new life in America, but end up in a barren, banal nowhere. Inevitably ending up alone and at bay, Bruno finally stages an elaborate gesture of despair. The film's final sequence—involving a ski lift, a pick-up truck, and a colony of performing animals in a roadside attraction—is one of the most savage and unforgiving endings on film.

Herzog's 1970s films are often lyrical, steeped in mystical German romanticism: *Stroszek* is a stark exception. This is a brutally lucid view of the dream of freedom; America is entirely stripped of mystique, presented as a spiritual wasteland and a trap for the unwary. And the final image of the chicken, dancing manically to a cacophony of harmonica and hillbilly whooping, is as unbearably cruel an image of the human condition—obsessive and out of control—as any filmmaker has asked an audience to watch.

What makes the picture truly phenomenal, however, is the way that Bruno S. commands the screen, with indomitable charm and verve. Despite the role of perennial holy fool, he embodies one of the distinctively strange intelligences of modern cinema. Because of its naturalistic approach and minor-key subject matter, *Stroszek* is less celebrated than Herzog's great visionary follies of the 70s—but it is among his best films and is certainly one of the most unpitying dramas ever made about Europe's dreams of America. **JRom**

**West Germany** (Skellig, Werner Herzog, ZDF) 108m Color

**Language:** English / German

**Director:** Werner Herzog

**Screenplay:** Werner Herzog

**Photography:** Stefano Guidi, Wolfgang Knigge, Edward Lachman, Thomas Mauch

**Music:** Chet Atkins, Sonny Terry

**Cast:** Pit Bedewitz, Burkhard Driest, Alfred Edel, Michael Gahr, Eva Mattes, Scott McKain, Ely Rodriguez, Bruno S., Clemens Scheitz, Clayton Szalpinski, Yuecsel Topcuguerler, Vaclav Vojta, Wilhelm von Homburg, Ralph Wade

**Poland** (Polski, Zespol) 165m BW/ Color

**Language:** Polish

**Director:** Andrzej Wajda

**Screenplay:** Aleksander Scibor-Rylski

**Photography:** Edward Klosinski

**Music:** Andrzej Korzynski

**Cast:** Jerzy Radziwilowicz, Krystyna Janda, Tadeusz Lomnicki, Jacek Lomnicki, Michal Tarkowski, Piotr Cieslak, Wieslaw Wójcik, Krystyna Zachwatowicz, Magda Teresa Wójcik, Boguslaw Sobczuk, Leonard Zajaczkowski, Jacek Domanski, Irena Laskowska, Zdzislaw Kozien, Wieslaw Drzewicz

**Cannes Film Festival:** Andrzej Wajda (FIPRESCI award), tied with *Miris Poljskog Cveca*

# CZLOWIEK Z MARMURU (1977)

## MAN OF MARBLE

One of the best movies ever made in Poland, Andrzej Wajda's *Man of Marble* is also an important testimony to the power of cinema. Recalling the puzzling structure of Orson Welles's *Citizen Kane* (1941), it tells the story of an ambitious film student, Agnieszka (the remarkably convincing Krystyna Janda), whose diploma film is dedicated to a forgotten "worker-hero of the State" during the 1950s, the bricklayer Birkut (Jerzy Radziwilowicz). In that Stalinist era he was transformed by the communist propaganda machine into a national myth. Despite her difficulties tracking down the witnesses of Birkut's "sanctification" two decades later, the stubborn young woman manages to meet with some of them and gets them to talk about the naïve worker.

It turns out that after being victimized by an act of sabotage, when someone placed a burning brick in his hands, the young Birkut lost his innocence and realized just how cynical was the idea of having been turned into a legend. To some extent a relative of Russian filmmaker Vsevolod Pudovkin's characters, Birkut began to experience an awakening of social conscience, though not in the revolutionary sense. After starting to ask the communist authorities challenging questions, Birkut was eliminated. This is the conclusion suggested by the movie's finale (though it was censured)—a daring expose of the communist state's tendency to "devour its beloved sons."

During the course of her investigations, Agnieszka meets Jerzy Burski (Tadeusz Lomnicki), an internationally renowned film director who participated, with his work, in the propagandistic creation of Birkut's heroic image: fragments of Burski's "documentaries" are important pieces in the narrative puzzle. Wajda depicts with admiration the young woman's battle, convincing us that it is the filmmaker's duty to always reveal the truth. This moral upshot to the story intensifies the film's importance, as was the case with Wajda's 1969 film, *Everything for Sale*, a parable about truth and falsity in the cinema.

*Man of Marble* may be deciphered at several levels: a meditation on cinema, it also is a complex depiction of the most horrid period in the history of communism, the Stalinist years. It also proved capable of anticipating social change, portraying as it did the beginning of an implacable process: The fall of communism. The film's sequel, *Man of Iron*, focuses on the workers' strikes in Gdansk and other Polish cities in the 1980s, casting the excellent Radziwilowicz once again, now in the role of Birkut's son.

*Man of Marble* consolidated Wajda's international status, sometimes unjustly judged as "academic." Together with Krzysztof Kielsowski and Krzysztof Zanussi, he became one of the protagonists of the so-called Cinema of Moral Anxiety, which held an enormous prestige and a subversive reputation in Poland. This film also confirms an assertion made by another important Polish film director, Janusz Zaorski, who noted near the beginning of the 1990s that, "We did our best films against the State, with the State's money." This paradoxical situation is what allowed for the appearance of masterpieces such as *Man of Marble*. An absolute must, especially for those who have a hard time understanding why Wajda was honored with a special Oscar in 2000. DD

# SATURDAY NIGHT FEVER (1977)

A movie phenomenon based on a magazine article, "Tribal Rites of the New Saturday Night," that author Nik Cohn has since admitted was fabricated. Whether discos in New York, or anywhere else in the world for that matter, were full of young people experiencing life, love, and the Hustle before the article came out isn't really the point. They took to the floor in droves after the film's success helped make disco the dance style of the late 1970s.

John Travolta, who had previously been a minor TV star in the series *Welcome Back, Kotter*, became the man to mob in the streets after he donned his white suit as Brooklyn boy Tony Manero, king of the local dancehall. Backed by the infectious Bee Gees song "Stayin' Alive," his opening scene walk down the street became the strut to emulate. His dance moves, which Travolta spent so long on he persuaded director John Badham to film from a distance rather than in close-up as originally planned, have been copied on many a dance floor and in many a movie since. **JB**

**U.S.** (Paramount, RSO) 118m Color

**Director:** John Badham

**Producer:** Milt Felsen, Kevin McCormick, Robert Stigwood

**Screenplay:** Norman Wexler, from the magazine article *Tribal Rites of the New Saturday Night* by Nik Cohn

**Photography:** Ralf D. Bode

**Music:** BeeGees, David Shire, Mussorgsky

**Cast:** John Travolta, Karen Lynn Gorney, Barry Miller, Joseph Cali, Paul Pape, Donna Pescow, Bruce Ornstein, Julie Bovasso, Martin Shakar, Sam Coppola, Nina Hansen, Lisa Peluso, Denny Dillon, Bert Michaels, Robert Costanzo

**Oscar nomination:** John Travolta (actor)

U.S. 83m BW
**Director:** Charles Burnett
**Producer:** Charles Burnett
**Screenplay:** Charles Burnett
**Photography:** Charles Burnett
**Cast:** Henry G. Sanders, Kaycee Moore, Charles Bracy, Angela Burnett, Eugene Cherry, Jack Drummond

# KILLER OF SHEEP (1977)

Charles Burnett's *Killer of Sheep* slid into the world between two popular waves of Black American cinema, the blaxploitation period of the early to mid 1970s and the Spike Lee–led charge of revitalized Black film of the 1980s. *Killer of Sheep* fits in neither camp, being both more daring and more quietly revolutionary than anything from those eras.

Writer/director Burnett anchored his exploration of Black-American, inner-city life on the story of Stan (Henry G. Sanders), a quiet, unexceptional man who works in a slaughterhouse to support his young family. They live in 1970 Watts, California, when urban struggle wasn't yet synonymous with the soul-crushing despair of drugs, drive-by shootings, and an unbreakable cycle of poverty. Although the bloody, backbreaking work that Stan does is what gives the film its title (a title that honors the fact that he does an honest day's work without complaint), the real thrust of the picture is in its nostalgia for a kind of innocence that was already fading by the time the film was made in 1977; it's in the celebration of the ordinariness of its characters. Children play in worn-down front yards, making toys out of whatever they find; a picnic is planned, and the plan goes hilariously astray on real life terms; Stan crawls under a kitchen sink to fix a broken pipe, and the camera lingers on his soft, curled body. It all sounds so unremarkable, but it's in that simplicity that the film sings.

Shot in raw black-and-white stock that imbues the movie with a gilded grace, *Killer of Sheep* is astonishing for being one of the few American films in which black characters are not metaphors for something or someone else. They're not simply some variation of stereotype, or merely passive victims of or snarling reactors to racism, class struggle, or the crush of American life. Burnett's camera pierces behind facades and public personas of American blackness to show the human beings beneath them. He paces the film leisurely so that we get to linger on faces and expressions. He captures intimacy—between husband and wife, parent and child, friends—with a documentarian's skill, so we feel as if we are privy to secrets, to sides of a black self that are not often displayed in cinema.

And they're not. So much film that is about African-Americans is filtered through both a horrible real-life history and an insidiously racist film industry that what is produced more often than not are ciphers with attitude who swagger, crack wise, and gun blast through one contrived scene after another. Burnett slows things down, peels back layers, creates settings that are purposefully banal, and illuminates the spirit behind the flesh and bone. He takes your breath away by not trying to take your breath away, by not trying to dazzle or overwhelm the viewer with a weighty political treatise—and yet his film is an example of the most radical, subversive art. It forces you to question all else you've seen or heard about blackness; it forces you to see and hear in all new ways. **EH**

**U.S.** (AFI) 90m BW

**Director:** David Lynch

**Producer:** David Lynch

**Screenplay:** David Lynch

**Photography:** Herbert Cardwell, Frederick Elmes

**Music:** Peter Ivers, David Lynch

**Nonoriginal music:** Fats Waller

**Cast:** Jack Nance, Charlotte Stewart, Allen Joseph, Jeanne Bates, Judith Anna Roberts, Laurel Near, V. Phipps-Wilson, Jack Fisk, Jean Lange, Thomas Coulson, John Monez, Darwin Joston, Neil Moran, Hal Landon Jr., Brad Keeler

# ERASERHEAD (1977)

The remarkable product of more than five years' worth of intermittent shooting and postproduction editing, *Eraserhead* was David Lynch's first feature after several promising but rarely seen shorts. A popular "midnight movie" and cult film phenomenon, this "dream of dark and troubling things," as Lynch himself has described it, assured a passionate fan base for the budding auteur, and anticipated the remarkable visuals of *The Elephant Man* (1980), *Dune* (1988), and *Wild at Heart* (1990), as well as the twisting, twisted narratives of *Twin Peaks: Fire Walk with Me* (1992), *Lost Highway* (1997), and *Mulholland Dr.* (2001).

With its unconventional plot, postindustrial wasteland setting, and black-and-white imagery that seems to have been extracted from the subconscious of a neurotic nebbish, *Eraserhead* has drawn comparisons to the Expressionist mises en scène of *The Cabinet of Dr. Caligari* (1919), the futuristic urban decay of *Metropolis* (1926), and the absurdist/surrealist dreamscape of *Un Chien Andalou* (1929)—and all with some justification, despite Lynch's insistence that none of these films was a direct influence. Additionally, although most commentators begin their discussions of the film by noting that the question "What is this movie about?" is misplaced if not wholly irrelevant, they typically proceed to argue that, despite its many idiosyncracies, *Eraserhead* is a narrative film with dialogue, a protagonist, and a more-or-less linear storyline.

This last claim isn't easy to support via conventional plot summary. *Eraserhead* opens with a strange-looking man (Jack Fisk) pulling levers inside a jagged planet, while out of the mouth of our floating "hero" Henry Spencer (Jack Nance) appears a wormlike creature, perhaps implying conception and birth. Arriving at his squalid apartment building, located in the midst of a desolate urban landscape, a neighbor informs him that his girlfriend Mary (Charlotte Stewart) wants him over to her parents' house for dinner. Over a meal consisting, among other things, of a miniature hen that hemorrhages blood and moves its legs up and down after he sticks a fork in it, Henry learns that he's the father of a premature baby still at the hospital. Mary moves in with Henry, but leaves shortly thereafter, as the malformed and apparently quadriplegic baby's constant crying keeps her awake all night.

The baby, which looks like a cross between an animatronic reptile and a calf fetus, becomes increasingly repulsive and disease-ridden. After fantasizing about a chipmunk-cheeked blonde woman (Laurel Near) who sings on a stage while stomping on umbilical wormies inside his radiator, and having a one-night stand with his seductive neighbor (Judith Anna Roberts), Henry imagines his own head popping off—replaced by that of his baby's—and then taken to a factory where it will be converted into the material for pencil-top erasers. Finally Henry cuts open his baby's full-body bandage, killing it and releasing mountains of foamy innards in the process. In a blinding flash of white, Henry embraces the Lady in the Radiator in what could be the afterlife.

No mere summation of *Eraserhead*'s plot, however "accurate" it may be, can possibly succeed in conveying the tone of this unique and challenging film. The feelings of unease, even horror, that result from watching it and that only increase in intensity upon repeated viewings are simply unforgettable. **SJS**

# CEDDO (1977)

In *Ceddo*, Ousmane Sembene's complex meditation on African history, the king of an African nation has converted to Islam, while members of the warrior class (the *ceddo*) retain the traditional religion. In protest of the religious constraints they are made to endure, a *ceddo* kidnaps the king's daughter. Successive men try and fail to rescue her, until civil war erupts.

Limpid, elegant, and direct, the film eliminates inessentials, showing people only as they appear while engaging in acts and debates of high political importance, establishing an equivalence between speech and action. In scenes of ritualized council meetings in public spaces, Sembene presents arguments, counter-arguments, and accusations through contrasting styles of speech and movement (the sour imam and his followers with their rote formulae and the king's childhood friend with his springy, expressive hand gestures).

Sembene's use of African-American spirituals, one of his most daring and brilliant strokes, widens the film's context to include the African diaspora and the future of the African villagers, destined for slavery, whom we see herded together, branded with a hot iron, waiting to be transported. Intercutting these scenes with the main narrative, *Ceddo* establishes a scathing tone and a crisp, intellectual atmosphere all its own. **CFu**

**Senegal** (Domireew, Sembene) 120m Eastmancolor

**Language:** French / Wolof

**Director:** Ousmane Sembene

**Screenplay:** Ousmane Sembene

**Photography:** Georges Caristan

**Music:** Manu Dibango

**Cast:** Tabata Ndiaye, Moustapha Yade, Ismaila Diagne, Matoura Dia, Omar Gueye, Mamadou Dioumé, Nar Modou, Ousmane Camara, Ousmane Sembene

**Berlin International Film Festival:** Ousmane Sembene (Interfilm award, forum of new cinema)

# DER AMERIKANISCHE FREUND (1977)
## THE AMERICAN FRIEND

A brilliant adaptation of Patricia Highsmith's 1974 novel *Ripley's Game* and one of the most eloquent expressions of Wim Wenders's existential universe, *The American Friend* casts Dennis Hopper as an American expatriate in Europe, luring a Hamburg picture framer (Bruno Ganz) who he's discovered has a possibly fatal illness into committing a murder. The financial reward will help out the man's wife and son.

The film works effectively as a thriller, with the muted expressionist colors of Robby Müller's wondrous camerawork and Jürgen Knieper's subtly urgent score contributing to the air of paranoid suspense. But *The American Friend* is also a marvelously astute psychological study, deftly delineating the fear, envy, wariness, and, finally, friendship that defines the relationship between the two men, each of them, in different ways, doomed.

Typically for Wenders at this highly productive stage in his career, the movie also speaks volumes about the symbiotic but troubled cultural relationship between America and Europe; in some respects not unlike a Jean-Pierre Melville film in its juxtaposition of Hollywood and European art-movie tropes and motifs, it pays tribute to those traditions with pleasing cameos for Nick Ray and Sam Fuller, Jean Eustache, Gérard Blain, and Lou Castel. **GA**

**West Germany / France** (Autoren, Losange, Moli Films, Road Movies, WDR, Wim Wenders) 127m Eastmancolor

**Language:** German / English

**Director:** Wim Wenders

**Producer:** Renée Gundelach, Wim Wenders

**Screenplay:** Wim Wenders, from the novel *Ripley's Game* by Patricia Highsmith

**Photography:** Robby Müller

**Music:** Jürgen Knieper

**Cast:** Dennis Hopper, Bruno Ganz, Lisa Kreuzer, Gérard Blain, Nicholas Ray, Samuel Fuller, Peter Lilienthal, Daniel Schmid, Jean Eustache, Rudolf Schündler, Sandy Whitelaw, Lou Castel

**Cannes Film Festival:** Wim Wenders nomination (Golden Palm)

# THE HILLS HAVE EYES (1977)

**U.S.** (Blood Relations) 89m Color
**Director:** Wes Craven
**Producer:** Peter Locke
**Screenplay:** Wes Craven
**Photography:** Eric Saarinen
**Music:** Don Peake
**Cast:** Susan Lanier, Robert Houston, Martin Speer, Dee Wallace-Stone, Russ Grieve, John Steadman, James Whitworth, Virginia Vincent, Lance Gordon, Michael Berryman, Janus Blythe, Cordy Clark, Brenda Marinoff, Peter Locke

Sandwiched between his notorious debut *Last House on the Left* (1972) and his supernatural slasher film *A Nightmare on Elm Street* (1984), Wes Craven's *The Hills Have Eyes* tends to get lost in critical discussion of America's reigning horror auteur. This may be truer today than ever, considering Craven's meteoric rise to mainstream respectability after the staggering box-office success of his *Scream* trilogy (1996, 1997, 2000). A relentless chronicle of violence against and within the bourgeois family unit, *Hills* usually occupies the role of Craven's "cult classic"—celebrated by the director's hard-core fans, appreciated for its low-budget aesthetic, generating semi-ironic readings which praise its archetypal allusions as well as its exploitation movie themes. Arguably, however, *Hills* warrants consideration as one of the richest and most perfectly realized films of Craven's career to date.

The plot moves inexorably toward establishing a structural correspondence between two superficially opposed families who face off in a battle to the death on the desolate site of a U.S. Air Force bomb-testing range. In one corner are the suburban middle-class Carters, headed for Los Angeles by car but making an unwise detour through the Yucca desert to locate a silver mine willed to Ethel (Virginia Vincent) and her husband "Big Bob" (Russ Grieve) by a deceased aunt. In the other corner is a clan of primitive scavengers who live in the surrounding hills and are ruled with an iron fist by a mutated monster-patriarch named Jupiter (James Whitworth). This group of cannibalistic guerillas—standing for any number of oppressed, embattled, and downtrodden minority/social/ethnic groups—manages to eke out a squalid existence by using discarded army surplus tools and weapons for the purpose of committing petty thievery.

When their car crashes in Jupiter's neck of the desert, the members of the Carter family reveal the extent of their ideologically inherited arrogance, repression, and capacity for denial, all of which makes them prime targets for victimization by their ruthless, unscrupulous enemies. Big Bob is crucified and eventually immolated by his counterpart Papa Jupiter in a highly symbolic act signifying utter repudiation of Judeo-Christian values—values which Big Bob himself hypocritically denounces in an earlier racist diatribe. Two of Jupiter's sons later raid the Carter's RV trailer, where they rape younger daughter Brenda (Susan Lanier) and murder her sister and mother. Stripped of all pretensions, desperate for survival, the remaining members of the Carter clan finally find within themselves the courage, craftiness, and rage to kill off their enemies. The film closes with a powerful red-filtered freeze-frame of son-in-law Doug (Martin Speer) in full fury, set to stab Jupiter's son Mars (Lance Gordon) in the chest—though Mars is surely already dead.

Craven's creativity is especially evident in his mixing and matching of different genres, including the horror film, the Western, the road movie, and the siege film. Stylistically, Craven makes innovative use of shock tactics and startle effects to keep the anxiety level high throughout. And the varied use of handheld camerawork, masked point-of-view shots, night photography, and rapid fire editing is all endowed with a strong sense of purpose, serving to sustain pace and tension in the narrative. SJS

Belgium / Netherlands (Excelsior, Holland, Rank, Rob Houwer) 167m Eastmancolor

**Language:** Dutch / English

**Director:** Paul Verhoeven

**Producer:** Rob Houwer

**Screenplay:** Kees Hollerhoek, Gerard Soeteman, Paul Verhoeven, from the book *Soldaat van Oranje '40 '45* by Erik Hazelhoff Roelfzema

**Photography:** Jost Vacano

**Music:** Rogier van Otterloo

**Cast:** Rutger Hauer, Jeroen Krabbé, Susan Penhaligon, Edward Fox, Lex van Delden, Derek de Lint, Huib Rooymans, Dolf de Vries, Eddy Habbema, Belinda Meuldijk, Peter Faber, Rijk de Gooyer, Paul Brandenburg, Ward de Ravet, Bert Struys

# SOLDAAT VAN ORANJE (1977)

## SOLDIER OF ORANGE

*Soldier of Orange* is Paul Verhoeven's most elaborate Dutch film—and the most spectacular and expensive film from that country at the time. It also announced themes that Verhoeven would return to in his later Hollywood career.

*Soldier* sketches the adventures of a group of Dutch students during World War II. Initially greeting the war with a shrugging "a bit of war would be nice," they soon find themselves forced to make choices—joining the Germans, the resistance movement, or going underground. Throughout the film, Erik Lanshof (Rutger Hauer) is at the center of things. While others around him are compelled to choose between different paths, Erik enjoys the freedom of letting chance make his decisions for him, jumping from one adventure to another.

*Soldier* is at its best when it addresses in minute detail the social issues dominating wartime Holland. Each character is a microcosm of Dutch society during the war. They are not only made human by connecting them to real people (the film features Queen Wilhelmina), but also used as a detailed reflection on how war changes people and their opinions—as if the film is asking us not to judge but to understand the motives of friend and foe. **EM**

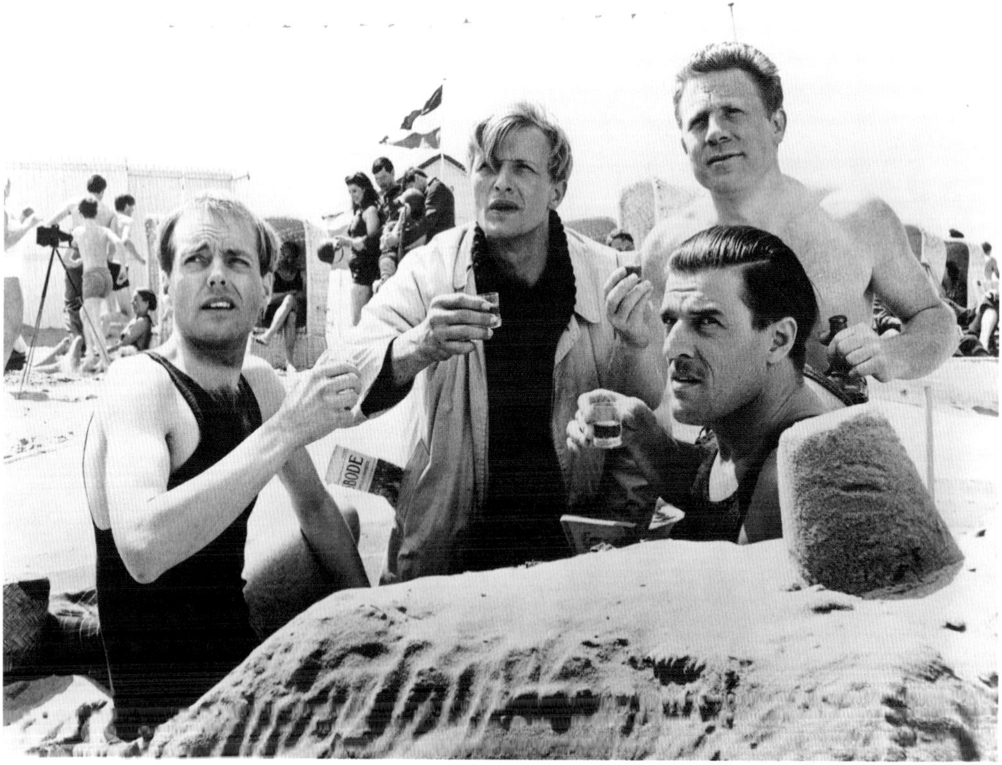

# SUSPIRIA (1977)

In its sheer enigmatic weirdness, Dario Argento's *Suspiria* serves to remind us that no film is ever really a text, but always an experience. Distinctly European in flavor, *Suspiria* begins as if it were an Italian *giallo* (pulp thriller)—with a series of spectacular murders staged with the baroque quality of a musical. But Argento soon switches gears, revealing a world not of masked or gloved human killers, but of supernatural forces, black magic, and malignant witches.

However, *Suspiria* is not only a late-ish entry in a European horror subgenre. It is also a product of particular stylistic influence, namely that of Argento's mentor, Mario Bava, a pioneer in multiple Italian genres whose highly visual effects were created with amazing intelligence and economy. Perhaps the most enduring contribution of Bava's style was the kind of relentless tracking shot which Argento makes outrageously his own, and which now, thanks to directors ranging from Martin Scorsese to Sam Raimi, has become a basic part of contemporary film language.

*Suspiria* takes place in a classically gothic setting—an old dance academy. The true nature of the instruction offered there is revealed in a rain of maggots that showers the girls one evening. In this pure gross-out lies a kind of key, as the big spectacular scenes themselves become tests of endurance. While the audience and the student protagonist, Susy Banyon (Jessica Harper), are drawn along by traces of mysterious and esoteric revelations, *Suspiria*'s intense array of audiovisual shocks and effects teeter on the very edge of unbearableness. This is the texture of the whole film, not only in its grand surreal deaths but even in its smallest gestures, as when a malevolent dance instructor pours water straight into Susy's mouth, the heavy glass pitcher rattling against her teeth.

Argento's film stands out even among the best of its form for the sheer intensity of the experience of watching—and hearing—it, the latter due to an almost overpowering score by the director and his frequent collaborators, the rock group Goblin. From beginning to end, this is a nightmarish fairy tale, culminating in a grotesque confrontation with the hideous elder of a witches coven. Finally, *Suspiria* reveals the horror film to be a kind of initiation ritual for protagonist and spectator alike—the horror genre itself as a kind of secular mystery religion. **AS**

**Italy / West Germany** (Seda Spettacoli) 98m Technicolor

**Language:** English / German / Latin

**Director:** Dario Argento

**Producer:** Claudio Argento, Salvatore Argento

**Screenplay:** Dario Argento, Daria Nicolodi, from the book *Suspiria de Profundis* by Thomas De Quincey

**Photography:** Luciano Tovoli

**Music:** Dario Argento, Agostino Marangolo, Massimo Morante, Fabio Pignatelli, Claudio Simonetti

**Cast:** Jessica Harper, Stefania Casini, Flavio Bucci, Miguel Bosé, Barbara Magnolfi, Susanna Javicoli, Eva Axén, Rudolf Schündler, Udo Kier, Alida Valli, Joan Bennett, Margherita Horowitz, Jacopo Mariani, Fulvio Mingozzi, Franca Scagnetti

**Australia** (Film House, VFC) 120m Eastmancolor

**Director:** Fred Schepisi

**Producer:** Fred Schepisi, Roy Stevens

**Screenplay:** Fred Schepisi, from novel by Thomas Keneally

**Photography:** Ian Baker

**Music:** Bruce Smeaton

**Cast:** Tommy Lewis, Freddy Reynolds, Ray Barrett, Jack Thompson, Angela Punch McGregor, Steve Dodds, Peter Carroll, Ruth Cracknell, Don Crosby, Elizabeth Alexander, Peter Sumner, Tim Robertson, Ray Meagher, Brian Anderson, Jane Harders

**Cannes Film Festival:** Fred Schepisi nomination (Golden Palm)

# THE CHANT OF JIMMIE BLACKSMITH
(1978)

Fred Schepisi's adaptation of Thomas Keneally's sensational novel about the plight of the Aborigine in late 19th-century Australia, as questions of federation and independence for the nation are coming to the fore, juxtaposes the marginalization, even destruction of the native peoples as the modern nation of white settlers is taking place.

*The Chant of Jimmie Blacksmith* traces the tragic situation of the half-caste main character (Tommy Lewis), who suffers ill treatment from white employers, even as his connection to his people weakens. Finally, he takes a job with a more brutal family, who try to starve him into submitting to their decision that his wife should leave him. Always patient and humble, Jimmie now explodes into a murderous rage. Crippled by a horrific gunshot, he is eventually captured and killed.

At the time, this was the most expensive picture made by the nascent Australian film industry. Despite praiseworthy reviews, it did not find much of an audience in its own country, though it was exhibited successfully abroad. Australian filmgoers perhaps found the subject matter too uncomfortable; its depiction of violence is shocking. It remains one of the cinema's most moving and effective treatments of racism and its horrific consequences. **RBP**

**Hong Kong** (Shaw Brothers) 98m Color

**Language:** Cantonese

**Director:** Chang Cheh

**Producer:** Mona Fong

**Screenplay:** Chang Cheh, Ni Kuang

**Photography:** To Kung Mo, Tsao Hui-chi

**Music:** Yu Chen Yung

**Cast:** Chiang Sheng, Philip Kwok, Lu Feng, Wei Pai, Sun Chien, Lo Meng, Wang Lung Wei, Ku Feng, Lung Tu, Sun Shu Pei, Shih Liu Huang, Shen Lao, Huang Lin Hui, Wang Ching-Ho, Cheng Wan Han

# WU DU (1978)
## FIVE DEADLY VENOMS

They may wear ridiculous masks, and they may be named after poisonous animals, but the lead actors in Chang Cheh's *Five Deadly Venoms* are nothing to be laughed at. They are, rather, the finest team of martial artists ever assembled in a single film. The icon/martyr status of Bruce Lee will never wane, Jackie Chan's combination of comedic and martial-arts skills is unparalleled, but, for the real deal, turn to the Venoms.

This team of actors—Kuo Choi (Lizard), Lo Meng (Toad), Sun Chien (Scorpion), Lu Feng (Centipede), Wei Pai (Snake), and Chiang Sheng ("Hybrid")—was schooled and groomed by Chang, who had a knack for developing new martial-arts heroes. They also assisted in choreographing some of the most remarkable fight scenes ever committed to film. Battles unfold with brutal grace and cleverness, each move more acrobatic than the next.

While the actors' physical talents are the main draw here, Chang does something very interesting with the story's structure, as well. The film unfolds like a cinematic balance sheet: if two bad guys beat up on one good guy, you can bet that, later, two good guys will exact violent, mathematical revenge. Charting these peculiar numerical structures in *Five Deadly Venoms* provides added pleasure to watching the film, as if the fight scenes weren't enough. **EdeG**

# L'ARBERO DEGLI ZOCCOLI (1978)
## THE TREE OF WOODEN CLOGS

In this elegiac recreation of the lives of Lombardy peasants, Ermanno Olmi offers a corrective to the anxiety of his earlier portraits of contemporary Italy: *The Job* (1961), *The Fiancés* (1962), *One Fine Day* (1968), *The Circumstance* (1973). Several stories emerge out of the details of the peasants' work and communal life: the courtship and marriage of a modest young couple; a father cutting down his landlord's tree to make shoes for his son to wear on his walk to school; an old man fertilizing tomatoes with chicken manure so they'll ripen quicker. The soft lighting, apparently almost entirely from "natural" sources, and, above all, the discrete, precise soundtrack give us the sense of assisting at an almost unmediated reality. The shortness of shots is a directorial statement, not letting us become involved for long in any one activity or point of view, allowing the film to expand, calmly, in multiple directions.

In a privileged sequence, a woman prays while walking, fills a wine bottle from a stream, and is finally seen silhouetted in the doorway of a church. It is here, perhaps (or in the use of Bach at several points of the film), that an unsympathetic viewer might accuse Olmi of aestheticism. But such criticism would miss the director's point about the positive role of religious faith in the peasants' lives. Its restrained treatment of this theme makes *The Tree of Wooden Clogs* one of the most touching and compelling of all films about religion.

If the cumulative emotional effect of *The Tree of Wooden Clogs* is close to that of *The Fiancés*, an earlier Olmi masterpiece set in an alienating, modern-day, industrial world, it shows how useless words like "humanism" (often invoked in reference to the director) are in trying to account for it. The combination of deep uncertainty and fervent idealism at the end of *The Fiancés* is extremely moving. This is also what we are left with after the more outwardly pessimistic ending of *The Tree*, and this may be what, above all, stamps Olmi's work with its poignancy and urgency. **CFu**

**Italy / France** (Gaumont, Gruppo Produzione Cinema, Italnoleggio, RAI, SACIS) 170m Gevacolor

**Language:** Italian

**Director:** Ermanno Olmi

**Screenplay:** Ermanno Olmi

**Photography:** Ermanno Olmi

**Nonoriginal music:** Johann Sebastian Bach

**Cast:** Luigi Ornaghi, Francesca Moriggi, Omar Brignoli, Antonio Ferrari, Teresa Brescianini, Giuseppe Brignoli, Carlo Rota, Pasqualina Brolis, Massimo Fratus, Francesca Villa, Maria Grazia Caroli, Battista Trevaini, Giuseppina Langalelli, Lorenzo Pedroni, Felice Cessi

**Cannes Film Festival:** Ermanno Olmi (Golden Palm), (Prize of the ecumenical jury)

# THE DEER HUNTER (1978)

**U.S.** (EMI, Universal) 183m
Technicolor

**Language:** English / Russian / Vietnamese / French

**Director:** Michael Cimino

**Producer:** Michael Cimino, Michael Deeley, John Peverall, Barry Spikings

**Screenplay:** Michael Cimino, Louis Garfinkle, Quinn K. Redeker, Deric Washburn

**Photography:** Vilmos Zsigmond

**Music:** Stanley Myers

**Cast:** Robert De Niro, John Cazale, John Savage, Christopher Walken, Meryl Streep, George Dzundza, Chuck Aspegren, Shirley Stoler, Rutanya Alda, Pierre Segui, Mady Kaplan, Amy Wright, Mary Ann Haenel, Richard Kuss, Joe Grifasi

**Oscar:** Barry Spikings, Michael Deeley, Michael Cimino, John Peverall (best picture), Michael Cimino (director), Christopher Walken (actor in support role), Peter Zinner (editing), Richard Portman, William L. McCaughey, Aaron Rochin, C. Darin Knight (sound)

**Oscar nomination:** Michael Cimino, Deric Washburn, Louis Garfinkle, Quinn K. Redeker (screenplay), Robert De Niro (actor), Meryl Streep (actress in support role), Vilmos Zsigmond (photography)

The second picture by Michael Cimino, originally a noted Hollywood screenwriter, *The Deer Hunter* was immediately declared both a cinematic masterwork and a hate film of gross historical distortion. Somewhere between these two extremes it also became a commercial hit despite being focused on the loss of American innocence during the Vietnam War.

Opening in a Pennsylvania steel town, three mill workers, Michael (Robert De Niro), Steven (John Savage), and Nick (Christopher Walken), are drafted for war. Before leaving their friends behind, however, Steven gets married with his wedding ceremony and ensuing reception doubling as a send-off party for the new recruits.

Jump cut in country. All three are made prisoners of war who finally escape their torment, albeit with several complications. Steven ends up a paraplegic, Nick flounders in Southeast Asia, an emotional cripple, and Michael returns home guilt-ridden for letting his friends fall in harm's way. His lot is further complicated when he falls in love with Linda (Meryl Streep), once Nick's betrothed, while struggling to live once again as a carefree civilian.

Over the course of more than three-hours of screen time, *The Deer Hunter* presents strong performances and a group of remarkably intense set pieces. First up the wedding, later supplanted by the now much discussed POW Russian roulette game. In between are various depictions of a collapsing community in the Pennsylvania hills, every scene of which features career-making moments from the likes of De Niro, Walken, and Streep.

Ironically and with an odd note of corny patriotism, the film's cast toasts their tenuous connection by singing "God Bless America" just before the closing credits roll. The sequence provides a broken-hearted, conciliatory commentary on the sad state of affairs that views the United States as the source of incredible heroism, cowardice, ignorance, and blind celebration. Sounding the false hope of a new day, *The Deer Hunter* is therefore a negative American classic.

Hindsight of and remove from the 1978 reflection on the war also demonstrates how the film is a provocative domestic melodrama. Running willy-nilly through a narrow view of historic facts, it offers a bravura depiction of the Vietnam experience channeled through individual men without concern for a wider social context. Most critics hold to this point, citing the film's simplistic, if not racist, depiction of Asians and the distorted use of Russian roulette in no less than two different narrative pivots. Still others focus on the homosocial, even homosexual, subtext concerning the warrior class and its assimilation of civilian life, read as the feminine sphere of influence.

The point may be most poignantly put, however, when recognizing *The Deer Hunter* was among the first mainstream American movies to focus on Vietnam. Simultaneously important for helping massage release patterns for so-called prestige pictures that screen only at the end of the year to qualify for Academy Award recognition, it provided indelible images for the pop imagination before earning a Best Picture Oscar. All this for presenting the seemingly banal story of working stiffs called up to their civic duty. **GC-Q**

U.S. (Paramount) 110m Metrocolor

**Director:** Randal Kleiser

**Producer:** Allan Carr, Neil A. Machlis, Robert Stigwood

**Screenplay:** Bronte Woodard, Allan Carr, from musical by Jim Jacobs and Warren Casey

**Photography:** Bill Butler

**Music:** John Farrar, John Farrar, Barry Gibb

**Nonoriginal Music:** Sylvester Bradford, Warren Casey, Sammy Fain, Jim Jacobs, Al Lewis, Richard Rodgers, Louis St. Louis, Mike Stoller, Ritchie Valens, David White

**Cast:** John Travolta, Olivia Newton-John, Stockard Channing, Jeff Conaway, Barry Pearl, Michael Tucci, Kelly Ward, Didi Conn, Jamie Donnelly, Dinah Manoff, Eve Arden, Frankie Avalon, Joan Blondell, Edd Byrnes, Sid Caesar

**Oscar nomination:** John Farrar (song)

# GREASE (1978)

A kitsch classic, *Grease* was to pubescent girls of the late 1970s what *Star Wars* was to young boys. Snake-hipped, slick-haired John Travolta shines as Danny Zuko, hip leader of the T-Birds at Rydell High in the fifties. He falls for sugary sweet out-of-town gal Sandy Olsson (Olivia Newton-John) during the holidays and is then mortified when she turns up at his school, her virginal image threatening to cramp his style.

Based on the Broadway musical by Jim Jacobs and Warren Casey, the film has an old-as-the-hills plot: cool boy won't date goody-two-shoes girl, boy gets jealous when she dates someone else. There are various misunderstandings thanks to their interfering friends, and then he realizes love is more important than being cool and it all ends happily ever after. However, the point here isn't the story—it's all the other ingredients that director Randal Kleiser throws into the mix that make this one of the best film musicals ever made. As well as finding two perfect leads in Travolta (who was hotter than hot, especially with teenage girls, in 1978 following the megasuccess of *Saturday Night Fever*) and Newton-John (in a role originally offered to Marie Osmond), each supporting cast member is well chosen, from Didi Conn as beauty-school dropout Frenchy to Stockard Channing as school tart Rizzo to Frankie Avalon as Frenchy's heavenly advisor.

There are also some great set pieces—the *Ben-Hur*–style Thunder Road car race, Travolta pouring his aching heart out at the drive-in while animated hot dogs dance on the screen behind him and, best of all, the toe-tappin', hand-jivin' song-and-dance numbers. Every one of them is a classic, from the sad songs of love, "Hopelessly Devoted to You" and "Sandy," to the sexy "You're the One That I Want" (in which Newton-John went from cutesy girl next door to black spray-on-trouser-clad vamp, a transformation some of her fans never quite got over), to the bouncy "Summer Nights." Best of all, of course, is "Greased Lightnin'"—the dance moves practiced in a million teenagers' homes in the decades ever since the film's release. **JB**

# DAYS OF HEAVEN (1978)

Terence Malick is the most unusual member of the generation of American directors usually termed the Hollywood Renaissance, with a strong interest in visual cinema that recalls the directors of classic Hollywood, particularly John Ford, whose fascination with symmetrical compositions and landscape vistas Malick shares. His first two feature films, *Badlands* and *Days of Heaven*, both follow very much in the tradition of outlaw couple narratives such as Arthur Penn's *Bonnie and Clyde*. But the crime narrative at the heart of each film—especially the complex love triangle in *Days of Heaven* between Richard Gere, Brooke Adams, and Sam Shepard—is hardly what is most memorable. Malick's interest in cinema as an intense, pictorial experience, is nowhere better illustrated than in this, his third film, which is memorable for its images of 19th-century American life. The misery and squalor of Eastern cities overpopulated by immigrants contrast with the vast, open spaces of the American prairie, the two settings linked by the inescapable fact of social class.

In the East, the upper class is represented impersonally by the factory system, but on the prairie, the house of the landowner, who hires workers directly and presides over them in the field, dominates the landscape, the one visible sign of human industry and wealth. Malick energizes this environment by putting a woman in the middle between two men, both of whom she loves, with the ultimate tragedy caused by their bitter rivalry, a search for exclusive ownership over someone who does not wish to be owned. Instead of relying on sequences heavy with dialogue to advance the story, Malick uses what are essentially silent-film techniques: well-designed images whose meaning can be fixed, as needed, by a memorable voiceover commentary that replaces the earlier device of title cards. Here, as in *Badlands*, the narrator is a female (17-year-old Linda Manz), called upon to describe and explain the behavior of men, especially their embracing of violence which seems so contrary to their better nature. Despite its beauty and pastoral evocation of an accommodating environment, *Days of Heaven* is filled with struggle, destruction, and ruminations on the vagaries of the human condition, much like the director's more recent *The Thin Red Line*. **RBP**

**U.S.** (Paramount) 95m Metrocolor

**Director:** Terrence Malick

**Producer:** Bert Schneider, Harold Schneider

**Screenplay:** Terrence Malick

**Photography:** Néstor Almendros

**Music:** Ennio Morricone

**Cast:** Richard Gere, Brooke Adams, Sam Shepard, Linda Manz, Robert J. Wilke, Jackie Shultis, Stuart Margolin, Tim Scott, Gene Bell, Doug Kershaw, Richard Libertini, Frenchie Lemond, Sahbra Markus, Bob Wilson, Muriel Jolliffe

**Oscar:** Néstor Almendros (photography)

**Oscar nomination:** Patricia Norris (costume), Ennio Morricone (music), John Wilkinson, Robert W. Glass Jr., John T. Reitz, Barry Thomas (sound)

# DAWN OF THE DEAD (1978)

**U.S. / Italy** (Target, Laurel) 126m Technicolor
**Director:** George A. Romero
**Producer:** Claudio Argento, Dario Argento, Alfredo Cuomo, Richard P. Rubinstein
**Screenplay:** George A. Romero
**Photography:** Michael Gornick
**Music:** Dario Argento, Agostino Marangolo, Massimo Morante, Fabio Pignatelli, Claudio Simonetti
**Cast:** David Emge, Ken Foree, Scott H. Reiniger, Gaylen Ross, David Crawford, David Early, Richard France, Howard Smith, Daniel Dietrich, Fred Baker, James A. Baffico, Rod Stouffer, Jesse Del Gre, Clayton McKinnon, John Rice

George Romero understands the metaphoric social impact of the horror film like no other writer-director. With his directorial debut, *Night of the Living Dead* (1968), he engaged race relations in the 1960s at an almost documentary level. Ten years later, *Dawn of the Dead* continued Romero's trend of refracting collective issues in the most unexpected of places. Within the vessel of the disturbing "living dead," Romero here explores the uncanny relationship between the zombie and the culture of capitalism, setting his flesh-eating horror in, of all places, a suburban shopping mall.

Four escapees of inner-city violence, zombie and otherwise, decide to take off in a helicopter for less dangerous surroundings. Running low on gas and supplies, they land on the roof of a mall inhabited by a mass of flesh-eating zombies. After securing a storage area, two members of the escape party decide to do a little looting. After their pleasant shopping experience, the group decides to remain in the mall, securing the exits, ridding themselves of the undead, and living out the American dream.

*Dawn of the Dead* provides a cunning critique of the American consumer: arms outstretched, feet shuffling to the mellow pop of Musak, the zombies wander stupidly around the mall, with only the most basic need for survival. Beyond these automatons, however, the mall's four human inhabitants add a complexity to Romero's assessment of capitalism. Spending months there, the survivors convert their storage area into a plush apartment, taking all they need and want. Nevertheless, the omnipresent views of the cavernous and deserted mall are a constant reminder that this excess of consumerism is only a distraction from the danger that exists just beyond the door, danger borne from humanity's own violence.

Romero's horror films have an enduring and eerie quality, perpetually jarring us from the fantasy of graphic zombie horror to remind us that real life is just as frightening. The mortal concerns of *Dawn of the Dead* unsettle us even after the living dead are left behind. **KB**

# SHAO LIN SAN SHIH LIU FANG (1978)
## SHAOLIN MASTER KILLER

Chia-Liang Liu is nothing less than the best fight choreographer ever to work in the Hong Kong film industry. After cutting his teeth as the martial arts director for many of Chang Cheh's best films, he made the move to the director's chair, bringing his unparalleled kinetic sense with him.

Nowhere are Liu's visual gifts more apparent than in *Shaolin Master Killer*. Like so many other martial arts movies, this is a simple revenge story, but one that is broken into three unusually discrete chunks. In the first, San Te's (Gordon Liu) family is killed by the Manchus, and he swears revenge; in the third, he exacts that revenge. But the second section is where the story, the action, and the visuals all come together in glorious fashion.

The middle hour is devoted entirely to San Te's laborious training sessions within the 36 chambers of the legendary Shaolin Temple, where he develops his mind as well as his body. Most memorably, San Te must haul heavy buckets of water up a steep incline with daggers strapped to his biceps: lower the arms, stab yourself in the brisket.

The film's star is the famously bald Gordon Liu. The intensity he brings to his performance serves to make *Shaolin Master Killer* stand out in yet another way. And this isn't even to mention the fight scenes. Suffice it to say, they can't possibly leave you disappointed. **EdeS**

**Hong Kong** (Shaw Brothers) 115m Color

**Language:** Cantonese / English

**Director:** Chia-Liang Liu

**Producer:** Mona Fong, Run Run Shaw

**Screenplay:** Kuang Ni

**Cast:** Lung Chan, John Cheung, Norman Chu, Hou Hsiao, Hoi San Lee, Chia Hui Liu, Chia Yung Liu, Lieh Lo, Casanova Wong, Yue Wong, Siu Tien Yuen

# UP IN SMOKE (1978)

It would be easy to dismiss *Up in Smoke* as a stoner comedy whose appeal is limited to midnight tokers and carefree college kids—and, surely, these groups remain the film's most ardent devotees—but to do so would be to ignore the inspired blend of improvisational comedy, absurdism, and free-wheeling nuttiness that makes the film far greater than the sum of its parts.

The first and best of the cinematic excursions of the wildly popular comedy duo, Cheech Marin and Tommy Chong, *Up in Smoke* boasts some of the most colorful characters in 1970s American comedy. Pedro (Cheech) is one of those rare protagonists who are played for both sympathy and mockery: he's a down-on-his-luck Mexican-American who lives in poverty but buys outrageous accoutrements for his beloved car. Man (Chong) is a burnout of the highest order, for whom a sausage-sized joint is but an appetizer. But the greatest performance is surely Stacy Keach as Sergeant Stedenko, the tightly wound, tic-ridden policeman whose determination is matched only by his incompetence.

One of *Up in Smoke*'s surprising pleasures is its use of the widescreen frame; one wouldn't expect such a low-budget effort to be so careful in its compositions. Not only is the film a hoot—it happens to be pretty well made, too. **EdeS**

**U.S.** (Paramount) 86m Metrocolor

**Language:** English / Spanish

**Director:** Lou Adler, Tommy Chong

**Producer:** Lou Adler, John Beug, Lou Lombardo

**Screenplay:** Tommy Chong, Cheech Marin

**Photography:** Gene Polito

**Music:** Tommy Chong, Danny Kortchmar, Cheech Marin, Waddy Wachtel

**Cast:** Cheech Marin, Tommy Chong, Strother Martin, Edie Adams, Harold Fong, Richard Novo, Jane Moder, Pam Bille, Arthur Roberts, Marian Beeler, Donald Hotton, John Ian Jacobs, Christopher Joy, Ray Vitte, Michael Caldwell

**U.S.** (Compass, Falcon) 91m Metrocolor
**Director:** John Carpenter
**Producer:** Debra Hill, Kool Lusby
**Screenplay:** John Carpenter, Debra Hill
**Photography:** Dean Cundey
**Music:** John Carpenter
**Cast:** Donald Pleasence, Jamie Lee Curtis, Nancy Kyes, P.J. Soles, Charles Cyphers, Kyle Richards, Brian Andrews, John Michael Graham, Nancy Stephens, Arthur Malet, Mickey Yablans, Brent Le Page, Adam Hollander, Robert Phalen, Tony Moran

# HALLOWEEN (1978)

No director since Alfred Hitchcock has managed to capture the delicious voyeurism of horror as well as John Carpenter in *Halloween*, a film so entrenched with our primordial anxieties that it continues to define the genre more than 20 years later. Indeed, the comparison between Hitchcock and Carpenter is no stretch; *Halloween* is saturated with Carpenter's tribute to Hitchcock, from character names—Sam Loomis and Tom Doyle, from *Psycho* (1960) and *Rear Window* (1954), respectively—to the casting of Jamie Lee Curtis, daughter of Janet Leigh, the ill-fated shower victim in *Psycho*.

*Halloween*'s plot is simple enough: a masked psychopath, Michael Myers, stabs and strangles his way through a group of teenage friends as they drink beer and pursue sexual encounters, until he finally comes up against the one pure force in the movie, the virginal babysitter Laurie Strode (Curtis). Despite its minimalism, the pronounced societal anxieties of *Halloween*'s good-versus-evil plot are left unresolved, a strategy repeated consistently in slasher films from *Friday the 13th* (1980) to *Scream* (1996). The intensity of Carpenter and Debra Hill's screenplay lies in situating the terror in the calm visage of suburbia, where one would (or at least used to) assume children were safe and sound.

Deconstructing notions of the protective homestead, *Halloween*'s camera work violates the fictitious town of Haddonfield with the roving point-of-view shot. The film's opening is itself a radiantly executed point-of-view take, peering through the eyes of the then-six-year-old killer. Carpenter constructs a purely aesthetic fear, separating *Halloween* from its own drudgingly expository progeny. Throughout the film, someone is always watching, be it predator or prey. The jolts of subjectivity in *Halloween* are entrancing, and as the film unravels we are left to peek around corners, over shoulders, through windows, and out of closets at what we are sure is impending doom.

The brilliant pacing and excruciatingly long takes manage to keep the adrenaline pumping, as Michael slinks in the shadows, rising from death again and again to chase the clever Laurie. In the end, we are left to wonder uncomfortably about the thread of separation between fact and fiction. **KB**

HALLOWEEN
The Night *He* Came Home!
MOUSTAPHA AKKAD PRESENTS DONALD PLEASENCE IN JOHN CARPENTER'S "HALLOWEEN"
WITH JAMIE LEE CURTIS, P.J. SOLES, NANCY LOOMIS · WRITTEN BY JOHN CARPENTER AND DEBRA HILL
EXECUTIVE PRODUCER IRWIN YABLANS · DIRECTED BY JOHN CARPENTER · PRODUCED BY DEBRA HILL
PANAVISION
A COMPASS INTERNATIONAL RELEASE
R RESTRICTED

**West Germany** (Albatros, Fengler, Autoren, Tango Film, Trio Film, WDR) 120m Fujicolor

**Language:** German

**Director:** Rainer Werner Fassbinder

**Producer:** Michael Fengler

**Screenplay:** Rainer Werner Fassbinder, Pea Fröhlich, Peter Märthesheimer

**Photography:** Michael Ballhaus

**Music:** Peer Raben

**Cast:** Hanna Schygulla, Klaus Löwitsch, Ivan Desny, Gisela Uhlen, Elisabeth Trissenaar, Gottfried John, Hark Bohm, George Byrd, Claus Holm, Günter Lamprecht, Anton Schiersner, Sonja Neudorfer, Volker Spengler, Isolde Barth, Bruce Low, Günther Kaufmann, Karl-Heinz von Hassel, Kristine De Loup, Hannes Kaetner

**Berlin International Film Festival:** Rainer Werner Fassbinder (reader jury of the Berliner Morgenpost), Hanna Schygulla (Silver Bear—actress), (outstanding single achievement—the whole team), Rainer Werner Fassbinder nomination (Golden Bear)

# DIE EHE DER MARIA BRAUN (1979)

## THE MARRIAGE OF MARIA BRAUN

Like many of German director Rainer Werner Fassbinder's other films, including *Effi Briest* (1974), *Lili Marleen* (1981), and *Veronika Voss* (1982), *The Marriage of Maria Braun* focuses on a female character whose fate reflects the history of his country. Married to a soldier, Hermann (Klaus Löwitsch), during World War II, Maria (Hanna Schygulla) believes her husband has died in battle; when peace is declared, she begins to work in a cabaret. Attacked by an American soldier who tries to rape her, she accidentally kills him during the struggle, which occurs on the very same night her husband returns. He takes responsibility for the crime, and while he remains in jail Maria works desperately to achieve redemption and to prepare a safe life for the days to come after his release. A decade of restless efforts turns her into a successful career woman, but happiness still seems impossible because, though liberated, Hermann feels uncomfortable in her presence. He leaves for South America to make his own fortune, and finally comes back near the end of the film. But Maria's fate again proves to be cruel as, on the night of their reconciliation, a gas line blows up and kills them both.

The melodramatic premises in no way diminish the force of this remarkable film, which analyzes, through a particular case, the "German miracle." Paid for with huge sacrifices, Germany's reconstruction rested mostly on the fragile shoulders of its women. Not unanimously accepted, Fassbinder's idea about this postwar boom was that, "If the walls were reconstructed, the hearts remained broken." *The Marriage of Maria Braun* speaks about the loss of the soul in a society exalting prosperity. Brightly performed by Schygulla, Maria is forced to suffer for seeking self-respect and dignity by inhuman means. Fascinated by money, she loses her feminine charm.

Convinced by Douglas Sirk that melodrama always works, Fassbinder managed to avoid sentimentalism by being rigorous and efficient. The famous "cold look" is still in place here, as a mark of his unmistakable seal. With *The Marriage of Maria Braun*, Fassbinder once again proves to be a master of the feminine portrait. **DD**

## REAL LIFE (1979)

Albert Brooks's debut feature, *Real Life*, has enjoyed a long life as a cult movie. Conceived in its day as a comedy inspired by a single, famous media event, the American "television verité" series *An American Family*, it has turned out to be an even more far-reaching satire of the entire, international phenomenon now known as "reality TV."

Developing the acerbic tone of his skits for *Saturday Night Live*, Brooks here again casts himself as the entirely unlovable center of a hilariously misanthropic, modern fable. Once Brooks moves himself and a crew (whose cameras are built into astronaut-like headgear) into the home of an "ordinary, typical" family, nothing remains real or sane for long. The seduction of glamorous showbiz and the lure of the almighty dollar control every transaction in this film, giving the story its brutal logic.

Outside America, Brooks is frequently hailed as an idiosyncratic, radical filmmaker; Stanley Kubrick was among his biggest fans. His ruthlessly pared-down style, serving a form of comedy that lets no one off the hook, is deliberately disquieting, almost anti-Woody Allen. But if Brooks had made only *Real Life*, his place in the annals of alternative American cinema would still be secure. **AM**

**U.S.** (Paramount) 99m Color

**Director:** Albert Brooks

**Producer:** Penelope Spheeris

**Screenplay:** Albert Brooks, Monica Mcgowan Johnson, Harry Shearer

**Photography:** Eric Saarinen

**Music:** Mort Lindsey

**Cast:** Dick Haynes, Albert Brooks, Matthew Tobin, J.A. Preston, Joseph Schaffler, Phyllis Quinn, James Ritz, Clifford Einstein, Harry Einstein, Mandy Einstein, Karen Einstein, James L. Brooks, Zeke Manners, Charles Grodin, Frances Lee McCain

## MY BRILLIANT CAREER (1979)

One of a series of international hits to come from Australia in the late 1970s and early 1980s, *My Brilliant Career* also reflects the feminist movement of that era. Based on a novel by an Australian female writer (Miles Franklin), and with prominent women serving as director, screenwriter, and producer, the film traces the coming of age of Sybylla (Judy Davis), an adolescent who lives in the outback near the turn of the century.

Sybylla, determined on a "brilliant career," pays little respect to the more restricted life that her parents and society expect her to lead. A bit of a tomboy, she is out of place at her grandmother's house, where the women are elegant and finely mannered. Courted by two interesting suitors, Sybylla is well matched with Harry Beecham (Sam Neill). In the end, however, she decides against marriage, knowing that she will not be able to endure life as the wife of a country farmer—even one who offers her the opportunity to pursue her interest in writing. The film ends with Sybylla mailing off the manuscript that will be published as *My Brilliant Career*. Excellent acting from a fine ensemble cast and an interesting presentation of early 20th-century sexual politics. **RBP**

**Australia** (GUO, Margaret Fink, NSWFC) 100m Eastmancolor

**Director:** Gillian Armstrong

**Producer:** Margaret Fink

**Screenplay:** Eleanor Witcombe, from novel by Miles Franklin

**Photography:** Donald McAlpine

**Music:** Nathan Waks

**Non-Original Music:** Robert Schumann (from "Kinderszenen")

**Cast:** Judy Davis, Sam Neill, Wendy Hughes, Robert Grubb, Max Cullen, Aileen Britton, Peter Whitford, Patricia Kennedy, Alan Hopgood, Julia Blake, David Franklin, Marion Shad, Aaron Wood, Sue Davies, Gordon Piper

**Oscar nomination:** Anna Senior (costume)

**West Germany/Soviet Union** (Mosfilm, ZDF) 163m BW/ Eastmancolor

**Language:** Russian

**Director:** Andrei Tarkovsky

**Producer:** Aleksandra Demidova

**Screenplay:** Arkadi Strugatsky, Boris Strugatsky, from the novel *The Roadside Picnic* by Arkadi and Boris Strugatsky

**Photography:** Aleksandr Knyazhinsky

**Music:** Eduard Artemyev

**Cast:** Aleksandr Kajdanovsky, Alisa Frejndlikh, Anatoli Solonitsyn, Nikolai Grinko, Natasha Abramova

**Cannes Film Festival:** Andrei Tarkovsky (prize of the ecumenical jury—special award)

# STALKER (1979)

Like Andrei Tarkovsky's earlier *Solaris* (1972), *Stalker* is adapted from a popular Eastern bloc science-fiction novel (*The Roadside Picnic*, by Arkadi and Boris Strugatsky) and uses genre trappings—again a mysterious, possibly alien phenomenon that debatably materializes the innermost wishes of flawed investigators—to ask fundamental questions about humanity, memory, desire, and desolation.

In an unnamed small country (the book is set in America), a Zone has appeared, perhaps as the result of a meteorite hit or a visitation from outer space, where the laws of physics and geography are suspended. Though the authorities police the borders of the Zone for the "protection" of the unwary, the title character (Aleksandr Kajdanovsky) is one of a small group of wounded sensitives who smuggle people past the barriers and guide them through the treacherous but magical space. Against the wishes of his wife (Alisa Frejndlikh), who has to care for their physically challenged but psychically gifted daughter, the Stalker takes two men—a writer in search of inspiration (Anatoli Solonitsyn), and a scientist with a covert mission (Nikolai Grinko)—into the Zone, past the rusting remains of a former military expedition, through perilous and often-changeable pathways, to "the Room," where wishes may come true.

It is not unthinkable that the Strugatskys' original novel could be remade one day as an action movie, but Tarkovky's version might more properly be tagged a reflection film: in the Zone, forward movement as often as not means doubling back, and we far more frequently see the travelers at rest, the camera at a respectful distance; long periods of speechlessness, marked by haunting music and a natural soundscape, are punctuated by intense, challenging, possibly futile debate among the characters. The Zone is one of cinema's great magical places: damp green and sylvan above-ground giving way to watery, muddy, uninhabited recent ruins as the party nears the perhaps-mythical Room. Like MGM's Oz, the Zone is colored amid drab, monochrome reality, though the Stalker's daughter—allegedly malformed by her father's exposure to the Zone—has her own color, notably in a breathtaking final shot that conveys her telekinetic powers with a simplicity as affecting in its own way as the bloody shocks of Brian De Palma in *Carrie* (1976) and *The Fury* (1978). **KN**

# ALIEN (1979)

"In space no one can hear you scream." *Alien*'s poster line was a classic come-on, but satisfyingly screams could be heard in cinemas. Defying the *Star Wars* craze, Ridley Scott resurrected the cheap genre of scary monsters from space, introduced it to exquisite, high-budget visuals, and created an arresting, nerve-wracking, adult-oriented science-fiction horror film.

Dan O'Bannon's hip screenplay is indebted to nifty 1950s schlocker *It! The Terror From Beyond Space* and follows the spooky manor formula of *The Cat And The Canary* or *Ten Little Indians*, but set aboard a spacecraft and with a much more alarming yuck factor. The Nostromo is a giant deep-space tug with a minimal (and offbeat) crew led by Captain Dallas (Tom Skerrit) and including sharp Warrant Officer Ripley (Sigourney Weaver) and ship's cat Jones. Responding to a distress call, they discover a derelict alien craft and strange eggs. One hatches a face-hugging parasite that attaches itself to John Hurt's Kane and wreaks gruesome havoc once Kane collapses shrieking at breakfast and the alien bursts out of his chest. The rest of the cast reportedly didn't know what was coming, making their shock and revulsion genuine. Scott produces thrills and makes tense dramatic use of dark corridors as the dwindling crew, never having seen a teen horror flick apparently, make their ways into the beast's double set of extending jaws. What elevated anxiety into art via Oscar-winning visual effects is *Alien*'s unique, awesome design and art direction mixing organic motifs with the metallic, and the sparingly-glimpsed alien designed by artist H.R. Giger, its terrible beauty given a startling grace by statuesque Masai dancer Bolaji Badejo.

Weaver became a star and icon overnight as gutsy survivor Ripley, making her stand in skimpy vest and panties. She was actually set to film the ending naked, emphasizing the frailty of the human against the perfect killing machine, but 20th Century Fox forbade it, anxious to secure an R rating. Unusually for a horror franchise, the sequels were all assigned to directors with strong reputations for distinctive visual styles—James Cameron, David Fincher, and Jean-Pierre Jeunet. **AE**

**G.B.** (Fox, Brandywine) 117m Color
**Director:** Ridley Scott
**Producer:** Gordon Carroll, David Giler, Walter Hill, Ivor Powell
**Screenplay:** Dan O'Bannon, Ronald Shusett, Dan O'Bannon, Walter Hill
**Photography:** Derek Vanlint
**Music:** Jerry Goldsmith
**Cast:** Tom Skerritt, Sigourney Weaver, Veronica Cartwright, Harry Dean Stanton, John Hurt, Ian Holm, Yaphet Kotto, Bolaji Badejo, Helen Horton
**Oscar:** H.R. Giger, Carlo Rambaldi, Brian Johnson, Nick Allder, Denys Ayling (special visual effects)
**Oscar nomination:** Michael Seymour, Leslie Dilley, Roger Christian, Ian Whittaker (art direction)

## BREAKING AWAY (1979)

**U.S.** (Fox) 100m Color

**Director:** Peter Yates

**Producer:** Peter Yates

**Screenplay:** Steve Tesich

**Photography:** Matthew F. Leonetti

**Music:** Patrick Williams

**Cast:** Dennis Christopher, Dennis Quaid, Daniel Stern, Jackie Earle Haley, Barbara Barrie, Paul Dooley, Robyn Douglass, Hart Bochner, Amy Wright, Peter Maloney, John Ashton, Lisa Shure, Jennifer K. Mickel, P.J. Soles, David K. Blasé

**Oscar:** Steve Tesich (screenplay)

**Oscar nomination:** Peter Yates (best picture), Peter Yates (director), Barbara Barrie (actress in support role), Patrick Williams (music)

Some of the most perceptive accounts of modern America have been made by filmmakers blessed with an outsider's eye. In *Breaking Away*, British director Peter Yates manages to invest what might have been a routine coming-of-age teen movie with persuasive insights into how class functions in that allegedly classless society.

On the surface, it's simply about cycling nut and Italianophile Dave (Dennis Christopher), torn between loyalty to his likewise just out-of-school pals, his working-class parents, and his attraction to a student at the university that sometimes seems to dominate his Indiana hometown. Will he get the girl, will he and his buddies beat the student teams in the Little Indy cycling race, will he pass—or even take—his exams? But for all the laughs and action (and the movie is very funny and very exciting), there's also a serious, intelligent, and surprisingly honest examination of how money, education, work prospects, and private aspirations combine to shape one's life and the person one shares it with.

One should also mention the expertise in the construction of the racing sequences (Yates made *Bullitt*, after all), the snappy dialogue, the Hawksian interweaving of ethics and relationships, the excellence of the cast (many of whom, like Paul Dooley as Dave's father, were never better), and the superb use of music. Huge fun. **GA**

## DIE BLECHTROMMEL (1979)
### THE TIN DRUM

**West Germany / France / Poland / Yugoslavia** (Argos, Artémis, Bioskop, Film Polski, Franz Seitz, GGB-14, Hallelujah, Jadran) 142m Eastmancolor

**Language:** German / Polish / Russian

**Director:** Volker Schlöndorff

**Producer:** Anatole Dauman, Franz Seitz

**Screenplay:** Jean-Claude Carrière, Günter Grass, Franz Seitz, Volker Schlöndorff, from novel by Günter Grass

**Photography:** Igor Luther

**Music:** Lothar Brühne, Maurice Jarre, Friedrich Meyer

**Cast:** Mario Adorf, Angela Winkler, David Bennent, Katharina Thalbach, Daniel Olbrychski, Tina Engel, Berta Drews, Roland Teubner, Tadeusz Kunikowski, Andréa Ferréol, Heinz Bennent, Ilse Pagé, Werner Rehm, Käte Jaenicke, Helmut Brasch

**Oscar:** West Germany (best foreign language film)

An allegory about infantilism, Volker Schlöndorff's *The Tin Drum* is told through the point-of-view of Oskar Metzerath (David Bennent), a German boy on the sideline of history. Omniscient before birth, his life becomes the frame for judging adult behavior, especially with regard to troublesome, obsessive sexuality. When he receives a tin drum for his third birthday, Oskar refuses to grow any bigger even as he grows older. Afterward observing the rise of Nazism, he bangs his drum and exhibits a scream to break glass whenever he feels libidinously challenged or disappointed. Gradually, however, Oskar's size reduces him to little more than a freak show simultaneously suggesting the absence of a moral conscience among people who supported the Third Reich.

Throughout its length the picture shocks and confuses. A midget circus act transforms into the headline of Parisian nightlife. Eels spill from a severed horse's head. A Nazi rally transforms into "The Blue Danube." Most disturbing, Oskar, the teenager trapped in a boy's body played by 12-year-old Bennent, makes love to his housemaid-turned-stepmother, possibly conceiving his child/brother.

A sensation ever since being released in 1979, *The Tin Drum* is a fantasy turned on end with unexpected jolts. **GC Q**

# ALL THAT JAZZ (1979)

"It's showtime, folks!" This fascinating, imaginative, and intimately autobiographical musical that still divides audiences is an American *8 1/2*, a startlingly candid testament from Bob Fosse, the gifted dancer, brilliant choreographer, multiple Tony award winner, and Oscar-winning director of *Cabaret*. Fosse's astonishingly frank dance drama—which he conceived, co-scripted, and made shortly after he had undergone open-heart surgery—has as his alter ego the Oscar-nominated Roy Scheider's chain-smoking, womanizing, pill-popping choreographer-director Joe Gideon. Too busy rehearsing his erotically-charged new show, browbeating backers, and chasing leggy showgirls to seriously heed his troubling chest pains, Joe is dying (flirtatious to the end in the operating theater with his attendant angel of death Jessica Lange) while contemplating personal failures, professional triumphs, and great showbiz moments. Brilliant or pretentious, according to taste, *All That Jazz* is savagely witty on backstage life and thrilling in how well it conveys the obsessive, all-consuming excitement of those passionately committed and driven in their work.

Sensational dancing in the jazzy signature Fosse style and eye-popping production numbers (the dazzling opener performed to George Benson's soulful version of "On Broadway," another featuring all-around entertainer *du jour* Ben Vereen) punctuate the confessional reminiscences of the arrogant, satirical theatrical eminence. These include flashes from his seedy burlesque roots and his insufficiently remorseful view of the women he has loved, exploited, adored, and discarded in his life (one of them obviously based on Fosse's third wife, dancer and Broadway star Gwen Vernon, another played by his protégé and latter-day partner Anne Reinking).

Audaciously structured and edited as well, *All That Jazz* won four deserved Oscars and stands alongside *Cabaret* as the best two musical dramas in thirty years. As it turned out, this undeniably self-indulgent celluloid epitaph was made nearly a decade before the fact. Fosse died suddenly if inevitably of a heart attack in 1987, at the moment his revival of his 1960s Broadway hit *Sweet Charity* (which had also provided his feature directorial debut) was opening. His legacy made itself felt in 2002's Oscar-winning *Chicago*, an old Kander-Ebb musical reworked into the dark razzmatazz *danse macabre* we know by Fosse in the 1970s. **AE**

**U.S.** (Fox, Columbia) 123m Technicolor

**Director:** Bob Fosse

**Producer:** Robert Alan Aurthur

**Screenplay:** Robert Alan Aurthur, Bob Fosse

**Photography:** Giuseppe Rotunno

**Music:** Ralph Burns, Peter Allen, Barry Mann, Mike Stoller, Antonio Vivaldi

**Cast:** Roy Scheider, Jessica Lange, Ann Reinking, Leland Palmer, Cliff Gorman, Ben Vereen, Erzsebet Foldi, Michael Tolan, Max Wright, William LeMassena, Irene Kane, Deborah Geffner, Kathryn Doby, Anthony Holland, Robert Hitt

**Oscar:** Philip Rosenberg, Tony Walton, Edward Stewart, Gary J. Brink (art direction), Albert Wolsky (costume), Alan Heim (editing), Ralph Burns (music)

**Oscar nomination:** Robert Alan Aurthur (best picture), Bob Fosse (director), Robert Alan Aurthur, Bob Fosse (screenplay), Roy Scheider (actor), Giuseppe Rotunno (photography)

**Cannes Film Festival:** Bob Fosse (Golden Palm), tied with Kagemusha

# BEING THERE (1979)

While this was not actually Peter Sellers's last movie—that was the less well remembered *The Fiendish Plot of Doctor Fu Manchu*—*Being There* is generally accepted as the swan-song to Sellers's career. Based on the 1971 novel by Jerzy Kosinski (who also wrote the screenplay), *Being There* was a labor of love for Sellers, who was obsessed with the book's central character, the simple gardener, Chance. In 1971, shortly after the book came out, Sellers sent Kosinski a telegram saying "AVAILABLE IN MY GARDEN OR OUTSIDE OF IT," followed by his telephone number.

Sellers's influence must have helped this film get made, as it is remarkably low-key and quirky even by 1970s' standards. The story is, aptly, a simple one: after the death of his wealthy employer Chauncey Gardiner, the almost retarded Chance (Sellers) is mistaken for Gardiner. Taken in by Senator Benjamin Rand (Melvyn Douglas) and his wife (Shirley Maclaine), his every utterance is taken as a profound remark about the state of human existence. Following a series of just-about-plausible events, he is seemingly about to become President of the United States when he vanishes in a suitably Christ-like manner.

In less capable hands, *Being There* might have been a clumsy parable or weak satire on human gullibility, but with carefully-paced direction by Hal Ashby (who gives the film a gentle, calm, and wintry feel throughout) and a superb central performance by Sellers, the movie works beautifully. This is also thanks to its often hilarious script, which constantly plays on verbal misunderstanding (most famously, Chance's unintentional sexual innuendo when, talking about television, he tells a pair of swingers that "I like to watch").

Sellers, who once said, "I have absolutely no personality at all. I am a chameleon. When I am not playing a role, I am nobody," brought a powerful passivity to the role, playing a polar opposite to his manic comic creations. Fittingly, after a long search for a suitable voice for Chance, he found one in the cautious, flat tones of another great British movie comic, Stan Laurel. **KK**

**U.S. /G.B. / West Germany / Japan** (BSB, CIP, Enigma, Fujisankei, Lorimar, NatWest, Northstar) 130m Technicolor

**Language:** English / Russian

**Director:** Hal Ashby

**Producer:** Andrew Braunsberg

**Screenplay:** Jerzy Kosinski, from his novel

**Photography:** Caleb Deschanel

**Music:** Johnny Mandel

**Cast:** Peter Sellers, Shirley MacLaine, Melvyn Douglas, Jack Warden, Richard A. Dysart, Richard Basehart, Ruth Attaway, David Clennon, Fran Brill, Denise DuBarry, Oteil Burbridge, Ravenell Keller, Brian Corrigan, Alfredine P. Brown, Donald Jacob

**Oscar:** Melvyn Douglas (actor in support role)

**Oscar nomination:** Peter Sellers (actor)

**Cannes Film Festival:** Hal Ashby nomination (Golden Palm)

## KRAMER VS. KRAMER (1979)

The 1970s began with Arthur Hiller's old-fashioned weepie *Love Story*, but ended with this very modern heart-wrencher from writer/director Robert Benton. When Joanna Kramer (Meryl Streep) realizes her marriage to Ted (Dustin Hoffman) isn't working, she walks away leaving him to bring up their young son Billy (a nice performance from Justin Henry, one that's not overly cute). Previously a working dad who had contributed more money than time and emotion to his child, Ted has to learn by trial and error how to raise his son alone. Of course, because nothing in movie life goes smoothly, he is just getting the hang of things when Joanna returns, wanting to sue him for custody.

Both Hoffman and Streep give strong, natural performances (they won Best Actor and Best Supporting Actress Oscars, and the movie won Best Picture), especially in the tense courtroom scenes, while director Benton shows restraint during the bonding moments between Ted and his son that could easily have become overwrought and overplayed. A fascinating and moving look at the true impact—on parents as well as children—of both separation and divorce. **JB**

**U.S.** (Columbia) 105m Technicolor

**Director:** Robert Benton

**Producer:** Stanley R. Jaffe

**Screenplay:** Robert Benton, from novel by Avery Corman

**Photography:** Néstor Almendros

**Music:** Herb Harris, John Kander

**Cast:** Dustin Hoffman, Meryl Streep, Jane Alexander, Justin Henry, Howard Duff, George Coe, JoBeth Williams, Bill Moor, Howland Chamberlain, Jack Ramage, Jess Osuna, Nicholas Hormann, Ellen Parker, Shelby Brammer, Carol Nadell

**Oscar:** Stanley R. Jaffe (best picture), Robert Benton (director), Robert Benton (screenplay), Dustin Hoffman (actor), Meryl Streep (actress in support role)

**Oscar nomination:** Justin Henry (actor in support role), Jane Alexander (actress in support role), Néstor Almendros (photography), Gerald B. Greenberg (editing)

## LIFE OF BRIAN (1979)

Beginning its life as a joke (when asked what the next Python movie would be, cast member Eric Idle said, "Jesus Christ: Lust For Glory"), the 1979 film *Life of Brian* evolved into a subtler vehicle. Subtle for the Monty Python team, that is.

While trying (unsuccessfully) to avoid accusations of blasphemy by clearly establishing that Graham Chapman's Brian is "not the Messiah, he's a very naughty boy," *Life of Brian* plays fast and loose with New Testament characters, and along the way makes both satirical and moral points. Although the movie, like all Python films, is essentially a collection of surreal, violent, and very funny sketches held together with a loose narrative thread, this one has—for obvious reasons—a strong story. The final scene, with a crucified Idle singing "Always look on the bright side of life," as Brian dies on the cross, deserted by family, supporters, and friends, was arguably the bleakest of any comedy since Stanley Kubrick's *Dr. Strangelove* (1964). A huge international hit, *Life of Brian* nevertheless nearly failed to get made, only going into production with money from ex-Beatle George Harrison's nascent production company, HandMade Films. **KK**

**G.B.** (HandMade, Python) 94m Eastmancolor

**Director:** Terry Jones

**Producer:** John Goldstone

**Screenplay:** Graham Chapman, John Cleese, Terry Gilliam, Eric Idle, Terry Jones, Michael Palin

**Photography:** Peter Biziou

**Music:** Geoffrey Burgon, Eric Idle, Michael Palin

**Cast:** Graham Chapman, John Cleese, Terry Gilliam, Eric Idle, Terry Jones, Michael Palin, Terence Bayler, Carol Cleveland, Kenneth Colley, Neil Innes, Charles McKeown, John Young, Gwen Taylor, Sue Jones-Davies, Peter Brett

**U.S.** (Omni, Zoetrope) 153m Technicolor

**Language:** English / French / Vietnamese / Khmer

**Director:** Francis Ford Coppola

**Producer:** Francis Ford Coppola, Gray Frederickson, Fred Roos, Tom Sternberg

**Screenplay:** John Milius, Francis Ford Coppola, from the novel *Heart of Darkness* by Joseph Conrad

**Photography:** Vittorio Storaro

**Music:** Carmine Coppola, Francis Ford Coppola, Mickey Hart, The Doors, Wagner

**Cast:** Marlon Brando, Robert Duvall, Martin Sheen, Frederic Forrest, Albert Hall, Sam Bottoms, Laurence Fishburne, Dennis Hopper, G.D. Spradlin, Harrison Ford, Jerry Ziesmer, Scott Glenn, Bo Byers, James Keane, Kerry Rossall

**Oscar:** Francis Ford Coppola, Fred Roos, Gray Frederickson, Tom Sternberg (best picture), Francis Ford Coppola (director), John Milius, Francis Ford Coppola (screenplay), Vittorio Storaro (photography), Walter Murch, Mark Berger, Richard Beggs, Nathan Boxer (sound)

**Oscar nomination:** Robert Duvall (actor in support role), Dean Tavoularis, Angelo P. Graham, George R. Nelson (art direction), Richard Marks, Walter Murch, Gerald B. Greenberg, Lisa Fruchtman (editing)

**Cannes Film Festival:** Francis Ford Coppola (FIPRESCI award), (Golden Palm), tied with *Die Blechtrommel*

# APOCALYPSE NOW (1979)

"The horror! The horror!" During the Vietnam War, Captain Willard (Martin Sheen) is ordered to find and "terminate with extreme prejudice" a Special Forces commander, Colonel Kurtz (Marlon Brando), who has turned renegade. Willard's journey is superficially an action adventure, but equally obviously an allegory of war's insanity and the journey of self-discovery. Finally, when Brando makes his appearance, the film becomes a philosophical search for a resolution to the insoluble mysteries of madness and evil.

Francis Coppola's epic was developed by gung-ho, prowar writer John Milius with Coppola's Zoetrope colleague and fellow antiwar guilty liberal George Lucas (originally set to direct) as a loose adaptation of Joseph Conrad's 1902 novel *Heart Of Darkness*, made pertinent to the war then being fought. The other main inspiration was Homer's *Odyssey*, prompting Coppola in a moment of levity to dub his movie "The Idiocy." The difficulties of filming are legend, the subject of several books and the 1991 documentary *Hearts of Darkness: A Filmmaker's Apocalypse*. A 16-week shoot in the Philippines became 238 days of principal photography. Sheen, only 36, suffered a near-fatal heart attack on location, but returned five weeks later. Brando showed up overweight and unprepared, forcing yet another re-think of how to end the picture before it killed them all.

Flawed but staggering cinema, the set pieces are unforgettable. *Apocalypse Now* opens (to The Doors' song, "The End") with an electrifying montage as the broken and wasted Willard's demons overwhelm him in a Saigon hotel room. His indispensable and highly quotable narration, an afterthought during editing, was written by Michael Herr, whose Vietnam reportage in Dispatches had provided another source for Milius. Heading up river aboard a patrol boat,

Willard and the crew rendezvous with their Air Cavalry escort, commanded by one of the great scary loonies of the screen, Colonel "I love the smell of napalm in the morning" Kilgore (Robert Duvall), a demented, charismatic surfer dude in a Stetson who orders a dawn raid on a Viet Cong-held coastal village, the film's tour de force. The unit takes off at sunrise as the bugler blows the traditional cavalry charge. Kilgore blasts Wagner's "The Ride of the Valkyries" from his chopper and dispenses "Death from Above" in fountains of smoke and fire. The scene concludes with Kilgore's notorious panegyric to jellied gasoline: "It smelled like . . . victory." This is but the first of several surreal, nightmarish, stoned rock-'n'-roll encounters vividly evoking fatal culture clashes and the psychoses of war, leading up to the "Gates of Hell," an engagement at the last outpost before Cambodia and the scene of an acid-trip frenzy of flares, screams, and gunfire.

On the other side, decapitated heads and the miasma enveloping Kurtz's compound await. Even more horrifically, so do the gibbering photojournalist (Dennis Hopper) and the ranting Brando, whose butchering is feverishly intercut with the sacrificial slaughter of an ox before Coppola surrenders to an unnervingly ambiguous ending. The ultimate horror of this hypnotic trip, though, is how closely it has been said to capture the reality of 'Nam. **AE**

U.S. (Aspen) 94m Technicolor

**Director:** Carl Reiner

**Producer:** William E. McEuen, David V. Picker

**Screenplay:** Steve Martin, Carl Gottlieb, Michael Elias

**Photography:** Victor J. Kemper

**Music:** Jack Elliott

**Cast:** Steve Martin, Bernadette Peters, Catlin Adams, Mabel King, Richard Ward, Dick Anthony Williams, Bill Macy, Dick O'Neill, Maurice Evans, Helena Carroll, Ren Woods, Pepe Serna, Sonny Terry, Brownie McGhee, Jackie Mason

# THE JERK (1979)

Even though largely misunderstood upon release, Carl Reiner's blissfully silly 1979 comedy turned out to be that year's third biggest box office draw. The debut feature film of comedian and writer Steve Martin, his concept of an idiot living his dream despite appearances was well ahead of its time. Years later, excessive stereotyping formed the backbone of successful comedies by the Farrelly Brothers—updating Martin only with their trademark obscene and overt sexual references for a more shock-resistant 1990s audience.

*The Jerk's* main character, a white-haired, thin, and pale Navin R. Johnson (Martin) was "raised a poor black child." It is funny because it is the bald and bland truth. Navin was abandoned as a baby and adopted by a black family who had love to spare. Shocked to learn that he isn't the Johnson's natural child, the naïf heads off to St. Louis to seek his destiny. The trip is serendipitous, leading the gullible but happy-go-lucky jerk to fame, fortune, and love. Romantically linked to Martin at the time, Bernadette Peters's quiet, creamy-limbed Gibson girl is a nifty foil to her leading man's riveting comedic skills. *The Jerk* led to a TV movie remake and a pilot for a television series, although both were unsuccessful. Hopes were high, but in vain, for the next pairing of Martin and Peters was in the grievously mistimed *Pennies from Heaven* (1981). **KK**

U.S. / G.B. (Henson, ITC) 97m Eastmancolor

**Director:** James Frawley

**Producer:** Jim Henson

**Screenplay:** Jack Burns, Jerry Juhl

**Photography:** Isidore Mankofsky

**Music:** Kenny Ascher, Paul Williams

**Cast:** Jim Henson, Frank Oz, Dave Goelz, Jerry Nelson, Richard Hunt, Charles Durning, Austin Pendleton, Scott Walker, Edgar Bergen, Milton Berle, Mel Brooks, James Coburn, Dom DeLuise, Elliott Gould, Bob Hope

**Oscar nomination:** Paul Williams, Kenny Ascher (music), Paul Williams, Kenny Ascher (song)

# THE MUPPET MOVIE (1979)

When is a road movie not a road movie? When the travelers along that road are a bunch of puppets—or, more specifically, Muppets, the creation of Jim Henson, whose eye for the absurd revolutionized children's programming. Although placing such "stars" as Kermit the Frog, Fozzy Bear, Ralph the Dog, and Miss Piggy in the real world (as opposed to the soundstage of "The Muppet Show") robs them of some of their magic, *The Muppet Movie* still has plenty of magic to go around. And, of course, silliness, because Muppets don't always agree with the laws of logic, let alone physics.

Kermit is a country frog out to make it big in Hollywood, and on the way he picks up a motley crew of companions, overcomes several obstacles, and evades capture by a villain who wants to exploit him as the mascot for his chain of Frog's Legs restaurants. But the plot comes a distant second to the songs and numerous celebrity cameos (some of them Muppets as well), culminating in an encounter with Orson Welles. The music is engaging, the voices (courtesy the likes of Henson and Frank Oz) expressive, and the whole exercise just so much giddy fun. **JKl**

# MANHATTAN (1979)

"Chapter One. He adored New York City. He idolized it all out of proportion." Satiric and lovely, *Manhattan* is the rapturous high point of Woody Allen's on-screen love affair with New York City and even opens like an expressive Valentine, with an affectionate montage of city images. His 1977 film *Annie Hall* won the major prizes, but this bittersweet follow-up film (also written by Allen and Marshall Brickman) is the perfect balancing act between wry, screamingly good wit ("When it comes to relationships with women, I ought to get the August Strindberg award") and well-aimed wounds. Allen's intellectual romantic Isaac Davis, a comedy writer, is hurt by Diane Keaton's pretentious WASP/Radcliffe tootsie Mary Wilke and runs back to the delightful and very fine, worryingly young Tracy (Mariel Hemingway) whom he has himself hurt.

*Manhattan* has some of the same *Annie Hall* elements that have come to be thought of as signature Woody. There are the psychoanalysis-dependent protagonists ("He's done a great job on you, you know . . . your self-esteem is like a notch below Kafka's") and the confidence-sharing, wisecracking relationship with a male buddy (here Michael Murphy). Among the pleasures that are distinctive to *Manhattan* are an early film role for Meryl Streep (as Ike's antagonistic ex-wife Jill), atmospheric wide shots like the dawn scene of Allen and Keaton sitting on a bench below the 52nd Street Bridge (the image used for the poster), or the compositions in their planetarium date, luminous black-and-white, widescreen cinematography by Gordon Willis, and a dazzlingly deployed George Gershwin score (played by the New York Philharmonic, conducted by Zubin Mehta).

There is a particularly great, revealing moment at the end of the film when Woody/Ike muses in monologue that Manhattanites create neuroses for themselves to avoid "more unsolvable, terrifying problems about the universe" and cheers himself (and the viewer) up by listing a captivating assortment of people and things—headed up by Groucho Marx, sports, music, literature, art, food, and not forgetting movies—that make life worth living. **AE**

**U.S.** (Rollins & Joffe) 96m BW

**Director:** Woody Allen

**Producer:** Charles H. Joffe

**Screenplay:** Woody Allen, Marshall Brickman

**Photography:** Gordon Willis

**Music:** George Gershwin

**Cast:** Woody Allen, Diane Keaton, Michael Murphy, Mariel Hemingway, Meryl Streep, Anne Byrne, Karen Ludwig, Michael O'Donoghue, Victor Truro, Tisa Farrow, Helen Hanft, Bella Abzug, Gary Weis, Kenny Vance, Charles Levin

**Oscar nomination:** Woody Allen, Marshall Brickman (screenplay), Mariel Hemingway (actress in support role)

**Australia** (Crossroads, Kennedy Miller) 93m Eastmancolor

**Director:** George Miller

**Producer:** Byron Kennedy

**Screenplay:** James McCausland, George Miller

**Photography:** David Eggby

**Music:** Brian May

**Cast:** Mel Gibson, Joanne Samuel, Hugh Keays-Byrne, Steve Bisley, Tim Burns, Roger Ward, Lisa Aldenhoven, David Bracks, Bertrand Cadart, David Cameron, Robina Chaffey, Stephen Clark, Mathew Constantine, Jerry Day, Reg Evans

# MAD MAX (1979)

Although the 1981 film *The Road Warrior*—the second installment of writer/director George Miller's postapocalyptic "trilogy" (*Mad Max Beyond Thunderdome* followed, and a fourth film is also in the works)—tends to receive most of the critical acclaim, the jaw-dropping *Mad Max*, released two years earlier, is where it all started. For it was here that Miller first brought to the screen his hellish vision of a barren, gang-ridden Australia, with the aid of a new young actor by the name of Mel Gibson.

Gibson was just 23 years old when he won the role of Max Rockatansky (as legend has it, Gibson auditioned the day after being in a bar fight and his distinctively black-and-blue face stuck in the mind of the casting director), and was such an unknown that when *Mad Max* was released in America, the preview trailers didn't even feature him but instead focused on the movie's explosions and car crashes. In retrospect, of course, Gibson's portrayal of a leather-jacketed antihero is an essential element of the picture.

In a desolate future Australia, Rockatansky is a motor cop trying to retain order in a quickly disintegrating society. Gangs race up and down the abandoned highways, raping and pillaging wherever they see fit, and one such group ends up at the door of Max's wife and child. When they are murdered, he seeks revenge, and so begins a violent rampage involving spectacular car chases, brutal fights, and relentless action.

What is even more impressive is the fact that the entire film cost just $400,000 to make—the budget was so tight that Miller is said to have crashed his own car for one scene—yet went on to make over $100 million, making it one of the most profitable movies of all time. *Mad Max* deservedly became a cult hit around the world (despite being dubbed into "American" in the United States, where it was thought audiences wouldn't understand the Australian accents) and remains to this day a striking, bleak, and memorable piece of cinema. **JB**

# NOSFERATU: PHANTOM DER NACHT (1979)
## NOSFERATU: PHANTOM OF THE NIGHT

Werner Herzog's remake of F.W. Murnau's 1922 adaptation of *Dracula* is at once an effective and touching tribute to the German silent classic and a remarkable work in its own right. Arriving almost simultaneously with John Badham's *Dracula* and the George Hamilton vampire comedy *Love at First Bite* (both 1979), *Nosferatu: Phantom der Nacht* retells Bram Stoker's story in a steady, almost hypnotic manner. Jonathan Harker (Bruno Ganz) travels through mistily beautiful yet threatening Carpathian mountainscapes, accompanied by a magical Popol Vuh score, to arrange for the relocation of the rat-faced, repulsive but melancholy Count Dracula (Klaus Kinski) from his castle fastness to the thriving city of Bremen. When his boat drifts into dock, the vampire unleashes a horde of white rats who bring plague to the community and cause far more death and devastation than his few petty predations.

In this version, Dr. Van Helsing (Walter Ladengast) is a petty irrelevance who is carried away by the police after Dracula's death, and—as for Murnau—humanity is represented by the heroine, the porcelain-fragile Lucy (Isabelle Adjani), whose self-sacrifice tempts the ancient creature to linger beyond sunrise. Adding in themes perhaps drawn from vampire films by Mario Bava (*Black Sabbath*, 1963) or Roman Polanski (*The Fearless Vampire Killers*, 1967), the coda has Jonathan transformed into Dracula reborn and galloping across a beach to spread the contagion further.

Opening with footage of Mexican mummies and slow-motion bats, Herzog's film is misty and suggestive, recreating famous images of the long-fingered, hollow-eyed bloodsucker from the original film as Kinski's slightly whiny, self-pitying, nevertheless vicious Dracula elaborates on the inhumanity of Max Schreck's Graf von Orlok. With the novelist Roland Topor (*The Tenant*) as a giggling Renfield and very strange, portrait-like readings of the traditional hero and heroine roles from Ganz and Adjani, this is unconventional as a horror movie—with scare scenes that are paced slowly, struck by magical or black-comic business (a town square cluttered with dignified funerals and scurrying rodents) rather than anything like action or even plot. If the original *Nosferatu* remains the most frightening screen version of *Dracula*, then this transformative rethinking is certainly the most mystic and mysterious. **KN**

**West Germany / France** (Gaumont, Werner Herzog) 107m Eastmancolor

**Language:** German

**Director:** Werner Herzog

**Producer:** Michael Gruskoff, Werner Herzog, Daniel Toscan du Plantier

**Screenplay:** Werner Herzog, from the novel *Dracula* by Bram Stoker

**Photography:** Jörg Schmidt Reitwein

**Music:** Popol Vuh

**Cast:** Klaus Kinski, Isabelle Adjani, Bruno Ganz, Roland Topor, Walter Ladengast, Dan van Husen, Jan Groth, Carsten Bodinus, Martje Grohmann, Rijk de Gooyer, Clemens Scheitz, Lo van Hensbergen, John Leddy, Margiet van Hartingsveld, Tim Beekman

**Berlin International Film Festival:** Henning von Gierke (Silver Bear—production design), Werner Herzog nomination (Golden Bear)

## ORDINARY PEOPLE (1980)

"We were going to our son's funeral and you were worrying what I wore on my feet!" It is still a source of indignation to some that Robert Redford's beautifully crafted and measured directorial debut should have bested Martin Scorsese's *Raging Bull* in the Academy Awards, taking the Oscars for Best Picture and Direction. Honors for *Ordinary People* also went to 19-year-old Timothy Hutton for Best Supporting Actor (making him the youngest man to date ever to win an acting Oscar), and to screenwriter Alvin Sargent for his sensitive, intelligent adaptation of Judith Guest's acclaimed novel about the impact of a teenaged son's death on a family. But those who don't "get" this movie are missing a remarkably fine, intimate personal drama about people unable to articulate the truth of their inner lives. Understandably, its appeal proved strongest in the United States, where its impressive commercial showing reflected 1980s America's receptiveness to the subject of getting in touch with one's feelings.

Hutton plays high-school teen Conrad Jarrett, overwhelmed by guilt and suicidal depression since his popular older brother drowned in the sailing accident he survived. There is no understanding or help for him from his distant, unsympathetic mother, Beth (Mary Tyler Moore), a control freak preoccupied with neatly ordered appearances and firmly in denial of her resentment. His successful, easygoing father, Calvin (Donald Sutherland), is concerned for the boy but doesn't know how to talk to him about what matters or express his own feelings. It falls to a frank, hands-on psychiatrist (Judd Hirsch) to reach Conrad and encourage him to acknowledge his deep distress and anger. Ultimately, only his father's love can save the boy, when connecting with him forces a painful choice.

Set in a wealthy Chicago suburb, the calm depiction of the Jarretts' social status and privileged comfort plays up the turbulence beneath the surface. The principals are superb, cast very much against type, particularly sitcom sweetheart Moore, and there is a radiant debut from Elizabeth McGovern as Conrad's sweet, awkward girlfriend. Redford's films are uniquely American and always graceful. This sincere, restrained, signature production epitomizes his liberal humanism. **AE**

**U.S.** (Paramount, Wildwood) 124m Technicolor

**Director:** Robert Redford

**Producer:** Ronald L. Schwary

**Screenplay:** Alvin Sargent, from novel by Judith Guest

**Photography:** John Bailey

**Music:** Marvin Hamlisch

**Cast:** Donald Sutherland, Mary Tyler Moore, Judd Hirsch, Timothy Hutton, M. Emmet Walsh, Elizabeth McGovern, Dinah Manoff, Fredric Lehne, James Sikking, Basil Hoffman, Scott Doebler, Quinn K. Redeker, Mariclare Costello, Meg Mundy, Elizabeth Hubbard

**Oscar:** Ronald L. Schwary (best picture), Robert Redford (director), Alvin Sargent (screenplay), Timothy Hutton (actor in support role)

**Oscar nomination:** Mary Tyler Moore (actress), Judd Hirsch (actor in support role)

## ATLANTIC CITY (1980)

A wonderfully hard-to-categorize combination of crime-thriller, love story, *Beauty and the Beast*-style fairy tale, and meditation on the changes affecting an American resort over half a century, Louis Malle's wry masterpiece centers on Burt Lancaster's aging numbers-runner, a garrulous romantic given to escaping the seedy circumstances of his current life with nostalgic fabulations of the way it was when he was big-time with the likes of Capone, Siegel, et al.

Suddenly an opportunity arises to revive his fortunes and self-respect in the shape of a feckless hippy coke-dealer (Robert Joy) who just happens to be the ex of a casino croupier (Susan Sarandon) the old man fancies from afar. Wealth and a young woman might be his again; trouble is, the coke really belongs to the Mob.

Malle and writer John Guare gently explore the gulf between dreams, delusion, and reality, making superb use of the fading glories of the titular playground, notching up the suspense here and there with expertly staged action sequences, and tethering the whole feather-light confection with solidly constructed performances from all involved. It's Lancaster, however, who finally steals the laurels in *Atlantic City*, with a career-best performance rivaled only by his J. J. Hunsecker in *Sweet Smell of Success*. **GA**

**U.S. / Canada / France** (Cine-Neighbor, Famous Players, International, Merchant, Paramount, Selta, CFDC) 104m Color

**Director:** Louis Malle

**Producer:** Denis Héroux

**Screenplay:** John Guare

**Photography:** Richard Ciupka

**Music:** Michel Legrand

**Cast:** Burt Lancaster, Susan Sarandon, Kate Reid, Michel Piccoli, Hollis McLaren, Robert Joy, Al Waxman, Robert Goulet, Moses Znaimer, Angus MacInnes, Sean Sullivan, Wallace Shawn, Harvey Atkin, Norma Dell'Agnese, Louis Del Grande

**Oscar nomination:** Denis Héroux (best picture), Louis Malle (director), John Guare (screenplay), Burt Lancaster (actor), Susan Sarandon (actress)

## LE DERNIER MÉTRO (1980)
### THE LAST METRO

There have been many French films about World War II and the German Occupation, but none as sumptuous as François Truffaut's *The Last Metro*. This is also Truffaut's film about the theater, the second installment in his unfinished trilogy about spectacle, after his film about filmmaking, *La Nuit Américaine* (aka *Day for Night*, 1973).

While Jewish director Lucas Steiner (Heinz Bennent) hides in the cellar for the duration of the war, his wife Marion (Catherine Deneuve) runs the theater, putting on a play with rising star Bernard Granger (Gérard Depardieu). Truffaut takes a few liberties with history, yet crams in myriad true details of everyday life in occupied France, from placating an influential fascist critic to smuggling black market ham. Above all, he vividly evokes the feel of the era through period songs, clothes, and objects, and recreates a picturesque theatrical milieu, with playful reverberations between the world of the film and the play-within-the-film.

Though Truffaut made two pictures afterward, *The Last Metro* remains his swansong before his premature death. The film's huge success, which also owed much to the romantic central star couple of Deneuve and Depardieu, crowned his brilliant career. A consensual view of a troubled period, no doubt, but a wonderful, uplifting, and glamorous movie. **GV**

**France** (Carrosse, SFP, Sédif, TF1) 128m Fujicolor

**Language:** French

**Director:** François Truffaut

**Producer:** François Truffaut

**Screenplay:** Jean-Claude Grumberg, Suzanne Schiffman, François Truffaut

**Photography:** Néstor Almendros

**Music:** Georges Delerue

**Cast:** Catherine Deneuve, Gérard Depardieu, Jean Poiret, Heinz Bennent, Andréa Ferréol, Maurice Risch, Paulette Dubost, Jean-Louis Richard, Sabine Haudepin, Jean-Pierre Klein, Renata, Marcel Berbert, Hénia Ziv, László Szabó, Martine Simonet

**Oscar nomination:** France (best foreign language film)

G.B. (Hawk, Peregrine, Producers Circle, Warner Bros.) 119m Color

**Director:** Stanley Kubrick

**Producer:** Stanley Kubrick

**Screenplay:** Stanley Kubrick, Diane Johnson, from novel by Stephen King

**Photography:** John Alcott

**Music:** Wendy Carlos, Rachel Elkind

**Cast:** Jack Nicholson, Shelley Duvall, Danny Lloyd, Scatman Crothers, Barry Nelson, Philip Stone, Joe Turkel, Anne Jackson, Tony Burton, Lia Beldam, Billie Gibson, Barry Dennen, David Baxt, Manning Redwood, Lisa Burns

# THE SHINING (1980)

Thanks to Stanley Kubrick's ingenious adaptation of Stephen King's novel of the same name, *The Shining* not only brought unfaltering fame to both writer and director—it also launched actor Jack Nicholson into the realm of superstardom. His eerie and blood-curdling *Tonight Show* cry "Heeeeeeeeere's Johnny!" has become one of the most memorable scenes in the history of cinema. Recovering alcoholic Jack Torrance (Jack Nicholson) takes his wife Wendy (Shelley Duvall) and young son Danny (Danny Lloyd) to live in the now empty Overlook Hotel, a palatial resort in the Colorado Rockies where he has been hired as off-season caretaker. As the weeks pass, each member of the family experiences some form of chilling hallucinatory episode. Danny, the most psychically gifted, is the first to catch glimpses of the bloody murders that occurred in the hotel many years before. Next, Jack begins a slow and inexorable plunge into madness. Though he doesn't consciously acknowledge his experiences, with each encounter his behavior becomes more erratic, violent, and abusive. Distracted by Danny's withdrawal and Jack's irrational behavior, Wendy is the last to succumb. In the end, she is painfully aware of her imminent danger and despite her near-hysteria manages to survive with her son.

In his own words, King's book is "just a little story about writer's block." Collaborating with novelist Diane Johnson, Kubrick strikes heavily upon the novel's themes of communication and isolation, reinforcing them with rich symbolism. These themes recur throughout the film, partly through the psychic ability of "shining," and partly through Jack's terrifying spiral into insanity.

The film is dark, disturbing, and claustrophobic. Kubrick demonstrates his mastery of the art, creating an atmosphere of great dread. Carefully selecting his camera angles and rhythms, he draws us into fear. Like all masterpieces, *The Shining* transcends its status as a literary adaptation to become not only vintage Kubrick—with spectacular aerial shots, a breathtaking and symbolic use of color, and recurrent mirror and labyrinth imagery, all enhanced by a memorable music score and Roy Walker's unforgettable production design—but a classic of modern horror cinema. Curiously, Stephen King was not particularly happy with Kubrick's interpretation of his tale of the deterioration of reality and gradual descent into madness. In 1997 he collaborated with Mick Garris on a TV mini-series that follows his original novel almost to the letter. **RDe**

# STAR WARS: EPISODE V—THE EMPIRE STRIKES BACK (1980)

**U.S.** (Lucasfilm Ltd.) 124m Color
**Director:** Irvin Kershner
**Producer:** Gary Kurtz, George Lucas
**Screenplay:** George Lucas, Leigh Brackett, Lawrence Kasdan
**Photography:** Peter Suschitzky
**Music:** John Williams
**Cast:** Mark Hamill, Harrison Ford, Carrie Fisher, Billy Dee Williams, Anthony Daniels, David Prowse, Kenny Baker, Peter Mayhew, Frank Oz, Alec Guinness, Jeremy Bulloch, John Hollis, Jack Purvis, Des Webb, Kathryn Mullen
**Oscar:** Bill Varney, Steve Maslow, Gregg Landaker, Peter Sutton (sound), Brian Johnson, Richard Edlund, Dennis Muren, Bruce Nicholson (special visual effects)
**Oscar nomination:** Norman Reynolds, Leslie Dilley, Harry Lange, Alan Tomkins, Michael Ford (art direction), John Williams (music)

"It is a dark time for the Rebellion . . . ." Darth Vader (David Prowse) searches obsessively for callow hero Luke Skywalker (Mark Hamill). Luke begins to discover his destiny. Roguish adventurer Han Solo (Harrison Ford) has bounty hunter Boba Fett (Jeremy Bulloch) snapping at his heels. Rebel princess Leia (Carrie Fisher) has unbraided her earmuff coiffure into a bun, and the evil Empire has a new array of techno-terrors with which to plague the gallant freedom fighters beleaguered in a galaxy far, far away.

The best picture in George Lucas's touchstone of modern cinema, the original *Star Wars* trilogy, this knockout sequel to the 1977 blockbuster and cultural phenomenon caps the first with more Oscar-winning special effects. Episode V has more personality: Romance blossoms in the lead trio, and strong new characters appear (like Billy Dee Williams's dashing scoundrel Lando Calrissian), all of them safely in the sure hands of studio workhorse Irvin Kershner. The action rages, from the spectacular ice planet Hoth, where Luke has a hypothermic misadventure, to the rebels fighting their first epic land battle. The battle drives on to the cliffhanging climax in Cloud City, where Han's past catches up with him—and arch-fiend Vader (memorably voiced by James Earl Jones) reveals to Luke the shocking truth at the heart of the Star Wars myth. Between these assaults, Luke continues to train as a Jedi knight, experiencing the Force in the swamps of Dagobah under the tutelage of quirky mystic master Yoda—a wizened puppet sage performed with startling expressiveness and exasperation by Muppeteer Frank "Miss Piggy" Oz.

Like its predecessor, *The Empire Strikes Back* incorporates all the hectic thrills of 1930s Saturday serials. The cracking screenplay by Leigh Brackett—noted for her collaborations with Howard Hawks and who died before the film went into production—and impressive newcomer Lawrence Kasdan, hurtles along with a spirited sense of romantic fun. One-liners became catchphrases—"I have a baaad feeling about this." Charming comic interplay for the scene-stealing androids C-3PO and R2-D2, and ever-weirder alien creatures wowed audiences the world over. Restored by Lucas in 1997 with digitally-enhanced effects and an additional three minutes, this rollicking popcorn adventure is arguably even slicker and just as entertaining today. **AE**

# THE ELEPHANT MAN (1980)

David Lynch's 1977 debut feature *Eraserhead* is a nightmarish vision of a heavily industrialized world full of hissing steam and polluting factories, perfect catalysts for Jack Nance's primal childbirth phobia. In *The Elephant Man*, Lynch works in many of those same themes and images, but this time they add up not to some weird, enigmatic metaphor but to a moving, humanistic statement.

Mel Brooks fought for years to bring the true story of John Merrick—cruelly nicknamed the "Elephant Man" due to his large tumors—to the big screen. He fought equally hard to bring Lynch on board. The director, working in beautiful widescreen black-and-white, depicts 19th-century London as an ugly, uncomfortable collision between squeamish Victorian sensibilities and the gritty, grungy realities of the industrial revolution.

Rescued from a sideshow by a well-intentioned surgeon (Anthony Hopkins), Merrick (John Hurt) tries fitting into a world whose first reaction to his deformed visage is shock and revulsion. Trained in the etiquette and formalities of the times, the gentle Merrick cannot overcome the prejudice and distaste of many of those around him.

Hurt plays Merrick with a sensitivity and dignity that radiates from beneath the tons of makeup that make him unrecognizable. Equally excellent is Hopkins, who realizes he may subconsciously be exploiting Merrick as a medical oddity despite his initial good intentions. It's a triumph all around but especially for Lynch, who earned numerous accolades that helped him escape from the art film ghetto. **JKl**

**G.B. / U.S.** (Brooksfilms Ltd) 124m BW

**Director:** David Lynch

**Producer:** Jonathan Sanger

**Screenplay:** Christopher De Vore, Eric Bergren, David Lynch, from books, *The Elephant Man and Other Reminiscences* by Sir Frederick Treves and *The Elephant Man: A Study in Human Dignity* by Ashley Montagu

**Photography:** Freddie Francis

**Music:** John Morris

**Cast:** Anthony Hopkins, John Hurt, Anne Bancroft, John Gielgud, Wendy Hiller, Freddie Jones, Michael Elphick, Hannah Gordon, Helen Ryan, John Standing, Dexter Fletcher, Lesley Dunlop, Phoebe Nicholls, Pat Gorman, Claire Davenport

**Oscar nomination:** Jonathan Sanger (best picture), David Lynch (director), Christopher De Vore, Eric Bergren, David Lynch (screenplay), John Hurt (actor), Stuart Craig, Robert Cartwright, Hugh Scaife (art direction), Patricia Norris (costume), Anne V. Coates (editing), John Morris (music)

U.S. (Lorimar Television) 113m
Metrocolor

**Language:** English / French / Italian

**Director:** Samuel Fuller

**Producer:** Gene Corman

**Screenplay:** Samuel Fuller

**Photography:** Adam Greenberg

**Music:** Dana Kaproff

**Cast:** Lee Marvin, Mark Hamill, Robert Carradine, Bobby Di Cicco, Kelly Ward, Stéphane Audran, Siegfried Rauch, Serge Marquand, Charles Macaulay, Alain Doutey, Maurice Marsac, Colin Gilbert, Joseph Clark, Ken Campbell, Doug Werner

**Cannes Film Festival:** Samuel Fuller nomination (Golden Palm)

# THE BIG RED ONE (1980)

The most ambitious war film in Samuel Fuller's career, a chronicle of his own First Infantry Division in World War II, *The Big Red One* was a long time coming. When it finally made it to the screen, a wholesale reediting by the studio and a tacked-on narration (by filmmaker Jim McBride) made it something less than Fuller had intended—he originally provided the studio with four-hour and two-hour cuts, both of which were rejected. Fuller enthusiasts still hold out hope that either or both of these versions might someday be restored. Nevertheless, it's a grand-style, idiosyncratic war epic, with wonderful poetic ideas, intense emotions, and haunting images rich in metaphysical portent.

The effective cast is headed by Lee Marvin (as the grim, hardened sergeant), with Mark Hamill, Bobby Di Cicco, and Robert Carradine (as the dogface who corresponds most closely to Fuller himself). Packed with energy and observation, it is full of unforgettable, spellbinding moments and haunting surrealist images: An inmate in an insane asylum grabbing and using a machine gun while declaring his enthusiasm for war; a protracted focusing on a corpse's wristwatch during the Normandy landing—a sequence that Steven Spielberg was well aware of when he made *Saving Private Ryan*; a soldier carrying a dead child after the liberation of one of the death camps—an uncanny sequence that indelibly evokes the homecoming of the hero to a ghost in Kenji Mizoguchi's *Ugetsu Monogatari*. **JRos**

**France** (Action, Gaumont) 110m
Eastmancolor

**Language:** French

**Director:** Maurice Pialat

**Producer:** Yves Gasser, Klaus Hellwig, Yves Peyrot

**Screenplay:** Arlette Langmann, Maurice Pialat

**Photography:** Pierre-William Glenn, Jacques Loiseleux

**Music:** Philippe Sarde

**Cast:** Isabelle Huppert, Gérard Depardieu, Guy Marchand, Humbert Balsan, Bernard Tronczak, Christian Boucher, Frédérique Cerbonnet, Jacqueline Dufranne, Willy Safar, Agnès Rosier, Patricia Coulet, Jean-Claude Meilland, Patrick Playez, Gérald Garnier, Catherine De Guirchitch

**Cannes Film Festival:** Maurice Pialat nomination (Golden Palm)

# LOULOU (1980)

This groundbreaking drama by Arlette Langmann and French realist Maurice Pialat is a scathing criticism of French society, in the guise of a sexually frank (and possibly titillating) look at relationship dynamics. Its lasting value goes well beyond that.

The simple story provides a framework for a meandering and somewhat confusing tale which nevertheless hangs together with the utmost credibility. Nelly (Isabelle Huppert) leaves her boor of a husband (Guy Marchard) for the lazy ex-con Loulou (Gerard Depardieu—completely absorbing as a rough but sensitive rogue). He won't work but he'll steal. She works but pops back and forth to her ex for any number of reasons, very few of them clear. Seemingly improvised, the dialogue still seems fresh and real even if the quality of the English translation varies greatly. The notion that a woman would, as Nelly succinctly puts it, "prefer a loafer who fucks, to a rich guy who bugs me," was shocking for its time. Two decades later, the language is still salty and direct and extremely enjoyable because of it. Famous for its "breaking bed" scene as well as an outtake where Huppert disappears between two parked cars, *Loulou* is compelling, intelligent, and very adult entertainment. **KK**

## AIRPLANE! (1980)

*Airplane!* was the third film credited to the producer/director/writing team of David and Jerry Zucker and Jim Abrahams, and the one that made their unique, parodic, detailed style part of the common consciousness. Essentially a parody of 1970s disaster films such as *The Towering Inferno*, *Earthquake!*, and *Airport*, *Airplane!* was largely based on one disaster movie in particular—the 1957 film *Zero Hour*. Zuckers and Abrahams bought the rights to *Zero Hour*, and *Airplane!* follows the original's story quite closely—thereby, as the Zuckers later admitted, accidentally giving the film a structure that their earlier efforts like *Top Secret* and *Kentucky Fried Movie* had lacked—to the point of containing some of that movie's dialogue (most famously Leslie Nielsen's line, "We have to find someone that not only can fly this plane but didn't have fish for dinner!"). But *Airplane!* adds other strands as well, taking what was by then an absurdly overwrought disaster film genre and playing upon all of its familiar conventions: a strained relationship, dangerously sick children, cowards who must face their weaknesses, a nun, blaxploitation jiveass dudes, as well as a wide streak of vulgarity.

While *Airplane!* may lack the R-rated humor of debtor movies like *Dumb And Dumber* and *Scary Movie*, it does have its share of close-to-the-bone moments, mostly in the form of Peter Grave's Captain Oveur, whose pedophiliac remarks to Little Joey (Rossie Harris) were, probably fortunately, toned down in the writing process. Most important of all, the film continued the trio's ruling that parody must be played straight, and while some characters—pilot Ted Striker (sitcom actor Robert Hays) being the most notable—veer from this wise path, veteran actors like Graves and Nielsen play their parts as though starring in the most serious of dramas. The exception that proves the rule here is the superb Stephen Stucker as air controller Johnny Hinshaw, who seems to inhabit his own deranged camp galaxy. The team has cited as their biggest influence *Mad Magazine*'s regular feature, "Scenes You'd Like to See," which parodied harrowing movie moments, but in a completely deadpan manner. **KK**

**U.S.** (Paramount) 88m Metrocolor

**Director:** Jim Abrahams, David Zucker, Jerry Zucker

**Producer:** Jon Davison, Howard W. Koch Jr.

**Screenplay:** Jim Abrahams, David Zucker, Jerry Zucker

**Photography:** Joseph F. Biroc

**Music:** Elmer Bernstein

**Nonoriginal music:** John Williams

**Cast:** Robert Hays, Julie Hagerty, Lloyd Bridges, Leslie Nielsen, Robert Stack, Peter Graves, Lorna Patterson, Stephen Stucker, Kareem Abdul-Jabbar, Jim Abrahams, Frank Ashmore, Jonathan Banks, Craig Berenson, Barbara Billingsley

**U.S.** (Chartoff-Winkler Productions) 129m BW/Technicolor

**Director:** Martin Scorsese

**Producer:** Robert Chartoff, Irwin Winkler

**Screenplay:** Paul Schrader, Mardik Martin, from book by Jake La Motta, Joseph Carter, Peter Savage

**Photography:** Michael Chapman

**Music:** Pietro Mascagni

**Cast:** Robert De Niro, Cathy Moriarty, Joe Pesci, Frank Vincent, Nicholas Colasanto, Theresa Saldana, Mario Gallo, Frank Adonis, Joseph Bono, Frank Topham, Lori Anne Flax, Charles Scorsese, Don Dunphy, Bill Hanrahan, Rita Bennett

**Oscar:** Robert De Niro (actor), Thelma Schoonmaker (editing)

**Oscar nomination:** Irwin Winkler, Robert Chartoff (best picture), Martin Scorsese (director), Joe Pesci (actor in support role), Cathy Moriarty (actress in support role), Michael Chapman (photography), Donald O. Mitchell, Bill Nicholson, David J. Kimball, Les Lazarowitz (sound)

# RAGING BULL (1980)

This boxing biopic was a personal project for actor Robert De Niro, who discovered the as-told-to autobiography of former middleweight champion Jake La Motta and persuaded director Martin Scorsese and writer Paul Schrader, his *Taxi Driver* collaborators, to commit to the intense, apparently unpromising material. With the *Rocky* movies—ironically also produced by Irwin Winkler and Robert Chartoff—celebrating the ring underdog who survives and triumphs standing as the most successful sports saga of all time, *Raging Bull* dares to deal with the anti-Rocky, a hungry contender who winds up a bloated has-been without really learning anything along the way, or finding satisfaction in his achievements.

After long years and many setbacks, La Motta (De Niro) wins the champion's belt, but in screen time a few minutes later he is clawing off the jewels to pawn so he can try to bribe his way out of a morals charge. *Raging Bull* is also a poetic, daring exploration of the soul of an inarticulate, violent man. It never excuses his many horrific flaws as it establishes the physical and psychological punishment he takes as well as dishes out, showing the deep-seated misogyny (and raging homophobia) that characterizes his whole Italian-American Bronx-limited world. The miracle is that De Niro, in a textbook example of masterly screen acting—augmented by much-publicized physical transformations—can find as much sympathy as he does for La Motta, showing how a jealous streak and in-the-ring aggression have appalling consequences for himself and his family. It's a remarkable feat, with the actor equally convincing as the wolverine-sleek, uncontrollably vicious punching machine of the early bouts and the fat-bellied, slow-thinking shambles La Motta becomes when his ring career is over and he can at last surrender to his uncontrollable lust for pastrami sandwiches.

Aside from the extraordinary fights—black-and-white hallucinations of popping flashbulbs, exploding body fluids, and brutal blows caught by cinematographer Michael Chapman on rollerskates—Scorsese stages many scenes that frighten or move: La Motta's brother Joey (Joe Pesci) hugging the sobbing boxer after he has been forced to throw a fight, a vignette which makes the Budd Shulberg "coulda been a contender" speech from *On the Waterfront* (rehearsed later as part of La Motta's nightclub act) seem hollow and contrived; La Motta needling his wife (Cathy Moriarty) about tiny imagined infidelities and becoming so ferociously abusive that anyone who loves him has to leave; a low point when he is dragged into prison and batters at the stone walls as if he were yet again matching himself against Sugar Ray Robinson; the rambling nightclub act La Motta performs as he tries to use words as viciously as he once used his fists, only to show how verbally punchy he has become as he struggles through his terrible act to the desperate catchphrase "That's entertainment."

*Raging Bull* is a film about masculinity that does not flinch from the collateral damage inflicted on women at the ringside—female spectators are seen trampled in a riot or receiving a face-full of blood splatter, and even in his nightclub days La Motta knocks a drink over into the lap of a visiting politician's wife. **KN**

EVERLAST

U.S. (Lucasfilm, Paramount) 115m Metrocolor

**Language:** English / German / French / Spanish

**Director:** Steven Spielberg

**Producer:** Frank Marshall

**Screenplay:** Lawrence Kasdan, George Lucas, Philip Kaufman

**Photography:** Douglas Slocombe

**Music:** John Williams

**Cast:** Harrison Ford, Karen Allen, Paul Freeman, Ronald Lacey, John Rhys-Davies, Denholm Elliott, Alfred Molina, Wolf Kahler, Anthony Higgins, Vic Tablian, Don Fellows, William Hootkins, Bill Reimbold, Fred Sorenson, Patrick Durkin

**Oscar:** Norman Reynolds, Leslie Dilley, Michael Ford (art direction), Richard Edlund, Kit West, Bruce Nicholson, Joe Johnston (special visual effects), Michael Kahn (editing), Bill Varney, Steve Maslow, Gregg Landaker, Roy Charman (sound), Ben Burtt, Richard L. Anderson (special sound effects)

**Oscar nomination:** Frank Marshall (best picture), Steven Spielberg (director), Douglas Slocombe (photography), John Williams (music)

# RAIDERS OF THE LOST ARK (1981)

A homage to rather than a spoof of the Saturday matinee serials of the 1930s, *Raiders of the Lost Ark* brought producer George Lucas (hot from *Star Wars*) together with director Steven Spielberg, for a movie combining excitement, special effects, and adventure, all played with a wry sense of humor.

Harrison Ford, in the role that suited him best in all his career, stars as Indiana Jones, a tweed-wearing professor of archaeology by day, who spends the rest of his time scouring the globe for treasures and artifacts—like the Lost Ark of the Covenant (the gold chest in which Moses supposedly stored the stone tablets inscribed with the Ten Commandments). Unfortunately, the Nazis are after it too, having heard that any army who carries the ark before it is indestructible.

With his trademark fedora, bullwhip, and rumpled clothes, Indy outruns a speeding boulder in a booby-trapped cavern, escapes from a pit of snakes, dodges sinister bandits in an African market, and hangs underneath a moving truck in a nail-biting chase through the desert. These are only some of the movie's impressive set pieces. Our dashing hero is no Superman, though, getting beaten and bashed up at every turn.

*Raiders* works on many levels, not only thanks to Ford's superb performance and Spielberg's skill at piling on the action and excitement, but also because Lawrence Kasdan (working from an outline by Lucas) delivers a script that is more than just an old-fashioned adventure. His hero is a complicated, less-than-perfect guy who walks the fine line between being a thief of priceless artifacts and protector of them. The villains—especially Indy's archaeological rival, Belloq (Paul Freeman)—aren't really that much different from the hero, except in their motivation (greed as opposed to historic preservation). The heroine, Marion (Karen Allen) isn't your archetypal girl-in-distress either, but a physically capable woman who (most of the time) can rescue herself and doesn't need the hero at all.

A perfect package of adventure, humor, effects, escapism, and terrific performances that has often been imitated (but never equaled) in films like *The Mummy* (1999), *Raiders* was followed by two fun sequels, and a third is rumored to be on the way. **JB**

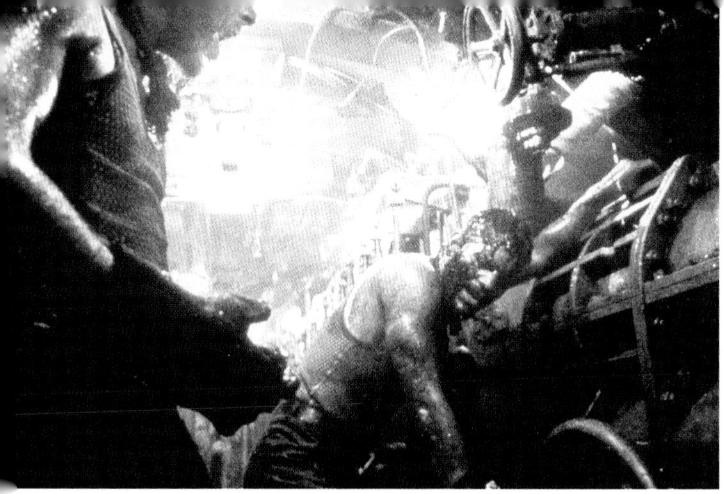

# DAS BOOT (1981)
## THE BOAT

Director Wolfgang Petersen's 1981 World War II drama *Das Boot* was nominated for six Academy Awards, a "mission impossible" for any foreign film. Capturing in authentic claustrophobic detail the sights and, most notably, the sounds of underwater warfare, the film sidelines issues of nationalism to focus on the dangerous task of manning a submarine in war-torn waters.

Following a single mission to hunt down Allied ships in the North Atlantic, the action takes place mostly in the filthy, mold-ridden stench of the cramped U96 submarine. In charge is Captain-Lieutenant Henrich Lehmann-Willenbrock, a veteran submariner at the age of 30. Blue-eyed leading man Jürgen Prochnow, until then unknown outside Germany, tempers the captain's expected ironclad professionalism with subtle, believable humanity. Although he acts as he must—letting enemy sailors drown rather than picking up prisoners, barking for clear reports even as his vessel sinks far below its depth capacity as the cabin rivets pop like gunfire—he is not without heart. The emotional truth of the terrible events lies between the lines of his daily diary entries. Prochnow, later embraced by Hollywood with appearances in *The Keep*, *The English Patient*, and others, so embodies the captain that it is unimaginable to think that both Robert Redford and Paul Newman were slated for this vital role when the film was a German-American concern. Within the superb supporting cast, Herbert Grönemeyer, now a well-known German rock musician, plays Lieutenant Werner, a character drawn from Lothar-Gunther Buchheim, the war correspondent upon whose best-selling 1973 memoirs the script for *Das Boot* was based.

Much of the nerve-shattering realism of *Das Boot* is due to the three scale-model U-boats built for the production. Taking up a large portion of the film's $14 million budget, they were later used in *Raiders of the Lost Ark*. As much a sonic as a visual experience, the entire film was shot silent; it was impossible to record live in the submarine interiors. The subtitled version is considered definitive, with all German and English dialogue added later—many of the German actors dubbing their own voices for the spoken English version. **KK**

**West Germany** (Bavaria, Radiant, SDR, WDR) 149m Technicolor
**Language:** German / English
**Director:** Wolfgang Petersen
**Producer:** Günter Rohrbach, Michael Bittins.
**Screenplay:** Wolfgang Petersen, from novel by Lothar G. Buchheim
**Photography:** Jost Vacano
**Music:** Klaus Doldinger
**Cast:** Jürgen Prochnow, Herbert Grönemeyer, Klaus Wennemann, Hubertus Bengsch, Martin Semmelrogge, Bernd Tauber, Erwin Leder, Martin May, Heinz Hoenig, Uwe Ochsenknecht, Claude-Oliver Rudolph, Jan Fedder, Ralf Richter, Joachim Bernhard, Oliver Stritzel
**Oscar nomination:** Wolfgang Petersen (director), Wolfgang Petersen (screenplay), Jost Vacano (photography), Mike Le Mare (special sound effects), Hannes Nikel (editing), Milan Bor, Trevor Pyke, Mike Le Mare (sound)

## GALLIPOLI (1981)

**Australia** (AFC, R & R, SAFC) 110m Eastmancolor
**Director:** Peter Weir
**Producer:** Patricia Lovell, Robert Stigwood
**Screenplay:** David Williamson, Peter Weir
**Photography:** Russell Boyd
**Music:** Brian May, Tomaso Albinoni, Georges Bizet, Jean Michel Jarre
**Cast:** Mark Lee, Bill Kerr, Harold Hopkins, Charles Lathalu Yunipingli, Heath Harris, Ron Graham, Gerda Nicolson, Mel Gibson, Robert Grubb, Tim McKenzie, David Argue, Brian Anderson, Reg Evans, Jack Giddy, Dane Peterson

Australian filmmaker Peter Weir re-created the tragic and notorious World War I debacle of Gallipoli—a blundered campaign that sent thousands of Anzac soldiers to slaughter in 1915—with atmosphere and harrowing action, producing one of the classic films on war's folly and waste. Sporting rivals and pals, two fleet-footed young Australian runners—Frank Dunne (Mel Gibson) the rough charmer, Archy Hamilton (Mark Lee) the sensitive idealist—enlist in the Great War and journey across the world for the British Empire, finding comradeship, courage, and horror in the trenches in the Dardanelles.

Weir distinguishes himself by creating a strong sense of time, place, culture clash, and intimate human drama while imbuing even simple acts with beauty and mystery, finding magical images that evoke excitement, high spirits, fear, and grief. Like much of Weir's work, *Gallipoli* radiates intelligence, humanity, and warmth through many such small moments. Charismatic Gibson, of course, is the one who went on to international superstardom, *Gallipoli* persuading Hollywood that Mad Max was not just a tough guy but one who looked like a romantic leading man. But the film's haunting last image is a freeze-frame of Lee—Weir's homage to a famous photograph taken by Robert Capa during the Spanish Civil War. **AE**

## CHARIOTS OF FIRE (1981)

**G.B.** (Allied Stars, Enigma, Goldcrest, Warner Bros.) 123m Color
**Director:** Hugh Hudson
**Producer:** David Puttnam
**Screenplay:** Colin Welland
**Photography:** David Watkin
**Music:** Vangelis
**Cast:** Nicholas Farrell, Nigel Havers, Ian Charleson, Ben Cross, Daniel Gerroll, Ian Holm, John Gielgud, Lindsay Anderson, Nigel Davenport, Cheryl Campbell, Alice Krige, Dennis Christopher, Brad Davis, Patrick Magee, Peter Egan
**Oscar:** David Puttnam (best picture), Hugh Hudson (director), Colin Welland (screenplay), Milena Canonero (costume), Vangelis (music)
**Oscar nomination:** Ian Holm (actor in support role), Terry Rawlings (editing)
**Cannes Film Festival:** Hugh Hudson (prize of the ecumenical Jury—special mention), Ian Holm (supporting actor), Hugh Hudson nomination (Golden Palm)

Opening on a beach with a group of barefoot runners, Hugh Hudson's *Chariots of Fire* made Vangelis a household name as his electronic score became synonymous with sporting excellence. Telling the story of two English runners, the film also won the Best Picture Academy Award despite being a British production.

The film centers on Harold Abrahams (Ben Cross), a Jewish sprinter, and Eric Liddell (Ian Charleston), his devoutly Christian rival, as they men struggle for national and personal honor following Word War I. As they train for the 1924 Summer Olympics, the values of sacrifice and fair play pepper their tale, although an ample reserve is set aside to exalt the brilliance of physical grace. Over the course of this journey, Abrahams hires Arab-Italian trainer Mussabini (Ian Holm), both sprinters confound their Cambridge Masters (played by John Gielgud and Lindsay Anderson), and the respective competition sparks the success of their teammates.

Ultimately concluded with triumph and redemption, *Chariots of Fire* equates athleticism with religious conviction, although Abrahams and Liddel are no mere figureheads. Instead they engage their times, wherein anti-Semitism, British classicism, and the lack of Hollywood high-concept technique mark this simple drama about seeking glory on the world's greatest stage for peaceful competition. **GCQ**

## BODY HEAT (1981)

**U.S.** (Ladd) 113m Technicolor
**Director:** Lawrence Kasdan
**Producer:** Fred T. Gallo
**Screenplay:** Lawrence Kasdan
**Photography:** Richard H. Kline
**Music:** John Barry
**Cast:** William Hurt, Kathleen Turner, Richard Crenna, Ted Danson, J.A. Preston, Mickey Rourke, Kim Zimmer, Jane Hallaren, Lanna Saunders, Carola McGuinness, Michael Ryan, Larry Marko, Deborah Lucchesi, Lynn Hallowell, Thom Sharp

The controversial directorial debut of *The Empire Strikes Back* (1980) and *Raiders of the Lost Ark* (1981) writer Lawrence Kasdan, *Body Heat* generated powerful and divergent reactions upon its initial release. David Chute called it "perhaps the most stunning debut movie ever," whereas Pauline Kael wrote a famously scathing review, deriding the film for its self-consciousness and neonoir pretensions.

*Body Heat* makes no effort to hide its indebtedness to noir tradition. Ned Racine (William Hurt) is a lazy, womanizing lawyer who works in a small town in Florida. In the midst of a terrible heat wave, he accidentally meets Maddy Walker (Kathleen Turner), a rich married woman from a nearby suburb. A steamy affair quickly develops. Soon enough, Maddy has convinced Ned to murder her husband so they can be together (and rich) forever—and to think it's his idea. After the murder, Ned gets double-crossed in various ways, discovering he was picked out and set up by Maddy from the very beginning. After Maddy fakes her own death, Ned is sent to jail, where he does some research and learns that she had actually taken on another woman's identity. But it's too late to do anything. The last shot shows Maddy sunbathing on an anonymous tropical island.

Besides the archetypal noir plot, in which a sexy mystery woman embroils a likeable, attractive but immoral male protagonist and brings him down, *Body Heat* is characteristically noirish in its rapid and super-snappy dialogue, and in its depiction of a femme fatale who is untrustworthy but enchanting nonetheless. Over time, positive response to Kasdan's film has won out, with subsequent neonoirs (such as *Blood Simple* [1984] and *The Last Seduction* [1994]) paying homage to *Body Heat*, much as *Body Heat* pays tribute to noirs such as *Double Indemnity* (1944) and *Out of the Past* (1947).

But there is also a subversive quality to *Body Heat*, which moves it away from classical noir. It is closer to the so-called erotic thriller. What was left implicit and suggestive in the earlier films is here foregrounded and made the visual focus. The extended soft-core sex scenes between Hurt and Turner are shocking and risqué even by today's more promiscuous standards. **SJS**

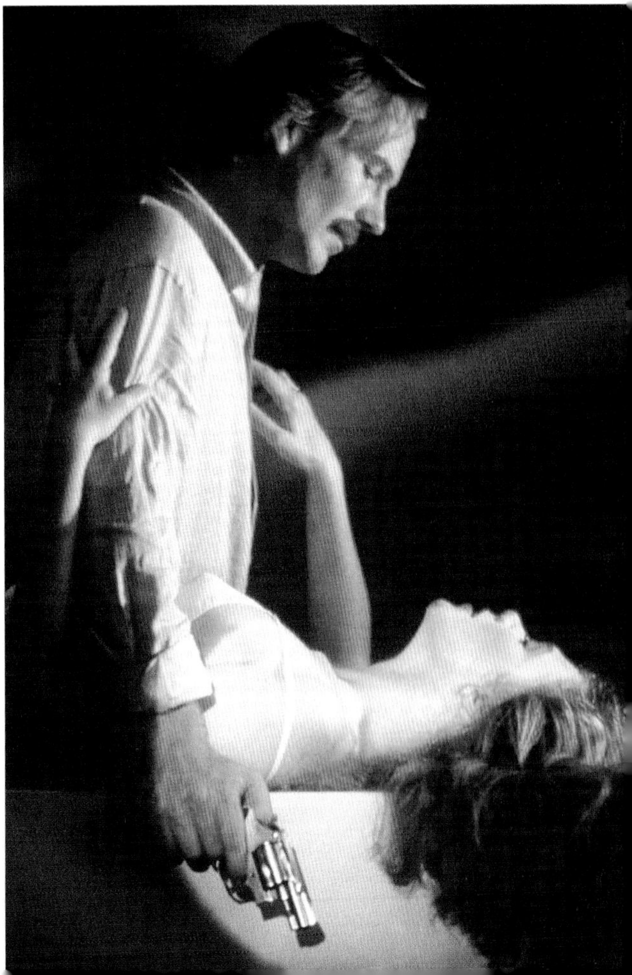

**U.S.** (Barclays, JRS, Paramount) 194m Technicolor

**Language:** English / Russian / German

**Director:** Warren Beatty

**Producer:** Warren Beatty

**Screenplay:** Warren Beatty, Trevor Griffiths, from the book *Ten Days That Shook the World* by John Reed

**Photography:** Vittorio Storaro

**Music:** Stephen Sondheim, Dave Grusin, Pierre Degeyter

**Cast:** Warren Beatty, Diane Keaton, Edward Herrmann, Jerzy Kosinski, Jack Nicholson, Paul Sorvino, Maureen Stapleton, Nicolas Coster, M. Emmet Walsh, Ian Wolfe, Bessie Love, MacIntyre Dixon, Pat Starr, Eleanor D. Wilson, Max Wright, George Plimpton, Harry Ditson, Leigh Curran, Kathryn Grody, Brenda Currin, Nancy Duiguid, Norman Chancer, Dolph Sweet, Ramon Bieri, Jack O'Leary, Gene Hackman, Gerald Hiken, William Daniels, Dave King, Joseph Buloff, Stefan Gryff, Denis Pekarev, Roger Sloman, Stuart Richman, Oleg Kerensky

**Oscar:** Warren Beatty (director), Maureen Stapleton (actress in support role), Vittorio Storaro (photography)

**Oscar nomination:** Warren Beatty (best picture), Warren Beatty, Trevor Griffiths (screenplay), Warren Beatty (actor), Diane Keaton (actress), Jack Nicholson (actor in support role), Richard Sylbert, Michael Seirton (art direction), Shirley Russell (costume), Dede Allen, Craig McKay (editing), Dick Vorisek, Tom Fleischman, Simon Kaye (sound)

# REDS (1981)

The commercial acceptability of the title alone signaled the end of Hollywood's fear of engaging meaningfully with leftist politics. Warren Beatty's tribute to journalist John Reed provides an intriguing look into American political radicals of the early 20th century and their fascination with the Bolshevik Revolution in Russia, and the improbable foundation of a communist state.

Beatty worked for years on *Reds*. His involvement in the finished product is substantial. He is credited, in the tradition of Orson Welles, as producer, director, screenwriter, and featured performer. The film was a daring venture, mostly because Reed, its central focus, was virtually unknown to the cinema public of the late 20th century. Limited by Hollywood conventions, Beatty is able only to suggest the complex and frenetic aspects of Reed's meteoric career: Front-line reporting from Europe; a fascination with Pancho Villa; involvement in union politics and World War I; his experiences at Harvard as a dandy and cheerleader; and his Byronic compulsion to seek out the unusual and the forbidden. The first half of *Reds* is devoted to Reed's love affair with feminist intellectual Louise Bryant (Diane Keaton). This part of the film is enlivened by some fine performances from secondary characters, with Maureen Stapleton as the anarchist Emma Goldman especially effective.

Once Reed leaves for Russia, *Reds* does an excellent job of delineating the epic events of the developing revolution, with its riotous parades and unruly mass meetings. Especially in the Russian scenes, Beatty conveys Reed's messianic enthusiasm and his deep commitment to political change after a period of self-absorbed adventurism (Beatty was especially suited to this role, given his own conversion to activism after a misspent youth). Wisely, Beatty gives the film a documentary flair by interspersing fictional sequences with short interviews featuring eyewitnesses of the period, including such luminaries as Will Durant and Henry Miller. These interviews not only provide a good deal of information about Reed but also argue for his importance in American history, which is the film's overall project. *Reds*, despite its concessions to entertainment cinema, is arguably Hollywood's most effective presentation of politics and ideological conflict in 20th-century America. **BP**

## AN AMERICAN WEREWOLF IN LONDON

(1981)

An imaginative and witty horror-comedy—written by director John Landis when he was just 19 years old—*An American Werewolf in London* revealed a more sinister side to England's capital city during the same year (1981) in which all news was devoted to the "fairy-tale" wedding of Charles and Diana that took place there. David Naughton and Griffin Dunne are two young American backpackers who venture onto the Yorkshire Moors one night despite being warned by the suspicious regulars of the Slaughtered Lamb pub not to, and find out why they should have listened when they are pursued by a hungry werewolf. Dunne meets a grisly end, while Naughton discovers the bite he has received has turned him into a half-wolf when he wakes up naked in London's Regents Park Zoo one morning with the taste of human flesh in his mouth.

Filled with gruesome, blackly comic scenes (most memorably, the werewolf pursuit through an underground tube station, and Naughton meeting his decaying—and rather annoyed—victims in a cinema), and great performances (including ex-*Railway Children* star Jenny Agutter as the nurse and Brian Glover as the grumpiest of the Slaughtered Lamb's patrons), the movie also boasts extraordinary werewolf effects from Rick Baker that prompted Michael Jackson to hire him and Landis to work on his classic video epic, *Thriller*. **JB**

**U.S. / G.B.** (American Werewolf, Guber-Peters, Lyncanthrope, PolyGram) 97m Technicolor

**Director:** John Landis

**Producer:** George Folsey Jr.

**Screenplay:** John Landis

**Photography:** Robert Paynter

**Music:** Elmer Bernstein

**Cast:** David Naughton, Jenny Agutter, Griffin Dunne, Don McKillop, Paul Kember, John Woodvine, Joe Belcher, David Schofield, Brian Glover, Lila Kaye, Rik Mayall, Sean Baker, Paddy Ryan, Anne-Marie Davies, Frank Oz

**Oscar:** Rick Baker (makeup)

## TRE FRATELLI (1981)

### THREE BROTHERS

In his film *Three Brothers*, loosely based on the Andrey Platonov short story *The Third Son*, director Francesco Rossi addresses a range of social issues in Italy, among them the exploitation of the working class, the effects of poverty on young people, and the rise in urban violence. The three Giuranna brothers, Raffaele (Philippe Noiret), Nicola (Michele Placido), and Rocco (Vittorio Mezzogiorno), representing three major facets of Italian society, return to their southern Italian village for their mother's funeral. Raffaele is a judge whose participation in an antiterrorist commission has put his life in jeopardy. Nicola is a factory worker and a member of a leftist group employing terrorist tactics in their fight for better conditions. Rocco is a social worker in an overcrowded, underfunded state correctional facility for juvenile delinquents.

The film's true power is apparent in the quiet, subtle moments when we gain insight into the psyches of the three brothers, who no longer feel connected to their home or their past, and whose feeble attempts to relive that past painfully highlight how much they have changed. Effectively blending melodrama and fantasy, Rossi allows us to see what the future may hold for each brother. These futures are presented as a flash-forward in the style of a film genre determined by each brother's respective personality. The film's ending serves as a powerful reminder of the importance of cherishing every moment we have on this earth. **RDe**

**Italy / France** (Gaumont, Iterfilm) 113m Technicolor

**Director:** Francesco Rosi

**Producer:** Antonio Macri, Giorgio Nocella

**Screenplay:** Tonino Guerra, Francesco Rosi

**Photography:** Pasqualino De Santis

**Music:** Pino Daniele, Piero Piccioni

**Cast:** Philippe Noiret, Michele Placido, Vittorio Mezzogiorno, Andréa Ferréol, Maddalena Crippa, Rosaria Tafuri, Marta Zoffoli, Tino Schirinzi, Simonetta Stefanelli, Pietro Biondi, Charles Vanel, Accursio Di Leo, Luigi Infantino, Girolamo Marzano, Gina Pontrelli

**Oscar nomination:** Italy (best foreign language film)

## CZLOWIEK Z ZELAZA (1981)
## MAN OF IRON

This sequel to the 1977 film *Man of Marble* confirmed director Andrzej Wajda's concern never to miss an opportunity to account for the major events in Poland's history. If the first film dealt mostly with the Stalinist era and its crimes, *Man of Iron* deals with the rousing of the Solidarity Movement, the strong union organization whose actions succeeded in blowing up the communist regime at the end of the 1980s.

Here again we meet documentary filmmaker Agnieszka (Krystyna Janda), who is now married to Mateusz (Jerzy Radziwilowicz), the son of former Polish worker-hero Birkut. Deeply involved in the organization of the 1980 strike in Gdansk, Mateusz is one of the Solidarity Movement's founders, and he tries to convince the intellectuals to join the union, too. A series of flashbacks shows us what was only suggested in the previous film: That Birkut was killed during the earlier strike in Gdansk in 1970, an insurrection that was savagely repressed by the communist Special Forces. However, this parallel between the events of the recent past and the new strike in Gdansk allows for the optimistic anticipation of a final victory.

Less intricately structured than *Man of Marble*, the sequel nevertheless provides worthy testimony of a decade that brought a surprising turn in the history of communism. The amazing documentary sequences shot in 1970 and then in 1980 intensify the film's national and international echoes. Western audiences, who were not too interested in movies coming from Eastern Europe, were especially shocked by what they saw: That is one reason why *Man of Iron* was awarded the Palme d'Or at the 1981 Cannes Film Festival. A brief appearance in the film by Lech Walesa, leader of the Solidarity Movement, as himself, also speaks to Wajda's sense of history and his uncanny ability to anticipate the future.

Determined to make a political movie with a strong impact, Wajda insisted on foregrounding the ideological message through dialogue—excessively so, in the opinion of some critics. Despite such remarks, however, *Man of Iron* fulfilled Wajda's commitment to "[put] myself, with my ideas, between the audience and history." His film is a moving tribute to the Polish citizens whose struggle enabled the freedom so cherished in this part of Europe. **DD**

**Poland** (Film Polski, Zespol Filmowy X) 153m BW/ Color

**Language:** Polish

**Director:** Andrzej Wajda

**Screenplay:** Aleksander Scibor-Rylski

**Photography:** Janusz Kalicinski, Edward Klosinski

**Music:** Andrzej Korzynski

**Cast:** Jerzy Radziwilowicz, Krystyna Janda, Marian Opania, Boguslaw Linda, Wieslawa Kosmalska, Andrzej Seweryn, Krzysztof Janczar, Boguslaw Sobczuk, Franciszek Trzeciak

**Oscar nomination:** Poland (best foreign language film)

**Cannes Film Festival:** Andrzej Wajda (Golden Palm), (prize of the ecumenical jury)

## ZU FRUH, ZU SPAT (1981)
### TOO EARLY, TOO LATE

This color documentary by Jean-Marie Straub and Danièle Huillet, one of their few works in 16mm, is almost certainly my favorite landscape film. There are no "characters" in this 105-minute feature about places, yet paradoxically it's the most densely populated work that they made. The first part shows a series of locations in contemporary France, accompanied by Huillet reading part of a letter Friedrich Engels wrote to Karl Kautsky describing the impoverished state of French peasants, and excerpts from the "Notebooks of Grievances," compiled in 1789 by the village mayors of those same locales in response to plans for further taxation.

The especially fine second section, roughly twice as long, does the same thing with a more recent Marxist text by Mahmoud Hussein about Egyptian peasants' resistance to English occupation before the "petit-bourgeois" revolution of Neguib in 1952. Both sections suggest that the peasants revolted too soon and succeeded too late. One of the film's formal inspirations is Beethoven's late quartets, and its slow rhythm is central to the experience it yields; what is so remarkable about Straub and Huillet's beautiful long takes is how their rigorous attention to both sound and image seems to open up an entire universe, whether in front of a large urban factory or out on a country road. As in Jacques Tati's studio-made *Playtime* (1967), the subject of *Too Early, Too Late* is the sheer richness of the world we live in. **JRos**

**Germany** 100m 16 mm Eastmancolor

**Language:** German

**Director:** Danièle Huillet, Jean-Marie Straub

**Screenplay:** Friedrich Engels, Danièle Huillet, Mahmoud Hussein, Jean-Marie Straub

**Photography:** Robert Alazraki, Caroline Champetier, William Lubtchansky, Marguerite Perlado

**Nonoriginal music:** Beethoven

## FAST TIMES AT RIDGEMONT HIGH (1981)

Just one short year after Bob Clark's gross-out classic *Porky's* set new (albeit short-lived) lows for Hollywood humor, Amy Heckerling's *Fast Times at Ridgemont High* brilliantly melded the teen comedy with the coming-of-age tale in this surprisingly sensitive take on suburban high school life in the early 1980s. Featuring a bevy of young actors, *Fast Times* holds up extraordinarily well under repeat viewings (spot the star!) and possesses strong nostalgic appeal for those who caught it on its initial release. In fact, a sweet sense of melancholy underlies this frequently side-splitting look at an adolescent American present fading all too quickly into the past—hardly surprising for a movie scripted by the future writer-director of such Gen-X hits as *Say Anything* (1989), *Singles* (1992), and *Almost Famous* (2000), ex-*Rolling Stone* reporter Cameron Crowe.

But Heckerling deserves at least as much credit as Crowe for seamlessly weaving together *Fast Times*'s multiple narratives, and for bringing out the humor in a story that sounds far more depressing than funny. Anticipating the touch she would later show in *Clueless* (1995), Heckerling mines the melodramatic material for laughs, avoids oversentimentality, and provides happy endings for everyone. Best line: perennially stoned surfer dude Jeff Spicoli (Penn, who almost steals the whole film from his peers) "All I need are some tasty waves, a cool buzz, and I'm fine," spoken in an ultra-lazy Southern California accent that predates *Bill & Ted's Excellent Adventure* (1989) by more than half a decade. **SJS**

**U.S.** (Refugee, Universal) 90m Technicolor

**Director:** Amy Heckerling

**Producer:** Irving Azoff, Art Linson

**Screenplay:** Cameron Crowe, from his novel

**Photography:** Matthew F. Leonetti

**Music:** Jackson Browne, Jimmy Buffett, Charlotte Caffey, Danny Elfman, Rob Fahey, Louise Goffin, Sammy Hagar, Don Henley, Danny Kortchmar, Giorgio Moroder, Graham Nash, Stevie Nicks, Tom Petty, Marv Ross, Billy Squier, Joe Walsh, Rusty Young, Charlotte Caffey, Jane Wiedlin

**Cast:** Sean Penn, Jennifer Jason Leigh, Judge Reinhold, Robert Romanus, Brian Backer, Phoebe Cates, Ray Walston, Scott Thomson, Vincent Schiavelli, Amanda Wyss, D.W. Brown, Forest Whitaker, Zoe Kelli Simon, Tom Nolan, Blair Ashleigh

U.S. (Amblin, Universal) 115m Technicolor
**Director:** Steven Spielberg
**Producer:** Kathleen Kennedy, Steven Spielberg
**Screenplay:** Melissa Mathison
**Photography:** Allen Daviau
**Music:** John Williams
**Cast:** Henry Thomas, Dee Wallace-Stone, Robert MacNaughton, Drew Barrymore, Peter Coyote, K.C. Martel, Sean Frye, C. Thomas Howell, David M. O'Dell, Richard Swingler, Frank Toth, Robert Barton, Michael Durrell
**Oscar:** Charles L. Campbell, Ben Burtt (special sound effects), Carlo Rambaldi, Dennis Muren, Kenneth Smith (special visual effects), John Williams (music), Robert Knudson, Robert J. Glass, Don Digirolamo, Gene S. Cantamessa (sound)
**Oscar nomination:** Steven Spielberg, Kathleen Kennedy (best picture), Steven Spielberg (director), Melissa Mathison (screenplay), Allen Daviau (photography), Carol Littleton (editing)

# E.T.: THE EXTRA-TERRESTRIAL (1982)

Despite Ridley Scott's *Alien* having convinced us that beings from outer space were something to be wary of, three years later Steven Spielberg showed that they could be cute and cuddly too, especially if they came in the form of pot-bellied creatures like E.T. His adorable, wide-eyed appearance was supposedly imagined after Spielberg's team superimposed Einstein's eyes and forehead onto the face of a baby.

A sci-fi adventure for the whole family, this was Spielberg's homage to childhood. A lonely little boy, Elliott (Henry Thomas), befriends the outer space being (played in many scenes by a small person in an E.T. suit) left behind by his pals. He introduces him to Earth customs such as how to communicate, drink beer, eat candy, and dress up in his little sister Gertie's (Drew Barrymore) clothes. Of course their secret friendship can't last for long, and soon the boy and his alien are under threat from government men wanting to experiment on the intergalactic traveler.

Based on an idea Spielberg had nurtured for a while and related to screenwriter Melissa Mathison after shooting *Raiders of the Lost Ark*, *E.T.* works as a delightful adventure that appeals to the child in all of us, also delivering enough sentimental moments to have the hardest viewer reduced to a blubbering mess before the end credits. That it doesn't become too sugary sweet comes from Spielberg's pacing and the mixture of humor and sadness in Mathison's script, coupled with Debra Winger and Pat Welsh's raspy vocalizations for *E.T.* and superb performances by the mainly young cast. Thomas—as the lucky boy whose imaginary friend is actually real—virtually carries the film on his own small shoulders, while Robert MacNaughton (as older brother Michael) and seven-year-old Drew Barrymore give terrific turns as the initially hesitant siblings won over by E.T.'s considerable charm.

Twenty years after the movie's original release, Spielberg brought out a special anniversary edition, featuring some computer alterations to E.T.'s facial expressions that he was unable to accomplish in 1982. The other notable change was the digital replacement of guns from the hands of the government agents (something Spielberg had never been comfortable with) with walkie-talkie radios. **JB**

## THE THING (1982)

A group of scientists (including Kurt Russell's protagonist) at an isolated outpost in Antarctica find themselves under siege by an alien lifeform that can take over their bodies. Cut off from the outside world, the men grow increasingly paranoid as they suspect each other of being taken over by the alien, and realize that they can't afford to let it venture beyond the outpost, lest it infect the entire world.

Based on the classic science-fiction story *Who Goes There?* by John W. Campbell, and having originally been adapted by Howard Hawks in 1951 as *The Thing From Another World*, this 1982 version by John Carpenter eschews the Boy's Own Adventure of the Hawks film and goes straight for claustrophobia and existential dread. Carpenter's *The Thing* proved to be one of the most influential horror movies of the '80s, much imitated but rarely bettered.

Along with the films of David Cronenberg, *The Thing* is one of the prime texts to explore the themes of bodily invasion that pervade horror and sci-fi movies of that decade. It is one of the first films to unflinchingly show the rupture and warp of flesh and bone into grotesque tableaus of surreal beauty, forever raising the bar on cinematic horror. **AT**

**U.S.** (Turman-Foster, Universal) 109m Technicolor

**Language:** English / Norwegian

**Director:** John Carpenter

**Producer:** David Foster, Lawrence Turman

**Screenplay:** Bill Lancaster, from the story *Who Goes There?* by John W. Campbell Jr.

**Photography:** Dean Cundey

**Music:** Ennio Morricone

**Cast:** Kurt Russell, Wilford Brimley, T.K. Carter, David Clennon, Keith David, Richard A. Dysart, Charles Hallahan, Peter Maloney, Richard Masur, Donald Moffat, Joel Polis, Thomas G. Waites, Norbert Weisser, Larry J. Franco, Nate Irwin

## POLTERGEIST (1982)

*Texas Chain Saw Massacre* helmsman Tobe Hooper gets on-screen credit for directing *Poltergeist*, but by all accounts producer Steven Spielberg played a more-than-supporting role in the film's creation. Indeed, the story of a suburban family disrupted and threatened by the increasingly malevolent unknown jibes with many of Spielberg's past and future scenarios, as does the somewhat playful casting of that modern bogeyman the television as the film's proxy villain, through which the malevolent spirits first make contact.

What begins as a wondrous encounter with the supernatural soon turns horrific, as the spooks manifest themselves in increasingly nasty ways (and via increasingly elaborate special effects). Copious movie magic and southern California family dynamics aside, *Poltergeist* proves far more terrifying than most of Spielberg's projects. This swings the see-saw of credit back to Hooper, who knows a thing or two about scaring audiences out of their wits: Skeletons start bobbing in the swimming pool, a boy is eaten by a tree, and a paranormal investigator tears off his own face. While anyone would be forgiven for asking why the family doesn't just pack their bags and leave, Hooper keeps the shocks and surprises coming at such a deviously steady pace that common sense plays second fiddle here to suspense and outright horror. **JKl**

**U.S.** (MGM) 114m Metrocolor

**Director:** Tobe Hooper

**Producer:** Steven Spielberg

**Screenplay:** Steven Spielberg, Michael Grais, Mark Victor

**Photography:** Mathew F. Leonetti

**Music:** Jerry Goldsmith

**Cast:** JoBeth Williams, Craig T. Nelson, Beatrice Straight, Dominique Dunne, Oliver Robins, Heather O'Rourke, Michael McManus, Virginia Kiser, Martin Casella, Richard Lawson, Zelda Rubinstein, Lou Perry, Clair E. Leucart, James Karen, Dirk Blocker

**Oscar nomination:** Stephen Hunter Flick, Richard L. Anderson (special sound effects), Richard Edlund, Michael Wood, Bruce Nicholson (special visual effects), Jerry Goldsmith (music)

**U.S.** (Blade Runner, Ladd) 117m Technicolor

**Language:** English / Japanese / Cantonese

**Director:** Ridley Scott

**Producer:** Michael Deeley

**Screenplay:** Hampton Fancher, David Webb Peoples, Roland Kibbee, from the novel *Do Androids Dream of Electric Sheep?* by Philip K. Dick

**Photography:** Jordan Cronenweth

**Music:** Vangelis

**Cast:** Harrison Ford, Rutger Hauer, Sean Young, Edward James Olmos, M. Emmet Walsh, Daryl Hannah, William Sanderson, Brion James, Joe Turkel, Joanna Cassidy, James Hong, Morgan Paull, Kevin Thompson, John Edward Allen, Hy Pyke

**Oscar nomination:** Lawrence G. Paull, David L. Snyder, Linda DeScenna (art direction), Douglas Trumbull, Richard Yuricich, David Dryer (special visual effects)

# BLADE RUNNER (1982)

Written in 1968, sci-fi author Philip K. Dick's *Do Androids Dream of Electric Sheep?* took 14 years to make it to the big screen, and it was another decade after that before Ridley Scott's jaw-dropping cinematic version—*Blade Runner* —was finally recognized as a masterpiece of science-fiction filmmaking. The $28 million movie was not well received on its original release and was a financial flop; only after the Director's Cut version was released in 1992 did critics and audiences fully embrace it.

Books have been devoted to the story behind the film itself. A tough production by all accounts, there were numerous reports of on-set bad feeling—star Harrison Ford reportedly didn't like costar Sean Young, the crew had T-shirts made to express their irritation at the punishing shooting schedule, and most notably, Ford and Scott didn't get along. Ford has rarely commented on the movie since its initial release, only remarking that it was the toughest movie he has ever worked on.

But what a movie it is. Justly acclaimed for its astonishing production design, Scott's vision of 2019 Los Angeles as bleak and neon-lit, with overcrowded streets and continual acid rain, has often been copied but never bettered. It is through this world that detective Rick Deckard (Ford) wanders, searching out "replicants"—mutinous androids masquerading as humans—while inadvertently falling for one such robot (Young). Packed with symbolism, *Blade Runner* has generated much debate over the years, with some fans arguing that the movie is subliminally about religion, citing examples such as replicant Roy Batty (Hauer) piercing his hand with a nail to possibly represent crucifixion, and Tyrell (Joe Turkel), creator of the replicants, serving as a God figure, keeping an eye over all his creations.

It is hard to imagine the film having the same impact with a different director (before Scott, Adrian Lyne, Michael Apted, and Robert Mulligan were all approached, and Martin Scorsese was interested in optioning the novel in 1969). As for the lead role, names mooted included Christopher Walken and even Dustin Hoffman. Scott's superb mix of 21st-century sci-fi and 1940s detective film noir makes for a stunning dystopia, while Ford, as the man sent to "retire" (i.e., execute) human-looking androids who have come to earth in search of their maker, may not have liked to "stand around and give some focus to Ridley's sets," as he told a journalist in 1991, but his bemusement works perfectly with the storyline.

One of the reasons *Blade Runner* has had such a cult following is the existence of more than one version of the film—the Director's Cut has added scenes, and leaves out Ford's voiceover narration along with the feel-good ending imposed by the studio. Another reason is the ongoing debate as to whether Deckard is actually a replicant himself. Whatever the answer—Scott has, on one occasion at least, hinted that Deckard may be an android—*Blade Runner* remains one of the most beautifully art-directed and visually stunning science-fiction movies ever made. **JB**

U.S. (MGM) 110m Metrocolor
**Director:** Barry Levinson
**Producer:** Jerry Weintraub
**Screenplay:** Barry Levinson
**Photography:** Peter Sova
**Music:** Bruce Brody, Ivan Kral
**Cast:** Steve Guttenberg, Daniel Stern, Mickey Rourke, Kevin Bacon, Timothy Daly, Ellen Barkin, Paul Reiser, Kathryn Dowling, Michael Tucker, Jessica James, Colette Blonigan, Kelle Kipp, John Aquino, Richard Pierson, Claudia Cron
**Oscar nomination:** Barry Levinson (screenplay)

# DINER (1982)

After the landmark of George Lucas's *American Graffiti*, the movieland zeitgeist preferred optimistic nostalgia for its maturing Baby Boomer audience. Responding to this cultural theme, Barry Levinson wrote and directed the 1982 Baltimore-based comedy classic *Diner* with a cast of unknowns, several of whom would move on to remarkable showbiz success in subsequent years.

*Diner*'s opening scene is Christmas night, 1959. The film tells the story of six twenty-somethings grappling with their intermingled friendship and the closing decade, all of it insinuated over the preparation for the marriage of one of their own on New Year's Eve. Interrupting these activities, the film's eponymous restaurant becomes the stars' home-away-from-home, their surrogate womb. Within its walls, ensconced among leather booths and eating off polished tabletops, they talk, talk, talk to retard the demands of the outside world and revel in one another's company.

Eddie (Steve Guttenberg) is an insecure loudmouth counting the days to his pending nuptials. Shrevie (Daniel Stern) is the hometown Everyman beholden to a steady job and a wife named Beth (Ellen Barkin), with whom he lacks an adult friendship. Boogie (Mickey Rourke) is a night-school law student, womanizer, and hairdresser with a gambling problem. Fenwick (Kevin Bacon) is the rich-kid dropout on the cusp of alcoholism, and Billy (Timothy Daly) is a graduate student with a long-time friendship-turned-pregnancy by way of his old friend Barbara (Kathryn Dowling). The last of the six is Modell (Paul Reiser), a hanger-on, but someone with an acute sense of comic timing.

## THE EVIL DEAD (1982)

**U.S.** (Renaissance) 85m Color
**Director:** Sam Raimi
**Producer:** Robert G. Tapert
**Screenplay:** Sam Raimi
**Photography:** Tim Philo
**Music:** Joseph LoDuca
**Cast:** Bruce Campbell, Ellen Sandweiss, Hal Delrich, Betsy Baker, Theresa Tilly, Philip A. Gillis, Dorothy Tapert, Cheryl Guttridge, Barbara Carey, David Horton, Wendall Thomas, Don Long, Stu Smith, Kurt Rauf, Ted Raimi

This "ultimate experience in grueling [sic] horror," as it immodestly bills itself in the end credits, changed the history of its genre. Sam Raimi took the gore of Italian horror movies and mixed it with a proudly juvenile sense of humor—making its teenage heroes so vapidly wholesome that we cannot wait, once they are holed up in a remote country shack, for them to die or be zombiefied. Such self-consciousness would subsequently come to dominate screen horror.

It is the ultimate "movie nerd" success story, flagrantly amateurish in many of its effects, but powered by a full-on soundtrack and ubiquitous, rapid, low-to-the-ground point of view shots. Raimi absorbed lessons from the 1970s generation of William Friedkin, Wes Craven, George Romero, and Brian De Palma, but added a down-home surrealism, somewhere between Jean Cocteau and Tex Avery. And in Bruce Campbell, Raimi found a sympathetically cartoonish star.

Today, it is hard to see anything but comedy in *The Evil Dead*, especially in the light of its sequels, *Evil Dead II* (1987) and *Army of Darkness* (1993). But we must remember that in 1982 the film had the same terrifying effect on audiences as *The Blair Witch Project* 17 years later—taking them, momentarily, out of their comfort zone. **AM**

## TOOTSIE (1982)

**U.S.** (Colum., Mir., Punch) 119m Color
**Director:** Sydney Pollack
**Producer:** Sydney Pollack, Dick Richards
**Screenplay:** Larry Gelbart, Don McGuire, Murray Schisgal
**Music:** Dave Grusin
**Cast:** Dustin Hoffman, Jessica Lange, Teri Garr, Dabney Coleman, Charles Durning, Bill Murray, Sydney Pollack, George Gaynes, Geena Davis
**Oscar:** Jessica Lange (actress in support role)
**Oscar nomination:** Sydney Pollack, Dick Richards (best picture), Sydney Pollack (director), Larry Gelbart, Murray Schisgal, Don McGuire (screenplay), Dustin Hoffman (actor), Teri Garr (actress in support role), Owen Roizman (photography), Fredric Steinkamp, William Steinkamp (editing), Dave Grusin, Alan Bergman, Marilyn Bergman (song), Arthur Piantadosi, Les Fresholtz, Rick Alexander, Les Lazarowitz (sound)

British critic Judith Williamson once disparaged the "Tootsie Syndrome" in contemporary culture—that device which decrees it only takes a few days in the shoes of your social "other" in order to completely understand and sympathize with their plight. The syndrome began with this film about a frustrated actor (Dustin Hoffman in a wonderful performance) who lands a role in a successful television soap opera by secretly impersonating a woman (who, these days, seems to resemble a Southern version of Dame Edna Everage).

The complications that follow for *Tootsie*—the frantic effort to maintain this masquerade, and the difficult attempt to romance a costar (Jessica Lange), including a mild lesbian complication—evoke the days of screwball sex-and-identity farce in the 1930s and '40s. But director Sydney Pollack (who also plays Tootsie's agent) has a keen sense of his contemporary moment, both in terms of behavioral detail and aesthetically.

*Tootsie*, alongside the work of James L. Brooks, pioneered a new style in mainstream cinema: Intensely busy, bristling with subplots, pop allusions (such as, here, a cameo from Andy Warhol), and jazzy montage sequences—raising dramatic complications and hinting at subversive implications while skating gracefully past them to an entertaining, happy ending. **AM**

## YOL (1982)

The story surrounding *Yol* is nearly as fascinating as the film itself. The director and writer, Yilmaz Güney, realized the film from prison. It was shot and overseen by Güney's assistant, Serif Gören, who worked from detailed notes and instructions written by Güney in his cell. The director subsequently escaped from jail and was present for the editing and postproduction. *Yol* went on to win the grand prize at the Cannes Film Festival and brought the world's attention to the violation of political prisoners' human rights in Turkey's right-wing dictatorship. Sadly, Güney died of cancer of a few years later after completing just one more film, *The Wall* (1983).

*Yol* is a deeply political film with an overt message and purpose that subordinates all the other elements. In each of the five prisoners' stories, hidebound traditions, religion, or the repression of the state are exposed. One of the prisoners must go back right away because of a petty rule. Another prisoner is cowed by his family, who want him to perform an honor killing on his unfaithful wife. A third convict who is happy to come home to his fiancée is soon disappointed because his family has selected a different woman for him to marry. A Kurdish prisoner returns to his native village after a long trip that takes nearly half of his leave, only to find that the Turkish army has completely wiped it out. Only one prisoner's story is hopeful, although he too suffers many setbacks and faces similar problems to the others.

*Yol* is deeply pessimistic and pulses with a palpable rage, making this otherwise fairly conventionally-structured film stirring and fresh. Güney's eye for detail, and his desire to expose the reactionary forces in his society, together provide a more intimate look into the life of a country than do most foreign films. Although *Yol*'s perspective is ultimately searing and critical, Güney takes pains to humanize his characters and make us care for them as individuals as well. Much of the credit for this must also go to the actors, who are uniformly excellent. Few better examples of engaged, political filmmaking exist. **RH**

**Turkey / Switzerland / France**
(Cactus, Films A2, Güney Film, Maran Film, Schweizer Fernsehen DRS) 114m Fujicolor Turkish

**Director:** Serif Gören, Yilmaz Güney

**Producer:** Edi Hubschmid, Yilmaz Güney

**Screenplay:** Yilmaz Güney

**Photography:** Erdogan Engin

**Music:** Sebastian Argol, Zülfü Livaneli

**Cast:** Tarik Akan, Serif Sezer, Halil Ergün, Meral Orhonsay, Necmettin Çobanoglu, Semra Uçar, Hikmet Celik, Sevda Aktolga, Tuncay Akça, Hale Akinli, Turgut Savas, Engin Çelike, Hikmet Tasdemir, Osman Bardakçi, Enver Güney

**Cannes Film Festival:** Serif Gören, Yilmaz Güney (FIPRESCI award) and (Golden Palm), tied with *Missing*, (prize of the ecumenical jury—special mention)

**U.S.** (MGM) 110m Metrocolor
**Director:** Barry Levinson
**Producer:** Jerry Weintraub
**Screenplay:** Barry Levinson
**Photography:** Peter Sova
**Music:** Bruce Brody, Ivan Kral
**Cast:** Steve Guttenberg, Daniel Stern, Mickey Rourke, Kevin Bacon, Timothy Daly, Ellen Barkin, Paul Reiser, Kathryn Dowling, Michael Tucker, Jessica James, Colette Blonigan, Kelle Kipp, John Aquino, Richard Pierson, Claudia Cron
**Oscar nomination:** Barry Levinson (screenplay)

# DINER (1982)

After the landmark of George Lucas's *American Graffiti*, the movieland zeitgeist preferred optimistic nostalgia for its maturing Baby Boomer audience. Responding to this cultural theme, Barry Levinson wrote and directed the 1982 Baltimore-based comedy classic *Diner* with a cast of unknowns, several of whom would move on to remarkable showbiz success in subsequent years.

*Diner's* opening scene is Christmas night, 1959. The film tells the story of six twenty-somethings grappling with their intermingled friendship and the closing decade, all of it insinuated over the preparation for the marriage of one of their own on New Year's Eve. Interrupting these activities, the film's eponymous restaurant becomes the stars' home-away-from-home, their surrogate womb. Within its walls, ensconced among leather booths and eating off polished tabletops, they talk, talk, talk to retard the demands of the outside world and revel in one another's company.

Eddie (Steve Guttenberg) is an insecure loudmouth counting the days to his pending nuptials. Shrevie (Daniel Stern) is the hometown Everyman beholden to a steady job and a wife named Beth (Ellen Barkin), with whom he lacks an adult friendship. Boogie (Mickey Rourke) is a night-school law student, womanizer, and hairdresser with a gambling problem. Fenwick (Kevin Bacon) is the rich-kid dropout on the cusp of alcoholism, and Billy (Timothy Daly) is a graduate student with a long-time friendship-turned-pregnancy by way of his old friend Barbara (Kathryn Dowling). The last of the six is Modell (Paul Reiser), a hanger-on, but someone with an acute sense of comic timing.

Well remembered for a few outstanding scenes, *Diner* is a bittersweet coming-of-age story beyond the confines of Los Angeles streets and movie studio sets or the skyscrapers and suburbs of New York City. The very act of filming in Baltimore gives the picture a more general sensibility and expands the horizon of such screen tales beyond cosmopolitan city-centers. Yet the humor of *Diner* is found in the set pieces constructed around an aspiring cast exhibiting a great deal of camaraderie and the production design elements that provide enough period details to seem utterly authentic. The cars are of the moment, and the music is too. A nascent sense of female political empowerment is in the air but so is the queasiness of these young men on the verge of either conforming to society's general consensus or else striking out on their own in stunningly new directions.

Laugh-out-loud moments appear alongside urgent dramatic vignettes. There is a spirited debate about Frank Sinatra and Johnny Mercer, for example, an unpleasant brotherly confrontation, and a penis in a popcorn bag.

Ending without a bang but a question mark, the structuring absence of the piece is undoubtedly Eddie's fiancée. She looms large and represents the entanglements of family and domesticity—in short, the final acceptance of adult responsibility. Altogether, these are the values all six characters in *Diner* seem to loathe but simultaneously long for in their last gasp of innocence at the end of 1959. **GC-Q**

# FITZCARRALDO (1982)

**West Germany/Peru** (Autoren, Project, Werner Herzog, Wildlife, ZDF) 158m Color

**Language:** English / German

**Director:** Werner Herzog

**Producer:** Werner Herzog, Lucki Stipetic

**Screenplay:** Werner Herzog

**Photography:** Thomas Mauch

**Music:** Popol Vuh

**Nonoriginal music:** Vincenzo Bellini, Giacomo Puccini, Richard Strauss, Giuseppe Verdi

**Cast:** Klaus Kinski, José Lewgoy, Miguel Ángel Fuentes, Paul Hittscher, Huerequeque Enrique Bohorquez, Grande Otelo, Peter Berling, David Pérez Espinosa, Milton Nascimento, Ruy Polanah, Salvador Godínez, Dieter Milz, William L. Rose, Leoncio Bueno, Claudia Cardinale

**Cannes Film Festival:** Werner Herzog (director), nomination (Golden Palm)

It is difficult to address *Fitzcarraldo* without first delving into the obsessive bent of its director Werner Herzog as well as his confounding collaboration with frequent (and frequently inscrutable) star Klaus Kinski. Their working relationship was predicated on mutual antagonism and outright aggression tempered by a mutual admiration, and that contradiction regularly manifested itself in their confrontational efforts. Needless to say, despite his unpredictable behavior Kinski often served as Herzog's first choice when it came time for casting. Or was it just that Herzog could rarely convince anyone else to commit to his infamous grueling projects?

Indeed, both Jason Robards and Mick Jagger were originally signed to the role, and it was only after both bowed out that Herzog contacted Kinski. And no wonder: The film's plot epitomizes both Herzog's and Kinski's legendary tenacity. Opera lover Brian Sweeney Fitzgerald (Kinski) vows to bring opera to remote Peru. But first he must make a fortune to fund the quixotic goal, and his plan involves hauling a huge steamboat over a mountain ridge to an isolated plot of land where he might harvest the rubber trees.

Fittingly, or perhaps typically, making a film depicting such a near-impossible feat encumbered by almost insurmountable obstacles indeed turned out to be an ordeal itself. It didn't help that Herzog approached the project with every bit the stubborn madness of his titular character. Injury, insanity, pain, illness, and even death in Herzog's quest to realize such a uniquely impressive vision in fact marred *Fitzcarraldo*'s production.

Herzog actually filmed deep in the jungles of Ecuador and Peru, dealing directly with all their inherent challenges, from mosquitoes to mudslides. To capture footage of a raft expedition threatened by tumultuous rapids, Herzog and a small crew ran the tumultuous rapids themselves. Most famously, to show the steamboat being transported over the mountain, Herzog did just that, depicting the effort with a documentary-like verisimilitude. In fact, much of the difficult process of making *Fitzcarraldo* is shown in Les Blank's equally riveting documentary *Burden of Dreams*, where a struggling Herzog teeters on the brink of a breakdown.

Yet *Fitzcarraldo*, the finished film, hardly comes across like Joseph Conrad's *Heart of Darkness*, let alone Francis Ford Coppola's *Apocalypse Now*, and Kinski is no Kurtz-like invader. Compared with Herzog and Kinski's bleak conquistador tale *Aguirre: The Wrath of God*, *Fitzcarraldo* is downright innocent. Kinski's optimistic opera lover, nicknamed "Fitzcarraldo" by the Peruvian locals, is driven by idealism as much as intransigence. The curious natives help him bring his dream to fruition in part because of his innocence, exuberance, and absolute passion for opera, which he plays on an old Victrola record player that he carries around with him. As the steamboat is dragged uphill, against all odds, Kinski's Fitzcarraldo stands on the top deck, beaming, as his Victrola blasts opera singer Enrico Caruso. It's a sight as surreal as it is inspiring, simultaneously announcing an accomplishment that is both dramatic (in terms of the narrative) and impressively tactile (in terms of filmmaking). **JKl**

# GANDHI (1982)

"The truth," Richard Attenborough said, "is that I never wanted to be a director at all. I just wanted to direct that film." For him, therefore, *Gandhi* represented a mission: Attenborough survived 20 years of delays, frustrations, ridicule, and personal financial risk to achieve his grand dream of recreating the life and times of Mohandas Kharamchand Gandhi (1869–1948), in a way that would touch audiences of East and West alike with the spiritual significance of the Mahatma.

Attenborough first conceived the project in 1962: His particular inspiration was Gandhi's dictum, "It has always been a mystery to me how men can feel themselves honored by the humiliation of their fellow beings." Already a producer, he was not to embark as a director until 1969, with *Oh! What a Lovely War*, and at various stages of his 18-year struggle to raise finances for *Gandhi*, Fred Zinnemann and David Lean were proposed as more likely and more marketable directors. Various writers, including Gerald Hanley, Donald Ogden Stuart, and Robert Bolt, tried their hand before John Briley's script masterfully captured the essence of Gandhi's life and achievement.

Over the years, generations of actors—including Alec Guinness, Dirk Bogarde, Peter Finch, Albert Finney, Tom Courtenay, Robert De Niro, Dustin Hoffman, John Hurt, and Richard Burton—were considered for the leading role. In the end the choice was the practically unknown Ben Kingsley, who had the advantage of facial features inherited from his Indian father. Kingsley dedicated himself to the role, shedding weight, taking up yoga, learning to spin cotton, and making a brave attempt to live life by Gandhi's example. The huge supporting cast included a remarkable display of stage and screen luminaries of the time.

Briley's script opens with the assassination and state funeral of Gandhi in 1948, and then flashes back to his beginnings as a young lawyer, protesting against racial discrimination in South Africa in 1893. From this it traces the main biographical landmarks of his battle against British imperial domination, and for an integrated Indian society and culture. Ironically, Gandhi's passionate commitment to peaceful protest often leads to violence and death, as well as his own lengthy imprisonment. Much of the action was filmed on the actual historic locations. The funeral scene, shot on the Rajpath using 11 camera crews, assembled an estimated 400,000 extras.

*Gandhi* triumphantly disproved the general tenet that films which are long in the making usually fall short of their ambition, losing the freshness of initial inspiration. *Gandhi* found an instant response in critical acclaim and a worldwide audience. Its eight Academy Awards marked a record, surpassed only by *Ben-Hur* (1959). For Attenborough a greater personal satisfaction was evidently the certainty that at least some of his audience felt themselves enriched by the encounter with Gandhi, through his screen portrait. For better or worse, *Gandhi* was to mark his future career as a director of inspirational film biographies. **DRos**

**G.B. / India** (Carolina Bank, Goldcrest, Indo-British, International, NFDC) 188m Technicolor

**Director:** Richard Attenborough

**Producer:** Richard Attenborough

**Screenplay:** John Briley

**Photography:** Ronnie Taylor, Billy Williams

**Music:** Ravi Shankar, George Fenton

**Cast:** Ben Kingsley, Candice Bergen, Edward Fox, John Gielgud, Trevor Howard, John Mills, Martin Sheen, Ian Charleson, Athol Fugard, Günther Maria Halmer, Saeed Jaffrey, Geraldine James, Alyque Padamsee, Amrish Puri, Roshan Seth

**Oscar:** Richard Attenborough (best picture), Richard Attenborough (director), John Briley (screenplay), Ben Kingsley (actor), Stuart Craig, Robert W. Laing, Michael Seirton (art direction), Billy Williams, Ronnie Taylor (photography), John Mollo, Bhanu Athaiya (costume), John Bloom (editing)

**Oscar nomination:** Tom Smith (makeup), Ravi Shankar, George Fenton (music), Gerry Humphreys, Robin O'Donoghue, Jonathan Bates, Simon Kaye (sound)

# LA NOTTE DI SAN LORENZO (1982)
## THE NIGHT OF THE SHOOTING STARS

*The Night of the Shooting Stars* is the masterwork of the Taviani Brothers, Paolo and Vittorio, and takes place on the Night of San Lorenzo, when all dreams come true. Narrated by a mother speaking to her sleeping baby, the story returns to 1944 when German invaders and fascist Italian collaborators controlled the then six-year-old narrator's village. With her hometown split between Nazi regulations and eventual liberation, a group of her townsfolk cross the Tuscan countryside seeking salvation.

Without either ignoring or dwelling on wartime terrors, this journey expresses civilian resistance. Daily struggles for food take priority over bullets or tactical advantage. Periodically the narrator's childhood perspective even shines through with tragicomically surreal images that discount the fearful quality of their odyssey.

Notable for its ensemble cast, *The Night of the Shooting Stars* also offers indelible images to salve the etched memory of unwanted conflict. A cathedral is bombed to kill worshippers. Wild watermelon is feasted upon in a field. Friends on opposite sides of a political divide murder one another. Two older people consummate a love affair decades in the making. Together these moments signify the gravity of World War II while remembering the dignity of everyday life. **GC-Q**

**Italy** (Ager, RAI) 105m Eastmancolor
**Language:** Italian
**Director:** Paolo Taviani, Vittorio Taviani
**Producer:** Giuliani G. De Negri
**Screenplay:** Paolo Taviani, Vittorio Taviani, Giuliani G. De Negri, Tonino Guerra
**Photography:** Franco Di Giacomo
**Music:** Nicola Piovani
**Cast:** Omero Antonutti, Margarita Lozano, Claudio Bigagli, Miriam Guidelli, Massimo Bonetti, Enrica Maria Modugno, Sabina Vannucchi, Giorgio Naddi, Renata Zamengo, Micol Guidelli, Massimo Sarchielli, Giovanni Guidelli, Mario Spallino, Paolo Hendel
**Cannes Film Festival:** Paolo Taviani, Vittorio Taviani (grand prize of the jury), (prize of the ecumenical jury), nomination (Golden Palm)

# DE STILTE ROND CHRISTINE M. (1982)
## A QUESTION OF SILENCE

A key moment in the history of women's filmmaking, Marleen Gorris's *A Question of Silence* charged and polarized audiences. The picture addressed women's submerged rage, reconnecting feminists with the anger that fueled the movements of the 1960s and 1970s while sparking, as *Thelma and Louise* (1991) would, accusations of reverse stereotyping.

Provoked by a news story about a working-class woman's arrest for shoplifting, *A Question of Silence* centers on three women, strangers to each other, who spontaneously kill a boutique manager as he superciliously confronts a frazzled housewife in the act. A unique mix of thriller, courtroom drama, black comedy, quasi-documentary, and political allegory, *A Question of Silence* is alternately riveting and distancing, mortifying and electrifying. The murder itself is heard rather than seen and embedded in a series of three flashbacks sequences, subverting the visual imperative.

In the film's courtroom climax, as Dr. van den Bos pronounces the women "completely sane," their act becomes politically charged. The concluding scene must be experienced rather than described—other than to say that the picture ends not in a bang or a whimper but in waves of raucous laughter, and finishes in silence. As one critic has asked, "Is it the murder that is so unsettling or is it the laughter?" Although Gorris's recent films are mellower and more popular, *A Question of Silence* makes ideology visceral and is a true shocker. **LB**

**Netherlands** (Sigma) 92m Color
**Language:** Dutch / English
**Director:** Marleen Gorris
**Producer:** Matthijs van Heijningen
**Screenplay:** Marleen Gorris
**Photography:** Frans Bromet
**Music:** Lodewijk de Boer, Martijn Hasebos
**Cast:** Edda Barends, Nelly Frijda, Henriëtte Tol, Cox Habbema, Eddie Brugman, Hans Croiset, Erik Plooyer, Anna van Beers, Noa Cohen, Kees Coolen, Edgar Danz, Diana Dobbelman, Miranda Frijda, Frederik de Groot, Noortje Jansen

Sweden / France / West Germany (Cin. AB, Gaumont, Persona, Swedish Film Inst., Sandrews, Svenska, TVI, Tobis) 188m Eastmancolor

**Language:** Swedish / German / Yiddish / English

**Director:** Ingmar Bergman

**Producer:** Jörn Donner

**Screenplay:** Ingmar Bergman

**Photography:** Sven Nykvist

**Music:** Daniel Bell

**Cast:** Erland Josephson, Jarl Kulle, Pernilla Allwin, Allan Edwall, Bertil Guve, Gunn Walgren, Ewa Fröling

**Oscar:** Sweden (best foreign language film), Anna Asp, Susanne Lingheim (art direction), Sven Nykvist (photography), Marik Vos-Lundh (costume)

**Oscar nomination:** Ingmar Bergman (director), Ingmar Bergman (screenplay)

**Venice Film Festival:** Ingmar Bergman (FIPRESCI award)

# FANNY OCH ALEXANDER (1982)
## FANNY AND ALEXANDER

Swedish director Ingmar Bergman's large body of work is so distinctive that it is frequently spoofed by comedians as well as imitated and cited by lesser filmmakers. Showing the deeper, darker side of the human spirit without flinching or resorting to melodrama, Bergman's dreamy, allegorical films present life as it is rather than how we wish it would be.

Announced as the director's penultimate film (he has since worked primarily in television), the autobiographical tale of *Fanny and Alexander* came as a jolt to fans of his brooding earlier films. Written by Bergman, and featuring many of Bergman's most talented, seasoned actors, including Erland Josephson, Harriet Andersson, and Gunnar Björnstrand, *Fanny* is considered his most accessible movie—it won four of its six Academy Award nominations, including Best Foreign Language Film.

This long part-autobiography spans an important and stormy year in the life of a brother and sister (Pernilla Allwin and Bertil Guve) born into an aristocratic family in turn-of-the-century Sweden. Filmed with an energy unseen in previous Bergman productions, the story is part Dickensian drama, part mystical fairy tale. Beginning at a luxurious family Christmas told from the boy's point of view, it switches to their miserable life after the death of the children's much-loved theater-owning father. By then, the usual Bergmanesque sense of foreboding has descended on the story, settling on life during the deeply unfortunate and terrifying remarriage of their mother to an awful bishop—Jan Malmsjö in a suitably hateful role.

*Fanny and Alexander*'s length and languorous, careful pace may put modern action viewers off, but Bergman's famous cinematographer Sven Nykvist uses lustrous lighting to make each frame a delight. The entire film has a dreamy sense of the unreal, a relief during its more tragic moments. Bergman, ever the master, wisely structures the tale to have its most horrific and most satisfying moment just when the story demands a resolution. By then the viewer is left breathless and waiting for the good times to return. Despite his life's work analyzing the frightening world of the living, Bergman here allows his audience some comfort—albeit with certain philosophical provisions. **KK**

# A CHRISTMAS STORY (1983)

It's the 1940s, a time when American families still eat dinner together, children walk long distances to school in well-bundled packs, and everyone knows their neighbors. For young Ralphie (Peter Billingsley) in *A Christmas Story*, life is good but not quite complete. Christmas is fast approaching and all he wants is a Red Ryder BB gun, the kind his radio hero hawks. Despite the opposition of his family and teacher, he's determined to come up with a scheme that will secure the toy by Christmas day.

This simple set-up gives director Bob Clark more than enough ammunition to lovingly but bitingly send up Christmas, family values, nostalgia for bygone eras, and the consumerism that has come to define the holiday season. Both droll and laugh-out-loud funny, this modern holiday classic resonates so deeply because it never becomes cruel or dismissive as it tackles its targets.

School bullies, a cantankerous dad and overworked mom, an odd younger sibling, and a posse of misfit friends all come to life in the voiceover by a grown-up Ralphie. Classic scenes (a schoolmate getting his tongue frozen to the flagpole; Christmas dinner at a Chinese restaurant) manage to be both uproarious and touching without ever sliding into schmaltz or sentimentality. For those who loathe the saccharine aspects of the holidays, but don't actually want to be Scrooge, *A Christmas Story* is a perfect fit. **EH**

**U.S. / Canada** (Christmas Tree, MGM) 94m Metrocolor

**Director:** Bob Clark

**Producer:** Bob Clark, René Dupont

**Screenplay:** Leigh Brown, Bob Clark, Jean Shepherd, from the novel *In God We Trust, All Others Pay Cash* by Jean Shepherd

**Photography:** Reginald H. Morris

**Music:** Paul Zaza, Carl Zittrer

**Cast:** Melinda Dillon, Darren McGavin, Peter Billingsley, Ian Petrella, Scott Schwartz, R.D. Robb, Tedde Moore, Yano Anaya, Zack Ward, Jeff Gillen, Colin Fox, Paul Hubbard, Leslie Carlson, Jim Hunter, Patty Johnson

# EL NORTE (1983)

Exploring illegal passage into the United States, *El Norte* brilliantly confronts the fantasy of First World comfort with the reality of Third World people. Written by the husband–wife team of Gregory Nava and Anna Thomas and directed by Nava, the film is significant for exposing the porous nature of national borders and the exploitation of nomadic workers. Praising the humanity of illegal immigrants eking out an existence beneath the American dream, *El Norte* further recognizes the context of such experience.

For Guatemalan siblings Enrique (David Villalpando) and Rosa (Zaide Silvia Gutiérrez), the issue is much simpler than geopolitics. When their father is murdered for organizing bean pickers and their mother "disappeared" by paramilitary functionaries, they flee for their lives. In Tijuana they struggle with that city's poverty and capture a coyote before arriving in Los Angeles. Realizing the rampant racism of their Northern employers, though now with the advantages of indoor plumbing and electricity, they work as day laborers with an insecure future.

Guatemala is herein characterized by green and yellow, Tijuana with tan, and the United States with blues and white. Music also cues the siblings' journey, but finally it's the total effect of their migration that registers the force of modern economic disparity. **GC-Q**

**U.S. / G.B.** (American Playhouse, Channel Four, Independent, Island Alive, PBS) 139m Color

**Language:** English / Spanish

**Director:** Gregory Nava

**Producer:** Trevor Black, Bertha Navarro, Anna Thomas

**Screenplay:** Gregory Nava, Anna Thomas

**Photography:** James Glennon

**Music:** The Folkloristas, Malecio Martinez, Linda O'Brien, Emil Richards

**Cast:** Zaide Silvia Gutiérrez, David Villalpando, Ernesto Gómez Cruz, Lupe Ontiveros, Trinidad Silva, Alicia del Lago, Abel Franco, Enrique Castillo, Tony Plana, Diane Civita, Mike Gomez

**Oscar nomination:** Gregory Nava, Anna Thomas (screenplay)

**U.S. / Canada** (Famous Players, Filmplan, Guardian, CFDC, Universal) 87m Color

**Director:** David Cronenberg

**Producer:** Claude Héroux

**Screenplay:** David Cronenberg

**Photography:** Mark Irwin

**Music:** Howard Shore

**Cast:** James Woods, Sonja Smits, Deborah Harry, Peter Dvorsky, Leslie Carlson, Jack Creley, Lynne Gorman, Julie Khaner, Reiner Schwartz, David Bolt, Lally Cadeau, Henry Gomez, Harvey Chao, David Tsubouchi, Kay Hawtrey

# VIDEODROME (1983)

A groundbreaking film of the commercial/independent movement of 1980s Hollywood, David Cronenberg's story about the horrible transformations wrought by exposure to televised violence wittily thematizes the very problems that the director's exploration of violent sexual imagery in his previous productions had caused with censors, Hollywood distributors, and feminist groups. Max Renn (James Woods) is a cable-station operator whose cynical marketing of sex and violence backfires on him when his abdomen suddenly grows a vagina-like opening into which, among other objects, audiocassettes can be inserted. The film, in which such sado-masochistic fantasy and transgendering play key roles, ends tragically, with Max's self-destruction.

In many ways the most audacious formal incarnation of Cronenberg's characteristic themes, *Videodrome* begins as a fairly standard commercial thriller, only to be transformed, at midpoint, into subjective fantasy of the most outrageous and unusual kind. Visually rich, *Videodrome* is also thought-provoking in its startling meditation on both polymorphous perversity and the interpenetration between the public and subjective realms of experience. Cronenberg has been both praised and condemned for his fluid treatment of gender (a closing sequence in which two female characters grow penises in a kind of riposte to Max's "vagination" was cut from the release print as too disturbing for mainstream audiences). Even in its edited form, *Videodrome* remains one of Hollywood's most unusual films, too shocking and idiosyncratic to be anything but a commercial failure. **RBP**

## STAR WARS: EPISODE VI—RETURN OF THE JEDI (1983)

The third installment, otherwise known as *Episode VI*, of George Lucas's original Star Wars trilogy picks up some time after the cliffhanger events of *The Empire Strikes Back* (1980). Luke Skywalker (Mark Hamill), an eager young Jedi trainee in the first installment, is now a brooding warrior (hence the black clothing). Skilled in the ways of the Force, he returns to his home planet of Tatooine to help his friends—Princess Leia (Carrie Fisher, clad in a sci-fi bikini male fans still rave about today), Lando Calrissian (Billy Dee Williams), and Chewbacca the wookie—rescue their frozen-in-carbonite pal Han Solo (Harrison Ford) from the clutches of Jabba the Hutt.

The main strand of the plot covers similar ground to *Star Wars* (1977). The evil Empire is constructing another Death Star, which our heroes have to destroy. Executive producer Lucas (who cowrote the script with Lawrence Kasdan) and director Richard Marquand introduce a new race of teddy-bear-like creatures, the Ewoks, to entertain younger members of the audience. The stars, meanwhile, are never eclipsed by cuddly muppets and impressive special effects, and skillfully bring Lucas's vision of intergalactic good-versus-evil to a close. **JB**

**U.S.** (Lucasfilm) 134m Color

**Director:** Richard Marquand

**Producer:** Howard G. Kazanjian

**Screenplay:** George Lucas, Lawrence Kasdan

**Photography:** Alan Hume

**Music:** John Williams, Joseph Williams

**Cast:** Mark Hamill, Harrison Ford, Carrie Fisher, Billy Dee Williams, Anthony Daniels, Peter Mayhew, Sebastian Shaw, Ian McDiarmid, Frank Oz, James Earl Jones, David Prowse, Alec Guinness, Kenny Baker, Michael Pennington, Kenneth Colley

**Oscar:** Richard Edlund, Dennis Muren, Ken Ralston, Phil Tippett (special visual effects)

**Oscar nomination:** Ben Burtt (special sound effects), Norman Reynolds, Fred Hole, James L. Schoppe, Michael Ford (art direction), John Williams (music), Ben Burtt, Gary Summers, Randy Thom, Tony Dawe (sound)

## THE BIG CHILL (1983)

Much imitated but never bettered—it is unlikely TV's *thirtysomething* would have existed without this movie—Lawrence Kasdan's nostalgic film about a handful of 1960s college friends, reunited in middle age for a funeral, manages to be both sharply witty and achingly moving.

Following the suicide of Alex—played by Kevin Costner, though only a scene in which he is already deceased and being prepared for his coffin remain in the final version—seven of his friends gather for a weekend to remember him. Sam (Tom Berenger), Michael (Jeff Goldblum), Nick (William Hurt), Karen (JoBeth Williams), and Meg (Mary Kay Place) are the pals, all dealing with their own midlife crises, who descend on married couple Sarah (Glenn Close) and Harold's (Kevin Kline) house, to reminisce, bicker, and open old wounds to a suitably '60s soundtrack.

Kasdan and Barbara Benedek's observant script captures all the idealistic feelings and disappointments of a '60s generation stuck in the far more materialistic '80s, while *The Big Chill*'s ensemble cast delivers just the right combination of sadness and humor, never lapsing into sentimentality. **JB**

**U.S.** (Carson, Columbia) 105m Metrocolor

**Director:** Lawrence Kasdan

**Producer:** Michael Shamberg

**Screenplay:** Barbara Benedek, Lawrence Kasdan

**Photography:** John Bailey

**Music:** Mick Jagger, Smokey Robinson, John Williams

**Cast:** Tom Berenger, Glenn Close, Jeff Goldblum, William Hurt, Kevin Kline, Mary Kay Place, Meg Tilly, JoBeth Williams, Don Galloway, James Gillis, Ken Place, Jon Kasdan, Ira Stiltner, Jake Kasdan, Muriel Moore

**Oscar nomination:** Michael Shamberg (best picture), Lawrence Kasdan, Barbara Benedek (screenplay), Glenn Close (actress in support role)

## SANS SOLEIL (1983)
### SUNLESS

**France** (Argos Film) 100m Color
**Language:** French
**Director:** Chris Marker
**Screenplay:** Chris Marker
**Photography:** Chris Marker
**Music:** Isao Tomita
**Nonoriginal music:** Modest Mussorgsky, Jean Sibelius
**Cast:** Florence Delay, Arielle Dombasle, Riyoko Ikeda, Charlotte Kerr, Alexandra Stewart
**Berlin International Film Festival:** Chris Marker (OCIC award—honorable mention, new cinema)

Chris Marker's masterpiece, whose title translates as *Sunless*, is one of the key nonfiction films of our time: a personal philosophical essay that concentrates mainly on contemporary Tokyo but also includes footage shot in Iceland, Guinea-Bissau, and San Francisco, where the filmmaker tracks down all the original locations in Hitchcock's *Vertigo* (1958), one of Marker's key cinematic obsessions. Difficult to describe and almost impossible to summarize, this poetic journal of a major French filmmaker and video artist radiates in all directions, exploring and reflecting on decades of experience all over the world.

A film about subjectivity, death, photography, social custom, and consciousness itself, *Sans soleil* registers like a poem one might find in a time capsule. Characteristically, it is a film of second thoughts by a photographer, a leftist, and a compulsive globe-trotter who remains haunted and transfixed by some of his own images. Significantly, as in his other films and videos, Marker refuses to take a directorial credit. It also seems pertinent that he assigns his own narration to an American woman (Alexandria Stewart) in the film's English-language version—he is quoted only in the third-person and past tense—marking him as a master of indirection. The wit and beauty of Marker's highly original form of discourse leave a profound aftertaste. **JRos**

## LE DERNIER COMBAT (1983)
### THE LAST BATTLE

**France** (Loup) 92m BW
**Language:** None / French
**Director:** Luc Besson
**Producer:** Luc Besson
**Screenplay:** Luc Besson, Pierre Jolivet
**Photography:** Carlo Varini
**Music:** Eric Serra
**Cast:** Pierre Jolivet, Jean Bouise, Fritz Wepper, Jean Reno, Christiane Krüger, Maurice Lamy, Pierre Carrive, Jean-Michel Castanié, Michel Doset, Bernard Havet, Marcel Berthomier, Petra Müller, Garry Jode

*Mad Max* style, Paris has been reduced to ruins in a desert landscape. Characters in this postapocalyptic sci-fi fantasy shot in black and white can no longer speak and must scavenge for water, food, and sex. The hero (Pierre Jolivet) frantically makes love to a rubber doll. Pursued by marauders, he takes off in his homemade plane, landing close to a derelict hospital. He is taken in by a doctor (Jean Bouise) who is sheltering one of the last women and who wants to start a new society with her and the hero as Adam and Eve and himself as God-voyeur. An evil giant (Jean Reno) also has designs on the woman; he besieges the doctor's compound, and rapes and kills the woman before being killed himself by the hero. The hero returns to confront the gang who drove him out, kills the leader, and appropriates the leader's woman, perhaps the last female on Earth.

Luc Besson's first film, made on a shoestring budget, *The Last Battle* combines cartoon-style humor, surreal touches (raining fish, for example), and violence, here to comment on youth alienation in the materialist 1980s where communication has been reduced to primitive urges, and the sophistication of urban Paris to the ruins of dystopia. **PP**

# L'ARGENT (1983)
## MONEY

An hour into *Money*, a sudden burst of whiteness introduces a new turn in the narrative. A gray-haired woman (Sylvie Van den Elsen) walks by, with a subtle glance passing between her and a criminal fugitive, Yvon (Christian Patey). A few moments later, everything is green and natural for the first time in the film.

Mystery is a watchword in the cinema of Robert Bresson, but the relationship that begins here between Yvon and his benefactress is the most mysterious of all. The woman seems to realize that she has a murderer on her hands. Her submission to him is masochistic, spiritual, and sexual all at once—not to mention, eventually, suicidal.

Is this woman a fool doomed by her code of misplaced goodness, or a saint who brings momentary grace to a damned soul? And what is Yvon by this stage of his harrowing journey—the premise, borrowed from Leo Tolstoy, of a 500-franc note forged by a trio of schoolboys triggering the inexorable dissolution of every structure in his life—an alienated madman, a cold manipulator, or a victim in search of his lost innocence?

The world of *Money* is barren and bare. The cold architecture of middle-class shops, courtrooms, and prisons is matched by an equally harsh sound-collage of sirens, cars, and machinery. Bodies are frequently pinned within the lines of doorways and windows.

Is *Money* Bresson's most secular, materialist work a logical culmination of the despair about modern industrialized life enacted in *The Devil Probably* (1977), or is there a glimmer of hope buried somewhere in its bleak vision? Some poignant details escape the determinist grid, like the shots of Yvon collecting hazelnuts from tree leaves and sharing them with the woman, as white sheets gently blow in the breeze—one of the simplest yet most beautiful passages in any Bresson film. Here we intuit the profound mystery of beings who move through landscapes of dehumanizing violence with their capacities for evil and goodness locked silently inside them—and we witness fleeting moments of absolute, natural purity in a world gone to hell. **AM**

**France / Switzerland** (EOS-Film, France 3 Cinéma, Marion's Films) 85m Eastmancolor

**Language:** French

**Director:** Robert Bresson

**Producer:** Jean-Marc Henchoz, Daniel Toscan du Plantier

**Screenplay:** Robert Bresson, from the short story *Faux billet* by Leo Tolstoy

**Photography:** Pasqualino De Santis, Emmanuel Machuel

**Nonoriginal Music:** Johann Sebastian Bach

**Cast:** Christian Patey, Vincent Risterucci, Caroline Lang, Sylvie Van den Elsen, Béatrice Tabourin, Didier Baussy, Marc Ernest Fourneau, Bruno Lapeyre, François-Marie Banier, Alain Aptekman, Jeanne Aptekman, Dominique Mullier, Jacques Behr, Gilles Durieux, Alain Bourguignon

**Cannes Film Festival:** Robert Bresson (director), tied with Andrei Tarkovsky for *Nostalghia*, nomination (Golden Palm)

**New Zealand** (Glitteron) 118m Fujicolor

**Director:** Geoff Murphy

**Producer:** Don Blakeney, Geoff Murphy

**Screenplay:** Keith Aberdein, Geoff Murphy

**Photography:** Graeme Cowley

**Music:** John Charles

**Cast:** Anzac Wallace, Bruno Lawrence, Tim Elliott, Kelly Johnson, Wi Kuki Kaa, Tania Bristowe, Ilona Rodgers, Merata Mita, Faenza Reuben, Tom Poata, Martyn Sanderson, John Bach, Dick Puanaki, Sean Duffy, Ian Watkin

# UTU (1983)

Te Wheke (Anzac Wallace) is a Maori tracker serving the British colonial machine in New Zealand. Turning tail when a branch of the army he serves overruns his village, he goes "native" and claims *utu*, or revenge. Thereafter he forms a band of marauders who tear up the countryside owned and protected by whites. In the end, another British-employed Maori tracker named Wiremu (Wi Kuki Kaa) kills him in a ritual fratricide, the likes of which are not often imagined outside Shakespearean adaptations.

Admirably representing the true Maori uprisings that forever changed New Zealand, *Utu* is the fictionalized account of perhaps the only successful indigenous resistance to British colonization. Connecting this tenacious ferocity with the personage of Te Wheke, a symbol of his historic brethren, the film's critical sensibility gathers moral strength while commenting on the urgency of self-determination. Further adding to its impact is the ambivalent development of different kinds of *utu* through an episodic plot that spirals to a quietly violent conclusion.

Enlisted by the blowhard Colonel Elliot (Tim Elliott), Lieutenant Scott (Kelly Johnson), a white New Zealander, is asked to apply his tactical experience of guerilla warfare. In the course of his pursuit, he falls in love with the Maori Kura (Tania Bristowe) before Wheke murders her, creating another *utu*. Director and coscreenwriter Geoff Murphy thus had conviction enough to make Wheke neither a renegade hero nor a criminal deviant. His transformation from Kiwi Uncle Tom to a bloodthirsty patriot is well motivated. So is the vengeful insanity of Williamson (Bruno Lawrence), a white settler whose plantation and wife are destroyed in one of Wheke's raids. Most memorably for the film's lasting resonance, though, is the pivotal role played by Wiremu. Recognizing the tides of change, he is Wheke's brother, and the task of justice falls to him in sacrificing kin on the way to a seemingly inevitable, integrated Euro-Kiwi future.

Throughout its running time, *Utu* is marvelously produced with rich New Zealand scenery, strong performances, gut-wrenching bursts of unanticipated violence, and a non-Eurocentric perspective. Admittedly a tragedy, Murphy's film is nonetheless brilliant drama and a brilliant achievement hailing from the Antipodes. **GC-Q**

# TERMS OF ENDEARMENT (1983)

From the author of *The Last Picture Show*, *Lonesome Dove*, and *Horseman Pass By* (upon which Martin Ritt's classic 1963 film *Hud* was based), Larry McMurty's novel of a strained, emotional, and difficult relationship between a mother and daughter was translated into a successful, award-winning Hollywood movie by screenwriter/director James L. Brooks. It remains a textbook example of how to make a successful mainstream American weepie.

Debra Winger, at the height of her career in the 1980s, stars as Emma, the stubborn daughter of possessive, often smothering mother Aurora (Shirley MacLaine). *Terms of Endearment* follows their relationship over a series of years, from Emma trying to extricate herself from her mother by marrying the laid back (and ultimately unfaithful) Flap Horton (Jeff Daniels), to mother and daughter reaching some sort of truce when Emma is dying of cancer. Although the film is a tearjerker of the highest order, Brooks manages to keep sickly sentiment at bay and in doing so helps his cast deliver one of the most moving deathbed scenes in recent cinema history.

The light relief—away from the mother/daughter harsh words and tears—is delivered in scenes by MacLaine, in an Oscar-winning turn, and Jack Nicholson, as astronaut Garrett Breedlove. It is during the moments between these two experienced actors that the film really sizzles, most notably as Garrett, displaying his devil-may-care attitude, drives himself and Aurora along the beach at the edge of the waves.

Subtly played by Winger, Daniels, John Lithgow (as the man Emma has an affair with following Flap's infidelity), and Danny DeVito (as another of Aurora's suitors), *Terms of Endearment* features scene-stealing performances from Nicholson and MacLaine that threaten to overtake the entire film. However, former television director Brooks (who reunited with Nicholson for the Oscar-winning *As Good As It Gets* in 1997) paces the movie in such a manner—cleverly mixing the humor and the tragedy—that their star turns only enhance this melancholy look at modern family relationships. **JB**

**U.S.** (Paramount) 132m Metrocolor

**Director:** James L. Brooks

**Producer:** James L. Brooks

**Screenplay:** James L. Brooks, from novel by Larry McMurtry

**Photography:** Andrzej Bartkowiak

**Music:** Michael Gore

**Cast:** Shirley MacLaine, Debra Winger, Jack Nicholson, Danny DeVito, Jeff Daniels, John Lithgow, Lisa Hart Carroll, Betty King, Huckleberry Fox, Troy Bishop, Shane Serwin, Megan Morris, Tara Yeakey, Norman Bennett, Jennifer Josey

**Oscar:** James L. Brooks (best picture), James L. Brooks (director), James L. Brooks (screenplay), Shirley MacLaine (actress), Jack Nicholson (actor in support role)

**Oscar nomination:** Debra Winger (actress), John Lithgow (actor in support role), Polly Platt, Tom Pedigo (art direction), Richard Marks (editing), Michael Gore (music), Donald O. Mitchell, Rick Kline, Kevin O'Connell, James R. Alexander (sound)

**Netherlands** (De Verenigde Nederlandsche) 105m Color

**Language:** Dutch

**Director:** Paul Verhoeven

**Producer:** Rob Houwer

**Screenplay:** Gerard Soeteman, from novel by Gerard Reve

**Photography:** Jan de Bont

**Music:** Loek Dikker

**Cast:** Jeroen Krabbé, Renée Soutendijk, Thom Hoffman, Dolf de Vries, Geert de Jong, Hans Veerman, Hero Muller, Caroline de Beus, Reinout Bussemaker, Erik J. Meijer, Ursul de Geer, Filip Bolluyt, Hedda Lornie, Paul Nygaard, Guus van der Made

# DE VIERDE MAN (1983)

## THE FOURTH MAN

Wrapping up his auspicious European period before heading to the fertile fields of Hollywood, Dutch director Paul Verhoeven reached some sort of trashy apotheosis in black comedy with *The Fourth Man*. Essentially a Hitchcock film had Hitchcock made more explicit his fear of female sexuality, *The Fourth Man* stars Jeroen Krabbé as a semicloseted, alcoholic gay writer who suspects his wealthy bisexual meal ticket Renée Soutendijk may have killed her previous three husbands. Krabbé hates his homosexuality yet can't resist seducing Soutendijk's boy toy, and leeches off her even as he thinks he could be murder victim number four.

Confused by self-loathing, Krabbé's suspicions deepen, but Verhoeven keeps the truth intentionally vague. He packs the film with overtly Catholic symbolism and premonitions of death, perversely toying with expectations. In fact, Verhoeven has since claimed that he and screenwriter Gerard Soeteman intentionally added superfluous and utterly extraneous symbolism just to throw off critics, and indeed the movie proceeds unpredictably. Verhoeven would later revisit essentially the same scenario with his Hollywood smash *Basic Instinct* (1992), but that far glossier film failed to recapture the humor and twisted energy of *The Fourth Man*. **JKl**

**U.S.** (Fox, Embassy) 101m Technicolor

**Director:** Martin Scorsese

**Producer:** Arnon Milchan

**Screenplay:** Paul D. Zimmermann

**Photography:** Fred Schuler

**Music:** Robbie Robertson

**Cast:** Robert De Niro, Jerry Lewis, Diahnne Abbott, Sandra Bernhard, Shelley Hack, Ed Herlihy, Lou Brown, Loretta Tupper, Peter Potulski, Vinnie Gonzales, Whitey Ryan, Doc Lawless, Marta Heflin, Katherine Wallach, Charles Kaleina

**Cannes Film Festival:** Martin Scorsese nomination (Golden Palm)

# THE KING OF COMEDY (1983)

Coming after *Taxi Driver* (1976) and especially *Raging Bull* (1980), Martin Scorsese's *The King of Comedy* might initially seem comparatively light. But while Scorsese does play the strange tale of loser Rupert Pupkin (Robert De Niro) who is obsessed with becoming a television host, for laughs, there's a queasy uneasiness to the film.

De Niro's confident smile packs as much menace as his far more imposing creations, while his unpredictable stalker associate Masha (Sandra Bernhard) comes across as so disconnected from reality that her appearances exude an aura of anxiety. Both are colorful reminders of the lonely and perhaps dangerous characters that exist in the periphery of any urban center. Still, the crucial key to *The King of Comedy* is Jerry Lewis as TV host Jerry Langford, playing, after all those years as a patsy, more or less an arrogant, bitter, and jaded version of himself. Lewis's dramatic break from his goofy public persona blurs the difference between fact and fiction, further highlighting the delusions of Pupkin and Masha. But Scorsese seems equally interested in the power and pitfalls of fame in general, offering *The King of Comedy* as a scathing indictment of the way our society overvalues celebrity. **JKl**

# THE RIGHT STUFF (1983)

High expectations for this celebratory, epic three-hour drama of America's early manned space program, with its ensemble of actors on the verge of stardom (Ed Harris, Dennis Quaid, and, in a small comic-relief role, Jeff Goldblum among them), were disappointed by its modest box-office return against a hefty budget. But writer-director Philip Kaufman's offbeat take on the heroics and striking treatment of the visuals saw *The Right Stuff* rewarded with eight Academy Award nominations (including Best Picture) and four wins, and an appreciative cult of admirers for whom the film's aerial and Earth-orbiting space sequences remain sheer bliss.

Adapted from Tom Wolfe's best-selling, tough, touching, and tale-telling nonfiction chronicle of the Mercury astronauts, the film contrasts the courageous but comparatively unsung exploits of sound-barrier-breaking test pilot Chuck Yaeger (Sam Shepard perfectly cast as the laid-back, ruggedly individualistic fly boy) with the selection, training, and media parading of more competitive, crewcut-wearing jocks into an elite, all-American cadre with "the right stuff." The admiring but good-humored and realistic, warts-and-all portrayals of the pilots is set against a distinctly satiric view of the Cold War's space race, with politicians desperate to minimize the Soviets' aerospace achievements by endangering and aggrandizing a batch of instant apple pie heroes.

There are many memorable moments: A race to find the crashed Yaeger has a searcher point to a speck and ask uncertainly "Is that a man?", cuts to the charred figure striding manfully from the smoking wreckage, and back to Yaeger's buddy (The Band's Levon Helm, also the film's narrator) exulting "You're damn right it is!"; Alan Shepard (Scott Glenn), equally anxious to pee and to make history while his vigil in the capsule atop a Saturn rocket is torturously protracted, John Glenn's (Harris) orbital flight graced with a mystical slant and a nail-biting reentry that explodes into his triumphal ticker-tape parade; Quaid's cocky, grinning Gordo Cooper awed by the "heavenly light" glowing across his helmet. The picture is consistently thrilling, including its use of Gustav Holst's powerful orchestral work *The Planets* with Bill Conti's exhilarating, Oscar-winning score.
**AE**

**U.S.** (The Ladd Co.) 193m Technicolor
**Director:** Philip Kaufman
**Producer:** Robert Chartoff, Irwin Winkler
**Screenplay:** Philip Kaufman, from book by Tom Wolfe
**Photography:** Caleb Deschanel
**Music:** Bill Conti
**Nonoriginal music:** Gustave Holst
**Cast:** Sam Shepard, Scott Glenn, Ed Harris, Dennis Quaid, Fred Ward, Barbara Hershey, Kim Stanley, Veronica Cartwright, Pamela Reed, Scott Paulin, Charles Frank, Lance Henriksen, Donald Moffat, Levon Helm, Mary Jo Deschanel
**Oscar:** Jay Boekelheide (special sound effects), Glenn Farr, Lisa Fruchtman, Stephen A. Rotter, Douglas Stewart, Tom Rolf (editing), Bill Conti (music), Mark Berger, Thomas Scott, Randy Thom, David MacMillan (sound)
**Oscar nomination:** Irwin Winkler, Robert Chartoff (best picture), Sam Shepard (actor in support role), Geoffrey Kirkland, Richard Lawrence, W. Stewart Campbell, Peter R. Romero, Jim Poynter, George R. Nelson (art direction), Caleb Deschanel (photography)

**U.S.** (Institute for Regional Education, Santa Fe) 87m Color

**Language:** English / Hopi

**Director:** Godfrey Reggio

**Producer:** Godfrey Reggio

**Screenplay:** Ron Fricke, Michael Hoenig, Godfrey Reggio, Alton Walpole

**Photography:** Ron Fricke

**Music:** Philip Glass, Michael Hoenig

**Berlin International Film Festival:** Godfrey Reggio nomination (Golden Bear)

# KOYAANISQATSI (1983)

As if a movie like *Koyaanisqatsi* weren't adventurous enough in its own right—an avant-garde feature with no story, nonstop minimalist music, and a serious sociopolitical message—director Godfrey Reggio announced from the start that this 1983 production was only the initial phase of a *qatsi* trilogy, all of which would be shot on commercial-grade 35mm film and aimed at mainstream theatrical release.

The series didn't continue until *Powaqqatsi* opened in 1988, and funding problems prevented Reggio from finishing it until 2002, when *Naqoyqatsi* finally arrived. Although all three installments have admirers, *Koyaanisqatsi* is easily the most fully realized of the bunch, retaining its power to tease the mind, tantalize the eye, and enchant the ear.

The film is rooted in three bold ideas. One is Reggio's wish to devise a new kind of sensuous, alluring cinema in which all the key creative partners—cinematographer Ron Fricke, composer Philip Glass, and himself as director—would be equal partners, making equal contributions to the finished film. Another is his conviction that general audiences will support nonnarrative cinema if it presents important ideas in an appealing, unpretentious manner. The third is his commitment to the message at the heart of the trilogy: That nature and culture have lost their ancient equilibrium in the modern era, and may spin out of control if humanity doesn't wake up to the dangers generated by its technological hubris.

True to its title—a word meaning "life out of balance" in the Hopi Indian language—the kaleidoscopic *Koyaanisqatsi* presents images of a world rendered incipiently unstable by all manner of human activities. The most memorable sequences use a diverse array of cinematic devices, from anamorphic lenses and freewheeling montage to time-lapse photography and varying camera speeds, to portray the world in fresh, original terms meant to spark fresh, original thinking about ecological and environmental issues.

Reggio's vision borrows important elements from earlier experimental filmmakers—the influences of Stan Brakhage and Hilary Harris are especially hard to miss—while reaching out to a wider audience than any avant-gardist had attracted before. The ongoing appeal of *Koyaanisqatsi* shows how well he succeeded. **DS**

# ONCE UPON A TIME IN AMERICA (1983)

Sergio Leone spent so much time luring actors to Italy for his spectacular string of Westerns that the setting of *Once Upon a Time in America* marked a radical change. Rather than the wide open spaces of the desert, Leone constructed an elaborate reproduction of New York's Lower East Side, the setting of his multigenerational story of Jewish gangsters (a wholly different kind of gunslinger) crossing paths and clashing over the years.

Beginning during Prohibition and leading up to the late 1960s, the film follows partners-in-crime Robert De Niro and James Woods as two gangland leaders whose different approaches inevitably lead to conflict. Noodles (De Niro) is quieter and prone to depression, whereas Max (Woods) is his hotheaded opposite. The film tracks the pair at three specific dates—1921, 1933, and 1968—and each time we catch up with the characters we are reminded of their inability to change.

At nearly four hours long, *Once Upon a Time in America* is Leone's longest and most languorous film. The patient narrative drifts along with the same narcotic haze of the opium den where Noodles reflects on his wayward life. As usual, Leone pays close attention to period details and composition, once again emphasizing his preference for the power of images over dialogue. His story plays out in simmering glances, scurrilous squinting, and barely concealed sneers. Helping this elegiac mood piece along is yet another brilliant score from longtime Leone collaborator Ennio Morricone, whose conspicuous use of the pan flute somehow suits the material.

Alas, Leone died shortly after the production of *Once Upon a Time in America*, but the film proved a fascinating conclusion to an iconic career. Lacking some of the force and invention of his more visceral and stylish Spaghetti Westerns, it nonetheless offers a different set of distinct pleasures, slower paced, but still representative of the director's unerring good taste and confident control of filmmaking's every parameter. **JKl**

**U.S. / Italy** (Embassy, PSO, Rafran, Warner Bros., Wishbone) 227m Technicolor

**Director:** Sergio Leone

**Producer:** Arnon Milchan

**Screenplay:** Leonardo Benvenuti, Piero De Bernardi, Enrico Medioli, Franco Arcalli, Franco Ferrini, Sergio Leone, Ernesto Gastaldi, from the novel *The Hoods* by Harry Grey

**Photography:** Tonino Delli Colli

**Music:** Ennio Morricone

**Cast:** Robert De Niro, James Woods, Elizabeth McGovern, Treat Williams, Tuesday Weld, Joe Pesci, Burt Young, Danny Aiello, William Forsythe, James Hayden, Darlanne Fluegel, Larry Rapp, Dutch Miller, Robert Harper, Richard Bright

# SCARFACE (1983)

Brian De Palma's updated remake of Howard Hawks's 1932 gangster classic *Scarface* is bloody, excessive, outrageous, and brilliantly crafted—and it sports an unforgettably histrionic performance from Al Pacino. When it first appeared, the film seemed like a striking departure for De Palma, away from Hitchcockian games with voyeurs, rear windows, and doppelgängers. Seen today, *Scarface* is quintessential De Palma, a treatise on the fragile conditions of male selfhood and power politics.

The film begins with documentary footage detailing the wave of Cuban refugees flooding into North America—adding a political dimension that completely transforms the template provided by Hawks's original. Tony Montana (Pacino) quickly realizes that crime and murder are his best ways out of the immigrant ghetto. His rise and fall as a modern gangster is rendered in a spectacular, garish style: De Palma takes every opportunity to heighten the fashions and musical crazes of the 1970s as a counterpoint to all the bloodshed and betrayal.

Commentators rushed to dub this take on Hawks's original (scripted by Oliver Stone) the first "postmodern" gangster epic. Tony even talks about himself in terms that recall Robert Warshow's classic essay "The Gangster as Tragic Hero"—"You need me, I'm the bad guy!". Yet, for all its dazzling self-consciousness, this is a grand narrative in the old style—and its cathartic, apocalyptic kick is tremendous.

De Palma takes to a new, melodramatic extreme one of the classic themes of the gangster genre: The hero's obsession with territorial control and the inexorable loss of this power. Tony dreams of absolute command—over his own body, over the hearts and allegiances of those close to him, and over the turf of his criminal empire. But after snorting mountains of cocaine, he cannot even see, on his own security cameras, those who come to kill him.

More than any disaster film made since the '70s, De Palma's controversial masterpiece gives us the subversive thrill of seeing a social microcosm explode into a thousand fragments—and all the while, a blimp flies above, heralding a bitterly mocking slogan in neon: "The World is Yours." **AM**

**U.S.** (Universal) 170m Technicolor
**Language:** English / Spanish
**Director:** Brian De Palma
**Producer:** Martin Bregman
**Screenplay:** Oliver Stone, from the novel *Armitage Trail* and 1932 screenplay *Scarface* by Howard Hawks
**Photography:** John A. Alonzo
**Music:** Giorgio Moroder
**Cast:** Al Pacino, Steven Bauer, Michelle Pfeiffer, Mary Elizabeth Mastrantonio, Robert Loggia, Miriam Colon, F. Murray Abraham, Paul Shenar, Harris Yulin, Ángel Salazar, Arnaldo Santana, Pepe Serna, Michael P. Moran, Al Israel, Dennis Holahan

# NARAYAMA BUSHI-KO (1983)
## THE BALLAD OF NARAYAMA

This strange film chronicles the lives and deaths of the inhabitants of a remote village, hidden in a mountainous region of 19th-century Japan. At age 70, each villager must be carried on a male relative's back over a rugged mountain path to the burial ground at Narayama, and left there to die.

*The Ballad of Narayama* centers around one family headed by a matriarch, Orin (Sumiko Sakamoto), who is approaching her 70th birthday. Director Shohei Imamura portrays village life both unsparingly and surrealistically, revealing the unvarnished desires and hardships that drive the villagers. In a time of famine, when a family takes more than their fair share of the food, they are buried alive. A sexually frustrated young man, unable to get a woman, finds relief with a neighbor's dog. The village and Orin's family are revealed like this, vividly existing in a brutal hand-to-mouth existence.

In the film's last segment, Orin reaches her 70th birthday and her oldest son, Tatsuhei (Ken Ogata), must carry her to Narayama. The trip over steep mountain passes is even more difficult than life in the village. As the journey continues Tatsuhei doggedly perseveres, and Orin gracefully faces her mortality. We come to realize that the fulfillment of this extravagantly useless ritual is what makes the villagers human. **RH**

**Japan** (Toei)130m Color

**Language:** Japanese

**Director:** Shohei Imamura

**Producer:** Goro Kusakabe, Jiro Tomoda

**Screenplay:** Shohei Imamura, from the novel *Narayama Bushi-Ko* by Shichirô Fukazawa

**Photography:** Masao Tochizawa

**Music:** Shinichirô Ikebe

**Cast:** Ken Ogata, Sumiko Sakamoto, Takejo Aki, Tonpei Hidari, Seiji Kurasaki, Kaoru Shimamori, Ryutaro Tatsumi, Junko Takada, Nijiko Kiyokawa, Mitsuko Baisho

**Cannes Film Festival:** Shohei Imamura (Golden Palm)

# AMADEUS (1984)

Czech director Milos Forman's casting of American Tom Hulce as the giggling Austrian composer Wolfgang Amadeus Mozart contrasts with the opulent sets and period details on display throughout the epic biopic *Amadeus*. But Hulce's wild, over-the-top performance as the brilliant enfant terrible jibes with the theory that larger-than-life music must flow from a larger-than-life personality.

Hulce cavorts and parades around as if anachronistically acknowledging the silliness of his frilly frocks and colored wigs. Nevertheless, he helps to propel the film forward at such a brisk pace that his clownish attitude and Yank accent hardly matter. Adapted by Peter Shaffer from his own play, *Amadeus* sets Mozart's effortless creative strides against the simplistic compositions of his envy-ridden rival Salieri (played by an appropriately sour F. Murray Abraham). Salieri's bitterness is introduced for laughs, whereas Mozart is depicted as a womanizing fool. Yet the proof is in the latter's achievements, as revealed via the film's thunderous score and a generous staging of *Don Giovanni*. Although seeing even a portion of such a stirring work in the context of what amounts to a piece of pop art may seem strange, that may also be the point. Forman seems nothing if not intent on contemporizing the life and accomplishments of one of history's greatest fonts of genius. **JKl**

**U.S.** (Saul Zaentz) 160m Color

**Director:** Milos Forman

**Producer:** Saul Zaentz

**Screenplay:** Peter Shaffer, from his play

**Photography:** Miroslav Ondrícek

**Nonoriginal music:** Johann Sebastian Bach, Wolfgang Amadeus Mozart, Antonio Salieri

**Cast:** F. Murray Abraham, Tom Hulce, Elizabeth Berridge, Simon Callow, Roy Dotrice, Christine Ebersole, Jeffrey Jones, Charles Kay, Kenny Baker

**Oscar:** Saul Zaentz (best picture), Milos Forman (director), Peter Shaffer (screenplay), F. Murray Abraham (actor), Patrizia von Brandenstein, Karel Cerny (art direction), Theodor Pistek (costume), Paul LeBlanc, Dick Smith (makeup), Mark Berger, Thomas Scott, Todd Boekelheide, Christopher Newman (sound)

**Oscar nomination:** Tom Hulce (actor), Miroslav Ondrícek (photography), Nena Danevic, Michael Chandler (editing)

**U.S.** (Cinema 84, Euro Film Fund, Hemdale, Pacific Western) 108m Color

**Language:** English / Spanish

**Director:** James Cameron

**Producer:** Gale Anne Hurd

**Screenplay:** James Cameron, Gale Anne Hurd, from the screenplays *Soldier* and *Demon with a Glass Hand* by Harlan Ellison

**Photography:** Adam Greenberg

**Music:** Brad Fiedel

**Cast:** Arnold Schwarzenegger, Michael Biehn, Linda Hamilton, Paul Winfield, Lance Henriksen, Rick Rossovich, Bess Motta, Earl Boen, Dick Miller, Shawn Schepps, Bruce M. Kerner, Franco Columbu, Bill Paxton, Brad Rearden, Brian Thompson

# THE TERMINATOR (1984)

This potential grade-Z kitsch candidate for the Golden Turkey Award actually became one of the surprise hits of 1984, and its popularity over the last two decades has established it as a genre classic. *The Terminator* is a triumph of style over plot, smartness over intelligence, and a combination of elements that outstrips its parts. Its circular narrative about the future trying to control the past in order to take control of itself—hence, changing the very premises of its own state—is a familiar one to all fans of postwar science-fiction literature (Harlan Ellison, Philip K. Dick, and others) and TV shows (such as *Outer Limits* and *Star Trek*).

Fresh from low-budget effects work for Roger Corman and John Carpenter, director-screenwriter James Cameron adapted the disarming humor of his mentors to deflect all possible objections to the film's many plot holes, head-on with a dumbfounded shrug or knowing wisecracks from the protagonists. The vision of a dark, dirty, and apocalyptic future was very much in vogue at the time, as witnessed by titles such as John Carpenter's *Escape from New York*, George Miller's *Mad Max II/The Road Warrior* (both 1981), Luc Besson's *The Last Combat* (1983), and Lars von Trier's *The Element of Crime* (1984).

Cameron's assured style—tech noir, as it was called after a nightclub in the film—and his kinetic energy combined with a sparse economy of narration in enfolding the many twists and turns, keep the viewer sufficiently distracted from the sheer absurdity of it all. Even Arnold Schwarzenegger—the very epitome of bad acting with his bland facial expression, heavy Austrian accent, and body language from the school of Frankenstein's monster—becomes a major asset to the film. All his violent acts and his ten or so lines are delivered with a mechanical dullness and a mock-grim look that makes them charged with an irresistible, multilayered irony. Virtually all his dialogue consists of short, unremarkable phrases. Yet, everybody who saw this sleeper phenomenon knows most of them by heart, down to Schwarzenegger's quirky pronunciation. "I'll be back" is probably the most quoted among them—frequently used as a catchphrase in radio and TV shows.

If *The Terminator*'s ability to engage the audience in such an interplay is reminiscent of *The Rocky Horror Picture Show*'s (1975) ritualistic cult following, then the nudging irony and frequent winks to the audience points forward to the *Scream* trilogy's (1999–2000) puns about generic clichés. The same goes for the sadistic but playful slapstick splatter-violence and the "final girl" twist at the end. Under the surface of this bric-a-brac of science-fiction elements actually lies an even less original slasher movie, complete with a (literally) mechanical killer and a tomboy (Linda Hamilton) discovering her resources to fight and overcome evil. But, as I remarked above, *The Terminator*'s unique combination strategy is greater than the sum of its parts. The response to the film, like that to all great genre movies, lies not in a presumed originality. Rather the opposite is true: It is in the way that the director fuses all these familiar elements and breathes new life into them that makes for such a memorable experience. **MT**

**G.B. / France / West Germany** (Fox, Argos, Channel Four, Pro-ject, Road Movies, WDR) 147m Color

**Director:** Wim Wenders

**Producer:** Anatole Dauman, Don Guest

**Screenplay:** L.M. Kit Carson, Sam Shepard

**Photography:** Robby Müller

**Music:** Ry Cooder

**Cast:** Harry Dean Stanton, Nastassja Kinski, Dean Stockwell, Aurore Clément, Hunter Carson, Socorro Valdez, Bernhard Wicki

**Cannes Film Festival:** Wim Wenders (Golden Palm), (prize of the ecumenical jury), (FIPRESCI award), tied with *Taxidi sta Kithira*

# PARIS, TEXAS (1984)

Who is that walking man? Travis (Harry Dean Stanton in his best role) emerges from the vast Texan desert, to the haunting strains of Ry Cooder's slide guitar. Instantly the possibility of a story seizes us: Where did he come from, where is he going? It turns out that Travis is fleeing a catastrophic family breakdown that left his wife, Jane (Nastassja Kinski), who has also since disappeared, and his young son, Hunter (Hunter Carson), in the care of Travis's brother, Walt (Dean Stockwell).

Travis does not want to stop walking. Walt and others slowly bring him back to language, to sociability, to a remembrance of home and belonging. But nothing will be right until Travis finds Jane. He discovers her in a strip club where she acts as a therapist to the often troubled and lonely customers. In a touching scene, he tells her his own story through a one-way mirror—he can see Jane but she is unable to see him.

Wim Wenders here made one of the archetypal films of the 1980s. His European, aesthetic vision—carried most powerfully by the landscape cinematography of Robby Müller—meshed perfectly with the American sensibility of writer Sam Shepard. It is an affecting story of "otherness," a man who cannot fit into the "symbolic order." In the course of his tentative reentry into civilization, Travis naturally bonds with other outsiders, such as a Latin American maid who teaches him eccentric lessons in dress and manners, and especially Hunter, with whom he shares a charmingly childlike rapport.

*Paris, Texas* was a pivotal film for Wenders. Just as Travis negotiates gingerly his relationship with society, Wenders was slowly coming to terms with the act of storytelling in cinema—an obligation he had hitherto suspended in the wandering, episodic era of his German-language *Alice in the Cities* (1974) and *Kings of the Road* (1976). He was also bringing himself to contemplate traditional values of marriage, family, and community. For some, he subsequently went too far in his embrace of both conventional cinema and traditional values. But *Paris, Texas*, like *Wings of Desire* (1987) captures the best of both phases in Wenders's career, both the longing for home and the recognition of a difficult, modern alienation from it. **AM**

# A NIGHTMARE ON ELM STREET (1984)

Wes Craven's signature film, *A Nightmare on Elm Street* was at once a critical and commercial success that managed to creatively combine horror and humor, Gothic literary motifs and slasher movie conventions, gory special effects and subtle social commentary. And it let loose a new monster in America's pop cultural consciousness: That wisecracking, fedora-wearing teen killer, Freddy Krueger.

Craven's first two films, *Last House on the Left* (1972) and *The Hills Have Eyes* (1977), had established the former English professor as a low-budget horror auteur along the lines of Tobe Hooper and George Romero. After his next few works failed to live up to this early potential, Craven developed the idea of a killer who claims his victims in their own dreams. Made for less than $2 million, *A Nightmare on Elm Street* was cast with unknown and B-movie actors (including a 21-year-old Johnny Depp in his film debut) and was completed in just 32 days. Not bad for a movie that would gross over $25 million at the box office, and which has inspired six sequels to date, making it one of the most profitable series in the history of horror cinema.

The film opens inside a surrealistic basement-cum-workshop, where a hideously scarred man wearing a red-and-green sweater and crusty old hat welds razor-sharp blades to metal fingertips and attaches these to a battered leather glove. As events unfold and long-repressed secrets are revealed, we learn that this inhuman dream invader is Freddy Krueger (Robert Englund), a former child killer who was burned to death by a mob of furious Elm Street parents after being released from prison on a technicality. Years later, Freddy has returned from the grave as evil incarnate, obsessed with taking revenge on the adolescent offspring of those who ended his mortal life. Residing in his young victims' subconscious, attacking them while they sleep, Freddy is virtually omnipotent, capable of rewriting the laws of physics and effecting all manner of grotesque yet creative killings. The film's spectacular set pieces, laden with special effects wizardry and gallons of fake blood, are balanced by an anxiety-inducing score and a gripping narrative, as we feel for the intended victims in their hopeless battle to stay awake.

Unlike earlier slasher films like *Halloween* (1978) and *Friday the 13th* (1980), *A Nightmare on Elm Street*'s monster-murderer is less a silent death machine than an archetypal "evil trickster," a kind of gothic antihero, a vicious killer who with charm, sense of humor, and flair for the dramatic, proves appealing to viewers. *Nightmare* combines elements of gothic literature—the seductive villain, the terrible place, the emphasis on dreams and subjective vision—with elements of the generic slasher movie—victims picked off one by one, the indestructible killer, the resourceful and virginal female survivor. **SJS**

**U.S.** (Media Home Entertainment, New Line, Smart Egg) 91m Color

**Director:** Wes Craven

**Producer:** Robert Shaye

**Screenplay:** Wes Craven

**Photography:** Jacques Haitkin

**Music:** Charles Bernstein, Steve Karshner, Martin Kent, Michael Schurig

**Cast:** John Saxon, Ronee Blakley, Heather Langenkamp, Amanda Wyss, Jsu Garcia, Johnny Depp, Charles Fleischer, Joseph Whipp, Robert Englund, Lin Shaye, Joe Unger, Mimi Craven, Jack Shea, Ed Call, Sandy Lipton

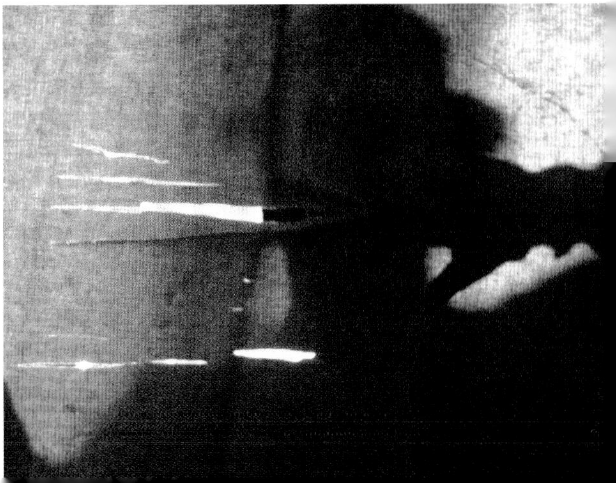

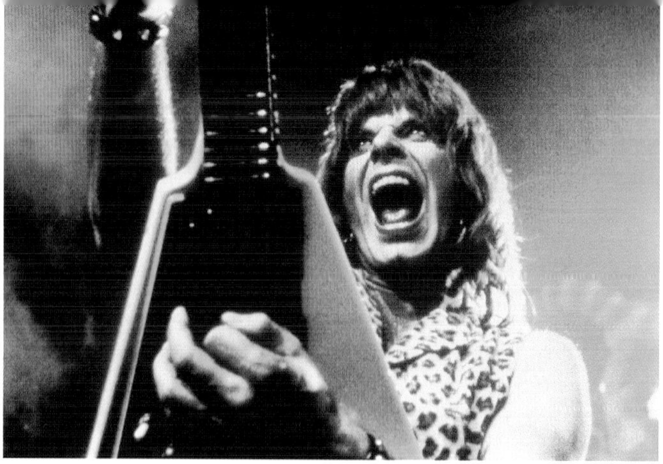

U.S. (Spinal Tap Prod.) 82m Color

**Director:** Rob Reiner

**Producer:** Karen Murphy

**Screenplay:** Christopher Guest, Michael McKean, Rob Reiner, Harry Shearer

**Photography:** Peter Smokler

**Music:** Christopher Guest, Michael McKean, Rob Reiner, Harry Shearer

**Cast:** Rob Reiner, Kimberly Stringer, Chazz Domingueza, Shari Hall, R.J. Parnell, David Kaff, Tony Hendra, Michael McKean, Christopher Guest, Harry Shearer, Bruno Kirby, Jean Cromie, Patrick Maher, Ed Begley Jr., Danny Kortchmar

# THIS IS SPINAL TAP (1984)

Rob Reiner's made-up documentary (if you will, "mockumentary") dances on that "fine line between stupid and clever," taking elements from real rock docs (*Don't Look Back*, *The Last Waltz*) and creating a new genre (later examples include *The Blair Witch Project* and *Bob Roberts*). *Tap* fans treasure favorite routines and lines: Derek Smalls (Harry Shearer) trapped in a stage pod or setting off an airport metal detector with the foil-wrapped pickle in his underpants; the band getting lost backstage as they try to reach an eager audience ("Hello, Cleveland!"); the undersized Stonehenge triptych descending to be "in danger of being crushed by a dwarf"; the blank looks of the band when confronted with their backlist of bad reviews or a radio DJ's classification of Spinal Tap as "currently residing in the 'Where Are They Now?' file"; the arguments over the offensive cover of the "Smell the Glove" album; Nigel's (Christopher Guest) tour of his guitar and amp collection ("These go to eleven"); "It's called 'Lick My Love Pump'."

And it's a collection of masterly cameos, from Fran Drescher as publicist Bobbi Flekman (her clones are still working in the business) to Bruno Kirby as the Sinatra-loving limo driver, with microbits from Billy Crystal and Dana Carvey as mime waiters ("Mime is money!"). Copping the Yoko thread from the 1970 film *Let It Be*, *Spinal Tap* delivers a genuine plot as childhood friends David St. Hubbins (Michael McKean) and Nigel Tufnel fall out when David's girlfriend Jeanine Pettibone (June Chadwick) worms her way into the band as manager, displacing the long-suffering Ian Faith (Tony Hendra), who memorably characterizes the dim girl as dressing "like an Australian's nightmare." It's an achievement that after an hour of jokes at the expense of the crassness and stupidity of Spinal Tap, with hideously accurate parodies of the strutting pretensions of the dinosaurs of rock ("Big Bottoms," "Sex Farm"), the film can manage to wring some emotion out of the threat that the band will break up. McKean, whose London accent is letter-perfect, has a great acting moment as he becomes so angry and hurt at his friend's betrayal that he can hardly speak. **KN**

## BEVERLY HILLS COP (1984)

What a different movie *Beverly Hills Cop* would have been had Sylvester Stallone, who was originally attached to the project, been the lead actor. The violent action would have been far bloodier no doubt, while the film would have lacked the rapid-fire comedy of its star, Eddie Murphy, that made it such a worldwide smash.

Murphy stars as Axel Foley, a smart-talking, streetwise Detroit cop who—like all the best movie cops—doesn't play by the rules. When an old friend is murdered, he heads to Los Angeles to unofficially investigate the crime, and inevitably causes a major upset among the Beverly Hills police department (who presumably spend most of their time arresting celebrities for minor misdemeanors) in the process.

Backed by a pop soundtrack and Harold Faltemeyer's annoyingly infectious "Axel F" theme, director Martin Brest (*Midnight Run*, *Scent of a Woman*) delivers a fast-paced fish-out-of-water action comedy that takes a few sharp digs at the all-style-and-no-substance LA lifestyle, while making the most of a charismatic star, who has never been better. Many police comedy/action movies have followed, including two sequels also featuring Murphy, but none have felt as fresh as this one. **JB**

**U.S.** (Paramount) 105m Technicolor

**Director:** Martin Brest

**Producer:** Jerry Bruckheimer, Don Simpson

**Screenplay:** Daniel Petrie Jr, Danilo Bach

**Photography:** Bruce Surtees

**Music:** Harold Faltermeyer

**Cast:** Eddie Murphy, Judge Reinhold, John Ashton, Lisa Eilbacher, Ronny Cox, Steven Berkoff, James Russo, Jonathan Banks, Stephen Elliott, Gilbert R. Hill, Art Kimbro, Joel Bailey, Bronson Pinchot, Paul Reiser, Michael Champion

**Oscar nomination:** Daniel Petrie Jr, Danilo Bach (screenplay)

## GHOST BUSTERS (1984)

Big-budget special effects and comedy are cleverly interwoven in this fantasy adventure written by two of the movie's stars, Harold Ramis and Dan Aykroyd. With Bill Murray they play a trio of paranormal "experts"—in reality, they are lazy, wisecracking ex-science professors, kicked off campus for their antics—who set up a ghost-busting business from an abandoned New York City firehouse. Their timing couldn't be better as the city is suddenly bursting with paranormal activity causing ghostly apparitions to run riot, terrorizing visitors to the library, ransacking an upscale hotel, and even taking up residence in a skeptical Sigourney Weaver's refrigerator.

Although Ramis (the serious, scientific nerd of the group), and Aykroyd (the bumbling dimwit), along with costars Weaver and Rick Moranis (as the "Key Master"), all have superb comic timing here, it is Murray's Dr. Peter Venkman, with his character's sleazy charm and cockiness, who steals every scene in *Ghost Busters*. And that is an impressive achievement indeed when you consider that his special effects costars include a gigantic, stampeding marshmallow man intent on reducing Manhattan to a pile of sugary rubble that would steal the movie away from a less skilled comic talent. **JB**

**U.S.** (Black Rhino, Columbia) 107m Metrocolor

**Director:** Ivan Reitman

**Producer:** Ivan Reitman

**Screenplay:** Dan Aykroyd, Harold Ramis

**Photography:** László Kovács

**Music:** Tom Bailey, Elmer Bernstein, Alannah Currie, Joe Leeway, Brian O'Neal, Kevin O'Neal, Ray Parker Jr, Diane Warren

**Cast:** Bill Murray, Dan Aykroyd, Sigourney Weaver, Harold Ramis, Rick Moranis, Annie Potts, William Atherton, Ernie Hudson, David Margulies, Steven Tash, Jennifer Runyon, Slavitza Jovan, Michael Ensign, Alice Drummond, Jordan Charney

**Oscar nomination:** Richard Edlund, John Bruno, Mark Vargo, Chuck Gaspar (special visual effects), Ray Parker Jr (song)

# A PASSAGE TO INDIA (1984)

David Lean's final film finds him just as obsessed with working with the widescreen tableau that defined *Lawrence of Arabia*, *The Bridge on the River Kwai*, and *Doctor Zhivago*, but *A Passage to India* (admittedly, not shot in 'Scope) is clearly more a movie of ideas than a movie of spectacle. More or less faithfully adapting E. M. Forster's story of class and cultural conflict in colonial India, the film by necessity loses some of the internalized thrust of the multi-perspective novel, and therefore misses some of the nuance of its characters' various motivations. Additionally, *A Passage to India* sometimes comes across as a story of mystery and vague sexual hysteria rather than a biting bid adieu to British colonialism. But in the hands of Lean—ever the consummate craftsman—the film blazes by, and if he too often relies on frequent collaborator Alec Guinness (conspicuously cast as an Indian) for humor and James Fox to make obvious the movie's themes, Lean's respect for the script and his actors allows them to transcend the sometimes fetishistic depiction of India.

Particularly strong is the wan Judy Davis, who in her search for the "real" India—the India neither homogenized nor shunned by her fellow Brits—gets more than she bargained for in the form of Victor Banerjee, whose obsequious and oblivious Dr. Aziz sparks in the mind of Davis's naïve Ms. Quested a primal aversion to "going native." As the relentless heat, claustrophobia, and chattering monkeys wear down Quested's banal enthusiasm, she grows increasingly unstable, leading to an encounter in the echo-enhancing Marabar caves that results in Aziz being accused of rape.

If Forster's collision of psychology and colonialism comes across almost as an afterthought, the film's disdain for English condescension ultimately lends the trial of Dr. Aziz an ironic inevitability, *A Passage to India* ends on an appropriately and satisfyingly ambivalent note, implying that some of the film's central characters still haven't learned their lesson. It's not as forceful or thought-provoking a conclusion as it could (or should) have been, but the film remains a strong effort all the same, and a fine conclusion to an illustrious career. **JKl**

**G.B.** (EMI, HBO, Thorn-EMI) 163m Technicolor

**Director:** David Lean

**Producer:** John Brabourne, Richard B. Goodwin.

**Screenplay:** David Lean, from novel by E.M. Forster

**Photography:** Ernest Day

**Music:** John Dalby, Maurice Jarre

**Cast:** Judy Davis, Victor Banerjee, Peggy Ashcroft, James Fox, Alec Guinness, Nigel Havers, Richard Wilson, Antonia Pemberton, Michael Culver, Art Malik, Saeed Jaffrey, Clive Swift, Anne Firbank, Roshan Seth, Sandra Hotz

**Oscar:** Peggy Ashcroft (actress in support role), Maurice Jarre (music)

**Oscar nomination:** John Brabourne, Richard N. Goodwin (best picture), David Lean (director), David Lean (screenplay), Judy Davis (actress), John Box, Hugh Scaife (art direction), Ernest Day (photography), Judy Moorcroft (costume), David Lean (editing), Graham V. Hartstone, Nicolas Le Messurier, Michael A. Carter, John W. Mitchell (sound)

# STRANGER THAN PARADISE (1984)

**U.S. / West Germany** (Cinesthesia, Grokenberger, ZDF) 89m BW
**Language:** English / Hungarian
**Director:** Jim Jarmusch
**Producer:** Sara Driver
**Screenplay:** Jim Jarmusch
**Photography:** Tom DiCillo
**Music:** John Lurie, Screamin' Jay Hawkins
**Cast:** John Lurie, Eszter Balint, Richard Edson, Cecillia Stark, Danny Rosen, Rammellzee, Tom DiCillo, Richard Boes, Rockets Redglare, Harvey Perr, Brian J. Burchill, Sara Driver, Paul Sloane
**Cannes Film Festival:** Jim Jarmusch (Golden Camera)

Several films down the line and Jim Jarmusch's modus operandi now seems pretty clear. His films reveal not just the way different cultures intersect, overlap, and interact in the modern world, but how, given the erosion of international borders, those differences often pale compared to the traits we all have in common. Regardless, *Stranger Than Paradise* is as weird as it is wonderful, a striking debut from a fiercely independent filmmaker.

Though it doesn't have much of a plot, *Stranger Than Paradise* is anything but loose. Willie, a New York slacker (played by musician John Lurie), is surprised by a visit from his Hungarian cousin Eva (Eszter Balint). Eva, stuck in his small apartment, then heads west to Cleveland to visit her Aunt Lotte (Cecillia Stark), and later, with nothing better to do, Willie and his pal Eddie (Richard Edson) follow her to Ohio. All three head to Florida together for one last stab at staving off boredom, but even the ocean can't stir them from their self-imposed stupor.

*Stranger Than Paradise* is like a parody of the American dream, with Eva's grass-is-always-greener view of the nation dashed by the harsh discovery that the States can be just as plain and uneventful as any other country. But Eva is the only one of the bunch willing to do anything about her stifling predicament. Willie and Eddie bring with them to Ohio, and then Florida, the same sense of monotony, like roving black holes sucking the life out of wherever they end up. Faced with such a fate, Eva has nothing better to do than escape, though Willie and Eddie realize she may be their own only escape as well.

Jarmusch sets most of his movie in claustrophobic rooms, keeping the camera relatively static as he captures the strange banalities of their exchanges. No one seems to be friends, yet since they're all in the same situation they make the most of their companionship. Nothing is keeping them in any one place, but then again nothing is drawing them out of their modest environs. Jarmusch's America seems like a vast cultural purgatory, and even the most ambitious of his characters don't seem especially eager to get out. **JKl**

**G.B.** (Enigma (First Casualty, Goldcrest, Intern'l Film Investors, Warner Bros.) 141m Color

**Language:** English / French / Khmer

**Director:** Roland Joffé

**Producer:** David Puttnam

**Screenplay:** Bruce Robinson

**Photography:** Chris Menges

**Music:** Mike Oldfield

**Nonoriginal music:** John Lennon, Paul McCartney, Giacomo Puccini, Francisco Tarrega

**Cast:** Sam Waterston, Haing S. Ngor, John Malkovich, Julian Sands, Craig T. Nelson, Spalding Gray, Bill Paterson, Athol Fugard, Graham Kennedy, Katherine Krapum Chey, Oliver Pierpaoli, Edward Entero Chey, Tom Bird, Monirak Sisowath, Lambool Dtangpaibool

**Oscar:** Haing S. Ngor (actor in support role), Chris Menges (photography), Jim Clark (editing)

**Oscar nomination:** David Puttnam (best picture), Roland Joffé (director), Bruce Robinson (screenplay), Sam Waterston (actor)

# THE KILLING FIELDS (1984)

Roland Joffé's morally earnest film depicting the disastrous aftermath of American involvement in Cambodian politics during the Vietnam War era offers a bravura performance by Sam Waterston as *New York Times* journalist Sydney Schanberg, whose dispatches from the country uncovered the dreadful results of the unacknowledged American bombing campaign against suspected communist bases.

*The Killing Fields* divides somewhat awkwardly into two parts, with Schanberg's brave, perhaps foolhardy decision to remain even after the Khmer Rouge take the country occupying the first part. Schanberg's Cambodian assistant, Dith Pran (Haing S. Ngor), assists the small group of Western journalists as they negotiate a series of harrowing encounters with the victors, but, despite their attempts to pass him off as a U.S. citizen, he is left behind when they leave. In the film's second part, Pran becomes the protagonist. With great ingenuity and fortitude, he endures harsh captivity and evades death, escaping through rice paddies filled with the corpses of his countrymen—the "killing fields" of the title—until he is brought to New York, there to be reunited with Schanberg. Although the film effectively evokes the atmosphere of terror, confusion, and dislocation that war brings, it does not dwell on international politics, but on the damage done to human dignity by impersonal violence. **BP**

**U.S.** (Delphi, TriStar) 134m Technicolor

**Director:** Barry Levinson

**Producer:** Mark Johnson

**Screenplay:** Roger Towne, Phil Dusenberry, from novel by Bernard Malamud

**Photography:** Caleb Deschanel

**Music:** Randy Newman

**Cast:** Robert Redford, Robert Duvall, Glenn Close, Kim Basinger, Wilford Brimley, Barbara Hershey, Robert Prosky, Richard Farnsworth, Joe Don Baker, John Finnegan, Alan Fudge, Paul Sullivan Jr., Rachel Hall, Robert Rich, Michael Madsen

**Oscar nomination:** Glenn Close (actress in support role), Mel Bourne , Angelo P. Graham, Bruce Weintraub (art direction), Caleb Deschanel (photography), Randy Newman (music)

# THE NATURAL (1984)

A baseball movie that succeeds in turning America's national pastime into a heroic myth, Barry Levinson's romantic adaptation of Bernard Malamud's novel traces the career of Roy Hobbs (Robert Redford), whose "gift" for the sport shows at an early age. Like all heroes, Hobbs acquires a magic weapon, a bat he makes from a tree hit by lightning and names "Wonder Boy." Though he shows great promise, his career is almost ended when a beautiful woman in black (Barbara Hershey), who sees his considerable talent, shoots him and then kills herself.

Roy becomes separated from Iris (Glenn Close), the good woman who loves him and bears his son, only, after years of drifting, to finally make it to the major leagues at age 38. There he struggles to get into the lineup of a last place team, which he soon turns around with his talent and charisma. Tempted by Memo (Kim Basinger), a big-city woman, Roy almost loses himself again, but in the end he not only rescues his team from defeat but is reunited with Iris and his son (the novel ends more bleakly, with Hobbs striking out).

Levinson's style is hardly realistic—Roy's final home run destroys a light tower and starts a storm of electric sparks—but the film features subtle, restrained performances from Redford and a fine ensemble cast (including Robert Duvall and Wilford Brimley). **BP**

# THE BREAKFAST CLUB (1985)

**U.S.** (A&M, Universal) 92m Technicolor

**Director:** John Hughes

**Producer:** John Hughes, Ned Tanen, Michelle Manning

**Screenplay:** John Hughes

**Photography:** Thomas Del Ruth

**Music:** Gary Chang, Wang Chung, Keith Forsey

**Cast:** Emilio Estevez, Paul Gleason, Anthony Michael Hall, John Kapelos, Judd Nelson, Molly Ringwald, Ally Sheedy, Perry Crawford, Mary Christian, Ron Dean, Tim Gamble, Fran Gargano, Mercedes Hall, John Hughes

In the 1960s, teen movies involved Frankie Avalon, Annette Funicello, lots of sand (no sex), and bouncy music, and in the 1970s being a teen was about being slaughtered in your bed in numerous horror movies. But in 1984 writer/director John Hughes revolutionized the teen genre with *Sixteen Candles*, and followed it a year later with *The Breakfast Club*, a movie credited with finally showing teens as they really speak and think.

No single film better epitomized the period, or has become more of a cult movie for teens, than *The Breakfast Club*, which not only made Hughes a name to watch—he went on to make the terrific *Ferris Bueller's Day Off* (1986) and hugely successful *Home Alone* (1990)—but also brought together a skilled group of young actors (as did Francis Coppola's *The Outsiders* two years before) that the media dubbed the "Brat Pack."

Five disparate teenagers are sentenced to a Saturday detention for various reasons and, despite their differences at the beginning of the day, have formed some sort of bond by the end. There's the school jock (Emilio Estevez), the weirdo with the heavy eye-liner (Ally Sheedy), the stuck-up princess (Molly Ringwald, a teen fave and muse of Hughes following her lead role in *Sixteen Candles*), the nerd (Anthony Michael Hall), and the rebel (Judd Nelson), all trying to entertain themselves under the watchful eye of anally-retentive teacher Vernon (Paul Gleason).

A film that relies on cleverly scripted banter rather than action, *The Breakfast Club* works in large part because of the characterizations of the cast as truths are revealed, grudges are aired, and each one gets their moment to shine. Much imitated in numerous films and TV series, this ultimate teen movie has never been bettered—be it because of its perfect timing, sharp performances, or the '80s time-capsule soundtrack, featuring that classic Simple Minds song (written for the film) "Don't You Forget About Me." **JB**

Japan / France (Greenwich, Herald Ace, Nippon Herald) 160m Color

**Language:** Japanese

**Director:** Akira Kurosawa

**Producer:** Masato Hara, Serge Silberman

**Screenplay:** Masato Ide, Akira Kurosawa, Hideo Ōguni, from the play *King Lear* by William Shakespeare

**Photography:** Asakazu Nakai, Takao Saitô, Masaharu Ueda

**Music:** Tôru Takemitsu

**Cast:** Tatsuya Nakadai, Akira Terao, Jinpachi Nezu, Daisuke Ryu, Mieko Harada, Yoshiko Miyazaki, Takashi Nomura, Hisashi Igawa, Peter, Masayuki Yui, Kazuo Kato, Norio Matsui, Toshiya Ito, Kenji Kodama, Takashi Watanabe

**Oscar:** Emi Wada (costume)

**Oscar nomination:** Akira Kurosawa (director), Yoshirô Muraki, Shinobu Muraki (art direction), Takao Saitô, Masaharu Ueda, Asakazu Nakai (photography)

# RAN (1985)

*Ran* was made at the time Akira Kurosawa was turning 75 years of age. It is important to understand the wisdom and artistry that those years brought to the creation of this film, quite possibly one of the greatest ever made. Of the 1,001 films one must see before dying, *Ran* is certainly in the top ten. The director has called it "a series of human events viewed from Heaven."

Kurosawa is unsurpassed in his mastery of film technique, and *Ran*'s battle sequences are unequaled to this day. They are like a cinematic ballet, violent and bloody yet filled with tremendous beauty. The story is adapted from Shakespeare's *King Lear*, combined with an ancient Japanese legend of three arrows. This decision moves the Bard's tragedy into distinctly new territory. Lear's daughters are now sons and the emphasis is on revenge rather than catharsis.

The performances range from brilliant to something resembling utter perfection. The standout without question is Mikeo Harada as Lady Kaede, one of Lord Hidetora's (Tatsuya Nakadai) daughters-in-law—watching her slink across the floor of her palace, her silk gowns rustling on the soundtrack, is unforgettable. Nakadai as Lord Hidetora displays a fierce defiance that melts into despair. And Lear's fool is transformed into the jester Kyoami, beautifully played by transvestite Shinnosuke Ikehata, an accomplished Noh actor—the makeup and much of *Ran*'s story is inspired by Noh drama and tradition.

Toru Takemitsu's minimalist score makes fine use of flute and percussion to accent the epic. A special emphasis is placed on silence during the battle scenes—a tactic far more effective than all the cannon roar of previous attempts at depicting war on screen.

*Ran* displays the wisdom of a lifetime in a "mere" two hours and forty minutes, during which time itself is simply suspended. As one character in the film declares, "Man is born crying; when he dies, enough, he dies." **DDV**

**U.S.S.R.** (Belarusfilm, Mosfilm, Sovexportfilm) 142m Color

**Language:** Russian

**Director:** Elem Klimov

**Screenplay:** Ales Adamovich, Elem Klimov

**Photography:** Aleksei Rodionov

**Music:** Oleg Yanchenko

**Nonoriginal music:** Wolfgang Amadeus Mozart, Richard Wagner

**Cast:** Aleksei Kravchenko, Olga Mironova, Liubomiras Lauciavicius, Vladas Bagdonas, Juris Lumiste, Viktor Lorents, Kazimir Rabetsky, Yevgeni Tilicheyev, Aleksandr Berda, G. Velts, V. Vasilyev, Igor Gnevashov, Vasili Domrachyov, G. Yelkin, Ye. Kryzhanovsky

# IDI I SMOTRI (1985)
## COME AND SEE

It's World War II in Belorussia, the countryside near the Polish border. A young boy (Aleksei Kravchenko) leaves his village to join the partisans fighting the invading Nazis. He gets separated from his unit and has to make his way home, only to find his entire village slaughtered, the bodies piled in a haphazard heap behind a farm. Lost, alone, and deafened, things can only get worse.

No other war movie matches Elem Klimov's *Come and See* for sheer nightmarish relentlessness. There is no plot, only a terrifying picaresque journey as the boy wanders the countryside and encounters one horrific scenario after another. There are no feats of heroism or sacrifice, nor any stirring jingoistic speeches exhorting the people to fight the enemy. There is only death and brutality and randomness and victimhood, where survival is utterly arbitrary, and possibly a cruel, cosmic joke.

You may ask why you should watch this movie, after the above description. The answer lies in the conviction and control Klimov exerts over the film and, thus, the viewer. There are surrealist tableaus at once alien and strangely familiar. There are bursts of visionary weirdness that take your breath away—a partisan soldier, using mud, sticks, and a discarded Nazi uniform, constructs a totem for a mob of grieving widows and mothers to attack and tear apart in an act of primitive violence and catharsis; or when a field is illuminated by enemy tracer fire, leaving the young hero with no place to take cover except behind a cow a pair a partisans had been fighting over as potential source for food. Events unfold like dream logic. There are moments when the movie switches to the boy's point of view and all sound collapses into a dull, hollow echo, duplicating his deafness after mortar shells explode around him.

Most war movies claim to be antiwar, but have their cake and eat it too by reveling in the gung-ho heroism of competent, can-do heroes. *Come and See* offers no such relief or comfort. It shows there are only victims in war. **AT**

# LA HISTORIA OFICIAL (1985)
## THE OFFICIAL STORY

After the military coup in Argentina in 1976, the forces of the state engaged in a so-called dirty war against civilian opposition. During this time thousands of people "disappeared" at the hands of the armed services and paramilitaries (estimates range between 9,000 and 30,000 deaths). Many of the children of these people were given away for adoption without their relatives' consent. *The Official Story* dramatizes these events in the story of Alicia (Norma Aleandro), a politically conservative high-school teacher of history who prefers to ignore pressing social conflicts in her version of Argentina's past. But she comes to suspect that her 5-year-old adopted daughter is the child of "disappeared" parents. It becomes clear that her husband Roberto (Héctor Alterio), a successful businessman, knows the whole story, and eventually Alicia confronts him.

Made in 1985, just after the collapse of military rule, Luis Puenzo's film is a brave attempt to face uncomfortable truths. Stylistically conventional, and the ending, in which Alicia's husband beats her, is fairly melodramatic, but the social anguish in *The Official Story* is certainly real. It was the film's political rather than artistic credentials that led the American Academy to award it the Oscar for Best Foreign Language Film. **EB**

**Argentina** (Hist. Cinemat., Progress Comm.) 112m Eastmancolor

**Language:** Spanish

**Director:** Luis Puenzo

**Producer:** Marcelo Piñeyro

**Screenplay:** Aída Bortnik, Luis Puenzo

**Photography:** Félix Monti

**Music:** Atilio Stampone

**Cast:** Héctor Alterio, Norma Aleandro, Chunchuna Villafane, Hugo Arana, Guillermo Battaglia, Chela Ruíz

**Oscar:** Argentina (best foreign language film)

**Oscar nomination:** Luis Puenzo, Aída Bortnik (screenplay)

**Berlin International Film Festival:** Luis Puenzo (Otto Dibelius film award)

**Cannes Film Festival:** Luis Puenzo (prize of the ecumenical jury), Norma Aleandro (actress), tied with Cher in *Mask*, Luis Puenzo nomination (Golden Palm)

# OUT OF AFRICA (1985)

Awesome landscapes nearly overpower this Best Picture winner shot on location in Kenya. "Nearly," however, is the operative word, because Meryl Streep and Robert Redford fulfill an uncommon love story to counterbalance this absurdly beautiful spectacle.

Truly every frame is a marvel, every set piece a gem. Produced as a memoir's translation to the big screen, *Out of Africa* also sidesteps charges of racism with fidelity to its source. Further demonstrating how First World storytelling technique can subdue all else in pursuit of profits and art, Sydney Pollack's epic exists as a sharply produced romance-cum-travelogue.

When the Danish lady Karen Blixen (Meryl Streep) is forced into a marriage of convenience with Baron Bror Finecke (Klaus Maria Brandauer), her dowry affords him a farm in Kenya. Afflicted with wanderlust he disregards her, so she finds sustenance in the adventurer Denys Hatton (Robert Redford). World War I interrupts the affair, as do certain other personal complications, after which the lovers continue falling in love. In the end, Bror's activities cause Karen's wealth to founder, and she is forced to bury Denys after a tragic accident.

Highlights include a safari via biplane, glimpses of naturally occurring wildlife, and the sweeping uplift of John Barry's thrilling score. **GC-Q**

**U.S.** 162m

**Director:** Sydney Pollack

**Producer:** Sydney Pollack

**Screenplay:** Kurt Luedtke, from memoirs by Isak Dinesen

**Photography:** David Watkin

**Music:** John Barry

**Nonoriginal music:** Mozart

**Cast:** Meryl Streep, Robert Redford, Klaus Maria Brandauer, Michael Kitchen, Joseph Thiaka, Stephen Kinyanjui, Michael Gough, Suzanna Hamilton, Rachel Kempson

**Oscar:** Sydney Pollack (best picture), Sydney Pollack (director), Kurt Luedtke (screenplay), Stephen B. Grimes, Josie MacAvin (art direction), David Watkin (photography), John Barry (music), Chris Jenkins, Gary Alexander, Larry Stensvold, Peter Handford (sound)

**Oscar nomination:** Meryl Streep (actress), Klaus Maria Brandauer (actor in support role), Milena Canonero (costume), Fredric Steinkamp, William Steinkamp, Pembroke J. Herring, Sheldon Kahn (editing)

# THE PURPLE ROSE OF CAIRO (1985)

**U.S.** (Jack Rollins & Charles H. Joffe, Orion) 84m BW/ Color

**Director:** Woody Allen

**Producer:** Robert Greenhut

**Screenplay:** Woody Allen

**Photography:** Gordon Willis

**Music:** Dick Hyman

**Cast:** Mia Farrow, Jeff Daniels, Danny Aiello, Irving Metzman, Stephanie Farrow, David Kieserman, Elaine Grollman, Victoria Zussin, Mark Hammond, Wade Barnes, Joseph G. Graham, Don Quigley, Maurice Brenner, Paul Herman, Rick Petrucelli

**Oscar nomination:** Woody Allen (screenplay)

**Cannes Film Festival:** Woody Allen (FIPRESCI award)

This sublime nostalgic comedy avoids the usual Allen formula of "goofy New Yorkers having trouble with relationships." Both Woody Allen and his famous neurotic monologue are absent this time, but fans of the writer-director needn't worry, because the hilarious one-liners and odd characters are still present. Above all, *The Purple Rose of Cairo* is about love, perhaps Allen's greatest love of all: for cinema.

A tribute to the magical powers of the screen, *The Purple Rose of Cairo* tells the story of Cecilia (Mia Farrow), a poor waitress who, during the Depression era, spends much of her time watching movies. "I forget my sorrows," confesses the young woman, who is terrorized by a rude and unemployed husband. Only by watching the brave and unbeatable heroes on screen can she resist the daily nightmare that is her life.

We know something about how much Americans needed the optimism imparted by movies during the Depression years from Preston Sturges's 1941 classic *Sullivan's Travels*. While Cecilia is watching, for the eighth time, a film entitled *The Purple Rose of Cairo*, the charming hero (Jeff Daniels) walks right off the screen to meet her, though the rest of the audience protests and asks for their money back. In their effort to prevent a financial fiasco, the film's Hollywood producers send the actor who performs the hero to seduce her. Although the fictitious character is gentle and romantic, the star who impersonates him is cynical and arrogant. Assuming both roles, Daniels ironically suggests the difference between the ideal and the real man. Charmed by both of them, Cecilia experiences an amazing metamorphosis from Cinderella to a beautiful princess, and Farrow's excellent performance makes us believe in a such a miraculous transformation.

*The Purple Rose of Cairo* is a meditation on illusion. The film's conclusion is not cynical, as with Allen's more recent *Deconstructing Harry* (1997). Fiction can save our lives, Allen argues in *Cairo*, managing to convince us. Among the lines, Cecilia's unforgettable remark: "I met a wonderful man. He's imaginary, but who cares? You can't have everything you want," recalling the famous closing line, "Nobody's perfect," from *Some Like It Hot* (1959), intensifying any belief we might have in the cinema's magical powers. **DD**

## BACK TO THE FUTURE (1985)

Michael J. Fox, already a TV heartthrob with the sitcom *Family Ties*, became a full-fledged movie star thanks to this time-traveling comedy adventure. Fox stars as Marty McFly, a 17-year-old who despairs of his pushover dad George (Crispin Glover), and so spends most of his time with eccentric inventor Emmett Brown (Christopher Lloyd). Doc Brown's latest invention is a time-travel machine in the shape of a DeLorean car, and soon enough Marty finds himself speeding backward in time to 1955, where his parents have barely met let alone started the relationship that will lead to Marty's very existence.

An extremely clever premise is further enlivened by quick-fire direction from Robert Zemeckis and a superb, witty script, as Marty—with the help of a much younger Doc Brown—tries to get back to the present without wreaking havoc on future events by altering the past (not as easy as it sounds when your unsuspecting mother-to-be has developed a crush on you). Fox is perfect as the teen trying to unite his parents so he can one day be born, Lloyd suitably foolish as the nutty scientist, while Glover and Lea Thompson (as Marty's mom) have a great time playing their characters as both middle-aged parents and teenagers. A timeless comedy adventure. **JB**

**U.S.** (Amblin, Universal) 116m Technicolor

**Director:** Robert Zemeckis

**Producer:** Neil Canton, Bob Gale

**Screenplay:** Robert Zemeckis, Bob Gale

**Photography:** Dean Cundey

**Music:** Alan Silvestri

**Cast:** Michael J. Fox, Christopher Lloyd, Lea Thompson, Crispin Glover, Thomas F. Wilson, Claudia Wells, Marc McClure, Wendie Jo Sperber, George DiCenzo, Frances Lee McCain, James Tolkan, J.J. Cohen, Casey Siemaszko, Billy Zane, Harry Waters Jr.

**Oscar:** Charles L. Campbell, Robert R. Rutledge (special sound effects)

**Oscar nomination:** Robert Zemeckis, Bob Gale (screenplay), Chris Hayes, Johnny Colla, Huey Lewis (song), Bill Varney, B. Tennyson Sebastian, Robert Thirlwell, William B. Kaplan (sound)

## TONG NIEN WANG SHI (1985)
### THE TIME TO LIVE AND THE TIME TO DIE

Taiwan in the 1950s: Young Ah Xiao's life is an apparently endless and uncomplicated round of playing marbles, chasing chums, and listening to his grandmother's plans to return home to mainland China. After a first, shocking taste of death, however, life darkens and the boy turns into a brutish teenager, trapped between feelings of familial duty and the need to prove his worth among the local street gangs.

In many respects, Hsiao-hsien Hou's autobiographical coming-of-age movie marked a distinct advance upon his earlier *A Summer at Grandpa's* (1984). It paved the way for the considerably more complex narrative structure of *City of Sadness* (1989), with its deployment of an individual character study to explore the dynamics of Taiwanese society at a precise moment in time. What shapes Ah Xiao's early life is a community unsure of its own identity and future since the separation from the communist mainland, with conflicting emotions potentially leading either to delinquency and crime or, as in Hou's case, a more fulfilling adulthood. The direction in *The Time to Live and the Time to Die* is understated, reflective, and measured, in the Ozu style, making all the more devastatingly powerful the paroxysms of agonized emotion when they are eventually allowed to ignite the screen. The film is a work of remarkable maturity, assurance, and clarity. **GA**

**Taiwan** (Central) 138m Color

**Language:** Mandarin

**Director:** Hsiao-hsien Hou

**Screenplay:** Chu T'ienwen, Hsiao-hsien Hou

**Photography:** Lee Pin Bing

**Music:** Wu Chuchu

**Cast:** Mei-Feng, Tang Yu-Yuen, Tien Feng, Xin Shufen, Yiu Ann-Shuln

**Berlin International Film Festival:** Hsiao-hsien Hou (FIPRESCI award—forum of new cinema)

**G.B.** (Embassy, Universal) 131m Technicolor

**Director:** Terry Gilliam

**Producer:** Arnon Milchan

**Screenplay:** Terry Gilliam, Charles McKeown, Tom Stoppard

**Photography:** Roger Pratt

**Music:** Michael Kamen

**Cast:** Jonathan Pryce, Robert De Niro, Katherine Helmond, Ian Holm, Bob Hoskins, Michael Palin, Ian Richardson, Peter Vaughan, Kim Greist, Jim Broadbent, Barbara Hicks, Charles McKeown, Derrick O'Connor, Kathryn Pogson, Bryan Pringle

**Oscar nomination:** Terry Gilliam, Tom Stoppard, Charles McKeown (screenplay), Norman Garwood, Maggie Gray (art direction)

# BRAZIL (1985)

The well-known history of bad feeling between *Brazil* creator Terry Gilliam and distributor Universal, in which the filmmaker resisted the studio's attempts to put out a severely truncated cut and eventually prevailed in getting his challenging picture released in the United States, has tended to soak up all the interest in this movie, which has its own unique strengths (and weaknesses) quite apart from any status it might retain as a near-political cause. Made significantly in 1984, and in parallel with the Michael Radford film of George Orwell's eponymous novel, *Brazil* is set "somewhere in the twentieth century," in an imaginary but credible oppressive state that combines the worst features of 1940s British bureaucracy, 1950s American paranoia, Stalinist or fascist totalitarianism, and the ills of the 1980s (e.g., an obsession with plastic surgery). Whereas Orwell's Air Strip One is built on an impossibly and horribly effective system of state surveillance, the worst aspect of Gilliam's invented dystopia is that it doesn't even work: the plot is kicked off by a farcical mistake as a squashed bug falls into a printer so that an arrest warrant intended for terrorist heating engineer Tuttle (Robert De Niro) is applied to an innocent Mr. Buttle (Brian Miller), and the grimly utilitarian city is falling apart even without the possibly state-sponsored terrorist bombs that periodically wreak appalling carnage.

Like *1984*'s Winston Smith, Sam Lowry (Jonathan Pryce) is a mid-level functionary of the brutal state who comes through a romantic attachment to align himself with rebellion and winds up squashed and broken by a friendly torturer. Gilliam, however, is far more concerned with the imaginary than Orwell, and delivers a fantastical setting that is escaped from only by even more fantasy. Sam enjoys romantic flights of imagination (scored with the Latin-flavored title tune) in which he is an angelic superhero knight facing up to Gilliamesque creations who seem like Pythonesque knock-offs from Japanese giant monster movies in order to rescue a dream girl (Kim Greist), one whose waking-life doppelganger is a lorry driver intent on shaking things up to redress the wrongs done Buttle and his family.

Perhaps thanks to the involvement of co-writer Tom Stoppard, *Brazil* is a more dramatically-engaging film than most of Gilliam's cartoonish efforts. The gruesome black humor and bizarre visuals (embodied by Katherine Helmond as a surgery-obsessed matron with a succession of shoe-shaped hats) exist alongside a credible—and horribly fact-based—depiction of a regime which charges its victims for the electricity and labor that goes into their own torture, as represented by the family man specialist from "Information Retrieval" (Michael Palin) and the desperate, middle-management paper-shuffler (Ian Holm). In one thing, at least, Universal had a point—the film does run a good reel beyond its optimum length, with a few too many slapstick routines that take it close to conventional knockabout. Brazil's home stretch includes a gruesome funeral scene that addresses various subplots that have been developing in the "real" world of the film, before it is revealed to be the *Owl Creek*-like fantasy of a dead man, as Sam's mind snaps under torture. **KN**

**Brazil / U.S. / Argentina** (HB, Sugarloaf) 119m Metrocolor

**Language:** English / Portuguese

**Director:** Hector Babenco

**Producer:** David Weisman

**Screenplay:** Leonard Schrader, from the novel *Beijo da Mulher Aranha* by Manuel Puig

**Photography:** Rodolfo Sánchez

**Music:** John Neschling

**Cast:** William Hurt, Raul Julia, Sonia Braga, José Lewgoy, Milton Gonçalves, Míriam Pires, Nuno Leal Maia, Fernando Torres, Patricio Bisso, Herson Capri, Denise Dumont, Antônio Petrin, Wilson Grey, Miguel Falabella, Walter Breda

**Oscar:** William Hurt (actor)

**Oscar nomination:** David Weisman (best picture), Hector Babenco (director), Leonard Schrader (screenplay)

**Cannes Film Festival:** William Hurt (actor), Hector Babenco nomination (Golden Palm)

# KISS OF THE SPIDER WOMAN (1985)

Based on a novel by Manuel Puig, Brazilian director Hector Babenco's courageous exploration of political, psychological, and sexual issues within the confines of a high-security South American prison thanks Burt Lancaster in its ending credits. The project was initiated by Lancaster, who was originally intending to star in the leading role which ultimately went to William Hurt. In a breakthrough performance, Hurt won an Oscar as Luis Molina, a window dresser imprisoned for homosexuality. Stagy and somewhat dated, the story itself still resonates, and Raul Julia's exceptionally believable performance is an even match for the high camp of Hurt's Luis.

Tall, mannered, and effeminate, Luis shares an enormous prison cell with heterosexual political prisoner Valentin Arregui (Julia). To pass the time, Luis recounts in intricate, almost maddening detail a melodrama he saw some years before. In a series of nostalgically colored flashbacks, Sonia Braga plays a stereotypical French singer during World War II. Braga, who didn't speak English at the time, phonetically sounded out her words, lending an unreal aspect to the arch-satire. Beautifully groomed and extremely sensitive, she falls for a handsome blonde Gestapo officer. Despite being a member of the French Resistance, she is convinced by her lover that the Nazis are good people who only want to rid the world of misery. Devoted to his politics, Valentin takes exception to the film, but is gradually lulled by its telling—as long as Luis doesn't concentrate on descriptions of food or naked women. Luis is only concerned about the film's romantic details but he has his own secret. The warden is promising him early release if he can draw valuable information from his cellmate, with whom Luis has fallen in love.

Although primarily of historical significance (homosexuality had rarely been portrayed in such terms in mainstream cinema), Hurt's performance goes beyond theatricality—his skill is keeping the character's real feelings hidden away under several layers of varying intensity. Even at the very end, the audience is unsure if he has betrayed Valentin or not. Considered the "gay" *Casablanca*, *Kiss of the Spider Woman*'s main virtue lies in its humanization of love in all forms. **KK**

# THE QUIET EARTH (1985)

Based on Craig Harrison's novel, Geoff Murphy's *The Quiet Earth* is a distinctly New Zealand take on the classic last-man-on-earth narrative. Scientist Zac Hobson (Bruno Lawrence) awakens one morning to discover that he is alone in the world following a scientific project gone awry. Lawrence's initial 36-minute solo performance is superb, as Zac vacillates between euphoria and despair at his isolation. Eventually he meets another survivor, Joanne (Alison Routledge), with whom he begins a relationship. Their idyll is disrupted by a third survivor, Api (Pete Smith), an aggressive Maori and the third point in the love triangle.

While the film's subject matter places it squarely within the sci-fi genre, its treatment of the material makes it less akin to dystopias such as *Mad Max* (1979) and closer to an investigation of human relationships and interracial concerns. What particularly sets the film apart is Murphy's depiction of the depopulated world. The entire soundtrack was redubbed in a studio to remove any trace of sound. Zac's gradual breakdown is conveyed via striking collages of images: Walking around in a ladies slip; driving trains as if they were part of a toy train set; a beautiful shot of him wandering in the rain playing the sax. *The Quiet Earth* does not appeal with ostentatious special effects—instead it is an intellectually stimulating, character-driven look into the human condition. **RDe**

**New Zealand** (Cinepro, Mr. Yellowbeard) 91m Color

**Director:** Geoff Murphy

**Producer:** Sam Pillsbury, Don Reynolds

**Screenplay:** Bill Baer, Bruno Lawrence, Sam Pillsbury, from novel by Craig Harrison

**Photography:** James Bartle

**Music:** John Charles

**Cast:** Bruno Lawrence, Alison Routledge, Pete Smith, Anzac Wallace, Norman Fletcher, Tom Hyde

## MISHIMA: A LIFE IN FOUR CHAPTERS (1985)

**U.S.** (American Zoetrope, Filmlink, Lucasfilm, M Co.) 120m BW/ Color

**Language:** Japanese / English

**Director:** Paul Schrader

**Producer:** Francis Ford Coppola, George Lucas, Tom Luddy, Mata Yamamoto

**Screenplay:** Leonard Schrader, Paul Schrader

**Photography:** John Bailey

**Music:** Philip Glass

**Cast:** Ken Ogata, Masayuki Shionoya, Hiroshi Mikami, Junya Fukuda, Shigeto Tachihara, Junkichi Orimoto, Naoko Otani, Gô Rijû, Masato Aizawa, Yuki Nagahara, Kyuzo Kobayashi, Yuki Kitazume, Haruko Kato, Yasosuke Bando, Hisako Manda, Roy Scheider

**Cannes Film Festival:** John Bailey, Eiko Ishioka, Philip Glass (best artistic contribution—photography, art direction, music), Paul Schrader nomination (Golden Palm)

Paul Schrader's extraordinary film about the Japanese writer-activist Yukio Mishima is an anomaly, a lavish American art movie in the Japanese language (although Roy Scheider provides some spare English voiceover). Mishima was a narcissist, a revolutionary patriot, a samurai manqué, and arguably the most important Japanese writer of the 20th century. The creator of *Taxi Driver*'s Travis Bickle clearly sees himself as a kindred spirit, although the film is more than mere homage. Schrader flips through Mishima's many masks with great intelligence and clarity.

The film interweaves the events leading up to Mishima's (Ken Ogata) final act of defiance—a grandstand attempt to reconcile art with action that involves kidnapping a general—with black-and-white biographical sequences showing the author's childhood, and three highly stylized, studio-bound dramatizations inspired by the writer's *Temple of the Golden Pavilion*, *Kyoko's House*, and *Runaway Horses*. Made under the auspices of executive producers Francis Ford Coppola and George Lucas (a noted sinophile), *Mishima* is a film as illuminating and coherent as it is intricate and involved, boasting breathtaking production design by Eiko Ishioka, gleaming cinematography by John Bailey, and a powerful, pulsing score by Philip Glass. **TCh**

## PRIZZI'S HONOR (1985)

**U.S.** (ABC) 130m Color

**Director:** John Huston

**Producer:** John Foreman

**Screenplay:** Richard Condon, Janet Roach, from novel by Richard Condon

**Photography:** Andrzej Bartkowiak

**Music:** Alex North, Gaetano Donizetti, Gioacchino Rossini

**Cast:** Jack Nicholson, Kathleen Turner, Robert Loggia, John Randolph, William Hickey, Lee Richardson, Michael Lombard, Anjelica Huston, George Santopietro, Lawrence Tierney, CCH Pounder, Ann Selepegno, Vic Polizos, Dick O'Neill, Sully Boyar

**Oscar:** Anjelica Huston (actress in support role)

**Oscar nomination:** John Foreman (best picture), John Huston (director), Richard Condon, Janet Roach (screenplay), Jack Nicholson (actor), William Hickey (actor in support role), Donfeld (costume), Rudi Fehr, Kaja Fehr (editing)

In 1985, director John Huston, despite waning health, embarked on his fortieth film—a black comedy that examines what might happen if two assassins fell in love. Jack Nicholson stars as Charley Partanna, a none-too-smart hitman for influential New York mob family the Prizzis. The godfather, Don Corrado (William Hickey), treats Charley like an adopted son since the Don's granddaughter Maerose (Anjelica Huston, daughter of the director and Nicholson's paramour at the time) did him wrong. Falling for smoldering blonde Irene Walker (Kathleen Turner) at a wedding, it turns out the lovers have been hired to kill each other.

Unusually—and refreshingly—the ending is what the story requires, not what the audience wants. Although the film was nominated for eight Oscars, Anjelica was the only one to win, for best supporting actress. But Hickey, who was nominated as well, is the film's stealthy dynamo; seemingly on his last legs he makes such lines as, "Would you like a cookie?" both threatening and hilarious. Lawrence Tierney (who played the eponymous Dillinger in Max Dosseck's 1945 film) also appears as a corrupt cop. Imperfect and ultimately depressing, *Prizzi's Honor* is nonetheless a comedic gem. **KK**

# SANS TOIT NI LOI (1985)
## VAGABOND

An erstwhile participant in the French New Wave, Agnès Varda lacked some of the credentials of her former film critic peers like François Truffaut and Jean-Luc Godard. Rather, she came from a photography background, and although she didn't know much about filmmaking when she began, Varda quickly demonstrated a style of her own. Perhaps best known for earlier films such as *Cleo from 5 to 7* (1962), a real-time wait for a woman to get the results of her cancer test, Varda actually veered back and forth between nonfiction and fiction filmmaking. *Vagabond* followed a long stretch of the former, which explains its hybrid merger of documentary style and more traditional cinematic techniques.

One morning, a farmer discovers the frozen body of a female drifter curled up in a field, her face blue and glazed with frost. Once the police arrive, Varda's own voice interrupts. She explains that little is known about the young woman, then proceeds to enact a series of faux interviews and flashbacks, each revealing small facts and passing details of the doomed girl. Nothing, of course, is really known about the woman Mona Bergeron (played with icy disaffection by Sandrine Bonnaire). She's merely a construct of Varda's elliptical narrative.

Yet Varda enlists the drifter as a metaphor for how little we ever actually know about many of the people we encounter on a day-to-day basis. Bonnaire's drifter comes across a number of people while in search of food and shelter, but she rarely makes an effort to know them. She's sullen and unthankful, slinking across the frigid French landscapes away from who knows what and toward her telegraphed tragic end. In the "interview" segments, characters recount bits and pieces of her behavior and demeanor but nobody can offer a complete picture of the enigmatic girl. Varda arranges each scene and bleak landscape with a photographer's eye, frequently placing her increasingly feral protagonist (and sometimes antagonist) at the margins of the frame just as the mysterious Mona herself exists in the periphery of the world itself. **JKl**

**G.B. / France** (Channel Four, Ciné Tamaris, Films A2, French Ministry of Culture and Communication) 105m Color

**Language:** French

**Director:** Agnès Varda

**Producer:** Oury Milshtein

**Screenplay:** Agnès Varda

**Photography:** Patrick Blossier

**Music:** Joanna Bruzdowicz, Fred Chichin

**Cast:** Sandrine Bonnaire, Setti Ramdane, Francis Balchère, Jean-Louis Perletti, Urbain Causse, Christophe Alcazar, Dominique Durand, Joël Fosse, Patrick Schmit, Daniel Bos, Katy Champaud, Raymond Roulle, Henri Fridlani, Patrick Sokol, Pierre Imbert

**Venice Film Festival:** Agnès Varda (FIPRESCI award), (Golden Lion), (OCIC award)

**France** (Les Films Adelph/Historia)
566m Color

**Language:** French

**Director:** Claude Lanzmann

**Photography:** Dominique Chapuis, William Lubtchansky

# SHOAH (1985)

On the one hand, it might seem absurd, even outrageous, to include Claude Lanzmann's *Shoah* with the other films selected here, using the regular number of words to describe and discuss it. But on the other hand, with all its particularities, including its nine-hour length and the authentic genius inhabiting it, it is vital to consider *Shoah* as a film among films.

Lanzmann traveled the world for nearly ten years discussing the Nazi extermination camps—not the concentration camps, not the Nazi system as a whole, not antisemitism as a process, but the specific places where death reigned, the inner circle of the Inferno. He collected testimonies from some of the very few survivors, several witnesses, and even former organizers of the mass-murdering process. He edited together these voices and images of the present (as filmed), showing the bodies, the faces, the landscapes as they look now, forever haunted by this tragic past. At the same time, he made every viewer aware of the absolute impossibility of representing what happened in such places as Auschwitz, Birkenau, Sobibor, Treblinka, and Chelmno, not because it's forbidden, just because it's impossible.

In doing all this, Lanzmann accomplished several things of great importance. He invented a way of bringing back memories of the Holocaust's horrors without distorting what these horrors had been. Consequently, he also succeeded in giving a name to this process—the "Shoah" of the film's title—which is now widely used. But on a wholly different level, Lanzmann also managed to achieve what one might call the essence of cinema: the highest degree of presence through a total absence. Absence of the millions of dead, of the past, of any evidence of remains, carefully eliminated by the murderers, of visual or audio archives.

Lanzmann's film stands as the absolute answer to Jean-Luc Godard's plea for "not a just image, just an image." *Shoah* was the film that demanded this radicalization of modern cinema; the extremism of idolatry and propaganda had led to the worst. It included some compromising links between filmmaking and the power of the industrial era. At its deepest roots, modern cinema stands as an ethical refusal of these links, and it needed to confront the most inhuman effects of the industrialization of representation to meet its highest expression. The discussion generated by *Shoah* confirms the importance of this extraordinary work of art—of which one might say that any projection is a victory for mankind, and its future. **J-MF**

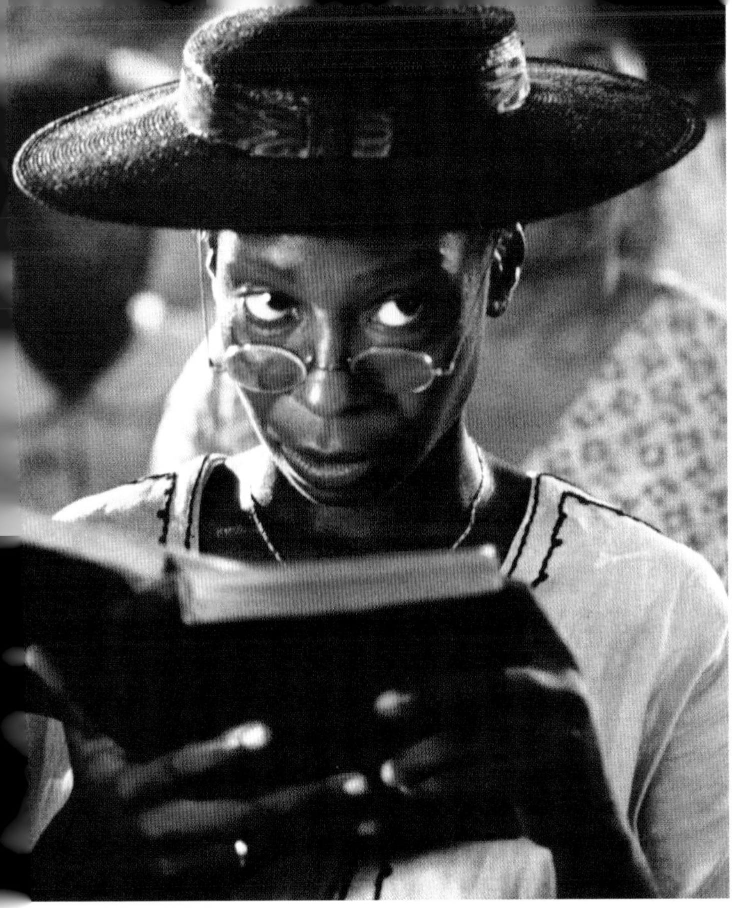

# THE COLOR PURPLE (1985)

Intent on dispelling his reputation strictly as a creator of popular youthful fantasies, Steven Spielberg chose Alice Walker's story of an impoverished rural black community in the early 20th-century American South as his vehicle for dramatic affirmation. Oddly enough, Spielberg's established skills as a director both help and hinder the project, as his knack for wry humor and glossy technical prowess fits uneasily with the material, which he toned down from Walker's novel.

But even if he bit off more than he could chew, *The Color Purple* still proved Spielberg's willingness to take risks. He gets strong performances out of Oprah Winfrey and Danny Glover, but in particular Spielberg's instincts once again proved invaluable in the casting of then relatively unknown Whoopi Goldberg. Her Celie rarely speaks but is full of emotion, relayed through Goldberg's impressive performance that does more with a well-timed wide smile than most actors do with a showy monologue. Spielberg too often falls back on sentimentality, but promising glimmers of the director who would graduate to more mature works like *Empire of the Sun* (1987), *Schindler's List* (1993), and *Artificial Intelligence: A.I.* (2001) are there to be studied. **JKl**

**U.S.** (Amblin, Guber-Peters Co., Warner Bros.) 154m Color

**Director:** Steven Spielberg

**Producer:** Quincy Jones, Kathleen Kennedy, Frank Marshall, Steven Spielberg

**Screenplay:** Menno Meyjes, from the novel by Alice Walker

**Photography:** Allen Daviau

**Music:** Quincy Jones

**Cast:** Danny Glover, Whoopi Goldberg, Margaret Avery, Oprah Winfrey, Willard E. Pugh, Akosua Busia, Desreta Jackson, Adolph Caesar, Rae Dawn Chong, Dana Ivey, Leonard Jackson, Bennet Guillory, John Patton Jr., Carl Anderson, Susan Beaubian, James Tillis, Phillip Strong, Laurence Fishburne, Sonny Terry

**Oscar nomination:** Steven Spielberg, Kathleen Kennedy, Frank Marshall, Quincy Jones (best picture), Menno Meyjes (screenplay), Whoopi Goldberg (actress), Margaret Avery (actress in support role), Oprah Winfrey (actress in support role), J. Michael Riva, Linda DeScenna (art direction), Allen Daviau (photography), Aggie Guerard Rodgers (costume), Ken Chase (makeup), Quincy Jones, Jeremy Lubbock, Rod Temperton, Caiphus Semenya, Andraé Crouch, Chris Boardman, Jorge Calandrelli, Joel Rosenbaum, Fred Steiner, Jack Hayes, Jerry Hey, Randy Kerber (music), Quincy Jones, Rod Temperton, Lionel Richie (song)

**U.S.** (De Laurentiis, *Red Dragon*) 119m Technicolor

**Director:** Michael Mann

**Producer:** Dino De Laurentiis, Richard A. Roth

**Screenplay:** Michael Mann, from the novel *Red Dragon* by Thomas Harris

**Photography:** Dante Spinotti

**Music:** Michel Rubini, Klaus Schulze

**Cast:** William L. Petersen, Kim Greist Joan Allen, Brian Cox, Dennis Farina, Stephen Lang, Tom Noonan, David Seaman , Benjamin Hendrickson, Michael Talbott, Dan Butler, Michele Shay, Robin Moseley, Paul Perri, Patricia Charbonneau

# MANHUNTER (1986)

Based on Thomas Harris's bestseller *Red Dragon*, this film introduced cannibalistic psychiatrist Hannibal Lecter (in the form of Brian Cox) five years before Anthony Hopkins's interpretation in the Oscar-winning *The Silence of the Lambs*.

Atmospherically and stylishly directed by *Heat*'s Michael Mann (who at that time was best known for *Miami Vice*), *Manhunter* focuses on FBI man Will Graham (William Petersen), who is coaxed out of breakdown-induced retirement so that his special talent of connecting with the psyche of killers can be put to good use in tracking down a particularly gruesome serial murderer. However, in order to do that, he has to confront the last man he helped catch—Lecter—in his prison cell, even though it was Lecter's mind games that endangered Graham's sanity in the first place.

One of the most tense and disturbing thrillers of the 1980s (and obviously a template for Chris Carter's TV series *Millennium*, among others), *Manhunter* features gripping performances, not only from the chilling Cox and intense Petersen, but also from the supporting cast, which includes Kim Greist, Joan Allen, and Dennis Farina. If you thought *The Silence of the Lambs* was scary, you ain't seen nothing yet. **JB**

**U.S.** (Act III, Columbia, *The Body*) 89m Technicolor

**Director:** Rob Reiner

**Producer:** Bruce A. Evans, Raynold Gideon, Andrew Scheinman

**Screenplay:** Raynold Gideon, Bruce A. Evans, from the novella *The Body* by Stephen King

**Photography:** Thomas Del Ruth

**Music:** Jack Nitzsche

**Cast:** Wil Wheaton, River Phoenix, Corey Feldman, Jerry O'Connell, Gary Riley, Kiefer Sutherland, Casey Siemaszko, Bradley Gregg, Jason Oliver, Marshall Bell, Frances Lee McCain, Bruce Kirby, William Bronder, Scott Beach, Richard Dreyfuss

**Oscar nomination:** Raynold Gideon, Bruce A. Evans (screenplay)

# STAND BY ME (1986)

Stephen King's short story *The Body*—a nonhorror ode to boyhood friendships—is beautifully adapted for the screen by director Rob Reiner and screenwriters Raynold Gideon and Bruce A. Evans. In *Stand by Me*, quiet Gordie (Wil Wheaton), daring Teddy (Corey Feldman), pudgy Vern (Jerry O'Connell), and group leader Chris (River Phoenix) are the four boys who spend the summer of 1959 doing nothing much more than hanging out at their treehouse until the day Vern announces that he knows where they can find a dead body. Intrigued to see what a corpse looks like, the friends set off on a long walk to find it.

A tale of friendships—related by a grown-up Gordie (an uncredited Richard Dreyfuss)—set against the beautiful Oregon scenery (standing in for the novel's Maine location), *Stand by Me* expertly depicts the fears, games, catchphrases, debates ("Mickey is a mouse, Donald is a duck, Pluto is a dog. What's Goofy?"), and secrets shared by young boys, whereas Kiefer Sutherland's older, meaner Ace gives a taste of what could be round the next corner in their lives. Beautifully played by the young cast, and lyrically directed by Reiner. **JB**

# BLUE VELVET (1986)

"It's a strange world, isn't it?" Graphic sexual violence and Dennis Hopper's shocking portrayal of a sadistic psychopath holding a singer's family hostage for her acquiescent brutalization provoked a storm of controversy around David Lynch's dark, disturbing, dreamlike mystery. Lynch's depiction of the cruelty, sickness, and horror lying just beneath the surface of nice, clean, white-picket-fenced middle America is not exactly subtle, but it is remorselessly gripping, bold, and stylish. *Blue Velvet* combines an air of twisted mystery with ironic, satiric Americana and a singular, chirpy, lightly stylized tone. The same winning mixture of the repulsively strange with the cozily familiar, the artful and the artless, made Lynch's television series *Twin Peaks* the cultural phenomenon of 1990 and strongly influenced numerous imitators.

Kyle MacLachlan and Laura Dern are engaging as Jeffrey Beaumont and Sandy Williams, the naïve youngsters caught up in the macabre relationship between Hopper's crazed, oxygen-tank-dependent kidnapper-killer (his insanely scary, obscenity-spewing Frank Booth providing one of the most unforgettable psychos of the screen) and brave Isabella Rossellini's bruised Dorothy Vallens, the tormented cabaret singer at his never- tender mercy while he holds her husband and little boy captive. Lumberton is a sunny, dreary American Everytown, with its neat lawns and flowerbeds, its industrial core, and the colorless diner where Jeffrey and Sandy combine forces as amateur sleuths while love blossoms. But everything is off-kilter—slightly or infamously—from curious college boy Jeffrey's discovery of a human ear in a field and his anxious, dangerous adventures as a crime-busting voyeur to his stunned arrival on a bizarre death tableau.

The scene in which Jeffrey, hiding in Dorothy's closet, witnesses Frank's frenzied rape of the blue-velvet-robed victim is most contentious but an undeniably arresting, classic example of Lynch's nerve. Clever use of innocuous pop ballads—most hauntingly the title song—laced through regular Lynch collaborator Angelo Badalamenti's creepy score heightens the atmosphere. And although he appears in only one scene, Dean Stockwell's performance as Frank's confederate Ben, with his deceptively camp bonhomie—miming to Roy Orbison's "In Dreams"—almost rivals Hopper's for spectacularly sinister weirdness. **AE**

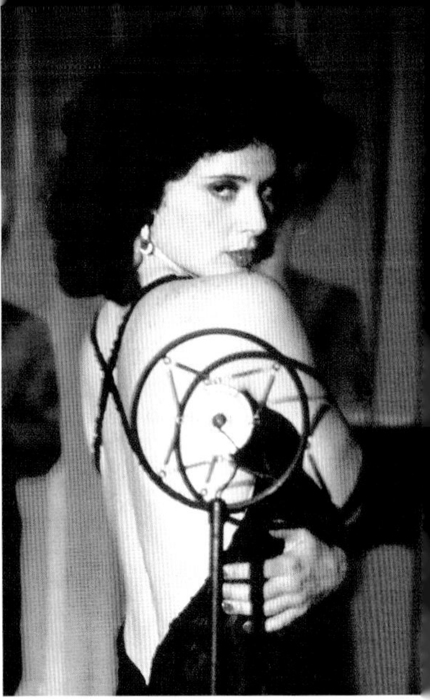

**U.S.** (De Laurentiis) 120m Color

**Director:** David Lynch

**Producer:** Fred C. Caruso

**Screenplay:** David Lynch

**Photography:** Frederick Elmes

**Music:** Angelo Badalamenti, David Lynch

**Nonoriginal music:** Roy Orbison, Bernie Wayne, Victor Young

**Cast:** Isabella Rossellini, Kyle MacLachlan, Dennis Hopper, Laura Dern, Hope Lange, Dean Stockwell, George Dickerson, Priscilla Pointer, Frances Bay, Jack Harvey, Ken Stovitz, Brad Dourif, Jack Nance, J. Michael Hunter, Dick Green

**Oscar nomination:** David Lynch (director)

**U.S.** (Orion, Charles H. Joffe & Jack Rollins) 103m Technicolor

**Director:** Woody Allen

**Producer:** Robert Greenhut

**Screenplay:** Woody Allen

**Photography:** Carlo Di Palma

**Music:** James V. Monaco

**Nonoriginal music:** Johann Sebastian Bach, Giacomo Puccini

**Cast:** Barbara Hershey, Carrie Fisher, Michael Caine, Mia Farrow, Dianne Wiest, Maureen O'Sullivan, Lloyd Nolan, Max von Sydow, Woody Allen, Daniel Stern, Julie Kavner, Joanna Gleason, Bobby Short, Lewis Black, Julia Louis Dreyfus

**Oscar:** Woody Allen (screenplay), Michael Caine (actor in support role), Dianne Wiest (actress in support role)

**Oscar nomination:** Robert Greenhut (best picture), Woody Allen (director), Stuart Wurtzel, Carol Joffe (art direction), Susan E. Morse (editing)

# HANNAH AND HER SISTERS (1986)

The last and most expansive of the remarkably fine run of Woody Allen pictures that began with *A Midsummer Night's Sex Comedy*, *Hannah and Her Sisters* is Bergmanesque in inspiration, perhaps, but Renoir-like in tone, betraying the influence of both of those masters as it traces the shifts in various tangled relationships over the space of a single year. Set, as some of his other films are, in arty, upper-crust Manhattan, the film centers on three sisters (Mia Farrow, Barbara Hershey, and Dianne Wiest), the partners of the first two (Michael Caine, Max von Sydow), the first's ex-husband (Allen), and a few other friends and colleagues brought in to complicate the romantic "roundelay." Allen himself is less to the fore than usual, his customarily neurotic hypochondriac taking up rather less time and sympathy than Caine, waivering in his fidelity to Farrow thanks to an infatuation with the younger Hershey. Indeed, one of the delights of the film is the way Allen handles this broader-than-usual canvas; the characters are if anything more rounded than previously, even as the wider focus gives us more of a sense of a world outside the rather limited one at the film's core.

In many respects, of course, it's the same old situations, types, even gags as before, yet there is something quite Chekhovian about the piece: The delicate poignancy of the various emotional dilemmas, the awareness of a very real pain underlying the jokes, the grim, inevitable fact of death hovering all the while just off-screen while Woody's own angst-filled jester faces a medical scare. The gags are not just one-liners, but wholly plausible in terms of character and plot—a quality done ample justice by one of the best casts Allen ever managed to put together. And unlike some of the other films, the tribute to the good things that make life just about worth living feels heartfelt in *Hannah and Her Sisters* rather than forced (even though Allen did indeed once consider a darker ending). A feel-good movie in the best sense of the word. **GA**

## SHE'S GOTTA HAVE IT (1986)

Spike Lee's debut feature, *She's Gotta Have It* is an exploration of the life of Nola Darling (Tracy Camilla Johns), a young black woman living in New York City who worries that her sexual appetites make her a "freak," and who juggles relationships with three different men, none of whom can entirely satisfy her. Whereas the self-regarding male model and "buppie" Greer (John Canada Terrell) and the gangly, irresponsible, pattering Mars Blackmon (Lee) are almost one-note comical caricatures, the decent, caring, poetic Jamie (Tommy Redmond Hicks) is positioned to win the girl.

Jamie disrupts the black-and-white movie by staging a full-color musical number as a birthday present, and is the one who forces the big, expected confrontation scene that makes Nola reassess her life and commit to him. But he also, in effect, rapes her to make a point, and the smothering "happy ending" is undercut by Nola's own narration, which concludes "I'm not a one-man woman . . . . There you have me." Usually characterized as a primarily an African-American filmmaker, Lee is certainly willing to explore strata of black American life neglected in all the hood movies, but his approach to chat, insight, New York, and the human heart makes him kin also to Eric Rohmer, Martin Scorsese, and Woody Allen. **KN**

**U.S.** (40 Acres & a Mule) 84m BW / Color

**Director:** Spike Lee

**Producer:** Spike Lee

**Screenplay:** Spike Lee

**Photography:** Ernest R. Dickerson

**Music:** Bill Lee

**Cast:** Tracy Camilla Johns, Tommy Redmond Hicks, John Canada Terrell, Spike Lee, Raye Dowell, Joie Lee, S. Epatha Merkerson, Bill Lee, Cheryl Burr, Aaron Dugger, Stephanie Covington, Renata Cobbs, Cheryl Singleton, Monty Ross, Lewis Jordan

**Cannes Film Festival:** Spike Lee (award of youth foreign film)

## LE DÉCLIN DE L'EMPIRE AMÉRICAIN (1986)
### THE DECLINE OF THE AMERICAN EMPIRE

The first international success of Canadian filmmaker Denys Arcand, *The Decline of the American Empire* is a sardonic study in sexual mores where the sex is much more in talk than in action. In a lakeside country house, four male French-Canadian academics are preparing a gourmet meal and talking about sex. Meanwhile, the four women who will be their guests meet at a health club in the city—and talk about sex. Then they all assemble for dinner where the conversations—and the revelations—continue.

Early on, in a radio interview, one of the women asks whether the "frantic drive for personal happiness" is "linked to the decline of the American empire." Arcand's film ironically explores this question. All the characters, it seems, are hell-bent on finding happiness; yet everyone is frustrated and desperate, and their relationships are disaster areas. This, Arcand hints, is the fallout of a society where sexual gratification is elevated over all other values. Interactions between the characters—especially during the dinner party—are filmed like a battle, with shot and countershot; the dialogue is witty, erudite, and oblique. *Decline* is at once bleak and funny; we may not like these people, but they're ceaselessly fascinating to watch. **PK**

**Canada** (Corporation Image M & M, Malofilm, NFB, Société Radio Cinema, Société Général du Cinéma du Québec, Téléfilm Canada) 101m Color

**Language:** French

**Director:** Denys Arcand

**Producer:** Roger Frappier, René Malo

**Screenplay:** Denys Arcand

**Photography:** Guy Dufaux

**Music:** François Dompierre

**Cast:** Dominique Michel, Dorothée Berryman, Louise Portal, Pierre Curzi, Rémy Girard, Yves Jacques, Geneviève Rioux, Daniel Brière, Gabriel Arcand, Évelyn Regimbald, Lisette Guertin, Alexandre Remy, Ariane Frédérique, Jean-Paul Bongo

**Oscar nomination:** Canada (best foreign language film)

**Cannes Film Festival:** Denys Arcand (FIPRESCI award)

## THE FLY (1986)

Even in his earliest films, director David Cronenberg imagined how advances in science, medicine, and technology (and often a fusion of the three) might alter human behavior. *The Fly* takes that fusion to its literal extreme, and while the movie exemplifies horror in the strictest sense, in actuality Cronenberg plays it like a twisted love story.

Retaining the bare-bones premise of the 1958 B-movie original with Vincent Price, *The Fly* stars Jeff Goldblum as a scientist who designs a matter transporter, a means to disassemble matter in one location and reassemble it in another. Much to the dismay of his lover, Geena Davis, one night Goldblum tests the machine on himself. Something goes wrong. Goldblum's DNA is accidentally fused with that of a common house fly, and while the genetic alteration at first enhances Goldblum's senses, it quickly results in a battle of genetic dominance between the two disparate species.

Cronenberg has never shunned visceral impact, and as Goldblum begins his transformation from human to human–fly hybrid, *The Fly* features a nonstop escalation of increasingly nasty special effects. Tough hair sprouts up in strange places. Goo oozes from every orifice. Body parts wither and fall off only to be replaced by mysterious new appendages.

Rob Bottin's array of repulsive prosthetics threatens to take center stage, and indeed his vomitous effects are played not only for shock but also for perverse humor. But as disgusting as this central transformation sounds (and is), Cronenberg and his capable cast somehow infuse it with real emotion. Davis struggles with Goldblum's gross transformation to connect with the man she once knew, while Goldblum struggles to retain his humanity as his free will is subsumed by instinct.

Alas, all of this can only end one way, as the sweet romance is destined to be squashed by fate's fly swatter. Cronenberg therefore plays his tragedy for maximum pathos, and thanks in no small part to the chemistry of its leads and the plausibility of their against-all-odds relationship, rarely has such a stomach-churning series of events resulted in so many shed tears. **JKl**

**U.S.** (Brooksfilms) 95m Color

**Director:** David Cronenberg

**Producer:** Stuart Cornfeld, Marc Boyman, Kip Ohman

**Screenplay:** David Cronenberg, George Langelaan, Charles Edward Pogue

**Photography:** Mark Irwin

**Music:** Howard Shore

**Cast:** Jeff Goldblum, Geena Davis, John Getz, Joy Boushel, Leslie Carlson, George Chuvalo, Michael Copeman, David Cronenberg, Carol Lazare, Shawn Hewitt

**Oscar:** Chris Walas, Stephan Dupuis (makeup)

## ALIENS (1986)

"Get away from her, you bitch!" Sigourney Weaver's Lt. Ellen Ripley gets madder when maternal and becomes the greatest sci-fi action heroine ever in James Cameron's sensational follow-up to *Alien*. One of cinema's greatest sequels, *Aliens* picks up Ripley (and Jones the cat) being recovered in the escape craft. The snag is that it's 57 years later and, besides having a trying time explaining what happened to the Nostromo, Ripley is appalled to learn that the site of their disastrous discovery (planet LV 426) has been colonized. Inevitably something bad happens there and the traumatized Ripley is sent back with an untrustworthy company man, a team of swaggering Marines (including Cameron favorites Michael Biehn, Bill "Game over!" Paxton, plus Jenette Goldstein's terrific tough cookie Vasquez), and another ambiguous android (Lance Henrikson as Bishop).

If *Alien* was a haunted house in space frightener, Cameron's relentless, furiously intense thrill-ride (winning the franchise's second effects Oscar) is the fort under siege in space, with the dwindling band and resourceful orphan Newt (Carrie Henn) beset by an implacable multiplicity of H. R. Giger's formidable, acid-drooling, giant foe and the mother of the species. The Director's Cut adds about 17 minutes without letting up. **AE**

**U.S./ G.B.** (Fox, Brandywine) 137m Eastmancolor

**Director:** James Cameron

**Producer:** Gale Anne Hurd

**Screenplay:** James Cameron, David Giler, Walter Hill

**Photography:** Adrian Biddle

**Music:** James Horner

**Cast:** Sigourney Weaver, Michael Biehn, Paul Reiser, Lance Henriksen, Carrie Henn, Bill Paxton, William Hope, Jenette Goldstein, Al Matthews, Mark Rolston, Ricco Ross, Colette Hiller, Daniel Kash, Cynthia Dale Scott, Tip Tipping

**Oscar:** Don Sharpe (special sound effects), Robert Skotak, Stan Winston, John Richardson, Suzanne M. Benson (special visual effects)

**Oscar nomination:** Sigourney Weaver (actress), Peter Lamont, Crispian Sallis (art direction), Ray Lovejoy (editing), James Horner (music), Graham V. Hartstone, Nicolas Le Messurier, Michael A. Carter, Roy Charman (sound)

## FERRIS BUELLER'S DAY OFF (1986)

Every male adolescent's dream—and every parent's nightmare—comes true on screen in writer/director John Hughes's teen comedy *Ferris Bueller's Day Off*, as the film's hero (Matthew Broderick) does all the things in just one day that most of us don't have the nerve to do in a lifetime.

Realizing one morning that "life moves pretty fast. If you don't stop and look around once in awhile, you could miss it," Ferris decides to skip school, and this time aims to make it count. Enlisting the help of his pal Cameron (Alan Ruck), Ferris "borrows" Cameron's father's prized Ferrari, performs "Twist and Shout" during a city parade (in one of the movie's most memorable scenes), catches a game at Chicago's Wrigley Field, and scams his way into a high-class restaurant.

Like previous Hughes movies such as *The Breakfast Club*, *Pretty in Pink*, and *Sixteen Candles*, adults here don't understand the teenagers in their care, be it Ferris's parents or the high school dean (Jeffrey Jones) who has made it his mission in life to catch Ferris in the act of doing something he shouldn't be doing. The grown-ups are just bystanders, the film really belonging to the supporting cast of Ruck (who was 30 playing the teenage role of Cameron), Jennifer Grey (as Ferris's bitter sister, who is sick of her popular brother), Mia Sara (Ferris's girlfriend Sloane), and, most of all, Matthew Broderick as the adorable, exuberant lead. **JB**

**U.S.** (Paramount) 102m Metrocolor

**Director:** John Hughes

**Producer:** John Hughes, Tom Jacobson

**Screenplay:** John Hughes

**Photography:** Tak Fujimoto

**Music:** Ira Newborn

**Cast:** Matthew Broderick, Alan Ruck, Mia Sara, Jeffrey Jones, Jennifer Grey, Cindy Pickett, Lyman Ward, Edie McClurg, Charlie Sheen, Ben Stein, Del Close, Virginia Capers, Richard Edson, Larry Flash Jenkins, Kristy Swanson

# DOWN BY LAW (1986)

**U.S. / West Germany** (Black Snake, Grokenberger, Island) 107m BW

**Director:** Jim Jarmusch

**Producer:** Alan Kleinberg Tom Rothman, Jim Stark

**Screenplay:** Jim Jarmusch

**Photography:** Robby Müller

**Music:** John Lurie, Tom Waits

**Cast:** Tom Waits, John Lurie, Roberto Benigni, Nicoletta Braschi, Ellen Barkin, Billie Neal, Rockets Redglare, Vernel Bagneris, Timothea, L.C. Drane, Joy N. Houck Jr., Carrie Lindsoe, Ralph Joseph, Richard Boes, Dave Petitjean

**Cannes Film Festival:** Jim Jarmusch nomination (Golden Palm)

Long recognized as a leading figure of American independent cinema, writer-director Jim Jarmusch is well known for highly idiosyncratic, noncommercial films. *Down by Law*, his landmark feature from 1986, epitomizes this counter-hegemonic interest and style and unwinds inside a hermetically sealed creative universe divorced from the demands of box-office receipts or the requirements of immediate audience gratification.

The story of chance encounters and luck, *Down by Law* draws on the interrelated lives of Jack (John Lurie), a pimp; Zack (Tom Waits), an unemployed DJ; and Bob (Roberto Benigni), an Italian tourist. Each of them ends up incarcerated, with Jack and Zack fall guys for crimes they didn't commit, and Bob serving time for committing murder in self-defense. At first not particularly fond of one another, they each nevertheless undertake a friendship of circumstance, eventually escaping into the relative calm of rural America. It's as straightforward as that, with little embellishment.

Still, Jarmusch's shorthand matters because his purposes are often deceptively simple. Long takes predominate with in-depth compositions showcasing wonderfully expressive black-and-white film. Time-killing activities like card games frame and support the characters' lives. Everywhere touched by a sense of farcical adventure, the movie is nominally set in Louisiana, though it clearly reflects the world we know, if only through other movies.

Often riding a thin line between amateur technique and professional brilliance, *Down by Law* avoids cliché-ridden expressions and the usual restrictions of space and place. In its length are domestic squabbles, the briefest of exposition to realize the prison setting, and an inexplicable escape through an underground sewer system, after which the film more or less works out a set of scenarios as if through improvisation.

For Jarmusch fans it's a must see. Even for his opponents it affirms the value of small-scale American film productions in opposition to the usual Hollywood fare. Regardless, Jarmusch draws his funding from German sources. Somehow his temperament, style, and commercial (dis)interests resonate within this looming Teutonic tradition, embellished here by the noted cinematographer Robby Müller, who transforms a relatively shapeless plot into something undeniably beautiful. **GC-Q**

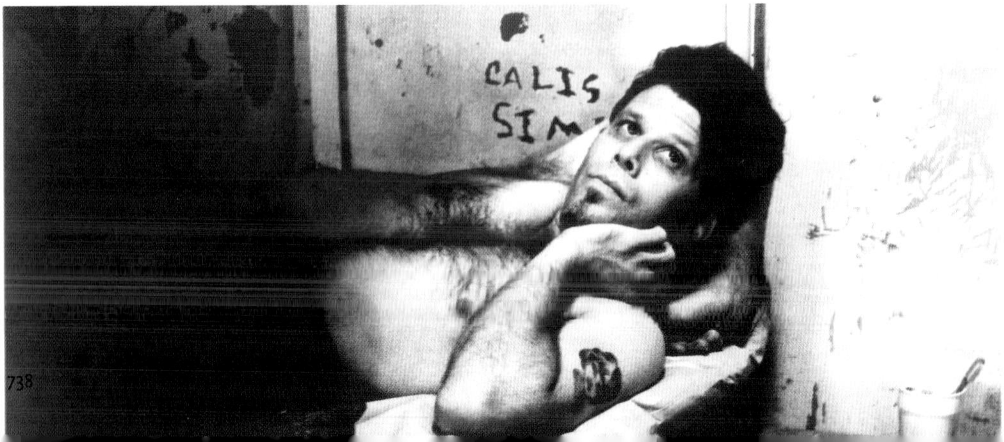

## A ROOM WITH A VIEW (1986)

Ismail Merchant and James Ivory had been working together since 1963, but it was *A Room with a View*, their 1985 adaptation of E. M. Forster's novel, that made the producing/directing team famous for a luxurious period style that would later be apparent in movies like *The Remains Of The Day* and *Howard's End*.

Much of the credit for revitalizing the cinematic period drama should also go to the third member of their team, Ruth Prawer Jhabvala, who had previously worked with Merchant Ivory on *Heat And Dust* and here beautifully adapted the tale of a young woman's awakening from the novel to the screen. Lucy (Helena Bonham Carter) is the woman in question, who discovers much about life and love in the Tuscan countryside as she decides between prospective suitors George (Julian Sands) and Cecil (Daniel Day-Lewis).

Sands, in his best screen performance, is passionate as George, kissing the demure Lucy in a yellow-tinted field of grass, while Day-Lewis hits just the right note as priggish Cecil (complete with oiled hair and annoying affectations). But it is Maggie Smith, as Lucy's dotty companion, and Denholm Elliott, as George's forward-thinking father, who stand out the most from a cast of superb actors in this stately and picturesque setting. **JB**

**G.B.** (Channel Four, Curzon, Goldcrest, Merchant-Ivory, National Film Finance) 117m Technicolor

**Director:** James Ivory

**Producer:** Ismail Merchant

**Screenplay:** Ruth Prawer Jhabvala, from novel by E.M. Forster

**Photography:** Tony Pierce-Roberts

**Music:** Richard Robbins

**Cast:** Maggie Smith, Helena Bonham Carter, Denholm Elliott, Julian Sands, Simon Callow, Patrick Godfrey, Judi Dench, Fabia Drake, Daniel Day-Lewis

**Oscar:** Ruth Prawer Jhabvala (screenplay), Gianni Quaranta, Brian Ackland-Snow, Brian Savegar, Elio Altramura (art direction), Jenny Beavan, John Bright (costume)

**Oscar nomination:** Ismail Merchant (best picture), James Ivory (director), Denholm Elliott (actor in support role), Maggie Smith (actress in support role), Tony Pierce-Roberts (photography)

## CHILDREN OF A LESSER GOD (1986)

On paper, this sounds like a disease-of-the-week TV movie, but thanks to a skillful adaptation of the stage play on which it is based, and two superb central performances, *Children of a Lesser God* is instead a thought-provoking film that is also a genuinely affecting love story.

Sign-language teacher James Leeds (William Hurt) goes to work at a school for the deaf, and encounters a former pupil, Sarah Norman (Marlee Matlin), who is now employed there as a janitor. An angry young woman who had been one of the school's brightest students, Sarah is initially resistant to James's charms and methods—he encourages his deaf students to use their voices—but eventually relents and becomes his lover.

Matlin, who is hearing-impaired, gives a superb performance as Sarah, signing with such furious intensity that Hurt's translation of her sign language is often unnecessary as we can see her meaning in her face. Hurt delivers an understated turn (which is exactly what is needed to prevent the film from becoming sentimental), while director Randa Haines (who had previously won an Emmy for the 1984 television drama *Something About Amelia*) beautifully explores Sarah's world of silence, especially in a scene between James and Sarah in a swimming pool, where James can finally experience the world the way Sarah does. Lovely. **JB**

**U.S.** (Paramount) 119m Color

**Director:** Randa Haines

**Producer:** Patrick J. Palmer, Burt Sugarman

**Screenplay:** Hesper Anderson, from play by Mark Medoff

**Photography:** John Seale

**Music:** Michael Convertino

**Cast:** William Hurt, Marlee Matlin, Piper Laurie, Philip Bosco, Allison Gompf, John F. Cleary, Philip Holmes, Georgia Ann Cline, William D. Byrd

**Oscar:** Burt Sugarman, Patrick J. Palmer (best picture), Hesper Anderson, Mark Medoff (screenplay), Marlee Matlin (actress)

**Oscar nomination:** William Hurt (actor), Piper Laurie (actress in support role)

**Berlin International Film Festival:** Randa Haines (reader jury of the Berliner Morgenpost), (Silver Bear—bringing a major theme to public attention), nomination (Golden Bear)

# PLATOON (1986)

A savage yet moving look at the Vietnam War, as seen through the eyes of a young soldier, *Platoon* remains one of the most powerful war movies ever made, and is one of writer/director Oliver Stone's most accomplished films.

The first of Stone's "Vietnam film trilogy"—the second and third installments being the 1989 film *Born on the Fourth of July* and the 1993 film *Heaven & Earth*—*Platoon* follows the experiences of 19-year-old Chris Taylor (Charlie Sheen), an idealistic, middle-class boy who volunteers for the army, unaware of the horrors to come. Once there, his letters home (narrated by Sheen, in a sometimes spookily similar fashion to how his father Martin narrated Francis Ford Coppola's 1979 Vietnam epic *Apocalypse Now*) detail his relationships with fellow grunts and the two sergeants who divide the platoon—hippie Elias Grodin (Willem Dafoe), who uses drugs to escape the nightmares taking place all around him, and dangerously violent Bob Barnes (Tom Berenger)—both of whom appear to be fighting each other for control of the platoon and for ownership of Chris's untainted soul.

*Platoon* has a unique perspective on war in general and the Vietnam War in particular, largely because Stone himself served in the conflict and uses the film to relate his own experiences as a young soldier. In each scene he directs from every point of view possible, so the audience is never sure where the next attack may come from, creating a feeling of unease and discomfort as if you were really there, watching this horrific, chaotic encounter unfold around you. With the help of military advisor Dale Dye, he delivers a series of blistering, messy images of war—a war where there is no Hollywood hero but instead just a patriotic boy who slowly becomes disillusioned with all he believed he was fighting for. For Stone, it was a personal triumph after fighting for ten years to get his script made; for the audience, it is an unforgettable, authentic, modern classic. **JB**

**U.S.** (Cinema 86, Hemdale) 120m Color

**Language:** English / Vietnamese

**Director:** Oliver Stone

**Producer:** Arnold Kopelson

**Screenplay:** Oliver Stone

**Photography:** Robert Richardson

**Music:** Georges Delerue

**Cast:** Tom Berenger, Willem Dafoe, Charlie Sheen, Forest Whitaker, Francesco Quinn, John C. McGinley, Richard Edson, Kevin Dillon, Reggie Johnson, Keith David, Johnny Depp, David Neidorf, Mark Moses, Chris Pedersen, Tony Todd

**Oscar:** Arnold Kopelson (best picture), Oliver Stone (director), Claire Simpson (editing), John Wilkinson, Richard D. Rogers, Charles Grenzbach, Simon Kaye (sound)

**Oscar nomination:** Oliver Stone (screenplay), Tom Berenger (actor in support role), Willem Dafoe (actor in support role), Robert Richardson (photography)

**Berlin International Film Festival:** Oliver Stone (Silver Bear—director), nomination (Golden Bear)

## CARAVAGGIO (1986)

In *Caravaggio*, Derek Jarman uses a studio in London and the sounds of contemporary Italy to create an astonishing portrait of the world of Renaissance art. The film opens with Caravaggio dying at Porto Ercole, looking back over his life in decadent Rome and entertaining his ruthless patrons with tales of energy and life stolen from his companions of bars and back rooms. The acting, from Nigel Terry and Tilda Swinton to Robbie Coltrane and Jonathan Hyde, is superb, Christopher Hobbs's sets are visually stunning, and Simon Fisher-Turner's music is utterly compelling. Art becomes life becomes art as Jarman breathes biographical life into Caravaggio's greatest paintings while the artist reflects without any mercy on his own life split between the braying snobbery of the art world, and the exciting danger of a universe where violence and sex intersect.

The film is remarkable for the set pieces that recreate Caravaggio's masterpieces, for the scenes of chilling hilarity as the cardinals plot their deadly strategems, and for the extraordinary triangle composed of Ranuccio (Sean Bean), the prostitute Lena (Swinton), and Caravaggio (Terry). One of the few biopics of an artist to really show what's on the end of an artist's brush. **CM**

**G.B.** (BFI) 93m Technicolor

**Director:** Derek Jarman

**Producer:** Sarah Radclyffe

**Screenplay:** Derek Jarman

**Photography:** Gabriel Beristain

**Music:** Simon Fisher-Turner

**Cast:** Noam Almaz, Dawn Archibald, Sean Bean, Jack Birkett, Sadie Corre, Una Brandon-Jones, Imogen Claire, Robbie Coltrane, Garry Cooper, Lol Coxhill, Nigel Davenport, Vernon Dobtcheff, Terry Downes, Dexter Fletcher, Michael Gough, Jonathan Hyde, Spencer Leigh, Emile Nicolaou, Gene October, Cindy Oswin, John Rogan, Zohra Sehgal, Tilda Swinton, Lucien Taylor, Nigel Terry, Simon Fisher-Turner

**Berlin International Film Festival:** Derek Jarman C.I.D.A.L.C. award, (Silver Bear—visual shaping), nomination (Golden Bear)

## TAMPOPO (1986)

The late Juzo Itami called his second comedy a "*ramen* Western"—*Ramen* are Chinese noodles, basically a Japanese fast food. It represents a quantum leap from his impressive first comedy, the 1984 *The Funeral*. Without abandoning his flair for social satire shown in that film, and in subsequent work, Itami expands his scope in *Tampopo* to encompass the kind of free-form narrative play we associate with the late work of Luis Buñuel. His subjects are food, sex, and death, his ostensible focal point the opening of a noodle restaurant. He takes us on a wild spree through an obsession, winding his way through various digressions with a dark, philosophical wit that is both hilarious and disturbing.

The title heroine (Nobuko Miyamoto), preoccupied only with food, is a widowed mother determined to master the art of *ramen* with the aid of a mentor named Goro (Tsutomu Yamazaki), a truck driver. Her story is interlaced with that of a nameless wealthy gangster dressed in white, accompanied by a white-clad mistress, who is preoccupied with food, sex, death, and cinema. We initially see the gangster sitting down in the front row of a movie theater before a sumptuous array of food, ostensibly preparing to watch the story of *Tampopo*. Various digressions extend these intertwining themes to incorporate such Japanese standbys as deception, poverty, family, and guilt.

As in *The Funeral*, Itami's ultimate interest appears to be exploring as well as ridiculing some of the paradoxes of Japanese society, including those involving class and etiquette, and he carries this off with energy and inventiveness. **JRos**

**Japan** (Itami P, New Century) 114m Color

**Language:** Japanese

**Director:** Juzo Itami

**Producer:** Seigo Hosogoe, Juzo Itami, Yasushi Tamaoki

**Screenplay:** Juzo Itami

**Photography:** Masaki Tamura

**Music:** Kunihiko Murai

**Cast:** Tsutomu Yamazaki, Nobuko Miyamoto, Ken Watanabe, Koji Yakusho, Mario Abe, Izumi Hara, Isao Hashizume, Hisashi Igawa, Toshimune Kato, Yoshi Kato, Yoshihiro Kato, Fukumi Kuroda, Nobuo Nakamura, Mariko Okada Shuji Otaki, Ryutaro Otomo, Yoshihei Saga, Kinzoh Sakura, Setsuko Shino, Hitoshi Takagi, Choei Takahashi, Akio Tanaka, Masahiko Tsugawa, Rikiya Yasuoka

## DO MA DAAN (1986)
### PEKING OPERA BLUES

**Hong Kong** (Cinema City) U.S.:104m Color
**Language:** Cantonese
**Director:** Tsui Hark
**Producer:** Claudie Chung Chun, Tsui Hark
**Screenplay:** Wai To Kwok
**Photography:** Poon Hang-Sang
**Music:** James Wong
**Cast:** Brigitte Lin, Cherie Chung, Sally Yeh, Kenneth Tsang, Wu Ma, Paul Chu, Hoi Ling Pak, Mark Cheng, Cheung Kwok Keung, Ku Feng, Lee Hoi San

When the post–New Wave Hong Kong cinema of the 1980s was embraced in the West, admirers were entranced by that film industry's ability to construct populist entertainment with imagination, wit, and intelligence—qualities largely absent from Hollywood products of the era. Perhaps no other title from the Hong Kong boom years of the '80s contains these elements in such abundance as *Peking Opera Blues*, director Tsui Hark's gloriously giddy and gravity-defying historical epic that unfolds in an opera house circa 1913.

Weaving the intersecting aspirations of three female protagonists—a general's daughter with secret revolutionary affiliations (Brigitte Lin), an aspiring acrobat who strives to infiltrate her father's all-male opera troupe (Sally Yeh), and a scheming mercenary on the hunt for stolen jewels (Cherie Chung)—as their destinies cross in the theater, Tsui also deftly interweaves a melange of film genres with impeccable skill, to encompasses historical melodrama, bedroom farce, and wirework action spectacular.

The political themes and gender issues at work within the narrative provide a fascinating subtext for this classic of contemporary Hong Kong film. One can only reflect back on such a burst of pure cinematic pleasure with bittersweet nostalgia—Tsui's recent output has been a dire mess, Peking's charming trio of leading ladies have all retired from the screen, and the early 21st-century Hong Kong film industry is in a catastrophic slump. **TCr**

## SALVADOR (1986)

**U.S.** (Hemdale) 123m Color
**Language:** English / Spanish
**Director:** Oliver Stone
**Producer:** Gerald Green, Oliver Stone
**Screenplay:** Oliver Stone, Rick Boyle
**Photography:** Robert Richardson
**Music:** Georges Delerue
**Photography:** Robert Richardson
**Cast:** James Woods, James Belushi, Michael Murphy, John Savage, Elpidia Carrillo, Tony Plana, Colby Chester, Cynthia Gibb, Will MacMillan, Valerie Wildman, José Carlos Ruiz, Jorge Luke, Juan Fernández, Salvador Sánchez, Rosario Zúñiga
**Oscar nomination:** Oliver Stone, Rick Boyle (screenplay), James Woods (actor)

Oliver Stone's directorial breakthrough came after a string of screenplays—including *Midnight Express*, *Scarface*, and *Year of the Dragon*—resulted in controversial box-office successes. In stark contrast to the racist and reactionary politics of these earlier films, *Salvador* is an openly leftist attack on the American support of brutal, fascist repression in Latin America. Written with shamelessly melodramatic plot points at every dramatic turn, triggering emotional responses from the audience, and directed with an engaging kinetic force from the first to the last image, it stands as a model for Stone's later films. It is also the first in his series of history lessons, where an American Everyman faces the truth behind the official lie—the American Dream, governmental propaganda, etc.—and gets to a point of no return at which he must reevaluate his world view.

*Salvador* follows true-life journalist Richard Boyle (James Woods) and his DJ friend Dr. Rock (James Belushi) traveling to what they expect to be a holiday in the sun with cheap sex, drugs, and rock-'n'-roll. Once there, however, they get caught up in a civil war so ugly that they cannot look away. Though the film fails to show the full scale of brutality in El Salvador during the "events that occurred in 1980–1981" (as is claimed by the opening notice), this journey into a living hell in the U.S. backyard stands as an uncompromising, shattering testimony to American foreign policy at its worst. **MT**

# TOP GUN (1986)

Applications to the U.S. Navy's fighter-pilot progam rose considerably after the release of this testosterone-fueled homage to the men who feel the need for speed, and it isn't hard to see why. Tom Cruise, in the role that turned him from teen pinup to megastar, is Maverick, a pilot at the Top Gun school in San Diego, California. He isn't great with authority, butting heads with superior officer Michael Ironside, and has intimacy issues, which cause problems when he falls for his aeronautics instructor (Kelly McGillis).

Cruise's macho but deep-down-I'm-sensitive performance appealed to the female audience, thanks especially to his barroom serenade of "You've Lost That Lovin' Feelin" to a bemused McGillis. But the impressive flight scenes are the real reason to appreciate the film. Director Tony Scott, at his best when directing fast-paced action (movies like *The Last Boy Scout* [1991] and *Days Of Thunder* [1990]), spends the briefest amount of time on the somewhat predictable romance and personal conflicts to pack the film with realistic dogfights and dazzling aeronautic displays. An enjoyable example of the archetypal 1980s action flick, *Top Gun* also contains a hit rock soundtrack and a host of young actors (including Meg Ryan, Val Kilmer, and *ER*'s Anthony Edwards) who all went on to become big stars. **JB**

**U.S.** (Paramount) 110m Metrocolor

**Director:** Tony Scott

**Producer:** Jerry Bruckheimer, Don Simpson

**Screenplay:** Jim Cash, Jack Epps Jr, from article by Ehud Yonay

**Photography:** Jeffrey L. Kimball

**Nonoriginal music:** Harold Faltermeyer, Giorgio Moroder (songs)

**Cast:** Tom Cruise, Kelly McGillis, Val Kilmer, Anthony Edwards, Tom Skerritt, Michael Ironside, John Stockwell, Barry Tubb, Rick Rossovich, Tim Robbins, Clarence Gilyard Jr., Whip Hubley, James Tolkan, Meg Ryan, Adrian Pasdar

**Oscar:** Giorgio Moroder, Tom Whitlock (song)

**Oscar nomination:** Cecelia Hall, George Watters (special sound effects), Billy Weber, Chris Lebenzon (editing), Donald O. Mitchell, Kevin O'Connell, Rick Kline, William B. Kaplan (sound)

**U.S.** (First Run Features) 157m Color
**Director:** Ross McElwee
**Screenplay:** Ross McElwee
**Photography:** Ross McElwee
**Cast:** Ross McElwee, Burt Reynolds, Charleen Swansea

# SHERMAN'S MARCH (1986)

Sometime around the mid-1950s, synchronous sound camera rigs, combining a 16mm camera with a magnetic tape recorder, were developed in both Europe and the United States. Finally, the recording of sound could have the immediacy of capturing real events on film. Thus was born that documentary film movement known as cinéma vérité, sometimes known as direct cinema, and sometimes abbreviated as CV. At first, the magnetic tape recorders were quite heavy (even if "portable"), but during the 1960s they became progressively smaller and lighter. In 1970, the Swiss manufacturer Nagra came out with the Nagra SN, a high-quality recorder small and light enough to be carried around in a filmmaker's (somewhat large) pocket. Two-person CV crews could now be reduced to a single filmmaker; not surprisingly, some of those new, self-contained filmmakers soon began focusing on themselves as the subjects of their films, and shortly thereafter the "diary film" became the newest documentary genre.

Ross McElwee's *Sherman's March* could be seen as the *Citizen Kane* of the diary film genre. Like *Kane, Sherman's March* was hailed by several mainstream critics as something utterly new in American cinema, but its greatest achievement lay less in its originality than in the way it brought together and perfected techniques and approaches already present in earlier film diaries. A student of Ricky Leacock and Ed Pincus at MIT, North Carolina native McElwee originally set out to make a film about the lingering effects of the South's defeat in the Civil War—and especially the devastation wrought by the infamous General William T. Sherman—on the contemporary South. Yet right before he was to start shooting, his long-time girlfriend broke up with him. His return home to find the traces of Sherman now became equally an attempt to find romance.

Unlike the CV films of the early 1960s, with their invisible camera crews, *Sherman's March* has McElwee constantly interacting with the subjects in front of his camera. Learning to hold his camera under his arm while maintaining eye contact with his subjects, McElwee is remarkably talented at making people amazingly unselfconscious as he films them. He never stoops to the cheap shot, or assumes an attitude of condescension toward even the most outlandish characters he encounters.

Over the course of the film, which took about five years to shoot and edit, he embarks on a few tentative attempts to create a relationship. None work out and some fail hilariously. His voiceover commentary becomes increasingly self-critical, until in an exceptionally poignant moment he finally wonders aloud whether he's filming his life or filming so he'll have a life.

Yet *Sherman's March* is never heavy, and one leaves it moved at the recognition of how effectively McElwee has captured the spirit of contemporary romance. It may look "simple," a kind of glorified home movie, but what makes it art is McElwee's generous spirit, good humor, and remarkable candor. **RP**

## DAO MA ZEI (1986)
### THE HORSE THIEF

Tian Zhuangzhuang's second feature (after the 1984 film *On the Hunting Ground*), set in the remote wilds of Tibet, is a breathtaking spectacle in scope and color. It is perhaps the most personal of all the "Fifth Generation" Beijing films to have emerged from the People's Republic of China, at least until Tian's subsequent *The Blue Kite* (1993). Tian's originality and mastery of sound and image communicate directly, beyond the immediate trappings of the film's slender plot (an occasional horse thief expelled from his clan for stealing temple offerings) and regional culture (with particular attention to Buddhist death rituals), expressing an environmental and ecological mysticism that suggests a new relationship between man and nature. The relatively small roles played by dialogue and story line, and the striking handling of composition and superimposition, make *The Horse Thief* evocative of certain Westerns of the 1920s, though it is far from being a silent film: The chants, percussion, and bells of Buddhist rituals and the beautiful music score are an essential part of the film's texture.

*The Horse Thief* suffered two minor forms of censorship from government authorities before its release. Tian's intention was to make the film timeless. However, the government changed the beginning of the film so that the date 1923 flashed on the screen before the first image, placing the action in a specific period. The other was the elimination of corpses from the first of the film's three "sky burials." But the story—a parable about a reluctant thief who, in order to feed his family, becomes a more methodical thief once he becomes a social outcast—remains intact, and the modernist style was similarly untampered with, despite the fact that the film was barely seen in mainland China because of its focus on a minority culture and its overall eclecticism. **JRos**

**China** (Xi'an) 88m Color
**Language:** Mandarin
**Director:** Tian Zhuangzhuang
**Producer:** Wu Tian-Ming
**Screenplay:** Zhang Rui
**Photography:** Zhao Fei, Hou Yong
**Music:** Qu Xiao-Song
**Cast:** Dan Jiji, Gaoba, Jayang Jamco, Tseshang Rinzim, Daiba

## YEELEN (1987)
### BRIGHTNESS

*Brightness*, an extraordinarily beautiful and mesmerizing fantasy by Souleymane Cissé, is set in the ancient Bambara culture of Mali (formerly French Sudan) long before it was invaded by Morocco in the 16th century. A young man named Niankoro (Issiaka Kane) sets out to discover the mysteries of nature—or *komo*, the science of the gods—with the help of his mother (Soumba Traore) and uncle (Ismaila Sarr). But Soma (Niamanto Sanogo), Niankoro's jealous and spiteful father, contrives to prevent him from deciphering the elements of the Bambara sacred rites and tries to kill him.

Apart from creating a dense and exciting universe that should make George Lucas green with envy, Cissé shoots his breathtaking images in Fujicolor and accompanies his story with a spare, hypnotic, percussive score. Quite possibly the greatest African film ever made, sublimely mixing the matter-of-fact with the uncanny, this wondrous work won the Jury Prize at the 1987 Cannes Film Festival. In all, *Brightness* provides an ideal introduction to a filmmaker who is, next to Ousmane Sembène, probably Africa's greatest director. **JRos**

**Mali** (Artificial Eye, Cissé, Souleymane) 105m Color
**Language:** Bambara / French
**Director:** Souleymane Cissé
**Producer:** Souleymane Cissé
**Screenplay:** Souleymane Cissé
**Photography:** Jean-Noël Ferragut, Jean-Michel Humeau
**Music:** Salif Keita, Michel Portal
**Cast:** Issiaka Kane, Aoua Sangare, Niamanto Sanogo, Balla Moussa Keita, Soumba Traore, Ismaila Sarr, Youssouf Tenin Cissé, Koke Sangare
**Cannes Film Festival:** Souleymane Cissé (prize of the ecumenical jury—special mention), (jury prize), tied with *Shinran: Shiroi michi*, nomination (Golden Palm)

West Germany / France (Argos, Road Movies, WDR) 127m BW / Color

**Language:** German / English / French

**Director:** Wim Wenders

**Producer:** Anatole Dauman, Wim Wenders

**Screenplay:** Peter Handke, Wim Wenders

**Photography:** Henri Alekan

**Music:** Jürgen Knieper

**Cast:** Bruno Ganz, Solveig Dommartin, Otto Sander, Curt Bois, Peter Falk, Hans Martin Stier, Elmar Wilms, Sigurd Rachman, Beatrice Manowski, Lajos Kovács, Bruno Rosaz, Laurent Petitgand, Chick Ortega, Otto Kuhnle, Christoph Merg

**Cannes Film Festival:** Wim Wenders (director), nomination (Golden Palm)

# DER HIMMEL ÜBER BERLIN (1987)

## WINGS OF DESIRE

Cowritten with Peter Handke, Wim Wenders's sumptuous fantasy *Wings of Desire* encompasses the division of Berlin, the effects of the Holocaust, and the ultimate beauty of life, daring to make a choice between two worlds—that of humans and that of their unseen but palpable guardian angels—via Damiel (Bruno Ganz), an angel who falls in love with a mortal. Atmospheric, elegiac, and patiently paced, the film was critically acclaimed and won honors at many film festivals, including the Best Director prize at Cannes upon its release.

As in Michael Powell and Emeric Pressburger's 1946 classic *A Matter of Life and Death*, Wenders's heaven is shown in crisp black-and-white, whereas the human world springs to life in vivid color, aided by the work of legendary cinematographer Henri Alekan, who also photographed Jean Cocteau's *Beauty and the Beast* (1946). High atop buildings or upon the shoulders of statues, angels are watching. Wearing trenchcoats and Mona Lisa smiles, they are invisible except to children and the occasional blind person who senses their presence. The angels see everything, feel everything, and so appear at mortals' sides at times of worry, frequenting lonely bedrooms, libraries, and accident scenes. Although unable to directly affect the actions of humans, the angels may lend a glimmer of hope where before there was only darkness.

But when the broad-faced angel Damiel goes to the aid of Marion (Solveig Dommartin), a beautiful trapeze artist who fears she will fall, he begins to long for the simple things humans take for granted: To touch, to hold, to be seen. On a dank film set around the ruins of Berlin, Peter Falk (playing himself) is a mysterious man: He is the actor famous for TV's *Columbo*, but he is also the only human who openly greets Damiel. At a coffee stand Falk extends his hand to the angel, saying "I can't see you, but I know you're here," without explaining how he knows the unknowable. Second-guessing the audience, Wenders allows Falk to be obliquely referred to twice as "Columbo," a device that amuses and jolts the viewer, making a soothing film experience suddenly less of a reverie and more of a reality. Inspired by Falk's recognition, Damiel decides "to take the plunge" and literally falls to his own mortality.

Inspired by the poetry of Rainer Maria Rilke, *Wings of Desire*'s slow heartbeat pace is essential to the feel of the story. It takes the time to fully examine questions only children ask, such as "Why am I me and not you? Why am I here and not there? When did time begin and where does space end?". Its slow tempo draws the audience inevitably into a world where priorities become clearer and life in general more hopeful. A languid, profound, and gentle "message" movie, its popularity demanded a sequel, *Faraway, So Close!* (1989), as well as an inevitable reshaping by Hollywood into the schematic romantic drama *City of Angels* (1998), starring Meg Ryan and Nicholas Cage. **KK**

Hong Kong (Golden Harvest) 101m Color

**Language:** Cantonese

**Director:** Jackie Chan

**Producer:** Willie Chan, David Lam, Edward Tang

**Screenplay:** Jackie Chan

**Photography:** Yiu-Tsou Cheung

**Cast:** Jackie Chan, Kenny Bee, Anthony Chan, Wai-Man Chan, John Cheung, Maggie Cheung, Mui Sang Fan, Kenny Ho, Ricky Hui, Regina Kent, Hoi-Shan Kwan, Rosamund Kwan, Benny Lai, Ben Lam, David Lam, Wai Lam, Carina Lau, Siu Ming Lau, Hoi San Lee, Siu-Tin Lei, Fong Liu, Ken Lo, Ray Lui, Sam Lui, Mars, Bozidar Smiljanic, Po Tai, Bill Tung, Lung Wei Wang

# 'A' GAI WAAK JUK JAAP (1987)

## PROJECT A, PART II

The setup is simple: Director/star Jackie Chan plays a hotshot in the Royal Hong Kong Navy at the turn of the last century. He sets out to quash a band of marauding pirates preying on ships off the South China coast and must uncover a traitor within his own ranks. That's it for the story—really. There are good guys and bad guys. There are no moral ambiguities, no gray areas. Do we doubt that the hero will triumph over the bad guys? Of course not. Let's face it, we don't watch a Jackie Chan movie for the plot. The plot is only a framework, the merest excuse for Chan to present us with one mind-blowing, outrageous set piece after another.

For Chan, his immediate environment—be it a cramped room, a rooftop, or a crowded marketplace—frequently becomes both playground and endurance course. The architecture and objects at hand might help or hurt him as he ducks, dodges, rolls, and weaves to get away from the inexhaustible supply of bad guys always in pursuit, always out to punch, kick, and generally beat him to a pulp. Watching him evade, jump, spin, and improvise his way out of a savage beating is to experience the joy and exhilaration of meticulous comic timing and old-fashioned slapstick. He makes it look easy, but the outtakes that run under the end credits (a tradition in Jackie Chan movies) reveal the set pieces to be painstaking, dangerous work. Chan has been injured on virtually every one of his movies. There is not a single bone in his body he has not broken at least once, all in pursuit of his art, which is to give us 90 minutes of unpretentious entertainment.

But why the sequel rather than the original movie? *Project A, Part II* follows the dictum of being "the same, only bigger," and it is here that one finds Chan at the peak of his powers as a filmmaker, a choreographer, and a martial artist, when he was still young, fast, and agile, before age and all those broken bones inevitably began slowing him down. **AT**

# BABBETES GAESTEBUD (1987)
## BABETTE'S FEAST

Those familiar with Isak Dinesen's story *Babette's Feast* will surely agree that Gabriel Axel's film—besides being a gem in many other respects—is a superb example of the art of adaptation. Relocating it from a Norwegian town to a tiny village on Denmark's windswept Jutland coast was simply a smart start to Axel's strategy of rethinking the whole relationship that exists between the austere lives led by two elderly sisters who are part of the village's devoutly religious community, and the sumptuous hedonism of the banquet cooked just once for the old folks and their fellow-believers by Babette (Stéphane Audran), the maid who ended up in Jutland as a refugee from the Paris Communes.

How and why Babette came to be there forms the first half of this consistently warm, witty, and wise contemplation of love, faith, and art. The second half comprises the preparation and (initially very wary) enjoyment of the unsung wizard's cuisine. Like Babette (and Prospero, who seems to have inspired Dinesen's creation), Axel proved himself something of a magician with this modest but enormously resonant, big-hearted movie; but he was helped no end by his actors, several of them familiar from Bergman and Dreyer classics. And Audran, herself famously a gourmet, clearly savors every moment of her mouth-wateringly exquisite performance. **GA**

**Denmark** (Det Danske, Panorama) 102m Eastmancolor
**Language:** Danish / Swedish / French
**Director:** Gabriel Axel
**Producer:** Just Betzer, Bo Christensen
**Screenplay:** Gabriel Axel, from novel by Isak Dinesen
**Photography:** Henning Kristiansen
**Music:** Per Nørgaard
**Cast:** Stéphane Audran, Birgitte Federspiel, Bodil Kjer, Jarl Kulle, Jean-Philippe Lafont, Bibi Andersson, Ghita Nørby, Asta Esper, Hagen Andersen, Thomas Antoni, Gert Bastian, Viggo Bentzon, Vibeke Hastrup, Therese Hojgaard Christensen, Pouel Kern, Cay Kristiansen
**Oscar:** Denmark (best foreign language film)
**Cannes Film Festival:** Gabriel Axel (prize of the ecumenical jury—special mention)

# RAISING ARIZONA (1987)

The Coen brothers' enormously inventive second feature abandoned the noir mood of *Blood Simple* (1984) for this larger-than-life (but likewise intricately plotted) comedy featuring cartoon-style caricature. Nicolas Cage is the convenience-store robber, forever in and out of jail, who falls for and weds prison-officer Holly Hunter; their somewhat improbably blissful trailer-park marriage is blighted when they find she's infertile and, to keep her happy, he kidnaps one of the quintuplets born to a local unpainted-furniture tycoon. As if it weren't bad enough that the father hires the biker from hell (Randall "Tex" Cob) to bring back his baby and wreak vengeance on the abductors, Cage's fortunes take a turn for the even worse. Much to his wife's anger, he is visited by escaped former cellmates John Goodman and William Forsythe, who have plans of their own for the famously missing infant.

The farcical improbabilities of *Raising Arizona* are as nothing to the absurdly overpoetic voiceover the Coens brilliantly concoct for their hapless and, despite his highfalutin turns of phrase, none-too-bright hero. The film is as fervently and intelligently in love with tacky excess as anything dreamed up by Preston Sturges. Indeed, some of the camera pyrotechnics may actually distract attention away from the deliciously witty dialogue, but overall the aura of heady hysteria is sustained with considerable expertise, not least in the perfectly pitched performances. **GA**

**U.S.** (Circle) 94m Color
**Director:** Joel Coen
**Producer:** Ethan Coen
**Screenplay:** Ethan Coen, Joel Coen
**Photography:** Barry Sonnenfeld
**Music:** Carter Burwell
**Cast:** Nicolas Cage, Holly Hunter, Trey Wilson, John Goodman, William Forsythe, Sam McMurray, Frances McDormand, Randall 'Tex' Cobb, T.J. Kuhn, Lynne Dumin Kitei, Peter Benedek, Charles 'Lew' Smith, Warren Keith, Henry Kendrick, Sidney Dawson

U.S. (Natant, Warner Bros.) 116m Color

**Language:** English / Vietnamese

**Director:** Stanley Kubrick

**Producer:** Stanley Kubrick

**Screenplay:** Gustav Hasford, Michael Herr, Stanley Kubrick, from the novel *The Short-Timers* by Gustav Hasford

**Photography:** Douglas Milsome

**Music:** Abigail Mead (Vivian Kubrick)

**Cast:** Matthew Modine, Adam Baldwin, Vincent D'Onofrio, R. Lee Ermey, Dorian Harewood, Arliss Howard, Kevyn Major Howard, Ed O'Ross, John Terry, Kieron Jecchinis, Bruce Boa, Kirk Taylor, Jon Stafford, Tim Colceri, Ian Tyler

**Oscar nomination:** Stanley Kubrick, Michael Herr, Gustav Hasford (screenplay)

# FULL METAL JACKET (1987)

In Stanley Kubrick's *Barry Lyndon*, the major battle scene depicts an engagement that the narrator tells us did not make the history books, "though it was memorable enough for those who took part." When he came to make a movie about Vietnam, a little after the various angst-ridden and fantastical takes by Francis Ford Coppola (*Apocalypse Now*) and Oliver Stone (*Platoon*) had established an acid/napalm-haze cinematic vocabulary for that war, Kubrick built on this approach. *Full Metal Jacket* presents a grunt-level world in which all officers, commissioned or not, are ridiculous but deadly alien beings (even hookers, we're told, are "serving officers in the Vietcong") and the trudging, heroic Marines of so many *Take the High Ground*-type pictures are nicknamed kids without a clue of where they are or what they're doing.

Based on *The Short-Timers*, an autobiographical novel by Gustav Hasford, with script input from Michael Herr (author of *Despatches* and the *Apocalypse Now* voiceover), *Full Metal Jacket* is ruthless, comic, horrific, and affecting in equal measure, depicting areas of the war rarely glimpsed in movies. A long opening act is set entirely on Parris Island, the induction-and-training center: After a montage in which long-haired young men are shorn to become bald drones no more distinguishable than the future folk of George Lucas's *THX 1138*, the film is commandeered by the astonishing R. Lee Ermey as drill sergeant Hartman, whose obscene, inventive, relentless abuse against all the recruits ("I bet you're the kind of guy that would fuck a person in the ass and not even have the goddamned common courtesy to give him a reacharound") is designed to break down the "maggots" totally before they can be rebuilt as killing machines. In a lecture, Hartman takes pride in the fact that Lee Harvey Oswald and Charles Whitman learned to shoot in the Marines. The horrible irony of this sequence—which closely parallels the gladiator-training regime of *Spartacus*—is that the logical payoff is the transformation of a pudgy foul-up (Vincent d'Onofrio) into one of Kubrick's grotesque ape-men, with a primal glare that echoes the droogs of *A Clockwork Orange* and Jack Torrance (Jack Nicholson) of *The Shining*. The first thing the new-made Marine does is murder his tormentor-creator and kill himself.

After this, the Vietnam sequences are almost a relief, as Pvt Joker (Matthew Modine), a journalist, unbends a little only to be confronted with even more demented individuals—when asked how he can kill women and children, a helicopter gunner gives a technical answer ("it's easy, don't lead them so much"), while a colonel remarks "Son, all I've ever asked of my marines is that they obey my orders as they would the word of God." The climax is a skirmish during a battle in the rubble of Hue City, in which Joker's platoon encounter a female Vietcong sniper: Nobody wins the encounter, and the Marines troop off into the night singing The Mickey Mouse Club Marching Song. Only Kubrick would dare tweak Disney like this. **KN**

G.B. (Handmade) 107m Color

**Director:** Bruce Robinson

**Producer:** Paul M. Heller

**Screenplay:** Bruce Robinson

**Photography:** Peter Hannan

**Music:** David Dundas, Rick Wentworth, Jimi Hendrix

**Cast:** Richard E. Grant, Paul McGann, Richard Griffiths, Ralph Brown, Michael Elphick, Daragh O'Malley, Michael Wardle, Una Brandon-Jones, Noel Johnson, Irene Sutcliffe, Llewellyn Rees, Robert Oates, Anthony Wise, Eddie Tagoe

# WITHNAIL AND I (1987)

Bruce Robinson's subsequent films may so far have proved a disappointment, but nothing can diminish the wonderfully idiosyncratic delights of his debut, a ruefully nostalgic comic account of living in partly self-imposed poverty and squalor in late-1960s Camden Town.

Richard Grant is appropriately and hilariously acerbic and theatrical as Withnail, the upper-middle-class reprobate slumming it while (vainly and not very often) trying to find work as an actor, and Paul McGann is equally effective as his quieter, slightly more conscientious and pretty young flatmate (the "I" of the title). Leaving behind the squalor of their unwashed North London slum for a cheap holiday in the Lake District in a cottage owned by Withnail's porcine gay uncle Monty (Richard Griffiths), the impoverished, booze-and-drugs obsessed pair find themselves bemused, bewildered, and even besieged by country ways and avuncular lusts.

*Withnail and I* is more or less a one-off, its representation of a story ("I" eventually sees the error of Withnail's eternally irresponsible ways and moves on toward a grown-up career) taking second place to the very funny verbal and visual gags, the oh-so-slightly grotesque exaggeration that underpins the comic remembrance of things past, and reveling in (revulsion for?) the colorful characters. Amazingly, it all—even the "Camberwell Carrot" joint—rings frighteningly true. **GA**

**U.S.** (Silver Screen, Touchstone) 119m Color

**Director:** Barry Levinson

**Producer:** Larry Brezner, Mark Johnson

**Screenplay:** Mitch Markowitz

**Photography:** Peter Sova

**Music:** Alex North

**Cast:** Robin Williams, Forest Whitaker, Tung Thanh Tran, Chintara Sukapatana, Bruno Kirby, Robert Wuhl, J.T. Walsh, Noble Willingham, Richard Edson, Juney Smith, Richard Portnow, Floyd Vivino, Cu Ba Nguyen, Dan Stanton, Don Stanton

**Oscar nomination:** Robin Williams (actor)

# GOOD MORNING, VIETNAM (1987)

Rapid-fire stand-up comic Robin Williams, who had been stifling his motor mouth on screen with disappointing results in movies like *Moscow on the Hudson* and *Popeye*, finally got the chance to let rip in Barry Levinson's comedy drama *Good Morning, Vietnam*. Williams plays real-life U.S. Armed Forces radio DJ Adrian Cronauer, who broadcasts his irreverent, wisecracking jokes (effectively Williams's stand-up routine, delivered sitting down), and Motown music from his base in Saigon to the troops fighting the Vietnam War. He also manages to annoy the military brass in the process, which includes a terrific turn from Bruno Kirby as a lieutenant who thinks he is funny but clearly isn't.

There are various subplots: Cronauer's butting heads with his superiors, a romance with a Vietnamese woman, and a friendship with her brother. This is one of the few American-made movies set during the Vietnam War that portrays the Vietnamese as real people. However, the real joy is in watching Williams deliver his manic monologues. Many of them were ad-libbed, and director Levinson made the wise decision to sit back and let the camera roll to capture each and every energetic outburst. **JB**

# AU REVOIR LES ENFANTS (1987)
## GOODBYE CHILDREN

How close this avowedly autobiographical film is to the precise facts can only be gauged by the intensity of the recollected emotion and guilt that it conveys. Julien (Gaspard Manesse) is a 12-year-old pupil in a Catholic boarding school in Nazi-occupied France. Apart from the welcome distractions of air-raid warnings, the war makes little impact on the daily routines of school life, and when three new kids arrive, they are submitted to the ritualistic antagonism of infant communities to strangers. Julien, himself something of an outsider, strikes up a friendship with one of the new boys, Jean (Raphael Fejtö). As they grow closer, he discovers that the newcomers have all adopted false names, though he only gradually and vaguely grows to understand the enormity of antisemitism, and that the Catholic fathers are endeavoring to shelter these endangered children. When the net grows tighter, it is an inadvertent action by Julien himself that betrays the Jewish children and sends them to an inconceivable fate. We realize that this moment will never cease to torment Julien.

Writer and director Louis Malle (*The Lovers* [1958], *Murmur of the Heart* [1971], *Atlantic City* [1980]), is not concerned with Hollywood-style war melodrama but with the life of the school—the daily drags and discoveries, the eccentric habits of schoolmasters, friendships, and suspicions. The war impinges in the air-raid warnings, and the puzzle that the occupying Nazis are, like any other group, a dangerous mix of goons and gentlemen.

Malle genuinely sees it all through the boys' own acute but still unformed vision, and the performances of Manesse and Fejtö are so moving precisely because of the open honesty that compensates for technical expertise. Malles's most personal film, *Au Revoir les Enfants* was the recipient of a slew of international awards (among them the Golden Lion at the 1987 Venice Film Festival), and represented a triumphant swan song in a career that had faltered somewhat since its brave beginnings in the era of the New Wave cinema. **DR**

**France / West Germany** (MK2, NEF, Nouvelles Éditions, Stella Films) 104m Color

**Language:** French / German

**Director:** Louis Malle

**Producer:** Louis Malle

**Screenplay:** Louis Malle

**Photography:** Renato Berta

**Music:** Camille Saint-Saëns, Franz Schubert

**Cast:** Gaspard Manesse, Raphael Fejtö, Francine Racette, Stanislas Carré de Malberg, Philippe Morier-Genoud, François Berléand, François Négret, Peter Fitz, Pascal Rivet, Benoît Henriet, Richard Leboeuf, Xavier Legrand, Arnaud Henriet, Jean-Sébastien Chauvin, Luc Etienne

**Oscar nomination:** France (best foreign language film), Louis Malle (screenplay)

**Venice Film Festival:** Louis Malle (Golden Lion), (OCIC Award)

U.S. (Fox, Amercent, Amer. Entert., Part., Gracie) 127m Color

**Director:** James L. Brooks

**Producer:** James L. Brooks

**Screenplay:** James L. Brooks

**Photography:** Michael Ballhaus

**Music:** Bill Conti

**Cast:** William Hurt, Albert Brooks, Holly Hunter, Robert Prosky, Lois Chiles, Joan Cusack, Peter Hackes, Christian Clemenson, Jack Nicholson, Robert Katims, Ed Wheeler, Stephen Mendillo, Kimber Shoop, Dwayne Markee, Gennie James

**Oscar nomination:** James L. Brooks (best picture), James L. Brooks (screenplay), William Hurt (actor), Holly Hunter (actress), Albert Brooks (actor in support role), Michael Ballhaus (photography), Richard Marks (editing)

**Berlin International Film Festival:** Holly Hunter(Silver Bear—actress), James L. Brooks nomination (Golden Bear)

# BROADCAST NEWS (1987)

An invitation to the 1984 Democratic Convention inspired the hectic spirit of James L. Brooks's fast-paced 1987 media romance. A former CBS television newsman himself, Brooks puts a career twist into the classic concept of screwball comedy. This time, the story centers on the unpredictable outcome of a love triangle between three ambitious and talented people who are made more emotionally fearful within the high-pressure confines of network news. A film about love, it is also about lovers who think that the only safe love affair is the one they have with their work.

Jane Craig (Holly Hunter) is a petite and tidy news producer who comes in early to have a cry at her desk every morning. Working in the Washington bureau of a TV network, she runs her newsroom as a meritocracy. Infatuated with Jane, Aaron Altman (Albert Brooks) is a good reporter with a few strikes against him: The camera doesn't love him, nor apparently, does Jane. Tom Grunick (William Hurt at his most affable and calculating) is everything Aaron is not—charming, telegenic, and not too smart. Jane, torn between both men emotionally, is forced to make a decision which lies at the heart of *Broadcast News*'s brilliance: When the going gets tough, the tough do nothing. Sometimes work is an easier option than being emotionally honest; in fact, loving work is often the most emotionally honest decision there is.

Co-starring Joan Cusack (famous for her bad hair and makeup as much as her memorably awkward, headlong dash to get a video tape to the newsroom in time), a delightfully slick Jack Nicholson appears in an uncredited supporting performance as the network's head anchorman, a professional who sees that Grunick is one of his own kind.

As "news" itself has become the show business of which Altman was so fearful, the earnestness and time devoted to TV stories seems to issue from another age. But the laughs are still there, and anyone who has ever been turned down for someone less intelligent will never forget Aaron's quip, "I say it here and it comes out there," when he calls the newsroom to update Grunick, his romantic nemesis, in an emergency broadcast. **RK**

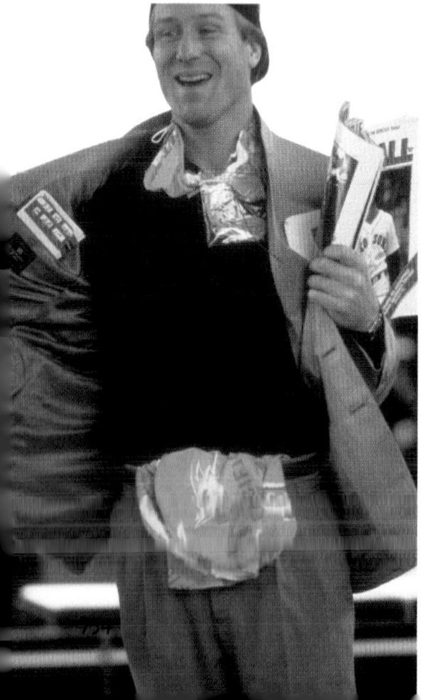

## HOUSEKEEPING (1987)

Bill Forsyth's first American movie deftly carries over to an alien environment the quirky, elliptical, bittersweet humor—the whimsy laced with melancholia—of his Scottish films. The setting of *Housekeeping* is somewhere in the Pacific Northwest where two small girls, after the death of their mother, are passed like unwanted gifts from relative to relative till they wind up in an isolated lakeside house in the care of their eccentric aunt Sylvie. Subtly played by Christine Lahti, Sylvie moves to an unheard music of her own, her gaze gentle but evasive, always responding in the least expected way. As the girls grow up, the elder (Andrea Burchill) comes to reject her embarrassing aunt; the younger sister (Sara Walker), as if in reaction, cleaves all the closer to her.

Forsyth rarely gives easy answers or passes judgment, and the film ends obliquely, with nothing neatly rounded off or resolved. The local women who come to visit, feeling the girls may need taking into care, aren't malicious—just bemused and concerned, unsure how to take this offbeat ménage. *Housekeeping* is a film of absences and half-felt loss, of unresolved myths and a sense of transience that darkens into more somber intimations of death. It is at last a sweet, wistful film that never raises its voice, but lingers in the mind like an insidious whisper. **PK**

**U.S.** (Columbia) 116m Rankcolor

**Director:** Bill Forsyth

**Producer:** Robert F. Colesberry

**Screenplay:** Bill Forsyth, from novel by Marilynne Robinson

**Photography:** Michael Coulter

**Music:** Michael Gibbs

**Cast:** Christine Lahti, Sara Walker, Andrea Burchill, Anne Pitoniak, Barbara Reese, Margot Pinvidic, Bill Smillie, Wayne Robson, Betty Phillips, Karen Austin, Dolores Drake, Georgie Collins, Tonya Tanner, Leah Penny, Brian Linds

## THE PRINCESS BRIDE (1987)

Rob Reiner's friendly fairy-tale adventure *The Princess Bride* delicately mines the irony inherent in its make-believe without ever undermining the effectiveness of the fantasy. The framing device is a grandfather (Peter Falk) reading a favorite book aloud to his skeptical grandson (Fred Savage), and Reiner uses the grandson's initial recalcitrance as both a challenge and a safety net. In the imaginary kingdom of Florin, the beautiful Buttercup (Robin Wright) is separated from the farmhand she loves (Cary Elwes), betrothed to the evil Prince Humperdinck (Chris Sarandon), and spirited away by the nefarious Vizzini (Wallace Shawn).

The colorful characters and adventures are, at their best, like live-action equivalents of Disney animated features, with lots of other fond Hollywood memories thrown in. Andre the Giant seems a cross between Andy Devine and Lumpjaw the Bear. Mandy Patinkin's engaging Inigo Montoya conjures up Gene Kelly in *The Pirate*. Not even the crude ethnic humor—Billy Crystal's Mel Brooks-ish Miracle Max—pricks the dream bubble, and the spirited cast has a field day. Adapted by William Goldman from his own novel, with Christopher Guest as a six-fingered sadist, Peter Cook as a lisping clergyman, and Carol Kane as Max's wife. **JRos**

**U.S.** (Act III, Buttercup, *Princess Bride*) 98m Color

**Director:** Rob Reiner

**Producer:** Rob Reiner, Andrew Scheinman

**Screenplay:** William Goldman , from his book

**Photography:** Adrian Biddle

**Music:** Willy De Ville, Mark Knopfler

**Cast:** Cary Elwes, Mandy Patinkin, Chris Sarandon, Christopher Guest, Wallace Shawn, André the Giant, Fred Savage, Robin Wright Penn, Peter Falk, Peter Cook, Mel Smith, Carol Kane, Billy Crystal, Anne Dyson, Margery Mason

**Oscar nomination:** Willy De Ville (song)

## MOONSTRUCK (1987)

**U.S.** (MGM) 102m Technicolor
**Director:** Norman Jewison
**Producer:** Norman Jewison, Patrick J. Palmer
**Screenplay:** John Patrick Shanley
**Photography:** David Watkin
**Music:** Dick Hyman
**Cast:** Cher, Nicolas Cage, Vincent Gardenia, Olympia Dukakis, Danny Aiello, Julie Bovasso, John Mahoney, Louis Guss, Feodor Chaliapin Jr., Anita Gillette, Leonardo Cimino, Paula Trueman, Nada Despotovich, Joe Grifasi, Gina DeAngeles
**Oscar:** Cher (actress), Olympia Dukakis (actress in support role), John Patrick Shanley (screenplay)
**Oscar nomination:** Patrick J. Palmer, Norman Jewison (best picture), Norman Jewison (director), Vincent Gardenia (actor in support role)
**Berlin International Film Festival:** Norman Jewison (Silver Bear—director) and nomination (Golden Bear)

A delightful tribute to the Italian-American family from director Norman Jewison, *Moonstruck* stars singer-turned-actress Cher as widow Loretta Castorini, who is about to be married to safe and reliable (read—dull and boring) Johnny Cammareri (Danny Aiello). While he is away tending to his ailing mother, Loretta takes it upon herself to contact Johnny's estranged brother Ronny (Nicolas Cage) and invite him to the wedding, but when they get to know each other the pair fall in love.

The central love story in this romantic comedy is fun and sparky thanks to two great central performances from Cage and especially Cher (a role for which she won an Oscar). She gets the opportunity to be a modern-day Cinderella, transforming from dowdy duckling to glamor queen after one trip to the hair salon. But it is the supporting players who add even more spice to the proceedings—especially Vincent Gardenia as Loretta's womanizing father Cosmo and Olympia Dukakis as her mother Rose—delivering scriptwriter John Patrick Shanley's words with zest. A much imitated treat that has yet to be bettered. **JB**

## THE UNTOUCHABLES (1987)

**U.S.** (Paramount) 119m Technicolor
**Director:** Brian De Palma
**Producer:** Art Linson
**Screenplay:** David Mamet, from novels by Oscar Fraley, Eliot Ness, Paul Robsky
**Photography:** Stephen H. Burum
**Music:** Ennio Morricone
**Cast:** Kevin Costner, Sean Connery, Charles Martin Smith, Andy Garcia, Robert De Niro, Richard Bradford, Jack Kehoe, Brad Sullivan, Billy Drago, Patricia Clarkson, Vito D'Ambrosio, Steven Goldstein, Peter Aylward, Don Harvey, Robert Swan
**Oscar:** Sean Connery (actor in support role)
**Oscar nomination:** Patrizia von Brandenstein, William A. Elliott, Hal Gausman (art direction), Marilyn Vance (costume), Ennio Morricone (music)

It's Prohibition-era Chicago, and someone has to sort out those pesky gangsters running around town. That man, of course, is Eliot Ness (Kevin Costner), a Treasury agent who sets up his own special unit, with the help of an assortment of cops and crime fighters, to bring down the bad guys and, most notably, the baddest of them all, Al Capone (Robert De Niro).

Director Brian De Palma's vision of the crime-ridden Windy City is bloodier than many that have gone before—including the TV drama on which this movie is loosely based—but he doesn't let the gore detract from the story, or from the performances of his cast. Costner successfully holds his own against two powerhouse turns from De Niro and Sean Connery. Connery, as world-weary cop Malone, has the best of David Mamet's dialogue, most notably the "he sends one of yours to the hospital, you send one of his to the morgue" speech. In another "method outing," De Niro packed on the pounds and wore suits (and, rumor has it, underpants) made by Capone's tailors to get a true feel for the character.

Filled with eye-widening set pieces—the Odessa Steps sequence at the train station and Capone's meeting that ends with punishment by baseball bat—*The Untouchables* remains a fascinating and gripping look at a particularly bloody piece of American history. **JB**

# HONG GAO LIANG (1987)
## RED SORGHUM

Winner of the Golden Bear at the 1988 Berlin International Film Festival, Zhang Yimou's feature from the People's Republic of China mixes local history and legend. It follows the adventures of a young girl (Gong Li) who is sold by her father to an elderly and wealthy leper, then carried off by a chair bearer posing as a highwayman, eventually becoming the head of a sorghum-wine distillery.

*Red Sorghum* is the first feature directed by the cinematographer of *Yellow Earth* (1984), *The Big Parade* (1986), and *Old Well* (1986). One of the leading members of the famous "Fifth Generation" of Chinese filmmakers, Zhang has been widely considered the most versatile of the group because of his background in cinematography and acting (he was the lead in *Old Well*). Many of *Red Sorghum*'s most striking virtues are visual: handsome 'Scope compositions of landscapes and sorghum waving in the wind, and a deft use of color filters.

Narrated offscreen by the heroine's grandson, the plot is set in the late 1920s and early 1930s and ends with the Japanese invasion. Although the action is often intriguing—lyrical in the early sections, whimsical toward the middle, and bloody and suspenseful toward the end—the overall narrative gets broken up quite a bit by the episodic structure, and the film registers mainly as detachable set pieces. The film presents the debut of Gong Li, who went on to become one of the major actresses of mainland Chinese cinema and starred in subsequent Zhang features. Like Zhang's early features with Gong, especially *Ju Dou* and *Raise the Red Lantern*, *Red Sorghum* is concerned both covertly and overtly with the persistence of feudalism in the life of mainland China. **JRos**

**China** (Xi'an) 91m Eastmancolor

**Language:** Mandarin

**Director:** Zhang Yimou

**Producer:** Tian-Ming Wu

**Screenplay:** Jianyu Chen, Wei Zhu, from the books *Red Sorghum* and *Sorghum Wine* by Yan Mo

**Photography:** Changwei Gu

**Music:** Jiping Zhao

**Cast:** Gong Li, Wen Jiang, Rujun Ten, Liu Jia, Cunhua Ji, Ming Qian, Zhang Yimou

**Berlin International Film Festival:** Zhang Yimou (Golden Bear)

# THE DEAD (1987)

The late John Huston devoted the better part of his career to a cinema predicated on the adaptation of literary works—informed by crafty casting and fluid storytelling, but often limited by the fact that his attraction to heavyweights like *The Maltese Falcon*, *The Red Badge of Courage*, *Moby Dick*, *The Man Who Would Be King*, *Wise Blood*, and *Under the Volcano* guaranteed "faithful" reductions at best. His last film, *The Dead*, which adapts the final story in James Joyce's *Dubliners*, represents the apotheosis of this position: isolating the story from the rest of the collection and most of its flawlessly composed language, and then doing his best with what remains.

Working with a script by his son Tony and starring his daughter Anjelica as Gretta Conroy, Huston hews to the original and much of its dialogue with rigorous affection, and within its acknowledged restrictions, the film's concentrated simplicity and purity achieve a kind of perfection. The lilting Irish flavor is virtually decanted, and Fred Murphy's gliding camera movements are delicately executed. There is also a rather awesome directness as well as calmness about the way that Huston contemplates his own rapidly approaching death. **JRos**

**G.B.** (Liffey, Zenith) 83m Color

**Director:** John Huston

**Producer:** Wieland Schulz-Keil, Chris Sievernich

**Screenplay:** Tony Huston, from story by James Joyce

**Photography:** Fred Murphy

**Music:** Alex North

**Cast:** Anjelica Huston, Donal McCann, Dan O'Herlihy, Donal Donnelly, Helena Carroll, Cathleen Delany, Ingrid Craigie, Rachael Dowling, Marie Kean, Frank Patterson, Maria McDermottroe, Sean McClory, Kate O'Toole, Maria Hayden, Bairbre Dowling

**Oscar nomination:** Tony Huston (screenplay), Dorothy Jeakins (costume)

**U.S.** (Paramount) 123m Technicolor

**Director:** Adrian Lyne

**Producer:** Stanley R. Jaffe, Sherry Lansing

**Screenplay:** James Dearden

**Photography:** Howard Atherton

**Music:** Maurice Jarre

**Cast:** Michael Douglas, Glenn Close, Anne Archer, Ellen Hamilton Latzen, Stuart Pankin, Ellen Foley, Fred Gwynne, Meg Mundy, Tom Brennan, Lois Smith, Mike Nussbaum, J.J. Johnston, Michael Arkin, Sam Coppola, Eunice Prewitt

**Oscar nomination:** Stanley R. Jaffe, Sherry Lansing (best picture), Adrian Lyne (director), James Dearden (screenplay), Glenn Close (actress), Anne Archer (actress in support role), Michael Kahn, Peter E. Berger (editing)

# FATAL ATTRACTION (1987)

Director Adrian Lyne made men all over the world squirm in their seats, and added the term "bunny boiler" to our vocabulary with this (let's face it misogynistic) nightmare film. Dan Gallagher (Michael Douglas) has a one-night stand with colleague Alex Forrest (Glenn Close) while his wife and kids are away. Alex wants more than a one-night stand, however, and her ever-increasing dementia about rejection finally erupts to destroy what she can never have: A proper, picket-fence, all-American family. It seems that all a high-powered independent woman in the 1980s really ever wanted was to be June Cleaver, but failing that, "June-with-a-cleaver" would do nicely.

*Fatal Attraction* is a wonderful example of what happens when big-budget Hollywood tries its hand at the exploitation market. With a less flashy, style-over-substance director like Lyne and without stars like Douglas and Close, this would be a typical run-of-the-mill, almost straight-to-video thriller, perhaps even marketed as a slasher film. But with typical Hollywood gloss, the film earns an aura of respectability—this appears not to be a horror movie, but a domestic drama-cum-suspense thriller, with (perhaps) erotic overtones. The ruse worked and this was one of the most successful films of 1987. **MK**

**Hong Kong** (Cinema City, Film Workshop) 98m Color

**Director:** Siu-Tung Ching

**Producer:** Hark Tsui

**Screenplay:** Kai-Chi Yun, from novel by Songling Pu

**Photography:** Poon Hang-Sang

**Music:** Romeo Díaz, James Wong

**Cast:** Leslie Cheung, Joey Wong, Wu Ma, Wang Zuxian, Liu Zhaoming

# SINNUI YAUMAN (1987)
## A CHINESE GHOST STORY

When it comes to fantasy filmmaking, Hong Kong can make Hollywood look imaginatively bankrupt. This 1987 cult classic suggests a combination of Sam Raimi, Jean Cocteau, Georges Méliès, and Tim Burton. It's a ghost story that is also a love story, a sword-and-sorcery tale, and a comedy. Leslie Cheung stars as a naïve young debt collector who falls in love with the enigmatic beauty (Joey Wong) haunting an abandoned temple. Unfortunately, she's a ghostly handmaiden for an ancient tree-spirit who feeds on living souls—so, with a Taoist swordsman (Wu Ma) protecting him, Cheung ventures into the netherworld to save his love from a fate worse than death. This picture is gorgeous to look at, especially in the velvety nocturnal sequences when skeletons stir, spirits come out to play, and it seems anything can happen and probably will. The special effects are indeed extraordinary: People fly through the air, their robes flowing, blades flashing in the moonlight (these are stunts, remember, not optical process shots); an evil tongue rolls out and slicks through the room like an obscene elastic slug; while hell itself is a bravura chamber of horrors. The film's broad, amiable slapstick doesn't really play, but its surprisingly lyrical, sensual romanticism is effective, and there's so much to enjoy that overlooking the sometimes clumsy storytelling is easy. **TCh**

# MUJERES AL BORDE DE UN ATAQUE DE NERVIOS (1988)
## WOMEN ON THE VERGE OF A NERVOUS BREAKDOWN

Thanks to the Oscar nomination it received for Best Foreign Language Film—the first in Pedro Almodóvar's career—*Women on the Verge of a Nervous Breakdown* confirmed the international status of the Spanish writer-director. The film certainly improves on the most worthy aspects of Almodóvar's previous works: the radical subjectivity of feelings, the exaggeration of emotions, and the bizarre mixture of melodrama and comedy.

The story's premises obviously belong to melodrama. Pepa Marcos (Carmen Maura) and her lover Iván (Fernando Guillén), a married man, make their living dubbing films. One day he announces that he wants to break things off, leaving a message on her answering machine. Deciding to meet him one last time for an explanation, Pepa investigates Iván's family life and discovers that his wife, recently released from a psychiatric hospital, plans on killing him. Despite his betrayal, Pepa runs to the airport, where he is about to take off with his new love, and saves his life. Expressing his gratitude to Pepa, Iván tries to make up with her, but she turns him down.

Although *Women on the Verge* is full of melodramatic situations, the way Almodóvar develops it reveals his particular sense of humor, based mostly on the eccentric characters populating the film. While Pepa is on the phone investigating her missing lover, her apartment fills with all sorts of people: Candela (María Barranco), a friend who is running from the police because she had an affair with a Shiite terrorist; a stuttering young man who wants to rent the apartment after Pepa moves out; and Iván's mad wife, with a gun in her purse. Everyone is so desperate, and the sheer accumulation of such despair in one place is so exaggerated we can only roar with laughter. The quid-pro-quos and the vaudeville situations might make the movie seem like a farcical comedy, but Almodóvar's sure touch is there to make the difference, with its exaltation of kitsch, excessive colors, and hyperbole.

Beyond its delirious humor, *Women on the Verge* is a moving female monologue about happiness and loneliness. Loosely inspired by Jean Cocteau's 1930 play *The Human Voice*, the film showcases the tremendous talent of Almodóvar's muse, Carmen Maura. Nor should we forget Antonio Banderas, who took an important step here toward international stardom. **DD**

**Spain** (El Deseo, Laurenfilm) 90m Eastmancolor
**Language:** Spanish
**Director:** Pedro Almodóvar
**Producer:** Pedro Almodóvar
**Screenplay:** Pedro Almodóvar
**Photography:** José Luis Alcaine
**Music:** Bernardo Bonezzi, C. Curet Alonso, Ventura Rodríguez
**Cast:** Carmen Maura, Antonio Banderas, Julieta Serrano, Rossy de Palma, María Barranco, Kiti Manver, Guillermo Montesinos, Chus Lampreave, Yayo Calvo, Loles León, Ángel de Andrés López, Fernando Guillén, Juan Lombardero, José Antonio Navarro, Ana Leza
**Oscar nomination:** Spain (best foreign language film)
**Venice Film Festival:** Pedro Almodóvar (Golden Osella—screenplay)

# SPOORLOOS (1988)
## THE VANISHING

**Netherlands / France** (Argos, Golden Egg, Ingrid, MGS, Movie Visions) 107m Color

**Language:** Dutch / French / English

**Director:** George Sluizer

**Producer:** George Sluizer, Anne Lordon

**Screenplay:** Tim Krabbé, George Sluizer, from the novel *The Golden Egg* by Tim Krabbé

**Photography:** Toni Kuhn

**Music:** Henny Vrienten

**Cast:** Bernard-Pierre Donnadieu, Gene Bervoets, Johanna ter Steege, Gwen Eckhaus, Bernadette Le Saché, Tania Latarjet, Lucille Glenn, Roger Souza, Caroline Appéré, Pierre Forget, Didier Rousset, Raphaeline, Robert Lucibello, David Bayle, Doumee

*The Golden Egg*, a best-selling novel published in 1984 by Dutch journalist and author Tim Krabbé, served as the source material for director George Sluizer's highly acclaimed thriller, *The Vanishing*. Like the book, the film tells the story of Rex Hofman (Gene Bervoets), a young Dutchman whose girlfriend Saskia (Johanna ter Steege) mysteriously disappears at a gas station in central France while the couple are on vacation. Obsessed with finding out what happened to her, tormented by the memory of her loss, Rex single-handedly launches an international missing-persons campaign that completely takes over his life.

Years later, long after the trail has gone cold and the police have closed the case, Rex still scours the countryside out of guilt and as a tribute to Saskia, alienating and eventually losing his new girlfriend in the process. Saskia's unlikely abductor, a French chemistry teacher named Raymond Lemorne (Bernard-Pierre Donnadieu) turns up with an offer to tell all, but only if Rex agrees in advance to undergo the exact same experience as his girlfriend. Rex hesitantly agrees because the worst thing of all is "not knowing." Raymond explains that he did indeed kill Saskia, not for sexual or personal reasons, but merely because he wanted to find out if he was capable of committing such an evil act. Rex willingly takes a sedative, and in the film's penultimate scene, awakens to find himself buried alive inside a narrow coffin. *The Vanishing* ends with a slow zoom in on a newspaper headline concerning the mysterious "double vanishing" of Rex and Saskia, while Raymond sits contemplatively at his cottage, his unsuspecting wife watering the plants that mark the couple's otherwise anonymous graves.

Despite its adherence to the mystery/horror/suspense form, and its international promotion and reception as an example of contemporary Hitchcockian moviemaking, *The Vanishing*'s plaintive score, melodramatic tone, and focus on subjectivity rather than detection all serve to make the film extremely difficult to analyze in traditional generic terms. Sluizer's picture fits most comfortably as part of a cycle of distinctively Dutch "thrillers," all of which possess an essentially national, culturally specific dimension. Other entries in this cycle include Paul Verhoeven's *The Fourth Man* (1983), Dick Maas's *The Lift* (1983) and *Amsterdamned* (1987), and, to some extent, Marleen Gorris's *Broken Mirrors* (1984). Despite their incorporation of conventions from disparate genres, and the undeniable presence of auteurist elements in each, it is possible to identify an underlying thematic preoccupation across all of these films. The male protagonists suffer an anxiety about being bound to a female partner in a normal relationship—the expectation or reality of marriage and all it legally and socially entails, namely monogamy, heterosexuality, and lifelong commitment. As with the Italian *giallo*, Dutch thriller cinema—*The Vanishing* is the most well-known and highly regarded example—is not so much a genre as a body of films resisting simple generic definition. **SJS**

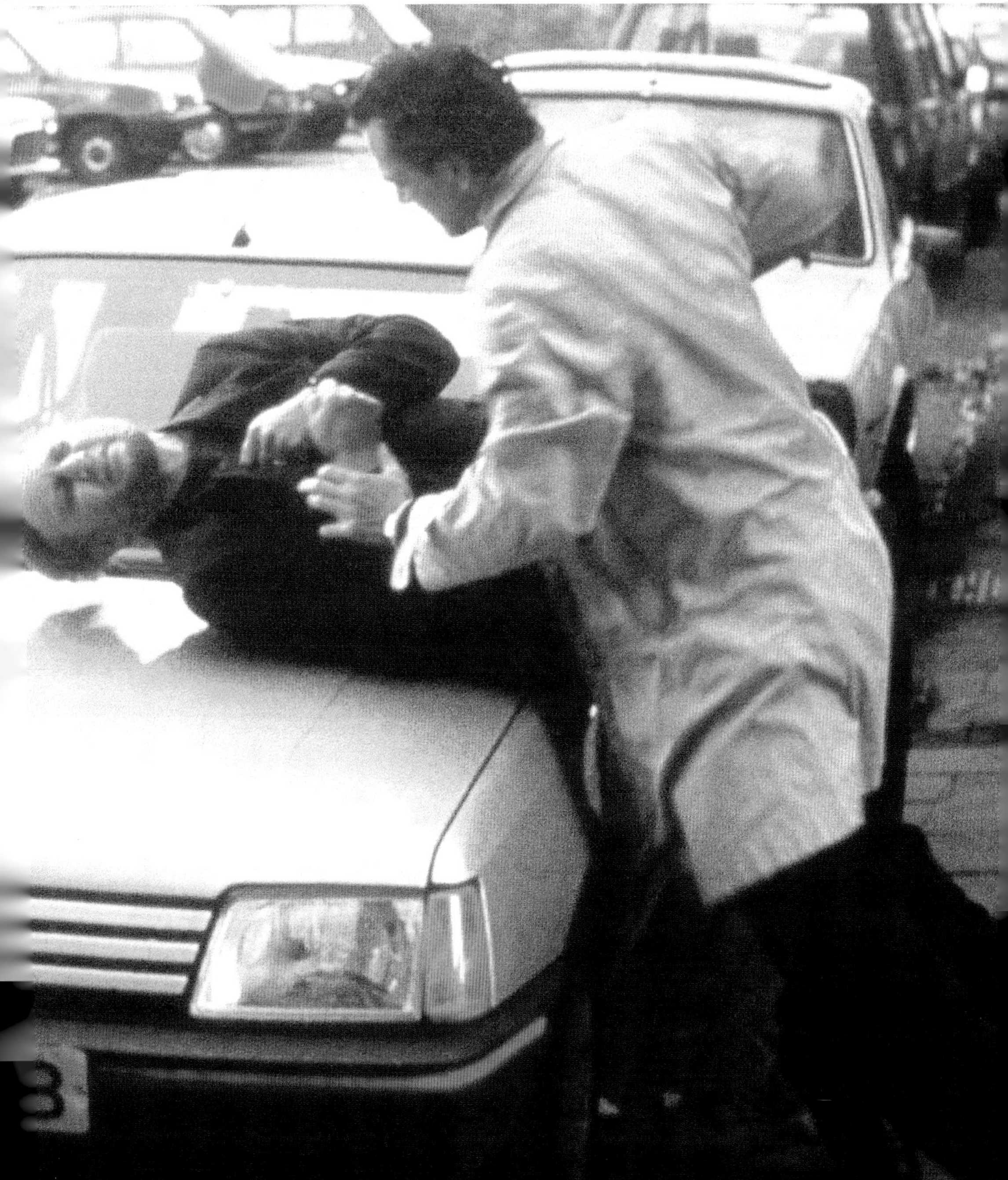

## BULL DURHAM (1988)

**U.S.** (Mount) 108m Color
**Director:** Ron Shelton
**Producer:** Mark Burg, Thom Mount
**Screenplay:** Ron Shelton
**Photography:** Bobby Byrne
**Music:** Michael Convertino
**Cast:** Kevin Costner, Susan Sarandon, Tim Robbins, Trey Wilson, Robert Wuhl, William O'Leary, David Neidorf, Danny Gans, Tom Silardi, Lloyd T. Williams, Rick Marzan, George Buck, Jenny Robertson, Gregory Avellone, Garland Bunting
**Oscar nomination:** Ron Shelton (screenplay)

Writer-director Ron Shelton brought his own experiences as a minor league ball player to this smart, madly sexy comedy, and used his directorial debut to share his passions for baseball, lusty women, and small-timers with big hearts.

The central character in *Bull Durham* is baseball groupie, amateur philosopher, and uninhibited, well-read Annie (Susan Sarandon). She selects a player from the Durham Bulls each year to share her bed and benefit from her life wisdom (sometimes tying her partner to the bed to read him Walt Whitman). Having chosen dim-witted rookie Ebby "Nuke" LaLoosh (Tim Robbins), a pitcher with "a million dollar arm and a five cent brain," she belatedly realizes that a veteran catcher nearing the end of his career, cynical Crash Davis (Kevin Costner), would have been the classier option. Meanwhile Crash gives Nuke manlier advice, providing several of the best laughs as he wearily expounds on meeting the media and avoiding foot fungus in curt, mid-game seminars on the pitcher's mound. Naturally this is really about the big game of life, with witty, sassy dialogue, highly engaging performances, an amusing soundtrack, and absolutely sizzling sex scenes between Sarandon and Costner (although it was Robbins who became her off-screen partner). **AE**

## ARIEL (1988)

**Finland** (Villealfa) 73m Eastmancolor
**Language:** Finnish
**Director:** Aki Kaurismäki
**Producer:** Aki Kaurismäki
**Screenplay:** Aki Kaurismäki
**Photography:** Timo Salminen
**Cast:** Turo Pajala, Susanna Haavisto, Matti Pellonpää, Eetu Hilkamo, Erkki Pajala, Matti Jaaranen, Hannu Viholainen, Jorma Markkula, Tarja Keinänen, Eino Kuusela, Kauko Laalo, Jyrki Olsonen, Esko Nikkari, Marja Packalén, Mikko Remes

A woman (Susanna Haavisto), impulsively quitting her job and going off with a retrenched miner (Turo Pajala), remarks: "Hopefully, I won't regret this." Later, as the man enters jail for a murder he didn't commit, he declares he has no religion, no fixed address, no family or friends. One of his newfound criminal colleagues dies trying to flee the country, uttering these famous last words: "Bury my heart on a tip."

If anyone has perfected the cinematic language to express drollness, it is Finnish director Aki Kaurismaki. His films have a sardonic, deadpan, couldn't-care-less air that belies the real depth of their commitment to society's marginals. *Ariel*, one of his best works of the 1980s, is a relentless parable of hard luck befalling ordinary people. Yet these characters never lament or protest their lot; the best they expect is a ticket to somewhere, anywhere, else.

At certain moments of his career, Kaurismaki has seemed, especially in his public pronouncements, incurably flip. But *Ariel*'s bleak outlook and its determinedly minimal means (approaching the austerity of Robert Bresson) reveal a more authentic engagement with his subject matter. *Ariel* makes for hypnotic viewing, forecasting the greatness that Kaurismaki would achieve in 2002's *Man Without a Past*. **AM**

# THE THIN BLUE LINE (1988)

Errol Morris's third documentary feature (after *Gates of Heaven* [1978] and *Vernon, Florida* [1981]) is an absorbing if problematic reconstruction of and investigation into the 1976 murder of a Dallas policeman. As an investigative detective-journalist who spent many years working on this case, Morris uncovered a disturbing miscarriage of justice in the conviction of Randall Adams—who came very close to being executed, but was saved as a result of this film. Morris goes so far in his talking-head interview technique that he eventually goads David Harris, Adams's companion on the night of the murder in question, into something very close to a confession.

It's the latter achievement that makes *The Thin Blue Line* as memorable and as important as it is. But it is worth bearing in mind that Morris's highly selective approach also leaves a good many questions unanswered. The issue of motive is virtually untouched, and the quasi-abstract re-creations of the crime, accompanied by what is probably the first effective film score ever composed by Philip Glass, give rise to a lot of metaphysical speculations that, provocative as they are, tend to overshadow many of the issues about what actually happened during the crime.

The results are compelling, even though they provide an object lesson in the dangers of being influenced by Werner Herzog; the larger considerations and the film noir overtones wind up distracting us from the facts of the case, and what emerges are two effective half-films, each of which is partially at odds with the other. Yet one can also see Morris honing his flair for juxtaposition and editing that would eventually bear fruit in his remarkable 1997 film *Fast, Cheap & Out of Control*, where he manages to juggle the continuities and discontinuities between four seemingly unrelated talking heads, and in the multiple achievements of his episodes in the TV series *First Person* (2000), which has already enjoyed two seasons. **JRos**

**U.S.** (American Playhouse) 103m Color

**Director:** Errol Morris

**Producer:** Mark Lipson

**Screenplay:** Errol Morris

**Photography:** Robert Chappell, Stefan Czapsky

**Music:** Philip Glass

**Cast:** Randall Adams, David Harris, Gus Rose, Jackie Johnson, Marshall Touchton, Dale Holt, Sam Kittrell, Hootie Nelson, Dennis Johnson, Floyd Jackson, Edith James, Dennis White, Don Metcalfe, Emily Miller, R.L. Miller

# AKIRA (1988)

**Japan** (Akira, Dragon, Nakamura, Telecom Animation, Tokyo Movie) 124m Color

**Language:** Japanese

**Director:** Katsuhiro Ôtomo

**Producer:** Shunzo Kato, Yoshimasa Mizuo, Ryohei Suzuki

**Screenplay:** Katsuhiro Ôtomo, Izô Hashimoto

**Photography:** Katsuji Misawa

**Music:** Shoji Yamashiro

**Cast:** Mitsuo Iwata, Nozomu Sasaki, Mami Koyama, Tesshô Genda, Hiroshi Ôtake, Kôichi Kitamura, Michihiro Ikemizu, Yuriko Fuchizaki, Masaaki Ôkura, Tarô Arakawa, Takeshi Kusao, Kazumi Tanaka, Masayuki Katô, Yôsuke Akimoto, Masato Hirano

Katsuhiro Ôtomo's animated masterpiece *Akira* is the pinnacle of Japanese apocalyptic science fiction. The plot is deceptively simple: in the chaotic future of Neo-Tokyo (named for its replacing the original Tokyo, destroyed by a mysterious cataclysm in the late 20th century), Kaneda, a teenage motorcycle gang member, finds his former best friend Tetsuo transformed into a homicidal telepath with the will and the power to kill hundreds. He reluctantly joins a group of antigovernment terrorists in their search for the mysterious Akira, a telepath even more powerful than Tetsuo.

Ôtomo's genius lies in linking the apocalypse with the rage of disaffected teenagers. After all, for a teenager, every emotion is apocalyptic. So imagine if a teenager had telekinetic powers that increase exponentially with his emotions, and imagine that this teenager were the most angry, resentful little bastard you've ever met. Think about that and then think about the most epic scenes of devastation you could possibly imagine, and you have this film. The energy-rush action of *Akira* is more than a 200 mph adrenaline ride. It provides the sugarcoating for some serious exploration of ideas and metaphors that preoccupy the Japanese psyche, namely social collapse, malaise, and the continuing ambivalence toward military power. It's not an accident that the chief opposing forces in the story are delinquent teenage bikers, would-be revolutionaries, and the military.

Most of all, *Akira*'s story is fueled by society's fear of its youth—wild, uncontrollable, chaotic youth. Tetsuo is the ultimate pissed-off teen, one with enough power to garner himself a body count in the dozens, and there's a reason the government and the army are terrified of the enigmatic Akira, forever frozen in an arrested childhood. This is adolescence causing destruction on an epic scale, drawing on memories of the atom bombs dropped on Japan in World War II, and our continuing collective fears of annihilation. The fascination that Japanese pop culture has with the Apocalypse goes beyond mere flirtation and leaps headlong into mad, dirty, monkey sex every chance it gets, which isn't necessarily very healthy, but certainly makes for some excellent stories. **AT**

# NUOVO CINEMA PARADISO (1988)
## CINEMA PARADISO

Marked by an autobiographical touch, this second movie by Italian director Giuseppe Tornatore is a nostalgic evocation of his childhood days, but also of those happy times before television when people used to go to the cinema. It tells the story of a filmmaker who, after being told by his mother that "Alfredo died," starts to remember the 1950s, when as a boy living in a small Sicilian village, he spent almost all his time in the Cinema Paradiso. While there he became friends with the projectionist Alfredo (Philippe Noiret, in one of his best roles), a father substitute who, after being blinded during a fire, continued to do his job with help from the child. Everything in their village spins around the cinema, a place of entertainment, but also of meeting and chatter.

The personalities of the Paradiso audience are quizzically charming, especially that of the priest who assumes the censor's role, cutting out the "daring" scenes. In the esteemed traditions of neorealism and Italian comedy, *Cinema Paradiso* finds an excellent balance between humor and nostalgia. Echoing François Truffaut's *The 400 Blows* (1959), the image of a happy childhood nurtured by the tones of movies reveals Tornatore's gratitude to the masters of cinema. The film is enjoyable and heartwarming, especially for the relationship between the boy and the projectionist. **DD**

**Italy / France** (Cristaldifilm, Ariane, RAI, TF1) 155m Color

**Language:** English / Italian

**Director:** Giuseppe Tornatore

**Producer:** Mino Barbera, Franco Cristaldi, Giovanna Romagnoli

**Screenplay:** Giuseppe Tornatore

**Photography:** Blasco Giurato

**Music:** Andrea Morricone, Ennio Morricone

**Cast:** Antonella Attili, Enzo Cannavale, Isa Danieli, Leo Gullotta, Marco Leonardi, Pupella Maggio, Agnese Nano, Leopoldo Trieste, Salvatore Cascio, Tano Cimarosa, Nicola Di Pinto, Roberta Lena, Nino Terzo

**Oscar:** Italy (best foreign language film)

**Cannes Film Festival:** Giuseppe Tornatore (grand prize of the jury), tied with *Trop belle pour toi*, nomination (Golden Palm)

# HÔTEL TERMINUS: KLAUS BARBIE ET SON TEMPS (1988)
## HOTEL TERMINUS: THE LIFE AND TIMES OF KLAUS BARBIE

Marcel Ophüls devised a new kind of Holocaust documentary in *The Sorrow and the Pity*, letting interviews and montages speak for themselves without the aid of voiceover narration, which Ophüls finds too redolent of groupthink and ideology.

He innovated further in *The Memory of Justice*, bringing in more of his personal reactions to the film's subject—the Nuremberg war-crimes trials. In *Hotel Terminus: The Life and Times of Klaus Barbie*, he took the radical step of centering a four-and-a-half-hour film on a Nazi who had successfully eluded photographers throughout his career. Equally uncompromising was Ophüls's decision not to use Holocaust atrocity footage, on the grounds that it has lost some of its impact after decades of exposure.

*Hotel Terminus* gains more than it loses from the near-invisibility of its protagonist and from Ophüls's insistence on evoking Holocaust evils through verbal testimony rather than filmic and photographic evidence. His choices have uncommon moral clarity if one believes that the enormity of Holocaust suffering ultimately defies media representation, and that cinema's big-screen charisma inevitably risks giving historical horrors a measure of aesthetic allure. A work of art in every sense, *Hotel Terminus* is among the most rigorous as well as the most accessible documentaries about the Nazi era. **DS**

**France / U.S.** (Samuel Goldwyn, Memory) 267m Color

**Language:** French / English / German / Spanish

**Director:** Marcel Ophüls

**Producer:** Marcel Ophüls

**Screenplay:** Marcel Ophüls

**Photography:** Reuben Aaronson, Pierre Boffety, Daniel Chabert, Michael J. Davis, Paul Gonon, Hans Haber, Lionel Legros, Wilhelm Rösing

**Cast:** Klaus Barbie, Claude Lanzmann, Jeanne Moreau, Marcel Ophüls

**Oscar:** Marcel Ophüls (documentary)

**Cannes Film Festival:** Marcel Ophüls (FIPRESCI award), tied with Krótki film *o zabijaniu*

**Berlin International Film Festival:** Marcel Ophüls (peace film award)

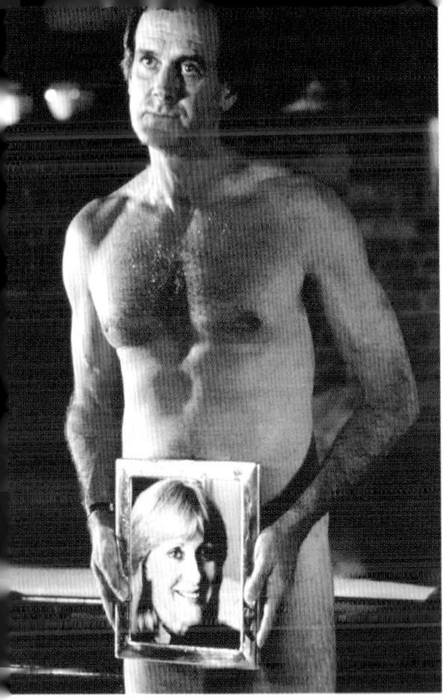

# A FISH CALLED WANDA (1988)

A Brit named George (Tom Georgeson), his American girlfriend Wanda (Jamie Lee Curtis), her Yankee lover Otto (Kevin Kline), and George's stuttering English minion Ken (Michael Palin) together rob a jewelry vault. Untrusting and untrustworthy, they're each criminal amateurs with secretly developed cross-purposes and internal alliances. So Wanda and Otto double-cross George by framing him for the crime, although Ken unwittingly intercedes and hides the ill-gotten treasure in his home aquarium.

When George is brought to trial and defended by Archie (John Cleese), a frustrated lawyer, Wanda resolves to seduce the good magistrate and learn the secret of her gang's stolen booty. Complications quickly develop, perhaps none more aggressively funny than Ken's several attempts to dispatch dog owner Mrs. Coady (Patricia Hayes), the one witness connecting George with the crime. Mixed in for good measure are Otto's play-acted gay come-ons to Ken, Archie's browbeaten home life, Archie and Wanda's developing love affair interrupted at every turn by Otto's bumbling jealousy, and an airport finale with flight to a leisurely future the prize for all comers.

A caper comedy of manners and not so subtle Anglo-American cultural disconnects, the success of Charles Crichton's *A Fish Called Wanda* lay in its treatment of stereotypical gangster types. First is the absurd motif of the piece that rests on the communications skills of a man with a lifetime stutter (Ken). Then there's a psycho killer (Otto) rendered as an oversensitive nincompoop manipulated by a femme fatale (Wanda) with a debilitating erotic weakness for romance languages. Last is the straight-laced hero (Archie), no more than a cloistered man with great passions, but also someone with an almost pathological knack for receiving the butt end of bad luck situations.

Laughs aside, *A Fish Called Wanda* offers a triumphant reappraisal of one-time scream queen Curtis as a comic actress while providing a launch pad for Kline's ascent into critical circles as an awards-worthy performer. Effortlessly, but most of all humorously, the film elevated the careers of Monty Python alums John Cleese and Michael Palin and made them Hollywood stars in the genre. **GCQ**

**U.S.** (MGM, Prominent, Star) 108m Technicolor

**Language:** English / Italian / Russian

**Director:** Charles Crichton

**Producer:** Michael Shamberg

**Screenplay:** John Cleese, Charles Crichton

**Photography:** Alan Hume

**Music:** John Du Prez

**Cast:** John Cleese, Jamie Lee Curtis, Kevin Kline, Michael Palin, Maria Aitken, Tom Georgeson, Patricia Hayes, Geoffrey Palmer, Cynthia Cleese, Mark Elwes, Neville Phillips, Peter Jonfield, Ken Campbell, Al Ashton, Roger Hume

**Oscar:** Kevin Kline (actor in support role)

**Oscar nomination:** Charles Crichton (director), John Cleese, Charles Crichton (screenplay)

# THE NAKED GUN (1988)

U.S. (Paramount) 85m Technicolor
**Director:** David Zucker
**Producer:** Robert K. Weiss
**Screenplay:** Jerry Zucker, Jim Abrahams, David Zucker, Pat Proft, from television series by Jerry Zucker, Jim Abrahams, David Zucker
**Photography:** Robert M. Stevens
**Music:** Ira Newborn
**Cast:** Leslie Nielsen, Priscilla Presley, George Kennedy, Ricardo Montalban, O.J. Simpson, Raye Birk, Susan Beaubian, Nancy Marchand, Jeannette Charles, Ed Williams, Tiny Ron, "Weird Al" Yankovic, Leslie Maier, Winifred Freedman, Joe Grifasi

David Zucker, Jim Abrahams, and Jerry Zucker, the team behind the 1980 blockbuster hit *Airplane!*, first introduced the world to bumbling cop Frank Drebin (Leslie Nielsen) with the comic TV series *Police Squad* in 1982. But it was this feature-length parody of the traditional cop show six years later that turned Nielsen's Drebin into a star, spawning two successful sequels.

The cop who always gets his man—usually by complete accident—is assigned to a new case: Investigating criminal mastermind Victor Ludwig (Ricardo Montalban), who plans to assassinate Queen Elizabeth II at a baseball game. (What, you expected the plot to make sense?!) Aiding him is the beautiful Jane (Priscilla Presley, showing a deft comic touch) and an assortment of oddballs including Police Captain Ed Hocken (George Kennedy) and Drebin's partner Nordberg (former football star O.J. Simpson, six years before his notorious trial).

The jokes are dumb and dumber, the spoofs and sight gags coming thick and fast as everything from the American National Anthem to classic movies like *Casablanca* (1942) are skewered by Zucker/Abrahams/Zucker's hilariously silly script. Stupid—but in a good way. **JB**

# BIG (1988)

U.S. (Fox, Gracie) 104m Color
**Director:** Penny Marshall
**Producer:** James L. Brooks, Robert Greenhut
**Screenplay:** Gary Ross, Anne Spielberg
**Photography:** Barry Sonnenfeld
**Music:** Howard Shore
**Cast:** Tom Hanks, Elizabeth Perkins, Robert Loggia, John Heard, Jared Rushton, David Moscow, Jon Lovitz, Mercedes Ruehl, Josh Clark, Kimberlee M. Davis, Oliver Block, Erika Katz, Allan Wasserman, Mark Ballou, Gary Howard Klar
**Oscar nomination:** Gary Ross, Anne Spielberg (screenplay), Tom Hanks (actor)

When young Josh (David Moscow) is refused a ride on a fairground rollercoaster, he puts a quarter in a carnival wishing machine and wishes he were big. Next morning, it seems Josh's dream has come true—sort of—when he wakes up to find himself in the body of a thirty-something (and definitely taller) man (Tom Hanks). Fleeing his home when his mother fails to recognize him (and in fact suspects him of being her son's abductor), big Josh has to go out into the adult world on his own with only his boyish innocence to help him.

While Hanks won Best Actor Academy Awards for his next two films (*Philadelphia* and *Forrest Gump*), this is arguably his best performance. Perfectly capturing the mannerisms of a pre-teen boy (Hanks watched his "younger self," Moscow, playing with costar Jared Rushton, and copied him), Hanks portrays overgrown Josh as a gangly innocent who believably charms his way into a job —at a toy company, of course. While the ending gets a little schmaltzy, director Penny Marshall otherwise keeps the three-hanky stuff to a minimum and gets maximum humor from her cast, especially in the pairing of Hanks and Rushton (as Josh's schoolboy pal), and the casting of Robert Loggia (as the toy firm's owner) and John Heard (as Josh's conniving business rival). **JB**

U.S. / G.B. (Lorimar, NFH, Warner Bros.) 119m Eastmancolor

**Director:** Stephen Frears

**Producer:** Norma Heyman, Hank Moonjean

**Screenplay:** Christopher Hampton, from novel by Choderlos de Laclos and play by Christopher Hampton

**Photography:** Philippe Rousselot

**Music:** George Fenton

**Cast:** Glenn Close, John Malkovich, Michelle Pfeiffer, Swoosie Kurtz, Keanu Reeves, Mildred Natwick, Uma Thurman, Peter Capaldi, Joe Sheridan, Valerie Gogan, Laura Benson, Joanna Pavlis, Nicholas Hawtrey, Paulo Abel Do Nascimento, François Lalande

**Oscar:** Norma Heyman, Hank Moonjean (best picture), Christopher Hampton (screenplay), Stuart Craig, Gérard James (art direction), James Acheson (costume)

**Oscar nomination:** Glenn Close (actress), Michelle Pfeiffer (actress in support role), George Fenton (music)

# DANGEROUS LIAISONS (1988)

Christopher Hampton translated his own acclaimed play *Les Liaisons Dangereuses* (itself based on a Choderlos de Laclos novel) into *Dangerous Liaisons*, a sumptuous, decadent drama of 18th-century French sexual intrigue, brought to life on screen by director Stephen Frears.

Glenn Close steals the show as the vicious and vindictive Marquise de Merteuil, whose main enjoyment in her bored, rich life is to conspire with the equally cynical Vicomte de Valmont (John Malkovich). Their latest scheme involves the virginal Cécile (Uma Thurman) and the pure Madame de Tourvel (Michelle Pfeiffer), but Valmont's attempts to ruin them both for his own pleasure is complicated when he falls for the unsuspecting Madame.

Frears leads us into the boudoirs and drawing rooms of the wealthy aristocracy, each one dripping with elegance and wickedness in equal measure. Close is perfectly acid tongued, Malkovich both seductive and slimy, and the cast rounded out by the unusual casting of Keanu Reeves (better known for more modern roles) as Chevalier Danceny, just one of the poor fellows caught up in Valmont's machinations. A handsome look at lust, betrayal, and guilt, *Dangerous Liaisons* is both lavishly mounted and beautifully portrayed. **JB**

**Japan** (Ghibli) 93m Technicolor

**Language:** Japanese

**Director:** Isao Takahata

**Producer:** Tohru Hara

**Screenplay:** Isao Takahata, from novel by Akiyuki Nosaka

**Music:** Yoshio Mamiya

**Cast:** Tsutomu Tatsumi, Ayano Shiraishi, Yoshiko Shinohara, Akemi Yamaguchi, Rhoda Chrosite, Amy Jones, J. Robert Spencer, Veronica Taylor

# HOTARU NO HAKA (1988)
## GRAVE OF THE FIREFLIES

With an attention to craft and design absent from so much mainstream Western animation, several Japanese animators have subverted the traditionally child-oriented nature of cartoons (at least that's how they're often perceived) into grand achievements equal to any big-budget live-action film. In fact, as Isao Takahata's *Grave of the Fireflies* readily attests, sometimes these animated films actually surpass their live-action equivalents, finding narrative freedom, emotional honesty, and a greater sense of artistic control on the plane of a two-dimensional set.

A harrowing and painful story of the horrors of war, *Grave of the Fireflies* follows two Japanese children orphaned after the firebombing of their village during World War II. Yet the film seems less interested in accusing the military of villainy in the name of battle and more interested in showing the often-silent victims of war, the innocent children left fending for themselves as hell rains down from above. Remarkably, *Grave of the Fireflies* debuted on a double-bill with Hayao Miyazaki's much lighter *My Neighbor Totoro*, and indeed it is hard to imagine audiences of children, let alone adults, making it through this powerful and disturbing film without being overwhelmed by sadness and disappointment in the seeming inevitability of human conflict. **JKI**

# TOPIO STIN OMICHLI (1988)
## LANDSCAPE IN THE MIST

In the opening shot of Theo Angelopoulos's *Landscape in the Mist*, a small boy, Alexandre (Michalis Zeke), and his pre-teen sister, Voula (Tania Palaiologou), emerge from the darkness and approach a spot near the camera. They stop. The camera slowly begins to circle them. She: "Are you afraid?" He: "No, I'm not." Suddenly they break away and walk, faster this time, toward a train station that we can now see in the distance.

This one-minute take is stunning, and sets the pattern for much of what is to follow. People and vehicles doggedly sticking to their paths, oblivious to all else, sometimes pausing, sometimes changing speed; barren or dark landscapes with a single stark, prominent feature; harsh, natural sound replaced, as a scene empties out, with Eleni Karaindrou's intense music. And, above all, Giorgos Arvinitis's camera circling, advancing, and withdrawing at a rhythm and with an intent always distinct from the action, always inscribing the curiosity, passion, wisdom, and pathos of Angelopoulos's gaze.

Such patterns give figure and form to the deliberately slim and open-ended plot events: The children run away from home and attempt to reach Germany by train to find a father who may not exist, encountering strangers helpful or menacing along the way. *Landscape in the Mist* is a bleak but exultant road movie somewhere between Roberto Rossellini's postwar chronicles of fragmentation and Chantal Akerman's landscape-centered panoramas of a hollow "new world order."

Almost nothing ever connects in these unnamed spaces and places between Athens and the German border: As Voula and Alexandre stand in a courtyard, in front of them a tractor unhitches a dying horse, and behind them a wedding party exits frame, singing and dancing. Only in the tentative relationship between Voula and traveling player Oreste (Stratos Tzortzoglou) does the image begin to hum with the tension of attraction and repulsion. But only for a precious little while: Once again these children will walk, pause, and walk away still faster down an endless highway, as the camera lifts high into the cold air and Oreste waves a forlorn farewell twice, to no one. **AM**

**France / Greece / Italy** (Basic, ETI, French Film Center, Paradise) 127m Color

**Language:** Greek

**Director:** Theo Angelopoulos

**Producer:** Theo Angelopoulos, Eric Heumann, Stéphane Sorlat

**Screenplay:** Theo Angelopoulos, Tonino Guerra, Thanassis Valtinos

**Photography:** Yorgos Arvanitis

**Music:** Eleni Karaindrou

**Cast:** Tania Palaiologou, Dimitris Kaberidis, Vassilis Kolovos, Gerasimos Skiadaressis, Stratos Tzortzoglou, Michalis Zeke

**Venice Film Festival:** Theo Angelopoulos (Silver Lion), (OCIC award), tied with *La Leggenda del Santo Bevitore*

**Berlin International Film Festival:** Theo Angelopoulos (interfilm award—forum of new cinema)

**Poland** (Polish TV) 53m color
**Language:** Polish
**Director:** Krzysztof Kieslowski
**Producer:** Ryszard Chutkowski
**Screenplay:** Krzysztof Kieslowski, Krzysztof Piesiewicz
**Photography:** Wieslaw Zdort
**Music:** Zbigniew Preisner
**Cast:** Henryk Baranowski, Wojciech Klata, Maja Komorowska, Artur Barcis, Maria Gladkowska, Ewa Kania, Aleksandra Kisielewska, Aleksandra Majsiuk, Magda Sroga-Mikolajczyk

# DEKALOG, JEDEN (1988)
## THE DECALOGUE

Polish director Krzysztof Kieslowski was that rare filmmaker who could mix politics, comedy, religion, tragedy, and metaphysics into his works without coming across as either pretentious or silly. But sadly, just as the director was finally beginning to taste the fruits of international success, he died unexpectedly in 1996 at the early age of 54. Without question, he accomplished more in his short career than most directors could ever hope to manage.

Although Kieslowski was the creator of many masterpieces, including *The Double Life of Veronique* (1991) and the *Three Colors* trilogy (*Blue* [1993], *White* [1994], and *Red* [1994]), *The Decalogue* may be his most profound, multifaceted, and perfect work. Originally filmed for Polish television, *The Decalogue* is a collection of ten hour-long short films, each ambitiously featuring a story based loosely on one of the Ten Commandments and all set in the same bleak Warsaw apartment complex.

Many of Kieslowski's earlier works obliquely addressed the political realities of Poland at the time, but with *The Decalogue* the director aims for something grander and more universal. The collection addresses the concepts of fate, chance, and faith through the intersection of different lives—children, parents, siblings, and strangers—seeking to illuminate the invisible threads that tie us together but also the feelings and beliefs that connect us to a higher power.

In one installment a father and son ponder the place of God in a time dominated by technology. In another, a doctor deliberates the ethics of keeping a patient on life support, when his life or death will forever alter the complicated future of the patient's troubled wife. Two brothers try to honor their estranged father's memory by caring for his priceless stamp collection. A horrifying murder calls into question the ethics of the death penalty. Each installment focuses on a mostly blameless domestic situation, profound quandaries with no right or wrong way out, and Kieslowski carefully follows the different paths his characters take.

Although each of *The Decalogue*'s segments may be attached to a specific Commandment, the connection is rarely clear or obvious. Kieslowski seems more interested in how those ancient rules apply when considered in the not always cut-and-dried context of contemporary, everyday life. Each installment shares certain thematic similarities, even if they possess slightly different aesthetics. As with his later *Three Colors* trilogy, the various episodes of *The Decalogue* sometimes also share the same actors, actors whose presence helps connect the disparate (and without exception compelling) stories.

Working in close tandem with his regular screenwriter Krzysztof Piesiewicz, composer Zbigniew Preisner (who created a sedate, minimal score), and nine different cinematographers, Kieslowski achieves that rare feat: A seamlessly unified diverse anthology that gets closer than almost any other film to what it means to be human. Compelling, intelligent, and poetic, *The Decalogue* is a true work of art that teaches even as it entertains. **JKl**

## DIE HARD (1988)

Before *Die Hard*, Bruce Willis was just an actor with one hit TV show (*Moonlighting*) and a flop movie (*Blind Date*) to his name, but following the movie's huge success, he deservedly became one of Hollywood's hottest stars.

His cocky charm breathes life into the character of John McClane, a New York cop visiting his estranged wife Holly (Bonnie Bedelia) at her office in Los Angeles, just as the building falls into the control of a group of ruthless terrorists led by Hans Gruber (Alan Rickman). While all the office workers—staying late for the company Christmas party—are herded into one area by the bad guys, our hero (who was in the bathroom when the assault begins) is off and running around the partially incomplete tower. In his own words being "a fly in the ointment, a monkey in the wrench, a pain in the ass" to the terrorists who aren't quite sure who is attacking them or how he got loose.

John McTiernan—who previously helmed the Arnold Schwarzenegger alien action movie *Predator* (Schwarzenegger, in fact, was originally tipped for the role of McClane)—packs his skyscraper adventure with explosions, fights, and relentless action, as our antihero (he smokes, curses, and bloodily despatches the bad guy) picks off the terrorists by listening in on their walkie-talkies in an attempt to figure out their nefarious plan.

McTiernan, along with writers Jeb Stuart and Steve DeSouza (adapting a Roderick Thorpe novel), effectively redefines the action movie as one-man-army. Willis quips his way through a series of clever setups and payoffs (when McClane takes his shoes and socks off at the beginning of the movie to combat jet lag, you just know his bare feet are going to be a plot device later, and they are), his undershirt getting dirtier by the second. His only pal is a flat-footed cop (Reginald Veljohnson) whom he communicates with by radio, whereas most of the other police officers and federal agents are either too dumb or too trigger-happy to realize what's really going on.

Superbly acted by Willis as a guy who really would rather be somewhere else, McClane is a hero for the '90s who has continued to mutter his "yippee-ki-yay motherfucker" catchphrase in two enjoyable sequels.

A true rollercoaster ride of a movie. **JB**

**U.S.** (Fox, Gordon, Silver) 131m Color

**Language:** English / German / Italian

**Director:** John McTiernan

**Producer:** Lawrence Gordon, Joel Silver

**Screenplay:** Jeb Stuart, Steven E. de Souza, from the novel *Nothing Lasts Forever* by Roderick Thorp

**Photography:** Jan de Bont

**Music:** Michael Kamen

**Cast:** Bruce Willis, Bonnie Bedelia, Reginald Veljohnson, Paul Gleason, De'voreaux White, William Atherton, Hart Bochner, James Shigeta, Alan Rickman, Alexander Godunov, Bruno Doyon, Andreas Wisniewski, Clarence Gilyard Jr., Joey Plewa, Lorenzo Caccialanza

**Oscar nomination:** Stephen Hunter Flick, Richard Shorr (special sound effects), Richard Edlund, Al Di Sarro, Brent Boates, Thaine Morris (special visual effects), Frank J. Urioste, John F. Link (editing), Don J. Bassman, Kevin F. Cleary, Richard Overton, Al Overton Jr. (sound)

**Netherlands / G.B. / France / Germany** (Air France, Capi, Channel Four, La Sept, NOS, NDR, Stichting, Documentaire, TF1, WDR) 80m Color

**Language:** French

**Director:** Joris Ivens

**Screenplay:** Joris Ivens, Marceline Loridan Ivens

**Photography:** Thierry Arbogast Jacques Loiseleux

**Music:** Michel Portal

**Cast:** Henxiang Han, Joris Ivens, Guilian Liu, Zhuang Liu, Hong Wang

# UNE HISTOIRE DE VENT (1988)

## A TALE OF THE WIND

Reading over the filmography of Joris Ivens, it's hard to believe that a single filmmaker made all his films. Here was an artist who was an active member of the first European avant-garde film movement; who filmed the first Soviet Five-Year Plan (*Komsomol*), the Spanish Civil War (*The Spanish Earth*), and the American New Deal (*Power and the Land*); and who made one of the first essential anticolonialist films (*Indonesia Calling*). Such a life was not without its contradictions—few artists could claim to have been awarded both the International Lenin Prize and the rank of Commander of the French Légion d'Honneur. Therefore, it's so wonderfully appropriate that his final film, *A Tale of the Wind*, codirected with his wife and filmmaking partner Marceline Loridan, is one of the most graceful and haunting works of self-reflection in cinema.

Having witnessed during his 90 years enough for ten lifetimes, this "flying Dutchman" turned his camera on perhaps his most elusive subject: himself. A lifelong asthmatic begins with some thoughts on the breath that sustains his and all life, and that is manifest in the world as the wind. Like Ivens's himself, the wind knows no boundaries, naturally linking peoples, cultures, and continents. Ivens' exploration eventually brings him back to China, site of several of his greatest films, where he sets out to find the Dragon, mythic representative of the wind, in order to learn its secret. There are bumps along the way; some Party officials do all they can to very politely stop him from shooting, while at times Nature has to be coaxed into cooperating with the filmmakers' project. Unable to film the magnificent terracotta warriors of the Qin Dynasty, Ivens and Loridan conjure up their own artifacts, even staging a Busby Berkeley-ish number with them. Moving between documentary, fiction, mythology, philosophy, and sheer whimsy, Loridan and Ivens created with their epitaph one of the most magnificently "free" films ever made, a fitting tribute to one of the cinema's true originals. **RP**

# WHO FRAMED ROGER RABBIT (1988)

Although live-action and animation had shared the screen before—most notably when animated mouse Jerry (of *Tom and Jerry* fame) danced with Gene Kelly in *Anchors Aweigh* (1945)—director Robert Zemeckis and animation director Richard Williams skillfully blended the two into this feature-length comedy thriller that still looks technically flawless over a decade after it was made.

Gruff, seedy-looking private eye Eddie Valiant, Bob Hoskins at his grumpy best, doesn't like Toons, the animated characters who live in the Toontown suburb of Los Angeles. So he is less than pleased when he is hired by film studio boss Marvin Acme (Stubby Kaye) to check into the activities of his star, a sexy cartoon named Jessica Rabbit (smokily voiced by Kathleen Turner). Eddie is even less impressed by her excitable rabbit husband, Roger (voice of Charles Fleischer), especially when the mismatched pair are plunged into a hilarious tangle of murder and blackmail.

Smartly characterized, by both the human and animated cast, and wittily scripted by Jeffrey Price and Peter S. Seaman, *Who Framed Roger Rabbit* is an action comedy just like the classic Warner cartoons it pays homage to: Bursting with fun, deliciously surreal, and watchable many times over. **JB**

**U.S.** (Amblin, Silver Screen, Touchstone) 103m Color

**Director:** Robert Zemeckis

**Producer:** Frank Marshall, Robert Watts

**Screenplay:** Jeffrey Price, Peter S. Seaman, from the novel *Who Censored Roger Rabbit?* by Gary K. Wolf

**Photography:** Dean Cundey

**Music:** Alan Silvestri

**Cast:** Bob Hoskins, Christopher Lloyd, Joanna Cassidy, Charles Fleischer, Stubby Kaye, Alan Tilvern, Richard LeParmentier, Lou Hirsch, Betsy Brantley, Joel Silver, Paul Springer, Richard Ridings, Edwin Craig, Lindsay Holiday, Mike Edmonds

**Oscar:** Charles L. Campbell, Louis L. Edemann (special sound effects), Ken Ralston, Richard Williams, Ed Jones, George Gibbs (special visual effects), Arthur Schmidt (editing), Richard Williams (special achievement award—animation direction and creation of the cartoon characters)

**Oscar nomination:** Elliot Scott, Peter Howitt (art direction), Dean Cundey (photography), Robert Knudson, John Boyd, Don Digirolamo, Tony Dawe (sound)

**U.S.** (Mirage, Star II) 133m Color

**Director:** Barry Levinson

**Producer:** Mark Johnson

**Screenplay:** Ronald Bass, Barry Morrow

**Photography:** John Seale

**Music:** Ian Gillan, Roger Glover, Doc Pomus, Hans Zimmer

**Cast:** Dustin Hoffman, Tom Cruise, Valeria Golino, Gerald R. Molen, Jack Murdock, Michael D. Roberts, Ralph Seymour, Lucinda Jenney, Bonnie Hunt, Kim Robillard, Beth Grant, Dolan Dougherty, Marshall Dougherty, Patrick Dougherty, John-Michael Dougherty

**Oscar:** Mark Johnson (best picture), Barry Levinson (director), Ronald Bass, Barry Morrow (screenplay), Dustin Hoffman (actor)

**Oscar nomination:** Ida Random, Linda DeScenna (art direction), John Seale (photography), Stu Linder (editing), Hans Zimmer (music)

**Berlin International Film Festival:** Barry Levinson (Golden Bear), (reader jury of the Berliner Morgenpost)

# RAIN MAN (1988)

Numerous writers and directors had tinkered with the script of *Rain Man* before director Barry Levinson came on board. Many believed the story of a used-car salesman trying to befriend his autistic brother on a cross-country journey so he can get his hands on the latter's multimillion dollar inheritance just too difficult to bring to the screen. Even the film's eventual stars, Dustin Hoffman and Tom Cruise, seemed worried about the movie's outcome when they dubbed it "Two Schmucks in a Car" during shooting.

Levinson luckily didn't balk at the idea of making a film with little dramatic story, instead focusing on the human development that is at the picture's heart. Traveling across country with the autistic Raymond (Hoffman) because Raymond won't fly, Charlie Babbitt (Cruise) gradually gets to understand the brother he hardly knows and in the process develops a sense of decency he didn't have before. Hoffman captures his character's autism without going overboard on the nervous tics, but most impressive here is Cruise, who holds his own alongside a more experienced actor and expertly depicts a shallow man who finally finds some depth in his life. **JB**

# UNE AFFAIRE DE FEMMES (1988)
## THE STORY OF WOMEN

A bit mislabeled—the French title is *Une Affaire de Femmes*, which translates better as "Women's Business"—Claude Chabrol's accomplished and generally uncharacteristic period film set in World War II occupied France and loosely adapted from a nonfiction book by lawyer Francis Szpiner, gives a plausible and wholly unsentimental account of a housewife and mother (Isabelle Huppert at her finest) in a small village near Dieppe who becomes an abortionist and is sent to the guillotine for it. Married to a French soldier (François Cluzet) who's in a POW camp, she doesn't want to sleep with him after his return; she soon becomes the family breadwinner—a tough survivor who is also helping other women out.

Cowritten by Chabrol and Colo Tavernier O'Hagan and based on actual events, The Story of Women more than makes up for Chabrol's *The Blood of Others* (1984), his worst film, adapted from a Simone de Beauvoir novel and set in Paris during the same period of the German Occupation—while looking forward to his excellent 1993 documentary, also about this period, *The Eye of Vichy*. Here his mise en scène and handling of the performances and setting are masterful. **JRos**

**France** (A2, Camélia, La Sept, MK2, Sofinergie) 108m Color

**Language:** French

**Director:** Claude Chabrol

**Producer:** Marin Karmitz

**Screenplay:** Claude Chabrol, Colo Tavernier, from novel by Francis Szpiner

**Photography:** Jean Rabier

**Music:** Matthieu Chabrol

**Cast:** Isabelle Huppert, François Cluzet, Nils Tavernier, Marie Trintignant, Dominique Blanc, Lolita Chammah, Aurore Gauvin, Guillaume Foutrier, Nicolas Foutrier, Marie Bunel, Dani, François Maistre, Vincent Gauthier, Franck de la Personne, Caroline Berg

**Venice Film Festival:** Isabelle Huppert (Volpi cup—actress), tied with Shirley MacLaine for *Madame Sousatzka*

# THE ACCIDENTAL TOURIST (1988)

Lawrence Kasdan's adaptation of Anne Tyler's 1988 bestseller captures the quirky, gentle humor of the novel itself. Reuniting *Body Heat*'s (1981) successful trio of Kasdan, William Hurt, and Kathleen Turner, *The Accidental Tourist* has been called "the saddest funny movie ever made."

The film follows the comfortably claustrophobic world of Macon Leary (Hurt). A business travel writer, his life is so carefully cushioned from even the mildest adventure that the logo of his book series is a winged armchair. After the shocking and poignant murder of their son, Macon's wife (Turner) can't take his emotional vacancy and leaves Macon with only the neurotic, nippy family dog for company. Only when he meets whacky dog trainer Muriell Pritchett (Geena Davis) does his life begin to change.

Although Davis won the Oscar for Best Actress in a Supporting Role, her performance seems almost garish next to the subtle comedy of the Leary siblings. Porter (David Ogden Stiers), Charles (Ed Begley Jr.), and sister Rose (Amy Wright) are a threesome straight from Grant Wood's painting *American Gothic*. Playing card games with rules so byzantine no nonfamily member can participate, their oddity extends even to the groceries, where all dry goods are stored in alphabetical order. Uniquely quiet, *The Accidental Tourist* is a somber drama lit from within by chunks of comedy. **KK**

**U.S.** (Warner Bros.) 121m Technicolor

**Director:** Lawrence Kasdan

**Producer:** Michael Grillo, Lawrence Kasdan, Charles Okun

**Screenplay:** Frank Galati, Lawrence Kasdan, from novel by Anne Tyler

**Photography:** John Bailey

**Music:** John Williams

**Cast:** William Hurt, Kathleen Turner, Geena Davis, Amy Wright, David Ogden Stiers, Ed Begley Jr., Bill Pullman, Robert Hy Gorman, Bradley Mott, Seth Granger, Amanda Houck, Caroline Houck, London Nelson, Gregory Gouyer, William Brown

**Oscar:** Geena Davis (actress in support role)

**Oscar nomination:** Lawrence Kasdan, Charles Okun, Michael Grillo (best picture), Frank Galati, Lawrence Kasdan (screenplay), John Williams (music)

Czechoslovakia / Switzerland / G.B. / Germany (Channel Four, Condor, Hessischer Rundfunk, SRG) 86m Eastmancolor

**Language:** Czech / English

**Director:** Jan Svankmajer

**Producer:** Peter-Christian Fueter

**Screenplay:** Jan Svankmajer, from the novel *Alice In Wonderland* by Lewis Carroll

**Photography:** Svatopluk Maly

**Cast:** Kristyna Kohoutová

# NECO Z ALENKY (1988)
## ALICE

In his characteristically bizarre and hyperimaginative manner, Czech filmmaker, animator, and puppet maker-extraordinaire Jan Svankmajer captures the feel of Lewis Carroll's children's tale *Alice in Wonderland* while still managing to convey several "adult" and culturally specific themes. The creative force behind many of his country's most celebrated shorts—including *Dimensions of Dialogue* (1982), *Down to the Cellar* (1983), and *The Pit, the Pendulum and Hope* (1983)—Svankmajer here finds ideal inspiration in the protosurrealist story of little Alice (played by young Kristyna Kohoutová, the only human member of the cast, save for those scenes in which she is transformed into a foot-tall china doll), who enters a world of strange creatures and animals and constantly questions the (il)logic of all she encounters.

In Svankmajer's conception, the disposable products of domestic life (such as rulers, socks, jars, and buttons) become the raw material for gothic splendor. And Lewis's familiar characters—such as the White Rabbit, the Mad Hatter, and the March Hare—are here more creepy than charming; as one critic writes, "they're partly enchanted, partly haunted, and there's a hint of the morphologist's lab in them, a trace of formaldehyde." Finally, however, *Alice* is less an adaptation than an exercise in auteurism, as Svankmajer finds new ways of treating his familiar obsessions with the inhumanness of routine and the vulgarity and danger of overeating. **SJS**

**U.S. / G.B.** (PolyGram, Warner Bros.) 126m Technicolor

**Director:** Tim Burton

**Producer:** Peter Guber, Jon Peters

**Screenplay:** Sam Hamm, Warren Skaaren, Bob Kane

**Photography:** Roger Pratt

**Music:** Danny Elfman, Prince

**Cast:** Michael Keaton, Jack Nicholson, Kim Basinger, Robert Wuhl, Pat Hingle, Billy Dee Williams, Michael Gough, Jack Palance, Jerry Hall, Tracey Walter, Lee Wallace, William Hootkins, Richard Strange, Carl Chase, Mac McDonald

**Oscar:** Anton Furst, Peter Young (art direction)

# BATMAN (1989)

In this blockbuster movie version of Bob Kane's classic comic, director Tim Burton reimagines eponymous superhero Batman (last seen on screen in a campy 1960s TV incarnation) as a dark and conflicted character.

Michael Keaton stars as tortured soul Bruce Wayne, a brooding man who as a child saw his parents killed by muggers in a darkened alleyway. Now a multimillionaire industrialist by day, at night he dons a cape, mask, and knee-high boots to become Batman and right the wrongs of bleak, gothic Gotham City. But is he a superhero or a crazed vigilante? Photojournalist Vicki Vale (Kim Basinger) and reporter Alex Knox (Robert Wuhl) are among those who want to discover Batman's secret identity and find out the truth.

While Burton gives his Caped Crusader depth, darkness, and even romance (in the form of Vicki), the show is almost stolen from his hero by the villain of the piece, The Joker, played with gusto by Jack Nicholson. Resplendent in purple suit and clown-like makeup, dancing to the Prince songs that pepper the soundtrack, he was surely the most enjoyably unlikeable bad guy to hit the big screen in a long time. **JB**

# WHEN HARRY MET SALLY (1989)

*When Harry Met Sally* provides indisputable proof, if it were needed, that all the right ingredients—a skilled, comic director (Rob Reiner), great script (Nora Ephron), and brilliant casting (Billy Crystal, Meg Ryan)—do add up to a damn-near perfect piece of film entertainment.

Sharing a postcollege car journey from Chicago to New York in 1977, smart-mouthed Harry (Crystal) announces to snobbish Sally (Ryan) that they will never be friends because, in his often skewed logic, "men and women can't be friends because the sex part always gets in the way." At the end of the trip, the pair go their separate ways only to cross paths a few years later in an airport and then again when she is on the verge of breaking up with her boyfriend and he has split up with his wife. Of course, they do eventually become friends, and it is inevitable that they become more than that before the movie's end—but that is half the fun.

A romantic comedy that tips its cap to Woody Allen movies like *Annie Hall* (1977), this is brought right up to date by Ephron's witty dialogue that accurately depicts the modern-day dating game. Harry learns the drawbacks of dating a younger woman when he asks a girl where she was when Kennedy was shot only to get the reply, "*Ted* Kennedy's been shot?". Against the backdrop of the most cinematic of cities, New York, scene upon scene is a classic or features memorable dialogue: Sally's fake orgasm in the deli, after which a woman at a neighboring table orders "I'll have what she's having" (the lady played by Reiner's own mother) and the store karaoke session when Harry bumps into his ex-wife are played expertly by the two leads, and support roles include Bruno Kirby as Harry's pal and Carrie Fisher as Sally's.

A triumph for all involved—Nora Ephron has yet to write a script that matches this one—the film turned Ryan into a highly sought-after leading lady and made Harry Connick, Jr., who performs the film's 1930s and '40s standards (including "It Had To Be You") on the soundtrack, a bonafide star. **JB**

**U.S.** (Castle Rock, Columbia, Nelson) 96m Color

**Director:** Rob Reiner

**Producer:** Rob Reiner, Andrew Scheinman

**Screenplay:** Nora Ephron

**Photography:** Barry Sonnenfeld

**Music:** Marc Shaiman

**Cast:** Billy Crystal, Meg Ryan, Carrie Fisher, Bruno Kirby, Steven Ford, Lisa Jane Persky, Michelle Nicastro, Gretchen Palmer, Robert Alan Beuth, David Burdick, Joe Viviani, Harley Jane Kozak, Joseph Hunt, Kevin Rooney, Franc Luz

**Oscar nomination:** Nora Ephron (screenplay)

# CRIMES AND MISDEMEANORS (1989)

Woody Allen in winning philosophical form (coming off two of his bleaker dramas, made back-to-back and both coolly received, *September* and *Another Woman*) tackles life, death, truth, love, God, and all things Dovstoyevskian in *Crimes and Misdemeanors*. A wonderful cast plays out a plot constructed like a set of Chinese boxes for a novel on film about close encounters of the Upper East Side kind. Handsomely shot by Ingmar Bergman's regular cinematographer Sven Nykvist, with Allen making striking use of music by Schubert and Bach as well as the jazz and swing favorites we associate with him.

Two apparently quite different stories dovetail at the last moment. Judah Rosenthal, a respected, socially prominent eye surgeon (played by Martin Landau in a brilliant, Oscar-nominated role), is an adulterer desperate to discard his angry mistress Dolores (Anjelica Huston) when she threatens to make a mess of his well-ordered, comfortable, and hypocritical life. Meanwhile Allen's documentary filmmaker Cliff Stern's attempts to woo Mia Farrow's Halley are frustrated by his insufferable brother-in-law, Lester (a marvelous turn by Alan Alda), a practiced charmer who makes sitcoms and is, incidentally, the subject of Cliff's current film. The big questions are Judah's to ponder when his shady brother (Jerry Orbach) offers to take the Dolores situation in hand—homicidally. Around his dilemma a network of family, friends, and brief acquaintances expose themselves, suffer, love, struggle, and crack deathless one-liners ("The last time I was inside a woman was when I visited the Statue of Liberty").

Allen in his familiar existentialist, angst-ridden Manhattan intellectual nebbish persona unsurprisingly delivers the best of these in the bittersweet comedic strand: "He wants to produce something of mine," trills Farrow. "Yes," worries Woody, "your first child!" More unusually, weighty, realistic, tragic drama and comedy of manners mingle in a uniquely sophisticated, ambitious discussion of values, morality, and law. Allen, firing on all cylinders, steers through pain, profundity, and outrageous humor with his inimitable, signature style, addressing good and evil, guilt and retribution, movies versus reality, and swell cocktail parties with wit and penetration. *Crimes and Misdemeanors* is intricate, adult, both dark and delightful, right up there among his very best work. **AE**

**U.S.** (Rank, Orion) 107m Color

**Director:** Woody Allen

**Producer:** Robert Greenhut

**Screenplay:** Woody Allen

**Photography:** Sven Nykvist

**Nonoriginal music:** Bach, Schubert

**Cast:** Bill Bernstein, Martin Landau, Claire Bloom, Stephanie Roth, Gregg Edelman, George J. Manos, Anjelica Huston, Woody Allen, Jenny Nichols, Joanna Gleason, Alan Alda, Sam Waterston, Zina Jasper, Dolores Sutton, Joel Fogel.

**Oscar nomination:** Woody Allen (director), Woody Allen (screenplay), Martin Landau (actor in support role)

## THE COOK, THE THIEF, HIS WIFE & HER LOVER (1989)

Taking his dissatisfaction with conservative politics to the extreme, Peter Greenaway devised *The Cook, the Thief, His Wife & Her Lover* as an opulent and decadent riposte to Margaret Thatcher's England. Michael Gambon plays Albert Spica, the monstrous, obnoxious, oafish thief of the title, holding court at a trendy London restaurant, decimating a disgustingly over-the-top banquet while surrounded by numerous sycophants and lackeys. Ignored for too long, his wife Georgina (Helen Mirren) initiates a passionate affair with a quieter, bookish patron (Alan Howard), facilitated by the accommodating chef back in the kitchen. So busy consuming and humiliating his hangers-on, Gambon at first doesn't notice his wife's deception, but once he discovers her adultery he concocts a cannibalistic revenge.

Greenaway directs his film like a tapestry gone wrong, revealing all manner of depravity as he pans back and forth between the kitchen and dining room in search of a smidgen of good will amidst the savagery. *The Cook, the Thief, His Wife & Her Lover* seethes anger and disgust, most of it directed toward the upper class, whose waste and barbarism is portrayed not just as a blight on society but frankly as an affront to good taste. **JKl**

**France / Neth. / G.B.** (Allarts, Elsevira, Erato, Erbograph, Films, Vendex) 124m Color

**Director:** Peter Greenaway

**Producer:** Kees Kasander

**Screenplay:** Peter Greenaway

**Photography:** Sacha Vierny

**Music:** Michael Nyman

**Cast:** Richard Bohringer, Michael Gambon, Helen Mirren, Alan Howard, Tim Roth, Ciarán Hinds, Gary Olsen, Ewan Stewart, Roger Ashton-Griffiths, Ron Cook, Liz Smith, Emer Gillespie, Janet Henfrey, Arnie Breeveld, Tony Alleff

## DRUGSTORE COWBOY (1989)

Gus van Sant's *Drugstore Cowboy* is a funny and very moving account of addiction. We follow a gang of junkies led by Bob (Matt Dillon) who feed their habits by robbing drugstores in Portland, Oregon. The petty crimes and the repetitive lives of the addicts are chronicled by the director without moralizing or comment. But the fragile nature of the relationships within the gang, and particularly the doomed love of Bob and his wife Dianne (Kelly Lynch), are as well observed as they are brilliantly acted.

While the plot may seem simple—run-ins with police and other junkies—there is real tragedy as the film moves toward its denoument. When one of the gang overdoses and Bob has to smuggle the body out of a motel hosting a sherriff's convention and then bury the body in the woods, he decides that he has to go straight. In the detox hostel he meets up with an old friend, a junkie priest played by William Burroughs, and their conversations punctuate his final encounters with the world he has left. The entire film is magnificent but these final conversations between Dillon and Burroughs are sublime. **CM**

**U.S.** (Avenue) 100m Color

**Director:** Gus Van Sant

**Producer:** Karen Murphy, Nick Wechsler

**Screenplay:** Gus Van Sant, Daniel Yost, from novel by James Fogle

**Photography:** Robert D. Yeoman

**Music:** Elliot Goldenthal

**Cast:** Matt Dillon, Kelly Lynch, James LeGros, Heather Graham, Eric Hull, Max Perlich, James Remar, John Kelly, Grace Zabriskie, George Catalano, Janet Baumhover, Ted D'Arms, Neal Thomas, Stephen Rutledge, Beah Richards

**Berlin International Film Festival:** Gus Van Sant (C.I.C.A.E. award—forum of new cinema)

# MY LEFT FOOT (1989)

Despite the strong potential for maudlin depression, *My Left Foot* emerged as a surprisingly entertaining, earthy, funny, and uplifting celebration of Irishman Christy Brown, who was born imprisoned in a body horrible crippled by cerebral palsy but won recognition and respect as an artist and writer. The concept of a disabled man with a surprising intellectual gift clearly has parallels with the fictional *Rain Man*, but *My Left Foot* is at least its equal in every department, not least in the principal performances. Daniel Day-Lewis is riveting in a role as far as he could get from his affected aesthete of *A Room with a View* (1986) or his gay opportunist in *My Beautiful Laundrette* (1985). Brenda Fricker is radiant as Christy's devout, careworn mam. Ray McAnally, who sadly died before the film's release, gave his last rich characterization as Christy's unpredictable, heavy-drinking da. And young Hugh O'Conor as the boy Christy conveys the nightmarish frustration of a bright child, presumed to be an idiot, struggling to communicate with his family.

First-time director Jim Sheridan and cowriter Shane Connaughton don't flinch from the tragedy and rage in Christy's life as a wheelchair-bound wit patronized and subjected to daily humiliations despite his considerable abilities. But their rounded impression of the man leaves an overwhelming sense of the miraculousness of life and of Christy's remarkable spirit. This is underlined by the magical quality injected into the smallest incidents—like the child Christy's wonder when he is borne by his brothers and sisters to their sweet, spooky Halloween street festivities.

The famous left foot, the only part of his body Christy could control, is featured in running jokes and dramatic episodes as Christy saves his mother's life, scores goals, paints, fells an adversary in a pub brawl, attempts suicide, lays bricks, and types his autobiography, all with the eponymous appendage. Day-Lewis proved the out-of-left-field Oscar winner who could not be denied. Having mastered the physical difficulties of a rigid, twisted body and impaired speech, he conveys a man whose cleverness brings him little relief, but whose humor, lust, and bloody-mindedness illuminate what might otherwise have been simply harrowing. **AE**

**Ireland / G.B.** (Ferndale, Granada, RTE) 98m Technicolor

**Director:** Jim Sheridan

**Producer:** Noel Pearson

**Screenplay:** Shane Connaughton, Jim Sheridan, from book by Christy Brown

**Photography:** Jack Conroy

**Music:** Elmer Bernstein

**Cast:** Daniel Day-Lewis, Brenda Fricker, Alison Whelan, Kirsten Sheridan, Declan Croghan, Eanna MacLiam, Marie Conmee, Cyril Cusack, Phelim Drew, Ruth McCabe, Fiona Shaw, Ray McAnally, Patrick Laffan, Derry Power, Hugh O'Conor

**Oscar:** Daniel Day-Lewis (actor), Brenda Fricker (actress in support role)

**Oscar nomination:** Noel Pearson (best picture), Jim Sheridan (director), Shane Connaughton (screenplay)

# DIE XUE SHUANG XIONG (1989)
## THE KILLER

Although director John Woo, producer Tsui Hark, and star Chow Yun-Fat had worked together previously—notably on the 1986 gangster drama *A Better Tomorrow*—and had each amassed a body of major work, it was the international success of *The Killer* that established Hong Kong action cinema as a distinct brand. Most of the major creatives then proceeded to up-and-down Hollywood careers, while Western filmmakers like Robert Rodriguez and Quentin Tarantino began lifting elements of their distinctive style—the popular flat-on-his-back, gun-in-each-hand slide is a favorite Chow Yun-Fat move, often imitated by pretenders—to enliven their own action pictures.

*The Killer* is an action melodrama about an honorable, sentimental hit man (Chow) trying to save enough money from a run of assassinations to pay for an operation to restore the sight of a singer (Sally Yeh) accidentally blinded during one of his hits, while a tough cop (Danny Lee) learns to respect the murderer he's required to track down and finally joins with him for a gruesome glorification. A genocidal film with more corpses than *Total Recall* and *Die Hard 2* combined—ironic in that the plot hinges on the lack of suitable cornea donors in Hong Kong—this is a literally astonishing mix of stunts, soap, and sly humor. The comic-book gunplay and violence of the action elements are mixed with an emotional strain that owes something to Douglas Sirk, but the real love story isn't the mild triangle between cop, killer, and blind victim but the almost-gay buddyship that works up between the two male leads.

The original Chinese title translates as *Bloodshed of Two Heroes*, which represents the film rather better than the export title, emphasizing its status as a relationship movie rather than privileging one of its main characters as a solitary figure. It winds up with a scene that establishes Woo's screen personality: A shoot-out in a chapel that sees candles, bullets, and bodies flying across the screen as doves flutter (sometimes in snatches of slow-motion) and liturgical music swells, with blotches of blood on bright-white clothes and tears flowing as freely as gore. **KN**

**Hong Kong** (Film Workshop, Golden Princess, Magnum) 111m Color

**Language:** Cantonese / Japanese

**Director:** John Woo

**Producer:** Tsui Hark

**Screenplay:** John Woo

**Photography:** Peter Pau, Wing-Hung Wong

**Music:** Lowell Lowe

**Cast:** Chow Yun-Fat, Danny Lee, Sally Yeh, Kong Chu, Kenneth Tsang, Fui-On Shing, Wing-Cho Yip, Fan Wei Yee, Barry Wong, Parkman Wong, Siu-Hung Ng, Sing Yeung, Siu Hung Ngan, Kwong Leung Wong

**U.S.** (40 Acres & a Mule) 120m Color
**Director:** Spike Lee
**Producer:** Spike Lee
**Screenplay:** Spike Lee
**Photography:** Ernest R. Dickerson
**Music:** Rubén Blades, Cathy Block, Chuck D, Flavor Flav, James Weldon Johnson, Rosamond Johnson, Raymond Jones, Bill Lee, Sami McKinney, Michael O'Hara, Lori Perry, Mervyn Warren, Public Enemy
**Cast:** Danny Aiello, Ossie Davis, Ruby Dee, Richard Edson, Giancarlo Esposito, Spike Lee, Bill Nunn, John Turturro, Paul Benjamin, Frankie Faison, Robin Harris, Joie Lee, Miguel Sandoval, Rick Aiello, John Savage
**Oscar nomination:** Spike Lee (screenplay), Danny Aiello (actor in support role)
**Cannes Film Festival:** Spike Lee nomination (Golden Palm)

# DO THE RIGHT THING (1989)

It's sometimes hard to remember, living now on a global, pop-culture landscape that has been so thoroughly sculpted by the language, music, aesthetics, and politics of hip-hop, that there was a time when the force of that youth movement hadn't yet been tapped, hadn't even begun to be realized by filmmakers (or the larger corporate-culture machine). At the same time, given the materialistic, shallow artistry that has come to define mainstream hip-hop and the music (rap) that is its soundtrack, it's sometimes just as hard to remember when the music was radical, subversive, and proudly revolutionary. Spike Lee's social protest film *Do the Right Thing* brilliantly captures that moment when rap was urgent and conscious; more impressively, it channels the issues of racism, race pride, class struggle, and the joys and grinds of everyday urban life into a paradoxically brightly colored snapshot. Incendiary and insightful, it's a film borne of hip-hop, when hip-hop had something to say.

The film's opening is set to the music—and assault of beats and booming voices—of hip-hop elders and icons, Public Enemy. Filled with a cast of vibrant characters whose intersecting day-in-the-life stories are used to illuminate larger sociopolitical points, *Do the Right Thing* is anchored by Mookie (Lee), a pizza delivery boy who canvases the neighborhood making his deliveries. The camera is all but perched on his shoulder as he makes his way across the local landscape. We meet his shrill, demanding girlfriend (Rosie Perez), cantankerous but loveable elders (Ruby Dee and Ossie Davis), and neighborhood youth as represented by, among others, Radio Raheem (Bil Nunn) and Buggin' Out (Giancarlo Esposito). We also meet the Italian pizzeria owner, Sal (Danny Aiello), whose ambivalence about his black clientele is forked in the differing attitudes of his racist son Pino (John Turturro) and more color-blind child Vito (Richard Edson). Rounding out the characters is a profane, hilarious Greek chorus of middle-aged and elderly black men whose scathing commentary on the day's events provides comic relief.

As the hot summer's day progresses and tempers flare, ordinary slights take on huge significance. Sexual and racial tensions that lie just below the surface of daily exchanges explode, and the resulting fiery violence (encapsulating police brutality and a fracturing of longtime relationships) is a clear metaphor for the state of late 20th-century American race relations. Controversial and frequently misrepresented by detractors (many of whom claimed that the film was a call to riot), *Do the Right Thing* is an unapologetic angry film. It's also filled with images of black love and camaraderie that continue to be so rare in American cinema that they're radical. Shot in bright colors that all but pop off the screen, filled with slightly skewed camera angles often suggesting the freewheeling style of comic books, and edited to reflect the energetic thrust of the most propulsive rap track, *Do the Right Thing* has become one of the most influential movies in the history of filmmaking, not only for its stylistic flourishes, but for giving filmmakers permission to draw from the experiences of lives previously ignored or distorted in both Hollywood and so-called independent film. It dares you to dismiss it. **EH**

**U.S.** (Dog Eat Dog, Warner Bros.) 91m Color

**Producer:** Michael Moore

**Director:** Michael Moore

**Screenplay:** Michael Moore

**Photography:** Chris Beaver, John Prusak, Kevin Rafferty, Bruce Schermer

**Music:** Buddy Kaye

**Cast:** James Bond, Pat Boone, Rhonda Britton, Anita Bryant, Karen Edgely, Bob Eubanks, Ben Hamper, Dinona Jackson, Timothy Jackson, Tom Kay, Michael Moore, Kaye Lani Rae Rafko, Ronald Reagan, Fred Ross, Robert Schuller, George Sells, Roger B. Smith, Steve Wilson

**Berlin International Film Festival:** Michael Moore (peace film award—honorable mention)

# ROGER & ME (1989)

Michael Moore's black-comedy documentary about the consequences of massive layoffs by General Motors in Flint, Michigan, and the writer-director's own unsuccessful attempts to meet with Roger Smith, GM's chairman, and bring him to Flint to see what his actions have wrought, is certainly impressive, as well as bracing proof that movies can be both hugely entertaining and politically sharp at the same time. Mixed in with Moore's justifiably lethal anger, however, is a certain sense of glib superiority over Flint's victims and corporate villains, which one is invited to share, but the breezy results, many of which are exhilarating and never boring, are not exactly devoid of cheap shots and journalistic oversimplifications. These qualities could be said to carry over into Moore's second big success, *Bowling for Columbine*, 13 years later. Thus the cheerful heartlessness of Reaganism that is the film's subject is not entirely irrelevant to its own methods, and critic Dave Kehr aptly dubbed *Roger & Me* around the time of its initial release, "the first feel-good atrocity film."

*Roger & Me*'s rather cavalier manner of juggling certain timeframes and sequences of events led at least one reviewer at the time to dismiss Moore as a charlatan. Despite this there are irrefutable facts in his muckraking. Moore's populist desire to entertain, which ensured his commercial success and the wider reach of his ideas, also entailed some self-aggrandizement as well as a certain number of journalistic shortcuts. In the final analysis it is worth asking which is more important: Corporate greed, or Moore's ego trip. **JRos**

**U.S.** (TriStar) 122m Technicolor

**Director:** Edward Zwick

**Producer:** Freddie Fields

**Screenplay:** Kevin Jarre, from the letters of Robert Gould Shaw, from the book *Lay This Laurel* by Lincoln Kirstein, and *One Gallant Rush* by Peter Burchard

**Photography:** Freddie Francis

**Music:** James Horner

**Cast:** Matthew Broderick, Denzel Washington, Cary Elwes, Morgan Freeman, Jihmi Kennedy, Andre Braugher, John Finn, Donovan Leitch, JD Cullum, Alan North, Bob Gunton, Cliff De Young, Christian Baskous

**Oscar:** Denzel Washington (actor in support role), Freddie Francis (photography), Donald O. Mitchell, Gregg Rudloff, Elliot Tyson, Russell Williams (sound)

**Oscar nomination:** Norman Garwood, Garrett Lewis (art direction), Steven Rosenblum (editing)

# GLORY (1989)

Following the bloom of American Civil Rights it became fashionable to resurrect little-known stories from the ravages of time. Edward Zwick's *Glory* is one such exercise meant to rewrite the blank slate of memory.

The film opens on a Civil War battlefield, where former slave John Rawlins (Morgan Freeman) labors to bury dead soldiers. Colonel Robert Shaw (Matthew Broderick), a liberal white blue blood, is thereafter placed in charge of the Union Army's first all-black volunteer company. Into his care are entrusted the raison d'être of the war, slaves and free blacks, each of whom is transformed into a fighting elite finally sent to their doom storming a fort.

Notable for being an inspirational alternative history, *Glory* more importantly showcased a group of outstanding young black actors. Foremost was Denzel Washington in his first Oscar-winning role as Private Trip. Other standouts include Jihmi Kennedy and Andre Braugher, although the sign of the times is surely the picture's eulogy of sacrifices made on behalf of racial harmony as the salve for present-day racial tensions.

True, *Glory* is consumed with sentimentalism and fatal purpose. But it is equally an antidote for contemporary cynicism, with a heroic true story and a winning score by James Horner. **GC-Q**

# ASTENICHESKIJ SINDROM (1989)
## THE ASTHENIC SYNDROME

A great movie about the contemporary world, but far from an easy one to take or understand, because it breaks so many rules about what films are supposed to be like. Directed in 1989 by the venerable (and venerably transgressive) Kira Muratova, who was then in her mid-50s, *The Asthenic Syndrome* has been perhaps rightly called the only "masterpiece of glasnost." It is also the only Russian film made during Perestroika that was banned by the Russian government—mainly, it would appear, for obscenity, though it wound up being shown anyway after the government sold the rights to a film club in Moscow. It begins with a powerful, 40-minute black-and-white narrative about a middle-aged woman doctor named Natasha (Olga Antonova) who is in an exploding, aggressive rage about the death of her husband. The film then eventually turns into an even more unorthodox tale in color about a disaffected high-school English teacher named Nikolai (played by cowriter Sergei Popov) who periodically falls asleep regardless of what is happening around him. The title alludes to a form of weakness or disability that presumably encompasses both the doctor's aggressiveness and the schoolteacher's passivity. Muratova evidently regards these two forms of behavior as emblematic of what is blighted about contemporary society in general: "I don't see any fundamental difference between us and the West," she has said. "Mankind is everywhere, in general, the same. I see in the world a level of suffering and cruelty which surpasses understanding."

In other words, though this tragicomic epic has plenty to say about postcommunist Russia, it is also one of the few recent masterpieces that deal more generally with the demons loose in today's world. It may drive you nuts—as it was undoubtedly meant to—but you certainly won't forget it. And it is interesting to add that at least two of Muratova's subsequent features, *Three Stories* (1987) and *Chekhov's Motifs* (2002), have continued the process of extreme stylization in the acting as well as the practice of squeezing together two or more fictions. Both factors sharply distinguish her late work from such relatively conventional and relatively naturalistic early features as *Brief Encounters* (1967), in which she acted. **JRos**

**Soviet Union** (Goskino, Odessa) 153m BW/Color

**Language:** Russian

**Director:** Kira Muratova

**Screenplay:** Aleksandr Chernykh, Kira Muratova, Sergei Popov

**Photography:** Vladimir Pankov

**Music:** Franz Schubert

**Cast:** Olga Antonova, Sergei Popov, Galina Zakhurdayeva, Natalya Buzko, Aleksandra Svenskaya, Pavel Polishchuk, Natalya Ralleva, Galina Kasperovich, Viktor Aristov, Nikolai Semyonov, Oleg Shkolnik, Vera Storozheva, Aleksandr Chernykh, Leonid Kushnir, Nadya Popova

**Berlin International Film Festival:** Kira Muratova (Silver Bear—special jury prize), nomination (Golden Bear)

## SEX, LIES, AND VIDEOTAPE (1989)

U.S. (Outlaw, Virgin) 100m Color
**Director:** Steven Soderbergh
**Producer:** John Hardy
**Screenplay:** Steven Soderbergh
**Photography:** Walt Lloyd
**Music:** Cliff Martinez
**Cast:** James Spader, Andie MacDowell, Peter Gallagher, Laura San Giacomo, Ron Vawter, Steven Brill, Alexandra Root, Earl T. Taylor, David Foil
**Oscar nomination:** Steven Soderbergh (screenplay)
**Cannes Film Festival:** Steven Soderbergh (Golden Palm), (FIPRESCI award), tied with *Yaaba*, James Spader (actor)

Writer/director Steven Soderbergh—now best known for *Erin Brockovich* (2000) and the Oscar-winning *Traffic* (2000)—made a striking debut with this drama that went on to win the *Palme D'Or* and Best Actor awards at the 1989 Cannes Film Festival.

Written in just eight days and filmed in five weeks on a budget of just $1.2 million, *Sex, Lies, and Videotape* has been credited with transforming the independent movie industry, enticing mainstream audiences to see small-scale indie films they otherwise would have missed. And this film is certainly unmissable, a sly, sexy, and intelligent look at modern-day relationships set in the steamy South.

Andie MacDowell, in her first leading role following appearances in *St. Elmo's Fire* (1985) and *Greystoke: The Legend of Tarzan* (1984), stars as Ann Millaney, a perfect wife stuck in a dull, almost sexless marriage to John (Peter Gallagher), an egotistical lawyer. Unbeknownst to Ann, John is having an affair with her feisty sister Cynthia (Laura San Giacomo), but all the secrets and lies in their combined relationships are revealed when John's former school friend Graham (James Spader) drives into town and forces the others to face truths about themselves and each other. Graham, of course, has surprises of his own to be exposed—he has a trunk full of videotapes, each featuring a woman talking openly about her sexual secrets. But how did he get all these women to open up to him?

Soderbergh's dialogue is breathtakingly frank, and he fills his film with skilled actors who deliver their lines brilliantly. Former model MacDowell—who has yet to give a better performance—is terrific as the prissy Southern flower, and San Giacomo a discovery as her uninhibited sibling. But the film really belongs to Spader—a former teen actor (*Pretty in Pink* [1986], *Less Than Zero* [1987]) who here shows an unexpected depth and sensitivity as he expertly portrays the most interesting of Soderbergh's repressed quartet. Superb. **JB**

# SAY ANYTHING (1989)

Former *Rolling Stone* writer Cameron Crowe captures teenage romance as it really is in his directorial debut. Having just graduated high school, young underachiever Lloyd Dobler (John Cusack) has the summer to spend as he wishes before he has to decide what to do with his life. And what he wants to do is spend it with focused straight A student Diane Court (Ione Skye), despite the objections of her divorced father (John Mahoney).

What raises *Say Anything* above other teen romantic comedies are the heartfelt performances, and Crowe's honest and unique look at the relationships. Traditionally it's the girl who spends the course of the film trying to make the man of her dreams love her. But here it's sensitive Lloyd (beautifully played by Cusack) who is the one truly invested in the relationship, while Diane remains aloof, fixated as she is on college and the approval of her father to whom she can "say anything." Crowe's script catches every moment of Lloyd's love and heartache perfectly, from the awkward first phone call when he asks Diane out on a date and she has to consult her high school yearbook to remember who he is, to every woman's favorite moment of the movie, when Lloyd stands outside Diane's home, an expression of ache on his face, while holding a boombox playing Peter Gabriel's "In Your Eyes" above his head. Perfect. **JB**

**U.S.** (Fox, Gracie) 100m Color
**Director:** Cameron Crowe
**Producer:** Polly Platt
**Screenplay:** Cameron Crowe
**Photography:** László Kovács
**Music:** Anne Dudley, Richard Gibbs, Nancy Wilson
**Cast:** John Cusack, Ione Skye, John Mahoney, Lili Taylor, Amy Brooks, Pamela Segall, Jason Gould, Loren Dean, Glenn Walker Harris Jr., Charles Walker, Russel Lunday, Polly Platt, Gloria Cromwell, Jeremy Piven, Patrick O'Neill

# THE UNBELIEVABLE TRUTH (1989)

*The Unbelievable Truth* is the highly intriguing if not always fully successful first feature by independent writer-director Hal Hartley. Shot in his hometown on Long Island, he gives us, among other characters, a mechanic mistaken for a priest (Robert Burke) returning from a prison sentence, a politically alienated teenager (Adrienne Shelly) who later finds work as a model for lingerie ads, and the teenager's mercenary redneck father (Christopher Cooke). Burke, Shelly, and Cooke would go on to work with Hartley again in subsequent features—Burke in *Simple Men* (1992) and *Flirt* (1993), Shelly in *Trust* (1990), and Cooke in *Trust* and *Simple Men*.

Fantasies about global annihilation obsess the teenager, fantasies about money obsess her father, and fantasies about a pair of murders apparently committed by the mechanic obsess almost everyone else in the film. The unvarnished quality of some of the acting limits this effort in spots, but the quirky originality of the story, characters, and filmmaking, and the offbeat, deadpan humor serve to keep the audience curious and alert. **JRos**

**U.S.** (Action) 90m Color
**Director:** Hal Hartley
**Producer:** Hal Hartley, Bruce Weiss
**Screenplay:** Hal Hartley
**Photography:** Michael Spiller
**Music:** Jim Coleman, Kendall Brothers, Philip Reed, Wild Blue Yonder
**Cast:** Adrienne Shelly, Robert John Burke, Chris Cooke, Julia McNeal, Katherine Mayfield, Gary Sauer, David Healy, Matt Malloy, Edie Falco, Jeff Howard, Kelly Reichardt, Ross Turner, Paul Schulze, Mike Brady, Bill Sage

## BEIQING CHENGSHI (1989)
### A CITY OF SADNESS

**Taiwan** (Artificial Eye, 3-H, Era) 157m Color

**Language:** Taiwanese / Mandarin / Japanese

**Director:** Hsiao-hsien Hou

**Producer:** Fu-Sheng Chiu

**Screenplay:** T'ien-wen Chu, Nien-jen Wu

**Photography:** Chen Huai'en

**Music:** Tachikawa Naoki

**Cast:** Wou Yi Fang, Nakamura Ikuyo, Jack Kao, Tony Leung Chiu Wai, Tianlu Li, Ikuyo Nakamura, Shufen Xin

**Venice Film Festival:** Hsiao-hsien Hou (Golden Lion)

There are two separate stories to tell here. One is this wonderful story which happens sometimes, somewhere, most of the time unpredictably: The rise of a New Wave, of an artistic movement in a country, and of the emergence of one or two (rarely more) exceptionally talented filmmakers. This occurred in the 1980s in Taiwan with the New Cinema movement, and one of the most talented directors who appeared at the time was Hsiao-hsien Hou. He began by making personal, autobiographical films (*The Boys from Fengkuei, A Summer at Grandpa's, Dust in the Wind, The Time to Live and The Time to Die*) which revealed his sense of pace, the physical intensity of his shots, the suggestive strength in the apparently indifferent way he filmed even the most simple situations.

Then there is a second story, concerning that inevitable moment when a nation needs its cinema to tell itself and the world its own tale—its collective autobiography, so to speak. In 1989, the vanishing of the military dictatorship which ruled the island for 40 years presented filmmakers the opportunity to tell the recent story of Taiwan. And this is what Hou, the "subjective avant-garde auteur," decided to do (and what he continued to do with *The Puppetmaster* and *Good Men, Good Woman*). *A City of Sadness*, which was clearly viewed in its own country as a huge step forward in the ability of cinema to look, finally, at Taiwan's recent past, constitutes a real turning point—a fact which also enabled the film to become a great public success.

A combination of historical fresco and modern film, the complex narrative structure of *A City of Sadness* (based upon the intricate lives of four brothers) and the enormous amount of historical information it embodies convey a beautiful and emotional sense of the period, the group, the individual, the inner feelings, and the demands of the various communities each brother belongs to—willingly or not. *A City of Sadness* is not only a masterpiece, it is a model for all those films which intend to show the major events of a country, most of the time becoming boring monuments instead. **J-MF**

## S'EN FOUT LA MORT (1990)
### NO FEAR, NO DIE

French director Claire Denis refers to her films *Chocolat* (1988), *No Fear No Die* (1990), and *I Can't Sleep* (1994) as her trilogy about colonialism and its aftermath. *No Fear, No Die* follows, in a quasidocumentary fashion, a few months in the lives of Dah (Isaach De Bankolé) and Jocelyn (Alex Descas), two black men training roosters for illegal cockfights in the basement of a shady suburban nightclub in France. Besides its underlying portrayal of exploitation of illegal immigrants, the film's claustrophobic, oppressive atmosphere is a fascinating ground for the dynamics of power, violence, desire, and cruelty enacted in this marginal world, as tensions gradually mount between Jocelyn and the nightclub owner's son Michel (Christopher Buchholz). Michel becomes jealous of the attention Jocelyn gets not only from his father, but also from his father's beautiful girlfriend Toni (Solveig Dommartin), whom both men covet.

The rivalry between Jocelyn and Michel, complicated by issues of race and power, finds its brutal resolution in a senseless murder at the end of *No Fear, No Die*, highlighting the absurdity of postcolonial violence. The close and raw filming of the ritual training of roosters, of the protagonists' faces and bodies, as well as the powerful performances of Descas and Bankolé, make this film an intense, intimate experience of a facet of human behavior triggered by circumstances in which "all men, whatever their race, color, or origins, are capable of anything and everything." **CO**

**France / Germany** (Cinéa, NEF) 97m Eastmancolor

**Language:** French

**Director:** Claire Denis

**Producer:** Francis Boespflug, Philippe Carcassonne

**Screenplay:** Claire Denis, Jean-Pol Fargeau

**Photography:** Pascal Marti

**Music:** Abdullah Ibrahim

**Cast:** Isaach De Bankolé, Alex Descas, Solveig Dommartin, Christopher Buchholz, Jean-Claude Brialy, Christa Lang, Gilbert Felmar, Daniel Bellus, François Oloa Biloa, Pipo Sarguera, Alain Banicles, Valérie Monnet

**Venice Film Festival:** Dominique Auvray (Silver Osella—editing)

## REVERSAL OF FORTUNE (1990)

There's nothing quite as fascinating as watching a rich, arrogant man fall from grace, and fall from favor with a crash Claus von Bülow most certainly did, both in real life and on screen as played here by Jeremy Irons in an Oscar-winning turn.

In one of the most famous trials of the 1980s, European aristocrat von Bülow was accused of the attempted murder of his very rich wife Sunny (Glenn Close), whom he supposedly sent into a permanent coma with an overdose of insulin. Barbet Schroeder's film, based on von Bülow lawyer Alan Dershowitz's book, cleverly guides us through the events leading up to the trial, using flashbacks and narration from the comatose Sunny, intercut with the two trials whose outcome has been well reported. Claus von Bülow was found guilty at his first trial and then acquitted on appeal at the next.

Sharply scripted by Nicholas Kazan, we get a look at how rich people with far too much time on their hands live (or, in Sunny's case, do not). This isn't a documentary of the case, but absorbing and beautifully played out drama. The film doesn't answer the question "Did he do it?", instead leaving you draw your own conclusions. **JB**

**U.S. / Japan** (Reversal, Shochiku-Fuji, Sovereign, Warner Bros.) 111m Technicolor

**Director:** Barbet Schroeder

**Producer:** Oliver Stone, Edward R. Pressman

**Screenplay:** Nicholas Kazan, from book by Alan M. Dershowitz

**Photography:** Luciano Tovoli

**Music:** Mark Isham

**Cast:** Glenn Close, Jeremy Irons, Ron Silver, Annabella Sciorra, Uta Hagen, Fisher Stevens, Jack Gilpin, Christine Baranski, Stephen Mailer, Christine Dunford, Felicity Huffman, Mano Singh, Johann Carlo, Keith Reddin, Alan Pottinger

**Oscar:** Jeremy Irons (actor)

**Oscar nomination:** Barbet Schroeder (director), Nicholas Kazan (screenplay)

**U.S.** (Warner Bros.) 145m Technicolor
**Director:** Martin Scorsese
**Producer:** Irwin Winkler
**Screenplay:** Nicholas Pileggi and Martin Scorsese, from the novel *Wise Guy* by Nicholas Pileggi
**Photography:** Michael Ballhaus
**Nonoriginal music:** Paul Anka, Jeff Barry, Eric Clapton, Ernie Erdman, Paul Evans, Claude François, George Harrison, Mick Jagger, Mel London, Elias McDaniel, McKinley, Harry Nilsson, Phil Spector, Pete Townshend
**Cast:** Robert De Niro, Ray Liotta, Joe Pesci, Lorraine Bracco, Paul Sorvino, Frank Sivero, Tony Darrow, Mike Starr, Frank Vincent, Chuck Low, Frank DiLeo, Henny Youngman, Gina Mastrogiacomo, Catherine Scorsese, Charles Scorsese
**Oscar:** Joe Pesci (actor in support role)
**Oscar nomination:** Irwin Winkler (best picture), Martin Scorsese (director), Nicholas Pileggi, Martin Scorsese (screenplay), Lorraine Bracco (actress in support role), Thelma Schoonmaker (editing)
**Venice Film Festival:** Martin Scorsese (Silver Lion—director)

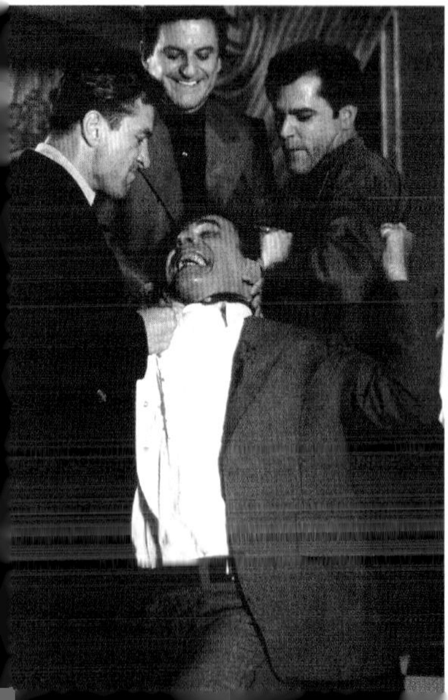

# GOODFELLAS (1990)

With this epic, Martin Scorsese returned to the world of tough-talking (mostly) Italian-American hoods featured in *Mean Streets* (1973), following 30 years in the lives of a group of neighborhood crooks. From hanging around the taxi rank, punk kid Henry Hill (Ray Liotta) progresses to hijacking, airport robberies, extortion, grievous bodily harm, drug dealing, and, finally, informing. Along the way, he gets a Jewish wife (Lorraine Bracco) who, unlike the Corleone women, finds it impossible to keep out of the wholesale sleaze that goes along with her husband's way of life. More important, of course, are Henry's close male relationships: with Jimmy (Robert De Niro), a coolly violent heist man, and Tommy (Joe Pesci), an unstable psychopath with hopes of getting "made." In the end, Hill is turned by the FBI and informs on his few surviving friends, winding up condemned to a Federal Witness Protection limbo where "if you ask for spaghetti bolognese they give you noodles with meatballs."

Drawn from cowriter Nicholas Pileggi's nonfiction book *Wiseguy*, this is more matter-of-fact in its insider's chattiness than the mythmaking *The Godfather* (1972). Indeed, *Goodfellas* is almost a companion piece to the comical *Married to the Mob* (1988) as it observes the manners and fashions of the organized crime world. Underlaid by a constant barrage of cunningly selected pop singles, from Tony Bennett to Phil Spector to Sid Vicious, this panorama of illegal America stays with a group of wholly repulsive, increasingly corrupt people for nearly two and a half hours but never loses its fascination. De Niro, underplaying in a secondary role, is quietly chilling as the repressed but unpredictable robber who sometimes seems to think he'll only be safe once he has killed everyone he knows. However, the show-off monster is Pesci, who plays the maniacal Tommy as a homicidal Lou Costello, segueing instantly from foul-mouthed rat-tat-tat wisecrack routines into mortifying threats or slap-in-the-face atrocities. Without moralizing, the film manages to convey the dead-end horrors of a life not just outside the law but outside all possible law. **KN**

## JACOB'S LADDER (1990)

*Jacob's Ladder* is a horror movie as ethereal journey. Most of the film takes place in the spiritual world reenvisioned as the concrete environment of New York City, where the soul of a dying man named Jacob Singer (Tim Robbins) is lost and confused in the fleeting moments before death. His journey to the afterlife stretches out into a tormenting series of flashbacks, visions, and eternal questioning.

Like Dante's *Inferno*, *Jacob's Ladder* is a downward spiral: As the film goes on, Jacob's visions become more and more horrifying. Though at first the demons are vaguely glimpsed or only hinted at, soon Jacob is enmeshed in hell on all sides.

Yet, despite the film's often terrifying and unsettling visuals, *Jacob's Ladder* is ultimately about coming to peace with one's life. It shows how Jacob, following the words of philosopher Meister Eckhart, burns away his memories and attachments so his soul can be freed. Director Adrian Lyne grounds this spiritual journey in the everyday world, thus allowing us to feel closer to the events. By taking the familiar and making it slightly discomforting or grotesque, he achieves a sublime cinematic state where nothing can be trusted and almost everything is unexpected. **JKe**

**U.S.** (Carolco) 115m Technicolor

**Director:** Adrian Lyne

**Producer:** Alan Marshall

**Screenplay:** Bruce Joel Rubin

**Photography:** Jeffrey L. Kimball

**Music:** Maurice Jarre

**Cast:** Tim Robbins, Elizabeth Peña, Danny Aiello, Matt Craven, Pruitt Taylor Vince, Jason Alexander, Patricia Kalember, Eriq La Salle, Ving Rhames, Brian Tarantina, Anthony Alessandro, Brent Hinkley, S. Epatha Merkerson, Suzanne Shepherd, Doug Barron

## KING OF NEW YORK (1990)

Abel Ferrara's *King of New York* is a chronicle of the downfall of New York drug kingpin Frank White (Christopher Walken), who, after years of illegal activity, decides to expiate his sins by building a hospital in an inner-city neighborhood. His attempts to give something back to the community encounter hostile resistance from every side—his Chinese drug partner (Joey Chin), the local Mafia, and an overzealous tough cop (David Caruso) ready to do anything to bring him down. Frank's futile efforts trigger an ethnically motivated gangster war that ends in a bloody showdown among the city's criminal factions.

Walken gives a tour de force performance in the lead as a ruthless killer with a twisted sense of morality, and Laurence Fishburne as White's henchman Jimmy Jump contributes to the film's frenetic energy. Like all of Ferrara's work, *King of New York* is not an easy movie to watch. It is violent and disturbing, with a high body count, further exploring the director's interest in characters who seek salvation against the backdrop of a drug-infested and violent New York City underground—depicted here as the archetypal Gotham City. Ferrara's 1992 follow-up, *Bad Lieutenant*, featuring Harvey Keitel as an unnamed cop who is as corrupt as Walken's White is devious, takes the director's bloody yet introspective examination of sin and redemption even further. **RDe**

**U.S. / Italy** (Caminito, Rank, Reteitalia, Scena) 103m Color

**Director:** Abel Ferrara

**Producer:** Augusto Caminito, Mary Kane

**Screenplay:** Nicholas St. John

**Photography:** Bojan Bazelli

**Music:** Joe Delia

**Cast:** Christopher Walken, David Caruso, Laurence Fishburne, Victor Argo, Wesley Snipes, Janet Julian, Joey Chin, Giancarlo Esposito, Paul Calderon, Steve Buscemi, Theresa Randle, Leonard L. Thomas, Roger Guenveur Smith, Carrie Nygren, Ernest Abuba

# DANCES WITH WOLVES (1990)

"I want to see the frontier . . . before it's gone." An idealistic Union soldier with a romantic dream of the frontier is rewarded for gallantry in the Civil War with his choice of assignment, an outpost in the Dakotas. There he is befriended by a tribe of Lakota Sioux and goes native, only to witness the encroachment of the white man and twilight falling on the great horse culture of the Plains.

Heartthrob Kevin Costner's directorial debut—ambitious, epic, some of it in Lakota with subtitles—*Dances with Wolves* had Hollywood wags predicting it would be another *Heaven's Gate*. But Costner had the last laugh, riding away with seven Oscars including Best Picture—the first Western to win since 1931—and Best Director (over Martin Scorsese for *Goodfellas*).

"Dances with Wolves" is the name the Indians give to Costner's Lieutenant John Dunbar. He is by stages terrified, intrigued, then captivated by his feather-decked neighbors and their way of life. And the story of how he finds himself and comes by his new name is as enchanting a Western as ever was—rich, lyrical, warm, full of unlooked-for laughs, heartbreaking, and spectacularly cinematic. Costner's direction is remarkably accomplished, taking each elegiac, mystical, or romantic interlude to an exciting action payoff, with battles, buffalo, the spectacular plains of South Dakota, and the handsome cast all gifts to Australian cinematographer and *Mad Max* veteran Dean Semler. The Indians are portrayed with unprecedented respect and affectionate intimacy as proud, quick, and humorous by Native Americans who are both magnificent looking and engaging, notably Graham Greene as shaman Kicking Bird and Rodney A. Grant as warrior Wind in His Hair.

Sentiment is strong, at times exhaustingly melodramatic. But the film's eloquence and evocative beauty make it enduringly enjoyable. A year later Costner presented the special edition, with an hour of additional material which expands the hero's romance with Stands with a Fist (Mary McDonnell) and shows the fate of captured white buffalo hunters. But there is no new major action scene and the added length, lovely and involving for devotees, does slow the pace. Action fans prefer the original, utterly enjoyable three-hour version. **AE**

U.S. (Tig, Majestic) 183m Color

**Language:** English / Sioux / Pawnee

**Director:** Kevin Costner

**Producer:** Kevin Costner, Jim Wilson

**Screenplay:** Michael Blake, from his novel

**Photography:** Dean Semler

**Music:** John Barry, Peter Buffett

**Cast:** Kevin Costner, Mary McDonnell, Graham Greene, Rodney A. Grant, Floyd "Red Crow" Westerman, Tantoo Cardinal, Robert Pastorelli, Charles Rocket, Maury Chaykin, Jimmy Herman, Nathan Lee Chasing His Horse, Michael Spears, Jason R. Lone Hill, Tony Pierce, Doris Leader Charge

**Oscar:** Jim Wilson, Kevin Costner (best picture), Kevin Costner (director), Michael Blake (screenplay), Dean Semler (photography), Neil Travis (editing), John Barry (music), Russell Williams, Jeffrey Perkins, Bill W. Benton, Gregory H. Watkins (sound)

**Oscar nomination:** Kevin Costner (actor), Graham Greene (actor in support role), Mary McDonnell (actress in support role), Jeffrey Beecroft, Lisa Dean (art direction), Elsa Zamparelli (costume)

**Berlin International Film Festival:** Kevin Costner (Silver Bear—outstanding single achievement, producing/directing/acting), nomination (Golden Bear)

# HITLERJUNGE SALOMON (1990)
## EUROPA EUROPA

Salomon Perel, played by Marco Hofschneider, changes uniforms, languages, and identities in an effort to survive the Holocaust. Renowned Polish filmmaker Agnieszka Holland refrains from passing judgment on her chameleon-like protagonist as she represents unspeakable psychological tortures and miraculous escapes from a matter-of-fact distance, not dwelling on agony or bloodbath. This is what renders this incredible story so shockingly believable and separates it from other films about the Holocaust.

Set between 1938 and 1945, *Europa Europa* is actually based on the real-life adventures of Salomon "Solly" Perel. Solly is a young Polish Jew from Germany, whose life takes a grotesque turn when the Nazis break into his family's apartment. With the family dispersed, Solly ends up alone, saved only by the Nazi uniform he puts on. This act launches his career as a performer. First, he winds up in a Russian orphanage in eastern Poland, where he receives a thorough education in communist dogma, renouncing his Jewish identity and denouncing religion as "the opiate of the masses." Hitler's troops take him back to Germany, where he is employed as a Russian interpreter, accepted as an Aryan. The irony and danger of his performance reach their epitome when he joins the Hitlerjugend, where he is taught how to recognize and kill Jews.

Hiding his circumcision becomes particularly dangerous when his good looks win the hearts of a gay Nazi officer and a desirable but excessively anti-semitic girl, played by Julie Delpy. As the only physical reminder of Solly's true identity, circumcision becomes a rich metaphor in the movie. Some of the most powerfully ambiguous moments of *Europa Europa* show Solly overidentifying with the role he is playing, suggesting that true identity might not be possible at all. Unsurprisingly, there is no catharsis or tragedy at the end; although when Solly is miraculously reunited with his lost brother Isaak (René Hofschneider), we sense that his performance is far from over. **AI**

**Germany / France / Poland** (CCC Filmkunst, Losange) 112m Eastmancolor

**Language:** German / Russian

**Director:** Agnieszka Holland

**Producer:** Artur Brauner, Margaret Ménégoz

**Screenplay:** Agnieszka Holland, from book by Salomon Perel

**Photography:** Jacek Petrycki, Jacek Zaleski

**Music:** Zbigniew Preisner

**Cast:** Marco Hofschneider, Salomon Perel, René Hofschneider, Piotr Kozlowski, Klaus Abramowsky, Michèle Gleizer, Marta Sandrowicz, Nathalie Schmidt, Delphine Forest, Andrzej Mastalerz, Wlodzimierz Press, Martin Maria Blau, Klaus Kowatsch, Holger Hunkel, Bernhard Howe

**Oscar nomination:** Agnieszka Holland (screenplay)

U.S. (Silver Screen, Touchstone) 119m Technicolor
**Language:** English / Italian
**Director:** Garry Marshall
**Producer:** Arnon Milchan, Steven Reuther
**Screenplay:** J.F. Lawton
**Photography:** Charles Minsky
**Music:** James Newton Howard
**Cast:** Richard Gere, Julia Roberts, Ralph Bellamy, Jason Alexander, Laura San Giacomo, Hector Elizondo, Alex Hyde-White, Amy Yasbeck, Elinor Donahue, Judith Baldwin, Jason Randal, Bill Applebaum, Tracy Bjork, Gary Greene, Billy Gallo
**Oscar nomination:** Julia Roberts (actress)

# PRETTY WOMAN (1990)

A 1940s-style romantic comedy given a modern twist, *Pretty Woman* came along as a refreshing antidote to the macho wham-bam movies that dominated Hollywood's output in the late '80s. One of the highest-grossing pictures of 1990, it succeeded in making the "date movie" popular again. Not bad for a film that was originally conceived as a depressing look at prostitution in Los Angeles, as based on the original script entitled *3 Thousand.*

*Pretty Woman* also gave huge career boosts to its two stars, Richard Gere (who hadn't had a hit since the mid-80s) and Julia Roberts, who earned an Oscar nomination for her performance. Gere is at his suave best as Edward Lewis, a business mogul on a trip to L.A. who winds up lost near Hollywood Boulevard, and asks hooker-with-a-heart-of-gold Vivian (Roberts in a miniscule miniskirt and PVC thigh boots) for directions back to his Beverly Hills hotel. Being the smart and sensible prostitute she is, Vivian offers to take him where he needs to go, and it's not long before she has charmed him into hiring her for the week to be his "beck-and-call girl." In return for her time and effort she gets unlimited use of his credit card to buy clothes and learns how to dine at a fancy restaurant (thanks to the friendly hotel concierge, played by Hector Elizondo). And, no surprise, Vivian falls in love with her benefactor.

The whole thing is highly improbable, of course. For starters, it's unlikely any Hollywood Boulevard streetwalkers look as nice and well groomed as Vivian. The huge success of Roberts in the role of a hooker is politically incorrect, but the sheer charm of *Pretty Woman* never fails to shine through. A modern-day treatment of *Pygmalion* and *Cinderella* rolled into one, the film is graced by first-class performances from two easy-on-the-eye stars, slick direction from Garry Marshall, and a sharp, funny script. **IB**

## ARCHANGEL (1990)

Guy Maddin, the underground cult wizard from Winnipeg responsible for *Tales From the Gimli Hospital*, followed this up with *Archangel*, an even stranger black-and-white feature made on a heftier budget. The film involves amnesiac victims of mustard gas during World War I and the Russian Revolution. The hero, a Canadian soldier (Kyle McCulloch), mistakes a nurse (Kathy Marykuca) for his dead love; she's married to a Belgian aviator (Ari Cohen) who can't remember he's married, and she gets so confused that she winds up mistaking the Canadian for the Belgian.

There are other complications, some of which, like the amnesia, suggest a deranged remake of *Random Harvest*, but *Archangel* often appears to be about nothing at all—except perhaps Maddin's obvious love for late silent and early talkie studio productions with kitschy pictorial effects, as well as offbeat surrealist conceits (such as a hailstorm of bunny rabbits falling into trenches). The results may not be consistently funny or affecting, but it never seems that Maddin is out to produce straight-out comedy or camp, much less serious drama. What comes across is a fascinating fetishist delirium, where memories of remote war movies get recycled into something that is alternately creepy and beautiful. **JRos**

**Canada** (Cinephile, Ordnance, Winnipeg) 90m BW

**Director:** Guy Maddin

**Producer:** Greg Klymkiw

**Screenplay:** Guy Maddin, George Toles

**Photography:** Guy Maddin

**Cast:** Kyle McCulloch, Kathy Marykuca, Sarah Neville, Ari Cohen, Michael Gottli, Victor Cowie, David Falkenburg, Michael O'Sullivan, Margaret Anne MacLeod, Ihor Procak, Robert Lougheed, Stephen Snyder, Michael Powell, Sam Toles, Lloyd Weinberg

## TRUST (1990)

Hal Hartley's second feature—a decided improvement over his first, *The Unbelievable Truth* (1989)—returns to the same basic turf, a Long Island commuter town, and features the same lead actress (Adrienne Shelly) as an alienated teenager. This time around, Shelly plays a high school student who finds herself pregnant, provokes her father's fatal heart attack, gets unceremoniously dumped by her boyfriend, and kicked out of the house by her mother (Merritt Nelson). Then she is assaulted, witnesses a kidnapping, and meets an angry and disgruntled electronics whiz (Martin Donovan), all in the same day.

It's a credit to the film that this overflow of incident neither strains credibility nor becomes exploited for facile comedy. In fact, the real story in *Trust* only begins once the heroine and the electronics whiz become involved and their mutual adjustments—including the strains represented by their difficult parents—gradually transform both of them. Unpredictable while remaining honest to both its characters and its milieu, this flaky comedy drama improves as it proceeds, much as Hartley's own body of work has often done. **JRos**

**U.S. / G.B.** (Channel Four, Republic, True Fiction, Zenith) 90m Color

**Director:** Hal Hartley

**Producer:** Hal Hartley, Bruce Weiss

**Screenplay:** Hal Hartley

**Photography:** Michael Spiller

**Music:** The Great Outdoors, Philip Reed

**Cast:** Adrienne Shelly, Martin Donovan, Merritt Nelson, John MacKay, Edie Falco, Gary Sauer, Matt Malloy, Suzanne Costollos, Jeff Howard, Karen Sillas, Tom Thon, Hannah Sullivan, Marko Hunt, Kathryn Mederos, Bill Sage

**Iran** (Institute for the Intellectual Development of Children & Young Adults) 97m Color

**Language:** Farsi

**Director:** Abbas Kiarostami

**Producer:** Ali Reza Zarrin

**Screenplay:** Abbas Kiarostami

**Photography:** Ali Reza Zarrindast

**Cast:** Hossain Sabzian, Mohsen Makhmalbaf, Abolfazl Ahankhah, Mehrdad Ahankhah, Manoochehr Ahankhah, Mahrokh Ahankhah, Nayer Mohseni Zonoozi, Ahmad Reza Moayed Mohseni, Hossain Farazmand, Hooshang Shamaei, Mohammad Ali Barrati, Davood Goodarzi, Haj Ali Reza Ahmadi, Hassan Komaili, Davood Mohabbat

# NEMA-YE NAZDIK (1990)

## CLOSE-UP

Based on a real incident, Abbas Kiarostami's masterly film first appears to present itself as a purely documentary reconstruction of events leading to the trial of the impoverished Hossein Sabzian for attempted fraud. After meeting an elderly woman on a bus and passing himself off as Mohsen Makhmalbaf (Iranian director of *The Cyclist* and *Kandahar*), Sabzian is invited to meet her family, and leads them to believe that, if they finance him, they'll appear in his next film. Eventually, they suspect he's an impostor planning to burgle their home, and call the police.

This would make merely for intriguing docudrama, were it not for Kiarostami's subtle approach to the narrative, which comprises a witty, illuminating, highly inventive exploration of the symbiotic relationships between truth and falsehood, appearance and reality, documentary and fiction. The characters—not only Sabzian and the Ahankhah family, but Kiarostami, Makhmalbaf, and a scoop-hungry journalist—are "played" by themselves. Some events are dramatically recreated, some simply described, others—like the trial itself (at which, strangely, Kiarostami is often allowed to take over questioning)—are presented as documentary footage. Though the narrative line, for all its flashbacks, is clear, the way in which it is presented and the status of what we're shown—is this for real, or acted out?—keep shifting, and the film becomes a multilayered investigation into that most elusive of phenomena: the Truth.

But even as he undermines our assumptions about objectivity, Kiarostami directs us toward one small, inescapable truth: That everyone, to quote Renoir, has his reasons. Sabzian, we discover as we delve deeper into this initially outlandish story, is neither con-man nor lunatic, but simply someone for whom cinema is of enormous value—and being viewed as a famous filmmaker makes him feel less insignificant, and more in control. Movies can help us dream and escape the constraints of our everyday lives. Besides being a funny, thought-provoking deconstruction of documentary conventions, *Close-Up* is a tribute both to the power of cinema and to the essential goodness—and imaginative capabilities—of ordinary people. The film's closing scene, which with one quiet image extols the virtues of kindness, humility, and forgiveness, is wholly characteristic of Kiarostami's unique brand of unsentimental humanism. **GA**

# EDWARD SCISSORHANDS (1990)

Rather than follow the hugely successful *Batman* (1989) with another special-effects-driven bonanza, director Tim Burton instead delivered a delightfully realized movie that was about as far from a mainstream Hollywood blockbuster as it was possible to get. The result is *Edward Scissorhands*, a decidedly left-of-center fairy tale that remains the most whimsical and touching film of Burton's career so far.

The Edward of the title (Johnny Depp) is not a man at all, but the creation of The Inventor (an all-too-brief cameo performance from the marvelous Vincent Price in his last film role). Edward looks human enough, except for one detail—he has scissors instead of hands—and he lives a solitary life in a crumbling mansion high above a neighborhood of pastel-colored houses. It is only when kindly Avon lady Peg Boggs (Dianne Wiest) discovers his hiding place that Edward descends to the "real" world below, and finds himself embraced by Peg's neighbors when he displays his special talent for hairdressing, dog grooming, and hedge shaping. Life for the trusting and innocent Edward is complicated, however, when he falls for Peg's cheerleader daughter Kim (Winona Ryder) and is soon coerced by her boyfriend (Anthony Michael Hall) into committing a crime.

One of the many successes Burton pulls off in this delightfully odd film is to cast his various players against type in this eccentric dreamlike world. Hall, best known for playing the nerd in John Hughes's *The Breakfast Club*, succeeds in showing a far nastier side in his role as oafish boyfriend Jim. Ryder, on the other hand, devoid of the ample cynicism she displayed in *Heathers*, brings a delicate touch to her role as the nice girl on the block. It is Depp, however, who impresses the most, creating a character trapped by his incomplete body, conveying Edward's frustration with few words, his pale, scarred face showing the hurt when he discovers that even his gentlest touch with his scissor hands can cause pain. An ambitious, beautifully conceived modern-day fairy tale. **JB**

**U.S.** (Fox) 105m Color
**Director:** Tim Burton
**Producer:** Tim Burton, Denise Di Novi
**Screenplay:** Tim Burton and Caroline Thompson
**Photography:** Stefan Czapsky
**Music:** Danny Elfman
**Cast:** Johnny Depp, Winona Ryder, Dianne Wiest, Anthony Michael Hall, Kathy Baker, Robert Oliveri, Conchata Ferrell, Caroline Aaron, Dick Anthony Williams, O-Lan Jones, Vincent Price, Alan Arkin, Susan Blommaert, Linda Perri, John Davidson
**Oscar nomination:** Ve Neill, Stan Winston (makeup)

# HENRY: PORTRAIT OF A SERIAL KILLER
(1990)

**U.S.** (Filmcat, Fourth World Media, MPI, Maljack) 83m Color
**Director:** John McNaughton
**Producer:** Lisa Dedmond, Steven A. Jones, John McNaughton
**Screenplay:** Richard Fire, John McNaughton
**Photography:** Charlie Lieberman
**Music:** Mic Fabus, Ken Hale, Steven A. Jones, Robert McNaughton
**Cast:** Mary Demas, Michael Rooker, Anne Bartoletti, Elizabeth Kaden, Ted Kaden, Denise Sullivan, Anita Ores, Megan Ores, Cheri Jones, Monica Anne O'Malley, Bruce Quist, Erzsebet Sziky, Tracy Arnold, Tom Towles, David Katz

Directed by John McNaughton, *Henry: Portrait of a Serial Killer* is loosely based on the story of real serial murderer Henry Lee Lucas. It is exceptional for its realism of style and amoral viewpoint. It remains with the viewer as one of the most disturbing movies ever made.

*Henry* flouts horror-film conventions with its flat narrative, an accumulation of episodes where the expected murders occur, but in unexpected ways—off-screen or on, but sudden, random, and casual. In one scene, Henry (Michael Rooker) snaps the necks of two prostitutes in his car and then goes with his roommate Otis (Tom Towles) to buy a hamburger.

The plot of *Henry* (insofar as it has one) follows events that occur after Otis's sister Becky (Tracy Arnold) moves into their small Chicago apartment, disrupting this pair's somewhat repressed homosexual partnership in crime. A low-budget movie, *Henry* excels in depicting the life of drifters amid a grubby lower-class milieu. At one point the film cuts from the corpse of a woman Henry has killed, to show a nasty matron in Becky's beauty salon spouting racist slurs.

Becky romanticizes about Henry when she hears how he killed his mother. Rooker brings a surly, Brando-esque appeal to the role of this psychopath, which helps to explain her bad choice of love objects. The film culminates in two especially upsetting murders. First, Henry and Otis kill a suburban family. After witnessing the mayhem, we suddenly realize that we have watched this footage alongside the killers, who are sitting on the sofa reviewing their home movie of the deed. Later, Henry kills Otis, whom he has caught raping Becky. Henry and Becky leave town, but the next morning, in the film's final sequences, Henry leaves their hotel room alone, pausing to drop off a heavy suitcase by the roadside.

*Henry* is so understated it might seem dull to younger viewers jaded by the gory excesses of other post-1980s horror flicks. Nor does it boast a charmingly elegant killer like Hannibal Lecter. Instead, Henry evokes horror through gritty realism and excellent acting. The film is not fun to watch, but important because it forces viewers into reflection, questioning our cultural fascination with serial killers. **CFr**

# TOTAL RECALL (1990)

Cult science-fiction author Philip K. Dick's story *We Can Remember It For You Wholesale* is impressively translated onto the screen with numerous jaw-dropping special effects and lashings of violence by Dutch director Paul Verhoeven, who had previously scored a similar sci-fi hit with the 1987 blockbuster *RoboCop*.

Arnold Schwarzeneggger stars as Doug Quaid, an everyday Joe (albeit one built like Hercules) who has recurring dreams about living on Mars. His wife (Sharon Stone) dismisses his fantasies, so Doug pays a visit to a virtual reality vacation company and gets hooked up to a machine that will simulate a trip to the red planet. Unfortunately, it also gives his brain a good zapping, and Doug wakes up from his virtual trip believing he is a secret agent, and soon finds himself pursued by various human and mutant heavies while he tries to work out in his head what is fact and what is fiction.

Many of Dick's favorite themes (also explored in *Do Androids Dream of Electric Sheep?*, which became Ridley Scott's classic sci-fi film *Blade Runner* in 1982) are explored in *Total Recall*—identity, perception, memories, real and manufactured—but never at the expense of action. And action there certainly is, from a fun fight between Stone and Schwarzenegger, their sparring dialogue an added bonus, to the final, gruesome but gripping showdown. **JB**

**U.S.** (Carolco, TriStar) 109m Technicolor

**Director:** Paul Verhoeven

**Producer:** Buzz Feitshans, Ronald Shusett

**Screenplay:** Ronald Shusett, Dan O'Bannon, Gary Goldman, from the short story *We Can Remember It For You Wholesale* by Philip K. Dick

**Photography:** Jost Vacano

**Music:** Jerry Goldsmith, Bruno Louchouarn

**Cast:** Arnold Schwarzenegger, Rachel Ticotin, Sharon Stone, Ronny Cox, Michael Ironside, Marshall Bell, Mel Johnson Jr., Michael Champion, Roy Brocksmith, Ray Baker, Rosemary Dunsmore, David Knell, Alexia Robinson, Dean Norris, Mark Carlton

**Oscar:** Eric Brevig, Rob Bottin, Tim McGovern, Alex Funke (special visual effects)

**Oscar nomination:** Stephen Hunter Flick (special sound effects), Nelson Stoll, Michael J. Kohut, Carlos DeLarios, Aaron Rochin (sound)

# WONG FEI-HUNG (1991)
## ONCE UPON A TIME IN CHINA

Hark Tsui was Hong Kong's reigning filmmaker in the 1980s and early '90s, deftly infusing his eye-popping action films with witty political commentary. *Once Upon a Time in China* finds him breathing new life into the chronicles of Chinese folk hero Wong Fei-Hung.

Wong, a legendary healer and martial artist, the subject of several of Hark's films dating back to the 1960s, is given a lavish reintroduction in this, the first episode in Hark Tsui's *Once Upon a Time* series. Set in 1875, Wong (Jet Li) faces off against British exploiters and corrupt Chinese businessmen in a wild and convoluted plot involving imperialism, the press-ganging of Chinese peasants into the building of America's railroads, arms smugglers, and disgraced martial artists forced to work as hired thugs.

This is popular Hong Kong cinema at its most breathless, aided by the superb athleticism of Li, who makes his entry into world stardom as the poised and stoical hero. He is the center of dazzling set pieces that include a gravity-defying duel fought with ladders, and a standoff between an unarmed Wong and an opponent with a gun. Underneath the twisting plot and relentless action, however, is a palpable melancholy—a lament for a China about to change forever under Western influences. **AT**

**Hong Kong** (Film Workshop) 134m Color

**Language:** Cantonese / English / Mandarin

**Director:** Hark Tsui

**Producer:** Hark Tsui

**Screenplay:** Yiu Ming Leung, Pik-yin Tang, Hark Tsui, Kai-Chi Yu

**Photography:** Tung-Chuen Chan, Wilson Chan, David Chung, Andy Lam, Arthur Wong, Bill Wong

**Music:** Romeo Díaz, James Wong

**Cast:** Jet Li, Biao Yuen, Rosamund Kwan, Jacky Cheung, Steve Tartalia, Kent Cheng, Yee Kwan Yan, Mark King, Jonathan Isgar, Shun Lau, Chi Yeung Wong, Ma Wu, Simon Yam, Cheung-Yan Yuen, Kam-Fai Yuen, Shun-Yee Yuen, Tony Yuen

U.S. (Columbia) 107m Color
**Director:** John Singleton
**Producer:** Steve Nicolaides
**Screenplay:** John Singleton
**Photography:** Charles Mills
**Music:** Stanley Clarke, Ice Cube
**Cast:** Hudhail Al-Amir, Laurence Fishburne, Lloyd Avery, Cuba Gooding Jr., Ice Cube, Mia Bell, Morris Chestnut, Lexie Bigham, Nia Long, Angela Bassett, Kenneth A. Brown, Nicole Brown, Tyra Ferrell, Ceal, Desi Arnez Hines
**Oscar nomination:** John Singleton (director), John Singleton (screenplay)

# BOYZ 'N THE HOOD (1991)

Given early 1970s heralds like Melvin Van Peebles and Gordon Parks, the 1980s saw a select few African-American filmmakers break into the mainstream. Foremost among them were Robert Townsend and Spike Lee, each crafting witty comedy-dramas about the condition of African America. Yet it was John Singleton's autobiographical debut, *Boyz 'N the Hood*, in 1991 that fully introduced a so-called Black American cinematic voice into the critical establishment. For his efforts Singleton earned two Academy Award nominations, and his film was a runaway hit that provided Columbia Pictures with a monster windfall.

Opening in the aftermath of the 1984 Los Angeles Olympiad, Singleton's drama settles on three 10-year-olds, Tre (Desi Arnez Hines II), Doughboy (Baha Jackson), and Ricky (Donovan McCrary). Raised in single-parent homes, their world is riven with gang violence, police brutality, and economic hardship. When Tre's mother Reva (Angela Bassett) deposits him at the front door of his father Jason "Furious" (Laurence Fishburne), he gets a crash course in masculinity and transforms into an upwardly mobile teen.

Flash forward seven years. Tre (now played by Cuba Gooding Jr.) is a high school senior with a part-time job, an application to a historic Black college, and a girlfriend named Brandi (Nia Long). Doughboy (Ice Cube) is a gangbanger and loafer trading on the patience of his mother, Mrs. Baker (Tyra Ferrell), while his brother Ricky (Morris Chestnut) builds himself up as a Division I college football draft prospect. Trying to escape the 'hood, Tre still remains connected to his neighborhood friends. When Doughboy's underworld connections threaten the trio, Ricky is killed in a drive-by shooting. Afterward Tre confronts his father's sage training and manages to avoid the mistakes of his downtrodden world. Through an ending scrawl we learn he escapes the trap of poverty and violence and accompanies Brandi to college.

Pedantic but expertly orchestrated through a moving depiction of intra-racial violence in the American inner city, *Boyz 'N the Hood* is a vividly memorable morality tale addressed to the same youth represented on screen. After a sobering dedication reminding us of the number of young black men killed by other young black men, it launches into a realistic, profanity-laden, and affecting coming-of-age story.

Especially noteworthy for the screen debut of rapper Ice Cube, Singleton's film evinces an awareness of Hollywood storytelling conventions and demonstrates a real affection for the topical influence of hip-hop music. Organized in a clear three-act structure and tending toward broad moralizing, the picture therefore exudes a professional polish. But it is also scored with the percussive beats and hypnotic raps of various chart-toppers lending their sounds to Tre's escape, making *Boyz 'N the Hood* the achievement of a career.

Despite occasional forays into larger projects, Singleton has struggled to repeat his early success. The artistic heft of his debut can perhaps be dismissed through hindsight and the lack of subsequent brilliance. However, the signal importance of *Boyz 'N the Hood* cannot be ignored when considering it as the origin of a wave of small-scale, black-centered inner-city and ghetto dramas that flourished in the 1990s. **GCQ**

China / Hong Kong / Taiwan (Palace, Era, China Film) 125m Eastmancolor

**Language:** Mandarin

**Director:** Yimou Zhang

**Producer:** Fu-Sheng Chiu

**Screenplay:** Ni Zhen, from novel by Su Tong

**Photography:** Zhao Fei, Lun Yang

**Music:** Naoki Tachikawa, Jiping Zhao

**Cast:** Li Gong, Caifei He, Jingwu Ma, Cuifen Cao, Qi Zhao, Jin Shuyuan, Ding Weimin, Cao Zhengyin, Zhihgang Cui, Chu Xiao, Lin Kong

**Oscar nomination:** Hong Kong (best foreign language film)

**Venice Film Festival:** Zhang Yimou (Silver Lion), tied with *The Fisher King* and *J'Entends Plus la Guitare*

# DA HONG DENG LONG GAO GAO GUA (1991)

## RAISE THE RED LANTERN

Completing a loose trilogy that began with *Red Sorghum* (1987) and *Ju Dou* (1990), Yimou Zhang's grim adaptation of a novel by Su Tong once again stars Li Gong as a young woman who marries a much older man. Once again he tells a story that explicitly critiques Chinese feudalism and indirectly contemporary China. This time, however, the style is quite different (despite another key use of the color red) and the vision much bleaker.

The heroine, a less sympathetic figure than her predecessors, is a university student in the 1920s who becomes the fourth and youngest wife of a powerful man in northern China after her stepmother can no longer afford to pay for her education. She quickly becomes involved in the various intrigues and rivalries between wives that rule her husband's world and family tradition. Each wife has her own house and courtyard within the palace, and whoever the husband chooses to sleep with on a given night receives a foot massage, several lighted red lanterns, and the right to select the following day's menu.

*Raise the Red Lantern* confines us throughout to this claustrophobic universe of boxes within boxes, where wives and female servants devote their lives to scheming against one another. Zhang confirms his mastery and artistry here in many ways, some relatively new (such as his striking soundtrack), though the cold, remote, and stifling world he presents here offers little emotional release. **JRos**

**France** (Constellation, Hachette, Sofinergie, UGC) 99m Color

**Language:** French

**Director:** Marc Caro, Jean-Pierre Jeunet

**Producer:** Claudie Ossard

**Screenplay:** Gilles Adrien, Marc Caro, Jean-Pierre Jeunet

**Photography:** Darius Khondji

**Music:** Carlos d'Alessio

**Cast:** Pascal Benezech, Dominique Pinon, Marie-Laure Dougnac, Jean-Claude Dreyfus, Karin Viard, Ticky Holgado, Anne-Marie Pisani, Boban Janevski, Mikael Todde, Edith Ker, Jacques Mathou, Rufus, Howard Vernon, Chick Ortega, Silvie Laguna

# DELICATESSEN (1991)

Creatively combining genres—postapocalyptic sci-fi, black comedy, and sweet romance—and offering audiences an impressively oddball collection of sounds, colors, actors, and images, Jean-Pierre Jeunet and Marc Caro's inspired film *Delicatessen* was the recepient of several European awards and anticipated the pair's subsequent collaboration, *The City of Lost Children* (1995). Jeunet would go on to direct *Alien: Resurrection* in 1997, which was followed with the international blockbuster *Amélie* in 2001.

The movie boasts an unforgettable opening: A mysterious figure covered from head to toe in an outfit made entirely of trash anxiously attempts to sneak away from a deli (located beneath a dilapidated apartment building) by hitching a ride in a garbage truck. Suddenly the lid to his can of freedom is violently ripped open and the menacing butcher-in-charge (Jean-Claude Drefyus) brings a huge meat cleaver down upon him. We soon learn that the butcher's specialty is human flesh, and once his new employee—the saw-playing ex-clown Louison (a beautifully smush-faced Dominique Pinon)—falls for his bespectacled cellist daughter (Marie-Laure Dougnac), the race to make Louison the special of the day is on. To save her clown boyfriend from her cannibal dad, Julie betrays the latter to a group of lentil-eating rebels who live underground. With an eccentric screenplay by comic book writer Gilles Adrien, and a number of darkly humorous set pieces, *Delicatessen* is a feast for the eyes and ears. **SJS**

# GULING JIE SHAONIAN SHA REN SHIJIAN (1991)

## A BRIGHTER SUMMER DAY

Epic in scope if not always in scale, Edward Yang's subtle and rich portrait of Taiwan fits so many details into its deceptively brisk four-hour running time that it's a wonder Yang delivered the film as short as it is. Set during a single Taipei school year in the early 1960s, *A Brighter Summer Day* depicts a country still reeling from the disruptive influx of Chinese Nationalists (led by the repressive Chiang Kai-shek) in 1948. Yang's Taiwan is torn between communism and democracy, nationalism and liberality, with confusion, alienation, and uncertainty leading to a sometimes debilitating anomie.

Yet as powerful as *A Brighter Summer Day* may be, Yang infuses it with touches of humor and humanism that temper the distressing atmosphere of impending doom. The direction is patient and serene; the film is like a masterful symphony of dozens of characters whose tone and tempo are deftly orchestrated by Yang. Favoring static or slow-moving long shots over close-ups, Yang gives his cast great freedom to explore their emotions (or apparent lack thereof), acting for the story and each other and not just the camera; yet Yang clearly wants the film to be about specific places and things as much as people. That *A Brighter Summer Day* reveals facts and plot points with the care, planning, and deliberation of a great novel therefore comes as no surprise.

Neither does the emotional weight of the film's tragic conclusion, the payoff of all of Yang's rigorous narrative design (itself the product of four years of preparation), which manages to seamlessly weave together the story of Taipei street gangs, puppy love, rock and roll, lost cultural signifiers, and the search for a national identity. While often compared loosely to Nicholas Ray's moody classic *Rebel Without A Cause*, *A Brighter Summer Day* is so much more. A masterpiece of the Taiwanese New Wave and a cinematic highpoint of the tail end of the 20th century, this is a film whose grasp of period and place is masterful almost beyond the realm of mere storytelling. It's like a multi-faceted photo album composed of truly moving, thought-provoking pictures. **JKl**

**Taiwan** (ICA, Jane Balfour, Yang & His Gang) 237m Color

**Language:** Mandarin

**Director:** Edward Yang

**Producer:** Yu Welyan

**Screenplay:** Yan Hongya, Lai Mingtang, Yang Shunqing, Edward Yang

**Photography:** Huigong Li, Longyu Zhang

**Music:** Zhan Hongda

**Cast:** Zhang Guozhu, Elaine Jin, Wang Juan, Zhang Han, Jiang Xiuqiong, Lai Fanyun, Lisa Yang, Zhang Zhen

# NAKED LUNCH (1991)

Defining the phrase *Naked Lunch*, as introduced in his book of the same name, writer William S. Burroughs matter-of-factly called it "a frozen moment when everyone sees what is on the end of every fork," as if that cleared up his confusing and confrontational antinarrative. David Cronenberg, in filming the movie version of Burroughs's often deliriously incoherent book, doesn't make things much clearer. Rather than faithfully adapt the book many said could never be adapted to the big screen, Cronenberg instead responded by intentionally making it even more complicated, incorporating elements not only from several of Burroughs's other works but from the author's life as well.

The movie of *Naked Lunch* combines Burroughs's novels *Naked Lunch*, *Junkie*, *Exterminator!* and *Queer*, with the perverse, William Tell-inspired death of Burroughs's wife. Cronenberg coheres a disorienting mishmash of fact and fiction with the rigid framework of film noir formalism. The result works more like a surreal portrait of Burroughs than as a traditional narrative, which should come as no surprise to anyone familiar with the iconoclastic bent of both Burroughs and Cronenberg.

Peter Weller is Bill Lee (a Burroughs pseudonym), an exterminator addicted to his own bug powder, who after accidentally killing his own wife, flees to the mysterious Tangiers-like Interzone. He is enlisted as a spy in a world of assorted creatures, spouting various spewing and oozing phallic appendages, live insect typewriters, and other weirdos. Just as Cronenberg combines fact and fiction, the film itself concerns that nether region between the real and the unreal, a place where drug-fueled hallucinations are not only the imaginative impetus for the creative process but the product of it.

Cronenberg's audacious subversion of narrative is admirable, as are the performances by Weller, Judy Davis, and Roy Scheider. But along with Peter Suschitzky's queasy green- and gray-tinged cinematography, of particular note is the astounding score, a collaboration between Cronenberg's composer of choice Howard Shore and legendary free jazz saxophone player Ornette Coleman. Like the film itself, it's a remarkable collision of different sensibilities, of composition, and of spontaneous expression. **JKl**

**Canada / G.B. / Japan** (Film Trustees, Nippon Film Develop. and Finance, RPC, The Ontario Film Develop. Corp., Téléfilm Canada) 115m Color

**Director:** David Cronenberg

**Producer:** Jeremy Thomas

**Screenplay:** David Cronenberg, from novel by William S. Burroughs

**Photography:** Peter Suschitzky

**Music:** Ornette Coleman, Howard Shore

**Cast:** Peter Weller, Judy Davis, Ian Holm, Julian Sands, Roy Scheider, Monique Mercure, Nicholas Campbell, Michael Zelniker, Robert A. Silverman, Joseph Scoren, Peter Boretski, Yuval Daniel, John Friesen, Sean McCann, Howard Jerome

**Berlin International Film Festival:** David Cronenberg nomination (Golden Bear)

# LA BELLE NOISEUSE (1991)
## THE BEAUTIFUL TROUBLEMAKER

Films about artists are risky, courting terrible clichés—romantic genius in the garret, tormented soul projected onto canvas—to show what someone goes through while shaping sensations and intuitions into pictures. Jacques Rivette accepts the challenge gleefully in *La Belle Noiseuse*, extrapolating from a short story by Balzac: This will be the story of an "unfinished masterpiece," produced and then hidden by a famous artist in his twilight years.

Rivette and his writers, Pascal Bonitzer and Christine Laurent, juggle many themes skillfully. On one level, the film offers a glimpse into the privileged world of art, where creators, dealers, and confidants weave a subtly erotic tangle. At the film's core, Rivette studies, with a minute attention to detail and duration, the dancelike rapport between an artist, Edouard Frenhofer (Michel Piccoli) and his mostly naked model, Marianne (Emmanuelle Béart). Their sessions wheel through many moods: Frustration, aggression, exuberance. The master-slave relationship shifts. Slowly, through many trials, an artistic work takes form.

As Frenhofer faces the disturbance in his marriage to Liz (Jane Birkin), warily watches the emergence of a new generation, and confronts the specter of his own mortality, it is hard not to see this melancholy hero as the director's own self-portrait. **AM**

**France / Switzerland** (CNC, France 3, George Reinhart, Canal+, Pierre Grisé, Region Languedes, Ronsillon Sofica 2, Sofica 3) 240m Eastmancolor

**Director:** Jacques Rivette

**Producer:** Martine Marignac

**Screenplay:** Pascal Bonitzer, Christine Laurent, Jacques Rivette, from the novella *Le Chef-d'Oeuvre Inconnu* by Honoré de Balzac

**Photography:** William Lubtchansky

**Nonoriginal music:** Igor Stravinsky

**Cast:** Michel Piccoli, Jane Birkin, Emmanuelle Béart, Marianne Denicourt, David Bursztein, Gilles Arbona, Marie Belluc, Marie-Claude Roger, Leila Remili, Daphne Goodfellow, Susan Robertson, Bernard Dufour

**Cannes Film Festival:** Jacques Rivette (grand prize of the jury), (prize of the ecumenical jury—special mention), nomination (Golden Palm)

# THE RAPTURE (1991)

Few movies have treated religion seriously, and fewer still have explored evangelical Christianity on its own theological terms. This is what Michael Tolkin does in *The Rapture*, which may be viewed with equal pleasure as a spiritual melodrama, a faith-based fable, and an eccentric fairy tale with roots in a real religious subculture.

Mimi Rogers plays Sharon, a swinging single who enjoys cruising for foursomes with a sleazy male friend. Then she hears about a religious movement that emphasizes a personal relationship with God, whose day of judgment—complete with a transcendent "Rapture" that will whisk good souls to heaven—is said to be coming soon. Her newfound faith helps her weather turbulent storms, such as her husband's death. When she thinks the end of times is imminent, she takes her daughter to a lonely patch of desert, where they await God's saving hand. In the film's most audacious twist, the Rapture actually does arrive, but by now suffering has led her to reject the idea of a just and merciful deity.

At once a psychological drama, a reflection on faith and free will, and a crisp 1990s variation on what Hollywood used to call the "woman's picture," this offbeat parable offers rich rewards for the open-minded moviegoer. **DS**

**U.S.** (New Line) 100m Color

**Director:** Michael Tolkin

**Producer:** Karen Koch, Nancy Tenenbaum, Nick Wechsler

**Screenplay:** Michael Tolkin

**Photography:** Bojan Bazelli

**Music:** Thomas Newman

**Cast:** Mimi Rogers, Darwyn Carson, Patrick Bauchau, Marvin Elkins, David Duchovny, Stephanie Menuez, Sam Vlahos, Rustam Branaman, Scott Burkholder, Vince Grant, Carole Davis, Patrick Dollaghan, James LeGros, Dick Anthony Williams, DeVaughn Nixon

**U.S.** (New Line) 102m Color
**Director:** Gus Van Sant
**Producer:** Laurie Parker
**Screenplay:** Gus Van Sant
**Photography:** John J. Campbell, Eric Alan Edwards
**Music:** Bill Stafford
**Cast:** River Phoenix, Keanu Reeves, James Russo, William Richert, Rodney Harvey, Chiara Caselli, Michael Parker, Jessie Thomas, Flea, Grace Zabriskie, Tom Troupe, Udo Kier, Sally Curtice, Robert Lee Pitchlynn, Mickey Cottrell
**Venice Film Festival:** River Phoenix (Volpi cup—actor)

# MY OWN PRIVATE IDAHO (1991)

In only his third feature, the follow-up to his 1989 breakthrough *Drugstore Cowboy* (his 1985 debut, the ultra-low-budget *Mala Noche*, is an unsung treasure still not available either on home video or DVD), Gus Van Sant's *My Own Private Idaho* remains the writer-director's most profound, moving, and complete film—what Desson Howe has called "an exquisite, cinematic poem . . . about the eternal search to belong somewhere, and the lonely landscape of the soul."

Without ever stifling his artistic, even avant-garde impulses for the sake of accessibility and mainstream appeal—something he would be angrily accused of doing after his maudlin middle-of-the-road dramas *Good Will Hunting* (1997) and *Finding Forrester* (2000)—Van Sant here manages to deliver a delightfully idiosyncratic story, one that relies on images at least as much as words to captivate viewers. True, the casting of teen heartthrobs Keanu Reeves (in what may be his finest performance to date) and River Phoenix (who would die tragically of a drug overdose at the age of 23, right on the cusp of a brilliant career) as the leads certainly didn't hurt *My Own Private Idaho*'s commercial prospects. But in explicitly thematizing homelessness, homosexuality, and teenage prostitution; by offering up a protagonist who suffers from narcolepsy and romanticized memories of a mother who abandoned him as a child; in paying extended homage to Orson Welles's adaption of Shakespeare's *Henry IV* plays, *Chimes at Midnight* (1965), via a self-consciously anachronistic use of bardspeak in several key scenes, no one can claim that Van Sant was unwilling to risk alienating—even incurring the wrath of—unsuspecting middle-American audiences. Though far too unconventional at both the narrative and stylistic levels to generate blockbuster appeal, the picture was lauded by critics, cherished by Van Sant enthusiasts, and awarded prizes at several international film festivals.

*My Own Private Idaho* (the title is taken from a B-52's song) centers on the relationship between Mike (Phoenix) and Scott (Reeves), two young hustlers living on the streets in Portland, Oregon. Members of a raucuous and libidinal family of social outcasts who congregate in a condemned building, the pair sell their bodies to whomever is buying in order to survive—though we eventually learn that Scott is actually the rebellious son of a well-to-do Portland family, who has chosen this lifestyle largely as a means of humiliating his father. With Mike, on the other hand, what you see is definitely what you get: A quiet, dreamy, gentle boy who is in love with his best friend, falls asleep at the drop of a hat—frequently at inopportune moments, a trait the director taps for both humor and pathos—and is obsessed with finding his long-lost mom. It is this latter quality that provides the impetus for the film's rambling (but never slow) road trip of a plot, as Scott accompanies his always-endangered buddy on excursions ranging from Idaho to Italy in search of a myth of maternal love that the audience sees as the scratchy home-video footage of Mike's mind.

In this tender yet unsentimental picture, Van Sant succeeds as few other filmmakers have in conveying the subjective experience of troubled, disaffected youth. **SJS**

## THELMA & LOUISE (1991)

**U.S.** (MGM, Pathé) 129m Color

**Director:** Ridley Scott

**Producer:** Mimi Polk, Ridley Scott

**Screenplay:** Callie Khouri

**Photography:** Adrian Biddle

**Music:** Hans Zimmer

**Cast:** Susan Sarandon, Geena Davis, Harvey Keitel, Michael Madsen, Christopher McDonald, Stephen Tobolowsky, Brad Pitt, Timothy Carhart, Lucinda Jenney, Jason Beghe, Marco St. John, Sonny Carl Davis, Ken Swofford, Shelly Desai, Carol Mansell

**Oscar:** Callie Khouri (screenplay)

**Oscar nomination:** Ridley Scott (director), Geena Davis (actress), Susan Sarandon (actress), Adrian Biddle (photography), Thom Noble (editing)

To call *Thelma & Louise* a feminist road movie is both accurate and a slight disservice to the film—the latter simply because you run the risk of minimizing the picture's far demographic reach. The story of a browbeaten housewife (Geena Davis) and her sardonic, world-weary waitress best friend (Susan Sarandon) who embark on a weekend getaway and end up fleeing the law after one of them kills a would-be rapist, this film struck a deep chord in audiences across gender, racial, and class lines when it was released. It continues to resonate with viewers because it not only confidently feminized a genre previously owned by men, but it did so by supplying details about social inequities that allowed a host of spectators to see themselves in the heroines, to identify with both the fright and flight of the women's journey.

As the titular characters, Sarandon and Davis embody everyday American women struggling against a host of obstacles (boorish men, dead-end jobs, joyless lives) while simply trying to survive. Director Ridley Scott captures a blue-skied, green-plain United States that is the stuff of myth and legend, promising freedom—but not to all. And it's the gap between that promise and the harsh reality that gives the film its punch, making it a biting commentary on America's dreams, truths, and limitations. **EH**

## TERMINATOR 2: JUDGMENT DAY (1991)

**U.S. / France** (Carolco, Canal+, Lightstorm, Pacific Western) 137m Color

**Language:** English / Spanish

**Director:** James Cameron

**Producer:** James Cameron,

**Screenplay:** James Cameron, William Wisher Jr.

**Photography:** Adam Greenberg

**Music:** Brad Fiedel

**Cast:** Arnold Schwarzenegger, Linda Hamilton, Edward Furlong, Robert Patrick, Earl Boen, Joe Morton, S. Epatha Merkerson, Castulo Guerra, Danny Cooksey, Jenette Goldstein

**Oscar:** Gary Rydstrom, Gloria S. Borders (special sound effects), Dennis Muren, Stan Winston, Gene Warren Jr, Robert Skotak (special visual effects), Stan Winston, Jeff Dawn (makeup), Tom Johnson, Gary Rydstrom, Gary Summers, Lee Orloff (sound)

**Oscar nomination:** Adam Greenberg (photography), Conrad Buff, Mark Goldblatt, Richard A. Harris (editing)

Arnold Schwarzenegger got the best role of his career in director James Cameron's 1984 movie *The Terminator* as a monosyllabic killer robot sent from the future, so it was hardly surprising he decided to reprise the role seven years later in Cameron's sequel. This time, Arnie's T-800 cyborg is the good guy, sent by rebel leader of the future John Connor (Michael Biehn's character from the original movie) to protect his younger self (Edward Furlong) and his mother Sarah (Linda Hamilton), so they can lead the fight that is to come against machines that will take over the earth.

It is what the T-800 is protecting them from that really impresses here—a new breed of Terminator, the far nastier T-1000 (Robert Patrick) that, thanks to some eye-popping special effects, is made of liquid metal and can morph into any shape, taking on the guise of another human or reforming from a puddle in his quest to terminate John and Sarah. In fact, everything in this sequel is bigger and better, from Hamilton's beefed-up physique to the multiple explosions, slick direction, and fast-paced action. A spectacular treat. **JB**

# THE SILENCE OF THE LAMBS (1991)

**U.S.** (Orion) 118m Color
**Director:** Jonathan Demme
**Producer:** Ronald M. Bozman, Edward Saxon, Kenneth Utt
**Screenplay:** Ted Tally, from novel by Thomas Harris
**Photography:** Tak Fujimoto.
**Music:** Howard Shore
**Cast:** Jodie Foster, Anthony Hopkins, Scott Glenn, Anthony Heald, Ted Levine, Frankie Faison, Kasi Lemmons, Brooke Smith, Paul Lazar, Dan Butler, Lawrence T. Wrentz, Don Brockett, Frank Seals Jr., Stuart Rudin, Masha Skorobogatov
**Oscar:** Edward Saxon, Kenneth Utt, Ronald M. Bozman (best picture), Jonathan Demme (director), Ted Tally (screenplay), Anthony Hopkins (actor), Jodie Foster (actress)
**Oscar nomination:** Craig McKay (editing), Tom Fleischman, Christopher Newman (sound)
**Berlin International Film Festival:** Jonathan Demme (Silver Bear—director), tied with *Ultrà* (1990), nomination (Golden Bear)

The first horror movie to win the Academy Award for Best Picture, *The Silence of the Lambs* also has the distinction of being only the third movie in history to win the five major Oscars after *It Happened One Night* (1934) and *One Flew Over the Cuckoo's Nest* (1975).

An adaptation of Thomas Harris's bestselling novel, the film was a deserved winner, featuring superb performances from Jodie Foster and Anthony Hopkins, with director Jonathan Demme, previously best known for comedy, delivering a continuous shiver down the spines of the audience without ever resorting to gore. Foster, as FBI recruit Clarice Starling, is asked by her superior Jack Crawford (Scott Glenn) to visit notorious serial killer Hannibal "The Cannibal" Lecter (Hopkins, in a role originally offered to Jeremy Irons), a former psychiatrist held in a subterranean prison who may have an insight into the psyche of a murderer named Buffalo Bill (creepily brought to life by Ted Levine) that will help the FBI catch him.

Of course, the witty, cultured Hannibal is too clever to give up such information easily. He draws Clarice into an uneasy, disturbing relationship in which he demands insight into her childhood in return for his opinions. It is their exchanges, in Hannibal's dark, gothic dungeon, separated only by glass, that are at the film's heart as Foster and, most notably Hopkins, give tour de force performances, delivering Ted Tally's often quotable words—"A census taker once tried to test me. I ate his liver with some fava beans and a nice Chianti"—with delicious (if that word can be used in reference to a movie about a cannibal) verve.

Since the movie's release in 1991, Hopkins's memorable character has taken on a life of its own, appearing in the disappointing 2001 sequel *Hannibal*—with the role of Clarice played by Julianne Moore—and more enjoyable prequel *Red Dragon* (2002), based on the same Harris novel as Michael Mann's superior, stylish *Manhunter* (1986). **JB**

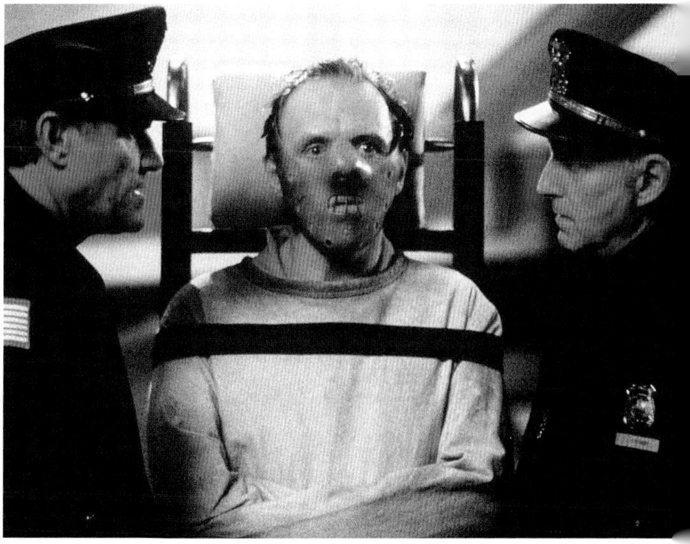

**U.S.** (Alcor, Camelot, Ixtlan, Canal+, Regency, Warner Bros.) 189m BW/Color

**Director:** Oliver Stone

**Producer:** A. Kitman Ho, Oliver Stone

**Screenplay:** Oliver Stone, Zachary Sklar, from the book *Crossfire: The Plot That Killed Kennedy* by Jim Marrs and *On the Trail of the Assassins* by Jim Garrison

**Photography:** Robert Richardson

**Music:** John Williams

**Cast:** Kevin Costner, Kevin Bacon, Tommy Lee Jones, Laurie Metcalf, Gary Oldman, Beata Pozniak, Michael Rooker, Jay O. Sanders, Sissy Spacek, Brian Doyle-Murray, Gary Grubbs, Wayne Knight, Jo Anderson, Vincent D'Onofrio, Pruitt Taylor Vince

**Oscar:** Robert Richardson (photography), Joe Hutshing, Pietro Scalia (editing)

**Oscar nomination:** A. Kitman Ho, Oliver Stone (best picture), Oliver Stone (director), Oliver Stone, Zachary Sklar (screenplay), Tommy Lee Jones (actor in support role), John Williams (music), Michael Minkler, Gregg Landaker, Tod A. Maitland (sound)

# JFK (1991)

Never a stranger to controversy, Oliver Stone followed up his powerful post-Vietnam movie *Born on the Fourth of July* with a film that angered and amazed people in equal measure—his questioning, overwhelming, urgent conspiracy movie *JFK*.

Of course, many people believe that we don't know the whole truth about the assassination of President John F. Kennedy on November 22, 1963. Do we really think Lee Harvey Oswald acted alone? Does the Warren Commission report, which attempted to come to a conclusion, really provide the answers? Although many people have debated whether there was more than one person that day who pulled a trigger, Stone went one further and committed some of the many theories to celluloid, and in doing so delivers a fascinating film that raises even more questions than it answers.

At the picture's heart is Jim Garrison (Kevin Costner), the real-life New Orleans District Attorney who had his own theories about who shot JFK and conducted an investigation into the matter from 1966 to 1969. Stone quite rightly doesn't buy into all of Garrison's theories—some believe he was a loose cannon who couldn't distinguish real clues from crackpot conspiracy ideas—but instead the director uses him as a push-off point, the symbolic center of a film simply because he is the only man in America who even attempted to bring anyone to justice for what must be the most famous murder of all time (and one that remains incompletely solved, shocking when you realize how many witnesses were present that day).

Using documentary footage—including the infamous home movie shot by Abraham Zapruder—as well as flashbacks, reconstructions, quick editing, and a skillful use of words and music, Stone weaves many ideas and theories together using the huge mountain of evidence and witness testimony without ever confusing or hoodwinking his audience. We don't get a result by the time the end credits roll three breathtaking hours later, but we do know—as if there was any doubt in our minds previously—that it was impossible for Lee Harvey Oswald to have acted alone.

And for those who were not alive or weren't old enough to remember the events of 1963, they are all here—the shooting of Kennedy during a cavalcade through Dallas, Jack Ruby's murder of Oswald, and so on. We see them as Garrison does, and Stone cleverly shows us what would convince this ordinary man to wade through so many reports and stories to seek out conspiracies that may have involved the CIA, Castro supporters, or various fringe groups. He would not succeed in getting us to care so completely about this search for truth without a strong central performance from Costner, who holds your attention throughout the film despite the numerous heavyweight actors who stroll in and out playing small roles—from Tommy Lee Jones as suspect Clay Shaw to Joe Pesci, Gary Oldman (as Oswald), Donald Sutherland, Jack Lemmon, Walter Matthau, Kevin Bacon, and Sissy Spacek, all of whom are superb.

A truly astonishing piece of filmmaking from a one-of-a-kind director. **JB**

**U.S.** (Detour) 97m Color
**Director:** Richard Linklater
**Producer:** Richard Linklater
**Screenplay:** Richard Linklater
**Photography:** Lee Daniel
**Cast:** Richard Linklater, Rudy Basquez, Jean Caffeine, Jan Hockey, Stephan Hockey, Mark James, Samuel Dietert, Bob Boyd, Terrence Kirk, Keith McCormack, Jennifer Schaudies, Dan Kratochvil, Maris Strautmanis, Brecht Andersch, Tommy Pallotta

# SLACKER (1991)

Richard Linklater's delightfully different and immensely enjoyable second feature—which is the first one that got any substantial distribution, after the more obscure and more obviously cinephiliac super-8-millimeter opus *It's Impossible to Learn to Plow by Reading Books* (1988)—takes us on a 24-hour tour of the flaky dropout culture of Austin, Texas, which has remained Linklater's headquarters ever since, throughout his multifaceted career. Unlike all his subsequent films to date, *Slacker* doesn't have anything resembling a continuous plot except in the most literal way that it moves chronologically and geographically through part of a day in Austin, but it's brimming with weird characters and wonderful talk (which often seems improvised, though it was all scripted by Linklater, apparently with the input of some of the participants, as in his 2001 animated film, *Waking Life*). The structure of dovetailing dialogues calls to mind an extremely laid-back variation of Luis Buñuel's *The Phantom of Liberty* (1974) or Jacques Tati *Playtime* (1967), in which various events are glued together simply by virtue of appearing in proximity within the same patch of time and space. Combining a certain formal logic with an illogical drive toward spinning out gratuitous fantasies and digressions is an impulse that follows Linklater through many of his subsequent pictures, but it's likely that this combination has never been displayed quite as brazenly as it is here.

"Every thought you have fractions off and becomes its own reality," remarks Linklater himself to a poker-faced cabdriver in the first (and in some ways funniest) sequence, again anticipating *Waking Life* by spouting fanciful philosophy from the back seat of a car. And the remainder of the movie amply illustrates this notion with its diverse paranoid conspiracy and assassination theorists, serial-killer buffs, musicians, cultists, college students, pontificators, petty criminals, street people, and layabouts (around 90 in all). Even if the movie goes nowhere in terms of narrative and winds up with a somewhat arch conclusion, the highly evocative scenes give an often hilarious sense of the surviving dregs of 1960s culture and a superbly realized sense of a specific community. **JRos**

# TONGUES UNTIED (1991)

The late Essex Hemphill's politically sparked, erotically charged poetry and defiant punk spirit deeply infuse Marlon Riggs's *Tongues Untied*, the groundbreaking, controversial documentary that vogued before Madonna, brought homo-thugs to light almost a decade before homophobic rappers and an idiotic mainstream media clumsily acknowledged their existence, and gave nuance and dignity to the degraded black sissy—all with humor and pathos. Performance footage, outrageous set pieces (the famous "snap off" scene), queen-on-the-street interviews, stinging critiques of homophobia in black films (using clips from Eddie Murphy's *Raw* and Spike Lee's *School Daze*), and talking heads either reciting poetry or simply testifying about their lives, add up to a portrait of both blackness and queerness that fairly seethes with energy.

Above all, what makes the film mandatory viewing is its deft juggling of personal/identity politics with a larger commentary on the public performance of persona, the way it critiques socially sanctioned bigotry while celebrating art (the creation of one's self and life) and Art (the creation of culture and its artifacts) that are produced within and beyond the confines of said bigotry. The depth and heart of *Tongues Untied* exposes the failings of both the largely white, theory-driven New Queer Cinema and the narrowly defined "authenticity" of most post-Spike Lee black cinema. Taking the viewer on a tour of a doubly marginalized subculture without pandering to the tourist's expectations or preconceptions, *Tongues Untied* transforms object into self-defining subject.

Riggs, whose other films also turn a piercing eye on issues of race and representation, is at his most raw and unapologetic here. *Tongues Untied* is a documentary that both perfectly captured an era (post-AIDS and pre-commodified queerness) and hugely influenced not only other filmmakers—documentarians and experimental film artists alike have borrowed from Riggs's blueprint—but also poets, novelists, and culture critics. The furor that erupted over government funding of the film helped make it notorious among people who never saw and never would deign to see it. That controversy has often overshadowed the artistry and social commentary contained within the film's frames: *Tongues Untied* is a seminal text on how to read between the lines of accepted cultural "truths," how to dismantle and see beyond stereotype—for both the watcher and the watched. **EH**

**U.S.** (Frameline) 55m Color
**Director:** Marlon Riggs
**Cast:** Essex Hemphill
**Berlin International Film Festival:** Marlon Riggs (Teddy documentary)

U.S. (American Zoetrope) 96m Color

**Director:** Fax Bahr, Eleanor Coppola, George Hickenlooper

**Producer:** Doug Claybourne, Les Mayfield, George Zaloom

**Screenplay:** Fax Bahr, George Hickenlooper

**Photography:** Larry Carney, Igor Meglic, Steven Wacks

**Music:** Todd Boekelheide, Carmine Coppola, Francis Ford Coppola, Mickey Hart

**Cast:** Sam Bottoms, Marlon Brando, Colleen Camp, Eleanor Coppola, Francis Ford Coppola, Gia Coppola, Roman Coppola, Sofia Coppola, Robert De Niro, Robert Duvall, Laurence Fishburne, Harrison Ford, Frederic Forrest, Albert Hall, Dennis Hopper, George Lucas, John Milius, Martin Sheen, G.D. Spradlin

# HEARTS OF DARKNESS: A FILMMAKER'S APOCALYPSE (1991)

During the 238 days it took for Francis Ford Coppola and company to finish principal shooting of *Apocalypse Now* in the Philippines, Coppola's wife Eleanor documented on camera and in writing the nightmarish trials experienced by the film's cast, crew, and, perhaps most profoundly (certainly on the most levels: physical, psychological, economic, spiritual), its renowned director. The astounding commercial and critical success of *Apocalypse Now* following its 1979 release resulted in its attaining the almost immediate status of a contemporary American classic. Contributing mightily to the legend is *Hearts of Darkness: A Filmmaker's Apocalypse*, directed by Fax Bahr with George Hickenlooper, which chronicles and reflects upon the turbulent making of Coppola's film. *Hearts of Darkness* seamlessly blends together the on- and off-set footage shot by Eleanor—as well as private conversations between her and her husband that Coppola was unaware at the time were being taped—with more standard "talking head" interviews with numerous people involved in the production (conducted by Bahr more than ten years later). Also punctuating the documentary are outtakes and scenes left on the cutting-room floor, as well as aural snippets of Orson Welles narrating Joseph Conrad's 1901 novel *Heart of Darkness* (upon which the *Apocalypse Now* screenplay was loosely based) for the Mercury Theater radio program in 1938.

*Hearts of Darkness* is widely considered among the very best entries in the subgenre loosely known as "making-of" documentaries, in large part because of its creators' access to primary source materials that would normally be extremely difficult to obtain. Among the highlights (lowlights for those involved): Interruptions on set by the Filipino military; increasingly grim confessions of insecurity and despair by the director to his wife; a heart attack suffered by the film's main actor, Martin Sheen, during the middle of shooting; and heated discussions between Coppola and two key cast members, Dennis Hopper (seemingly stoned the entire time and incapable of remembering his lines) and Marlon Brando (who showed up on set grossly overweight, without having read Conrad's novel). Add to all this the sacking of the originally contracted lead, Harvey Keitel; a massive typhoon that destroyed numerous sets;

Coppola's endless dissatisfaction with his film's conclusion; and the fact that a project originally scheduled for 16 weeks of shooting ended up taking more than three years to complete, and one has to figure the creators of *Hearts of Darkness* knew they had a "making-of" gold mine on their hands.

One of the documentary's most fascinating aspects is the way it effectively (though unintentionally) reveals the paradoxical nature of auteurism as a critical concept in film scholarship, as well as in popular thinking about Coppola's career as a maverick director with a unique and uncompromising artistic vision. On the one hand, and as *Hearts of Darkness* labors to make clear beyond the shadow of a doubt, *Apocalypse Now* could only ever have been a Coppola picture. On the other hand, it is just as clear that *Apocalypse Now* could never have been the masterpiece it turned out to be had Coppola not received such magnificent contributions from his cast and crew. Not to mention from Eleanor, who, if *Hearts of Darkness* is at all to be trusted, had much more faith in her husband than he had in himself. **SJS**

**France / Poland / Norway** (L Studio, Canal+, Norsk, Sidéral, Tor) 98m Color

**Language:** French / Polish

**Director:** Krzysztof Kieslowski

**Producer:** Leonardo De La Fuente

**Screenplay:** Krzysztof Kieslowski, Krzysztof Piesiewicz

**Photography:** Slavomir Idziak

**Music:** Zbigniew Preisner

**Cast:** Irène Jacob, Halina Gryglaszewska, Kalina Jedrusik, Aleksander Bardini, Wladyslaw Kowalski, Jerzy Gudejko, Janusz Sterninski, Philippe Volter, Sandrine Dumas, Louis Ducreux, Claude Duneton, Lorraine Evanoff, Guillaume De Tonquedec, Gilles Gaston-Dreyfus, Alain Frérot

**Cannes Film Festival:** Krzysztof Kieslowski (FIPRESCI award), (prize of the ecumenical jury), Irène Jacob (actress), Krzysztof Kieslowski nomination (Golden Palm)

# LA DOUBLE VIE DE VÉRONIQUE (1991)
## THE DOUBLE LIFE OF VERONIQUE

Krzysztof Kieslowski's first feature after his ten-part masterpiece *Decalogue* (1988), launching the European coproduction mode of making films that would lead to his *Three Colors* trilogy (*Blue* [1993], *White* [1994], and *Red* [1994]), *The Double Life of Veronique* is an exquisite enigma following the parallel lives of two 20-year-old women, one in Poland and one in France, both played by the beautiful Irène Jacob. As in *Three Colors*, European coproduction becomes not only a means of financing but also part of the formal and thematic conceptualization of the project.

The Polish Veronika is a talented singer with a heart condition; the French Véronique quits her voice lessons and gets involved with a puppeteer (Philippe Volter) who writes children's books. Masterfully directed, this rather dreamlike film is simultaneously an effort on Kieslowski's part to hold onto to his Polish identity and an equally determined effort to move beyond it—almost as if the filmmaker were dreaming of a resurrected artistic identity for himself as Polish state financing went the route of Polish communism. **JRos**

**Australia** (M & A, AFFC, Beyond, Rank) 94m Eastmancolor

**Director:** Baz Luhrmann

**Producer:** Tristram Miall

**Screenplay:** Baz Luhrmann, from story by Andrew Bovell, Baz Luhrmann

**Photography:** Steve Mason

**Music:** David Hirschfelder

**Cast:** Paul Mercurio, Tara Morice, Bill Hunter, Pat Thomson, Gia Carides, Peter Whitford, Barry Otto, John Hannan, Sonia Kruger, Kris McQuade, Pip Mushin, Leonie Page, Antonio Vargas, Armonia Benedito, Jack Webster

**Cannes Film Festival:** Baz Luhrmann (award of the youth—foreign film)

# STRICTLY BALLROOM (1992)

Before writer/director Baz Luhrman made the frenetic bauble *Moulin Rouge*, he deftly captured the magic and power of old-fashioned Hollywood musicals with *Strictly Ballroom*. He did so by intertwining two classic themes: The rebel who eventually triumphs over adversity and naysayers, and the ugly duckling who blossoms into a swan—and gets the prince in the end.

When promising dancer Scott Hastings (a devastatingly sexy Paul Mercurio) defies the ballroom dancing community and its rules, his shrieking stage mother (Pat Thomson) nearly disowns him and resorts to all manner of trickery to rein him back in. Simultaneously, one of the mother's beginning dance students, the mousy Fran (Tara Morice, sweetly affecting) develops a crush on Scott, a man seemingly far out of her league in every way. Defying odds and doubters, the two become a couple, both on and off the dance floor. Fast moving, romantic, funny, and full of wit, *Strictly Ballroom* is sterling escapist fare.

What makes the film work is that beneath the fast edits, swooning soundtrack, and gloriously garish costumes (and even more hysterically garish secondary characters) is an enormous heart, a depth of soul. Its knowing evocation of what it means and costs to be both a dreamer and an outcast makes the couple's heart-stopping finale a lump-in-the-throat triumph. **EH**

# THE PLAYER (1992)

At the start of *The Player*, two fast-talking Hollywood types amble out the front door of a studio office, trading one-liners about films that begin with spectacular "long takes." As the camera fluidly leaves these characters and picks up others, the joke becomes knowingly clear: This is the ultimate such take, a parody of modern cinema's jazzy, showy moments.

*The Player* was touted as Robert Altman's comeback—his recovery 12 years after the commercial disaster of *Popeye* (1980). This claim is far from correct—Altman never stopped working in film, theater, and TV. But *The Player*, displaying a mastery and modernity that are breathtaking, brought Altman back to mainstream attention. It is fabulously cynical entertainment.

The witty script (by Michael Tolkin, from his novel of the same name) resembles a more successful screen adaptation of Tom Wolfe's *The Bonfire of the Vanities* than Brian De Palma's official 1990 version. Griffin Mills, played with icy charm by Tim Robbins, is a slick studio executive. He evaluates pitches—brief verbal synopses of often absurdly high-concept film ideas (such as *The Graduate II*). Griffin is being made increasingly nervous by the power plays in his company, and especially by the death threats he is receiving from a disgruntled, ignored scriptwriter.

Here begins a thriller plot involving mysterious identity, accidental murder, deception, bluff, coincidence, physical danger, and sexual intrigue. Altman carries it all off faultlessly, yet his true interest lies elsewhere. As usual, Altman delights in the painting of a detailed mosaic, a world in miniature. The oddball minor characters, fleeting incidents, overheard conversations, strange digressions—these are what make *The Player* marvelous.

Altman effortlessly encapsulates modern Hollywood filmmaking, while providing a radical alternative to it. Against all those feel-good movies with strong heroes, clear conflicts, and clear-cut motivations, *The Player* offers a shifty hero, fuzzy situations, and ambiguous motives—sliced and diced with the purest irony. By the end, you'll be wondering how the cream of Hollywood's stars—from Jack Lemmon to Julia Roberts—ever agreed to be a part of this supreme exercise in subversive mischief. **AM**

**U.S.** (Avenue, Guild, Spelling) 124m Color

**Director:** Robert Altman

**Producer:** David Brown, Michael Tolkin, Nick Wechsler

**Screenplay:** Michael Tolkin, from his novel

**Photography:** Jean Lépine

**Music:** Thomas Newman

**Cast:** Tim Robbins, Greta Scacchi, Fred Ward, Whoopi Goldberg, Peter Gallagher, Brion James, Cynthia Stevenson, Vincent D'Onofrio, Dean Stockwell, Richard E. Grant, Sydney Pollack, Lyle Lovett, Dina Merrill, Angela Hall, Leah Ayres

**Oscar nomination:** Robert Altman (director), Michael Tolkin (screenplay), Geraldine Peroni (editing)

**Cannes Film Festival:** Robert Altman (director), Tim Robbins (actor), Robert Altman nomination (Golden Palm)

U.S. (Dog Eat Dog, Live) 99m
Eastmancolor

**Director:** Quentin Tarantino

**Producer:** Lawrence Bender

**Screenplay:** Quentin Tarantino

**Photography:** Andrzej Sekula

**Cast:** Harvey Keitel, Tim Roth, Michael Madsen, Chris Penn, Steve Buscemi, Lawrence Tierney, Randy Brooks, Kirk Baltz, Edward Bunker, Quentin Tarantino, Rich Turner, David Steen, Tony Cosmo, Stevo Polyi, Michael Sottile

# RESERVOIR DOGS (1992)

Self-confessed video geek Quentin Tarantino was just 28 when he wrote the script for this groundbreaking—and much imitated—movie, the title of which apparently came from a patron of the video store where Tarantino used to work who referred to *Au Revoir les Enfants* as "that reservoir dog movie," a phrase Tarantino liked so much he decided to use it for his first film as director.

Dripping with quotable dialogue and superb performances from the almost totally male cast, *Reservoir Dogs* tells the story of the bloody aftermath of a diamond heist gone wrong. In flashback, we see the criminals as they are brought together by Joe Cabot (Lawrence Tierney)—none of whom know each other's real identities (making it impossible for anyone to rat their accomplices out) and are given new monikers: Mr. Brown (Tarantino), the jerky Mr. Pink (Steve Buscemi), young Mr. Orange (Tim Roth), world-weary Mr. White (Harvey Keitel), and violent Mr. Blonde (Michael Madsen, in a creepily mesmerizing performance); and in a series of revealing scenes we learn about the events that have led to the film's blood-soaked climax in a warehouse.

But it isn't just the clever plotting that makes this film such a 1990s classic. Like the second film that Tarantino directed, *Pulp Fiction* (1994), the movie is cleverly cast (Madsen, Keitel, and Roth all giving career-best performances) and packed with memorable scenes that have become part of cinematic history, each containing pop culture references that are now recognized as a trademark of his scripts. Whether it's a scene in which the men—convening in a coffee shop before the heist—discuss everything from the etiquette of tipping to the real meaning of Madonna's "Like a Virgin" (their conclusion being unprintable here), or the shocking "ear" tableau with Madsen (featuring the unforgettable use of Steeler's Wheel classic "Stuck in the Middle with You"), Tarantino choses his words and actions so cleverly that much is revealed about each character's personality no matter how trivial the words are that they speak. A superb debut from one of the most individual cinematic talents to come out of the '90s. **JB**

## ROMPER STOMPER (1992)

*Romper Stomper* ignited a passionate debate in Australia about whether it was a racist or antiracist tract. The passage of time allows us to judge the qualities of Geoffrey Wright's impressive feature debut more clearly.

Set within the skinhead subculture of the Melbourne suburb of Footscray, *Romper Stomper* vividly details the disintegration of a gang led by Hando (Russell Crowe in an early role)—from bashing up Vietnamese Australians to being picked off like scared animals by the law and aggrieved citizens alike.

The central focus of the film is a violently melodramatic love triangle, involving Gabe (Jacqueline McKenzie) and her shifting intimacies with the bullish Hando and the more sensitive Davey (the remarkable Daniel Pollock). The influences of Stanley Kubrick and Martin Scorsese are palpable, especially in set pieces like the *Clockwork Orange*-style siege on a bourgeois home.

*Romper Stomper* does not pretend to offer a sophisticated commentary on the complexities of multicultural Australia. These "skins" are what gangsters or juvenile delinquents so often are in cinema—a flamboyant metaphor for a life lived at the edge of society. Both Wright and Crowe strive to give these events a Shakespearean grandeur, à la *Richard III*, and they largely succeed. **AM**

**Australia** (AFC, Film Victoria, Romper Stomper P/L, Seon) 94m Eastmancolor

**Language:** English / Vietnamese

**Director:** Geoffrey Wright

**Producer:** Ian Pringle, Daniel Scharf

**Screenplay:** Geoffrey Wright

**Photography:** Ron Hagen

**Music:** John Clifford White

**Cast:** Russell Crowe, Daniel Pollock, Jacqueline McKenzie, Alex Scott, Leigh Russell, Daniel Wyllie, James McKenna, Eric Mueck, Frank Magree, Christopher McLean, Josephine Keen, Samantha Bladon, Tony Lee, John Brumpton, Don Bridges

## GLENGARRY GLEN ROSS (1992)

With the 1992 film *Glengarry Glen Ross*, James Foley crafts the ultimate black comedy about selling. Adapted for the screen by David Mamet from his own 1984 Pulitzer Prize-winning play, Mamet's trademark repeating dialogue not only keeps the story at one remove from reality but keeps the viewer in a tension-filled holding pattern as well.

In a depressingly functional real-estate office on a rainy New York night, a team of desperate salesmen are given an ultimatum: sell dubious property to "dead leads"—people who have no history of land investment—by morning or else be fired. Those who succeed will be given the "Glengarry leads," a list of genuine buyers. As for the actors—Jack Lemmon, Al Pacino (nominated for a supporting actor Oscar here, he won it for his lead in *Scent of a Woman* the same year), Kevin Spacey, Alan Arkin, Jonathan Pryce, and Alex Baldwin—*Glengarry Glen Ross* doesn't have a cast, it has a pantheon. Baldwin in particular gives a supporting yet pivotal performance as the hardline company man, a role created expressly for the film. Director Foley makes *Glengarry Glen Ross* into more than an updated *Death of a Salesman*: It's the only film for which antacids should be taken before viewing. **KK**

**U.S.** (GGR, New Line, Zupnik II) 100m Color

**Director:** James Foley

**Producer:** Jerry Tokofsky, Stanley R. Zupnik

**Screenplay:** David Mamet, from his play

**Photography:** Juan Ruiz Anchía

**Music:** James Newton Howard

**Cast:** Jack Lemmon, Al Pacino, Ed Harris, Alan Arkin, Kevin Spacey, Alec Baldwin, Jonathan Pryce, Bruce Altman, Jude Ciccolella, Paul Butler, Lori Tan Chinn, Neal Jones, Barry Rossen, Leigh French, George Cheung

**Oscar nomination:** Al Pacino (actor in support role)

**Venice Film Festival:** Jack Lemmon (Volpi cup—actor)

U.S. (Malpaso, Warner Bros) 131m Technicolor

**Director:** Clint Eastwood

**Producer:** Clint Eastwood

**Screenplay:** David Webb Peoples

**Photography:** Jack N. Green

**Music:** Clint Eastwood, Lennie Niehaus

**Cast:** Clint Eastwood, Gene Hackman, Morgan Freeman, Richard Harris, Jaimz Woolvett, Saul Rubinek, Frances Fisher, Anna Levine, David Mucci, Rob Campbell, Anthony James, Tara Dawn Frederick, Beverley Elliott, Liisa Repo-Martell, Josie Smith

**Oscar:** Clint Eastwood (best picture), Clint Eastwood (director), Gene Hackman (actor in support role), Joel Cox (editing)

**Oscar nomination:** David Webb Peoples (screenplay), Clint Eastwood (actor), Henry Bumstead, Janice Blackie-Goodine (art direction), Jack N. Green (photography), Les Fresholtz, Vern Poore, Rick Alexander, Rob Young (sound)

# UNFORGIVEN (1992)

Clint Eastwood's last Western is a grand one to have ridden out on: dark, gripping, and embracing complex themes, *Unforgiven* is a saga of melancholy beauty and unflinching moral, physical, and historical realism. Eastwood received his belated due as a filmmaker with this, his sixteenth feature, winning Oscars for Best Picture and Best Director. It's a radical revision of his younger, iconic, "supercool" man with no name and few words. Acknowledged as the great antiromantic Western, from a script that did the rounds for 20 years before Eastwood seized on it to play against his own myth. Graying gunmen, oppressed women, and the painful ugliness of death provide the dark matter. Debunking Western heroics, and a dime novelist rewriting and glamorizing the bloody events he witnesses, adds sardonic humor to *Unforgiven*'s mix.

Eastwood's weather-beaten William Munny is a retired killer, reformed by the love of a good woman who has died, leaving him struggling to raise two children on a failing farm. Unlike Eastwood's Josey Wales, Munny doesn't need to redeem his humanity but struggle to retain it when he teams with old sidekick Ned (Morgan Freeman) to claim a bounty offered by brothel women. Their task: to avenge a knifed whore in bleak Big Whiskey, where brutal sheriff Little Bill (Gene Hackman) is indifferent to the women's demands for justice. Meanwhile, Richard Harris's flamboyant killer English Bob arrives to take up the prostitutes' reward himself, traveling with his biographer, one of those Eastern journalists who transformed some of the scum of the earth into the libertarian outlaw heroes of penny dreadful novellas.

*Unforgiven* is most fascinating in its revisionist approach to the mythology of the Old West, of dashing desperados and daring deeds, juxtaposed with the realities as recalled by Munny and Ned concerning the discomfort of sleeping on the trail, the misery of riding through the rain, and the ugly actuality of shooting a man—preferably when he's down. In another sharp contrast, the settings are gorgeous (Alberta, Canada spectacularly doubling for the mid-western frontier). The film is punctuated with grim scenes of horror from the slashing of the young prostitute to the inevitable final showdown.

Both Hackman's and Freeman's performances stand out, but there is an interesting dichotomy in Eastwood's own. Munny's pious utterances and his professed loss of appetite for killing do not ring entirely true, and when he is at last aroused to rage the result is what Eastwood devotees have been awaiting with inappropriate anticipation. In the end, Munny becomes an amalgam of all the violent avenging riders Eastwood has portrayed over the years.

This is as fine a piece of craftsmanship as one would expect from Eastwood, who brings to the film all his understanding of a genre he single-handedly kept alive for 20 years when it was out of fashion. Hackman won an Oscar for his sadistic Little Bill, having turned down the script years before Eastwood bought it. Touchingly, in its final grace note the film is dedicated "to Sergio and Don"—Eastwood's late directorial mentors Leone and Siegel. He did them proud. **AE**

CLINT EASTWOOD
GENE HACKMAN
RICHARD HARRIS
MORGAN FREEMAN
UNFORGIVEN
15
WARNER BROS. PRESENTS
MALPASO PRODUCTION CLINT EASTWOOD GENE HACKMAN MORGAN FREEMAN AND RICHARD HARRIS "UNFORGIVEN
MUSIC BY LENNIE NIEHAUS PRODUCTION DESIGNED BY HENRY BUMSTEAD DIRECTOR OF PHOTOGRAPHY JACK N. GREEN
WRITTEN BY DAVID WEBB PEOPLES EXECUTIVE PRODUCER DAVID VALDES PRODUCED AND DIRECTED BY CLINT EASTWOOD

# BRAM STOKER'S DRACULA (1992)

Over 100 movies and TV series have been based (some, like *Blacula*, less closely than others) on the Dracula legend as written by Bram Stoker. This 1992 adaptation, sporting the author's name because another movie studio owned the rights to the single-word title *Dracula*, is more a love story than a horror film, telling the story of a man searching for his lost love across time. The perfect man, it would seem, if one can ignore the pointy teeth and thirst for human blood.

*Bram Stoker's Dracula* begins with Vlad the Impaler (Gary Oldman), who returns from fighting in the Crusades to discover that his beloved wife, believing he had died, has flung herself off a parapet to certain death below. Understandably annoyed with God (whose battles he had effectively been fighting) at this turn of events, Vlad renounces the Creator and becomes a bloodthirsty creature of the night, rampaging through 15th-century Transylvania and leaving a trail of gore in his wake. Fast forward a few hundred years, and young English lawyer Jonathan Harker (Keanu Reeves) is instructed to visit Count Vlad Dracula at his remote East European castle, where he discovers a pale-skinned, ancient looking creature who is just a little too interested in a picture of Harker's fiancée Mina (Winona Ryder). Believing her to be a reincarnation of his dead wife Elizabeta, Vlad heads for London to meet his love, leaving a distracted Jonathan in the capable hands of his friendly Brides.

Director Francis Ford Coppola fills his operatic movie with stunning images—the beautiful castle, Vlad's red cloak slithering across the cobblestones, the vampire's horrific rampage against a blood-red sky—while Oldman delivers an effective, haunting central performance as the creature of the night bored by his own immortality. Anthony Hopkins provides some nice sarcasm as vampire hunter Van Helsing, and Ryder (who had to pull out of Coppola's previous movie, *The Godfather Part III*, due to illness), is an ethereal heroine one can well imagine Dracula wishing for across oceans of time. **JB**

**U.S.** (American Zoetrope , Columbia, Osiris) 130m Technicolor

**Director:** Francis Ford Coppola

**Producer:** Francis Ford Coppola, Fred Fuchs, Charles Mulvehill

**Screenplay:** James V. Hart, from novel by Bram Stoker

**Photography:** Michael Ballhaus

**Music:** Wojciech Kilar, Annie Lennox

**Cast:** Gary Oldman, Winona Ryder, Anthony Hopkins, Keanu Reeves, Richard E. Grant, Cary Elwes, Bill Campbell, Sadie Frost, Tom Waits, Monica Bellucci, Michaela Bercu, Florina Kendrick, Jay Robinson, I.M. Hobson, Maud Winchester

**Oscar:** Eiko Ishioka (costume), Tom C. McCarthy, David E. Stone (special sound effects), Greg Cannom, Michèle Burke, Matthew W. Mungle (makeup)

**Oscar nomination:** Thomas E. Sanders, Garrett Lewis (art direction)

# CANDYMAN (1992)

Bernard Rose's undoubted talents have rarely been seen to better effect than in this most grown-up of horror films adapted by the writer-director from a Clive Barker short story. We are used to slasher movies in which adolescent girls turn at the end on their attackers, but *Candyman* has a sexually mature woman stalking the murderer from the opening scenes.

Helen Lyle (Virginia Madsen) is a graduate student in anthropology doing work on urban legends. She stumbles across rumors of Candyman, a being who slices his victims with a hook. Increasingly convinced of the reality of Candyman (played by gravel-voiced Tony Todd), Helen is ignored by her husband and his academic friends and finds herself suspected of Candyman's crimes. In an astonishing finale, Helen bargains her life against a baby that Candyman has stolen and then takes spectacular revenge on her cheating husband.

What gives the film its real bite and edge is that Candyman, the being with a hook for a hand, is black—the product of a turn-of-the-century murder punishing interracial sex. It is the introduction of race into questions of sexuality which gives the film its real purchase on the fantasies of middle America. The spectacular ending which fuses male and female, black and white in an ultimate act of miscegenation remains as powerful today as when the film was shot in the early 1990s. **CM**

**U.S.** (PolyGram, Propaganda) 99m Color

**Director:** Bernard Rose

**Producer:** Steve Golin, Alan Poul, Sigurjon Sighvatsson

**Screenplay:** Bernard Rose, from the story *The Forbidden* by Clive Barker

**Photography:** Anthony B. Richmond

**Music:** Philip Glass

**Cast:** Virginia Madsen, Tony Todd, Xander Berkeley, Kasi Lemmons, Vanessa Williams, DeJuan Guy, Marianna Elliott , Ted Raimi, Ria Pavia, Mark Daniels, Lisa Ann Poggi, Ada Philipson, Eric Edwards, Carolyn Lowery, Barbara Alston

# CONTE D'HIVER (1992)
## A TALE OF WINTER

The second film in Eric Rohmer's "Contes des quatre saisons" ("Tale of Four Seasons") series begins a little disconcertingly with a summer romance (featuring equally surprising explicit sex) between a young hairdresser (Charlotte Véry) and the handsome hero she meets while vacationing in Brittany (Frédéric van den Driessche). That brief prologue over, however, the rest of the film is a more familiarly cool Christmas-period conversation piece as, five years later, the heroine dithers between two stolid suitors, perversely still believing that the holiday lover—who unwittingly fathered her daughter and to whom she accidentally gave an incorrect home address with which to contact her—will reappear as if by magic out of the blue.

With its witty but wintry study of seemingly forlorn faith and lost love reminiscent of *My Night With Maud*, and the almost irritatingly indecisive and self-centered heroine recalling *The Green Ray*, this is archetypal Rohmer territory, down to the beautifully judged nod to Shakespeare's play and, consequently, a miraculous but extremely satisfying ending. As ever, too, the naturalistic performances are entirely plausible, the use of place—Paris and Burgundy—evocative, and the characterizations (including an intellectual librarian and the girl's more pragmatic boss as her admirers) precisely representative of the choices she faces. Quietly brilliant, and finally very moving. **GA**

**France** (C.E.R., Canal+, Losange, Sofiarp, Soficas) 114m Color

**Language:** French

**Director:** Eric Rohmer

**Producer:** Margaret Ménégoz

**Screenplay:** Eric Rohmer

**Photography:** Luc Pagès

**Music:** Sébastien Erms

**Cast:** Charlotte Véry, Frédéric van den Driessche, Michael Voletti,Hervé Furic, Ava Loraschi, Christiane Desbois, Rosette, Jean-Luc Revol, Haydée Caillot, Jean-Claude Biette, Marie Rivière, Claudine Paringaux, Roger Dumas, Danièle Lebrun, Diane Lepvrier

**Berlin International Film Festival:** Eric Rohmer (FIPRESCI award), (prize of the ecumenical jury—special mention), nomination (Golden Bear)

G.B. (Strand) 87m Color

**Director:** Nick Broomfield

**Photography:** Barry Ackroyd

**Cast:** Nick Broomfield, Arlene Pralle, Aileen Wuornos

## AILEEN WUORNOS: THE SELLING OF A SERIAL KILLER (1992)

Was Aileen Wuornos—lesbian, prostitute, serial killer—a misunderstood victim of circumstance or a cold-hearted killer? Or both? Was she railroaded by an American judicial system anxious to convict one of history's few documented female serial killers, or was justice served? Nick Broomfield, the British documentary filmmaker with a penchant for tabloid tactics, set out to answer those questions in taking on the Wuornos case. In the process, however, he uncovered a real-life cast of characters whose duplicity, greed, psychobabble, and posturing for the camera don't do much to definitively clear or condemn Wuornos, but shed a piercing light on the underbelly of the American character.

Wuornos, with her pudgy, pasty face, flashing eyes, and limp hair, is not a conventional heroine. The film makes it clear that her life was undoubtedly hard and unfair; the anger that flushes her face speaks volumes about deprivation and struggle. Class struggle, sexual abuse, queer sexuality, a tainted and corrupt judicial system, and the celebrity-bestowing gaze of the camera are all cogs in the machine of this riveting, hop-scotching documentary that, like the best efforts in the genre, speaks to concerns and questions beyond those specifically raised within its borders. But the film's greatest observation is that in America, even the poor and loveless—not to mention the criminal—can be commodified and pimped by someone, and seemingly everyone. **EH**

**G.B. / Japan** (Brit. Screen, Channel Four, Eurotrustees, Nippon Film Dev. Finance, Palace) 112m Color

**Director:** Neil Jordan

**Producer:** Stephen Woolley

**Screenplay:** Neil Jordan

**Photography:** Ian Wilson

**Music:** Simon Boswell, Anne Dudley

**Cast:** Forest Whitaker, Miranda Richardson, Stephen Rea, Adrian Dunbar, Breffni McKenna, Joe Savino, Jaye Davidson, Andrée Bernard, Jim Broadbent, Ralph Brown, Tony Slattery

**Oscar:** Neil Jordan (screenplay)

**Oscar nomination:** Stephen Woolley (best picture), Neil Jordan (director), Stephen Rea (actor), Jaye Davidson (actor in support role), Kant Pan (editing)

## THE CRYING GAME (1992)

*The Crying Game*'s big, infamous twist is actually far less interesting than the more radical depiction that it offers: Forest Whitaker's character, Jody, whose queerness is so removed from most people's preconceptions that few critics or viewers ever even seem to notice the slyly drawn man's tiered sexuality. Writer/director Neil Jordan crafts an often droll, frequently melodramatic essay on the unfathomable laws of desire in this layered tale of a mysterious "woman" (the aloof and beautiful Jaye Davidson, reviving the tragic mulatto), her lover who is murdered under bizarre circumstances (Whitaker), and a man involved with the murder (Stephen Rea). It's all wrapped in a bow of political intrigue that's centered on longstanding tensions between the British army and the Irish Republican Army.

As the love triangle between the deceased man, his faux widow, and his assassin deepens, all sorts of secrets come tumbling out; the movie abandons what the story first appeared to be about for a new tale altogether, this one about sexual intrigue. A landmark film for the convergence of marketing chutzpah and layered sexual subversiveness that made it a hit, *The Crying Game* proved that there was an audience for audacious, nervy independent cinema. With its varying takes on race, sexuality, and gender, it kicked open the doors for discussions on the complexities of attraction and erotic longing. Its extraordinary box office success, for better or worse, helped transform independent film from a cult item to a highly profitable market share. **EH**

# C'EST ARRIVÉ PRÈS DE CHEZ VOUS (1992)
## MAN BITES DOG

*Man Bites Dog* is probably the most controversial film in the history of Belgian cinema. It rose to instant fame after critics all over the world denounced its portrayal of on-screen violence, linking it to contemporary films such as *Reservoir Dogs* (1992) and *Henry: Portrait of a Serial Killer* (1990). Although *Man Bites Dog* shares some features with these other movies, it is also very different.

Shot in grainy black-and-white stock, employing handheld camera work and direct sound (there is no music), *Man Bites Dog* has the look of a cinéma vérité documentary. The story concerns a film crew who are following around a self-proclaimed serial killer named Ben (played by cowriter and codirector Benoît Poelvoorde). As Ben goes about his business, he slowly makes the crewmen accomplices to his crimes. He takes them out to a copious meal, they start helping him dispose of bodies, and he even helps them out financially.

Ben's running commentary—on his "craft"; on his victims and their social peculiarities; and on the crew (suggesting camera angles and condemning their shabby looks)—invests *Man Bites Dog* with a surprisingly humorous tone. Here we are, enjoying a serial killer's work, because he is so funny, upbeat, and unpredictable. While murdering a man in his bathroom, Ben abruptly stops and asks the crew which French film this scene reminds them of; during shooting, the crew's successive sound operators all end up getting killed—a homage to the combustible drummers in Rob Reiner's classic mockumentary, *This Is Spinal Tap* (1984).

Then the laughter stops. The turning point in *Man Bites Dog* is an elaborate, and gruesomely explicit, rape scene. Here the film stops being a black comedy, becoming instead a bleak criticism of our desire to watch everyday life tilt out of balance. The impact of the rape scene is so shocking that it forces us to rethink our earlier pleasures, and changes the status of the narrative.

According to the creators of *Man Bites Dog*, the idea for the film stemmed from a Belgian tabloid journalism TV series, one which blew small stories out of proportion and intruded on people's private lives. This underlying concept helped guarantee the film's success, and secured its status as an all-time cult favorite. **EM**

**Belgium** (Artistes Anonymes) 92m BW

**Language:** French

**Director:** Rémy Belvaux, André Bonzel, Benoît Poelvoorde

**Producer:** Rémy Belvaux, André Bonzel, Benoît Poelvoorde

**Screenplay:** Rémy Belvaux, André Bonzel, Benoît Poelvoorde, Vincent Tavier

**Photography:** André Bonzel

**Music:** Jean-Marc Chenut, Laurence Dufrene

**Cast:** Benoît Poelvoorde, Jacqueline Poelvoorde-Pappaert, Nelly Pappaert, Hector Pappaert, Jenny Drye, Malou Madou, Willy Vandenbroeck, Rachel Deman, André Laime, Edith Lemerdy, Sylviane Godé, Zoltan Tobolik, Valérie Parent, Alexandra Fandango, Olivier Cotica.

**Cannes Film Festival:** Rémy Belvaux, André Bonzel, Benoît Poelvoorde (SACD award—best feature), Rémy Belvaux, André Bonzel, Benoît Poelvoorde (special award of the youth)

**Hong Kong** (Swift) 167m Color
**Language:** Cantonese
**Director:** Stanley Kwan
**Producer:** Jackie Chan, Leonard Ho
**Screenplay:** Chiu Tai An Ping
**Photography:** Poon Hang-Sang
**Music:** Huang Jin Chen
**Cast:** Maggie Cheung, Han Chin, Carina Lau, Shin Hong, Tony Leung, Lawrence Ng
**Berlin International Film Festival:** Maggie Cheung (Silver Bear—actress), Stanley Kwan nomination (Golden Bear)

# YUEN LING-YUK (1992)
## THE ACTRESS

Stanley Kwan's 1992 masterpiece is still quite possibly the greatest Hong Kong film I've seen; perhaps only some of the masterpieces of Wong Kar-wai, such as *Days of Being Wild* (1991) and *In the Mood for Love* (2000)—both of these also significantly period films—are comparable in depth and intensity. Yet it must be acknowledged that the shortening of the original 167-minute running time to 126 minutes has been harmful. Adding insult to injury, the Hong Kong producers destroyed the original negative, apparently the uncut version survives only on Australian television. The story of silent film star Ruan Ling-yu (1910–1935), known as the Garbo of Chinese cinema, *The Actress* combines documentary footage with period re-creation, biopic glamor with profound curiosity, and ravishing historical clips with color simulations of the same sequences being shot—all to explore a past that seems more complex, sexy, and mysterious than the present.

Maggie Cheung won a well-deserved best actress prize at Berlin for her classy performance in the title role, despite the fact that her difference from Ryan Ling-yu as an actress is probably more important than any similarities. In fact, she was basically known as a comic actress in relatively lightweight Hong Kong entertainment before this film, and *The Actress* proved to be a turning point in her career toward more dramatic and often meatier parts. But the gap between her own polished star image and that of Ruan as a more unbridled tragedienne is crucial, and much of Kwan's work as a director goes into creating a kind of nimbus around Cheung's poise and grace. George Cukor comes to mind as a Hollywood equivalent. Kwan also creates a labyrinth of questions around who Ruan was and why she committed suicide—a labyrinth both physical (with beautifully ambiguous uses of black-and-white movie sets) and metaphysical.

Highlights include the stylish beauty of an imagined Shanghai film world of the 1930s and the flat abrasiveness of Kwan chatting with Cheung on video about what all this means and coming up with damn little. Any historical movie worth its salt historicizes the present along with the past, and this movie implicitly juxtaposes our own inadequacy with those potent clips of Ling-yu herself. **JRos**

# BA WANG BIE JI (1993)
## FAREWELL MY CONCUBINE

First of the "Fifth Generation" of Chinese filmmakers to emerge onto the world scene from the Beijing Film Academy since it reopened its doors in 1978, Kaige Chen bravely invoked his own bitter memories of the Cultural Revolution. An exquisite, fascinating drama of the 50-year relationship between two male Beijing Opera singers that spans China's turbulent 20th century through convulsive collective and personal betrayals.

China's first Palme d'Or winner at Cannes (to the dismay of officials provoked by elements of homosexuality and recent history), *Farewell My Concubine* is an impassioned, sumptuous epic and a stunning achievement, particularly because it was made in a troubled, censorious environment. Hong Kong pop star Leslie Cheung plays the abandoned boy sexually abused and groomed to become a star in female roles—most significantly as a tragic royal concubine in a popular classic. Fengyi Zhang is his lifelong intimate, the less artistic and less idealistic costar whose marriage to conniving prostitute Li Gong is a catalyst for jealousy, denunciation, and haunted self-preservation during upheavals in the company and society. Rare indeed is a film on this scale that balances exotic culture and thrilling spectacle (the opera, civil war, and revolutionary mobs) with intimate and universally powerful human experience. **AE**

**China / Hong Kong** (Beijing Film, China Film, Maverick, Tomson) 171m Color

**Language:** Mandarin

**Director:** Kaige Chen

**Producer:** Feng Hsu

**Screenplay:** Wei Lu, from novel by Lillian Lee

**Photography:** Changwei Gu

**Music:** Jiping Zhao

**Cast:** Leslie Cheung, Fengyi Zhang, Li Gong, Qi Lu, Da Ying, You Ge, Chun Li, Han Lei, Di Tong, Mingwei Ma, Yang Fei, Zhi Yin, Hailong Zhao, Dan Li, Wenli Jiang

**Oscar nomination:** Hong Kong (best foreign language film), Changwei Gu (photography)

**Cannes Film Festival:** Kaige Chen (FIPRESCI award), (Golden Palm), tied with *The Piano*

# THIRTY TWO SHORT FILMS ABOUT GLENN GOULD (1993)

Glenn Gould was the brilliant, eccentric Canadian pianist who retired from the concert stage young and spent the rest of his driven, reclusive but remarkable life making acclaimed recordings, experimental radio programs, a fortune on the commodities market, and legendarily bizarre telephone calls until his death at age 50 in 1982. An entirely appropriate acknowledgment of his otherworldly genius was the inclusion of Gould's performance of a Bach prelude in the Voyager spacecraft's message to the stars from planet Earth.

Young French-Canadian writer-director François Girard adroitly juggles dramatic fiction, documentary realism, humor, and even animation with insight into the artist's agony and ecstasy in a beguiling, dazzlingly adventurous series of vignettes—the playful structure of 32 short films a witty mimicking of Bach's "Goldberg Variations"—for a unique, funny, tender, and exhilarating biopic. "Diary of One Day," for example, is an X-ray film of a pianist's skeleton, musculature, and nerve endings at work; "Truck Stop" observes Gould mentally orchestrating conversations around him in a café into a pleasing rhythmic arrangement. Colm Feore gives a wonderful, commanding performance of this rare individual, suggesting all the complexities of a gifted, multifaceted, and idiosyncratic character. And the soundtrack, compiled from Gould's own repertoire, is glorious. **AE**

**Canada / Portugal / Netherlands / Finland** (CBC, Glenn Gould, NOS, Rhombus, Samuel Goldwyn., Société Radio-Canada, The Ontario Film Development Corp.,Téléfilm Canada, YLE) 92m Color

**Director:** François Girard

**Producer:** Michael Allder, Niv Fichman, Barbara Willis Sweete, Larry Weinstein

**Screenplay:** François Girard, Don McKellar

**Photography:** Alain Dostie

**Nonoriginal music:** Johann Sebastian Bach, Richard Wagner

**Cast:** Colm Feore, Derek Keurvorst, Katya Ladan, Devon Anderson, Joshua Greenblatt, Sean Ryan, Kate Hennig, Sean Doyle, Sharon Bernbaum, Don McKellar, David Hughes, Carlo Rota, Peter Millard, John Dolan, Allegra Fulton

U.S. (Columbia) 101m Technicolor
**Director:** Harold Ramis
**Producer:** Trevor Albert
**Screenplay:** Danny Rubin, Harold Ramis
**Photography:** John Bailey
**Music:** George Fenton
**Cast:** Bill Murray, Andie MacDowell, Chris Elliott, Stephen Tobolowsky, Brian Doyle-Murray, Marita Geraghty, Angela Paton, Rick Ducommun, Rick Overton

# GROUNDHOG DAY (1993)

Comic actor Bill Murray gives what may be the best and warmest performance of his career in this genius comedy—arguably the best of the 1990s—from writers Harold Ramis (who also directs) and Danny Rubin.

Murray plays Phil Connors, a grumpy weatherman who is dispatched with producer Rita (Andie MacDowell) and cameraman Larry (Chris Elliott) to the friendly little town of Punxsutawney, Pennsylvania, to witness the annual Groundhog Day ceremony. A groundhog named Punxsutawney Phil emerges and, depending on whether or not he sees his shadow, predicts if the town will experience a few more weeks of winter. Disparaging and self-centered, Phil doesn't want to be there at all, so when he wakes up the next morning to discover he is reliving Groundhog Day all over again, he isn't exactly thrilled. Especially when he relives it again the next day, and the next, and seems to be the only person who is experiencing, and remembering, the same events over and over (and over) again.

It's a terrific conceit (one that is never explained, which makes it even better) that first causes the scheming Phil to take advantage of the situation. He asks a woman one day what she looks for in a man, and the following day embodies all those attributes to the unwitting lady. It then drives him to attempt suicide in various ways (until he discovers that he will inevitably wake up alive again the next/same morning). Eventually he is led to improve his behavior as well as his people skills in an effort to redeem himself in the eyes of Rita, who sees him only as the grouch he has always been. In between, there are delicious running gags including waking up to the same banter and Sonny and Cher song ("I've Got You Babe") on the radio; seeing Stephen Tobolowsky in a superb turn as irritating insurance salesman Ned Ryerson, and knowing what is going to happen before it does.

*Groundhog Day* is both wonderfully clever and hysterically funny—comedy is rarely this perfect. **IB**

## SHORT CUTS (1993)

One of the shortest-seeming long movies of the 1990s, this is Robert Altman's braiding-together of a fistful of Raymond Carver stories. *Short Cuts* follows various plot and character threads through a Los Angeles blighted by insects and earthquake, where everyone is on the point of cracking up and random tragedy is always impending.

Altman assembles a once-in-a-lifetime cast, but also manages to give them all things worth doing: Jack Lemmon as an estranged father, Julianne Moore naked from the waist down, Anne Archer as a party clown, Bruce Davison and Andie MacDowell shocked by grief, Jennifer Jason Leigh as a phone-sex operator, Robert Downey Jr. and Chris Penn as casually awful men, Tim Robbins as a callous cop, Peter Gallagher wrecking his wife's home, Lily Tomlin and Tom Waits drinking. On repeated viewings, the overlaps become more fun to spot and individual performances take the spotlight. In the end, the film is especially notable for its mosaic portrait of Altman's sparkly, haunted, corrupt Los Angeles (a very different place from Carver's drier Midwest).

An interesting counterpart to Altman's insider's vision of *The Player* (1992), *Short Cuts* gets away from the arena of the movie business (only a brief presence here) into the strange little lives of other involved Angelinos. **KN**

**U.S.** (Avenue, Fine Line, Spelling) 187m Color

**Director:** Robert Altman

**Producer:** Cary Brokaw

**Screenplay:** Robert Altman, Frank Barhydt, from stories by Raymond Carver

**Photography:** Walt Lloyd

**Music:** Gavin Friday, Mark Isham, Doc Pomus

**Cast:** Ensemble cast including: Andie MacDowell, Bruce Davison, Jack Lemmon, Julianne Moore, Matthew Modine, Anne Archer, Jennifer Jason Leigh, Chris Penn, Lili Taylor, Robert Downey Jr., Madeleine Stowe, Tim Robbins, Peter Gallagher, Lily Tomlin, Tom Waits, Lori Singer, Lyle Lovett, Huey Lewis, Darnell Williams

**Oscar nomination:** Robert Altman (director)

**Venice Film Festival:** Robert Altman (Golden Lion), tied with *Trois couleurs: Bleu*, entire ensemble cast (Volpi cup)

## PHILADELPHIA (1993)

Although AIDS had been tackled on TV, most notably in the acclaimed 1985 drama *An Early Frost*, and in independent cinema (the 1990 film *Longtime Companion*), Jonathan Demme's *Philadelphia* was the first mainstream Hollywood movie about the disease. Tom Hanks, in a role that won him his first Best Actor Oscar, stars as Andrew Beckett, a homosexual Philadelphian lawyer who is fired by his firm after they discover he has AIDS. They claim they dismissed him for incompetence at work, so he hires a hotshot lawyer to defend him in a suit against them. Of course, the lawyer he hires, Joe Miller (Denzel Washington), is homophobic and harbors misconceptions about the disease, but in the course of their fight he learns from Andrew and comes to respect him.

Demme fills his heartfelt drama with accomplished actors, from Hanks (who pulls off an opera-appreciation scene lesser actors would have fumbled) and Washington to Jason Robards, as the firm's bigoted boss, and Antonio Banderas as Andrew's companion. Some may argue that Demme sanitizes the ravages AIDS inflicts on a person in the film, but Hanks's sympathetic, passionate performance more than makes up for any attempts at softening the subject matter for a mainstream audience. **JB**

**U.S.** (Clinica Estetico, TriStar) 125m Technicolor

**Director:** Jonathan Demme

**Producer:** Edward Saxon

**Screenplay:** Ron Nyswaner

**Photography:** Tak Fujimoto

**Nonoriginal music:** Howard Shore, Bruce Springsteen, Neil Young

**Cast:** Tom Hanks, Denzel Washington, Antonio Banderas, Roberta Maxwell, Buzz Kilman, Karen Finley, Daniel Chapman, Jeffrey Williamson, Joanne Woodward, Jason Robards

**Oscar:** Tom Hanks (actor), Bruce Springsteen (song)

**Oscar nomination:** Ron Nyswaner (screenplay), Carl Fullerton, Alan D'Angerio (makeup), Neil Young (song)

**Berlin International Film Festival:** Tom Hanks (Silver Bear—actor), Jonathan Demme nomination (Golden Bear)

**U.S.** (Universal, Amblin) 127m Color

**Director:** Steven Spielberg

**Producer:** Kathleen Kennedy, Gerald R. Molen

**Screenplay:** Michael Crichton, David Koepp, from novel by Michael Crichton

**Photography:** Dean Cundey

**Music:** John Williams

**Cast:** Sam Neill, Laura Dern, Jeff Goldblum, Richard Attenborough, Bob Peck, Martin Ferrero, B.D. Wong, Joseph Mazzello, Ariana Richards, Samuel L. Jackson, Wayne Knight, Gerald R. Molen, Miguel Sandoval, Cameron Thor, Christopher John Fields

**Oscar:** Gary Rydstrom, Richard Hymns (special sound effects), Dennis Muren, Stan Winston, Phil Tippett , Michael Lantieri (special visual effects), Gary Summers, Gary Rydstrom, Shawn Murphy, Ron Judkins (sound)

# JURASSIC PARK (1993)

The same year that saw his "grown-up" war drama *Schindler's List* win vast critical acclaim, Steven Spielberg also delivered the kind of movie we had come to expect from the director of *Raiders of the Lost Ark*—a rip-roaring adventure of dinosaurs and disaster based on Michael Crichton's best-selling novel, *Jurassic Park*.

Slightly bonkers millionaire John Hammond (Richard Attenborough) has created the ultimate theme park on a remote island, and he wants to offer a sneak preview to a few carefully selected people: paleontologists Alan Grant (Sam Neill) and Ellie Sattler (Laura Dern), mathematician Ian Malcolm (Jeff Goldblum), and Hammond's own grandchildren Tim (Joseph Mazzello) and Lex (Ariana Richards). What they find is a luscious isle populated by real-life dinosaurs recreated using DNA found in pieces of long-buried amber. A perfect sanctuary, in theory, but because the dinosaur breeds they have "made" include the infamous tyrannosaurus and some nasty, toothy creatures named velociraptors, it's obvious that the whole scheme is going to end in tears—and screaming and dying.

Part monster movie and part disaster movie as the island is thrashed by a storm and the assembled characters find there is nowhere to hide from giant rampaging (and, one assumes, hungry) prehistoric creatures, *Jurassic Park* is packed with so many thrills and jaw-dropping dino effects it isn't hard to see why the movie went on to gross over $900 million worldwide. Cleverly building up to the revelation of the "monsters" by stunning us with the visual treat of cuddly, friendly, vegetarian dinosaurs first, when we do finally meet the ass-kicking T-Rex it is in one of the movie's fabulous set pieces. The imperiled adults and children are stranded in the broken-down "ride" (jeeps on a track taking them through the park) as the storm hits, the electric fences malfunction, and the scariest dinosaur of them all gets loose.

There are many other impressive moments in Crichton and Spielberg's fable of science gone out of control, from the raptors in the kitchen to the T-Rex/raptor showdown. The actors, while realizing the true stars of the film are computer generated, have fun with their performances (especially Goldblum as the "I-told-you-so" chaos theorist). But ultimately this is Spielberg's show, and what an impressive, edge-of-the-seat show it is. **JB**

## THE AGE OF INNOCENCE (1993)

Martin Scorsese's brilliant adaptation of Edith Wharton's novel of manners, set in late 19th-century New York, offers a carefully conceived and finely detailed reconstruction of a distant time and place. Newland Archer (Daniel Day Lewis), ready to take his place among the small circle of fabulously wealthy socialites who dominate the city, contemplates marriage to the lovely, innocent, but conventional May Welland (Winona Ryder). But his plan for a predictable life is suddenly interrupted by the arrival of Ellen Olenska (Michelle Pfeiffer), a member of the same social set who, married to a European count, has just returned to New York to divorce her husband. Shunned by this society for her presumptive behavior and general heedlessness of stuffy customs, the glamorous and sexy Ellen is championed by Newland. Against his better judgment, however, Newland does marry May and, later thinking of leaving her for Ellen, is prevented by his wife's announcement of a pregnancy. He stays with May, lives a life of solid accomplishment, only to discover years later that everyone knew of his feelings.

Scorsese's evocation of a highly structured society is exquisite, with a concentration on social rituals (archery at Newport, the opera season, lavish private entertainment) and the narrow range of freedoms they permit. Day-Lewis and Pfeiffer are excellent as the lovers doomed to separation and frustration. **BP**

**U.S.** (Cappa, Columbia) 139m Technicolor

**Director:** Martin Scorsese

**Producer:** Barbara De Fina

**Screenplay:** Jay Cocks, Martin Scorsese, from novel by Edith Wharton

**Photography:** Michael Ballhaus

**Music:** Elmer Bernstein

**Cast:** Daniel Day-Lewis, Michelle Pfeiffer, Winona Ryder, Alexis Smith, Geraldine Chaplin, Mary Beth Hurt, Alec McCowen, Richard E. Grant, Miriam Margolyes, Robert Sean Leonard, Siân Phillips, Jonathan Pryce, Michael Gough, Joanne Woodward, Stuart Wilson

**Oscar:** Gabriella Pescucci (costume)

**Oscar nomination:** Jay Cocks, Martin Scorsese (screenplay), Winona Ryder (actress in support role), Dante Ferretti, Robert J. Franco (art direction), Elmer Bernstein (music)

## HSIMENG JENSHENG (1993)
### THE PUPPETMASTER

Part of a loosely connected trilogy on the history of Taiwan that includes *City of Sadness* (1989) and *Good Men, Good Women* (1995), *The Puppetmaster* is set during the Japanese occupation, which lasted from 1895 to 1945. Based on fact, it recounts the life story of Li Tianlu, recollected in old age, with Li himself appearing occasionally as an on-screen narrator. Li is apprenticed to a puppeteer, and as he develops his skills we witness the events of his life. The film weaves together the personal and the political, as Li gets married and acquires a mistress, as well as negotiating other family complications. At times the Japanese are presented as oppressors—in one scene they arrive to demand that the men in his grandfather's family cut their pigtails. But Li manages an accommodation with them, even working as a puppeteer for the Japanese propaganda service. At the end of the war the Japanese commander invites him to lunch and tells him how much he will miss him.

Director Hou Hsiao-Hsien has an unhurried style, with long shots that calmly observe the interaction of the characters. If the narrative method, with its frequent ellipses, requires attention, audiences will be well rewarded by a deeply felt portrait of Taiwanese life. **EB**

**Taiwan** (ERA, Nian Dai, Qiu Fusheng) 142m Color

**Language:** Mandarin / Taiwanese / Japanese

**Director:** Hou Hsiao-hsien

**Producer:** Chiu Fu-Sheng, Zhang Huakun

**Screenplay:** Chu T'ien-wen, Li Tianlu, Wu Nien-Jen

**Photography:** Lee Pin Bing

**Music:** Chen Ming Chang, Zhang Hongda

**Cast:** Li Tianlu, Lim Giong, Lin Chung, Bai Ming Hwa, Cheng Fue Choung, Liou Hung, Tsai Chen-Nan, Yang Lai-Yin

**Cannes Film Festival:** Hou Hsiao-hsien (jury prize), nomination (Golden Palm)

U.S. (Amblin, Universal) 197m BW/Color

**Director:** Steven Spielberg

**Producer:** Branko Lustig, Gerald R. Molen, Steven Spielberg

**Screenplay:** Steven Zaillian, from the novel *Schindler's Ark* by Thomas Keneally

**Photography:** Janusz Kaminski

**Music:** John Williams

**Cast:** Liam Neeson, Ben Kingsley, Ralph Fiennes, Caroline Goodall, Jonathan Sagall, Embeth Davidtz, Malgoscha Gebel, Shmulik Lev, Mark Ivanir, Béatrice Macola, Andrzej Seweryn, Friedrich von Thun, Krzysztof Luft, Harry Nehring, Norbert Weisser

**Oscar:** Steven Spielberg, Gerald R. Molen, Branko Lustig (best picture), Steven Spielberg (director), Steven Zaillian (screenplay), Allan Starski, Ewa Braun (art direction), Janusz Kaminski (photography), Michael Kahn (editing), John Williams (music)

**Oscar nomination:** Liam Neeson (actor), Ralph Fiennes (actor in support role), Anna B. Sheppard (costume), Christina Smith, Matthew W. Mungle, Judith A. Cory (makeup), Andy Nelson, Steve Pederson, Scott Millan, Ron Judkins (sound)

# SCHINDLER'S LIST (1993)

Working from a well-constructed script by Steven Zaillian (*Searching for Bobby Fischer*), adapting Thomas Keneally's nonfiction novel—a fascinating account of the Nazi businessman Oskar Schindler, who saved the lives of over 1,100 Polish Jews—Spielberg does an uncommonly good job both of holding our interest over 185 minutes and of showing more of the nuts and bolts of the Holocaust than we usually get from fiction films. One enormous plus is the rich and beautiful black-and-white cinematography by one-time Chicagoan Janusz Kaminski. Spielberg's capacity to milk the maximal intensity out of the existential terror and pathos conveyed in Keneally's book—Polish Jews could be killed at any moment by the capriciousness of a labor camp director (Ralph Fiennes)—is complemented and even counterpointed by his capacity to milk the glamor of Nazi high life and absolute power. Significantly, each emotional register is generally accompanied by a different style of cinematography, and much as Liam Neeson's effective embodiment of Schindler works as our conduit to the Nazis, Ben Kingsley's subtle performance as his Jewish accountant, right-hand man, and mainly silent conscience provides our conduit to the Polish Jews.

What is unfortunately missing, and therefore distorted, are many of the more fascinating elements in the real-life story that don't match Spielberg's pious, patriarchal scenario—such as the major role that Schindler's wife, Emilie, played in saving Jewish lives after he resumed living with her while he was establishing a mock munitions plant in Moravia, or the fact that he continued to betray her with other women. One also wonders how Spielberg might have coped with the bribes that were necessary for many of the Polish Jews to find their way onto Schindler's list and thus survive. If he had dealt with this sort of material, though, the film would have probably lost some of its moral directness even while gaining in moral complexity. JRos

# TROIS COULEURS: BLEU (1993)
## THREE COLORS: BLUE

*Blue*, the first film in Krzysztof Kieslowski's "Three Colors" trilogy, may be inspired by the meaning of the first color in the French flag (liberty), but the irascible director would never be so literal. Instead he keeps the movie mysterious and oblique, with both beautiful and haunting results. Juliette Binoche plays a widow who reacts to the death of her composer husband and daughter by withdrawing from the world. Yet memories of her past, as well as the secrets her husband left behind, interrupt her selfish emotional isolation, leading her to complete unfinished business.

Along with a top-tier score and evocative cinematography, *Blue* benefits most from Kieslowski's sharp eye and unerring feel for the fleeting emotions, enigmatic actions, and minute details that comprise human nature. Thanks to his perceptive script and careful control of the story, Kieslowski creates a film whose richness and honesty offer a glimpse into the enigmatic workings of the soul. He fills every frame of *Blue* with meaning, enhanced and accented in no small part by Binoche's brave and powerful performance, which hinges on subtle tics and other physical nuances in its depiction of a broken spirit slowly pulling herself back together. **JKl**

**France / Poland / Switzerland** (CAB, CED, Eurimages, France 3, MK2, Tor) 100m Eastmancolor

**Language:** French

**Director:** Krzysztof Kieslowski

**Producer:** Marin Karmitz

**Screenplay:** Agnieszka Holland, Slavomir Idziak, Krzysztof Kieslowski, Krzysztof Piesiewicz, Edward Zebrowski

**Photography:** Slavomir Idziak

**Music:** Zbigniew Preisner

**Cast:** Juliette Binoche, Benoît Régent, Florence Pernel, Charlotte Véry, Hélène Vincent, Philippe Volter, Claude Duneton, Hugues Quester, Emmanuelle Riva, Florence Vignon, Daniel Martin, Jacek Ostaszewski, Yann Trégouët, Alain Ollivier

**Venice Film Festival:** Krzysztof Kieslowski (Golden Lion), tied with *Short Cuts*, Slavomir Idziak (Golden Osella—photography), Juliette Binoche (Volpi cup—actress)

# THE PIANO (1993)

*Sweetie* (1989) and *An Angel at My Table* (1990) taught us to expect startling as well as beautiful things from Jane Campion, and this assured and provocative third feature offers yet another lush parable about the perils and paradoxes of female self-expression.

Set during the 19th century, this original story by Campion—which evokes at times some of the romantic intensity of Emily Brontë—focuses on a Scottish widow (Holly Hunter) who hasn't spoken since her childhood, presumably by choice, and whose main form of self-expression is her piano playing. She arrives with her nine-year-old daughter (Anna Paquin) in the New Zealand wilds to enter into an arranged marriage, which gets off to an unhappy start when her husband-to-be (Sam Neill) refuses to transport her piano. A local white man living with the Maori natives (Harvey Keitel) buys the piano from him and, fascinated by and attracted to the mute woman, agrees to "sell" it back to her a key at a time in exchange for lessons—lessons that have ultimately traumatic consequences.

Setting out to be politically correct, erotic, and romantic at the same time, *The Piano* inevitably bites off more than it can possibly chew, but winds up stimulating passionate feelings nonetheless. **JRos**

**Australia / NZ / France** (AFC, CiBy NSW Film & TV Office) 121m Eastmancolor

**Director:** Jane Campion

**Producer:** Jan Chapman

**Screenplay:** Jane Campion

**Photography:** Stuart Dryburgh

**Music:** Michael Nyman

**Cast:** Holly Hunter, Harvey Keitel, Sam Neill, Anna Paquin, Kerry Walker, Geneviève Lemon, Tungia Baker, Ian Mune, Peter Dennett, Te Whatanui Skipwith, Pete Smith, Bruce Allpress

**Oscar:** Jane Campion (screenplay), Holly Hunter (actress), Anna Paquin (actress in support role)

**Oscar nomination:** Jan Chapman (best picture), Jane Campion (director), Stuart Dryburgh (photography), Janet Patterson (costume), Veronika Jenet (editing)

**Cannes Film Festival:** Jane Campion (Golden Palm), tied with *Ba wang bie ji*, Holly Hunter (actress)

China / Hong Kong (Beijing Film, Longwick) 138m Color

**Language:** Mandarin

**Director:** Tian Zhuangzhuang

**Producer:** Luo Guiping, Cheng Yongping

**Screenplay:** Xiao Mao

**Photography:** Hou Yong

**Music:** Yoshihide Otomo

**Cast:** Yi Tian, Zhang Wenyao, Chen Xiaoman, Lu Liping, Zhong Ping, Chu Quanzhong, Song Xiaoying, Zhang Hong

# LAN FENG ZHENG (1993)
## THE BLUE KITE

Banned in China, the powerful eighth feature of Tian Zhuangzhuang (*The Horse Thief*, *Li Lianying*, *The Imperial Eunuch*) follows its fictional hero, Tietou, and his family in Beijing from 1953 to 1968, through the Cultural Revolution and its ensuing repercussions and purges. Tietou's father is a librarian, and in one unforgettable and disquieting postrevolution scene, the hero's father, attending a meeting for library staff, briefly leaves the room to go to the toilet. Upon his return he finds that he's been branded a reactionary, leading to his banishment to a collective farm for "reeducation" and a radical change in his entire family's fortunes.

*The Blue Kite* offers a sublime and often subtle look at how history and politics disrupt ordinary lives, with a memorable use of its central courtyard location and a keen feeling for everyday life within that space. One comes away from this film with a profound sense of how individuals strive to maintain a sense of ethics within a changing society that periodically confounds those ethics or makes them irrelevant. **JRos**

**Taiwan / U.S.** (Central Motion Pictures Corp., Good Machine) 106m Color

**Language:** Mandarin / English

**Director:** Ang Lee

**Producer:** Ted Hope, Ang Lee, James Schamus

**Screenplay:** Ang Lee, Neil Peng, James Schamus

**Photography:** Jong Lin

**Music:** Mader

**Cast:** Dion Birney, Jeanne Kuo Chang, Winston Chao, Paul Chen, May Chin, Chou Chung-Wei

**Oscar nomination:** Taiwan (best foreign language film)

**Berlin International Film Festival:** Ang Lee (Golden Bear), tied with *Xian hun nu*

# HSI YEN (1993)
## THE WEDDING BANQUET

A young Taiwanese businessman living in New York and sharing an apartment with his physical therapist boyfriend, decides to marry a Chinese artist who needs a green card. The next thing he knows, his parents from Taiwan, not knowing he's gay, have decided to come to the wedding, leading to a good many predictable if enjoyable comic complications. Director Ang Lee collaborated on the script for *The Wedding Banquet* with Neil Feng and producer James Schamus—the latter of whom has continued to work with the director ever since as both producer and cowriter.

This 1993 feature, Lee's second, is a clever and entertaining social comedy that helped to establish him as a commercial director long before such more obvious mainstream crowd pleasers as *The Ice Storm* (1997) and *Crouching Tiger, Hidden Dragon* (2000). Satire about—yet also clearly for—the middle class, *The Wedding Banquet* has a lot more heart than edge, and is pitched mainly at liberal straight people, though the Chinese cultural details should be fascinating to all non-Chinese viewers. **JRos**

# TROIS COULEURS: ROUGE (1994)
## THREE COLORS: RED

The third color of the French flag stands for fraternity, and although the last film of Krzysztof Kieslowski's "Three Colors" trilogy again remains only loosely connected to that theme, he somehow gets to the heart of brotherhood via the sometimes tenuous and often-impossible-to-comprehend ties that connect all of humanity. If each of the "Three Colors" films ends up much more than the sum of their ambiguous parts, then *Red* provides the grand and illuminating summation of all three entries. Like the closing chapter of a great philosophical novel, *Red* parcels out its details patiently and elliptically, drawing power from the mysterious plot machinations that connect a good-natured model (the ineffable Irène Jacob) with a cynical, retired judge (Jean-Louis Trintignant). Both lead empty lives yet express their loneliness in completely different ways, but the judge sees something intriguing in the model that draws him out of his shell of self-hatred.

Like many of Kieslowski's works, *Red* runs deep with chance and coincidence, and although the metaphysical director rarely addresses spirituality in his work per se, his final film (Kieslowski retired after directing *Red* and died shortly later) often seems a meditation on not just earthly bonds but also our place in the universe. In lesser hands such subject matter would no doubt have gotten bogged down in New Age musings, but Kieslowski is smarter than that. His characters develop and interact organically, as if tapping into a script made entirely of emotional cues rather than mere words. His camera captures places and moments that appear insignificant yet whose importance is inevitably born out. In *Red* he even manages to almost magically make manifest the very fabric of our existence, as the metaphors and symbolic touches of all three films—*Blue* (1993), *White* (1994), and *Red*—blur together during the challenging and undeniably moving conclusion, which casts the entire trilogy in a new light. Rarely has a film so brilliantly fused together so many ideas, images, and emotions into one masterful whole, a life primer and work of art posing as a mere movie. **JKl**

**France / Poland / Switzerland** (CAB, France 3, Canal+, MK2, Tor, TSR) 99m Eastmancolor

**Language:** French

**Director:** Krzysztof Kieslowski

**Producer:** Marin Karmitz

**Screenplay:** Krzysztof Kieslowski, Krzysztof Piesiewicz

**Photography:** Piotr Sobocinski

**Music:** Bertrand Lenclos, Zbigniew Preisner

**Cast:** Irène Jacob, Jean-Louis Trintignant, Frédérique Feder, Jean-Pierre Lorit, Samuel Le Bihan, Marion Stalens, Teco Celio, Bernard Escalon, Jean Schlegel, Elzbieta Jasinska, Paul Vermeulen, Jean-Marie Daunas, Roland Carey, Brigitte Raul, Leo Ramseyer

**Oscar nomination:** Piotr Sobocinski (cinematography), Krzysztof Kieslowski (director), Krzysztof Piesiewicz, Krzysztof Kieslowski (screenplay)

**Cannes Film Festival:** Krzysztof Kieslowski (Golden Palm)

**U.S.** (KTCA-TV, Kartemquin) 170m Color

**Director:** Steve James

**Producer:** Peter Gilbert, Steve James, Frederick Marx

**Screenplay:** Steve James, Frederick Marx

**Photography:** Peter Gilbert

**Music:** Ben Sidran

**Cast:** William Gates, Arthur Agee, Emma Gates, Curtis Gates, Sheila Agee, Arthur "Bo" Agee, Earl Smith, Gene Pingatore, Isiah Thomas, Sister Marlyn Hopewell, Bill Gleason, Patricia Weir, Marjorie Heard, Luther Bedford, Aretha Mitchell

**Oscar nomination:** Frederick Marx, Steve James, William Haugse (editing)

# HOOP DREAMS (1994)

*Hoop Dreams* follows the true story of a pair of inner-city Chicago teens, Arthur Agee and William Gates, and their pursuit of NBA fame. Straight out of grammar school the two boys are recruited by an athletic scout, literally pulled off the streets and placed in a predominately white college preparatory school, St. Joseph High. Following in the footsteps of their basketball idol and St. Joseph's alumnus Isiah Thomas, both boys are inundated with the intense demands of maturation, academia, and, of course, athletics.

Within the first year documented by the film, only one of the boys survives the rigors of the prep school. In an attempt to continue following his basketball dreams the other returns to the city and attends a public high school. Although separated by different basketball programs, we continue to watch the boys mature and grow into athletic powerhouses over a five-year period. Such a concentrated time span allows a personal look into these two boys' lives, showing that their pursuit of basketball glory is not just their passion, but their respective families' dream.

Keeping in step with their failures and successes, director and narrator Steve James unravels a unique story of inner-city struggles. As the film's layers become more apparent, intricate subplots make us intimately familiar with the other players in their lives. The constant ebb and flow of life plays on the boys' emotions and fate. Basketball functions not only as a game for Arthur and William, but as a way for their instructors and family members to play out their own dreams and desires. The film thus allow us to peer into the world of competitive high school basketball through the eyes of young men, torn families, and passionate coaches.

*Hoop Dreams* represents five years of painstaking dedication by both of the featured boys, as well as by the filmmakers. Following both Arthur and William from their boyish scrawny days of grammar school to their highs and lows as prized high school basketball players, this film questions and contemplates inner-city life, family, sacrifices, success, and failure. **AK**

RAMS
30

# FORREST GUMP (1994)

A brisk trot through events in American history from the 1950s until the 1980s as seen through the eyes of one man, *Forrest Gump* succeeds as both epic and character study. This is thanks to clever, if occasionally sentimental, direction from Robert Zemeckis and a sensitive central performance from Tom Hanks, who won his second Best Actor Academy Award in as many years for the role.

We first meet Forrest, an amiable idiot savant with an IQ of 75, sitting on a park bench, waiting for a bus to take him to meet his childhood friend Jenny (Robin Wright Penn). While lingering there, he relates his life story to a succession of people who share the bench—and what a story it is. Raised by a mother (Sally Field) who corrected his gait with leg braces but never attempted to correct his mind ("Stupid is as stupid does" being her motto), Forrest went on to experience many of America's most famous events of the 20th century. This begins on the day he discovered that he could run (outrunning bullies, his braces fly off and he speeds into the distance) when he uses his new talent to become a football star. Over the next three decades, this simple man meets John F. Kennedy, Lyndon Johnson, and Richard Nixon; becomes a Vietnam war hero (saving "Lieutenant Dan," his grumpy superior brilliantly portrayed by Gary Sinise); and later a shrimp tycoon. All the while he dreams that he will be reunited with Jenny, whose life takes a different path from his. Where Forrest experiences many cultural historical moments, Jenny is deep into American counterculture, protesting the war and embracing alcohol and drugs.

The love story between Jenny and Forrest is somewhat unconvincing—she seems to turn up only when she needs help, which makes her character less sympathetic. However, this adaptation of Winston Groom's novel works best as the moving story of an honest, innocent man (superbly played by Hanks, who modeled his distinctive accent on that of Michael Conner, who plays Forrest as a boy), and as a meditation on the latter half of the last century, made possible by computer trickery that places Hanks—to often hilarious effect—in old footage of notable events. **JB**

**U.S.** (Paramount) 142m BW/ Color

**Director:** Robert Zemeckis

**Producer:** Wendy Finerman, Steve Starkey, Steve Tisch

**Screenplay:** Eric Roth, from novel by Winston Groom

**Photography:** Don Burgess

**Music:** Alan Silvestri

**Cast:** Tom Hanks, Robin Wright Penn, Gary Sinise, Mykelti Williamson, Sally Field, Rebecca Williams, Michael Conner Humphreys, Harold G. Herthum, George Kelly, Bob Penny, John Randall, Sam Anderson, Margo Moorer, Ione M. Telech, Christine Seabrook

**Oscar:** Wendy Finerman, Steve Starkey, Steve Tisch (best picture), Robert Zemeckis (director), Eric Roth (screenplay), Tom Hanks (actor), Ken Ralston, George Murphy, Stephen Rosenbaum, Allen Hall (special visual effects), Arthur Schmidt (editing)

**Oscar nomination:** Gary Sinise (actor in support role), Rick Carter, Nancy Haigh (art direction), Don Burgess (cinematography), Gloria S. Borders, Randy Thom (special sound effects), Daniel C. Striepeke, Hallie D'Amore, Judith A. Cory (makeup), Alan Silvestri (music), Randy Thom, Tom Johnson, Dennis S. Sands, William B. Kaplan (sound)

## CLERKS (1994)

Writer/director Kevin Smith stepped forward in 1994 as the most promising Generation X newcomer with this impressive debut film. Set in a New Jersey convenience store, Smith's *Clerks* is a day-in-the life tale of two shopworkers, Dante (Brian O'Halloran) and his reckless friend Randal (Jeff Anderson), who works at the video store next door. As various oddballs come into the store, Dante tries to sort out relationship problems, while Randal spends most of the day bored, insulting customers, watching porn movies, and discussing important matters like the true meaning of the destruction of the Death Star in *Return Of The Jedi*.

Shot in black-and-white, the $27,500-budget movie was filmed over 21 days at the QuickStop Groceries store where Smith had worked since he was 19, and where he edited the film each night. Anchored by a pair of great central performances, and packed with witty dialogue, the film also introduced the two hilarious characters Smith has used in his subsequent movies *Mallrats*, *Chasing Amy*, *Dogma*, and *Jay And Silent Bob Strike Back* (all of which are at least partly set in Smith's homestate of New Jersey): Stoner Jay (Jason Mewes) and his aptly named pal Silent Bob (played by Smith himself). **JB**

**U.S.** (Miramax, View Askew) 92m BW
**Director:** Kevin Smith
**Producer:** Scott Mosier, Kevin Smith
**Screenplay:** Kevin Smith
**Photography:** David Klein
**Music:** Scott Angley
**Cast:** Brian O'Halloran, Jeff Anderson, Marilyn Ghigliotti, Lisa Spoonhauer, Jason Mewes, Kevin Smith, Scott Mosier, Walter Flanagan, Scott Schiaffo, Al Berkowitz, Ed Hapstak, Lee Bendick, David Klein, Pattijean Csik, Ken Clark
**Cannes Film Festival:** Kevin Smith (award of the youth foreign film), (Mercedes-Benz award)

## FOUR WEDDINGS AND A FUNERAL (1994)

Hugh Grant is the perennial best man in this hugely successful British comedy set at various social functions from director Mike Newell and *Blackadder* writer Richard Curtis.

Grant—in the part that propelled him from stiff upper-lipped roles in movies like *Bitter Moon* and *The Remains of the Day* to Hollywood megastar—is perfect as the chronically late Charles, who falls for Carrie (Andie MacDowell) at one wedding and then spends the rest of the film awkwardly attempting to woo her. In between, this richly humorous look at the British upper middle class at play features all those classic wedding nightmares (the bumbling priest, a tactless toast from the best man, the awkwardness of being seated at a table with all your ex-girlfriends) dressed up in lovely hats and gowns. However, it is the funeral of the title that provides the movie with its poignant heart.

Some may argue that the rarely expressive MacDowell was miscast as the love interest (perhaps so the British filmmakers could boast a Hollywood name). However, she sensibly takes a backseat to the wonderful supporting cast of characters, including Simon Callow, John Hannah, and Kristin Scott Thomas, who provide *Four Weddings and a Funeral* with its charm and funniest moments. **JB**

**U.K.** (Channel Four, PolyGram, Working Title) 117m Eastmancolor
**Director:** Mike Newell
**Producer:** Duncan Kenworthy
**Screenplay:** Richard Curtis
**Photography:** Michael Coulter
**Music:** Richard Rodney Bennett
**Cast:** Hugh Grant, James Fleet, Simon Callow, John Hannah, Kristin Scott Thomas, David Bower, Charlotte Coleman, Andie MacDowell, Timothy Walker, Sara Crowe, Ronald Herdman, Elspet Gray, Philip Voss, Rupert Vansittart, Nicola Walker
**Oscar nomination:** Duncan Kenworthy (best picture), Richard Curtis (screenplay)

**U.S.** (Walt Disney) 89m Technicolor
**Language:** English / Swahili
**Director:** Roger Allers, Rob Minkoff
**Producer:** Don Hahn
**Screenplay:** Irene Mecchi, Jonathan Roberts, Linda Woolverton
**Music:** Hans Zimmer, Elton John, Tim Rice, Lebo M., Joseph Williams
**Cast (voices):** Matthew Broderick, Joseph Williams, Jonathan Taylor Thomas, Jason Weaver, James Earl Jones, Jeremy Irons, Moira Kelly, Niketa Calame, Laura Williams, Ernie Sabella, Nathan Lane, Robert Guillaume, Rowan Atkinson, Madge Sinclair, Zoe Leader
**Oscar:** Hans Zimmer (music), Elton John, Tim Rice (song)
**Oscar nomination:** Elton John, Tim Rice (songs)

# THE LION KING (1994)

In 1991, Disney released the magical *Beauty and the Beast*—the first animated movie to be nominated for a Best Picture Academy award—and brought their animation right up to date with its beautiful mix of traditional and computer-generated cartooning. *The Lion King* followed three years later and not only improved on the standards set by *Beauty* but also instantly became a Disney classic, to be ranked alongside other tearjerkers like *Snow White and the Seven Dwarfs* (1937) and, of course, *Bambi* (1942).

Young Simba the lion cub (voiced by Jonathan Taylor Thomas as a cub and Matthew Broderick as an adult lion) is exiled by his evil uncle Scar—a creepily effective vocal performance from Jeremy Irons—following his father Mufasa's (James Earl Jones) death. Forced to fend for himself, he befriends two odd characters, Pumbaa (Ernie Sabella) and Timon (Nathan Lane), and also falls for a lioness named Nala (voiced by Niketa Calane and later by Moira Kelly) before returning to regain his place as head of the pride.

This animated adventure works so well because it has all the elements of a terrific movie and plenty of action and adventure. The lion cub scenes appeal to small children and the impressive animation causes even adult jaws to drop. The film has a classic story arc as the carefree cub becomes a wise and respected lion. Backed by a catchy score by Elton John—including the hits "Circle of Life" and "Can You Feel the Love Tonight"—*The Lion King* is surprisingly moving, relating as we are only to cartoon characters, particularly in the relationship between Simba and his father and the ending to turn-grown-men-into-a-blubbering-pile-of-mush. Luckily, the vocal talents of Lane, Rowan Atkinson (as wisecracking bird Zazu), Cheech Marin, and Whoopi Goldberg (as cackling hyenas) are on hand for some side-splitting light relief, otherwise we would all demand that the video or DVD of the film should come with a box of tissues. **JB**

## SÁTÁNTANGÓ (1994)

How can one do justice to this grungy seven-hour black comedy, which in many ways is among the most impressive films of the 1990s? Adapted by Hungarian director Béla Tarr and László Krasznahorkai from the latter's 1985 novel, *Sátántangó* is a diabolical piece of sarcasm about the dreams, machinations, and betrayals of a failed farm collective, set during two consecutive rainy fall days (rendered more than once from the perspectives of different characters), and later the same month. The form of the novel was inspired by the steps of the tango—six forward, six backward—an idea reflected by the film's overlapping time structure, its 12 sections, and its remarkably choreographed long takes and camera movements, which often suggest a despiritualized Andrei Tarkovsky with the hothouse intensity of a John Cassavetes. Each section ends powerfully with offscreen third-person narration—eloquent, poetic commentary on the characters and their world that comes directly from the novel.

*Sátántangó* makes us share a lot of time as well as space with its characters, and the overall effect is to give a moral weight as well as a narrative weight to every shot: As detestable as these people are, we're so fully with them for such extended stretches that we cannot help but feel deeply involved, even implicated, in their various maneuvers. Among the extraordinary sequences—and there are indeed many—is a riveting tour de force charting for a full hour the chiefly solitary movements of an aging doctor lost in an alcoholic haze, hilariously detailing the amount of exertion required for an overweight man to drink himself into near-oblivion. It's important to add that the apparent cruelty shown to a cat in another sequence is as expertly faked as the nearly continuous rain; for all the apparent gritty realism, Tarr is a master of artifice.

The story may seem to comment indirectly on the collapse of communism, but it has just as much to say about the subsequent degradations of capitalism; as Tarr has pointed out, the police—and human nature—are the same everywhere. The subject of this brilliantly constructed narrative is nothing less than the world today, and its 431-minute running time is necessary not so much because Tarr has so much to say, but because he wants to say it right. **JRos**

**Hungary/ Germany / Switzerland**
(Mafilm, Vega Film, Von Vietinghoff)
450m BW

**Language:** Hungarian

**Director:** Béla Tarr

**Producer:** György Fehér, Ruth Waldburger, Joachim von Vietinghoff

**Screenplay:** Béla Tarr, from novel by László Krasznahorkai

**Photography:** Gábor Medvigy

**Music:** Mihály Vig

**Cast:** Mihály Vig, Putyi Horváth, László Lugossy, Éva Almássy Albert, János Derzsi, Irén Szajki, Alfréd Járai, Miklós Székely B., Erzsébet Gaál, Erika Bók

**Berlin International Film Festival:** Béla Tarr (Caligari film award)

## NATURAL BORN KILLERS (1994)

**U.S.** (Alcor, Ixtlan, J D, Regency, Warner Bros.) 118m BW/ Technicolor

**Director:** Oliver Stone

**Producer:** Jane Hamsher, Don Murphy, Clayton Townsend

**Screenplay:** David Veloz, Richard Rutowski, Oliver Stone, from story by Quentin Tarantino

**Photography:** Robert Richardson

**Music:** Zack De La Rocha, Peter Gabriel, Tom Hajdu, Brent Lewis, Andy Milburn, Trent Reznor, Eric Avery Weiss, Leonard Cohen, Dr. Dre, Bob Montgomery, Patti Smith

**Cast:** Tommy Lee Jones,Woody Harrelson, Juliette Lewis, Rodney Dangerfield, Robert Downey Jr.

**Venice Film Festival:** Oliver Stone (special jury prize), Juliette Lewis (Pasinetti Award—actress)

Never one to avoid controversy with films like *Platoon* (1990) and *JFK* (1991), Oliver Stone caused his biggest storm yet with this superb, satirical comment on the relationship between the media and violence. Using diverse film techniques and styles—animation, video, back and front projection, black-and-white and color film—*Natural Born Killers* tells the story of Mickey (Woody Harrelson) and Mallory (Juliette Lewis) Knox on a cross country murder spree. The lurid tale soon comes to the attention of the media, and is related to an eager public by sleazy TV host Wayne Gale (Robert Downey Jr.).

The movie is graphically violent as the white-trash lovers slaughter their way across the United States, but Stone should be commended for this provocative tale rather than condemned for it. Many acclaimed actors believed in his clever, stylized, and striking movie enough to appear in it, from Tommy Lee Jones (as a particularly smarmy prison governor) to Tom Sizemore (as the dogged cop on Mickey and Mallory's trail), and lead actors Harrelson, Lewis, and Downey Jr. all deliver searing performances that are among the best of their respective careers. **JB**

## THE LAST SEDUCTION (1994)

**U.S.** (ITC) 110m Color

**Director:** John Dahl

**Producer:** Jonathan Shestack

**Screenplay:** Steve Barancik

**Photography:** Jeff Jur

**Music:** Joseph Vitarelli

**Cast:** Linda Fiorentino, Peter Berg, Bill Pullman, Michael Raysses, Bill Nunn, Zack Phifer, J.T. Walsh, Brien Varady, Dean Norris, Donna Wilson, Mik Scriba, Erik-Anders Nilsson, Patricia R. Caprio, Herb Mitchell, Renee Rogers

Made for U.S. cable TV company HBO (who broadcast it before giving the film a theatrical release, thus sadly making it ineligible for the Academy Awards), *The Last Seduction* was director John Dahl's third, and best, venture into the film noir genre.

Linda Fiorentino positively sizzles across the screen as femme fatale Bridget, whom we first meet when she cons her husband (Bill Pullman) into making a large drug deal, only to run off with the money and leave him behind. She then slithers into a small town and into the life of sweet, infatuated Mike (Peter Berg), who has no clue just what he has let himself in for.

Simmering with steamy sexuality, Dahl's thriller is deliciously bitter and twisted as Fiorentino twirls unsuspecting men around her little finger then casts them aside just as quickly. Pullman—best known for kinder roles—is a revelation as Fiorentino's almost-as-nasty-as-she-is spouse, while Berg hits the right note as the poor guy who never quite realizes how deep he is being dragged in. But the true star of the film is Fiorentino, who chews up and spits out Steve Barancik's delicious dialogue, reducing men to quivering, whimpering victims in the process. **JB**

# PULP FICTION (1994)

A couch potato's paradise, this clever and immensely entertaining 1994 second feature by Quentin Tarantino (after *Reservoir Dogs* and before *Jackie Brown*) is a chronologically scrambled collection of interrelated and interlocking crime stories. Apart from its ingenious structure, *Pulp Fiction* extracts nearly all its kicks from allusions to and echoes of other movies and TV shows. Despite all its thematic nudges about redemption and second chances its true agenda is only the flip side of *Forrest Gump*: to make the escapist, media-savvy viewer the real hero of the story. Taken on its own crass terms, Tarantino's mock-tough narrative—which derives most of its titillation from farcical mayhem, drugs, deadpan macho monologues, evocations of anal penetration, and terms of racial abuse—resembles a wet dream for 14-year-old male closet queens (or, perhaps more accurately, the 14-year-old male closet queen in each of us), and his command of this smart-alecky mode is so sure and confident that this nervy movie sparkles throughout with canny twists and turns.

John Travolta, Samuel L. Jackson, Bruce Willis, and Harvey Keitel all vibrate with high-voltage star power, while the rest of the film's cast (including Uma Thurman, Ving Rhames, Maria de Medeiros, Tim Roth, Amanda Plummer, Eric Stoltz, Rosanna Arquette, Christopher Walken, Steve Buscemi, and Tarantino himself) amply fill out the remaining scenery. Only occasionally—as in an overloaded and ugly basement episode and some anemic love scenes—does Tarantino seem to be straining, though even here his overall project is evident: to evict real life and real people from the art film once and for all and replace them with generic teases and assorted hommages, infused with hype and attitude, building a veritable monument to the viewer's assumed cinema connoisseurship. The references range from Douglas Sirk to Howard Hawks to *Saturday Night Fever* to kung fu by way of Godard, but one shouldn't expect any of the life experiences of the old movie sources to leak through; punchy, flamboyant surface is all. **JRos**

**U.S.** (Band Apart, Jersey, Miramax) 154m Color

**Director:** Quentin Tarantino

**Producer:** Lawrence Bender

**Screenplay:** Quentin Tarantino, Roger Avary

**Photography:** Andrzej Sekula

**Nonoriginal music:** Dick Dale and his Del-tones, Kool and the Gang, Al Green, Tornadoes, Ricky Nelson, Dusty Springfield, Centurians, Chuck Berry, Urge Overkill, Maria McKee, Revels, Statler Brothers, Lively Ones

**Cast:** Tim Roth, Amanda Plummer, Laura Lovelace, John Travolta, Samuel L. Jackson, Phil LaMarr, Frank Whaley, Burr Steers, Bruce Willis, Ving Rhames, Paul Calderon, Bronagh Gallagher, Rosanna Arquette, Eric Stoltz, Uma Thurman

**Oscar:** Quentin Tarantino, Roger Avary (screenplay)

**Oscar nomination:** Lawrence Bender (best picture), Quentin Tarantino (director), John Travolta (actor), Samuel L. Jackson (actor in support role), Uma Thurman (actress in support role), Sally Menke (editing)

**Cannes Film Festival:** Quentin Tarantino (Golden Palm)

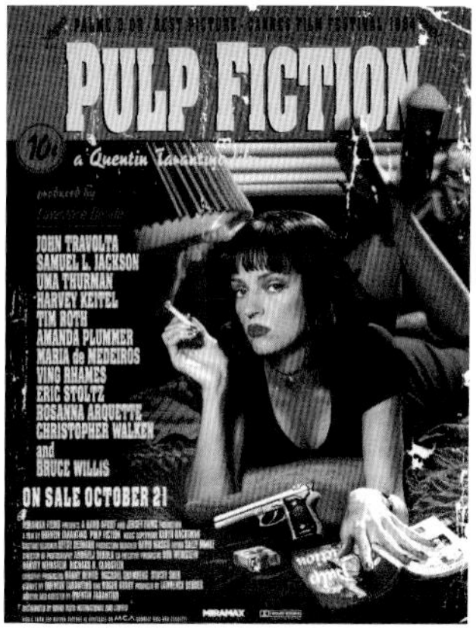

U.S. (Castle Rock, Columbia) 142m Technicolor
**Director:** Frank Darabont
**Producer:** Niki Marvin
**Screenplay:** Frank Darabont, from the short story *Rita Hayworth and the Shawshank Redemption* by Stephen King
**Photography:** Roger Deakins
**Music:** Doris Fisher, Thomas Newman, Allan Roberts
**Cast:** Tim Robbins, Morgan Freeman, Bob Gunton, William Sadler, Clancy Brown, Gil Bellows, Mark Rolston, James Whitmore, Jeffrey DeMunn, Larry Brandenburg, Neil Giuntoli, Brian Libby, David Proval, Joseph Ragno, Jude Ciccolella

# THE SHAWSHANK REDEMPTION (1994)

Much of horror writer Stephen King's work has been successfully translated to the screen (including *Misery*, *Carrie*, and *The Shining*), but the best adaptations are arguably those of his nonhorror short stories, like *Stand By Me* and this reworking of a tale originally titled *Rita Hayworth and the Shawshank Redemption*.

In 1946, quiet young banker Andy Dufresne (Tim Robbins) is sent to Shawshank Prison for the murder of his wife and her lover. While there he slowly builds a friendship with another long term prisoner, Red (Morgan Freeman, who narrates Andy's story). Over a period of 20 years, Andy gradually learns the prison system and wins the respect of the governor and guards by using his banking skills to do their tax returns and business dealings for them, but he never stops wishing for his freedom.

Simply and movingly played by Freeman and Robbins, and beautifully scripted by director Frank Darabont (who keeps close to the source material, the only major change being that Red was an Irishman in King's story), *Shawshank* is an intelligent, engrossing tale, rich with characterization that, although not a box-office success on its initial release in 1994, has deservedly become a must-see movie thanks to word of mouth in the years since. **JB**

**France** (IMA, Alain Sarde, Strand) 110m Color
**Language:** French
**Director:** André Téchiné
**Producer:** Georges Benayoun, Alain Sarde
**Screenplay:** Olivier Massart, Gilles Taurand, André Téchiné
**Photography:** Jeanne Lapoirie
**Cast:** Élodie Bouchez, Gaël Morel, Stéphane Rideau, Frédéric Gorny, Michèle Moretti, Jacques Nolot, Eric Kreikenmayer, Nathalie Vignes, Michel Ruhl, Fatia Maite, Claudine Taulère, Elodie Soulinhac, Dominique Bovard, Monsieur Simonet, Chief Officer Carre

# LES ROSEAUX SAUVAGES (1994)
## THE WILD REEDS

This wonderful and masterful feature from Andre Téchiné, his twelfth, is one of the best movies from an excellent French television series of fiction features on teenagers from the 1960s to early '80s. As Téchiné's *French Provincial* (1974) evokes in some ways the Bernardo Bertolucci of *The Conformist* (1970), this account of kids living in southwest France in 1962 toward the end of the Algerian war has some of the feeling, lyricism, and sweetness of Bertolucci's *Before the Revolution* (1964). Though *Wild Reeds* is clearly the work of someone much older and wiser.

The main characters are all completing their baccalaureate examination at a boarding school. They include a boy struggling with his homosexual desire for a close friend (Gael Morel), an older student who is a right-wing opponent of Algerian nationalism (Frederic Gorny), and a communist daughter of one of the teachers (Elodie Bouchez), who befriends the homosexual and falls for the older student in spite of their political differences. One comes to regard these characters and others as old friends, and Téchiné's handling of pastoral settings is as exquisite as his feeling for period. *Wild Reeds* was the winner of Cesar awards (the French equivalent of the Oscars) for best picture, director, screenplay, and "new female discovery" (for Bouchez). **JRos**

# CHONG QING SEN LIN (1994)
## CHUNGKING EXPRESS

Hong Kong (Jet Tone) 97m Color
**Language:** Cantonese / Mandarin
**Director:** Kar-wai Wong
**Producer:** Yi-kan Chan
**Screenplay:** Kar-wai Wong
**Photography:** Christopher Doyle, Wai Keung Lau
**Music:** Frankie Chan, Roel A. García
**Cast:** Brigitte Lin, Tony Leung Chiu Wai, Faye Wong, Takeshi Kaneshiro, Valerie Chow, Chen Jinquan, Huang Zhiming, Liang Zhen, Zuo Songshen

Kar-wai Wong's preference to work without a script gives his films some brilliantly off-kilter cadences. That the results are just as often as beautiful and touching as they are challenging stands as a testament to his choice of collaborators and his trust in the same. *Chungking Express* tells two unconventional (and barely related) love stories, each involving a lonely policeman and set in the bustling urban epicenter of Hong Kong. In the first, young detective Takeshi Kaneshiro pledges to find a new girlfriend before an arbitrary can of pineapples reaches its expiration date. He thinks he succeeds when he comes across Brigitte Chin-Hsia Lin, who (unbeknownst to him) happens to be a drug dealer in search of a lost shipment. Then the director suddenly shifts gears to the laconic Tony Leung, a beat cop who catches the eye of counter-girl Faye Wong at his regular eating spot. Frustrated by his apparent lack of interest, Wong expresses her affection by breaking into Leung's apartment, cleaning and redecorating it, relishing the chance (however fleeting and furtive) to live in his world and absorb his essence.

Both stories are as funny as they are oddly compelling. Yet the real star of *Chungking Express* is neither the actors nor the story, but the way they're presented. Working with talented cinematographer and frequent collaborator Christopher Doyle, Kar-wai Wong transforms Hong Kong into a blur of orange neon lights and disjointed, distorted images, playing with film stock, exposure, and speed the way others might fiddle with a script. Add to this a keen understanding of the power of song—in the case of *Chungking Express*, the Mamas and the Papas's quirkily incongruous "California Dreamin'"—and Wong reveals himself as one of the more pop savvy and iconoclastic of Hong Kong's new generation of filmmakers. While other films by Wong may pack more emotional resonance, *Chungking Express* gets by and gets off on sheer innocence, exuberance, and cinematic freedom, a striking triumph of style over substance that gives life to the grunge and chaos at the heart of contemporary Hong Kong. **JKl**

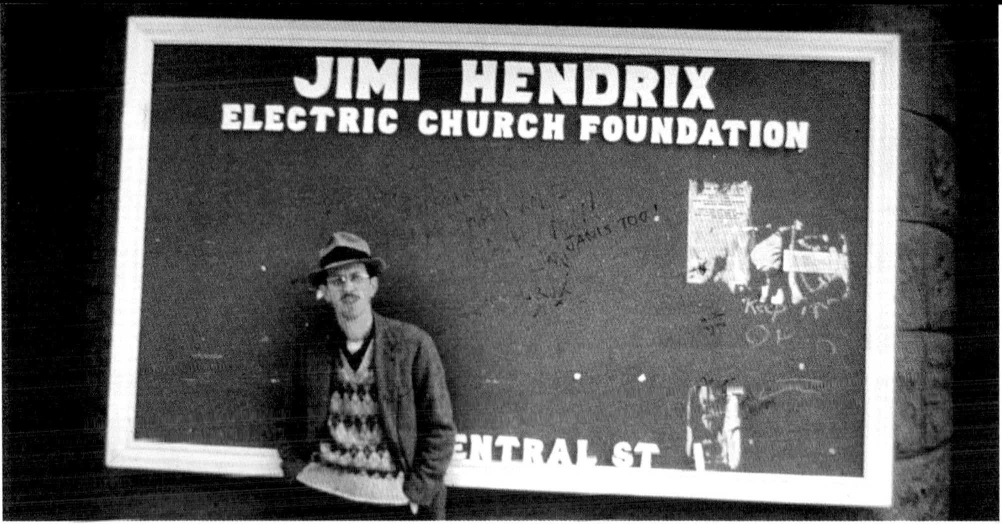


**U.S.** (Superior) 119m Color

**Director:** Terry Zwigoff

**Producer:** David Lynch, Lynn O'Donnell, Terry Zwigoff

**Photography:** Maryse Alberti

**Music:** David Boeddinghaus

**Cast:** Robert Crumb, Aline Kominsky, Charles Crumb, Maxon Crumb, Robert Hughes, Martin Muller, Don Donahue, Dana Crumb, Trina Robbins, Spain Rodriguez, Deirdre English, Peggy Orenstein, Beatrice Crumb, Kathy Goodell, Dian Hanson

## CRUMB (1994)

Anyone familiar with the work of underground comic artist R. Crumb might assume that he has a few screws loose, and indeed they might be right. But the most remarkable discovery made by Terry Zwigoff's sad, fascinating documentary is that R. Crumb is actually the least strange and best adjusted of three siblings, all of whom reveal an offhand brilliance and creativity yet channel that brilliance into radically contrasting outlets and lifestyles. One spends much of his time meditating on the streets of San Francisco. The other spends most of his time a recluse, holed up at home with his mother as he battles clinical depression and madness. Both exhibit an artistic inclination and talent at least equal to R. Crumb's, and the film spends much of its time revealing how a relatively inconsequential shared childhood steered each sibling in different directions.

*Crumb*, of course, spends most of its duration tracking the rise of R. Crumb as an underground comic icon during the heyday of the American Haight-Ashbury hippie culture in the late 1960s. Through a series of revealing and shockingly honest interviews, Zwigoff shows Crumb to be contrary at heart. He is a rebel against seemingly arbitrary (and often infuriatingly politically correct) rules of art and behavior with a taste for vintage jazz, fashions, and affectations that existed before American culture was gripped tighter by its corporate overseers. Crumb is the quintessential rebel whose form of passive resistance—comics—ironically transformed him into an underground icon.

*Crumb* marked an auspicious debut for Zwigoff, a longtime fan of vintage jazz and underground comics who eventually parlayed his success as a documentary filmmaker into a feature film, directing *Ghost World* (which happened to be based on an underground comic by Daniel Clowes, another vintage jazz obsessive). Needless to say, *Crumb* has as much to say about the lifestyle and attitude of eccentrics like Zwigoff in general as it does about R. Crumb. Specifically, his portrayal of the jaded Crumb in the months before his retirement remains an invaluable document (and in some ways outcome) of the underground '60s comics scene. JKl

# HEAVENLY CREATURES (1994)

**G.B. / Germany / NZ** (Fontana, Miramax , N.Z. F.C , Senator, WingNut) 99m Eastmancolor
**Director:** Peter Jackson
**Producer:** Jim Booth
**Screenplay:** Frances Walsh, Peter Jackson
**Photography:** Alun Bollinger
**Music:** Peter Dasent
**Cast:** Melanie Lynskey, Kate Winslet, Sarah Peirse, Diana Kent, Clive Merrison, Simon O'Connor, Jed Brophy, Peter Elliott, Gilbert Goldie, Geoffrey Heath, Kirsti Ferry, Ben Skjellerup, Darien Takle, Elizabeth Moody, Liz Mullane
**Oscar nomination:** Frances Walsh, Peter Jackson (screenplay)
**Venice Film Festival:** Peter Jackson (Silver Lion)

More often than not, filmmakers wilt into reverence or undue solemnity when they take on fact-based movies rooted in tragedy. Not Peter Jackson, who, though now famous for his *Lord of the Rings* trilogy, was already hedging the lines between good and evil, innocence and sin, comedy and drama in his early film *Heavenly Creatures*. A gleefully free interpretation of a 1952 murder case in which two schoolgirls in New Zealand, Pauline Parker and Juliet Hulme, conspired to kill Pauline's mother (prophetically named Mrs. Rieper) in hopes of avoiding being separated from one another.

At once prankish and moving, the film tells the girls' story as a parable of teenage puppy love gone awry between two bookish misfits. Juliet (Kate Winslet, in the role that launched her career), a smart-mouthed poor little rich girl from England who's cursed with callously neglectful parents, bonds with the shy, dowdy but intelligent Pauline (Melanie Lynskey). The more the girls' parents, disturbed by the homoerotic intensity of their friendship, try to pry them apart, the more they retreat into a florid dream universe, driven by their journals and populated by avenging princes and princesses. Each girl jacks up the other's obsessive imagination until they have abolished the line between reality and desire—as does Jackson in gorgeous fantasy sequences filled with digitally manipulated clay figures and featuring—hilariously—the girls' idols, Mario Lanza and Orson Welles.

Jackson's use of the ominously warped close-up sets off Lynskey's adolescent snarl (what became of this promising young actress?) against Winslet's luscious charisma, the dominatrix curl of her lip crumpling on a dime into the pathos of the abandoned child. This tough-minded, yet enormously sympathetic movie is less a critique of lesbian teen hysteria than an indictment of adult bourgeois hysteria about sexuality of any kind in the 1950s. Jackson didn't know it when he began shooting the film, but Juliet, who disappeared into England after her release from prison, resurfaced years later with a new identity as the best-selling mystery writer Anne Perry. **ET**

**France / Iran** (Abbas Kiarostami, CiBy 2000, Farabi, Miramax) 103m Color

**Language:** Farsi

**Director:** Abbas Kiarostami

**Producer:** Abbas Kiarostami

**Screenplay:** Abbas Kiarostami

**Photography:** Hossein Djafarian, Farhad Saba

**Cast:** Mohamad Ali Keshavarz, Farhad Kheradmand, Zarifeh Shiva, Hossein Rezai, Tahereh Ladanian, Hocine Redai, Zahra Nourouzi, Nasret Betri, Azim Aziz Nia, Astadouli Babani, N. Boursadiki, Kheda Barech Defai, Ali Ahmed Poor, Babek Ahmed Poor, Mahbanou Darabi

**Cannes Film Festival:** Abbas Kiarostami nomination (Golden Palm)

# ZIRE DARAKHATAN ZEYTON (1994)

## THROUGH THE OLIVE TREES

The social status of filmmaking among ordinary people, central to Abbas Kiarostami's wonderful movies *Close-Up* (1990) and *Life, and Nothing More* (1991) is equally operative in this entertaining and sometimes beautiful film. *Through the Olive Trees* concludes an unofficial trilogy begun with *Where Is the Friend's Home?* (1987), which focused on the adventures of a poor schoolboy in a mountainous region of northern Iran. *Life, and Nothing More*, the second of the three, fictionally re-created Kiarostami and his son's return to the area, which had recently been devastated by an earthquake, to look for two child actors from the earlier film. *Through the Olive Trees* is a comedy about the making of a movie, mostly emphasizing the persistent efforts of a young actor to woo an actress who won't even speak to him. Like Kiarostami's subsequent *Taste of Cherry* (1997), all three films in the trilogy strategically leave out certain information about the characters, inviting audiences to fill in the blanks and in this case yielding a mysteriously beautiful and open-ended conclusion. If you've seen the two earlier pictures, some details are enhanced: The child actors who are never found in *Life, and Nothing More*, for instance, turn up as gofers here, carrying flower pots to a location.

On the other hand, if you're unfamiliar with Kiarostami—one of our greatest living filmmakers and certainly the greatest in Iran—this is an excellent introduction, and it has served that function for many viewers across the globe (excluding, for the most part, the United States, where the distributor Miramax picked up the film only to bury it, making it the hardest to see of Kiarostami's late features). It was the first of his European coproductions and has the only professional actor he's ever hired for any of his films, Mohammad-Ali Keshavarz, as the director. It's an especially effective showcase for Kiarostami's gifts as a landscape artist, having been shot exclusively in exteriors, and the beautiful ways that he interweaves conversations in cars moving through this mountainous region, and the people and other sights that they pass on the road are often breathtaking. **JRos**

# RIGET (1994)
## THE KINGDOM

**Denmark / France / Germany / Sweden** (Coproduction, DR, Greco, MEDIA, NOS, Nordic Film & TV, SVT, TV Collab. Fund, WDR, Zentropa, arte) 280m Color

**Language:** Danish / Swedish

**Director:** Morten Arnfred, Lars von Trier

**Producer:** Sven Abrahamsen, Philippe Bober, Peter Aalbæk Jensen, Ole Reim, Ib Tardini

**Screenplay:** Tomas Gíslason, Lars von Trier, Niels Vørsel

**Photography:** Eric Kress

**Music:** Joachim Holbek

**Cast:** Ernst-Hugo Järegård, Kirsten Rolffes, Holger Juul Hansen, Søren Pilmark, Ghita Nørby, Jens Okking, Otto Brandenburg, Annevig Schelde Ebbe, Baard Owe, Birgitte Raaberg, Peter Mygind, Vita Jensen, Morten Rotne Leffers, Solbjørg Højfeldt, Udo Kier

A medical horror epic, *The Kingdom* was originally a four-part TV miniseries: Sewn together into two parts for theatrical showings, it ends tantalizingly with a "To Be Continued" caption setting up the similarly inconclusive *Kingdom 2* (1997). Dr. Stig Helmer (Ernst-Hugo Järegård), an arrogant Swedish neurosurgeon in exile after plagiarizing research, is in trouble in the eponymous Copenhagen hospital because his botched brain operation has left little Mona (Laura Christensen) a babbling imbecile. Helmer's Danish nemeses are spiritualist malingerer Mrs. Drusse (Kirsten Rolffes), pompous administrator Moesgaard (Holger Juul Hansen), and Bilko-esque fixer Hook (Troels Lyby).

Mrs. Drusse fakes illness so she can get into the Kingdom to investigate the haunting of the hospital by Mary, a little girl murdered in 1919. The blithely cheerful Moesgaard's "Operation Morning Air" program of staff singsongs and being nice to patients infuriates Helmer. His son, intern Mogge (Peter Mygind), is worried because a severed head he has given as a love gift to a doctor with whom he is smitten has gone missing. Hook, who keeps a record of medical accidents to blackmail, has just fallen in love with Judith (Birgitte Raaberg), a doctor unnaturally pregnant by a departed boyfriend Agge, recognizable in a photo-strip as Udo Kier. Also involved: A voodoo curse and a doctor so desperate to get hold of a diseased liver that he has it transplanted into his own body.

*The Kingdom*'s spare, but escalating, supernatural manifestations are genuinely eerie, sometimes magical: Mary's waxen ghost in the elevator shaft; a little quake as water eats away at the foundations (Helmer thinks Denmark was "shat out of water and chalk"); a discarnate spirt communicating with Mrs. Drusse through flickering fluorescent lights; a bloody hand waving in intense light inside a driverless ambulance. Throughout, von Trier (with codirector Morten Arnfred and longtime collaborator Niels Vørsel sharing the Mark Frost role) seamlessly blends the distinctive look of his early films (rust-colored filters, lots of water, muted or brown-toned color, suppurating unpleasantnesses) with the mock-documentary aesthetic of irony-laden 1990s soap: Jittery handheld camera work, deliberately rough edits, alternating vignettes of satire and sickness, cross-cut subplots, catch-phrases ("Danish scum"), likably obsessive characters, and out-of-left-field plot developments. **KN**

**Italy / France** (Banfilm, La Sept, Canal+, Rai Uno, Sacher) 100m Technicolor

**Language:** Italian / English / Mandarin

**Director:** Nanni Moretti

**Producer:** Nella Banfi, Angelo Barbagallo, Nanni Moretti

**Screenplay:** Nanni Moretti

**Photography:** Giuseppe Lanci

**Music:** Nicola Piovani, Keith Jarrett, Angélique Kidjo

**Cast:** Nanni Moretti, Giovanna Bozzolo, Sebastiano Nardone, Antonio Petrocelli, Giulio Base, Italo Spinelli, Carlo Mazzacurati, Jennifer Beals, Alexandre Rockwell, Renato Carpentieri, Raffaella Lebboroni, Marco Paolini, Claudia Della Seta, Lorenzo Alessandri, Antonio Neiwiller

**Cannes Film Festival:** Nanni Moretti (director), nomination (Golden Palm)

# CARO DIARIO (1994)

## DEAR DIARY

Nanni Moretti has attracted the label of the "Italian Woody Allen," but this description is woefully inadequate. In *Dear Diary* he turns to the genre of the diary film. Yet this is not a spontaneous, cinéma vérité piece; everything we see is carefully scripted and staged.

The film is in three sections. The first and best is "On My Vespa," a glimpse at Moretti's daily travels. The second, "Islands," is the most overtly comic, showing Moretti and a friend in search of an ever elusive quiet island on which to work. The third, "Doctors," is a sobering and unforgettable account of Moretti's brush with cancer.

*Dear Diary* teems with marvelous digressions, reflections, and cinema quotations. Exercises in personal filmmaking are sometimes narcissistic and cloying, but that is not the case here. Moretti's hatred of pathos and easy spectacle serve him well. Everything in the film—from chemotherapy to a visit to the place where Pasolini was murdered—is presented with utter simplicity and directness.

*Dear Diary* is a glorious movie about everyday experience—about traveling, dancing, thinking, getting sick, drinking a glass of water. Few films give such a grounded and joyous sense of what it is to live in the material world. **AM**

**U.S. / France** (De Fina-Cappa, Légende, Syalis, Universal) 178m Technicolor

**Language:** English / Farsi / French

**Director:** Martin Scorsese

**Producer:** Barbara De Fina

**Screenplay:** Nicholas Pileggi, from his book

**Photography:** Robert Richardson

**Cast:** Robert De Niro, Sharon Stone, Joe Pesci, James Woods, Don Rickles, Alan King, Kevin Pollak, L.Q. Jones, Dick Smothers, Frank Vincent, John Bloom, Pasquale Cajano, Melissa Prophet, Bill Allison, Vinny Vella

# CASINO (1995)

Something of a companion piece to Martin Scorsese's 1990 masterpiece *Goodfellas* (stars Robert De Niro and Joe Pesci and writer Nicolas Pileggi reuniting here), *Casino* focuses on the lives of Las Vegas mobsters during the 1970s, when the Mafia's involvement in the gambling city was at its heyday.

De Niro stars as Sam "Ace" Rothstein, a character based on real-life mobster Frank "Lefty" Rosenthal. Ace is a bookie turned successful casino manager who falls for you-just-know-she'll-be-trouble call girl Ginger (Sharon Stone, in a role originally earmarked for Madonna), allowing his love for her to affect his head for business. And if Ginger and her ex-boyfriend/pimp Lester (James Woods) weren't danger enough, Ace's old pal Nicky (Pesci) arrives in town to mess up Ace's nice little earner once and for all.

This three-hour drama has all the trademarks of a Scorsese film—lovingly staged set pieces, eye-boggling tracking shots, a hit-filled soundtrack, Pesci as a trigger-happy psycho—mixed with interesting historical fact about the Mob's involvement in America's most famous gambling town. Scorsese's Vegas is violent, sexy, and fascinating, making Ace's narration about the city today almost poignant. "The big corporations took over," he observes. "Today, it works like Disneyland." **JB**

# DESERET (1995)

**Director:** James Benning
**Producer:** James Benning
**Writer:** James Benning
**Photography:** James Benning
**Cast:** Fred Gardner (narrator)

The better-known work of experimental/structuralist filmmaker James Benning (*One Way Boogie Woogie* [1977], *Landscape Suicide* [1986], *North on Evers* [1992]), *Deseret* became an undisputed succès d'estime when it was premiered at Sundance in 1996. The title is an allusion to the name proposed by the Mormons when applying for statehood for the territory in which they were settling—later to become Utah. The film combines 92 *New York Times* excerpts from 1852 to 1991 with magnificently composed static shots taken throughout the territory.

Benning recorded images at different moments of the year over 18 months with his 16mm camera, pared them down to 92 shots of one minute each, and then reorganized them to "match," one shot per sentence, a prerecorded soundtrack of the *New York Times* stories boiled down to a few lines. Creating sometimes mysterious correspondences between image and text, the film leaves the viewer free to make his or her own connections, as the wealth of information provided on the soundtrack is offset by the still beauty of the landscapes: Deserts, plains of snow, lonely trails, trees in bloom, cemeteries, ruins, unfriendly rocks, empty settlers' houses, roads that seem to be leading nowhere. With a few exceptions, the human figure is kept off-screen, yet one is subtly aware of the presence, and the emotion of the filmmaker when composing the shots.

The text recounts the turbulent genesis of Utah—from the frontier days of settlement, persecutions, massacres, and retaliation, to the containment of the Indians, the access to statehood, the transformation of the Mormon Church into a wealthy, conservative corporation, and the use of the land as a testing ground for nuclear power. Apart from a spectacular instance—when the newspaper stories reach the turn of the century, the black-and-white footage turns to color—image and sound are at odds with each other, the East Coast style of the *New York Times* seemingly missing the point of the real drama that took place there. The landscapes resist the inscription of official history, yet they are haunted by its imperfect traces. Never have Benning's images been so beautiful, so starkly composed, and so sad. Their deceptively still surface hides troubled waters, but the emotion is kept at bay. **BR**

**Australia / U.S.** (Kennedy Miller, Universal) 89m Color

**Director:** Chris Noonan

**Producer:** Bill Miller, George Miller, Doug Mitchell

**Screenplay:** George Miller, Chris Noonan, from the novel *The Sheep-Pig* by Dick King-Smith

**Photography:** Andrew Lesnie

**Music:** Nigel Westlake

**Cast:** Christine Cavanaugh, Miriam Margolyes, Danny Mann, Hugo Weaving, Miriam Flynn, Russi Taylor, Evelyn Krape, Michael Edward-Stevens, Charles Bartlett, Paul Livingston, Roscoe Lee Browne, James Cromwell, Magda Szubanski, Zoe Burton, Paul Goddard

**Oscar:** Scott E. Anderson, Charles Gibson, Neal Scanlan, John Cox (special visual effects)

**Oscar nomination:** George Miller, Doug Mitchell, Bill Miller (best picture), Chris Noonan (director), George Miller, Chris Noonan (screenplay), James Cromwell (actor in support role), Roger Ford, Kerrie Brown (art direction), Marcus D'Arcy, Jay Friedkin (editing)

# BABE (1995)

"That'll do, pig." Described by one critic as "The *Citizen Kane* of talking pig movies," this joyous fable of a pig who becomes a champion sheep-herder makes previously unrepentant carnivores seriously contemplate vegetarianism. Babe is an innocent, irresistible piglet whisked from breeding pen to the barnyard of an eccentric man of few words, Farmer Hoggett (James Cromwell), who develops an affectionate bond with the creature. The farmer's fat, rosy wife (Magda Szubanski) unsentimentally eyes the piggy as a Christmas dinner of roast pork. But Babe has "an unprejudiced heart," unfailing courtesy, curiosity, and courage, affecting every life on the farm and reshaping his ultimately heroic destiny.

Ten years passed from the time Australian producer and cowriter George Miller—doctor, vegetarian, and creator-director of the *Mad Max* trilogy—became captivated with British farmer turned teacher and author Dick King-Smith's charming children's book *The Sheep-Pig* to the film's production. Miller waited for the development of the technology he required. Now he could seamlessly mix real livestock (including large numbers of piglets who were each coiffed with Babe's distinctive black tuft of toupee) with uncanny animatronic doubles. Plausible dubbing of voice performances (notably those by Christine Cavanaugh as Babe and Miriam Margolyes and Hugo Weaving as Hoggett's sheepdogs) set a new standard for anthropomorphic entertainment. Within moments, the illusion that the animals are talking completely takes over, giving credibility to the impulses of human behavior they display, from generosity and selflessness to neuroses to spite, bigotry, and criminality.

Longtime Miller colleague Chris Noonan made his feature directorial debut with witty invention, delightful pace, emotive use of music from Charles Camille Saint-Saens's "Carnival of the Animals," and the serenity of a St. Francis in choreographing his four-footed and feathered company to wildly hilarious and exciting effect. The story, narrated by Roscoe Lee Browne and a zany chorus of singing mice, has sweet, touching simplicity to enchant children while operating as beautifully on a more mature level. We hear and see gentle echoes of George Orwell's *Animal Farm*, whose satire was reproduced more faithfully in the darker, underrated sequel *Babe: Pig In The City*. **AE**

## TOY STORY (1995)

The first feature-length blockbuster from Pixar, the production company that would go on to make *A Bug's Life* (1998) and *Monsters, Inc.* (2001), *Toy Story* is a rip-roaring, computer-animated kids' adventure that is, quite frankly, far too intelligent, funny, and beautifully made to be just for a junior audience.

Six-year-old Andy doesn't know that his playthings come alive when he's not in the room. Led by Woody (voiced by Tom Hanks), a cowboy doll that's always been Andy's favorite, the toys (including Bo Peep, Mr. Potato Head, and Rex the dinosaur) gather to await Andy's birthday, where he may get—oh no!—a new toy that he likes more than all of them. And this year, Andy gets the most super-duper toy ever: Buzz Lightyear (Tim Allen), a space ranger complete with high-tech gadgets. Woody realizes he has to get rid of Buzz to be Andy's favorite once again, and his machinations lead the pair into terrible danger in the world outside Andy's bedroom.

A witty script—the authors included Joel Cohen and *Buffy the Vampire Slayer* creator Joss Whedon—and wonderful, almost 3-D animation, plus Hanks's and Allen's absolutely perfect characterizations, make this a hugely enjoyable comic treat that deservedly became an instant classic. **JB**

**U.S.** (Pixar Animation, Walt Disney) 81m Technicolor
**Language:** English / Spanish
**Director:** John Lasseter
**Producer:** Bonnie Arnold, Ralph Guggenheim
**Screenplay:** John Lasseter, Andrew Stanton, Peter Docter, Joe Ranft, Joss Whedon, Andrew Stanton, Joel Cohen, Alec Sokolow
**Music:** Randy Newman
**Cast (voices):** Tom Hanks, Tim Allen, Don Rickles, Jim Varney, Wallace Shawn, John Ratzenberger, Annie Potts, John Morris, Erik von Detten, Laurie Metcalf, R. Lee Ermey, Sarah Freeman, Penn Jillette, Jack Angel, Spencer Aste
**Oscar nomination:** Randy Newman (music), Randy Newman (song), Joel Cohen, Peter Docter, John Lasseter, Joe Ranft, Alec Sokolow, Andrew Stanton, Joss Whedon (screenplay)

## STRANGE DAYS (1995)

A movie that gives new meaning to the word "punchy," Kathryn Bigelow's hyperventilating and violent thriller—entertaining if occasionally over the top—is set in Los Angeles on New Year's Eve in the year 1999 and has a plot involving snuff tapes (with several nods to Michael Powell's 1960 film *Peeping Tom*), racial violence, and police corruption. One feels at times that these matters have been worked into James Cameron and Jay Cocks's script like fashionable teasers rather than as subjects the filmmakers have much to say about, but they are certainly part of the punchiness.

Ralph Fiennes stars as a disgraced former cop, Lenny Nero, now a black marketer who trafficks illicit virtual-reality tapes. It's impossible to be bored by this film, and Angela Bassett's charisma as an action heroine is readily apparent. Besides the refreshing interracial relationship between Fiennes and Bassett, *Strange Days* offers the sights and sounds of a dystopic Los Angeles, suffering more than a few premillennial jitters. **JRos**

**U.S.** (Lightstorm) 145m Color
**Director:** Kathryn Bigelow
**Producer:** James Cameron, Steven-Charles Jaffe
**Screenplay:** James Cameron, Jay Cocks
**Photography:** Matthew F. Leonetti
**Music:** Graeme Revell
**Cast:** Ralph Fiennes, Angela Bassett, Juliette Lewis, Tom Sizemore, Michael Wincott, Vincent D'Onofrio, Glenn Plummer, Brigitte Bako, Richard Edson, William Fichtner, Josef Sommer, Joe Urla, Nicky Katt, Michael Jace, Louise LeCavalier

## BRAVEHEART (1995)

**U.S.** (Fox, B.H. Finance, Icon, Paramount, Ladd) 177m Color
**Language:** English/ French / Latin
**Director:** Mel Gibson
**Producer:** Bruce Davey, Mel Gibson, Alan Ladd Jr.
**Screenplay:** Randall Wallace
**Photography:** John Toll
**Music:** James Horner
**Cast:** Mel Gibson, James Robinson, Sean Lawlor, Sandy Nelson, James Cosmo, Sean McGinley, Andrew Weir, Gerda Stevenson, Brian Cox, Patrick McGoohan, Sophie Marceau
**Oscar:** Mel Gibson, Alan Ladd Jr, Bruce Davey (best picture), Mel Gibson (director), John Toll (cinematography), Lon Bender, Per Hallberg (special sound effects), Peter Frampton, Paul Pattison, Lois Burwell (makeup)
**Oscar nomination:** Randall Wallace (screenplay), Charles Knode (costume), Steven Rosenblum (editing), James Horner (music), Andy Nelson, Scott Millan, Anna Behlmer, Brian Simmons (sound)

Producer, director, and star Mel Gibson's gigantic historical epic combines brutal action, heaps of derring-do, and romantic tragedy so wholeheartedly that both the testosterone-crazed action crowd and women who love a good cry are pleased by at least one or the other half of its ruggedly handsome three hours.

Financed heavily by Gibson himself, whose attractions in tartan skirt and blue dye are matched by one of his most appealing and heroic performances, *Braveheart* is a panegyric for Scottish warrior William Wallace, whose loss of his love (stunning Catherine McCormack) triggers a hanky-wringing sequence of events in spectacular locations with a cast of thousands. Wallace's grassroots revolt against Edward I (dastardly Patrick McGoohan) at the turn of the 14th century climaxed with the Scots' victory at Stirling but ended in tears, betrayal, and butchery. Punctuated by battle sequences that run from thrilling to repulsively gory, the story is a good old-fashioned swashbuckler with vengeance and historical figures. Gibson took Best Picture and Director Oscars among *Braveheart*'s five wins for a film made with passionate gusto and heart which retains a sense of humor and exhibits a flair for the mythic that balances the sadistic and partisan excesses. **AE**

## SAFE (1995)

**U.S. / G.B.** (Metro Tartan, American Playhouse, Channel Four, Chemical, Good Machine, Kardana) 119m Color
**Director:** Todd Haynes
**Producer:** Christine Vachon, Lauren Zalaznick
**Screenplay:** Todd Haynes
**Photography:** Alex Nepomniaschy
**Music:** Brendan Dolan, Ed Tomney
**Cast:** Julianne Moore, Peter Friedman, Xander Berkeley, Susan Norman, Kate McGregor-Stewart, Mary Carver, Steven Gilborn, April Grace, Peter Crombie, Ronnie Farer, Jodie Markell, Lorna Scott, James LeGros, Dean Norris, Julie Burgess

Even though it arrived a few years early, Todd Haynes's *Safe* epitomized America's pre-millennial tension in the days leading toward the year 2000. Julianne Moore plays a vapid and materialistic suburban housewife who develops a severe allergic reaction to the world around her, starting with a rash and lethargy but leading ultimately to more violently disruptive responses. Desperate, she ensconces herself in a holistic retreat for people with the same problem. But is the ailment just a figment of Moore's atrophied imagination, a by-product of her tedious, banal existence? Or has her body truly revolted against modernity?

Haynes coyly keeps the exact nature of her illness ambiguous, depicting Moore's syndrome as very real while at the same time implying that her descent into sickness and subsequent embrace of New Age treatment may just be a search for something to fill a void in her life. Moore's performance is increasingly wrought with anxiety, panic, and fear, as she realizes that everything she knows—her home, her routine, her family—may have to be sacrificed for the sake of her well-being. *Safe* offers a lot of questions but few answers, bravely subverting sickness-of the week tropes by withholding the promise of a miracle cure. It's a thoroughly modern horror film whose threat seems to be civilization itself. **JKl**

# CLUELESS (1995)

When Jane Austen wrote the novel *Emma*, it is unlikely the 19th-century author ever imagined her tale of a meddling young romantic heroine would be transplanted to late-20th-century Beverly Hills, but that is precisely what writer/director Amy Heckerling did with *Clueless*.

The film made a star of young Alicia Silverstone (who previously was best known as the star of the Aerosmith video "Crazy"). She plays Cher, a 90210 teen whose mother, as she tells us, "died in a freak accident during a routine liposuctioning," leaving Cher to be raised by her wealthy father (Dan Hedaya) in their vast Beverly Hills home. Although she does go to school with her pal Dionne (Stacey Dash), much of Cher's life is spent shopping on Rodeo Drive, coordinating her humongous wardrobe, and matchmaking for her friends, including school newcomer Tai (Brittany Murphy), who soon becomes something of a clone of her more savvy pal.

Like the Austen book on which it is (very loosely) based, there is a central love story. While interfering in other people's love lives, Cher barely notices her stepbrother Josh (Paul Rudd) as a possible romantic entanglement until it is almost too late. However, the film works best as a sharply funny satire on 20th-century teens, complete with its own language (good-looking men are "Baldwins"—a nod to the handsome acting family led by Alec and Billy), blistering asides ("searching for a boy in high school is like searching for meaning in a Pauly Shore movie"), and well-aimed jabs at contemporary LA culture (Cher points out that she doesn't need to practice parking beacuse everywhere she goes there is valet parking).

Heckerling keeps everything moving at a brisk pace, skewering fashion victims while making her heroine one of the most devoted, and Silverstone proves to be the perfect muse, fitting the role of the chic but dippy Cher to perfection. A funny, touching, and biting movie. **JB**

**U.S.** (Paramount) 97m Color
Director: Amy Heckerling
**Producer:** Robert Lawrence, Scott Rudin
**Screenplay:** Amy Heckerling
**Photography:** Bill Pope
**Music:** David Kitay
**Cast:** Alicia Silverstone, Paul Rudd, Brittany Murphy, Stacey Dash, Donald Adeosun Faison, Dan Hedaya, Breckin Meyer, Justin Walker, Wallace Shawn, Jeremy Sisto, Twink Caplan, Elisa Donovan, Aida Linares, Sabastian Rashidi, Herb Hall

## HEAT (1995)

**U.S.** (Forward Pass, Monarchy, Regency, Warner Bros.) 171m Color

**Director:** Michael Mann

**Producer:** Art Linson, Michael Mann

**Screenplay:** Michael Mann

**Photography:** Dante Spinotti

**Music:** Elliot Goldenthal

**Cast:** Al Pacino, Robert De Niro, Val Kilmer, Jon Voight, Tom Sizemore, Diane Venora, Amy Brenneman, Ashley Judd, Mykelti Williamson, Wes Studi, Ted Levine, Dennis Haysbert, William Fichtner, Natalie Portman, Tom Noonan

In Michael Mann's telemovie *L.A. Takedown* (1987), there is a scene in which a cop and the criminal he has been obsessively tracking happen to bump into each other while shopping. There is a tense pause, and then the criminal breaks the ice with a classic invitation: "Coffee?"

That scene reappears in Mann's *Heat*, a film whose richly deserved cult following has steadily grown since 1995. Set in Los Angeles, it takes a well-worked theme—the symbiotic relationship between cop Vincent (Al Pacino) and criminal Neil (Robert De Niro)—and meditates moodily upon it. Mann combines a flamboyant, epic style with a manic attention to realistic detail—resulting in indelible set pieces like the street shoot out.

In its exploration of family and intimacy, *Heat* treats a founding theme of noir fiction: The danger of bonding with another person. Agonizing scenes dramatize Neil's assertion that a "professional" should be able to walk away from everything in his life within 30 seconds.

These professionals are almost automatons: Hard-driven, single-minded, married to their unsavory work (rather than their teary, long-suffering companions). But they are also proud, stoic men, and in their determination lies a lofty splendor to which Mann pays immortal tribute. **AM**

## KJÆRLIGHETENS KJØTERE (1995)
### ZERO KELVIN

**Norway / Sweden** (Norsk, Sandrews) 118m Color

**Language:** Norwegian

**Director:** Hans Petter Moland

**Producer:** Bent Rognlien

**Screenplay:** Lars Bill Lundholm, Hans Petter Moland, from the novel *Larsen* by Peter Tutein

**Photography:** Philip Øgaard

**Music:** Terje Rypdal

**Cast:** Stellan Skarsgård, Gard B. Eidsvold, Bjørn Sundquist, Camilla Martens, Paul-Ottar Haga, Johannes Joner, Erik Øksnes, Lars Andreas Larssen, Juni Dahr, Johan Rabaeus, Frank Iversen, Tinkas Qorfiq

Hans Petter Moland's *Zero Kelvin* has the crisp economy of a tough, knotty thriller by Roman Polanski. The story occurs in a grimly circumscribed setting: a shack in Greenland where three men hired as seal hunters quickly go crazy. Larsen (Garb B. Eidsvold) is a dandy; Holm (Bjorn Sundquist) is the quiet, scientific type; and Randbaek (Stellan Skarsgård) is a raging bull. For a while, dramatic tension occurs only between Larsen and Randbaek, as they seesaw between violence and boyish, petulant displays. But then Holm makes a sudden, decisive intervention—propelling the characters out of the shack and into the ice and snow. Now Moland can produce his most striking images and most ingenious narrative moves.

Although they are stranded in a landscape where all traces of civilization are absent, the characters' social values do not disappear, but instead are placed into stark relief by the monumental setting. Moland's ultimate concern is with the ethical dilemmas of human behavior under pressure. *Zero Kelvin* brilliantly examines what a normally civilized person will do in extreme circumstances, with all restraints removed. It asks what can separate men from beasts. And it coolly probes the constant claims of its characters to moral superiority or lofty idealism. **AM**

## SE7EN (1995)

Who would have guessed that a grisly and upsetting serial-killer police procedural costarring Brad Pitt and Morgan Freeman as detectives, written by a Tower Records cashier (Andrew Kevin Walker), and directed by David Fincher (*Alien*) would bear a startling resemblance to a serious work of art? One can already tell that this film is on to something special during the opening credits, which formally echo several classic American experimental films and thematically point to the eerie kinship between the serial killer (Kevin Spacey) and the police—not to mention the kinship between murder and art-making that the movie is equally concerned with. The detectives are trying to solve a series of hideous murders based on the seven deadly sins, and the sheer foulness and decay of the nameless city that surrounds them—which makes those of *Taxi Driver* and *Blade Runner* seem almost like children's theme parks—conjures up a metaphysical mood that isn't broken even when the film moves to the countryside for its climax.

Admittedly, designer unpleasantness is a hallmark of our era, and this movie may be more concerned with wallowing in it than with illuminating what it means politically. In this respect, it shares some of the duplicity of *Taxi Driver*—another film that derives much of its power from this country's love-hate relationship with fundamentalism, although it should be added that America is hardly alone in experiencing this ambivalence. *Se7en* is one of the only Hollywood films to have shown widely in postrevolutionary Iran (along with the *Godfather* trilogy and *Dances with Wolves*). It likely showed there in censored form; one can't account for its appeal in that country simply by noting that its highly skilled cinematographer, Darius Khondji, is Iranian.

The filmmakers stick to their vision with such dedication and persistence that something indelible comes across—something ethically and artistically superior to *The Silence of the Lambs* that refuses to exploit suffering for fun or entertainment and leaves you wondering about the world we're living in. Paradoxically, however, one should note that the film originally had a much grimmer ending—available now as a DVD bonus—which preview audiences resisted. **JRos**

**U.S.** (New Line) 127m Color

**Director:** David Fincher

**Producer:** Phyllis Carlyle, Arnold Kopelson

**Screenplay:** Andrew Kevin Walker

**Photography:** Darius Khondji

**Music:** Howard Shore

**Cast:** Morgan Freeman, Brad Pitt, Kevin Spacey, Gwyneth Paltrow, R. Lee Ermey, Andrew Kevin Walker, Daniel Zacapa, John Cassini, Bob Mack, Peter Crombie, Reg E. Cathey, George Christy, Endre Hules, Hawthorne James, William Davidson

**Oscar nomination:** Richard Francis-Bruce (editing)

## SMOKE (1995)

**U.S. / Germany** (Eurospace, Internal, Miramax, NDF, Smoke) 112m BW/Color
**Director:** Wayne Wang, Paul Auster
**Producer:** Kenzo Hirikoshi, Greg Johnson, Hisami Kuroiwa, Peter Newman
**Screenplay:** Paul Auster
**Photography:** Adam Holender
**Music:** Rachel Portman
**Cast:** Giancarlo Esposito, José Zúñiga, Stephen Gevedon, Harvey Keitel, Jared Harris, William Hurt, Daniel Auster, Harold Perrineau Jr., Cole/Paul Benjamin, Deirdre O'Connell, Victor Argo, Michelle Hurst, Forest Whitaker, Stockard Channing, Vincenzo Amelia, Erica Gimpel
**Berlin International Film Festival:** Wayne Wang, Harvey Keitel (Silver Bear—special jury prize), Wayne Wang nomination (Golden Bear)

Centered on a Brooklyn tobacco shop that also serves as a meeting place for colorful eccentrics representing a cross-section of New York society, this collaboration between director Wayne Wang and author Paul Auster wobbles intriguingly between an intricate character study and an improvisational comedy. But given the film's general emotional pay-off, punctuated with a bravura Harvey Keitel monologue, *Smoke* ultimately falls closer to the former, especially considering the heavy themes of trust, regret, and responsibility.

Keitel, William Hurt, Forest Whitaker, and Stockard Channing are all great here, and Wang weaves their interrelated tales into a single impressive tapestry. *Smoke*'s diverse plotlines are in fact all held together by tiny thematic threads: Many of the characters dwell on some significant loss in their life, others reflect on unrequited love, and still others try to restore a frayed bond between child and parent. Each thread connects one character to the other in subtle ways, and while the fabric of society may for better or worse be in constant flux or full of gaps, Wang and Auster optimistically imply that it's the inherent goodness of man which keeps it all from unraveling. **JKl**

## BADKONAKE SEFID (1995)
### THE WHITE BALLOON

**Iran** (Ferdos Films) 85m Color
**Language:** Farsi
**Director:** Jafar Panahi
**Producer:** Kurosh Mazkouri
**Screenplay:** Abbas Kiarostami
**Photography:** Farzad Jadat
**Cast:** Aida Mohammadkhani, Mohsen Kalifi, Fereshteh Sadr Orfani, Anna Borkowska, Mohammad Shahani, Mohammed Bakhtiar, Aliasghar Smadi, Hamidreza Tahery, Asghar Barzegar, Hasan Neamatolahi, Bosnali Bahary, Mohammadreza Baryar, Shaker Hayely, Homayoon Rokani, Mohammad Farakani
**Cannes Film Festival:** Jafar Panahi (Golden Camera)

This fresh and unpredictable comic "thriller" from Iran is the first feature of Jafar Panahi, a former assistant to the great Iranian filmmaker Abbas Kiarostami, who's credited, along with Panahi and Parviz Shahbazi, with the screenplay. *The White Balloon* describes in real time the adventures of a seven-year-old girl named Razieh (Aida Mohammadkhani) and her older brother in the streets of Tehran during the 85 minutes that elapse immediately before the celebration of the Iranian New Year.

After convincing her mother she needs another goldfish for the celebration, Razieh sets off to buy one, but twice en route to the store she loses the banknote she's been given. Most of the remainder of the film is devoted to her efforts to get the money back. If the plot sounds slender, the movie is both gripping and charming, with well-sketched characters and expert storytelling—and Panahi's efforts to redefine our sense of time along the way are remarkable. Bit by bit, we're drawn into this child's perception of time passing, focused on her desire for the goldfish and the various obstacles standing in the way of her acquiring it.

No less important is *The White Balloon*'s abrupt, last-minute revelation of middle class snobbery on Razieh's part after a soldier goes to significant trouble to help her recover her money. This points one toward the more obvious ethical concerns of Panahi's next two features, *The Mirror* (1997) and *The Circle* (2000). **JRos**

# XICH LO (1995)
## CYCLO

We enter a world that is at once familiar yet strange. We feel like we've been here before. We are told it's 1990s Hanoi, a city we haven't seen since the news footage of the Vietnam War in the 1970s.

A young rickshaw rider (Le Van Loc) has his bicycle stolen, which puts him in debt to the woman who rented it out to him. She sends him to the silent gangster and pimp Poet (Tony Leung Chiu Wai), who puts him to work committing acts of vandalism and petty larceny to pay off his debt. What he doesn't know is that Poet has also persuaded his sister into working as a prostitute, servicing rich clients who pay with U.S. dollars. Brother and sister, both innocents, are put on the path to corruption under the guidance of the same man.

*Cyclo's* story may sound like a recipe for melodrama, but director Tran Ahn Hung is after something else altogether. His approach is measured and considered. His focus is on color and silence as his camera lurks around the characters, discreetly awaiting the smallest flicker in their faces as thoughts and emotions shift and turn. The plot may take its starting point from Vittorio De Sica's *The Bicycle Thief*, but it is not an exercise in neorealism. Rather, the tone is almost magical realist, focusing on unexpected eruptions of odd beauty, as when the characters suddenly pause in their lives to look at a military helicopter falling off its ground transport in heavy traffic, or when the film suddenly centers on Poet's (living up to his name) minimalist poetry, matching the stanzas with images of elliptical stillness. It's strange to see so many moments of beauty in a story about corruption, lost innocence, violence, drugs, and death. There's a sense of director Tran striving for a new form of storytelling, eschewing commercial genre conventions. The film could easily have been a thriller or a gangster movie, but *Cyclo* is a film in tune with the rhythms of the city it's set in, preparing to quietly re-acquaint us with a place and a people we haven't see for more than 20 years. **AT**

**Vietnam / France** (Entertainment, Lazannec, Lumière, La Sept, SFP) 120m Color

**Language:** Vietnamese / Italian

**Director:** Anh Hung Tran

**Producer:** Christophe Rossignon

**Screenplay:** Trung Binh Nguyen, Anh Hung Tran

**Photography:** Benoît Delhomme, Laurence Trémolet

**Music:** Tôn-Thât Tiêt

**Cast:** Le Van Loc. Tony Leung Chiu Wai, Tran Nu Yên-Khê, Nhu Quynh Nguyen, Hoang Phuc Nguyen, Ngo Vu Quang Hal, Tuyet Ngan Nguyen, Doan Viet Ha, Bjuhoang Huy, Vo Vinh Phuc, Le Kinh Huy, Pham Ngoc Lieu, Le Tuan Anh, Le Cong Tuan Anh, Van Day Nguyen

**Venice Film Festival:** Anh Hung Tran (FIPRESCI award), (Golden Lion)

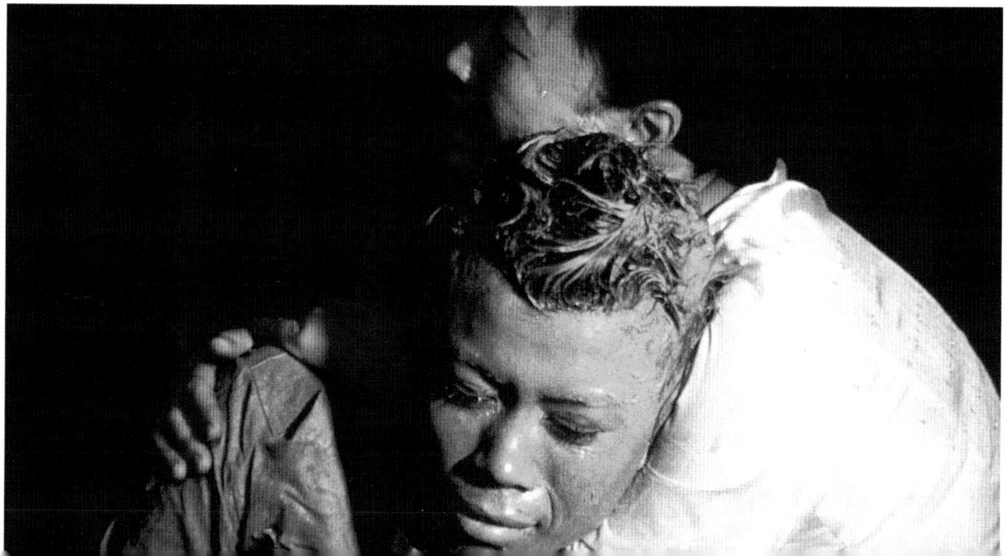

## UNDERGROUND (1995)

**France / Yugoslavia / Germany / Hungary** (CiBy 2000) 192m Color

**Language:** Serbo-Croatian / German

**Director:** Emir Kusturica

**Screenplay:** Dusan Kovacevic, Emir Kusturica, from the novel *Bila jednom jedna zemlja* by Dusan Kovacevic and play *Prolece u januaru* by Dusan Kovacevic and Emir Kusturica

**Photography:** Vilko Filac

**Music:** Goran Bregovic

**Cast:** Miki Manojlovic, Lazar Ristovski , Mirjana Jokovic, Slavko Stimac, Ernst Stötzner, Srdjan Todorovic, Mirjana Karanovic, Milena Pavlovic, Danilo 'Bata' Stojkovic, Bora Todorovic, Davor Dujmovic, Dr. Nele Karajlic, Branislav Lecic, Dragan Nikolic, Erol Kadic

**Cannes Film Festival:** Emir Kusturica (Golden Palm)

Though slightly trimmed by director-writer Emir Kusturica for American consumption, this riotous 167-minute satiric and farcical allegory about the former Yugoslavia from World War II to the postcommunist present is still marvelously excessive. The outrageous plot of *Underground* involves a couple of anti-Nazi arms dealers and gold traffickers who gain a reputation as communist heroes. One of them (Miki Manojlovic) installs a group of refugees in his grandfather's cellar, and on the pretext that the war is still raging upstairs he gets them to manufacture arms and other black-market items until the 1960s, meanwhile seducing the actress (Mirjana Jokovic) whom his best friend (Lazar Ristovski) hoped to marry.

Loosely based on a play by cowriter Dusan Kovacevic, this sarcastic, carnivalesque epic won the *Palme d'Or* at Cannes in 1995 and has been at the center of a furious controversy ever since for what's been called its pro-Serbian stance. (Kusturica himself is a Bosnian Muslim.) However one chooses to take its jaundiced view of history, it is probably the best film to date by the talented filmmaker (*Time of the Gypsies*, *Arizona Dream*), a triumph of mise en scène mated to a comic vision that keeps topping its own hyperbole. **JRos**

## DILWALE DULHANIYA LE JAYENGE (1995)
### THE BRAVE HEART WILL TAKE THE BRIDE

**India** (Eros) 192m Color

**Language:** Hindi

**Director:** Aditya Chopra

**Producer:** Yash Chopra

**Screenplay:** Aditya Chopra, Javed Siddiqi

**Photography:** Manmohan Singh

**Music:** Jatin Pandit, Lalit Pandit

**Credited cast:** Shahrukh Khan, Kajol, Amrish Puri, Farida Jalal, Anupam Kher, Karan Johar, Pooja Ruparel, Satish Shah, Anaita, Mandira Bedi, Arjun Sablok, Achla Sachdev, Parmeet Sethi, Himani Shivpuri, Lalit Tiwari

In the 1990s, Hindi film reinvented itself as a slicker, younger, and more stylish form, the new cable and satellite television channels setting the pace for a new look and the growth in advance music sales allowing budgets to rise. This resulted in a return to the cinema halls of the middle-class audience which had deserted it for VHS. This decade also saw more films about the Indian diaspora—people of Indian origin settled overseas—and *The Brave Heart Will Take the Bride* was as much a hit with this audience as in its home country, making it one of the biggest hits in Indian film history.

Londoners Shah Rukh and Kajol, one of the decade's most popular screen pairs, meet on an a holiday in Switzerland but are separated when her family takes her to Punjab for a marriage arranged at the time of her birth. Although the girl is ready to run away with her lover, he insists her father should give her away; so he persuades her family to accept him by showing them he knows how an Indian boy should behave. The tight script and hit music made it clear that Aditya Chopra, though very much his own director, was set to follow in the footsteps of his famous filmmaker father, Yash Chopra. **RDw**

# DEAD MAN (1995)

At the beginning of Jim Jarmusch's *Dead Man*, a timid, bespectacled, hypercivilized clerk, William Blake (Johnny Depp), is heading west to take up a career in the frontier town of Machine. The journey seems endless, and once he arrives he discovers that his position was filled months ago. Feeling dejected, he beds a prostitute, only to be interrupted by her fiancé who shoots her dead, wounds William, and is shot by him in return. William flees, beginning a journey through the wilderness of the American West in which, with an enigmatic Indian named Nobody (Gary Farmer) at his side, and progressively suffering from his untreated wound, he navigates toward his death. Nobody is his guide: "Do you know how to use that weapon?" he asks, "It will replace your tongue."

An essay on contemplation, this film charms through Robby Müller's black-and-white cinematography (influenced by Ansel Adams), the exquisitely simple guitar score by Neil Young, Depp's gentle performance poetry—typified when he lies down to embrace a dead fawn. Bizarre support roles by John Hurt, Iggy Pop, Lance Henriksen, Gabriel Byrne, and lanky, towering, Robert Mitchum, in his last screen appearance, a smoking cigar between his lips—persuading Blake to leave his office by pointing a double-gage shotgun into his face—fill out the almost plotless scenery.

Much of the narrative and violence in *Dead Man* is flat and unromantic, especially the perverse, almost catatonic behavior of Cole Wilson (Henriksen)—a killer not so much cold-blooded as bloodless. The pervading silences of the great Western emptiness, the silver birch gliding by as William rides through the forest, Nobody's matter-of-factness as he performs not entirely comprehensible rituals upon a man not entirely conscious, all lead to an almost meaningless evocation of person, place, and moment. When at the end Nobody pushes William off on a great lake, the spirit-canoe glides away into the other world in a vision that recalls the Death of King Arthur at Avalon. **MP**

**U.S. / Germany / Japan** (12 Gauge, JVC, Miramax, Newmarket, Pandora) 121m BW

**Director:** Jim Jarmusch

**Producer:** Demetra J. MacBride

**Screenplay:** Jim Jarmusch

**Photography:** Robby Müller

**Music:** Neil Young

**Cast:** Johnny Depp, Gary Farmer, Lance Henriksen, Michael Wincott, Mili Avital, Iggy Pop, Crispin Glover, Eugene Byrd, Michelle Thrush, Jimmie Ray Weeks, Mark Bringleson, Gabriel Byrne, John Hurt, Alfred Molina, Robert Mitchum

**Cannes Film Festival:** Jim Jarmusch nomination (Golden Palm)

**U.S. / Germany** (PolyGram, Spelling, Blue Parrot, Bad Hat Harry, Rosco) 106m Technicolor

**Language:** English / Hungarian / Spanish / French

**Director:** Bryan Singer

**Producer:** Michael McDonnell, Bryan Singer

**Screenplay:** Christopher McQuarrie

**Photography:** Newton Thomas Sigel

**Music:** John Ottman

**Cast:** Gabriel Byrne, Kevin Spacey, Stephen Baldwin, Chazz Palminteri, Pete Postlethwaite, Kevin Pollak, Benicio Del Toro, Suzy Amis, Giancarlo Esposito, Dan Hedaya, Paul Bartel, Carl Bressler, Phillip Simon, Jack Shearer, Christine Estabrook

**Oscar:** Kevin Spacey (actor in support role), Christopher McQuarrie (screenplay)

# THE USUAL SUSPECTS (1995)

"The greatest trick the devil ever pulled was convincing the world he didn't exist." *The Usual Suspects* is an absorbing confidence trick concerning the identification of a criminal archfiend: Who is Keyser Soze? With its convoluted plotting, macho repartee, and Bryan Singer's confident direction, the great trick the filmmakers pulled was convincing audiences to see the movie again immediately. The illusion is that repeated viewing of what comes before the shock revelation can unravel the mystery to complete satisfaction. But screenwriter Christopher McQuarrie, who won the Oscar, and Singer revel in twists and turns, not reason.

Spacey, snatches his first Oscar, as Verbal "people say I talk too much" Kint, a con man and the talkative cripple, whose narrative is the thread to which we cling. Five criminals are placed in a holding cell to appear in a lineup, although none were actually involved with the crime for which they have been arrested. The seemingly chance meeting, however, inspires them to team up on a heist, which sets them up for blackmail and betrayal.

A hip, urban *Rashômon* (1950) with staccato bursts of violent, beautifully choreographed action, *The Usual Suspects*, actually opens on a scene of carnage in which a mystery man executes Byrne's Keaton. This "objective" sequence will recur, revised, as remembered by Verbal and as imagined by his interrogator, a Federal agent (Chazz Palminteri) too fixated on his own theory of why these men came together in a homicidal fiasco to "stand back from it" and "look at it right." The viewer makes the same mistake, cleverly misdirected.

Singer delights in sleights of hand, like a camera dissolve into a swirling cup of coffee and a thrilling elevator shaft assassination, that make one forgetful of loose ends. The contribution of John Ottman, performing the unusual double of editing labyrinthine scenes and composing the brooding score, shouldn't be underestimated either. The ultimate accolade is that one can't say the film doesn't hold up. It may not add up, but it remains a madly intriguing puzzle. **AE**

# THE PILLOW BOOK (1996)

*The Pillow Book* has a fanciful plot typical of Peter Greenaway's cinema. Nagiko (Vivian Wu) has a taste for having her body written upon in various calligraphic styles by men, including Jerome (Ewan McGregor). This began in childhood, thanks to her father—as did a passion for ancient Japanese erotic literature. When Nagiko grows up, she comes into intense conflict with an old, sinister publisher also associated with her father—at which point the film becomes a rather gruesome revenge tale.

Since the mid 1990s, Greenaway's imaginative powers have been channeled into the exploration of digital technologies—often with unsatisfying results, at least on the levels of storytelling and emotional involvement. *The Pillow Book*, however, rates as one of his most pleasurable films because it achieves a lightness, a lyricism, a grace. It works out many variations on the theme of the twin pleasures of flesh and writing. The "boutique culture" milieu is intoxicating; there is even pop music in place of the usual Michael Nyman score. And emotion is not absent. Throughout, there are lists and inventories, slow montage sequences devoted to "things that make the heart quicken"—and the beauty of these passages manages to overpower Greenaway's standard misanthropy. **AM**

**France / G.B. / Netherlands** (Alpha, Channel Four, Delux, Eurimages, Kasander & Wigman, Canal+, Nederlands Fonds voor de Film, Woodline)126m BW / Color

**Language:** English / Cantonese / Italian / Japanese / Mandarin

**Director:** Peter Greenaway

**Producer:** Kees Kasander

**Screenplay:** Peter Greenaway, from book by Sei Shonagon

**Photography:** Sacha Vierny

**Cast:** Vivian Wu, Yoshi Oida, Ken Ogata, Hideko Yoshida, Ewan McGregor, Judy Ongg, Ken Mitsuishi, Yutaka Honda, Barbara Lott, Miwako Kawai, Chizuru Ohnishi, Shiho Takamatsu, Aki Ishimaru, Hisashi Hidaka, Dehong Chen

# TROIS VIES & UNE SEULE MORT (1996)

## THREE LIVES AND ONLY ONE DEATH

Perhaps the most accessible movie of the Chilean-born Raul Ruiz (who has more than a hundred titles to his credit), *Three Lives and Only One Death* provides a sunny showcase for the charismatic talents of the late Marcello Mastroianni, who plays four separate roles, and stands as a testament to the filmmaker's imaginative postsurrealist talents as a yarn spinner and a weaver of magical images and ideas.

Mixing together ideas borrowed liberally and freely from stories by Nathaniel Hawthorne and Isak Dinesen with whimsical notions that could belong to no one but Ruiz (such as the tale of a millionaire who willingly and successfully turns himself into a beggar), *Three Lives and Only One Death* is a French comedy with a Paris setting, which often resembles a kind of euphoric free fall through the works and fancies of a writer like Jorge Luis Borges. Among the spirited cast members are Mastroianni's daughter Chiara, and Melvil Poupaud (who played in Ruiz's 1983 film *City of Pirates*). **JRos**

**France / Portugal** (CNC, Gémini, La Sept, Le Groupement National des Cinémas de Recherche, Canal+ Madragoa) 123m Eastmancolor

**Language:** French

**Director:** Raoul Ruiz

**Producer:** Paulo Branco

**Screenplay:** Pascal Bonitzer, Raoul Ruiz

**Photography:** Laurent Machuel

**Music:** Jorge Arriagada

**Cast:** Marcello Mastroianni, Anna Galiena, Marisa Paredes, Melvil Poupaud, Chiara Mastroianni, Arielle Dombasle, Féodor Atkine, Jean-Yves Gautier, Jacques Pieiller, Pierre Bellemare, Smaïn, Lou Castel, Roland Topor, Jacques Delpi, Jean Badin

**Cannes Film Festival:** Raoul Ruiz nomination (Golden Palm)

**U.S. / G.B.** (Gramercy, PolyGram, Working Title) 98m Color

**Director:** Joel Coen

**Producer:** Ethan Coen

**Screenplay:** Joel Coen and Ethan Coen

**Photography:** Roger Deakins

**Music:** Carter Burwell

**Cast:** William H. Macy, Steve Buscemi, Frances McDormand, Peter Stormare, Kristin Rudrüd, Harve Presnell, Tony Denman, Gary Houston, Sally Wingert, Kurt Schweickhardt, Larissa Kokernot, Melissa Peterman, Steve Reevis, Warren Keith, Steve Edelman, Sharon Anderson

**Oscar:** Ethan Coen, Joel Coen (screenplay), Frances McDormand (actress)

**Oscar nomination:** Ethan Coen (best picture), Joel Coen (director), William H. Macy (actor in support role), Roger Deakins (photography), Ethan Coen, Joel Coen (editing)

**Cannes Film Festival:** Joel Coen (director), nomination (Golden Palm)

# FARGO (1996)

"I guess that was your accomplice, in the wood chipper?" One specialty of sibling partners Joel and Ethan Coen is twisting time-honored Hollywood genres—noir thriller, screwball comedy, gangster drama, or the fugitive-from-a-chain-gang flick—into flamboyant, contemporary delights. The foremost filmmakers to emerge from America in the 1980s, their best films still look great, and devilishly clever *Fargo* is among their very best. It's a wicked tale (as ever, cowritten by the brothers, produced by Ethan, directed by Joel) which provokes gasps of admiration and rapt shock along with belly laughs. Embezzlement, abduction, deceit, misunderstanding, and murder are all in the frame, as is another regular feature of the Coenesque experience—a crime that gets totally out of control.

*Fargo* takes place in North Dakota, where oppressed car salesman Jerry Lundergaard (William H. Macy in the anxious performance that lifted him from ever-useful character actor to eagerly sought character actor) arranges a meeting with the two ex-cons he hires to abduct his wife. But most of the film, impishly introduced as a true story in the first of its macabre deceptions, is set in the austere, snowy landscapes of the Coens's native Minnesota (where the exaggerated regional dialect amusingly employed in hilariously banal chitchat is a flat, singsong relic of the area's Scandinavian immigrant pioneers, and at absurd odds with the heinous goings-on).

The desperately in debt Lundergaard cuts a supposedly simple, "no rough stuff" deal. His wife's ransom is to be paid by her rich, bullying father (Harve Presnell) and split between hubby and his hired thugs, with the woman going free none the wiser. Only things go horribly and grotesquely awry in the hands

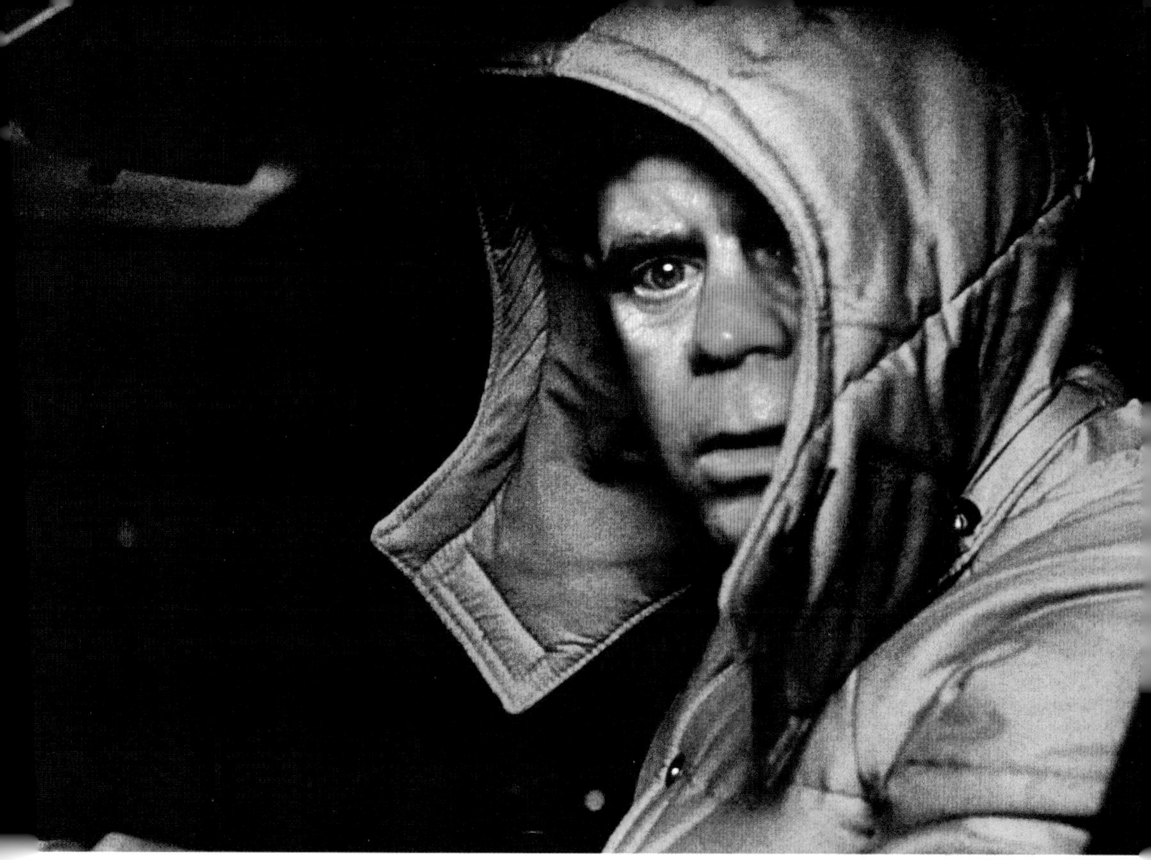

of the psychopath (Peter Stormare's Grimsrud) with a craving for pancakes, and the agitated bungler ("funny lookin' little fella" Steve Buscemi's Showalter) who can't control him or events. Enter Frances McDormand (Mrs. Joel Coen), absolutely fantastic as the very pregnant, comically ordinary but sharp small-town police chief, Marge Gunderson. Resolutely conducting her first triple homicide investigation with unhurried waddle and droll aplomb, Marge is easily the most engaging character ever conceived by the Coens (along with, later, Jeff Bridge's "The Dude" Lebowski).

The Coens's witty expertise results in a quirky, bizarre tragi-comedy that manages to be wildly funny and violently distressing by neatly accomplished turns, the essential innocence and simplicity of some characters contrasted effectively with the depravity of others. Hapless criminals and victims are there not to be empathized with but to be cruelly toyed with for our wincing pleasure. That cold, malevolent streak that has recurred in much of their work is what prompted one detractor famously to dub them "arty nuisances." But it does not diminish their flagrant talent to dazzle, bemuse, and amuse. Against its icy visuals, *Fargo* contains some of their warmest work, full of signature Coen brothers' set pieces and running jokes but also the surprisingly redemptive comfort of simple, straightforward decency. McDormand and the Coens's screenplay won Oscars for breaking the mold in a unique case of murder. **AE**

**U.S.** (Fox, Centropolis) 145m Color

**Director:** Roland Emmerich

**Producer:** Dean Devlin

**Screenplay:** Dean Devlin, Roland Emmerich

**Photography:** Karl Walter Lindenlaub

**Music:** David Arnold

**Cast:** Bill Pullman, Mary McDonnell, Mae Whitman, Jeff Goldblum, Judd Hirsch, Will Smith, Vivica A. Fox, Ross Bagley, Margaret Colin, Robert Loggia, James Rebhorn, Randy Quaid, James Duval, Lisa Jakub, Giuseppe Andrews

**Oscar:** Volker Engel, Douglas Smith, Clay Pinney, Joe Viskocil (special visual effects)

**Oscar nomination:** Chris Carpenter, Bill W. Benton, Bob Beemer, Jeff Wexler (sound)

# INDEPENDENCE DAY (1996)

Special effects movies don't get much bigger than *Independence Day*, a sci-fi bonanza that oozes American patriotism from every frame. Jeff Goldblum is the satellite whizz who picks up a transmission from outer space that seems to be counting down to zero. He heads off to Washington D.C. to warn President Bill Pullman (a very Clintonesque leader, with Mary McDonnell his Hillary-like wife) that spaceships appearing all over the planet may not be filled with fuzzy and friendly E.T.s, but are actually hostile aliens planning to devastate Earth.

Director Roland Emmerich and producer Dean Devlin pack their movie with humorous actors—Will Smith, Robert Loggia, Judd Hirsch, Harvey Fierstein—playing the action with tongue planted firmly in cheek, though the real star here is not any of the actors, but the brilliant special effects. From alien spaceships reminiscent of cult television series *V*, to the attacks on Earth (almost too realistic), we watch in horror as once great landmarks—the Empire State Building and the White House—are reduced to piles of smoking rubble. All in all, a great example of what edgy fun a sci-fi extravaganza can be. **JB**

**France / G.B.** (Channel Four, CiBy 2000, Thin Man) 142m Metrocolor

**Director:** Mike Leigh

**Producer:** Simon Channing-Williams

**Screenplay:** Mike Leigh

**Photography:** Dick Pope

**Music:** Andrew Dickson

**Cast:** Timothy Spall, Phyllis Logan, Brenda Blethyn, Claire Rushbrook, Marianne Jean-Baptiste, Elizabeth Berrington, Michele Austin, Lee Ross, Lesley Manville, Ron Cook, Emma Amos, Brian Bovell, Trevor Laird, Claire Perkins, Elias Perkins McCook

**Oscar nomination:** Simon Channing-Williams (best picture), Mike Leigh (director), Mike Leigh (screenplay), Brenda Blethyn (actress), Marianne Jean-Baptiste (actress in support role)

**Cannes Film Festival:** Mike Leigh (Golden Palm), (prize of the ecumenical jury), Brenda Blethyn (actress)

# SECRETS AND LIES (1996)

*Secrets and Lies*, Mike Leigh's gripping, multifaceted comedy-drama, winner of the grand prize at Cannes in 1996, may well be his most accessible and optimistic film. This helps to explain why it possibly remains the celebrated work of a writer-director for stage and screen who is often best known for his anger and merciless skewering of class differences in Thatcherite and post-Thatcher England.

Hortense, a young black optometrist (Marianne Jean-Baptiste), seeks out her white biological mother (Brenda Blethyn), a factory worker who put her up for adoption at birth. As the two become acquainted, tensions build between the mother and another illegitimate daughter (Claire Rushbrook), between the mother and her younger brother (Timothy Spall), and between him and his wife (Phyllis Logan), everything leading to a ferocious climax.

The dense, Ibsen-like plotting of family revelations in *Secrets and Lies* is dramatically satisfying in broad terms, though it leaves a few details unaccounted for. But the acting is so strong—with Spall a particular standout—that you're carried along as if by a tidal wave. **JRos**

# BREAKING THE WAVES (1996)

Before issuing a manifesto that urged subscribing to a dogma, Danish filmmaker Lars Von Trier made a film about the ambiguous horrors of living by dogma. Set in remote Scotland in the 1970s, *Breaking the Waves* leaves behind the slickly-designed, highly-wrought artifice of the often-monochrome magical worlds of earlier Von Trier productions (*The Element of Crime, Europa*) to experiment with the edgy, hand-held, rough-around-the-edges look typical of his *The Idiots* and Dogme95 pictures by other directors (such as Thomas Vinterberg's *Festen* and Joren Kragh-Jacobsen's *Mifune*). However, this is by no means a dogma or dogmatic film, as scenes are set with computer-augmented haunted landscapes and deeply-unfashionable '70s pop music selections.

Von Trier was obsessed as a child with a fairy-tale book called "Golden Heart," about a good little girl who gives away so much that she uses herself up—though his copy was missing a crucial happy ending. *Breaking the Waves* is the first of a trilogy, followed by *The Idiots* and the musical *Dancer in the Dark*, extrapolating from this theme. Here, the heroine is Bess (Emily Watson), a withdrawn, almost childish young woman raised in an austere, horrifyingly religious community in the Outer Hebrides. She begins to emerge from her shell when she impulsively marries Jan (Stellan Skarsgård), a Swede who works on an oil rig in the North Sea, but her new life is fractured when Jan is crippled by an industrial accident. Replacing her cold religion with extreme love, Bess takes a peculiar path to sainthood and martyrdom, discovering that she can only reach the bedridden Jan by recounting to him tales of sexual adventures, which leads her to comic, tragic, and ultimately fatal encounters.

Ostracized as a whore by village elders who routinely stand over the graves of women and curse them to hell for causing the fall of man, Bess is drawn out to sea to a boat captained by a Satanic Udo Kier, but the final moments of the film present her posthumous influence as genuinely miraculous. The plot takes a difficult but rewarding path, and it might shade into gimmickry were it not for a startlingly real, affecting, and strange central performance from Watson. **KN**

**Denmark / Sweden / France / Netherlands / Norway** (Argus, Canal+, CoBo, Det Danske, Eurimages, European Script Fund, Finnish Film Foundation, La Sept, Liberator, Lucky Red, Media Investment Club, Nederlands Fonds voor de Film, Nordic Film & TV Fund, Northern Lights, Norwegian Film Institute, October, Philippe Bobor, SVT Drama, Swedish Film Institute, TV1000 AB, Icelandic Film Corporation, Trust Film Svenska, VPRO TV, Villealfa, YLE, Zentropa, ZDF, arte) 159m Color (Eastmancolor)

**Director:** Lars von Trier

**Producer:** Peter Aalbæk Jensen, Vibeke Windeløv

**Screenplay:** Lars von Trier, Peter Asmussen

**Photography:** Robby Müller

**Music:** Joachim Holbek

**Cast:** Emily Watson, Stellan Skarsgård, Katrin Cartlidge, Jean-Marc Barr, Adrian Rawlins, Jonathan Hackett, Sandra Voe, Udo Kier, Mikkel Gaup, Roef Ragas, Phil McCall, Robert Robertson, Desmond Reilly, Sarah Gudgeon, Finlay Welsh

**Oscar nomination:** Emily Watson (actress)

**Cannes Film Festival:** Lars von Trier (grand prize of the jury), nomination (Golden Palm)

# THE ENGLISH PATIENT (1996)

**U.S.** (J&M, Miramax, Tiger Moth) 160m Color

**Language:** English / German

**Director:** Anthony Minghella

**Producer:** Saul Zaentz

**Screenplay:** Anthony Minghella, from novel by Michael Ondaatje

**Photography:** John Seale

**Music:** Gabriel Yared

**Cast:** Ralph Fiennes, Juliette Binoche, Willem Dafoe, Kristin Scott Thomas, Naveen Andrews, Colin Firth, Julian Wadham, Jürgen Prochnow, Kevin Whately, Clive Merrison, Nino Castelnuovo, Hichem Rostom, Peter Rühring, Geordie Johnson, Torri Higginson

**Oscar:** Saul Zaentz (best picture), Anthony Minghella (director), Juliette Binoche (actress in support role), Stuart Craig, Stephanie McMillan (art direction), John Seale (photography), Ann Roth (costume), Walter Murch (editing), Gabriel Yared (music), Walter Murch, Mark Berger, David Parker, Christopher Newman (sound)

**Oscar nomination:** Anthony Minghella (screenplay), Ralph Fiennes (actor), Kristin Scott Thomas (actress).

**Berlin International Film Festival:** Juliette Binoche (Silver Bear—actress), Anthony Minghella nomination (Golden Bear)

"Every night I cut my heart out, but by morning it was full again." Anthony Minghella's epic adaptation of Michael Ondaatje's Booker Prize–winning novel owned Oscar night, winning nine Academy Awards in the most sweeping victory since the 1987 film *The Last Emperor*. It was particularly remarkable for a film that the writer-director had almost despaired of making. Having been "intoxicated" by the poetic book, he spent over three years restructuring it, greatly expanding the doomed love story at its heart. The independent producer Saul Zaentz (*One Flew Over the Cuckoo's Nest* [1975], *Amadeus* [1984]) originally found backing from 20th-Century Fox. But disagreements, about casting Kristin Scott Thomas rather than an American actress for example, culminated in the studio pulling out. Production was halted before Miramax stepped in with the finance.

A severely burned and disfigured pilot (Ralph Fiennes) is found in the wreckage of his biplane in North Africa near the end of World War II. Apparently amnesiac, unidentified but presumed to be English, he is dying and in the care of French-Canadian nurse Hana (Juliette Binoche). Taking refuge in a devastated Italian monastery, they are joined by Willem Dafoe's vengeful Canadian torture victim and two bomb disposal experts for intimate explorations of memory, loss, and healing. The mystery patient—revealed as Hungarian Count Laszlo Almásy—recalls his past gradually between the late 1930s and 1945, in Tuscany, Cairo, and the Sahara Desert. Almásy's love affair with the married Katharine Clifton (Kristin Scott Thomas) unfolds with tragic consequences.

The film has two strong elements to captivate. The story is convoluted but classically, passionately romantic. And the production is meticulously artful, repeatedly likened to the style of David Lean, from dreamlike aerial sequences and a dramatic sandstorm to sensuous love scenes and enchanting effects—cave paintings examined by torchlight, church frescoes illuminated by a flare). *The English Patient*'s scale, its majesty on big screens, and its sense of importance demanded recognition for its artistic and technical achievements. **AE**

# GABBEH (1996)

Mohsen Makhmalbaf's *Gabbeh* is an overwhelmingly gorgeous film. From its first bold strokes—when a young woman (Shaghayeh Djodat) seems to spring to life from a figure in a Persian carpet—the colors, sounds, and rapid associative editing are entrancing. But *Gabbeh* is much more than another quaint, pretty, exotic, touristic, pseudo-peasant exercise in the vein of, say, *Il Postino* (1994). The mournful story of deferred love that fills the film offers a profound humanist panorama of love and longing, birth and death, nature and culture, magic and loss.

The images in the carpet provide an ancient, immemorial point of origin for this tale, but the weave of its telling crosses and combines many times, places, and situations. Past and present moments, old and young people, the rich arts of everyday life, as well as the sanctioned arts of a painting or a film: Makhmalbaf covers a rich and varied territory of vital sensations and experiences.

These days, every film with a few red-tinted sunset shots is lazily labeled "poetic." *Gabbeh* is an authentic expression of the "cinema of poetry." Every word, sight, sound, gesture, and color comes to resonate metaphorically with something else: The gesture of an animal resembles the motions of carpet makers; rapidly flowing water is like a field of grass sent dancing by the wind.

Within the context of burgeoning Western appreciation of the "New Iranian Cinema," *Gabbeh* has been faulted in comparison with the sublimely neorealist films of Abbas Kiarostami, such as the 1994 film *Through the Olive Trees*. But Makhmalbaf is to Kiarostami what Prince is to Michael Jackson—a dark, perverse cousin. *Gabbeh* shows a special aspect of Makhmalbaf's prodigious talent—a hushed, patient, timeless aspect. The breathtaking style he adopts here—modeled partly on that of Georgian screen master Sergei Paradjanov—fuses folk and modernist elements in a way that refuses any absolute distinction between them.

For all its spellbinding complexity, this is a film which has a limpidity and directness which are truly sublime. For those open to the experience, *Gabbeh* is a movie which makes its way straight into the soul. **AM**

**Iran / France** (MK2, Sanaye Dasti) 75m Color

**Language:** Farsi

**Director:** Mohsen Makhmalbaf

**Producer:** Khalil Daroudchi, Khalil Mahmoudi

**Screenplay:** Mohsen Makhmalbaf

**Photography:** Mahmoud Kalari

**Music:** Hossein Alizadeh

**Cast:** Abbas Sayah, Shaghayeh Djodat, Hossein Moharami, Rogheih Moharami, Parvaneh Ghalandari

U.S. (Castle Rock, Columbia, Rio Dulce) 135m Color

**Director:** John Sayles

**Producer:** R. Paul Miller, Maggie Renzi

**Screenplay:** John Sayles

**Photography:** Stuart Dryburgh

**Music:** Mason Daring

**Cast:** Stephen Mendillo, Stephen J. Lang, Chris Cooper, Elizabeth Peña, Oni Faida Lampley, Eleese Lester, Joe Stevens, Gonzalo Castillo, Richard Coca, Clifton James, Tony Frank, Miriam Colon, Kris Kristofferson, Jeff Monahan, Matthew McConaughey

**Oscar nomination:** John Sayles (screenplay)

# LONE STAR (1996)

John Sayles's wise and witty study of interconnected lives down by the Texan border with Mexico is about crossing lines, digging up the past, learning lessons, and moving on. It proffers a garrulous gallery of characters, all somehow connected with or investigated by Rio County Sheriff Sam Deeds (Chris Cooper) after a skeleton is discovered in the desert just outside of town. Deeds privately reckons it may have something to do with the ongoing battle his late dad (Matthew McConaughey)—for years a local hero—had with a notoriously corrupt and racist lawman (Kris Kristofferson) several decades previously. What happened way back then? And how has it affected the present town, with its uneasy mix of whites, Hispanics, and blacks all keen to rewrite history as well as claim the future? How does the personal affect the political, and vice versa?

On the surface, *Lone Star* might be seen as a cross between a detective story and a modern Western, but it's more pertinently the kind of kaleidoscopic survey of a society in the process of change at which Sayles has been excelling for years—ever since *Matewan* (1987) and *City of Hope* (1991), in fact. Here, however, for the first time he adds flashbacks (sometimes as private memories, sometimes as shared experience) to include time as an extra ingredient in a heady brew already made up of class, money, sex, friendship, family, and race. Inevitably, given the border setting, the last figures heavily in terms of fear, hatred, desire, immigration, job prospects, and prejudice; mercifully, Sayles never sermonizes, but simply shows us how things function (or not, as the case may be). The dialogue is witty and colorful but naturalistic, the performances are excellent throughout, the use of music is characteristically sly and expressive, and Stuart Dryburgh's camera work eloquently conveys the various allegiances and divisions in the community on view. And watch out for that quietly subversive (albeit eminently justifiable) ending—forget the Alamo, indeed! GA

# TRAINSPOTTING (1996)

G.B. (Channel Four, Figment, PolyGram, Noel Gay) 94m Color

**Director:** Danny Boyle

**Producer:** Andrew Macdonald

**Screenplay:** John Hodge, from novel by Irvine Welsh

**Nonoriginal music:** Johann Sebastian Bach, Georges Bizet, Brian Eno, Iggy Pop

**Photography:** Brian Tufano

**Cast:** Ewan McGregor, Ewen Bremner, Jonny Lee Miller, Kevin McKidd, Robert Carlyle, Kelly Macdonald, Peter Mullan, James Cosmo, Eileen Nicholas, Susan Vidler, Pauline Lynch, Shirley Henderson, Stuart McQuarrie, Irvine Welsh, Dale Winton

**Oscar nomination:** John Hodge (screenplay)

The team behind the 1994 British cult hit *Shallow Grave*—producer Andew Macdonald, writer John Hodge, director Danny Boyle, and star Ewan McGregor—reunited for this punchy, grim look at the Edinburgh drug scene, based on offbeat writer Irvine Welsh's controversial novel.

McGregor stars as Mark "Rent Boy" Renton, an addict with a collection of misfit pals: Casual dealer Sick Boy (Jonny Lee Miller); Spud (Ewen Bremner), a character who is destined to be one of life's losers; and Begbie (Robert Carlyle in a scary stand-out performance), a violent psycho who picks fights with anyone and everyone.

Boyle uses a clever cinematic imagination to bring these losers' lives onto the screen, from the show-stopping opening moment as Renton runs down the street, to his infamous "Choose life" speech narrated as he is pursued for yet another petty crime committed to pay for his habit. Drug abuse here isn't depicted as a glamorous option—Renton's horrific hallucinations include a dive into possibly the most disgusting toilet in Scotland in an attempt to retrive lost narcotics, and the unforgettable images of a dead baby that haunt him when he is trying to detox.

At the time of its release, some critics of the film complained that although *Trainspotting* doesn't glamorize drugs, it also doesn't pass any moral judgments on its drug-addicted characters. But Boyle and Hodge's refusal to take a moral stance is in fact one of the movie's many attributes—we are not there to judge Renton and his pals; we are just there to watch as, in a bleakly humorous fashion, their lives fizzle away to nothing. A fascinating, highly charged, and brilliantly played movie, *Trainspotting* is rightly regarded as one of the best British films of the 1990s. It features some of the country's most startling young talent: Carlyle, McGregor, writer Hodge, and director Boyle (who went on to work with McGregor again two years later in the interesting but uneven *A Life Less Ordinary*). **JB**

# SCREAM (1996)

**U.S.** (Dimension, Woods) 111m Color
**Director:** Wes Craven
**Producer:** Cathy Konrad, Cary Woods
**Screenplay:** Kevin Williamson
**Photography:** Mark Irwin
**Music:** Marco Beltrami
**Cast:** David Arquette, Neve Campbell, Courteney Cox, Skeet Ulrich, Rose McGowan, Matthew Lillard, Jamie Kennedy, W. Earl Brown, Drew Barrymore, Joseph Whipp, Lawrence Hecht, Roger L. Jackson, David Booth, Liev Schreiber, Carla Hatley

In 1996, Wes Craven—director of such modern horror classics as *The Hills Have Eyes* (1978) and *A Nightmare on Elm Street* (1984)—shocked everyone who thought his career was over by initiating one of the most popular and successful horror series of all time. *Scream*, featuring a bevy of talented young actors (including Drew Barrymore, Neve Campbell, Skeet Ulrich, David Arquette, Rose McGowan, and Jamie Kennedy), took the United States by storm, bringing in over $103 million at the box office and kicking off a new wave of hip and reflexive slasher movies. *Urban Legend* (1998), *I Know What You Did Last Summer* (1997), *Valentine* (2001), and of course *Scream 2* (1997), *Scream 3* (2000), and the stalker parody *Scary Movie* (2000) all owe much of their success to Craven's original.

*Scream*'s intense ten-minute prologue is among the most talked-about horror scenes in recent memory. An anonymous caller threatens the lives of high school cutie Casey Becker (Barrymore) and her boyfriend unless she can answer such questions as "Who was the killer in *Friday the 13th?*" Like everyone else in *Scream*, Casey has seen most of the classic slasher movies: *Halloween* (1978), *Prom Night* (1980), etc. But only the most hardcore horror fans have a chance to live here and even that's not always enough. The main story concerns the efforts of virginal heroine Sidney Prescott (Campbell) to survive the attacks of a slasher film fanatic with a ghost mask and a very sharp knife. Only the timely help of dirt-seeking news reporter Gail Weathers (Courteney Cox) is enough to save Sidney, who is shocked to discover that her enemy is really a *pair* of close male friends (including her sometimes boyfriend) who seem to get off on the fact that they kill without reason.

Among the reasons for *Scream*'s outstanding success is an often hilarious script (written by Kevin Williamson, who would go on to create the hit teen TV show, *Dawson's Creek*), the numerous jokey references to earlier horror movies, and Craven's expert direction, which manages to frighten audiences even while they're laughing. **SJS**

## DECONSTRUCTING HARRY (1997)

**U.S.** (Jean Doumanian, Sweetland) 96m Technicolor
**Director:** Woody Allen
**Producer:** Jean Doumanian
**Screenplay:** Woody Allen
**Photography:** Carlo Di Palma
**Cast:** Caroline Aaron, Woody Allen, Kirstie Alley, Bob Balaban, Richard Benjamin, Eric Bogosian, Billy Crystal, Judy Davis, Hazelle Goodman, Mariel Hemingway, Amy Irving, Julie Kavner, Eric Lloyd, Julia Louis-Dreyfus, Tobey Maguire
**Oscar nomination:** Woody Allen (screenplay)

Woody Allen vents some shocking spleen toward women—one candidate in particular springs to mind—as an all-star cast reenacts scenes from the life and work of a neurotic, sex-obsessed, self-absorbed, constantly quipping and kvetching writer, Harry Block (Allen). Allen's 27th film as writer-director, *Deconstructing Harry* is brilliantly clever, unnervingly vicious, and nakedly self-confessional.

Harry has made a career of turning his life into thinly disguised fiction. Six analysts and three wives later he still isn't taking responsibility and deceives himself that his relationship with a much younger woman is appropriate: "Because of my immaturity I have a boyish charm." Extracts from Harry's work interweave with the "real" counterparts of his "fictional" characters, disputing his interpretation of relationships. Comedy and drama collide in surreal heights, such as Harry's anxious visit to Hell and his confrontations with his literary creations. Among some dazzling conceits is the plight of a movie star in one of Harry's short stories, with Robin Williams as the actor who literally goes out of focus. Along with all the pithy one-liners a fan could hope for there is shrewd, honest insight here, but there are those bound to agree with Woody/Harry's anguished climactic wail: "I'm OD'ing on myself!" **AE**

## L.A. CONFIDENTIAL (1997)

**U.S.** (Monarchy, Regency, Warner Bros.) 138m Technicolor
**Director:** Curtis Hanson
**Producer:** Curtis Hanson, Arnon Milchan, Michael G. Nathanson
**Screenplay:** Brian Helgeland, Curtis Hanson, from novel by James Ellroy
**Photography:** Dante Spinotti
**Music:** Jerry Goldsmith
**Cast:** Kevin Spacey, Russell Crowe, Guy Pearce, James Cromwell, Kim Basinger, Danny DeVito
**Oscar:** Brian Helgeland, Curtis Hanson (screenplay), Kim Basinger (actress in support role)
**Oscar nomination:** Arnon Milchan, Curtis Hanson, Michael G. Nathanson (best picture), Curtis Hanson (director), Jeannine Claudia Oppewall, Jay Hart (art direction), Dante Spinotti (photography), Peter Honess (editing), Jerry Goldsmith (music)
**Cannes Film Festival:** Curtis Hanson nomination (Golden Palm)

Set in 1950s Los Angeles, a festering swamp of corrupt cops dallying with freshly minted mobsters and fledgling tabloids, Curtis Hanson's smart and soulful movie trims James Ellroy's heavily plotted pulp bestseller to its emotional heart. Hanson's pacing is exquisite, his casting impish and inspired, as he traces the morally ambiguous alliance between three radically incompatible cops roped together in a multiple-murder investigation. Kevin Spacey cooks as a celebrity cop refusing to snitch on his mates. Russell Crowe is ardent and thuggish as a crusading policeman vying with up-tight career cop Guy Pearce for the affections of a classy hooker, played by Kim Basinger (a career-making performance she subsequently failed to top).

Dressed in the sumptuous chocolate browns of warm film noir, *L.A. Confidential* is hot, funny, and sorrowful. Though it teases brash '50s optimism with glum '30s cynicism and tars both with the brush of the knowing '90s, the film is also wildly romantic—perhaps the last great mounting of American film noir's feverish chase for and destruction of dreams. Dicks and dames collide in a grandiose lament for the loss of true love, moral courage, and, while we're at it, hope in our civic culture. **ET**

# CHEUN GWONG TSA SIT (1997)
## HAPPY TOGETHER

Hong Kong wunderkind writer/director Wong Kar Wai's elegiac look at the demise of a love affair is a nervy, shimmering mood piece, with the mood being indigo. Ironically titled, *Happy Together* is set primarily in Argentina, where Chinese emigrants and lovers Li Fai (Tony Leung) and Poh Wing (Leslie Cheung) have settled in the hopes of finding a place where they can forge a life with one another. It's a futile dream, though, as their wildly opposing personalities (quiet and responsible versus impetuous and flamboyant) are quickly fanned into irreconcilable differences.

Using long shots, sparse music, carefully composed scenes, and deeply evocative stretches of silence and stillness, Wong takes the viewer right to the serrated heart of this disintegrating relationship; the journey is hypnotic. Much credit has to be given to legendary cinematographer Christopher Doyle, whose masterful use of light and color renders every frame a work of art. The air of melancholy that cast, crew, and director evoke fairly wafts off the screen, and scenes such as the one where two men tango in a dilapidated old kitchen take your breath away with the depth of their beauty. Leung and Cheung slip seamlessly into their characters; there are moments when the pain they convey is so dead-on that you almost have to turn away. The anguish as they go back and forth is revealed through the petulance of one and the quiet suffering of the other, with the actors speaking volumes in their eyes, gestures, and postures.

The seesaw between betrayal and excruciating tenderness (a shared cigarette in the back of a taxi, with one lover's head slowly finding a resting place on the other's shoulder; Li spooning soup into the mouth of Poh, whose bandaged, broken limbs render him helpless and wholly dependent on Li, bringing their emotional positioning/roles in the relationship into the realm of the physical via rich metaphor) makes it clear that there is no easy way to severe the ties that bind and choke. The sweetest sadness walks with the viewer out of the theater after the closing credits roll. An absolutely perfect film. **EH**

**Hong Kong** (Block 2, Jet Tone, Prénom H, Seowoo) 96m BW/Color

**Language:** Cantonese / Mandarin / Spanish

**Director:** Wong Kar-wai

**Producer:** Ye-cheng Chan, Chan Yecheng

**Screenplay:** Wong Kar-wai

**Photography:** Christopher Doyle

**Music:** Danny Chung

**Cast:** Leslie Cheung, Tony Leung Chiu Wai, Chen Chang, Gregory Dayton

**Cannes Film Festival:** Wong Kar-wai (director), nomination (Golden Palm)

# MONONOKE HIME (1997)
## PRINCESS MONONOKE

**Japan** (Dentsu, Nippon TV, Ghibli, Tokuma Shoten) 133m Fujicolor
**Language:** Japanese
**Director:** Hayao Miyazaki
**Producer:** Toshio Suzuki
**Screenplay:** Hayao Miyazaki
**Photography:** Atsushi Okui
**Music:** Jô Hisaishi
**Cast:** Yôji Matsuda, Yuriko Ishida, Yûko Tanaka, Kaoru Kobayashi, Masahiko Nishimura, Tsunehiko Kamijoe, Sumi Shimamoto, Tetsu Watanabe, Mitsuru Satô, Akira Nagoya, Akihiro Miwa, Mitsuko Mori, Hisaya Morishige

There are many reasons to discuss the extent to which cartoons, or animated movies, belong to the field of cinema or, no matter how brilliant they might be, whether they belong to a specific artform of their own. The animated movies of Hayao Miyazaki, especially *Princess Mononoke*, his most accomplished masterpiece, simultaneously challenge this discussion and transcend it. *Princess Mononoke* poses a challenge insofar as it elaborates an incredibly complex, graphically creative, and ideologically demanding legend, using the tools of drawing and modeling far more than those of traditional filmmaking. Nevertheless, the film's power to evoke strong emotion, the depth and ambiguity of its main characters, the striking multiplicity of its secondary characters, and the search for something that lies beyond what is (so beautifully) drawn—all of this somehow results in a meeting between animation, which is used to fulfill its more powerful capabilities, and filmmaking, which serves as a portal to the invisible dimensions of the world through the mechanical recording of reality.

Mythical warriors and doomed princess, archaic beasts and industrial devils, desirable figures of evil and magic rainbows—all can run and thunder, fight and love, jump to the stars, and, suddenly but temporarily, disappear in the reification of the childish design of human faces by Japanese cartoonists. In this film, very unusually for an animated production, blood refers to real blood, love and death are realized through colored ink, and everything has a presence that belongs to the actual world. Fantastic animals and today's ecological issues interact like elements of the same nature. If Miyazaki succeeds in creating this unique encounter between animation and filmmaking, it has to do with the energy of both the storytelling and the artwork, the astonishing tension that exists through *Princess Mononoke*'s entire running time, from the first to the last image. Don't tell Miyazaki that the films he makes are not real, because he is convinced the opposite is true. And he is as brave as his characters. One can only hope he will stay this way. **J-MF**

## FAST, CHEAP, AND OUT OF CONTROL (1997)

As a documentary filmmaker, Errol Morris doesn't just "document" in the bare-bones, cinéma vérité sense of the term. Rather, he depicts people, places, and ideas in an entirely different (and often stylishly artificial) light, making the familiar appear unusual, and the unusual seem reasonable or at least accessible.

*Fast, Cheap, And Out of Control* focuses on a quartet of disparate and distinctive professionals: A lion tamer, a topiary gardener, a robot designer, and an expert on naked mole rats. Yet somewhere between his footage of roaring cats, elaborate hedges, self-propelled masses of wires and metal, and remarkably ugly rodents, Morris gets at something far grander and more profound than a traditional documentary. His subjects all dedicate their lives to studying and sometimes shaping the world around them, in a sense plying the oddities and uncertainties of life into a more practical form. Whether training lions to suppress their carnivorous instincts or sculpting shrubs and bushes into elaborate creations, the four eccentric foci of Morris's film gradually appear more and more "normal." Eventually they are just average guys fascinated with their place in a universe that grows stranger and more wondrous the more we learn about it. **JKl**

**U.S.** (American Playhouse, Fourth Floor) 80m BW/Color

**Director:** Errol Morris

**Producer:** Errol Morris

**Photography:** Robert Richardson

**Music:** Caleb Sampson

**Cast:** Dave Hoover, George Mendonça, Ray Mendez, Rodney Brooks

## THE BUTCHER BOY (1997)

One of Neil Jordan's finest and most intimate movies, *The Butcher Boy* is adapted, in a wonderfully wicked screenplay by Jordan and Patrick McCabe, from McCabe's novel of the same name. The film is set in rural Ireland in the 1960s and tells the story of a young boy who, dogged by inconstancy and abandonment, retreats into a fantasy world of adventure fed by television and Cold War images. Left to his own devices by his unstable mother (Aisling O'Sullivan) and his alcoholic wreck of a father (Stephen Rea), and hounded by the town busybody (a very funny Fiona Shaw), young Francie, played with astonishing vibrancy by first-time actor Eamonn Owens, spirals into madness and rage in a cycle of explosive episodes that alienate even his devoted best friend.

When the comfort Francie draws from a vision of an earthy Virgin Mary (a capriciously cast Sinead O'Connor) turns sour, the boy seals his fate with an act of breathtaking vindictiveness. For all its somber themes, there is nothing mawkish about *The Butcher Boy*. Shot in quick, febrile takes, the movie builds, with its cocksure tone and jaunty score, to a pitch of menace laced with sadness, mimicking Francie's erratic inner state and his gift for self-immolation. **ET**

**Ireland / U.S.** (Geffen, Warner Bros.) 109 min Technicolor

**Director:** Neil Jordan

**Producer:** Redmond Morris, Stephen Woolley

**Screenplay:** Neil Jordan, Pat McCabe, from novel by Pat McCabe

**Photography:** Adrian Biddle

**Music:** Elliot Goldenthal

**Cast:** Eamonn Owens, Sean McGinley, Peter Gowen, Alan Boyle, Andrew Fullerton, Fiona Shaw, Aisling O'Sullivan, Stephen Rea, John Kavanagh, Rosaleen Linehan, Anita Reeves, Gina Moxley, Niall Buggy, Ian Hart, Anne O'Neill

**Berlin International Film Festival:** Neil Jordan (Silver Bear—director), nomination (Golden Bear), Eamonn Owens (special mention)

**U.S.** (Canal+ Droits Audiovisuels, Fox Searchlight, Good Machine) 112 min Technicolor

**Director:** Ang Lee

**Producer:** Ted Hope, Ang Lee, James Schamus

**Screenplay:** James Schamus, from novel by Rick Moody

**Photography:** Frederick Elmes

**Music:** Mychael Danna

**Cast:** Kevin Kline, Joan Allen, Henry Czerny, Adam Hann-Byrd, David Krumholtz, Tobey Maguire, Christina Ricci, Jamey Sheridan, Elijah Wood, Sigourney Weaver, Kate Burton, William Cain, Michael Cumpsty, Maia Danziger, Michael Egerman

**Cannes Film Festival:** James Schamus (screenplay), Ang Lee nomination (Golden Palm)

# THE ICE STORM (1997)

Novelist Rick Moody captured the mood of the 1970s with *The Ice Storm*, a mesmerizing tale of two suburban families in emotional free fall. Making a film of the book in 1997, Taiwanese director Ang Lee elicited deftly controlled performances from a stellar ensemble cast of Kevin Kline, Joan Allen, Sigourney Weaver, Christina Ricci, Elija Wood, Adam Hann-Byrd, and Tobey Maguire. The limited plot of a story of tragedies, both small and large, is less told than felt, through the staging of a series of moody and atmospheric scenes.

Set in New Canaan, Connecticut, 1973, a suburban satellite of New York City—finally getting what the city has had for some time, a sense of being ill at ease—neighboring families the Hoods and the Carvers lead almost identical lives. The adults drink and smoke too much and talk about porn films or Watergate. Benjamin Hood (Kline) conducts a strangely dispassionate affair with Janey Carver (Weaver, wearing the wild clothing of a '70s suburban seductress), while Hood's wife (Allen, her hair in a controlled, precise bob), suspecting as much, is unable to coerce an admission of truth from her husband. Meanwhile, their children (Ricci, Hann-Byrd, and Wood) experiment with sex and booze in such a detached manner—going through the motions without emotion. Paul Hood (Maguire), the film's main and most vibrant character, is a young man who makes sense of his family in terms of the Fantastic Four, a group of dysfunctional comic superheros. The weather, a deus ex machina so disliked by certain script theorists, works as another mysterious and deadly force the two couples can only handle after it has struck.

As the director of art-house favorites *The Wedding Banquet* (1993) and *Eat Drink Man Woman* (1994), Ang Lee proved his ability to handle social and emotional subtlety with his startlingly fresh English-language debut *Sense and Sensibility* (1995). *The Ice Storm* showcases Lee's abilities even more. His unusually perceptive use of detailed period décor and wardrobe—just the right colors—sets a cool setting for heated emotions so disturbing in revelation that they can be glanced at only obliquely. **KK**

## BOOGIE NIGHTS (1997)

Risk is not exactly a quality that one tends to associate with the American cinema, yet every now and then a true daredevil comes along and shakes things up. For the 1990s odds are that the name of this savior is Paul Thomas Anderson. *Boogie Nights*, his second feature after the neglected *Hard Eight* (1996), is a mesmerizing epic of the pornography industry in the late 1970s and early 1980s. Mark Wahlberg stars as a Southern California teenager who parlays his prodigious endowment into stardom as porn icon "Dirk Diggler." Brilliantly recreating an era of bellbottoms, disco, and wretched pharmaceutical and sexual excess, Anderson shocks and surprises us with a view of the porn world that is both satiric and compassionate, yet it's no exaggeration to call *Boogie Nights* effective social history as well.

Anderson sets his movie right at the moment when celluloid pornography was beginning to give way to newer, cheapskate video formats, yet the change being chronicled here is more than merely technological. As François Truffaut himself once claimed, porn in the '70s was on the verge of becoming another genre, with movies like *Deep Throat*, *Behind the Green Door*, and *The Devil in Miss Jones* drawing enormous audiences of middle class and middlebrow hipsters. Yet along came video, and suddenly the porn star system and the cinematic fantasies it inspired were brutally replaced by an aesthetic that emphasized the ordinariness of the bodies on screen—an anticipation perhaps of what lay ahead for American TV in the 1990s.

Burt Reynolds gives his best performance maybe ever as the filmmaker/patriarch of an oddball sex-movie "family" that includes Julianne Moore, William H. Macy, John C. Reilly, Phillip Seymour Hoffman, and others who would soon be known as Anderson's stock company. Like other filmmakers of his generation, Anderson has a penchant for sweeping, seemingly impossible Steadicam shots. Yet in his work they never feel gratuitous. Rather, they serve to constantly reinforce the complexity of his storytelling, as each layer of the narrative is shown to constantly be impacting and influencing the others. **RP**

**U.S.** (Ghoulardi, Lawrence Gordon, New Line) 152m Color

**Director:** Paul Thomas Anderson

**Producer:** Paul Thomas Anderson, Lloyd Levin, John S. Lyons, Joanne Sellar

**Screenplay:** Paul Thomas Anderson

**Photography:** Robert Elswit

**Music:** Michael Penn

**Cast:** Mark Wahlberg, Burt Reynolds, Luis Guzmán, Julianne Moore, Don Cheadle, Philip Baker Hall, Heather Graham, Philip Seymour Hoffman, Thomas Jane, William H. Macy, Ricky Jay, John C. Reilly, Robert Ridgely, Alfred Molina, Nicole Ari Parker

**Oscar nomination:** Paul Thomas Anderson (screenplay), Burt Reynolds (actor in support role), Julianne Moore (actress in support role)

**U.S.** (De Fina-Cappa, Refuge, Touchstone, Walt Disney) 128m Technicolor

**Language:** English / Tibetan

**Director:** Martin Scorsese

**Producer:** Barbara De Fina

**Screenplay:** Melissa Mathison

**Photography:** Roger Deakins

**Music:** Philip Glass

**Cast:** Tenzin Thuthob Tsarong, Gyurme Tethong, Tulku Jamyang Kunga Tenzin, Tenzin Yeshi Paichang, Tencho Gyalpo, Tsewang Migyur Khangsar, Geshi Yeshi Gyatso, Sonam Phuntsok, Lobsang Samten, Gyatso Lukhang, Jigme Tsarong, Tenzin Trinley, Robert Lin, Vyas Ananthakrishnan, Kim Chan, Yoon C. Joyce, Ken Leung, Ben Wang

**Oscar nomination:** Dante Ferretti, Francesca LoSchiavo (art direction), Roger Deakins (photography), Dante Ferretti (costume), Philip Glass (music)

# KUNDUN (1997)

An Italian-American filmmaker best known for his depiction of New York's mean streets may not at first seem the most obvious choice to bring *Kundun*, the story of the Dali Lama, to the big screen. Yet ironically, as with his equally incongruous Edith Wharton adaptation *The Age of Innocence*, Martin Scorsese proves the perfect shepherd for such a difficult tale.

With his impeccable research and keen attention to detail, Scorsese pays deference to the factual nature of the story, but he approaches the epic material with the same energy and enthusiasm that he brings to his somewhat more terrestrial urban dramas. Propelled in part by a hypnotic Philip Glass score, *Kundun* follows the birth of the Dali Lama through his conflicts with the Chinese and eventually to his exile, fostering along the way an oddly appropriate Zen-like air of inevitability. Shot mostly with indigenous (albeit English-speaking) actors on location in Asia, *Kundun* features spectacular mountain-filled vistas that continually emphasize the smallness of man in the universe, even a man of such esteem as the Dali Lama. That Scorsese's film manages to maintain the modesty the Dali Lama exudes even while featuring him as the lead character in an epic movie is a great achievement in and of itself. **JKl**

**Canada** (Alliance, Canadian Film and Video Production Tax Credit, Ego Gort, Harold Greenberg Fund, TMN, Téléfilm Canada) 112 min Color

**Director:** Atom Egoyan

**Producer:** Atom Egoyan, Camelia Frieberg

**Screenplay:** Atom Egoyan, from novel by Russell Banks

**Photography:** Paul Sarossy

**Music:** Mychael Danna, Sarah Polley

**Cast:** Ian Holm, Caerthan Banks, Sarah Polley, Tom McCamus, Gabrielle Rose, Alberta Watson, Maury Chaykin, Stephanie Morgenstern, Kirsten Kieferle, Arsinée Khanjian

**Oscar nomination:** Atom Egoyan (director), Atom Egoyan (screenplay)

**Cannes Film Festival:** Atom Egoyan (FIPRESCI award), (grand prize of the jury), (prize of the ecumenical jury), nomination (Golden Palm)

# THE SWEET HEREAFTER (1997)

Truly the exception to the rule when it comes to literary adaptations, *The Sweet Hereafter* handles author Russell Banks's novel so intelligently that even Banks has conceded the film improves on the book. Toning down his trademark diced-up time lines and fascination with multimedia, director Atom Egoyan creates a stunningly direct, almost fablelike exploration of loss. In fact, Egoyan brilliantly incorporates "The Pied Piper of Hamlin" into his film, eventually lending the wrenching events a reflective and somber thematic unity.

When a school bus crashes and sinks below the ice, killing most of its young passengers, the residents of a small town must find ways to deal with issues of grief, exacerbated by the presence of an outsider lawyer (Ian Holm) who believes only the assignation of blame can alleviate the town's feelings of collective guilt. Egoyan reveals the tragedy itself only in bits and pieces, and as the events of that day grow clearer and clearer, so does the director's depiction of the heartbreaking accident. As Holm's drive for financial and emotional reward draws to a close, the testimony of one survivor (Sarah Polley) becomes more and more integral to his case, but he soon learns that in the face of unthinkable despair, sometimes honesty comes second to reconciliation. **JKl**

# FUNNY GAMES (1997)

In this brutal and provocative "home invasion" movie—a subgenre traceable as far back as D.W. Griffith and familiar today from such films as *A Clockwork Orange* (1971), *Straw Dogs* (1971), and *Panic Room* (2002)—Michael Haneke pushes viewers to the limit, forcing us to contemplate the senselessness of random violence, as well as our seemingly ceaseless fascination with watching it on-screen.

A well-to-do family of three go on vacation to their lakeside cottage. Shortly after their arrival, a chubby, clean-cut young man (Frank Giering) knocks on the door, politely asking to borrow an egg. He is quickly joined by a thinner and more refined companion (Arno Frisch, star of Haneke's earlier, equally troubling *Benny's Video* [1992]). Initially fooled by the young men's polished appearance and their claim to be friends of the neighboring family, wife Anna (Susanne Lothar) allows them into the house. Once inside, however, the boys proceed to disable the husband (Ulrich Mühe), force Anna to strip, and shoot the couple's young son (Stefan Clapczynski).

While the sadistic teens play not-so-funny games with their victims—all of whom end up dead by the end—the director plays games with his audience: At one point, after Anna manages to kill one of her captors, Haneke interrupts the diegesis, allowing the boy's friend to "rewind" the film, thereby saving his partner in crime. There is no happy ending here, only troubling questions and the inevitability of future mayhem. **SJS**

**Austria** (Wega) Color 108m
**Language:** German / French
**Director:** Michael Haneke
**Producer:** Veit Heiduschka
**Screenplay:** Michael Haneke
**Photography:** Jürgen Jürges
**Nonoriginal Music:** Georg Friedrich Händel, Pietro Mascagni, Wolfgang Amadeus Mozart
**Cast:** Susanne Lothar, Ulrich Mühe, Arno Frisch, Frank Giering, Stefan Clapczynski, Doris Kunstmann, Christoph Bantzer, Wolfgang Glück, Susanne Meneghel, Monika Zallinger
**Cannes Film Festival:** Michael Haneke nomination (Golden Palm)

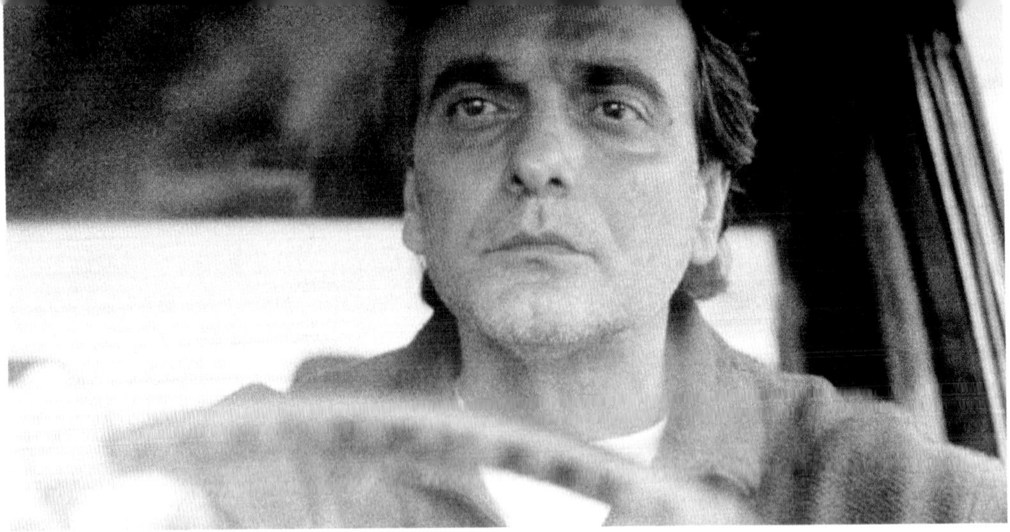

France / Iran (Abbas Kiarostami, CiBy 2000) 95m Color

**Language:** Farsi

**Director:** Abbas Kiarostami

**Producer:** Abbas Kiarostami

**Screenplay:** Abbas Kiarostami

**Photography:** Homayun Payvar

**Cast:** Homayon Ershadi, Abdolrahman Bagheri, Afshin Khorshid Bakhtiari, Safar Ali Moradi, Mir Hossein Noori

**Cannes Film Festival:** Abbas Kiarostami (Golden Palm), tied with *Unagi*

# TA'M E GUILASS (1997)
## TASTE OF CHERRY

A middle-aged man (Homayon Ershadi) who is contemplating suicide drives around the hilly, dusty outskirts of Tehran, trying to find someone who will bury him if he succeeds and retrieve him if he fails. This minimalist yet powerful and life-enhancing feature by Abbas Kiarostami never explains why the man wants to end his life, and is even inconclusive about whether or not he succeeds. Yet every moment in his daylong odyssey carries a great deal of poignancy and philosophical weight. *Taste of Cherry* has remained in many ways Kiarostami's most controversial film ever since it shared the 1997 *Palm d'or* at Cannes with Shohei Imamura's *The Eel*. In part this is because the film entrusts so much of its meaning and power to the audience and the nature of its own investment in what it's watching. Like many of Kiarostami's other films, it is centered around the simultaneously private and public experience of a character in a car giving rides to others. And just as the experience of watching a movie in a theater combines private responses with public reactions, this is a film that speaks to both of these situations. We attend to *Taste of Cherry* alone, and with others.

Kiarostami—working without a script, yet constructing his story basically out of dialogues taking place in a car—filmed each of his actors separately while himself occupying either the driver's seat or the passenger's seat, provoking the nonprofessional actors' lines as if interviewing them. Thus the subject of isolation that lies at the heart of *Taste of Cherry* is integral to the way it was filmed. Does one identify with the unhappy hero, with the Iranian soldier, Afghan seminarian, and Turkish taxidermist he converses with, or with all four?

Kiarostami is a master at filming landscapes and constructing parable-like narratives whose missing pieces solicit the viewer's active imagination. This extends even beyond the film's plot and characters to its surprisingly cheerful, self-referential coda. An epilogue centered on camaraderie that follows this story about profound isolation radiates with wonder and euphoria. **JRos**

# ABRE LOS OJOS (1997)
## OPEN YOUR EYES

**Spain / France / Italy** (Escorpión, Alain Sarde, Lucky Red, Sogetel) 117m Color

**Language:** Spanish

**Director:** Alejandro Amenábar

**Producer:** Fernando Bovaira, José Luis Cuerda

**Screenplay:** Alejandro Amenábar, Mateo Gil

**Photography:** Hans Burman

**Music:** Alejandro Amenábar, Mariano Marín

**Cast:** Eduardo Noriega, Penélope Cruz, Chete Lera, Fele Martínez, Najwa Nimri, Gérard Barray, Jorge de Juan, Miguel Palenzuela, Pedro Miguel Martínez, Ion Gabella, Joserra Cadiñanos, Tristán Ulloa, Pepe Navarro, Jaro, Walter Prieto.

**Berlin International Film Festival:** Alejandro Amenábar (C.I.C.A.E. Award—Panorama honorable mention—direction).

Alejandro Amenábar's *Open Your Eyes* may be best known as the Spanish film Cameron Crowe remade with Tom Cruise as *Vanilla Sky* (2001), but it deserves to be seen for the virtuoso piece and true original it is. Intrigued with cryogenics and virtual reality, Amenábar has said he intended to make a "realistic" science-fiction movie out of mere "camera angles" instead of mind-blowing special effects. But *Open Your Eyes* transcends such easy classification unless viewed as a precursor to such films as *eXistenZ* (1999), *The Matrix* (1999), *Fight Club* (1999), *The Sixth Sense* (1999), *Memento* (2000), and *Mulholland Dr.* (2001)—dark films that, constructed like paranoia-inducing puzzles, peel away in layers, present identity as performance or virtual experience, question the nature of time and reality, and must be seen at least twice.

The film opens as narcissistic, well-off César (Eduardo Noriega) ditches his latest one-night stand, meets his "dream girl" Sophia (Penélope Cruz), and betrays his best friend the night before he awakens, after a hideously disfiguring automobile accident, in a psychiatric prison, accused of murder. There, in what for a time seems to be reality, he projects a present and future out of remnants of his past life and previously-viewed films. Breaking down, he becomes unable to distinguish life from dream—that is, until the labyrinthine series of twists and revelations leading to the conclusion, in which the "reality" of everything that has gone before is chillingly undermined. **LB**

# MAT I SYN (1997)
## MOTHER AND SON

**Germany / Russia** (Zero, O-Film, Severnij Fund) 73m Color

**Language:** Russian

**Director:** Aleksandr Sokurov

**Producer:** Aleksandr Golutva, Thomas Kufus

**Screenplay:** Yuri Arabov

**Photography:** Aleksei Fyodorov

**Music:** Mikhail Ivanovich, Otmar Nussio

**Cast:** Aleksei Ananishnov, Gudrun Geyer

Organized around two characters, very little dialogue, long takes, and frequent cuts between scenes shot with anamorphic and then conforming lenses, Aleksandr Sokurov's *Mother and Son* is a beautiful and haunting visual essay masquerading as a feature film. Nominally set in the 20th century, judging by a steam locomotive and the two characters' costumes, the picture concerns an ailing Mother (Gudrun Geyer) and her doting Son (Aleksei Ananishnov). No names are exchanged and little other background information is given. Instead the piece builds through careful observation to an ever-so-brief reminiscence about familial sympathy.

An ailing heart is what threatens the chaste love affair during Mother's last day alive, often in the arms of Son. Together they pause for the mysteries of creation, his pain stemming from apathy and hers born from being afraid to die. Between them are hinted the enduring connections of blood, first mother to son, then son to mother. Yet the eerie quality of the film—its lasting impression—is of landscapes that are as isolating as they are breathtaking.

Not an easy allegory binding flora and fauna to family dynamics, but it's nonetheless a tone poem with loneliness and loss as themes around the edges of every frame. **GC-Q**

## TITANIC (1997)

The story behind director James Cameron's labor of love is almost more dramatic than the tale that unfolds on screen. With a reported budget of over $200 million, even before its release *Titanic* was given the dubious honor of being the most expensive production of all time. Much of the cost went to a six-month shoot in Mexico involving a 775-foot replica of the famous boat, which sank when it hit an iceberg back in 1912. It was a shoot dogged with problems—including delays to filming when the cast and crew were poisoned by PCP laced food in Nova Scotia. Rumors that Cameron was a crazed perfectionist emerged. His attention to detail included hiring the original companies that provided the real Titanic's furnishings as supervisors so that every chandelier and plate was a perfect replica. But, following the film's stupendous box-office success (more than $1 billion worldwide) and the most Academy Awards (11) since Ben-Hur (1959), he was rechristened a genius, and is now deservedly considered one of the most successful directors of all time.

Cameron's vision is half *Poseidon Adventure* and half *Love Boat*, as both romance and deep-sea disaster are explored in equal measure. Kate Winslet stars as Rose, the young socialite who is to marry dastardly Cal (Billy Zane) but falls for steerage passenger Jack (Leonardo DiCaprio) just before the world's most famous ship plunges into its watery grave. Their forbidden romance gives the movie its heart. Cameron piles on the special effects to truly convey the terror that is to come, forcing his actors to spend days in freezing cold water filming the scary scenes when the supposedly "unsinkable" ship begins to sink and then horrifically splits in half.

A blockbuster if ever there was one, *Titanic* made a superstar/teen heartthrob of DiCaprio. The film boasts one of the biggest-selling soundtracks of all time—a number one hit for Celine Dion with the theme "My Heart Will Go On." In terms of production size and sheer epic scale, *Titanic* remains one of the most impressive films of all time. **JB**

**U.S.** (Fox, Lightstorm, Paramount) 194 min Color

**Language:** English / French / German / Swedish

**Director:** James Cameron

**Producer:** James Cameron, Jon Landau

**Screenplay:** James Cameron

**Photography:** Russell Carpenter

**Music:** James Horner

**Cast:** Leonardo DiCaprio, Kate Winslet, Billy Zane, Kathy Bates, Bill Paxton, Gloria Stuart, Frances Fisher, Bernard Hill, Jonathan Hyde, David Warner, Victor Garber, Danny Nucci, Lewis Abernathy, Suzy Amis, Nicholas Cascone

**Oscar:** James Cameron, Jon Landau (best picture), James Cameron (director), Peter Lamont, Michael Ford (art direction), Russell Carpenter (photography), Deborah Lynn Scott (costume), Tom Bellfort, Christopher Boyes (special sound effects), Robert Legato, Mark A. Lasoff, Thomas L. Fisher, Michael Kanfer (special visual effects), Conrad Buff, James Cameron, Richard A. Harris (editing), James Horner (music), James Horner, Will Jennings (song), Gary Rydstrom, Tom Johnson, Gary Summers, Mark Ulano (sound)

**Oscar nomination:** Kate Winslet (actress), Gloria Stuart (actress in support role), Tina Earnshaw, Greg Cannom, Simon Thompson (makeup)

# TETSUO (1998)

An exceptionally kinky and violent Japanese experimental feature by Shinya Tsukamoto, *Tetsuo* is a prime candidate for midnight cult status. The dialogue is minimal, but the principal meanings are clear enough, in a highly fragmented, frequently pixilated account of a man and woman, both partially transformed into metal, copulating and mutilating each other with passion and energy. Over the top in every respect, basically a surreal heavy-metal fantasy like the *Mad Max* pictures, with gory, slimy textures that recall David Lynch's *Eraserhead* (1977), *Tetsuo* contains enough frenetic motion that you certainly won't be bored. Though you may find yourself worn out before the 67 minutes are over.

This is obviously not for every taste—but if you like it, there's a fair chance you'll like it a lot. Japanese critics have reportedly described Tsukamoto as Japan's answer to Sam Raimi, David Cronenberg, and David Lynch. Asian film critic Tony Rayns has aptly noted that the movie "springs from all the fantasy entertainment Japanese kids grow up with: Godzilla movies, sci-fi animation, manga comic strips and 'hardcore' rock music," despite the relatively grown-up fantasies that Tsukamoto makes out of them. Shortly thereafter, he turned out a "sequel" called *Tetsuo II: Body Hammer* that was actually closer to a color remake—more conventional in terms of plot and consequently less interesting and memorable. **JRos**

**Japan** (JHV, K2 Spirit, Kaijyu Theater, SEN) 67m BW
**Language:** Japanese
**Director:** Shinya Tsukamoto
**Producer:** Shinya Tsukamoto
**Screenplay:** Shinya Tsukamoto
**Photography:** Kei Fujiwara, Shinya Tsukamoto
**Music:** Chu Ishikawa
**Cast:** Tomorowo Taguchi, Kei Fujiwara, Nobu Kanaoka, Renji Ishibashi, Naomasa Musaka, Shinya Tsukamoto

# FESTEN (1998)
## THE CELEBRATION

On balance, "Dogma 95"—a Danish film manifesto that calls for location shooting, handheld cameras, direct sound, and an avoidance of special effects—probably has more significance as a highly successful publicity stunt than as an ideological breakthrough, judging especially from the first two features that emerged under its ground rules, Lars von Trier's *The Idiots* (1988) and Thomas Vinterberg's *The Celebration*. Both films, in fact, are apparent acts of rebellion and daring that are virtually defined by their middle-class assumptions and dogged apoliticism. Vinterberg's work, which is even more conventional in inspiration than von Trier's—think Ibsen, Strindberg, Bergman—is genuinely explosive and powerfully executed.

Shot with the smallest and lightest digital video camera then available, *The Celebration* chronicles the acrimonious and violent family battles that ensue at a country manor house where the 60th birthday of the family patriarch is being observed, not long after the eldest son's twin sister has committed suicide. The extreme forms of aggressive behavior that emerge from the onset and Vinterberg's jagged style of crosscutting disguise the fact that this is basically a very well written, acted, and directed piece of psychodrama rather than the revolutionary experiment it was proclaimed to be. But the sheer dramatic power derived from the gradual unveiling of family secrets eventually and justifiably wins one over. **JRos**

**Denmark** (DR, Nimbus Film, SVT Drama) 105m Color
**Language:** Danish / German / English
**Director:** Thomas Vinterberg
**Producer:** Birgitte Hald
**Screenplay:** Thomas Vinterberg, Thomas Vinterberg, Mogens Rukov
**Photography:** Anthony Dod Mantle
**Music:** Lars Bo Jensen
**Cast:** Ulrich Thomsen, Henning Moritzen, Thomas Bo Larsen, Paprika Steen, Birthe Neumann, Trine Dyrholm, Helle Dolleris, Therese Glahn, Klaus Bondam, Bjarne Henriksen, Gbatokai Dakinah, Lasse Lunderskov, Lars Brygmann, Lene Laub Oksen, Linda Laursen
**Cannes Film Festival:** Thomas Vinterberg (jury prize), tied with *La Classe de neige*, nomination (Golden Palm)

**U.S.** (Amblin, DreamWorks, Mark Gordon, Mutual, Paramount) 170m Technicolor

**Language:** Czech / English / French / German

**Director:** Steven Spielberg

**Producer:** Ian Bryce, Mark Gordon, Gary Levinsohn, Steven Spielberg

**Screenplay:** Robert Rodat

**Photography:** Janusz Kaminski

**Music:** John Williams

**Cast:** Tom Hanks, Edward Burns, Tom Sizemore, Matt Damon, Jeremy Davies, Adam Goldberg, Barry Pepper, Giovanni Ribisi, Vin Diesel, Ted Danson, Max Martini, Dylan Bruno, Joerg Stadler, Paul Giamatti, Dennis Farina

**Oscar:** Steven Spielberg (director), Janusz Kaminski (photography), Gary Rydstrom, Richard Hymns (special sound effects), Michael Kahn (editing), Gary Rydstrom, Gary Summers, Andy Nelson, Ron Judkins (sound)

**Oscar nomination:** Steven Spielberg, Ian Bryce, Mark Gordon, Gary Levinsohn (best picture), Robert Rodat (screenplay), Tom Hanks (actor), Thomas E. Sanders, Lisa Dean (art direction), Lois Burwell, Conor O'Sullivan, Daniel C. Striepeke (makeup), John Williams (music)

# SAVING PRIVATE RYAN (1998)

From his very first works, Steven Spielberg displayed an almost preternatural gift for filmmaking and specifically the machinations of suspense and special effects, a skill that movie audiences responded to in droves. But the massive success of such early films as *Jaws* (1975) and *Close Encounters of the Third Kind* (1977)—which helped congeal the blockbuster mentality of modern Hollywood—in some ways hurt Spielberg's reputation. Craving respect, he knew his movies would always be dismissed as merely popular entertainment and technical exercises.

Spielberg nonetheless tried to broaden his range with such mature experiments as *The Color Purple* (1985) and *Empire of the Sun* (1987), but it wasn't until the harrowing Holocaust film *Schindler's List* (1993) that he finally made a movie that satisfied both the critics and the public. With the exception of his two thrill-ride *Jurassic Park* (1993, 1997) films, Spielberg has remained more or less in serious mode ever since.

*Saving Private Ryan* introduced something new to the director's vocabulary: A visceral, violent intensity. Spielberg had dealt with violence before, of course, but typically it was either cartoonish or carefully moderated (and then milked) as a dramatic beat punctuating moments of maximum horror. The opening battle sequence of *Saving Private Ryan*, however, is absolutely relentless. No sooner have American boats landed on the beaches of Normandy, than young men are mowed down by incessant bursts of machine-gun fire, the bullets piercing their useless helmets with a sickening "ping." And it doesn't stop there. Soldiers are blown to bits. Body parts fly through the air and litter the ground. The sea turns a squeamish blood red. The camera lurches wildly, the desaturated film stock the color of death. The "new" Spielberg takes no prisoners.

Admittedly, the Spielberg of old can't always resist falling back on unabashed sentimentality. A pair of flimsy bookends start and end the film on purely manipulative notes, and Spielberg encourages his composer of choice John Williams to indulge in his worst heartstring-tugging tendencies. More uncomfortably, the same techniques Spielberg uses to depict the horrors of the war in his truly awe-inspiring opening battle scene he later enlists to propel the more traditional good-versus-evil conflict of the conclusion.

But the familiar good guy/bad guy dichotomy actually twists the antiwar message into something more challenging. War is hell, Spielberg acknowledges, except when you're winning, since victory is ultimately what accords the right to dictate the rules of morality. *Saving Private Ryan* contains just enough darkness lurking in the fog of war to stave off accusations it supports blind patriotism. Looking over thousands of graves, a soldier asks of his wife, "Was I a good man?" That's a more ambiguous way of asking not just "was it worth it?" but "was it justified?" These are questions that no doubt haunt all those left standing when the shooting stops, surveying the death and destruction around them wrought for even the noblest of purposes. **JKl**

**U.S.** (CFP, Lions Gate, Muse) 110m Color

**Director:** Vincent Gallo

**Producer:** Chris Hanley

**Screenplay:** Vincent Gallo, Alison Bagnall

**Photography:** Lance Acord

**Music:** Vincent Gallo

**Cast:** Vincent Gallo, Christina Ricci, Ben Gazzara, Mickey Rourke, Rosanna Arquette, Jan-Michael Vincent, Anjelica Huston, Kevin Pollak, Alex Karras, John Sansone, Manny Fried, John Rummel, Bob Wahl, Penny Wolfgang, Anthony Mydcarz

# BUFFALO 66 (1998)

Actor Vincent Gallo (*Palookaville*, *The Funeral*) wrote, directed, and stars in this independent comic drama, which he has described as his masterpiece—an arrogant statement, perhaps, but one that's not too far from the truth. He stars as Billy, a sleazy ex-con who kidnaps a feisty young girl (Christina Ricci, in tight skirt and fairy-tale slippers) and gets her to pretend she's his loving wife on a visit to his wacked-out parents (Anjelica Huston and Ben Gazzara), who are unaware he's been away in jail. Billy has told them his absence was because he was working as an undercover operative for the government.

Wonderfully quirky stuff, this low-budget bizarre romance boasts suitably eccentric performances from the four leads (Gazzara as Gallo's pervy dad deserves a special mention, while Huston is a hoot as his football-obsessed wife), and some neat cameos from Mickey Rourke, Jan-Michael Vincent, and Rosanna Arquette. Gallo, meanwhile, multitasks superbly (he even wrote the film's music and used his parents' Buffalo home as the main location), delivering an ironic look at relationships and disillusionment with a variety of visual styles and images. **JB**

**G.B.** (Handmade, PolyGram, SKA, Steve Tisch, Summit) 105m Color

**Director:** Guy Ritchie

**Producer:** Matthew Vaughn

**Screenplay:** Guy Ritchie

**Photography:** Tim Maurice-Jones

**Music:** David A. Hughes, John Murphy

**Cast:** Jason Flemyng, Dexter Fletcher, Nick Moran, Jason Statham, Steven Mackintosh, Nicholas Rowe, Nick Marcq, Charles Forbes, Vinnie Jones, Lenny McLean, Peter McNicholl, P.H. Moriarty, Frank Harper, Steve Sweeney, Huggy Leaver

# LOCK, STOCK AND TWO SMOKING BARRELS (1998)

A sharply funny British gangster flick, *Lock, Stock and Two Smoking Barrels* showcased the talents of debut writer/director Guy Ritchie and his young British cast, which includes Nick Moran, Jason Flemyng, and, in a convincing and thoroughly enjoyable performance, footballer-turned-actor Vinnie Jones.

Mates Tom (Flemyng), Bacon (Jason Statham), Soap (Dexter Fletcher), and Eddy (Moran) find themselves up to their necks in trouble after they invest their hard-earned cash into raising a £100,000 stake for a card game, only for hotshot card player Eddy to be set up to lose by the game's host Hatchet Harry (P.H. Moriarty). Leaving the game owing Harry a half million quid, Eddy has a week to raise the money before he and his pals start losing fingers, with the only alternative being that Harry will accept Eddy's dad's (a surprisingly believable turn from musician/actor Sting) bar to cancel the debt.

Throw in confusion over a pair of antique guns, debt collector Big Chris (Jones), violent thugs, henchmen, and a bizarre scheme for the boys to get rich quick involving a marijuana den, and you have a smartly paced, sharply scripted, and wittily played—if occasionally over-the-top—drama boosted by an excellent soundtrack. **JB**

# LOLA RENNT (1998)
## RUN LOLA RUN

A visually inventive, kinetically exciting movie, Tom Tykwer's *Run Lola Run* is an exercise in surprises, beginning right from the opening credits where a crowd scene turns into an aerial shot from above in which the assembled people spell out the movie's title.

The plot itself is simple—young, shockingly flame-haired Lola (Franke Potente) receives a telephone call from her boyfriend Manni (Moritz Bleibtreu). Manni explains that he was supposed to deliver 100,000 deutschemarks to a gangster, but he left the bag containing the loot on the subway. He has 20 minutes to find the money before the bad guys will kill him, so his plan is to rob a bank—Lola's is to find the money some other way, and the film follows her high-speed adventure to save Manni as the minutes tick away.

It's the way young German director Tykwer shows us Lola's mission that is different and inventive. Her 20-minute story is told three different times, each subtly different in a manner that delivers three different outcomes. Twyker uses animation, camera tricks, color and black-and-white film, music video effects, and instant replays to tell each adventure as Lola runs, Manni runs, and the film becomes a human obstacle course they both have to carefully maneuver in order to survive.

Potente, who would go on to appear alongside Matt Damon in the Hollywood blockbuster *The Bourne Identity* (2002), provides a striking cinematic image as she runs down the movie's various streets and avenues, arms pumping and distinctive red hair flying, but she also delivers a warm, more in-depth performance in scenes such as one between Lola and her wealthy father (Herbert Knaup), whom she visits asking for money only to learn that he plans to leave her mother and marry his mistress.

An interesting, unusual filmmaking experiment that has humor, breathless excitement, and a tremendous energy, all tightly packaged into an MTV-generation movie by the fresh talent of its writer-director. **JB**

**Germany** (Bavaria Film, German Independents, WDR, X-Filme, arte) 81m Color

**Language:** German

**Director:** Tom Tykwer

**Producer:** Stefan Arndt

**Screenplay:** Tom Tykwer

**Photography:** Frank Griebe

**Music:** Reinhold Heil, Johnny Klimek, Franka Potente, Tom Tykwer

**Cast:** Franka Potente, Moritz Bleibtreu, Herbert Knaup, Nina Petri, Armin Rohde, Joachim Król, Ludger Pistor, Suzanne von Borsody, Sebastian Schipper, Julia Lindig, Lars Rudolph, Andreas Petri, Klaus Müller, Utz Krause, Beate Finckh

**Venice Film Festival:** Tom Tykwer nomination (Golden Lion)

## RUSHMORE (1998)

**U.S.** (American Empirical, Touchstone) 93m Color
**Director:** Wes Anderson
**Producer:** Barry Mendel, Paul Schiff
**Screenplay:** Wes Anderson, Owen Wilson
**Photography:** Robert D. Yeoman
**Music:** Mark Mothersbaugh
**Cast:** Jason Schwartzman, Bill Murray, Olivia Williams, Seymour Cassel, Brian Cox, Mason Gamble, Sara Tanaka, Stephen McCole, Connie Nielsen, Luke Wilson, Dipak Pallana, Andrew Wilson, Marietta Marich, Ronnie McCawley, Keith McCawley

When director Wes Anderson and his cowriter Owen Wilson carved a new niche with the 1996 film *Bottle Rocket*, it single-handedly revived the then-exhausted realm of low-budget independent American comedies. Their second entry in this genre, the adorably miserable *Rushmore*, takes another look at the losers and oddballs they so adore.

Max Fischer (played by Jason Schwartzman, the son of Talia Shire and nephew to Frances Ford Coppola) is a bespectacled, intellectual geek. As a scholarship student at Rushmore Academy he is profoundly unpopular. Verging on flunking out, he manages to be president of virtually every extracurricular activity there is on campus. Doomed by his social skills, he nevertheless falls for a beautiful teacher (Olivia Williams) and finds a mentor in wealthy if depressed Herman J. Blume (Bill Murray). This slow turn-of-the-screwball comedy is Murray's finest dramatic hour, allowing him at last to be profound, wounded, and funny, all at the same time. And the soundtrack of mostly 1960s rock music gives *Rushmore* a sense of being somewhere other than in its obviously contemporary setting. **KK**

## PI (1998)

**U.S.** (Harvest, Plantain, Protozoa, Truth and Soul) 84m BW
**Director:** Darren Aronofsky
**Producer:** Eric Watson
**Screenplay:** Darren Aronofsky, Sean Gullette, Eric Watson
**Photography:** Matthew Libatique
**Music:** Clint Mansell
**Cast:** Sean Gullette, Mark Margolis, Ben Shenkman, Pamela Hart, Stephen Pearlman, Samia Shoaib, Ajay Naidu, Kristyn Mae-Anne Lao, Espher Lao Nieves, Joanne Gordon, Lauren Fox, Stanley Herman, Clint Mansell, Tom Tumminello, Ari Handel

Writer/director Darren Aronofsky's explosive debut comes across like David Lynch's *Eraserhead* reworked by cyberpunk author William Gibson. Sean Gullette plays a mathematical genius beset by debilitating headaches and an insatiable quest for a numerical series that links everything in the world, from the stock market to The Bible. After a breakthrough that costs him his homemade computer, Gullette is approached by members of a radical Jewish Kabbalah sect, as well as armed Wall Street goons, both after the mysterious numbers in his head. As Gullette's headaches worsen, his quest becomes more and more maddening. But what does this numerical code of the universe mean, and why are so many people interested in it?

Strikingly shot in high-contrast black and white with various novel and visceral camera techniques, *Pi* evokes the paranoia of Poe and Kafka within the fuzzy framework of science fiction. Aronofsky lets most of the questions hang until the film's conclusion, and keeping the audience in the dark is just another way to heighten the chaotic, exhilarating, frequently imposing mood of the picture. His ability to capture the rush and confusion of racing down a time line toward infinity, only to suddenly slam into a dead end, makes for impressive and occasionally disturbing stuff. **JKl**

# HAPPINESS (1998)

Few filmmakers can invoke so many varied emotional responses—laughter, disgust, sympathy, just to name a few—from their audiences as contemporary American independent filmmaker Todd Solondz with his highly controversial *Happiness*. There is no way to concisely sum up the happenings of this film, which involves a first-rate ensemble cast including audacious performances by Dylan Baker, Philip Seymour Hoffman, Ben Gazzara, Lara Flynn Boyle, Camryn Manheim, and Jon Lovitz. Suffice it to say that *Happiness* is about relationships—all of them painfully flawed—and takes us into territory few filmmakers dare to (or want to) brave. One of the picture's most memorable scenes depicts a father answering, in utterly frank and matter-of-fact terms, questions from his young son about his acts of pederasty.

*Happiness* is perhaps best described as an indictment of the modern American family and suburban living (both on-screen and off), suggesting that perversion lurks around every corner, inside every family's four walls. Solondz, who is evolving into a postmodern and more disturbed Woody Allen, has taken this perhaps exaggerated notion as his cinematic credo; he succeeds, in part, because he refuses to allow his flawed characters to spin off into the realm of one-dimensionality. **MO**

**U.S.** (Good Machine, Killer) 134m Color

**Language:** English / Russian

**Director:** Todd Solondz

**Producer:** Ted Hope, Christine Vachon

**Screenplay:** Todd Solondz

**Photography:** Maryse Alberti

**Music:** Robbie Kondor

**Cast:** Jane Adams, Jon Lovitz, Philip Seymour Hoffman, Dylan Baker, Lara Flynn Boyle, Justin Elvin, Cynthia Stevenson, Lila Glantzman-Leib, Gerry Becker, Rufus Read, Louise Lasser, Ben Gazzara, Camryn Manheim, Arthur J. Nascarella, Molly Shannon

**Cannes Film Festival:** Todd Solondz (FIPRESCI award—parallel sections)

**Canada / U.S.** (Fox 2000, Geisler-Roberdeau, Phoenix) 170m Color

**Director:** Terrence Malick

**Producer:** Robert Michael Geisler, Grant Hill, John Roberdeau

**Screenplay:** Terrence Malick, from novel by James Jones

**Photography:** John Toll

**Music:** Hans Zimmer

**Cast:** Sean Penn, Adrien Brody, James Caviezel, Ben Chaplin, George Clooney, John Cusack, Woody Harrelson, Elias Koteas, Jared Leto, Dash Mihok, Tim Blake Nelson, Nick Nolte, John C. Reilly, Larry Romano, John Savage.

**Oscar nomination:** Robert Michael Geisler, John Roberdeau, Grant Hill (best picture), Terrence Malick (director), Terrence Malick (screenplay), John Toll (photography), Billy Weber, Leslie Jones, Saar Klein (editing), Hans Zimmer (music), Andy Nelson, Anna Behlmer, Paul Brincat (sound)

**Berlin International Film Festival:** Terrence Malick (Golden Bear), 3rd place (reader jury of the Berliner Morgenpost), John Toll (honorable mention)

# THE THIN RED LINE (1998)

After making the highly acclaimed and influential *Badlands* (1973) and *Days of Heaven* (1978), Terrence Malick did something unheard of for a prominent director: He vanished without a trace. Rumors abounded: Malick was living life as a recluse in some remote locale. Or maybe he was hiking across Texas, bird watching. Wherever he disappeared to, word of his late 1990s return to filmmaking came just as suddenly. Details of Malick's new project were closely guarded and sketchy at best, but two things were clear: it was an adaptation of James Jones's World War II novel *The Thin Red Line*, and it reportedly featured a massive cast of several prominent actors and promising newcomers alike.

Both rumors proved correct, but the film still surprised many as unexpected. Especially coming after Steven Spielberg's own World War II drama *Saving Private Ryan* (1998), Malick's *The Thin Red Line* seemed particularly cerebral. The two films couldn't have been more different, and the reactions they provoked reflected those discrepancies. Audiences left visceral *Saving Private Ryan* shaken to the core. Audiences left the more philosophical *The Thin Red Line* scratching their heads.

Yet there's no question which film leaves the stronger impression. *The Thin Red Line* addresses the madness of war from a distinctly theoretical, even theological vantage. War, the film seems to say, is more than just a conflict between two groups of men. War is depicted in *The Thin Red Line* as an affront to nature, and in turn an affront to God himself.

Malick's film delves into the collective consciousness of the troops as it struggles to reconcile the fragility of life with the recklessness of their behavior. Daringly, *The Thin Red Line* flits from soldier to soldier, getting into their heads and amplifying their thoughts as part of an ongoing internal dialogue, but otherwise retaining a sense of anonymity among the soldiers.

The men are highly aware of the exotic world around them and in particular its beauty: When the film begins, one soldier (Jim Caviezel) has gone AWOL, living a life of simplicity and innocence among a South Pacific tribe until his Eden-like existence is disrupted. Even as the soldiers slink through the forest, Malick can't resist training his camera on the colorful wildlife around them, or capturing the light streaming through the leaves of the towering trees. It's as if God and all of his creatures are watching this strange species at work destroying all that is good in the world, and wondering what free will hath wrought.

Several performances do stick out in the film—Elias Koteas's sensitive Captain; Nick Nolte's callous, career-minded colonel; Sean Penn's cynical Sergeant—but Malick keeps the narrative elliptical. *The Thin Red Line* has no real beginning or end, and although it is punctuated by dramatic beats and thrilling battle scenes, they serve as interruptions of no less a profound meditation than Malick's quest for the meaning of life. **JKl**

France / Italy / Denmark / Netherlands (3 Emme, Argus, CoBo Fund, DR, Jennie Cinematografica, La Sept, Canal+, Liberator, Nordic Film & TV Fund, October, PGO TV Holland, Rai, SVT, VPRO TV, Zentropa, ZDF, arte) 117m Color

**Language:** Danish

**Director:** Lars von Trier

**Producer:** Vibeke Windeløv

**Screenplay:** Lars von Trier

**Photography:** Casper Holm, Jesper Jargil, Kristoffer Nyholm, Lars von Trier

**Cast:** Bodil Jørgensen, Jens Albinus, Anne Louise Hassing, Troels Lyby, Nikolaj Lie Kaas, Louise Mieritz, Henrik Prip, Luis Mesonero, Knud Romer Jørgensen, Trine Michelsen, Anne-Grethe Bjarup Riis, Paprika Steen, Erik Wedersøe, Michael Moritzen, Anders Hove

**Cannes Film Festival:** Lars von Trier nomination (Golden Palm)

# IDIOTERNE (1998)

## THE IDIOTS

*The Idiots* is a film for anyone who's ever been caught in the middle of a joke by an authority figure declaring "That's not funny, that's sick!". Von Trier's low-budget, mostly improvised comedy-drama follows a group of intelligent, middle-class people who live in a hippie-ish commune and engage in "spassing," pretending in public to be mentally disabled. Karen (Bodil Jørgensen)—a meek, obviously traumatized woman—falls in with the spassers, not realizing that they are faking, then becomes the most devoted seeker of her "inner idiot."

Fragmentary glimpses reveal pranks, complicated interrelationships, parties, and arguments, interspersed with talking-head interviews in which the protagonists seem as puzzled as anyone else by what they have got into. *The Idiots* is full of funny, disturbing, even suspenseful scenes: One spasser turning up at a friend's ad agency and acting mentally challenged while posing as an important client; a spasser left alone with a biker gang who will certainly beat him if they catch on that they're being set up; a visit to Karen's home that reveals how near the edge she really is. The thesis is that you really are what you pretend to be, as the unleashed inner idiots of all the characters reflect deeper, sometimes disturbing truths about them. **KN**

**France** (CNC, Canal+, Monteurs, Procirep, Zeie, Zélie, arte) 112m Color

**Language:** French

**Director:** Philippe Grandrieux

**Producer:** Catherine Jacques

**Screenplay:** Sophie Fillières, Philippe Grandrieux, Pierre Hodgson

**Photography:** Sabine Lancelin

**Music:** Alan Vega

**Cast:** Marc Barbé, Elina Löwensohn, Géraldine Voillat, Coralie, Maxime Mazzolini, Alexandra Noël, Annick Lemonnier, Sadija Sada Sarcevic, Lea Civello, Astrid Combes, Sylvie Granato, Tony Baillargeat, Marc Berman, Martine Vandeville, Antoine Debilly

# SOMBRE (1998)

*Sombre* lives up to its name, the screen shrouded for much of the time in a darkness that defies the viewer to scan its depths. It is morally dark too, leaving us with a feeling of disturbance and unease, and an obscure sense of having watched something we should not have. Philippe Grandrieux's first cinema feature—after two decades working in video—is about a solitary man (Marc Barbé), who travels France killing young women. The film shows us a series of his murders, through which he remains impassively enigmatic. One day, however, he meets Claire (former Hal Hartley player Elina Löwensohn), who finds herself drawn into a perverse relation with him.

*Sombre* would be challenging for its subject matter alone, a woman readily entering into complicity with her aggressor. But Grandrieux's style forces us to suspend our habitual judgments. The film's claustrophobic darknesses, oblique continuity, and minimum of explanatory dialogue oblige us to find our way—as the characters do—through an atmosphere dominated by will, desire, and the death wish. Grandrieux remains less feted than more publicity-hungry contemporaries such as Gaspar Noé, but he represents one of the most challenging and uncompromising new visions in French cinema. **JRom**

# RING (1998)

It's a deceptively simple premise for a ghost story: There is a cursed videotape being circulated. Anyone who watches it will die seven days afterward.

When TV reporter Reiko Asakawa (Nanako Matsushima), while working on a story about urban legends, discovers that her niece is one of the victims of the videotape, she sets out to find it. When she watches it, the odd and mysterious images convince her the curse is true, and she asks her estranged ex-husband Ryuji Takayama (Hiroyuki Sanada) for help. They have seven days to decipher the images on the video and find a way to break the curse, especially after their four-year old son watches it as well.

Director Hideo Nakata achieves a steady sense of mounting disquiet thoughout the film as Reiko and Ryuji try to unravel the mystery of the videotape's images. What they find is a decades-old tragedy involving the death of a girl with unusual psychic abilities. There are no cheap shock effects here. Instead, Nakata relies on sound and atmosphere to suggest the presence of the unquiet dead hovering over the living, poised to strike.

*Ring* succeeds in isolating the mood of the late 1990s: the pervasive sense of uncertainty; anxiety about the break-up of the nuclear family; the pervasiveness of technology in our lives subverted to unfathomable, dangerous ends; the sense of being implicated in an endless, inescapable cycle of Life and Death, and how we have no choice but to continue to go on.

In movies, the popularity of genres comes in cycles. A particular genre becomes relevant when it captures the anxieties and preoccupations of the society at large. *Ring* singlehandedly revived the horror genre for the end of the 20th century, spawning two sequels, a prequel, a Korean remake, and an overcooked but hugely successful Hollywood remake (directed by Gore Verbinski), not to mention directly and indirectly influencing dozens of horror films from all over Asia and, soon enough, America. **AT**

**Japan** (Kadokawa Shoten, Omega) 96m BW / Color

**Language:** Japanese

**Director:** Hideo Nakata

**Producer:** Shinya Kawai, Takenori Sento, Takashige Ichise

**Screenplay:** Hiroshi Takahashi, from the novel *Ringu* by Kôji Suzuki

**Photography:** Junichirô Hayashi

**Music:** Kenji Kawai

**Cast:** Nanako Matsushima, Miki Nakatani, Hiroyuki Sanada, Yuko Takeuchi, Hitomi Sato, Yoichi Numata, Yutaka Matsushige, Katsumi Muramatsu, Rikiya Otaka, Masako, Daisuke Ban, Kiyoshi Risho, Yuurei Yanagi, Yôko Ôshima, Kiriko Shimizu

## THERE'S SOMETHING ABOUT MARY (1998)

**U.S.** (Fox) 119m Color

**Director:** Bobby Farrelly, Peter Farrelly

**Producer:** Frank Beddor, Michael Steinberg, Bradley Thomas, Charles B. Wessler

**Screenplay:** Ed Decter, John J. Strauss, Peter Farrelly, Bobby Farrelly

**Photography:** Mark Irwin

**Music:** Jonathan Richman

**Cast:** Cameron Diaz, Matt Dillon, Ben Stiller, Lee Evans, Chris Elliott, Lin Shaye, Jeffrey Tambor, Markie Post, Keith David, W. Earl Brown, Sarah Silverman, Khandi Alexander, Marnie Alexenburg, Danny Murphy, Richard Tyson

Despite any earlier reservations I may have had about Bobby and Peter Farrelly, the brothers behind *Dumb & Dumber* (1994) and *Kingpin* (1996), they're progressively winning me over, partly because they keep getting better. *There's Something about Mary* often had me in stitches. For all their tweaking of PC attitudes, the brothers' brand of gross-out humor is basically sweet-tempered, and though this film looks a bit slapdash, its script (by the Farrellys, Ed Decter, and John J. Strauss) is surprisingly well put together.

Victimized hero Ted Stroehmann (Ben Stiller) nurtures a 13-year infatuation with the title heroine (Cameron Diaz), who'd moved away to Miami soon after graduating from high school in Rhode Island. He hires a shady detective (Matt Dillon) to track her down, and the detective falls in love with her himself. This movie's unforced feeling for lower-middle-class disaffection is worthy at times of W. C. Fields, and there are some worst-case-scenario sequences involving a prom date, a dog, and masturbation that are convulsively hilarious. I also grew inordinately fond of Jonathan Richman and his drummer, the two klutzy musicians who periodically reappear, like the minstrels in *Cat Ballou* (1965). **JRos**

## MAGNOLIA (1999)

**U.S.** (Ghoulardi, New Line) 188m Color

**Director:** Paul Thomas Anderson

**Producer:** Paul Thomas Anderson, Joanne Sellar

**Screenplay:** Paul Thomas Anderson

**Photography:** Robert Elswit

**Music:** Jon Brion

**Cast:** John C. Reilly, Tom Cruise, Julianne Moore, Philip Baker Hall, Jeremy Blackman, Philip Seymour Hoffman, William H. Macy, Melora Walters, Jason Robards, Melinda Dillon, Michael Bowen, Ricky Jay, Felicity Huffman, April Grace, Pat Healy

**Oscar nomination:** Paul Thomas Anderson (screenplay), Tom Cruise (actor in support role), Aimee Mann (song).

**Berlin International Film Festival:** Paul Thomas Anderson (Golden Bear), (reader jury of the Berliner Morgenpost)

"As we move through life, we should try to do good." In telling a sprawling story of family—the betrayal, secrets, heartaches, and disappointments contained within—writer-director Paul Thomas Anderson jumps back and forth between a sleazy, misogynistic television huckster (Tom Cruise); a lonely child prodigy (Jeremy Blackman); an elderly, dying misanthrope (Jason Robards) and his trophy wife (Julianne Moore); a boozing, drug-addled young woman (Melora Walters); a popular, dying quiz-show host (Philip Baker Hall); and a bumbling, lonely, big-hearted cop (John C. Reilly). The various connections between these people, the coincidences and twists of fate that link them, are what drives this epically structured film.

Filled with biblical references and allusions, *Magnolia* makes no secret of grappling with large themes and issues—the meaning of life, the nature of evil, the terms of human connection. What makes this hugely ambitious picture work so well is Anderson's ability to portray these themes by staying focused on the minute details of his characters' bruised inner lives. Frogs fall mysteriously from the sky in a downpour, a car crashes into a storefront while the radio churns out the pop hit "Dreams," and people fall apart. The whole while, Anderson maintains an unwavering empathy with his broken characters, humanizing the villains while clearly siding with the victimized and misunderstood. *Magnolia* seethes with anger and pain, staggering toward hope—something like redemption—the whole time. **EH**

# BEAU TRAVAIL (1999)

Claire Denis is one of the most audacious, talented directors in the world, and *Beau Travail* may well be her crowning glory. Based on Herman Melville's literary classic, *Billy Budd*, the film is set in the rugged outback of Africa, where the French Foreign Legion—men of every race and hue—are undergoing rigorous training. The stark desert, with its endless stretch of sand and jagged rocks set beneath a rolling blue sky, provides a breathtaking canvas for Denis, who captures the rituals of men exercising, marching, showering, and bonding with a poet's eye. In her carefully constructed scenes, the routines of everyday life are transformed into gracefully choreographed dances. But while this ode to masculinity and male beauty is unfolding, the jealousy of a military official, Sergeant Galoup (Denis Lavant) toward one of his underlings, Sentain (Gregoire Colin), builds toward a tragic ending.

Galoup narrates the tale in voiceover. The homoeroticism of the military experience is neither forced nor shied away from, and it doesn't really qualify *Beau Travail* as an example of queer cinema, as so many of both the film's fans and detractors declared upon its release. Denis's interests are broader than that. In brief but powerful strokes, she raises questions about the relationships of whites to blacks, especially in former European colonies; connections between gender and racial politics are made in scenes where the men go into town on leave and mingle with local women. But the film remains steadfastly ambiguous throughout, never taking any specific stance on these issues. Most importantly, what Denis does, with a minimum of dialogue and with a primary focus on hypnotic visuals that fill the screen in long takes, is capture the beauty of ritual and repetition—as well as the power of monotony to break spirit, which is as much the reason behind military ritual as the aim of physical conditioning.

In terms of sheer beauty, *Beau Travail* pays off frame for frame, whether it's the sight of the men in formation performing calisthenics, or the happy accident of Denis capturing a ray of sun as it's refracted in the window of a moving train—or finally, the disgraced officer, dancing beneath a spinning disco ball at film's end. Denis tells her stories through images rather than through dialogue and plot, with a gift for color, lighting, and composition that is unsurpassed. **EH**

**France** (La Sept-Arte, SM, Tanaïs) 92m Color

**Language:** French

**Director:** Claire Denis

**Producer:** Patrick Grandperret

**Screenplay:** Claire Denis, Jean-Pol Fargeau, from the story *Billy Budd, Sailor* by Herman Melville

**Photography:** Agnès Godard

**Music:** Charles Henri de Pierrefeu, Eran Zur

**Cast:** Denis Lavant, Michel Subor, Grégoire Colin, Richard Courcet, Nicolas Duvauchelle, Adiatou Massudi, Mickael Ravovski, Dan Herzberg, Giuseppe Molino, Gianfranco Poddighe, Marc Veh, Thong Duy Nguyen, Jean-Yves Vivet, Bernardo Montet, Dimitri Tsiapkinis

**Berlin International Film Festival:** Claire Denis (reader jury of the Berliner Zeitung—special mention)

# THE BLAIR WITCH PROJECT (1999)

**U.S.** (Blair Witch, Haxan) 86m BW/Color

**Director:** Daniel Myrick, Eduardo Sánchez

**Producer:** Robin Cowie, Gregg Hale

**Screenplay:** Daniel Myrick, Eduardo Sánchez

**Photography:** Neal Fredericks

**Music:** Tony Cora

**Cast:** Heather Donahue, Joshua Leonard, Michael C. Williams, Bob Griffin, Jim King, Sandra Sánchez, Ed Swanson, Patricia DeCou, Mark Mason, Jackie Hallex

**Cannes Film Festival:** Daniel Myrick, Eduardo Sánchez (award of the youth foreign film)

"In October of 1994, three student filmmakers disappeared in the woods near Burkittsville, Maryland while shooting a documentary . . . . A year later their footage was found." Thus begins *The Blair Witch Project*, Daniel Myrick and Eduardo Sánchez's shoestring-budgeted horror "mockumentary," which parlayed an innovative marketing campaign and incredible word-of-mouth into more than $140 million in the United States alone—making it one of the most profitable independent films of all time.

Led by aspiring director Heather, the three "student filmmakers" mentioned above make their way to Burkittsville (formerly Blair), Maryland to shoot footage for a documentary they are making about a local legend, the so-called Blair Witch. Rumor has it this mysterious figure has been haunting the nearby Black Hills forest since the 18th century, and is responsible for a number of heinous murders. After conducting interviews with some of the locals, the trio hikes into the forest to gather additional footage. None of them experienced campers, they soon get lost, and their once-cheery demeanor deteriorates into an increasingly volatile mixture of fear, blame, frustration, and panic. To make matters worse, ominous signs begin to appear, including piles of stones carefully positioned outside their tent and wooden effigies hanging in the trees. Then Josh silently disappears. In the film's harrowing finale, Michael and Heather stumble across a decrepit house. Hoping to find Jeff, they enter; what they discover is a nightmare. Through the lens of her camcorder, we see what Heather sees: first darkness and ruins and children's handprints on the walls; then, after someone or something knocks her unconscious, just a blank ceiling, which lasts until the tape—and the film itself—runs out.

Despite criticisms directed toward the film's sometimes slow pace and reliance on nausea-inducing handheld camera work, *The Blair Witch Project* clearly succeeds in its use of documentary techniques as a means of instilling terror in viewers. Myrick and Sánchez's unique production method has itself become the stuff of legend: The actors not only were responsible for shooting the entire film themselves (over the course of eight consecutive days and nights), but also had to carry their own equipment, and improvise almost all of their lines. Several times a day, the directors would write notes to each cast member, sealing them in tubes for their eyes only. By achieving such a high degree of realism, Myrick and Sánchez took their product a step beyond earlier horror films with mockumentary aspirations, such as Wes Craven's *The Last House on the Left* (1972) and Tobe Hooper's *The Texas Chain Saw Massacre* (1974).

By exploiting some of our most basic fears—of the dark, of the unknown, of strange sounds—*The Blair Witch Project* manages to elicit intense emotional responses. Some of the most terrifying moments occur when all we are able to see is a black/blank screen and what our imagination conjures up is far more frightening than anything the most sophisticated special effects or makeup can produce. It is to their credit that those involved in the making of this film were well aware of this often ignored fact. **SJS**

## GOHATTO (1999)
### TABOO

**U.K. / France / Japan** (BS Asahi, Bac, Eisei Gekijo, Imagica, Kadokawa Shoten, Canal+, Oshima, RPC, Shochiku) 100m Color

**Language:** Japanese

**Director:** Nagisa Oshima

**Producer:** Shigehiro Nakagawa, Eiko Oshima, Kazuo Shimizu

**Screenplay:** Nagisa Oshima, from the novellas *Maegami No Sozaburo* and *Sanjogawara Ranjin* by Ryotaro Shiba, and TV series *Shinsengumi Keppuroku*

**Photography:** Toyomichi Kurita

**Music:** Ryuichi Sakamoto

**Cast:** Takeshi Kitano, Ryuhei Matsuda, Shinji Takeda, Tadanobu Asano, Koji Matoba, Masa Tommies, Masatô Ibu, Uno Kanda, Kazuko Yoshiyuki, Tomorowo Taguchi, Yoichi Sai, Jiro Sakagami, Zakoba Katsura, Kei Sato

A leading figure in the Japanese—and international—cinematic new wave of the 1960s, Nagisa Oshima returned to the cinema in 2000, 14 years after his previous film, the ape-love comedy *Max, mon amour*, crashed and burned at the Cannes Film Festival. Hobbled by serious health problems, Oshima somehow still found the strength to create what is surely one of his most personal works. *Gohatto*—which in all probability will be the still-ailing Oshima's final work—exudes the autumnal quality of the late works of the great masters; it is both a distillation of much of his earlier style and themes, as well a suggestion of a possible cinema for others to create.

In 1865, a militia is selecting recruits to train as samurai warriors. A powerful attraction grows between Tashiro (Tadanobu Asano) and his rival for the coveted samurai role, the bewitching Kano (Ryuhei Matsuda); the desire between the two will infect the rest of the militia, revealing long suppressed tensions and emotions. Using a highly theatrical mise en scène, Oshima creates an effective vision of a world as rigidly structured as it is artificial; as so often in his work, the outbreak of raw, physical desire pushes his characters into actions of which they would have never believed themselves capable. **RP**

## ROSETTA (1999)

**France / Belgium** (ARP Sélection, CNC, Cen. de Cin. et de l'Audiovisuel de la Comm. Française de Belgique, Laterne, Wallone, Canal+, Fleuve, October, RTBF) 95m Color

**Language:** French

**Director:** Jean-Pierre Dardenne, Luc Dardenne

**Producer:** Jean-Pierre Dardenne, Luc Dardenne, Laurent Pétin, Michèle Pétin

**Screenplay:** Jean-Pierre Dardenne, Luc Dardenne

**Photography:** Alain Marcoen

**Music:** Jean-Pierre Cocco

**Cast:** Émilie Dequenne, Fabrizio Rongione, Anne Yernaux, Olivier Gourmet, Bernard Marbaix

**Cannes Film Festival:** Jean-Pierre Dardenne, Luc Dardenne (Golden Palm), (ecumenical jury—special mention), Émilie Dequenne (actress), tied with Séverine Caneele for *L'Humanité*

From its opening seconds, this feature from Belgian brothers Jean-Pierre and Luc Dardenne, winner of the Palme d'Or at the 1999 Cannes Film Festival, was surely the most visceral filmgoing experience of that year, including all of Hollywood's explosions and special-effects extravaganzas. It concerns the desperate efforts of the 18-year-old heroine of the title to find a steady job. Played by Émilie Dequenne, (a remarkable nonprofessional), Rosetta lives in a trailer park with her alcoholic mother and suffers from stomach cramps. She particularly hopes to work at a waffle stand whose current employee has romantic designs on her. This may sound like the grimmest sort of neo-realism, but the Dardennes keep the story so ruthlessly unsentimental and physical that it would be a disservice to describe it as neo-anything.

You feel *Rosetta* in your nervous system before you get a chance to reflect on its meaning, almost as if the Dardenne brothers were intent on converting an immediate experience of the contemporary world into a breathless theme-park ride. It makes just about every other form of movie "realism" look like trivial escapism. The film is certainly not devoid of psychological nuance either, and it had such an impact in Belgium that a wage law for teenagers, passed in November 1999, is known as "the Rosetta plan." **JRos**

**Spain / France** (El Deseo, France 2, Renn, Vía Digital) 101m Eastmancolor

**Language:** Spanish / Catalan / English

**Director:** Pedro Almodóvar

**Producer:** Agustín Almodóvar, Michel Ruben

**Screenplay:** Pedro Almodóvar

**Photography:** Affonso Beato

**Music:** Alberto Iglesias

**Cast:** Cecilia Roth, Marisa Paredes, Candela Peña, Antonia San Juan, Penélope Cruz, Rosa Maria Sardà, Fernando Fernán Gómez, Fernando Guillén, Toni Cantó, Eloy Azorín, Carlos Lozano, Manuel Morón, José Luis Torrijo, Juan José Otegui, Carmen Balagué

**Oscar:** Spain (best foreign language film)

**Cannes Film Festival:** Pedro Almodóvar (director), (prize of the ecumenical jury), nomination (Golden Palm)

# TODO SOBRE MI MADRE (1999)
## ALL ABOUT MY MOTHER

Pedro Almodóvar's 1999 film opens on a handsome boy, Esteban (Eloy Azarín), who's very close to his single mother, Manuela (Cecilia Roth), and for a while (given some sly references to Truman Capote and Tennessee Williams) it looks as though we're about to see a thinly disguised gay autobiopic. In a way we are, for although Esteban is killed off on his 17th birthday and the focus shifts to Manuela, *All About My Mother*—like all Almodóvar films—constructs femininity through the irreverent, loving gaze of a gay man who grew up surrounded by adoring women on the verge. Crazed with grief, Manuela travels to Barcelona and finds herself playing den mother to a pregnant nun with AIDS (a dewy Penelope Cruz, in one of the great Spanish roles she traded away to become a Hollywood pin-up), a beat-up transgendered prostitute (Antonia San Juan) who stage manages her every moment, and a lesbian actress (the great Marisa Paredes) who is playing Blanche Dubois in more ways than one. The plot, elaborately structured and layered with significance, is an excuse to throw together a bunch of throaty-voiced women (with or without their own breasts) to talk dirty, booze, weep, and prop each other up.

When a woman in an Almodóvar film cries, it's a heaving, gasping, aristocratic happening. Still, in his court-jester way, Almodóvar is the most enthusiastic of social levelers. A nun can fall, a hooker can rise, and though both may rail at their fates, their suffering lacks all bitterness or rage. Even the color scheme is egalitarian, and trash has its own beauty: The circling cars of

johns trawling for hookers at night beneath a Barcelona bridge are bathed in the same moonlit loveliness as the city's floodlit old buildings.

Toward the end of *All About My Mother*, the prostitute steps onto a stage and, having itemized the cost of her many surgeries to an appalled audience of bourgeois theatergoers, enchants them with her ad-libbed thoughts on what it takes to be real. "You are more authentic," she says, "the more you resemble the things you've dreamed of." For Almodóvar, nature is overrated, while acting —lying included—is the cover that frees us to be our worst and best selves. This wonderfully seductive set piece summarizes the exuberantly humane credo that animates every movie he makes. Though *All About My Mother* contains scenes as candid and uproarious as any of the director's early films, it sustains the quieter, sadder, and more reflective tone that began in his 1995 film *The Flower of My Secret*, and continued in the lovely *Talk to Her* (2003). As the movie closes, this alluring coven of women shakes out into fresh unions, cemented not only by Almodóvar's elastic definition of womanhood, but by his conciliatory spirit, assuring us that though anatomy may not be destiny, the kindness of female strangers is irreducible. Given the pap that is currently most studios' idea of a "women's movie," gay filmmakers like Almodóvar and Todd Haynes may be providing a last refuge for strong female roles, as well as for wholehearted melodrama in our hyper-ironic age. **ET**

## THREE KINGS (1999)

**U.S.** (Atlas, Coast Ridge, Junger Witt, Village Roadshow, Warner Bros.) 114m Technicolor
**Language:** English / Arabic
**Director:** David O. Russell
**Producer:** Paul Junger Witt, Edward McDonnell
**Screenplay:** John Ridley, David O. Russell
**Photography:** Newton Thomas Sigel
**Music:** Carter Burwell
**Cast:** George Clooney, Mark Wahlberg, Ice Cube, Spike Jonze, Cliff Curtis, Nora Dunn, Jamie Kennedy, Saïd Taghmaoui, Mykelti Williamson, Holt McCallany, Judy Greer, Christopher Lohr, Jon Sklaroff, Liz Stauber, Marsha Horan

*Three Kings* is a millennium-capping antiwar film that employed what were then state-of-the-art tools (fast edits, dizzying camera work, color schemes that pop off the screen) and combined them with old-fashioned—if not out-of-style—leftist politics.

Writer-director David O. Russell tells the tale of the first Gulf War (1991) through the eyes of three American soldiers whose ignorance, greed, and naïveté is slowly wiped away as they are dragged deeper into the political and cultural trappings behind the war, forced to humanize their enemies and demystify their own country and military. In the process, the audience is exposed to a version of Gulf War I that the media (particularly the American media) did not and never would report—the deaths of innocents, the corruption and posturing of high-ranking military officials, the co-option of "objective" media to spin the story. It's heady, even dense, stuff made accessible and urgent through a snappy script, relentlessly energetic pacing, dazzling visuals and props, and taut acting from the leads (George Clooney, Mark Wahlberg, Ice Cube). An assured juggling of genre and tone shifts—it's part war story, part heist thriller, and wholly an antiwar creed—the film should fall apart at the seams but doesn't strike a single false note. **EH**

## BAD MA RA KHAHAD BORD (1999)
### THE WIND WILL CARRY US

**Iran / France** (MK2 Productions) 118m Color
**Language:** Farsi
**Director:** Abbas Kiarostami
**Producer:** Marin Karmitz, Abbas Kiarostami
**Screenplay:** Abbas Kiarostami
**Photography:** Mahmoud Kalari
**Music:** Peyman Yazdanian
**Cast:** Behzad Dourani, Noghre Asadi, Roushan Karam Elmi, Bahman Ghobadi, Shahpour Ghobadi, Reihan Heidari, Masood Mansouri, Ali Reza Naderi, Frangis Rahsepar, Masoameh Salimi, Farzad Sohrabi, Lida Soltani
**Venice Film Festival:** Abbas Kiarostami "CinemAvvenire" award, best film), (FIPRESCI award), (grand special jury prize), nomination (Golden Lion)

Like all Abbas Kiarostami's films, *The Wind Will Carry Us* unfolds in an eternal present and is structured, much like life only more so, not by plot as such but by the obsessive repetitions of everyday activity.

An excitable engineer arrives from Tehran with his crew in a remote mountain village of Iranian Kurdistan to record a mourning ritual. Reliant on the villagers' matter-of-fact hospitality, the engineer waits impatiently for a terminally ill woman to die, befriending a small boy in return for bulletins on the woman's condition. He spends his time rushing up and down a hill to improve the reception on his endless phone calls to the city. We hear the voices of his crew as they work, but never see their faces. The engineer argues with his Tehran handlers about issues that never become clear.

What passes for event in *The Wind Will Carry Us* is the progress of a dung beetle and a man falling down a hole, all observed with Kiarostami's customary tranquility. Time slows down for the engineer, and for the audience—our Western sense of drama is negated and redefined. The gaps in this wonderfully pregnant half-story are for us to fill in. **ET**

# ODISHON (1999)
## THE AUDITION

One year after Hideo Nakata's *Ringu* (1998) proved beyond the shadow of a doubt that contemporary Japanese horror was a force to be reckoned with in world cinema, Takashi Miike's *Audition* effectively reworked the genre by masking its true intentions behind a wall of melodrama until the film's terrifying final third—culminating in a staggering scene of sexualized torture that had many audience members hiding their eyes, if not running from the theater.

Shigeharu Aoyama (Ryo Ishibashi), the lonely, middle-aged owner of a video production company, worries about finding the right woman to replace his adolescent son's mother, who died seven years earlier. That all changes after he holds a fake audition for actresses seeking a role in a made-up project. Instantly attracted to the beautiful and engimatic Asami (Eihi Shiina), who initially proves as dutiful as she is beautiful, Aoyoma soon proposes marriage at a picturesque seaside resort. From there, *Audition* drastically shifts gears as various aspects of Asami's disturbing past and monstrous personality are revealed.

Sex in Miike's cinema is frequently depicted as a weapon. In *Audition*'s shocking denouement, a now dominatrix-like Asami sits astride the temporarily paralyzed Aoyoma and penetrates his body—including his eyeballs—with needles, all the while cooing "kiri, kiri, kiri" ("deeper, deeper, deeper"). Never have such sweet words caused so much pain to protagonist and viewer alike. **SJS**

**Japan / South Korea** (AFDF, Omega Project) 115m Color

**Language:** Japanese

**Director:** Takashi Miike

**Producer:** Satoshi Fukushima, Akemi Suyama

**Screenplay:** Daisuke Tengan, from novel by Ryu Murakami

**Photography:** Hideo Yamamoto

**Music:** Kôji Endô

**Cast:** Ryo Ishibashi, Eihi Shiina, Tetsu Sawaki, Jun Kunimura, Renji Ishibashi, Miyuki Matsuda, Toshie Negishi, Ren Osugi, Shigeru Saiki, Ken Mitsuishi, Yuriko Hirooka, Fumiyo Kohinata, Misato Nakamura, Yuuto Arima, Ayaka Izumi

# LE TEMPS RETROUVÉ (1999)

## TIME REGAINED

**France / Italy / Porrtugal** (Blu CNC, France 2, Gémini, Canal+, Lendemain, Madragoa) 169m Color

**Language:** French

**Director:** Raoul Ruiz

**Producer:** Paulo Branco

**Screenplay:** Raoul Ruiz, from novel by Marcel Proust

**Photography:** Ricardo Aronovich

**Music:** Jorge Arriagada

**Cast:** Catherine Deneuve, Emmanuelle Béart, Vincent Perez, John Malkovich, Pascal Greggory, Marcello Mazzarella, Marie-France Pisier, Chiara Mastroianni, Arielle Dombasle, Edith Scob, Elsa Zylberstein, Christian Vadim, Dominique Labourier, Philippe Morier-Genoud, Melvil Poupaud

**Cannes Film Festival:** Raoul Ruiz nomination (Golden Palm)

One of the most willful and prolific of all filmmakers, the Chilean exile Raul Ruiz reinvented himself as a French avant-gardist in the 1970s and never looked back. Many of Ruiz's films were destined only for the most specialist audience, but he unexpectedly made a breakthrough into the art-house mainstream in the late '90s, mostly without diluting his neosurrealist vision. Perversely, Ruiz's big crossover hit—a huge commercial success in France—was a seemingly impossible project, an adaptation of Marcel Proust (and more perversely still, of the last volume of *In Search of Lost Time*).

Ruiz's free-associative style leads us through a construction of time and memory even more labyrinthine than Proust's own—from the dreams of the child Marcel to more elusive passages where the self-reflexive aspects of Proust are filtered through the self-reflexity of Ruiz's own filmmaking.

*Time Regained* is as visually sumptuous as one could wish costume drama to be, Ruiz exploring the costume tradition (here surely with a glance at Luchino Visconti) rather than subverting it. An eminent cast adds to Ruiz's perspective on Proust's commentary on perception and memory, its players (including Catherine Deneuve, Emmanuelle Béart, and John Malkovich as a marvellously skittish Baron de Charlus) becoming the glittering "stars" of Proust's salon world. **JRos**

# FIGHT CLUB (1999)

**U.S.** (Art Linson, Fox 2000, Regency, Taurus) 139m Color

**Director:** David Fincher

**Producer:** Ross Grayson Bell, Ceán Chaffin, Art Linson

**Screenplay:** Jim Uhls, from novel by Chuck Palahniuk

**Photography:** Jeff Cronenweth

**Music:** Dust Brothers

**Cast:** Edward Norton, Brad Pitt, Helena Bonham Carter, Meat Loaf, Zach Grenier, Richmond Arquette, David Andrews, George Maguire, Eugenie Bondurant, Christina Cabot, Sydney Colston, Rachel Singer, Christie Cronenweth, Tim De Zarn, Ezra Buzzington

**Oscar nomination:** Ren Klyce, Richard Hymns (special sound effects)

"The first rule about Fight Club is that you don't talk about Fight Club. The second rule about Fight Club is that you don't talk about Fight Club." Based on the novel by Chuck Palahniuk, David Fincher's film stakes out manly territory in 1999's most intriguing, angry, yet witty cinematic fantasy. Spectacularly popular, *Fight Club* is nevertheless as morally challenging as it is visually memorable.

Edward Norton plays the mild-mannered narrator who, tortured by his empty office life, goes to 12-Step support group meetings just to feel something. At one of these meetings, Jack meets and falls for Marla (Helena Bonham Carter), and later hooks up with the dangerously wild Tyler Durden (Brad Pitt). Tyler convinces Norton that his life can be better lived by learning how to fight. Soon enough, their street fighting antics attract other men, giving them all something that their ordinary lives are lacking—a sort of dirty, aggressive dignity which is eventually reorganized into a virtual terrorist cell.

With astonishing camera and special effects work, *Fight Club* moves at rocketlike pace and is the kind of exciting, distressingly inspiring movie that makes even the strangest event seem normal, including Meat Loaf as a cancer patient with enormous mammary glands. Look out for the big twist in the ending. **RK**

# BEING JOHN MALKOVICH (1999)

Acclaimed video director, Spike Jonze, (whose previous works include the music videos to Fatboy Slim's "Weapon Of Choice" and the Beastie Boys' "Sabotage") turned filmmaker successfully turns one of the oddest concepts for a movie (as perceived by writer Charlie Kaufman) into one of the most inventive Hollywood films in recent history.

Craig Schwartz (John Cusack) is a disheveled puppeteer barely scraping together a living with his dark (and quite traumatic to children) street puppet shows. His dowdy wife Lotte (an almost unrecognizable Cameron Diaz) spends what little they have on raising the menagerie of animals she has living in their small home. To earn extra cash, Craig takes a job as a filing clerk in a strange company that is located on the 7 ½ floor of a big Manhattan office building. The legend of how an office could exist between the 7th and 8th floors makes for a movie in itself, but it is what Craig discovers hidden behind a filing cabinet that sets this film's quirky events in motion. For behind the cabinet is a door, and when Craig crawls through it he discovers it is actually some sort of metaphysical portal that sends him hurtling into the brain of actor John Malkovich (playing himself here). Here, he experiences the things Malkovich does for just 15 minutes before being expelled abruptly onto the side of the New Jersey Turnpike.

Kaufman cleverly weaves an intricate plot around this outstanding idea, beginning when Craig lets fellow office worker Maxine (Catherine Keener) in on his discovery and she convinces him to charge people to try this demented ride for themselves. Jonze dazzles at every turn as he tells this smart, subversive, and darkly comic tale, and he has assembled a cast—Cusack and Diaz especially—who beautifully translate his skewed vision to the screen. Of course, *Being John Malkovich* wouldn't have worked at all without the eponymous actor himself, who parodies his public image brilliantly, especially in a truly wonderful scene when he tries the portal himself and ends up in his own bizarre world, eating dinner in a restaurant populated by numerous Mr. Malkovichs. Wonderfully hip, utterly marvelous. **JB**

**U.S.** (Gramercy, Propaganda, Single Cell) 112m Technicolor

**Director:** Spike Jonze

**Producer:** Steve Golin, Vincent Landay, Sandy Stern, Michael Stipe

**Screenplay:** Charlie Kaufman

**Photography:** Lance Acord

**Music:** Carter Burwell

**Cast:** John Cusack, Cameron Diaz, Ned Bellamy, Eric Weinstein, Madison Lanc, Octavia Spencer, Mary Kay Place, Orson Bean, Catherine Keener, K.K. Dodds, Reginald C. Hayes, Byrne Piven, Judith Wetzell, John Malkovich, Kevin Carroll

**Oscar nomination:** Spike Jonze (director), Charlie Kaufman (screenplay), Catherine Keener (actress in support role)

# AMERICAN BEAUTY (1999)

**U.S.** (DreamWorks SKG, Jinks/Cohen) 122m Color

**Director:** Sam Mendes

**Producer:** Bruce Cohen, Dan Jinks

**Screenplay:** Alan Ball

**Photography:** Conrad L. Hall

**Music:** Thomas Newman

**Cast:** Kevin Spacey, Annette Bening, Thora Birch, Wes Bentley, Mena Suvari, Peter Gallagher, Allison Janney, Chris Cooper, Scott Bakula, Sam Robards, Barry Del Sherman, Ara Celi, John Cho, Fort Atkinson, Sue Casey

**Oscar:** Bruce Cohen, Dan Jinks (best picture), Sam Mendes (director), Alan Ball (screenplay), Kevin Spacey (actor), Conrad L. Hall (photography)

**Oscar nomination:** Annette Bening (actress), Tariq Anwar (editing), Thomas Newman (music)

If *Blue Velvet* peeked behind the curtains of modern-day suburbia back in 1986, 13 years later *American Beauty* yanked them completely away from the windows and gave us all an unsettling, unnerving full view of what goes on inside.

"This is my neighborhood, this is my street, this is my life," says Lester Burnham (Kevin Spacey) in voiceover as the camera moves over his town before reaching his house at the start of the film. "I'm 42 years old. In less than a year, I'll be dead. Of course I don't know that yet. In a way, I am dead already." Like Joe Gillis (William Holden) in *Sunset Boulevard*, Lester and the audience know his fate from the beginning, but we realize that is just one small part of his story, especially when we meet his wife, daughter, and assorted neighbors.

*American Beauty* is a dark, bleak comedy about what life is really like for those people supposedly living the American Dream—people who don't lack for anything material but who are unhappy, unfulfilled, and dissatisfied. As well as Lester, who tells us that the high point of his day is masturbating during his morning shower, there is his wife Carolyn (Annette Bening, in a career-best performance), a real-estate agent obsessed with her picture-perfect home and garden, and their sulky, unhappy, dark daughter Jane (Thora Birch) living out this suburban nightmare. This extends to other people in the neighborhood, especially the dysfunctional Fitts family. Led by a retired military man (Chris Cooper) who rules over his almost catatonic wife (Allison Janney) and their strange son Ricky (Wes Bentley), whom we first meet behind a video camera, filming the rows and silences of the Burnham household. In fact, the only

family who seem happy and well-adjusted are the gay couple who, in ex-Colonel Fitts's eyes at least, are the least outwardly "normal" family of all.

Mainly, of course, this is Lester's story, and with Spacey in the role it is an extremely fascinating one—that is, on the surface, a tale of one man's midlife crisis as he tries to rediscover the freedom he has lost in the face of marital and parental responsibility. Forced to accompany his wife to a school basketball game to watch his cheerleader daughter perform, he becomes transfixed by the Lolita-esque Angela (Mena Suvari). He is soon having erotic visions of her (the most memorable being her naked but for a cover of red rose petals) that lead him to completely change his life in the hope that he will be able to seduce her.

Written by Alan Ball, who went on to create the acclaimed HBO television series *Six Feet Under*, this is a funny, sad, wistful, and even hopeful movie that never goes quite where you think it will. Director Sam Mendes takes the viewer on a journey filled with fine acting and memorable images that is surprisingly cinematic for a first-time filmmaker whose previous work was in the theater. Beautiful and brooding, *American Beauty* is a truly remarkable debut. **JB**

**South Korea** (Fun & Happiness Film) 113m Color

**Language:** Korean

**Director:** Sang-Jin Kim

**Producer:** Kwan Soo Lee

**Photography:** Jung Woo Choi

**Music:** Mu-hyeon Son

**Cast:** Sung-jae Lee, Oh-seong Yu, Seong-jin Kang, Ji-tae Yu, Yeong-gyu Park, Jun Jeong, Yu-won Lee, Jeong-ho Lee, Su-ro Kim, Won-jong Lee, So-yeong Jeong

# JUYUSO SEUBGYUKSAGEUN (1999)

## ATTACK THE GAS STATION!

A gang of street punks attack a gas station and trash the place for the sheer hell of it. The next evening, bored and pissed off, they decide to trash the same gas station again. The tightwad manager sees them coming and hides the money, telling them that there weren't any takings that day because the damage the punks inflicted on the place had turned customers away. Instead of leaving, the gang decides to stay and pump gas for the evening, pocketing the earnings for themselves. This brings them into contact with nearly every stratum of modern Korean society—anyone with a car who might need gas, a tune-up, or an oil-check, including cops, yuppies, and celebrity baseball players.

Since the gang has a zero tolerance policy toward anyone who's rude or obnoxious to them, the number of hostages in the station's upper office increases exponentially as the night wears on. Along the way, the punks teach the teenage gas jockeys the finer points of standing up to authority (namely their boss), how to develop a little more self-respect, how to confront a gang of bullies (by beating them up and taking them hostage), and generally trashing just about every notion of Confucian piety and social repression that governs Korean society.

This is only Kim Sang-Jin's second movie, his first being the sequel to a cop comedy franchise, and it is here that his voice comes out cranked to eleven. *Attack the Gas Station!* burst onto the scene with the anarchic force of the first Sex Pistols single. Kim takes what appears to be a simple premise and blows it up into an epic state-of-the-nation allegorical farce. Boasting a gleeful and witty script filled with twists and a sense of escalating insanity, Kim has the conviction to take the story as far as it can go, only to push it even further over the edge. This is surely the funniest, brainiest comedy set in a gas station ever made. **AT**

# EYES WIDE SHUT (1999)

*Eyes Wide Shut* is the perfect postscript to the oeuvre of Stanley Kubrick, who died within days of completing the film, in that it is signature Kubrick: intriguing, intellectual, intent, fastidiously crafted, and commanding to direct. It is also arguably portentous, remote, and labored. It enjoyed a big opening, thanks in part to sexy trailers of the reigning "world's most glamorous couple" and costars Tom Cruise and Nicole Kidman. However, box-office sales dropped significantly when word got around that the film is not so much an erotic drama as a psychodrama that probes marriage, fidelity, desire, jealousy, and sexual paranoia. Adapted by Kubrick and Frederic Raphael from Arthur (*La Ronde*) Schnitzler's *Dream Story*, it is about the reality of sexual love versus its romantic illusions.

Cruise's William Harford is a prosperous Manhattan doctor with a lovely wife, Alice (Kidman), a child, and demanding society patients (including one played by filmmaker Sydney Pollack). Frustrated Alice runs an unsuccessful art gallery, leaving her too much time to get high and confrontational about a marriage that looks perfect from the outside. During a fight with her overconfident, comfortable husband she makes a disclosure that sends him into the night. On his dreamlike odyssey he meets people with sad fixations or dirty secrets and a jazz musician with a bizarre story to tell, all of which convince him that everyone else is having a hot time while he is haunted by images of his wife. The central, strange, and striking centerpiece in his wanderings is a mysterious, ritualistic orgy of masked swingers (digitally amended in the United States to obscure the more graphic sexual images). A scene that is more theatrical than erotic and makes the point that dispassionate sexual adventure is a melancholy, hollow pursuit.

Cruise's performance was overshadowed by Kidman's smaller but more emotionally outspoken role, but his presence in virtually every scene gives the film an essential humanity. His palpably wounded male pride, pain, vulnerability, and bewilderment provide a sympathetic connection to what otherwise is a cold and cynical observation of relationships. But, as ever, Kubrick's uncomfortable personal vision is conveyed with distinctive and stunning style. **AE**

**U.S.** (Hobby, Pole Star, Warner Bros.) 159m Color

**Director:** Stanley Kubrick

**Producer:** Stanley Kubrick

**Screenplay:** Stanley Kubrick, Frederic Raphael, from the novel *Traumnovelle* by Arthur Schnitzler

**Photography:** Larry Smith

**Music:** Jocelyn Pook

**Cast:** Tom Cruise, Nicole Kidman, Madison Eginton, Jackie Sawiris, Sydney Pollack, Leslie Lowe, Peter Benson, Todd Field, Michael Doven, Sky Dumont, Louise J. Taylor, Stewart Thorndike, Randall Paul, Julienne Davis, Lisa Leone

**Venice Film Festival:** Stanley Kubrick (Filmcritica Bastone Bianco award)

# THE SIXTH SENSE (1999)

**U.S.** (Hollywood, Spyglass, Kennedy/Marshall) 107m Technicolor
**Language:** English / Spanish / Latin
**Director:** M. Night Shyamalan
**Producer:** Kathleen Kennedy, Frank Marshall, Barry Mendel
**Screenplay:** M. Night Shyamalan
**Photography:** Tak Fujimoto
**Music:** James Newton Howard
**Cast:** Bruce Willis, Haley Joel Osment, Toni Collette, Olivia Williams, Trevor Morgan, Donnie Wahlberg, Peter Anthony Tambakis, Jeffrey Zubernis, Bruce Norris, Glenn Fitzgerald, Greg Wood, Mischa Barton, Angelica Torn, Lisa Summerour, Firdous Bamji
**Oscar nomination:** Frank Marshall, Kathleen Kennedy, Barry Mendel (best picture), M. Night Shyamalan (director), M. Night Shyamalan (screenplay), Haley Joel Osment (actor in support role), Toni Collette (actress in support role), Andrew Mondshein (editing)

Writer/director M. Night Shyamalan, aged just 29 and making his second film, virtually reinvented the drama thriller with this love story/ghostly chiller that is now infamous for its twist ending.

A year after being shot in his home by a former patient, child psychologist Malcolm Crowe (Bruce Willis) attempts to understand a new, troubled boy, Cole (Haley Joel Osment). Cole, it seems, can see dead people: ghosts of those who left matters unresolved before their deaths and who visit the boy searching for some resolution. Meanwhile, as he tries to help Cole, Malcolm's own life is in disarray, his loving marriage to wife Anna (Olivia Williams) now distant and cold.

A ghost story of the highest order, *The Sixth Sense* works on many levels. The spooks are there as Cole is visited by tormented apparitions, but this is more emotional drama than scary suspense film, focusing on the relationships between boy and psychologist, Malcolm and his wife, and Cole and his mother (Toni Collette). Osment is a terrific discovery in a role that, had it been played too cute, would have wrecked the entire film, and Collette delivers the right amount of confusion and love for her unusual son in each scene. Willis, however, is the true revelation, giving a whispered, understated performance that is the heart of the film.

Of course, it is Shyamalan who deserves the most praise for putting all the elements of the film together. His clever use of muted colors and subtle hints of what is to come—the temperature dropping when a ghost is present, the use of the color red—and the aforementioned twist in the tail is so neatly done that, although the audience has effectively been hoodwinked throughout, it makes you want to reappraise the film a second, third, and fourth time rather than be annoyed that you have been led down a completely different path than the one you thought you were on.

A modern, emotionally complex classic that is as achingly poignant as it is chillingly tense. **JB**

# THE MATRIX (1999)

A sci-fi blockbuster that manages to effectively fuse pop-philosophical themes with skillfully choreographed action sequences and state-of-the-art special effects, *The Matrix* was conceived of and written and directed by Chicago-based brothers Andy and Larry Wachowski. As former comic book writers, they threw just about everything into the mix, including *The Wizard of Oz* and *The Wild Bunch, Alice in Wonderland* and *Hard Target, Sleeping Beauty* and the *Bible*.

*The Matrix* stars Keanu Reeves as a dutiful company man who doubles at night as a hacker named Neo. His Cartesian skepticism concerning the true nature of reality is validated after a beautiful mystery woman, Trinity (Carrie-Anne Moss), introduces him to legendary zen-hacker Morpheus (Laurence Fishburne). Accepting Morpheus's invitation to take a mind/brain opening techno-drug trip, Neo discovers that the world in which he previously "existed" is nothing but a computer-generated virtual reality program controlled by the very artificial-intelligence machines developed by mankind years before. It seems that the machines, which require endless supplies of electrical current to survive, keep the entire human population—save for a smattering of rebels and one underground city—in a state of perpetual hallucination. Lying unconscious in automated incubators, humans are deceived into believing that they are actually living and leading productive lives, while in reality vampire-like computers are siphoning off their precious mojo. Morpheus is certain that Neo is the Messianic "One," who, according to legend, will show up one day to save the human race from eternal subjugation. Although initially dissuaded by a surprisingly domestic soothsayer (Gloria Foster), Neo manages to summon the inner fortitude necessary to defeat the waspy Artificial Intelligence defense squad, with the help of John Woo-style martial arts ballet, Sam Peckinpah-inspired slow-motion gunfighting, and repeated self-affirmations.

What separates *The Matrix* from other virtual reality science-fiction fare, are its epic pretensions, apocalyptic overtones, and breathtaking visuals. New technologies such as "Bullettime" super slo-mo photography, wire-enhanced gymnastics, and Woo-Ping Yuen (*Fist of Legend, Black Mask*) choreographed kung fu fight scenes all served to raise the bar significantly for big-budget Hollywood action sequences. One of the most fascinating things about the film is the manner in which it attempts to negotiate between progressive messages of nonconformity and self-realization on the one hand, and the generic imperatives imposed by Hollywood's conservative studio system on the other. As one critic wrote, "It's cruel, really, to put tantalizing ideas on the table and then ask the audience to be satisfied with a shoot-out and a martial arts duel." Others praised the Wachowski brothers for beginning their film with an extended fight scene starring Trinity, only to note her relegation to "Neo's love interest" for the rest of the picture.

Such mixed messages reappear at the level of narrative. Considering that what remains of postwar planet Earth is a bleak, inhospitable "desert of the real," and that the virtual world in which Neo grew up is not without advantages, it isn't entirely clear what the human resistance hopes to gain by its struggles. Clearly such quandaries were not a turnoff for viewers. **SJS**

**U.S.** (Groucho II, Silver, Village Roadshow)136m Technicolor

**Director:** Andy Wachowski, Larry Wachowski

**Producer:** Joel Silver

**Screenplay:** Andy Wachowski, Larry Wachowski

**Photography:** Bill Pope

**Music:** Paul Barker, Don Davis

**Cast:** Keanu Reeves, Laurence Fishburne, Carrie-Anne Moss, Hugo Weaving, Gloria Foster, Joe Pantoliano, Marcus Chong, Julian Arahanga, Matt Doran, Belinda McClory, Anthony Ray Parker, Paul Goddard, Robert Taylor, David Aston, Marc Gray

**Oscar:** Zach Staenberg (editing), Dane A. Davis (special sound effects), Editing, John Gaeta, Janek Sirrs, Steve Courtley, Jon Thum (special visual effects), John T. Reitz, Gregg Rudloff, David E. Campbell, David Lee (sound)

## NUEVE REINAS (2000)
### NINE QUEENS

**Argentina** (FX SOUND, Audiovisuales Argentinas, J.Z., Kodak, Naya, Patagonik) 114m Color
**Language:** Spanish
**Director:** Fabián Bielinsky
**Producer:** Cecilia Bossi, Pablo Bossi
**Screenplay:** Fabián Bielinsky
**Photography:** Marcelo Camorino
**Music:** César Lerner
**Cast:** Gastón Pauls, Ricardo Darín, Leticia Brédice, Tomás Fonzi, Graciela Tenembaum, María Mercedes Villagra, Gabriel Correa, Pochi Ducasse, Luis Armesto, Ernesto Arias, Amancay Espíndola, Isaac Fajm, Jorge Noya, Óscar Núñez, Ignasi Abadal

A lot of walking occurs in this engaging Argentinean crime lark. The on-foot journey of two swindlers, Marcos (Ricardo Darin) and Juan (Gastón Pauls) offers, in passing, an understated documentary on Buenos Aires in the 21st century. But as these characters imagine the scams they might pull, their steps propel them into the charged space of a fiction.

Debut director Fabián Bielinsky maintains a firm balance between the mundane and the thrilling. Much of the film eschews a musical score, giving extra weight to the passing seconds. But when music is finally allowed in, the effect carries a more energetic wallop than in most bigger-budget caper movies.

Bielinsky clearly adores the Hollywood classics by directors such as Billy Wilder and Joseph Mankiewicz concerning elaborate, double-crossing deceits. Juan learns early on not to take at face value whatever misfortune occurs around him, because it could so easily be a con engineered by the shifty Marcos. Such a tricky narrative courts the risk, inherent in this type of story, of creating an ever-escalating spiral of one-upmanship. But Bielinsky has a special trump card up his sleeve, and that is the reality factor. The moment in which Argentina's dire economic crisis intervenes is a real highlight. **AM**

## LA CAPTIVE (2000)
### THE CAPTIVE

**France / Belgium** (CNC, Gimages 3, Gémini, Canal+, Paradise, arte) 118m Color
**Language:** French
**Director:** Chantal Akerman
**Producer:** Paulo Branco
**Screenplay:** Chantal Akerman, Eric De Kuyper, from the novel *La prisonnière* by Marcel Proust
**Photography:** Sabine Lancelin
**Cast:** Stanislas Merhar, Sylvie Testud, Olivia Bonamy, Liliane Rovère, Françoise Bertin, Aurore Clément, Vanessa Larré, Samuel Tasinaje, Jean Borodine, Anna Mouglalis, Bérénice Bejo, Adeline Chaudron, Sophie Assante, Christopher Gendreau, Sébastien Haddouk

Inspired by *La Prisonnière*, the fifth volume of Marcel Proust's novel *Remembrance of Things Past*, Chantal Akerman's film *La Captive* is eerily reminiscent of Hitchcock's *Vertigo* (1958). Twisting themes of obsession, passion, and desire, Akerman focuses on Simon (Stansilas Merhar), a man who seeks total possession of his love, Ariane (Sylvie Testud). Consumed with desire, Simon views Ariane not only as a companion but also as an object about whom he craves an understanding of her very being—her past, her present, and her future. Convinced that Ariane is leading a double life with a lesbian counterpart, Andrée (Olivia Bonamy), Simon's fixation grows increasingly stronger, eventually stifling Ariane's every move.

Fully addressing the complexities of sexuality and longing, Akerman crafts an exceptional story of love and obsession. Patterning *The Captive* after one of her most common film motifs, the impossible desire to comprehend "otherness," Akerman masterfully uses clean, medium-long shots of landscapes to enhance her themes of isolation and separation. Working with gifted cinematographer Sabine Lancelin, the pair create a simple yet elegant story of a woman exposed to the suppressive force of male jealousy. **AK**

# DUT YEUNG NIN WA (2000)
## IN THE MOOD FOR LOVE

*In the Mood for Love* takes place in a tiny and tightly packed tenement house in Hong Kong during the 1960s, where two neighbors spend so much time in close proximity that it's no wonder their lives ultimately cross. Tony Leung and Maggie Cheung suspect that their respective spouses are having an affair, but they're not sure if they should follow suit with an affair of their own. Instead they meet for quiet meals and shy discussions, passing the time together as it dawns upon them that maybe they really are meant for each other.

However, director Wong, working as usual without a script, allows the tale of infidelity to play out in an oddly reserved and unpredictable manner. Where the viewer might sense simmering romance, Wong sees sad resignation. The two potential lovers cling near one another like satellites, but they seem to understand that they may never be able to share the same orbit. This is not unrequited love but resisted love, as Leung and Cheung struggle to stay apart even though they seem destined to be together. Wong choreographs this strange relationship with the grace and rhythm of a waltz. Working with his usual director of photography Christopher Doyle, he tracks the couple in slow motion as they pass each other on the tiny staircases, fret about the weather on the shadowy streets, and cryptically act out the kind of arguments they might have were they actually lovers.

Once again Wong also brilliantly uses music, in this case a Nat King Cole instrumental cue that grows in mysterious power the more the theme is replicated. Each scene is luminous, spilling over with carefully researched but understated period details captured in a dreamlike haze by an eavesdropping camera. Cheung, clad in a series of beautiful dresses, is stunning, the perfect counterpart to the handsome and tasteful Leung, so in many ways you are rooting for the two to end up together. That they don't doesn't come as a surprise, but the emotional power of their nonrelationship proves remarkably effective. **JKl**

**France / Hong Kong** (Block 2, Jet Tone, Paradis) 98m BW/ Color

**Language:** Cantonese / French / Mandarin / Spanish

**Director:** Kar-wai Wong

**Producer:** Kar-wai Wong

**Screenplay:** Kar-wai Wong

**Photography:** Christopher Doyle, Pin Bing Lee

**Music:** Mike Galasso, Shigeru Umebayashi

**Cast:** Maggie Cheung, Tony Leung Chiu Wai, Ping Lam Siu, Tung Cho Cheung, Rebecca Pan, Lai Chen, Man-Lei Chan, Kam-wah Koo, Roy Cheung, Chi-ang Chi, Hsien Yu, Po-chun Chow, Tony Leung Chiu-wai, Maggie Cheung Man-yuk, Paulyn Sun, Man-lei Wong

**Cannes Film Festival:** Tony Leung Chiu Wai (actor), Christopher Doyle, Pin Bing Lee, William Chang (grand technical prize), Kar-wai Wong nomination (Golden Palm)

**Morocco / Tunisia / France / Belgium** (2M, Ace, Alexis, Ali'n, Gimages 3, Canal+, Playtime, TF1, TPS) 99m Color

**Language:** Arabic / French

**Director:** Nabil Ayouch

**Producer:** Etienne Comar, Jean Cottin, Antoine Voituriez

**Screenplay:** Nabil Ayouch, Nathalie Saugeon

**Photography:** Vincent Mathias

**Music:** Krishna Levy

**Cast:** Mounïm Kbab, Mustapha Hansali, Hicham Moussoune, Abdelhak Zhayra, Saïd Taghmaoui, Amal Ayouch, Mohamed Majd, Hicham Ibrahimi, Nadia Ould Hajjaj, Abdelkader Lofti, Khalil Essaadi, Abdessamad Tourab Seddam, Ahmed Lahlil, Karim Merzak, Halima Frizi

# ALI ZAOUA, PRINCE DE LA RUE (2000)

## ALI ZAOUA, PRINCE OF THE STREETS

The lives and fates of street children, society's castaways, are an ongoing source of fascination for filmmakers, and given the ever-growing gap between rich and poor around the globe, there's no end of fresh material in sight. In *Ali Zaoua, Prince of the Streets*, director and co-screenwriter Nabil Ayouch tells the story of a trio of homeless Moroccan boys whose lives on the mean streets of Casablanca consist of stealing, hustling, and trying to stay one step ahead of certain death. That last item is most likely to come in the form of Dib (Saïd Taghmaoui), the self appointed, cruel young leader of a huge posse of Lost Boys. Dib's sadistic power plays and fulfilled threats keep his sprawling gang under his control and give the boys (albeit, perversely) what they otherwise lack: a family.

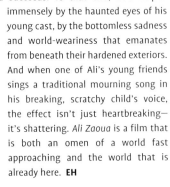

The titular character (Abdelhak Zhayra) dies early in the film, leaving his comrades to try to bury him in a way suitable for the young boy who, in his fantasies, was a powerful sailor. They want to honor their friend by letting him be, in death, what he likely would never have been in life. Working with a cast that is comprised largely of nonactors, Ayouch achieves a powerful documentary feel with the film, whose grit and grime is depressingly realistic. Young Ali's fantasies are illustrated in bright, colorful animation that counteracts the bleakness of his realities—a bleakness that cinematographer Vincent Mathias captures with great skill, occasionally alleviating it with unexpected snatches of beauty (such as the twinkling, inky night sky.) What makes the film so powerful is Ayouch's deft juggling of his characters' harsh lives with both humor and unabashed sentimentality. He wants to break your heart, is determined to do so, and succeeds. To that end, he's helped immensely by the haunted eyes of his young cast, by the bottomless sadness and world-weariness that emanates from beneath their hardened exteriors. And when one of Ali's young friends sings a traditional mourning song in his breaking, scratchy child's voice, the effect isn't just heartbreaking—it's shattering. *Ali Zaoua* is a film that is both an omen of a world fast approaching and the world that is already here. **EH**

## GLADIATOR (2000)

Hot off filming *The Insider*, Russell Crowe lost 40 lbs of weight and built up his muscles to play thinking women's sex object Maximus, the Roman general turned gladiator, in Hollywood's first true Roman epic for over three decades. Exiled when his mentor, Caesar Marcus Aurelius (Richard Harris) dies and is succeeded by his power-hungry son, Commodus (Joaquin Phoenix), Maximus, now in exile, trains as a gladiator and swears his revenge—understandable when you consider that Commodus not only kicked Maximus out of the bosom of Rome and tried to kill him, but also had his family murdered.

As you would expect from director Ridley Scott, the movie is epic not only in scale but also in imagery, as the majesty that was Rome is re-created superbly on screen (much praise is due here to Scott's cinematographer, John Mathieson). But Scott doesn't lose sight of the human side of the story amid the computer trickery, brilliantly staged battle sequences, and spectacular sets, delivering a fascinating, grisly, and heroic tale. With skilled actors, most notably Crowe, a wonderfully preening Phoenix and, in his final role, Oliver Reed who sadly died during filming—his remaining scenes were generated using a stand-in and computer-enhanced filmwork. **JB**

**G.B. / U.S.** (DreamWorks SKG, Scott Free, Universal) 155m Technicolor

**Director:** Ridley Scott

**Producer:** David Franzoni, Branko Lustig, Douglas Wick

**Screenplay:** David Franzoni, John Logan, William Nicholson

**Photography:** John Mathieson

**Music:** Hans Zimmer

**Cast:** Russell Crowe, Joaquin Phoenix, Connie Nielsen, Oliver Reed, Richard Harris, Derek Jacobi, Djimon Hounsou, David Schofield, John Shrapnel, Tomas Arana, David Hemmings, Ralf Moeller, Spencer Treat Clark, Tommy Flanagan, Sven-Ole Thorsen

**Oscar:** Douglas Wick, David Franzoni, Branko Lustig (best picture), Russell Crowe (actor), Janty Yates (costume), John Nelson, Neil Corbould, Tim Burke, Rob Harvey (special visual effects), Scott Millan, Bob Beemer, Ken Weston (sound)

**Oscar nomination:** Ridley Scott (director), David Franzoni, John Logan, William Nicholson (screenplay), Joaquin Phoenix (actor in support role), Arthur Max, Crispian Sallis (art direction), John Mathieson (photography), Pietro Scalia (editing), Hans Zimmer (music)

**France / Israel** (Agav Hafakot, Canal+, MP, R&C, Telad, Tele Plus, arte) 123m Color

**Language:** Hebrew

**Director:** Amos Gitai

**Producer:** Amos Gitai, Michel Propper, Laurent Truchot

**Screenplay:** Amos Gitai, Marie-Jose Sanselme

**Photography:** Renato Berta

**Music:** Jan Garbarek

**Cast:** Liron Levo, Tomer Russo, Uri Ran-Klausner, Yoram Hattab, Guy Amir, Juliano Mer, Ran Kauchinsky, Kobi Livne, Liat Glick, Pini Mittleman, Meital Barda, Gidi Gov

**Cannes Film Festival:** Amos Gitai nomination (Golden Palm)

# KIPPUR (2000)

Since his debut in the early 1980s with a series of documentaries that ran afoul of Israeli television, Amos Gitai has become known as Israel's most provocative filmmaker. Despite his courage and good instincts, at times his films can feel somewhat clumsy and inept—but not *Kippur*. In this haunting remembrance of things past, Gitai conjures up a shattering vision of the 1973 Yom Kippur War, in which he himself was seriously wounded. Two friends head for the Golan Heights to join up with their unit, but are deflected into a medical team that helicopters in to rescue the wounded. From the moment the reservists begin driving out of peacetime to the front lines, literally searching for the location of war, Gitai edges us into ever more lunar landscapes where time, flesh, the very earth, are fatally susceptible to distortion and/or disintegration.

*Kippur* is less about a specific struggle between enemy forces than it is an evocation of the hallucinatory state of war: confusion, shock, numbing fatigue, constant cacophony. There's at least one sequence that is truly the stuff from which nightmares are made: A rescue team tries to carry away a seriously wounded soldier from a battlefield knee-deep in mud, only to have the body keep slipping off the stretcher. In one horrifying, gruesomely funny moment, Gitai makes us experience bone deep the impact of the war—personal and cosmic, realistic and surreal. **RP**

**Taiwan / Japan** (Atom, Nemuru Otoko Seisaku Iinkai, Omega, Pony Canyon) 173m Color

**Language:** English / Hokkien / Mandarin

**Director:** Edward Yang

**Producer:** Shinya Kawai, Osamu Kunota, Naoko Tsukeda, Wei-yen Yu

**Screenplay:** Edward Yang

**Photography:** Wei-han Yang

**Music:** Kai-Li Peng

**Credited cast:** Wu Nien-Jen, Elaine Jin, Issey Ogata, Kelly Lee, Jonathan Chang, Hsi-Sheng Chen, Su-Yun Ko, Michael Tao, Shu-shen Hsiao, Adrian Lin, Pang Chang Yu, Ru-Yun Tang, Shu-Yuan Hsu, Hsin-Yi Tseng, Yiwen Chen

**Cannes Film Festival:** Edward Yang (director), nomination (Golden Palm)

# YI YI (2000)
## A ONE AND A TWO

Edward Yang's most accessible movie and probably his best since *A Brighter Summer Day*, this 2000 feature follows three generations of a contemporary Taipei family from a wedding to a funeral, and although it takes almost three hours to unfold, not a single moment seems gratuitous.

Working once again with nonprofessional actors, Yang coaxes a standout performance from Wu Nien-jen—a substantial writer and director in his own right—as N.J., a middle-aged partner in a failing computer company who hopes to team up with a Japanese game designer, and who has a secret rendezvous in Tokyo with a woman (Su-Yun Ko) he jilted 30 years earlier. Other major characters in *Yi Yi* include the hero's eight-year-old son (Jonathan Chang), teenage daughter (Kelly Lee), spiritually traumatized wife (Elaine Jin), comatose mother-in-law (Ru-Yun Tang), and debt-ridden brother-in-law (Hsi-Sheng Chen). The son—a comic and unsentimental marvel named Yang-Yang—becomes obsessed with photographing what people can't see, like the backs of their heads, because to him it's the half of reality that's missed. He may come closest to being a mouthpiece for Yang, who seems to miss nothing as he interweaves shifting viewpoints and poignant emotional refrains, creating one of the richest family portraits in modern cinema. **JRos**

# REQUIEM FOR A DREAM (2000)

U.S. (Artisan, Bandeira, Protozoa, Sibling, Industry, Thousand Words Truth & Soul) 102m Color

**Director:** Darren Aronofsky

**Producer:** Eric Watson, Palmer West

**Screenplay:** Hubert Selby Jr., Darren Aronofsky, from novel by Hubert Selby Jr.

**Photography:** Matthew Libatique

**Music:** Clint Mansell

**Cast:** Ellen Burstyn, Jared Leto, Jennifer Connelly, Marlon Wayans, Christopher McDonald, Louise Lasser, Marcia Jean Kurtz, Janet Sarno, Suzanne Shepherd, Joanne Gordon, Charlotte Aronofsky, Mark Margolis, Michael Kaycheck, Jack O'Connell, Chas Mastin

**Oscar nomination:** Ellen Burstyn (actress)

Darren Aronofsky's follow-up to his acclaimed debut *Pi* (1998) is nothing short of remarkable. *Requiem for a Dream* follows four characters—Harry Goldfarb (Jared Leto), his mother (Ellen Burstyn), girlfriend (Jennifer Connelly), and best friend (Marlon Wayans)—through the nightmare world of drug addiction. Each has their own drug, their own way of handling their addiction, and they all end up in different situations, but these addictions are all caused by the same thing, the failure of the American Dream. For Aronofsky, the Dream is dead and his film is a nightmarish mourning for its victims.

Visually, *Requiem* owes much to both Danny Boyle's *Trainspotting* (1996) and the films of Spike Lee; but unlike Boyle, whose own drug movie included sequences of hallucinogenic subjectivity, Aronofsky resists grounding the audience in any kind of objective position. The entire film is shot within this drug-addled subjective tense. And from Lee, Aronofsky takes a hyperkinetic visual sensibility used to represent a Brooklyn state-of-mind, though *Requiem* makes thematic use of these elements, rather than just employing them for surface style.

The acting is uniformly magnificent, with Leto, Connelly, and Wayans giving surprisingly strong performances. But it is Burstyn's role as Harry's diet-pill addicted mom that is nothing short of astonishing, and if one had to pick a single reason to see the film it would have to be for this performance. Although nominated for a Best Actress Oscar, Burstyn lost to Julia Roberts (*Erin Brockovich*) and no disrespect to either the film or Ms. Roberts, but come on! Granting that Roberts's performance was the best of her career, Burstyn's Sara is the best of her career—and that's hardly a fair comparison.

But missing from this discussion—and the real reason to see *Requiem for a Dream*, beyond its intelligent ideas, amazing use of narcotic subjectivity, meaningful stylistics, and magnificent performances—is the film's remarkable balance of horror (the final sequences of drug madness are some of the scariest moments I've seen in years) and great Jewish comedy. Just imagine Woody Allen directing *Naked Lunch*. **MK**

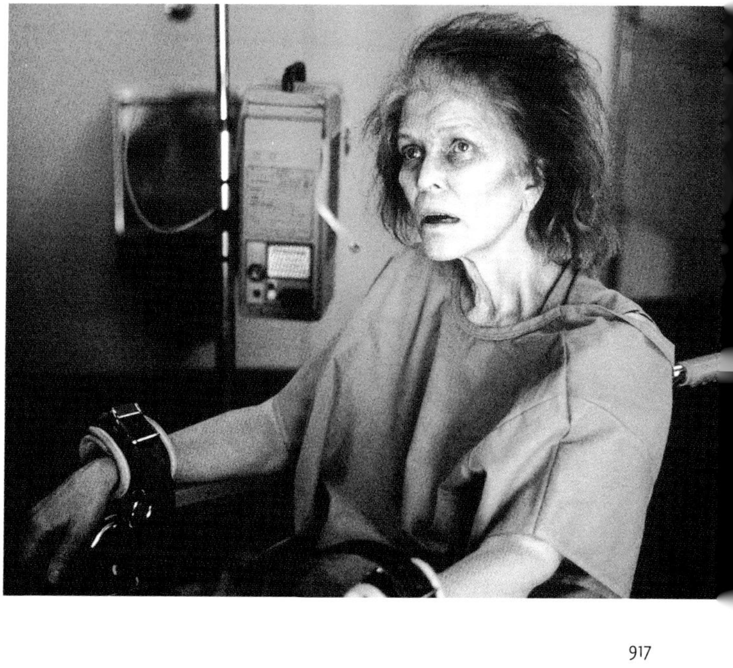

**Mexico** (Altavista, Zeta) 153m Color
**Language:** Spanish
**Director:** Alejandro González Iñárritu
**Producer:** Alejandro González Iñárritu
**Screenplay:** Guillermo Arriaga
**Photography:** Rodrigo Prieto
**Music:** Gustavo Santaolalla
**Cast:** Emilio Echevarría, Gael García Bernal, Goya Toledo, Álvaro Guerrero, Vanessa Bauche, Jorge Salinas, Marco Pérez, Rodrigo Murray, Humberto Busto, Gerardo Campbell, Rosa María Bianchi, Dunia Saldívar, Adriana Barraza, José Sefami, Lourdes Echevarría
**Cannes Film Festival:** Alejandro González Iñárritu (critics week grand prize), (young critics award, best feature)

# AMORES PERROS (2000)

Quentin Tarantino had such a pronounced and immediate effect on American filmmakers that it was only a matter of time before his influence stretched into other countries. *Amores Perros*—which translates roughly to "Love's a Bitch"—shows that by 2000 the Tarantino model of stylish violence and jumbled narratives had made its way south of the U.S. border, to Mexico. *Amores Perros* marked the feature debut of Mexican director Alejandro Gonzalez Iñárritu, and if the film ultimately offers nothing particularly new, his vibrant filmmaking still manages to inject the somewhat familiar scenarios with energy, humor, intelligence, and warmth.

Shot as three interlocking stories whose central characters overlap at one key juncture, *Amores Perros* remains faithful to the canine theme of its title, as each segment of the film features a dog or dogs in a prominent role. In the first, a boy cheats with his brother's wife while entering his prized dog into grisly (and viscerally effective) fights, hoping to raise money so that he and his sister-in-law can run off together. In the second Edgar Allen Poe by way of Luis Buñuel segment, a vain, crippled supermodel loses her dog in the crawlspace beneath the floorboards of her apartment, and is tormented by the sounds of its incessant suffering as well as her inability to alleviate it. In the final segment, a homeless hit man seeks redemption for the life he has led and recognition from his estranged family.

All three segments ironically illustrate man's inhumanity to man via his treatment of animals, which incidentally fare so poorly in the film that *Amores Perros* infamously sports a prominent and preemptive disclaimer at its start noting that no animals were harmed during the making of the film. In fact, the frequent dog violence (and violence to dogs) is depicted so realistically that at times it does threaten to overwhelm the picture. But Iñárritu succeeds in delivering his message of bloody disloyalty, chilling [illegible], and [illegible] disjunction with an abundance of style, revealing in the process a strong trust for the instincts of his [illegible] as well as the intelligence of his audience. **JKl**

## MEET THE PARENTS (2000)

If proof were needed, *King of Comedy*, *Midnight Run*, and *Analyze This* removed all doubt—Robert De Niro isn't just a serious Method actor, he is also a great comic talent. In *Meet The Parents* he not only raises a laugh but also matches seasoned comedian Ben Stiller scene for scene.

Male nurse Greg Focker (Stiller) decides to propose to his girlfriend Pam (Teri Polo), but when he learns her sister's fiancé asked her father for permission to marry, Greg realizes he'll have to do the same thing. So begins a comedy of errors as Greg accompanies Pam to her family home for the first time and discovers that whatever could go wrong does, and disastrously so. As he tries to impress Pam's parents, her ex-CIA agent father Jack (De Niro) in particular, accidents escalate: first involving the beloved family pet, then the ashes of Jack's mother, a flammable gazebo, and an overflowing septic tank, all catastrophes just waiting to happen. And matters get even worse for Greg after he meets Pam's favored ex-fiancé (Owen Wilson).

Stiller, in a role originally intended for Jim Carrey, is utterly believable as the well-meaning guy who just can't get it right. But the real applause should go to De Niro, who on the basis of this performance might consider ditching "serious" acting altogether and taking up a new career as one of the best funnymen around. **JB**

**U.S.** (DreamWorks SKG, Nancy Tenenbaum, Tribeca, Universal) 108m Color

**Language:** English / Spanish / Hebrew / French

**Director:** Jay Roach

**Producer:** Robert De Niro, Jay Roach, Jane Rosenthal, Nancy Tenenbaum

**Screenplay:** Jim Herzfeld, John Hamburg

**Photography:** Peter James

**Music:** Randy Newman

**Cast:** Robert De Niro, Ben Stiller, Teri Polo, Blythe Danner, Nicole DeHuff, Jon Abrahams, Owen Wilson, James Rebhorn, Thomas McCarthy, Phyllis George, Kali Rocha, Bernie Sheredy, Judah Friedlander, Peter Bartlett, John Elsen

**Oscar nomination:** Randy Newman (song)

## SIGNS & WONDERS (2000)

Director Jonathan Nossiter and screenwriter James Lasdun, who collaborated on the very promising *Sunday* (1997), reunite for this ambitious and ambiguous thriller involving an Americanized businessman in Athens, Alec (Stellan Skarsgård), who has twice left his Greek-American wife Marjorie (Charlotte Rampling at her best) and their two children for another woman (Deborah Kara Unger), but who still hasn't given up on their marriage.

Shot in digital video as if it were a documentary, *Signs & Wonders* at separate junctures evokes Nicolas Roeg, Graham Greene, and Richard Lester's *Petulia* (1968), even as it takes up multinational corporations, political amnesia, the mixed blessing of American idealism, and some of the monstrous ways love can turn sour. Clearly the film bites off more than it can possibly chew, and ultimately it winds up risking pretentiousness. But Nossiter, an American who grew up in Europe, and Lasdun (who also wrote the 1998 Bernardo Bertolucci film, *Besieged*), an Englishman who currently lives in the United States, share a sense of cultural displacement that allows them to create something original and provocative. **JRos**

**France** (Goatworks, Ideefixe, Industry, MK2, Sunshine Amalgamedia) 105m Color

**Language:** English / Greek

**Director:** Jonathan Nossiter

**Producer:** Marin Karmitz

**Screenplay:** James Lasdun, Jonathan Nossiter

**Photography:** Yorgos Arvanitis

**Music:** Adrian Utley

**Cast:** Stellan Skarsgård, Charlotte Rampling, Deborah Unger, Dimitri Katalifos, Ashley Remy, Dave Simonds, Arto Apartian, Alexandros Mylonas, Dimitris Kaberidis, Themis Bazaka, Michael Cook, Peggy Gennatiempo, Steven Goldstein, Steven Edward Zate

**Berlin International Film Festival:** Jonathan Nossiter nomination (Golden Bear)

**U.S. / Hong Kong / China / Taiwan** (Asia Union, China Film, Columbia, EDKO, Good Machine, Sony, United China, Zoom Hunt) 120m Technicolor

**Language:** Mandarin

**Director:** Ang Lee

**Producer:** Li-Kong Hsu, William Kong, Ang Lee

**Screenplay:** Hui-Ling Wang, James Schamus, Kuo Jung Tsai, from book by Du Lu Wang

**Photography:** Peter Pau

**Music:** Jorge Calandrelli, Yong King, Tan Dun

**Cast:** Chow Yun-Fat, Michelle Yeoh, Zhang Ziyo, Chen Chang, Sihung Lung, Pei-pei Cheng, Fa Zeng Li, Xian Gao, Yan Hai, De Ming Wang, Li-Li Li, Su Ying Huang, Jin Ting Zhang, Rei Yang, Kai Li

**Oscar:** Taiwan (best foreign language film), Timmy Yip (art direction), Peter Pau (photography), Tan Dun (music)

**Oscar nomination:** William Kong, Li-Kong Hsu, Ang Lee (best picture), Ang Lee (director), Hui-Ling Wang, James Schamus, Kuo Jung Tsai (screenplay), Timmy Yip (costume), Tim Squyres (editing), Jorge Calandrelli, Tan Dun, James Schamus (song)

# WO HU CANG LONG (2000)
## CROUCHING TIGER, HIDDEN DRAGON

Director Ang Lee has said that his intention with *Crouching Tiger, Hidden Dragon* was quite simply to make the best martial arts movie possible, and the artistic success and popularity of the end result indicates he achieved just that. Working from a script by his longtime collaborator James Schamus, who borrowed heavily from Chinese folk tales in the creation of the hybrid action/fantasy/romance, Lee convened an international cast of Asian action superstars who also possessed the requisite acting skills to deliver the story.

Lee also made a brilliant decision by bringing in famed fight choreographer Lee Wu-Ping, a pioneer in the martial arts world. Taking inspiration from the physicality of the Chinese theater, Wu-Ping ignores the laws of physics by hoisting the actors up on wires so that they may fight on treetops, skip across water like stones, run up walls, and often clash in midair. For Western audiences perhaps unaccustomed to these aerial ballets, the sight of an opening foot chase over the rooftops of a village on a moonlit night proved immediately and irresistibly enticing.

Chow Yun Fat, Michelle Yeow, and relative newcomer Ziyo Zhang easily handle the supernatural physicality of their respective roles, but their acting never proves subservient to the impressive action scenes. In fact, one reason *Crouching Tiger, Hidden Dragon* became such a sensation was its attention to plot and character development, two rarities even in the most ambitious martial arts films, which typically stress stunts and fighting sequences over acting chops.

Chow Yun Fat plays a warrior in search of a stolen sword, the Green Dragon. Aided in his quest by Yeow, a former love interest, he discovers that the theft of the sword by Ziyo Zhang is connected to and clouded by longstanding issues of honor and revenge. For all the gravity-defying stunts and fitful bursts of

inventive violence, Lee keeps the focus firmly on the film's three central characters, whose philosophies on the utility of fighting and bloodshed have been shaped by their radically different experiences in life.

A strong feminist undercurrent also runs through *Crouching Tiger, Hidden Dragon*, adding another layer of intelligence to the film. The various female characters fight for different reasons, but most of them seem to be fighting for respect in a man's world. Having run away from home, the tiny Zhang, posing as a warrior, finds herself beset in a bustling way station by several unsavory fighters. Lee plays the inevitable thrashing of these few dozen would-be assailants for laughs, like a hyperkinetic variation on the old bar fight. But part of Zhang's passionate and over-the-top response seems to stem from simmering resentment, her understanding that were it known that she is female she would have been dismissed outright rather than respected (or feared) as a formidable opponent.

Lee modulates each scene of the movie with a similar nuance and sensitivity. His fight sequences play like psychological confrontations as much as sword fights, the clash of innocence and experience, of peace and anger. Even so, Lee leaves as much room for levity as he does for visual poetry, achieving a rare balance of thrills, beauty, humor, and smarts. **JKl**

## TRAFFIC (2000)

It took until 2000 for Hollywood to realize what a talent it had in director Steven Soderbergh, despite his superb 1989 debut, *Sex, Lies, and Videotape*, and masterful follow-ups like *Out Of Sight* (1998) and *The Limey* (1999). Although *Erin Brockovich* (2000) finally got him noticed, it was with *Traffic* that he was at last recognized as one of the most interesting directors of his generation.

Loosely based on the acclaimed 1989 British TV series *Traffik*, the film explores various areas of the drug trade in a gritty, almost documentary style, focusing on different people in the chain that fuels America's drug culture, from the judge (Michael Douglas, who turned down the role when he first saw the script, only to change his mind when the role was expanded) spearheading the President's war against drugs while encountering drug problems in his own middle-class home, to the Mexican cop (a mesmerizing Benicio Del Toro, who won an Oscar for his performance) using his own questionable methods to get the same job done south of the border, to the shell-shocked pregnant mother (Catherine Zeta-Jones, giving one of the best performances of her career) forced to cope when her drug-trafficking hubby (Steven Bauer) is carted off to jail.

The supporting cast is equally impressive (many signed up purely for the opportunity to work with Soderbergh)—Don Cheadle and Luis Guzmán as Drug Enforcement Administration agents determined to get the dealer they have been tracking; Dennis Quaid, as Jones's lawyer; and most notably, Erika Christensen as Douglas's heroin-addicted daughter—while other actors deliver small cameos (Amy Irving, James Brolin, Albert Finney) and make the most of their screen time with powerful performances.

Tautly scripted by Stephen Gaghan (who had previously written episodes of *NYPD Blue* and *American Gothic*), the movie is perfectly realized by Soderbergh, who ambitiously used more than 130 actors in 110 locations, filming them with handheld cameras and imaginative editing and cinematography techniques to deliver a truly awe-inspiring and thought-provoking picture. **JB**

**Germany / U.S.** (Bedford Falls, Compulsion, IEG, Splendid, US) 147m Color

**Language:** English / Spanish

**Director:** Steven Soderbergh

**Producer:** Laura Bickford, Marshall Herskovitz, Edward Zwick

**Screenplay:** Stephen Gaghan, from miniseries *Traffik* by Simon Moore

**Photography:** Steven Soderbergh

**Music:** Brian Eno, Cliff Martinez

**Cast:** Benicio Del Toro, Michael Douglas, Catherine Zeta-Jones, Denis Quaid, Alec Roberts, Miguel Ferrer, Luis Guzmán, Don Cheadle, Topher Grace, Erika Christensen, Jacob Vargas, Amy Irving, Tomas Milian, Majandra Delfino, Albert Finney, James Brolin, Steven Bauer

**Oscar:** Steven Soderbergh (director), Stephen Gaghan (screenplay), Benicio Del Toro (actor in support role), Stephen Mirrione (editing)

**Oscar nomination:** Edward Zwick, Marshall Herskovitz, Laura Bickford (best picture)

**Berlin International Film Festival:** Benicio Del Toro (Silver Bear—actor), Steven Soderbergh nomination (Golden Bear)

# LES GLANEURS ET LA GLANEUSE (2000)
## THE GLEANERS AND I

Digital technology has revolutionized filmmaking by making it more democratic and less expensive—the merits, fall-out from, and worthiness of that revolution can still be rigorously debated. What has so often been lacking in digital movies though is any sense of beauty or style, any *eye* for making movies. Even more, the "personal" films that have come out of the digital revolution have often been sophomoric and self-indulgent. Leave it to the mother of the French New Wave, Agnès Varda, to show all the upstarts how it should be done.

Unapologetically and unflinchingly leftist in its politics, swerving from musings on life and mortality to the role of art in society, all while paying tribute to society's outcasts and marginalized, *The Gleaners and I* is all over the map. Yet Varda doesn't let the film get away from her; the viewer never feels anything other than that they're in the passenger seat on an eye-opening journey that's being navigated by a master. There's a wonderful moment in the film in which director Varda, picking overripe figs from a tree and eating them on the spot, launches a tirade about the greed of those who are both wealthy and selfish. Rather than spout threadbare Marxist theory, she simply observes, "They don't want to be nice." That raw truth resonates throughout the documentary, at the center of which are modern-day gleaners, people who salvage scraps after open-air markets close, or pick through dumpsters to find food. Varda lets these marginalized people speak for themselves, and they eloquently address everything from world politics to personal tragedies, while the film shows that those two poles are not so far apart.

Tough questions of social inequity are smoothly juxtaposed against the salvelike qualities of art, and the necessity of finding beauty where you live, actively seeking it out just as you would food or shelter. The result is a protest film that's part social critique, part travelogue, but always an unsentimental celebration of human resilience. Threaded throughout *The Gleaners and I* are Varda's musings on her own mortality. Rather than being pitying or sentimental, though, those moments capsulize the film's assertion that everyone who clears life's hurdles is an artist of sorts. **EH**

**France** (Tamaris) 82m Color

**Language:** French

**Director:** Agnès Varda

**Photography:** Didier Doussin, Stéphane Krausz, Didier Rouget, Pascal Sautelet, Agnès Varda

**Screenplay:** Agnès Varda

**Music:** Agnès Bredel, Joanna Bruzdowicz, Richard Klugman, Isabelle Olivier

**Cast:** Bodan Litnanski, Agnès Varda, François Wertheimer

# MEMENTO (2000)

Based on his brother Jonah's story *Memento Mori*, British director Christopher Nolan's second feature is a near-perfect psychological puzzle. Known to movie buffs as "the film filmed backward," this modern film noir is told in stops and starts. Scenes appear in reverse chronological order then move forward again, presenting information that is useless until another parcel of the plot is supplied. An annoying gimmick in another director's hands, Nolan makes the chronological scene shifting an effective way to unfold what is essentially a misguided murder mystery where the hero may or may not know that his facts are not "the facts." Following a long tradition of memory loss within the noir genre—*Blue Dahlia* (1945) and *Suture* (1993)—the main character's amnesia is yet another exciting factor within a film that has many.

Australian actor Guy Pearce stars as Leonard, a nervy and smug ex-insurance investigator. He wears nice suits and drives a nice car but stays in rundown motels, an indication of the self-imposed gumshoe he has become. Suffering from a rare form of amnesia (a real condition called anterograde amnesia, the inability to make new memories), Leonard keeps track of his actions through sticky notes and polaroids, tattooing his body with the more important "truths" of the matter. His one aim is to avenge the rape and murder of his wife, a near-impossible task considering he has the slenderest of leads and can't remember anything from the immediate past. The people around him, bedmate Natalie (Carrie-Anne Moss) or chirpy Teddy (Joe Pantoliano), could be friends or could be the killer—he has no idea.

In virtually every scene, Pearce gives a compelling, nervy performance as the man who is haplessly fanatical about his mission yet so incapable of making the decisions he needs to make. How the threads of the story are unraveled and reorganized is an impressive feat of logic minding and script continuity. This technical ploy demands the audience's vigilance yet, in true film noir form, doesn't reward it. In the end, it is the way the tale is told that is memorable, not the story itself. **KK**

**U.S.** (Remember, Newmarket, Todd) 113m BW/Color

**Director:** Christopher Nolan

**Producer:** Jennifer Todd, Suzanne Todd

**Screenplay:** Christopher Nolan, Jonathan Nolan

**Photography:** Wally Pfister

**Music:** David Julyan

**Cast:** Guy Pearce, Carrie-Anne Moss, Joe Pantoliano, Mark Boone Junior, Russ Fega, Jorja Fox, Stephen Tobolowsky, Harriet Sansom Harris, Thomas Lennon, Callum Keith Rennie, Kimberly Campbell, Marianne Muellerleile, Larry Holden

**Oscar nomination:** Christopher Nolan, Jonathan Nolan (screenplay), Dody Dorn (editing)

## DANCER IN THE DARK (2000)

This self-referential musical plays for the most part in director Lars von Trier's Dogme95 style, with edgy camera work and improv-seeming performances. But it repeatedly segues into fantasized songs that don't look like any other musical numbers in film, with their video blur look—brighter than the film's "reality," but still not MGM glam—and growth out of rhythmic factory or scratch noises (even the battering of a murder victim's head).

Sometime in the 1960s, in an America created in Europe (because the director refuses to fly), Czech single mother Selma (Björk) works in a basin factory and takes on extra jobs to raise the money she needs so that her son can have an operation which will forestall the hereditary blindness that is already beyond help in her. She dreams musical numbers, and goes to the movies with her friend Kathy (Catherine Deneuve, brilliantly cast)—who explains the images to her—but gently (if devastatingly) resists the courtship of nice guy Jeff (Peter Stormare). Instead, she focuses on holding off the effects of her handicap until she can pay Dr. Porkorny (Udo Kier) for her son's eye operation.

If Selma dreams of an unreal musical world, one with a dancing shop floor straight out of *The Pajama Game*, her "real" life is just as fable-like, albeit on the miserable side as her troubles mount. Her landlord, local cop Bill (David Morse), is in debt but has made a show of being rich for his wife, and learns about Selma's stash, which he connives to steal. She confronts him and he forces her to kill him to get the money, which she then passes to Dr. Porkorny—we are supposed to believe a huge eye hospital is located in the nearby woods just off the bus stop—before being arrested, tried, convicted, and, in the end, hanged. It is as unreal as a Guy Maddin movie, but the scenes all work, and Björk is marvelous in a difficult role, conveying exactly the prisons into which she forces herself for a love she can barely express in person ("I just wanted to hold the little baby"). **KN**

**Denmark / Germany / Netherlands / U.S. / G.B. / France / Sweden / Finland / Iceland / Norway**
(Zentropa, Svenska, Väst, Liberator, Pain Unlimited, Cinematograph A/S, What Else? B.V., Icelandic Film Corp., Blind Spot, France 3, DR, arte, SVT Drama, Angel, Canal+, FilmFour, Constantin, Lantia Cinema, TV 1000, VPRO TV, WDR, YLE) 140m Color

**Director:** Lars von Trier

**Producer:** Vibeke Windeløv

**Screenplay:** Lars von Trier

**Photography:** Robby Müller

**Music:** Björk

**Cast:** Björk, Catherine Deneuve, David Morse, Peter Stormare, Joel Grey, Cara Seymour, Vladica Kostic, Jean-Marc Barr, Vincent Paterson, Siobhan Fallon, Zeljko Ivanek, Udo Kier, Jens Albinus, Reathel Bean, Mette Berggreen

**Cannes Film Festival:** Lars von Trier (Golden Palm), Björk (actress)

# O BROTHER, WHERE ART THOU? (2000)

**G.B. / France / U.S.** (Buena Vista, Mike Zoss, Canal, Touchstone, Universal, Working Title) 106m Color
**Director:** Joel Coen
**Producer:** Ethan Coen
**Screenplay:** Ethan Coen, Joel Coen, from the *The Odyssey* by Homer
**Photography:** Roger Deakins
**Music:** T-Bone Burnett
**Cast:** George Clooney, John Turturro, Tim Blake Nelson, John Goodman, Holly Hunter, Chris Thomas King, Charles Durning, Del Pentecost, Michael Badalucco, J.R. Horne, Brian Reddy, Wayne Duvall, Ed Gale, Ray McKinnon, Daniel von Bargen
**Oscar nomination:** Ethan Coen, Joel Coen (screenplay), Roger Deakins (photography)
**Cannes Film Festival:** Joel Coen nomination (Golden Palm)

Titled after a fictitious film mentioned by the hero of Preston Sturges's 1941 classic, *Sullivan's Travels*, and based loosely on Homer's *Odyssey*, Joel and Ethan Coen's arch period comedy is a journey through the marvels and the madness of America's Deep South during the Great Depression.

Overarticulate, vain ex-convict Ulysses Everett McGill (George Clooney) breaks out of a prison chain gang with Delmar (Tim Blake Nelson) and Pete (John Turturro) in tow. Tracked by a lawman who seems to be the devil himself, their journey to find McGill's hidden bankroll takes them to a back-country recording studio. The trio hook up with a young guitarist (blues musician Chris Thomas King), who sold his soul to Satan; befriend manic-depressive (and real-life) bankrobber Babyface Nelson (Michael Badalucco); and have some terrifying encounters with the law, the devil, the Klu Klux Klan, and a one-eyed bible salesman (John Goodman).

Making the most threatening situation look ridiculous, some of the most emotive elements of the Depression Era mutate here into folksy humor. At its heart, *O Brother, Where Art Thou?* is a surreal and sincere romp that brings with it a wealth of folk music from the American 1920s and '30s. The soundtrack, a blend of bluegrass and spirituals, proved so popular that it single-handedly spawned a full-blown country music revival. **KK**

# LE FABULEUX DESTIN D'AMÉLIE POULAIN (2001)

## AMÉLIE

**France / Germany** (Filmstiftung Nordrhein-Westfalen, France 3, La Sofica Sofinergie 5, Canal+, MMC Independent, Tapioca, UGC Images, Victoires ) 122m BW/ Color

**Language:** French

**Director:** Jean-Pierre Jeunet

**Producer:** Jean-Marc Deschamps, Arne Meerkamp van Embden, Claudie Ossard

**Screenplay:** Guillaume Laurant, Jean-Pierre Jeunet

**Photography:** Bruno Delbonnel

**Music:** Yann Tiersen

**Cast:** Audrey Tautou, Mathieu Kassovitz, Rufus, Yolande Moreau, Artus de Penguern, Urbain Cancelier, Dominique Pinon, Maurice Bénichou, Claude Perron, Michel Robin, Isabelle Nanty, Claire Maurier, Clotilde Mollet, Serge Merlin, Jamel Debbouze

**Oscar nomination:** France (best foreign language film), Guillaume Laurant, Jean-Pierre Jeunet (screenplay), Aline Bonetto, Marie-Laure Valla (art direction), Bruno Delbonnel (photography), Vincent Arnardi, Guillaume Leriche, Jean Umansky (sound)

Debuting and succeeding as it did not long before the terrorist attacks of 2001, Jean-Pierre Jeunet's *Amélie* nonetheless gained even more attention and acclaim after it went into wider release in the months immediately following September 11th. The right movie at the right time, *Amélie* was immediately received not as mindless escapism but as a fantastic and idealized respite from the horrors and rigors of the real world. Hence the film's fanciful French title, *Le Fabuleux destin d'Amélie Poulain*—which translates literally to *The Fabulous Destiny of Amelie Poulain*—remains a far more colorful and helpful title than the simple international truncation.

*Amélie* could probably also go by the title *The Fabulous Destiny of Jean-Pierre Jeunet*. The writer/director had already revealed himself a gifted creator (with regular collaborator Marc Caro) of fantastic, half-familiar worlds. His dark comedy *Delicatessen* was set in the future, where food shortages lead to some creative cannibalistic solutions at a strange, funhouse-like inn. The even better *The City of Lost Children* focused on an alternate world, where the dreams of oddly mature children are harvested by a decrepit and dastardly mad scientist who is unable to generate dreams of his own. On its face, *Amélie* takes place in the real world. But using a remarkable array of playful (and often playfully literal) effects, Jeunet transforms contemporary France into a beautiful and surreal reflection of reality, in which the wide-eyed and idealistic titular character spreads love and happiness to the frowning faces all around her.

Amélie herself, however, is in a funk, and so decides to expend some of her remarkable energy in search of true love. Played with innocent, imp-like precision by Audrey Tautou, Amélie doesn't just sob; she is reduced to a puddle of tears. The city doesn't just glow metaphorically; it's given a preternatural tint and perpetually perfect weather thanks to some savvy computer effects. In lesser hands, *Amélie* could have been bogged down in sappiness and misused sentimentality, but Jeunet wisely retains just enough of the pain and disappointment of real life to temper his fairy-tale-like fantasy. And the film—like its central character—is obsessed with tiny details and whimsical minutiae that keep the viewer tied to the quirky tall tale.

Jeunet's best decision was casting Tautou, who radiates good nature but also displays a mischievous streak that goes with her sly smile and keeps the performance from becoming too saccharine. Amélie's feelings run dramatically hot and cold, and Tautou so capably regulates the way her character radiates emotions that you can't help but seesaw back and forth along with her. Indeed, unlike most fantasy directors, Jeunet seems more interested in how people feel and how they in turn make other people feel than in the world in which they live. As fantastical as that world may be in *Amélie*, you never get the impression the film is about anything other than the way two hearts beating on opposite sides of a vast metropolis can somehow find a way to interlink and beat as one. **JKl**

**France / Taiwan** (Arena, Homegreen) 116m Color

**Language:** Mandarin / French / Taiwanese

**Director:** Ming-liang Tsai

**Producer:** Bruno Pesery, Chinlin Hsieh

**Screenplay:** Ming-liang Tsai, Pi-ying Yang

**Photography:** Benoît Delhomme

**Credited cast:** Kang-sheng Lee, Shiang-chyi Chen, Yi-Ching Lu, Tien Miao, Cecilia Yip, Chao-jung Chen, Guei Tsai, Arthur Nauzyciel, David Ganansia, Jean-Pierre Léaud, Li-Ching Lu

**Cannes Film Festival:** Ming-liang Tsai nomination (Golden Palm)

# NI NEIBIAN JIDIAN (2001)

## WHAT TIME IS IT THERE?

In many ways, *What Time Is It There?* is Ming-liang Tsai's most exciting and original film to date. The obsessive constants in his first five features—the same actors playing similar roles in some of the same locations, the quirky preoccupation with water and alienation—may make him seem like a minimalist. But here he branches out beautifully by adding another city and country to his repertory—Paris, France, which alternates with Taipei—without compromising any of his formal rigor or playfulness. In the 1998 film *The Hole*, a young man and woman occupy flats on separate floors of the same building; here the pair (Kang-sheng Lee and Shiang-chyi Chen) occupy separate countries and time zones. They remain basically strangers, apart from fleeting encounters, but the intricate formal rhyme schemes devised by Tsai as he oscillates between the two are even more inventive than those in *The Hole*—one of the many things evoking Jacques Tati here. There is also some play in *What Time Is It There?* between the young man watching François Truffaut's *The 400 Blows* (1959) on video in Taipei and the young woman encountering Truffaut's star, Jean-Pierre Léaud, in a Paris graveyard.

Though lack of human connection remains a constant in Tsai's work—the various kinds of formal connectedness that he reveals here, not only across cities but between different parts of the planet, feel somehow hopeful. **JRos**

**U.S. / Mexico** (Anhelo, Besame Mucho) 105m Color

**Language:** Spanish

**Director:** Alfonso Cuarón

**Producer:** Alfonso Cuarón, Jorge Vergara

**Screenplay:** Alfonso Cuarón, Carlos Cuarón

**Photography:** Emmanuel Lubezki

**Music:** Natalie Imbruglia

**Cast:** Ana López Mercado, Diego Luna, Gael García Bernal, Nathan Grinberg, Verónica Langer, María Aura, Giselle Audirac, Arturo Ríos, Andrés Almeida, Diana Bracho, Emilio Echevarría, Marta Aura, Maribel Verdú, Juan Carlos Remolina, Liboria Rodríguez

**Oscar nomination:** Carlos Cuarón, Alfonso Cuarón (screenplay)

**Venice Film Festival:** Alfonso Cuarón, Carlos Cuarón (screenplay), Gael García Bernal, Diego Luna (Marcello Mastroianni award), Alfonso Cuarón nomination (Golden Lion)

# Y TU MAMÁ TAMBIÉN (2001)

## AND YOUR MOTHER TOO

Even fans of this deceptively simple, multilayered film often reduce it down to one of its two primary genre blueprints in order to praise it: Teen coming-of-age film or raunchy road flick. On the surface, *Y tu mamá también* is the story of what happens when childhood friends Tenoch (Diego Luna) and Julio (Gael Garcia Bernal) embark on a road trip with an older woman (Ana Morelos). The trio trek across Mexico in pursuit of a mythological beach, encountering the land and people in ways that depict the country as a more sociologically complex and dynamic entity than is usually represented on film.

Beneath the coming-of-age/road-trip fusion, however, Alfonso Cuarón's film is an artful, insightful essay on class, capitalism, and globalization, and on the ways that the dynamics of those items play out in everything from the ability to feed one's family to the shaping of our sexual desires. The simmering tensions between the two boys are ultimately rooted in their conflicting class status, in their resentments and hidden prejudices. With its unflinching politics, swooning sensuality, and unabashed celebration of sexuality, *Y tu mamá también* is one of the best examples of the revitalized Mexican cinema of the late 20th/early 21st centuries. **EH**

## SAFAR E GHANDEHAR (2001)
### KANDAHAR

There is a deliciously surreal moment in *Kandahar* in which artificial legs are dropped by airplane down to a makeshift medical treatment center that's set up in the middle of the Afghanistan desert. The sight of the parachuted plastic limbs drifting slowly from the clouds is both hilarious and horrifying—and oddly beautiful. Hybridism and contradiction define the film. Nafas (Niloufar Pizira) was born in Afghanistan but fled to Canada as a youth, eventually becoming a successful reporter. She returns to her homeland to find the sister (who lost her legs to a land-mine explosion) who was unfortunately left behind. The sister's letters have detailed a repressive, nightmarish existence under Taliban rule that has led her to plan her suicide, timed to take place during an upcoming eclipse. The panicked, Westernized Nafas decides to sneak into the country to try to rescue her sibling, with the clock ticking.

Iranian writer-director Mohsen Makhmalbaf combines actual, original documentary footage with a fictional narrative to illustrate the horrors of a society ruled by madmen who have distorted religion and cultural tradition to suit their own narrow world view. *Kandahar*'s great strength is that Makhmalbaf knows to let drama, tragedy, and even humor coexist on the same plane; they're organic components that underscore and complement one another. As Nafas navigates her way across the country, the viewer glimpses the ravages of war and tyranny—immense poverty and suffering, families ripped apart, the constant threat of violence and reprisal. Unexpectedly beautiful images and complex characters constantly jolt us.

Ultimately, the human survival instinct driving the film is captured in the telling. And it's the collapse of that instinct in Nafas's sister that is so heartbreaking, even as the film outlines how and why that collapse finally occurred. *Kandahar* exposed to the world a real-life nightmare of religious/political/cultural turmoil that many of us were wholly unaware of, even as that turmoil was reshaping the world we live in, foreshadowing global strife to come. The most unsettling aspect of this fantastic picture is the fact that it will be timely and pressingly relevant for many, many years to come. **EH**

**Iran / France** (Bac, Makhmalbaf, Studio Canal) 85m Color
**Language:** Farsi / English / Polish
**Director:** Mohsen Makhmalbaf
**Producer:** Mohsen Makhmalbaf
**Screenplay:** Mohsen Makhmalbaf
**Photography:** Ebrahim Ghafori
**Music:** Mohammad Reza Darvishi
**Cast:** Niloufar Pazira, Hassan Tantai, Sadou Teymouri, Hoyatala Hakimi, Monica Hankievich, Zahra Shafahi, Safdar Shodjai, Mollazaher Teymouri
**Cannes Film Festival:** Mohsen Makhmalbaf (prize of the ecumenical jury), nomination (Golden Palm)

**U.S. / Japan** (Dentsu, Mitsubishi, NTV, Ghibli, Tokuma Shoten, Touhoku Shinsha Walt Disney) 125m Color

**Language:** Japanese

**Director:** Hayao Miyazaki

**Producer:** Toshio Suzuki

**Screenplay:** Hayao Miyazaki

**Music:** Jô Hisaishi

**Cast:** Daveigh Chase, Rumi Hiiragi, Miyu Irino, Jason Marsden, Mari Natsuki, Suzanne Pleshette, Michael Chiklis, Takashi Naitô, Lauren Holly, Yasuko Sawaguchi, Tatsuya Gashuin, John Ratzenberger, Ryunosuke Kamiki, Tara Strong, Susan Egan

**Oscar:** Hayao Miyazaki (animation)

**Berlin International Film Festival:** Hayao Miyazaki (Golden Bear), tied with *Bloody Sunday*

## SEN TO CHIHIRO NO KAMIKAKUSHI (2001)
### SPIRITED AWAY

With every film that he makes, Hayao Miyazaki sets the standard for animated features higher and higher. Yet he possesses such a singular vision that it's hard to tell just where to place him on the pantheon. He isn't a throwback to the past, because no one in the past made movies quite like Miyazaki's. And he certainly isn't a precursor of things to come, because it's hard to imagine anybody but Miyazaki doing what he does. He is one of a kind, and as such his films hold a special place in the heart of movie lovers.

This is especially true in his native Japan, where each of his features exceeds the box office tally of its predecessor, with many of them eclipsing the take of even the most prominent Hollywood blockbusters. This is because Miyazaki creates fantastic worlds somehow free from the cloying characters and patronizing tone of so many mainstream animated features. Not surprisingly, his unfailingly intelligent films appeal to both children and adults, simple enough for the former to enjoy yet complex enough for the latter to appreciate on a different level.

The shy and nervous Chihiro (voice by Daveigh Chase in the English-language version) and her parents are on their way to their new home when they take a detour through a mysterious tunnel. When they emerge on the other side, they discover a seemingly deserted town, but things aren't what they seem. Chihiro's parents gorge themselves on food and magically transform into a pair of pigs, and that's when Chihiro realizes they're not alone. When night falls, the town becomes populated with hundreds of spirits, and Chihiro must overcome her fears to rescue her parents and find their way home. Guided by a more benevolent spirit named Haku (Jason Marsden), Chihiro sneaks her way into the inner workings of the town, where she discovers a witch named Yubaba (Suzanne Pleshette) who runs the spirit city like a booming business with an elaborate spa resort as its main draw. It's only by ingratiating herself to the enigmatic crone and her unpredictable cronies that Chihiro can even hope to escape.

*Spirited Away* is in many ways Miyazaki's *Alice in Wonderland*. The writer/director's hand-drawn scenes burst with energy and invention, and Miyazaki takes full advantage of the fantastical story to devise dozens of unique spirits and creatures that roam this world of utterly inscrutable rules and impenetrable logic. Giant babies throw destructive temper tantrums. Evil spirits offer gifts of gold as bait before devouring everything in sight. Characters change shapes (and sometimes personalities) with no warning: One appears alternately as a boy, a dragon, and a river spirit. Chihiro reacts to each of these creatures first with confusion then with fear and ultimately with courage. She soon realizes that she must master this strange world if she ever hopes to get home, and just as the spirits she encounters change her outlook on life, so does Chihiro affect the behavior of the spirits. She's a stranger in a strange land whose denizens consider her the strangest of them all. **JKl**

WALT DISNEY STUDIOS PRESENTS
A STUDIO GHIBLI FILM
MIYAZAKI'S
SPIRITED AWAY
WINNER
AUDIENCE AWARD
BEST NARRATIVE FEATURE
The 45th San Francisco Film Festival
WINNER
GOLDEN BEAR AWARD
BEST PICTURE
The 52nd Berlin International Film Festival
WINNER
BEST PICTURE
BEST ORIGINAL SONG
The 25th Nippon Academy Awards

France / Austria (CNC, Eurimages, Canal+, Alain Sarde, MK2, WFF, Wega Film, arte, ORF) 130m Color

**Language:** French

**Director:** Michael Haneke

**Producer:** Yvon Crenn, Christine Gozlan, Veit Heiduschka

**Screenplay:** Michael Haneke, from novel by Elfriede Jelinek

**Photography:** Christian Berger

**Cast:** Isabelle Huppert, Annie Girardot, Benoît Magimel, Susanne Lothar, Udo Samel, Anna Sigalevitch, Cornelia Köndgen, Thomas Weinhappel, Georg Friedrich, Philipp Heiss, William Mang, Rudolf Melichar, Michael Schottenberg, Gabriele Schuchter, Dieter Berner

**Cannes Film Festival:** Michael Haneke (grand prize of the jury), Benoît Magimel (actor), Isabelle Huppert (actress), Michael Haneke nomination (Golden Palm)

# LA PIANISTE (2001)

## THE PIANO TEACHER

In the clinical, highly formalized manner that has become his signature in such films as *Benny's Video* (1992), Michael Haneke strips away from *The Piano Teacher* the romantic lushness of the generic melodrama to expose a cold, alienated social structure founded on abuse. Adapted from Elfriede Jelinek's 1983 novel, the film delves into the psychosexual neuroses underlying, even generating, the intensity of classical art and the rituals we build around it.

Isabelle Huppert gives the performance of her life as Erika Kohut, a respected but professionally unfulfilled piano teacher. Erika pursues illicit behavior that society considers masculine, from gazing at hardcore porn to insisting on her sexual preferences. But at every turn she is shunned or reviled, leading to extreme alienation and perversion.

From the point that Erica and her infatuated student Walter (Benoit Magimel) connect, the film embarks on a relentless demonstration of the ways in which a man and a woman manage not to coalesce. We witness a grim parade of refusals, frustrations, misunderstandings, and violations. Throughout, Haneke engineers an odd, compelling kind of sympathy for Erika.

The triumph of *The Piano Teacher* is to carefully place this interpersonal tragedy within the social contexts of patriarchy and high culture. **AM**

France / Italy (Bac, Canal+, Rai, Sacher, Telepiù) 99m Color

**Language:** Italian / Latin

**Director:** Nanni Moretti

**Producer:** Angelo Barbagallo, Nanni Moretti

**Screenplay:** Nanni Moretti, Linda Ferri, Heidrun Schleef

**Photography:** Giuseppe Lanci

**Music:** Nicola Piovani

**Cast:** Nanni Moretti, Laura Morante, Jasmine Trinca, Giuseppe Sanfelice, Sofia Vigliar, Renato Scarpa, Roberto Nobile, Paolo De Vita, Roberto De Francesco, Claudio Santamaria, Antonio Petrocelli, Lorenzo Alessandri, Alessandro Infusini, Silvia Bonucci, Marcello Bernacchini

**Cannes Film Festival:** Nanni Moretti (FIPRESCI award), (Golden Palm)

# LA STANZA DEL FIGLIO (2001)

## THE SON'S ROOM

Alongside such distinguished dramas as Atom Egoyan's *The Sweet Hereafter* (1998) and Pedro Almodovar's *All About My Mother* (1999), Nanni Moretti's *The Son's Room* is another film that tackles the difficult subject of a child's tragic death and its consequent devastating effects on remaining family members.

Moretti—after 20 years of unusual, hybrid work—raised suspicion when he chose this as his first foray into mainstream drama. Was it a bid for cultural respectability? Happily, the film rises far above such knee-jerk reactions. Although a death is at its center, grieving—and the difficult matter of getting beyond grieving—is its true subject. Moretti's masterstroke is to make the family's father (played by the director) a psychotherapist. It is in the interactions—some hilarious, some shocking—between Moretti and his patients that we grasp the film's complex, empathetic understanding of human behavior.

After his brush with mortality, the therapist finds that he can no longer dispense advice, no longer make love, or even sing to himself in mindless joy. *The Son's Room* offers a moving study of how this man and those around him slowly revitalize themselves and return to the Eden of everyday life. **AM**

# NO MAN'S LAND (2001)

A warrior's term associated with World War I, "no man's land" connotes the uninhabitable kill zone between opposing forces. Complicating the term with an absurdist drama designed around a "Mexican standoff" forms the purpose of Danis Tonivic's *No Man's Land*, a drama set in the Balkans.

It's 1993 and a relief platoon of Bosnian soldiers gets lost in the night on their way to the front. Ambushed by a Serbian patrol, the group is decimated, save for two of their number. Chiki (Branko Djuric) suffers a glancing bullet wound before finding the safety of trenches, and his friend Cera (Filip Sovagovic) is knocked unconscious. Sent to survey the trench, a Serbian veteran and his new partner Nino (Rene Bitorajac) set a bouncing Betty beneath Cera's body, just before Chiki kills the veteran. When Cera wakes up, unable to move, the three are forced to cooperate to survive because they're equally cut off from either side's rear guard and leadership.

Artillery shells drop from the sky. Guns stand at the ready. Tempers rise and fall. Meanwhile the closely quartered enemies try complying with United Nations peacekeepers, themselves prodded by a band of rabid journalists waiting for a break in the story. Ever the tragedy, and no matter how well-meaning the interlopers, *No Man's Land* ends with escalating acts of individual violence hopeless enough to affirm the futility of war. Beginning with men on patrol and ending with Cera waiting to die, Tonivic's film is a riveting portrait of military purposes run amuck at the very point of conflict. Which is to say that Chiki, Nino, and Cera bear the ravages of a much greater agenda, namely the combination of religious, political, ethnic, but most of all, nationalist impulses.

At the point of bullet shells, in the spark of a blasting cap, all is lost save for the oldest cliché of war. Young men die, unavoidably sacrificed to the unnatural grasp of strategy. A bleak affair, indeed, but a meaningful cinematic experience exchanged for the duration of a dark, dark comedy of errors wherein forthright patriots festoon one another on the symbolic bayonets of their rifles. **GC-Q**

**Bosnia-Herzegovina / Slovenia / Italy / France / G.B. / Belgium** (Casablanca, Counihan Villiers, Eurimages, Fabrica, Fonds Slovène, Man's, Noé, Maj, Centre du Cinema et de l'Audiovisuel de la Communauté Française de Belgique, Wallons) 98m Color

**Language:** Serbo-Croatian / English / French

**Director:** Danis Tanovic

**Producer:** Marc Baschet, Frédérique Dumas-Zajdela, Cédomir Kolar

**Screenplay:** Danis Tanovic

**Photography:** Walther van den Ende

**Music:** Danis Tanovic

**Cast:** Branko Djuric, Rene Bitorajac, Filip Sovagovic, Georges Siatidis, Serge-Henri Valcke, Sacha Kremer, Alain Eloy, Mustafa Nadarevic, Bogdan Diklic, Simon Callow, Katrin Cartlidge, Tanja Ribic, Branko Zavrsan, Djuro Utjesanovic, Mirza Tanovic

**Oscar:** Bosnia (best foreign language film)

**Cannes Film Festival:** Danis Tanovic (screenplay), nomination (Golden Palm)

**U.S. / Australia** (Bazmark) 127m Color

**Director:** Baz Luhrmann

**Producer:** Fred Baron, Martin Brown, Baz Luhrmann

**Screenplay:** Baz Luhrmann, Craig Pearce

**Photography:** Donald McAlpine

**Music:** Craig Armstrong

**Cast:** Nicole Kidman, Ewan McGregor, John Leguizamo, Jim Broadbent, Richard Roxburgh, Garry McDonald, Jacek Koman, Matthew Whittet, Kerry Walker, Caroline O'Connor, Christine Anu, Natalie Jackson Mendoza, Lara Mulcahy, David Wenham, Kylie Minogue

**Oscar:** Catherine Martin, Brigitte Broch (art direction), Catherine Martin, Angus Strathie (costume)

**Oscar nomination:** Fred Baron, Martin Brown, Baz Luhrmann (best picture), Nicole Kidman (actress), Donald McAlpine (photography), Jill Bilcock (editing), Maurizio Silvi, Aldo Signoretti (makeup), Andy Nelson, Anna Behlmer, Roger Savage, Guntis Sics (sound)

**Cannes Film Festival:** Baz Luhrmann nomination (Golden Palm)

# MOULIN ROUGE! (2001)

Writer/director Baz Luhrmann effectively reinvented the movie musical with this brash, fast, gaudy, and unique tale that is the third of his "Red Curtain" trilogy which began with *Strictly Ballroom* (1992) and continued with *Romeo & Juliet* (1996).

A 21st-century MTV version of an 1890s Paris romance, *Moulin Rouge!* begins by assaulting your senses and never once stops until the final scene is through. As the theatrical curtain rises, we are introduced to the story of Christian (Ewan McGregor), a young Englishman who comes to Paris to be a writer. He soon makes contact with a group of artists led by Toulouse Lautrec (John Leguizamo) who want to stage a show, and who enlist Christian to write it. They also ask him to approach Moulin Rouge owner Harold Zidler (Jim Broadbent) for funds and it is while visiting Zidler's club that Christian lays eyes upon—and instantly falls in love with—the beautiful star of the Moulin Rouge, Satine (Nicole Kidman). Of course, in the tradition of the best tortured romances, their love may never be, because she is betrothed to the slimy Duke (Richard Roxburgh) and, unbeknownst to Christian (though the delicate coughing should have tipped him off), she is also dying of consumption.

Critics could argue that the plot is a melodramatic, clichéd affair, but they would be missing the point of Luhrmann's luxurious spectacle. The romance is set against the backdrop of the Moulin Rouge, a place where aristocracy,

bohemia, criminals, the rich, and the working class mixed together in absinthe-soaked decadence. It gives some hint as to what Luhrmann is trying (and largely succeeds) to bring to the screen: A celebration of show business, of life, and of color. Of course, *Moulin Rouge!* is also a celebration of music, which Luhrmann uses to ingenious effect. The featured songs are all recognizable but used in an unusual manner: Christian serenades Satine with a mishmash of quotes from love songs as varied as "Your Song" and "Up Where We Belong"; she performs "Diamonds are a Girl's Best Friend" at the club, while the assembled male crowd demands entertainment to the tune of Nirvana's "Smells Like Teen Spirit." And, in perhaps the most bizarre scene in the film, Zidler convinces the Duke to remain interested in Satine by performing a quite unique version of Madonna's "Like A Virgin."

It's all very inventive and as sparkling as the diamonds Satine sings about (every cent of the $52 million budget up onscreen). McGregor is wide-eyed, charismatic, and sensitive as struggling writer Christian, and Kidman is a joy to watch as Satine—sexy, strong, and ravishing. And each member of the supporting cast is fun to watch, too, from red-cheeked Broadbent to the hilarious Leguizamo, and, in a small cameo role, singing star Kylie Minogue as the green absinthe fairy. Love or loathe this visual masterpiece, you could never say you have ever seen anything quite like it before. **JB**

# MONSOON WEDDING (2001)

Mira Nair has addressed life in India from radically different vantages, whether via the street kids of *Salaam Bombay*! or the regal focus of her opulent fantasy *Kama Sutra*. Yet *Monsoon Wedding* is both the most vibrant of all her works and perhaps her most emotionally satisfying, in part due to its relatively uncluttered narrative and universal subject matter.

Flitting from English to Hindi to Punjabi, often over the course of a single scene, *Monsoon Wedding* shows the irrelevance of language and background when it comes to something as familiar as the mysteries and foibles of romance. Scattered members of an upper-class family return to India from around the globe for a wedding. But in the chaotic days leading up to the event, relationships fizzle, new connections rise, and long suppressed family secrets finally surface.

Shot on digital video, *Monsoon Wedding* actually benefits from this oft-derided format, which has the tendency to cloak actors and action in a blurry fog. Here, however, the DV enhances the colorful settings, and the handheld camera work is useful in capturing the constant flurry of disparate characters. If a subplot involving child abuse comes off as somewhat contrived, more often than not the film wonderfully celebrates the blossoming of love. **JKl**

**India / U.S. / France / Italy** (Delhi Dot Com, IFC, Keyfilms Roma, Mirabai, Pandora, Paradis)114m Color

**Language:** English / Hindi / Punjabi

**Director:** Mira Nair

**Producer:** Caroline Baron, Mira Nair

**Screenplay:** Sabrina Dhawan

**Photography:** Declan Quinn

**Music:** Mychael Danna

**Cast:** Naseeruddin Shah, Lillete Dubey, Shefali Shetty, Vijay Raaz, Tilotama Shome, Vasundhara Das, Parvin Dabas, Kulbhushan Kharbanda, Kamini Khanna, Rajat Kapoor, Neha Dubey, Kemaya Kidwai, Ishaan Nair, Randeep Hooda, Roshan Seth

**Venice Film Festival:** Mira Nair (Golden Lion ), (laterna magica prize)

# À MA SOEUR! (2001)
## FAT GIRL

**France / Italy** (Catherine Breillat, CNC, Flach, Immagine, Canal+, Urania, arte) 93m Color
**Language:** French / Italian
**Director:** Catherine Breillat
**Producer:** Conchita Airoldi, Jean-François Lepetit
**Screenplay:** Catherine Breillat
**Photography:** Yorgos Arvanitis
**Cast:** Anaïs Reboux, Roxane Mesquida, Libero De Rienzo, Arsinée Khanjian, Romain Goupil, Laura Betti, Albert Goldberg, Odette Barrière, Ann Matthijsse, Pierre Renverseau, Jean-Marc Boulanger, Frederick Bodin, Michel Guillemin, Josette Cathalan, Claude Sese
**Berlin International Film Festival:** Catherine Breillat (Manfred Salzgeber award), nomination (Golden Bear)

French writer/director Catherine Breillat is the brilliant madwoman of world cinema. But she's far from crazy. Her unbridled, unconventional, and at times confrontational unsavory examinations of female sexuality via the cinema are violent. They're graphic. And no matter how downtrodden or humiliated the female characters may be, their idiosyncratic creator wholly resists notions of women as inherent victims passive to fate and masculinity.

*Fat Girl* is Breillat's vaguely autobiographical study on female adolescence, on both the teenaged body and its newly amassed libidinal power and on those who have such power denied them. Anaïs Pingot (Anaïs Reboux) is 12, fat, sulky, shrewdly intelligent, and the black sheep of her well-to-do family. Her weight is both source of and buffer from their contempt. Her 15-year-old sister Elena (Roxane Mesquida) is thin, gorgeous, and the apple of their parents' eyes. When the quartet go to a placid resort for a family vacation, Elena soon begins an affair with an older man while Anaïs takes it all in, measuring herself against her sister, caught in a blur of love/hate emotion that spills into her everyday exchanges. It's a character study about angst and longing and burgeoning sexuality that has been stripped of all sentimentality. It's filled instead with standard-issue Breillat shock tactics—a fully erect penis, nudity from unexpected characters, and an act of violence at the film's end that is edge-of-the-seat shocking in its intensity and randomness.

In *Fat Girl* Breillat detonates several genres all at once—the family drama, coming-of-age films, the woman's movie. Her only fidelity is to her vision; her shattering of cinematic conventions mirrors the turbulence of the inner life of her plump young heroine, who herself fits neatly within no outlines. *Fat Girl* is a tough-minded film that gets inside the heads and desires of its two young female leads in a way that is all its own, with its obvious favor shown on the outcast. There are no obvious cinematic blueprints for this picture (save, perhaps, previous Breillat works), and it takes everything that viewers may have thought they knew about the above-mentioned genres and twists them into a feminist howl of rage, power, and resistance. **EH**

# MULHOLLAND DR. (2001)

**U.S. / France** (Asymmetrical, Imagine, Canal+, Alain Sarde, Picture, Touchstone) 145m Color

**Language:** English

**Director:** David Lynch

**Producer:** Neal Edelstein, Tony Krantz, Michael Polaire, Alain Sarde, Mary Sweeney

**Screenplay:** David Lynch

**Photography:** Peter Deming

**Music:** Angelo Badalamenti

**Cast:** Naomi Watts, Jeanne Bates, Laura Elena Harring, Scott Wulff, Robert Forster, Brent Briscoe, Maya Bond, Patrick Fischler, Michael Cooke, Bonnie Aarons, Michael J. Anderson, Joseph Kearney, Enrique Buelna, Richard Mead, Ann Miller

**Oscar nomination:** David Lynch (director)

**Cannes Film Festival:** David Lynch (director), tied with Joel Coen for *The Man Who Wasn't There*, nomination (Golden Palm)

Fans of David Lynch—and his twisting, odd, and addictive television series *Twin Peaks* in particular—quite rightly love *Mulholland Dr.* because it captures all that series' weirdness, dreamlike feel, and creepiness in one film. In fact, *Mulholland Dr.* actually started out in Lynch's head as a TV series like *Twin Peaks*, but after he made the pilot episode it was deemed too expensive for a full series to be made. So instead, the writer/director got his cast back together, added more scenes (including an ending), and released it as a feature-length movie.

And what a movie. Beautifully made and almost infuriatingly impossible to figure out, it begins with a beautiful young woman (Laura Harring) staggering from the wreckage of a car crash on Hollywood's Mulholland Drive, unable to remember who she is or how she got there. Somehow she makes her way into the apartment of Betty Elms (Naomi Watts), and Betty decides to help her recover her identity (for now, the woman calls herself "Rita," after Rita Hayworth). So far, so straightforward? Well, not really. We then seem to be pulled through Lynch's warped looking glass, where Betty is actually a struggling actress named Diane and the lover of a star named Camilla (who looks remarkably like Rita). Camilla, in turn, is preparing to leave Diane for a young director (Justin Theroux).

One of the joys of *Mulholland Dr.* is that Lynch doesn't give us all the answers. Is the film's first part a dream Diane is having as she dies? Which story is real and which one is not? Head-scratching stuff, though Lynch has hinted that certain clues in the mise en scène might assist us in solving the puzzle: his use of a red lampshade, for instance, and a key (who gives it and why), and the location of the accident. And for keen-eyed viewers there are apparently two clues to the true meaning of the movie located at the very beginning, even before the opening credits have rolled.

Like *Twin Peaks*, *Eraserhead* (1977), *Blue Velvet* (1986), *Wild at Heart* (1990), *Twin Peaks: Fire Walk With Me* (1992, a "prequel" to the TV series), and *Lost Highway* (1997), the confusion, surrealness, and blurred lines between dreams and reality are part of what makes *Mulholland Dr.* so addictive. Some viewers may get impatient that the end doesn't resolve what has gone before, but the beauty of Lynch's luscious visuals, Angelo Badalementi's haunting score, and the superb performances more than make up for any such frustration. Interestingly, Lynch cast a series of actors who had previously appeared in daytime soaps—Laura Harring was in *Sunset Beach*, Melissa George and Naomi Watts in Australia's *Home and Away*—and all give impressive performances here. Watts, especially, is a discovery as Betty/Diane, playing the ingenue and the jealous, vindictive lover with equal conviction.

A superb, engrossing, annoying, and dazzling film that is Lynch's best work since *Blue Velvet*. **JB**

# THE ROYAL TENENBAUMS (2001)

U.S. (American Empirical, Touchstone) 109m Technicolor
**Director:** Wes Anderson
**Producer:** Wes Anderson, Barry Mendel, Scott Rudin
**Screenplay:** Wes Anderson, Owen Wilson
**Music:** Mark Mothersbaugh
**Photography:** Robert D. Yeoman
**Cast:** Gene Hackman, Anjelica Huston, Gwyneth Paltrow, Ben Stiller, Luke Wilson, Owen Wilson, Danny Glover, Bill Murray, Alec Baldwin, Seymour Cassel, Kumar Pallana, Grant Rosenmeyer, Jonah Meyerson, Aram Aslanian-Persico, Irene Gorovaia
**Oscar nomination:** Wes Anderson, Owen Wilson (screenplay)
**Berlin International Film Festival:** Wes Anderson nomination (Golden Bear)

Clearly inspired by back issues of *The New Yorker* magazine, with a streak of arch whimsy running through it, Wes Anderson's whimsical ensemble piece *The Royal Tenenbaums* did not disappoint fans of his two previous films, *Bottle Rocket* (1996) and *Rushmore* (1998). Decorated with Edmund Gorey-like drawings and narrated by a deadpan Alex Baldwin, this oddball fantasy hangs on the mannered performances of a stellar cast. With a script that's laden with visual gags (characters are outfitted in adult versions of the clothes they wore as children, guns go off comically, and a droll stabbing takes place) and nifty, oblique quips, the straightforward emotional content is virtually nil. Despite its flaws, Anderson has yet again come up with a fresh take on the dysfunctional-family-as-comedy genre. Based on a nonexistent book, the script earned Academy Award nominations for Anderson and his cowriter Owen Wilson. Wilson also costars, but not as one of the Tenenbaum brothers, even though his real-life brother Luke plays a Tenenbaum, yet another askew aspect of an elliptical movie.

Estranged from his exotic wife Etheline (Anjelica Huston) for years, disbarred lawyer Royal Tenenbaum (Gene Hackman) has fallen on hard times. His three grown children were prodigies—Richie (Luke Wilson) is a former tennis pro, his adopted sister Margot (Gwyneth Paltrow) a renowned writer, and Chas (Ben Stiller) a financial genius. Now, wary of him and dealing with crises of their own, the trio have moved back in with their mother to the family's five-story corner house (which has, naturally, a turret sporting the family banner, all in contemporary New York). Etheline finds herself in love with her business partner (Danny Glover, resplendent in tweeds and corduroys). Royal, ever the con artist, feigns cancer to win back their affections, supported by his untrustworthy manservant Pagoda (Kumar Pallana), who loves Royal but tries to kill him, giving rise to Royal's quip, "That is the last time you stab me." Bill Murray and Owen Wilson also provide fittingly quirky supporting performances as Margot's clueless psychiatrist husband and her suitor, the neighboring cowboy author Eli.

A colorful if sad and vaguely surreal examination of a family circling life in their own eccentric fugue pattern, *The Royal Tenenbaums* is peopled with two-dimensional characters who amount to little more than collections of odd habits and extraordinary talents, only Stiller's character having any genuine emotional weight. Hackman reigns supreme, however, in his fully realized and comparatively natural performance as a man who is calm and self-possessed on the surface but who isn't really attentive to anyone's needs but his own. Underneath, he is desperately grasping at anything that might win back his family on his terms. Hackman gets the best lines of the script—when Eli says, "I always wanted to be a Tenenbaum," Royal puzzlingly answers, "Me too. Me too."

Ultimately, *The Royal Tenenbaums* is also an extremely satisfying hybrid that is far too funny to be wholly tragic and far too glib to be profound. What lingers are glancing sensations of joy and pain from a family gifted but doomed. **KK**

New Zealand / U.S. (New Line, Saul Zaentz, Tolkien Ent.,WingNut ) 178m Color

**Language:** English / Sindarin

**Director:** Peter Jackson

**Producer:** Peter Jackson, Barrie M. Osborne, Fran Walsh

**Screenplay:** Fran Walsh, Philippa Boyens, Peter Jackson, from the novel *The Fellowship of the Ring* by J.R.R. Tolkien

**Photography:** Andrew Lesnie

**Music:** Howard Shore

**Cast:** Elijah Wood, Ian McKellen, Viggo Mortensen, Sean Astin, Cate Blanchett, Sean Bean, Liv Tyler, John Rhys-Davies, Billy Boyd, Dominic Monaghan, Orlando Bloom, Christopher Lee, Hugo Weaving, Ian Holm, Andy Serkis

**Oscar:** Andrew Lesnie (photography), Jim Rygiel, Randall William Cook, Richard Taylor, Mark Stetson (special visual effects), Peter Owen, Richard Taylor (makeup), Howard Shore (music)

**Oscar nomination:** Peter Jackson, Barrie M. Osborne, Frances Walsh (best picture), Peter Jackson (director), Frances Walsh, Philippa Boyens, Peter Jackson (screenplay), Ian McKellen (actor in support role), Grant Major, Dan Hennah (art direction), Ngila Dickson, Richard Taylor (costume), John Gilbert (editing), Enya, Nicky Ryan, Roma Ryan (song), Christopher Boyes, Michael Semanick, Gethin Creagh, Hammond Peek (sound)

# THE LORD OF THE RINGS: THE FELLOWSHIP OF THE RING (2001)

One of the most ambitious productions in movie history, Peter Jackson's movie trilogy beginning with *The Fellowship of the Ring* is a masterpiece of traditional direction and performance mixed with computer-generated imagery. It deserves to be remembered not just for its scale but also for the truly amazing piece of cinema that it is.

Based on J.R.R. Tolkien's classic books of hobbits, elves, and other creatures who populate the land known as Middle Earth, the trilogy (*The Lord of the Rings*) was filmed over 16 months in New Zealand with a huge cast and crew assigned to make three movies for a $300 million budget. Planned to appeal to audiences who had never read Tolkien's work, it would also feature all the detail and minutae fans of the books would demand. Jackson succeeded at both, delivering an old-fashioned series of epics—the trilogy released over three years—created using the best of modern moviemaking. He was perhaps the perfect man to bring Tolkien's world to the screen, having delivered darkly fascinating movies like *Heavenly Creatures* (1994) and *The Frighteners* (1996), after his earlier experiments in gory schlock horror—*Bad Taste* (1987), *Meet the Feebles* (1989), and *Braindead* (1992)—before taking on this huge project. *The Fellowship of the Ring* is black, twisting and dark and sinister and scary, richly detailed, so real you feel you could reach into the movie screen and touch the hilltop house at Bag End or the elegant trees of Rivendell.

The story begins with a hobbit—a small in stature, hairy-footed creature—named Frodo Baggins (Elijah Wood), who is entrusted with a ring that gives the wearer great power. It is also a dangerous ring, so Frodo and his friend Sam (Sean Astin) must leave their home and travel great distances to the one place, Mordor, where it can be destroyed. They are accompanied on their journey by a fellowship elected to protect them: Wizard Gandalf (Ian McKellen), warriors Aragorn (Viggo Mortensen) and Boromir (Sean Bean), elf Legolas (Orlando Bloom), and dwarf Gimli (John Rhys-Davies).

The Middle Earth cast strides through spectacular imagery as the group goes on its perilous journey across snowcapped mountains, through the threatening Caves of Moria, along rivers, and through valleys, creating a living, breathing world as they go. A much-loved story, this is a classic quest and a wondrous moral tale of how power corrupts, beautifully realized by a wonderful cast and a visionary director. **JB**

# A.I: ARTIFICIAL INTELLIGENCE (2001)

A pet project of Stanley Kubrick's for over 20 years, this thoughtful piece of science fiction is based on a 1969 short story by Brian Aldiss, and was to be the director's next film after *Eyes Wide Shut*. Following Kubrick's death in 1999, his widow asked Steven Spielberg, who had spoken at length with Kubrick over the years about the project, to step in and bring Stanley's vision to the screen. The result is a film that is both Spielberg and Kubrick—a meeting of two disparate cinematic minds which makes for an unusual and visually stunning production that is also the most uncommercial movie Spielberg has directed to date.

In the near future, robots (named "mechas") look and act as humans. One technological company has gone a step further and invented an android—in the form of a child named David (Haley Joel Osment)—who not only looks like a real boy but can feel and give love like one as well. Brought home by Henry (Sam Robards) for his wife Monica (Frances O'Connor) as a sort of replacement for their own son who is in a coma, David initially (and understandably) unnerves Monica, but she eventually warms to him and decides to activate the circuits that will make David love her. Unfortunately, once the program has been turned on, it can't be switched off—meaning that David will forever be devoted to her, which becomes a problem when Monica's own son recovers and returns home.

Although at times reminiscent of Spielberg's most famous childhood fantasy, *ET: The Extra Terrestrial*, and that other tale of a man-made creature wanting to be a real boy, *Pinocchio*, *A.I.* is far from cuddly as it tackles deeper issues when David is abandoned by his "mother" in a deeply disturbing scene and finds himself in a grim outside world filled with outcast mechas (including Jude Law's Gigolo Joe). Underlying questions such as *What makes us real?* and *Is it the capacity to love and be loved that makes us human?* make this one of the most thought-provoking, and definitely darkest, films of Spielberg's career. **JB**

**U.S.** (Amblin, DreamWorks SKG, Stanley Kubrick, Warner Bros.) 146m Technicolor

**Director:** Steven Spielberg

**Producer:** Bonnie Curtis, Kathleen Kennedy, Steven Spielberg

**Screenplay:** Ian Watson, Steven Spielberg, from the short story *Supertoys Last All Summer Long* by Brian Aldiss

**Photography:** Janusz Kaminski

**Music:** John Williams

**Cast:** Haley Joel Osment, Jude Law, Frances O'Connor, Brendan Gleeson, Sam Robards, William Hurt, Jake Thomas, Ken Leung, Michael Mantell, Michael Berresse, Kathryn Morris, Adrian Grenier, Clark Gregg, Kevin Sussman, Tom Gallop

**Oscar nomination:** Dennis Muren, Scott Farrar, Stan Winston, Michael Lantieri (special visual effects), John Williams (music)

**Venice Film Festival:** Steven Spielberg (future film festival digital award)

# GANGS OF NEW YORK (2002)

**U.S. / Germany / Italy / G.B. / Netherlands** (Cappa, ITC, IEG, Meespierson, Miramax, P.E.A., Q&Q, Splendid) 166m Color

**Language:** English / Gaelic

**Director:** Martin Scorsese

**Producer:** Alberto Grimaldi, Harvey Weinstein

**Screenplay:** Jay Cocks, Steven Zaillian, Kenneth Lonergan

**Photography:** Michael Ballhaus

**Music:** Bono, Peter Gabriel, Howard Shore

**Cast:** Leonardo DiCaprio, Daniel Day-Lewis, Cameron Diaz, Jim Broadbent, John C. Reilly, Henry Thomas, Liam Neeson, Brendan Gleeson, Gary Lewis, Stephen Graham, Eddie Marsan, Alec McCowen, David Hemmings, Larry Gilliard Jr., Cara Seymour.

**Oscar nomination:** Alberto Grimaldi, Harvey Weinstein (best picture), Martin Scorsese (director), Jay Cocks, Steven Zaillian, Kenneth Lonergan (screenplay), Daniel Day-Lewis (actor), Dante Ferretti, Francesca LoSchiavo (art direction), Michael Ballhaus (photography), Sandy Powell (costume), Thelma Schoonmaker (editing), Bono, The Edge, Adam Clayton, Larry Mullen Jr. (song), Tom [illegible] Sharrock (sound)

Martin Scorsese's 2002 brutal but memorable epic has its setting in 19th-century New York, specifically Lower Manhattan in 1846, but in feeling may as well be the Middle Ages. The result of three decades of research inspired by Herbert Asbury's 1928 book of the same name, *Gangs of New York* is unique in its depiction of the era. Its visual imagery, as well as the persecution endured by the city's immigrants, is accurate, although the deaths and amount of bloodshed is overdramatized for effect.

The story opens as members of weirdly named Irish gangs gather in Paradise Square. Priest Vallon (Liam Neeson), an Irish gang chieftain, dies in battle and his young son Amsterdam (Leonardo DiCaprio) escapes the carnage. 16 years later, Amsterdam returns to avenge his father's death by infiltrating the ranks of the infamous Bill Cutting (Daniel Day-Lewis). Called The Butcher, he is a terrifying gang leader who celebrates the anniversary of his adversary's death. As perhaps the final phase in Scorsese's overweening interest in urban violence, the unusual period setting is at least as arresting as the story itself. Although the love interest between a beautiful thief (Cameron Diaz) and Amsterdam doesn't always work, Day-Lewis's characterization of The Butcher is riveting. Ambitiously designed to show where modern America has come from, *Gangs of New York* is a film that will grow in importance with passing time. **KK**

## THE PIANIST (2002)

A drama about the survival of Polish-Jewish pianist Wladyslaw Szpilman in the Warsaw ghetto, *The Pianist* is not an ideas movie. It has no particular "angle" on the Holocaust, nor is it noticeably a Roman Polanski film. Yet the movie is made with humility and intelligence, and though it's not the director's own Holocaust story, one can hardly doubt it's the movie he's been waiting to make all his life.

Though laboring under an awkwardly expository screenplay by Ronald Harwood, the movie is gorgeously shot by Pawel Edelman. Rich dark browns with an edge of sepia—the colors of old photos, the color of history—will break your heart many times over. A wonderfully restrained Adrien Brody plays the rather chilly Szpilman, who evades the Nazis in a series of astonishing narrow escapes that nevertheless confirm his intolerable isolation as a fugitive dependent on the good will of strangers. The movie is particularly good at revealing the terrifying blend of arbitrary personal sadism of individual German soldiers and the institutional brutality of the Nazi machine. Wisely, Polanski doesn't comment: He seems to have decided that in the face of such meticulously planned horror, the best one can do is get the details right. **ET**

**G.B. / France / Germany / Netherlands / Poland** (Agencja Produkcji Filmowej, Beverly Detroit, Canal+ Polska, FilmFernsehFonds Bayern, FBB, FFA, Héritage, Interscope, Canal+, Mainstream, Meespierson, R.P., Runteam, Studio Babelsberg, Studio Canal, TVP) 148m Color

**Language:** English / German

**Director:** Roman Polanski

**Producer:** Robert Benmussa, Roman Polanski, Alain Sarde

**Screenplay:** Ronald Harwood, from book by Wladyslaw Szpilman

**Photography:** Pawel Edelman

**Music:** Wojciech Kilar

**Cast:** Adrien Brody, Emilia Fox, Michal Zebrowski, Ed Stoppard, Maureen Lipman, Frank Finlay, Jessica Kate Meyer, Julia Rayner, Wanja Mues, Richard Ridings, Nomi Sharron, Anthony Milner, Lucy Skeaping, Roddy Skeaping, Ben Harlan

**Oscar:** Roman Polanski (director), Ronald Harwood (screenplay), Adrien Brody (actor)

**Oscar nomination:** Roman Polanski, Robert Benmussa, Alain Sarde (best picture), Pawel Edelman (photography), Anna B. Sheppard (costume), Hervé de Luze (editing)

**Cannes Film Festival:** Roman Polanski (Golden Palm)

# HABLE CON ELLA (2002)
## TALK TO HER

**Spain / France** (El Deseo, France 2, Renn, Vía Digital) 101m Eastmancolor
**Language:** Spanish / Catalan / English
**Director:** Pedro Almodóvar
**Producer:** Agustín Almodóvar, Michel Ruben
**Screenplay:** Pedro Almodóvar
**Photography:** Affonso Beato
**Music:** Alberto Iglesias
**Cast:** Cecilia Roth, Marisa Paredes, Candela Peña, Antonia San Juan, Penélope Cruz, Rosa María Sardà, Fernando Fernán Gómez, Fernando Guillén, Toni Cantó, Eloy Azorín, Carlos Lozano, Manuel Morón, José Luis Torrijo, Juan José Otegui, Carmen Balagué
**Oscar:** Spain (best foreign language film)
**Cannes Film Festival:** Pedro Almodóvar (director), (prize of the ecumenical jury), nomination (Golden Palm)

*Talk to Her* provides a counterpoint to the human warmth and emotional messiness of Pedro Almodóvar's joyously cathartic previous film, *All About My Mother* (1999). Although it retains some of the bright appearances of the director's earlier, more vibrant work, *Talk to Her*, Almodóvar's fourteenth feature, can be regarded as his most controlled and sustained picture. It is also his most melancholy, coolly distant, and disconcerting film, especially in its treatment—or "silencing"—of women. Whereas Almodóvar's films generally embrace the untidiness of life and cinema, *Talk to Her* is extremely elegant, complex, and even classical in its structure, with various motifs (as well as images within images, performances within performances) connecting across it. The corporeality of his earlier, often manic pictures is displaced here by a curiously bloodless, clinical, and evasive tone.

The film opens with a performance by Pina Bausch that sets the tone for what is to follow, a complex "dance" of competing and merging identities that rarely allows characters to meet or address each other on equal ground. The contrasting responses—one almost hysterical, the other distracted—of the two male protagonists to Bausch's performance intimate that we are entering a world of subjective motivations, responses, and actions.

Most of Almodóvar's previous films focus on female characters and their complex, and often contradictory, interactions with each other and the world around them. *Talk to Her* concentrates on its male protagonists and their increasingly insular dialogues with the women "in" their lives—both of whom end up in comas. One of the most remarkable aspects of Almodóvar's film is the way in which he is able to subtly manipulate and direct the audience, shifting emphasis away from—at least for a time—the more disturbing connotations of the actions the picture represents. In what may be the boldest move in the director's cinema, he "shows" a rape through a deft parody of a silent surrealist film called *The Shrinking Lover*. The most significant achievement of *Talk to Her* lies in the ways in which it plays with and challenges audience identification. It is a profound meditation on the way in which we talk to and *through* the people, objects, and texts that express our lives. **AD**

# CIDADE DE DEUS (2002)
## CITY OF GOD

There are films that capture the zeitgeist perfectly; there are films that give a peek at, if not warning of, the world to come. Fernando Meirelles' *City of God* does both with aplomb. With its dizzying pace, fast edits, hand-held camera, quick-shift changes in point of view, and obvious nods to Quentin Tarentino, the film is clearly rooted in both the tone and tempo of late 20th/early 21st-century American filmmaking.

At its core, *City of God* is about the devolution of a Brazilian housing project that is tracked from its relatively idyllic 1960s beginnings to its 1980s destination as a violent, poverty-ridden domain where each successive generation becomes less connected to the human traits of empathy, conscience, and hope. Based on a true story, *City of God* is narrated by the teenaged Buscape (Alexandre Rodrigues), whose gentle disposition prevents him from becoming a gangster, but whose artistic bent leads him to become a celebrated photographer/documentarian of his surroundings. If there's a lead in the ensemble of motley characters (the cast is comprised of nonactors, real-life street kids) and intertwined storylines, it's the hyper-violent Lil' Ze, whose propensity for violence and complete lack of remorse make him a terrifying figure. It's the open-ended final minutes, in which a generation of almost feral homeless kids takes over the projects, which makes the film's point crystal clear: This is a horror movie of the first order. **EH**

**Brazil / France / U.S.** (Globo, Lumiere, O2, Studio Canal, VideoFilmes, Wild Bunch) 130m Color

**Language:** Portuguese

**Director:** Fernando Meirelles

**Producer:** Andrea Barata Ribeiro, Mauricio Andrade Ramos

**Screenplay:** Bráulio Mantovani, from novel by Paulo Lins

**Photography:** César Charlone

**Music:** Ed Cortês, Antonio Pinto

**Cast:** Matheus Nachtergaele, Seu Jorge, Alexandre Rodrigues, Leandro Firmino da Hora, Philippe Haagensen, Johnathan Haagensen, Douglas Silva, Roberta Rodriguez Silvia, Alice Braga, Gero Camilo, Darlan Cunha, Renato de Souza, Karina Falcão, Graziela Moretto

**Russia / Germany** (Egoli Tossell, Fora, The Hermitage Bridge Studio) 99m Color

**Language:** Russian

**Director:** Aleksandr Sokurov

**Producer:** Andrei Deryabin, Jens Meuer, Jens Meurer, Karsten Stöter

**Screenplay:** Boris Khaimsky, Anatoli Nikiforov, Svetlana Proskurina, Aleksandr Sokurov

**Photography:** Tilman Büttner

**Music:** Sergei Yevtushenko

**Cast:** Sergei Dontsov, Mariya Kuznetsova, Leonid Mozgovoy, David Giorgobiani, Aleksandr Chaban, Maksim Sergeyev, Anna Aleksakhina, Konstantin Anisimov, Aleksei Barabash, Vladimir Baranov, Valentin Bukin, Kirill Dateshidze, Mikhail Dorofeyev, Yevgeni Filatov, Svetlana Gajtan, Vadim Gushchin, Oleg Khmelnitsky, Yuri Khomutyansky, Aleksandr Kulikov, Tamara Kurenkova, Vladimir Lisetsky, Vadim Lobanov, Oleg Losev, Aleksandr Malnykin, Kirill Miller, Sergei Muchenikov, Sergei Nadporozhny, Natalya Nikulenko, Yuri Orlov, Alla Osipenko, Mikhail Piotrovsky, Aleksandr Razbash, Yelena Rufanova, Vladimir Sevastyanikhin, Ilya Shakunov, Anatoli Shvedersky, Svetlana Smirnova, Boris Smolkin, Yelena Spiridonova, Artyom Strelnikov, Svetlana Svirko, Valentina Yegorenkova, Lev Yeliseyev, Yuli Zhurin

**Cannes Film Festival:** Aleksandr Sokurov nomination (Golden Palm)

# RUSSKIJ KOVCHEG

## RUSSIAN ARK (2002)

This Alexander Sokurov feature is one of the most staggering technical achievements in the history of cinema—a single shot lasting 95 minutes while moving through 33 rooms in the world's largest museum, the Hermitage in Saint Petersburg (which also encompasses the Winter Palace). Part pageant and museum tour, part theme-park ride and historical meditation, it covers two centuries of czarist Russia as smoothly as it crosses the Hermitage and even periodically moves outside of it, with the offscreen Sokurov engaged in an ongoing dialogue with an on-screen 19th-century French diplomat (apparently suggested by Adolphe, marquis de Custine).

Sokurov used close to 2,000 actors and extras and three live orchestras in making what may be the world's only unedited single-take feature as well as the longest Steadicam sequence ever shot. (Reportedly only one previous take of the sequence was even attempted, after lengthy and detailed rehearsals of all the participants, and it apparently failed due to the subdegree temperature outside.) *Russian Ark* is also the first uncompressed high-definition film recorded on a portable hard-disk system rather than on film or tape before being transferred to 35mm, and, along with Sokurov's earlier innovative experiments with optical distortions and perspective in features such as *Whispering Pages* (1993) and *Mother and Son* (1997), it marks him as a kind of 19th-century modernist—a filmmaker who, like Manoel De Oliveira in a very different way, combines an acute sense of the past with a very up-to-date sense of how to convey it.

As one critic has suggested, *Russian Ark* is an anti-*October*, challenging Sergei Eisenstein's reliance on montage while using the Winter Palace as a gigantic set. All of which is to say that we are only just starting to grasp the dimensions of this formidable achievement, although it is worth adding that the surprising and virtually unprecedented commercial success of this film in the United States strongly indicates that Sokurov's technical mastery is not merely an achievement to be enjoyed by specialists of cinema or Russian history. **JRos**

# ADAPTATION (2002)

Though it spawns plots and meta-plots like a bunny rabbit, this divinely nutty second collaboration between writer Charlie Kaufman and director Spike Jonze (the team behind *Being John Malkovich*) is not one of those irritating hipster ur-narratives that keeps winking at the audience. The movie is based on a pair of true stories—*New Yorker* writer Susan Orlean's nonfiction best-seller *The Orchid Thief*, about her encounter with a crazed Florida orchid poacher (played in the movie with manic avidity by Chris Cooper), and Kaufman's struggle to turn the book into a viable screenplay. On paper the two writers, portrayed in the movie with admirable lack of Method by Meryl Streep and Nicolas Cage (who also plays Charlie's untalented but wildly successful brother), are a match made in heaven. Both are skittish about plot, preferring the mad illogic of real life as source material; both are fascinated by people who live sexier, more emotional lives than they do.

A joyless, balding bag of nerves, Charlie is the most maladapted creature in a movie rife with hardy perennials—from the sexy orchid, to the poacher, a survivor who retools from orchid collector to porno-site operator without blinking, to Hollywood, seen early on in the movie as a creature rising from primordial slime. Charlie thrives nowhere, but unlike Woody Allen, whose schlubs have become a vanity project—they always come fortified with successful careers and babes panting for them—Kaufman takes his self-exposure right down to the bone. Desperate to find a narrative, Charlie sullenly succumbs to his brother's entreaties to attend Robert McKee's famed story-structure seminar, where, to his astonishment, the spell is broken. He finds himself elaborating a film that plays like some dementedly overstuffed music video, stitched together by a hurricane of movie clichés—drugs, sex, violence, the works. It's hard to imagine audiences—even those indifferent to the travails of screenwriters—not warming to this soulful, willfully romantic movie's broader themes: Love, incompleteness, envy, longing for family, and the desire to find comfort and structure in a comfortless, disorganized world. **ET**

**U.S.** (Beverly Detroit, Clinica Estetico, Good Machine, Intermedia, Magnet, Propaganda) 114m Color

**Language:** English / Latin

**Director:** Spike Jonze

**Producer:** Jonathan Demme, Vincent Landay, Edward Saxon

**Screenplay:** Charlie Kaufman, Donald Kaufman, from the book *The Orchid Thief* by Susan Orlean

**Photography:** Lance Acord

**Music:** Carter Burwell

**Cast:** Nicolas Cage, Tilda Swinton, Meryl Streep, Chris Cooper, Jay Tavare, Litefoot, Roger Willie, Jim Beaver, Cara Seymour, Doug Jones, Stephen Tobolowsky, Gary Farmer, Peter Jason, Gregory Itzin, Curtis Hanson

**Oscar:** Chris Cooper (actor in support role)

**Oscar nomination:** Charlie Kaufman, Donald Kaufman (screenplay), Nicolas Cage (actor), Meryl Streep (actress in support role)

**Berlin International Film Festival:** Spike Jonze (Silver Bear—jury grand prix), nomination (Golden Bear)

# FAR FROM HEAVEN (2002)

**U.S. / France** (Clear Blue Sky, John Wells, Killer, Section Eight, TF1, US, Vulcan) 107m Color

**Director:** Todd Haynes

Producer: Jody Patton, Christine Vachon

**Screenplay:** Todd Haynes

**Photography:** Edward Lachman

**Music:** Elmer Bernstein

**Cast:** Julianne Moore, Dennis Quaid, Dennis Haysbert, Patricia Clarkson, Viola Davis, James Rebhorn, Bette Henritze, Michael Gaston, Ryan Ward, Lindsay Andretta, Jordan Puryear, Kyle Timothy Smith, Celia Weston, Barbara Garrick, Olivia Birkelund

**Oscar nomination:** Todd Haynes (screenplay), Julianne Moore (actress), Edward Lachman (photography), Elmer Bernstein (music)

**Venice Film Festival:** Julianne Moore (Volpi cup—actress), (audience award—actress), Edward Lachman (outstanding individual contribution), Todd Haynes (SIGNIS award—honorable mention), Todd Haynes nomination (Golden Lion)

A sumptuously autumnal tale of grand passion brewed in a suffocating climate of repression and desire, Todd Haynes's melodrama *Far from Heaven* is also an unabashedly loving, yet slyly subversive homage to the maternal weepies of the 1950s—in particular Douglas Sirk's *All That Heaven Allows*, his race drama *Imitation of Life*, and Max Ophüls's *The Reckless Moment*.

Made for $12 million, a princely budget for a director who cast his first film (*Superstar: The Karen Carpenter Story*) with Barbie dolls, the film is less a departure for Haynes than an integral part of his ongoing, intensely politicized project, which is to seize on a cultural moment and read it back to us on its own terms, but with a stylistic edge that nudges us to read the present from the past. *Far From Heaven* is set in the 1950s, a decade we've learned to remember at best with knowing amusement, at worst with outright contempt. That isn't Haynes's game at all. His muse, Julianne Moore, is incandescent as Cathy Whitaker, a homemaker and pillar of Hartford, Connecticut society whose cushy life unravels when she stumbles upon her sales-executive husband (wonderfully played by the hyper-masculine Dennis Quaid) in the arms of a male hustler. Struggling to hold together her "ideal marriage," Cathy grows more and more attracted to her black gardener (the excellent Dennis Haysbert), whose serene self-possession stands in painful contrast to her churning agitation. The opprobrium they suffer merely by being seen together rains down from both black and white communities.

*Far From Heaven* is fiercely unredemptive—its ending offers a revealingly pessimistic variation on the tacked-on happy ending of *All That Heaven Allows*, suggesting that racial and sexual inequalities have changed little since the 1950s. For all the movie's political ambitions, you can lose yourself (as Haynes clearly intends) in the swoony sadness of the mother's story, feel the deliciously weepy rush of the victim, and salivate over the film's luscious look, from the production and costume designs, with their wildly operatic reds and oranges, to Elmer Bernstein's swelling, plaintive score, to Moore declaiming her lines in letter-perfect mimicry of the breath cadences affected by diva actresses of the period. **ET**

# CHICAGO (2002)

One of the most successful musical movies of all time, *Chicago* also has the distinction of being the first musical to win the Best Picture Academy Award since 1968's *Oliver!*. A triumph for a project that had been doing the rounds in Hollywood for years, with stars including Madonna, Goldie Hawn, and John Travolta all tipped for roles before Miramax and director Rob Marshall took it on with the perfect combination of Renee Zellweger, Catherine Zeta-Jones (who won Best Supporting Actress for her performance), and Richard Gere.

A tale of fame and infamy (perfect for the 21st century, an era in which you can become a celebrity by surviving a few weeks in a camera-filled jungle or revive your acting career by being arrested) based on Bob Fosse, John Kander, and Fred Ebb's stage musical, *Chicago* is set in the jazz age Windy City of the 1920s, where the men can be bad but the girls even badder. Roxie Hart (Zellweger) is one such gal, sent to jail for shooting the lover who had promised to make her a singing star. She enlists the help of showman lawyer Billy Flynn (Gere) to get her off. He also represents Velma Kelly (Zeta-Jones), who murdered her sister and husband, washed the blood off her hands, then performed "All That Jazz" on stage before being arrested.

Mixing jailhouse and courtroom scenes with show-stopping musical numbers like "When You're Good To Mama" and "Razzle Dazzle" as they are imagined in Roxie's head, director and choreographer Marshall gives the traditional musical an MTV-generation update with quick cuts and pared-down musical numbers (no high-kicking chorus girls here, apart from Flynn's fawning follies during "All I Care About") that make the film more mainstream and accessible than Baz Lurhmann's more daring *Moulin Rouge!*. Marshall's charismatic cast clearly have a ball, too—especially the always wonderful John C. Reilly (as Roxie's husband), Oscar-nominated Queen Latifah (as prison warden "Mama" Morton), and the two actors who both performed in musical theater early in their careers, Gere and Zeta-Jones. Being bad has never been so good. **JB**

**U.S. / Canada** (Loop, Miramax, Producers Circle) 113m BW/Color

**Language:** English / Hungarian

**Director:** Rob Marshall

**Producer:** Marty Richards

**Screenplay:** Bill Condon, from play by Maurine Dallas Watkins, from musical by Bob Fosse, Fred Ebb

**Photography:** Dion Beebe

**Music:** Danny Elfman, John Kander

**Cast:** Renée Zellweger, Catherine Zeta-Jones, Richard Gere, Queen Latifah, John C. Reilly, Lucy Liu, Taye Diggs, Colm Feore, Christine Baranski, Dominic West, Mya, Deirdre Goodwin, Ekaterina Chtchelkanova, Denise Faye, Susan Misner

**Oscar:** Marty Richards (best picture), Catherine Zeta-Jones (actress in support role), John Myhre, Gordon Sim (art direction), Colleen Atwood (costume), Martin Walsh (editing), Michael Minkler, Dominic Tavella, David Lee (sound)

**Oscar nomination:** Rob Marshall (director), Bill Condon (screenplay), Renée Zellweger (actress), John C. Reilly (actor in support role), Queen Latifah (actress in support role), Dion Beebe (photography), John Kander, Fred Ebb (song)

# FILM INDEX


12 Angry Men 337
1900 620
2 ou 3 Choses Que Je Sais D'Elle 467
2001 498-499
39 Steps, The 128
400 Blows, The 360
42nd Street 108-109
8 1/2 416-417

**A**

'A' Gai Waak Juk Jaap 748
À Ma Soeur! 937
À Nous la liberté 89
A One and a Two 916
Abre Los Ojos 883
Accidental Tourist, The 775
Actor's Revenge, An 428
Actress, The 826
Adam's Rib 249
Adaptation 947
Adventure, The 382-383
Adventures of Robin Hood, The 146
Affair to Remember, An 340
Affaire de Femmes, Une 775
African Queen, The 267
Age d'or, L' 84-85
Age of Gold, The 84-85
Age of Innocence 831
Aguirre, Der Zorn Gottes 552
Aguirre: The Wrath of God 552
Ai No Corrida 619
Aileen Wuornos: The Selling of a Serial Killer 824
Airplane! 671
Akira 764
Albero degli Zoccoli, L' 641
Ali Zaoua, Prince de la Rue 914
Ali Zaoua, Prince of the Streets 914
Ali: Fear Eats the Soul 594
Alice 776
Alien 653
Aliens 737
All About Eve 259
All About My Mother 900-901
All Quiet on the Western Front 89
All That Heaven Allows 332-333
All That Jazz 655
All the President's Men 614
Alphaville 448
Alphaville, une Étrange Aventure de Lemmy Caution 448
Amadeus 707
Amarcord 580-581
[illegible]
American Beauty 906-907
American Friend, The 635
American Graffiti 568
American In Paris, An 268
American Werewolf in London 679
Amerikanische Freund, Der 635
Amores Perros 918
Anatomy of a Murder 364
And Your Mother Too 928
Andalusian Dog, An 74
Andrei Rublev 518
Andrei Rublyov 518
Angel Face 273
Angels with Dirty Faces 146
Angst Essen Seele Auf 594
Animal Farm 299
Année dernière à Marienbad, L' 393
Annie Hall 626-627
Aparajito 344
Apartment, The 390-391
Apocalypse Now 658-659
Apur Sansar 368-369
Archangel 795
Argent, L' 699
Ariel 762
Artificial Intelligence: A.I. 941
Artists and Models 310
Ascent, The 619
Ashes and Diamonds 356
Asphalt Jungle, The 255
Astenicheskij Sindrom 785
Asthenic Syndrome, The 785
Atalante, L' 120
Atlantic City 665
Attack the Gas Station! 908
Au Hasard Balthazar 466
Au revoir les enfants 753
Audition, The 903
Autumn Afternoon, An 405
Avventura, L' 382-383
Awful Truth, The 144

**B**

Ba Wang Bie Ji 827
Bab El Hadid 352
Babbete's Gaestebud 749
Babe 852
Babes in Arms 152
Babette's Feast 749
Back to the Future 723
Bad and the Beautiful, The 278
Bad Day at Black Rock 314
Bad Ma Ra Khahad Bord 902
Badkonake Sefid 858
Badlands 566-567
Baker's Wife, The 148
Ballad of Narayama, The 707
Balthazar 466
Band Wagon, The 282
Bank Dick, The 171
Barefoot Contessa, The 302
Barren Lives 424
Barry Lyndon 602
Batman 776
Battaglia di Algeri, La 446
Battle of Algiers, The 446
Battle of San Pietro, The 207
Battleship Potemkin 58-59
Beat the Devil 295
Beau travail 897
Beautiful Troublemaker, The 805
Beauty and the Beast 221
Before the Revolution 438
Being John Malkovich 905
Being There 656
Beiqing Chengshi 788
Belle de Jour 472-473
Belle noiseuse, La 805
Ben-Hur 371
Best Years of Our Lives, The 215
Beverly Hills Cop 713
Bharat Mata 346
Bicycle Thief, The 233
Big 767
Big Carnival, The 263
Big Chill, The 697
Big Heat, The 290
Big Parade, The 61
Big Red One, The 670
Big Sky, The 279
Big Sleep, The 222
Bigamist, The 281
Bigger Than Life 335
Bird with the Crystal Plumage, The 533
Birds, The 413
Birth of a Nation, The 30-31
Biruma No Tategoto 327
Bitch, The 98
Bitter Tea of General Yen, The 116
Bitter Tears of Petra von Kant, The 561
Bitteren Tränen der Petra von Kant, Die 561
Black Cat, The 121
Black God, White Devil 441
Black Narcissus 227
Black Orpheus 366
Black Sunday 388
Blackmail 77
Blade Runner 684-685
Blair Witch Project, The 898
Blaue Engel, Der 82-83
Blazing Saddles 591
Blechtrommel, Die 654
Blonde Cobra 415
Blowup [illegible]
Blue Angel, The 82-83
Blue Kite, The 831
Blue Velvet 733
Boat, The 675
Bob le flambeur 318
Bob the Gambler 318
Body Heat 677
Bonnie and Clyde 480-481
Boogie Nights 879
Boot, Das 675
Boucher, Le 519
Boudu Sauvé des Eaux 101
Boudu Saved from Drowning 101
Boyz N the Hood 800-801
Bram Stoker's Dracula 822
Braveheart 854
Brave-Hearted Will Take the Bride, The 860
Brazil 724-725
Breakfast at Tiffany's 396
Breakfast Club, The 717
Breaking Away 654
Breaking the Waves 867
Breathless 370
Bride of Frankenstein 129
Bridge on the River Kwai, The 345
Brief Encounter 216
Brighter Summer Day, A 803
Brightness 745
Bring Me the Head of Alfredo Garcia 595
Bringing Up Baby 149
Broadcast News 754
Broken Blossoms 38
Bronenosets Potyomkin 58-59
Büchse der Pandora, Die 80-81
Buffalo 66 888
Bull Durham 762
Buono, Il Brutto, Il Cattivo, Il 458-459
Burmese Harp, The 327
Butch Cassidy and the Sundance Kid 506
Butcher Boy, The 877
Butcher, The 519

**C**

Cabaret 553
Cabinet of Dr. Caligari, The 36-37
Cairo Station 352
Camille 135
Campanadas a Medianoche 449
Candyman 823
Captain Blood 126
Captains Courageous 138
Captive, La 912
Captive, The 912
Caravaggio 741
Carmen Jones 307
Caro Diario 850
Carrie 613

Carrosse d'or, Le 281
Casablanca 184-185
Casino 850
Cat People 187
Ceddo 635
Celebration, The 885
Celine and Julie Go Boating 590
Céline et Julie Vont en Bateau 590
C'era Una Volta il West 489
C'est arrivé près de chez vouz 825
Chagrin et la Pitié, Le 538
Chant of Jimmy Blacksmith, The 640
Chariots of Fire 676
Charme Discret de la Bourgeoisie, Le 560
Chelovek s kinoapparatom 78-79
Chicago 949
Chienne, La 98
Children of a Lesser God 739
Children of Paradise, The 210
Chimes at Midnight 449
Chinatown 588-589
Chinese Ghost Story, A 758
Chong Qing Sen Lin 845
Christmas Story, A 695
Chronicle of a Summer 401
Chronique d'un été 401
Chuen Gwong Tsa Sit 875
Chungking Express 845
Cidade de Deus 945
Cinema Paradiso 765
Citizen Kane 172-173
City Lights 95
City of God 945
City of Sadness, A 788
Cléo de 5 à 7 404
Cleo from 5 to 7 404
Clerks 839
Clockwork Orange, A 536-537
Close Encounters of the Third Kind 624
Closely Watched Trains 486-487
Close-up 796
Cloud-Clapped Star, The 384
Clueless 855
Color of Pomegranates, The 520
Color Purple, The 731
Come and See 720
Come Drink With Me 460
Condamné à Mort s'échappé ou Le Vent Souffle où Il Veut, Un 330
Conformist, The 511
Conformista, Il 511
Conte d'hiver 823
Contempt 418
Conversation, The 584
Cook, the Thief, His Wife, & Her Lover, The 779
Cool Hand Luke 476-477
Cool World, The 415
Cow, The 489
Cranes are Flying, The 347
Cría Cuervos 609
Cria! 609
Cries and Whispers 559
Crimes and Misdemeanors 778
Crouching Tiger Hidden Dragon 920-921
Crowd, The 72
Crumb 846
Crying Game, The 824
Csillagosok, Katonák 482
Cyclo 859
Czlowiek Z Marmuru 630
Czlowiek z Zelaza 680

**D**

Da Hong Deng Long Gao Gao Gua 802
Da Zui Xia 460
Daisies 460
Dance, Girl, Dance 169
Dancer in the Dark 925
Dances with Wolves 792
Dangerous Liaisons 768
Dao Ma Zei 745
David Holzman's Diary 496
Dawn of the Dead 646
Day for Night 573
Day in the Country, A 130
Day the Earth Stood Still, The 270
Daybreak 160
Days of Heaven 645
De Man Die Zijin Haar Kort Liet Knippen 455
Dead Man 861
Dead, The 757
Dear Diary 850
Decalogue, The 770
Déclin de l'Empire Américain, Le 735
Decline of the American Empire 735
Deconstructing Harry 874
Deep End 526
Deer Hunter, The 642-643
Deewar 600
Defiant Ones, The 353
Dekalog, Jeden 770
Delicatessen 802
Deliverance 555
Demoiselles de Rochefort, Les 474
Der Himmel über Berlin 746-747
Dernier Combat, Le 698
Dernier Metro, Le 665
Dersu Uzala 583
Deseret 851
Deserto Rosso, Il 437
Destry Rides Again 156
Detour 214
Deus E O Diabo Na Terra Do Sol 441
Diaboliques, Les 298
Diary of a Country Priest 268
Die Hard 771
Die Xue Shuang Xiong 781
Dilwale Dulhaniya le Jayenge 860
Diner 688-689
Dirty Harry 547
Discreet Charm of the Bourgeoisie, The 560
Do Ma Daan 742
Do the Right Thing 782-783
Docks of New York, The 73
Dodsworth 136
Dog Day Afternoon 595
Dog Star Man 404
Dog's Life, A 403
Dolce Vita, La 378-379
Don't Look Now 574
Double Indemnity 204-205
Double Life of Veronique, The 816
Double Vie de Véronique, La 816
Down By Law 738
Dr. Mabuse, der Spieler 43
Dr. Mabuse, Parts 1 and 2 43
Dr. Strangelove 434-435
Dr. Zhivago 444
Dracula 357
Dracula 92-93
Drugstore Cowboy 779
Duck Soup 112-113
Dumbo 178
Dut Yeung Nin Wa 913

**E**

E.T. the Extra-Terrestrial 682
Ear, The 528-529
Earth 86-87
Earth Entranced 485
Easy Rider 512-513
Eclipse, The 405
Eclisse, L' 405
Edward Scissorhands 797
Ehe Der Maria Braun, Die 650
El Norte 695
El Topo 523
Elephant Man, The 669
Empire Strikes Back, The 668
Enfants du Paradis, Les 210
English Patient, The 868
Enter the Dragon 569
Eraserhead 634
Espíritu del la Colmena, El 579
Europa '51 277
Europa Europa 793
Evil Dead, The 686
Exorcist, The 576-577
Eyes Wide Shut 909
Eyes Without a Face 365

**F**

Fabuleax Destin d'Amélie Poulain 927
Faces 491
Fanny and Alexander 694
Fantasia 166
Fantastic Planet 579
Far from Heaven 948
Farewell My Concubine 827
Farewell My Lovely 206
Fargo 864-865
Fast Times at Ridgemont High 681
Fast, Cheap & Out of Control 877
Faster Pussycat! Kill, Kill! 453
Fat City 560
Fat Girl 937
Fatal Attraction 758
Faustrecht Der Freiheit 603
Femme du Boulanger, La 148
Ferris Bueller's Day Off 737
Festen 885
Fight Club 904
Firemen's Ball, The 484
Fires Were Started 192
Fish Called Wanda, A 766
Fitzcarraldo 690-691
Five Deadly Venoms 640
Five Easy Pieces 522
Flaming Creatures 420
Floating Weeds 377
Fly, The 736
Foolish Wives 49
Footlight Parade 110
Forbidden Games 272
Forbidden Planet 326
Force of Evil 237
Forrest Gump 838
Four Weddings and a Funeral 839
Fourth Man, The 702
Fox and His Friends 603
Frankenstein 94
Freaks 106
Freedom for Us 89
French Connection, The 545
Frenzy 562
From Here to Eternity 284
Full Metal Jacket 750-751
Funny Games 881

**G**
Gaav 489
Gabbeh 869
Gallipoli 676
Gangs of New York 942
Garden of the Finzi-Continis, The 535
Gaslight 202
Gattopardo, Il 422-422
General, The 66
Gentlemen Prefer Blondes 289
Gertrud 439
Get Carter 544
Ghandi 692
Ghost and Mrs. Muir, The 232
Ghost Busters 713
Giant 331
Giardino dei Finzi-Contini, Il 535
Gigi 353
Gilda 230
Gimme Shelter 532
Giulietta deglie Spiriti 451
Gladiator 915
Glaneurs et la Glaneuse, Les 923
Gleaners and I, The 923
Glengarry Glen Ross 819
Glory 784
Godfather, Part II, The 592-593
Godfather, The 558
Godson, The 475
Gohatto 899
Gold Diggers of 1933 110
Gold Rush, The 60
Golden Coach, The 281
Golden River 454
Goldfinger 429
Gone with the Wind 158-159
Good Morning Vietnam 752
Good, the Bad, and the Ugly, The 458-459
Goodbye Children 753
Goodfellas 790
Gospel According to St. Matthew, The 440
Graduate, The 468-469
Grand Illusion 140
Grande Illusion, La 140
Grapes of Wrath, The 168
Grave of the Fireflies 768
Grease 644
Great Escape, The 421
Great Expectations 224-225
Great Train Robbery, The 28-29
Greed 52-53
Groundhog Day 828
Guling Jie Shaonian Sha Ren Shijian 803
[illegible]
Gunfight at the OK Corral 345
Gunga Din 161
Guys and Dolls 311

**H**
Hable con ella 944
Halloween 648-649
Hannah and Her Sisters 734
Happiness 891
Happy Together 875
Hard Day's Night, A 436
Harder They Come, The 582
Harold and Maude 542-543
Haunting, The 426-427
Häxan 48
Hanyo 385
Heartbreak Kid, The 551
Hearts of Darkness: A Filmmaker's Apocalypse 814-815
Heat 856
Heaven and Earth Magic 412
Heavenly Creatures 847
Heiress, The 246
Henry V 202
Henry: Portrait of a Serial Killer 798
High Noon 279
High Plains Drifter 554
High School 514
High Sierra 179
High Society 336
Hill 24 Doesn't Answer 315
Hills Have Eyes, The 636-637
Hiroshima mon amour 374
His Girl Friday 164
Histoire de Vent, Une 772
Hitlerjunge Salomon 793
Hold Me While I'm Naked 455
Hole, The 376
Hombre 471
Hong Gao Liang 757
Hoop Dreams 836-837
Horí, Má Panenko 484
Horse Thief, The 745
Hotaru No Haka 768
Hôtel Terminus:Klaus Barbie et Son Temps 765
Hotel Terminus:The Life and Times of Klaus Barbie 765
Hour of the Wolf 500
House is Black, The 425
Housekeeping 755
Housemaid, The 385
How Green Was My Valley 182
Hsi Yen 834
Hsia Nu 505
Hsimeng Jensheng 831
Hud 419
Hurdes, Las 114
Hustler, The 402

**I**
I Am a Fugitive from a Chain Gang 101
I Know Where I'm Going! 214
I Walked with a Zombie 194
Ice Storm, The 878
Idi I Smotri 720
Idioterne 894
Idiots, The 894
If.... 494
Ikiru 276
In a Lonely Place 263
In the Heat of the Night 461
In the Mood for Love 913
In the Realm of the Senses 619
In the Year of the Pig 515
Incredible Shrinking Man, The 343
Independence Day [illegible]
India Song 604
Intolerance 34-35
Invasion of the Body Snatchers 334
It Happened One Night 122-123
It's a Gift 117
It's a Wonderful Life 228-229
Ivan Groznyj I 203
Ivan the Terrible, I 203

**J**
Jacob's Ladder 791
Jalsaghar 358-359
Jaws 612
Jazz Singer, The 70
Jean Dielman... 597
Jerk, The 660
Jetée, La 394
Jeux interdits 272
Jezebel 145
JFK 810-811
Johnny Guitar 295
Jour se lève, Le 160
Journal d'un curé de campagne 268
Joven, La 384
Judge Priest 121
Jules and Jim 398
Jules et Jim 398
Juliet of the Spirits 451
Jungle Book, The 483
Jurassic Park 830
Juyuso Seubgyuksageun 908

**K**
Kabinett des Doktor Caligari, Das 36-37
Kandahar 929
Keeper of Promises 410
Kes 521
[illegible]
Kid Brother, The 71
Killer of Sheep 632-633
Killer, The 781
Killers, The 223
Killing Fields, The 716
Killing of a Chinese Bookie, The 613
Kind Hearts and Coronets 247
King Kong 115
King of Comedy, The 702
King of New York 791
Kingdom, The 849
Kippur 916
Kiss Me Deadly 319
Kiss of the Spider Woman 726
Kjælighetens Kjøtere 856
Klute 541
Körkarlen 41
Koyaanisqatsi 704
Kramer vs. Kramer 657
Kumonosu Jo 343
Kundun 880

**L**
L.A. Confidential 874
La Belle et la Bête 221
Ladies Man, The 399
Ladri di biciclette 233
Lady Eve, The 174
Lady from Shanghai, The 240
Ladykillers, The 316
Lan Feng Zheng 834
Land Without Bread 114
Landscape in the Mist 769
Last Battle, The 698
Last Chants for a Slow Dance 628
Last Laugh, The 56
Last Metro, The 665
Last Picture Show, The 549
Last Seduction, The 842
Last Tango in Paris 553
Last Wave, The 625
Last Year at Marienbad 393
Laura 201
Lavender Hill Mob, The 266
Lawrence of Arabia 406-407
Le Mépris 418
Leopard, The 422-422
Letjat Zhuravli 347
Letter from an Unknown Woman 234-235
Letzte Mann, Der 56
Life and Death of Colonel Blimp, The 193
Life of Emile Zola, The 141
Lion King, The 840
Little Big Man 527
Little Caeser 88
Lock, Stock, and Two Smoking Barrels [illegible]
Lola 396
Lola Montès 326
Lola Rennt 889
Lolita 409

Lone Star 870
Long Goodbye, The 572
Lord of the Rings: The Fellowship of the Ring, 940
Lost Weekend, The 212-213
Louisiana Story 245
Loulou 670
Love Me Tonight 100
Lucía 504

**M**

M 96-97
M*A*S*H* 530
M. Hulot's Holiday 291
Ma Nuit Chez Maud 504
Madame de... 283
Mad Masters, The 315
Mad Max 662
Magnificent Ambersons, The 188-189
Magnolia 896
Maîtres fous, Les 315
Make Way for Tomorrow 142
Maltese Falcon, The 176-177
Maman et la Putain, La 565
Man Bites Dog 825
Man Escaped, A 330
Man From Laramie, The 319
Man in Grey, The 193
Man of Iron 680
Man of Marble 630
Man of the West 349
Man Who Fell to Earth, The 621
Man who had his hair cut short, The 455
Man Who Knew Too Much, The 331
Man Who Shot Liberty Valance, The 410
Man with a Movie Camera, The 78-79
Manchurian Candidate, The 409
Manhattan 661
Manhunter 732
Manila in the Claws of Brightness 605
Marketa Lazarová 483
Marnie 432
Marriage of Maria Braun, The 650
Marty 316
Maschera del Demonio, La 388
Masculine-Feminine 466
Masculin-Féminin 466
Masque of the Red Death, The 438
Mat I Syn 883
Matrix, The 911
Matter of Life and Death, A 223
Maynila: Sa Mga Kuko Ng Liwanag 605
McCabe and Mrs. Miller 539
Me and My Gal 107
Mean Streets 570-571
Méditerranée 425
Meet Me in St. Louis 198-199
Meet the Parents 919
Még Kér A Nép 544
Meghe Dhaka Tara 384
Memento 924
Memorias del Subdesarrollo 495
Memories of Underdevelopment 495
Meshes of the Afternoon 191
Metropolis 62-63
Midnight Cowboy 507
Midnight Song 139
Mildred Pierce 208-209
Million, Le 90
Million, The 90
Mirror 586
Mishima: A Life in Four Chapters 728
Modern Times 131
Mon oncle 357
Mondo cane 403
Money 699
Mononoke Hime 876
Monsieur Verdoux 230
Monsoon Wedding 936
Monty Python and the Holy Grail 601
Monty Python's Life of Brian 657
Moonstruck 756
Mortal Storm, The 170
Mother and Son 883
Mother and the Whore, The 565
Mother India 346
Moulin Rouge! 934-935
Mr. Deeds Goes to Town 134
Mr. Smith Goes to Washington 153
Mujeres al Borde de un Ataque de Nervios 759
Mulholland Dr. 938
Muppet Movie, The 660
Murder, My Sweet 206
Murmur of the Heart 547
Music Room, The 358-359
Mutiny on the Bounty 126
My Brilliant Career 651
My Darling Clementine 218-219
My Fair Lady 433
My Left Foot 780
My Life to Live 412
My Man Godfrey 133
My Night with Maud 504
My Own Private Idaho 806-807
My Uncle 357

**N**

Naked Gun, The 767
Naked Lunch 804
Naked Spur, The 288
Nanook of the North 44-45
Napoléon 71
Narayama Bushi-Ko 707
Nashville 608
Nattvardsgästerna 419
Natural Born Killers 842
Natural, The 716
Neco z Alenky 776
Nema-Ye Nazdik 796
Network 618
Neuve Reinas 912
Ni Neibian Jidian 928
Night and Fog 323
Night at the Opera, A 127
Night of the Hunter, The 324-325
Night of the Living Dead 502-503
Night of the Shooting Stars, The 693
Night, The 397
Nightmare on Elm Street, A 711
Nights of Cabiria, The 342
Nine Queens 912
Ninotchka 161
No Fear, No Die 789
No Man's Land 933
North By Northwest 361
Nosferatu, a Symphony of Terror 46-47
Nosferatu, eine Symphonie des Grauens 46-47
Nosferatu: Phantom der Nacht 663
Notorious 226
Notte di San Lorenzo, La 693
Notte, La 397
Notti of Cabiria, Le 342
Novecento 620
Now, Voyager 183
Nuit Américaine, La 573
Nuit et Brouillard 323
Nuovo Cinema Paradiso 765
Nutty Professor, The 414

**O**

O Brother, Where Art Thou? 926
O Pagador De Promessas 410
O Thiassos 610-611
Obchod Na Korze 443
October 68-69
Odd Man Out 232
Odishon 903
Official Story, The 721
Oktyabr 68-69
Olvidados, Los 262
Olympia 1: Teil - Fest Der Volker & Olympia 2: Teil - Fest Der Schönheit 147
Olympia Part 1: Festival of the Nations & Part 2: Festival of Beauty 147
On the Town 254
On the Waterfront 296-297
Once Upon a Time in America 705
Once Upon a Time in China 799
Once Upon a Time in the West 489
One Flew Over the Cuckoo's Nest 596
One-Eyed Jacks 395
Onibaba 442
Only Angels Have Wings 157
Open City 211
Open Your Eyes 883
Ordet 317
Ordinary People 664
Orfeu Negro 366
Orphans of the Storm 42
Orphée 255
Orpheus 255
Ossessione 197
Ostre Sledované Vlaky 486-487
Our Hospitality 49
Out of Africa 721
Out of the Past 231
Outlaw Josey Wales, The 614
Ox-Bow Incident, The 195

**P**

Paisà 217
Paisan 217
Paleface, The 241
Palm Beach Story, The 183
Pandora and the Flying Dutchman 266
Pandora's Box 80-81
Papillon 569
Parapluies de Cherbourg, Les 431
Paris, Texas 710
Partie de Campagne, Une 130
Pasazerka 418
Passage to India, A 714
Passenger 418
Passion de Jeanne d'Arc, La 75
Passion of Joan of Arc, The 75
Pat Garrett and Billy the Kid 582
Pather Panchali 312-313
Paths of Glory 348
Patton 530
Peeping Tom 389
Peking Opera Blues 742
Pépé le Moko 145
Performance 531

Persona 464-465
Phantom Carriage, The 41
Phantom of the Opera, The 57
Phenix City Story, The 322
Philadelphia 829
Philadelphia Story, The 167
Pi 890
Pianist, The 943
Pianiste, La 932
Piano Teacher, The 932
Piano, The 833
Pickpocket 372-373
Pickup on South Street 288
Picnic at Hanging Rock 604
Pier, The 394
Pierrot le Fou 452
Pillow Book, The 863
Pink Flamingos 563
Pinocchio 169
Place in the Sun, A 269
Planet of the Apes 490
Planète Sauvage, La 579
Platoon 740
Player, The 817
Playtime 470
Point Blank 478
Poltergeist 683
Popiól I Diament 356
Postman Always Rings Twice, The 217
Potomok Chingis-Khana 76
Pretty Woman 794
Prima Della Rivoluzione 438
Princess Bride, The 755
Princess Mononoke 876
Prizzi's Honor 728
Producers, The 496
Project A, Part II 748
Psycho 386-387
Public Enemy, The 95
Pulp Fiction 843
Puppetmaster, The 831
Purple Rose of Cairo, The 722

**Q**

Quatre Cent Coups, Les 360
Queen Christina 114
Question of Silence, A 693
Quiet Earth, The 727
Quiet Man, The 271

**R**

Raging Bull 672-673
Raiders of the Lost Ark 674
Rain Man 774
Raise the Red Lantern 802
Raising Arizona 749
Ran 718-719
[illegible]
Rashomon 256-257
Real Life 651
Rear Window 300-301
Rebecca 165
Rebel Without a Cause 320-321
Reckless Moment, The 251
Red and the White, The 482
Red Desert, The 437
Red Psalm 544
Red River 238
Red Shoes, The 242-243
Red Sorghum 757
Règle du Jeu, La 162-163
Rekopis Znaleziony w Saragossie 447
Report 471
Repulsion 450
Requiem for a Dream 917
Resevoir Dogs 818
Return of the Jedi 697
Reversal of Fortune 789
Ride Lonesome 366
Riget 849
Right Stuff, The 703
Ring 895
Rio Bravo 375
Rio Grande 258
Rocco and his Brothers 377
Rocco e i suoi fratelli 377
Rocky 615
Rocky Horror Picture Show, The 598-599
Roger & Me 784
Roma, Città Aperta 211
Roman d'un tricheur, Le 138
Roman Holiday 286
Romper Stomper 819
Room with a View, A 739
Rope 239
Roseaux Sauvages, Les 844
Rosemary's Baby 492-493
Rosetta 899
Roue, La 50
Royal Tennenbaums, The 939
Rules of the Game, The 162-163
Run Lola Run 889
Rushmore 890
Russian Ark 946
Russkij Kovcheg 946

**S**

Sabotage 135
Safar e Ghandehar 929
Safe 854
Salaire De La Peur, La 287
Salò o le centoventi giornate di sodoma 606-607
Salo, or The 120 days of Sodom 606-607
Salt of the Earth 310
Salvador 742
Samouraï, Le 475
Sanma No Aji 405
Sans Soleil 698
Sans Toit Ni Loi 729
Sanshô Dayû 308-309
Sansho the Baliff 308-309
Saragossa Manuscript 447
Såsom I En Spegel 400
Sátántangó 841
Saturday Night and Sunday Morning 380
Saturday Night Fever 631
Satyricon 508-509
Saving Private Ryan 886-887
Say Anything 787
Sayat Nova 520
Scarface 706
Scarface: The Shame of a Nation 104
Schindler's List 832
Scorpio Rising 430
Scream 872-873
Se7en 857
Searchers, The 328-329
Seconds 461
Secret Beyond the Door 236
Secrets & Lies 866
Sedmikrasky 460
S'en Fout La Mort 789
Sen To Chihiro No Kamikakushi 930-931
Senso 306
Sergeant York 178
Serpico 575
Servant, The 428
Seven Brides for Seven Brothers 298
Seven Chances 56
Seven Samurai, The 304-305
Seventh Seal, The 338-339
Seventh Victim, The 194
Sex, lies, and videotape 786
Shadow of a Doubt 196
Shadows 367
Shadows of Our Forgotten Ancestors 437
Shaft 546
Shame 497
Shane 294
Shanghai Express 105
Shao Lin San Shih Liu Fang 647
Shaolin Master Killer 647
Shawshank Redemption, The 844
She Done Him Wrong 111
Sherlock Jr. 54-55
Sherman's March 744
She's Gotta Have It 735
Shining, The [illegible]
Shoah 730
Shock Corridor 421
Shoot the Piano Player 381
Shop on Main Street, The 443
Short Cuts 829
Signs & Wonders 919
Silence of the Lambs, The 809
Silver Lode 307
Sin of Lola Montes, The 326
Singin' in the Rain 274-275
Sinnui Yauman 758
Sixth Sense, The 910
Sjunde Inseglet, Det 338-339
Skammen 497
Slacker 812
Sleeper 575
Sleuth 554
Smiles of a Summer Night 322
Smiling Madame Beudet, The 42
Smoke 858
Smultronstället 341
Snake Pit, The 240
Snow White and the Seven Dwarfs 143
Solaris 556-557
Soldaat Van Oranje 638
Soldier of Orange 638
Solyaris 556-557
Sombre 894
Some Like it Hot 362-363
Sommarnattens Leede 322
Sons of the Desert 116
Son's Room, The 932
Sorrow and the Pity, The 538
Souffle Au Coeur, Le 547
Sound of Music, The 447
Souriante Madame Beudet, La 42
Spartacus 392
Spellbound 207
Spider's Stratagem, The 526
Spirit of the Beehive, The 579
Spirited Away 930-931
Splendor in the Grass 392
Spoorloos 760-761
Spring in a Small Town 237
Stachka 51
Stagecoach 150-151
Stalker 652
Stand By Me 732
Stanza del Figlio, La 932
Star is Born, A 302
Star Wars 622-623
Steamboat Bill, Jr. 76
Stella Dallas 141
Stilte Rond Christine M., De 693
Sting, The 564
Storm over Asia 76
Story of a Cheat, The 138
Story of the Late Chrysanthemums, The 152
Story of Women, The 775
Strada, La 303

Strange Days 853
Stranger than Paradise 715
Stranger, The 220
Strangers on a Train 265
Strategia del Ragno, La 526
Straw Dogs 550
Streetcar Named Desire, A 264
Strictly Ballroom 816
Strike 51
Stroszek 629
Subarnarekha 454
Sullivan's Travels 180-181
Suna No Onna 433
Sunless 698
Sunrise 64-65
Sunset Blvd. 260-621
Superfly 564
Suspiria 639
Sweet Hereafter, The 880
Sweet Smell of Success 348
Sweet Sweetback's Badasssss Song 548
Swing Time 132

T

Tabu 91
Tale of the Wind, A 772
Tale of Winter, A 823
Tales of Ugetsu 293
Talk to Her 944
Ta'm e Guilass 882
Tampopo 741
Targets 501
Taste of Cherry 882
Taxi Driver 616-617
Temps retrouvé, Le 904
Ten Commandments, The 336
Terminator 2: Judgment Day 808
Terminator, The 708-709
Terms of Endearment 701
Terra Em Transe 485
Tetsuo 885
Texas Chainsaw Massacre, The 585
Thelma and Louise 808
There's Something About Mary 896
Thief of Bagdad, The 50
Thin Blue Line, The 763
Thin Man, The 124-125
Thin Red Line, The 892-893
Thing, The 683
Things to Come 137
Third Man, The 252-253
Thirty Two Short Films About Glenn Gould 827
This is Spinal Tap 712
Three Brothers 679
Three Colors: Blue 833
Three Colors: Red 835
Three Kings 902
Three Lives and Only One Death 863
Throne of Blood 343
Through a Glass Darkly 400
Through the Olive Trees 848
Time Regained 904
Time to Live and the Time to Die, The 723
Tin Drum, The 654
Tini Zabutykh Predkiv 437
Tirez sur le pianiste 381
Titanic 884
To Be or Not to Be 186
To Have and Have Not 200
To Kill A Mockingbird 408
To Live 276
Todo Sobre Mi Madre 900-901
Tokyo Olympiad 445
Tokyo Orimpikku 445
Tokyo Story 285
Tong Nien Wang Shi 723
Tongues Untied 813
Too Early, Too Late 681
Tootsie 686
Top Gun 743
Top Hat 130
Topio Stin Omichli 769
Total Recall 799
Touch of Evil 350-351
Touch of Zen, A 505
Toy Story 853
Traffic 922
Trainspotting 871
Travelling Players 610-611
Tre Fratelli 679
Treasure of the Sierra Madre, The 244
Tree of Wooden Clogs, The 641
Trip to the Moon, A 26-27
Tristana 521
Triumph des Willens 118-119
Triumph of the Will 118-119
Trois Couleurs: Bleu 833
Trois Couleurs: Rouge 835
Trois Vies & Une Seule Mort 863
Trou, Le 376
Trouble in Paradise 102-103
Trust 795
Turkish Delight 578
Turks Fruit 578
Two or Three Things I Know About Her 467
Two-Lane Blacktop 551

U

Uccello dalle Piume di Cristallo, L' 533
Ucho 528-529
Ugetsu Monogatari 293
Ukigusa 377
Ultimo Tango a Parigi 553
Umberto D 280
Umbrellas of Cherbourg, The 431
Un chien andalou 74
Unbelievable Truth, The 787
Underground 860
Unforgiven 820-821
Unknown, The 67
Untouchables, The 756
Unvanquished, The 344
Up in Smoke 647
Usual Suspects, The 862
Utu 700

V

Vacances de M. Hulot, Les 291
Vagabond 729
Vampire, The 99
Vampires, Les 32-33
Vampyr 99
Vangelo Secondo Matteo, Il 440
Vanishing, The 760-761
Vargtimmen 500
Vertigo 354-355
Vidas Secas 424
Videodrome 696
Vierde Man, De 702
Vij 488
Vinyl 442
Viridiana 399
Viskingar och Rop 559
Vivre Sa Vie: Film en Douze Tableaux 412
Voskhozhdenie 619
Voyage dans la Lune, Le 26-27
Voyage in Italy 292

W

Wages of Fear 287
Walkabout 540
Wall, The 600
Wanda 535
War Game, The 445
Wavelength 479
Way Down East 39
Wedding Banquet, The 834
Week End 474
West Side Story 402
What Ever Happened to Baby Jane? 411
What Time Is It There? 928
Wheel, The 50
When Harry Met Sally 777
Whiskey Galore! 250
White Balloon, The 858
White Heat 251
Who Framed Roger Rabbit 773
Who's Afraid of Virginia Woolf 462-463
Wicker Man, The 572
Wild Bunch, The 516-517
Wild Reeds 844
Wild Strawberries 341
Willy Wonka and the Chocolate Factory 538
Winchester '73 258
Wind Will Carry Us, The 902
Wings of Desire 746-747
Winter Light 419
Within Our Gates 40
Withnail and I 752
Wizard of Oz, The 154-155
Wo Hu Cang Long 920-921
Wolf Man, The 175
Woman in the Dunes, The 433
Woman Under the Influence, A 587
Women on the Verge of a Nervous Breakdown 759
Wong Fei-Hung 799
Woodstock 524-525
World of Apu, The 368-369
Written on the Wind 330
W.R.—Misterje Organizma 534
W.R.:Mysteries of the Organism 534
Wrong Man, The 335
Wu Du 640
Wuthering Heights 164

X

Xiao cheng zhi chun 237
Xich Lo 859

Y

Y tu mama tambien 928
Yankee Doodle Dandy 190
Ye Ban Ge Sheng 139
Yeelen 745
Yeux Sans Visage, Les 365
Yi yi 916
Yol 687
Young and the Damned, The 262
Young Frankenstein 587
Young Girls of Rochefort, The 474
Young One, The 384
Yuen Ling-yuk 826
Yukinojo Henge 428

Z

Z 510
Zabriskie Point 533
Zangiku monogatari 152
Zemlya 86-87
Zerkalo 586
Zéro de conduite 107
Zero for Conduct 107
Zero Kelvin 856
Zire Darakhatan Zeyton 848
Zu Fruh, Zu Spat 681

# DIRECTOR INDEX


**A**
Abrahams, Jim 671
Ackerman, Chantal 597, 912
Adler, Lou 647
Aldrich, Robert 319, 411
Alea, Tomás Gutiérrez 495
Allen, Woody 575, 626-627, 661, 722, 734, 778, 874
Allers, Roger 840
Almodovar, Pedro 759, 900 901, 944
Altman, Robert 530, 539, 572, 608, 817, 829
Amenabar, Alejandro 883
Anderson, Lindsay 494
Anderson, Paul Thomas 879, 896
Anderson, Wes 890, 939
Angelopolous, Theo 610-611, 769
Anger, Kenneth 430
Antonioni, Michaelangelo 382-383, 397, 405, 437, 456-457, 533
Arcand, Denys 735
Argento, Dario 533, 639
Arliss, Leslie 193
Armstrong, Gillian 651
Arnold, Jack 343
Aronofsky, Darren 890, 917
Arzner, Dorothy 169
Ashby, Hal 542-543, 656
Attenborough, Richard 692
Avildsen, John 615
Axel, Gabriel 749
Ayouch, Nabil 914

**B**
Babenco, Hector 726
Bacon, Lloyd 108-109, 110
Badham, John 631
Bahr, Fax 814-815
Batchelor, Joy 299
Bava, Mario 388
Beatty, Warren 678
Becker, Jacques 385
Belvaux, Remy et al. 825
Benning, James 851
Benton, Robert 657
Bergman, Ingmar 328, 338-339, 341, 400, 419, 464-465, 497, 500, 559, 694
Berkeley, Busby 152
Bertolucci, Bernardo 438, 511, 526, 553, 620
Besson, Luc 698
Biberman, Howard J. 310
Bielinsky, Fabian 912
Bigelow, Kathryn 853
Boetticher, Budd 366
Bogdanovich, Peter 501, 549
Boorman, John 478, 555
Borzage, Frank 170
Boyle, Danny 871
Brakhage, Stan 404
Brando, Marlon 395
Breillat, Catherine 937
Bresson, Robert 268, 330, 372-373, 461, 699
Brest, Martin 713
Brocka, Lino 605
Brooks, Albert 651
Brooks, James L. 701, 754
Brooks, Mel 496, 587, 591
Broomfield, Nick 824
Browning, Tod 67, 92-93, 106
Bunuel, Luis 71, 84-85, 114, 161, 384, 399, 472-473, 521, 560
Burnett, Charles 632-633
Burton, Tim 776, 797

**C**
Cameron, James 708-709, 737, 808, 884
Cammell, Donald 531
Campion, Jane 833
Camus, Marcel 366
Capra, Frank 116, 122-123, 134, 153, 228-229
Carne, Marcel 160, 210
Caro, Marc 802
Carpenter, John 683, 648-649
Cassavetes, John 367, 491, 587, 613
Chabrol, Claude 519, 775
Chahine, Youssef 352
Chan, Jackie 748
Chaplin, Charlie 60, 95, 131, 230
Cheh, Chang 640
Chen, Kaige 827
Chia-Liang, Liu 647
Chong, Tommy 647
Chopra, Aditya 860
Chopra, Yash 600
Christensen, Benjamin 48
Chytilova, Vera 460
Cimino, Michael 642-643
Cisse, Souleymane 745
Clair, Rene 89, 90
Clark, Bob 695
Clarke, Shirley 415
Cleese, John 766
Clement, Rene 272
Cline, Edward 171
Clouse, Robert 569
Clouzot, Henri-Georges 287, 298
Cocteau, Jean 221, 255
Coen, Ethan 749, 864-865
Coen, Joel 749, 864-865, 926
Conner, Bruce 471
Cooper, Merian C. 115
Coppola, Francis Ford 558, 584, 592-593, 658-659, 822
Corman, Roger 438
Costa-Gavras, 510
Costner, Kevin 792
Craven, Wes 711, 636-637, 872-873
Crichton, Charles 266
Cronenberg, David 696, 736, 804
Crosland, Alan 70
Crowe, Cameron 787
Cuaron, Alfonso 928
Cukor, George 135, 167, 202, 249, 302, 433
Curtiz, Michael 126, 146, 184-185, 190, 208-209

**D**
Dahl, John 842
Darabont, Frank 844
Dardenne, Jean-Pierre 899
de Antonio, Emile 515
De Sica, Vittorio 233, 280, 535
Delvaux, Andre 455
DeMille, Cecile B. 336
Demme, Jonathan 809, 829
Demy, Jacques 396, 431, 474
Denis, Claire 789, 897
DePalma, Brian 613, 706, 756
Deren, Maya 191
Dickinson, Thorold 315
Diterle, William 141
Dmytryk, Edward 206
Donen, Stanley 298, 254, 274-275
Dovzhenko, Alexander 86-87
Dreyer, Carl 75, 99, 317, 439
Duarte, Anselmo 410
Dulac, Germaine 42
Duras, Marguerite 604
Duvivier, Julien 145
Dwan, Allan 307

**E**
Eastwood, Clint 554, 614, 820-821
Edwards, Blake 396
Egoyan, Atom 880
Eisenstein, Sergei 51, 58-59, 68-69, 203
Emmerich, Roland 866
Erice, Victor 579
Eustache, Jean 565

**F**
Farrelly, Bobby 896
Farrokhzad, Forugh 425
Fassbinder, Rainer Werner 581, [illegible]
Fellini, Federico 305, 342, 451, 378-379, 416-417, 508-509, 580-581
Ferrara, Abel 791
Feuillade, Louis 32-33
Fincher, David 857, 904
Fisher, Terence 357
Flaherty, Robert 44-45, 91, 245
Fleming, Victor 138, 154-155, 158-159
Foley, James 819
Ford, John 121, 150-151, 168, 182, 218-219, 258, 271, 328-329, 410
Forman, Milos 484, 484, 596, 707
Forsyth, Bill 755
Fosse, Bob 553, 655
Franju, Georges 365
Frankenheimer, John 409, 466
Frawley, James 660
Frears, Stephen 768
Friedkin, William 545, 576-577
Fuller, Samuel 288, 423, 670

**G**
Gallo, Vincent 888
Gance, Abel 50, 71
Garnett, Tay 217
Ghatak, Ritwak 384, 454
Gibson, Mel 854
Gilliam, Terry 601, 724-725
Girard, Francois 827
Gitai, Amos 916
Godard, Jean-Luc 370, 412, 418, 448, 452, 461, 467, 474
Gorris, Marleen 693
Grandrieux, Philippe 894
Greenaway, Peter 779, 863
Griffith, D.W. 30-31, 34-35, 38, 39, 42
Guitry, Sacha 138
Guney, Yilmaz 687

**H**
Haines, Randa 739
Halas, John 299
Hamer, Robert 247
Hamilton, Guy 429
Haneke, Michael 881, 932
Hanson, Curtis 874
Hardy, Robin 572
Hark, Tsui 742, 758, 799
Hartley, Hal 787, 795
Has, Wojech 447
Hawks, Howard 104, 149, 157, 164, 178, 200, 222, 238, 279, 289, 375
Haynes, Todd 854, 948
Heckerling, Amy 681, 855
Hellman, Monte 551
Henzell, Perry 582
Herzog, Werner 552, 629, 663, 690-691

Hill, George Roy 506, 564
Hitchcock, Alfred 77, 128, 135, 165, 196, 207, 226, 239, 265, 300-301, 331, 334-335, 355, 361, 386-387, 413, 432, 562
Hodges, Mike 544
Holland, Agnieszka 793
Hooper, Tobe 585, 683
Hopper, Dennis 512-513
Hou, Hsiao-hsien 831
Howe, J.A. 71
Hsiao-hsien, Hou 723, 788
Hu, King 460, 505
Hudson, Hugh 676
Hughes, John 717, 737
Huillet, Daniele 681
Hung Tran, Anh 859
Huston, John 176-177, 207, 244, 255, 267, 295, 560, 728, 757

I
Ichikawa, Kon 327, 428, 445
Imamura, Shohei 707
Inarritu, Alejandro 918
Itami, Juzo 741
Ivens, Joris 772
Ivory, James 739

J
Jackson, Peter 847, 940
Jacobs, Ken 415
Jacopetti, Gualtiero 403
Jaffe, Roland 716
James, Steve 836-837
Jansco, Miklos 482, 544
Jarman, Derek 741
Jarmusch, Jim 715, 738, 861
Jennings, Humphrey 192
Jeunet, Jean-Pierre 802, 927
Jewison, Norman 466, 756
Jodorowsky, Alejandro 523
Jones, Terry 601, 657
Jonz, Spike 905, 947
Jordan, Neil 824, 877
Jost, Jon 628
Julian, Rupert 57

K
Kachyna, Karel 528-529
Kadar, Jan 443
Kalatozov, Mikhail 347
Karlsen, Phil 322
Kar-Wai, Wong 845, 875, 913
Kasdan, Lawrence 677, 697, 775
Kaufman, Philip 703
Kaurismaki, Aki 762
Kazan, Elia 264, 296-297, 392
Keaton, Buster 49, 54-55, 56, 66, 76
Kelly, Gene 254, 274
Khan, Mehboob 346
Kiarostami, Abbas 796, 848, 882, 902
Kieslowski, Krzysztof 770, 816, 833, 835
Kim, Sang-Jin 908
Ki-Young, Kim 377
Kleiser, Randal 644
Klimov, Elem 720
Kramer, Stanley 353
Kropachyov, Georgi 488
Kubrick, Stanley 348, 392, 409, 434-435, 498-499, 536-537, 602, 666-667, 750-751, 909
Kuchar, George 455
Kurosawa, Akira 256-257, 276, 304-305, 343, 583, 718-719
Kusturica, Emir 860
Kwan, Stanley 826

L
La Cava, Gregory 133
Laloux, Rene 579
Landis, John 679
Lang, Fritz 43, 62-63, 96-97, 236, 290
Lanzmann, Claude 730
Lasseter, John 853
Laughton, Charles 324-325
Lean, David 216, 224-225, 345, 406-407, 444, 714
Lee, Ang 834, 878, 920-921
Lee, Spike 735, 782-783
Leigh, Mike 866
Leone, Sergio 489, 458-459, 705
LeRoy, Mervyn 88, 101, 110
Lester, Richard 436
Levinson, Barry 688-689, 716, 752, 774
Lewin, Albert 266
Lewis, Jerry 399, 414
Lewis, Joseph H. 248
Linklater, Richard 812
Litvak, Anatole 240
Lloyd, Frank 126
Loach, Ken 521
Loden, Barbara 535
Losey, Joseph 428
Lubitsch, Ernst 161, 186, 102-103
Lucas, George 568, 622-623, 668, 697
Luhrmann, Baz 816, 934-935
Lumet, Sidney 337, 575, 595, 618
Lund, Katia 945
Lupino, Ida 281
Lynch, David 634, 669, 733, 938
Lyne, Adrian 758, 791

M
Mackendrick, Alexander 250, 316, 348
Maddin, Guy 795
Makavejev, Dusan 534
Makhmalbaf, Mohsen 869, 929
Malick, Terrence 566-567, 645, 892-893
Malle, Louis 547, 665, 753
Mamoulian, Rouben 100, 114
Mankiewicz, Joseph 232, 259, 302, 311
Mankiewicz, Joseph L. 554
Mann, Anthony 258, 288, 319, 349
Mann, Delbert 316
Mann, Michael 732, 856
Marker, Chris 394, 698
Marshall, Garry 794
Marshall, George 152
Marshall, Penny 767
Marshall, Rob 949
May, Elaine 551
Maysles, Albert 532
Maysles, David 532
McBride, Jim 496
McCarey, Leo 112-113, 142, 144, 340
McElwee, Ross 744
McLeod, Norman Z. 117, 241
McNaughton, John 798
McTiernan, John 771
Mehrjui, Dariush 489
Meirelles, Fernando 945
Melies, Georges 26-27
Melville, Jean-Pierre 318, 475
Mendes, Sam 906-907
Menzel, Jiri 486-487
Menzies, William Cameron 137
Meyer, Russ 453
Micheaux, Oscar 40
Miike, Takashi 903
Milestone, Lewis 89
Miller, George 662
Minghella, Anthony 868
Minkoff, Rob 840
Minnelli, Vincente 198-199, 268, 278, 282, 353
Miyazaki, Hayao 876, 930-931
Mizoguchi, Kenji 156, 293, 308-309
Moland, Hans Petter 856
Moore, Michael 784
Moretti, Nanni 850, 932
Morin, Edgar 401
Morris, Errol 763, 877
Mu, Fei 237
Mulligan, Robert 408
Munk, Andrzej 418
Muratova, Kira 785
Murnau, F.W. 56, 46-47, 64-65, 91
Murphy, Geoff 700, 727
Myrick, Daniel 898

N
Nair, Mira 936
Nakata, Hideo 895
Nava, Gregory 695
Newell, Mike 839
Nichols, Mike 462-463, 468-469
Nolan, Christopher 924
Noonan, Chris 852
Nossiter, Jonathan 919

O
Olivier, Laurence 202
Olmi, Ermanno 641
Ophuls, Marcel 538, 765
Ophuls, Max 234-235, 251, 283, 326
Oshima, Nagisa 619, 899
Otomo, Katsuhiro 764
Ozu, Yasujiro 285, 376, 405

P
Pabst, G.W. 80-81
Pagnol, Marcel 148
Pakula, Alan 541, 614
Panahi, Jaffar 858
Paradjanov, Sergei 437, 520
Parks Jr., Gordon 546, 564
Pasolini, Pier Paolo 440, 606-607
Peckinpah, Sam 516-517, 550, 582, 595
Penn, Arthur 480-481, 527
Pereira dos Santos, Nelson 424
Petersen, Wolfgang 675
Pialat, Maurice 670
Polanski, Roman 450, 492-493, 588-589, 943
Pollack, Sydney 686, 721
Pollet, Jean-Daniel 425
Polonsky, Abraham 237
Pontecorvo, Gillo 446
Porter, Edwin S. 28-29
Powell, Michael 193, 214, 223, 227, 242-243, 389
Preminger, Otto 201, 273, 307, 364
Pressburger, Emeric 193, 214, 223, 227, 242-243
Pudovkin, Vsevolod 76
Puenzo, Luis 721

R
Rafelson, Bob 522
Raimi, Sam 686
Ramis, Harold 828
Rapper, Irving 183
Ray, Nicholas 263, 295, 320-321, 335
Ray, Satyajit 312-313, 344, 358-359, 368-369
Redford, Robert 664

Reed, Carol 232, 252-253
Reggio, Godfrey 704
Reiner, Carl 660
Reiner, Rob 712, 732, 755, 777
Reisz, Karel 380
Reitherman, Wolfgang 483
Reitman, Ivan 713
Renoir, Jean 98, 101, 130, 140, 162-163, 281
Resnais, Alain 323, 374, 393
Riefenstal, Leni 118-119, 147
Riggs, Marlon 813
Ritchie, Guy 888
Ritt, Martin 419, 471
Rivette, Jacques 590, 805
Roach, Jay 919
Robinson, Bruce 752
Robson, Mark 194
Rocha, Glauber 441, 485
Roeg, Nicholas 531, 540, 574, 621
Rohmer, Eric 504, 823
Romero, George 502-503, 646
Rose, Bernard 823
Rosenberg, Stuart 476-477
Rosi, Francesco 679
Rossellini, Roberto 211, 217, 277, 292
Rossen, Robert 402
Rouch, Jean 315, 401
Ruiz, Raoul 863, 904
Russell, David O. 902

S
Sanchez, Eduardo 898
Sandrich, Mark 130
Saura, Carlos 609
Sayles, John 870
Schaffner, Franklin J. 490, 530, 569
Schepisi, Fred 640
Schlesinger, John 507
Schlondorff, Volker 654
Schrader, Paul 728
Schroeder, Barbet 789
Scorcese, Martin 570-571, 616-617, 672-673, 702, 790, 831, 850, 880, 942
Scott, Ridley 653, 684-685, 808, 915
Scott, Tony 743
Seiter, William A. 116
Sembene, Ousmane 635
Sharman, Jim 598-599
Sharpstein, Ben 143, 166, 169, 178
Shelton, Ron 762
Shepitko, Larisa 614
Sheridan, Jim 700
Sherman, Lowell 111
Shindo, Kaneto 442
Shymalayan, M. Knight 910
Siegel, Don 334, 547
Singer, Bryan 862
Singleton, John 800-801
Siodmak, Robert 223
Sirk, Douglas 330, 332-333
Sjostrom, Victor 41
Skolimowski, Jerzy 526
Sluizer, George 760-761
Smith, Harry 412
Smith, Jack 420
Smith, Kevin 839
Snow, Michael 479
Soderbergh, Steven 786, 922
Sokurov, Aleksandr 883, 946
Solas, Humberto 504
Solondz, Todd 891
Spielberg, Steven 612, 624, 674, 682, 731, 830, 832, 886-887, 941
Stevens, George 132, 161, 269, 294, 331
Stone, Oliver 740, 742, 810-811, 842
Straub, Jean-Marie 681
Stuart, Mel 538
Sturges, John 314, 345, 421
Sturges, Preston 174, 180-181, 183
Svankmajer, Jan 776

T
Takahata, Isao 768
Tanovic, Danis 933
Tarantino, Quentin 818, 843
Tarkovsky, Andrei 518, 556-557, 586, 652
Tarr, Bela 841
Tashlin, Frank 310
Tati, Jacques 291, 357, 470
Taviani, Vittorio 693
Taviani, Paolo 693
Techine, Andre 844
Teshigahara, Hiroshi 433
Tian, Zhuangzhuang 745
Tolkin, Michael 805
Tornatore, Giuseppe 765
Tourneur, Jacques 187, 194, 231
Truffaut, Francois 360, 381, 398, 573, 665
Tsai, Ming-liang 928
Tsukamoto, Shinya 769
Tykwer, Tom 889

U
Ulmer, Edgar G. 121, 214

V
Van Dyke, W.S. 124-125
Van Peebles, Melvin 548
Van Sant, Gus 779, 806-807
Varda, Agnes 404, 729, 923
Verhoeven, Paul 578, 638, 702, 799
Vertov, Dziga 78-79
Vidor, Charles 230
Vidor, King 61, 72, 141
Vigo, Jean 107, 120
Vinterberg, Thomas 885
Visconti, Luchino 197, 306, 376, 422-423
Vlacil, Frantisek 483
von Sternberg, Josef 73, 82-83, 105
von Stroheim, Erich 49, 52-53
von Trier, Lars 849, 867, 894, 925

W
Wachowski, Andy 911
Wachowski, Larry 911
Wadleigh, Michael 524-525
Waggner, George 175
Wajda, Andrzej 356, 630, 680
Walsh, Raoul 50, 107, 179, 251
Wang, Wayne 858
Warhol, Andy 442
Waters, Charles 336
Waters, John 563
Watkins, Peter 445
Weibang, Maxu 139
Weine, Robert 36-37
Weir, Peter 604, 625, 676
Welleman, William 95, 195
Welles, Orson 172-173, 188-189, 220, 240, 350-351, 449
Wenders, Wim 635, 710, 746-747
Whale, James 94, 129
Wilcox, Fred 326
Wilde, Ted 71
Wilder, Billy 204-205, 212-213, 260-261, 263, 362-363, 390-391
Wise, Robert 270, 402, 447, 426-427
Wiseman, Frederick 514
Woo, John 781
Wood, Sam 127
Wright, Geoffrey 819
Wyler, William 136, 145, 164, 215, 246, 286, 371

Y
Yang, Edward 803, 916
Yates, Peter 654

Z
Zemeckis, Robert 723, 773, 838
Zhang, Yimou 757, 802
Zhuangzhuang, Tian 834
Zinnemann, Fred 170, 184
Zucker, David 671, 767
Zwick, Edward 784
Zwigoff, Terry 846

# PICTURE ACKNOWLEDGEMENTS

*All the images that appear in this volume are from the archives of The Kobal Collection which seeks to collect, organize, preserve, and make available the publicity images issued by the film production and distribution companies to promote their films. We apologize in advance for any unintentional omissions or errors and will be pleased to insert the appropriate acknowledgment to any companies or individuals in any subsequent edition of this work.*

1 20th Century Fox / Douglas Kirkland; 4 Paramount; 5 Miramax / David James; 6 United Artists; 7 Universal; 8 Warner Bros.; 9 Universal; 10 Embassy; 11 Columbia / Sony; 12 Dreamworks / Jinks / Cohen / Lorey Sebastian; 15 Amblin / Universal / Murray Close; 17 Columbia / Sony / Chan Kam Chuen; 19 Amblin / Universal; 20 New Line / Saul Zaentz / Wing Nut / Pierre Vinet; 24 Lucasfilm / 20th Century Fox / John Jay; 26 Méliès / StarFilm; 27 Méliès / StarFilm; 28 Edison; 29 Edison; 30 Epoch / Griffith Prods; 31 Epoch / Griffith Prods; 32 Gaumont; 33 Gaumont; 35 Wark Prods / Griffith Prods; 36 Decla-Bioscop; 37 Decla-Bioscop; 38 Griffith Prods; 41 Svensk Filmindustri; 43 Uco-Film; 44 Flaherty; 45 Flaherty; 46 Prana-Film; 47 Prana-Film; 48 Svensk Filmindustri; 51 Goskino; 52 MGM; 53 MGM; 54 Metro; 55 Metro; 57 Universal; 58 Goskino / Mosfilm; 59 Goskino / Mosfilm; 60 UA / Charles Chaplin; 61 MGM; 62 UFA; 63 UFA; 64 Karl Struss, Fox Films; 65 Karl Struss, Fox Films; 66 United Artists; 67 MGM; 68 Sovkino; 69 Sovkino; 70 Warner Bros. / First National; 72 MGM; 73 Paramount; 74 Bunuel-Dali; 75 Société Générale des Films; 77 Gainsborough / BIP; 79 VUFKU; 80 Nero-Film; 81 Nero-Film; 82 Universum / UFA; 83 Universum / UFA; 84 Vicomte / CDN; 85 Vicomte / CDN; 86 VUFKU Ukraine; 87 VUFKU Ukraine; 88 Warner Bros. / First National; 90 Tobis Film; 92 Universal; 93 Universal; 94 Roman Freulich, Universal; 96 Nero-Film; 97 Nero-Film; 98 Braunberger-Richebe; 99 Tobis / Dreyer / Klangfilm; 100 Paramount; 102 Paramount; 103 Paramount; 104 Gene Kornman United Artists; 105 Paramount; 106 MGM; 108 Warner Bros. / First National; 109 Warner Bros. / First National; 111 Paramount; 112 Paramount; 113 Paramount; 115 RKO; 115 RKO; 117 Paramount; 118 NSDAP; 119 NSDAP; 120 Gaumont / Nounez; 122 Irving Lippman, Columbia; 123 Irving Lippman, Columbia; 124 MGM; 125 MGM; 127 MGM; 128 Gaumont / British; 129 Roman Freulich, Universal; 131 UA / Charles Chaplin; 132 RKO; 133 Universal; 134 Irving Lippman, Columbia; 136 Goldwyn; 140 Réalisations D'art Cinématographique; 142 Paramount; 144 Columbia; 147 Olympia-Film; 148 Films Marcel Pagnol; 149 top RKO; 150 Ned Scott, UA / Walter Wagner; 151 Ned Scott, UA / Walter Wagner; 153 Irving Lippman, Columbia; 154 MGM; 155 MGM; 156 Universal / Ray Jones; 157 Irving Lippman, Columbia; 158 Selznick / MGM; 159 Selznick / MGM; 160 Raymond Voinquel Sigma Prods; 162 Nouvelle Edition Française; 163 Nouvelle Edition Française; 165 Selznick / UA; 167 James Manatt, MGM; 168 20th Century Fox; 170 MGM; 171 Universal; 172 RKO; 173 RKO; 174 A.L. 'Whitey' Schafer, Paramount; 175 Universal; 176 Warner Bros. / First National; 177 Warner Bros. / First National; 179 (t) Bert Six, Warner Bros. / First National; 179 (b) Warner Bros. / First National; 180 A.L. 'Whitey' Schafer, Paramount; 181 Paramount; 182 Gene Kornman 20th Century Fox; 184 Warner Bros.; 185 Warner Bros.; 186 United Artists; 187 RKO; 188 RKO; 189 RKO; 190 Warner Bros.; 192 Crown Film Unit; 195 20th Century Fox; 196 Universal; 197 ICI; 199 MGM; 200 Warner Bros.; 201 20th Century Fox; 203 Alma Ata / Mosfilm; 204 Paramount; 205 Paramount; 206 RKO; 208 Warner Bros.; 209 Warner Bros.; 210 Pathé; 211 Excelsa / Minerva; 212 Paramount; 213 Paramount; 215 Goldwyn; 216 Rank / Cineguild; 218 20th Century Fox; 219 20th Century Fox; 220 Haig / International / RKO; 221 G.R. Aldo, Discina / Andre Paulvé; 222 Warner Bros.; 224 Rank / Cineguild; 225 Rank / Cineguild; 226 (t) Ernest Bachrach, RKO / Vanguard; 226 (b) RKO / Vanguard; 227 The Archers / Rank / Independent; 228 RKO; 229 RKO; 231 RKO; 233 De Sica; 234 Rampart / Universal; 235 Rampart / Universal; 236 Diana / Universal; 238 Monterey / UA; 239 Transatlantic / WB; 241 Paramount; 242 The Archers / Rank / Independent; 243 The Archers / Rank / Independent; 244 Warner Bros.; 245 Robert Flaherty; 247 Ealing; 248 United Artists; 249 MGM; 250 Ealing / Rank; 252 Len Lee, British Lion / London Films; 253 Len Lee, British Lion / London Films; 254 MGM; 256 Daiei; 257 Daiei; 259 20th Century Fox; 260 Paramount; 261 Paramount; 262 Ultramar; 264 (t) Jack Albin, Warner Bros. / Feldman; 264 (b) Warner Bros. / Feldman; 265 Warner Bros.; 267 Horizon / Romulus; 269 Paramount; 270 20th Century Fox; 272 Silver; 273 RKO; 274 MGM; 275 MGM; 276 Toho; 277 Ponti / De Laurentiis; 278 MGM; 282 MGM; 283 Rizzoli / Indus; 284 Columbia; 285 Shochiku; 286 Paramount; 289 20th Century Fox; 290 Irving Lippman, Columbia; 293 Daiei; 294 Paramount; 296 Columbia; 297 Columbia; 299 Halas and Batchelor; 300 Paramount; 301 Paramount; 303 Ponti / De Laurentiis; 304 Toho; 305 Toho; 306 Lux; 308 Daiei; 309 Daiei; 311 Goldwyn; 312 Govt. of W.Bengal; 313 Govt. of W.Bengal; 314 MGM; 317 Palladium; 320 Floyd McCarty, Warner Bros.; 321 Floyd McCarty, Warner Bros.; 324 United Artists; 325 United Artists; 328 Whitney / Warner Bros.; 329 Whitney / Warner Bros.; 332 Universal; 333 Ray Jones, Universal; 334 Allied Artists; 337 Orion-Nova / UA; 338 Svensk Filmindustri; 339 Svensk Filmindustri; 340 20th Century Fox; 341 Svensk Filmindustri; 342 De Laurentiis / Marceau; 344 Epic; 345 Columbia / Horizon; 346 Mehboob; 347 Mosfilm; 349 Ashton / UA; 350 Universal; 351 Universal; 354 Paramount / Hitchcock; 355 Paramount / Hitchcock; 356 Film Polski / ZRF; 358 Aurora; 359 Aurora; 361 MGM; 363 Bernie Abramson, Ashton / Mirisch / UA; 364 Carlyle / Columbia; 367 Lion; 368 Satyajit Ray; 369 Satyajit Ray; 371 MGM; 372 Lux; 373 Lux; 375 Armada / WB; 378 Riama-Pathé; 379 Riama-Pathé; 380 Woodfall; 382 Cino Del Duca / PCE / Lyre; 383 Cino Del Duca / PCE / Lyre; 386 Shamley / Hitchcock / Universal; 387 Shamley / Hitchcock / Universal; 388 Galatea / Jolly; 389 Anglo-Amalgamated; 390 Mirisch / UA; 391 Mirisch / UA; 394 Argos; 395 Paramount / Pennebaker; 397 Nepi / Silver / Sofitepid; 400 Svensk Filmindustri; 403 Cineriz; 406 Horizon / Columbia; 407 Horizon / Columbia; 408 Universal; 411 Warner Bros.; 413 Universal / Hitchcock; 414 Lewis / Paramount; 416 Cineriz / Francinex; 417 Cineriz / Francinex; 423 SGC / Pathé / Titanus; 426 Argyle / MGM; 429 EON / Danjaq; 430 Puck; 432 Universal; 434 Hawk / Columbia; 435 Bob Penn, Hawk / Columbia; 436 Shensoa / Proscenium; 439 Palladium; 440 Arco / Lux; 443 Barrandov; 444 MGM; 446 Casbah / Igor; 449 Alpine / Espanola; 451 Rizzoli / Eichberg / Federiz; 453 Eve / RM Film; 456 Bridge / Ponti / MGM; 457 Bridge / Ponti / MGM; 458 Gonzalez / PEA / Constantin / Grimaldi; 459 Gonzalez / PEA / Constantin / Grimaldi; 462 Chenault / WB; 463 Chenault / WB; 464 Svensk Filmindustri; 465 Svensk Filmindustri; 468 Embassy / Deg; 469 Embassy / Deg; 473 Five / Paris; 476 Jalem / WB; 477 Jalem / WB; 478 MGM; 480 Penn / Beatty / WB; 481 Penn / Beatty / WB; 482 Mafilm / Mosfilm; 484 Barrandov / Ponti; 486 Barrandov; 487 Barrandov; 489 Paramount / Rafran; 490 20th Century Fox; 492 Paramount; 493 Paramount; 494 Memorial; 497 Svensk Filmindustri; 498 MGM; 499 MGM; 500 Svensk Filmindustri; 501 Saticoy / Bogdanovich; 502 Image Ten; 503 Image Ten; 505 Lian Bang / Union; 506 20th Century Fox; 507 Florin / Hellman / UA; 508 PEA / Grimaldi; 509 PEA / Grimaldi; 511 Maran / Marianne / Mars; 512 BBS / Columbia; 513 BBS / Columbia; 515 Pathé; 516 Warner Bros. / Seven Arts; 517 Bernie Abramson, Warner Bros. / Seven Arts; 518 Mosfilm; 520 Armenfilm; 522 Bernie Abramson, Columbia; 523 Panicas; 524 Wadleigh-Maurice / Warner Bros.; 525 Wadleigh-Maurice / Warner Bros.; 527 Stockbridge-Hiller Prods / CBS; 528 Barrandov; 529 Barrandov; 531 Goodtimes; 532 Maysles Films; 534 Neoplanta / Telepool; 536 Hawk / Polaris / Warner Bros.; 537 Hawk / Polaris / Warner Bros.; 539 Warner Bros.; 540 Dean Goodhill, Raab-Litinoff Films; 542 Paramount; 543 Paramount; 545 20th Century Fox; 546 MGM; 548 Yeah; 549 Columbia; 550 ABC / Amerbroco / Talent; 552 Werner Herzog; 555 Elmer / Warner Bros.; 556 Mosfilm; 557 Mosfilm; 558 Paramount; 559 Bo-Erik Gyberg, Svenska Filminstitutet / Cinematograph AB; 561 Autoren / Tango;

562 Universal; 563 John Waters / Dreamland; 566 Pressman-Williams; 567 Pressman-Williams; 568 Universal; 570 Scorsese / Warner Bros.; 571 Scorsese / Warner Bros.; 574 DLN / Paramount / British Lion; 576 Josh Weiner, Hoya / Warner Bros.; 577 Hoya / Warner Bros.; 578 VNF; 580 FC / PECF; 581 FC / PECF; 583 Daiei / Mosfilm / Atelier; 584 Brian Hamill, Zoetrope / Paramount / Coppola; 585 Vortex; 586 Mosfilm; 588 Paramount / Long Rd / Penthouse; 589 Paramount / Long Rd / Penthouse; 591 Warner Bros.; 593 Paramount; 594 Peter Gauhe, Autoren / Tango / RUFF; 596 Peter Sorel, Fantasy / NV Zvaluw; 598 John Jay 20th Century Fox; 599 John Jay 20th Century Fox; 601 White / National Film Trustee / Python; 602 Hawk / Peregrine / Warner Bros.; 603 City / Tango; 605 Lino Brocka; 606 Artistes Associés; 607 Artistes Associés; 608 ABC / Paramount; 609 Querejeta y Garate; 610 Papalios; 611 [illegible] Universal / Zanuck-Brown; 615 Elliott Marks, Chartoff-Winkler; 616 Columbia / Bill / Phillips / Judeo; 617 Columbia / Bill / Phillips / Judeo; 618 Michael Ginsburg, MGM / UA; 620 Angelo Novi, Artistes Associés / Artemis / PEA; 621 David James, British Lion; 622 (l) John Jay, Lucasfilm / 20th Century Fox; 622 (r) Lucasfilm / 20th Century Fox; 623 John Jay, Lucasfilm / 20th Century Fox; 624 Columbia / EMI; 625 Last Wave / Ayer Prods; 626 Brian Hamill, Rollins-Joffe / UA; 627 Brian Hamill, Rollins-Joffe / UA; 629 Skellig / Werner Herzog / ZDF; 631 Paramount; 632 Charles Burnett; 633 Charles Burnett; 634 AFI / David Lynch; 636 Blood Relations; 637 Blood Relations; 638 Rob Houwer Film; 639 Seda Spettacoli; 641 Gaumont; 642 EMI; 643 EMI; 644 Dave Friedman, Paramount; 645 Paramount; 646 Katherine Kolbert, MKR / Dawn Associated; 649 Compass / Falcon; 650 R.W. Fassbinder Foundation; 652 Vadim Murashko, Mosfilm / ZDF; 653 Bob Penn 20th Century Fox; 655 Josh Weiner, Columbia; 656 Sidney Baldwin, Lorimar / Fernsehproduktion; 658 Omni / Zoetrope / UA; 659 Omni / Zoetrope / UA; 661 Brian Hamill, Rollins-Joffe / UA; 662 Chic Stringer, Kennedy-Miller / Crossroads; 663 Claude Chiarini, Gaumont / Werner Herzog; 664 Marcia Reed, Paramount / Wildwood; 666 Hawk Films / Warner Bros.; 667 Hawk Films / Warner Bros.; 668 Terry Chostner, Lucasfilm / 20th Century Fox; 669 Frank Connor, Brooksfilms Ltd; 671 John Monte, Paramount; 672 Chartoff-Winkler / UA; 673 Chartoff-Winkler / UA; 674 Lucasfilm / Paramount; 675 Karl-Heinz Vogelman, Bavaria / Radiant / SDR / WDR; 677 Ladd Co.; 678 David Appleby, Barclays / JRS / Paramount; 680 Film Film Polski / Zespol Filmowy X; 682 Amblin / Universal; 684 Stephen Vaughan, Blade Runner Partnership / Ladd Co.; 685 Stephen Vaughan, Blade Runner Partnership / Ladd Co.; 687 Cactus Film; 688 Catharine Bushnell, MGM; 689 Catharine Bushnell MGM; 690 Beat Presser, Autoren / Herzog / Wildlife / ZDF; 691 Beat Presser, Autoren / Herzog / Wildlife / ZDF; 692 Columbia / Indo-British / NFDC; 694 Arne Carlsson, Svenska Filminstitutet; 696 Filmplan / Guardian Trust / Universal; 701 Zade Rosentha,l, Paramount; 703 Ron Grover, Ladd Co.; 704 Institute of Regional Education / Santa Fe; 705 Angelo Novi, Embassy International; 706 Sidney Baldwin, Universal; 708 Joyce Rudolph, Cinema '84; 709 Cinema '84; 710 Robin Holland, Road Movies / 20th Century Fox; 711 (t) Michael Leshnov, New Line / Smart Egg; 711 (b) Joyce Rudolph, New Line / Smart Egg; 712 Embassy Pictures; 714 Frank Connor, HBO / Thorn-EMI; 715 Cinesthesia Prods; 717 A&M / Universal; 718 Greenwich / Nipon Herald; 719 Greenwich / Nipon Herald; 722 Brian Hamill, Orion / Rollins-Joffe; 724 David Appleby, Embassy / Universal; 725 David Appleby, Embassy / Universal; 726 HB / Sugarloaf; 727 Mr Yellowbeard; 730 Les Films Adelph / Historia; 731 John Shannon, Warner Bros.; 733 Umberto Montiroli, De Laurentiis; 734 Brian Hamill, Orion; 736 Attila Dory, Brooksfilms / 20th Century Fox; 738 Black Snake Inc.; 740 Hemdale; 743 Paramount / Ralph Nelson Jr.; 746 Ralf Strathmann, Argos / Road Movies; 747 Ralf Strathmann, Argos / Road Movies; 750 Natant / Warner Bros.; 751 [illegible] / Warner Bros.; [illegible] 20th Century Fox; 759 Macusa Cores, El Deseo / Laurenfilm; 760 Argos / Golden Egg / MGS / Movie Visions; 761 Argos / Golden Egg / MGS / Movie Visions; 763 Third Floor Prods; 764 Akira Committee; 766 David James, MGM; 771 20th Century Fox; 773 Amblin / Touchstone; 774 Stephen Vaughan, UA; 777 Castle Rock Ent; 778 Brian Hamill, Orion; 780 Jonathan Hession, Ferndale / Granada / RTE; 781 Film Workshop / Golden Princess / Magnum; 782 David Lee, Universal / 40 Acres & a Mule; 783 David Lee, Universal / 40 Acres & a Mule; 786 Diana Gary, Outlaw Prods; 788 Artificial Eye / 3-H / Era; 790 Barry Wetcher, Warner Bros.; 792 Ben Glass, Orion / Tig / Majestic; 793 Renata Paschel, CCC / Filmkunst / Losange; 794 Ron Batzdorff, Touchstone; 797 Zade Rosenthal, 20th Century Fox; 798 Maljack Prods; 801 Darren Stevens, Columbia; [illegible] ICA / Balfour / Yang & His Gang; 803 ICA / Balfour / Yang & His Gang; 804 Attila Dory, Recorded Picture Co / Naked Lunch; 806 New Line; 807 New Line; 809 Ken Regan, Orion; 810 Ben Glass, Warner Bros. / Regency / Le Studio Canal; 811 Ben Glass, Warner Bros. / Regency / Le Studio Canal; 812 Detour; 814 American Zoetrope; 817 Lorey Sebastian, Avenue / Guild / Spelling; 818 (t) Dog Eat Dog / Live; 818 (b) Linda R Chen, Dog Eat Dog / Live; 820 Bob Akester, Malpaso / Warner Bros.; 821 Bob Akester, Malpaso / Warner Bros.; 822 Ralph Nelson Jr, American Zoetrope / Columbia / Orion; 825 Jean Claude Moschetti, Artistes Anonymes; 826 Swift; 828 Louis Goldman, Columbia; 830 Murray Close, Universal / Amblin; 832 David James, Universal / Amblin; 836 KTCA-TV / Kartemquin; 837 KTCA-TV / Kartemquin; 838 Phillip Caruso, Paramount; 843 (t) Linda R Chen, Miramax; 843 (b) Miramax; 845 Jet Tone; 846 Superior; 847 Pierre Vinet, Wingnut Films; 848 CiBy 2000; 849 Nordic Film / Zentropa; 852 Jim Townley, Kennedy Miller / Universal; 855 (t) Paramount; 855 (b) Elliott Marks, Paramount; 857 Peter Sorel, New Line; 859 Productions Lazennec; 861 Christine Parry, 12 Gauge prods; 862 Linda R Chen, Rosco / Bad Hat Harry / Polygram; 864 Michael Tackett, Gramercy / Polygram / Working Title; 865 Michael Tackett, Gramercy / Polygram / Working Title; 867 Zentropa / Sept Cinema; 868 Phil Bray, J&M / Miramax / Tiger Moth; 869 Mohamad Ahmadi, MK2 / Sanaye Dasti; 870 Alan Pappe, Castle Rock; 871 Liam Longman, Channel Four / Figment / Polygram / Noel Gay; 872 David M. Moir, Miramax Film Corp; 873 David M. Moir, Miramax Film Corp; 875 Block 2 / Jet Tone / Prénom H / Seowoo; 876 (t) Tokuma Shoten; 876 (b) Tokuma Shoten; 878 20th Century Fox; 879 G. Lefkowitz, New Line; 881 Wega; 882 CiBy 2000; 884 Merie W. Wallace, 20th Century Fox / Paramount; 886 David James, Dreamworks / Amblin / Paramount; 887 David James, Dreamworks / Amblin / Paramount; 889 Bernd Spauke, X Filme / Creative Pool; 891 Henny Garunkel, Good Machine / Killer Films; 892 Merie W. Wallace, 20th Century Fox; 893 Merie W. Wallace, 20th Century Fox; 898 Haxan Films; 900 Teresa Isasi, Renn / El Deseo; 901 Teresa Isasi, Renn / El Deseo; 903 AFDF / Omega; 905 (l) Melissa Moseley, Polygram Holding; 905 (r) Polygram Holding; 906 Lorey Sebastian, Dreamworks LLC; 907 Lorey Sebastian, Dreamworks LLC; 909 Hobby / Pole Star / Warner Bros.; 910 Ron Phillips, Spyglass Ent; 911 Jasin Boland, Warner Bros. / Village Roadshow; 913 Block 2 / Jet Tone / Paradis; 915 Jaap Buitendijk, Dreamworks / Universal; 917 John Baer, Requiem for a Dream; 918 Altavista; 920 Chan Kam Chuen, United China; 921 United China; 922 Bob Marshak, Bedford Falls / Compulsion / Splendid; 924 Danny Rothenberg, Remember Prods; 925 Zentropa / Svenska Film; 926 Melinda Sue Gordon, Touchstone / Universal; 929 Bac / Makhmalbaf / Studio Canal; 931 Studio Ghibli; 933 Dejan Vekic, Eurimages / Fonds Slovene; 934 Bazmark / 20th Century Fox; 935 Douglas Kirkland, Bazmark / 20th Century Fox; 936 (t) Mirabai Films; 936 (b) Nan Goldin, Mirabai Films; 938 Melissa Moseley, Studio Canal / Alain Sardé; 939 James Hamilton, American Empirical / Touchstone; 940 New Line / Saul Zaentz / Wingnut; 941 (t) David James, Amblin / Kubrick / Dreamworks / Warner Bros.; 941 (b) Amblin / Kubrick / Dreamworks / Warner Bros.; 942 Mario Tursi, Initial / Miramax; 943 Guy Ferrandis, Studio Canal; [illegible] / Lumière / Studio Canal; 947 (l) Ben Kaller, Columbia; 947 (r) Columbia; 948 Killer Films / Vulcan / Clear Blue Sky; 949 (t) David James, Loop / Miramax / Producers Circle; 949 (b) Loop / Miramax / Producers Circle.